and

ALPHABETICAL INDEX

OF

PATENTEES OF INVENTIONS,

From March 2, 1617 (14 James I.) to October 1, 1852 (16 Victoriæ).

BENNET WOODCROFT

ALPHABETICAL INDEX
OF
PATENTEES
OF INVENTIONS

*with an Introduction and Appendix of additions and corrections
compiled in the Patent Office Library*

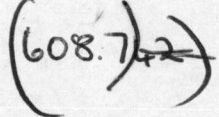

LONDON: EVELYN, ADAMS & MACKAY

First published in 1854

This edition © 1969 by Evelyn, Adams & Mackay Ltd. All rights reserved
S.B.N. 238. 78913. 6

The Publishers wish to thank Mr. H. Harding for his valuable assistance

(608·7)

Published by Evelyn, Adams & Mackay Ltd, 9 Fitzroy Square, London W.1
Printed in England by the Redwood Press, Trowbridge, Wiltshire

INTRODUCTION

THIS INDEX is a remarkable work. Its pages carry some of the most splendid names in the history of the industrial development of Great Britain. It carries, too, the rare distinction that an Act of Parliament was passed to secure it for the nation. But above all, it is remarkable for the vision and determination of its compiler, Bennet Woodcroft.

The index is concerned with patents granted for inventions in Great Britain from 1617 up to the time the Patent Office was reconstituted in October, 1852. The British method for rewarding and encouraging inventors through the grant to them of limited monopolies—the 'patenting' system—became part of civil law upon the enactment of the celebrated Statute of Monopolies in 1624. This Statute defined the principle which has remained fundamental to the granting of patents for inventions; but as to the means and manner by which this principle should be put into effect, the Statute was silent. In practice, the detailed business of adjudicating on the merits of every petition for an invention patent was left to lawyers, judges, and the Law Officers of the Crown. For over 200 years, until Parliament eventually passed the Patent Law Amendment Act of 1852 to overhaul the system, anyone seeking the protection of a patent for his invention had to negotiate a legal obstacle course. By the early 1800's the complexities of this process had become absurdly irrelevant to the realities of a period in which the growth in scientific knowledge and of technical invention had created the industrial revolution. Charles Dickens pilloried the system with its 'gang of Hanapers and Chaffwaxes' in his *Poor man's tale of a patent;* while the impatience of inventors and professional men with its anachronisms and frustrations grew to a respectable clamour for reform. It was to this campaign that Bennet Woodcroft added all the persuasiveness of his experience as an engineer, inventor and patentee.

Woodcroft had been born in Stockport on 29 December 1803; his father a successful dyer and velvet finisher. His education had a technical bias: he studied chemistry under Dalton and he also served a youthful apprenticeship as a weaver in Failsworth, near Manchester, after a time joining his father in the business. He later described himself as a 'silk manufacturer.' During his years around Manchester he formed friendships with several eminent engineers of the day, including Whitworth, Nasmyth, and Fairbairn. The latter described Woodcroft as 'an original inventor,' for he was already displaying gifts as an innovator. During his life, Woodcroft was granted 13 patents for inventions: at least two of these were technically of first importance—his variable pitch marine propeller, and the ingenious loom tappet—the second proving a considerable commercial success. But it was the personal experience and detailed knowledge that Woodcroft thereby gained of the British patenting system, his appreciation of its many shortcomings, and his understanding of both what inventors needed from patenting and the country's need for invention, that, in the long term, emerged as the lasting benefits of Woodcroft's involvements as a patentee.

About 1843, Woodcroft set up in Manchester as a consulting engineer, moving his consultancy to London in 1846, where he took an office in Furnival's Inn, opposite what later was to be the site of the Patent Office. The following year, 1847, he was appointed Professor of Machinery at University College, London; but in this role he was not well suited and he resigned in 1851. If this proved an unsatisfactory episode, there succeeded the long period of intense and dedicated activity which was to be the principal achievement of his working life.

From his first encounter, in 1826, with the obstacles that then confronted the would-be patentee, Woodcroft had seen that a major failing was the absence of published descriptions—'specifications'—of previously patented inventions and of adequate indexes. Twelve years later, when next he was 'bitten by the mania of invention,' as he put it, he set out with characteristic industry to remedy the situation. With the aid of a complete list of patents, which he somehow procured from the Lord Chancellor's clerk, Woodcroft began to compile the remarkable trio of indexes to all of the patents which had been granted for inventions since 1617—the earliest date in the Lord Chancellor's list. One of these was a Chronological Index, which listed patents progressively in order of their dates of grant and gave for each a title or brief description. A second was a Subject Index, listing patents under main and sub-headings. Third was this Name Index, which presented in one cumulated alphabetical order the names of all patentees since 1617.

Continued agitation for patent reform led to the appointment by the Government of a Select Committee of enquiry in 1851 and to which Woodcroft was among the several eminent persons concerned in some way with patents who were invited to give evidence. In the opening part of his evidence, Woodcroft condemned a situation in which, through the lack of published specifications and the absence of necessary indexes, inventors were virtually kept in ignorance of what had previously been patented; and he deplored the difficulties that lay in the path of anyone who attempted to unearth this information. Woodcroft described his own efforts at repairing these deficiences and urged the Committee that the publishing of specifications, and of indexes such as those he had himself compiled, should be an essential part of any reformed patents system.

Woodcroft can scarcely have been more gratified at the results of his appearance before the Select Committee. The Patent Law Amendment Act which followed in the next year ordered the publication of specifications in future; while in 1853 a further Act authorised the purchase of Woodcroft's three indexes for public use, which enabled them to be published. And Bennet Woodcroft himself was appointed as Superintendent of the Specifications of the newly-established Office of the Commissioners of Patents for Invention in November 1852, at what was then the substantial salary of £1000 per annum.

The new Superintendent turned to his duties with typical energy. 'Mr. Woodcroft,' it was said later, 'was no ordinary Government official; being unfettered by any tradition of routine he set himself, immediately upon his appointment, to carry out the Patent Act not in the spirit of doing as little as he must, but as much as he could.'

In directing that the specifications of patents for invention be published, the Act of 1852 made no mention of those granted *before* 1852—although these represented the 'prior art' at that period and it had been one of the points strongly pressed upon the Select Committee by Woodcroft that the specifications of these patents should be available in print to inventors. However, the difficulties in the way of achieving this were considerable. Not least among them was the fact that the several thousand specifications involved were dispersed at random on rolls held by three separate Government offices, situated at opposite ends of Chancery Lane; and the Act gave the new Patent Office neither direction nor statutory right over these old specifications. Woodcroft was undeterred. He first overcame official obstruction, and then, with access to the documents achieved, proceeded to organise a major printing effort so that all of the 14,359 specifications or enrolments of the period up to the inception of the Patent Office were published in a mere five years. During this time he succeeded, too, in bringing out for sale, at 'the cost of printing and paper only,' his trio of subject, name and chronological indexes for the 1617-1852 era. It must not be forgotten, moreover, that concurrently with the project of publishing this old-law material, Woodcroft had to provide for publishing the specifications and indexes for inventions which it was expected the new law would encourage inventors to patent. And in the early years following the 1852 Act, about 3,000 specifications were being published by the Patent Office annually.

In one respect, Woodcroft was out of sympathy with later practice. He was opposed to an official examination of patent applications, but was instead a life-long advocate of publishing specifications and indexes and of then leaving inventors to make their own searches. It was in accord with this thinking that immediately the issue of the old-law specifications had been completed, in 1857, Woodcroft launched another important innovation with the publishing of the first abridgments of specifications. These summarised the essence of inventions and their publication in a series of subject volumes it was hoped would, in Woodcroft's words, 'prevent the misapplication of time and labour in re-inventing what is already known.' The first Abridgments were textual only and dealt with the 1617-1852 period; thereafter, the individual summaries were frequently illustrated. They continue in unbroken series to this day and in substantially unaltered form, representing a massive subject summary of invention patents published in this country, and an acknowledgement to the vision of their originator.

Yet perhaps nothing better illustrates Woodcroft's farsightedness than the proposal he made to the Select Committee that patent specifications should not only be published for sale, but ought to be freely available in public libraries throughout the country. This was dissemination of technical information in a modern sense, but advocated when the public-library movement was barely struggling into existence and against a tradition of charging for the most meagre search facilities—and these available in London alone. Providentially, his proposal found expression in the Act of 1852, and we find the Commissioners of Patents reporting as early as 1857 that gifts of complete sets of specifications and indexes had been made to the principal towns in the country, with the interesting observation that 'in many of them this had been the foundation of free libraries where previously none had existed.'

Woodcroft was also directly responsible for setting up in the Patent Office a public reference library of scientific literature—books and periodicals, as well as British and foreign patent publications—for the use of inventors and anyone else. From modest beginnings in 1855, the Library of the Patent Office gradually came to rank with the foremost scientific research libraries of the world, until in 1966 the library founded by Woodcroft formally became the National Reference Library of Science and Invention.

All of the publishing activity that enlivened the reformed patenting system from October 1852 was done in the name of the Commissioners of the Patent Office: but the driving force behind it, in the important first years of the Office, as well as much of its direction, came from Bennet Woodcroft. In Woodcroft the Commissioners had made a wise choice. He retired from their service in April 1876 and died three years later.

D. R. JAMIESON

APPENDIX

Additional and corrected entries

This appendix includes additions and corrections noted in their use of the Index by the staff of the Patent Office Library (now the National Reference Library of Science and Invention), and also incorporates the date corrections by A. A. Gomme (see *Transactions of the Newcomen Society*, vol. 13, 1932-33, pp. 159-164).

Page	Name	Progressive number	Date and Title
16	Ayloffe, Sir George	15	25th April 1620. Employing pit and other coal etc. in smelting ore and manufacturing metals.
29	Bastone, Joseph	3467	24th July 1811. Bedsteads and other articles of furniture.
84	Burnett, Robert	2245	13th June 1798. Utensils and apparatus for brewing, etc.
94	Cartright, Edmund	2524	16th December 1801. Machinery for combing fibrous materials.
142	Dason, John	222	31st July 1682. Manufacture of salt, etc.
152	De Meckenheim, Louis Nicolas	11620	10th March 1847. Machinery for making nails, screw blanks, rivets, bolts and pins.
153	De Normandy, Alphone Rene Le Mire	10632	22nd April 1845. Dissolving Lac, shellac, rendering fabrics waterproof.
		10743	28th June 1845. Manufacture of thimbles and finger shields.
187	Fauche Borel, Louis	4069	25th October 1816. Making boots and shoes without sewing and impervious to wet; applicable to other purposes.
		4410	18th November 1819. Moveable and inodorous conveniences.
199	Fourdrinier, Henry *and* Sealy	3068	14th August 1807. Machinery for making paper.
207	Gamble, John	3068	14th August 1807. Machinery for making paper.

Page	Name	Progressive number	Correction
38	Bennett, Thomas	328	*Before* 1693 *insert* 14th September.
41	Berks, Thomas, Earl of	102	*For* 1637 *read* 1638.
52	Blood, Edmond	165	*For* 1671 *read* 1672.
57	Borel, Lewis Fauche	4069	*For* Lewis *read* Louis.
69	Brooks, Isaac	14032	*For* Brooks *read* Brookes.
			For March *read* May.
74	Brown, Thomas Beal	12680	*For* Brown *read* Browne; re-position entry.
77	Brunker, Sir William	54	*For* 1631 *read* 1632.
80	Budding, Edward	5990	*For* Edward *read* Edwin.
	Budding, Edwin	8860	*For* 8860 *read* 8660.
83	Burges, Roger	1	*For* 2nd March 1617 *read* 11th March 1618.
84	Burneby, Eustace	155	*For* 1667 *read* 1668.
		159	*For* 1670 *read* 1671.
	Burrell, Andrews	42	*For* January 1628 *read* 2nd January 1629.
85	Burtonshaw, John	3935	*For* Burtonshaw *read* Burtenshaw; re-position entry.
86	Bushby, Charles Augustin	3683	*For* Bushby *read* Busby; re-position entry.
	Bushnell, John	321	*For* 29th April *read* 27th April.
87	Butler, James	250	*For* 23rd June *read* 25th June.
89	Calthorp, Richard	152	*For* 19th February 1667 *read* 29th February 1668.
94	Cason, John	3	*For* Cason *read* Gason; re-position entry.
95	Castle, William	197	*For* 20th March 1676 *read* 10th March 1677.
96	Chamberlayne, Peter	157	*For* 1668 *read* 1669.
97	Champion, John	569	*For* 10th September *read* 13th September.
	Champion, John, junior	1239	*Delete* junior; re-position entry.
103	Chikley, Thomas, Sir	162	*For* 1671 *read* 1672.
104	Chriscel, Christopher	1056	*For* Chriscel *read* Chrysel; re-position entry.
110	Clauss, Christian	1394	*For* 5th November *read* 2nd October.
111	Clay, William Neale	8459	*For* 1864 *read* 1840.
112	Clerk, Samuel	6017	*For* Clerk *read* Clarke; re-position entry.
113	Clifford, Martin	134	*For* 1661 *read* 1662.
	Cloudesley, Paulo	261	*For* 4th November *read* 23rd November; *for* Cloudesley *read* Clowdesly; re-position entry.
116	Coffey, Aeneas	5974	*For* 1833 *read* 1830.
117	Cole, Richard	372	*For* 29th July *read* 9th July.
118	Colladon, John	138	*For* 1662 *read* 1663.
119	Collinge, John	4617	*For* 1812 *read* 1821.
	Collier, George	14140	*For* too lsor *read* tools for
121	Combs, Benjamin Merriman	5547	*For* Combs *read* Coombs; re-position entry.

Page	Name	Progressive number	Correction
126	Corcellis, Charles	**247**	*For* 15th October *read* 17th October.
127	Cottam, Edward	**11241**	*For* July *read* June.
128	Cotton, Samuel	**12**	*For* 1619 *read* 1620.
133	Crofts, Francis	**38**	*For* 1627 *read* 1628.
137	Crupley, John	**127**	*For* 24th June *read* 28th June.
	Culpepper, Sir Thomas	**80**	*For* 1635 *read* 1636.
138	Curtis, Joseph	**7792**	*Before* Joseph *insert* William; re-position entry.
139	Curtis, Edmund	**163**	*For* 16th March 1671 *read* 7th March 1672.
	Cuttler, John	**3873**	*For* Cuttler *read* Cutler; re-position entry.
141	Daniell, Frederick	**5454**	*For* Frederick *read* John Frederic.
142	Darby, William	**380**	*For* William *read* Abraham; re-position entry.
146	Dawson, Emerson	**4001**	Delete whole entry.
150	De Colmar, Charles Xavier Thomas	**13504**	*For* De Colmar *read* Thomas, Charles Xavier de Colmar; re-position entry.
152	De Mechenheim, Louis Nicolas	**9373**	*For* De Mechenheim *read* De Meckenheim.
154	Deacon, James *and* Thomas	**5753**	*For* Deacon *read* Deakin; re-position entry.
	Deacon, Thomas	**5753**	Delete whole entry.
156	Degeldew, Cornelius	**210**	*For* 4th May 1680 *read* 4th March 1681.
158	Derosne, Charles	**10380**	Delete whole entry.
159	Dewey, James	**145**	*For* 1664 *read* 1665.
	Dewhurst, Thomas	**1131**	*For* 23rd August *read* 16th July.
160	Dickens, Jones	**463**	*For* Dickens *read* Dickins; re-position entry.
165	Dodd, Barrodall Robert	**2839**	Re-position entry.
	Dodd, Thomas	**6337**	*For* Dodd *read* Todd; re-position entry.
166	Dolland, George	**3540**	
	Dolland, John	**721**	
		752	*For* Dolland *read* Dollond.
	Dolland, Peter	**1017**	
	Dollman, Thomas Francis	**3561**	Re-position entry.
169 to 176	Dorila, Andrew *to* Dundonald, Thomas		It should be noted that the duplicated page numbers were distinguished by the use of square brackets.
and			
[169] to [176]	Dundonald, Thomas *to* Edwards, Samuel		
169	Dotchin, Samuel	**9488**	*For* 1482 *read* 1842
	Doughty, Robert	**309**	*Before* 1692 *insert* 18th March.
174	Duesburg, William	**5797**	*For* 5797 *read* 5397.
[169]	Dundonald, Thomas, Earl of	**12064**	*For* 11th February *read* 10th February.
[170]	Dunning, Richard	**451**	*For* 23rd September *read* 23rd August.
	Dupin, Nicholas	**248**	*For* 248 *read* 249.
[171]	Duvivion, Anthony	**290**	*For* Duvivion *read* Duvivier.
[175]	Edisbury, Kendrick	**277**	*For* 1st October *read* 7th October.

Page	Name	Progressive number	Correction
178	Elliot, Arthur *to*		} Re-position entries.
179	Elliott, William Gilbert		
182	Etherington, John	**11**	*For* 1619 *read* 1620.
	Evance, Sir Stephen	**279**	*Before* October *insert* 17th.
183	Ewbanke, Collowell Henry	**197**	*For* 29th March *read* 10th March.
187	[Faucon, Joseph Seraphin]	**11529**	*For* [Faucon] *read* [Fancon].
	Februe, Peter Le	**62**	*For* 1833 *read* 1633.
189	Freguson, Patrick	**1139**	*For* Freguson *read* Ferguson; re-position entry.
194	Fontainemoreau, Pierre	**11968**	*For* 11968 *read* 11969.
196	Ford, Edward	**126**	*For* 1640 *read* 1642.
198	Fouillet, Charles	**11388**	*For* Fouillet *read* Pouillet; re-position entry.
200	Franke, Thornesse	**48**	*For* 31st July 1629 *read* 30th July 1630
	Franke, Major Thornes	**129**	*For* 13th July 1660 *read* 23rd July 1662.
207	Gamble, Josias Christopher	**5327**	*For* 7th February *read* 11th February.
209	Gaskins, Joshua	**241**	*For* Gaskins *read* Haskins; re-position entry.
214	Gifford, Nathaniel	**284**	*Before* November *insert* 6th.
		305	*For* 18th October *read* 19th October.
216	Gladwin, Thomas	**287**	*For* 2nd January *read* 11th January.
226	Greaves, William	**6340**	*For* Greaves, William *read* North, William Greaves; re-position entry.
228	Greenburg, Edward	**99**	*For* 1636 *read* 23rd March 1637.
230	Grent, Thomas	**59**	*For* 20th July *read* 20th June.
232	Grosse, Tobias Le	**309**	*Before* 1692 *insert* 18th March.
239	Hale, Thomas	**145**	*For* 1664 *read* 1665.
250	Harding, William	**433**	*For* 17th July *read* 12th July.
251	Harrington, William	**210**	*For* 1680 *read* 1681.
253	Harrison, George	**7834**	*For* 1831 *read* 1838.
259	Hayes, James	**139**	*For* August 1662 *read* 17th September 1663.
	Hayes, Richard	**166**	*For* 1672 *read* 1673.
261	Heathcoat, George	**6267**	*For* George *read* John.
265	Heming, Edmund	**364**	*For* 21st June *read* 20th June.
267	Henshaw, Thomas	**145**	*For* 1664 *read* 1665.
	Henson, Samuel	**9478**	*Before* Samuel *insert* William.
273	Hildeyerde, Charles	**147**	*For* 1665 *read* 1666.
	Hill, Abraham	**143**	*For* 1664 *read* 1665.
274	Hill, Symon	**64**	*For* 30th May *read* 31st May.
275	Hillyard, Nicholas	**2**	*For* 1st May *read* 5th May.
281	Holland, Thomas	**410**	*For* 8th November *read* 28th November.
	Hollingsworth, Tomas	**10865**	*For* 10865 *read* 10864.
284	Hopkins, John	**19749**	*For* 19749 *read* 10749.
288	Howard, Charles	**130**	*For* 1660 *read* 1661.
289	Howard, Sir Phillip	**154**	*For* 1667 *read* 1668.
289	Howard, Sir Phillip	**158**	*For* 1668 *read* 1669.
291	Hughes, Henry	**100**	*For* 1637 *read* 1638.
294	Hutchins, Samuel	**523**	*For* 2nd November *read* 7th November.
	Hutchinson, Samuel	**146**	*For* 1664 *read* 1665.

Page	Name	Progressive number	Correction
	Hutton, Thomas	**307**	*Before* 1692 *insert* 24th March.
296	Ions, James	**2918**	Delete whole entry.
305	Johnes, Roger	**23**	*For* Johnes *read* Jones; re-position entry.
312	Jones, Williams Lutyche	**14032**	*For* 24th March *read* 24th May.
313	Joyce, Thomas	**9649**	*For* 9649 *read* 8649.
314	Judson, Joseph Edwards	**10866**	*For* 10866 *read* 10865.
315	Kearsly, John	**148**	*For* 1665 *read* 1666.
317	Keir, James	**2926**	*For* 2926 *read* 2927.
320	Kinder, Robert	**3069**	*For* 3069 *read* 3969.
322	Knappe, Edward	**31**	*For* 1625 *read* 1626.
329	Lane, Ralph	**343**	*For* 2nd August *read* 6th August.
332	Le Blon, James	**492**	*For* 1st May *read* 1st June 1727.
	Le Februe, Peter	**62**	*For* 12th April *read* 13th April.
334	Lee, Edward	**168**	*For* 1672 *read* 1673.
	Lee, John	**9432**	*For* 9432 *read* 9437.
335	Leighton, Sir Ellis	**153**	*For* 1667 *read* 1668.
338	Lardet, John	**1040**	*For* Lardet *read* Liardet; re-position entry.
343	Lockhead, James	**12081**	*For* Lockhead *read* Lochhead; re-position entry.
355	MacInnes, John	**12831**	*For* 12831 *read* 12381.
360	Malzel, John	**3966**	*For* Malzel *read* Maelzel; re-position entry.
364	Marshall, Ralph	**286**	*For* 2nd January *read* 11th January.
369	Matthew, Daniel Dering	**3125**	*For* Matthew *read* Mathew; re-position entry.
375	Mell, James	**309**	*Before* 1692 *insert* 18th March.
376	Merchant, Alexander	**138**	*For* 1662 *read* 1663.
377	Merryweather, John	**4006**	*For* 1316 *read* 1816.
379	Miller, John	**4**	*For* 1st July *read* 3rd November.
384	Mollerston, Charles	**2814**	*For* Mollerston *read* Mollersten.
385	Moore, Bryan	**498**	*For* 21st May *read* 21st June.
388	Morland, Sir Samuel	**151**	*For* 1667 *read* 1668.
398	Neade, William	**69**	*For* 16th May *read* 12th May.
	Neale, Thomas	**273**	*For* 15th September *read* 5th September.
		292	*Before* 1692 *insert* 17th February.
408	Newton, William Edward	**12791**	*For* 12791 *read* 11791.
409	Newton, William Edward	**13974**	*For* 1851 *read* 1852.
410	Nickels, Christopher	**80021**	*For* 80021 *read* 8002; *for* 1838 *read* 1839.
415	Nott, Benedict	**6205**	*Before* Benedict *insert* Joel.
	Nott, Joel Benedick	**6026**	*For* Benedick *read* Benedict.
420	Osborn, William Henry	**4105**	*Delete* William.
422	Palmer, Andrew	**23**	*For* 1623 *read* 1624.
423	Palmer, Mathew	**457**	*For* 22nd September 1723 *read* 4th September 1722.
426	Parker, Thomas	**49**	*For* 1630 *read* 1631.
428	Parkin, Thomas	**6940**	*For* 1855 *read* 1835.

Page	Name	Progressive number	Correction
433	Pease, Robert	**383**	*Before* 1708 *insert* 27th August.
446	Pitts, Nicholas	**144**	*For* 1664 *read* 1665.
	Plant, Reuben	**12705**	*For* 12705 *read* 12706
457	Poyntz, Captain John	**320**	*For* 17th April *read* 27th April.
		327	*For* 24th October *read* 24th November.
462	Puckle, Thomas	**317**	*For* 7th March *read* 10th March.
466	Ramsey, David	**6**	*For* 1618 *read* 1619.
		49	*For* 1630 *read* 1631.
		50	*For* 1630 *read* 1631.
		68	*For* 1634 *read* 1635.
		78	*For* 1635 *read* 1636.
468	Rapburne, Aaron	**1**	*For* Rapburne *read* Rathburne; *for* 2nd March 1617 *read* 11th March 1618.
477	Richardson, Charles	**6823**	*For* Richardson *read* Rickards; re-position entry.
478	Riddele, William	**12383**	*For* Riddele *read* Riddle.
491	Rowe, Jacob	**431**	*For* 20th October *read* 12th October.
494	Rupert, His Highness Prince	**161**	*For* 1670 *read* 1671.
		162	*For* 1671 *read* 1672.
502	Savery, Thomas	**379**	*For* 1706 *read* 20th February 1707.
	Sawton, Samuel	**210**	*For* 1680 *read* 1681.
	Scandalarus, Nicholas	**80**	*For* 1635 *read* 1636.
506	Searle, Henry	**214**	*For* Searle *read* Serle; re-position entries.
		215	
511	Sharpey, Sir Robert	**52**	*For* September 1630 *read* 2nd October 1630.
512	Shawe, John	**251**	*For* Shawe *read* Chater; re-position entry.
	Shawe, Ralph	**541**	*For* 24th May *read* 24th April.
514	Sherrard, William	**261**	*For* 4th November *read* 23rd November.
515	Shipman, William	**28**	*For* 27th January 1624 *read* 22nd January 1625.
524	Smith, Anthony Forester	**310**	*Before* 1692 *insert* 24th March.
526	Smith, James	**160**	*For* 1670 *read* 1671.
532	Sneath, William	**7326**	*For* 7326 *read* 7236.
	Sorocold, George	**369**	*For* 1703 *read* 1704.
	Spears, Alexander	**9980**	*For* 9980 *read* 9880.
535	Spencer, Arnold	**36**	*For* 1627 *read* 1628.
539	Stapleton, John	**318**	*For* 17th March *read* 13th April.
552	Sutton, William	**275**	*Before* 1691 *insert* 15th September.
554	Sylvanus, George	**322**	*Before* April *insert* 22nd.
563	Teshmaker, John Englebert	**286**	*For* 2nd January 1962 *read* 11th January 1762.
567	Thomson, Tully	**7872**	*For* Tully *read* Sally.
	Thomson, William	**8878**	*For* 8878 *read* 8778.
570	Tilson, Thomas	**140**	*For* 1662 *read* 1663.
571	Togood, Thomas	**132**	*For* 1661 *read* 1662.

Page	Name	Progressive number	Correction
572	Togood, Thomas	139	*For* August 1662 *read* 17th September 1663.
		142	*For* 1663 *read* 1664.
	Tomlyn, George	128	*For* 5th February 1660 *read* 1st February 1661
		137	*For* 1662 *read* 1663.
	Tookey, Thomas	103	*For* 1637 *read* 1638.
580	Tyssen, Francis	279	*Before* October *insert* 17th.
	Tyzacke, John	309	*Before* 1692 *insert* March.
		331	*For* February *read* January.
587	Vincent, Henry	215	*For* 29th August *read* 19th August.
	Vivyan, Hannyball	67	*For* Vivyan Hannyball *read* Vyvyan Haniball; re-position entry.
589	Wagoner, Fredericke	119	*For* 18th July *read* 18th June.
593	Walter, Robert	9733	*For* Walter *read* Walker; re-position entry.
594	Walton, Samuel	156	*For* 1668 *read* 1669.
598	Watson, Francis	145	*For* 1664 *read* 1665.
		154	*For* 1667 *read* 1668.
600	Wayne, Ralphe	135	*For* 19th March 1662 *read* 12th March 1663.
600	Weale, John	215	*For* 29th August *read* 19th August.
	Weale, Samuel	215	*For* 29th August *read* 19th August.
604	Wells, John	167	*For* 1672 *read* 1673.
	Wemis, James	136	*For* 1662 *read* 1663.
608	Wheeler, William	127	*For* 24th June *read* 28th June.
614	Wigley, Thomas	6437	*For* Wigley *read* Wrigley; re-position entry.
615	Wildgoose, Thomas	6	*For* 1618 *read* 1619.
620	Williams, John	308	*Before* 1692 *insert* 24th March.
623	Willis, Richard	29	*For* 1624 *read* 1625.
	Willoughby, Lord Francis	141	*For* 1663 *read* 1664.
628	Winchester, James	9560	*For* 1741 *read* 1842
631	Wolfen, John Jasper	4	*For* 1st July *read* 3rd November.
637	Worcester, Edward	131	*For* 1661 *read* 1662.

ALPHABETICAL INDEX

OF

PATENTEES OF INVENTIONS,

FROM MARCH 2, 1617 (14 JAMES I.) TO OCTOBER 1, 1852 (16 VICTORIÆ).

ALPHABETICAL INDEX

OF

PATENTEES OF INVENTIONS.

Name of Patentee.	Progressive Number.	Date.		Subject-matter of Patent.

A.

Name of Patentee.	Progressive Number.	Date.		Subject-matter of Patent.
ABBÉ ALLANSON - - -	10,801	4th Aug.	1845	Apparatus for preventing and alleviating spinal disorders.
ABBEY, RICHARD - - -	6035	21st Feb.	1831	Preparing the leaf of a British plant for producing a healthy beverage by infusion.
ABBEY, RICHARD - - -	12,227	29th July	1848	Preserving fermented and other liquids and matters in vessels.
ABBOTT, BENJAMIN - -	6240	8th March	1832	Machinery for making stockings, stocking net or frame-work knitting, warp web, warp net, and point net.
ABBOTT, WILLIAM, junior -	8176	1st Aug.	1839	Manufacture of felt.
ABERY, JOHN - - -	1405	8th Dec.	1783	Coach-box, to be fixed to the bodies of coaches, chariots, and other carriages.
ABLON, EUGENE - - -	12,112	8th April	1848	Increasing the draft in chimneys of locomotive or other engines.
ABRAHAM, HENRY ROBERT -	7685	14th June	1838	Apparatus for regulating the supply of water and other liquids, and the quantity delivered into receivers.
ABRAHAM, HENRY ROBERT -	7921	3rd Jan.	1839	Apparatus applicable to steam-boilers.
ACKERMAN, PAUL - -	10,914	3rd Nov.	1845	Harpoons and other similar instruments.
ACKERMANN, RUDOLPH -	2491	28th April	1801	Waterproofing woollen-cloths, cotton, linen, silk, hats, paper, and other manufactures.
ACKERMANN, RUDOLPH [Akerman, Rudolph.]	4212	27th Jan.	1818	Axletrees for four-wheeled carriages.
ACKROYD, WILLIAM -	12,903	19th Dec.	1849	Dressing and cleaning worsted, and worsted mixed with cotton and other fabrics, after they have been woven.
ACKROYD, WILLIAM -	14,250	31st July	1852	Manufacture of yarn and fabrics, when cotton-wool and silk are employed.
ACRAMAN, DANIEL WADE -	4499	16th Oct.	1820	Manufacturing chains and chain-cables, and forming materials for the purpose.
ACRAMAN, DANIEL WADE -	4774	12th April	1823	Preparation of iron for chains and chain-cables.
ACRAMAN, WILLIAM -	4499	16th Oct.	1820	Manufacturing chains and chain-cables, and forming materials for the purpose.
ADAM, JAMES - - -	3509	26th Nov.	1811	Drying malt and all kinds of grain and seeds.
ADAM, QUINTIN MC -	2924	26th March	1806	Dressing yarns for weaving, by means of a machine.
ADAMS, BENJAMIN - -	2011	13th Sept.	1794	Making shoe-catches with spring straps, to be used with buckle rings.
ADAMS, DUDLEY - -	2155	23rd Jan.	1797	Spectacles, removing all pressure from the temple and nose.
ADAMS, DUDLEY - -	2407	30th May	1800	Making telescopes portable.

Name of Patentee.	Progressive Number.	Date.	Subject-matter of Patent.
ADAMS, DUDLEY - - -	3889	7th March 1815	Construction of paper and vellum tubes for telescopes; optical parts of telescopes.
ADAMS, GEORGE - - -	656	25th May 1750	Quadrant for taking the altitude of the sun or moon by refraction; also a refracting telescope with four spherical lenses.
ADAMS, GEORGE - - -	3350	19th June 1810	Feeding cattle and sheep in houses built for their protection from the weather, and moveable by means of wheels and slides, iron railways or otherwise; preserving the manure from such cattle and sheep, and applying it in the cultivation of land.
ADAMS, HENRY W. - -	13,645	29th May 1851	Means of generating galvanic electricity; of decomposing water or various electrolytes; of collecting hydrogen; of burning it, or atmospheric air, separately or in combination.
ADAMS, ROBERT - - -	3716	7th July 1813	Preparing blacking.
ADAMS, ROBERT - - -	13,527	24th Feb. 1851	Rifles and other fire-arms.
ADAMS, SAMUEL - - -	12,328	16th Nov. 1848	Mills for grinding.
ADAMS, STEDMAN - - -	3299	1st Feb. 1810	Steam-engines; and distillation.
ADAMS, STEDMAN - - -	3441	1st May 1811	Application of mechanical powers to the propelling of ships and vessels through the water.
ADAMS, THOMAS - - -	5648	6th May 1828	Instruments, trusses, or apparatus, for the relief or cure of hernia or rupture.
ADAMS, WILLIAM BRIDGES -	6790	13th March 1835	Construction of wheels for carriages in which springs are used.
ADAMS, WILLIAM BRIDGES -	7212	20th Oct. 1836	Wheel-carriages.
ADAMS, WILLIAM BRIDGES -	8197	16th Aug. 1839	Construction of wheel-carriages;—partly applicable to machinery for propelling, and also for the purpose of securing ships and other vessels, and for communicating motion between different portions of machinery.
ADAMS, WILLIAM BRIDGES -	8756	28th Dec. 1840	Construction of wheel-carriages, and appendages thereto.
ADAMS, WILLIAM BRIDGES -	11,445	12th Nov. 1846	Construction of wheel-carriages, and engines moved or retarded by animal or mechanical agency;—partly applicable to other like purposes.
ADAMS, WILLIAM BRIDGES -	11,715	24th May 1847	Construction of railways; engines, and carriages used thereon; also transport and storage arrangements for the conveyance, management, and preservation of perishable articles.
ADAMS, WILLIAM BRIDGES -	13,653	3rd June 1851	Construction of roads and ways, buildings, bridges, locomotive engines, and carriages;—partly applicable to other purposes.
ADAMSON, DANIEL - -	14,259	12th Aug. 1852	Construction of steam-engines and steam-boilers, also method of using and rarifying steam;—partly applicable to marine, locomotive, and other boilers and marine architecture, as well as in cisterns, tanks, and similar articles.
ADAMSON, WILLIAM - -	3972	22nd Dec. 1815	Application of water to move an horizontal wheel about its axis, with more power than if applied in any other position.
ADCOCK, HENRY - - -	4901	19th Feb. 1824	Making umbilical, ventral, lumbar, and spinal bandages or supporters to be permanently or occasionally fixed to clothes.

Name of Patentee.	Progressive Number.	Date.	Subject-matter of Patent.
ADCOCK, HENRY - - -	6924	5th Nov. 1835	Docks and quays, to facilitate the importation and exportation of merchandise.
ADCOCK, HENRY - - -	6997	5th Feb. 1836	Loading and unloading ships, brigs, schooners, and other vessels, especially colliers.
ADCOCK, HENRY - - -	7248	9th Dec. 1836	Raising water from mines and deep places.
ADCOCK, HENRY - - -	7272	11th Jan. 1837	Construction of furnaces for the reduction of metallic ores, which furnaces are applicable to other purposes; processes in the iron manufacture.
ADCOCK, HENRY - - -	7648	22nd May 1838	Raising water from mines, and other deep places, or from a lower level to a higher;—applicable to raising liquids generally, and to other purposes.
ADCOCK, HENRY - - -	8759	30th Dec. 1840	Apparatus for condensing, concentrating, and evaporating aëriform and other fluids.
ADCOCK, HENRY - - -	12,174	3rd June 1848	Furnaces and fireplaces.
ADCOCK, HENRY - - -	13,788	23rd Oct. 1851	Manufacture of pipes, chimney-pots, and hollow vessels; also bricks, tiles, copings, columns, and other articles.
ADDAMS, ROBERT - -	5310	14th Dec. 1825	Propelling carriages on turnpike, rail, or other roads.
ADDENBROOKE, JOSEPH -	13,891	8th Jan. 1852	Manufacture of envelopes; machinery used therein.
ADDISON, THOMAS - -	291	29th Feb. 1692	Use of sea-coal and pit coal for smelting iron ore, stone, flags, cinders, old iron and other materials, and for refining and making the same into good bar iron, also into guns, bullets, and other utensils.
ADDISON, WILLIAM BROOK -	9253	10th Feb. 1842	Machinery for spinning worsted and woollen yarn.
ADEY, GEORGE - -	4158	12th Aug. 1817	Frames for shearing or cropping woollen and other cloths; and fixing the shears in said frames.
ADIE, ALEXANDER - - -	4323	23rd Dec. 1818	Sympiesometer, or improved air barometer.
ADKIN, JOSEPH, jun. - -	1007	14th March 1772	Machine or engine for stamping and printing paper, also silk, woollen, cotton, and linen cloths, and other fabrics of silk, wool, cotton, or linen.
ADKIN, JOSEPH, sen. - -	1007	14th March 1772	Machine or engine for stamping and printing paper, also silk, woollen, cotton, and linen cloths, and other fabrics of silk, wool, cotton, or linen.
ADOR, AMBROISE - - -	7547	20th Jan. 1838	Producing or obtaining motive-power.
ADOR, AMBROISE - - -	7576	24th Feb. 1838	Lamps or apparatus for producing or affording light.
ADOR, AMBROISE - - -	7803	13th Sept. 1838	Lamps or apparatus for producing or affording light.
ADOR, AMBROISE - - -	12,863	24th Nov. 1849	Producing light.
ADORNO, JUAN NEPOMUCENO -	11,094	17th Feb. 1846	Manufacturing cigars and other similar articles.
ADORNO, JUAN NEPOMUCENO -	11,593	24th Feb. 1847	Manufacturing cigars and other similar articles.
ADORNO, JUAN NEPOMUCENO -	13,203	31st July 1850	Manufacturing cigars and other similar articles.
ADORNO, JUAN NEPOMUCENO -	13,481	31st Jan. 1851	Construction of maps and globes; apparatus for mounting the same.
AERSKIN, WILLIAM - -	177	24th Dec. 1674	Engine without oars, for lowering ships and vessels out of and into rivers and harbours, when obstructed by contrary winds.

Name of Patentee.	Progressive Number.	Date.	Subject-matter of Patent.
AFFLECK, THOMAS - - -	6367	19th Jan. 1833	Means and machinery for deepening and excavating the beds of rivers, removing sandbanks, bars, and other obstructions to navigation.
AFFLECK, THOMAS - - -	6522	11th Dec. 1833	Means and machinery for deepening and excavating the beds of rivers, removing sandbanks, bars, and other obstructions to navigation.
AFLECK, ALEXANDER - -	2469	3rd Feb. 1801	Preparing and manufacturing flax, hemp, silk, and other materials.
AFLECK, ALEXANDER - -	2607	8th April 1802	Preparing and manufacturing flax, hemp, silk, and other materials.
AGAR, THOMAS - - -	254	13th Aug. 1687	Manufacture of milled lead, for sheathing and preservation of ships or any other thing.
AIKEN, ARTHUR - - -	4456	11th May 1820	Preventing mildew in sailcloth and other canvas, and in other manufactures made of vegetable fibre.
AIKMAN, JAMES - - -	13,897	20th Jan. 1852	Treating or finishing textile fabrics and materials.
AINGWORTH, BENJAMIN - -	6155	30th Aug. 1831	Making and constructing buttons.
AINGWORTH, BENJAMIN - -	9115	7th Oct. 1841	Manufacture of buttons.
AINGWORTH, BENJAMIN - -	9378	4th June 1842	Manufacture of glass to be used for purposes to which plate-glass and window glass are usually applied.
AINGWORTH, BENJAMIN - -	10,036	6th Feb. 1844	Manufacturing buttons for wearing-apparel.
AINGWORTH, BENJAMIN - -	12,732	1st Aug. 1849	Ornamenting iron and other metals for use in the manufacture of gun-barrels and other articles.
AINSLIE, JOHN - - -	8965	22nd May 1841	Moulding tiles, bricks, retorts, and similar articles, from clay and other plastic substances.
AINSLIE, JOHN - - -	9886	30th Sept. 1843	Drying tiles, bricks, retorts, and similar articles made from clay and other plastic substances.
AINSLIE, JOHN - - -	10,481	18th Jan. 1845	Apparatus and arrangements for the manufacture of tiles and similar articles from clay and other plastic matter.
AINSLIE, JOHN - - -	11,155	31st March 1846	Apparatus for the manufacture of bricks; arrangements for the manufacture of bricks, tiles, and similar articles from clay and other plastic substances.
AINSLIE, JOHN - - -	13,376	30th Nov. 1850	Arrangements and apparatus for the manufacture of bricks, tiles, and other articles made from clay and other plastic substances;—partly applicable to the treatment and preparation of earths, minerals, and animal and vegetable matters.
AINSWORTH, JOHN HORROCKS	7948	24th Jan. 1839	Machinery or apparatus for stretching, drying, and finishing woven fabrics.
AITCHISON, JOHN - - -	5848	15th Sept. 1829	Concentrating and evaporating cane-juice, solutions of sugar, and other fluids.
AITCHISON, JOHN - - -	8550	24th June 1840	Generating and condensing steam; heating, cooling, and evaporating fluids.
AITKEN, JOHN - - -	1270	5th Dec. 1780	Loading guns or fire-arms with two or more charges of gunpowder and shot, or balls, and discharging the same successively.
AITKEN, JOHN - - -	10,078	24th Feb. 1844	Atmospheric railways.
AITKEN, JOHN - - -	10,141	10th April 1844	Water-engines and steam-engines, and the mode of traction on or in canals, waters, or ways.

Name of Patentee.	Progressive Number.	Date.	Subject-matter of Patent.
AITKEN, JOHN - - -	11,713	22nd May 1847	Steam engines, and atmospheric engines; distilling, and pumping water.
AITKEN, THOMAS - - -	7073	26th April 1836	Preparation of cotton and other fibrous substances; and conveyance of the same to roving-frames, mules, throstles, &c.
AITKEN, THOMAS - - -	8363	28th Jan. 1840	Machinery for drawing cotton and other fibrous substances.
AITKEN, WILLIAM - - - [Aitkin, William.]	5924	30th March 1830	Preservation of beer, ale, and other fermented liquors.
AITKEN, WILLIAM - - -	6772	25th Feb. 1835	Construction of carriages to be propelled by animal or other power.
AITKEN, WILLIAM - - -	11,336	15th Aug. 1846	Two and four wheeled carriages.
AITKEN, WILLIAM COSTON -	10,701	3rd June 1845	Ornamenting cornices, ends for cornice poles and other rods, curtain bands, and other articles.
ALBANO, BENEDICT - -	9890	5th Oct. 1843	Preparing materials and applying them to the manufacture of ornamental mouldings.
ALBEMARLE, His Grace the [Duke of.	255	23rd Aug. 1687	Saw-mills, or engines for clearing timber from off the ground.
ALBERT, DOMINIC FRICK -	8826	1st Feb. 1841	Combination of materials, and processes in the manufacture of fuel.
ALBERT, DOMINIC FRICK -	9442	10th Aug. 1842	Combination of materials for manufacturing a manuring powder.
ALBERT, DOMINIC FRICK -	10,598	7th April 1845	Manufacture of candles.
ALBERT, DOMINIC FRICK -	10,741	28th June 1845	Application of materials to the manufacture of soap.
ALBRIGHT, ARTHUR - -	13,695	17th July 1851	Manufacture of phosphorus; apparatus to be used therein.
ALCOCK, GEORGE BARTON -	2903	23rd Jan. 1806	Lamps.
ALCOCK, THOMAS - - -	6059	13th Jan. 1831	Machinery for making lace called bobbin-net.
ALCOCK, THOMAS - - -	6197	15th Dec. 1831	Machinery for making bobbin-net lace.
ALCOCK, THOMAS - - -	6343	8th Dec. 1832	Machinery for making bobbin-net lace.
ALCOCK, THOMAS - - -	6344	8th Dec. 1832	Machinery for making bobbin-net lace.
ALCOCK, THOMAS - - -	6764	12th Feb. 1835	Machinery for making bobbin-net lace.
ALCOCK, THOMAS - - -	7032	17th March 1836	Machinery for making ornamental bobbin-net lace.
ALDERSEY, ROBERT - -	219	17th June 1682	Engine for raising water out of wells, pits, or mines.
ALDERSEY, ROBERT - -	377	6th June 1706	Floating dam for carrying lighters and other vessels, over flats and shallows in rivers.
ALDERSEY, THOMAS - -	983	26th Feb. 1771	Machine for grinding and polishing plate-glass.
ALDERSEY, WILLIAM - -	4534	3rd Feb. 1821	Steam-engine, and other machinery where the crank is used.
ALDERSON, GEORGE - -	2749	26th Jan. 1804	Manufacture of metal pipes, the same being lead lined with tin.
ALDERSON, HENRY - -	12,393	28th Dec. 1848	Smelting copper.
ALDOUS, JAMES - - -	6770	25th Feb. 1835	Steam-engines.
ALDRICH, HORATIO NELSON -	7341	15th April 1837	Spinning, twisting, doubling, or otherwise preparing cotton, silk, and other fibrous substances.
ALEGRE, PIERRE - - -	5006	7th Oct. 1824	Generating steam.
ALEXANDER, GEORGE - -	3646	4th Feb. 1813	Suspending the card of the mariner's compass.
ALEXANDER, ISAAC - -	13,847	8th Dec. 1851	Preparing and treating certain kinds of cheese, to render the same applicable to a variety of culinary and other domestic purposes.

Name of Patentee.	Progressive Number.	Date.		Subject-matter of Patent.
ALISON, WILLIAM - - -	2285	4th Jan.	1799	Making Spanish or Morocco leather.
ALLABONE, RICHARD - -	6392	27th Feb.	1833	Machinery used in the manufacture of bobbin-net lace for the purpose of producing ornamental lace.
ALLAIRE, RENE - - -	10,156	24th April	1844	Cleansing gentlemen's garments.
ALLAN, ALEXANDER - -	11,718	27th May	1847	Turn-tables on or in connection with railways;—applicable to the construction of tubular boilers.
ALLAN, THOMAS - - -	13,352	16th Nov.	1850	Electric-telegraphs; application of electric currents for deflecting magnets, or producing electro-magnets.
ALLAN, THOMAS - - -	13,446	11th Jan.	1851	Paving or covering roads, streets, and other surfaces.
ALLAN, THOMAS - - -	14,190	24th June	1852	Producing and applying electricity; apparatus employed therein.
ALLARTON, GEORGE - -	9151	11th Nov.	1841	Balling and blooming iron.
ALLEMAND, CHARLES - -	13,347	14th Nov.	1850	Apparatus for producing light.
ALLEN, GEORGE NECKLESON -	1535	27th Feb.	1786	Capstan.
ALLEN, JOHN - - -	513	7th Aug.	1729	Heating water for driving engines, and for brewing, distilling, &c.; application of powers to move engines for navigating ships, and draining mines; drying malt.
ALLEN, MATTHEW - - -	10,503	30th Jan.	1845	Stoves, and apparatus for heating.
ALLEN, SAMUEL, junior -	13,487	1st Feb.	1851	Manufacture of buttons.
ALLEN, WILLIAM - - -	3640	15th Jan.	1813	Machinery to be worked by wind.
ALLEN, WILLIAM - - -	4431	15th Jan.	1820	Pianofortes.
ALLEN, WILLIAM - - -	6140	20th July	1831	Pianofortes.
ALLIER, THOMAS VICTOR -	10,998	10th Dec.	1845	Breaks or machinery for stopping or retarding carriages.
ALLINGHAM, JAMES - -	11,162	7th April	1846	Steam-engines.
ALLINGHAM, THOMAS - -	4228	19th Feb.	1818	Economical and universal lamp.
ALLIOTT, ALEXANDER - -	9652	2nd March	1843	Apparatus for drying woollen, cotton, silk, and different fibrous materials and other substances, and stretching certain fibrous materials.
ALLIOTT, ALEXANDER - -	10,059	19th Feb.	1844	Fulling, stretching, drying, and dressing goods made of cotton-wool, silk, and other fibrous materials.
ALLIOTT, ALEXANDER - -	10,070	24th Feb.	1844	Scouring, bleaching, and dyeing.
ALLIOTT, ALEXANDER - -	12,090	8th March	1848	Apparatus used in the working of steam-boilers; apparatus for cleaning flues.
ALLIOTT, ALEXANDER - -	12,095	14th March	1848	Spring apparatus and balances; breaks, and the means of working them.
ALLIOTT, ALEXANDER - -	12,575	17th April	1849	Apparatus for registering the force of wind, water and steam, weight of goods, and velocity of carriages.
ALLIOTT, ALEXANDER - -	13,490	3rd Feb.	1851	Cleaning, dyeing, and drying machines, and machinery used in sugar, soap, metal, and colour manufacturing.
ALLISON, JAMES - - -	8523	30th May	1840	Iron knees for ships and vessels.
ALLMAN, FENNEL - - -	9755	3rd June	1843	Apparatus for the production and diffusion of light.
ALLMAN, FENNELL - - -	11,690	4th May	1847	Making, forming, or shaping candles.
ALLMAN, FENNELL - - -	12,276	28th Sept.	1848	Apparatus for the production of light from electricity.

Name of Patentee.	Progressive Number.	Date.	Subject-matter of Patent.
ALLPORT, SAMUEL - - -	12,608	14th May 1849	Manufacturing a part or parts of looms used in weaving.
ALLWRIGHT, JAMES - -	4637	14th Jan. 1822	Keyed musical instrument.
ALMONDE, OTTO C. VON -	8701	12th Nov. 1840	Production of mosaic work from wood.
ALPHEY, GODFREY - - -	2547	3rd Nov. 1801	Waterproofing hats and caps; also leather, cotton, linen, silks, stuffs, pasteboard, and other manufactures and substances, for the purpose of being worked up into shoes, boots, hats, bonnets, and other wearing-apparel.
ALPIN, THOMAS MC - -	13,055	23rd April 1850	Machinery for washing cotton, linen, and other fabrics.
ALSOP, ROBERT - • -	955	22nd March 1770	Loom-embroidery, manufactured in gold or silver, on silk ribbon and woollen, linen, cotton, or mohair.
ALSOP, WILLIAM - • -	10,407	25th Nov. 1844	Manufacture of elastic fabrics; making articles from elastic fabrics; weaving fabrics for driving-bands of machinery and other uses.
ALSTON, JAMES - - -	1511	19th Nov. 1785	Lining, edging, plating, and covering buckles and other articles made of iron, copper, or other metals or mixed metals, with silver or gold, by the application of tin or alloyed tin.
ALSTON, JAMES - - -	1624	30th Oct. 1787	Making buttons of iron or steel covered with tin and other metal, or tin alone.
ALTREE, FREDERICK - -	13,842	5th Dec. 1851	Means of and apparatus for heating ovens.
ALZARD, GILBERT CLAUDE -	9498	22nd Oct. 1842	Bread, biscuits, macaroni, vermicelli and pastry, and mode of making the same.
AMATT, ANTHONY - - -	2059	3rd Aug. 1795	Machine for combing wool and heckling flax and hemp, which machine may be worked by water, steam, or horse-mills, or any other moving power.
AMBERGER, JEAN PIERRE PAUL	13,269	3rd Oct. 1850	Application of magnetic power for moving and stopping carriages, for giving adherence to wheels upon rails, and for transmitting motion.
AMBLER, JAMES - - -	10,102	14th March 1844	Machinery for applying fringes to shawls and other articles.
AMBLER, JAMES - - [Ambler, James, senior.]	10,646	1st May 1845	Preparing and combing wool.
AMBLER, JAMES - - -	13,950	2nd Feb. 1852	Preparing and combing wool and other fibrous materials.
AMBROSE, SAMUEL - - -	924	5th May 1769	Pump worked by a roll or sheave placed in an aperture in the spear.
AMESBURY, JOSEPH - -	7337	4th April 1837	Apparatus for relief of stiffness, weakness, or distortion of the human spine, chest, or limbs.
AMESBURY, JOSEPH - -	8008	20th March 1839	Apparatus for the support of the human body.
AMESBURY, JOSEPH - -	10,659	6th May 1845	Apparatus for the relief of stiffness, weakness, or distortion in the human body.
AMIES, JOSEPH - - -	6312	29th Sept. 1832	Construction of apparatus to be employed in making paper.
AMIES, NATHANIEL JONES -	13,488	1st Feb. 1851	Manufacture of braid; machinery connected therewith.
AMIES, NATHANIEL JONES -	14,261	12th Aug. 1852	Manufacture of braid; machinery connected therewith.
AMMONETT, FRANCIS - -	221	29th July 1682	Manufacture of draped milled stockings.
AMOS, CHARLES EDWARDS -	8698	10th Nov. 1840	Manufacture of paper.

Name of Patentee.	Progressive Number.	Date.	Subject-matter of Patent.
AMOS, CHARLES EDWARDS	12,836	10th Nov. 1849	Manufacture of paper; apparatus and machinery used therein;—part of which machinery is applicable for regulating the pressure of fluids for various purposes.
ANASPIE, PATRICK Mᶜ	14,339	2nd Nov. 1852	Manufacture of Portland stone, cement and other composition, for general building purposes and hydraulic works.
ANDERSON, ADAM	3287	14th Dec. 1809	Portable stove or furnace, of cast-iron, forged or plate-iron, or other metals.
ANDERSON, ALFRED GEORGE	13,051	20th April 1850	Treatment of a substance produced in soap-making, and its application to useful purposes.
ANDERSON, DAVID	6798	25th March 1835	Machinery for making healds.
ANDERSON, FREDERICK BUO-[NAPARTE.	13,367	30th Nov. 1850	Spectacles.
ANDERSON, JAMES	2474	10th Feb. 1801	Economizing fuel in the heating of houses; improving the construction of hothouses.
ANDERSON, JAMES	8916	5th April 1841	Windlasses.
ANDERSON, JAMES	12,324	11th Nov. 1848	Separating different qualities of potatoes and other vegetables.
ANDERSON, JOHN BARKER	10,400	25th Nov. 1844	Manufacture of soap.
ANDERSON, Sir JAMES CALEB	6147	3rd Aug. 1831	Machinery for propelling vessels on water, and for other purposes.
ANDERSON, Sir JAMES CALEB	7407	19th July 1837	Locomotive-engines;—partly applicable to other purposes.
ANDERSON, Sir JAMES CALEB	11,273	29th June 1846	Obtaining motive-power, and applying it to propel carriages and vessels, and drive machinery.
ANDERSON, SPOLE ROSENBORGH	6869	28th July 1835	Hand and power looms.
ANDERSON, WILLIAM	11,423	22nd Oct. 1846	Machinery for preparing and spinning cotton and other fibrous substances.
ANDERTON, GEORGE	5343	4th March 1826	Combing or dressing wool and waste silk.
ANDREW, CHARLES	12,978	21st Feb. 1850	Method of and machinery for preparing warps for weaving.
ANDREW, JAMES	9255	15th Feb. 1842	Dressing yarns or warps for weaving.
ANDREW, JOHN	1053	31st Aug. 1773	Balance (static and hydrostatic) for weighing without weight or scale, and finding the value of gold.
ANDREW, JONATHAN	5079	11th Jan. 1825	Construction of a machine for throstle and water spinning of yarn from cotton, flax, silk, wool, or other fibrous substances.
ANDREWS, FREDERICK	5438	20th Dec. 1826	Construction of carriages, and engines to propel the same by steam, or other suitable power.
ANDREWS, JOHN	1719	23rd Dec. 1789	Fish-hooks of a superior strength, colour, and polish.
ANDREWS, JOHN	14,210	6th July 1852	Coke-ovens, and apparatus connected therewith.
ANDREWS, JONATHAN	1134	11th Sept. 1776	Powder for cleansing woollen-cloth, and extracting paint stains and grease.
ANDREWS, PHINEAS	3176	31st Oct. 1808	Thrashing corn, grain, pulse, and all kinds of seed.
ANDREWS, SOLOMON	14,315	7th Oct. 1852	Machinery for cutting, punching, stamping, forging, and bending metals, and other substances;—applicable to driving piles, and other similar purposes, also crushing and pulveriring ores and other hard substances.

Name of Patentee.	Progressive Number.	Date.	Subject-matter of Patent.
ANDREWS, WILLIAM - -	13,598	24th April 1851	Steam-engines, boilers, pumps, safety valves, and wheels and axles.
ANDREWS, WILLIAM WARD -	8328	2nd Feb. 1841	Raising and lowering windows and window-blinds, opening and shutting doors;—applicable to raising and lowering maps, curtains, and other articles.
ANDREWS, WILLIAM WARD -	9035	21st July 1841	Coffee-pot.
ANGEL, LAWRENCE - -	4822	24th July 1823	Bleaching linen or cotton yarn or cloth.
ANGELL, ALBERT - - -	1277	24th Jan. 1781	Elastic gum for making colours durable, dressing silk, linen and cotton, in the loom, rendering clay or composition used in modelling, supple, and preventing the same from drying too fast.
ANGELL, JAMES - - -	1636	15th Jan. 1788	Hanging and fixing bells, bolts, and door-latches, with wheels and chains instead of cranks.
ANGELL, JUSTINIAN - -	183	25th Oct. 1675	Maintenance of two lighthouses.
ANGELY, PAUL D' - - -	13,097	4th June 1850	Construction of privies and urinals; apparatus and machinery for cleansing privies, cess-pools, and other places; deodorising the matter extracted therefrom, and rendering it available for agricultural purposes.
ANGILBERT, PIERRE ANTOINE	6432	1st June 1833	Preserving animal and vegetable substances.
ANNES, JOHN - - -	8795	16th Jan. 1841	Making paint from materials not before used for that purpose.
ANNESLEY, WILLIAM - -	4240	8th April 1818	Construction of ships, boats, and other vessels.
ANNESLEY, WILLIAM - -	4549	5th April 1821	Construction of ships, boats, and other vessels.
ANNESS, SAMUEL - - -	2900	26th Nov. 1805	Preparing enamel colours, and applying them so prepared to ornamenting vessels of glass.
ANSELL, JAMES - - -	13,319	7th Nov. 1850	Obtaining and applying motive-power; pumps.
ANSELL, ROBERT - - -	1594	20th March 1787	Mixing and preparing colours for printing.
ANSTEY, GEORGE - - -	13,447	11th Jan. 1851	Consuming smoke, and regulating the draft in chimneys.
ANTES, JOHN - - - -	1835	3rd Nov. 1791	Locks, latches, and bolts that strike and catch by means of a spring.
ANTES, JOHN - - - -	2388	10th April 1800	Machine to turn over the leaves of music-books by means of a pedal.
ANTHONY, CHARLES JAMES	12,647	7th June 1849	Means of treating unctuous animal matter.
ANTHONY, WILLIAM - -	2266	10th Nov. 1798	Facilitating the draught of carriages, fixing carriage bodies, tents, and marquees.
ANTLEY, JOSEPH - - -	1541	27th March 1786	Spur, upon an entirely new principle.
APPEL, RUDOLPH - - -	13 717	14th Aug. 1851	Treatment of paper or fabrics, to prevent copies or impressions being taken of any writing or printing thereon.
APPLEBY, CHARLES - -	6891	25th Aug. 1835	Manufacturing files.
APPLEBY, EDWIN - - -	6376	29th Jan. 1833	Steam-engines.
APPLEBY, THOMAS - -	902	13th Aug. 1768	Balsam for the cure of sand or gravel in the bladder or kidneys, also green wounds, and other casualties.
APPLEGATH, AUGUSTUS - [Applegarth, Augustus.]	4249	23rd April 1818	Casting stereotype or other plates for printing; construction of plates for printing bank-notes, or other printed impressions where difficulty of imitation is a desideratum.
APPLEGATH, AUGUSTUS - [Applegarth, Augustus.]	4640	14th Jan. 1822	Printing-machines.

Name of Patentee.	Progressive Number.	Date.		Subject-matter of Patent.
APPLEGATH, AUGUSTUS -	4757	18th Feb.	1823	Printing-machines.
APPLEGATH, AUGUSTUS -	4850	9th Oct.	1823	Machinery for casting types.
APPLEGATH, AUGUSTUS - [Applegarth, Augustus.]	4902	19th Feb.	1824	Machines for printing.
APPLEGATH, AUGUSTUS - [Applegarth, Augustus.]	5613	26th Jan.	1828	Block printing.
APPLEGATH, AUGUSTUS - [Applegarth, Augustus.]	5988	31st Aug.	1830	Printing-machines.
APPLEGATH, AUGUSTUS -	6310	22nd Sept.	1832	Machinery for cutting out wood for carriage wheels, and for cutting and shaping the wheels.
APPLEGATH, AUGUSTUS - [Applegarth, Augustus.]	6318	29th Sept.	1832	Steam-carriages.
APPLEGATH, AUGUSTUS - [Applegarth, Augustus.]	6438	20th June	1833	Construction of railroads, bridges, piers, jetties, and aqueducts.
APPLEGATH, AUGUSTUS -	6450	18th July	1833	Letterpress and block printing; and machinery for the same.
APPLEGATH, AUGUSTUS -	7225	15th Nov.	1836	Printing calicoes and other fabrics.
APPLEGATH, AUGUSTUS -	7647	22nd May	1838	Apparatus for block printing.
APPLEGATH, AUGUSTUS -	11,505	21st Dec.	1846	Machines for printing paper and other fabrics.
APPLEGATH, AUGUSTUS -	13,879	24th Dec.	1851	Machinery used for printing.
APPLETRE, JOHN -	420	23rd May	1718	Raising silk in Great Britain to as great perfection as in any part of Europe.
APPOLD, JOHN GEORGE -	13,586	9th April	1851	Machinery for regulating and ascertaining the labour performed by manual or other power.
APRICE, JOHN -	39	6th Aug.	1627	Engine for the earing, ploughing, and tilling of land, without the use of oxen or horses.
APSDIN, JOSEPH -	5022	21st Oct.	1824	Producing an artificial stone.
APSDIN, JOSEPH -	5180	7th June	1825	Making lime.
APSEY, JOSEPH -	5569	27th Nov.	1827	Substitute for the crank.
APSEY, JOSEPH -	8923	6th April	1841	Construction of flues for steam-boiler and other furnaces.
APSEY, JOSEPH -	12,829	2nd Nov.	1849	Steam-engines; and propelling vessels.
ARCHBALD, WILLIAM AUGUSTUS	6009	13th Oct.	1830	Preparing and making sugar.
ARCHBALD, WILLIAM AUGUSTUS	6569	27th Feb.	1834	Making sugars.
ARCHBOLD, FREDERICK -	3225	18th April	1809	Converting sea or salt water into fresh water, both on land and on board ship.
ARCHBOLD, JOHN FREDERICK	3186	20th Dec.	1808	Distilling brandy from wine, and rectifying the spirit.
ARCHBOLD, JOHN FREDERICK	3240	8th June	1809	Distilling, rectifying, and brewing.
ARCHBOLD, JOHN FREDERICK	4605	1st Nov.	1821	Ventilation of close carriages.
ARCHBOLD, THOMAS -	8948	4th May	1841	Producing ornamental or tambour work in the manufacture of gloves.
ARCHER, HENRY -	12,192	24th June	1848	Matches and the production of light; apparatus to be used therewith.
ARCHER, HENRY -	12,340	23rd Nov.	1848	Facilitating the division of sheets or pieces of paper, parchment, or similar substances.
ARCHER, JOHN ALEXANDER -	13,443	11th Jan.	1851	Manufacture of tobacco.
ARCHER, SAMUEL -	1039	3rd April	1773	Making mock pearl from mother of pearl, shell, and glass.
ARCHER, SAMUEL -	9934	9th Nov.	1843	Manufacture of flannel.
ARCHER, WILLIAM -	14,037	24th March	1852	Preventing accidents on railways.
ARCHIBALD, CHARLES DIXON	13,890	8th Jan.	1852	Manufacture of bricks and other articles made of plastic materials; cutting, shaping, and dressing the same, also stone, wood, and metals; machinery used therein.

Name of Patentee.	Progressive Number.	Date.	Subject-matter of Patent.
ARCHIBALD, JOHN - - -	7161	4th Aug. 1836	Machinery for carding wool, and doffing, straightening, piecing, roving, and drawing, cardings of wool.
ARCY, JOSEPH D' - - -	5719	29th Nov. 1828	Construction of steam-engines; apparatus connected therewith.
ARD, CHARLES - - -	710	9th Sept. 1756	Manufacturing salt.
ARDESORF, CHARLES - -	341	2nd Aug. 1695	Composition for preserving ships from worms.
ARDIT, JEAN MARIE ETIENNE	6149	10th Aug. 1831	Apparatus for drawing, copying, and reducing drawings, and for taking panoramas.
ARGAND, AMI - - - -	1425	15th March 1784	Lamp, producing neither smoke nor smell, and giving more light than any before known.
ARIELL, WILLIAM - - -	3578	25th June 1812	Machinery for extracting corroded iron and other nails and bolts, from ships' bottoms, masts, decks, and any other part thereof.
ARKELL, PETER - - -	13,050	20th April 1850	Manufacture of candle-wicks.
ARKWRIGHT, RICHARD -	931	3rd July 1769	Machinery for the making of weft or yarn from cotton, flax, and wool.
ARKWRIGHT, RICHARD - -	1111	16th Dec. 1775	Preparing silk, cotton, flax, and wool for spinning.
ARMAND, ETIENNE ALEXANDER	13,855	10th Dec. 1851	Distilling and treating organic substances and bituminous matters, and treatment of their products; apparatus used in these processes.
ARMENGAUD, CHARLES - -	10,264	18th July 1844	Apparatus for heating apartments; apparatus for cooking.
ARMITAGE, WILLIAM - -	1907	7th Sept. 1792	Kitchen ranges, stoves, and grates.
ARMITAGE, WILLIAM - -	14,123	8th May 1852	Safety envelope; machinery to be used the manufacture of the same.
ARMSTRONG, GEORGE - -	12,351	2nd Dec. 1848	Steam-engines.
ARMSTRONG, JOHN - - -	12,350	2nd Dec. 1848	Waterclosets
ARMSTRONG, ROBERT - -	7239	3rd Dec. 1836	Water-pressure engine, for raising water and other substances.
ARMSTRONG, WILLIAM - -	7425	28th Aug. 1837	Ploughs.
ARMSTRONG, WILLIAM - -	8083	30th May 1839	Harrows
ARMSTRONG, WILLIAM - -	9474	22nd Sept. 1842	Machinery for ploughing, harrowing, and raking land, and for cutting food for animals.
ARMSTRONG, WILLIAM GEORGE	11,319	31st July 1846	Apparatus for lifting, lowering, and hauling.
ARMSTRONG, WILLIAM GEORGE	12,157	11th May 1848	Water-pressure engine.
AMATT, ANTHONY - - -	2059	3rd Aug. 1795	Machine for combing wool, and heckling flax and hemp.
ARNEY, GERARD ANDREW -	11,045	20th Jan. 1846	Gelatine; and fining or clarifying liquids.
ARNIER, LOUIS - - -	14,341	6th Nov. 1852	Steam-boilers.
ARNOLD, JOHN - - -	1113	30th Dec. 1775	Pendulum spring for time-keepers; and compensating the effects of heat and cold on the same.
ARNOLD, JOHN - - -	1328	2nd May 1782	Escapement and balance, to compensate the effects of heat and cold in pocket-chronometers or watches, also for incurvating the two ends of the helical spring, to render the expansion and contraction of the spring concentric with the centre of the balance.
ARNOLD, JOHN ROGER - -	4531	27th Jan. 1821	Expansion balance for chronometers.
ARNOLD, JOHN - - -	5886	26th Jan. 1830	Spring-latch or fastens for doors.
ARNOLD, MICHAEL - - -	78	17th Feb. 1635	Heating vessels used by brewers, dyers, soap-boilers, salt and saltpetre makers; also drying bricks and tiles, with sea-coals; making and drying tiles, stone-jugs, bottles, melting-pots for goldsmiths, and other earthen commodities, also with sea-coals.

Name of Patentee.	Progressive Number.	Date.	Subject-matter of Patent.
ARNOLD, SAMUEL - - -	1435	19th May 1784	Printing vocal and instrumental music with types.
ARNOLD, STUART - - -	2833	26th March 1805	Chimney safe-guard for the preservation of houses and buildings from fire, robbery, and foul air.
ARNOLD, THOMAS - -	5792	26th May 1829	Gauge for denoting the strength of fluids or spirituous liquors, and for measuring the quantity.
ARNOTT, NEIL - - -	4615	14th Nov. 1821	Production and agency of heat in furnaces, steam and air engines, and in distilling, evaporating, and brewing apparatus.
ARNOTT, NEIL - - -	6459	25th Jan. 1834	Metallic pens and pen-holders.
ARNOUX, CLAUDE - - -	14,177	24th June 1852	Construction of railway-carriages.
ARNOUX, JEAN - - -	1811	28th May 1791	Spinning-wheel for spinning, and, at the same time, reeling or winding flax, hemp, rope-yarn and other articles, from the smallest thread to the largest cable.
ARROTT, ALEXANDER ROBERT-[SON.	10,296	29th Aug. 1844	Recovery of manganese used in making bleaching-powder.
ARROTT, ALEXANDER ROBERT-[SON.	12,016	5th Jan. 1848	Manufacturing common salt.
ARROWSMITH, JOHN - -	4899	10th Feb. 1824	Diorama.
ARROWSMITH, JOHN - -	8130	25th June 1839	Steam-engines.
ARTER, CHARLES - - -	6659	12th Aug. 1834	Taps for drawing off liquids.
ARTENN, JOSE FRANCISCO [CARLOS D'	8022	5th April 1839	Machinery for transmitting power.
ARTHUR, WILLIAM - -	7461	4th Nov. 1837	Spinning hemp, flax, and other fibrous substances.
ASAERT, JOSEPH EUGENE -	12,293	19th Oct. 1848	Obtaining motive-power.
ASCOUGH, JOHN - - -	923	22nd March 1769	Machine for manufacturing combs.
ASDA, AUGUSTE VICTOR JOSEPH [D'.	6591	10th April 1834	Pumps, or machinery for raising water.
ASDA, AUGUSTE VICTOR JOSEPH [Baron D'	7989	6th March 1839	Producing light. ("Solar" light.)
ASH, GEORGE CLAUDIUS -	8986	12th June 1841	Apparatus for fastening candles in candle-sticks.
ASH, HENRY CLARKE - -	9823	6th July 1843	Tea-pots.
ASH, ROBERT - - - -	1300	27th July 1781	Machine fixed to a stocking-frame for making fastened platted work, in silk, cotton, thread, and worsted, or other materials.
ASH, WILLIAM - - -	8552	24th June 1840	Augers or tools for boring.
ASHBURY, JOHN - - -	12,094	11th March 1848	Construction and manufacture of wheels used on railways and common roads; preparing and constructing the tyres used thereon.
ASHBY, JOHN - - -	12,283	12th Oct. 1848	Machinery for cleaning grain and dressing meal.
ASHBY, WILLIAM - - -	11,176	25th April 1846	Manufacture of flour.
ASHDOWNE, JOHN - - -	7093	13th May 1836	Apparatus to be added to wheels, to facilitate the draught of carriages on turnpike and common roads.
ASHE, EDWARD DAVID - -	13,345	14th Nov. 1850	Nautical instrument or instruments; applicable especially to great circle sailing.
ASHE, WILLIAM - - -	11,456	19th Nov. 1846	Cleansing privies, sewers, and drains.
ASHLEY, JOHN - - -	1875	12th May 1792	Self-acting watercloset.
ASHLEY, JOHN - - -	2256	7th Aug. 1798	Raising water from wells.
ASHLEY, JOHN - - -	3472	7th Aug. 1811	Filtering-vessels, for purifying and cleansing water.

Name of Patentee.	Progressive Number.	Date.	Subject-matter of Patent.
ASHLEY, JOHN - - -	3554	15th April 1812	Horizontal and vertical moving roaster.
ASHLEY, ANTHONY Lord -	162	8th Jan. 1671	*Authority to take security from and to administer an oath to workmen not to divulge the patent granted to Prince Rupert. (No. 161, 8th January 1671.)*
ASHMORE, THOMAS -	3957	9th Sept. 1815	Making leather.
ASHTON, ISAAC - - -	1793	24th Feb. 1791	Resisting or sustaining weight or pressure in any lateral or anti-vertical direction.
ASHTON, JOHN - - -	4238	14th March 1818	Apparatus for ascertaining the strength of spirituous liquors, and also the specific-gravity of fluids and metals.
ASHTON, JOHN - - -	7930	11th Jan. 1839	Manufacturing plush of silk and other fibrous materials.
ASHTON, JOHN - - -	8710	21st Nov. 1840	Hat bodies.
ASHTON, JOSEPH - - -	938	7th Nov. 1769	Casting and making coffin-nails and tacks from pig-iron, and tinning the same.
ASHTON, JOSEPH - - -	992	25th June 1771	Casting and making nails, vizt. sheathing, rose, sharp, trunk, bullen, hob, scupper, clout, Flemish, and sparables, from cast-iron.
ASHTON, JOSEPH - - -	1553	5th Aug. 1786	Making and casting buttons and button-shanks.
ASHTON, JOSEPH - - -	3721	14th July 1813	Beaver-hats or light elastic waterproof hats.
ASHTON, SAMUEL - - -	1977	16th Jan. 1794	Tanning hides and skins.
ASHURST, WILLIAM HENRY -	13,046	18th April 1850	Manufacture of varnishes.
ASHWORTH, EDMUND -	6996	5th Feb. 1836	Machinery for preparing and spinning cotton, silk, wool, and other fibrous materials.
ASHWORTH, GEORGE LEACH -	10,992	10th Dec. 1845	Machinery for preparing and spinning cotton and other fibrous substances.
ASHWORTH, JAMES - -	1640	4th March 1788	Towing of ships, sloops, barges and all other vessels upon the water.
ASHWORTH, JAMES - -	1674	6th Nov. 1788	Steam or fire engine with three or more cylinders, and appendages.
ASHWORTH, JAMES - -	2597	24th March 1802	Making iron liquor for the use of dyers and printers.
ASHWORTH, JAMES - -	13,085	29th May 1850	Machinery or apparatus for preparing, spinning, and weaving cotton-wool and other fibrous materials.
ASHWORTH, JOHN - - -	2328	16th July 1799	Stiffening, drying, and finishing dyed muslins.
ASHWORTH, JOHN - - -	13,647	29th May 1851	Method of preventing and removing incrustation in steam-boilers.
ASPINWALL, THOMAS -	4141	16th July 1817	Elliptic valve pump-box.
ASPINWALL, THOMAS -	5658	22nd May 1828	Mechanical type-caster.
ASPINWALL, THOMAS -	10,013	16th Jan. 1844	Cannon of wrought-iron or steel, or both combined; machinery used in the making; method of making.
ASPINWALL, THOMAS -	10,728	23rd June 1845	Ordnance-carriage; apparatus for governing the recoil and moving the piece backwards and forwards.
ASTELL, WILLIAM - -	38	20th March 1627	Melting of iron-ore and making the same into cast works and bars, with sea-coal and pit-coal.
ASTLEY, JOSEPH - - -	3065	28th July 1807	Manufacture of sal ammoniac.
ASTLEY, PHILIP - - -	1335	1st Aug. 1782	Rendering horses tractable and docile, capable of standing the firing of ordnance, beating of drums, music, also the recoil of small ordnance fired from the saddle, or other causes of disturbance.

Name of Patentee.	Progressive Number.	Date.		Subject-matter of Patent.
ASTON, JOHN - - - -	6641	10th July	1834	Manufacture of buttons.
ASTON, JOHN - - - -	9386	4th April	1843	Manufacture of covered buttons.
ASTON, JOHN - - - -	11,227	28th May	1846	Buttons and ornaments for dress.
ASTON, JOHN - - - -	13,679	3rd July	1851	Buttons and ornaments for dress, and the machinery for making the same respectively.
ATHA, RICHARD - - -	10,920	4th Nov.	1845	Atmospheric-engines.
ATHERLEY, EDMUND GIBSON -	5664	12th June	1828	Apparatus for generating power, applicable to various purposes.
ATHERTON, CHARLES - -	12,930	7th Feb.	1850	Machinery for regulating the admission of steam to the cylinders of steam-engines.
ATHERTON, PETER - - -	1179	5th Feb.	1778	Making screws, and machines for dividing of instruments, from the said screws.
ATHERTON, PETER - - -	1896	6th July	1792	Twisting, winding, and doubling silk, cotton, and wool.
ATHERTON, PETER - - -	2036	29th Jan.	1795	Twisting, winding, and doubling cotton and wool.
ATKINS, GEORGE - - -	4374	18th May	1819	Meridian declination dial, for ascertaining the variation of the compass.
ATKINS, GEORGE - - -	5190	18th June	1825	Stoves or grates.
ATKINS, HENRY - - -	10,381	5th Nov.	1844	Manufacture of net-lace.
ATKINS, ROBERT - - -	2737	31st Oct.	1803	Construction of hydrometers for ascertaining the strength of spirituous liquors; adapting a sliding rule to the same.
ATKINS, WILLIAM - - -	3054	16th June	1807	Weaving borders or stripes of different colours, on shawls or other goods of cotton, silk, linen, worsted, or any mixture of the same.
ATKINSON, GEORGE - -	4271	10th June	1818	Manufacturing an article to resemble bombasin, from a combination of materials.
ATKINSON, JOHN - - -	1996	18th June	1794	Making colours or paints from certain materials.
ATKINSON, JOHN - - -	2094	9th March	1796	Making white paint or colour from certain materials. (A substitute for white lead).
ATKINSON, JONATHAN - -	11,677	27th April	1847	Manufacturing soap.
ATKINSON, JOSEPH - -	8417	7th March	1840	Thrashing and winnowing machines.
ATKINSON, RICHARD - -	6225	16th Feb.	1832	Raising or brushing woollen-cloths and other goods.
ATKINSON, SAMUEL - -	283	19th Oct.	1691	Engine made of timber, with glass windows, door, air pipes, leather sleeves, and braces affixed; to enable a man to work under water for many hours.
ATKINSON, SAMUEL - -	10,090	4th March	1844	Carriage wheels.
ATKINSON, WILLIAM - -	4016	9th April	1816	Forming blocks with bricks and cement, to resemble stone for building.
ATLEE, JAMES FALCONER -	5073	11th Jan.	1825	Process by which planks and other scantlings of wood will be prevented from shrinking, and improved in their durability, closeness of grain, and power of resisting moisture, and thus better adapted for ship or other building purposes, for the construction of furniture, and other purposes where compact wood is desirable. "Condensed wood."
ATLEE, JAMES FALCONER -	5593	22nd Dec.	1827	Construction of made masts.
ATLEE, JAMES FALCONER -	5607	15th Jan.	1828	Bands or hoops for securing made and other masts, bowsprits, and yards.
ATLEE, JOHN FALCONER -	2163	7th Feb.	1797	Condensing and cooling spirits in the process of distillation.

Name of Patentee.	Progressive Number.	Date.	Subject-matter of Patent.
ATLEE, JOHN FALCONER -	3017	7th March 1807	Apparatus to be used in fermenting liquors.
ATTERBURY, EDWARD JOHNSON [COLE.	11,614	10th March 1847	Gearing machinery.
ATTWOOD, CHARLES - -	4148	5th Aug. 1817	Manufacture of crown glass, or German sheet glass.
ATTWOOD, CHARLES - -	4383	22nd June 1819	Mode of manufacturing mineral and vegetable alkali; and the application so far as regards mineral alkali, as an improvement on the modes now in use, particularly in the manufacture of kelp.
ATTWOOD, CHARLES - -	6490	19th Oct. 1833	Manufacturing or purifying soda.
ATTWOOD, CHARLES - -	6542	16th Jan. 1834	Making a certain pigment or pigments.
ATTWOOD, CHARLES - -	10,651	3rd May 1845	Manufacturing iron.
ATTWOOD, CHARLES - -	12,128	18th April 1848	Manufacture of iron.
ATTWOOD, CHARLES - -	12,793	5th Oct. 1849	Manufacture of iron.
ATTWOOD, GEORGE - -	13,042	15th April 1850	Method of making tubing of copper, or alloys of copper.
ATTWOOD, HENRY - - -	12,763	13th Sept. 1849	Manufacture of starch and other like articles from farinaceous and leguminous substances.
ATTWOOD, THOMAS - -	3460	27th June 1811	Combination of metals, or metal and wood.
ATTWOOD, THOMAS - -	4798	3rd June 1823	Making cylinders for printing cottons, calicoes, and other articles.
ATTWOOD, THOMAS - -	5110	26th Feb. 1825	Nibs and slots in copper cylinders, for printing cottons, linen, silk, stuffs, and other articles.
AUBE, BERNARD - - -	8496	7th May 1840	Preparation of wool for the manufacture of woollen and other stuffs.
AUBREY, LEWIS - - -	5380	4th July 1826	Web or wire for making paper.
AUBREY, LEWIS - - -	6025	1st Nov. 1830	Cutting paper.
AUBRIL, ADOLPHE - - -	9522	25th Nov. 1842	Refining sugar.
AUCHTERLONIE, THOMAS -	12,961	7th Feb. 1850	Production of ornamental fabrics.
AUDLEY, LORD BARON - -	6694	11th Oct. 1834	Lock protector, as a substitute for, or to be attached to locks or other fastenings.
AUGHTIE, GABRIEL - -	2128	20th July 1796	Making coffins.
AULAS, CHARLES FRANCOIS [EDWARD.	7316	6th March 1837	Preparing writing paper to prevent the discharge of the ink without detection, also to prevent the falsification of writing thereon.
AULAS, CHARLES FRANCOIS [EDWARD.	7322	15th March 1837	Cutting and working wood by machinery.
AULAS, CHARLES FRANCOIS [EDWARD.	7462	7th Nov. 1837	Preparing writing paper to prevent the discharge of the ink wishout detection, also to prevent the falsification of writing thereon.
AULAS, CHARLES FRANCOIS [EDWARD.	7465	7th Nov. 1837	Cutting and working wood by machinery.
AULD, ANDREW - - -	10,386	9th Nov. 1844	Regulating the pressure and generation of steam, in steam boilers and generators.
AULD, DAVID - - - -	10,386	9th Nov. 1844	Regulating the pressure and generation of steam, in steam boilers and generators.
AULD, DAVID - - - -	13,419	19th Dec. 1850	Steam-engines;—working of steam-boilers, and apparatus connected therewith.
AURIOL, JAMES - - -	942	2nd Dec. 1769	Making soap without boiling.
AUSTIN, CHARLES EDWARD -	9181	16th Dec. 1841	Apparatus for changing the line on railways.
AUSTIN, EDWARD - - -	7372	12th May 1837	Raising sunken vessels and other bodies.
AUSTIN, GEORGE - - -	3960	23rd Nov. 1815	Fulling woollen-cloths; fulling-mills.

Name of Patentee.	Progressive Number.	Date.	Subject-matter of Patent.
AUSTIN, HENRY - - -	9737	25th May 1843	Wood pavements, floorings, and veneers.
AUSTIN, HENRY - - -	9763	10th June 1843	Glueing or ornamenting certain materials for building and other purposes.
AUSTIN, HENRY - - -	9846	20th July 1843	Waterclosets.
AUSTIN, HENRY - - -	10,794	31st July 1845	Construction and working of atmospheric-railways.
AUSTIN, HENRY - - -	11,134	11th March 1846	Construction of railways and railway carriages and conveyances.
AUSTIN, HENRY - - -	11,248	22nd June 1846	Wood, mosaic, and tessellated work.
AUSTIN, HUMPHREY -	4979	22nd June 1824	Shearing-machines.
AUSTIN, JAMES - - -	316	5th March 1693	Chariot of artillery, musket proof, holding two small field-pieces and two hand mortars.
AXON, CHARLES - - -	6264	1st May 1832	Throstles and doubling-frames for spinning, doubling, and twisting yarns of cotton, silk, linen, wool, and other fibrous substances.
AXON, JAMES - - - -	1935	27th Feb. 1793	Cleaning and fining raw cotton, silk, and wool.
AYERS, CHARLES ROBERT -	9424	23rd July 1842	Ornamenting and colouring glass, earthenware, porcelain, and metals.
AYLIFFE, JOHN - - -	78	17th Feb. 1635	Heating vessels used by brewers, dyers, soap-boilers, salt and saltpetre makers; also drying bricks and tiles, with sea-coals; making and drying tiles, stone-jugs, bottles, melting-pots for goldsmiths, and other earthen commodities, also with sea-coals.
AYRE, JOHN - - - -	10,942	15th Nov. 1845	Fabric for sail-cloth.
AYRE, WILLIAM, junior -	11,900	14th Oct. 1847	Propelling vessels.
AYRES, PHILIP BARNARD -	11,668	20th April 1847	Preparing putrescent organic matters, as night-soil, the matter held in suspension in the water of sewers, and other similar matters, for the purpose of manure or for other purposes; apparatus for the same.
AYSCOGHE, HENRY - -	256	26th Aug. 1687	An ablution, enabling persons to walk and remain under water three hours, with no covering over their heads.
AYTON, JAMES - - -	5102	19th Feb. 1825	Spring to be applied to bolting-mills for the dressing of flour and other substances.
AZULAY, BONDY - - -	11,737	10th June 1847	Charcoal and other fuel.
AZULAY, BONDY - - -	12,165	26th May 1848	Manufacture of gas, tar, charcoal, and certain acids.

B.

BAADER, JOSEPH DE - -	3959	14th Nov. 1815	Constructing railroads and carriages to be used on them.
BABB, GEORGE - - -	3526	23rd Jan. 1812	Files, plane-irons, fire-irons, and other articles.
BABINGTON, BENJAMIN GREY	12,106	27th March 1848	Manufacture of metallic-pens.
BABINGTON, BENJAMIN GREY	13,322	7th Nov. 1850	Preventing incrustation of steam and other boilers.
BABU, CHARLES NICHOLAS [MICHEL.	853	12th July 1766	Pump; also an engine for extinguishing fires.

Name of Patentee.	Progressive Number.	Date.	Subject-matter of Patent.
BACCHUS, JOHN OGDEN - -	6671	1st Sept. 1834	Manufacture and working of plate-glass and other glass.
BACHE, WILLIAM - - -	1255	4th May 1780	Propeller, or machine for improving the power of mills and forges.
BACHELARD, JOHN LOUIS -	8531	30th July 1840	Manufacture of beds, mattrasses, chairs, sofas, cushions, pads, and other articles of a similar nature.
BACHHOFFNER, GEORGE HENRY	12,317	4th Nov. 1848	Conveying intelligence.
BACHHOFFNER, GEORGE HENRY	13,414	19th Dec. 1850	Obtaining light and heat; apparatus connected therewith.
BACKHOUSE, HENRY - -	7317	7th March 1837	Block-printing.
BACON, HUGH FORD - -	5807	2nd July 1829	Gas lamp or burner.
BACON, HUGH FORD - -	6810	9th April 1835	Apparatus for producing a uniform supply of gas to gas-burners, through pipes.
BACON, HUGH FORD - -	7536	11th Jan. 1838	Apparatus for regulating the supply of gas through pipes, to gas-burners.
BACON, HUGH FORD - -	7868	10th Nov. 1838	Construction of the glass holders and glass chimneys of gas-burners.
BACON, HUGH FORD - -	7939	17th Jan. 1839	Apparatus for regulating the supply of gas through pipes to gas-burners, for uniformity of supply.
BACON, JOHN - - - -	1208	20th Jan. 1779	Medicinal preparation for the cure of intermitting fevers, consumptive and many other disorders.
BACON, JOSHUA BUTTERS -	6785	11th March 1835	Construction of locomotive steam-engines for railways and common roads.
BACON, JOSHUA BUTTERS -	7171	13th Aug. 1836	Structure and combination of apparatus employed in the generation and use of steam.
BACON, RICHARD MACKENZIE	3757	23rd Nov. 1813	Apparatus for printing from types, blocks, or plates.
BACON, WILLIAM - - -	11,838	19th Aug. 1847	Steam-engines.
BADAMS, JOHN - - -	5174	16th May 1825	Extracting certain metals from their ores, and purifying certain metals.
BADDELEY, JAMES HENRY -	13,288	17th Oct. 1850	Manufacture of ornamental articles of earthenware.
BADDELEY, RICHARD - -	445	22nd May 1722	Making streaks for binding cart and waggon wheels, also box smoothing irons, of pig iron.
BADDELEY, WILLIAM - -	9981	8th Dec. 1843	Rotatory engines.
BADGER, HENRY - - -	11,185	28th April 1846	Manufacture of glass.
BADGER, JONATHAN - -	9628	11th Feb. 1843	Construction of bedsteads for invalids.
BADGER, JONATHAN - -	10,918	4th Nov. 1845	Construction of easy chairs.
BADINI, CHARLES FRANCIS -	2074	17th Nov. 1795	Plan for detecting and preventing all kinds of written forgeries.
BADNALL, RICHARD, the younger [Badnell, Rich., the younger.]	4762	18th March 1823	Throwing, twisting, or spinning sewing silk, organzine, Bergam, and other silks.
BADNALL, RICHARD - -	4797	3rd June 1823	Dyeing.
BADNALL, RICHARD - -	5092	10th Feb. 1825	Winding, doubling, spinning, throwing, or twisting of silk, wool, cotton, or other fibrous substances.
BADNALL, RICHARD - -	5230	30th July 1825	Manufacture of silks.
BADNALL, RICHARD - -	6306	8th Sept. 1832	Construction of trams of rail or tramroads, on which locomotive-engines can work.
BADNALL, RICHARD - -	7711	27th June 1838	Manufacture of carpets, and other similar woven fabrics, by the introduction of an article not before used in the manufacture.

Name of Patentee.	Progressive Number.	Date.		Subject-matter of Patent.
BADSTONE, JOSEPH	3467	24th July	1811	Improvements applicable to bedsteads and various other things.
BAGGALY, JOHN JAMES	9233	27th Jan.	1842	Metallic dies and plates for stamping, pressing, or embossing.
BAGGALY, JOHN JAMES	9241	29th Jan.	1842	Combs for the hair;—applicable to combing other fibrous substances.
BAGGS, ISHAM	8434	17th March	1840	Engraving;—applicable to lithography.
BAGGS, ISHAM	8809	23rd Jan.	1841	Printing.
BAGGS, ISHAM	9251	9th Feb.	1842	Obtaining motive-power by carbonic acid, and by a peculiar application of heated air.
BAGGS, ISHAM	9527	25th Nov.	1842	Producing light.
BAGGS, ISHAM	10,738	26th June	1845	Obtaining motive-power by air.
BAGGS, ISHAM	11,696	7th May	1847	Production and management of artificial light.
BAGGS, ISHAM	13,939	29th Jan.	1852	Crushing gold quartz and metallic ores.
BAGLEY, JOHN WOODHOUSE	10,390	13th Nov.	1844	Manufacture of lace, and other weavings.
BAGLEY, JOHN WOODHOUSE	13,122	11th June	1850	Lace' and other weaving.'
BAGLEY, JOHN WOODHOUSE	13,880	24th Dec.	1851	Manufacture of knitted, looped, and other elastic fabrics.
BAGNALL, JOSEPH	3464	11th July	1811	Making bridle-bits, snaffles, and bradoons for horses, also martingale hooks and rings.
BAGNALL, THOMAS	2505	21st May	1801	Mill to chop, grind, riddle and pound bark, also to work green hides out of the drench, and make them fit for the bark liquor.
BAGOT, THOMAS	3904	4th April	1815	Machine for passing boats, barges, and other vessels from a higher level to a lower, and the contrary, without loss of water.
BAGSHAW, SAMUEL	4576	26th July	1821	Making vases, urns, basins, and other ornamental articles.
BAGSHAW, SAMUEL	5232	8th Aug.	1825	Manufacturing pipes for conveyance of water, gas, and other fluids.
BAGSHAW, SAMUEL	6708	6th Nov.	1834	Filter for water or other liquids.
BAHRE, JOACHIM	702	22nd July	1755	Liquid composition for printing and painting paper, silk, cloth and canvas, in divers colours.
BAILDON, HENRY CRAVEN	13,688	7th July	1851	Writing, printing, or marking letters, characters or figures on paper, parchment, or other material prepared for the purpose.
BAILEY, ALEXANDER MABYN	1163	19th July	1777	Making salt from sea-water or brine springs, also fresh water from sea-water.
BAILEY, BENJAMIN	9576	29th Dec.	1842	Machinery employed in the manufacture of stockings, gloves, and other framework knitted fabrics.
BAILEY, BENJAMIN	10,075	24th Feb.	1844	Machinery for manufacturing looped fabrics.
BAILEY, BENJAMIN	11,835	6th Aug.	1847	Manufacturing knitted fabrics.
BAILEY, BENJAMIN	13,639	23rd May	1851	Manufacture of looped fabrics.
BAILEY, CHARLES	6077	15th Feb.	1831	Machinery for making bobbin-net.
BAILEY, CRAWSHAY	9582	11th Jan.	1843	Construction of rails for tramways and railways.
BAILEY, HENRY	12,696	4th July	1849	Constructing articles of wearing-apparel;—applicable to fastenings for the same.
BAILEY, ISAAC	13,822	20th Nov.	1851	Preparing, combing, and spinning wool, alpaca, mohair, and other fibrous materials.
BAILEY, JOSEPH SHARP	12,281	5th Oct.	1848	Preparing, combing, and drawing wool, alpaca, mohair, and other fibrous substances.

Name of Patentee.	Progressive Number.	Date.	Subject-matter of Patent.
BAILEY, JOSEPH SHARP -	13,822	20th Nov. 1851	Preparing, combing, and spinning wool, alpaca, mohair, and other fibrous materials.
BAILEY, MICHAEL - -	5081	13th Jan. 1825	Spinning, doubling, throwing, and twisting silk, wool, cotton, flax, hemp, and such like materials.
BAILEY, NATHAN - - -	7158	1st Aug. 1836	Machinery for manufacturing stocking fabric.
BAILEY, THOMAS - - -	973	7th Dec. 1770	Making saddles and saddle-cloths.
BAILEY, THOMAS - - -	5826	5th Aug. 1829	Machinery for making lace.
BAILEY, THOMAS - - -	6077	15th Feb. 1831	Machinery for making bobbin-net.
BAILEY, WILLIAM - - -	575	9th May 1741	Engine for making bricks and pantiles.
BAILEY, WILLIAM - - -	4277	11th July 1818	Sashes, skylights, and frames for containing glass, and for making roofs of houses and of various other buildings.
BAILEY, WILLIAM - -	4765	18th March 1823	Metallic window-frames, and metallic mouldings for ornamenting furniture.
BAILEY, WILLIAM - -	4977	15th June 1824	Gas consumer, for consuming the smoke from gas burners and lamps.
BAILLIE, BENJAMIN - -	7307	20th Feb. 1837	Ventilation of buildings ("Baillie's patent ventilation").
BAILLIE, BENJAMIN - -	8747	23rd Dec. 1840	Locks, and the fixings and fastenings thereto belonging.
BAILLIE, BENJAMIN - -	10,402	25th Nov. 1844	Regulating the ventilation of buildings.
BAILLIE, JOHN - - -	6963	21st Dec. 1835	Propelling vessels and other floating bodies, by steam or other power.
BAILLIEU, WILLIAM - -	9209	23rd Dec. 1841	Apparatus to expand the human chest.
BAIN, ALEXANDER - -	8783	11th Jan. 1841	Application of moving power to clocks and timepieces.
BAIN, ALEXANDER - -	8996	21st June 1841	Inkstands and inkholders.
BAIN, ALEXANDER - -	9204	21st Dec. 1841	Application of electricity to control railway-engines, mark time, give signals, and print intelligence at distant places.
BAIN, ALEXANDER - -	9745	27th May 1843	Production and regulation of electric currents; electric time-pieces, and electric printing and signal telegraphs.
BAIN, ALEXANDER - -	10,450	31st Dec. 1844	Apparatus for ascertaining and registering the progress and direction of ships, for ascertaining the temperature of the holds, and for taking soundings at sea.
BAIN, ALEXANDER - -	10,838	25th Sept. 1845	Electric clocks and telegraphs;—partly applicable for other purposes.
BAIN, ALEXANDER - -	11,480	12th Dec. 1846	Transmitting and receiving electric-telegraphic communications; apparatus connected therewith.
BAIN, ALEXANDER - -	11,584	19th Feb. 1847	Timekeepers and clocks; and apparatus connected therewith.
BAIN, ALEXANDER - -	11,886	7th Oct. 1847	Musical instruments; and means of playing on musical instruments.
BAIN, ALEXANDER - -	14,146	29th May 1852	Electric-telegraphs and electric clocks and timekeepers; apparatus connected therewith.
BAINBRIDGE, EDWARD THOMAS	8467	13th April 1840	Obtaining power.
BAINBRIDGE, EDWARD THOMAS	14,134	22nd May 1852	Obtaining power when fluids are used
BAINBRIDGE, JOHN - -	4738	16th Dec. 1822	Rotatory steam-engines.
BAINBRIDGE, JOHN - -	4825	31st July 1823	Machines for shearing wool or fur from skins, and for shearing woollen, silk, cotton, or other cloths and velvets, also for shaving pelts.

Name of Patentee.	Progressive Number.	Date.	Subject-matter of Patent.
BAINBRIDGE, WILLIAM - -	2963	1st April 1803	Flageolet or English flute.
BAINBRIDGE, WILLIAM - -	3043	14th May 1807	Flageolet or English flute.
BAINBRIDGE, WILLIAM - -	3308	26th Feb. 1810	English flute or flageolet.
BAINBRIDGE, WILLIAM - -	4399	4th Oct. 1819	Double and single flageolet or English flute.
BAINES, ROBERT RAINES -	3934	22nd June 1815	Vertical windmill sails.
BAINES, ROBERT RAINES -	4082	16th Nov. 1816	Perpetual log or sea perambulator.
BAINES, WILLIAM - - -	11,819	29th July 1847	Manufacture of parts of railways; bearings of machinery; apparatus used in constructing railways.
BAIRD, JAMES - - -	12,508	7th March 1849	Manufacturing iron.
BAIRD, JOHN - - -	4276	11th July 1818	Making cast-iron boilers for evaporating the juice of sugar cane (annealing them in a furnace).
BAIRD, RICHARD - - -	12,004	22nd Dec. 1847	Method of communication between persons in charge of railway trains; and between passengers and engine drivers and other servants in charge of such trains.
BAISLER, FRANCIS - -	4180	28th Nov. 1817	Machinery for cutting paper,—" Patent paper plough."
BAKER, ABRAM - - -	7	16th Feb. 1618	Making, working, and compounding smalt.
BAKER, CHARLES - - -	2193	11th Oct. 1797	Preventing the smut in wheat.
BAKER, HENRY - - -	1293	25th June 1781	Ornamenting glass by a composition of colours impressed on the glass by copper plates and wooden blocks.
BAKER, HENRY F. - - -	12,003	22nd Dec. 1847	Steam-boiler furnaces.
BAKER, JAMES HANMER -	5139	29th March 1825	Vegetable materials for dyeing and calico printing.
BAKER, JOHN - - -	642	3rd April 1749	Refining lees produced after the boiling or bucking of linens and cottons, and making the same again available for the same purpose, also for making soap, and for other purposes where vegetable ashes are used.
BAKER, JOHN - - -	663	18th April 1751	Making pearl-ashes.
BAKER, JOHN - - -	674	13th Jan. 1753	Saving the oily particles formed in boiling tar, and the soot formed in burning tar into pitch.
BAKER, JOHN - - -	812	30th April 1764	Making salt equal to that imported from France or Spain.
BAKER, JOHN - - -	937	7th Nov. 1769	Making baize for the Spanish and Portuguese trade, to imitate French baize.
BAKER, JOSEPH - - -	3508	23rd Nov. 1811	Machinery for kneading dough without manipulation.
BAKER, THOMAS - - -	1178	3rd Feb. 1778	Machine for making stockings, waistcoat and breeches pieces, caps, gloves, mits, purses, and all sorts of hosiery, in silk, cotton, thread, and worsted.
BAKER, THOMAS - - -	6581	20th March 1834	Mechanism of chronometers, watches, and clocks;—applicable to other mechanical purposes.
BAKER, THOMAS CHARLES -	2577	20th Jan. 1802	Vanes or sails for windmills.
BAKER, WALTER - - -	633	12th July 1748	Medicine called "Schwanberg's liquid shell."
BAKER, WHITMORE - -	7403	19th July 1837	Truss, applicable to the nicking of horses' tails.
BAKER, WILLIAM - - -	1178	3rd Feb. 1778	Machine for making stockings, waistcoat and breeches pieces, caps, gloves, mits, purses, and all sorts of hosiery, in silk, cotton, thread, and worsted.

Name of Patentee.	Progressive Number.	Date.		Subject-matter of Patent.
BAKER, WILLIAM - - -	9232	27th Jan.	1842	Manufacture of boots and shoes.
BAKER, WILLIAM - - -	12,384	21st Dec.	1848	Railway wheels and turn-tables;—applicable to shafts or axles driven by steam or other power.
BAKEWELL, FREDERICK COL-[LIER.	6238	8th March	1832	Machinery for making soda-water, and other aërated waters or liquids.
BAKEWELL, FREDERICK COL-[LIER.	11,957	11th Nov.	1847	Machinery for making soda-water, and other aërated waters and liquids.
BAKEWELL, FREDERICK COL-[LIER.	12,352	2nd Dec.	1848	Making communications from place to place, by electricity.
BAKEWELL, JOHN - - -	6059	13th Jan.	1831	Machinery for manufacturing bobbin-net.
BAKEWELL, JOSEPH - -	8711	21st Nov.	1840	Preventing ships and other vessels from foundering; also raising vessels when sunk.
BAKEWELL, SAMUEL ROSCOE -	5985	18th Aug.	1830	Machinery to be used in the manufacture of bricks, tiles, and other articles to be made of clay or other plastic substance;—partly applicable to other purposes.
BALDEN, SAMUEL - - -	3935	24th June	1815	Machine for heating ovens.
BALDWIN, ETHAN - - -	13,141	19th June	1850	Generating and applying steam in propelling vessels, locomotives, and stationary machinery.
BALDWIN, JOSEPH - - -	13,402	12th Dec.	1850	Manufacture of carpets and other fabrics.
BALE, THOMAS SAUNDERS -	13,692	17th July	1851	Method of treating, ornamenting, or preserving buildings, and edifices;—also applicable to other similar purposes.
BALFOUR, ALEXANDER - -	12,327	16th Nov.	1848	Apparatus for cutting metal washers and other articles; construction of buffers.
BALL, EDMUND RICHARD -	4157	9th Aug.	1817	Manufacturing paper for bills, notes, or other uses requiring strength.
BALL, EDWARD - - -	51	13th Aug.	1630	Melting, making, fining, and burning iron, lead, tin, salt, bricks, tiles, lime, and other things (glass excepted) with peat or turf prepared for the purpose.
BALL, FRANCIS - - -	316	6th March	1693	Chariot of artillery, musket proof.
BALL, JAMES - - - -	1784	16th Nov.	1790	Square and other pianofortes.
BALL, JOHN - - - -	2819	5th Feb.	1805	Machine for thrashing corn and pulse.
BALL, JOHN - - - -	3444	7th May	1811	Cooking stove.
BALL, JOHN - - - -	7631	3rd May	1838	Carriages.
BALL, JOHN - - - -	13,339	12th Nov.	1850	Applying heat to bakers' ovens and their appendages.
BALL, SAMUEL - - -	1517	19th Dec.	1785	Apparatus for making, inlaying, and working of hose-pieces and other work usually made on the stocking frame, of silk, worsted, thread, cotton, and other materials.
BALL, THOMAS - - -	13,880	24th Dec.	1851	Manufacture of knitted, looped, and other elastic fabrics.
BALMAIN, WILLIAM HENRY -	12,505	5th March	1849	Manufacture of glass, and preparation of certain materials to be used therein;—in part applicable to the manufacture of alkalies.
BALMANNO, MORTON - -	7794	6th Sept.	1838	Making paper, pasteboard, felt, and tissues.
BANCE, JOHN - - -	6142	27th July	1831	Construction of heads or hoods for such cabriolets, gigs, and open carriages, as require the heads to fold down behind, when not in use.
BANCKS, ROBERT OLDDISS -	13,375	30th Nov.	1850	Manufacture of paper.

Name of Patentee.	Progressive Number.	Date.	Subject-matter of Patent.
BANCROFT, EDWARD　-　-	1103	23rd Oct. 1775	Use of certain vegetables for dyeing, staining, printing, painting, or otherwise colouring wool, hair, fur, silk, hemp, cotton, linen, skins, leather, paper, and wood.
BANCROFT, PETER -　-　-	8461	31st March 1840	Renovating animal charcoal after use, so as to render it fit for use a second time.
BANCROFT, PETER -　-　-	11,112	25th Feb. 1846	Refining and purifying animal and vegetable oils and grease.
BANES, SAMUEL　-　-	13,976	23rd Feb. 1852	Apparatus to be applied to or connected with the cables of ships or other vessels, when riding at anchor.
BANFIELD, JOHN　-　-　-	11,133	11th March 1846	Making signals and communications on railways, and between railway engines, carriages, and trains.
BANISTER, JAMES -　-　-	12,812	12th Oct. 1849	Tubes for locomotive and other boilers.
BANISTER, JAMES -　-　-	13,656	7th June 1851	Manufacture of metallic tubes for steam-boilers, and other uses.
BANISTER, JOSEPH -　-　-	7083	7th May 1836	Watches, and other timekeepers.
BANKART, FREDERICK　-　-	10,805	7th Aug. 1845	Treating certain metallic ores, and refining the products therefrom.
BANKS, CHRISTOPHER PIGGETT	6445	29th June 1833	Manufacture of certain culinary and chemical utensils and vessels.
BANKS, RICHARD　-　-　-	1834	31st Oct. 1791	Machine for sinking shafts in mines.
BANKS, RICHARD　-　-　-	4022	4th May 1816	Wheel-carriages.
BANKS, RICHARD　-　-　-	4207	23rd Jan. 1818	Wheeled-carriages.
BANKS, ROBERT RICHARDSON	11,914	21st Oct. 1847	Drying-apparatus, for artificially curing and preserving the berries of coffee.
BANKS, SAMUEL　-　-　-	12,506	5th March 1849	Mills for grinding wheat and other grain.
BANKS, SAMUEL MARLOW　-	8479	16th April 1840	Manufacture of iron.
BANKS, THOMAS　-　-　-	5855	30th Sept. 1829	Steam-engines.
BANKS, THOMAS　-　-　-	9390	13th June 1842	Construction of wheels and tires of wheels, for use on railways.
BANKS, WILLIAM -　-　-	6886	17th Aug. 1835	Machinery, pens, and presses, for ruling and pressing paper.
BANNISTER, JOHN -　-　-	2024	22nd Nov. 1794	Driving and working mills and engines moved by wheelwork, and increasing their powers.
BANTON, EDWARD -　-　-	9888	5th Oct. 1843	Saddles and horse-harness.
BANTON, EDWARD -　-　-	10,865	9th Oct. 1845	Covering rollers used in spinning cotton and other threads; covering mill-straps.
BAPAUME, PIERRE AUGUSTE　-	11,882	7th Oct. 1847	Preparing and engraving plates adapted to printing cotton stuffs, paper, and other substances.
BARANOWSKI, JOSEPH JEAN　-	11,806	19th July 1847	Ready reckoning machine.
BARANOWSKI, JOSEPH JEAN　-	11,955	11th Nov. 1847	Ready reckoning machine.
BARANOWSKI, JOSEPH JEAN　-	13,063	23rd April 1850	Machinery for counting, numbering, and labelling.
BARBAR, THOMAS　-　-　-	114	14th Dec. 1637	Engine for turning corn and seed mills, fulling and paper mills, and mills for drawing up water; also carriages and wheel-works turned by wind, water, man, or beast.
BARBAR, THOMAS　-　-　- [Barber, Thomas.]	124	8th Feb. 1640	Making candles, taps, links, and torches, with oil and other things.
BARBE, CHARLES LOUIS　-　-	13,969	12th Feb. 1852	Reproducing of drawings; obtaining designs, to be principally used in the engraving of surfaces for printing fabrics.

Name of Patentee.	Progressive Number.	Date.	Subject-matter of Patent.
BARBER, EDMUND - - -	10,880	11th Oct. 1845	Graining and decorating in oil, distemper, and other colours; imitating marbles, granites, fancy and other woods; apparatus and instruments to be used therein.
BARBER, HARLEY - - -	11,572	8th Feb. 1847	Manufacture of looped and woven fabrics.
BARBER, JOHN - - -	885	26th Nov. 1766	Raising water out of mines and ships, and for supply of cities; also raising ponderous weights, particularly coals, out of mines (by fire or water or both jointly).
BARBER, JOHN - - -	1041	21st April 1773	Machine and apparatus to purify fossil-coal, extract metals from their ores, and collect their particles when volatilized, by means of fire, water, air, and steam.
BARBER, JOHN - - -	1118	12th March 1776	Machine for draining mines, and raising coals, ores, and minerals, from great depths.
BARBER, JOHN . - -	1833	31st Oct. 1791	Procuring motion, and facilitating metallurgical operations, by inflammable air.
BARBER, JOHN - - -	1928	22nd Dec. 1792	Smelting and purifying fossil-coal, iron-stone, iron-ore, and other metallic ores, and the calx thereof, by steam, air, and fire; and impregnating the same, and the matrix thereof, with inflammable air, thereby producing a tough metal.
BARBER, JOHN - - -	8800	19th Jan. 1841	Machinery for tracing or etching designs or patterns on cylindrical surfaces.
BARBER, RICHARD - - -	6910	22nd Oct. 1835	Reels for reeling.
BARBER, RICHARD - - -	9546	8th Dec. 1842	Manufacture of boots, shoes, and clogs.
BARBER, RICHARD - - -	10,140	10th April 1844	Apparatus for giving quick rotatory motion to mops and such like instruments.
BARBER, RICHARD - - -	13,370	30th Nov. 1850	Manufacture of reels for reeling, and stands for reels;—applicable to the manufacture of desk or wafer seals.
BARBER, ROBERT - - -	1083	20th Oct. 1774	Machine for heckling, twining, dressing, dividing, spinning, and twisting into threads or wires, vegetable, animal, and fossil substances, and which, by being connected with a weaving-loom, may be applied to working, warping, and weaving various patterns.
BARBER, ROBERT - - -	1154	8th May 1777	Machine for making, drawing, sizing, and proportioning threads of silk, worsted, hemp, flax, gold and silver wire, and other materials, and for weaving the same, plain or figured, at the same time or separately.
BARBER, ROBERT - - -	1880	15th May 1792	Machine for making lace-work, fish-nets, garden-nets, horse-nets, rabbit-nets, and game-nets, in gold, silver, brass, iron, silk, mohair, cotton, thread, worsted, yarn, and hemp.
BARBER, ROBERT - - -	1923	8th Dec. 1792	Gigger stocking-frame, and mode of using the same.
BARBER, ROBERT - - -	2175	25th March 1797	Gigger stocking-frames.
BARBER, ROBERT - - -	2858	14th June 1805	Making and shaping stockings and pieces; stocking-stitch, and warp-work.
BARBER, THOMAS - - -	1083	20th Oct. 1774	Machine for heckling, twining, dressing, dividing, spinning, and twisting into threads or wires, vegetable, animal, and fossil substances, and which, by being connected with a weaving-loom, may be applied to working, warping, and weaving various patterns.

Name of Patentee.	Progressive Number.	Date.		Subject-matter of Patent.
BARBER, THOMAS - - -	1365	3rd May	1783	Machine for reducing and spinning wool, flax, cotton-wool, mohair, and other animal and vegetable substances, into thread.
BARBER, THOMAS HUNT -	11,889	7th Oct.	1847	Machinery for propelling vessels.
BARBER, THOMAS HUNT -	12,171	1st June	1848	Machinery for sawing wood.
BARBERIS, ANTHONY - -	12,419	16th Jan.	1849	Spinning silk; construction of swifts; arrangement of apparatus for winding silk, and other fibrous substances.
BARBON, NICHOLAS - -	338	18th Dec.	1694	Mill for raising water from the Thames or other river, without use of horses or other beasts.
BARBOR, ROBERT - - -	12,932	17th Jan.	1850	Artificial fuel; and machinery used for making the same.
BARBOR, WILLIAM - - -	1851	11th Feb.	1792	Machinery for hanging doors, windows, and lights, particularly those of carriages.
BARCLAY, ALEXANDER - -	862	21st Nov.	1766	Friction-wheels for sugar-mills.
BARCLAY, ANDREW - -	9675	24th March	1843	Lustres, chandeliers, pendants, and apparatus connected therewith, to be used with gas, oil, and other substances;—applicable to other purposes.
BARCLAY, ANDREW - -	12,928	15th Jan.	1850	Smelting iron and other ores; working iron and other metals; rotary-engines, and fans connected therewith.
BARCLAY, ANDREW - -	13,245	5th Sept.	1850	Smelting iron and other ores; manufacture of iron and other metals; rotary-engines, fans, and other machinery or apparatus connected therewith.
BARCLAY, DAVID - - -	4573	26th July	1821	Spiral lever, or rotary standard press.
BARCLAY, HENRY - - -	9337	30th April	1842	Compositions for cutting, grinding, or polishing glass, porcelain, stones, metals, and other hard substances.
BARCLAY, HUGH - - -	13,636	19th May	1851	Extracting fatty and oily matters; refining and bleaching fatty matters and oils, animal and vegetable, wax, and resins; making candles and soap.
BARCLAY, JAMES - - -	3789	12th March	1814	Wheels and axletrees for carriages.
BARCLAY, ROBERT - - -	1766	28th July	1790	Making punches for stamping and punching the matrices of printing types for letters and devices, and impressing on copper cuts, or other printing plates, and on dies, precious metals, or other substances, certain marks, which marks, letters, and devices cannot be counterfeited.
BARCLAY, WILLIAM - -	2634	14th July	1802	Medicinal compound, or "Barclay's Antibilious deobstruent Pills."
BARCLAY, WILLIAM, Rev. -	5229	30th July	1825	Instrument to determine angles of altitude, without a view of the horizon.
BARD, NATHANIEL - - -	360	16th Feb.	1699	Engine for levelling and preserving roads and highways.
BAREAU, PIRIE HENRI - -	14,020	8th March	1852	Manufacture of carpets, velvets, and other fabrics.
BARFORD, JOHN - - -	578	18th July	1741	Making moccadoes or French carpeting.
BARING, JOHN - - -	5669	3rd July	1828	Machine for cutting fur from skins, for the use of hatters ("Cant twist blades fur cutter.")
BARING, JOHN - - -	6914	23rd Oct.	1835	Machine for combing or brushing wool, flax, and other fibrous materials into teeth set in a cylinder, to separate the longer from the shorter fibres.
BARING, JOHN - - -	6994	3rd Feb.	1836	Machinery for combing, or brushing, or separating wool.

Name of Patentee.	Progressive Number.	Date.	Subject-matter of Patent.
BARKER, CHARLES MATHEW -	10,631	22nd April 1845	Manufacture of matches for obtaining instantaneous light;—partly applicable to sawing wood.
BARKER, CHARLES MATHEW -	12,837	10th Nov. 1849	Sawing or cutting wood and metals.
BARKER, EDWARD - - -	11,924	26th Oct. 1847	Preparation of manure.
BARKER, JOHN - - -	663	18th April 1751	Making pearl-ashes.
BARKER, JOHN - - -	3631	21st Dec. 1812	Surgical instruments to prevent hemorrhage of the sub-clavian artery, in amputation of the arm.
BARKER, JOHN - - -	6300	8th Sept. 1832	Process for making malleable iron.
BARKER, JOHN JACOB - -	6288	26th July 1832	Fountain pens.
BARKER, JOSEPH - - -	3931	6th Feb. 1816	Continuing the motion of machinery.
BARKER, JOSEPH - - -	4084	19th Nov. 1816	Method of acting upon machinery.
BARKER, JOSEPH - - -	6797	25th March 1835	Constructing umbrellas and parasols.
BARKER, JOSEPH - - -	7357	29th April 1837	Construction of umbrellas and parasols.
BARKER, JOSEPH - - -	8754	23rd Dec. 1840	Gas-meters.
BARKER, JOSEPH - - -	8928	20th April 1841	Measuring aëriform or fluid substances.
BARKER, JOSEPH - - -	12,487	28th Feb. 1849	Constructing umbrellas and parasols.
BARKER, ROBERT - - -	1612	19th June 1787	Apparatus, called "La nature à coup d'œil," for displaying views of nature, at large, by oil painting, fresco, water colours, crayons, or other mode of painting or drawing.
BARKER, THOMAS - - -	4574	26th July 1821	Clearing furs and wools used in hat-making, from kemps and hairs.
BARKER, WILLIAM - -	9671	20th March 1843	Construction of metallic pistons.
BARKER, WILLIAM - -	13,594	7th April 1851	Machinery for chipping, rasping, and shaving dyewood and other materials; apparatus connected therewith.
BARKSTEAD, JOHN - -	265	10th Nov. 1690	Engine for winding and throwing silk.
BARKSTEAD, JOHN - -	276	22nd Sept. 1691	Making calicoes, muslins, and other fine cloths, out of West-Indian cotton-wool.
BARLING, JOSEPH - -	9422	16th July 1842	Producing rotary motion in machinery worked by manual labour.
BARLOW, ALFRED - -	12,833	2nd Nov. 1849	Weaving.
BARLOW, ANTHONY - -	450	12th July 1722	Wheel, iron bars, plates, pins, &c. to be fixed to coaches, waggons, or carts, for preserving the roads from being cut and worn.
BARLOW, CHARLES - -	12,868	29th Nov. 1849	Manufacture of a certain pigment.
BARLOW, CHARLES - -	13,451	11th Jan. 1851	Propelling.
BARLOW, CHARLES - -	13,452	14th Jan. 1851	Machinery for the manufacture of railway-chairs.
BARLOW, CHARLES - -	13,686	3rd July 1851	Rotary-engines.
BARLOW, CHARLES - -	13,702	31st July 1851	Saws.
BARLOW, HENRY BERNOULLI	12,430	20th Jan. 1849	Manufacture of cut piled fabrics; and machinery applicable thereto.
BARLOW, HENRY BERNOULLI	13,290	17th Oct. 1850	Spinning cotton and other fibrous materials.
BARLOW, JAMES - - -	8049	25th April 1839	Construction of candlesticks.
BARLOW, JOHN - - -	4044	2nd July 1816	Cooking-apparatus.
BARLOW, JOHN HAWKINS -	4043	27th June 1816	Tea-urns, tea-pots, tea-boards, or tea-trays.
BARLOW, JOSEPH - - -	5127	15th March 1825	Bleaching, clarifying, and improving the quality and colour of bastard and piece sugars.
BARLOW, PETER WILLIAM -	12,659	14th June 1849	Parts of the permanent ways of railways.
BARLOW, PETER WILLIAM -	12,917	3rd Jan. 1850	Permanent ways of railways.
BARLOW, ROBERT - - -	526	22nd March 1731	Machine for cleaning wheat.

Name of Patentee.	Progres-sive Number.	Date.	Subject-matter of Patent.
BARLOW, ROBERT - - -	3053	16th June 1807	Artificial marbles and stones, or aromatic chemical compositions for moulding brooches, amulets, rings, lockets, or other ornaments.
BARLOW, ROBERT - - -	3856	22nd Nov. 1814	Instrument named "hydrostatic self-blowing machine."
BARLOW, ROBERT - - -	5453	1st Feb. 1827	Combination of machinery, to supersede the crank in steam-engines.
BARLOW, ROBERT JOSEPH -	6722	25th Nov. 1834	Springs applicable to carriages and to other purposes.
BARLOW, THOMAS GREAVES -	13,593	15th April 1851	Treatment of substances used in the production of gas, and of some of the products of the said substances; apparatus for making gas; discharging and giving motion to gas.
BARLOW, WILLIAM HENRY -	10,093	6th March 1844	Construction of keys, wedges, or fastenings for engineering purposes.
BARLOW, WILLIAM HENRY -	12,046	27th Jan. 1848	Manufacture of railway keys.
BARLOW, WILLIAM HENRY -	12,136	27th April 1848	Electric-telegraphs, and apparatus connected therewith.
BARLOW, WILLIAM HENRY - [Barlow, Henry.]	12,438	23rd Jan. 1849	Construction of the permanent ways of railways.
BARLOW, WILLIAM HENRY -	12,917	3rd Jan. 1850	Permanent ways of railways.
BARNARD, CHARLES - -	7541	13th Jan. 1838	Mangle.
BARNARD, EDWARD - -	5687	19th Aug. 1828	Weaving and preparing cloth.
BARNARD, GEORGE - -	6116	23rd May 1831	Locks and other spring-fastenings, for doors and other places.
BARNARD, WILLIAM HENRY -	6466	20th Aug. 1833	A solvent not hitherto used in the arts.
BARNES, JOHN - - -	9517	10th Nov. 1842	Manufacture of articles used in printing and dyeing cotton, silk, woollen, and other fabrics.
BARNES, JOHN - - -	10,757	8th July 1845	Manufacture of certain chemical agents used in dyeing and printing cottons, woollens, and other fabrics.
BARNES, JOSEPH - - -	9221	13th Jan. 1842	Working of steam-engines.
BARNES, JOSEPH - - -	12,461	8th Feb. 1849	Apparatus for bleaching, dyeing, clearing, and steaming animal or vegetable fibrous substances, either in a raw or manufactured state.
BARNES, RICHARD - -	6487	19th Oct. 1833	Machine and apparatus for producing, by the combustion of gas or oil, heated air for warming the interior of buildings; applicable at the same time, to purposes of giving light.
BARNES, RICHARD - -	8889	22nd March 1841	Machinery for raising or drawing water or other fluids.
BARNES, RICHARD - -	12,176	6th June 1848	Apparatus for making gas for illumination;—applicable to retorts for distilling pyroligneous acid.
BARNETT, DAVID - - -	11,441	5th Nov. 1846	Machines for effecting or facilitating certain arithmetical processes or computations.
BARNETT, GEORGE - -	7609	7th April 1838	Button for protecting the thread or shank from friction and wear.
BARNETT, GEORGE - -	8565	11th July 1840	Fastenings for wearing-apparel.
BARNETT, JOHN - - -	2668	21st Dec. 1802	Making parasols and umbrellas.
BARNETT, JOSEPH - - -	2374	4th Feb. 1800	Making buttons for wearing-apparel.
BARNETT, JOSEPH - - -	2668	21st Dec. 1802	Making parasols and umbrellas.
BARNETT, THOMAS - -	2656	6th Nov. 1802	Ventilation of vessels containing fluids.

Name of Patentee.	Progressive Number.	Date.		Subject-matter of Patent.
BARNETT, THOMAS	13,892	8th Jan.	1852	Machinery for grinding wheat and other grain.
BARNETT, WILLIAM	7129	22nd June	1836	Apparatus for generating and purifying gas for illumination.
BARNETT, WILLIAM	7615	18th April	1838	Production of motive-power.
BARNETT, WILLIAM	7727	10th July	1838	Manufacture of iron.
BARR, JOHN	5192	21st June	1825	Production of steam, applicable to steam-engines or other purposes.
BARRACLOUGH, WILLIAM	4810	5th July	1823	Looms for weaving fabrics composed wholly or partly of woollen, worsted, cotton, linen, silk, or other materials; and machinery and implements for, and method of working the same.
BARRANS, JOSEPH	12,862	24th Nov.	1849	Axles and axle-boxes of locomotive-engines and other railway-carriages.
BARRAT, PIERRE PHILIPPE [CELESTIN.	11,977	25th Nov.	1847	Machinery for tilling and working land.
BARRATT, OGLETHORPE WAKE-[LIN.	7742	24th July	1838	Coating and colouring (qy. *covering*) certain metals.
BARRATT, OGLETHORPE WAKE-[LIN.	7942	19th Jan.	1839	Decomposing muriate of soda for manufacturing mineral alkali, and other valuable products.
BARRATT, OGLETHORPE WAKE-[LIN.	9077	8th Sept.	1841	Precipitation or deposition of metals.
BARRATT, OGLETHORPE WAKE-[LIN.	9786	15th June	1843	Gilding, plating, and coating various metallic surfaces.
BARRATT, OGLETHORPE WAKE-[LIN.	10,519	10th Feb.	1845	Manufacture of acids; treating noxious vapours given off from chimneys and from chemical and other works.
BARRATT, THOMAS	5987	31st Aug.	1830	Machinery for making paper.
BARRATT, THOMAS	8715	25th Nov.	1840	Manufacture of paper.
BARRATT, ZACHARIAH	2540	18th Sept.	1801	Mill for grinding corn, to be worked by water, wind, horses, hand, or otherwise.
BARRATT, ZACHARIAH	3175	31st Oct.	1808	Machine for washing linen and cotton clothes, and pressing the water from them.
BARRATT, ZACHARIAH	4225	10th Feb.	1818	Machine for curing, cleaning, sweeping, and ventilating chimneys, or extinguishing fires therein.
BARRÉ, MATHIAS NICHOLAS [LA ROCHE.	9112	7th Oct.	1841	Manufacture of a fabric applicable to sails and other purposes.
BARRETO, JOSEPH DE OLI-[VEIRA.	2644	30th Aug.	1802	Treating and curing ruptures.
BARRETO, MARY DE LIMA	2644	30th Aug.	1802	Treating and curing ruptures.
BARRETT, JAMES	2816	29th Jan.	1805	Construction of malt-kilns, so as to prevent damages from fire, and to save fuel in the drying of malt.
BARRETT, JOHN	1422	12th March	1784	Chandelier girandole lustre.
BARRETT, JOHN	7918	20th Dec.	1838	Printing.
BARRINGTON, CHARLES	14,223	15th July	1852	Steam-boiler water-feeding apparatus, and furnace.
BARRON, JAMES	3282	5th Dec.	1809	Apparatus used for rollers for window-blinds, maps, and other similar objects.
BARRON, JAMES	3976	23rd Jan.	1816	Castors.
BARRON, JAMES	4320	10th Dec.	1818	Making and fixing knobs used on drawers, doors, and cabinet furniture.
BARRON, JAMES	4828	11th Aug.	1823	Construction and manufacture of window-blinds.

27

Name of Patentee.	Progressive Number.	Date.	Subject-matter of Patent.
BARRON, JAMES - - -	5391	24th July 1826	Combination of machinery for feeding fire with fuel;—which machinery is applicable to other purposes.
BARRON, JAMES - - -	7014	26th Feb. 1836	Bedsteads, and apparatus to be used with or for bedsteads.
BARRON, ROBERT - - -	1200	31st Oct. 1778	Lock.
BARROS, IGNACIO DE - -	11,880	30th Sept. 1847	Machinery for making lasts for boots and shoes, butts or stocks for fire-arms, and other irregular forms.
BARROS, IGNACIO DE - -	12,519	14th March 1849	Machinery for making lasts for boots and shoes, butts or stocks for fire-arms, and other irregular forms.
BARROW, JOHN - - -	3818	25th June 1814	Securing carriage-glasses.
BARROW, JOHN - - -	9615	28th Jan. 1843	Manufacture and hanging of window-sashes.
BARROWS, WILLIAM - -	7778	21st Aug. 1838	Manufacture of iron.
BARRUEL, JEAN JOSEPH ERNEST	11,123	11th March 1846	Working certain sulphurets to transform them into oxydes, and to collect the latter; collecting oxydes from oxydised ores, equivalent to these sulphurets.
BARRY, JOHN RICHARD -	4575	26th July 1821	Wheeled-carriages.
BARRY, JOHN THOMAS -	4376	24th May 1819	Apparatus for distillation, evaporation, exsiccation, and for preparation of colours.
BARRY, RICHARD - - -	309	— 1692	Tanning skins for leather, and making imitation Russian leather.
BARRY, THOMAS - - -	12,758	6th Sept. 1849	Locomotive-engines; and construction of railways.
BARSHAM, JAMES - - -	11,459	21st Nov. 1846	Manufacturing brooms and brushes.
BARSHAM, JOHN - - -	7010	20th Feb. 1836	Manufacture of oxalic acids and salacetecella.
BARSHAM, JOHN - - -	10,884	16th Oct. 1845	Manufacture of mattrasses, cushions, brushes, and brooms; machinery for preparing materials for such purposes.
BARSHAM, JOHN - - -	12,586	26th April 1849	Separating the fibre from cocoa-nut husks.
BARSHAM, WILLIAM JAMES -	8917	5th April 1841	Fastening buttons and other articles on to wearing-apparel, and other descriptions of goods.
BARSHAM, WILLIAM JAMES -	12,172	1st June 1848	Manufacture of mats.
BARSTON, JOHN - - -	566	21st Dec. 1738	Universal astronomical quadrant for taking altitudes.
BARTHELEMEY, JOHN PETER -	2763	18th May 1804	Shield or protection for the human body, against sword, bayonet, or pike, also proof against musket-balls.
BARTHOLOMEW, VALENTINE -	5441	21st Dec. 1826	Shades for lamps and other lights.
BARTHOLOMEWE, JOHN - -	57	17th April 1632	Engine for draining water out of mines.
BARTLETT, HENRY VALENTINE	11,209	15th May 1846	Artificial palates, teeth, and gums; and machinery employed in the manufacture thereof.
BARTLETT, JOHN - - -	5666	17th June 1828	Process for preparing flax thread or yarn, for use in the manufacture of boots, shoes, saddlery, sailcloth, and other cloth or bagging.
BARTLETT, THOMAS - -	2514	18th June 1801	Elastic trusses for ruptures.
BARTLETT, JOHN, junior - -	7795	6th Sept. 1838	Construction of wheels for railroads and other roads;—applicable to wheels in general.
BARTON, JOHN - - -	3230	25th April 1809	Machine for raising weights or water.
BARTON, JOHN - - -	3272	2nd Nov. 1809	Lamps, with wicks constantly supplied with oil from a reservoir below the flame.

Name of Patentee.	Progressive Number.	Date.	Subject-matter of Patent.
BARTON, JOHN	3482	9th Sept. 1811	Sawing-machine.
BARTON, JOHN	3745	1st Nov. 1813	Construction and application of steam-engines.
BARTON, JOHN	4062	31st Aug. 1816	Pistons.
BARTON, JOHN	4462	15th May 1820	Propelling; also construction of engines and boilers applicable to propelling, and to other purposes.
BARTON, JOHN	4678	4th June 1822	Process for the application of prismatic colours to the surface of steel and other metals, and using the same in the manufacture of various ornaments.
BARTON, JOHN	6430	1st June 1833	Construction and application of pumps and machinery for raising fluids, and for other purposes.
BARTON, JOHN	6885	1st July 1834	Construction and application of pumps and machinery for raising fluids, and for other purposes.
BARTON, JOHN	13,231	19th Sept. 1850	Machinery or apparatus for printing calicoes and other surfaces; manufacture of copper and other metallic rollers employed therein; machinery or apparatus connected with such manufacture.
BARTON, JOSEPH	2176	25th March 1797	Preparing indigo for dyeing wool, silk, linen, cotton, and goods made from them.
BARTON, JOSEPH	2291	29th Jan. 1799	Medicine or chemical preparation; (" Compound concentrated fluid vital air.")
BARTON, JOSEPH	3997	14th March 1816	Truss.
BARTON, LUKE	7545	20th Jan. 1838	Machinery for framework knitting.
BARTON, WILLIAM	79	9th March 1635	Engines to cause and maintain their own motion, without aid of man, horse, wind, river, or brook;
BARTON, WILLIAM	525	17th Dec. 1730	Pens of silver, brass, steel, or other metals, for harpsichords and spinnets, in lieu of crow quills.
BARWISE, JOHN	8783	11th Jan. 1841	Application of moving-power to clocks and timepieces.
BASFORD, WILLIAM	10,020	20th Jan. 1844	Manufacturing bricks, tiles, quarries, and other articles composed of brick-earth; burning and firing the same, and certain articles of pottery and earthenware.
BASKERVILLE, JOHN	582	16th Jan. 1742	Making and flat-grinding thin metal plates; and rolling the same into mouldings or level plates.
BASS, JOHN HOLMES	5939	3rd June 1830	Machinery for cutting corks and bungs.
BASTER, JOHN	1600	8th May 1787	Apparel, for a protection to the breeches and upper part of the stockings, against wet.
BASTIER, JULES LE	12,800	12th Oct. 1849	Machinery for printing.
BATCHELER, JOHN	652	6th Feb. 1750	Manufacturing brocades and tissues of gold, silver and silk, or silk only.
BATE, GEORGE	9790	15th June 1843	Apparatus for raising and lowering window-blinds and maps.
BATE, JOHN	6254	9th April 1832	Machinery applicable to the imitation of medals, sculpture, and other works of art in relief.
BATE, RICHARD	1836	26th Nov. 1791	Machine to pump water, and for other useful purposes.
BATE, ROBERT BRETTELL	4659	21st March 1822	Hydrometers and saccharometers.
BATE ROBERT BRETTELL [Bate, R. Bretel.]	5124	15th March 1825	Frames of eye-glasses.

Name of Patentee.	Progressive Number.	Date.	Subject-matter of Patent.
BATE, ROBERT BRETTELL - [Bate, R. Brettel.]	7035	21st March 1836	Hydrometers and saccharometers.
BATE, WILLIAM - - -	4467	3rd June 1820	Combination of and additions to machinery, to increase power.
BATE, WILLIAM - - -	4468	3rd June 1820	Preparing hemp, flax, or other fibrous material for spinning.
BATE, WILLIAM - - -	7553	27th Jan. 1838	Obtaining and regulating power.
BATEMAN, JOHN - - -	3765	9th Dec. 1813	Musical instruments.
BATEMAN, JOHN FREDERIC -	12,032	18th Jan. 1848	Valves or plugs for the passage of water or other fluids.
BATEMAN, JONAS - - -	5108	26th Feb. 1825	Portable life-boat.
BATEMAN, JONAS - - -	6634	30th June 1834	Apparatus for saving human life in cases of shipwreck or other disasters by water.
BATEMAN, JONAS - - -	13,307	2nd Nov. 1850	Life-boats.
BATES, JOHN - - -	4610	9th Nov. 1821	Machinery for feeding furnaces, steam-engines and other boilers with coal, coke, and fuel of every kind.
BATES, JOSHUA - - -	5823	1st Aug. 1829	Steam-boilers or generators.
BATES, JOSHUA - - -	5824	1st Aug. 1829	Whitening sugars.
BATES, JOSHUA - - -	6068	31st Jan. 1831	Refining and clarifying sugars.
BATES, JOSHUA - - -	6185	27th Oct. 1831	Machinery for roving, twisting, or spinning cotton, silk, wool, hemp, flax, or other fibrous substances.
BATES, JOSHUA - - -	6459	13th Aug. 1833	Machinery for cleaning and combing wool, or such other fibrous substances.
BATES, JOSHUA - - -	6539	13th Jan. 1834	Condensing aëriform substances; and refrigerating fluids.
BATES, JOSHUA - - -	7082	16th April 1836	Machinery for cleaning and preparing wool.
BATES, JOSHUA - - -	7185	15th Sept. 1836	Machinery for making metal hinges.
BATES, WILLIAM - - -	7017	8th March 1836	Finishing hosiery and other goods made from lambs' wool, angola, and worsted yarn.
BATES, WILLIAM - - -	7187	16th Sept. 1836	Reels for reeling cotton.
BATES, WILLIAM - - -	8089	4th June 1839	Finishing hosiery and other looped fabrics.
BATES, WILLIAM - - -	9597	19th Jan. 1843	Dressing and getting-up hosiery goods, comprising shirts, drawers, stockings, socks, gloves, and other looped fabrics made from merino, lambs' wool, cotton, and other yarns; machinery for raising the nap or pile on the same.
BATES, WILLIAM - - -	10,113	19th March 1844	Dressing and getting-up hosiery goods manufactured from lambs' wool and other yarns; machinery to raise the nap of the same; construction of legs for stockings, and other articles of hosiery.
BATHER, GEORGE - - -	6608	22nd May 1834	Weighing-machine.
BATHO, NATHANIEL - -	8720	25th Nov. 1840	Machinery for planing, turning, boring, or cutting, metals and other substances.
BATLEY, BENJAMIN - -	2441	11th Sept. 1800	Curing and preserving herrings and sprats.
BATLEY, BENJAMIN - -	2465	25th Jan. 1801	Curing and preserving herrings, sprats, and other fish.
BATLEY, BENJAMIN - -	2866	8th July 1805	Refining sugar.
BATLEY, WILLIAM - -	2123	28th June 1796	Working steam-engines.
BATTEN, WILLIAM - -	6138	13th July 1831	Apparatus for checking or stopping chain-cables;—applicable to other purposes.
BATTISCOMBE, CHRISTOPHER -	885	11th Nov. 1767	Machine for avoiding the danger which would attend a person, who in falling from his horse, entangles his feet in the stirrups.

Name of Patentee.	Progressive Number.	Date.	Subject-matter of Patent.
BATTYE, THOMAS - - -	11,861	9th Sept. 1847	Retaining the waist in a desirable form, without producing the inconvenience of tight lacing of stays or corsets, or buckling of belts, waistbands, or girdles.
BAUER, GEORGE FREDERICK -	2615	5th May 1802	Carriages, and the wheels of carriages.
BAUGH, ROWLAND - - -	116	6th April 1638	Burning tiles with sea-coals.
BAXTER, GEORGE - - -	6916	23rd Oct. 1835	Producing coloured steel-plate, copper-plate and other impressions.
BAXTER, GEORGE - - -	12,753	30th Aug. 1849	Producing coloured steel-plate, copper-plate and other impressions.
BAXTER, SAMUEL - - -	13,409	12th Dec. 1850	Apparatus for lifting ; and for facilitating the working or steering of ships or vessels.
BAYLES, NATHANIEL - -	1367	7th May 1783	Harpoon.
BAYLEY, JAMES - - -	1921	28th Nov. 1792	Machine for dyeing, staining, or printing silk handkerchiefs, calicoes, muslins, and other articles.
BAYLEY, JOHN - - -	11,321	1st Aug. 1846	Machinery for spinning or twisting cotton and other fibrous substances.
BAYLEY, THOMAS - - -	3293	15th Jan. 1810	Sliding pullies for window-blinds and for other purposes.
BAYLEY, WILLIAM - -	981	17th Jan. 1771	Preparing a composition or blacking, in cakes, rolls, or balls, or other soilid form.
BAYLIFFE, EDWARD - -	5389	14th July 1826	Machinery for drawing, roving, and spinning sheep's wool and lambs' wool.
BAYLIS, BENJAMIN - -	4761	18th March 1823	Impelling machinery.
BAYLIS, CHARLES WINTERTON	8734	16th Dec. 1840	Metallic pen and penholder ("Patent flexion Pen").
BAYLIS, THOMAS - - -	7361	6th May 1837	Evaporating and heating fluids.
BAYLIS, WILLIAM - - -	1963	12th Oct. 1793	Glass, tin and other metal, lamps, lanterns, burners, and frames, with lens glasses.
BAYLIS, WILLIAM - - -	2052	30th May 1795	Lamp for streets, houses, shops, and various other purposes.
BAYLIS, WILLIAM - - -	4620	27th Nov. 1821	Machine for washing and cleaning clothes.
BAYLISS, WILLIAM - -	11,589	24th Feb. 1847	Machine for flattening and turning iron links for flat wood stub-chains.
BAYLY, ABRAHAM - - -	362	12th April 1699	Drawing low wines and spirits from turnips, carrots, and parsnips.
BAYLY, ANSELM (Rev. Doctor)	1615	20th July 1787	Elastic girdles, bandages, or rollers, to relieve ruptures, fractures, sprains, and swellings.
BAYLY, GEORGE PHILLIPS -	9611	26th Jan. 1843	Brushes.
BAYLY, JOHN - - - -	362	10th April 1699	Drawing low wines and spirits from turnips, carrots, and parsnips.
BAYLY, LEWIS - - - [Baylie, Lewis.]	150	16th May 1666	Engine for cutting drains, lines, or trenches; and making rivers navigable.
BAYLY, LEWIS - - -	169	3rd April 1673	Mill for grinding rapeseed, linseed, and hard woods ; press for extracting oil from rape-seed and linseed ; also an engine for cleansing and digging rivers, harbours, and havens.
BAYLY, LEWIS - - -	196	15th March 1676	Engine with nets, for raising gravel, sand, shingle, and other ballast from under water, and removing obstructions in rivers without making holes ; engine for driving piles for securing piers and defences against the violence of the sea.
BAYLY, WILLIAM - - -	296	22nd April 1692	Glazed printed hangings of cotton, worsted, or woollen yarn.

Name of Patentee.	Progressive Number	Date.	Subject-matter of Patent.
BAYLY, WILLIAM - - -	804	18th Oct. 1692	Printing paper in various figures and colours, by means of engines made of brass or other metal, without paint or stain (with fire).
BAYNES, JOHN - - -	669	25th Feb. 1752	Sash-frames.
BAYNES, JOHN - - -	1713	8th Dec. 1789	Soup-ladles, tureens, gravy-spoons, ladles, and skimmers.
BAYNES, JOHN - - -	4398	27th Sept. 1819	Machinery to be attached to carriages to give them motion by manual labour.
BAZILE. EUGENE - - -	11,477	7th Dec. 1846	Obtaining heat during the manufacture of coke; its application to various purposes.
BAYZILLE, THEOPHILE GERVAIS	8386	12th Feb. 1840	Producing soda and other articles obtained from the decomposition of common salt.
BAZLEY, THOMAS - - - [Bazley, Thomas, junior.]	10,676	22nd May 1845	Tube flyers, used in machinery for roving and slubbing cotton and other fibrous substances.
BAZLEY, THOMAS - - -	14,188	24th June 1852	Machines for combing cotton, flax, silk, and other fibrous materials.
BEACH, MOSES SPERRY - -	9308	23rd March 1842	Machinery for printing with type; construction of type for printing.
BEACHAM, JOHN - - -	5101	19th Feb. 1825	Waterclosets.
BEADON, GEORGE - - -	6643	10th July 1834	Apparatus for preventing boats or other floating bodies from capsizing when oppressed by too much sail, and for easing off ropes and sheets of different descriptions of vessels.
BEADON, GEORGE - - -	10,372	31st Oct. 1844	Life-boats or rafts; apparatus for raising or lowering the masts of vessels.
BEADON, GEORGE - - -	10,789	29th July 1845	Propelling vessels and land carriages; raising and drawing off water for driving machinery.
BEADON, GEORGE - - -	11,538	21st Jan. 1847	Warping or hauling vessels;—applicable to moving other bodies.
BEADON, GEORGE - - -	11,727	3rd June 1847	Wheel-carriages.
BEADON, SARAH - - -	9740	25th May 1843	Apparatus for regulating the inclination of vessels for drawing off liquids contained therein; construction of casks; means of drawing off liquids;—partly applicable for regulating the inclination of looking-glasses and other articles.
BEADON, WILLIAM - - -	12,935	19th Jan. 1850	Conveying away or decomposing smoke and products of combustion from stoves or grates; ventilating rooms.
BEADON, WILLIAM, Jun. -	13,518	18th Feb. 1851	Improvements applicable to the roofing of houses, buildings, and other structures.
BEAL, WILLIAM LANGLEY -	11,792	13th July 1847	Construction of anchors.
BEAL BENJAMIN - - -	9027	13th July 1841	Engines to be worked by steam, water, gas, or vapours.
BEALE, JOHN - - - -	1560	6th Oct. 1786	Umbrella with joints, flat springs and tops, worm springs, and bolts, slip bolts, screws, slip rivet, cross stop, and square slips.
BEALE, JOHN - - - -	3523	23rd Jan. 1812	Engine for cutting trunnels and spiles, and other articles.
BEALE, JOSHUA TAYLOR -	4708	27th Sept. 1822	Steam-engines.
BEALE, JOSHUA TAYLOR -	5809	19th Jan. 1828	Communicating heat for various purposes.
BEALE, JOSHUA TAYLOR -	6110	30th April 1831	Apparatus for separating a portion of the aqueous vapour from the vapour of alcohol, in distilling and rectifying spirituous liquors.

Name of Patentee.	Progressive Number.	Date.	Subject-matter of Patent.
BEALE, JOSHUA TAYLOR -	6227	23rd Feb. 1832	Steam-engines.
BEALE, JOSHUA TAYLOR -	6252	28th March 1832	Steam-engines.
BEALE, JOSHUA TAYLOR -	6537	4th Jan. 1834	Lamps for burning substances not hitherto usually burnt in such vessels.
BEALE, JOSHUA TAYLOR -	6777	27th Feb. 1835	Steam-engine (simplified and economical);— may be used for other purposes.
BEALE, JOSHUA TAYLOR -	7501	7th Dec. 1837	Lamp for burning substances not hitherto usually burnt in such vessels.
BEALE, JOSHUA TAYLOR -	8564	10th July 1840	Steam-engines.
BEALE, JOSHUA TAYLOR -	12,185	13th June 1848	Construction and arrangement of engines and machinery for propelling boats or vessels on water; means of preventing incrustation in the boilers ;—parts of the improvements are applicable to land purposes.
BEALE, WILLIAM - - -	32	31st Aug. 1625	Cement to preserve ships, pinnaces and other vessels, from fire, also from barnacles.
BEALEY, RICHARD - - -	14,235	20th July 1852	Apparatus used in bleaching.
BEAMAN, JOSEPH - - -	9568	22nd Dec. 1842	Manufacture of malleable iron.
BEAN, THOMAS - - -	1184	6th March 1778	Shoes, clogs, and pattens.
BEAR, HENRY - - -	11,816	28th July 1847	Manufacture of tobacco.
BEARD, CHARLES - -	6235	1st March 1832	Taps or cocks for drawing off liquids.
BEARD, JOHN - - -	6370	1st Sept. 1834	Machinery for dressing woollen-cloth.
BEARD, RICHARD - - -	8109	17th June 1839	Printing calicoes and other fabrics.
BEARD, RICHARD - - -	8466	6th April 1840	Printing calicoes and other fabrics.
BEARD, RICHARD - - -	8546	13th June 1840	Apparatus for taking likenesses, representations of nature, drawings, and other objects.
BEARD, RICHARD - - -	9292	10th March 1842	Taking likenesses and representations of nature and of other objects.
BEARD, RICHARD - - -	9908	13th Oct. 1843	Printing calicoes and other fabrics.
BEARDMORE, NATHANIEL -	12,199	3rd July 1848	Founding and constructing walls, piers, and breakwaters;—in part applicable to other structures.
BEARE, JOHN - - -	6592	12th April 1834	Engines for raising or conveying water or other fluids.
BEART, ROBERT - - -	6426	25th May 1833	Tiles for draining land.
BEART, ROBERT - - -	6738	23rd Dec. 1834	Apparatus for making bricks.
BEART, ROBERT - - -	7855	6th Nov. 1838	Apparatus for filtering liquids.
BEART, ROBERT - - -	8379	8th Feb. 1840	Apparatus for filtering fluids.
BEART, ROBERT - - -	10,258	12th July 1844	Apparatus for boring in the earth and in stone.
BEART, ROBERT - - -	10,636	24th April 1845	Manufacture of bricks and tiles.
BEART, ROBERT - - -	11,288	10th July 1846	Tilling land.
BEART, ROBERT - - -	13,275	10th Oct. 1850	Manufacture of bricks and tiles.
BEASLEY, WILLIAM - -	14,163	10th June 1852	Manufacture of metal tubes and solid forms ; machinery employed therein.
BEATER, JAMES GOLLOP -	9845	20th July 1843	Fastenings for trouser-straps, and fastenings for wearing-apparel generally.
BEATSON, DONALD - -	12,949	29th Jan. 1850	Instruments for taking, measuring, and computing angles.
BEATSON, ROBERT - - -	2200	31st Oct. 1797	Applying the power of wind or water to horizontal mills.
BEATTIE, GEORGE - - -	12,200	6th July 1848	Air spring, and atmospheric resisting power.
BEATTIE, JOHN - - -	13,250	5th Sept. 1850	Steering vessels.

Name of Patentee.	Progressive Number.	Date.	Subject-matter of Patent.
BEATTIE, JOSEPH - - -	8741	16th Dec. 1840	Locomotive-engines, carriages, chairs, and wheels used on railways; machinery for their construction.
BEATTIE, JOSEPH - - -	13,782	22nd Oct. 1851	Construction of railways; locomotive-engines and carriages used thereon; machinery by which some of the improvements are effected.
BEATTY, ROBERT - - -	1220	22nd April 1779	Machine for steering ships by a horizontal wheel, quadrants, pinion, and spindles.
BEAUCHAMP, GEORGE - -	1323	15th April 1782	Fire-escape.
BEAUMONT, GEORGE - -	2703	17th May 1803	Mixture used in preparing sheep's wool and lambs' wool for various purposes.
BEAUMONT, GEORGE DUCKETT [BARBER.	10,660	8th May 1845	Propelling carriages.
BEAUMONT, JOHN - - -	531	1st June 1731	Compound of sundry wholesome ingredients, for the feeding of swine.
BEAUMONT, JOHN - - -	1649	5th May 1788	Machine for raising coals from the pit, drawing water, driving waggons, and working mills, without aid of horses, fire, wind, or water.
BEAUMONT, WALTER - -	2703	17th May 1803	Mixture used in preparing the wool of sheep and lambs for various purposes.
BEAUREGARD, FELIX ALEX-[ANDER TESTUD DE	12,209	11th July 1848	Generating steam, and obtaining power from steam-engines.
BEAUVALET, JEAN ERNEST -	14,167	12th June 1852	Manufacture of iron and steel.
BEAVAN, JOHN PHILLIPS -	5307	7th Dec. 1825	Cement for building and other purposes.
BEAVAN, MARTIN - - -	3938	12th July 1815	Construction of furnaces and apparatus for smelting copper and other ores, and making copper and other metals.
BEAVAN, WILLIAM - -	3938	12th July 1815	Construction of furnaces and apparatus for smelting copper and other ores, and making copper and other metals.
BECHER, JOHN JOACHIM -	213	2nd Aug. 1681	Instrument for winding silk.
BECHER, JOHN JOACHIM -	214	29th Aug. 1681	Making pitch and tar from pit-coals.
BECHER, JOHN JOACHIM -	215	29th Aug. 1681	Engine to raise and throw out water from deep mines.
BECHER, JOHN JOACHIM -	217	28th April 1682	Floating mills for grinding all sorts of grain.
BECK, GEORGE - - -	1274	16th Dec. 1780	Apparatus for planning and surveying by land or sea.
BECK, RICHARD THOMAS -	7255	15th Dec. 1836	Mechanism for obtaining power and motion, to be used as a general mechanical agent (Rotæ vivæ").
BECK, RICHARD THOMAS -	7415	8th Aug. 1837	Mechanism for obtaining power and motion, to be used as a general mechanical agent (" Rotæ vivæ").
BECK, RICHARD THOMAS -	7670	5th June 1838	Mechanism for obtaining power and motion, to be used as a general mechanical agent (" Rotæ vivæ")
BECK, STEPHEN - - -	1413	16th Jan. 1784	Ship's hearth or stove, with copper and iron kettles.
BECK, STEPHEN - - -	1463	28th Jan. 1785	Ship's hearth or stove, with copper or iron kettles.
BECK, THOMAS - - -	7099	18th May 1836	Mechanism for obtaining power and motion, to be used as a general mechanical agent.
BECKER, ANDREW - - -	398	10th Feb. 1715	Machine for raising ships from the bottom of the sea.
BECKER, JOHN CONRAD - -	2551	7th Nov. 1801	Musical instruments, chiefly harps and piano-fortes.

Name of Patentee.	Progressive Number.	Date.	Subject-matter of Patent.
BECKETT, THOMAS	868	10th Feb. 1767	Medicine called "-beaume de vie"; making the same from scarce and valuable drugs.
BECKETT, WILLIAM	12,550	28th March 1849	Making certain articles of wearing-apparel.
BECKHAM, DANIEL	7708	27th June 1838	Obtaining castings in gold, silver, and albata.
BECKWITH, THOMAS	1301	28th July 1781	Crayons of various colours, for drawing and other purposes.
BEDELLS, CALEB	7945	21st Jan. 1839	Gloves, stockings, and other articles of hosiery.
BEDELLS, CALEB	8799	19th Jan. 1841	Manufacture of braids and plats.
BEDELLS, CALEB	9220	13th Jan. 1842	Manufacture of elastic fabrics, and articles of elastic fabrics.
BEDELLS, CALEB	9472	15th Sept. 1842	Fabrics produced by lace-machinery.
BEDELLS, CALEB	9782	15th June 1843	Manufacture of boots, shoes, slippers, overalls, and clogs; apparatus for the same; preparing materials for the purpose.
BEDELLS, CALEB	10,060	19th Feb. 1844	Manufacture of elastic fabrics.
BEDELLS, CALEB	10,076	24th Feb. 1844	Manufacture of bonnets, collars, capes, shawls, caps, coats, cloaks, gaiters, scarfs, stockings, gloves, and mits.
BEDELLS, CALEB	10,482	21st Jan. 1845	Manufacture of braces.
BEDELLS, CALEB	10,791	29th July 1845	Weaving.
BEDELLS, CALEB	14,310	30th Sept. 1852	Manufacture of articles of dress where looped fabrics are used; preparing looped fabrics for making articles of dress, and parts of garments.
BEDELLS, JOSEPH	9220	13th Jan. 1842	Manufacture of elastic fabrics, and articles of elastic fabrics.
BEDFORD, ISAAC HAWKER	11,002	12th Dec. 1845	Manufacture of window and other glass.
BEDFORD, STEPHEN	737	10th Feb. 1759	Impressing on varnish laid on copper, iron, paper, and other bodies, to be used in coach panels, snuff-boxes, and merchandise and devices.
BEDFORD, STEPHEN	4382	22nd June 1819	Preparation of iron and other metals; converting British iron into steel.
BEDFORD, WILLIAM	8631	17th Sept. 1840	Machinery employed in manufacturing hosiery goods, or frame-work knitting.
BEDINGTON, WILLIAM, junior	10,254	10th July 1844	Construction of furnaces.
BEDWELL, MARTIN	508	19th April 1729	Spinning, working, and weaving, hemp, flax, and hair.
BEER, WILLIAM	2667	9th Dec. 1802	Medicine for the cure of gout, rheumatism, &c., and method of administering the same.
BEESLEY, JAMES	1795	3rd March 1791	Plated tongs, pokers, shovels, and fenders.
BEETSON, WILLIAM	8494	5th May 1840	Stuffing-boxes;—applicable to waterclosets, pumps, and cocks.
BEETSON, WILLIAM	8590	5th Aug. 1840	Waterclosets and stuffing-boxes;—applicable to pumps and cocks.
BEETSON, WILLIAM	13,188	23rd July 1850	Waterclosets, pumps, and cocks.
BEEVER, JOHN	5305	3rd Dec. 1825	Gun-barrel.
BEILBY, JONATHAN	8919	5th April 1841	Brewing.
BEKAERT, FRANCIS BERNARD	11,726	29th May 1847	Preserving milk, and increasing the quantity of cream obtained therefrom.
BEKAERT, FRANÇOIS BERNARD	14,262	12th Aug. 1852	Manufacture of zinc-white.
BELFOUR, JOHN DANIEL	1939	16th March 1793	Machinery for making all kinds of cordage.
BELFOUR, JOHN DANIEL	2233	3rd May 1798	Machine for making cordage.
BELFOUR, JOHN DANIEL	2313	30th April 1799	Manufacturing cordage of all kinds.

Name of Patentee.	Progressive Number.	Date.		Subject-matter of Patent.
BELL, ALEXANDER - - -	6029	4th Nov.	1830	Machinery for removing wool or hair from skins.
BELL, CHARLES WILLIAM -	13,195	25th July	1850	Apparatus connected with waterclosets, drains, and cesspools, and gas and air traps.
BELL, EDWARD - - -	9477	29th Sept.	1842	Applying heat in making artificial fuel;—applicable to the preparation of asphalt, and for other purposes.
BELL, ELIZABETH - - -	2702	10th May	1803	Sweeping chimneys, and constructing them so as to lessen inconvenience from fire or smoke.
BELL, ELIZABETH - - -	3019	7th March	1807	Sweeping chimneys; machinery for making pieces of pottery used in constructing chimneys.
BELL, GEORGE - - -	6302	8th Sept.	1832	Making pill-boxes and other boxes from pasteboard, paper, or other materials.
BELL, GEORGE - - -	9648	1st March	1843	Machines for drying wheat, malt, seeds, and corn, and for bolting, dressing, and separating flour, meal, and other like substances.
BELL, GEORGE - - -	10,459	11th Jan.	1845	Drying malt, grain, and seeds.
BELL, GEORGE - - -	11,870	23rd Sept.	1847	Gas-tar as a substitute for oil paint (" Patent mineral paint ").
BELL, GEORGE - - -	12,017	7th Jan.	1848	Arrangements of wheels and axles of steam and other carriages;—in part applicable to other machinery.
BELL, HUGH - - - -	12,337	23rd Nov.	1848	Aërial-machines, and machinery in connection with the buoyant power produced by gaseous matter.
BELL, ISAAC LOWTHIAN -	13,529	24th Feb.	1851	Manufacture of sulphuric-acid.
BELL, JAMES - - -	1527	31st Jan.	1786	Making a vegetable acid or vinegar from refuse malt-wash, after distillation.
BELL, JAMES - - -	2347	4th Nov.	1799	Pocket fastening.
BELL, JAMES - - -	3338	17th May	1810	Refining sugar, and forming sugar-loaves.
BELL, JAMES - - -	3425	26th March	1811	Cutting, shaving, or scraping sugar-loaves and lumps; pulverising sugar-loaves, lumps, and bastard-sugar.
BELL, JAMES ALEXANDER HA-[MILTON.	13,107	8th June	1850	Dressing bran, pollard, and sharps.
BELL, JAMES THOMAS - -	5314	6th Jan.	1826	Construction or manufacture of watches.
BELL, JONATHAN, junior -	9916	27th Oct.	1843	Machinery for manufacturing elastic braid.
BELL, SAMUEL - - -	510	— May	1729	Making a red marble stoneware with mineral earth, capable of receiving a gloss, to imitate ruby.
BELL, THOMAS - - -	1378	17th July	1783	Printing with one or various colours at one time, linens, lawns, cambrics, cottons, calicoes, muslins, woollen-goods, silks, &c.
BELL, THOMAS - - -	1443	9th July	1784	Printing five colours (more or less) at once, on linens, cottons, calicoes, muslins, woollens, silks, stuffs, gauzes, or other goods.
BELL, THOMAS - - -	7365	8th May	1837	Manufacture of sulphate of soda;—applicable to other purposes.
BEEL, THOMAS - - -	8151	13th July	1839	Obtaining copper from copper slag.
BELL, THOMAS - - -	9429	29th July	1842	Manufacture of copper.
BELL, THOMAS - - -	10,916	3rd Nov.	1845	Processes in the manufacture of alkali;—applicable to purposes of condensation.
BELL, THOMAS - - -	11,307	23rd July	1846	Smelting copper ores.
BELL, THOMAS - - -	14,039	24th March	1852	Manufacture of sulphuric-acid.
BELL, THOMAS - - -	14,185	24th June	1852	Manufacture of sulphuric-acid.

Name of Patentee.	Progressive Number.	Date.	Subject-matter of Patent.
BELL, WILLIAM - - -	1242	26th Dec. 1779	Affixing impressions from dies, on gold, silver, or metals, by means of rolling cylinders on which such dies are engraved.
BELL, WILLIAM - - -	1990	17th May 1794	Making buckles and shoe-fastenings.
BELL, WILLIAM - - -	2063	8th Sept. 1795	Manufacturing needles, bodkins, knitting-pins, fish-hooks, netting-needles, mesh-pins, and sail-needles.
BELL, WILLIAM - - -	2829	9th March 1805	Manufacturing blanks or moulds for knife, razor and scissor blades, and for other edge-tools, also for forks, files, and nails.
BELL, WILLIAM - - -	2997	22nd Dec. 1806	Smoothing-irons, planing-irons, and various edge-tools.
BELL, WILLIAM - - -	3127	30th April 1808	Pipes or pumps for conducting water and other fluids.
BELL, WILLIAM - - -	3352	19th June 1810	Machine for cutting pasteboard, or cards out of pasteboard or paper, and for cutting various other articles.
BELL, WILLIAM - - -	3896	14th March 1815	Apparatus for copying manuscripts or other writings or designs.
BELL, WILLIAM - - -	3907	18th April 1815	Making wire of every description.
BELL, WILLIAM - - -	5697	4th Sept. 1828	Filtering water and various other liquids.
BELL, WILLIAM - - -	7371	11th May 1837	Evaporating and heating fluids.
BELL, WILLIAM HEWARD -	11,174	21st April 1846	Working coal, or coal-mines.
BELLAMY, JOHN - -	1975	9th Jan. 1794	Waterproofing leather and various other articles.
BELLAMY, SAMUEL - -	1165	1st Aug. 1777	Stamping upon plated-metal, gilt and other metals, hat and cloak pins, various decorations or devices for furniture and lock furniture.
BELLEMOIS, MARIN HYPPOLITE	7895	6th Dec. 1838	Treating massicot, litharge, and other compounds of lead, for the purpose of obtaing therefrom silver and certain other products.
BELLFORD, AUGUSTE EDOUARD [LORADOUX.	14,244	29th July 1852	Manufacture of sheet-iron.
BELLFORD, AUGUSTE EDOUARD [LORADOUX.	14,275	26th Aug. 1852	Machinery and apparatus for printing fabrics and other surfaces.
BELLFORD, AUGUSTE EDOUARD [LORADOUX.	14,305	30th Sept. 1852	Manufacture of boots and shoes;—partly applicable to the manufacture of various articles of dress.
BELLFORD, AUGUSTE EDOUARD [LORADOUX.	14,347	25th Nov. 1852	Construction of springs for railway and other carriages.
BELLHOUSE, DAVID - -	10,221	6th June 1844	Construction of boilers for evaporating saline and other solutions, for crystallization.
BELLI, NICHOLAS - - -	608	6th Sept. 1744	Use of a vegetable productive of sweet, fine, and wholesome oil; especially useful for the manufacturing of wool, and which may be cultivated in Engand.
BELLINGHAM, JOHN - -	209	6th Dec. 1679	Making Normandy window-glass.
BELLINGHAM, JOHN - -	244	7th Jan. 1685	Making square window-glasses for chaises and coaches.
BELLINGHAM, JOHN - -	3589	28th July 1812	Make and construction of axletrees for all descriptions of carriages.
BELLINGHAM, JOHN - -	5346	18th April 1826	Construction of cooking-apparatus.
BELTZUNG, FRANÇOIS JOSEPH	14,059	15th April 1852	Manufacture of bottles and jars, of glass, clay, gutta-percha, or other plastic material; caps and stoppers for the same; machinery for pressing and moulding the said materials.

Name of Patentee.	Progres- sive Number.	Date.	Subject-matter of Patent.
BEMETZRIEDER, ANTONIUS　-	2552	10th Nov. 1801	Making pianofortes.
BEMMAN, ROBERT WILLIAM　-	3955	23rd Aug. 1815	Ploughs.
BENBOW, THOMAS MOORCROFT	11,037	13th Jan.　1846	Fastenings for surgical and other bandages, and for articles of dress.
BENCRAFT, STEPHEN　-　-	9387	9th June　1842	Construction of saddle-trees.
BENCRAFT, STEPHEN　-　-	10,246	3rd July　1844	Making and fitting up hames, for prevention and cure of galled shoulders in draught horses.
BENDALL, JAMES　-　-　-	13,362	23rd Nov. 1850	Certain agricultural implements.
BENECKE, FREDERICK　-　-	5005	7th Oct.　1824	Making, preparing, or producing spelter or zinc.
BENECKE, WILLIAM　-　-	3853	12th Nov. 1814	Manufacturing verdigris.
BENECKE, WILLIAM　-　-	5466	20th Feb. 1827	Machine for grinding or crushing seeds or other oleaginous substances, for the purpose of obtaining oil therefrom.
BENHAM, JOHN LEE　-　-	6051	13th Dec. 1830	Shower and other baths.
BENHAM, JOHN LEE　-　-	8113	18th June 1839	Apparatus for correctly ascertaining the number of passengers conveyed in omnibuses and other public carriages.
BENINGFIELD, THOMAS TI- [MOTHY.	4708	27th Sept. 1822	Steam-engines.
BENIOWSKI, BARTHOLOMEW -	11,451	17th Nov. 1846	Apparatus for, and process of, printing.
BENIOWSKI, BARTHOLOMEW -	11,905	14th Oct.　1847	Apparatus for, and process of, printing.
BENIOWSKI, BARTHOLOMEW -	12,589	26th April 1849	Apparatus for, and process of, printing.
BENJAMIN, HENRY　-　-	9240	27th Jan.　1842	Preserving animal and vegetable matter.
BENJAMIN, NATHANIEL -　-	9010	28th June 1841	Manufacture of type.
BENJAMIN, WOLF -　-　-	4255	5th May　1818	Composition, and its application to render canvas, linen and cloth durable, pliable, and waterproof.
BENNET, JAMES　-　-　-	2688	10th March 1803	Felting woollen-cloth, and cloth of sheep's wool and other combined materials.
BENNET, ISAAC　-　-　-	362	10th April 1699	Drawing low wines and spirits from turnips, carrots, and parsnips.
BENNET, JAMES　-　-　-	2417	20th June 1800	Manufacturing, cutting, dressing, dyeing, and finishing cloth.
BENNETT, JOHN　-　-　-	3677	7th April　1813	Metal dovetail joint, for furniture and any kind of framework.
BENNETT, JOHN　-　-　-	4289	31st Aug.　1818	Filtering-vessels, and the filtering medium thereof.
BENNETT, JOSEPH -　-　-	7733	12th July 1838	Machinery for carding wool, cotton, flax, or other fibrous substances;—partly applicable to machinery for drawing, doubling, roving, and spinning the same.
BENNETT, JOSEPH -　-　-	8580	29th July 1840	Machinery for cutting rags, ropes, waste hay, straw, or other soft or fibrous substances;—partly applicable to tearing or opening rags, ropes, or other tough materials.
BENNETT, JOSHUA -　-　-	1437	19th June 1784	Manufacturing stuffs called " Prince's everlasting Union" plain, pearled, striped, figured, cut, or uncut.
BENNETT, SAMUEL　-　-	2789	20th Oct. 1804	Making or casting razors.
BENNETT, THOMAS　-　-	328	— Oct.　1693	Making salt.
BENNETT, THOMAS　-　-	1215	22nd March 1779	Compound metal for lining copper, brass, and iron vessels.
BENNETT, THOMAS　-　-	4578	4th Aug.　1821	Steam-engines or steam-apparatus.

Name of Patentee.	Progressive Number.	Date.	Subject-matter of Patent.
BENNETT, THOMAS WILLIAM -	9595	19th Jan. 1843	Paving or covering roads, streets, and other ways or surfaces.
BENNETTS, GEORGE　-　-	9866	15th Aug. 1843	Steam-engines and boilers; and generating steam.
BENNOCH, JOHN　-　-　-	2482	17th Feb. 1801	Machine for making nails, bolts, rods, watch-springs, and metal plates,
BENSON, EDWARD WHITE　-	7046	29th March 1836	Making ceruse or white-lead.
BENSON, EDWARD WHITE　-	7710	27th June 1838	Manufacture of carbonate of lead.
BENSON, THOMAS　-　-	487	5th Nov. 1726	Engine for working and preparing flint stones, for the manufacture of white pots.
BENSON, THOMAS　-　-　-	536	14th Jan. 1732	Engine for grinding flint stones, for the manufacture of white wares, as pots and other vessels.
BENSON, WILLIAM　-　-	11,041	15th Jan. 1846	Machines for the manufacture of tiles and other plastic substances.
BENT, WILLIAM　-　-　-	1204	23rd Dec. 1778	Stove grates, with front bars of cast iron.
BENT, WILLIAM　-　-　-	1205	23rd Dec. 1778	Ship-blocks, which turn on iron or steel pins or axles cased with metals.
BENTALL, EDWARD HAMMOND	8982	10th June 1841	Ploughs.
BENTALL, EDWARD HAMMOND	9789	15th June 1843	Ploughs, and apparatus which may be attached thereto, for ascertaining the draft of instruments used in tilling land.
BENTALL, EDWARD HAMMOND	10,442	18th Dec. 1844	Implements for sowing seed or grain.
BENTALL, EDWARD HAMMOND	11,311	23rd July 1846	Implements for ploughing, and clearing land of weeds.
BENTALL, EDWARD HAMMOND	14,043	24th March 1852	Construction of ploughs.
BENTALL, EDWARD HAMMOND	14,082	22nd April 1852	Chilling cast iron.
BENTHAM, JOSEPH　-　-	8929	22nd April 1841	Weaving.
BENTHAM, SAMUEL　-　-	1838	26th Nov. 1791	Planing wood.
BENTHAM, SAMUEL　-　-	1947	12th April 1793	Making fire-irons.
BENTHAM, SAMUEL　-　-	1951	23rd April 1793	Mode of working wood, metal, and other materials.
BENTHAM, SAMUEL　-　-	2035	24th Jan. 1795	Method of performing and facilitating divers manufacturing and economical processes.
BENTHAM, SAMUEL　-　-	3429	2nd April 1811	Laying the foundations of works of stone, brick, or other artificially composed materials;—applicable to the projection of wharfs and piers into deep water, the construction of bridges, the formation of harbours, and the erection of heavy buildings on bad ground.
BENTHAM, SAMUEL　-　-	3544	5th March 1812	Excluding the water of the sea, of rivers, or of lakes, during the erection of masonry under water, or for security of the foundations of sea-walls or similar works.
BENTINCK, JOHN　-　-　-	982	17th Jan. 1771	Chain pump for raising water out of ships, draining lands, or for other purposes.
BENTLEY, DAVID　-　-　-	5497	8th May 1827	Carriage wheel.
BENTLEY, DAVID　-　-　-	5620	21st Feb. 1828	Bleaching linen or cotton yarn and goods; machinery adapted for bleaching and finishing the same.
BENTLEY, HENRIETTE CAROLINE.	2005	7th Aug. 1794	Bed for invalids, which may be made and the linen changed, without inconveniencing the patient.
BENTLEY, JOSEPH -　-　-	8024	9th April 1839	Guns, pistols, and other fire-arms.
BENTLEY, JOSEPH -　-　-	10,280	30th July 1844	Fire-arms.
BENTLEY, NATHANIEL　-　-	1932	23rd Jan. 1793	Machine for scouring, milling, and washing hosiery, linen and woollen cloths, clothing, and other manufactures or raw materials.

Name of Patentee.	Progressive Number.	Date.	Subject-matter of Patent.
BENTLEY, THOMAS - -	7311	25th Feb. 1837	Fulling woollen-cloths.
BENTLEY, TIMOTHY - -	2773	19th June 1804	Seasoning and purifying casks.
BENTON, ROBERT - - -	9421	16th July 1842	Propelling, retarding, and stopping carriages on railways.
BERANGER, JOSEPH - -	12,525	19th March 1849	Weighing-machines.
BERENGER, CHARLES RANDOM [DE. [*Berenger, Chas. Random.*]	2385	31st March 1800	Printing and colouring transparencies on silk, cotton, linen, and other woven goods, for carriage and window blinds, also for screens and other ornamental purposes.
BERENGER, CHARLES RANDOM [DE. [*Berenger, Charles de.*]	2949	24th July 1806	Animal substance and method of preparing and manufacturing the same, whereby the said substance becomes applicable as a substitute for horse and other hair, for stuffing cushions, mattrasses, carriages, sofas and chairs, and for other purposes where flock, wool, or hair are now applied.
BERENGER, CHARLES RANDOM [DE.	3507	21st Nov. 1811	Producing a valuable oil, soap, and barilla, and a black colour or pigment.
BERENGER, CHARLES RANDOM [DE. [*Berenger, Charles Random, Baron de.*]	4990	27th July 1824	Applying percussion to the purpose of igniting charges in fire-arms generally.
BERENGER, CHARLES RANDOM, [DE. [*Berenger, Charles Random, Baron de.*]	5439	20th Dec. 1826	Gunpowder-flasks, powder-horns, or other utensils of different shapes used for the purpose of carrying gunpowder therein, in order to load therefrom guns, pistols, blunderbusses and other fire-arms.
BERENGER, CHARLES RANDOM [DE. [*Berenger, Charles Random, Baron de.*]	5905	27th Feb. 1830	Fire-arms, and certain other weapons of defence.
BERFORD, MICHAEL LAWRENCE	1117	11th March 1776	Nautical-windlass, adapted for applying the labour of men to various mechanic powers; but more peculiarly adapted to the use of navigation, such as rowing, craning, &c.
BERGER, CHRISTOPHER -	1233	7th Sept. 1779	Spiral wedge for elevating, pointing, and lowering cannon and all other pieces of ordnance.
BERGER, SAMUEL BENJAMIN [EDWARD:	11,732	3rd June 1847	Construction of railway-carriages.
BERGER, THOMAS - - -	12,947	26th Jan. 1850	Manufacture of starch.
BERGER, WILLIAM THOMAS -	9013	28th June 1841	Manufacture of starch.
BERGIN, THOMAS FLEMING -	6781	4th March 1835	Railway-carriages;—applicable to other purposes.
BERGIN, THOMAS FLEMING -	6840	27th May 1835	Suspending and adjusting the bodies of railway and all other wheeled-carriages.
BERGIN, THOMAS FLEMING -	7352	25th April 1837	Propulsion on railways.
BERGUE, CHARLES DE - -	6714	15th Nov. 1834	Machinery for spinning cotton, flax, silk, and other fibrous substances.
BERGUE, CHARLES DE - -	7048	29th March 1836	Machinery for spinning and doubling yarn or thread made from cotton or other fibrous materials.
BERGUE, CHARLES DE - -	8691	7th Nov. 1840	Machinery for making reeds used in weaving.
BERGUE, CHARLES DE - -	9052	21st Aug. 1841	Axletrees and axle-boxes.
BERGUE, CHARLES DE - -	10,782	24th July 1845	Rollers and other machinery to be employed in flattening, preparing, and polishing wire, for the construction or manufacture of reeds for weaving;—the rollers being applicable to other like purposes.

Name of Patentee.	Progres- sive Number.	Date.	Subject-matter of Patent.
BERGUE, CHARLES DE　-　-	11,184	28th April 1846	Atmospheric railways.
BERGUE, CHARLES DE　-　-	11,649	8th April　1847	Wheeled-carriages.
BERGUE, CHARLES DE　-　-	11,815	26th July　1847	Buffing-apparatus and springs.
BERGUE, CHARLES DE　-　-	12,013	5th Jan.　1848	Railway-carriages.
BERGUE, CHARLES DE　-　-	12,286	12th Oct.　1848	Bridges, girders, and beams.
BERGUE, CHARLES DE　-　-	12,435	23rd Jan.　1849	Steam-engines; pumps; springs for railways.
BERGUE, CHARLES DE　-　-	13,043	15th April 1850	Locomotive and other steam-engines; also buffers for railway purposes.
BERGUE, CHARLES DE　·　-	13,493	7th Feb.　1851	Construction of the permanent way of rail- ways.
BERINGTON, JAMES　-　-	7514	19th Dec.　1837	Curing smoky chimneys;—applicable to purposes of ventilation.
BERINGTON, JAMES　-　-	7853	3rd Nov.　1838	Knapsacks.
BERKENHOUT, JOHN　-　-	886	7th Dec.　1767	Making, dicing, or flowering playing-cards.
BERKS, THOMAS Earl of -　-	102	7th Feb.　1637	Kilns for drying grain, flax, yarn, hats and hops, with sea-coal, turf, or peat; also ovens for cooking, drying linen, and other purposes, at one fire and at the same time.
BERNARD, JULIAN -　-　-	13,272	4th Oct.　1850	Pneumatic springs, buffers, pumps, and stuffing-boxes.
BERNARD, JULIAN -　-　-	13,382	4th Dec.　1850	Manufacture or production of boots and shoes; and materials and machinery to be employed therein.
BERNARD, JULIAN -　-　-	13,808	13th Nov.　1851	Manufacture of leather or dressed skins, and of materials to be used in lieu thereof; machinery employed in such manufacture.
BERNARD, JULIAN -　-　-	13,931	27th Jan.　1852	Manufacture or production of boots and shoes; materials, machinery, and appa- ratus connected therewith.
BERNARD, JULIAN -　-　-	14,287	10th Sept. 1852	Manufacture or production of boots and shoes; materials, machinery, and appa- ratus connected therewith.
BERNEY, THOMAS FRENCH　- [Berney, Thomas Trench.]	7875	15th Nov.　1838	Cartridges.
BERNEY, THOMAS FRENCH　-	8143	6th July　1839	Cartridges.
BERNHARD, ANTON　-　-	5677	24th July　1828	Apparatus for raising water or other fluids.
BERNHARD, ANTON　-　-	5737	15th Dec.　1828	Apparatus or wheels for propelling vessels, and for other purposes.
BERNHARDT, FRANZ ANTON　-	6726	4th Dec.　1834	Warming and airing buildings.
BERNON, ALFRED -　-　-	5181	7th June　1825	Fulling and washing woollen-cloths, or other fabrics requiring fulling.
BERRIE, JAMES　-　-	6798	25th March 1835	Machinery for making healds.
BERRIMAN, ROBERT　-　-	1508	10th Nov.　1785	Apparatus for greasing carriage and other wheels, without taking them from the axle.
BERRIMAN, ROBERT　-　-	2905	23rd Jan.　1806	Machine for preparing land for the reception of seed.
BERROLLAS, ANTHONY　-　-	5586	13th Dec.　1827	Winding-up a pocket watch or clock, without key; detached alarum watch.
BERROLLAS, JOSEPH ANTHONY	3174	31st Oct.　1808	Making infallible repeating watches.
BERROLLAS, JOSEPH ANTHONY	3342	26th May　1810	Warning watch.
BERROLLAS, JOSEPH ANTHONY	5489	28th April 1827	Detached alarum watches.
BERRY, HENRY　-　-　-	4927	20th March 1824	Apparatus for producing light.
BERRY, HENRY　-　-　-	5304	3rd Dec.　1825	Securing volatile or other fluids and concrete or other substances, in bottles and vessels.
BERRY, MILES　-　-　-	6172	28th Sept. 1831	Boilers and steam-engines for propelling or actuating machinery and boats; mode of condensing the steam.

Name of Patentee.	Progressive Number.	Date.	Subject-matter of Patent.
BERRY, MILES - - -	6289	26th July 1832	Construction of presses applicable to various purposes.
BERRY, MILES - - -	6398	19th March 1833	Making or constructing gas-meters.
BERRY, MILES - - -	6479	5th Oct. 1833	Construction of weighing-machines.
BERRY, MILES - - -	6558	19th Feb. 1834	Machinery for shaping metal into bolts, rivets, nails, and other articles;—partly applicable for other purposes.
BERRY, MILES - - -	6676	13th Sept. 1834	Mills for grinding wheat and other grain;—applicable to other purposes.
BERRY, MILES - - -	6808	8th April 1835	Construction of rotary steam-engines.
BERRY, MILES - - -	6809	9th April 1835	Construction of printing-machinery or presses.
BERRY, MILES - - -	6944	5th Dec. 1835	Power-looms for weaving.
BERRY, MILES - - -	7058	12th April 1836	Mechanism for registering the notes played on the keys of pianofortes, organs, or such like instruments.
BERRY, MILES - - -	7111	7th June 1836	Machinery for cleansing, purifying, and drying wheat or other grain or seeds.
BERRY, MILES - - -	7115	13th June 1836	Apparatus for cooking vegetable substances;—with modifications and additions, applicable to evaporating and concentrating saccharine juices and other liquids.
BERRY, MILES - - -	7146	13th July 1836	Machinery for forming staves for barrels, casks, and for other purposes.
BERRY, MILES - - -	7203	6th Oct. 1836	Machinery for making metal screws.
BERRY, MILES - - -	7291	28th Jan. 1837	Machinery for making metal screws;—applicable to shaping metal for other purposes.
BERRY, MILES - - -	7330	27th March 1837	Machinery for heckling or combing, and preparing and roving hemp, flax, tow, and other vegetable fibres.
BERRY, MILES - - -	7353	27th April 1837	Machinery for making bricks, tiles, and other such articles.
BERRY, MILES - -	7354	27th April 1837	Machinery for making horse-shoes.
BERRY, MILES - - -	7386	6th June 1837	Obtaining motive-power for propelling or working machinery.
BERRY, MILES - - -	7451	26th Oct. 1837	Preparation of palm-oil for use in woollen manufactures, for lubricating machinery, and for other purposes.
BERRY, MILES - - -	7452	26th Oct. 1837	Machinery for heckling or combing, and preparing and roving hemp, flax, tow, and such other vegetable fibres.
BERRY, MILES - - -	7630	3rd May 1838	Alloying metals by cementation;—applicable to the preservation of copper, iron, and other metals.
BERRY, MILES - - -	7639	14th May 1838	Applying certain textile and exotic plants as substitutes for flax, hemp, cotton, and silk.
BERRY, MILES - - -	7656	31st May 1838	Economizing heat and fuel in furnaces or closed fireplaces.
BERRY, MILES - - -	7785	30th Aug. 1838	Looms for producing metallic tissues, and improvements in such tissues;—applicable for making buttons, epaulets, and tassels, and for other purposes, in place of braiding, also for making imitations of jewellery, and other fancy articles.
BERRY, MILES - - -	7796	6th Sept. 1838	Making and refining sugars.
BERRY, MILES - - -	7899	6th Dec. 1838	Means and apparatus for making gaseous liquids; filling bottles with the same; retaining or emptying the contents.

Name of Patentee.	Progressive Number.	Date.		Subject-matter of Patent.
BERRY, MILES - - -	7925	4th Jan.	1839	Rotatory-engines, to be worked by steam or other fluids.
BERRY, MILES - - -	8194	14th Aug.	1839	Spontaneous reproduction of all the images received in the focus of the camera obscura.
BERRY, MILES - - -	8273	19th Nov.	1839	Applying certain fibrous plants to making paper, spinning yarn, and weaving cloth, in place of flax, hemp, cotton, or similar fibrous materials.
BERRY, MILES - - -	8289	2nd Dec.	1839	Machinery for making pins, and sticking them in paper.
BERRY, MILES - - -	8357	21st Jan.	1840	Manufacture of prussiate of potash and prussiate of soda.
BERRY, MILES - - -	8500	9th May	1840	Treating, refining, and purifying oils.
BERRY, MILES - - -	8603	14th Aug.	1840	Arrangement, construction, and mode of applying certain apparatus for propelling ships and other vessels.
BERRY, MILES - - -	8725	27th Nov.	1840	Looms for weaving.
BERRY, MILES - - -	8946	4th May	1841	Machinery for making nails and brads.
BERRY, MILES - - -	8978	5th June	1841	Machinery for ruling paper.
BERRY, MILES - - -	9004	23rd June	1841	Apparatus for producing motive-power by gases or vapour produced by combustion.
BERRY, MILES - - -	9029	14th July	1841	Construction of locks, latches or such kind of fastenings for doors and gates, and for other purposes.
BERRY, MILES - - -	9056	27th Aug.	1841	Means and apparatus for obtaining motive-power, and rendering more effective the use of known agents of motion.
BERRY, MILES - - -	9076	8th Sept.	1841	Apparatus for, and means of, cleansing forms of type after being used in printing.
BERRY, THOMAS - - -	402	18th Feb.	1716	Curing the sweepings of ships, and thereby rendering them useful and saleable.
BERTE, ANTHONY FRANCIS -	2931	29th April	1806	Machine for casting or founding types, letters, and ornaments used in printing.
BERTE, ANTHONY FRANCIS -	3033	15th April	1807	Casting printers' types, sorts, and other articles of metal.
BERTHON, EDWARD LYON -	12,667	20th June	1849	Instrument to show the velocity of a vessel propelled through the water, by wind, steam, or other moving power.
BERTHON, EDWARD LYON -	12,901	19th Dec.	1849	Ascertaining and indicating the course, velocity, trim, and draught of ships, and rate of currents; discharging water from ships; and taking altitudes and levels at sea and on land.
BERTHON, EDWARD LYON -	13,659	12th June	1851	Boats; and instruments for sounding and indicating the rise, fall, and rate of currents.
BERTIE, JOHN - - -	6621	5th June	1834	Texture of bobbin-net or twist net; also machinery to produce lace-net with the said improved texture.
BERTIE, JOHN - - -	6950	9th Dec.	1835	Machinery for making ornamental bobbin-net lace.
BERTRAM, CHARLES - -	9847	20th July	1843	Mastic or cement; may be also employed as artificial stone, and for coating metals and other substances.
BERTRAM, CHARLES - -	11,219	26th May	1846	Manufacture of artificial fuel; and the application of the residual products to useful purposes.
BERTRAND, ISIDORE - -	12,754	30th Aug.	1849	Protecting persons and property from accidents in carriages.

Name of Patentee.	Progressive Number.	Date.	Subject-matter of Patent.
BESANT, JOHN - - -	1574	29th Nov. 1786	Wheeled-carriages.
BESANT, JOHN - - -	1767	28th July 1790	Carriage for the conveyance of merchandise or passengers.
BESNARD, PHILLIP - -	1332	20th July 1782	Alembical lamp or lantern.
BESSEMER, HENRY - -	7585	8th March 1838	Machinery for casting printing-types, spaces, and quadrats; means of breaking off and counting the same.
BESSEMER, HENRY - -	8777	6th Jan. 1841	Checking or stopping railroad carriages, under certain circumstances.
BESSEMER, HENRY - -	9100	23rd Sept. 1841	Manufacture of "certain glass."
BESSEMER, HENRY - -	9775	15th June 1843	Manufacture of bronze and other metallic powders.
BESSEMER, HENRY - -	10,011	13th Jan. 1844	Pigment or paint, and method of preparing the same;—partly applicable to preparing and treating oils, turpentine, varnishes, and gold size, when employed to fix metallic powders and metal leaf.
BESSEMER, HENRY - -	10,981	5th Dec. 1845	Atmospheric propulsion, and apparatus connected therewith;—partly applicable to the manufacture of columns, pipes and tubes, and partly to exhausting and impelling air and other fluids.
BESSEMER, HENRY - -	11,317	30th July 1846	Manufacture of glass; machinery and apparatus connected therewith; also silvering and coating glass;—partly applicable to the manufacture of tinfoil and thin sheets of other metal or alloys of metal.
BESSEMER, HENRY - -	11,352	26th Aug. 1846	Railway engines and carriages;—partly applicable to propelling steam-vessels, and to motive purposes generally.
BESSEMER, HENRY - -	11,794	17th July 1847	Manufacture of plates, sheets, or panes of glass.
BESSEMER, HENRY - -	12,101	22nd March 1848	Manufacture of glass.
BESSEMER, HENRY - -	12,450	31st Jan. 1849	Manufacture of glass, apparatus connected therewith.
BESSEMER, HENRY - -	12,578	17th April 1849	Extracting saccharine juices from the sugar-cane; making sugar; machinery employed therein.
BESSEMER, HENRY - -	12,611	15th May 1849	Expressing and treating oils; manufacture of varnishes, pigments, and paints.
BESSEMER, HENRY - -	12,669	23rd June 1849	Machinery for raising and forcing water.
BESSEMER, HENRY - -	12,780	20th Sept. 1849	Preparation of fuel; apparatus for supplying furnaces with the same.
BESSEMER, HENRY - -	13,183	22nd July 1850	Figuring and ornamenting surfaces; blocks, plates, rollers, implements, and machinery employed therein.
BESSEMER, HENRY - -	13,202	31st July 1850	Apparatus acting by centrifugal force, in the manufacture of sugar; treatment of saccharine matter by such apparatus.
BESSEMER, HENRY - -	13,560	20th March 1851	Manufacture and refining of sugar; machinery used in such manufacture for producing a vacuum;—applicable also for exhausting and forcing fluids.
BESSEMER, HENRY - -	13,819	19th Nov. 1851	Producing ornamental surfaces on woven fabrics and leather; and rendering the same applicable to bookbinding, and other uses.
BESSEMER, HENRY - -	13,988	24th Feb. 1852	Expressing saccharine fluids; manufacture refining, and treating of sugar.

Name of Patentee.	Progressive Number.	Date.	Subject-matter of Patent.
BESSEMER, HENRY - -	14,239	24th July 1852	Manufacture, refining, and treating of sugar;—applicable in part for evaporating other fluids.
BESWICK, ROBERT - -	13,803	4th Nov. 1851	Making bricks and tiles or quarries; constructing ovens or kilns for burning or firing the same, and other articles of pottery and earthenware.
BETHELL, JOHN - - -	6599	24th April 1834	Machinery for making metal screws, pins, bolts, and rivets.
BETHELL, JOHN - - -	6757	31st Jan. 1835	Apparatus for diving and working under water, and inspecting from above objects under the surface of the water.
BETHELL, JOHN - - -	7731	11th July 1838	Rendering wood, cork, leather, woven and felted fabrics, ropes, stones, and plasters or compositions, more durable, less pervious to water, or less inflammable.
BETHELL, JOHN - - -	8456	28th March 1840	Treating and preparing certain oils and fatty matters.
BETHELL, JOHN - - -	12,250	21st Aug. 1848	Preserving animal and vegetable substances, also stone, chalk, and plaster, from decay.
BETJEMANN, HENRY JOHN -	13,588	15th April 1851	Connecting parts of bedsteads and other frames; machinery employed therein.
BETTELEY, JOSEPH - -	9444	11th Aug. 1842	Windlasses, and machinery for moving weights.
BETTERIDGE, JOHN - -	5137	29th March 1825	Preparing and working pearl shell, for the purpose of applying it to ornamental uses in the manufacture of japan ware, and other wares and articles.
BETTLESTON, JOHN - -	4478	20th June 1820	Construction and application of spring trusses or bandages, for the relief or cure of hernia.
BETTON, MICHAEL - -	587	14th Aug. 1742	Oil extracted from a flinty rock for the cure of rheumatism, also scorbutic, and other complaints.
BETTON, THOMAS - - -	587	14th Aug. 1742	Oil extracted from a flinty rock for the cure of rheumatism, also scorbutic, and other complaints.
BETTRIDGE, JOSEPH - -	8972	27th May 1841	Manufacturing pâpier-maché, pearl, china, ivory, horn, wood, and composition, into pillars and stands for lamps, and other articles of domestic furniture.
BETTS, JOHN - - - -	807	28th March 1764	Machine to be fixed to a stocking frame, to make eyelet-holes in mits, gloves, and other goods usually made on such frames.
BETTS, JOHN THOMAS - -	6963	22nd Dec. 1835	Preparing spirituous liquors in the making of brandy.
BETTS, JOHN THOMAS - -	7159	3rd Aug. 1836	Preparing spirituous liquors in the making of brandy.
BETTS, JOHN THOMAS - -	7310	25th Feb. 1837	Preparing spirituous liquors in the making of brandy.
BETTS, JOHN THOMAS - -	7444	5th Oct. 1837	Preparing spirituous liquors in the making of brandy.
BETTS, JOHN THOMAS - -	7577	24th Feb. 1838	Manufacture of gin (" Betts' patent stomachic Gin ").
BETTS, JOHN THOMAS - -	7728	10th July 1838	Preparing spirituous liquors in the making of brandy.
BETTS, JOHN THOMAS - -	7817	21st Sept. 1838	Manufacture of gin (" Betts' patent stomachic Gin ")
BETTS, JOHN THOMAS - -	7967	11th Feb. 1839	Preparing spirituous liquors in the making of brandy.

Name of Patentee.	Progres-sive Number.	Date.	Subject-matter of Patent.
BETTS, JOHN THOMAS - -	9445	11th Aug. 1842	Covering and stopping the necks of bottles.
BETTS, JOHN THOMAS - -	9665	16th March 1843	Manufacture of metal covers for bottles and other vessels; manufacture of sheet metal for the purpose.
BETTS, JOHN THOMAS - -	9805	27th June 1843	Covering and stopping the tops of boxes, jars, pots, and other vessels.
BETTS, WILLIAM - - -	807	28th March 1764	Machine to be fixed to a stocking frame, to make eyelet-holes in mits, gloves, and other goods usually made on such frames.
BETTS, WILLIAM - - -	1161	14th July 1777	Machine for weaving hose, caps, mits, pieces, gloves, and other hosiery, in silk, cotton, and wool.
BETTS, WILLIAM - - -	1265	23rd Sept. 1780	Machine for weaving silk, thread, cotton, and worsted, also woollen and all other kinds of yarn.
BETTS, WILLIAM - - -	9659	8th March 1843	Making bricks and tiles.
BETTS, WILLIAM - - -	10,449	30th Dec. 1844	Bottles, jars, pots, and other similar vessels; mode of manufacturing, stoppering, and covering the same.
BETTS, WILLIAM - - -	10,886	16th Oct. 1845	Manufacture of brandy, gin, rum, and other British spirits and compounds.
BETTS, WILLIAM - - -	11,981	30th Nov. 1847	Manufacture of capsules; and application of designs to certain surfaces.
BETTS, WILLIAM - - -	12,415	13th Jan. 1849	Manufacture of capsules; material to be employed therein, and for other purposes.
BEURET, EUGENE DE - -	7766	10th Aug. 1838	Construction of railroads and tramroads, to facilitate the ascent and descent of hills.
BEVAN, EDWARD - - -	945	11th Dec. 1769	Venetian window-blinds.
BEVAN, JOHN - - -	9312	6th April 1842	Expelling air from cases or vessels, used for the preservation of various articles of food.
BEVAN, RICHARD - - -	9508	5th Nov. 1842	Arrangements connected with the circulation of steam in pipes, for producing heat; and application of the same.
BEVANS, JAMES - - -	2742	19th Nov. 1803	Application of machinery for striking mouldings, and for grooving, fluting, and excavating wood.
BEVANS, JOHN - - -	1799	4th April 1791	Circular wooden sash-frames, sashes, and soffits; fanlights, doors, mouldings, and handrails for stairs.
BEVANS, JOHN - - -	2852	27th May 1805	Window-frame and sashes.
BEVERIDGE, ELIZABETH -	3893	14th March 1815	Bedstead.
BEVINGTON, RICHARD - -	2925	26th March 1806	Machine for splitting hides, skins, pelts, or leather.
BEVINGTON, SAMUEL - -	2925	26th March 1806	Machine for splitting hides, skins, pelts, or leather.
BEWLEY, HENRY - -	9401	23rd June 1842	Chalybeate water.
BEWLEY, HENRY - - -	10,265	20th July 1844	Confining corks, or substitutes for corks, in bottles and other vessels, of glass, earthenware or stoneware, containing liquids.
BEWLEY, HENRY - - -	10,825	4th Sept. 1845	Flexible syringes, tubes, bottles, hose, and other like vehicles and vessels.
BEWLEY, THOMAS - - -	507	10th March 1729	Machine for raising water by alternate exhaustion and pressure of the air, without the help of fire; for supply of towns, gardens, &c., also for draining mines, fens, and other places.
BEWLEY, THOMAS - - -	4895	24th Jan. 1824	Wheeled-carriages.

Name of Patentee.	Progressive Number.	Date.	Subject-matter of Patent.
BEWLEY, WILLIAM -	10,376	2nd Nov. 1844	Fastenings of doors, windows, and other places.
BEX, HENRI AUGUSTE - -	10,985	10th Dec. 1845	Polishing, dyeing, and colouring, marble, stone, and other materials used in the construction or decoration of houses.
BIAGGINI, MICHAEL - -	1221	29th April 1779	Stamping and painting silk tiffany, gauze, and other goods, in imitation of lace.
BICKES, FRANCOIS HENRI -	11,310	23rd July 1846	Distillation.
BICKES, FRANCOIS HENRI -	11,758	19th June 1847	Treating, manuring or preparing, corn, seeds, plants and trees ; fertilizing land.
BICKFORD, JOHN SOLOMON -	10,928	6th Nov. 1845	Manufacturing the miner's safety fuze.
BICKFORD, WILLIAM - -	6159	6th Sept. 1831	Instrument for igniting gunpowder when used in blasting rocks, and in mining. (" Miner's safety Fuze.")
BICKNELL, ELHANAN -	8444	25th March 1840	Separating the solid from the liquid parts of tallow and other fatty matters.
BICKNELL, WILLIAM -	2490	28th April 1801	Covering felt for making caps and helmets, and for other useful purposes.
BICKNELL, WILLIAM GEORGE	13,108	7th June 1850	Machinery or apparatus for cleaning, purifying and drying wheat and other grain or seeds. (*M. Berry's extension for six years from 6th June 1850*).
BIDAULT, JACQUES - -	10,263	17th July 1844	Applying heat for generating steam and for other purposes ; may also be employed to obtain power.
BIDDELL, ARTHUR - -	9842	15th July 1843	Machinery for ploughing and scarifying land, and for raking ; also machinery used in thrashing, cutting, and grinding, for agricultural purposes ; construction of whippletrees.
BIDDELL, GEORGE ARTHUR -	12,312	2nd Nov. 1848	Gas-burners.
BIDDELL, WILLIAM ADOLPHUS	13,791	29th Oct. 1851	Moulding, casting, ornamenting and finishing, articles and surfaces.
BIDDER, GEORGE PARKER -	9608	26th Jan. 1843	Cutting roofing-slates.
BIDDLE, EDWARD - - -	89	18th March 1636	Extracting tallow or other liquid substance, from bones.
BIDDLE, JOHN - - -	5204	8th July 1825	Machine for making, repairing, and cleansing, roads and paths ;—applicable, or partly so, to other purposes.
BIDDLE, RICHARD - - -	10,910	3rd Nov. 1845	Driving mills and other machinery by the power of the wind.
BIELEFELD, CHARLES FRE-[DERICK.	9601	26th Jan. 1843	Suspending swing looking-glasses, and other articles requiring like movements.
BIELEFELD, CHARLES FRE-[DERICK. [*Bielefield Charles Frederick.*]	10,935	11th Nov. 1845	Manufacture of embossed or pressed paper, calico, leather, and other fabrics and articles.
BIELEFELD, CHARLES FRE-[DERICK.	11,289	14th July 1846	Making moulds or dies used in the manufacture of articles of pâpier-maché, and other matters ; moulding articles from certain plastic materials.
BIELEFELD, CHARLES FRE-[DERICK.	13,531	24th Feb. 1851	Manufacturing sheets of pâpier-maché, or substances in the nature thereof.
BIGELOW, ERASTUS B. - -	11,128	11th March 1846	Looms for weaving certain kinds of carpets, or other fabrics of like character.
BIGG, JOHN - - - -	2040	28th Feb. 1795	Bleaching paper.
BIGGS, EDWARD - - -	3758	23rd Nov. 1813	Working a stamp by a steam-engine, or by water or horse-power.
BIGGS, EDWARD - -	4055	14th Aug. 1816	Machinery for making pans and stales of various kinds.

Name of Patentee.	Progressive Number.	Date.	Subject-matter of Patent.
BIGGS, EDWARD - - -	4159	12th Aug. 1817	Making pans and stales of various kinds.
BIGGS, JOHN - - - -	10,133	30th March 1844	Manufacture of looped, woven, and elastic fabrics.
BIGGS, THOMAS - - -	9114	7th Oct. 1841	Securing hats, caps, and bonnets, from being lost by the effect of wind or other causes.
BILEY, EDWARD - - -	1965	2nd Nov. 1793	Machine for mashing malt, in brewing.
BILL, ROBERT - - -	3418	26th March 1811	Machine for washing clothes, and for other processes in family and other establishments.
BILL, ROBERT - - -	4461	15th May 1820	Constructing beams, masts, yards, bowsprits, and other parts of vessels ; also parts of the rigging of such vessels.
BILL, ROBERT - - -	4624	5th Dec. 1821	Construction of certain descriptions of boats and barges.
BILL, ROBERT - - -	4644	5th Feb. 1822	Manufacturing metallic tubes, cylinders, cones, or other forms adapted for the construction of masts, yards, booms, bowsprits, or casks, or for other purposes to which they may be applicable.
BILL, WILLIAM - - -	798	3rd Nov. 1763	Machine for making chocolate.
BILLIN, THOMAS - - -	452	17th Oct. 1722	Manufacture of earthenware from a peculiar clay ; also engines and tools used in the said manufacture.
BILLINGSLEY, CASE - -	496	6th May 1728	Engine for raising water to supply cities, extinguish fires, drain mines, and for other purposes.
BILLINGSLEY, MICHAEL -	2673	22nd Dec. 1802	Machine to be worked by steam, water, or horses, for the purpose of boring cylinders.
BILLINGSLEY, MICHAEL -	3908	20th April 1815	Steam-engine.
BILLINGSLEY, WILLIAM -	121	10th Dec. 1638	Printing or stamping cabinets, bedsteads, playing-tables and other things, with liquid gold and silver.
BILLITER, RICHARD HENRY -	9746	27th May 1843	Filtering oils.
BILLSON, CHARLES -	14,310	30th Sept. 1852	Manufacture of articles of dress where looped fabrics are used ; also preparing looped fabrics for making articles of dress, and parts of garments.
BINGHAM, JAMES - - -	8131	26th June 1839	Compositions to resemble ivory, bone, horn, mother-of-pearl, and other substances, applicable to the manufacture of handles of knives, forks, and razors, pianoforte keys, snuff-boxes, and various other articles.
BINGHAM, JAMES - - -	8361	25th Jan. 1840	Compositions to resemble ivory, bone, horn, mother-of-pearl, and other substances, applicable to the manufacture of handles of knives, forks, and razors, pianoforte keys, snuff-boxes, and various other articles.
BINGHAM, JAMES - - -	8616	3rd Sept. 1840	Compositions to resemble ivory, bone, horn, mother-of-pearl, and other substances, applicable to the manufacture of handles of knives, forks, and razors, pianoforte keys, snuff-boxes, and various other articles.
BINGHAM, WILLIAM - -	6166	24th Sept. 1831	Fire-arms of different descriptions.
BINGLEY, MARK - - -	11,495	15th Dec. 1846	Bookbinding ; and weaving materials used in bookbinding, applicable to other weaving ; preparing for, and making, alphabets for books ; inking type ; preparing mottled paper for bookbinders and others, applicable also for graining leather.
BINKS, CHRISTOPHER - -	7963	8th Feb. 1839	Obtaining and rendering useful, chlorine, also the chlorides of lime and soda, and other compounds of chlorine, for bleaching.

Name of Patentee.	Progressive Number.	Date.	Subject-matter of Patent.
BINKS, CHRISTOPHER - -	10,604	7th April 1845	Application and use of certain compounds as manure; manufacture of such compounds.
BINKS, CHRISTOPHER - -	10,911	3rd Nov. 1845	Manufacturing cyanogen, ammonia, and their compounds; and the use in these manufactures, of substances not hitherto so employed.
BINKS, HENRY - - -	4165	28th Aug. 1817	Axletrees of carriages.
BINNS, JONAS - - -	4712	18th Oct. 1822	Propelling vessels; construction of steam-engines and boilers applicable to propelling vessels, and to other purposes.
BINNS, JOSHUA VICKERMAN -	13,150	24th June 1850	Piecing wool-cardings; also a machine for the purpose.
BINNS, THOMAS - - -	1937	15th March 1793	Apparatus to be attached to waterclosets.
BINNS, THOMAS - - -	2332	20th July 1799	Movement, producing a retrograde motion, capable of being applied to mangles and calenders.
BINNS, THOMAS - - -	2352	4th Nov. 1799	Machine answering the several purposes of a portable watercloset or bidet, and easy chair.
BINNS, THOMAS - - -	2445	27th Oct. 1800	Applying heat for melting and manufacturing animal fat and other solid substances.
BINNS, THOMAS - - -	2488	23rd April 1801	Making candles of wax, spermaceti, tallow, or other solid inflammable substance.
BINNS, THOMAS - - -	4712	18th Oct. 1822	Propelling vessels; construction of steam-engines and boilers applicable to propelling vessels, and to other purposes.
BINNS, THOMAS - - -	7163	6th Aug. 1836	Railways; and steam-engines to be used thereon, and for other purposes.
BIRAM, BENJAMIN - - -	9249	8th Feb. 1842	Construction and application of rotary engines.
BIRAM, BENJAMIN - - -	10,445	21st Dec. 1844	Oscillating engines worked by steam, water, or other fluids, applicable to the raising or propelling of fluids.
BIRAM, BENJAMIN - - -	12,489	28th Feb. 1849	Miners' lamps.
BIRCH, CHARLES LUCAS - -	3063	21st July 1807	Construction of the roofs and upper quarters of landaus, barouches, and other carriages.
BIRCH, EDWARD - - -	12,625	31st May 1849	Constructing and propelling ships or other vessels.
BIRCH, EUGENIUS - - -	8699	12th Nov. 1840	Railroads; and the engines and carriages worked thereon.
BIRCH, JAMES - - -	2608	8th April 1802	Furnace for smelting and making pig-iron.
BIRCH, RICHARD COMYNS -	2259	11th Aug. 1798	Purifying, refining and preparing indigo, for the use of dyers.
BIRCH, THOMAS - - -	7481	18th Nov. 1837	Carding-engines, for carding cotton and other fibrous substances.
BIRCH, WILLIAM - - -	2259	11th Aug. 1798	Purifying, refining and preparing indigo, for the use of dyers.
BIRCHALL, THOMAS - -	11,832	5th Aug. 1847	Folding newspapers and other papers.
BIRD, JAMES - - -	12,051	8th Feb. 1848	Liquid measures.
BIRD, JOHN - - -	6908	15th Oct. 1835	Making and compounding printers' ink and other pigments.
BIRD, JOHN - - -	9411	7th July 1842	Machinery for raising or forcing water and other fluids;—applicable as an engine to be worked by steam, for propelling vessels, and for other purposes.
BIRD, MICHAEL - - -	394	1st Dec. 1713	Engine for drying malt and hops.

Name of Patentee.	Progressive Number.	Date.		Subject-matter of Patent.
BIRD, MOSES - - - -	1778	29th Oct.	1790	Guarded lock, bolt, or box to be applied to the bolt, for the greater security of door and other locks.
BIRD, OLIVER - - -	7148	13th July	1836	Machinery applicable to the dressing of woollen and other cloths.
BIRKBY, JOHN - - -	6917	29th Oct.	1835	Machinery for pointing wire;—applicable for making cards and pins.
BIRKBY, JOHN - - -	7034	17th March	1836	Machinery for making needles.
BIRKBY, JOHN - - -	9267	25th Feb.	1842	Manufacture of wire cards.
BIRKETT, WILLIAM - -	13,663	12th June	1851	Obtaining soap from washwaters.
BIRKIN, RICHARD - - -	7090	11th May	1836	Machinery for making ornamented bobbin-net lace.
BIRKINSHAW, JOHN - -	4503	23rd Oct.	1820	Manufacturing, and construction of, a wrought or malleable iron rail-road or way.
BIRKMYRE, WILLIAM - -	10,320	19th Sept.	1844	Manufacture of potash, soda, alum, sulphuric-acid, and sulphate of soda.
BIRKMYRE, WILLIAM - -	11,966	16th Nov.	1847	Smelting copper and other ores.
BIRKMYRE, WILLIAM - -	12,888	12th Dec.	1849	Making and refining sugar.
BIRLEY, THOMAS HORNBY -	12,641	5th June	1849	Machinery for preparing, roving, and spinning cotton, and wool (*J. G. Bodmer's Extension for 5 years, from 27th May 1849*).
BIRNIE, SAMUEL - - -	1661	12th Aug.	1788	Preparing calx of lead and restoring the same into pig-lead, after being used in extracting mineral alkali from common salt.
BIRT, ISAIAH - - - -	2967	18th Sept.	1806	Black paint, composed chiefly of earthy and mineral substances.
BIRT, THOMAS PARRANT -	5366	23rd May	1826	Wheel-carriages.
BISHOP, JAMES - - -	11,348	25th Aug.	1846	Passenger carriages.
BISHOP, JOHN - - -	2341	23rd Sept.	1799	Producing a power, to move machinery and reduce labour, by means of fire, water, and steam with or without condensation.
BISHOP, JOHN - - -	9355	23rd May	1842	Construction of break apparatus, applicable to railway-carriages.
BISHOP, JOHN - - -	9581	29th Dec.	1842	Apparatus for portioning steam power : also improvements in plugs, cocks, or taps for steam, gases, and liquids.
BISHOP, JOHN - - -	9979	8th Dec.	1843	Paving roads, streets, and other places.
BISHOP, PETER - - -	11,173	21st April	1846	Manufacture of bayonets.
BISHOP, SAMUEL HUNTON [TOWNSEND	11,601	2nd March	1847	Construction of the upper part of chimneys.
BISHOP, THOMAS - - -	694	26th Nov.	1754	Liquid blue for dyeing linens, cottons, &c.
BISHOPP, GEORGE DANIEL -	10,846	2nd Oct.	1845	Machines for obtaining mechanical power, and for raising and impelling fluids.
BISSE, EDWARD - - -	49	21st Jan.	1630	Barrel engine, for raising water out of mines, graffs, coalpits, or any other place.
BISSELL, LEVI - - -	13,710	5th Aug.	1851	Means of sustaining travelling carriages and other vehicles;—applicable to other like purposes.
BISSY, STEPHEN Baron DE -	884	11th Nov.	1767	Oar, for men of war, merchantmen, and other rowing vessels.
BITTLESTON, JOHN - -	4478	20th June	1820	Construction and application of spring trusses or bandages for the relief or cure of hernia.
BLACHE, LOUIS GOY LA -	719	12th Nov.	1757	Royal military drops.
BLACK, BENJAMIN - -	3579	25th June	1812	Lamps for coaches, chariots, and other carriages.

Name of Patentee.	Progres-sive Number.	Date.	Subject-matter of Patent.
BLACK, BENJAMIN - -	4963	25th May 1824	Carriage lamps.
BLACK, CHARLES - - -	10,620	15th April 1845	Manufacture of horse-shoes.
BLACK, GEORGE - - -	1071	27th May 1774	Lock and latch to be affixed to a door, for the purpose of raising it from the floor over a carpet, or to give air to a room without opening the door.
BLACK, HORATIO - - -	12,065	14th Feb. 1848	Evaporation.
BLACK, JAMES - - -	13,315	7th Nov. 1850	Machine for folding.
BLACKEY, JOHN HERBERT	10,644	29th April 1845	Spinning-throstles.
BLACKMORE, BENJAMIN - -	1412	19th Dec. 1783	Bolting-cloths, to be used by millers for the purpose of dressing flour.
BLACKMORE, BENJAMIN -	2386	31st March 1800	Elastic spring, for making bolting-cloths without seams.
BLACKWELL, BENJAMIN BRUN-[TON.	9641	21st Feb. 1843	Coating iron nails, screws, nuts, bolts, and other articles made of iron, with certain other metals.
BLACKWELL, JAMES - -	12,049	2nd Feb. 1848	Evaporating-furnaces.
BLACKWELL, JOHN - -	6059	13th Jan. 1831	Machinery for making lace called bobbin-net.
BLADEN, NATHANIEL - -	220	10th July 1682	Mill for making paper and pasteboard.
BLADES, JOSEPH - -	5604	15th Jan. 1828	Waterproof stiffening for hats.
BLAIKIE, FRANCIS - -	1653	11th June 1788	Preparing an ingredient to be used as a substitute for gum, in thickening colours for printing.
BLAIR, ARCHIBALD - -	2623	31st May 1802	Machinery for pressing all sorts of substances.
BLAIR, ARCHIBALD - -	2643	19th Aug. 1802	Retaining cotton and other elastic substances when pressed.
BLAIR, ARCHIBALD - -	2828	9th March 1805	Retaining cotton and other elastic bodies (when pressed) by means of wrappers.
BLAIR, HARRISON - - -	8465	6th April 1840	Manufacture of sulphuric-acid, crystallized soda, and soda-ash; recovery of the residue for various useful purposes.
BLAIR, JOHN - - -	13,742	11th Sept. 1851	Beds or couches, and other articles of furniture.
BLAIR, ROBERT - - -	1473	26th April 1785	Refracting telescope and other optical instruments.
BLAIR, ROBERT - - -	1800	4th April 1791	Reflecting telescopes, and other dioptrical instruments.
BLAKE, FRANCIS STILES -	6461	14th Aug. 1833	Fids for the upper masts, running bowsprits, and jib-booms, of ships and other vessels.
BLAKE, JAMES PARTRIDGE -	7382	30th May 1837	Apparatus for hulling, cleansing, preparing, or dressing paddy or rough rice; and for hulling, dressing, and preparing oats and other such grain;—applicable to other purposes.
BLAKE, JONATHAN - -	12,743	16th Aug. 1849	Lamps.
BLAKE, OBED - - -	12,414	11th Jan. 1849	Ventilators for ships, vehicles, houses, or other buildings.
BLAKE, OBED - - -	12,486	28th Feb. 1849	Process of manufacturing and finishing plates, sheets, or panes, of glass.
BLAKEMORE, RICHARD - -	4284	24th July 1818	Amorphous metal-plates; also crystallizing, or rendering crystallizable, the surface of tin plates, or iron or copper plates tinned. (Morphous metal plates.)
BLAKEMORE, RICHARD - -	13,366	30th Nov. 1850	Construction of ploughs.
BLAKEY, THOMAS - - -	14,202	6th July 1852	Mills for grinding.
BLAKEY, WILLIAM - -	848	10th June 1766	Machine which performs its operations, either by the agency of fire, fall of water, or both, with reduced friction.

Name of Patentee.	Progressive Number.	Date.		Subject-matter of Patent.
BLANC, ANTOINE　-　-　-	8386	12th Feb.	1840	Producing soda and other articles obtained from the decomposition of common salt.
BLANCH, JOHN　-　-　-	1072	17th June	1774	Hydrostatic pump, answering the purposes of a common pump, and for extinguishing fires, watering roads, gardens, &c. ; also useful in ships as a head pump.
BLANCHARD, PETER　-　-	493	30th May	1727	Engine for making sapping silk lacing both round and flat.
BLANCHARD, RICHARD　-	493	30th May	1727	Engine for making sapping silk lacing, both round and flat.
BLAND, JOHN -　-　-　-	4824	31st July	1823	Steam-engines, such as condense out of the cylinder (rendering the air-pump unnecessary).
BLASHFIELD, JOHN MARRIOTT	12,790	27th Sept.	1849	Manufacture of manure.
BLAXLAND, GEORGE　-　-	8729	28th Nov.	1840	Propelling ships and vessels, at sea and in navigable rivers.
BLEASDALE, HENRY　-　-	11,489	14th Dec.	1846	Apparatus employed in making rollers used in machinery for preparing and spinning cotton, and other fibrous substances.
BLEASDALE, RICHARD　-　-	11,683	4th May	1847	Machinery for preparing and spinning cotton-wool, and other fibrous substances.
BLENKINSOP, JOHN　-　-	3431	10th April	1811	Mechanical means whereby the conveyance of coals, minerals, and other articles, is facilitated, and the expense reduced.
BLEWITT, REGINALD JAMES -	11,723	27th May	1847	Manufacture of malleable iron.
BLEWSTON, Dr. FREDERICK DE	198	25th Oct.	1677	Melting down, forging, extracting, and reducing iron and all metals and minerals, by the use of pit-coal and sea-coal.
BLIGHT, RICHARD -　-　-	1218	10th April	1779	Construction of cannons, guns, and gun-carriages.
BLIGNY, JOSEPHINE JULIE [BESNIER DE.	8086	3rd June	1839	Umbrellas and parasols.
BLINKHORN, WILLIAM -　-	12,966	11th Feb.	1850	Machinery to be used in the manufacture of glass.
BLOCKLEY, THOMAS　-　-	740	14th July	1759	Polishing and rolling malleable metal, and making tire for wheel-carriages.
BLON, JAMES CHRISTOPHER, LE	423	5th Feb.	1719	Multiplying pictures and draughts by natural colours with impression.
BLON, JAMES CHRISTOPHER, LE	492	1st May.	1727	Weaving tapestry in the loom.
BLONK, BENJAMIN　-　-	1507	8th Nov.	1785	Stamping, impressing, or rolling scissors out of a bar, sheet, plate, or string of steel, by means of stamps, fly or screw presses, or by rolling with cylinders.
BLOOD, EDMOND　-　-　-	165	7th Nov.	1671	Making a silk shag, suitable for garments, from silk waste prepared by teasels or rowing cards.
BLOXAM, JAMES MACKENZIE -	9793	20th June	1843	Meridian instruments.
BLUETT, JAMES　-　-　-	5747	22nd Dec.	1828	Producing a reciprocating action by means of rotatory motion ; to be applied to the working of pumps and other machinery.
BLUMBERG, HENRY　-　-	10,923	4th Nov.	1845	Purification of spirits for the use of brewing distillers, and rectifiers.
BLUNDELL, GEORGE　-　-	2235	3rd May	1798	Machine for saving fuel, and preventing dirt and dust from fires (economical receiver).
BLUNDELL, HENRY　-　-	6043	6th Dec.	1830	Machine for grinding or crushing seeds and other oleaginous substances, for the purpose of abstracting oil therefrom ;—applicable, with certain modifications, to other purposes.

Name of Patentee.	Progressive Number.	Date.	Subject-matter of Patent.
BLUNDELL, HENRY - -	7184	15th Sept. 1836	Operating on certain vegetable and animal substances, in the process of making candles therefrom.
BLUNDELL, JOSEPH BIRKBECK	13,720	14th Aug. 1851	Machines for sweeping and cleansing roads and ways.
BLUNT, CHARLES FLY - -	3556	21st April 1812	Arrangements of machinery for improvement of ships' fire-hearths, and for other purposes.
BLUNT, JOHN - - - -	2853	27th May 1805	Apparatus fixed to stirrups, for the purpose of detaching the same from the stirrup leather, in cases of accident.
BLUNT, RICHARD TILLYER -	1625	30th Oct. 1787	Making yeast for purposes of fermentation.
BLURTON, WILLIAM - -	7045	26th March 1836	Method of, and apparatus for, extracting milk from cows and other animals.
BLYDESTEIN, ISAAC - -	1745	21st April 1790	Perpetual motion or self-moving principle.
BLYTH, ALFRED - - -	10,558	13th March 1845	Steam-engines, steam boilers, and machinery for propelling vessels, for steam navigation, and for other purposes.
BLYTH, ALFRED - - -	11,862	9th Sept. 1847	Apparatus for distilling and rectifying.
BLYTH, GEORGE - - -	6,700	22nd Oct. 1834	Saddles for horses.
BLYTH, JOHN - - -	6972	31st Dec. 1835	Retarding the progress of carriages in certain cases.
BLYTH, JOHN - - - -	10,558	13th March 1845	Steam-engines, steam-boilers, and machinery for propelling vessels, for steam navigation, and for other purposes.
BLYTH, JOHN - • - -	11,011	20th Dec. 1845	Diminishing the risk of accidental explosions of gunpowder and other substances liable to explode by contact with fire.
BLYTH, JOHN - - - -	11,229	28th May 1846	Closing the orifices of bottles or other vessels;—applicable to inkholders.
BLYTH, JOHN - - - -	11,862	9th Sept. 1847	Apparatus for distilling and rectifying.
BLYTHE, WILLIAM - -	8183	1st Aug. 1839	Processes to be used in the printing, dyeing, or colouring of cotton, woollen, silk, and other cloths and yarns.
BLYTHE, WILLIAM - -	12,807	12th Oct. 1849	Certain materials used in the processes of dyeing and printing.
BOARDER, WILLIAM - -	7298	16th Feb. 1837	Steam-engines.
BOASE, JOHN - - -	5728	10th Dec. 1828	Machinery for scraping, sweeping, cleaning, and watering streets, roads, and other ways.
BOASE, JOHN - - - -	5923	30th March 1830	Steam-boilers; and a mode of quickening the draft for furnaces connected therewith.
BOASE, JOHN - - -	5956	19th July 1830	Steam-carriages; boilers.
BOAZ, JAMES - - -	2564	3rd Dec. 1801	Communicating intelligence to and from different places, by signs produced by means of lights and otherwise.
BOAZ, JAMES - - -	2804	2nd July 1805	Raising water, and working machinery, by steam.
BOAZ, JAMES - - -	3695	15th May 1813	Instruments to prevent doors and window-shutters being broken open, or forced in by the wind.
BOCCIUS, GOTTLIEB - -	9237	27th Jan. 1842	Gas and gas-burners.
BOCCIUS, GOTTLIEB - -	9647	28th Feb. 1843	Arrangements and apparatus for the production and distribution of light.
BOCHE, MICHEL - -	10,683	22nd May 1845	Apparatus for measuring charges of powder and shot.
BOCHET, HENRY DU - -	9631	11th Feb. 1843	Making pianofortes.

Name of Patentee.	Progressive Number.	Date.	Subject-matter of Patent.
Bock, Henry － － －	5788	2nd May 1829	Machinery for embroidering or ornamenting cloths, stuffs, and other fabrics.
Boddy, William Barnard －	9619	31st Jan. 1843	Apparatus and means for opening shutters, and fastening window-sashes, windows, and window-shutters.
Bode, Henry (Baron De) －	7107	4th June 1836	Capstans.
Bode, Henry (Baron De) －	7379	23rd May 1837	Apparatus for retarding and stopping chain or other cables or ropes, on board ships or vessels.
Bode, Henry (Baron De) －	8096	8th June 1839	Means of rendering magnetic-needles less prejudicially influenced by local attraction ;— applicable to other magnetic objects for the same purpose.
Boden, Henry － － －	10,214	4th June 1844	Manufacture of bobbin net or twist lace.
Boden, John Amory － －	8131	26th June 1839	Compositions to resemble ivory, bone, horn, mother of pearl, and other substances applicable to the manufacture of handles of knives, forks, and razors, pianoforte-keys, snuff boxes, and various other articles.
Boden, John Amory － －	8361	25th Jan. 1840	Compositions to resemble ivory, bone, horn, mother of pearl, and other substances, applicable to the manufacture of handles of knifes, forks, and razors, pianoforte-keys, snuff boxes, and various other articles.
Bodley, George － － －	2537	3rd Sept. 1801	Mill for grinding bark.
Bodley, George － － －	2585	27th Feb. 1802	Portable stove or kitchen for dressing victuals.
Bodley, George － － －	4019	27th April 1816	Metallic engine, to work by steam or water.
Bodmer, Frederick William	12,741	16th Aug. 1849	Machinery for letter-press printing.
Bodmer, James － － －	3755	23rd Nov. 1813	Loading at the breach, fire-arms with a rifled bore ; also a touch-hole, and moveable sight for fire-arms.
Bodmer, John George －	5016	14th Oct. 1824	Machinery for cleaning, carding, drawing, roving, and spinning cotton and wool.
Bodmer, John George －	6616	24th May 1834	Steam-engines and boilers applicable to fixed and locomotive engines.
Bodmer, John George －	6617	24th May 1834	Construction of grates, stoves, and furnaces applicable to steam-engines, and to other purposes.
Bodmer, John George －	6841	27th May 1835	Machinery for preparing, roving, and spinning cotton and wool.
Bodmer, John George －	7388	12th June 1837	Machinery for spinning and doubling cotton, silk, flax, and other fibrous materials.
Bodmer, John George －	7837	22nd Oct. 1838	Machinery for carding, drawing, roving, and spinning cotton, flax, wool, silk, and other fibrous substances.
Bodmer, John George －	7881	22nd Nov. 1838	Machinery, tools, or apparatus, for cutting, planing, turning, drilling, and rolling metals, and other substances.
Bodmer, John George －	8070	20th May 1839	Machinery, tools, or apparatus, for cutting, planing, turning, drilling, and rolling metals, and other substances.
Bodmer, John George －	8579	29th July 1840	Machinery for cleaning, carding, roving, drawing, and spinning, cotton and wool.
Bodmer, John George －	8912	3rd April 1841	Construction of screwing-stocks, taps, and dies, or other tools ; apparatus or machinery for cutting and working in metals.
Bodmer, John George －	8981	10th June 1841	Machinery for propelling vessels on water ;— partly applicable to steam-engines on land.

Name of Patentee.	Progressive Number.	Date.	Subject-matter of Patent.
BODMER, JOHN GEORGE -	9279	7th March 1842	Machinery for cleaning, carding, roving, and spinning cotton and other fibrous substances.
BODMER, JOHN GEORGE -	9547	8th Dec. 1842	Manufacture of metallic hoops and 'tires for wheels; method of fixing the same; machinery employed therein.
BODMER, JOHN GEORGE -	9702	20th April 1843	Locomotive steam-engines and carriages for railways; marine engines and vessels; apparatus for propelling the same; stationary engines for pumping water, raising bodies, and blowing or exhausting air.
BODMER, JOHN GEORGE -	9899	5th Oct. 1843	Grates, furnaces, and boilers; working iron or other metals; machinery connected therewith.
BODMER, JOHN GEORGE -	10,243	3rd July 1844	Locomotive steam-engines and carriages for railways; marine-engines and vessels; apparatus for propelling the same; stationary engines and apparatus connected therewith.
BODMER, JOHN GEORGE -	12,641	5th June 1849	Machinery for preparing, roving, and spinning cotton and wool.
BOGAERTS, JOHN - - -	4302	10th Nov. 1818	Raising and lowering water in canal locks.
BOGARDUS, JAMES - - -	8208	26th Aug. 1839	Applying labels, stamps, or marks, to letters and other such documents.
BOGGETT, WILLIAM - -	12,429	20th Jan. 1849	Machinery for obtaining and applying motive power.
BOGGETT, WILLIAM - -	12,787	27th Sept. 1849	Heating and evaporating fluids.
BOGGETT, WILLIAM - -	13,271	3rd Oct. 1850	Producing and applying heat; engines to be worked by steam or other elastic fluid; which engines are also applicable as pumps.
BOGGETT, WILLIAM - -	13,783	22nd Oct. 1851	Obtaining and applying heat and light.
BOGGETT, WILLIAM - -	14,333	21st Oct. 1852	Obtaining and applying heat and light.
BOILEAU, PETER - - -	2234	3rd May 1798	Manufacture of straw into hats, bonnets, and other articles.
BOIS, PHILIP HENRY DU	11,448	12th Nov. 1846	Producing ornamental metal surfaces.
BOISSIMON, CHARLES HEARD [DE.	11,226	28th May 1846	Making corks and bungs.
BOLAND, RICHARD - -	13,609	29th April 1851	Chains, chain-pins, swivels, brooches, and other fastenings for wearing-apparel.
BOLD, JOHN - - - -	4500	20th Oct. 1820	Printing-presses.
BOLD, JOHN - - - -	4690	4th July 1822	Printing.
BOLTON, GEORGE - - -	2041	28th Feb. 1795	Gun-lock for muskets, pistols, and other fire-arms.
BOLTON, HUGH - - -	6274	5th June 1832	Machinery for carding cotton and other fibrous materials.
BOLTON, JOHN - - -	9214	11th Jan. 1842	Tapes for measuring, and boxes for containing the same.
BOLTON, WILLIAM - -	2222	10th March 1798	Capstan.
BOLTON, WILLIAM - -	2519	23rd June 1801	Rudder, and means of preserving the same.
BOLTS, WILLIAM - - -	2343	26th Sept. 1799	Form, quality, and use of, candles and other lights made of tallow, wax, spermaceti, or other inflammable substance.
BOMMENAER, ADRIANUS VAN- [DEN.	563	27th June 1738	Machine for twining and twisting yarn into thread, for the making of superfine lace or cambric.
BOMPAS, CHARLES CARPENTER	5644	29th April 1828	Propelling locomotive-carriages and machines, boats, and other vessels.

Name of Patentee.	Progressive Number.	Date.	Subject-matter of Patent.
BOMPAS, GEORGE GIVINETT -	6031	4th Nov. 1830	Preserving copper and other metals from corrosion or oxydation.
BOND, GEORGE ALEXANDER -	2834	26th March 1805	Construction of clocks and other timepieces.
BOND, JOHN - - - -	13,990	26th Feb. 1852	Machinery for preparing cotton and other fibrous substances; apparatus applicable to looms for weaving; tools employed therein.
BOND, JOHN LINNELL - -	5119	9th March 1825	Construction of windows, casements, folding sashes and doors, which are hung so as to exclude rain and wind, and to afford ventilation.
BONELL, CORNELIUS - -	12,810	12th Oct. 1849	Rotatory engines; construction of carriages, vessels, or other vehicles, to be worked or propelled by means of the said improvements in rotatory engines, by or other motive-power; machinery connected therewith.
BONELLI, GAETAN - - -	11,437	3rd Nov. 1846	Bridges, viaducts, aqueducts, and other similar erections.
BONEUIL, ANTHONY BOURBOU- [LONDE.	1677	11th March 1789	Apparatus and processes for making fossi alkali.
BONEUIL, ANTHONY BOURBOU- [LONDE.	1678	25th March 1789	Apparatus and processes used in whitening hemp, flax, cotton, wax, and other articles; also goods manufactured from the same.
BONHAM, THOMAS - - -	7030	14th March 1836	Vices.
BONNER, CHARLES - -	5334	18th Feb. 1826	Securing and suspending windows, gates, doors, shutters, blinds, and other apparatus.
BONNER, THOMAS - - -	5571	4th Dec. 1827	Safety-lamps.
BONNIN, GOUSSE - - -	919	5th March 1769	Manufacturing certain materials into crucibles, named black-lead crucibles.
BONSER, THOMAS - - -	11,297	15th July 1846	Machinery for tilling land.
BOOKER, NUGENT - - -	3234	9th May 1809	Lime-kilns.
BOOKER, THOMAS WILLIAM -	7495	4th Dec. 1837	Preparing iron to be coated with tin or other metals.
BOOKER, THOMAS WILLIAM -	8855	22nd Feb. 1841	Manufacture of iron.
BOOND, WILLIAM - - -	2694	5th April 1803	Manufacture of cotton pile goods or fustians.
BOORN, MOSES - - -	1698	27th Aug. 1789	Engine for sowing grain in rows or drills.
BOOT, JARVIS - - -	4881	13th Dec. 1823	Apparatus for singeing lace, and for other purposes.
BOOT, JOHN - - - -	9061	4th Sept. 1841	Machinery for making figured fabrics in warp and bobbin-net lace machines.
BOOTE, RICHARD - - -	9889	5th Oct. 1843	Pottery and mosaic-work.
BOOTH, EDWARD - - -	344	23rd Sept. 1695	Watch or clock, with the balance-wheel flat or hollow, to work within and cross the centre of the verge, with teeth like tenter-hooks to move the balance or pendulum, the pallets of the verge to be circular, concave and convex.
BOOTH, EDWARD - - -	359	1st Dec. 1698	Engine for draining water, which, with ladles or forcers turning circularly, drives the water to the desired place or height.
BOOTH, GEORGE ROBINS -	9784	15th June 1843	Applying heat from various combustibles, to manufacturing and other purposes.
BOOTH, GEORGE ROBINS -	13,334	12th Nov. 1850	Manufacture of gas.
BOOTH, GEORGE ROBINS -	13,547	10th March 1851	Generating and applying heat.
BOOTH, GEORGE ROBINS -	14,116	8th May 1852	Manufacture of gas.
BOOTH, HENRY - - -	4367	6th May 1819	Propelling boats and other vessels.

Name of Patentee.	Progressive Number.	Date.	Subject-matter of Patent.
BOOTH, HENRY - - -	6814	14th April 1835	Composition for greasing axle-bearings of carriages, and the axle-spindles and bearing parts of machinery. ("Patent axle grease and lubricating fluid.")
BOOTH, HENRY - - -	6961	16th Dec. 1835	Method of attaching railway-carriages together, for obtaining steadiness and smoothness of motion.
BOOTH, HENRY - - -	6989	23rd Jan. 1836	Locomotive steam-engines and railway-carriages.
BOOTH, HENRY - - -	7244	3rd Dec. 1836	Construction and arrangement of railway tunnels, to be worked by locomotive-engines.
BOOTH, HENRY - - -	7335	4th April 1837	Construction of locomotive-engine boiler furnaces;—applicable to other furnaces.
BOOTH, HENRY - - -	9184	16th Dec. 1841	Propelling vessels through water.
BOOTH, HUGH - - -	9126	21st Oct. 1841	Looms for weaving.
BOOTH, JAMES - - -	9824	6th July 1843	Means of converting rectilinear into rotary motion, and the reverse.
BOOTH, JOHN - - -	230	27th Nov. 1683	Engine for sawing timber, boards, and stones, without the aid of wind or water.
BOOTH, JOHN PETER - -	9152	11th Nov. 1841	Manufacture of a compound fabric for making quilts, coverlets, and wadding, for clothing or furniture.
BOOTH, JOHN PETER - -	9414	9th July 1842	Machinery for working in mines;—applicable to raising, lowering, and transporting heavy bodies, and promoting a more perfect ventilation of the mine.
BOOTH, JOHN PETER - -	13,578	31st March 1851	Manufacture of fabric applicable to the construction of muffs, boas, tippets, and other articles, and for ornamenting dress furniture, and for other similar uses.
BOOTH, JOSEPH - - -	1846	23rd Jan. 1792	Apparatus and chemical compositions for the purpose of making woollen-cloths, linens, and various other fabrics.
BOOTH, JOSEPH - - -	1888	12th June 1792	Apparatus and chemical compositions for the purpose of making woollen-cloths, linens, and various other fabrics.
BOOTH, TEMPEST - - -	13,174	15th July 1850	Obtaining and applying motive-power; apparatus for the purpose.
BOOTH, WILLIAM - - -	2112	31st May 1796	Making stays and corsets.
BOOTH, WILLIAM - - -	4244	8th April 1818	Machine for making wooden-clogs, for pattens, clog-soles, and Devonshire clogs.
BOOTH, WILLIAM - - -	5081	13th Jan. 1825	Spinning, doubling, throwing, and twisting silk, wool, cotton, flax, hemp, and such like materials.
BOOTHBY, BENJAMIN - -	4705	27th Sept. 1822	Manufacturing cannon-shot.
BOOTHMAN, WILLIAM -	1344	16th Nov. 1782	Making iron liquor.
BOOTIE, JOHN - - -	901	13th Aug. 1763	Tinning copper and brass vessels, to prevent the formation of verdigris.
BORDEN, EARL, junior -	13,741	5th Sept. 1851	Treatment of certain animal and vegetable substances, to render them more convenient for use as articles of food, and for their better preservation.
BORDIER, JULIUS - -	9219	13th Jan. 1842	Preparing skins and hides, and converting them into leather.
BOREL, LEWIS FAUCHE -	4069	25th Oct. 1816	Making boots and shoes without sewing, and impervious to wet;—applicable to other purposes.

Name of Patentee.	Progressive Number.	Date.		Subject-matter of Patent.
BOREL, LOUIS FAUCH　-　-	4410	18th Nov.	1819	Moveable and inodorous conveniences.
BORGOGNON, JEAN MICHEL　-	11,333	11th Aug.	1846	Producing artificial basaltic lavas.
BORIE, HENRY JULES　-　-	13,369	30th Nov.	1850	Manufacture of bricks.
BORLAND, JOHN　-　-	13,311	2nd Nov.	1850	Weaving-machinery.
BORRIE, PETER　-　-	9859	3rd Aug.	1843	Steam-engines, boilers, and propelling-machinery.
BORRIE, PETER　-　-	10,351	17th Oct.	1844	Machinery for the manufacture of sugar.
BORRIE, PETER　-　-	10,493	23rd Jan.	1845	Construction and equipment of ships or vessels.
BORRIE, PETER　-　-	11,499	21st Dec.	1846	Construction of piers and harbours.
BORRODAILE, GEORGE　-　-	5295	17th Nov.	1825	Making or setting up hats, or hat bodies.
BOSLEY, JOSEPH　-　-	698	1st March	1755	New movement in watches; also a slide for regulating watches.
BOSQUET, ABRAHAM　-　-	2242	8th June	1798	Method, by the application of which ships are rendered durable, sound, and free from bilge water.
BOSS, ISAAC ABRAHAM　-　-	10,478	16th Jan.	1845	Manufacture of parasols and umbrellas.
BOSSY, ANTOINE　-　-	10,760	10th July	1845	Manufacture of waterproof paper.
BOSTWICK, LEONARD　-　-	10,134	2nd April	1844	Machinery for sewing all kinds of cloth or other materials.
BOSVILLE, LENNARD　-　-	194	28th Jan.	1677	Mills for making cider and perry.
BOSWELL, JOHN WHITLEY　-	2621	20th May	1802	Building ships or vessels.
BOSWORTH, JOHN　-　-　-	3336	9th May	1810	Carriages to facilitate the unloading of heavy coals and other things.
BOTFIELD, THOMAS　-　-	3246	26th July	1809	Constructing an iron or metal roof for houses or other buildings.
BOTFIELD, THOMAS　-　-	5596	2nd Jan.	1828	Smelting and making iron.
BOTTEN, CHARLES -　-　-	8739	16th Dec.	1840	Gas-meters.
BOTTOM, JOHN　-　-	9214	11th Jan.	1842	Tapes for measuring; and boxes for containing the same.
BOTTOM, JOHN　-　-	10,526	20th Feb.	1845	Carpenters' stocks and braces.
BOTTOM, JOHN FRANCIS -　-	12,426	18th Jan.	1849	Dressing or getting-up fabrics of cotton or silk, or of both combined.
BOTTOMLEY, EDWIN　-　-	7806	13th Sept.	1838	Power and hand looms.
BOTTOMLEY, JOHN -　-　-	12,484	22nd Feb.	1849	Machinery for weaving.
BOTTURE, SEBASTIANO -　-	13,418	19th Dec.	1850	Machinery and apparatus for elevating fluids;—application of fluids as a motive-power.
BOUCHER, EUGENE ALEXANDRE DESIRE.	12,720	1st Aug.	1849	Manufacture of cards.
BOUCHET, MICHAEL JOSEPH ISIDOR.	1406	9th Dec.	1783	Lamp and lantern, producing neither smoke nor smell.
BOUCICAULT, DION DE -　-	12,496	28th Feb.	1849	Modes to be used for transmitting and distributing liquids and fluids for agricultural purposes; apparatus connected therewith.
BOUISSON, JOSEPH MARIE DU	5902	12th Feb.	1830	Extracting colour from dye-woods and other substances, for purposes of dyeing.
BOULAY, JOHN DU -　-　-	11,565	8th Feb.	1847	Fitting up granaries and warehouses, and getting into condition and preserving therein, grain, pulse, seeds, malt, and other perishable articles.
BOULAY, THOMAS DU　-　-	7420	24th Aug.	1837	Drying and screening malt.
BOULAY, THOMAS DU　-　-	11,565	8th Feb.	1847	Fitting up granaries and warehouses, and getting into condition and preserving therein, grain, pulse, seeds, malt, and other perishable articles.

Name of Patentee.	Progressive Number.	Date.	Subject-matter of Patent.
BOULD, JOHN - - - -	9192	16th Dec. 1841	Condensing steam-engines.
BOULNOIS, WILLIAM - -	6992	30th Jan. 1836	Combination of springs for carriages.
BOULNOIS, WILLIAM - -	11,935	2nd Nov. 1847	Draught-harness.
BOULTON, MATTHEW - -	1757	8th July 1790	Application of the powers of water-mills, cattle-mills, and steam-engines, either simply or combined with the pressure of the atmosphere, and with weights and springs, to the working of fly-presses or stamps.
BOULTON, MATTHEW - -	2207	30th Dec. 1797	Apparatus for raising water and other fluids.
BOULTON, SAMUEL - - -	13,987	23rd Feb. 1852	Treatment of metallic ores, and certain salts and residuary matters; obtaining products therefrom.
BOUND, WILLIAM - - -	3057	4th July 1807	Receiver for the cinders and ashes of register and other stoves.
BOUND, WILLIAM - - -	4122	17th May 1817	Application of apparatus for converting fuel used for heating gas-retorts, into coke or charcoal.
BOUNSALL, JAMES - - -	3753	16th Nov. 1813	Rope-making, and machinery for the same.
BOUNSALL, JAMES - - -	4160	12th Aug. 1817	Machinery used for tarring, reeling, and twisting yarn, and forming the strands of cables and other cordage, and manufacturing rope of every size.
BOURA, AIME - - - -	11,844	19th Aug. 1847	Extracting colouring matters.
BOURCART, JEAN JACQUES -	14,045	27th March 1852	Preparing, combing, and spinning wool and other fibrous materials.
BOURDIEU, JOHN - - -	4704	27th Sept. 1822	Preparation of colours for printing woven cloth.
BOURDIEU, JOHN - - -	4789	29th April 1823	Preparation of a mucilage to be used in printing linen, woollen, and cotton cloths, and silks.
BOURJOT, CHARLES - -	7762	3rd Aug. 1838	Manufacture of iron.
BOURJOT, CHARLES - -	9862	8th Aug. 1843	Apparatus for obtaining the profile of various forms or figures.
BOURLIER, JOHN STEPHEN -	9577	29th Dec. 1842	Machinery for printing calicoes, silks, paper-hangings, and other fabrics.
BOURN, DANIEL - - -	628	20th Jan. 1748	Machine for carding wool and cotton by hand or water.
BOURNE, JOHN - - -	6326	22nd Oct. 1832	Machine for scraping or cleaning roads and other ways.
BOURNE, JOHN - - -	7824	8th Oct. 1838	Steam-engines; and construction of boilers, furnaces, and stoves.
BOURNE, JOHN FREDERICK -	7795	6th Sept. 1838	Construction of wheels for railways and other roads;—applicable to the construction of wheels in general.
BOURNE, JOSEPH - - -	4871	22nd Nov. 1823	Burning stone-ware and brown-ware, in kilns or ovens.
BOURNE, JOSEPH - - -	11,831	4th Aug. 1847	Construction of kilns for burning stone-ware and brown-ware.
BOURNE, THOMAS - - -	2945	24th June 1806	Engine for roasting meat by steam, and for other purposes.
BOURNE, WILLIAM - - -	7139	2nd July 1836	Producing and transferring patterns, in one or more colours or metallic preparations, to surfaces of metal, wood, cloth, paper, or other suitable substance.
BOUSFIELD, FREDERICK -	13,869	19th Dec. 1851	Manufacture of manure.
BOUSIE, WILLIAM - - -	1428	17th April 1784	Refining sugar, also making sugar from the cane-juice.

Name of Patentee.	Progressive Number.	Date.	Subject-matter of Patent.
BOUSSOIS, EDWARD JOSEPH [FRANÇOIS DUCLOS DE.	9154	11th Nov. 1841	Manufacture of copper.
BOUSSOIS, FDWARD JOSEPH [FRANÇOIS DUCLOS DE.	9764	10th June 1843	Manufacture of lead, tin, tungsten, copper, and zinc, from ores, slags, and other products; and manufacture of their alloys with other metals.
BOUVEIRON, HENRI ALPHONSE [BOUNEVIALLE.	9205	21st Dec. 1841	Axletrees.
BOVILL, GEORGE HINTON -	10,734	23rd June 1845	Construction of parts of apparatus for propelling carriages and vessels by air; propelling carriages and vessels by atmospheric pressure.
BOVILL, GEORGE HINTON -	11,067	31st Jan. 1846	Manufacture of iron.
BOVILL, GEORGE HINTON -	11,129	11th March 1846	Apparatus for working atmospheric and other railways, canals, and mines; transmitting gas for lighting railways and other places.
BOVILL, GEORGE HINTON -	11,342	18th Aug. 1846	Manufacturing wheat and other grain, into meal and flour.
BOVILL, GEORGE HINTON -	12,636	5th June 1849	Manufacturing wheat and other grain, into flour.
BOVILL, GEORGE HINTON -	14,220	15th July 1852	Manufacturing wheat and other grain, into meal and flour.
BOWDEN, ANTHONY - -	2523	1st July 1801	Engine for batting or beating and cleansing cotton.
BOWDEN, CHARLES DOUGLAS	837	13th Jan. 1766	Hydraulic engine for raising water.
BOWDEN, JOSIAH - - -	12,685	4th July 1849	Manufacture of soap.
BOWDEN, WILLIAM - -	11,132	11th March 1846	Machinery for washing and cleansing cotton, linen, and woollen fabrics.
BOWER, DAVID FARRAR - -	13,570	24th March 1851	Preparing, rotting, and fermenting flax, line, grasses, and other fibrous vegetable substances.
BOWER, JOSEPH - - -	4824	31st July 1823	Steam-engines, such as condense out of the cylinder (rendering the air pump unnecessary).
BOWER, JOSEPH - - -	8413	4th March 1840	Manufacture of carbonate of soda.
BOWER, LEONARD - - -	13,187	23rd July 1850	Machinery for manufacturing screws, bolts, rivets, and nails.
BOWER, MANOAH - - -	6700	22nd Oct. 1834	Saddles for horses.
BOWER, MANOAH - - -	7108	7th June 1836	Improvements applicable to various descriptions of carriages.
BOWEN, SAMUEL - - -	878	1st July 1767	Making sago, vermicelli, and soy, from American plants, equal in goodness to those from the East Indies.
BOWIE, ROBERT - - -	6985	21st Jan. 1836	Distillation and decoction;—applicable to heating fluids, and the purification of oleaginous bodies, both animal and vegetable.
BOWLAS, DAVID - - -	13,712	7th Aug. 1851	Apparatus for manufacturing weavers' healds or harness.
BOWLER, JOHN - - -	2105	26th April 1796	Making and working presses, particularly packing presses and hot presses.
BOWLER, JOHN - - -	5248	27th Aug. 1825	Manufacture of hats.
BOWLER, JOHN - - -	6028	4th Nov. 1830	Machinery employed in the process of dyeing hats.
BOWLES, FREDERICK - -	9471	15th Sept. 1842	Preparing flour from grain and potatoes by machinery, for making starch, bread, biscuit, and pastry.

Name of Patentee.	Progressive Number.	Date.	Subject-matter of Patent.
BOWLES, JOSEPH - - -	4003	23rd March 1816	Oil-mills.
BOWMAN, FREDERICK - -	6883	17th Aug. 1835	Process for renewing the virtues of animal charcoal, when exhausted or impaired.
BOWMAN, JAMES WILLIAM -	11,376	17th Sept. 1846	Reburning animal charcoal.
BOWMAN, KEMP - - -	689	21st Feb. 1754	Application and adaptation of a machine for making salt from sea water.
BOWMAN, MICHAEL - -	2093	1st March 1796	Truss with a jointed and spring pad, elastic understrap, and circular band.
BOWMAN, ROBERT - - -	2985	30th Oct. 1806	Making of whalebone, hats, caps, and bonnets; harps for cleaning corn; bottoms of sieves, and girths for horses; also a cloth for making hats, caps, &c., and for backs of chairs and carriages, bottoms of beds, and weavers' reeds.
BOWMAN, ROBERT - - -	4488	20th July 1820	Construction of looms for weaving various sorts of cloths.
BOWMAN, ROBERT - - -	5052	9th Dec. 1824	Apparatus for stopping, releasing, and regulating, chain and other cables of vessels.
BOWMAN, THOMAS - - -	2444	21st Oct. 1800	Making perukes or wigs, with fastenings made of elastic compressed steel springs.
BOWN, WILLIAM - - -	10,105	14th March 1844	Weaving elastic fabrics.
BOWNSALL, JAMES - - -	4160	12th Aug. 1817	Machinery used for tarring, reeling, and twisting yarn, also for forming the strands of cordage, and manufacturing rope.
BOWRA, EDWARD - - -	8653	1st Oct. 1840	Manufacture of boas, muffs, cuffs, flounces, and tippets.
BOWRING, EDWARD - -	5292	10th Nov. 1825	Working, weaving, or preparing, silk and other fibrous materials used in making hats, bonnets, shawls, and other articles.
BOWSER, GEORGE - - -	692	3rd July 1754	Embossing, printing, or staining, callimancoes and other woollen goods.
BOWSER, WILLIAM - -	10,576	27th March 1845	Ships' fire hearths.
BOWSER, WILLIAM, junior -	10,576	27th March 1845	Ships' fire hearths.
BOWYER, JOSEPH - - -	3046	29th May 1807	Manufacturing carpeting, for carpets and carpet bags.
BOWYER, JOSEPH - - -	4290	31st Aug. 1818	Machinery for making Wilton carpeting, figured and imperial rugs.
BOYCE, JOSEPH - - -	2324	4th July 1799	Machine for cutting wheat, and all other corn.
BOYD, JOHN - - - -	8052	30th April 1839	Spinning-frame used for spinning flax, hemp, and tow, upon the wet principle.
BOYDELL, JAMES, junior - -	6815	14th April 1835	Apparatus for tracking or towing boats and other vessels.
BOYDELL, JAMES, junior - -	7370	11th May 1837	Propelling carriages.
BOYDELL, JAMES, junior - -	8673	2nd Nov. 1840	Stopping railway and other carriages, and preventing them running off the rails.
BOYDELL, JAMES, junior - -	9365	24th May 1848	Manufacture of keel-plates for vessels; iron gates, gate-posts, fencings, and gratings.
BOYDELL, JAMES, junior - -	9607	26th Jan. 1843	Manufacture of metals for edge tools.
BOYDELL, JAMES, junior - -	9635	17th Feb. 1843	Apparatus for retaining the wheels of carriages on the breaking of an axle, or otherwise.
BOYDELL, JAMES, junior - -	9690	7th April 1843	Manufacturing bars of iron with other metals.
BOYDELL, JAMES, junior - -	9816	6th July 1843	Manufacture of metallic roofs and joists, and joining sheets or plates of metal for various purposes.

Name of Patentee.	Progressive Number.	Date.	Subject-matter of Patent.
BOYDELL, JAMES, junior - -	10,945	17th Nov. 1845	Manufacture of hinges and handles for knives and other instruments.
BOYDELL, JAMES, junior -	10,946	17th Nov. 1845	Building ships and other vessels.
BOYDELL, JAMES, junior - [Boydell, James.]	11,357	29th Aug. 1846	Applying apparatus to carriages, to facilitate the draft.
BOYES, JOHN - - -	11,309	23rd July 1846	Machines for thrashing and winnowing grain and other seeds.
BOYLE, ARTHUR - -	11,830	4th Aug. 1847	Manufacture of buttons.
BOYNTON, JAMES - -	6543	18th Jan. 1834	Apparatus for producing light.
BOYS, EDWARD, junior -	6406	4th April 1833	Apparatus for preventing accidents with carriages, in descending hills, or in other perilous situations.
BOZEK, JOSEPH ROMUALD -	11,028	6th Jan. 1846	Construction and application of railroad carriage-wheels.
BRABY, JAMES - -	7279	11th Jan. 1837	Construction of carriages.
BRADBURY, JOHN LEIGH -	3094	24th Dec. 1807	Spinning cotton, flax, and wool.
BRADBURY, JOHN LEIGH -	3555	15th April 1812	Machine for heading pins.
BRADBURY, JOHN LEIGH -	3990	9th March 1816	Machinery for spinning cotton, flax, wool, tow, worsted, or any other fibrous substance.
BRADBURY, JOHN LEIGH -	4525	9th Jan. 1821	Engraving and etching metal rollers used for printing woollen, cotton, linen, paper, cloth, silk, and other substances.
BRADBURY, JOHN LEIGH -	4813	15th July 1823	Printing, painting, or staining, silks, cottons, woollen and other cloths, and paper, parchment, vellum, leather, and other substances, by means of blocks, or surface printing.
BRADBURY, JOHN LEIGH -	4984	3rd July 1824	Twisting, spinning, or throwing, silk, cotton, wool, linen, or other fibrous substances.
BRADFORD, DANIEL DUNSCOMB	6175	4th Oct. 1831	Lamps.
BRADFORD, JAMES - -	13,184	22nd July 1850	Locks and other fastenings.
BRADFORD, WILLIAM - -	686	12th Dec. 1753	Machine for weighing gold coin, rings, and all utensils made of gold ; also a sliding rule for taking the contents of solids and superficials.
BRADLEY, GEORGE - -	5210	16th July 1825	Construction of looms for weaving woollen cloths.
BRADLEY, HENRY - -	3255	8th Aug. 1809	Preparing hemp, flax, hurds, short tow, and clearing, for spinning into yarn, alone or mixed with cotton ; and mode of spinning the same.
BRADLEY, JOHN - -	3437	24th April 1811	Manufacturing gun-skelps.
BRADLEY, RICHARD - -	7778	21st Aug. 1838	Manufacture of iron.
BRADLY, JAMES - -	3061	13th July 1807	Iron bar for fireplaces, boilers, furnaces, hot-houses, &c.
BRADLY, JOHN - -	1362	25th March 1783	Forge black, tue iron and frame for conveying wind by the blast of bellows, or otherwise.
BRADSHAW, GEORGE -	13,483	31st Jan. 1851	Fastenings for garments.
BRADSHAW, JAMES -	12,368	15th Dec. 1848	Looms for weaving various plain and ornamental textile fabrics.
BRADSHAW, PETER -	8506	12th May 1840	Dibbling corn and seeds.
BRADSHAW, WILLIAM -	12,368	15th Dec. 1848	Looms for weaving various plain and ornamental textile fabrics.
BRADY, JOHN DRUMGOLLE -	14,029	22nd March 1852	Helmets, cartridge-boxes, and other military accoutrements.
BRAGG, WILLIAM ALLEN -	12,520	14th March 1849	Propelling by atmospheric pressure.

Name of Patentee.	Progressive Number.	Date.	Subject-matter of Patent.
BRAIN, RICHARD FARMER -	4139	10th July 1817	Apparatus to generate gas, from coal or other substance, for lighting or heating houses, manufactories, and other places.
BRAITHWAITE, AUGUSTUS SEPTIMUS.	10,680	22nd May 1845	Buckles, clasps, and other fastenings.
BRAITHWAITE, FREDERICK -	9661	16th March 1843	Machinery for splitting wood for fuel, and other purposes.
BRAITHWAITE, GEORGE MOTT	8634	17th Sept. 1840	Tinning metals.
BRAITHWAITE, JOHN - -	2065	18th Sept. 1795	Smoke-jacks.
BRAITHWAITE, JOHN - -	5763	31st Jan. 1829	Converting liquids into vapour or steam.
BRAITHWAITE, JOHN - -	5903	27th Feb. 1830	Manufacturing salt.
BRAITHWAITE, JOHN - -	11,046	20th Jan. 1846	Heating, lighting, and ventilating.
BRAITHWAITE, JOHN - -	11,546	28th Jan. 1847	Heating, lighting, and ventilating.
BRAMAH, JOSEPH - - -	1177	27th Jan. 1778	Watercloset.
BRAMAH, JOSEPH - - -	1402	1st Dec. 1783	Water-cock, with a plug or valve.
BRAMAH, JOSEPH - - -	1430	23rd April 1784	Lock for doors, cabinets, and other things on which locks are used (without wheels or ward.)
BRAMAH, JOSEPH - - -	1478	9th May 1785	Hydrostatical machine and boiler, for working all kinds of mechanical and other engines.
BRAMAH, JOSEPH - - -	1720	15th Jan. 1790	Machine, constructed on a rotative principle, for raising, pumping, or forcing air, water, or other fluids.
BRAMAH, JOSEPH - - -	1948	18th April 1793	Fire-engine, easily portable, and containing a reservoir of water, with means for more easily dispersing the same.
BRAMAH, JOSEPH - - -	2045	31st March 1795	Producing and applying more power to all machinery requiring motion and force.
BRAMAH, JOSEPH - - -	2196	31st Oct. 1797	Retaining, clarifying, preserving, and drawing off, malt and other liquors; casks, and implements for the purpose.
BRAMAH, JOSEPH - - -	2232	3rd May 1798	Locks for doors, cabinets, &c., and keys for the same.
BRAMAH, JOSEPH - - -	2560	28th Nov. 1801	Construction of steam-engines and boilers used for generating steam.
BRAMAH, JOSEPH - - -	2652	30th Oct. 1802	Machine for producing straight, smooth, and parallel surfaces, on wood and other materials.
BRAMAH, JOSEPH - - -	2840	25th April 1805	Making paper.
BRAMAH, JOSEPH - - -	2977	15th Oct. 1806	Printing-machines.
BRAMAH, JOSEPH - - -	3260	23rd Sept. 1809	Making pens for writing.
BRAMAH, JOSEPH - - -	3270	2nd Nov. 1809	Making carriage-wheels; locking the same when passing down declivities.
BRAMAH, JOSEPH - - -	3611	31st Oct. 1812	Constructing, laying, and organizing pipes for conveyance of water for the supply of cities, towns or other places where public water-works are adopted;—applying the water so conveyed to other useful purposes.
BRAMAH, JOSEPH - - -	3616	26th Nov. 1812	Construction of parts of wheeled-carriages;—partly applicable to machinery where a rotary motion is necessary.
BRAMAH, JOSEPH - - -	3780	10th Feb. 1814	Application of a species of earth to destroy the dry rot; may be also employed as a substitute for lead, in oil paints, and for other purposes.
BRAMLEY, THOMAS - -	6027	4th Nov. 1830	Locomotive and other carriages applicable to rail and other roads;—also partly applicable for moving bodies on water, and working other machinery.

Name of Patentee.	Progressive Number.	Date.	Subject-matter of Patent.
BRAMWELL, FREDERICK - -	12,341	23rd Nov. 1848	Feeding furnaces with fuel.
BRAMWELL, FREDERICK JO-[SEPH.	13,820	20th Nov. 1851	Working the valves of steam-engines, for marine and other purposes; paddle-wheels.
BRAMWELL, THOMAS - -	11,553	30th Jan. 1847	Furnaces and apparatus, to render atmospheric air available in producing cyanides, and other compounds; applicable to other purposes.
BRAND, ROBERT - - -	996	10th Aug. 1771	Traverse elastic truss, for the relief of persons afflicted with ruptures in the groin or navel.
BRANDEIS, JOSEPH - -	14,168	12th June 1852	Manufacture of raw and refined sugar.
BRANDLING, ROBERT WILLIAM	5148	12th April 1825	Construction of railroads, and carriages employed thereon, or elsewhere.
BRANDLING, ROBERT WILLIAM	6507	19th Nov. 1833	Applying steam and other power to ships, boats, and other purposes.
BRANDLING, ROBERT WILLIAM	10,901	31st Oct. 1845	Railways and railway-carriages, for the security and convenience of the public.
BRANDON, RICHARD - -	2831	26th March 1805	Pills and liquid, also a botanic ointment, for the cure of the evil, scrofula, scurvy, leprosy, gout, and rheumatism.
BRANDRETH, THOMAS SHAW -	5281	8th Nov. 1825	Constructing wheel-carriages.
BRANDRETH, THOMAS SHAW -	5840	9th Sept. 1829	Application of animal power to machinery.
BRANDT, CHARLES - - -	6982	19th Jan. 1836	Heating, evaporating, and cooling fluids.
BRANDT, CHARLES - - -	7157	27th July 1836	Evaporating and cooling fluids.
BRANDT, GASPARD - - -	12,563	13th April 1849	Construction of the bearings of railway-engines, and railway and other carriages.
BRANWHITE, THOMAS - -	11,442	5th Nov. 1846	Machinery for obtaining, applying, accelerating, and retarding, motive power also for giving notice of alarm in cases of danger.
BRAYSHAY, RICHARD - -	2546	30th Oct. 1801	Machine for increasing speed and power to mechanical operations, by land and water.
BRAZIL, JOHN - - -	13,673	24th June 1851	Dyeing, and preparation of dye woods.
BRAZIL, JACOB - - -	3736	4th Sept. 1813	Machine for working capstans and pumps on board ships;—applicable to other purposes.
BRAZIL, JACOB - - -	8312	16th Dec. 1839	Obtaining motive-power.
BRECK, JAMES - - -	3089	16th Dec. 1807	Manufacturing iron straps or girdles into various articles, as substitutes for those now made of hemp.
BREIDENBACK, THOMAS - -	5491	28th April 1827	Parts of bedsteads.
BREIDENBACK, THOMAS - -	5538	13th Aug. 1827	Beasteads, and manufacturing articles to be used with them, from materials not before used for the purpose.
BREIDENBACK, THOMAS - -	5641	26th April 1828	Machine for manufacturing tubes or rods, and for other purposes.
BREMNER, JAMES - - -	10,195	22nd May 1844	Arrangements for constructing harbours, piers, and buildings, in water; cleansing harbours; raising sunken vessels.
BRENT, JOHN - - - -	471	26th Oct. 1724	Wind-engine for giving motion to mill-work, with fanes moving horizontally.
BRENT, ROBERT - - -	253	25th Jan. 1687	Furnaces, vessels, ways and means, for extracting gold, silver, copper, lead and tin, from their ores and minerals, and reducing them to malleable metals, by which means gold and silver are taken from lead and its ore, without the lead being diminished in value.

Name of Patentee.	Progressive Number.	Date.		Subject-matter of Patent.
BRENT, WILLIAM BRENT -	10,705	3rd June	1845	Machinery for cutting or excavating, and removing earth.
BRETT, ALFRED - - -	11,576	11th Feb.	1847	Electric-telegraphs; arrangements and apparatus used therewith;—applicable to timekeepers, and to other purposes.
BRETT, JACOB - - -	10,662	10th May	1845	Railways; propelling railway-carriages.
BRETT, JACOB - - -	10,758	8th July	1845	Propelling carriages on railways and other roads and ways.
BRETT, JACOB - - -	10,779	21st July	1845	Atmospheric propulsion; manufacture of tubes for atmospheric railways, and other purposes.
BRETT, JACOB - - -	10,939	13th Nov.	1845	Printed communications made by electric-telegraphs.
BRETT, JACOB - - -	12,C54	8th Feb.	1848	Electric, printing, and other telegraphs.
BRETT, RICHARD - - -	239	28th Aug.	1684	Melting or smelting copper and tin ores in furnaces, with sea-coal or pit-coal.
BRETT, THOMAS WATKINS, [BENJAMIN.	14,166	12th June	1852	Electric-telegraphs.
BREWER, ALFRED - - -	9633	11th Feb.	1843	Machinery for manufacturing paper.
BREWER, HENRY - - -	6243	15th March	1832	Machinery for making paper.
BREWER, HENRY NEWSON -	8362	3rd March	1841	Wooden blocks for ships' rigging tackle, and other purposes where pullies are used.
BREWER, RICHARD - -	817	14th Nov.	1764	Quadrant of altitude, applicable chiefly to the uses of navigation.
BREWER, WILLIAM - -	12,471	12th Feb.	1849	Manufacture of paper and cardboard, and producing watermarks thereon; machinery for these purposes.
BREWIN, AMBROSE - - -	9646	28th Feb.	1843	Manufacture of ornamented net or lace.
BREWIN, FRANCIS - - -	2319	18th June	1799	Tanning hides and skins.
BREWIN, FRANCIS - - -	2550	3rd Nov.	1801	Tanning.
BREWIN, FRANCIS - - -	6977	11th Jan.	1836	Processes of tanning.
BREWIN, FRANCIS - - -	7933	11th Jan.	1839	Using materials employed in tanning; and preparing the same for other useful purposes.
BREWSTER, DAVID - -	3453	21st May	1811	Optical instruments for measuring angles; telescopes, and other instruments.
BREWSTER, DAVID - -	4136	10th July	1817	Optical instrument or " kaleidescope."
BREYNTON, WILLIAM - -	10,788	25th July	1845	Rotatory steam-engines.
BREYNTON, WILLIAM - -	11,541	23rd Jan.	1847	Rotatory steam-engines.
BREZA, EUGENE RICHARD [LADISLAS DE.	7570	20th Feb.	1838	Chemical compound, to render cloth, wood, paper and other substances, indestructible by fire, and to preserve them from the ravages of insects.
BRIAND, GEORGE - - -	13,507	11th Feb.	1851	Obtaining fresh and pure water, from salt, sea, and other waters.
BRIDE, JOHN Mc - - -	9032	21st July	1841	Machinery and apparatus for dressing and weaving cotton, silk, flax, wool, and other fibrous substances.
BRIDE, JOHN Mc - -	10,259	15th July	1844	Machinery and apparatus for weaving by hand, steam, or other power.
BRIDE, JOHN Mc - -	11,444	12th Nov.	1846	Weaving.
BRIDE, WILLIAM, junior - -	12,556	2nd April	1849	Apparatus and process for converting salt water into fresh water; oxygenating water.
BRIDGE, THOMAS - - -	720	12th Jan.	1758	Machine for making rivers navigable.

Name of Patentee.	Progres-sive Number.	Date.	Subject-matter of Patent.
BRIDGE, THOMAS - - -	1022	11th Aug. 1772	Producing an essence or extract, from which fine spruce beer may be made.
BRIDGEMAN, WILLIAM - -	226	9th June 1683	Engine for rendering salt and brackish water sweet and fit for drinking, cooking, washing, and other uses.
BRIDGES, DANIEL - - -	631	16th April 1748	Refining, purifying, and meliorating, rape oil.
BRIDGES, DANIEL - - -	966	10th Aug. 1770	Refining spermaceti, and making candles of the same.
BRIDGES, HENRY - - -	11,463	1st Dec. 1846	Railway-wheels.
BRIDGES, WILLIAM - -	9566	22nd Dec. 1842	Buttons.
BRIDGMAN, EDWARD LILLIE -	4250	23rd April 1818	Making coffins; machines for conveying coffins; appendages for the same.
BRIDGMAN, JESSE - - -	10,127	28th March 1844	Separating the fatty and oily from the membranous portions of animal and vegetable substances.
BRIDSON, HENRY - - -	14,111	1st May 1852	Machinery for stretching, drying, and finishing woven fabrics.
BRIDSON, THOMAS RIDGWAY -	6624	10th June 1834	Machinery for drying cotton, linen, and other similar manufactured goods.
BRIDSON, THOMAS RIDGWAY -	7056	7th April 1836	Expediting the bleaching of linen and other vegetable fibres.
BRIDSON, THOMAS RIDGWAY -	7653	26th May 1838	Machinery for stretching, drying, and finishing woven fabrics.
BRIDSON, THOMAS RIDGWAY -	7655	29th May 1838	Construction and arrangement of machinery for stretching, mangling, drying, and finishing woven goods or fabrics;—partly applicable to other purposes.
BRIERLEY, HENRY - - -	10,802	5th Aug. 1845	Machinery for spinning.
BRIERLEY, HENRY - - - [*Brierly, Henry.*]	11,602	2nd March 1847	Machinery for spinning.
BRIERLEY, JOHN - - -	3190	17th Jan. 1809	Setting blue lead for corroding the same into white-lead.
BRIERLEY, SAMUEL - -	4628	19th Dec. 1821	Preparing and cleansing raw silk for dyeing and manufacturing.
BRIGGS, EDWARD - - -	10,220	6th June 1844	Manufacture of hats; and machinery connected with such manufacture.
BRIGGS, HENRY - - -	4810	5th July 1823	Construction of looms for weaving fabrics composed wholly, or partly, of woollen, worsted, cotton, linen, silk, or other materials; machinery and implements for, and method of, working the same.
BRIGGS, HENRY - -	13,767	9th Oct. 1851	Oil-lamps; and apparatus for lubricating machinery.
BRIGGS, JOHN GEORGE - -	9887	5th Oct. 1843	Axles.
BRIGHT, CHARLES TILSON -	14,331	21st Oct. 1852	Making telegraphic communications; instruments and apparatus employed therein and connected therewith.
BRIGHT, EDWARD BRAILSFORD	14,331	21st Oct. 1852	Making telegraphic communications; instruments and apparatus employed therein and connected therewith.
BRIGHT, RICHARD - - -	7539	13th Jan. 1838	Apparatus for effecting the more complete combustion of candles, and superseding the necessity of snuffing.
BRIGHT, RICHARD - -	12,305	2nd Nov. 1848	Lamps, wicks, and covers, for vessels for holding oil and other fluids.
BRIGHTLY, CHARLES - -	4202	17th Jan. 1818	Printing-press, for printing from types, plates, or blocks.

Name of Patentee.	Progressive Number.	Date.	Subject-matter of Patent.
BRINDLEY, JAMES - - -	730	27th Sept. 1758	Fire-engine for drawing water out of mines, draining lands, and other purposes.
BRINDLEY, JOSEPH - -	2646	20th Sept. 1802	Securing ships' beams to their sides.
BRINDLEY, STEPHEN - -	4717	18th Oct. 1822	Building ships, boats, barges, and other vessels.
BRINDLEY, WILLIAM - -	7049	29th March 1836	Manufacture of tea-trays and other japanned ware, and the board or material used therein and for other purposes.
BRINDLEY, WILLIAM - -	7522	23rd Dec. 1837	Construction of presses.
BRINDLEY, WILLIAM - -	8396	25th Feb. 1840	Apparatus for pressing cotton-wool, and goods of various descriptions.
BRINDLEY, WILLIAM - -	10,653	6th May 1845	Manufacture of trays and other japanned wares, also various other articles made of pulp.
BRINDLEY, WILLIAM - -	12,175	6th June 1848	Manufacture of articles of pâpier-mâché.
BRINDLEY, WILLIAM - -	12,494	28th Feb. 1849	Manufacture of waterproof paper.
BRINDLEY, WILLIAM - -	12,850	17th Nov. 1849	Producing ornamental designs on pâpier-mâché; preserving vegetable matters.
BRINDLEY, WILLIAM - -	13,923	27th Jan. 1852	Manufacture of flocked fabrics; manufacture of buttons.
BRINE, EDWARD - - -	2664	29th Nov. 1802	Machinery for dragging or locking wheels of carriages, and disengaging the horses therefrom.
BRISBANE, SAMUEL - -	13,260	19th Sept. 1850	Looms for weaving.
BRISCO, JOHN - - -	246	4th July 1685	Making paper as white and good as French or Dutch, for writing, printing, and other purposes.
BRISTOW, JAMES - - -	4450	19th April 1820	Application of machinery for propelling boats or other vessels floating in or on water, and for attaining other purposes, by means of a hydro-pneumatic apparatus, acted upon by a steam-engine, or other adequate power.
BRITTEN, JOHN - - -	11,111	25th Feb. 1846	Applying heat for heating, cooking, and evaporating; apparatus connected therewith.
BRITTEN, JOHN - - -	11,526	12th Jan. 1847	Machinery for printing, ruling, and damping paper for various purposes.
BRITTEN, JOHN - - -	11,992	8th Dec. 1847	Apparatus for cooking, preparing, and containing food, and opening and closing oven doors;—partly applicable to other purposes.
BRITTEN, JOHN - - -	12,129	20th April 1848	Heating, lighting, and ventilating, closing, and securing doors; lighting and ventilating carriages;—partly applicable to other like purposes.
BRITTEN, JOHN - - -	12,548	28th March 1849	Apparatus for cooking, preserving, preparing, and storing food and drinks; preparing materials for constructing the same; also constructing vertical roasting-jacks and chains for the same;—applicable to other chains, and partly applicable to other purposes.
BRITTER, WILLIAM - -	12,202	6th July 1848	Manufacture of tobacco-pipes.
BROAD, ROBERT - -	11,679	28th April 1847	Turn-tables for railways.
BROADBENT, WILLIAM - -	11,833	5th Aug. 1847	Manufacture of paper.
BROADMEADOW, SIMEON -	4893	19th Jan. 1824	Manufacturing and purifying inflammable gases by admission and admixture of atmospheric air.

Name of Patentee.	Progressive Number.	Date.		Subject-matter of Patent.
BROADMEADOW, SIMEON -	5146	2nd April	1825	Apparatus for exhausting, condensing, or propelling air, smoke, gas, or other aëriform products.
BROADWOOD, HENRY FOWLER	9245	2nd Feb.	1842	Name-board of a pianoforte, harpsichord, or other like instrument.
BROADWOOD, JAMES SHUDI -	5261	6th Oct.	1825	Square pianofortes.
BROADWOOD, JAMES SHUDI -	5485	9th April	1827	Grand pianofortes.
BROADWOOD, JOHN -	1379	18th July	1783	Pianoforte.
BROCKEDON, WILLIAM -	4395	20th Sept.	1819	Wire-Drawing.
BROCKEDON, WILLIAM -	6163	20th Sept.	1831	Construction of writing pens and penholders; and method of using them.
BROCKEDON, WILLIAM -	7832	17th Oct.	1838	Combination of materials for forming a substitute for corks and bungs.
BROCKEDON, WILLIAM -	8369	31st Jan.	1840	Retaining fluids in bottles, decanters, and other vessels.
BROCKEDON, WILLIAM -	9303	21st March	1842	Manufacturing fibrous materials for the cores of stoppers, to be coated with India-rubber, and used for stopping bottles and other vessels.
BROCKEDON, WILLIAM -	9712	25th April	1843	Manufacture of wadding for fire-arms.
BROCKEDON, WILLIAM -	9977	8th Dec.	1843	Manufacture of pills and medicated lozenges; preparing or treating black-lead.
BROCKEDON, WILLIAM -	10,270	24th July	1844	Covering roofs of houses and other buildings; covering valves used when propelling by atmospheric pressure; covering railway-sleepers; and covering stringed and keyed musical instruments.
BROCKEDON, WILLIAM -	11,455	19th Nov.	1846	Manufacture of articles where India-rubber or gutta-percha is used.
BROCKEDON, WILLIAM -	11,865	9th Sept.	1847	Heating rooms or apartments.
BROCKEDON, WILLIAM -	13,674	24th June	1851	Surgical instruments.
BROCKLEHURST, JOHN -	11,090	11th Feb.	1846	Hanging and disconnecting window sashes and frames.
BROCKSOPP, THOMAS -	4344	23rd Feb.	1819	Application of machinery for breaking or crushing sugar.
BROCQ, PHILIP LE -	1513	5th Dec.	1785	Rearing, cultivating, training, and bringing to perfection, all kinds of fruit-trees and plants; protecting their leaves, blossoms, flowers, and fruit.
BROCQ, PHILIP LE -	1894	5th July	1792	Portable mangles.
BRODERIP, CHARLES -	3506	2nd Nov.	1811	Constructing steam-engines.
BRODERIF, CHARLES -	3690	5th May	1813	Vessels to be used for heating fluids and other substances.
BRODERIP, CHARLES -	3702	31st May	1813	Raising and lowering vessels, from one level to another of navigable waters.
BRODERIP, CHARLES -	4622	5th Dec.	1821	Construction of steam engines.
BRODIE, ALEXANDER -	880	14th July	1767	Making fire-stoves and registers.
BRODIE, ALEXANDER -	1271	8th Dec.	1780	Ship stove, kitchen, or hearth, with a smoke-jack and iron boilers.
BRODIE, ALEXANDER -	1599	8th May	1787	Making iron tire for all sorts of wheel-carriages.
BRODIE, ALEXANDER -	2856	31st May	1805	Making boilers for steam-engines and for other purposes, and constructing flues for conveying heat to the same.
BRODUM, WILLIAM -	2303	10th April	1799	"Botanical syrup," for the cure of scorbutic, leprous, and scrofulous complaints; "Nervous cordial," for the cure of consumptive, nervous and debilitated constitutions.

Name of Patentee.	Progressive Number.	Date.	Subject-matter of Patent.
BROGUETTE, CHARLES ALEX- [ANDER.	12,581	21st April 1849	Printing and dyeing fibrous and other materials.
BROMWICH, BRYAN I'ANSON -	7859	8th Nov. 1838	Machinery to be worked by the application of the expansive force of air or other elastic fluid, to obtain motive-power.
BROMWICH, BRYAN I'ANSON -	8110	17th June 1839	Machinery to be worked by the application of the expansive force of air or other elastic fluid, to obtain motive-power.
BROMWICH, BRYAN I'ANSON -	8510	13th May 1840	Stirrup-irons.
BROOK, BARNARD HENRY -	5624	6th March 1828	Construction and setting of ovens and retorts, for carbonizing coal for use in gas works.
BROOK, CHARLES - - -	5800	4th June 1829	Machinery for spinning cotton and other fibrous substances.
BROOK, CHARLES - - -	9637	17th Feb. 1843	Apparatus for purifying gas.
BROOK, CHARLES - - -	9905	12th Oct. 1843	Machinery for spinning and twisting cotton and other fibrous substances.
BROOKE, JAMES WILLIAMSON	10,619	15th April 1845	Lamps.
BROOKE, JAMES WILLIAMSON	12,513	14th March 1849	Lamps.
BROOKE, JOHN EDWARD -	5224	26th July 1825	Machinery used in scribbling and carding wool or other fibrous substances.
BROOKES, PHILLIP - -	5195	21st June 1825	Preparation of a certain composition ; and its application to making dies, moulds, matrices, smooth surfaces, &c.
BROOKES, SAMUEL - -	3178	3rd Nov. 1808	Splitting raw hides of bulls, oxen, and cows.
BROOKING, SAMUEL - -	5650	6th May 1828	Shipping fid, for securing and releasing the upper masts of ships and vessels.
BROOKING, SAMUEL - -	5695	4th Sept. 1828	Making sails of ships and other vessels.
BROOKS, ISAAC - - -	14,032	24th March 1852	Stoves and other apparatus for heating.
BROOKS, JOSEPH - - -	1788	14th Jan. 1791	Machine for raising water, boats, and weights, from a lower to a higher level, without aid of fire or wind.
BROOKS, RICHARD - - -	591	7th July 1743	Machine for manufacturing wool yarn, and woollen cloths, in several branches.
BROOKS, ROBERT, junior - -	10,719	12th June 1845	Apparatus for facilitating the playing on stringed musical instruments.
BROOMAN, RICHARD ARCHI- [BALD.	9833	10th Aug. 1843	Manufacture of paper, cordage, matting, and other textile fabrics, from vegetable matters not before used for that purpose;—application of the said materials for stuffing cushions and mattrasses.
BROOMAN, RICHARD ARCHI- [BALD.	9994	28th Dec. 1843	Figure-weaving machinery.
BROOMAN, RICHARD ARCHI- [BALD.	10,550	11th March 1845	Preparation and application of artificial fuels, mastics, and cements.
BROOMAN, RICHARD ARCHI- [BALD.	10,582	27th March 1845	A thread made from a substance not hitherto applied to that purpose; also its application for making piece-goods, ribbons, paper, and other articles.
BROOMAN. RICHARD ARCHI- [BALD.	10,724	18th June 1845	Machinery for weaving.
BROOMAN, RICHARD ARCHI- [BALD.	10,783	25th July 1845	Dyeing.
BROOMAN, RICHARD ARCHI- [BALD.	10,908	3rd Nov. 1845	Printing and figuring silk, cotton, and other textile fabrics.
BROOMAN, RICHARD ARCHI- [BALD.	10,909	3rd Nov. 1845	Gas-meters.

Name of Patentee.	Progressive Number.	Date.		Subject-matter of Patent.
BROOMAN, RICHARD ARCHI-[BALD.	11,048	20th Jan.	1846	Railway and common road carriages.
BROOMAN, RICHARD ARCHI-[BALD.	11,680	29th April	1847	Turn-tables for railways.
BROOMAN, RICHARD ARCHI-[BALD.	11,724	29th May	1847	Processes and machinery employed in scouring and bleaching.
BROOMAN, RICHARD ARCHI-[BALD.	12,304	2nd Nov.	1848	Manufacture of hinges, and machinery used therein.
BROOMAN, RICHARD ARCHI-[BALD.	12,444	27th Jan.	1849	Manufacture of artificial limbs.
BROOMAN, RICHARD ARCHI-[BALD.	12,665	20th June	1849	Apparatus for transferring liquids from one vessel to another, and for filling bottles and other vessels with liquids.
BROOMAN, RICHARD ARCHI-[BALD.	12,688	4th July	1849	Steam generators.
BROOMAN, RICHARD ARCHI-[BALD.	12,742	16th Aug.	1849	Machinery, apparatus and processes, for extracting, depurating, forming, drying, and evaporating substances.
BROOMAN, RICHARD ARCHI-[BALD.	12,765	13th Sept.	1849	Draught-horse saddlery, harness, and saddle trees.
BROOMAN, RICHARD ARCHI-[BALD.	12,995	7th March	1850	Types, stereotype plates, and other figured surfaces for printing from.
BROOMAN, RICHARD ARCHI-[BALD.	13,053	23rd April	1850	Manufacture of zinc, and apparatus employed therein.
BROOMAN, RICHARD ARCHI-[BALD.	13,200	31st July	1850	Abdominal supporters.
BROOMAN, RICHARD ARCHI-[BALD.	13,256	19th Sept.	1850	Purifying water, and preparing it for engineering, manufacturing, and domestic uses.
BROOMAN, RICHARD ARCHI-[BALD.	13,316	7th Nov.	1850	Railways.
BROOMAN, RICHARD ARCHI-[BALD.	13,398	7th Dec.	1850	Agricultural machines.
BROOMAN, RICHARD ARCHI-[BALD.	13,557	15th March	1851	Manufacturing screws.
BROOMAN, RICHARD ARCHI-[BALD.	13,583	2nd April	1851	Machinery for the manufacture of rope and cordage.
BROOMAN, RICHARD ARCHI-[BALD.	13,753	25th Sept.	1851	Presses, and pressing.
BROOMAN, RICHARD ARCHI-[BALD.	13,771	10th Oct.	1851	Preparation and treatment of fibrous and membranous substances, both in the raw and manufactured state, whereby they are cleaned, and rendered more durable, capable of contraction or expansion, of resisting decomposition, and of receiving and retaining colours.
BROOMAN, RICHARD ARCHI-[BALD.	13,845	8th Dec.	1851	Applying electro-chemical action to manufacturing purposes.
BROOMAN, RICHARD ARCHI-[BALD.	13,846	8th Dec.	1851	Manufacture of sugar, preparation of certain substances for such manufacture; machinery and apparatus employed therein.
BROOMAN, RICHARD ARCHI-[BALD.	13,876	19th Dec.	1851	Sounding-instruments.
BROOMAN, RICHARD ARCHI-[BALD.	13,946	31st Jan.	1852	Purification and decolouration of oils; apparatus employed therein.
BROOMAN, RICHARD ARCHI-[BALD.	13,981	23rd Feb.	1852	Windmills.
BROOMAN, RICHARD ARCHI-[BALD.	14,008	8th March	1852	Presses, and pressing.

Name of Patentee.	Progressive Number.	Date.		Subject-matter of Patent.
BROOMAN, RICHARD ARCHI- [BALD.	14,114	4th May	1852	Paddle-wheels.
BROOMAN, RICHARD ARCHI- [BALD.	14,173	18th June	1852	Manufacture of wheels, tires, and hoops,
BROOMAN, RICHARD ARCHI- [BALD.	14,255	10th Aug.	1852	Manufacture of manure.
BROOMAN, RICHARD ARCHI- [BALD.	14,317	7th Oct.	1852	Knitting-machinery.
BROOMAN, RICHARD ARCHI- [BALD.	14,318	7th Oct.	1852	Manufacture of sugar; machinery and apparatus employed therein.
BROOMAN, RICHARD ARCHI- [BALD.	14,321	14th Oct.	1852	Mowing, cutting, and reaping machines.
BROOMFIELD, JOHN - -	5153	20th April	1825	Machinery for propelling vessels;—applicable to other purposes.
BROQUETTE, CHARLES ALEX- [ANDER.	12,581	21st April	1849	Printing and dyeing fibrous and other materials.
BROTHERHOOD, ROWLAND -	12,713	10th Nov.	1849	Apparatus for covering trucks and waggons on railways, also road waggons, and canal boats.
BROTHERS, ORLANDO - -	11,840	19th Aug.	1847	Manufacturing retorts; machinery connected therewith.
BROTHERSTON, PETER - -	1073	22nd June	1774	Machine for making all kinds of lace; also a machine for making nets of all kinds, from various materials.
BROTHERSTON, PETER - -	1357	20th Feb.	1783	Machine for spinning woollen yarn, and spinning cotton-wool into yarn, for weft.
BROUGHTON, CHARLES - -	3354	3rd July	1810	Construction of organs.
BROUGHTON, WILLIAM - -	3647	4th Feb.	1813	Making canvas for military and other purposes.
BROUGHTON, WILLIAM - -	10,776	21st July	1845	Machinery for grinding grain, drugs, colours, or other substances.
BROUILLET, PAUL PREVOST -	9685	30th March	1843	Apparatus for warming apartments.
BROUNCKER, WILLIAM - -	39	6th Aug.	1627	Engine for earing, ploughing, and tilling land, by the labour of two men without the aid of oxen.
BROUNCKER, Sir WILLIAM, [Knight.	90	26th March	1636	Drawing double the quantity of aqua vitæ from a given quantity of liquor; also extracting a larger quantity of strong water from malt than has hitherto been usual.
BROWELL, JAMES - - -	3150	11th July	1808	Chemical preparation for preserving woollen and vegetable substances from mildew, rot, or fermentation; and also for rendering cloths, and other fabrics, impervious to rain.
BROWN, CHARLES - - -	9897	5th Oct.	1843	Manufacture of dip candles.
BROWN, DAVID STEPHENS -	12,764	13th Sept.	1849	Apparatus for the fumigation of plants.
BROWN, DAVID STEPHENS -	13,757	25th Sept.	1851	Agricultural implement.
BROWN, EDWARD - - -	8127	22nd June	1839	Roasting and refining copper, to reduce the oxydation of the metal, and render it more pure and ductile.
BROWN, EDWARD - - -	8157	20th July	1839	Apparatus for cooking.
BROWN, EDWARD - - -	11,587	20th Feb.	1847	Carbonic compounds, formed of earthy, vegetable, animal, and mineral rubbish, fecal substances, the waste of manufactories, and certain acids and alkalies, applicable as manure.
BROWN, FREDERICK - -	8215	9th Sept.	1839	Stoves or fire-places.
BROWN, FREDERICK - -	9103	24th Sept.	1841	Stoves or fire-places.

Name of Patentee.	Progressive Number.	Date.	Subject-matter of Patent.
BROWN, FREDERICK - -	10,138	10th April 1844	Stoves.
BROWN, FREDERICK - -	11,375	17th Sept. 1846	Ovens for kitchen ranges.
BROWN, GEORGE - -	10,530	20th Feb. 1845	Manufacture of soda.
BROWN, GEORGE - -	10,810	9th Aug. 1845	Drill-plough for seed and manure.
BROWN, GEORGE BEALE -	6444	27th June 1833	Machinery for making pins used for fastening wearing-apparel.
BROWN, HENRIETTA -	13,180	17th July 1850	Manufacture of metallic casks and vessels.
BROWN, HENRY - -	733	22nd Dec. 1758	Dyeing, staining, and stamping, stockings and other apparel, in all colours.
BROWN, HENRY - -	8193	13th Aug. 1839	A new covering or plating for household furniture, picture-frames, cabinet and fancy work, and other articles of domestic or personal use; and mode of making such covering or plating.
BROWN, HENRY - - -	8930	22nd April 1841	Manufacture of steel.
BROWN, HENRY - - -	9493	20th Oct. 1842	Woollen carding-engines.
BROWN, HENRY - - -	10,074	24th Feb. 1844	Carding silk, cotton, and other fibres.
BROWN, HENRY - - -	12,694	4th July 1849	Rolls for rolling flat and half-round file and other iron and steel.
BROWN, HOUSTOWN RIGG	3474	7th Aug. 1811	Construction of wheel-carriages, wheels, axles, and boxes.
BROWN, ISAAC - - -	5851	23rd Sept. 1829	Watches, and other horological machines.
BROWN, JAMES - - -	1916	2nd Nov. 1792	Machine for cutting fustian and other goods, of cotton, silk, woollen, or any mixture of them.
BROWN, JAMES - - -	1967	3rd Dec. 1793	Machine for cutting fustian or other goods of cotton, silk, woollen, or any mixture of them.
BROWN, JAMES - - -	1999	15th July 1794	Machine for opening velverets and other goods, after being cut.
BROWN, JAMES - - -	6385	14th Feb. 1833	Capstans, and apparatus used therewith.
BROWN, JAMES - - -	7098	18th May 1836	Machinery for making paper.
BROWN, JAMES - - -	9551	8th Dec. 1842	Steam-engines, and steam propelling-machinery.
BROWN, JAMES - - -	9868	16th Aug. 1843	Tackle and apparatus for working and using chain-cables, in ships and other vessels; tillers for rudders of ships and other vessels.
BROWN, JAMES - - -	11,061	29th Jan. 1846	Weaving.
BROWN, JEREMIAH - -	6995	3rd Feb. 1836	Machinery and process for manufacturing metallic tubes; machinery or process for forging or rolling metal for other purposes.
BROWN, JEREMIAH - -	11,781	3rd July 1847	Rolls and machinery used in the manufacture of iron, also rolls and machinery for shaping iron for various purposes.
BROWN, JOHN - - -	2777	4th Aug. 1804	Wheels of carriages;—applicable also to windlasses, capstans, and to various other purposes.
BROWN, JOHN - - -	3047	2nd June 1807	Construction of a press for printing books and other articles;—partly applicable to presses in common use.
BROWN, JOHN - - -	3279	28th Nov. 1809	Machine for letter-press printing, also for printing ornaments and figures;—partly applicable to presses now in use.
BROWN, JOHN - - -	3434	24th April 1811	Machine for making bobbin-lace, or twist-net.
BROWN, JOHN - - -	3527	25th Jan. 1812	Pocket, to be used about the person or otherwise.
BROWN, JOHN - - -	6305	8th Sept. 1832	Machinery for spinning cotton, silk, flax, and other fibrous substances ("throstles.")

Name of Patentee.	Progressive Number.	Date.	Subject-matter of Patent.
Brown, John - - -	6742	23rd Dec. 1834	Instrument for ascertaining levels.
Brown, John Bower - -	10,343	10th Oct. 1844	Combining blast steel with iron; constructing carriage springs.
Brown, John Harcourt -	11,113	25th Feb. 1846	Securing letters, envelopes, covers, despatches, packets, and parcels.
Brown, John Harcourt -	13,441	7th Jan. 1851	Manufacture of wafers.
Brown, John Harcourt -	13,503	10th Feb. 1851	Construction and building of ships, boats, buoys, rafts, and other vessels.
Brown, John Harcourt -	14,131	22nd May 1852	Manufacture of paper, and articles of paper.
Brown, Joseph - - -	7793	8th Sept. 1838	Beds, sofas, chairs, and other furniture, to render them more suitable for travelling, and for other purposes.
Brown, Peter Joseph - -	3379	26th Sept. 1810	Construction of buoys for ships or vessels, and for mooring chains, or for similar purposes.
Brown, Richard - - -	2898	26th Nov. 1805	Construction of several parts of tables, and other household furniture supported on feet.
Brown, Robert - - -	2571	16th Jan. 1802	Manufacturing nets of all kinds.
Brown, Robert - - -	2760	14th May 1804	Machine to affix to Vandyke knitting-frames, for manufacturing lace or net-work of various figures and qualities, with thread, silk, cotton, worsted, or other materials.
Brown, Robert - - -	3928	14th June 1815	Swing wheel ploughs, plough-carriages, and plough-shares.
Brown, Robert - - -	7423	24th Aug. 1837	Construction of Cockle's stoves, or apparatus for drying or stoving hops, malt, grain, or seeds.
Brown, Robert - - -	9518	15th Nov. 1842	Manufacture of garden pots.
Brown, Robert - - -	12,462	8th Feb. 1849	Machinery for perforating, sewing, stitching, pegging, and rivetting.
Brown, Robert - - -	13,359	19th Nov. 1850	Pumps, and their application for raising or forcing water.
Brown, Samuel - - -	3107	4th Feb. 1808	Rigging of ships or vessels.
Brown, Samuel - - -	3408	6th March 1811	Machinery for making casks and other vessels.
Brown, Samuel - - -	3888	28th Feb. 1815	Rudder, and apparatus connected therewith.
Brown, Samuel - - -	4004	23rd March 1816	Swing and wheel plough-carriages, and plough-shares.
Brown, Samuel - - -	4090	19th Dec. 1816	Chain manufactured by a new process; and apparatus and improvements in performing and executing the same.
Brown, Samuel - - -	4137	10th July 1817	Construction of a bridge by the formation and uniting of its component parts.
Brown, Samuel - - -	4874	4th Dec. 1823	Engine for effecting a vacuum, and thus producing powers by which water may be raised, and machinery set in motion.
Brown, Samuel - - -	5126	15th March 1825	Apparatus for giving motion to vessels employed in inland navigation.
Brown, Samuel - - -	5282	8th Nov. 1825	Machinery for making casks and other vessels.
Brown, Samuel - - -	5350	25th April 1826	Engine for effecting a vacuum, and thus producing powers by which water may be raised, and machinery set in motion.
Brown, Samuel - - -	5929	24th April 1830	Making bolts and chains.
Brown, Samuel - - -	6045	6th Dec. 1830	Drawing up ships and other vessels from the water on to the land; moving ships, vessels, and other bodies on land, from one place to another.

Name of Patentee.	Progressive Number.	Date.		Subject-matter of Patent.
BROWN, SAMUEL - - -	7151	14th July	1836	Generating gas.
BROWN, SAMUEL - - -	8346	21st Jan.	1840	Making casks and other vessels, of iron and other metals.
BROWN, SAMUEL - - -	9045	11th Aug.	1841	Manufacture of metallic casks or vessels; tinning or zincing metal for such and other purposes.
BROWN, SAMUEL - - -	9792	17th June	1843	Manufacture of casks and other vessels.
BROWN, SAMUEL - - -	11,072	3rd Feb.	1846	Gas-engines; and propelling carriages and vessels.
BROWN, SAMUEL - - - [Brown, Samuel, junior.]	12,431	20th Jan.	1849	Apparatus for measuring and registering the flow of liquids; — in part applicable to motive purposes.
BROWN, SAMUEL - - -	13,094	1st June	1850	Engines for measuring and registering the flow of fluids and substances in a fluid state; — applicable to steam and other motive-engines.
BROWN, SAMUEL Sir - -	8994	19th June	1841	Drawing carriages or other machines along inclined planes, railways and other roads, and drawing or propelling vessels in canals, rivers, and other navigable waters.
BROWN, SAMUEL Sir - -	9680	27th March	1843	Construction of breakwaters; constructing and erecting light-houses and beacons, fixed and floating; apparatus connected therewith; anchors for mooring the same, applicable also to ships.
BROWN, SAMUEL Sir - -	10,790	29th July	1845	Formation of embankments for canals, docks, or sea-walls; propulsion of locomotive-engines and other carriages or bodies, on canals and other inland waters, and on rail and other roads; propelling vessels on the ocean and navigable rivers.
BROWN, SAMUEL Sir - -	11,295	14th July	1846	Railways and railway-carriages; construction and arming of ships or vessels.
BROWN, SAMUEL Sir - -	11,887	7th Oct.	1847	Propelling and steering vessels; mariners' compass.
BROWN, THOMAS - - -	2716	21st June	1803	Machine for cutting tobacco, and tallow for tallow-chandlers and soap-boilers; also for cutting turnips, cabbages, carrots, and other kinds of roots, for feeding cattle.
BROWN, THOMAS - - -	5827	5th Aug.	1829	Coach for public conveyance and luggage.
BROWN, THOMAS - - -	11,666	20th April	1847	Machinery for raising and lowering weights.
BROWN, THOMAS BEAL -	12,680	29th June	1849	Looms, and manufacture of woven and twisted fabrics.
BROWN, WILLIAM - - -	6277	9th June	1832	Steam-engines.
BROWN, WILLIAM - - -	9127	26th Oct.	1841	Process of dyeing various matters, whether the raw material of wool, silk, flax, hemp, cotton, or other similar fibrous substances, or the same in any stage of manufacture; preparation of pigments or painters' colours.
BROWN, WILLIAM - - -	9757	3rd June	1843	Manufacture of porcelain, china, pottery, and earthenware; — partly applicable to the manufacture of paper, and the preparation of certain pigments or painters' colours.
BROWN, WILLIAM - - -	11,765	23rd June	1847	Communicating intelligence by means of electricity; apparatus relating thereto; — partly applicable to other purposes.
BROWN, WILLIAM - - -	12,294	26th Oct.	1848	Manufacturing elastic stockings, and other elastic bandages and fabrics.

Name of Patentee.	Progressive Number.	Date.	Subject-matter of Patent.
BROWN, WILLIAM - - -	12,711	18th July 1849	Communicating intelligence by electricity; electric clocks.
BROWN, WILLIAM - - -	12,991	7th March 1850	Electric and magnetic apparatus, for indicating and communicating intelligence.
BROWN, WILLIAM - - -	13,013	23rd March 1850	Preparing and combing wool.
BROWN, WILLIAM - - -	14,325	18th Oct. 1852	Machinery and apparatus for preparing and spinning wool, hair, flax, silk, and all other fibrous materials.
BROWN, WILLIAM ALEXANDER	6247	23rd March 1832	Making prussiates of potash, soda, and iron; construction of machinery used in the said manufacture; employing prussiates of iron as substitutes for indigo in dyeing materials and fabrics.
BROWN, WILLIAM HENRY -	12,694	4th July 1849	Rolls for rolling flat and half round file and other iron and steel.
BROWN, WILLIAM HENRY -	13,623	6th May 1851	Manufacture of helves.
BROWN, WILLIAM SMITH, [junior.	11,029	6th Jan. 1846	Manufacture of square and quadrilateral sails, for ships and other vessels.
BROWNE, HENRY - - -	435	12th Aug. 1721	Engine for beating raw hemp.
BROWNE, HENRY - - -	503	5th Oct. 1728	Making cannon or great guns, of iron or brass.
BROWNE, HENRY - - -	2315	28th May 1799	Making and preparing extract of zinc, for medicinal purposes.
BROWNE, HENRY - - -	4544	16th March 1821	Construction of boilers, to effect a saving of fire, and the consumption of smoke.
BROWNE, HENRY NIBBS -	10,510	4th Feb. 1845	Manufacture of sugar.
BROWNE, JAMES HAMILTON -	13,280	10th Oct. 1850	Separation and disinfection of fecal matters; apparatus employed therein.
BROWNE, JOHN - - -	1138	25th Nov. 1776	Engine for forming iron vessels, and for planishing and burnishing the same when tinned.
BROWNE, JOHN - - -	5496	5th May 1827	Composition or substance which may be manufactured or moulded into bricks or blocks for building, or moulded and made applicable to ornamental, architectural, and other purposes.
BROWNE, JOHN - - -	7863	8th Nov. 1838	Paving roads and streets.
BROWNE, JOHN - - -	8050	25th April 1839	Saddles and stirrups for horses and other animals;—applicable to apparatus for carrying packs.
BROWNE, JOHN - - -	9349	12th May 1842	Manufacture of mud boots and overalls.
BROWNE, JOHN - - -	10,104	14th March 1844	Urinary utensils.
BROWNE, JOHN - - -	10,180	14th May 1844	Apparatus for protecting the human face, or part of the human face, from the inclemency of the weather;—partly applicable for protecting birds in cages.
BROWNE, JOHN - - -	12,326	11th Nov. 1848	Fire-escapes; also apparatus to be used by persons cleaning windows.
BROWNE, JOHN - - -	12,452	6th Feb. 1849	Constructing and rigging vessels; atmospheric and other railways.
BROWNE, JOHN - - -	12,686	4th July 1849	Apparatus to assist combustion in stoves or grates.
BROWNE, MARK - - -	2530	31st July 1801	Instrument or engine, possessing power to work engines on water or land, and for other purposes.

Name of Patentee.	Progressive Number.	Date.	Subject-matter of Patent.
BROWNE, PETER - - -	804	18th Jan. 1764	Painting silks and satins in oil colours.
BROWNE, ROBERT FREDERICK	10,545	8th March 1845	Construction of chairs and couches.
BROWNE, THOMAS BEALE -	13,294	24th Oct. 1850	Weaving and preparing fibrous materials; staining or printing fabrics.
BROWNE, WILLIAM -	12,789	27th Sept. 1849	Preparing for pulverization, flint stone, china stone, ores, minerals, spars, sands, earths, and other substances,
BROWNHILL, JONATHAN - [Brownill, Jonathan.]	4474	8th June 1820	Securing the blades of knives and forks in the handles, by caps of iron, steel, or other materials, soldered on the tangs after the handles are upon them.
BROWNHILL, JONATHAN -	5646	1st May 1828	Transferring vessels from one level to another, on canals; raising or lowering weights, carriages, or goods, on railroads.
BROWNHILL, JONATHAN - [Brownill, Jonathan.]	5748	23rd Dec. 1828	Table-forks.
BROWNRIGG, JOHN STUDHOLME	9874	24th Aug. 1843	Preparation of a material from a vegetable substance, and its application for affording light, and for other uses.
BROWSER, WILLIAM - -	5111	26th Feb. 1825	Uniting and plating or coating iron with copper, or with any other composition whereof copper is the principal ingredient.
BRUCE, DUNCAN - - -	13,237	22nd Aug. 1850	Construction of rotatory engines.
BRUCE, WILLIAM - - -	2918	18th March 1806	Day or night telescopes.
BRUCE, WILLIAM - - -	6661	14th Aug. 1834	Machinery for making ship and other biscuit or bread.
BRUCE, WILLIAM - - -	11,640	25th March 1847	Constructing piers, breakwaters, and other submarine works of stone.
BRUFF, PETER - - -	14,093	29th April 1852	Construction of the permanent way of rail, tram, or other roads; rolling-stock or apparatus used thereon.
BRUGES, PIERRE THEODORE DE	1104	27th Oct. 1775	Making salt-petre.
BRUMBY, MARTIN - - -	907	28th Nov. 1768	Liquor for tanning thread sail-cloth, and mode of preserving the sail-cloth or "tanned canvas" from mildewing and rotting.
BRUNEL, MARC ISAMBARD -	2305	11th April 1799	Writing and drawing machine, for making two or three similar writings or drawings at the same time, and by the same person.
BRUNEL, MARC ISAMBARD -	2478	10th Feb. 1801	Machine for cutting one or more mortices forming the sides of the shells of blocks, and cutting the pin-hole of the same.
BRUNEL, MARC ISAMBARD -	2663	27th Nov. 1802	Trimmings and borders of muslin, lawn, and cambric.
BRUNEL, MARC ISAMBARD -	2844	7th May 1805	Saws, and machinery for sawing timber.
BRUNEL, MARC ISAMBARD -	2968	23rd Sept. 1806	Cutting veneers or thin boards.
BRUNEL, MARC ISAMBARD -	3116	14th March 1808	Circular saws for sawing wood.
BRUNEL, MARC ISAMBARD -	3369	2nd Aug. 1810	Machinery for making shoes and boots.
BRUNEL, MARC ISAMBARD -	3384	1st Oct. 1810	Apparatus for giving motion to machinery;— partly applicable to hydraulic and pneumatic purposes.
BRUNEL, MARC ISAMBARD -	3529	28th Jan. 1812	Saw-mills.
BRUNEL, MARC ISAMBARD -	3643	26th Jan. 1813	Saw-mills.
BRUNEL, MARC ISAMBARD -	3791	12th March 1814	Mode of giving durability to certain descriptions of leather.
BRUNEL, MARC ISAMBARD -	3993	14th March 1816	Knitting-machine or "tricoteur."

Name of Patentee.	Progressive Number.	Date.	Subject-matter of Patent.
BRUNEL, MARC ISAMBARD -	4204	20th Jan. 1818	Forming tunnels or drifts under ground.
BRUNEL, MARC ISAMBARD -	4301	5th Nov. 1818	Tin-foil, capable of large and varied crystallization.
BRUNEL, MARC ISAMBARD -	4434	25th Jan. 1820	Making stereotype-plates.
BRUNEL, MARC ISAMBARD -	4522	22nd Dec. 1820	Copying-presses, and pocket copying-press.
BRUNEL, MARC ISAMBARD -	4683	26th June 1822	Steam-engines.
BRUNEL, MARC ISAMBARD -	5212	16th July 1825	Mechanical arrangements for obtaining powers from certain fluids, and applying them to useful purposes.
BRUNET, JAMES JOSEPH -	9826	6th July 1843	Propelling.
BRUNET, JAMES JOSEPH -	13,928	27th Jan. 1852	Combinations of materials in ship-building.
BRUNET, JEAN BAPTISTE AL-[PHONSE.	13,550	10th March 1851	Manufacture of coverings for roofs, walls, partitions, furniture, and other similar articles; boxes, tubes, and other hollow articles; preparation of materials for such purposes; also machinery to be employed in such or similar manufactures.
BRUNET, PIERRE - - -	5037	11th Nov. 1824	Furnace.
BRUNETT, WILLIAM SHELTON	5043	25th Nov. 1824	Ship's tackle.
BRUNIER, LOUIS - - -	6305	8th May 1834	Hydraulic machine (of a centrifugal force) applicable to the raising or forcing of water.
BRUNIER, LOUIS - - -	13,579	31st March 1851	Obtaining power by the use of steam or compressed air.
BRUNKER, SIR WILLIAM, Kⁿᵗ -	54	24th Jan. 1631	Making kersey and twill sieves, and beads of bone and wood.
BRUNTON, FREDERICK -	4145	19th July 1817	Mode of employing silk or other materials, in making hats and bonnets.
BRUNTON, JOHN - - -	5712	2nd Oct. 1828	Apparatus for making coal-gas and coke; method of arranging the same.
BRUNTON, JOHN - - -	6799	25th March 1835	Construction of retorts for generating gas for the purpose of illumination.
BRUNTON, JOHN - - -	11,138	23rd March 1846	Construction, and mode of opening and closing moveable bridges or arches, for carrying railways, tramways, or other roads, across canals, docks, or other open cuttings.
BRUNTON, THOMAS - -	3671	26th March 1813	Manufacturing ships' anchors, windlasses, and chain-cables or moorings.
BRUNTON, THOMAS - -	4649	13th Feb. 1822	Ships' anchors.
BRUNTON, THOMAS - -	5943	19th June 1830	Mechanical power, applicable to machinery of different descriptions.
BRUNTON, THOMAS - -	6099	28th March 1831	Apparatus rendered applicable for distilling.
BRUNTON, THOMAS - -	6106	14th April 1831	Apparatus rendered applicable to steam-engines.
BRUNTON, THOMAS - -	6107	14th April 1831	Apparatus rendered applicable for making or refining sugar.
BRUNTON, THOMAS - -	6189	15th Nov. 1831	Adaptation of certain apparatus for heating fluids or liquids, and generating steam.
BRUNTON, THOMAS - -	6190	15th Nov. 1831	Mechanical apparatus for raising water, and for other useful purposes.
BRUNTON, WILLIAM - -	3700	22nd May 1813	Method and machinery for drawing or propelling carriages on roads or railways, also vessels on water, by levers acting alternately or conjointly upon such roads, railways, canals or navigations, or upon machinery attached thereto.
BRUNTON, WILLIAM - -	4387	29th June 1819	Steam-engines, and furnaces of steam-engines.

Name of Patentee.	Progressive Number.	Date.	Subject-matter of Patent.
BRUNTON, WILLIAM　-　-	4449	19th April 1820	Fire-grates.
BRUNTON, WILLIAM　-　-	4685	26th June 1822	Fire-grates, and means of introducing coal thereon.
BRUNTON, WILLIAM　-　-	5621	21st Feb.　1828	Furnaces for the calcination, sublimation, or evaporation of ores, metals, or other substances.
BRUNTON, WILLIAM　-　-	5722	4th Dec.　1828	Apparatus to ascertain and register the specific-gravity and temperature of certain fluids in transit;—partly applicable to other purposes.
BRUNTON, WILLIAM　-　.	6500	2nd Nov.　1833	Apparatus for excavating the ground, and forming embankments.
BRUNTON, WILLIAM　-　-	9135	2nd Nov.　1841	Dressing ores, and separating metals or minerals from other substances.
BRUNTON, WILLIAM　-　-	9351	19th May　1842	Dressing ores, and separating metals or minerals from other substances.
BRUNTON, WILLIAM, junior　-	10,295	29th Aug.　1844	Manufacture of shovels for mining purposes.
BRUNTON, WILLIAM, junior　-	10,378	2nd Nov.　1844	Apparatus for dressing ores.
BRUNTON, WILLIAM, junior　-	11,967	16th Nov.　1847	Apparatus for dressing ores or minerals.
BRYANT, AMOS　-　-	11,698	8th May　1847	Preparing, constructing, and draining land; implements to be used therein.
BRYANT, THOMAS BARBER　-	1631	30th Nov.　1787	Pumps and pumping.
BRYANT, THOMAS BARBER　-	1634	20th Dec.　1787	Whale-oil.
BRYANT, WILLIAM　-　-	7246	3rd Dec.　1836	Manufacture of liquid and paste blacking, by introducing india-rubber, oil, and other articles and things.
BRYANT, ZACHARIAH　-　-	8915	3rd April　1841	Manufacturing cloth and other fabrics from wool, cotton, flax, silk, and other substances.
BRYCE, ALEXANDER　-　-	2567	2nd Jan.　1802	Drying yarns of linen, cotton, or silk, or composed of all or any of these articles, also piece goods.
BRYDONE, WALTER MARR　-	13,908	22nd Jan.　1852	Apparatus for signal and other lights for railways.
BRYERE, PIERRE　-　-	11,392	2nd Oct.　1846	Manufacture of boots, shoes, and clogs.
BUCHAN, ALEXANDER　-	1853	13th Feb.　1792	Stocking-frame for ribbed and plain work.
BUCHANAN, ARCHIBALD-　-	4854	16th Oct.　1823	Construction of weaving-looms, impelled by machinery.
BUCHANAN, ARCHIBALD-　-	4875	4th Dec.　1823	Machinery for carding cotton and other wool, whereby the top cards are regularly stripped and kept clean, without the aid of hand labour.
BUCHANAN, GEORGE　-　-	12,875	3rd Dec.　1849	Cocks, valves, or stoppers; use of flexible substances for regulating or stopping the passage of fluids; making joints of tubes and pipes, or other vessels.
BUCHANAN, JAMES -　-　-	8514	22nd May 1840	Machinery for and mode of, preparing, twisting, and spinning hemp, flax, and other fibrous substances; applying tar or other preservatives to rope and other yarns.
BUCHANAN, JAMES -　-　-	9313	6th April　1842	Preparing and spinning cotton-wool, flax, hemp, and other fibrous substances.
BUCHANAN, JOHN -　-　-	6834	13th May　1835	Construction of cylinder printing-machines used for printing paper, calico, and other fabrics.
BUCHANAN, JOHN -　-　-	7229	22nd Nov. 1836	Apparatus for dyeing, and performing similar operations.

Name of Patentee.	Progressive Number.	Date.	Subject-matter of Patent.
BUCHANAN, JOHN - - -	8197	16th Aug. 1839	Construction of wheel-carriages;—partly applicable to machinery for propelling and also for securing ships and other vessels; and for communicating motion between different portions of machinery.
BUCHANAN, JOHN - - -	8755	28th Dec. 1840	Wheel-carriages for rail or other roads.
BUCHANAN, JOHN - - -	11,335	15th Aug. 1846	Ships or vessels; propelling thereof, and securing from floatal damage;—parts of the machinery may be used for motion on land.
BUCHANAN, ROBERTSON - -	2097	8th March 1796	Pump for raising water, particularly on board ship;—may be converted into an engine for extinguishing fires.
BUCHANAN, ROBERTSON - -	3741	18th Oct. 1813	Impelling vessels, boats, barges, and rafts;—may also be applied for moving mills, raising water, dredging, cleansing, or deepening rivers and harbours, and impelling other machinery.
BUCHHOLZ, GUSTAV ADOLPH	12,061	9th Feb. 1848	Obtaining motive-power.
BUCHHOLZ, GUSTAV ADOLPH	13,453	16th Jan. 1851	Printing; manufacture of printing-apparatus, also folding and cutting apparatus.
BUCHHOLZ, GUSTAV ADOLPH	13,515	17th Feb. 1851	Motive-power and propulsion.
BUCHLER, EDWARD - -	12,423	16th Jan. 1849	Manufacture of boots and shoes;—applicable to other fabrics.
BUCK, GEORGE WATSON -	10,467	14th Jan. 1845	Manufacture for, and method of, sustaining the rails of railways.
BUCKINGHAM, JAMES - -	7394	17th June 1837	Combinations of machinery, to be applied as mechanical agents where toothed gear and other mechanism have hitherto been used.
BUCKINGHAM, JAMES - -	7480	16th Nov. 1837	Ventilating mines, ships, and other places; apparatus for effecting the same.
BUCKLE, JOHN WILLIAM -	4652	2nd March 1822	Machinery for cutting out irregular forms in wood or any other substance, by tools with continuous or reciprocating circular motion.
BUCKNAL, WILLIAM - -	528	30th April 1731	Mathematical machine in two parts, for the improvement of astronomy and navigation, by applying its uses to various new problems.
BUCKNALL, WILLIAM - -	7007	17th Feb. 1836	Machinery for propelling vessels, and for water-wheels.
BUCKNELL, WILLIAM - -	8895	2nd March 1841	Applying heat for hatching eggs;—applicable to other purposes where heat is required.
BUCKTON, RICHARD - -	14,237	21st July 1852	Adaptation and application of a new manufactured material, to certain articles of dress.
BUCKWELL, WILLIAM - -	9190	16th Dec. 1841	Scaffolding or framework for building purposes.
BUCKWELL, WILLIAM - -	12,544	28th March 1849	Compressing or solidifying fuel and other materials.
BUCKWELL, WILLIAM - -	12,829	2nd Nov. 1849	Steam-engines; and propelling vessels.
BUCKWELL, WILLIAM - -	12,851	17th Nov. 1849	Manufacturing pipes and other structures, artificially in moulds, when using stone and other matters.
BUCKWELL, WILLIAM - -	12,912	3rd Jan. 1850	Compressing or solidifying fuel.

Name of Patentee.	Progres-sive Number.	Date.		Subject-matter of Patent.
BUCKWELL, WILLIAM - -	13,045	18th April	1850	Construction and means of applying carriage and certain other springs.
BUDD, EDWARD - - -	9999	28th Dec.	1843	Reducing copper ores; construction of furnaces for treating copper ores;—partly applicable to other ores.
BUDD, JAMES PALMER - -	9495	20th Oct.	1842	Manufacture of iron.
BUDD, JAMES PALMER - -	10,475	16th Jan.	1845	Manufacture of iron.
BUDD, JAMES PALMER - -	11,078	11th Feb.	1846	Manufacture of iron.
BUDD, JAMES PALMER - -	13,121	11th June	1850	Manufacture of coke.
BUDD, JOHN - - - -	6754	27th Jan.	1835	Printing silk, cotton, calico, or other fabrics; manufacture of blocks, cylinders, or rollers used for such purposes.
BUDDING, EDWARD - -	5990	31st Aug.	1830	Combination and application of machinery for shearing lawns and grass-plats (in place of scythes.)
BUDDING, EDWIN - - -	8860	15th Oct.	1840	Machinery for cutting vegetable and other substances.
BUDDING, EDWIN - - -	9788	15th June	1843	Covering the cylinders of carding and scribbling engines; condensing the rovings delivered from such engines; apparatus for grinding the points of the cards, which apparatus may also be employed for grinding other articles.
BUDDLE, JOHN - - -	3783	21st Feb.	1814	Fire-pan or fire-lamp; also fire-grate or fire-stove, capable of consuming small coals.
BUDGE, JOHN - - -	1025	5th Nov.	1772	Machine for raising metals, minerals, or other heavy materials, from great depths, by aid of horses, or by water movement, by means of a double barrel on an inserted principle, having at the same time an increasing and decreasing power, gathering strength as it draws.
BUDGEN, JOHN - - -	3979	3rd Feb.	1816	Reducing rags of silk, linen or cotton, to their original state, so that the materials can be re-manufactured.
BUFFINGTON, JACOB - -	2791	30th Oct.	1804	Straining or stretching woollen-cloth for cropping or shearing; straining other piece-goods.
BUFFUM, ARNOLD - - -	5337	18th Feb.	1826	Making and dyeing hats.
BUFFUM, ARNOLD - - -	5356	6th May	1826	Steam-engines.
BUGBY, JOSEPH - - -	2944	19th June	1806	Machine for spinning hemp, flax, tow, and wool.
BUISSON, JOSEPH MARIE UR-[SULE LA RIGANDELLE DU.	5902	12th Feb.	1830	Extracting colour from dye-woods and other substances, for the use of dyers.
BUISSON, MICHEL ANTOINE [BERTIN BURIN DU.	10,726	23rd June	1845	Distillation of bituminous shistus, and other bituminous substances; purification, rectification, and preparation of the productions for various useful purposes.
BULKELEY, JOHN - - -	1695	30th July	1789	Heel-case of silver, gold, plated iron, or other metal, for shoes, boots, and slippers.
BULKELEY, THOMAS - -	5888	26th Jan.	1830	Making or manufacturing candles.
BULKELEY, THOMAS - -	5957	19th July	1830	Propelling vessels;—applicable to other purposes.
BULL, DEKINS - - -	63	25th May	1633	Making platforms, terraces, and rooms of buildings, so that fire or water will not injure them.

Name of Patentee.	Progressive Number.	Date.	Subject-matter of Patent.
BULL, JOHN - - - -	1526	31st Jan. 1786	Machine for paring, trimming, friezing, and grounding leather, used in manufacturing gloves, breeches, and shoes, and for binding books; cutting out shoes, slippers, gloves, mits and muffs, and embellishing the same with ornaments in gold, silver, and colours.
BULL, MARK - - - -	1264	15th Sept. 1780	Machine to support an umbrella, to be fixed in a saddle or phaeton or any other carriage.
BULL, REUBEN - - -	7340	15th April 1837	Chimney caps, to facilitate the discharge of smoke and prevent its return.
BULL, RICHARD - - -	373	22nd Dec. 1704	Roasting coffee in a furnace with a barrel, box, and flue, and without the use of a charcoal or wood fire.
BULLER, THOMAS WENTWORTH	12,599	3rd May 1849	Manufacture of earthenware.
BULLOCK, HUGH - - -	45	— Jan. 1629	Engine for cutting timber into plank, board, and other squares.
BULLOCK, JOHN LLOYD -	11,204	12th May 1846	Manufacture of quinine.
BULLOCK, WILLIAM - -	2542	8th Oct. 1801	Fastening to be applied to sashes or dining tables.
BULLOCK, WILLIAM - -	3695	15th May 1813	Instruments to prevent doors and window-shutters being broken open, or violently driven in by the wind.
BULLOUGH, ADAM - -	11,462	1st Dec. 1846	Looms for weaving.
BULLOUGH, JAMES - -	6900	1st Oct. 1835	Hand-looms and power-looms.
BULLOUGH, JAMES - -	8790	14th Jan. 1841	Machinery for weaving.
BULLOUGH, JAMES - -	9507	3rd Nov. 1842	Construction of looms for weaving.
BULLOUGH, JAMES - -	11,462	1st Dec. 1846	Looms for weaving.
BULMER, JOHN - - -	73	18th July 1634	Engines for raising ships and goods sunk in the sea.
BUMPSTEAD, ROBERT - -	472	4th Nov. 1724	Machine for raising water to supply cities, float ships, drain and cleanse lands, docks, rivers, and ponds, or irrigate dry lands.
BUNDY, WILLIAM - - -	2119	28th June 1796	Machine for cutting and making combs.
BUNDY, WILLIAM - - -	2932	1st May 1806	Machine for making leaden bullets, and other shot.
BUNDY, WILLIAM - - -	3268	28th Sept. 1809	Heading pins.
BUNDY, WILLIAM - - -	3436	24th April 1811	Stringed musical instruments.
BUNDY, WILLIAM - - -	3638	15th Jan. 1813	Manufacture of lint.
BUNDY, WILLIAM - - -	4099	1st Feb. 1817	Machinery for breaking and preparing flax and hemp.
BUNDY, WILLIAM - - -	4354	1st April 1819	Machinery for breaking hemp and flax.
BUNDY, WILLIAM - - -	4734	16th Dec. 1822	Machine for breaking, cleaning, and preparing flax, hemp, and other vegetable substances containing fibre.
BUNDY, WILLIAM - - -	4858	1st Nov. 1823	Anti-evaporating cooler, to regulate the temperature of worts or wash in fermentation.
BUNDY, WILLIAM - - -	6001	21st Sept. 1830	Machinery for spinning and twisting silk and wool; also for roving, spinning, and twisting cotton, flax, hemp, and other fibrous substances.
BUNN, JOHN - - - -	3601	25th Sept. 1812	Manufacturing rods and hoops from old iron hoops.
BUNN, LOCKINTON LAWRENCE. [ST.	13,713	7th Aug. 1851	Manufacture of kamptulicon.

Name of Patentee.	Progres-sive Number.	Date.	Subject-matter of Patent.
BUNNETT, JACOB - - -	1540	18th March 1786	Machine for printing paper hangings, calicoes, cottons, and linens, by means of which any number of colours may be printed thereon at one and the same time.
BUNNETT, JOSEPH - - -	7123	18th June 1836	Window-shutters;—also applicable to other purposes.
BUNNETT, JOSEPH - - -	7689	14th June 1838	Steam-engines.
BUNNETT, JOSEPH - - -	8831	3rd Feb. 1841	Locomotive engines and carriages.
BUNNETT, JOSEPH - - -	9397	21st June 1842	Pavements for streets, roads, and other surfaces; machinery for producing and repairing the same.
BUNNETT, JOSEPH - - -	11,164	15th April 1846	Water-closets;—partly applicable to other purposes.
BUNNETT, JOSEPH - - -	13,411	12th Dec. 1850	Doors, windows, shutters, and blinds.
BUNNETT, JOSEPH - - -	13,473	23rd Jan. 1851	Public carriages for the conveyance of passengers.
BUNTING, EDMUND - -	2174	25th March 1797	Producing a forward and retrograde motion, capable of being applied to mangles, pumps, calenders, rolling presses or other mechanism.
BUNYAN, ARTHUR - - -	408	12th Sept. 1716	Expressing sweet oil from a certain English seed, for use in the woollen manufacture, also for painters, leather dressers, &c.
BURCH, JOSEPH - - -	7937	15th Jan. 1839	Printing cotton, woollen, paper, and other fabrics and materials.
BURCH, JOSEPH - - -	9728	16th May 1843	Machinery for printing cotton, silk, woollen, paper, oil-cloth, and other fabrics and materials; apparatus for preparing moulds, and casting surfaces for printing; preparing surfaces previous to the design being delineated thereon.
BURCH, JOSEPH - - -	10,657	6th May 1845	Machinery for printing calico and other fabrics;—partly applicable to other purposes where resistance to heat is required.
BURCH JOSEPH - - -	12,658	14th June 1849	Printing on cotton, woollen, silk, paper, and other fabrics and materials.
BURCH, JOSEPH - - -	13,266	28th Sept. 1850	Printing terry and pile carpets, woollen, silk, and other materials.
BURCH, JOSEPH - - -	13,866	19th Dec. 1851	Printing and ornamenting cut pile and other fabrics and yarns.
BURCH, RICHARD - - -	7301	16th Feb. 1837	Locomotive steam-engines to be used on rail or other roads;—applicable to marine and stationary steam-engines.
BURCH, RICHARD - -	7454	2nd Nov. 1837	Manufacturing gas from coals.
BURCH, RICHARD - -	13,677	3rd July 1851	Looms for weaving.
BURCH, WILLIAM - -	6987	23rd Jan. 1836	Machinery for printing silk and cotton net or lace.
BURCH, WILLIAM - -	11,809	20th July 1847	Railways; carriages to be used on railways; giving signals on railways.
BURDON, ROWLAND - -	2066	18th Sept. 1795	Making, uniting, and applying cast-iron blocks in lieu of key-stones, in the construction of arches.
BURDON, ROWLAND - -	2635	23rd July 1802	Uniting, combining, and connecting the "metallic patent blocks" for the construction of arches.
BURETT, BAPTISTE - - -	10,031	30th Jan. 1844	Manufacture of gas.
BURGE, WILLIAM - - -	3752	16th Nov. 1813	Construction of fireplaces.
BURGE, WILLIAM - - -	9206	21st Dec. 1841	Propelling vessels.

Name of Patentee.	Progres-sive Number.	Date.	Subject-matter of Patent.
BURGES, CAROLINE ELIZA ANN	6301	8th Sept. 1832	Apparatus for sketching, drawing, or deli-neating.
BURGES, GEORGE - - -	5500	26th May 1827	Construction of wheeled-carriages, and wheels for the same or other purposes.
BURGES, MATHIAS - - -	114	14th Dec. 1637	Making an engine for working all kinds of mills, also for carriages and wheel works turned by wind, water, man, or beast.
BURGES, MATHIAS - - -	124	8th Feb. 1640	Making candles, taps, links, and torches, with oil and other things.
BURGES, ROGER - - -	1	2nd March 1617	Making, describing, carving, graving, and printing, maps of London, Westminster, Bristol, Norwich, Canterbury, Bath, Oxford, Cambridge, and Windsor.
BURGES, THOMAS - - -	1686	9th June 1789	Producing rotary motion from the action of an alternate movement in any direction, effected by a steam-engine or other ma-chine.
BURGESS, HENRY - - -	4701	3rd Sept. 1822	Wheeled-carriages.
BURGESS, RICHARD - -	6080	21st Feb. 1831	A drink for the cure of gout, gravel, and other diseases;—applicable to other cases.
BURGESS, WILLIAM -	13,466	21st Jan. 1851	Machinery for cutting turnips, and other substances.
BURGESS, WILLIAM -	14,175	21st June 1852	Manufacture of gutta-percha tubing.
BURGIS, JOHN - - -	5768	5th Feb. 1829	Gilding or silvering certain woven fabrics, in burnished and dead burnished or matted gold and silver, for borderings and other purposes.
BURKE, WILLIAM HENRY -	8231	3rd Oct. 1839	Constructing vessels for containing air, ap-plicable to the purpose of raising bodies in or under water; fastening such vessels to chains or other apparatus for raising or lifting such bodies.
BURKE, WILLIAM HENRY -	10,110	19th March 1844	Machinery for cutting India-rubber and other elastic substances, into balls and other solid figures.
BURKE, WILLIAM HENRY -	11,055	20th Jan. 1846	Manufacture of fabrics which may, if re-quired, be made airproof and waterproof;—parts of the materials employed, when com-bined with other matters, being intended to produce coverings for vessels of capacity.
BURKE, WILLIAM HENRY -	12,591	26th April 1849	Manufacture of waterproof and airproof fabrics; preparation of caoutchouc and gutta-percha, alone, or in combination, applicable to wearing-apparel, bands, straps, and other purposes.
BURKINYOUNG, FREDERICK [HANDELL.	11,242	16th June 1846	Pianofortes.
BURLEIGH, RICHARD CLARKE	11,355	28th Aug. 1846	Artificial light.
BURLEIGH, RICHARD CLARKE	12,053	8th Feb. 1848	Burners for obtaining light and heat; appa-ratus to be used therewith.
BURLINGHAM, JOHN - -	6331	8th Nov. 1832	Mills or machinery worked by wind, appli-cable to grinding corn, and other pur-poses.
BURMAN, SAMUEL - - -	1870	18th April 1792	Lap half-boot.
BURN, JAMES - - - -	1858	2nd March 1792	Composition for making hats.
BURN, JOHN - - - -	4941	14th April 1824	Apparatus for dressing various kinds of cotton, flaxen, woollen, or silk manufac-tures.

Name of Patentee.	Progressive Number.	Date.	Subject-matter of Patent.
BURN, ROBERT - - -	12,348	2nd Dec. 1848	Roller gin, used in separating the seed from cotton.
BURN, ROBERT - - -	14,353	21st Dec. 1852	Steam-engines.
BURNE, CHARLES - - -	785	3rd March 1763	Keels or vessels for taking ballast out of ships, sand-beds out of rivers, and for other purposes.
BURNBY, EUSTACE - - - [Burnby, Eustace.]	133	31st Oct. 1662	Preparation of British barley, in the manner of French barley and pease barley.
BURNEBY, EUSTACE - -	155	24th Dec. 1667	Preparing steel-hemp.
BURNEBY, EUSTACE - -	159	3rd Feb. 1670	Husbanding, ordering, and preparing rice and safflower.
BURNEBY, EUSTACE - -	178	21st Jan. 1675	Making white paper for writing and printing.
BURNELL, JOHN, junior - -	9148	9th Nov. 1841	Manufacture of lantern-leaves from horn; construction of lanterns.
BURNETT, FREDERICK JOSEPH	7720	4th July 1838	Manufacture of soap.
BURNETT, HENRY - - -	5100	19th Feb. 1825	Machinery for a rotary or endless lever action.
BURNETT, JOHN - - -	4042	20th June 1816	Convolving iron axletree, to reduce friction and animal labour, and prevent wheels of carriages from coming off.
BURNETT, Sir WILLIAM, Knight	7747	26th July 1838	Preserving wood and other vegetable matters from decay.
BURNETT, Sir WILLIAM, Knight	8437	19th March 1840	Preserving animal, woollen, and other fibrous substances from decay.
BURNETT, Sir WILLIAM, K.C.B.	14,232	20th July 1852	Preserving wood and other vegetable matters from decay. (Extension for 7 years from 26th July 1852.)
BURNETT, WILLIAM HICKLING [Burnett, Hickling.]	7926	8th Jan. 1839	Machinery for sawing, planing, grooving, and otherwise preparing or working wood for certain purposes.
BURNETT, WILLIAM HICKLING	8551	24th June 1840	Machinery for cutting or working wood.
BURNETT, WILLIAM HICKLING	9083	9th Sept. 1841	Machinery for cutting wood; apparatus connected therewith;—partly applicable to other purposes.
BURNETT, WILLIAM SHELTON	5078	11th Jan. 1825	Lessening the drift of ships at sea, and protecting them in gales of wind.
BURNS, JAMES - - -	2358	23rd Nov. 1799	Fire-grates, stoves, furnaces, and chimneys.
BURR, THOMAS - - -	4445	11th April 1820	Machinery for manufacturing lead and other metal into pipes and sheets.
BURR, THOMAS - - -	7234	24th Nov. 1836	Manufacture of sheets and pipes or tubes and other articles, of lead and other metals.
BURR, THOMAS - - -	8189	8th Aug. 1839	Rolling lead and other soft metals.
BURRELL, ANDREWS - -	42	— Jan. 1628	Engines for draining marsh and fen grounds.
BURRELL, CHARLES - -	14,219	15th July 1852	Reaping-machines.
BURRELL, JOSEPH - - -	2757	10th May 1804	Thrashing-machine.
BURRELL, JOSEPH - - -	3836	21st Feb. 1815	Safeguard to be used in getting in and out of chairs, curricles, and other two-wheeled carriages.
BURRELL, SAMUEL - -	6767	16th Feb. 1835	Manufacturing buttons for clothes.
BURRIDGE, JOHN - - -	5184	9th June 1825	Bricks, stones, or other materials, for the better ventilation of houses and other buildings.
BURROWS, BASSETT - -	3563	5th May 1812	Manufacturing waterproof hats.
BURROWS, BENJAMIN - -	14,308	30th Sept. 1852	Weaving.

Name of Patentee.	Progressive Number.	Date.		Subject-matter of Patent.
BURROWS, EZRA WASHINGTON	10,028	30th Jan.	1844	Construction of engines for producing and communicating motive-power by the elastic force of steam, or by manual or animal labour.
BURROWS, JAMES - - -	12,300	26th Oct.	1848	Steam-engines, and machinery or apparatus belonging thereto ; construction and arrangement of boilers for generating steam ; furnaces and flues used in connection therewith ;—partly applicable to other similar purposes.
BURROWS, JOHN - - -	1008	17th March	1772	Medicine called Velno's vegetable syrup ; making the same from vegetables and drugs.
BURROWS, SAMUEL - -	11,517	7th Jan.	1847	Manufacture of knives.
BURSILL, GEORGE HENRY -	8522	28th May	1840	Weighing, and weighing-machines.
BURSILL, GEORGE HENRY -	11,948	6th Nov.	1847	Envelopes, wrappers, and covers ; and machinery for the manufacture thereof.
BURSILL, GEORGE HENRY -	12,159	22nd May	1848	Treating malt-liquors and other liquids or fluids ; machinery for effecting such treatment.
BURSTALL, TIMOTHY - -	5090	3rd Feb.	1825	Locomotive or steam carriage, for conveyance of mails, passengers, and goods.
BURSTALL, TIMOTHY - -	5405	22nd Aug.	1826	Machinery for propelling locomotive-carriages.
BURSTALL, TIMOTHY - -	7797	6th Sept.	1838	Steam-engines, and apparatus used therewith ;—partly applicable to water-power.
BURSTALL, THOMAS - -	13,839	1st Dec.	1851	Machinery for manufacturing bricks and other articles, from clay, alone or mixed with other materials.
BURT, HENRY POTTER - -	4937	14th April	1824	Construction of cranks for bells, and for other purposes.
BURT, HENRY POTTER - -	13,378	30th Nov.	1850	Manufacture of window-blinds.
BURT, PETER - - - -	5535	4th Aug.	1827	Steam-engine.
BURTON, BENNETT ALFRED -	12,645	7th June	1849	Manufacture of pipes, tiles, bricks, stairs, copings and other articles, from plastic materials ; machinery employed therein.
BURTON, BENNETT ALFRED -	12,922	11th Jan.	1850	Apparatus connected with sewers, drains, and cesspools ; suction and delivery pipes ; connecting such pipes or hose ;—the apparatus for sewers being applicable to other like purposes.
BURTON, GEORGE - - -	208	23rd May	1679	Pipes, engines, and vessels (by way of hydragogy), for raising water out of ships and mines, for draining land, and for supplying, even in the drought of summer, all sorts of mills, whether undershot or overshot ; also for raising the Thames-water in larger quantity than is now raised by the water-mill houses, without the great charge and labour of men and horses.
BURTON, JOSEPH - - -	1210	3rd Feb.	1779	Women's clogs.
BURTONSHAW, JOHN - -	3935	24th June	1815	Machine or instrument for heating ovens.
BURY, ABRAHAM - - -	7843	3rd Nov.	1838	Printing, colouring or dyeing cotton or other fabrics ; producing acids applicable to these and other purposes.
BURY, CHARLES - - -	13,273	10th Oct.	1850	Machinery or apparatus for cleaning, spinning, doubling, and throwing raw silk.

Name of Patentee.	Progressive Number.	Date.		Subject-matter of Patent.
BURY, CHARLES - - -	13,274	10th Oct.	1850	Machinery or apparatus for preparing and spinning, doubling or twisting, silk-waste, cotton-wool, flax, or other fibrous substances.
BURY, EDWARD - - -	10,601	7th April	1845	Locomotive-engines, carriages or waggons running on railways or common roads, for the prevention of accidents.
BURY, SAMUEL - - -	1637	15th Jan.	1788	Organ, pianoforte, and other musical instruments; conveyance of music or the sound of the voice to a distance.
BURY, THOMAS - - -	4758	18th Feb.	1823	Dyeing or producing a permanent nankeen colour on cotton-wool, skein-yarn, and certain other articles.
BURY, THOMAS - - -	12,956	31st Jan.	1850	Construction of machines for glazing, embossing, and finishing, woven fabrics, and paper.
BUSBY, CHARLES AUGUSTIN -	6268	15th May	1832	Producing the circulation of fluids through pipes, cisterns or other vessels, applicable for warming or cooling the interior of buildings, and for other purposes.
BUSBY, JOHN - - - -	429	10th May	1720	Kiln to dry malt with hot air.
BUSH, MATTHEW - - -	3639	15th Jan.	1813	Machine for printing calicoes.
BUSH, MATTHEW - - -	4489	20th July	1820	Machine for printing silks, linens, calicoes, woollens, and other similar fabrics, whereby one or more colours may be printed on handkerchiefs and shawls, linens, calicoes, and fabrics of a like nature.
BUSH, MATTHEW - - -	5011	7th Oct.	1824	Machinery for printing calicoes and other fabrics.
BUSH, MATTHEW - - -	5479	27th March	1827	Machinery for printing calico and other fabrics.
BUSH, MATTHEW - - -	5938	24th May	1830	Machinery for printing calicoes and other fabrics.
BUSH, MATTHEW - - -	6626	14th June	1834	Machinery for drying and printing calicoes and other fabrics.
BUSH, WILLIAM - - -	3911	29th April	1815	Method of preventing accidents arising from horses falling when harnessed to two-wheeled carriages.
BUSH, WILLIAM - - -	4254	5th May	1818	Drying and preparing malt, wheat, and other grain.
BUSH, WILLIAM - - -	7180	3rd Sept.	1836	Apparatus for, and means of, building and working under water;—partly applicable to other purposes.
BUSH, WILLIAM - - -	8513	20th May	1840	Fire-arms and cartridges.
BUSH, WILLIAM - - -	9094	21st Sept.	1841	Apparatus for, and means of, building and working under water.
BUSH, WILLIAM - - -	9932	9th Nov.	1843	Rendering magnetic-needles less prejudicially influenced by local attraction.
BUSH, WILLIAM - - -	12,692	4th July	1849	Lamps and lighting.
BUSHBY, CHARLES AUGUSTIN	3683	14th April	1813	Constructing locks of canals, docks, and navigations, so as to lessen the loss of water when vessels pass the same.
BUSHNELL, JOHN - - -	321	29th April	1693	Machine to drain mines and meads, and raise ships sunk at sea.
BUSK, ROBERT - - -	5409	30th Aug.	1826	Machinery for heckling or dressing, breaking, scutching and cleaning, hemp, flax, and other fibrous substances.
BUSK, ROBERT - - -	5891	26th Jan.	1830	Apparatus used for distilling and rectifying.

Name of Patentee.	Progressive Number.	Date.	Subject-matter of Patent.
BUSK, WILLIAM - - -	4183	5th Dec. 1817	Making pipes or tubes of porcelain, clay, or other ductile substances.
BUSK, WILLIAM - - -	4981	29th June 1824	Propelling ships, boats, or other floating bodies.
BUSK, WILLIAM - - -	5002	16th Sept. 1824	Propelling ships, boats, or other vessels.
BUSK, WILLIAM - - -	5035	11th Nov. 1824	Propelling ships, boats, or other vessels or floating bodies.
BUSK, WILLIAM - - -	5419	18th Oct. 1826	Propelling boats, ships, and other vessels or floating bodies.
BUSK, WILLIAM - - -	6859	10th July 1835	Propelling boats, ships, or other floating bodies.
BUTLER, JAMES - - -	250	23rd June 1686	Woven wire-engines for bolting, dressing, sifting, and chaffing meal, and cleansing dross from metals.
BUTLER, JAMES - - -	1026	13th Nov. 1772	Wheels, the spokes of which are constructed of springs for coaches and carriages.
BUTLER, JAMES - - -	5239	12th Aug. 1825	Making coffins so as to prevent the removal of the bodies therefrom, after interment.
BUTLER, JOHN - - -	1536	4th March 1786	Making ships' bolts and rods, from iron, copper, brass, or iron shearings.
BUTLER, RICHARD - - -	6375	29th Jan. 1833	Obtaining oil from certain substances, and gas from the same, or from the oil produced therefrom.
BUTLER, SAMUEL - - -	687	22nd Jan. 1754	Making coaches and other wheel-carriages.
BUTT, JOHN - - - -	10,119	22nd March 1844	Candlesticks.
BUTTAL, SAMUEL - - -	349	6th March 1696	Raising and discharging water out of mines, meres, ponds, or vessels; pipes and other instruments employed for the purpose.
BUTTERS, JAMES - - -	2565	3rd Dec. 1801	Machine for saving persons from drowning, though ignorant of the art of swimming, ("collinette.")
BUTTERWORTH, JOHN HOLLAND.	10,117	20th March 1844	Apparatus applicable to preparation machines used in spinning cotton and other fibrous materials.
BUTTERY, GEORGE - - -	1847	26th Jan. 1792	Construction of pianofortes and other musical instruments where hammers are or can be used.
BUTTON, CHARLES - - -	7521	23rd Dec. 1837	Manufacture of white-lead.
BUTTON, CHARLES - - -	13,363	23rd Nov. 1850	Means or appliances used in conveying telegraphic intelligence between different places.
BUXTON, EDWARD - - -	9941	16th Nov. 1843	Spinning wool, cotton, and other fibrous materials.
BUXTON, JOHN - - -	3816	7th June 1814	Twisting and laying cotton, silk, and various other articles.
BUZAGLO, ABRAHAM - -	826	25th April 1765	Machine for warming rooms equally in every part, and without offensive smell, by means of a coal fire.
BUZAGLO, ABRAHAM - -	928	8th June 1769	Warming-machine made either of copper, brass, tin, pewter, lead, steel, iron-plate, bell or other metal, and acting without fire, for the purpose of warming the feet of persons riding in carriages.
BUZAGLO, ABRAHAM - -	1211	11th Feb. 1779	Machines, instruments, and necessaries, for exercise (muscular strength and health restoring exercise).

Name of Patentee.	Progressive Number.	Date.	Subject-matter of Patent.
By, William - - - -	4938	14th April 1824	Apparatus for the preservation or protection of books and covers.
Bycroft, Richard - -	13,459	18th Jan. 1851	Apparatus to be used by persons to secure warmth and dryness when travelling.
Byerley, Anne Bird - -	7871	13th Nov. 1838	Obtaining motive-power.
Byerley, John, Sir - -	6818	22nd April 1835	Composition, which will effect a saving in oil and soap used in woollen manufactories.
Byfield, Timothy - -	388	22nd Oct. 1711	Sal oleosum volatile,—a chemical preparation or medicine.
Bynner, Jeremiah - -	7503	9th Dec. 1837	Lamps.
Bynner, Jeremiah - -	9136	2nd Nov. 1841	Gas burners.
Byrne, Alexander, Samuel	8234	7th Oct. 1839	Paints or pigments, and vehicles; and modes of applying paints, pigments, and vehicles.
Byrne, Charles - - -	1003	4th Feb. 1772	Construction of guns and all other fire-arms.
Byrne, Oliver - - -	7591	10th March 1838	Instrument for gauging malt, and the fluid or solid contents of casks and other vessels.
Byrom, James - - -	9700	19th April 1843	System of connection for working the cranks of direct action steam-engines.
Bywater, John - - -	2782	14th Sept. 1804	Clothing and unclothing the sails of windmills while in motion.
Bywater, John - - -	2959	22nd Aug. 1806	Sails of ships and other navigable vessels; and mode of working them.
Bywater, John - - -	3048	6th June 1807	Construction of windlasses for weighing the anchors of ships and navigable vessels, and for other purposes.

C.

Caan, Charles le - -	3311	26th Feb. 1810	Apparatus to be added and united to the axletrees and wheels, or naves of wheels of carriages, so as to impede, resist, or check their motion.
Cabanel, Rudolphe - -	3039	5th May 1807	Construction of wheels and axletrees.
Cabanel, Rudolphe - -	5143	30th March 1825	Machinery for raising water;—partly applicable to other purposes.
Cadby, Charles - -	13,221	12th Aug. 1850	Stringed musical instruments.
Cademan, Thomas - -	81	25th March 1635	Distilling strong waters, and making vinegars of cider, perry, and buck or French wheat.
Cairncross, William -	1579	19th Dec. 1786	Securing the joints between the legs and rails of chairs, tables, &c. in cabinet work, by metal screws applied on the inner side.
Calcina, Comte Melano de -	9097	21st Sept. 1841	Paving or covering roads and other ways or surfaces.
Caldecott, William Lloyd	10,566	17th March 1845	Manufacture of soap.
Calder, George - - -	8122	22nd June 1839	Stoves or apparatus for roasting, baking, or cooking ("plantanum roaster.")

Name of Patentee.	Progressive Number.	Date.	Subject-matter of Patent.
CALDERBANK, THOMAS - -	4208	23rd Jan. 1818	Working pumps and other machinery.
CALDWELL, CHARLES ANDREW	8095	6th June 1839	Furnaces and apparatus for applying the heat of fuel.
CALDWELL, JAMES - - -	6435	6th June 1833	Cranes, vessels, and apparatus, for delivering coals from shipping, to wharfs, warehouses, waggons, or carts, without employing lighters;—applicable to other purposes.
CALDWELL, JAMES - - -	8469	15th April 1840	Cranes, windlasses, and capstans.
CALDWELL, JAMES - - -	10,835	18th Sept. 1845	Ships' riding-bits, and windlasses.
CALDWELL, SAMUEL -	2788	17th Oct. 1804	Machinery and apparatus to be annexed to warp-frames, whereby these frames will work, make, or manufacture all kinds of thread-lace.
CALDWELL, SAMUEL - -	2879	21st Sept. 1805	Machinery and apparatus to be annexed to stocking-frames or other plain frames, for the purpose of manufacturing plain hose, or other plain piece-work of silk, cotton, mohair, worsted, or other material.
CALLAWAY, GEORGE - -	12,860	24th Nov. 1849	Propelling ships and other vessels; apparatus for ploughing land.
CALLEN, ARTHUR WELLINGTON	13,973	14th Feb. 1852	Manufacture of certain parts of machinery used in paper-making; certain parts of railways; railway and other carriages.
CALLET, LOUIS CYPRIEN -	7729	11th July 1838	Machinery for producing motive-power, applicable for propelling boats and other vessels, carriages, and machines, also for other purposes.
CALLOW, EDWARD - - -	13,215	6th Aug. 1850	Muskets, cannon, and other firearms; explosive compositions and instruments.
CALTHROP, RICHARD - -	152	19th Feb. 1667	Engine for working, sawing, and polishing marble.
CALVERT, EDWARD - -	746	21st Feb. 1760	" Violet cordial."
CALVERT, FRANCIS ALTON -	12,427	18th Jan. 1849	Machinery for cleaning and preparing cotton-wool, and other fibrous substances.
CALVERT, FREDERICK CRACE -	11,126	11th March 1846	Preparing " jute " for various purposes.
CALVERT, FREDERICK CRACE -	13,658	12th June 1851	A new application of certain fluids for making extracts, applicable to the processes of dyeing, printing, and tanning; apparatus connected therewith.
CALVERT, FREDERICK CRACE -	13,793	30th Oct. 1851	Manufacturing iron; manufacturing and purifying coke.
CALVERT, JAMES - - -	12,568	16th April 1849	Looms for weaving.
CALVERT, HENRY - - -	6021	26th Oct. 1830	Making saddles so as to avoid the danger arising from their slipping forward.
CAMBIS, LOUIS JOSEPH MARIE, [Marquis DE.	5372	23rd May 1826	Construction of rotatory steam-engines, and apparatus connected therewith.
CAMBRIDGE, WILLIAM COL-[BORNE.	10,172	30th April 1844	Machinery for rolling or crushing ground; cutting and thrashing agricultural products; adaptation of horse-power to thrashing machinery;—may also be applied to other uses.
CAMERON, CHARLES - -	8791	14th Jan. 1841	Engines to be actuated by steam or other elastic fluid.
CAMERON, CHARLES - -	10,014	16th Jan. 1844	Extinguishing fires in buildings.

Name of Patentee.	Progressive Number.	Date.	Subject-matter of Patent.
CAMERON, JOHN - - -	13,996	4th March 1852	Obtaining copper from ores.
CAMERON, ROBERT - -	1414	17th Jan. 1784	Steam-engine or fire-engine.
CAMERON, ROBERT - -	1452	30th Sept. 1784	Sawing-machines; and working the same.
CAMERON, ROBERT - -	1525	28th Jan. 1786	Raising coals, ores, and water.
CAMERON, ROBERT - -	1702	5th Sept. 1789	Machines for raising coals, ores, and water from mines; also machinery used in coal-mines.
CAMERON, ROBERT, junior -	4002	23rd March 1816	Machine for manufacturing paper.
CAMPBELL, ALEXANDER FRAN-[CIS.	8004	18th March 1839	Ploughs.
CAMPBELL, ALEXANDER FRAN-[CIS.	8108	17th June 1839	Ploughs, harrows, scarifiers, cultivators, and horse-hoes.
CAMPBELL, ALEXANDER FRAN-[CIS.	8517	28th May 1840	Ploughs and other agricultural implements.
CAMPBELL, ALEXANDER FRAN-[CIS.	12,663	20th June 1849	Wheels, ploughs, and harrows; steam-boilers, and machinery for propelling vessels.
CAMPBELL, EDWARD - -	509	8th May 1729	Remedy for smoky chimneys, by fixing on the top a " mantle chimney " without doors, made of brick and lime, or other building materials.
CAMPBELL, ETHEN - -	12,815	18th Oct. 1849	Generating and applying motive-power; and propelling vessels.
CAMPBELL, GEORGE - -	416	— Aug. 1717	Making salt, and removing the corrosive nature of the same, by a separate preparation of the brine.
CAMPBELL, HECTOR - -	1922	28th Nov. 1792	Destroying and taking away the carbonic, oleaginous, and colouring elements in rags and other materials used for making paper.
CAMPBELL, JOHN - - -	10,929	6th Nov. 1845	Machinery for drying and finishing bleached cotton and other goods.
CAMPBELL, JOHN - - -	14,121	8th May 1852	Manufacture and treatment or finishing of textile fabrics and materials; machinery used therein.
CAMPBELL, JOHN GEORGE [TRUSCOTT.	8995	19th June 1841	Propelling vessels.
CAMPBELL, JOHN GORDON -	7228	19th Nov. 1836	Manufacture of silk, and silk in combination with certain other fibrous substances.
CAMPBELL, ROBERT - -	1086	11th Nov. 1774	Making library-steps, to be contained in writing-tables, library-tables, and dining-tables, with or without hand-rail, and with or without desks on the top, also in card-tables, breakfast-tables, dressing or other tables, and in chairs or stools.
CAMPIN, FREDERICK WILLIAM	11,058	22nd Jan. 1846	Obtaining and applying motive-power.
CAMPION, JEREMIAH - -	11,493	15th Dec. 1846	Soldiers' belts, and carrying of knapsacks.
CAMPION, JOHN - - -	1247	4th March 1780	Formation and construction of locks and latches, so as to prevent their being picked, and to exclude dust.
CAMPION, ROBERT - - -	3682	13th April 1813	Making double canvas and sail-cloth, with hemp and flax or either of them, without starch.
CANEY, JOHN HOPPER - -	5761	23rd Jan. 1829	Construction of umbrellas and parasols.
CANNON, WILLIAM JEARY -	12,063	10th Feb. 1848	Construction of carriages for the conveyance of sheep and other animals on railways.

Name of Patentee.	Progressive Number.	Date.	Subject-matter of Patent.
CANOLLE, JEAN DE - -	1386	12th Sept. 1783	A new invented factitious coal, to be used instead of charcoal.
CANT, JOHN - - - -	2624	31st May 1802	Tanning leather.
CANTELO, JAMES - - -	11,102	25th Feb. 1846	Apparatus for hatching eggs and rearing the young; and for heating hot-houses and other buildings.
CAPARN, JAMES - - -	2980	30th Oct. 1806	Machine for discharging smoke from smoky chimneys.
CAPELAIN, PHILLIP LE - -	9030	15th July 1841	Meters for measuring gas and other aëriform fluids.
CAPLIN, JEAN FRANCOIS ISI-[DORE.	7640	14th May 1838	Stays or corsets, and other parts of dress where lacing is employed; instruments for measuring for the same, also for the bodies of dresses.
CAPPER, CHARLES HENRY -	10,255	10th July 1844	Manufacture of palisades, gates, and fences;—applicable to other purposes.
CAPPER, CHARLES HENRY -	12,184	13th June 1848	Preparing and cleaning minerals and other substances.
CARASS, JOHN - - -	818	14th Nov. 1764	Marine collar and belt.
CARBINES, HENRY - -	10,364	24th Oct. 1844	Fusees, cartridges, and other like explosive instruments.
CARCANO, JEAN BAPTISTE -	10,443	18th Dec. 1844	Working atmospheric-railways.
CARCO, DENNIS - - -	1340	1st Nov. 1782	Composition for covering leather hats, and all other sorts of hats.
CARD, NATHANIEL - - -	9074	8th Sept. 1841	Manufacture of wicks for candles, lamps, and other similar purposes; apparatus connected therewith.
CARD, NATHANIEL - - -	9590	14th Jan. 1843	Manufacture of candlewick; machinery for producing such manufacture.
CARD, NATHANIEL - - -	11,580	16th Feb. 1847	Machinery for twisting, twining, or manufacturing cords, band, twine, and other similar articles, from cotton, flax, hemp, silk, and other fibrous yarns or threads.
CARDIFFE, CHARLES - -	216	16th Feb. 1682	Making muskets, carbines, and pistols, so as to discharge several shots in a single barrel and lock, with one priming.
CARDONELES, ADAM DE - -	249	9th Jan. 1686	Making writing and printing paper; imprinting His Majesty's arms thereon; mills and engines for the purpose.
CARDWELL, THOMAS - -	9556	15th Dec. 1842	Construction of presses for compressing cotton and other articles.
CAREY, CHARLES - - -	11,923	26th Oct. 1847	Obtaining infusions or extracts from coffee and other matters.
CAREY, GEORGE DANIEL -	6705	23rd Oct. 1834	Machinery employed in the manufacture of hats.
CAREY, JOHN - - - -	2963	30th Aug. 1806	Preventing fires, and preserving persons and property therefrom, by improved alarms, chimneys, cisterns, fire-screens, and other articles.
CAREY, ROBERT - - -	7957	29th Jan. 1839	Paving or covering streets, roads, or other ways.
CARLOTTI, MARC - - -	9318	8th April 1842	Construction and manufacture of boots, half boots, shoes, clogs, and goloshes.

Name of Patentee.	Progressive Number.	Date.		Subject-matter of Patent.
CARMICHAEL, PETER - -	11,193	5th May	1846	Heckling or dressing flax, hemp, and other fibrous substances; machinery for rubbing, stretching, and equalizing the breadth of cloth made from flax, hemp, jute, and other fibrous substances.
CARMICHAEL, PETER - -	11,393	2nd Oct.	1846	Machinery for drawing, roving, and spinning flax, hemp, silk, and other fibrous substances.
CARNE, JOHN - - - -	1440	3rd July	1784	Machine on an inverted principle, for raising and removing earth, sand, stone, and other materials.
CARON, LOUIS - - -	3076	21st Oct.	1807	Weaving hair with silk or other materials, and making the same into perukes or wigs; instrument for taking the measure or section of the head;—applicable to other purposes.
CARPENTER, EDWARD JOHN -	8545	13th June	1840	Application of machinery for assisting vessels in their evolutions on the water, especially in tacking, veering, propelling, steering, casting or winding and backing astern.
CARPENTER, EDWARD JOHN -	13,632	13th May	1851	Construction of ships and vessels; machinery for propelling and directing the same.
CARPENTER, ELIAS - -	2075	19th Nov.	1795	Bleaching paper in the water leaf or sheet, and sizing it without drying.
CARPENTER, JAMES - -	3956	23rd Aug.	1815	Curry-comb; (inverting the handle over the back.)
CARPENTER, JAMES - -	5880	18th Jan.	1830	Locks and other securities applicable to doors, and to other purposes.
CARPENTER, JOHN - - -	3877	20th Jan.	1815	Knapsack, with a pouch suspended in front to counteract its weight.
CARPENTER, SAMUEL ALFRED	12,558	3rd April	1849	Buckles or substitutes for buckles.
CARPENTER, WILLIAM - -	11,153	25th March	1846	Thrashing-machines.
CARPMAEL, WILLIAM - -	6955	16th Dec.	1835	Locomotive steam-carriages;—partly applicable to steam-engines and boilers in general.
CARR, HENRY - - -	10,709	5th June	1845	Construction of temporary roofs or coverings.
CARR, JOHN - - - -	9141	9th Nov.	1841	Operating in certain processes for ornamenting glass.
CARR, JOHN - - - -	11,785	3rd July	1847	Looms for weaving.
CARR, JOHN, junior - -	8961	20th May	1841	Apparatus for retarding and stopping railway-carriages.
CARR, JOHN THOMAS - -	9050	21st Aug.	1841	Steam-engines.
CARR, RILEY - - -	6521	11th Dec.	1833	Machinery for cutting, cropping, and dressing, woollen and cotton cloths.
CARRON, WILLIAM - -	9201	21st Dec.	1841	Construction of clogs and pattens.
CARSON, JAMES - -	7900	12th Dec.	1838	Slaughtering animals for human food.
CARSON, SAMUEL - -	8376	5th Feb.	1840	Apparatus for withdrawing air or vapours.
CARSON, SAMUEL - -	9435	3rd Aug.	1842	Purifying and preserving animal substances.
CARSON, SAMUEL - -	10,922	4th Nov.	1845	Treating eggs for the purposes of food.
CART, EDWARD - -	12,066	14th Feb.	1848	Manufacture of gas.
CARTALI, THEODORE - -	13,099	4th June	1850	Treatment or preparation of yarns or threads for weaving.

Name of Patentee.	Progressive Number.	Date.	Subject-matter of Patent.
CARTE, RICHARD - - -	12,996	7th March 1850	Flutes, clarionets, hautboys, and bassoons.
CARTER, EDWARD - - -	12,879	5th Dec. 1849	Printing calico and other fabrics.
CARTER, ELIAS - - -	5552	11th Oct. 1827	Covering for the roofs of houses and other buildings.
CARTER, ELIAS - - -	6851	22nd June 1835	Apparatus for regulating the supply of gas to burners, and stopping off the same;—applicable also as a cock in drawing off or regulating the flow of other fluids.
CARTER, GEORGE - - -	6431	1st June 1833	Paddle-wheels.
CARTER, GEORGE - - -	7717	2nd July 1838	Saw-mills.
CARTER, GEORGE - - -	10,611	15th April 1845	Locks and latches.
CARTER, HORATIO - - -	13,015	23rd March 1850	Production of light from ordinary coal-gas, by the use of burners of more than one ring or sheet of flame, with a suitable chimney supplied with air.
CARTER, JAMES - - -	10,333	27th Sept. 1844	Cutting slate for roofing and other purposes.
CARTER, JAMES - - -	11,487	14th Dec. 1846	Lubricator.
CARTER, JOHN - - -	11,195	5th May 1846	Paddle-wheels.
CARTER, JOHN THOMPSON -	11,558	1st Feb. 1847	Machinery for crushing, bruising, and preparing, flax, hemp, and other fibrous materials.
CARTER, JOSEPH - - -	5218	16th July 1825	Apparatus for giving a new motion to "mules" and " billies."
CARTER, JOSEPH THRELFALL -	11,387	1st Oct. 1846	Propelling carriages on railways.
CARTER, THOMAS - - -	14,323	14th Oct. 1852	Propelling.
CARTER, WILLIAM - - -	4327	6th Jan. 1819	Preparing cork-bark for making corks.
CARTER, WILLIAM - - -	4421	9th Dec. 1819	Manufacture of measures of capacity.
CARTER, WILLIAM - - -	4517	11th Dec. 1820	Steam-engines.
CARTERON, JEAN ADOLPHE -	12,451	5th Feb. 1849	Dyeing.
CARTHY, DENNIS, Mc -	841	6th March 1766	Composition or cement. " Pietra Cotta."
CARTHY, JOHN JAMES ALEX-[DER MC.	4239	8th April 1818	Applying granite or other material in the making or forming of pavement for streets, roads, ways, and places.
CARTLEDGE, JOSEPH - -	1374	31st May 1783	Glazing earthenware.
CARTLEDGE, JOSEPH - -	1418	5th Feb. 1784	Glazing earthenware.
CARTMELL, THOMAS - -	5033	6th Nov. 1824	Cock to be applied to the lock of fire-arms or ordnance, for firing the same by percussion, and whereby the priming is rendered impervious to wind, rain, or damp.
CARTWRIGHT, BENJAMIN -	639	31st Jan. 1749	Steel candle-snuffers and stand; also a secret spring to secure a watch in a man's fob, or by a lady's side.
CARTWRIGHT, EDMUND - -	1470	4th April 1785	Machine for weaving.
CARTWRIGHT, EDMUND - -	1565	30th Oct. 1786	Machine for weaving.
CARTWRIGHT, EDMUND - -	1616	1st Aug. 1787	Machine for weaving.
CARTWRIGHT, EDMUND - -	1676	13th Nov. 1788	Machine for weaving.

Name of Patentee.	Progressive Number.	Date.		Subject-matter of Patent.
CARTWRIGHT, EDMUND - -	1696	3rd Aug.	1789	Machinery for breaking, combing, heckling, preparing, spinning, sizing, dressing, and winding wool, tow, hemp, flax, and cotton.
CARTWRIGHT, EDMUND - -	1747	27th April	1790	Machinery for dressing, heckling, combing, and preparing hemp, flax, wool, hair, silk, and cotton.
CARTWRIGHT, EDMUND - -	1787	11th Dec.	1790	Machinery for dressing, combing, heckling, and preparing wool, hemp, flax, silk, hair, and cotton.
CARTWRIGHT, EDMUND - -	1876	15th May	1792	Machinery for manufacturing wool, hemp, flax, silk, hair, and cotton, into yarn, twist, cords, ropes and cables, and until perfected in the loom, and cut for raising a pile.
CARTWRIGHT, EDMUND - -	2046	14th April	1795	Formation of bricks, stones, or other building materials.
CARTWRIGHT, EDMUND - -	2194	11th Oct.	1797	Incombustible substitute for certain building materials, to render dwelling-houses and other buildings secure from fire.
CARTWRIGHT, EDMUND - -	2202	11th Nov.	1797	Construction, working, and application of steam-engines.
CARTWRIGHT, EDMUND - -	2471	5th Feb.	1801	Framing, combining, and organizing, the parts and mechanism of steam-engines; regulating their velocities, and lessening the waste of power.
CARTWRIGHT, EDWARD -	4992	27th July	1824	Roller printing-presses.
CARTWRIGHT, HENRY - -	10,464	11th Jan.	1845	Construction of paddle-wheels.
CARTWRIGHT, JOHN -	8832	4th Feb.	1841	Stocking-frames, or framework knitting machinery.
CARTWRIGHT, JOHN -	12,377	16th Dec.	1848	Brace for the use of carpenters and others.
CARTWRIGHT, JOSEPH -	3528	28th Jan.	1812	Material applicable to the manufacture of table and other spoons.
CARTWRIGHT, RICHARD -	1984	7th May	1794	Thread or yarn produced by mixing and spinning together certain materials into one single thread, for making hosiery, flannels, cassimeres, cloths, and all or most other articles into which the materials of which it is composed are capable of being separately manufactured or worked.
CARVALHO, DAVID NIMES -	7238	3rd Dec.	1836	Propelling or moving vessels and other floating bodies on water, and carriages on land:—applicable to windmills, and other purposes.
CARWOOD, MARTIN - - -	2935	15th May	1806	Manufacturing metallic cocks for conveying and stopping fluids.
CASLON, WILLIAM - - -	3439	27th April	1811	Register belonging to a mould for casting types.
CASLON, WILLIAM - - -	3610	31st Oct.	1812	Printing-type.
CASLON, WILLIAM - - -	4790	10th May	1823	Construction of gasometers.
CASON, JOHN - - - -	3	1st July	1617	Making locks, sluices, bridges, cuts, cranes, mills, dams, and other inventions necessary and convenient for grinding corn, raising water, and making rivers navigable.

Name of Patentee.	Progressive Number.	Date.	Subject-matter of Patent.
Cason, John - - - -	14	2nd June 1619	Engines for raising water, and making rivers navigable.
Cason, John - - - -	34	5th Sept. 1626	Draining marshes, whether fresh or salt.
Cassell, Edwin Edward -	7908	17th Dec. 1838	Lamps.
Cassell, Edwin Edward -	10,327	26th Sept. 1844	Combination of materials suitable for paving, piping, roofing, and most other purposes to which wood and iron are applicable.
Cassell, John Henry - -	6596	18th April 1834	Cement or combination of materials, applicable to the purposes for which cement, stone, brick, or other similar substances may be used.
Casson, John - - -	3729	9th Aug. 1813	Machine for teaching languages, music, arithmetic, &c. to the blind, by the touch or feeling. ("Panagram.")
Castelain, Leon - - -	9522	25th Nov. 1842	Refining or manufacturing sugar.
Castelain, Leon - - -	12,208	11th July 1848	Manufacture of soap.
Castle, William - - -	197	20th March 1676	Ships' fire-hearths made of iron, copper, or other metals.
Castley, James - - -	12,409	11th Jan. 1849	Manufacture of varnishes from resinous substances.
Catford, William - -	9290	8th March 1842	Machinery for making lace or other netted fabrics.
Cathery, George - - -	2721	6th July 1803	Eradicating smut from wheat.
Catherwood, William -	689	21st Feb. 1754	Applying and adapting a machine to make salt from sea-water.
Catlin, George - - -	9878	4th Sept. 1843	Construction of vessels for navigation, designed to prevent the loss of life in case of shipwreck or other accident at sea.
Cattle, Robert - - -	6340	4th Dec. 1832	Construction of fire-engines.
Cavaignac, Godefroy - -	7896	6th Dec. 1838	Apparatus for transporting materials for various purposes from place to place;—applicable to road cutting, and embankments.
Cavaillon, Florentin Jo-[seph de.	12,718	1st Aug. 1849	Obtaining carbonated hydrogen-gas, and applying the products resulting therefrom to various useful purposes.
Cavaillon, Joseph de - -	4093	23rd Jan. 1817	Preparing, clarifying, and refining sugar and other vegetable, animal, and mineral substances; machinery and utensils used therein.
Cave, Thomas John - -	7431	14th Sept. 1837	Construction of paddle-wheels applicable to ships, boats, and vessels, propelled by steam or other mechanical power.
Cawkwell, Richard - -	3641	15th Jan. 1813	Machine for washing, cleansing, and scouring linen, woollen goods, and other articles.
Cawood, Martin - - -	10,308	12th Sept. 1844	Power-looms.
Cayley, George, Sir -	5260	6th Oct. 1825	New locomotive-apparatus.
Cayley, Sir George, Bart. -	7351	25th April 1837	Apparatus for propelling carriages on common roads or railways;—partly applicable to other purposes.
Ceal, Alfred - - -	11,816	28th July 1847	Manufacture of tobacco.
Cederbarg, Andrew - -	2218	28th Feb. 1798	Machine for glazing, polishing, and graining divers sorts of leather, and other articles.

Name of Patentee.	Progressive Number.	Date.	Subject-matter of Patent.
CELARIER, CHARLES WILLIAM	7320	10th March 1837	Lamps, causing the oil to ascend;—applicable to the raising of water, and other liquids.
CERRETI, NICHOLAS - -	603	9th May 1744	Greek-water, for the cure of venereal distemper.
CHABANNES, JEAN FREDERIC - [Chabannes, John Frederick.]	2364	16th Dec. 1799	Machine for separating coals; a composition for making small coals into cakes or bricks to be used for fuel.
CHABANNES, JEAN FREDERIC [Marquis DE.	3875	16th Jan. 1815	Extracting from fuel a larger quantity of caloric than ordinary, and applying it to warm several rooms by one fire.
CHABANNES, JEAN FREDERIC [Marquis DE [Chabanns, Jean Frederick Marquis de.]	3933	5th Dec. 1815	Conducting air, and regulating the temperature, in houses and other buildings, and warming and cooling either air or liquids;—applicable to various purposes.
CHABANNES, JEAN FREDERIC [Marquis DE. [Chabannes, Jean Frederick Marquis de.]	4191	19th Dec. 1817	Constructing pipes or tubes of tin, copper, sheet-lead, sheet-iron, or other metals or mixture of metals capable of being reduced into sheets.
CHABANNES, JEAN FREDERIC [Marquis DE. [Chabannes, Jean Frederick Marquis de.]	4192	19th Dec. 1817	Warming, cooling, or conducting air in houses and other buildings; warming, cooling, evaporating, condensing, and taking the residuum from liquids;—applicable to other purposes.
CHABANNES, JEAN FREDERIC [Marquis DE. [Chabannes, Jean Frederick Marquis de.]	4582	14th Aug. 1821	Method and apparatus for attracting and catching fish.
CHABERT, JOSEPH EUGENE -	10,344	10th Oct. 1844	Preparing materials to be used in making picture and other frames, and for architectural and other purposes.
CHABERT, JOSEPH EUGENE -	13,372	30th Nov. 1850	Machinery for washing and drying linen and other fabrics.
CHABOT, CHARLES - - -	11,847	2nd Sept. 1847	Railway-carriages, and buffers and other apparatus connected with such carriages.
CHADLEY, JAMES - - -	5998	13th Sept. 1830	Making or forming bricks, tiles, and chimney bars;—applicable to the building or erecting the flues of chimneys.
CHADWICK, CHARLES - -	1093	28th Dec. 1774	Flowering and figuring velvets, velverets, cottons, silks, satins, corduroys, jeans, dimities, or other piece-goods, after the same are made in the piece.
CHALKLEN, JOHN - - -	4051	3rd Aug. 1816	Valve-waterclosets, and the frames or stools thereof.
CHALKLEN, JOHN - - -	7030	14th March 1836	Vices.
CHALMIN, JEAN BAPTISTE -	13,829	22nd Nov. 1851	Preparing and weaving cotton.
CHAMBERLAIN, WILLIAM, jun.	12,188	13th June 1848	Apparatus for recording votes at elections.
CHAMBERLAINE, PETER - -	157	18th Feb. 1668	Navigating vessels in a straight line, in all winds, favourable or adverse.
CHAMBERLAYNE, WILLIAM -	171	12th Nov. 1673	Plating and tinning iron, copper, steel, and brass; compressing and plating all other metals.
CHAMBERS, ABRAHAM HENRY	4441	18th March 1820	Preparing substances for forming highways and other roads;—applicable to other purposes.
CHAMBERS, ABRAHAM HENRY	4527	15th Jan. 1821	Manufacture of building cement, composition, stucco, or plaster, by the application and combination of materials not hitherto used for the purpose.

Name of Patentee.	Progressive Number.	Date.	Subject-matter of Patent.
CHAMBERS, ABRAHAM HENRY	4906	28th Feb. 1824	Preparing and paving horse and carriage ways.
CHAMBERS, ABRAHAM HENRY	5114	5th March 1825	Filtering-apparatus.
CHAMBERS, DANIEL - -	7110	7th June 1836	Pumps.
CHAMBERS, ENNIS - - -	5114	5th March 1825	Filtering-apparatus.
CHAMBERS, ENOCH - -	12,839	10th Nov. 1849	Manufacture of wheels.
CHAMBERS, THOMAS - -	9058	27th Aug. 1841	Manufacture of buttons and fastenings for wearing-apparel.
CHAMBERS, WILLIAM - -	2945	24th June 1806	Machine for roasting meat by the power of steam, and for other purposes where small powers are necessary.
CHAMEROY, EDMÉ AUGUSTIN -	12,767	13th Sept. 1849	Heliacal railway ("helicoide") and a circular chariot.
CHAMEROY, EDMÉ AUGUSTIN -	13,037	15th April 1850	Manufacture of boilers and of pipes of malleable substances, as well as of elastic matter.
CHAMEROY, EDMÉ AUGUSTIN -	13,228	22nd Aug. 1850	Paving streets and other surfaces.
CHAMEROY, EDMÉ AUGUSTIN -	14,157	8th June 1852	Steam-engines.
CHAMFLOWER, THOMAS - -	466	15th April 1724	Machine called a syphon or an attracting-engine, that acts without friction or solids, partly by friction and partly by force, of great use for preserving ships of war in engagements, and merchant ships in diversity of distress at sea; also for draining mines, moors, and marshes, and for raising water to extinguish fires.
CHAMIER, FREDERICK - -	12,747	23rd Aug. 1849	Manufacture of ships' blocks.
CHAMPION, CONSTANT - -	10,561	17th March 1845	Burning animal charcoal.
CHAMPION, JAMES - - -	6974	6th Jan. 1836	Machinery for spinning, twisting, and doubling, cotton and other fibrous substances.
CHAMPION, JAMES - - -	10,001	28th Dec. 1843	Drawing and spinning cotton and other fibrous substances.
CHAMPION, JOHN - - -	568	10th Sept. 1739	Making tough and brittle metals from sulphurous minerals; mixing the same with other metals.
CHAMPION, JOHN - - -	726	28th July 1758	Preparing spelter and brass made from a mineral not before used for the purpose.
CHAMPION, JOHN - - -	950	9th Jan. 1770	Hatching and rearing domestic fowls and other birds, by artificial heat.
CHAMPION, JOHN - - -	2239	2nd June 1798	Making wire from rolled and slit iron, either Foreign or English.
CHAMPION, JOHN, junior -	1224	17th May 1779	Extracting tar out of coal, in the operation of making coke for blast furnaces.
CHAMPION, JOHN, junior -	1239	24th Nov. 1779	Making brass and spelter.
CHAMPION, NEHEMIAH - -	454	20th April 1723	Converting copper into brass.
CHAMPION, NEHEMIAH - -	567	8th June 1739	Machine or model, for more advantageously applying the fall of water on a wheel engine.
CHAMPION, WILLIAM - -	564	1st July 1738	Reducing sulphurous British minerals into a body of metallic sulphur.
CHAMPION, WILLIAM - -	867	26th Jan. 1767	Refining copper for making brass, by wrought iron; making brass, by using black-jack instead of calamy; manufacturing brass wire, by using coal instead of wood.

Name of Patentee.	Progressive Number.	Date.	Subject-matter of Patent.
CHAMPION, WILLIAM DUDE- [RIDGE.	5496	20th April 1827	Composition suitable for moulding into bricks or blocks of any form, for building, and for ornamental, architectural, and other purposes.
CHAMPNESS, JAMES MASON -	4165	28th Aug. 1817	Axletrees of carriages.
CHANCE, EDWARD - - -	12,067	14th Feb. 1848	Furnaces; manufacture of glass.
CHANCE, JAMES TIMMINS -	7618	21st April 1838	Manufacture of glass.
CHANCE, JAMES TIMMINS -	9407	7th July 1842	Manufacture of glass.
CHANCE, JAMES TIMMINS -	11,185	28th April 1846	Manufacture of glass.
CHANCE, JAMES TIMMINS -	11,749	15th June 1847	Manufacture of glass.
CHANCE, JAMES TIMMINS -	12,067	14th Feb. 1848	Furnaces; manufacture of glass.
CHANCE, JAMES TIMMINS -	13,699	29th July 1851	Manufacture of glass.
CHANCE, JAMES TIMMINS -	14,048	29th March 1852	Manufacture of glass.
CHANCE, ROBERT LUCAS -	7596	19th March 1838	Manufacture of glass.
CHANCELLOR, JOHN - -	3487	9th Sept. 1811	Mechanical musical instrument, applicable to clocks or other machinery.
CHANCELLOR, JOHN - -	4314	21st Nov. 1818	Instrument, with or without pedal-work, for turning the leaves of music-books.
CHANDLER, THOMAS - -	11,983	1st Dec. 1847	Machinery for applying liquid manure.
CHANDOIS, ACHILLE - -	12,477	14th Feb. 1849	Extracting and preparing the colouring matter from orchil.
CHANGY, CHARLES EDOUARD FRANCOIS CONSTANT PROS- PERE DE.	12,855	20th Nov. 1849	Preparation and manufacture of flax, hemp, and other like fibrous substances.
CHANTER, JOHN - - -	6653	26th July 1834	Abstracting heat from steam, or other vapours and fluids;—applicable to stills, breweries, and to other purposes.
CHANTER, JOHN - - -	6672	2nd Sept. 1834	Furnaces.
CHANTER, JOHN - - -	6920	2nd Nov. 1835	Combination of parts forming an improved furnace for consuming smoke and economizing fuel, and which furnace is applicable to locomotive carriages, steamboats, and to other purposes.
CHANTER, JOHN - - -	"7306	17th Feb. 1837	Furnaces for locomotive-engines and other purposes.
CHANTER, JOHN - - -	7805	13th Sept. 1838	Furnaces for steam-boilers.
CHANTER, JOHN - - -	10,309	12th Sept. 1844	Furnaces, fire-bars, hot-air generators, and flues.
CHANTER, JOHN - - -	12,726	1st Aug. 1849	Preparation of materials for coating ships and other vessels.
CHANTRELL, WILLIAM - -	10,764	12th July 1845	Weaving-machinery.
CHANU, ADOLPHE LUDOVIC -	14,065	15th April 1852	Explosive compounds and fusees; also methods of firing the same.
CHAPEAUROUGE, PHILIP AU- [GUSTUS DE.	6614	24th May 1834	Machine or apparatus for producing motive-power.
CHAPEAUROUGE, PHILIP AU- [GUSTUS.	6802	31st March 1835	Machine or apparatus for producing motive-power.
CHAPLIN, FREDERICK - -	7008	18th Feb. 1836	Tanning hides and skins of certain descriptions.
CHAPLIN, FREDERICK - -	11,771	29th June 1847	Wheels of railway-carriages.
CHAPLIN, JEAN FRANCOIS [ISIDORE.	7640	14th May 1838	Stays or corsets, and other parts of the dress where lacing is employed; instruments for measuring for corsets or stays, and for the bodies of dresses.

Name of Patentee.	Progressive Number.	Date.	Subject-matter of Patent.
CHAPLIN, WILLIAM - -	6241	8th March 1832	Wheeled-carriages, and constructing the same.
CHAPMAN, CHARLES - -	1326	18th April 1782	Silver, brass, or steel spring, inserted in the boot above the calf of the leg, in order to keep the boot in its proper position.
CHAPMAN, CHARLES PEARSE -	6933	24th Nov. 1835	Printing silks, calicoes, and other fabrics.
CHAPMAN, CHARLES PEARSE - [*Chapman, Charles Pearce.*]	7128	22nd June 1836	Printing silks, calicoes, and other fabrics.
CHAPMAN, EDWARD WALTON	2326	16th July 1799	Making cord, ropes, and cordage, tarred and untarred, from the spinning of the yarn to the finishing of the rope or cordage.
CHAPMAN, EDWARD WALTON	3078	30th Oct. 1807	Making belts or flat bands for drawing coals and other minerals out of pits and mines, and for raising weights.
CHAPMAN, EDWARD WALTON	3632	30th Dec. 1812	Facilitating and reducing the expense of carriage on railways and other roads.
CHAPMAN, GEORGE - -	7542	13th Jan. 1838	Steam-engines.
CHAPMAN, GEORGE - -	10,213	4th June 1844	Steam-engines.
CHAPMAN, HENRY - -	9603	26th Jan. 1843	Fabric for maps, charts, prints, drawings, and other purposes.
CHAPMAN, JOHN - - -	1136	31st Oct. 1776	Chemical preparation of iron equal in hardness to the best blister-steel, retaining at the same time the toughness and properties of iron.
CHAPMAN, JOHN - - -	7266	21st Dec. 1836	Cabs.
CHAPMAN, JOHN MELLAR -	10,663	10th May 1845	Manufacture of rails and other parts of railways.
CHAPMAN, JOHN TIMOTHY -	13,052	20th April 1850	Apparatus for setting-up ships' rigging, and for raising weights.
CHAPMAN, THOMAS - -	2317	6th June 1799	Taking the wool or fur from seals' and other skins, for manufacturing the same into hats or other clothing.
CHAPMAN, THOMAS - -	2871	29th July 1805	Mill for tearing, crushing, and preparing oak-bark, for the use of tanners.
CHAPMAN, THOMAS - -	3423	26th March 1811	Conveying vessels of any burden through the water, without the help of oars or sails.
CHAPMAN, WILLIAM - -	500	27th July 1728	Chaise or chair with two wheels, drawn by one horse between a pair of shafts.
CHAPMAN, WILLIAM - -	2191	13th Sept. 1797	Making ropes of any number of yarns and strands, tarred or untarred.
CHAPMAN, WILLIAM - -	2219	6th March 1798	Making ropes of any number of yarns and strands, tarred or untarred; coiling up the same while making.
CHAPMAN, WILLIAM - -	2265	8th Nov. 1798	Making ropes of any number of yarns and strands, tarred or untarred; coiling up the same.
CHAPMAN, WILLIAM - -	2326	16th July 1799	Making cord, ropes, and cordage, tarred and untarred, from the spinning of the yarn to the finishing of the rope or cordage.
CHAPMAN, WILLIAM - -	2513	5th June 1801	Preserving cordage by the application of certain substances, separately or combined.

Name of Patentee.	Progressive Number.	Date.	Subject-matter of Patent.
CHAPMAN, WILLIAM - -	3026	8th April 1807	Reducing the wear and prolonging the duration of ropes for drawing coals or other minerals from pits or mines.
CHAPMAN, WILLIAM - -	3030	11th April 1807	Putting coals on board ships, lighters, and other vessels, so as to prevent breakage.
CHAPMAN, WILLIAM - -	3078	30th Oct. 1807	Making belts or flat bands for drawing coals and other minerals out of pits and mines, and for raising weights.
CHAPMAN, WILLIAM - -	3126	27th April 1808	Conveying coals and other minerals in the working of mines; returning the empty carriages.
CHAPMAN, WILLIAM - -	3335	9th May 1810	Wheels for mechanical movements, which wheels are to be worked by water, steam, or other suitable fluids or gases.
CHAPMAN, WILLIAM - -	3632	30th Dec. 1812	Facilitating and reducing the expense of carriage on railways and other roads.
CHAPMAN, WILLIAM - -	4550	12th April 1821	Transferring the ladings of lighters and barges, into ships or vessels, and vice versâ.
CHAPMAN, WILLIAM - -	5330	7th Feb. 1826	Machinery for loading or unloading ships, vessels, or craft.
CHAPMAN, WILLIAM - -	5540	14th Aug. 1827	Construction of waggons for railways or tramways.
CHAPPÉ, JEAN BAPTISTE PAUL [Chappé, Paul.]	7841	31st Oct. 1838	Consuming smoke in steam-engine or other furnaces or fireplaces.
CHAPPÉ, JEAN BAPTISTE PAUL	10,354	17th Oct. 1844	Machinery for spinning and doubling cotton and other fibrous substances.
CHAPPELL, DANIEL - -	586	7th Aug. 1742	Printing goods made of wool, worsted and silk, mohair and silk, or mohair alone.
CHAPPEL, GRAHAM - -	3557	28th April 1812	Lamp, and method of using oil and wick therein.
CHAPPEL, NATHANIEL - -	10,962	20th Nov. 1845	Manufacture of worts.
CHARLESWORTH, JOSEPH -	5743	18th Dec. 1828	Improvements on or additions to gig-mills, for raising and finishing woollen-cloths and other fabrics.
CHARLESWORTH, JOSHUA -	5743	18th Dec. 1828	Improvements on or additions to gig-mills, for raising and finishing woollen-cloths and other fabrics.
CHARLETON, GEORGE - -	5233	10th Aug. 1825	Building ships or other vessels.
CHARLIEU, ANDRÉ DROUET DE [Charlieu André Dronot de.]	8941	27th April 1841	Preparation of matters to be consumed in obtaining light; construction of burners for the same.
CHARLIEU, ANDRÉ DROUET DE	10,115	20th March 1844	Rails for railways; and wheels for locomotive-carriages.
CHARLTON, ALFRED - -	6870	28th July 1835	Machinery for stiffening and finishing woven or manufactured goods.
CHARLTON, GEORGE - -	7561	8th Feb. 1838	Anchors, capstans, and windlasses; and means of mooring and riding ships at anchor.
CHARLTON, JOHN - - -	2609	10th April 1802	Punch or prop, for supporting the roofs of mines.
CHARLTON, JOHN - - -	9870	17th Aug. 1843	Castors for furniture.
CHARLTON, ROBERT - -	6870	27th July 1835	Machinery for stiffening and finishing woven or manufactured goods.

Name of Patentee.	Progressive Number.	Date.		Subject-matter of Patent.
CHARPILLON, LOUIS CESAIRES	12,911	29th Dec.	1849	Locks for guns and pistols.
CHARSLEY, JOHN - - -	25	31st July	1623	Making engines for bolting and dressing meal.
CHASE, SAMUEL - - -	1005	12th Feb.	1772	Medical cure for scorbutic disorders by administering an electuary and drops internally, and applying a digestive liniment and cerate externally.
CHASE, SAMUEL - - -	1531	7th Feb.	1786	Medicine for relieving bilious complaints, indigestion, and obstructions in the bowels (" stomach drops").
CHASTEL, CHARLES BARON DE	1363	28th April	1783	Machine for separating gold and silver from earth, scoriæ, and impurities, by trituration, mercury, and amalgams.
CHATAUVILLARD, LOUIS ALFRED DE.	12,613	15th May	1849	Fire-arms, cartridges, bullets, bayonets, and ordnance.
CHATER, JAMES - - -	1495	5th Aug.	1785	Instrument for preventing robbery from the person. (" Watch and note guard.")
CHATER, JOHN - - -	9006	29th June	1841	Machinery for making lace and other fabrics, traversed, looped, or woven.
CHATRE, RAOUL AMAND [JOSEPH JEAN COMPTE DE LA.	9331	26th April	1842	Preparing surfaces of fabrics for covering roofs, floors, and other surfaces.
CHATTEN, JAMES PERKINS -	10,194	22nd May	1844	Manufacture of dead-eyes for setting up the rigging of ships and other sailing vessels.
CHATTERTON, JOHN -	13,660	12th June	1851	Protecting insulated electro-telegraphic wires; methods and machinery used for the purpose.
CHATTERTON, RICHARD DOVER	9217	11th Jan.	1842	Propelling.
CHATWIN, JOHN - - -	9423	16th July	1842	Manufacture of covered buttons.
CHATWIN, JOSEPH - - -	9384	9th June	1842	Construction of cocks.
CHATWIN, THOMAS TURNER -	10,484	21st Jan.	1845	Manufacture of covered buttons.
CHAUDOIS, ACHILLE - -	12,477	14th Feb.	1849	Extracting and preparing the colouring matter from orchil.
CHAUFFOURIER, PIERRE AUGUSTIN.	12,522	14th Mar.	1849	Manufacture of watches.
CHAUFFOURIER, PIERRE AUGUSTIN.	12,695	4th July	1849	Castors.
CHAUGY, CHARLES EDWARD FRANCOIS CONSTANT PROSPERE DE.	12,855	20th Nov.	1849	Preparation and manufacture of flax, hemp, and other like fibrous substances.
CHAUMETTE, ISAAC DE LA -	434	12th Aug.	1721	Cannon, fusees, and pistols; swords which serve for bayonets; powder-flasks; machine to cure smoky chimneys; snuff boxes; penknife and pocket-knife; buckles; machine for drawing lotteries; two cases of pistols of which a carbine may be made; turning-mattrass for armies and hospitals; coaches and chaises; preventing shipwreck; bomb or grenade; breastplates; candlesticks and rings; pocket-scissors; machine for holding glasses at table; picture, serving as a tester to a bed, and an ornament to a room; lantern; fusee-lock; firing fusees horizontally; double counters for drawing lotteries.

Name of Patentee.	Progressive Number.	Date.	Subject-matter of Patent.
CHAUSSENOT, HENRY BERNARD.	6868	28th July 1835	Construction of gas-lamps, so as to produce a better combustion of the gas.
CHAUVIER, HYPPOLITE - -	10,622	17th April 1845	Manufacture of soap.
CHEAPE, WILLIAM - - -	1237	23rd Nov. 1779	Weaving diaper and damask linens, for table-cloths, and for other purposes, also figured silks, cottons, and worsteds, without the assistance of draw boys.
CHEESE, GRIFFITH JAMES -	1539	11th Mar. 1786	Musical instrument called the "grand harmonica."
CHEETHAM, DAVID - [Cheetham, David, junior.]	7669	5th June 1838	Machinery applicable to the preparation of cotton and other fibrous substances for spinning.
CHEETHAM, DAVID - [Cheetham, David, junior.]	7769	14th Aug. 1838	Consuming smoke in steam-engine or other furnaces or fire-places.
CHEETHAM, DAVID - -	10,106	14th Mar. 1844	Machinery for preparing and spinning cotton-wool and other fibrous substances.
CHEETHAM, DAVID - -	10,220	6th June 1844	Manufacture of hats, and machinery connected with such or similar manufacture.
CHEETHAM, DAVID - -	11,271	29th June 1846	Machinery to be used for preparing and spinning cotton and other fibrous substances.
CHEETHAM, DAVID - -	13,072	7th May 1850	Machinery and operations connected with the manufacture of cotton-wool, silk, and other fibrous substances and fabrics; application of certain materials to the manufacture of textile fabrics.
CHEETHAM, DAVID - -	13,313	2nd Nov. 1850	Manufacture of cotton and other fibrous materials, and fabrics composed of such materials.
CHEETHAM, DAVID - -	13,435	2nd Jan. 1851	Steam-engines; apparatus for generating and indicating the pressure of steam, and for filtering water for boilers; steam vessels or ships.
CHEETHAM, JAMES, junior -	13,569	24th March 1851	Manufacture of bleached, coloured or particoloured threads or yarns.
CHELL, PHILIP - - -	2255	3rd Aug. 1798	Machine for raising or lowering boats, vessels, or other things, from one level to another on canals or rivers, to save water, and prevent the necessity of tunnelling.
CHELL, PHILIP - - -	3530	28th Jan. 1812	Giving motion to machinery; raising water or other fluids from a lower to a higher level.
CHELL, PHILIP - - -	4756	18th Feb. 1823	Machinery for drawing, roving, and spinning hemp, flax, and waste silk.
CHELL, PHILIP - - -	5015	14th Oct. 1824	Machinery for drawing, roving, and spinning flax, wool, waste silk, or other fibrous substances.
CHEMANT, NICHOLAS DUBOIS [DE.	1803	11th May 1791	Composition for making artificial teeth; springs for fastening the same.
CHEMANT, NICHOLAS DUBOIS [DE.	2167	15th Feb. 1797	Table, with a stove placed in the centre.
CHENOT, ADRIEN - - -	11,515	31st Dec. 1846	Treatment of metallic oxydes and their compounds; apparatus for the purpose.

Name of Patentee.	Progressive Number.	Date.	Subject-matter of Patent.
CHÉROT, AUGUSTE - - -	10,723	17th June 1845	Machinery for spinning flax, hemp, and other fibrous materials.
CHERRY, FREDERICK - -	3759	23rd Nov. 1813	Construction of various articles of an officer's field equipage.
CHERRY, FREDERICK CLIFFORD	4335	20th Jan. 1819	Box, case, or frame forge, applicable to shipping, agriculture, and other purposes.
CHERRY, JAMES - - -	6746	15th Jan. 1835	Bedsteads, or apparatus applicable to the ease and comfort of invalids and others.
CHESSHIRE, EDWIN - -	11,071	3rd Feb. 1846	Apparatus to be applied to railway-carriages to reduce the effects of collisions.
CHESTERMAN, JAMES - -	5817	14th July 1829	Apparatus for measuring land, and for other purposes.
CHESTERMAN, JAMES - -	9214	11th Jan. 1842	Tapes for measuring, and boxes for containing the same.
CHESTERMAN, JAMES - -	11,962	13th Nov. 1847	Tape-measures, and cases for containing the same; also machinery for making such measures and cases, or parts thereof.
CHESTERMAN, JAMES - -	12,843	13th Nov. 1849	Carpenters' braces, and other tools used for drilling and boring.
CHESTERMAN, WILLIAM - -	8268	12th Nov. 1839	Stoves.
CHESTERMAN, WILLIAM - -	9001	23rd June 1841	Filtering liquids.
CHESTON, THOMAS - -	1549	1st July 1786	Making elastic spring-buckles and spurs, of gold, silver, iron, steel, copper, pinchbeck, or other mixed metals, also of metals plated with gold and silver.
CHEVERTON, BENJAMIN - -	10,015	16th Jan. 1844	Machinery for cutting wood and other materials.
CHEVERTON, BENJAMIN - -	13,137	19th June 1850	Methods of imitating ivory and bone.
CHIDLEY, JOHN JAMES - -	11,805	19th July 1847	Printing-presses.
CHIFNEY, BARKER - - -	2498	2nd May 1801	Preparing and laying slates for covering houses and other buildings, and preparing slates for other purposes.
CHIFNEY, BARKER - - -	2687	8th March 1803	Manufacturing, preparing, and laying roofing-slates.
CHIFNEY, BARKER - - -	2781	14th Sept. 1804	Composition for washing muslins and linens, and for other purposes.
CHIFNEY, SAMUEL - -	2809	16th Jan. 1805	Bits for bridles.
CHIKLEY, THOMAS, Sir - -	162	8th Jan. 1671	Authority to take security from and to administer an oath to workmen not to divulge the patent granted to Prince Rupert. (No. 161, 8th January 1671.)
CHILD, GEORGE - - -	6667	23rd Aug. 1834	Machinery for raising water and other liquids.
CHILD, GEORGE - - -	8772	6th Jan. 1841	Manufacture of bricks and tiles;—partly applicable to compressing peat and other materials.
CHILD, WILLIAM DIMSDALE -	10,818	21st Aug. 1845	Manufacture of sugar.
CHILDS, JAMES - - -	12,564	16th April 1849	Manufacture of candles, night-lights, and candle-lamps.

Name of Patentee.	Progressive Number.	Date.	Subject-matter of Patent.
CHILDS, JAMES - - -	13,795	3rd Nov. 1851	Presses and matting; treating fatty and oily matters, and apparatus for the purpose; manufacture of candles and nightlights.
CHILDS, SAMUEL - - -	10,899	27th Oct. 1845	Manufacture of candles.
CHILDS, SAMUEL - - -	11,656	15th April 1847	Manufacture of candles; preparing and combining animal, vegetable, and mineral substances, applicable to the manufacture of candles, and to other uses.
CHILTON, CHARLES - -	9661	16th March 1843	Machinery for cutting or splitting wood for fuel and other purposes.
CHING, JOHN - - -	2121	28th June 1796	Medicine for destroying worms.
CHING, REBECCA - -	3129	7th May 1808	Medicine called "Ching's worm-destroying Lozenges."
CHINNOCK, CHARLES - -	11,031	12th Jan. 1846	Construction and method of extending and compressing articles of furniture and domestic use;—applicable to cutlery, workmen's tools, window-blinds, shutters, and to similar purposes.
CHINNOCK, CHARLES - -	11,385	24th Sept. 1846	Folding and securing letters, envelopes, and covers.
CHINNOCH, CHARLES - -	11,706	22nd May 1847	Regulating motion and controlling friction in the joints and other parts of furniture, machinery, and carriages.
CHIRM, JOSEPH - - -	2499	12th May 1801	Machine for boring timber, for pumps, water-pipes, and other purposes.
CHISHOLM, JOHN - - -	3953	21st Aug. 1815	Constructing register and other stoves.
CHISHOLM, JOHN - - -	7895	6th Dec. 1838	Obtaining silver and other products from massicott, litharge, and other compounds of lead.
CHISHOLM, JOHN - - -	8094	6th June 1839	Obtaining sulphur from pyrites, or certain native sulphurets.
CHIVER, ROBERT - - -	105	17th May 1637	Ways, arts, engines, and inventions for husbandry, raising water, draining land, liming or gravelling land, planting and producing hops, and planting trees in dry and barren grounds.
CHIVER, ROBERT - - -	125	12th March 1640	Ways and inventions for the better cultivation of land, by improved methods of raising water by means of hatches, bays, engines, wheels, pumps, and other instruments; also by altering the superficies of some grounds, enlarging rivers, and draining and raising low and marshy grounds.
CHOICE, WILLIAM - -	5353	27th April 1826	Machinery for making bricks.
CHOUMERT, GEORGE - -	1382	7th Aug. 1783	Machine for cutting, splitting, and dividing hides and skins, or leather.
CHOWNE, WILLIAM DINGLE -	12,391	28th Dec. 1848	Ventilating rooms and apartments.
CHREES, ELIZABETH - -	12,258	29th Aug. 1848	Manufacture of sealing-wax.
CHRIMES, EDWARD - -	10,837	25th Sept. 1845	Cocks and taps.
CHRISCEL, CHRISTOPHER -	1056	17th Nov. 1773	Constructing and setting boilers, for fire-engines, salt-works, brewhouses, distilleries, soap-houses, sugar-houses, and sugar-works.

Name of Patentee.	Progressive Number.	Date.		Subject-matter of Patent.
CHRIST, JOHN GEORGE - -	5463	14th Feb.	1827	Copper and other plate printing.
CHRISTEN, HENRI JEREMY -	13,257	19th Sept.	1850	Cylinder-printing.
CHRISTIAN, CHARLES TOWNS- [END.	9803	27th June	1843	Construction of steam-engines.
CHRISTIAN, JOHN TEMPEST -	804	18th Jan.	1764	Painting silks and satins, in oil colours.
CHRISTIE, DAVID - -	12,882	10th Dec.	1849	Machinery for preparing, assorting, straightening, tearing, teasing, doubling, twisting, braiding, and weaving cotton-wool and other fibrous substances.
CHRISTIE, DAVID - -	13,325	7th Nov.	1850	Machinery or apparatus for preparing, carding, spinning, doubling, twisting, weaving, and knitting, cotton-wool and other fibrous substances; also for sewing and packing.
CHRISTIE, JOHN - - -	4848	9th Oct.	1823	Combining and using fuel in stoves, furnaces, boilers, and steam-engines.
CHRISTIE, JOHN - - -	4909	28th Feb.	1824	Combining and applying certain kinds of fuel.
CHRISTIE, JOHN HOUGHTON -	12,883	10th Dec.	1849	Construction of wrought-iron wheels; machinery for effecting the same.
CHRISTOPHERS, JOHN -	4599	18th Oct.	1821	Anchors, or substitutes for anchors.
CHRISTOPHERS, JOHN - [Christopher, John.]	6177	7th Oct.	1831	Clothes-buttons.
CHRISTOPHERS, JOHN -	6291	3rd Aug.	1832	Clothes-buttons.
CHRISTOPHERS, JOHN -	6443	27th June	1833	Anchors.
CHRISTOPHERS, JOHN -	6601	26th April	1834	Anchors.
CHRISTOPHERS, JOHN -	12,803	12th Oct.	1849	Naval architecture.
CHRYSEL, CHRISTOPHER LE- [BRECHT.	735	24th Jan.	1759	Taking the wool from off sheep-skins.
CHUBB, CHARLES - -	4972	15th June	1824	Construction of locks.
CHUBB, CHARLES - - -	5656	17th May	1828	Construction of latches which may be used for fastening doors or gates.
CHUBB, CHARLES - - -	6527	20th Dec.	1833	Locks used for fastening and security.
CHUBB, CHARLES - - -	6832	13th May	1835	Making secure, receptacles for property, strong doors, safes, chests, and boxes.
CHUBB, CHARLES - - -	8100	11th June	1839	Apparatus and machinery for preserving books and other papers, documents, and articles, from fire.
CHUBB, JEREMIAH - - -	4219	3rd Feb.	1818	Construction of locks.
CHUBB, JEREMIAH - - -	8100	11th June	1839	Apparatus and machinery for preserving books and other papers, documents, and articles, from fire.
CHUBB, JOHN - - -	11,491	14th Dec.	1846	Locks and latches.
CHUBB, JOHN - - -	11,523	11th Jan.	1847	Latches, latch-locks, and other locks.
CHUBB, WILLIAM - - -	7401	10th July	1837	Night commode-pans.
CHURCH, JABEZ - - -	11,010	20th Dec.	1845	Manufacture of coke; and ovens for producing the same.
CHURCH, JOHN - - -	3756	23rd Nov.	1813	Saponaceous compounds, for deterging in sea-water, hard water, and soft water.
CHURCH, WILLIAM - -	4245	8th April	1818	Steam-engine.
CHURCH, WILLIAM - -	4258	7th May	1818	Machinery for making nails and spikes, also wire and screws, of iron, copper, brass, or other metal.
CHURCH, WILLIAM - -	4565	3rd July	1821	Apparatus for printing.
CHURCH, WILLIAM - -	4664	21st Mar.	1822	Apparatus for printing.

Name of Patentee.	Progressive Number.	Date.	Subject-matter of Patent.
CHURCH, WILLIAM - -	4760	18th Feb. 1823	Apparatus for printing, to be used for type, block, or plate printers.
CHURCH, WILLIAM - -	4903	19th Feb. 1824	Machinery for printing.
CHURCH, WILLIAM - -	4953	15th May 1824	Apparatus used in casting iron and other metals.
CHURCH, WILLIAM - -	5030	4th Nov. 1824	Augers and bits for boring, and apparatus for making the same.
CHURCH, WILLIAM - -	5084	18th Jan. 1825	Casting cylinders, tubes, and other articles, of iron, copper, and other metals.
CHURCH, WILLIAM - -	5417	18th Oct. 1826	Printing.
CHURCH, WILLIAM - -	5524	13th July 1827	Apparatus for spinning fibrous substances.
CHURCH, WILLIAM - -	5777	26th March 1829	Buttons, and machinery for manufacturing the same.
CHURCH, WILLIAM - -	5857	15th Oct. 1829	Machines for propelling vessels, and other machines capable of being propelled by steam; boilers applicable to the same, and other purposes.
CHURCH, WILLIAM - -	5858	15th Oct. 1829	Instruments for sharpening knives and other edge tools; machinery for manufacturing the same.
CHURCH, WILLIAM - -	6000	21st Sept. 1830	Construction of boats and other vessels;—partly applicable to the construction of carriages.
CHURCH, WILLIAM - -	6041	29th Nov. 1830	Apparatus for propelling boats and driving machinery by steam;—partly applicable to the purposes of evaporation.
CHURCH, WILLIAM - -	6145	27th July 1831	Machinery for making nails.
CHURCH, WILLIAM - -	6220	9th Feb. 1832	Apparatus to be used in the transportation of goods or passengers;—partly applicable to steam-engines.
CHURCH, WILLIAM - -	6232	25th Feb. 1832	Machinery for making nails.
CHURCH, WILLIAM - -	6469	7th Sept. 1833	Apparatus to be used in the transportation of goods or passengers;—partly applicable to steam-engines.
CHURCH, WILLIAM - -	6791	16th March 1835	Apparatus for conveying goods and passengers by land or water;—partly applicable to steam-engines, and other steam-apparatus.
CHURCH, WILLIAM - -	8609	27th Aug. 1840	Fastenings for wearing-apparel; apparatus for making the same and similar articles; preparing the said articles for sale.
CHURCH, WILLIAM - -	9187	16th Dec. 1841	Manufacturing metallic tubes; and mode of joining them or other tubes or pieces.
CHURCH, WILLIAM - -	11,197	5th May 1846	Machinery for making candlestick-pans and other articles produced by stamping; machinery for making sockets or tubes for candlesticks, and tubes or tubular articles applicable to other purposes.
CHURCH, WILLIAM - -	12,298	26th Oct. 1848	Machinery for making playing and other cards, or articles made wholly or in part of paper or pasteboard;—partly applicable to other purposes where pressure is required.
CHURCH, WILLIAM - -	12,994	7th March 1850	Machinery to be employed in manufacturing cards and other articles composed wholly or in part of paper, or pasteboard;—part being applicable to printing the same, and part to other purposes where pressure is required.

Name of Patentee.	Progres-sive Number.	Date.	Subject-matter of Patent.
CHURCH, WILLIAM - -	14,087	24th April 1852	Fire-arms, ordnance, and projectiles to be used therewith; machinery for the manufacture of parts of such fire-arms, ordnance, and projectiles.
CHURCHMAN, WALTER -	514	24th Jan. 1730	Engine for making chocolate.
CHURCHMAN, WALTER -	539	21st March 1733	Machine, worked by the united power of weight and draught, for raising water, draining lands, coal-pits, and mines, and for grinding, stamping, or other work where mechanical power may be applied.
CLAEYS, THEODORE - -	11,784	3d July 1847	Manufacture of various articles from cork.
CLAGGETT, CHARLES - -	1140	7th Dec. 1776	Violins and other instruments played on finger-boards.
CLAGGETT, CHARLES - -	1664	15 Aug. 1788	Constructing and tuning musical instruments.
CLAGGETT, CRISPUS - -	1248	16th March 1780	Travelling-machine, named the "Imperial Mercury."
CLAIS, JOHN SEBASTIAN -	1014	30th April 1772	Index-balance, for weighing money or other materials, without shifting the weights.
CLANRICARDE, JOHN DE BURGH, [Marquis of.	6139	15th July 1831	Fire-arms, and the projectiles used therewith.
CLARE, JOHN, junior - -	13,323	7th Nov. 1850	Manufacture of metallic-casks.
CLARE, PETER - - -	975	28th Dec. 1770	Smoke-jack, to roast horizontally and perpendicularly.
CLARENDON, THOMAS - -	9933	9th Nov. 1843	Shoeing horses.
CLARIDGE, RICHARD TAPPIN -	7489	25 Nov. 1837	Mastic cement, applicable to paving and road-making, covering buildings, and to various other purposes.
CLARIDGE, RICHARD TAPPIN -	9331	26th April 1842	Preparing surfaces of fabrics to be used in roofs, floors, and other surfaces.
CLARK, ALEXANDER - -	4665	21st March 1822	Boilers and condensers of steam-engines.
CLARK, ALEXANDER - -	6365	15th Jan. 1833	Blowing-machines.
CLARK, BENJAMIN - - -	5688	19th Aug. 1828	Machinery for shearing, cropping, or cutting and finishing, woollen and other cloths and cassimeres.
CLARK, BRACY - - -	2923	26th March 1806	Horse-shoes.
CLARK, CHARLES - • -	8080	25th May 1839	Glazing and enamelling cast-iron hollow ware, and other metallic substances.
CLARK, CHARLES - -	9623	31st Jan. 1843	Pyro-hydro pneumatic-apparatus for generating, purifying, and condensing steam and other vapours; also for extracting from vegetables the soluble portions thereof;—application of parts of said apparatus to other heating, evaporating, and distilling purposes.
CLARK, CHARLES - - -	11,275	29th June 1846	Pyro-hydro pneumatic-apparatus for generating, purifying, and condensing steam and other vapours, and for obtaining vegetable extracts.
CLARK, CHARLES WEARG -	10,311	12th Sept. 1844	Manufacture of bricks and tiles for chimneys and flues, and for other purposes.
CLARK, EDWIN - - -	13,336	12th Nov. 1850	Electric-telegraphs, and apparatus connected therewith.
CLARK, GEORGE DELIANSON -	8686	5th Nov. 1840	Purifying tallow, fat, and oils, by depriving them of offensive smell, and by solidifying such as are fluid, also giving additional hardness to such as are solid; separating stearine or stearic-acid from claine in such substances.

Name of Patentee.	Progressive Number.	Date.		Subject-matter of Patent.
CLARK, GEORGE JAMES - -	4308	12 Nov.	1818	Apparatus for applying the drag to a carriage-wheel.
CLARK, HENRY - - -	10,903	31st Oct.	1845	Preparation of materials to be employed for producing illumination.
CLARK, JAMES - - -	9624	1st Feb.	1843	Manufacturing certain descriptions of cloth.
CLARK, JAMES - - -	10,522	14th Feb.	1845	Weaving.
CLARK, JAMES - - -	10,682	22nd May	1845	Manufacture of fabrics from fibrous materials.
CLARK, JAMES - - -	12,296	26th Oct.	1848	Manufacture of boots, shoes, and clogs.
CLARK, JOHN - - - -	3718	14th July	1813	Making beds, pillows, hammocks, cushions, and various other articles of the kind, in a different manner, and of different materials from any hitherto used.
CLARK, JOHN - - - -	7607	4th April	1838	Machinery for turning;—in part applicable to other purposes.
CLARK, JOHN - - - -	7993	6th March	1839	Construction of a leg and foot for propelling carriages on rail or common roads; combination or arrangement of machinery for locomotive-carriages, rendering the weight of the load partly applicable as the moving power.
CLARK, JOHN - - - -	10,318	14th Sept.	1844	Printing and calendering.
CLARK, JOHN JAMES - -	6257	13 April	1832	Machinery for, and process used in, the manufacture of tiles, bricks, bread, biscuits, and other articles formed of plastic materials;—applicable to other purposes.
CLARK, LAWRENCE - -	413	17th May	1717	Making starch from potatoes.
CLARK, MATTHEW - - -	5572	4th Dec.	1827	Apparatus for the better manufacture of sugar from the canes.
CLARK, MOSES - - -	12,836	10th Nov.	1849	Manufacture of paper; apparatus and machinery used therein;—partly applicable to regulating the pressure of fluids.
CLARK, RICHARD - - -	11,734	7th June	1847	Production of artificial light; burners, lamps, and candlesticks.
CLARK, RICHARD - - -	12,194	26th June	1848	Gas-burners, candle-lamps, and other lamps.
CLARK, ROBERT - - -	2691	23rd March	1803	Construction of trusses for ruptures.
CLARK, ROBERT - - -	10,847	2nd Oct.	1845	Steering vessels.
CLARK, SQUIRE - - -	3900	21st March	1815	Making a swift and other apparatus thereto belonging, for winding silk.
CLARK, THOMAS - - -	708	3rd March	1756	Making leather-boxes and other articles.
CLARK, THOMAS - - -	1675	8th Nov.	1788	Machine for weaving cotton, worsted, flax, hemp, or any yarn, into calicoes, cloths, buntings, or other fabrics.
CLARK, THOMAS - - -	6488	19th Oct.	1833	Apparatus to produce or evolve chlorine for manufacturing purposes.
CLARK, THOMAS - - -	7440	30th Sept.	1837	Apparatus to be used in manufacturing sulphuric-acid.
CLARK, THOMAS - - -	8080	25th May	1839	Glazing and enamelling cast-iron hollow ware, and other metallic substances.
CLARK, THOMAS - - -	8666	22nd Oct.	1840	Construction of locks, latches, and such like fastenings, applicable for securing doors, gates, windows, shutters, and for such like purposes.
CLARK, THOMAS - - -	8875	8th March	1841	Purifying and softening certain waters, for the use of manufactories, villages, towns, and cities.
CLARK, THOMAS - - -	10,328	26th Sept.	1844	Domestic-convenience.

Name of Patentee.	Progressive Number.	Date.	Subject-matter of Patent.
CLARK, WILLIAM　-　-　-	2944	19th June 1806	Machine for spinning hemp, flax, tow, and wool.
CLARK, WILLIAM　-　-　-	4101	8th Feb. 1817	Safeguard to locks.
CLARK, WILLIAM　-　-	5688	19th Aug. 1828	Machinery for shearing, cropping, or cutting and finishing, woollen and other cloths and cassimeres.
CLARKE, DUGALD　-　-　-	949	5th Jan. 1770	Constructing and hanging the boiler of steam-engines; also applying the powers of the steam-engine to the working of mills.
CLARKE, GEORGE　-　-　-	8359	23rd Jan. 1840	Construction of looms for weaving.
CLARKE GEORGE MILLER　-	10,029	30th Jan. 1844	Night-lights, and apparatus used therewith.
CLARKE GEORGE MILLER　-	10,536	3rd March 1845	Construction of lamps and apparatus to be used therewith.
CLARKE, HENRY　-　-	9643	22nd Feb. 1843	Machinery for lapping and folding woven textures, and surface-fabrics.
CLARKE, JEAN GEORGE SUE　-	9315	6th April 1842	Supplying and regulating the supply of air to the furnaces of locomotive-engines.
CLARKE, JOHN　-　-　-	8385	5th Nov. 1840	Hydraulic double-action force and lift pump.
CLARKE, JOHN WERE　-	5503	8th June 1827	Fixing the dead-eyes to the channel and sides of ships or vessels.
CLARKE, JOSEPH　-　-　-	8388	14th Feb. 1840	Pianofortes.
CLARKE, JOSIAH　-　-　-	10,160	27th April 1844	Wheels to be used in slubbing or bobbin frames, roving or jack frames; engine for cutting such wheels.
CLARKE, RICHARD　-　-　-	1395	14th Nov. 1783	Malt and oat kiln of cast-metal; bottoms for bakers' ovens of the same metal.
CLARKE, RICHARD　-　-	2956	1st Aug. 1806	Cementing flock on walls of plaster, wood, linen, or paper, to serve as a decoration for apartments, in imitation of fine cloth.
CLARKE, RICHARD　-　-　-	12,154	11th May 1848	Chronometers, clocks, watches, or other time-keepers.
CLARKE, THOMAS　-　-　-	5501	26th May 1827	Manufacturing carpets.
CLARKE, THOMAS　-　-　-	10,731	23rd June 1845	Atmospheric system of propulsion;—applicable to other motive purposes.
CLARKE, THOMAS　-　-　-	11,077	11th Feb. 1846	Obtaining and applying motive-power;—partly applicable to regulating and controlling fluids.
CLARKE, THOMAS　-　-　-	12,514	14th March 1849	Obtaining and applying motive-power; railroads and other roads; supporting pressure, resisting strain, and protecting against fire.
CLARKE, THOMAS HARDEMAN	8330	24th Dec. 1839	Fastenings for window-sashes, tables, and for such like purposes.
CLARKE, URIAH　-　-　-	9599	21st Jan. 1843	Machinery for framework knitting; framework knitted fabric.
CLARKE, URIAH　-　-　-	9695	18th April 1843	Manufacture of narrow elastic and non-elastic fabrics of fibrous material.
CLARKE, URIAH　-　-　- [Clark, Uriah.]	10,926	5th Nov. 1845	Manufacturing and making looped fabrics.
CLARKE, URIAH　-　-　-	11,572	8th Feb. 1847	Manufacture of looped and woven fabrics.
CLARKE, WILLIAM -　-　-	10,163	30th April 1844	Machinery for manufacturing ornamented bobbin-net or twist-lace.
CLARKE, WILLIAM -　-　-	10,350	14th Oct. 1844	Machinery for manufacturing ornamented bobbin-net or twist-lace, and other fabrics.
CLARKE, WILLIAM -　-　-	10,401	25th Nov. 1844	Manufacture of ornamental lace or net.

Name of Patentee.	Progressive Number.	Date.		Subject-matter of Patent.
CLARKE, WILLIAM - - -	11,042	17th Jan.	1846	Manufacturing lace and other fabrics by lace machinery.
CLARKE, WILLIAM - -	11,277	30th June	1846	Weighing-machines, steel-yards, and scale-beams.
CLARKSON, JAMES - - -	2672	21st Dec.	1802	"Tatham's clumps" for constructing water-pipes, sewers, tunnels, wells, conduits, reservoirs, or other circular walls, shells, or buildings.
CLARKSON, THOMAS CHARLES	12,466	8th Feb.	1849	Manufacture and application of leather, and vegetable substances in combination with leather, india-rubber, canvas, silk, cotton-wool, and other fibrous substances, in the manufacture of waterproof articles.
CLARKSON, WILLIAM - -	1217	3rd April	1779	Spring, to be fitted in with hats, bonnets, or other articles of dress, for their firm retention.
CLARRANT, ANTHONY DE -	259	19th May	1688	Making tar or pitch for the preservation of wood from putrefaction and worms, also to resist fire and the heat of the sun, and for the better preservation of ropes.
CLATWORTHY, JOHN - -	3213	1st March	1809	Shears for shearing sheep.
CLATWORTHY, THOMAS -	3213	1st March	1809	Shears for shearing sheep.
CLAUDE, LOUIS JAMES - -	12,089	8th March	1848	Locomotive-engines.
CLAUDET, ANTOINE JEAN [FRANÇOIS.	9193	18th Dec.	1841	Process or means of, and apparatus for, obtaining images or representations of nature or art.
CLAUDET, ANTOINE JEAN [FRANÇOIS. [Claudet, Antoine François Jean.]	9957	21st Nov.	1843	Process and means of obtaining the representation of objects of nature and art.
CLAUSS, CHRISTIAN - -	1394	5th Nov.	1783	Guitar.
CLAUSSEN, PETER - - -	11,100	20th Feb.	1846	Machinery for weaving; preparing materials for weaving.
CLAUSSEN, PETER - - -	11,303	23d July	1846	Apparatus for propelling, exhausting, and compressing air and aëriform bodies.
CLAUSSEN, PETER - - -	11,658	15th April	1847	Weaving-machinery; preparation of materials employed in weaving.
CLAUSSEN, PETER - - -	13,224	16th Aug.	1850	Bleaching; preparation of materials for spinning and felting; yarns and felts.
CLAUSSEN, PETER - - -	13,956	3d Feb.	1852	Manufacture of saline and metallic compounds.
CLAY, HENRY - - -	1027	20th Nov.	1772	Making japanned high varnished panels in paper, for carriages and sedan-chairs, also for rooms, doors, and cabins of ships, as well as for cabinets, screens, chimney-pieces, tables, trays, caddies, tea-chests, and dressing-boxes.
CLAY, HENRY - - -	1180	5th Feb.	1778	Making buttons of paper japanned, with or without shanks of metal or catgut, or set in cups or sockets of metal.
CLAY, HENRY - - -	1572	9th Nov.	1786	Manufacturing buttons of dyed materials.
CLAY, HENRY - - -	1729	23rd Feb.	1790	Manufacturing buttons of a material not before used for the purpose.
CLAY, HENRY - - -	1918	20th Nov.	1792	Manufacturing panels for coaches and other carriages, also for tables, cabinets, pictures, and other furniture.
CLAY, HENRY - - -	2092	27th Feb	1796	Carriage for conveying and discharging coals, lime, soil, manure, stones, gravel, sand, rubbish, and other materials.

Name of Patentee.	Progressive Number.	Date.	Subject-matter of Patent.
CLAY, HENRY - - -	2213	1st Feb. 1798	Saving part of the water, heretofore wasted, in passing boats or barges through locks on navigable canals.
CLAY, JOHN - - -	7572	22d Feb. 1838	Machinery for shearing or cropping, and dressing and finishing, woollen and other cloths.
CLAY, JOHN - - -	8726	27th Nov. 1840	Arranging and setting up types for printing.
CLAY, JOHN - - -	9300	21st March 1842	Arranging and setting up types for printing.
CLAY, JOHN - - -	10,491	23rd Jan. 1845	Apparatus for consuming smoke.
CLAY, PHILIP HUTCHINSON -	4125	22nd May 1817	Combination of machinery for repairing turnpike and other roads and highways, and for keeping them in order.
CLAY, WILLIAM - - -	12,373	16th Dec. 1848	Machinery for rolling iron or other metals ;— partly applicable to other machinery in which cylinders or rollers are used.
CLAY, WILLIAM NEALE - -	7196	28th Sept. 1836	Manufacture of sulphate of soda.
CLAY, WILLIAM NEALE - -	7477	16th Nov. 1837	Manufacture of glass.
CLAY, WILLIAM NEALE - - [*Clay, Neale.*]	7518	19th Dec. 1837	Manufacture of iron.
CLAY, WILLIAM NEALE - -	8459	31st March 1804	Manufacture of iron.
CLAYFIELD, WILLIAM HENRY	2680	10th Feb. 1803	Reducing and extracting lead and other metals from regulus and regule.
CLAYFIELD, WILLIAM HENRY	2793	22nd Nov. 1804	Processes for separating the alkalies of potash and soda from their sulphates and sulphites.
CLAYPOLE, HENRY KREBS -	11,954	9th Nov. 1847	Process, apparatus, and machinery, for making sugar.
CLAYTON, EDWIN - -	5992	31st Aug. 1830	Manufacturing dough or paste for baking into bread.
CLAYTON, HENRY - -	10,132	30th March 1844	Manufacture of tiles, drain-pipes or tubes, and bricks.
CLAYTON, HENRY - -	13,864	19th Dec. 1851	Manufacture of tubes, pipes, tiles, and other articles made from plastic materials.
CLAYTON, ROBERT - -	4064	30th Sept. 1816	Preparing, making, and finishing, metal and composition blocks, plates, and rollers, also types and dies, by which patterns, devices, and compositions can be imprinted and impressed upon cloths, paper, leather, and earthenware.
CLAYTON, ROBERT - -	4247	16th April 1818	Depositing or inserting metals, or a mixture of metals, in wood, ivory, bone, horn, paper, and pottery-ware, to supersede inlaying.
CLEAVER, JOHN - -	9903	12th Oct. 1843	Furnace for subliming ores of zinc. or reducing them to a metallic state.
CLEGG, JOHN - - -	11,519	7th Jan. 1847	Looms for weaving.
CLEGG, ROBERT - - -	12,568	16th April 1849	Looms for weaving.
CLEGG, SAMUEL - - -	3247	26th July 1809	Rotative-engine, with a piston which makes a complete revolution at a distance from the revolving axis, shaft, or cylinder.
CLEGG, SAMUEL - - -	3968	9th Dec. 1815	Gas-apparatus.
CLEGG, SAMUEL - - -	4283	24th July 1818	Gasometer.
CLEGG, SAMUEL - - -	5629	20th March 1828	Construction of steam-engines, boilers, and generators.
CLEGG, SAMUEL - - -	6020	20th Oct. 1830	Gas-meter.
CLEGG, SAMUEL - - -	7674	7th June. 1838	Gas-meters.

Name of Patentee.	Progressive Number.	Date.		Subject-matter of Patent.
CLEGG, SAMUEL - - -	7920	3rd Jan.	1839	Valves, and their combination with machinery.
CLEGG, SAMUEL - - -	12,131	20th April	1848	Gas-meters.
CLELAND, WILLIAM - -	4193	22nd Dec.	1817	Bleaching flax and hemp, also yarns and cloth or other goods, made of either of these articles.
CLELAND, WILLIAM - -	4696	17th Aug.	1822	Apparatus for evaporating liquids.
CLELAND, WILLIAM - -	4949	6th May	1824	Manufacturing sugar from cane-juice, and refining sugar and other substances.
CLELAND, WILLIAM - -	5394	24th July	1826	Evaporation.
CLELAND, WILLIAM - -	5520	4th July	1827	Preparing, refining, and evaporating sugar.
CLELLAN, CAREY MC. -	12,424	16th Jan.	1849	Corn-mill.
CLEMENT, JAMES - - -	8029	10th April	1839	Preparing mouldings, and producing the effect of chasing or embossing devices or patterns on frames and other work.
CLEMENT, JAMES - - -	9275	4th March	1842	Composition for ornamenting glass, picture-frames, and articles for interior and other decorations, also for manufacture of toys and other fancy articles.
CLEMENT, JEAN LEANDRE -	7780	21st Aug.	1838	Ascertaining and indicating the rate of vessels passing through the water.
CLEMENT, JEAN LEANDRE -	9418	12th July	1842	Apparatus for ascertaining the temperature of fluids, and the pressure of steam.
CLEMENT, WILLIAM HOOD -	12,335	21st Nov.	1848	Manufacture of sugar;—partly applicable to evaporation generally; apparatus for preparing cane trash as fuel.
CLEMETSHAW, WILLIAM -	1042	23rd April	1773	Iron-oven with a grate and regulator, to be placed behind a common range fire, for culinary purposes.
CLENCHARD, JOSEPH THEODORE	13,026	26th March	1850	Application of orchil to the processes of dyeing and printing in colours; apparatus employed in dyeing.
CLERK, SAMUEL - - -	6017	20th Oct.	1830	Making saddle-lining, saddle-cloth, and girths fore keping saddles in their proper place on horses and other animals of burden.
CLERK, WILLIAM - - -	3331	2nd May	1810	Preventing dust, smoke, and the danger of fire, also increasing and regulating the heat, from stoves and chimney fire-places for heating public buildings and dwelling-houses, without obstructing the view of the burning fuel.
CLERKE, ROBERT - - -	20	10th May	1622	Making soap, soap-ashes, pot-ashes, and salts for soaps.
CLERKE, ROBERT, SIR - -	253	25th Jan.	1687	Furnaces for extracting gold, silver, copper, lead, and tin, from their ores, and reducing them to malleable metals.
CLERKE, TALBOT - - -	253	25th Jan.	1687	Furnaces for extracting gold, silver, copper, lead, and tin, from their ores, and reducing them to malleable metals.
CLEVELAND, CHARLES - -	6759	9th Feb.	1835	Pens, penholders, and apparatus for supplying ink to pens; also apparatus for making pens.
CLIFF, JOSEPH - - -	10,708	5th June	1845	Manufacture of alum and aluminous compounds from a new substance; and production of fire-clay from the residuum.
CLIFFE, JOE - - -	12,797	12th Oct.	1849	Furnaces, or the means of consuming smoke.
CLIFFE, WASTEL - - -	1969	9th Dec.	1793	Making plane-irons, also making hoes and trowels from rolled steel, and fastening them to handles.

Name of Patentee.	Progres-sive Number.	Date.		Subject-matter of Patent.
CLIFFE, WASTEL	2336	2nd Aug.	1799	Grinding corn, malt, and other grain by steel or iron-hardened plates.
CLIFFORD, MARTIN	134	10th Nov.	1661	Making crystal glass.
CLIFFORD, THOMAS	1762	17th July	1790	Manufacturing nails by machinery.
CLIFFORD, THOMAS	1785	4th Dec.	1790	Manufacturing nails.
CLIFT, SAMUEL	11,479	8th Dec.	1846	Distillation of tar and pitch.
CLIFT, SAMUEL	13,470	21st Jan.	1851	Manufacture of potash, soda and glass.
CLIFTON, FRANCIS	459	5th Dec.	1723	Engines to spin wool, flax, cotton, silk, &c. into a fine thread, and mix in the first thread, by certain multiplying wheels.
CLIGNETT, JOHN	236	19th June	1684	Carriage with two or more wheels, and not liable to overturn.
CLINK, GEORGE	7936	1st March	1839	Process and apparatus for producing regular figures or patterns in carpets and other fabrics; mode of producing parti-colours on yarns or threads.
CLINTON, JOHN	12,378	16th Dec.	1848	Flutes.
CLIVE, JOHN HENRY	5950	1st July	1830	Construction of, and machinery for, locomotive ploughs, harrows, and other machines and carriages.
CLIVE, THOMAS	9316	7th April	1842	Construction of candlesticks.
CLOSE, VALENTINE	2127	5th July	1796	Constructing and erecting ovens, kilns, and fire-places, so as to effect a saving in fuel, and in the firing, hardening and baking of porcelain, chinaware, and earthenware.
CLOSE, WILLIAM	3505	2nd Nov.	1811	Trumpet, French horn, and bugle.
CLOUDESLEY, PAULO	261	4th Nov.	1688	Making, dressing, and instrating black plain silks, called alamodes, ranforsees, and lutestrings.
CLOUGH, CHARLES BUTLER	14,268	19th Aug.	1852	Machinery or apparatus applicable to the purposes of brushing and cleaning.
CLOUGH, HENRY GORE	2919	21st March	1806	Trusses for compressing and supporting ruptured parts of the human body.
CLOUGH, PETER	329	9th Dec.	1693	Making three sorts of tar or pitch: one that preserves wood from putrefaction and the gnawing of worms; another that resists fire, and will not melt by the heat of the sun; and another that preserves ropes a long time either in water or air.
CLOUGH, RICHARD	1106	16th Nov.	1775	Making warps with silk selvages, for velverets and other kinds of cotton goods, from cotton prepared in a particular manner.
CLOUGH, ROBERT	5976	5th Aug.	1830	Supporting-block, to be used in graving docks, and for other purposes.
CLOUGH, WILLIAM THOMPSON	7793	31st Aug.	1838	Manufacture of sulphuric-acid from copper ore, copper-regulus, and sulphuret of zinc.
CLOUGH, WILLIAM THOMPSON	8886	17th March	1841	Manufacture of the carbonates of soda and potash.
CLUBB, STEPHEN	2881	27th Sept.	1805	Mangle.
CLULEY, FRANCIS	3387	8th Oct.	1810	Making and adjusting bedsteads on a double frame, with a fourfold method, for the relief of sick, lame, infirm, and aged persons.
CLUNIE, ALEXANDRE	873	26th March	1767	Machine for working cranes used in landing goods from ships and other craft.
CLUTTERBUCK, WILLIAM	5874	21st Nov.	1829	Shears used for cutting or cropping woollen-cloth and other fabrics.
CLYBURN, RICHARD	6986	21st Jan.	1836	Power-looms.

Name of Patentee.	Progres-sive Number.	Date.	Subject-matter of Patent.
CLYBURN, RICHARD - -	8660	15th Oct. 1840	Machinery for cutting vegetable and other substances.
CLYBURN, RICHARD - -	9828	10th July 1843	Machinery for beating, cleansing, and crushing various animal and vegetable substances.
CLYBURN, RICHARD - -	13,314	2nd Nov. 1850	Wheel-carriages.
CLYMER, GEORGE - - -	4174	1st Nov. 1817	Printing-presses.
CLYMER, GEORGE - - -	4313	21st Nov. 1818	Ships' pumps.
CLYMER, GEORGE - - -	4809	5th July 1823	Agricultural ploughs.
CLYMER, GEORGE - - -	5550	6th Sept. 1827	Typographic printing, between plain or flat surfaces.
COAD, RICHARD - - -	6858	10th July 1835	Apparatus for consuming smoke and economizing fuel in furnaces, particularly applicable to those of steam-engines.
COAD, RICHARD - - -	11,976	25th Nov. 1847	Combustion of fuel, and applying the heat so obtained.
COAD, RICHARD - - -	12,323	9th Nov. 1848	Construction of blast and other furnaces and fire-places.
COATS, THOMAS - - -	13,350	16th Nov. 1850	Turning, cutting, and shaping wood and other materials.
COATES, EZRA JENKS - -	8544	13th June 1840	Propelling canal and other boats.
COATES, EZRA JENKS - -	8822	30th Jan. 1841	Forging bolts, spikes, and nails.
COATES, EZRA JENKS - -	10,040	8th Feb. 1844	Apparatus for facilitating the reduction of fractures and dislocations of bones, and for maintaining the parts in their just positions.
COATES, EZRA JENKS - -	10,065	21st Feb. 1844	Forging bolts, spikes, and nails.
COATES, EZRA JENKS - -	13,089	1st June 1850	Manufacture of bolts, spikes, and nails.
COATES, GEORGE - - -	1717	12th Dec. 1789	Machine for washing, scouring, or cleansing linen, cotton, and woollen cloths, or other woven or knit fabric.
COATES, GEORGE - - -	2161	31st Jan. 1797	Machine for making horse-shoe nails, brads, and several other articles, of iron and other metals.
COATES, JOHN - - -	11,678	27th April 1847	Machinery for cleaning the surface of woven fabrics, or removing loose fibres from the same, previous to printing.
COATES, JOHN - - -	12,107	3rd April 1848	Machinery for printing calicoes and other surfaces.
COATHUPE, CHARLES THORN-[TON	7281	11th Jan. 1837	Manufacture of certain descriptions of glass.
COBB, THOMAS - - -	2147	19th Nov. 1796	Making coloured paper for rooms, also for writing, printing, drawing, and for various other purposes.
COBB, THOMAS - - -	2681	21st Feb. 1803	Manufacturing shag or plush.
COBB, THOMAS - - -	3084	4th Dec. 1807	Making paper in separate sheets.
COBB, THOMAS - - -	3580	16th July 1812	Making paper in separate sheets.
COBB, THOMAS - - -	5849	15th Sept. 1829	Manufacture of paper for covering walls and rooms; apparatus for effecting the same.
COBB, WILLIAM - - -	808	31st March 1764	Making an air-jacket with proper shoes for the use of shipwrecked persons.
COBB, WILLIAM - - -	881	30th July 1767	Machine for catching fish.
COBBING, JAMES - - -	5889	26th Jan. 1830	Skates.
COBBOLD, EDWARD - -	7613	10th April 1838	Manufacture of certain pigments or paints, or such like substances.

Name of Patentee.	Progressive Number.	Date.	Subject-matter of Patent.
COBBOLD, EDWARD - -	7632	5th May 1838	Manufacturing gas for affording light and heat; application of certain products thereof to useful purposes.
COBBOLD, EDWARD - -	9428	28th July 1842	Supporting and propelling human and other bodies, on and in the water.
COBBOLD, EDWARD - -	9531	3rd Dec. 1842	Instruments for writing or marking;—partly applicable to brushes for water-colour drawing.
COBBOLD, EDWARD - -	9704	20th April 1843	Supporting and propelling human and other bodies, on and in the water.
COBBOLD, EDWARD - -	10,162	27th April 1844	Preparation of peat, rendering it applicable for fuel and for various other purposes.
COCHAUX, JOSEPH - -	5930	24th April 1830	Apparatus for preventing the explosion of boilers, in generating steam.
COCHRAN, JOHN - - -	2258	7th Aug. 1798	Spinning flax, hemp, and tow, by means of machinery wrought by water, horse, steam, or other power.
COCHRAN, JOHN WEBSTER -	11,235	2nd June 1846	Machinery for cutting and shaping wood for shipbuilding and other purposes.
COCHRAN, MATHEW - -	12,130	20th April 1848	Production of coloured patterns or designs on warps of carpets, velvets, or on other textile materials;—partly applicable for the same purpose on woven fabrics or other plain surfaces.
COCHRAN, MATHEW - -	12,980	27th Feb. 1850	Machinery for the production of, and for ornamenting, fabrics and tissues generally;—partly applicable to the regulation of other machinery, and to other similar purposes.
COCHRANE, ALEXANDER -	6150	10th Aug. 1831	Machinery for propelling or moving locomotive-carriages, and giving motion to mills, and other machinery.
COCHRANE, ALEXANDER -	7735	13th July 1838	Umbrellas and parasols.
COCHRANE, ALEXANDER -	8140	3rd July 1839	Lock.
COCHRANE, ALEXANDER BRODIE	12,918	3rd Jan. 1850	Manufacture of iron pipes or tubes.
COCHRANE, CHARLES STUART -	6037	13th Nov. 1830	Preparing and spinning cashmere wool.
COCHRANE, Sir THOMAS - -	3657	3rd March 1813	Lighting cities, towns, and villages.
COCHRANE, Sir THOMAS, Knight	3772	24th Dec. 1813	Regulating atmospheric pressure in lamps, globes, and other transparent cases; supplying combustible matter to flames, and preserving uniform intensity of light.
COCHRANE, Sir THOMAS, Knight	4217	3rd Feb. 1818	Purifying oil of tar.
COCHRANE, Sir THOMAS, Knight	4241	8th April 1818	Making street-lamps adapted for the combustion of purified oil of tar; arrangement of parts of lamps, rendering *them* also capable of producing a clear light by the combustion of the said oil; the use thereof in such lamps.
COCHRANE, Sir THOMAS, Knight	4253	4th May 1818	Machine for removing the smoke or gases generated in stoves, furnaces, or fire places; also in certain cases for directing the heat, and applying such smoke or gases to useful purposes.
COCHRANE, Sir THOMAS, Knight	5256	15th Sept. 1825	Propelling ships, vessels, and boats at sea.
COCHRANE, Sir THOMAS, Knight	6018	20th Oct. 1830	Apparatus to facilitate excavating, sinking, and mining.
COCHRANE, Sir THOMAS, Knight	6036	11th Nov. 1830	Rotary-engine to be impelled by steam.

Name of Patentee.	Progressive Number.	Dat	Subject-matter of Patent.
COCHRANE, WILLIAM ERSKINE	4476	17th June 1820	Construction of lamps.
COCHRANE, WILLIAM ERSKINE	4651	22nd Feb. 1822	Lamps rendered capable of burning concrete oils, animal fat, and other similar substances.
COCHRANE, WILLIAM ERSKINE	5283	8th Nov. 1825	Cooking-apparatus.
COCHRANE, WILLIAM ERSKINE	5608	15th Jan. 1828	Cooking-apparatus.
COCHRANE, WILLIAM ERSKINE	5758	14th Jan. 1829	Paddle-wheels for propelling boats and other vessels.
COCHRANE, WILLIAM ERSKINE	5921	20th March 1830	Cooking-apparatus.
COCHRANE, WILLIAM ERSKINE	13,246	5th Sept. 1850	Propelling, steering, and ballasting vessels; pistons of steam-engines; fire-bars of furnaces; railway-sleepers.
COCK, ALEXANDER -	3786	12th March 1814	Prevention and cure of dry rot and common decay in timber; preserving woollen, linen, and other articles from mildew.
COCK, DAVID - - -	3296	1st Feb. 1810	Vessels for melting metals and heating fluids.
COCKBURNE, ALEXANDER -	793	29th July 1763	Composition for and method of curing salmon with spices.
COCKER, SAMUEL - -	7488	25th Nov. 1837	Making needles.
COCKER, THOMAS FILDES -	14,355	11th Jan. 1853	Annealing or softening metallic wires and sheets of metal; reducing, compressing, or drawing metallic wires; manufacture of metal rolls.
COCKERELL, JOHN - -	9874	24th Aug. 1843	Preparation of a certain material produced from a vegetable substance; application of the same for affording light, and for other uses.
COCKING, SEPTIMUS - -	9330	26th April 1842	Production of light by the burning of oil, tallow, and wax; apparatus for regulating and extinguishing such light.
COCKS, HENRY VENNER -	8257	2nd Nov. 1839	Stoves and furnaces.
COCKSEY, THOMAS - -	12,565	16th April 1849	Machinery for washing and cleansing cotton and other fabrics;—applicable to operations in bleaching, dyeing, printing, and sizing warps and piece-goods.
COCKSHOTT, WILLIAM -	2078	18th Dec. 1795	Cotton goods wherein the warp and weft are combined, and the colour thrown up into diamonds, waves, spots, sprigs, flowers, and other figures, with cotton, silk, linen, or worsted.
COCKSHUTT, JOHN - -	988	2nd May 1771	Making malleable iron directly from the ore, with coal; refining pig-iron with charcoal; finery for the purpose.
COE, CHARLES - -	2823	12th Feb. 1805	Flue for heating ovens, &c. uniformly.
COFFEY, ÆNEAS - -	5974	5th Aug. 1833	Machinery used in brewing and distilling.
COFFIN, GUY CARLETON -	10,239	3rd July 1844	Locomotive, marine, and stationary engines.
COFFIN, Sir ISAAC, Bart. -	3337	15th May 1810	Perpetual oven for making bread.
COFFIN, Sir ISAAC, Bart. -	4815	15th July 1823	Catching mackerel and other fish.
COFFYN, AUGUSTUS -	10,567	17th March 1845	Pumps.
COGAN, HUGH - -	10,762	12th July 1845	Weaving fabrics in patterns or various colours.
COGAN, ROBERT - -	13,458	16th Jan. 1851	Application of plain or ornamental glass, alone or in combination, to new purposes of construction or manufacture.
COGAN, WILLIAM - -	583	10th April 1742	Use of a seed to obtain oil applicable to house painting; cultivating the vegetable producing such seed.

Name of Patentee.	Progressive Number.	Date.	Subject-matter of Patent.
COGGIN, THOMAS PATRICK -	5498	19th May 1827	Machine for dibbling grain of all sorts.
COHEN, ABRAHAM - -	7882	26th Nov. 1838	Construction of railway-carriages; connecting and retarding railway-trains.
COLBERT, JAMES GERARD -	4117	13th May 1817	Making screws of iron, brass, steel, or other metals, for use in woodwork.
COLCHESTER, WILLIAM - -	8170	29th July 1839	Soap-frame.
COLDRIDGE, CHARLES - -	3940	18th July 1815	Grate and apparatus.
COLE, JAMES - - -	9228	15th Jan. 1842	Construction of brushes.
COLE, JAMES FERGUSON -	4530	27th Jan. 1821	Chronometers.
COLE, JOHN - - - -	381	10th Sept. 1707	Drawing burdens on wheel-carriages.
COLE, JOHN LAWES - -	12,105	22nd Mar. 1848	Steam-engines.
COLE, MICHAEL - - -	382	7th Aug. 1708	New kind of light.
COLE, RICHARD - - -	372	29th July 1704	Forming glasses into conical figures and lamps, for the better dispersing and casting light.
COLE, RICHARD - - -	1936	15th March 1793	Constructing certain parts and movements of watches, clocks, and timepieces.
COLE, RICHARD - - -	2619	18th May 1802	Leghorn and chip hats.
COLE, WILLIAM - - -	911	16th Dec. 1768	Chain-pump for raising water out of ships, draining land, or for other purposes.
COLE, WILLIAM - - -	982	17th Jan. 1771	Chain-pump for raising water out of ships, draining lands, or for other purposes.
COLE, WILLIAM - - -	11,018	23rd Dec. 1845	Looms.
COLE, WILLIAM - - -	14,042	24th March 1852	Preventing and removing the deposit of sand, mud, or silt, in tidal rivers, also in docks, harbours, and other channels communicating with the sea, through tidal rivers.
COLEBANK, HENRY - -	4677	4th June 1822	Engine for cutting, twisting, and spreading wick for candles.
COLEGRAVE, FRANCIS EDWARD	12,615	22nd May 1849	Means of communicating between the passengers and guard of a railway-train, or between the guard and engine-driver;—parts of which are applicable to working signals.
COLEGRAVE, FRANCIS EDWARD	12,953	29th Jan. 1850	Saddles;—partly applicable to the standing rigging and other furniture of ships or vessels, and to the connecting links or chains of railway-carriages, and to other purposes.
COLEGRAVE, FRANCIS EDWARD	13,163	3rd July 1850	Valves of steam and other engines; causing driving-wheels of locomotive-engines to bite the rails; supplying water to steam-boilers.
COLEMAN, EDWARD - -	668	11th Feb. 1752	Machine for draining or flooding lands, and for other purposes.
COLEMAN, EDWARD - -	2370	1st Feb. 1800	Artificial frogs to be applied to horses' feet, for prevention of contracted hoofs, thrushes, and canker.
COLEMAN, EDWARD - -	3128	30th April 1808	Construction and application of horse-shoes, to prevent diseases to which the feet of horses are subject, especially contraction of the hoof.
COLEMAN, EDWARD - -	4446	15th April 1820	Constructing horse-shoes.
COLEMAN, EZRA - - -	10,792	30th July 1845	Moving locomotive-engines on inclined planes of railways.
COLEMAN, JAMES EDWARD -	14,193	28th June 1852	Application of india-rubber and gutta-percha, and of compounds thereof.
COLEMAN, OBED MITCHELL -	10,341	10th Oct. 1844	Pianofortes.
COLEMAN, RICHARD - -	10,685	22nd May 1845	Construction of harrows and sheepfolds.

Name of Patentee.	Progressive Number.	Date.	Subject-matter of Patent.
COLEMAN, THOMAS - -	6100	29th March 1831	Roller for horses.
COLES, CHARLES BARWELL -	5465	20th Feb. 1827	Constructing gasometers, or machines for holding and distributing gas for illumination.
COLES, CHARLES BARWELL -	8205	23rd Aug. 1839	Fixing and carrying fire-arms on horseback.
COLES, EDWARD ROBERT -	10,397	21st Nov. 1844	Construction of buildings generally.
COLES, JAMES - - -	11,364	3rd Sept. 1846	Apparatus for the prevention and treatment of distortions of the spine and chest, also for treatment of diseases of the spine, and other disorders where a recumbent position of the patient is required.
COLES, JOSHUA - - -	552	14th Feb. 1735	Liquid blue for blueing washed linen.
COLES, RICHARD - - -	8746	23rd Dec. 1840	Making tanks and other vessels, of slate, stone, marble, and other materials; fitting and fastening such materials together.
COLES, WILLIAM - - -	4567	5th July 1821	Braces or instruments for the relief of hernia or ruptures.
COLES, WILLIAM - - -	6650	26th July 1834	Specific remedy for the cure, alleviation, or prevention, of rheumatic, gouty, or other affections arising from colds, or other causes.
COLES, WILLIAM - - -	6957	16th Dec. 1835	Locomotive-carriages.
COLES, WILLIAM - - -	7472	14th Nov. 1837	Gunnery, gun and other carriages, and means of connecting the same.
COLES, WILLIAM - - -	8204	23rd Aug. 1839	Reducing friction in machinery used for propelling vessels, lathes, and other machines.
COLLADON, JOHN - - -	138	2nd May 1662	Curing smoky chimneys by altering the course of the smoke towards the top, or by inserting tunnels with checks within the chimneys.
COLLARD, WILLIAM FREDERICK	3481	9th Sept. 1811	Upright pianoforte.
COLLARD, WILLIAM FREDERICK	4542	8th March 1821	Pianofortes.
COLLEN, ARTHUR - - -	8284	25th Nov. 1839	Pumps.
COLLETT, CHARLES MINORS -	11,659	15th April 1847	Apparatus and arrangements for affording additional security in locks.
COLLETT, JOSEPH - - -	600	17th Feb. 1744	Elixir for the cure of dropsy and jaundice, and for relief of the stone and gravel.
COLLETT, JOSEPH - - -	673	3rd July 1752	Medicine called "oleum anedinum," or "British balsam of health."
COLLETT, JOSEPH - - -	695	2nd Dec. 1754	Medicine called "oleum vitæ," or the "Ladies' nervous and cordial drops."
COLLETT, JOSEPH - - -	728	16th Aug. 1758	Medicine for the cure of gout (anti-arthritic wine and powder).
COLLETT, JOSEPH - - -	828	5th June 1765	Making catheters and bougies of fine leather, for curing the stone in the bladder.
COLLETTE, THOMAS - -	7955	29th Jan. 1839	Children's cots.
COLLIER, ELISHA HAYDON - [Collyer, Elisha Hayden.]	4315	24th Nov. 1818	Fire-arms;—also applicable to cannon.
COLLIER, ELISHA HAYDON -	7145	13th July 1836	Steam-boilers.
COLLIER, ELISHA HAYDON -	7482	21st Nov. 1837	Machinery applicable to the raising of fluids and other bodies.
COLLIER, ELISHA HAYDON - [Collier, Elisha Hoydon.]	8001	14th March 1839	Machinery for manufacturing nails.
COLLIER, ELISHA HAYDON -	9885	28th Sept. 1843	Construction of furnaces and flues.
COLLIER, ELISHA HAYDON -	10,828	11th Sept. 1845	Manufacture of nails; machinery for the purpose.

Name of Patentee.	Progressive Number.	Date.	Subject-matter of Patent.
COLLIER, GEORGE - - -	7533	11th Jan. 1838	Power-looms.
COLLIER, GEORGE - - -	8412	4th March 1840	Looms for weaving figured and twilled fabrics.
COLLIER, GEORGE - - -	12,535	26th March 1849	Machinery for preparing and spinning cotton and other fibrous materials; preparation of yarns; machinery for weaving the same.
COLLIER, GEORGE - - -	13,267	28th Sept. 1850	Printing yarns for, and weaving, carpets and other fabrics.
COLLIER, GEORGE - - -	13,402	12th Dec. 1850	Manufacture of carpets and other fabrics.
COLLIER, GEORGE - - -	13,408	12th Dec. 1850	Preparing cotton and other textile materials for spinning; tools or apparatus for making cards and other parts of such preparing machinery; engines for giving motion to the same;—applicable also in other cases where motive-power is required.
COLLIER, GEORGE - - -	13,888	31st Dec. 1851	Manufacture of carpets and other fabrics.
COLLIER, GEORGE - - -	14,140	22nd May 1852	Preparing, spinning, twisting, doubling, and weaving, cotton-wool and other fibrous materials;—tools or apparatus for constructing parts of machines used in such manufactures.
COLLIER, JAMES - - -	704	10th Sept. 1755	Engine for draining water from fenny, moorish, and drowned lands.
COLLIER, JAMES - * -	3829	4th Aug. 1814	Machine for combing wool, hemp, flax, waste silk, cotton, hair, or any other substance or material capable of being reduced to a sliver by the operation of combing.
COLLIER, JAMES - - -	3874	16th Jan. 1815	Apparatus or instrument called "Criopyrite," for obtaining and applying power to the raising of water.
COLLIER, JAMES - - -	5926	5th April 1830	Generating gas for illumination; apparatus for the purpose.
COLLIER, JAMES - - -	6121	2nd June 1831	Manufacture of useful products from a certain oleaginous substance.
COLLIER, JAMES - * -	7871	13th Nov. 1838	Obtaining motive-power.
COLLIER, JOHN - - -	4020	1st May 1816	Machine for shearing woollen-cloths.
COLLIER, JOHN - - -	4195	15th Jan. 1818	Machinery for cropping or shearing woollen-cloths.
COLLIER, JOHN - - -	4702	27th Sept. 1822	Machines for shearing cloth.
COLLIER, JOSHUA - - -	2279	12th Dec. 1798	Freeing fish-oils from their impurities; strainers for oils and other liquids; instruments for ascertaining their qualities and assisting their burning.
COLLIER, WILLIAM - -	5561	10th Nov. 1827	Power-looms for weaving.
COLLINGE, CHARLES - -	6415	2nd May 1833	Making or manufacture of axletrees.
COLLINGE, JOHN - -	1626	2nd Nov. 1787	Construction of carriage and other wheel-boxes, and axletrees.
COLLINGE, JOHN - -	1899	17th July 1792	Carriage and other wheel-boxes and axletrees, to lessen the draught and friction.
COLLINGE, JOHN - - -	2019	30th Oct. 1794	Sugar-mills.
COLLINGE, JOHN - - -	3410	9th March 1811	Carriage and other wheel-boxes and axletrees.
COLLINGE, JOHN - - -	4583	14th Aug. 1821	Cast-iron rollers for sugar-mills, by more permanently fixing them to their gudgeons.
COLLINGE, JOHN - - -	4617	22nd Nov. 1812	Hinges.
COLLINGE, JOHN - - -	5123	15th March 1825	Springs and other apparatus used for closing doors and gates.
COLLINGE, JOHN - * -	6023	1st Nov. 1830	Apparatus for suspending the rudders of ships or other vessels.

Name of Patentee.	Progressive Number.	Date.	Subject-matter of Patent.
COLLINS, BENJAMIN - -	1030	18th May 1773	Cordial cephalic snuff.
COLLINS, BENJAMIN CHARLES	1798	18th March 1791	Construction of a grate with air-flues in the cheeks and back.
COLLINS, CHARLES HENRY -	10,902	31st Oct. 1845	Atmospheric railways.
COLLINS, FREDERICK WILLIAM [MICHAEL	12,097	14th March 1848	Ornamenting china, earthenware, and glass.
COLLINS, HENRY GEORGE -	7515	19th Dec. 1837	Bookbinding;—partly applicable to cutting paper for other purposes.
COLLINS, JOHN - - -	12,043	27th Jan. 1848	Furnaces, stoves, grates, and fire-places, kilns, and other apparatus, for preparing vegetable and other substances; generation and application of heat.
COLLINS, LAWRENCE - -	2565	3rd Dec. 1801	Machine for saving persons from drowning. ("Collinette.")
COLLINS, ROBERT NELSON ·	12,354	2nd Dec. 1848	Compounds for the prevention of injury to health under certain circumstances.
COLLINS, THOMAS - - -	3370	10th Aug. 1810	Making ladders in different pieces, capable of being immediately put together by means of socket-joints.
COLLINS, WILLIAM - -	1187	20th March 1778	Preparing, gilding, polishing, or burnishing metals plated with silver, or otherwise, for making buttons or other articles in the toy way, by laying on the gold when the metals are much thicker than has heretofore been used.
COLLINS, WILLIAM - - -	1388	2nd Oct. 1783	Making and preparing bolts to fasten ships' timbers together.
COLLINS, WILLIAM - -	1704	19th Sept. 1789	Construction of pumps, and the chambers, pistons, and boxes of the same, so as to prevent their being choked with gravel, sand, and filth, on shipboard, and for raising water with less power than those now in use.
COLLINS, WILLIAM - -	1739	31st March 1790	Covering and combining copper or brass sheets with a semi-metallic substance, to prevent corrosion.
COLLINS, WILLIAM - -	1926	20th Dec. 1792	Metal-sheets, and fastening for sheets, intended for the sheathing of ships, as also the rudder-furniture.
COLLINS, WILLIAM - -	2390	23rd April 1800	Application of sundry articles and materials for the preservation of shipping, and for marine purposes.
COLLINS, WILLIAM - -	2860	20th June 1805	Ventilator for the purpose of ventilating tents and marquees.
COLLINS, WILLIAM - -	2874	9th Aug. 1805	Ventilator for use in close carriages, sedan-chairs, rooms, or cabins, and for conveyance of sound.
COLLINS, WILLIAM - -	4115	6th May 1817	Composition and preparation of a metal to make sheets or plates, and the application of the same for sheathing ships' bottoms; chain-pump used on board ships.
COLLINS, WILLIAM - -	4438	10th March 1820	Carriage and other lamps.
COLLINS, WILLIAM WHITAKER	14,033	24th March 1852	Manufacture of steel.
COLLINSON, EDWARD - -	1940	18th March 1793	Lamp for lighting streets, houses, halls, and shops, and for other purposes.
COLLISON, JOHN - - -	1341	4th Nov. 1782	Making mineral and vegetable alkali.
COLLYER, JAMES - - -	4230	19th Feb. 1818	Machine for dressing and gigging woollen and other cloths.
COLMAN, JAMES - - -	9166	9th Dec. 1841	Manufacture of starch.
COLMAN, JAMES - - -	13,110	8th June 1850	Manufacture of starch.

Name of Patentee.	Progressive Number.	Date.		Subject-matter of Patent.
COLMAR, CHARLES XAVIER DE	13,504	10th Feb.	1851	Calculating machine. (" Arithmometer.")
COLOMBIER, RENÉ JOSEPH LE [COMTE DU	10,414	2nd Dec.	1844	Machinery for splitting and cutting skins and hides.
COLQUHOUN, JAMES NISBET -	4583	7th June	1821	Art of killing and capturing whales and other animals.
COLSON, MELCHIOR - -	14,258	12th Aug.	1852	Construction of vehicles.
COLT, SAMUEL - -	6909	22nd Oct.	1835	Fire-arms.
COLT, SAMUEL - -	12,668	20th June	1849	Fire-arms.
COLT, SAMUEL - -	13,823	22nd Nov.	1851	Fire-arms.
COLTMAN, WILLIAM - -	8351	21st Jan.	1840	Machinery employed in making frame-work knitting, or stocking frabrics.
COLTMAN, WILLIAM - -	8619	7th Sept.	1840	Machinery employed in frame-work knitting, or stocking fabrics.
COLTON, WILLIAM - -	9392	13th June	1842	Weighing-machine.
COMBE, JAMES - -	9891	5th Oct.	1843	Heckling, cleaning, preparing, and carding flax and other fibrous substances.
COMBE, JAMES - -	12,832	2nd Nov.	1849	Machinery for heckling hemp and flax; machinery for producing flax yarns.
COMBE, JOHN - - -	12,693	4th July	1849	Machinery for heckling, carding, winding, dressing, and weaving flax, cotton, silk, and other fibrous substances.
COMBS, BENJAMIN MERRIMAN	5547	30th Aug.	1827	Pully-machinery and apparatus, for securing and removing curtains, and roller and other blinds.
COMPTISE, LEWIS - -	3923	8th June	1815	Machinery for extracting gold and silver from the cinders of gold-refines, and other substances.
CONDER, FRANCIS ROUBILIAC	9644	23rd Feb.	1843	Cutting and shaping wood; machinery for the purpose.
CONDER, FRANCIS ROUBILIAC	11,009	20th Dec.	1845	Propelling.
CONDIE, JOHN - -	8727	27th Nov.	1840	Applying springs to locomotive-engines, and railway and other carriages.
CONDIE, JOHN - -	11,411	15th Oct.	1846	Machinery used in manufacturing malleable iron.
CONGREVE, WILLIAM - -	3134	24th May	1808	Gun-carriage, for land or sea service.
CONGREVE, WILLIAM - -	3164	24th Aug.	1808	Measuring time; constructing clocks and chronometers.
CONGREVE, WILLIAM - -	3201	7th Feb.	1809	Construction or arrangement of buildings, so as to afford security against fire.
CONGREVE, WILLIAM (Colonel)	3565	11th May	1812	Gun and carronade carriages.
CONGREVE, WILLIAM (Colonel)	3606	31st Oct.	1812	Securing buildings, towns, dockyards, and ships from fire, combining a power for the raising of water to the tops of buildings.
CONGREVE, WILLIAM (Colonel)	3670	23rd March	1813	Constructing the locks and sluices of canals, basins, or docks.
CONGREVE, WILLIAM (Sir) -	3937	3rd July	1815	Manufacturing gunpowder.
CONGREVE, WILLIAM (Sir) -	4298	19th Oct.	1818	Constructing steam-engines.
CONGREVE, WILLIAM (Sir) -	4404	1st Nov.	1819	Inlaying or combining different metals, or other hard substances.
CONGREVE, WILLIAM (Sir) -	4419	4th Dec.	1819	Manufacture of bank-note paper, for the prevention of forgery.
CONGREVE, WILLIAM (Sir) -	4521	22nd Dec.	1820	Printing in one, two, or more colours.
CONGREVE, WILLIAM (Sir) -	4563	7th June	1821	Art of killing and capturing whales and other animals.
CONGREVE, WILLIAM (Sir) -	4593	28th Sept.	1821	Constructing steam-engines.
CONGREVE, WILLIAM (Sir) -	4642	29th Jan.	1822	Multiplying fac-simile impressions to any extent.

Name of Patentee.	Progressive Number.	Date.	Subject-matter of Patent.
CONGREVE, WILLIAM (Sir) -	4853	16th Oct. 1823	Fireworks.
CONGREVE, WILLIAM (Sir) -	4898	7th Feb. 1824	Stamping.
CONGREVE, WILLIAM (Sir) -	5054	14th Dec. 1824	Gas-meter.
CONGREVE, WILLIAM (Sir) -	5461	8th Feb. 1827	Motive-power.
CONNE, NICHOLAS - - -	4388	30th June 1819	Lamps for domestic purposes.
CONNELDON, WILLIAM - -	26	20th Sept. 1623	Furnace for melting lead by means of sea-coal or other fuel, wood excepted.
CONNELL, JAMES - - -	9959	24th Nov. 1843	Manufacturing candles and candlewicks.
CONNELL, JAMES EDWARD Mc-	12,231	7th Aug. 1848	Steam-engines; means of retarding the same on railways; connecting railway-carriages together; effecting communication by signals or otherwise.
CONNELL, JAMES EDWARD Mc -	13,729	28th Aug. 1851	Locomotive steam-engines and railway-axles;—partly applicable to stationary and marine steam-engines.
CONNELL, JAMES EDWARD Mc -	14,182	24th June 1852	Steam-engines, boilers, and other vessels for containing fluids; railways; materials and apparatus employed therein.
CONNISON, ALEXANDER - -	9655	3rd March 1843	Steam-engines.
CONNOP, JACOB - - -	13,172	10th July 1850	Melting, moulding, and casting sand, earth, and argillaceous substances, for paving, building, and other purposes.
CONNOP, THOMAS - - -	2029	12th Jan. 1795	Machine for batting cotton and wool.
CONNOP, THOMAS - - -	2602	30th March 1802	Machine for batting, opening, and cleansing cotton-wool and sheep's wool.
CONOCHIE, JOHN Mc -	12,089	8th March 1848	Locomotive-engines.
CONOCHIE, JOHN Mc -	14,189	24th June 1852	Locomotive and other steam-engines and boilers; railways; railway carriages and their appurtenances; also machinery and apparatus for producing parts of such improvements.
CONSITT, JOHN - - -	7319	8th March 1837	Machinery for spinning, doubling, and twisting cotton and other fibrous substances.
CONSTABLE, JOHN - - -	10,171	30th April 1844	Manufacture of sugar.
CONSTABLE, JOHN - - -	10,690	24th May 1845	Manufacture of gas for lighting and heating.
CONSTANT, LOUIS HONORÉ [GERMAIN	3541	27th Feb. 1812	Refining sugars.
CONTE, GRAZIANO - - -	10,850	3rd Oct. 1845	Machinery for cutting, carving, and sculpturing marble, stone, wood, and other like substances.
CONTI, GASPARE - - -	9873	22nd Aug. 1843	Hydraulic-machinery to be applied as a motive-power.
CONTI, GASPARE - - -	10,077	24th Feb. 1844	Hydraulic-machinery to be used as a motive-power.
CONVERSE, SHERMAN - -	6317	29th Sept. 1832	Making metallic-rails for the construction of railways.
CONVERSE, SHERMAN - [Converse, Shearman.]	6324	22nd Oct. 1832	Making fire-grates.
CONWAY, HENRY SEYMOUR -	1310	1st Jan. 1782	Kiln and oven for burning lime, also for distilling and brewing purposes.
CONWAY, HENRY SEYMOUR, [Right Honourable	1689	23rd June 1789	Conveying the heat arising from the fires of coke-ovens, and adapting the same to the working of steam-engines, to cooking, also to calcining and fusing ores, and making brass and steel, and to heating buildings, or heating water for baths, also applicable to other purposes requiring fire or heat.
CONWELL, WILLIAM EUGENE-	4660	21st March 1822	Preparation and application of a certain purgative vegetable oil.

Name of Patentee.	Progressive Number.	Date.	Subject-matter of Patent.
COOCH, JOHN - - -	2416	17th June 1800	Machine for winnowing or dressing corn or grain for making bread, also for the use of cattle, or for seed.
COOCH, JOSHUA - - -	12,235	10th Aug. 1848	Sack-holders.
COODE, GEORGE - - -	12,093	11th Mar. 1848	Distributing over land, liquids and other substances in a liquid or fluent state; apparatus and machinery employed therein.
COODES, JAMES JAMIESON -	7486	25th Nov. 1837	Mortar for dressing rough rice or paddy, or re-dressing rice.
COOK, BENJAMIN - - -	3122	26th March 1808	Making barrels and ramrods for fowling-pieces, muskets, pistols, and other fire-arms.
COOK, BENJAMIN - - -	3460	27th June 1811	Combining and connecting different metals, or metals and wood, so as to make the combinations have the same appearance.
COOK, BENJAMIN - - -	3609	31st Oct. 1812	Making window-blinds, fire-screens, chimney-pieces, sashes, doors, picture-frames, frames for pier and other glasses, and various other useful and ornamental articles and things.
COOK, BENJAMIN - - -	4123	17th May 1817	Making and constructing solid and hollow cylinders or rollers.
COOK, BENJAMIN - - -	4668	16th April 1822	Mixture or preparation which may be used in preventing the damage arising from accidents by fire.
COOK, BENJAMIN - - -	5178	31st March 1825	Production and purification of coal-gas.
COOK, BENJAMIN - - -	5288	10th Nov. 1825	Rendering ships' cables and anchors more secure and less liable to strain and injury while the ships lay at anchor.
COOK, BENJAMIN - - -	5289	10th Nov. 1825	Binding books and portfolios.
COOK, BENJAMIN - - -	5322	19th Jan. 1826	Making hinges.
COOK, BENJAMIN - - -	5331	7th Feb. 1826	Making files.
COOK, BENJAMIN - - -	5782	23rd April 1829	Making rollers or cylinders of copper and other metals or a mixture of metals, for printing calicoes, silks, cloths, and other articles.
COOK, BENJAMIN - - -	6024	1st Nov. 1830	Making nebs and slots in hollow cylinders of copper, brass, or other metals, for printing calicoes, muslins, cloths, silks, and other articles.
COOK, BENJAMIN - - -	6248	22nd Mar. 1832	Application of a material for making paints and varnishes, and for other purposes.
COOK, BENJAMIN - - -	6260	13th April 1832	Manufacturing various articles from a metal not hitherto used for the purpose.
COOK, BENJAMIN - - -	6756	31st Jan. 1835	Beds and mattrasses.
COOK, BENJAMIN - - -	7504	9th Dec. 1837	Gas-burners ("Argand burners").
COOK, BENJAMIN - -	13,438	2nd Jan. 1851	Manufacture of metallic tubes.
COOK, BENJAMIN, junior -	9358	23rd May 1842	Construction of bedsteads, both in metal and wood.
COOK, BENJAMIN, junior -	9991	18th Dec. 1843	Coating the surfaces of metals of various forms, and applying them to useful purposes.
COOK, EDWARD - - -	2087	9th Feb. 1796	Instruments for taking observations and altitudes by sea and land, without dependence on the visible or sensible horizon.
COOK, HENRY - - -	1185	16th March 1778	Composition to be used as a substitute for lead, slates, or tiles, in covering churches, houses, and all other buildings.
COOK, HENRY - - -	1668	26th Aug. 1788	Elastic sponge for sponging great guns and other fire-arms, and not liable to damage by vermin or water.

Name of Patentee.	Progressive Number.	Date.	Subject-matter of Patent.
COOK, JAMES - - - -	4960	20th May 1824	Making locks for guns, pistols, and other fire-arms.
COOK, JAMES - - - -	7294	2nd Feb. 1837	Gas-burners.
COOK, JOHN - - - -	937	7th Nov. 1769	Making baize.
COOK, JOSEPH - - -	6756	31st Jan. 1835	Beds and mattrasses.
COOK, ROBERT - - -	4560	9th May 1821	Machinery for raising water ("Hydragogue").
COOK, ROBERT - - -	8897	22nd Mar. 1841	Manufacture of bricks.
COOK, ROBERT - - -	9254	14th Feb. 1842	Machinery for spinning flax, hemp, and tow.
COOK, THOMAS - - -	4452	29th April 1820	Cooking - apparatus, or "philosophical cookery."
COOK, THOMAS - - -	5216	16th July 1825	Construction of carriages and harness.
COOK, THOMAS - - -	5932	24th April 1830	Construction and fitting up of boats of various descriptions.
COOK, WILLIAM - - -	5996	7th Sept. 1830	Cocks for supplying kitchen-ranges or cooking-apparatus with water, and for other purposes, "Fountain cocks."
COOK, WILLIAM - - -	8392	22nd Feb. 1840	Carriages.
COOK, WILLIAM - - -	10,795	31st July 1845	Stoves.
COOK, WILLIAM - - -	13,893	12th Jan. 1852	Construction of steam-engines, being a rotatory circular valve, for the regular admission of steam from the boiler, alternately into the chambers of the two cylinders of double-acting engines.
COOKE, JAMES - - -	1349	13th Jan. 1783	Machine for ploughing or drilling land, planting and sowing grain, pulse, and seeds, mixed with manure, or without manure, and for harrowing the same.
COOKE, JAMES - - -	1659	12th Aug. 1788	Machine for ploughing and drilling land, planting or sowing grain, pulse, and seeds, mixed with manure, or without manure, and for harrowing the same.
COOKE, JAMES - - -	1973	8th Jan. 1794	Knife-plate, weight, and regulator, to be used with a machine for cutting straw and hay into chaff.
COOKE, JAMES - - -	2290	29th Jan. 1799	Apparatus for applying fire to boilers, ovens, and other caldronic implements ("Carbo frugalist.")
COOKE, LAYTON - - -	3694	11th May 1813	Gaiters, and mode of fastening the same.
COOKE, MASTA JOSCELIN -	9651	2nd March 1843	Manufacture of artificial fuel.
COOKE, OSMOND - - -	660	2nd Feb. 1751	Cleansing and improving British spirits.
COOKE, WILLIAM - - -	2971	2nd Oct. 1806	Construction of waggons, and other carriages with more than two wheels.
COOKE, WILLIAM - - -	3708	15th June 1813	Making and working ploughs.
COOKE, WILLIAM - - -	3869	24th Dec. 1814	Apparatus for the detection of depredators. ("Thieves' Alarum.")
COOKE, WILLIAM - - -	13,620	3rd May 1851	Manufacture of soda and the carbonate thereof.
COOKE, WILLIAM FOTHERGILL	7174	17th Aug. 1836	Winding-up springs to produce continuous motion.
COOKE, WILLIAM FOTHERGILL	7390	12th June 1837	Giving signals and sounding alarums at distant places, by means of electric-currents transmitted through metallic-circuits.
COOKE, WILLIAM FOTHERGILL	7614	18th April 1838	Giving signals and sounding alarums at distant places, by means of electric-currents transmitted through metallic-circuits.
COOKE, WILLIAM FOTHERGILL	8345	21st Jan. 1840	Giving signals and sounding alarums at distant places, by means of electric-currents.

Name of Patentee.	Progressive Number.	Date.	Subject-matter of Patent.
COOKE, WILLIAM FOTHERGILL	9465	8th Sept. 1842	Apparatus for transmitting electricity;—applicable to apparatus for giving signals and sounding alarums at distant places, by means of electric-currents.
COOKE, WILLIAM FOTHERGILL	10,655	6th May 1845	Electric-telegraphs and apparatus relating thereto;—partly applicable to other purposes.
COOKSON, WILLIAM ISAAC -	8374	5th Feb. 1840	Processes for obtaining copper and other metals, from metallic ores.
COOKSON, WILLIAM ISAAC -	10,116	20th March 1844	Apparatus for burning sulphur in the manufacture of sulphuric-acid.
COOKWORTHY, WILLIAM -	898	17th March 1768	Making porcelain from moorstone, growan, and growan clay.
COOMBS, BENJAMIN MERRI- [MAN	3661	9th March 1813	Apparatus for cooking victuals.
COOPER, ALFRED - - -	12,924	11th Jan. 1850	Steam and other power engines; application thereof to motive purposes; method and machinery for arresting or checking the progress of locomotive-engines, and other carriages.
COOPER, EDWARD - - -	7617	21st April 1838	Making soap.
COOPER, EDWARD - - -	7850	3rd Nov. 1838	Manufacture of paper.
COOPER, GEORGE PATE - -	14,169	12th June 1852	Fastenings for garments.
COOPER, HENRY - - -	10,315	12th Sept. 1844	Machinery for doubling cotton, worsted, and other fibrous materials.
COOPER, JAMES - - -	1603	15th May 1787	Application of water or any fluid, to turn mills or machinery.
COOPER, JAMES - - -	9970	5th Dec. 1843	Vessels of peculiar construction, and an apparatus, for preserving provision for the use of families.
COOPER, JOHN - - -	1482	24th May 1785	Japanning or blueing buckles or clasps for mourning, the same being made of tin, pewter, lead, or mixture or composition of the said metals.
COOPER, JOSEPH - - -	10,125	28th March 1844	Purification and clarification of sugar;—applicable to the purification or clarification of other articles.
COOPER, JOSEPH - - -	11,057	22nd Jan. 1846	Separating the fluid and soluble parts of certain vegetable substances from the solid parts.
COOPER, JOSEPH - - -	12,318	4th Nov. 1848	Fastenings for wearing-apparel.
COOPER, JOSEPH ROCK - -	7610	10th April 1838	Fire-arms.
COOPER, JOSEPH ROCK - -	8347	21st Jan. 1840	Fire-arms, and balls to be used therewith.
COOPER, JOSEPH ROCK - [Cooper, Joseph Rocke.]	12,781	20th Sept. 1849	Fire-arms.
COOPER, LEONARD - - -	14,259	12th Aug. 1852	Construction of steam-engines and steam-boilers; using and rarefying steam;—applicable to marine, locomotive, and other boilers, marine-architecture, cisterns, tanks, and articles of the like nature.
COOPER, ROBERT - - -	8480	16th April 1840	Ploughs.
COOPER, ROBERT BURTON -	4540	3rd March 1821	Stoppers, covers or lids, for bottles, tobacco and snuff boxes, ink-holders, and other articles (or a substitute for them.)
COOPER, ROBERT BURTON -	6113	18th May 1831	Tap for fluids, liquids, and gases;—applying the improvements to other purposes.
COOPER, ROBERT BURTON -	6485	12th Oct. 1833	Instrument for pointing pencils and for certain other purposes.

Name of Patentee.	Progressive Number.	Date.	Subject-matter of Patent.
COOPER, ROBERT BURTON -	10,930	6th Nov. 1845	Manufacture of taps or cocks; stopping bottles and other vessels.
COOPER, SAMUEL - - -	4570	17th July 1821	Printing.
COOPER, THOMAS - - -	2136	9th Sept. 1796	Machine for mashing or mixing malt or other grain or meal, for brewing or distilling.
COOPER, THOMAS WILLIS -	3413	14th March 1811	Apparatus to be fixed on the naves of wheels, and the beds of axletrees of carriages, to prevent accidents.
COOPER, WILLIAM - -	1619	11th Aug. 1787	Machine for cleaning, spreading, twisting, and cutting cotton, and making wicks for candles.
COOPER, WILLIAM - -	7270	10th Jan. 1837	Executing ornaments, devices, colours, or stains, on glass.
COOPER, WILLIAM - -	8808	21st Jan. 1841	Constructing thrashing-machines and other agricultural implements.
COOPER, WILLIAM - -	11,512	31st Dec. 1846	Manufacture of caps, bonnets, book-covers, curtains and hangings, show-cards, labels, theatrical decorations, and coffins.
COOPER, WILLIAM ARCHIBALD	10,202	23rd May 1844	Machinery for spinning cotton-wool and other fibrous substances.
COOPER, WILLIAM EARNSHAW	14,053	2nd April 1852	Manufacture of candles and candle-wicks; and machinery or apparatus employed therein.
COOTE, SARAH - - -	10,267	24th July 1844	Calking ships, boats, and other vessels.
COPESTAKE, WILLIAM - -	6833	13th May 1835	Making lace.
COPLAND, ROBERT - -	3941	21st July 1815	Effecting a saving in the consumption of fuel.
COPLAND, ROBERT - - -	4024	9th May 1816	Effecting a saving in the consumption of fuel.
COPLAND, ROBERT - - -	4364	1st May 1819	Combinations of apparatus for gaining power.
COPLAND, ROBERT - - -	4749	16th Jan. 1823	Combinations of apparatus for gaining power.
COPLAND, ROBERT - - -	5452	16th Jan. 1827	Combinations of apparatus for gaining power.
COPLAND, ROBERT - - -	7057	9th April 1836	Combinations of apparatus for gaining power.
COPLAND, ROBERT - - -	7216	5th Nov. 1836	Combinations of apparatus for gaining power.
COPLAND, ROBERT - - -	7950	24th Jan. 1839	Water-wheels.
COPLEY, JOHN - - -	38	20th March 1627	Melting iron ore, and making cast iron work and bars, with sea-coals and pit-coals.
COPLEY, JOHN - - -	52	20th March 1630	Making white and bay salt, with sea water and brine, without such pans, furnaces, or other means as are now used.
COPPIN, ELIZABETH - -	532	8th Oct. 1731	Fluxing and fixing mundic into a metal, and extracting silver from it.
COQUATRIX, JEAN BENJAMIN -	13,927	27th Jan. 1852	Apparatus for lubricating machinery.
CORBAUX, MARIE FRANCOIS [CATHERINE DOETZER	8234	7th Oct. 1839	Paints or pigments and vehicles; modes of applying the same.
CORBETT, JAMES - - -	7241	3rd Dec. 1836	Producing harmonic sounds on the harp.
CORBETT, ROSS - - -	5194	21st June 1825	Coach or carriage steps.
CORBETT, THOMAS - - -	7768	10th Aug. 1838	Heating hot-houses and other buildings.
CORCELLIS, CHARLES - -	247	15th Oct. 1685	Making pitch or tar which will preserve ships from the ravages of worms, without sheathing or careening.

Name of Patentee.	Progressive Number.	Date.	Subject-matter of Patent.
CORCORAN, BRYAN - - -	9876	25th Aug. 1843	Grinding wheat and other substances.
CORDEN, ROBERT - - -	10,170	30th April 1844	Apparatus for making gas for illumination.
CORDES, JAMES JAMIESON -	6575	18th March 1834	Machinery for making nails.
CORDES, JAMES JAMIESON -	6576	18th March 1834	Machinery for making rivets and screw-blanks or bolts.
CORDES, JAMES JAMIESON -	6686	8th Oct. 1834	Machinery for making nails.
CORDES, JAMES JAMIESON -	6687	8th Oct. 1834	Machinery for making rivets and screw-blanks or bolts.
CORDES, JAMES JAMIESON -	7486	25th Nov. 1837	Mortar for dressing rough rice or paddy, or redressing rice.
CORDES, JAMES JAMIESON -	8572	18th July 1840	Rotary-engine.
CORMACK, WILLIAM - -	10,289	15th Aug. 1844	Purifying coal-gas.
CORMACK, WILLIAM - -	10,607	10th April 1845	Purifying gas.
CORMACK, WILLIAM - -	11,245	17th June 1846	Obtaining motive-power.
CORMACK, WILLIAM - -	12,975	21st Feb. 1850	Purifying gas; — applicable in obtaining certain products from gas-water, and other similar fluids.
CORNTHWAITE, THOMAS -	1692	7th July 1789	Locks and keys.
CORNWELL, BRYAN - -	1403	1st Dec. 1783	Medicine called " Oriental vegetable cordial ;" making the same from herbs, flowers, and roots.
CORPE, ALFRED RICHARD -	13,919	24th Jan. 1852	Trousers' strap fasteners.
CORRY, JOHN - - -	13,437	2nd Jan. 1851	Machinery for weaving figured fabrics;— applicable to other purposes where Jacquard apparatus is employed.
CORT, HENRY - - -	1351	17th Jan. 1783	Machinery, furnace, and apparatus; for preparing, welding, and working various sorts of iron.
CORT, HENRY - - -	1420	14th Feb. 1784	Shingling, welding, and manufacturing iron and steel into bars, plates, and rods of purer quality and in larger quantity, than heretofore, by a more effectual application of fire and machinery.
CORTY, JOSEPH - - -	4203	20th Jan. 1818	Stills; process of distilling and rectifying.
CORY, HORACE - - -	7846	3rd Nov. 1838	Manufacture of white-lead.
COSNAHAN, MARK - - -	5130	17th March 1825	Apparatus for ascertaining the way or leeway of ships and other vessels;—applicable to other purposes.
COSNAHAN, MARK - - -	6164	20th Sept. 1831	Apparatus for converting salt, brackish, turbid, or impure water, into purified or fresh water; — applicable to other purposes.
COSTA, SOLOMON ISRAEL DE -	12,616	22nd May 1849	Vessels for holding solids or fluids; machinery for manufacturing such vessels.
COSTER, JOHN - - -	397	27th May 1714	Engine for drawing water out of deep mines.
COSTER, JOHN, junior - -	397	27th May 1714	Engine for drawing water out of deep mines.
COSTIGIN, JOHN - - -	5429	13th Dec. 1826	Steam machinery or apparatus.
COTELLE, THEODORE - -	7887	1st Dec. 1838	Extracting the salt from sea-water, and rendering it pure and drinkable; purifying other water.
COTGREAVE, ROBERT - -	13,076	22nd May 1850	Machinery or apparatus to be used in draining land.
COTTAM, ADAM - - -	12,823	2nd Nov. 1849	Machinery to be used in preparing and spinning cotton and other fibrous substances.
COTTAM, EDWARD - - -	11,241	16th July 1846	Bedsteads.

Name of Patentee.	Progres-sive Number.	Date.	Subject-matter of Patent.
COTTAM, EDWARD - - -	12,704	12th July 1849	Machinery for cutting straw, clover, and hay; for grinding, and for sawing wood; apparatus for ascertaining the power employed in working machines.
COTTAM, ELIZABETH - -	10,281	30th July 1844	Heating Italian-irons.
COTTAM, GEORGE - - -	7497	5th Dec. 1837	Construction of wheels for railway and other carriages.
COTTAM, GEORGE - - -	12,704	12th July 1849	Machinery for cutting straw, clover, and hay; for grinding, and for sawing wood; apparatus for ascertaining the power employed in working machines.
COTTAM, SAMUEL FLETCHER -	12,441	25th Jan. 1849	Machinery for preparing, spinning, and doubling cotton-wool, flax, silk, and similar fibrous materials.
COTTER, JOHN BERKELEY -	10,330	26th Sept. 1844	Preparation and manufacture of woven fabrics or tissues;—applicable to various purposes.
COTTER, JOSEPH ROGERSON -	4849	9th Oct. 1823	Wind musical instruments.
COTTERILL, CHARLES FORSTER	9714	27th April 1843	Progressive manufacture of grain into flour or meal.
COTTERILL, EDWIN - -	11,152	25th March 1846	Articles applied to windows, doors, and shutters.
COTTON, SAMUEL - - -	12	28th Jan. 1619	Erecting mills on barges or lighters in the River Thames.
COTTON, WILLIAM - - -	3291	15th Jan. 1810	Regulating the texture of cloth in the process of weaving.
COTTON, WILLIAM - - -	9392	13th June 1842	Weighing-machine.
COTTON, WILLIAM - - -	11,255	22nd June 1846	Knitting-machinery.
COTTY, ABEL - - -	345	15th Nov. 1695	Engine for cutting and rasping logwood and other dyewoods, to be worked either by water, or by hand or horse labour.
COUCH, JAMES - - -	6723	25th Nov. 1834	Ships' channels.
COULLON, JEAN CHARLES [VICTOR	11,936	2nd Nov. 1847	Propelling vessels.
COULON, AUGUSTE - - -	7602	26th March 1838	Block-printing.
COULSON, THOMAS LANE -	11,264	29th June 1846	Construction of chairs.
COUPIER, JEAN THEODORE -	13,979	23rd Feb. 1852	Manufacture of paper.
COUPLAND, FREDERICK - -	3684	28th April 1813	Manufacture of shawls, cords, brunswicks, ribbed and plain cassimeres, and milled cloths, from mixtures of animal and vegetable wool, spun into yarn without oil.
COUPLAND, MICHAEL - -	9063	4th Sept. 1841	Furnaces.
COUPLAND, RICHARD - -	3684	28th April 1813	Manufacture of shawls, cords, brunswicks, ribbed and plain cassimeres, and milled cloths, from mixtures of animal and vegetable wool, spun into yarn without oil.
COURAN, IGNATIUS - - -	578	18th July 1741	Making carpeting, named moccadoes, moucades, or mouquets.
COURNIER, LOUIS - - -	6473	21st Sept. 1833	Curing certain maladies of the head.
COURT, ALEXANDER ALLARD [DE LA	5359	6th May 1826	Instrument applicable to the organ of sight.
COURT, WILLIAM - - -	4967	15th June 1824	Manufacturing salt.
COURTAULD, GEORGE - -	3834	4th Aug. 1814	Spindle for the manufacture of silk thread.
COUTANT, ANTOINE VICTOR -	13,592	15th April 1851	Mode of partially hardening iron for various purposes.
COVE, WILLIAM - - -	378	8th June 1706	Making lampblack.
COWAN, CHARLES - - -	8334	3rd Jan. 1840	Machinery used in the manufacture of paper.
COWAN, CHARLES - - -	11,063	29th Jan. 1846	Manufacture of paper, mill-board, and other similar substances.

Name of Patentee.	Progressive Number.	Date.	Subject-matter of Patent.
COWAN, MALCOLM - - -	2857	11th June 1805	Construction of sails for ships and other vessels.
COWDEN, JOHN - - -	3114	3rd March 1808	Register and other stoves.
COWDEROY, JOHN - - -	5866	2nd Nov. 1829	Machinery for making bricks.
COWDEROY, JOHN - - -	6183	14th Oct. 1831	Machinery to be used in the process of making bread and biscuits.
COWEN, GEORGE - - -	1920	28th Nov. 1792	Construction of cisterns or reservoirs for filtering, cleansing, and purifying water.
COWEN, JOSEPH - - -	10,215	4th June 1844	Making retorts for generating gas for illumination.
COWELL, HENRY BRIDGE -	7738	18th July 1838	Apparatus for retaining leaves or pieces of paper or cloth, or of other thin substances, folded or unfolded, in a flattened condition under gentle pressure.
COWELL, HENRY BRIDGE -	8730	2nd Dec. 1840	Taps for drawing off and stopping the flow of fluids.
COWING, HENRY - - -	12,930	17th Jan. 1850	Obtaining motive-power; steam and other ploughs; land-carriages; fire-engines; raising water for draining and other agricultural purposes; apparatus for evaporating saccharine and other liquors.
COWLEY, JOHN - - -	12,821	2nd Nov. 1849	Manufacture of bedsteads, chairs, tables, couches, and tubular or hollow articles.
COWLING, SAMUEL - -	7435	21st Sept. 1837	Raising water;—applicable to various purposes.
COWPER, CHARLES - - -	12,746	23rd Aug. 1849	Machinery for raising and lowering weights and persons in mines; arrangement and construction of steam-engines employed to put such machinery in motion;—partly applicable to steam-engines generally.
COWPER, CHARLES - - -	12,827	2nd Nov. 1849	Treatment of coal, and separating coal and other substances from foreign matters; manufacture of artificial fuel and coke; distillation and treatment of tar and other products from coal; machinery and apparatus employed for the said purposes.
COWPER, CHARLES - - -	12,844	14th Nov. 1849	Manufacture of sugar.
COWPER, CHARLES - - -	12,856	20th Nov. 1849	Manufacture of sugar.
COWPER, CHARLES - - -	12,861	24th Nov. 1849	Piling, faggoting, and forging iron, for plates, bars, shafts, axles, tires, cannons, anchors, and other similar purposes.
COWPER, CHARLES - - -	12,889	15th Dec. 1849	Instruments for measuring, indicating, and regulating the pressure of air, steam, and other fluids; instruments for measuring and regulating the temperature of the same; and instruments for obtaining motive-power from such fluids.
COWPER, CHARLES - - -	13,417	19th Dec. 1850	Manufacture of files.
COWPER, CHARLES - - -	13,455	16th Jan. 1851	Construction of apparatus for manufacturing, and apparatus for retaining and drawing off, soda-water and other aërated liquors.
COWPER, CHARLES - - -	13,513	17th Feb. 1851	Moulds for electro-metallurgy.
COWPER, CHARLES - - -	13,616	3rd May 1851	Coverings for buildings.
COWPER, CHARLES - - -	13,683	3rd July 1851	Preparation of cotton for dyeing and bleaching.
COWPER, CHARLES - - -	13,705	31st July 1851	Locomotive-engines and boilers, and carriages;—partly applicable to other similar purposes.

Name of Patentee.	Progressive Number.	Date.		Subject-matter of Patent.
COWPER, CHARLES - - -	13,849	8th Dec.	1851	Separating coal from foreign matters, and apparatus for that purpose.
COWPER, CHARLES - - -	13,942	31st Jan.	1852	Multiplying motion; applicable to steam-engines, saw-mills, and other machinery in which an increase of velocity is required.
COWPER, CHARLES - - -	13,977	23d Feb.	1852	Machinery for combing and preparing wool and other fibrous substances.
COWPER, CHARLES - - -	14,278	26th Aug.	1852	Application of iron to building purposes.
COWPER, EBENEZER - -	5955	19th July	1830	Printing-machines.
COWPER, EDWARD - - -	3696	20th May	1813	Machines for cutting the edges of paper and books.
COWPER, EDWARD - - -	3974	10th Jan.	1816	Printing paper for paper-hanging and other purposes.
COWPER, EDWARD - - -	4194	7th Jan.	1818	Printing-presses.
COWPER, EDWARD - - -	4801	10th June	1823	Machines and apparatus for printing calico, linen, silk, wool, paper, or other substances.
COWPER, EDWARD - - -	5484	5th April	1827	Printing music.
COWPER, EDWARD - - -	5631	26th March	1828	Cutting-paper.
COWPER, EDWARD - - -	5900	12th Feb.	1830	Manufacture of gas.
COWPER, EDWARD - - -	5955	19th July	1830	Printing-machines.
COWPER, EDWARD ALFRED -	11,222	26th May	1846	Manufacture of railway-chairs.
COWPER, EDWARD ALFRED -	13,353	19th Nov.	1850	Machinery for loading and discharging certain descriptions of cargo in ships and other vessels; construction of such vessels.
COWPER, TEW - - -	4372	18th May	1819	Machines or ploughs for under-draining land.
COX, CAROLINE JULIA SOPHIA	8416	7th March	1840	Fastening and uniting the edges of the divided parts of shoes, boots, bandages, packages, and other articles of dress or utility.
COX, EDWARD - - -	712	23rd Feb.	1757	Machine for unlading coal-ships in the Pool of the River Thames.
COX, GABRIEL - - -	182	30th July	1675	Working and weaving point-laces after the manner of point de Bouise and point d'Espagne.
COX, GEORGE - - - -	10,042	8th Feb.	1844	Manufacture of leather and gelatine.
COX, GEORGE - - - -	10,477	16th Jan.	1845	Tanning, and leather-dressing.
COX, HENRY - - - -	11,739	10th June	1847	Preserving and preparing wood, bricks, tiles, and other substances.
COX, JAMES FITCHEW -	7478	16th Nov.	1837	Process of tanning.
COX, JOHN - - - -	7042	22nd March	1836	Manufacture of soap;—applicable to the fulling of woollen-cloths.
COX, JOHN - - - -	8709	21st Nov.	1840	Construction of coke-ovens.
COX, JOHN - - - -	8802	19th Jan.	1841	Apparatus for assisting persons to swim or float and progress in water.
COX, JOHN - - - -	9199	21st Dec.	1841	Processes of tanning.
COX, JOHN - - - -	10,042	8th Feb.	1844	Manufacture of leather and gelatine.
COX, JOHN - - - -	10,477	16th Jan.	1845	Tanning and leather-dressing.
COX, PETER - - - -	3294	23rd Jan.	1810	Thrashing-machine.

Name of Patentee.	Progressive Number.	Date.	Subject-matter of Patent.
Cox, Robert Albion - -	894	14th March 1768	Smelting and refining gold, silver, copper, lead and its ores, also the waste and sweepings, as well as the slags, by grinding, washing, and working the same; constructing the smelting and testing furnaces.
Cox, William - - -	13,125	11th June 1850	Machinery or apparatus for manufacturing aërated waters or other such liquids.
Cox, William Hinckes -	7183	15th Sept. 1836	Tanning hides and skins.
Coxe, Matthew - - -	82	6th June 1635	Making wafer-seals.
Coxon, Peter Britus - -	11,629	19th March 1847	Embossing, raising, and forming ornamental figures and designs on intertwined textile fabrics.
Craanen, Daniel - - -	2666	30th Nov. 1802	Making verdigris, in lumps or powder, with ingredients the produce of Great Britain.
Crabb, Isaac - - -	362	10th April 1699	Drawing low wines and spirits from turnips, carrots, and parsnips.
Crabb, Lawrence - -	233	6th March 1684	Grinding logwood and other dyewoods.
Crabtree, Robert - -	5808	4th July 1829	Apparatus for propelling carriages, vessels, and locomotive bodies.
Crackles, Samuel - -	3177	3rd Nov. 1808	Making brushes from whalebone.
Craddock, Thomas -	8432	16th March 1840	Steam-engines and steam-boilers.
Craddock, Thomas -	11,473	3rd Dec. 1846	Steam-engines and boilers, and machinery connected therewith.
Cragg, Edward - - -	3239	8th June 1809	Making or preparing salt.
Cragg, John - - -	3277	21st Nov. 1809	Casting iron-roofs for buildings, and covering them with slate.
Cragg, John - - -	3761	29th Nov. 1813	Facing walls of Gothic or other structures with slates, secured by mouldings, grooves, and tyes of cast iron, so as to have (when sanded) the appearance of finely wrought stone work; also ceilings of the same materials; capping buttresses in Gothic architecture with pinnacles of cast-iron; spiral-stair of cast-iron, for the interior of a tower, wall, or turret.
Cragg, William - - -	3239	8th June 1809	Making or preparing salt
Craig, Alexander - -	6013	20th Oct. 1830	Machinery for cutting timber into veneers or other useful forms.
Craig, Alexander - -	6720	25th Nov. 1834	Steam-engines.
Craig, James - - -	8283	25th Nov. 1839	Machinery for manufacturing paper.
Craig, John - - -	5206	8th July 1825	Manufacture of salt.
Craig, William - - -	8411	3rd March 1840	Machinery for preparing, spinning, and doubling cotton, flax, wool, and other fibrous substances.
Craig, William - - -	9044	11th Aug. 1841	Machinery for preparing and spinning hemp, flax, wool, and other fibrous materials.
Craigie, John - - -	3298	1st Feb. 1810	Making a kitchen fire-place.
Craigie, John - - -	3421	26th March 1811	Waggons, carts, and other wheel-carriages.
Cramer, Jean Michael -	6712	13th Nov. 1834	Steam-engine.
Crampton, Thomas Russell	9261	15th Feb. 1842	Steam-engines and railway-carriages.
Crampton, Thomas Russell	10,768	12th July 1845	Match-boxes for the production of instantaneous light; machinery for manufacturing the same.
Crampton, Thomas Russell	10,854	6th Oct. 1845	Locomotive-engines; and railways.
Crampton, Thomas Russell	11,349	25th Aug. 1846	Locomotive-engines.
Crampton, Thomas Russell	11,760	19th June 1847	Locomotive-engines.

Name of Patentee.	Progressive Number.	Date.	Subject-matter of Patent.
CRAMPTON, THOMAS RUSSELL	12,627	2nd June 1849	Locomotive, marine, and stationary engines; also connecting-apparatus of marine engines.
CRANAGE, GEORGE	851	17th June 1766	Making pig-iron or cast-iron malleable in a reverberatory or air-furnace, with pit-coal only.
CRANAGE, THOMAS	851	17th June 1766	Making pig-iron or cast-iron malleable in a reverberatory or air-furnace, with pit-coal only.
CRANE, CHARLES	12,028	18th Jan. 1848	Manufacture of certain acids and salts, and apparatus applicable for the purpose.
CRANE, GEORGE	7195	28th Sept. 1836	Manufacture of iron.
CRANE, HENRY	6580	20th March 1834	Making and forming iron for hoops of casks, and for other purposes.
CRANE, HENRY SAMUEL	4808	30th June 1823	Manufacture of inflammable gas.
CRANE, JOSIAH	940	16th Nov. 1769	Machine, on which is fixed a set of sliders, to be attached to a stocking-frame, for shading and brocading, working, and making flowers in gold, silver, silk, worsted, cotton, and thread, on silk, thread, cotton, and worsted-pieces, for waistcoats, breeches, stockings, gloves, mits, and all goods made on stocking-frames.
CRANE, JOSIAH	2755	1st May 1804	Double-seaming and uniting the insides of stocking network together.
CRANE, PATRICK MOIR	11,653	8th April 1847	Manufacture of iron.
CRANFIELD, THOMAS	3445	7th May 1811	Machines for spinning and roving cotton, flax, tow, hemp, wool, and silk, and for twisting thread.
CRANNIS, JOSEPH	9640	21st Feb. 1843	Wood-paving.
CRAUFURD, HENRY WILLIAM	7355	29th April 1837	Coating iron and copper, to prevent oxydation.
CRAVEN, THOMAS	678	29th March 1753	Pair of pumps for the use of merchant-ships and colliers.
CRAWFORD, DALRYMPLE	10,807	7th Aug. 1845	Dibbling-machine.
CRAWFORD, DALRYMPLE	10,906	31st Oct. 1845	Machinery for arresting the progress of railway carriages and trains.
CRAWFORD, MAURICE	967	10th Aug. 1770	Tinning copper-work.
CRAWFORD, ROBERT RUMNEY	13,171	10th July 1850	Drying paper.
CRAWFORD, THOMAS	974	20th Dec. 1770	Engine for winding silk-thread and yarn and for framing at the same time, and also for winding single, double, and several threads together at once.
CRAWHALL, JOSEPH	6294	8th Aug. 1832	Manufacture of flat rope for use in mines.
CRAWHALL, JOSEPH	10,086	2nd March 1844	Machinery for manufacturing ropes and cordage.
CRAWSHAY, WILLIAM	4248	18th April 1818	Making bar or other iron, from slag or cinders produced in smelting copper ores and manufacturing copper.
CREASE, HAROLD	11,306	23rd July 1846	Preparation of paints and colours for decorative and other similar purposes.
CREASE, JAMES	1336	1 Aug. 1782	Pot or pan applied to a night-stool to prevent offensive smell.
CREED, JAMES	579	9th Sept. 1741	Three engines for cutting sheet-lead for water-pipes, and for covering buildings; pump with a perpendicular stroke for raising water or for extinguishing fires.
CREED, SIR JAMES	651	13th Dec. 1749	Making white-lead; casting lead to be used for milling, for the covering of churches or other buildings.

Name of Patentee.	Progres-sive Number.	Date.	Subject-matter of Patent.
CREIGHTON, HENRY - -	4282	22nd July 1818	Regulating the admission of steam into pipes or other vessels used for heating buildings, or other places.
CRELLIN, JAMES - - -	7421	24th Aug. 1837	Waterclosets.
CRESSWELL, JOSEPH - -	1759	10th July 1790	Engine for washing linen, woollen, or any other article.
CRESSWELL, JOSEPH - -	2085	4th Feb. 1796	"Quadrant pump."
CRICKMER, FREDERICK WIL-[LIAM.	13,682	3rd July 1851	Packing stuffing-boxes and pistons.
CRICKMER, RICHARD JEX -	13,682	3rd July 1851	Packing stuffing-boxes and pistons.
CRIGHTON, JOHN - -	4764	18th March 1823	Construction of the cylinders of carding-engines, and other machines used in preparing for spinning cotton, flax, wool, silk, and mixtures of such substances.
CRIGHTON, JOHN - - -	7262	21st Dec. 1836	Construction of cylinders used in carding-engines for carding cotton-wool, silk, and other fibrous materials.
CRIGHTON, JOHN, junior -	8057	7th May 1839	Machinery for weaving single, double, and treble cloths, by hand or power.
CRIGHTON, JOHN, junior -	8317	16th Dec. 1839	Machinery for weaving single, double, and treble cloths, by hand or power.
CRIGHTON, WILLIAM -	4764	18th March 1823	Construction of the cylinders of carding-engines, and other machines used in preparing for spinning cotton, flax, wool, silk, and mixtures of such substances.
CRISPE, WILLIAM - -	572	9th Aug. 1740	Double shaft and pole carriage, with two wheels, and drawn by two horses harnessed a-breast.
CRISPIN, WILLIAM - -	2713	14th June 1803	Making and working windlasses.
CROCKFORD, JOSHUA -	8165	20th July 1839	Applying cotton and other wicks to tallow, and other like substances used for candles.
CROCKFORD, JOSHUA -	14,006	8th March 1852	Brewing, and brewing-apparatus.
CROFTS, FRANCIS - -	38	20th March 1627	Melting iron ore, and making cast-iron work and bars, with sea-coals and pit-coals.
CROFTS, WILLIAM - -	6229	23rd Feb. 1832	Machinery for making bobbin-net lace.
CROFTS, WILLIAM - -	6349	18th Dec. 1832	Machinery for making bobbin-net lace.
CROFTS, WILLIAM - -	6382	11th Feb. 1833	Machinery for making bobbin-net lace.
CROFTS, WILLIAM - -	6383	11th Feb. 1833	Combining and actuating machinery for making bobbin-net lace.
CROFTS, WILLIAM - -	6447	4th July 1833	Machinery for making bobbin-net.
CROFTS, WILLIAM - -	6618	27th May 1834	Machinery for making bobbin-net lace.
CROFTS, WILLIAM - -	6717	20th Nov. 1834	Machinery for making ornamented bobbin-net lace.
CROFTS, WILLIAM - -	6739	23rd Dec. 1834	Machinery for making ornamented bobbin-net lace.
CROFTS, WILLIAM - -	6854	26th June 1835	Machinery for making ornamented bobbin-net lace.
CROFTS, WILLIAM - -	6871	30th July 1835	Machinery for making ornamented bobbin-net lace.
CROFTS, WILLIAM - -	6921	4th Nov. 1835	Machinery for making bobbin-net lace, parts of which are for making ornamented bobbin-net lace.
CROFTS, WILLIAM - -	7190	22nd Sept. 1836	Machinery for making bobbin-net lace or twist net, parts of which are for making ornamented bobbin-net lace or twist lace.
CROFTS, WILLIAM - -	7345	18th April 1837	Manufacture of figured and ornamented bobbin-net or twist lace, or other fabrics.

Name of Patentee.	Progres-sive Number.	Date.	Subject-matter of Patent.
CROFTS, WILLIAM - - -	7638	10th May 1838	Manufacture of lace.
CROFTS, WILLIAM - - -	8038	20th April 1839	Machinery used in making ornamented bob-bin-net lace, and lace or net of various sorts.
CROFTS, WILLIAM - - -	8430	16th March 1840	Machinery for making ornamented bobbin-net or twist lace, and other ornamented fabrics looped or woven.
CROFTS, WILLIAM - - -	8690	7th Nov. 1840	Machinery for making figured bobbin-net or twist lace, and other ornamental fabrics looped or woven.
CROFTS, WILLIAM - - -	9467	8th Sept. 1842	Manufacture of figured or ornamented lace.
CROFTS, WILLIAM - - -	10,370	31st Oct. 1844	Manufacture of figured or ornamented lace or net of various textures.
CROFTS, WILLIAM - - -	10,390	13th Nov. 1844	Manufacture of lace and other weavings.
CROFTS, WILLIAM - - -	11,344	20th Aug. 1846	Manufacture of lace and other fabrics.
CROLL, ALEXANDER - -	7748	26th July 1838	Manufacture of gas for affording light.
CROLL, ALEXANDER ANGUS -	8253	2nd Nov. 1839	Manufacture of gas; reconverting salts used in purifying gas; manufacture of am-moniacal salts.
CROLL, ALEXANDER ANGUS -	8577	29th July 1840	Manufacture of gas for illumination; prepa-ration of materials for the purification of gas.
CROLL, ALEXANDER ANGUS -	9663	16th March 1843	Manufacture of gas for illumination; ap-paratus used when transmitting and measuring gas or other fluids.
CROLL, ALEXANDER ANGUS -	10,096	7th March 1844	Manufacture of gas for illumination; ap-paratus used when transmitting and measuring gas.
CROLL, ALEXANDER ANGUS -	10,739	26th June 1845	Manufacturing, measuring, and transmitting gas; obtaining ammoniacal and other products from the refuse.
CROLL, ALEXANDER ANGUS -	11,205	13th May 1846	Gas-meters.
CROLL, ALEXANDER ANGUS -	12,251	22nd Aug. 1848	Manufacture of gas; apparatus for trans-mitting gas.
CROMPTON, THOMAS BONSOR -	4509	1st Nov. 1820	Drying and finishing paper.
CROMPTON, THOMAS BONSOR -	5655	13th May 1828	Cutting paper.
CROMPTON, THOMAS BONSOR -	8027	9th April 1839	Manufacture of paper.
CROMWELL, SAMUEL THOMAS	10,937	11th Nov. 1845	Apparatus to be applied to piano-fortes.
CRONIER, PIERRE MARCISSE -	8296	4th Dec. 1839	Filters; cleansing the same; separating colouring and tanning matters by filtra-tion; employing such matters.
CROOK, JEREMIAH - - -	7214	28th Oct. 1836	Machinery for manufacturing hat-bodies.
CROOK, JOHN ROWLAND -	13,743	11th Sept. 1851	Hats, caps, and bonnets.
CROOK, THOMAS - - -	2032	12th Jan. 1795	Machine for the prevention and cure of smoky chimneys.
CROOK, THOMAS - - -	13,667	17th June 1851	Looms for weaving.
CROOK, WILLIAM - - -	10,832	18th Sept. 1845	Looms for weaving.
CROOKER, MATTHEW AUGUS-[TUS.	14,192	28th June 1852	Paddles for steam-vessels.
CROOKS, JOHN - - -	2204	12th Dec. 1797	Making soap, and bleaching by means and use of mineral and vegetable alkalies.
CROOKS, JOHN - - -	2342	23rd Sept. 1799	Manufacture of soap; bleaching by volatile, mineral, and vegetable alkalies, either conjointly or alone; killing vermin.
CROOKSHANK, JAMES - -	912	21st Dec. 1768	Manufacturing a silk-stuff equal in quality to Italian crapé or tiffany.

Name of Patentee.	Progressive Number.	Date.	Subject-matter of Patent.
CROOTE, FRANCIS - - -	46	13th April 1629	Making white and bay salt from sea-water, sea-sand, and other materials.
CROPPER, EDWARD - - -	831	18th June 1765	Making alum from liquor obtained from copperas materials and uncalcined ore.
CROPPER, JAMES - - -	6931	14th Nov. 1835	Machinery for embroidering bobbin-net or lace, and cloths, stuffs, or other fabrics made from silk, cotton-wool, flax or hemp.
CROPPER, JAMES - - -	6937	3rd Dec. 1835	Machinery for making bobbin-net lace.
CROSBY, BENJAMIN - -	3153	25th July 1808	Stand for books, with cases to receive books and other articles.
CROSBY, THOMAS - - -	2031	12th Jan. 1795	Regulating-machine for fire-places and flues.
CROSFIELD, JOSEPH -	8448	25th March 1840	Manufacture of plate-glass.
CROSHER, WILLIAM -	9210	24th Dec. 1841	Bolt for building and other purposes.
CROSLAND, JAMES STEAD -	8463	2nd April 1840	Locomotive and other steam-engines.
CROSLEY, HENRY - - -	6590	8th April 1834	Arrangement and combination of apparatus, with certain agents used therewith, for the evaporation of fluids and solutions, and for other purposes.
CROSLEY, HENRY - - -	8032	15th April 1839	Manufacture of paper.
CROSLEY, HENRY - - -	8258	7th Nov. 1839	Battery, or arrrangement of apparatus for the manufacture of sugar.
CROSLEY, HENRY - - -	9574	28th Dec. 1842	Manufacture of sugar, and the products of sugar.
CROSLEY, HENRY - - -	11,158	3rd April 1846	Manufacture of sugar; machinery and apparatus employed therein.
CROSLEY, HENRY - - -	12,491	28th Feb. 1849	Mode and apparatus for heating and lighting, for drying substances, and for employing air for manufacturing purposes.
CROSLEY, JOHN - - -	4947	5th May 1824	Construction of lamps or lanterns so as to protect the light from wind or motion.
CROSLEY, JOHN - - -	5027	4th Nov. 1824	Egress of smoke and rarefied air in certain situations.
CROSLEY, SAMUEL - - -	5088	1st Feb. 1825	Apparatus for measuring and registering the quantity of liquids passing from one place to another.
CROSLEY, SAMUEL - - -	5089	1st Feb. 1825	Construction of gas-regulators or governors.
CROSLEY, SAMUEL - - -	5530	1st Aug. 1827	Constructing and working an engine for producing power and motion.
CROSLEY, SAMUEL - - -	6174	3rd Oct. 1831	Gas-meter.
CROSS, CHRISTOPHER - -	13,249	5th Sept. 1850	Manufacture of textile fabrics; also manufacture of wearing-apparel and other articles from textile materials; machinery for effecting the same.
CROSS, CHRISTOPHER - -	13,585	8th April 1851	Textile fabrics, and manufacture of wearing-apparel from textile materials.
CROSS, ROBERT - - -	2179	26th April 1797	Tan-pit, and mode of tanning.
CROSS, ROBERT - - -	2746	31st Dec. 1803	Heating pans, vats, cisterns, and other vessels used for working steam-engines, also used in calico-printing, dyeing, brewing, paper-making, bleaching, salt-making, tanning and for other purposes.
CROSSE, ANDREW - - -	11,604	2nd March 1847	Precipitating- or extracting impurities from fermentable and other liquids.
CROSSE, ANDREW - - -	12,618	24th May 1849	Tanning hides and skins; dyeing fabrics and substances.
CROSSE, ANDREW - - -	14,280	26th Aug. 1852	Extraction of metals from their ores.
CROSSKILL, WILLIAM - -	9082	8th Sept. 1841	Machinery for rolling and crushing land; machinery for the culture of grass-land.

Name of Patentee.	Progressive Number.	Date.	Subject-matter of Patent.
CROSSKILL, WILLIAM - -	10,131	30th March 1844	Machinery for making wheels for carriages.
CROSSKILL, WILLIAM - -	13,214	6th Aug. 1850	Mills for grinding, splitting, pulverizing, and crushing grain, bones, bark, ore, and other hard substances, grinding paint and other soft substances, shelling rice and other grain; machinery for giving rotary-motion to mills, thrashing-machines, and other machinery worked by animal power.
CROSSLEY, HENRY - - -	7469	11th Nov. 1837	Obtaining saccharine-matter from beet-root and other vegetable substances.
CROSSLEY, JOSEPH - - -	13,267	28th Sept. 1850	Printing yarns for carpets and other fabrics; weaving such fabrics.
CROSSLEY, JOSEPH - - -	13,474	28th Jan. 1851	Manufacture of carpets, rugs, and other fabrics.
CROSSLEY, WILSON - -	10,992	10th Dec. 1845	Machinery for preparing and spinning cotton and other fibrous substances.
CROUCHER, JOSEPH - -	10,355	17th Oct. 1844	Construction and arrangement of machinery for clearing, cleansing, watering, breaking up and raking, streets, roads, lands, and other ways.
CROUÉE, JULES THIEBEAULD [DE LA	10,114	19th March 1845	Apparatus for purifying, clarifying, and refining vegetable extracts.
CROUTELLE, EMANUEL CHARLES [THEODORE.	13,953	3rd Feb. 1852	Machinery for preparing woollen threads, and other filamentous substances, for weaving.
CROUY, HENRY DE - - -	7902	12th Dec. 1838	Filtration.
CROUY, NICOLAS HENRI JEAN [FRANCOIS Comte de.	9678	25th March 1843	Rotary-pumps, and rotary steam-engines.
CROW, FRANCIS - - -	3644	30th Jan. 1813	Mariners' compass, or boat-compass.
CROWDER, JOSEPH - - -	5179	31st May 1825	Pusher bobbin-net machine.
CROWLEY, THOMAS - -	1153	26th April 1777	Machine for splitting, cutting, paring, shreading, or dividing in length and breadth, hides, skins, and leather; also cutting, sawing, splitting or dividing, wood, cork, bone, horn, ivory or other substances.
CROWLEY, THOMAS - -	1280	26th July 1780	Engine to cut, split and divide asunder, hides, skins, and leather, in length and breadth.
CROWTHER, JOHN - - -	14,340	2nd Nov. 1852	Self-acting hydraulic crane or engine for lifting weights (such weights when lifted to be used as motive-power), and for loading and unloading vessels and vehicles.
CROWTHER, PHINEHAS - -	2378	28th Feb. 1800	Applying the power of a reciprocating steam-engine to the crank or rotative axis, for drawing coals, lead, tin, &c. out of mines, or for carrying or drawing machinery for any other purpose.
CROXTON, REBECCA - -	182	30th July 1675	Working and weaving point-laces after the manner of point de Bouise and point d'Espagne.
CRUCKSHANKS, ALEXANDER -	8141	3rd July 1839	Producing certain inflammable substances; applying the heat and light obtained from the same to various useful purposes.
CRUDGINGTON, CHARLES -	10,038	8th Feb. 1844	Manufacture of iron and steel.
CRUM, WALTER - - -	12,871	3rd Dec. 1849	Finishing woven fabrics.
CRUMPE, ROBERT - - -	8	9th Jan. 1618	Erecting a tunnel or pipe of timber or lead, with engines for draining and drawing water from mines, coal-pits, or other minerals, and for raising water for towns, castles, and houses.

Name of Patentee.	Progressive Number.	Date.	Subject-matter of Patent.
CRUMPE, ROBERT	29	4th March 1624	Three engines for draining water out of mines, minerals, and coal-pits, and for raising and bringing water into towns, castles, and houses.
CRUMPLER, JOHN	814	18th June 1764	Weaving gold and silver wire and copper wire gilt, either with cotton, silk, thread, or yarn.
CRUMPLER, JOHN	1013	15th April 1772	Throwing silk to make tiffany and crape; engine for dressing such silk when thrown and woven, and for finishing the same.
CRUNDWELL, JOHN	5845	15th Sept. 1829	Apparatus to be applied to fowling-pieces in place of locks.
CRUPLEY, JOHN	127	24th June 1642	Raising water to great heights to bore timber with a wooden augur; laying piles without driving; raising weights.
CRUTCHETT, JAMES	9416	12th July 1842	Manufacturing gas; apparatus for consuming gas.
CUBITT, WILLIAM	3041	9th May 1807	Equalizing the motion of windmill-sails.
CUBITT, WILLIAM	8371	31st Jan. 1840	Roofing.
CUERTON, RICHARD, jun.	8390	22nd Feb. 1840	Manufacture of cornices, mouldings, and window-sashes.
CUERTON, RICHARD, jun.	8419	7th March 1840	Extracting and concentrating the colour, tannin, and other matter contained in vegetable and animal substances.
CUFF, JOSEPH	3165	25th Aug. 1808	Machinery for slaughtering hogs, bullocks, and other cattle.
CULLIN, ABRAHAM	35	24th Oct. 1626	Making stone-pots, stone-jugs, and stone-bottles.
CULLIN, THOMAS	12,331	18th Nov. 1848	Apparatus for steering ships and other vessels.
CULLOCH, JOHN Mc	11,862	9th Sept. 1847	Apparatus for distilling and rectifying.
CULPEPPER, SirTHOMAS, Knight	80	10th March 1635	Making salt; with power to erect works for the purpose, on waste land near the sea coast.
CUMBERLAND, JOHN	427	14th April 1720	Heating, drying, seasoning, and bending wood, plank, or board, also ships' timbers.
CUMING, WILLIAM	3789	12th March 1814	Wheels and axle-trees for carriages.
CUMMEROW, CHARLES	5730	10th Dec. 1828	Propelling vessels.
CUMMING, ALEXANDER	1105	11th Nov. 1775	Water-closet.
CUMMING, DONALD	3468	26th July 1811	Machine for cutting and reaping grass, corn, and other articles.
CUMMING, JOHN	14,102	29th April 1852	Production of surfaces for printing or ornamenting fabrics.
CUMMINGS, GEORGE	809	31st March 1764	Composition to be laid on skins, paper, or linen, for drawing or writing on with pen and ink, or pencil, and rubbing off clean.
CUMMINS, CHARLES	8462	2nd April 1840	Barometers and sympiesometers.
CUNDELL, HENRY	2429	16th July 1800	Composition for destroying rats or other vermin ("Cundell's Myoctonus").
CUNDY, THOMAS SYSON	10,248	3rd July 1844	Construction and arrangement of stoves and fire-places.
CUNINGHAME, ALEXANDER	14,013	8th March 1852	Treatment and application of slag, or the refuse matter of blast-furnaces.
CUNLIFFE, JOHN TATTERSALL	11,701	14th May 1847	Pickers for power-looms; apparatus for manufacturing the same.
CUNNINGHAM, ALBERT RO-[BERT.	11,387	1st Oct. 1846	Propelling carriages on railways.

Name of Patentee.	Progressive Number.	Date.	Subject-matter of Patent.
Cunningham, Andrew -	8897	22nd March 1841	Manufacture of bricks.
Cunningham, Henry Duncan Preston.	13,368	30th Nov. 1850	Reefing sails.
Cunningham. William -	2026	28th Nov. 1794	Manufacturing paper of various sorts.
Curdy, John Mᶜ - - -	6368	22nd Jan. 1833	Machinery for acquiring power in rivers and currents.
Curdy, John Mᶜ - - -	6819	23rd April 1835	Generating steam.
Curdy, John Mᶜ - - -	7890	1st Dec. 1838	Generating steam, and applying the same to the evaporation and boiling of fluids;—applicable to steam-engines, and for other purposes.
Curr, John - - - -	1660	12th Aug. 1788	Raising coals, lead, and other minerals out of mines, so as to prevent the corves running foul of each other; platform for landing and delivering.
Curr, John - - - -	1924	17th Dec. 1792	Applying ropes for raising coals, metals, or minerals out of mines, or for conveying goods in situations where ropes are worked over wheels, rollers, sheaves, or pullies.
Curr, John - - - -	2270	17th Nov. 1798	Making flat rope, for use in drawing coals and other materials out of pits or mines.
Curr, John - - - -	2891	16th Nov. 1805	Laying ropes.
Curr, John - - - -	2914	8th March 1806	Spinning hemp for making ropes or cordage.
Curr, John - - - -	2947	4th July 1806	Applying cables of ships and vessels upon the windlasses, capstans, or drums.
Curr, John - - - -	2960	23rd Aug. 1806	Laying and twisting yarns for making ropes.
Curr, John - - - -	3157	30th July 1808	Applying flat ropes and flat bands or belts to capstans and windlasses of ships and vessels, for towing the same; applying flat or round ropes, lines, bands, or belts, for catching and detaining whales.
Curr, John - - - -	3502	30th Oct. 1811	Laying ropes.
Curr, John - - - -	3711	29th June 1813	Applying flat ropes to horse-gins and perpendicular drum-shafts of steam-engines, for mining purposes.
Currie, Donald - - -	5614	31st Jan. 1828	Preserving grain, and other vegetable and animal substances and liquids.
Currie, Henry William -	12,646	7th June 1849	Manufacture of coach-lace, and other similar looped or cut pile fabrics.
Curtain, William - -	12,388	21st Dec. 1848	Manufacturing Brussels tapestry, Turkey and velvet or cut-pile carpets, also velvets and silk, linen, and mixed cloths, and rugs.
Curtis, Charles Berwick -	8803	19th Jan. 1841	Making signals by self-acting apparatus, to be used on railways to obviate collisions.
Curtis, James - - -	2958	20th Aug. 1806	Boilers for manufacturing sugar; fixing the same.
Curtis, Joseph - - -	7792	31st Aug. 1838	Machinery and apparatus for facilitating travelling and transport on railways;—partly applicable to other purposes.
Curtis, Matthew - - -	9798	22nd June 1843	Looms for weaving.
Curtis, Matthew - - -	11,902	14th Oct. 1847	Machines for preparing and spinning cotton and other fibrous substances; preparing to be woven and weaving such substances when spun.
Curtis, Richard Gill -	6007	6th Oct. 1830	Glazing horticultural and other buildings; sash-bars and rafters.
Curtis, William Joseph -	7436	21st Sept. 1837	Boiler or apparatus for generating steam.

Name of Patentee.	Progres-sive Number.	Name.	Subject-matter of Patent.
CURTIS, WILLIAM JOSEPH -	13,014	23rd March 1850	Machinery and apparatus adapted for the manufacture of sugar.
CURZON, HENRY - - -	8034	16th April 1839	Presses.
CURZON, HENRY - - -	8365	28th Jan. 1840	Steam-engines.
CURZON, HENRY - - -	13,766	9th Oct. 1851	Manufacture of carpets and rugs.
CUSSONS, THOMAS - - -	13,761	2nd Oct. 1851	Ornamenting woven fabrics for book-binding.
CUSTIS, EDMUND - - -	163	16th March 1671	Discovery of wrecks and vessels sunk, also taking out of them goods, treasures, merchandise, guns, and ships' furniture.
CUTHBERT, JOHN - - -	298	31st May 1692	Diving-habit, for enabling a man to work one hour under water, by means of an air-pump.
CUTLER, JOB - - - -	7732	12th July 1838	Condensing steam in steam-engines; and supplying the boilers of the same with the water obtained.
CUTLER, JOB - - - -	7909	17th Dec. 1838	Combinations of metals for making tubes or pipes, and for other purposes; making the said tubes; applicable to the making of tubes or pipes from other metals and combinations of metals.
CUTLER, JOB - - - -	7999	12th March 1839	Constructing chains for suspension-bridges, cables, mining and other purposes; making the bars, links, and bolts thereof.
CUTLER, JOB - - - -	8232	3rd Oct. 1839	Combinations of metals to be used for various purposes.
CUTLER, JOB - - - -	8395	22nd Feb. 1840	Cutting corks, and constructing the necks of bottles.
CUTLER, JOB - - - -	9140	6th Nov. 1841	Construction of the tubular-flues of steam-boilers.
CUTLER, JOB - - - -	9707	20th April 1843	Machinery to be used in manufacturing pipes and bars; application of such pipes or bars to various purposes.
CUTLER, JOB - - - -	12,021	13th Jan. 1848	Welded iron pipes or tubes to be used as the flues of steam-boilers.
CUTLER, JOB - - - -	12,500	28th Feb. 1849	Manufacture of metal pipes or tubes.
CUTTEAN, PETER JAMES -	2491	28th Aug. 1801	Waterproofing woollen-cloths, cotton, linen, silk, hats, paper, and other substances.
CUTTEL, JOSHUA - - -	7290	26th Jan. 1837	Producing slubbings of wool; spinning wool.
CUTTEN, JOHN - - -	8254	2nd Nov. 1839	Garden-pots.
CUTTLER, JOHN - - -	3873	6th Jan. 1815	Fire-places, stoves, &c.
CUTTS, JOHN - - - -	8326	21st Dec. 1839	Machinery for making wire-cards for carding cotton, silk, wool, and other fibrous substances.
CYNELME, LEMUEL DOLE -	1082	12th Sept. 1774	Alarm, whereby sedan-chairs, coaches, chariots, post-chaises and other carriages, may be immediately stopped and their attendants summoned, in case of danger.

D.

DAALEN, JAMES VAN - -	353	25th Feb. 1698	Engine or carriage with four wheels and double troubles, which open in the middle, shoot the load at once, and return into their places again.

Name of Patentee.	Progressive Number.	Name.		Subject-matter of Patent.
DACIE, JOHN - - - -	11,478	7th Dec.	1846	Apparatus to be fixed to boots and shoes, for protecting the wearer from splashes in walking.
DA COSTA, SOLOMON ISRAEL -	12,616	22nd May	1849	Vessels for holding solids or fluids; machinery for manufacturing such vessels.
DACRE, RICHARD LORD - -	33	8th April	1626	Making steel; apparatus for the purpose.
DAFT, THOMAS BARNABAS -	7959	2nd Feb.	1839	Inkstands; materials and apparatus for fastening and sealing letters or other documents.
DAFT, THOMAS BARNABAS -	8584	1st Aug.	1840	Inkstands.
DAFT, THOMAS BARNABAS -	10,568	17th March	1845	Springs to be applied to girths, belts, and bandages; manufacture of elastic bands.
DAFT, THOMAS BARNABAS -	11,554	1st Feb.	1847	Constructing inkstands; fastenings to elastic bands.
DAFT, THOMAS BARNABAS -	11,808	20th July	1847	Manufacture of elastic fabrics and articles.
DAILEY, WILLIAM JAMES -	12,104	22nd March	1848	Machinery for propelling.
DAIN, CHRISTOPHER - -	8532	2nd June	1840	Construction of vessels for containing and supplying ink and other fluids.
DAKEYNE, DANIEL - -	1961	16th Sept.	1793	Machine applied to and used with rollers, wheels, or any other instruments, for preparing and spinning flax, hemp, tow, wool, jersey-hair, or other animal, vegetable, or fossil substance into yarn, or thread. ("Equalinum.")
DAKEYNE, EDWARD - -	5882	21st Jan.	1830	Hydraulic-engine, for applying the pressure of water, steam, and other elastic fluids, to the working of machinery and other uses requiring power;—applicable to raising or forcing fluids.
DAKEYNE, JAMES - -	5882	21st Jan.	1830	Hydraulic-engine, for applying the pressure of water, steam, and other elastic fluids, to the working of machinery and other uses requiring power;—applicable to raising or forcing fluids.
DAKIN, ELIZABETH - -	12,198	3rd July	1848	Cleaning and roasting coffee; apparatus and machinery used therein; apparatus for making infusions and decoctions of coffee.
DAKIN, WILLIAM - - -	11,988	8th Dec.	1847	Cleaning and roasting coffee; apparatus and machinery used therein; apparatus for making infusions and decoctions of coffee.
DAKING, THOMAS - - -	3692	8th May	1813	Heating liquors for the manufacture of leather and other manufactures.
DALE, JOHN - - - -	1950	18th April	1793	Conducting and generating steam for steam-engines.
DALE, JOHN - - - -	4167	3rd Oct.	1817	Application of a certain material to the making of rollers or cylinders.
DALE, JOSEPH - - -	2295	19th Feb.	1799	Tambourines.
DALE, WILLIAM - - -	7592	14th March	1838	Constructing columns, pillars, bed-posts, and other like articles.
DALGLISH, ROBERT - [Dalglish, Robert, junior.]	6042	6th Dec.	1830	Machinery or apparatus for printing calicoes and other fabrics.
DALGLISH, ROBERT - -	13,068	7th May	1850	Printing; application of colours to silk, cotton, linen, woollen, and other textile fabrics.
DALLAS, ALEXANDER - -	4944	27th April	1824	Machine to pick and dress stones, particularly granite.
DALLOW, EDWARD - - -	212	25th Jan.	1681	Draining mines.
DALLOWS, PHILLIP - -	303	22nd Sept.	1692	Making Granado-shells, of glass.

Name of Patentee.	Progressive Number.	Date.	Subject-matter of Patent.
DALTON, ALFRED - - -	12,895	15th Dec. 1849	Reverberatory and other furnaces.
DALTON, DANIEL - - -	13,602	26th April 1851	Railroads.
DALTON, JAMES FORBES -	3034	21st April 1807	Construction of four-wheel carriages.
DALTON, JOHN - - -	12,597	1st May 1849	Printing calicoes and other surfaces.
DALTON, JOHN - - -	12,942	26th Jan. 1850	Machinery for bleaching, dyeing, printing, and finishing textile and other fabrics; engraving copper-rollers and other metallic bodies.
DALTON, THOMAS - - -	12,180	8th June 1848	Manufacture of fringes, gimps, and bullions.
DALVIGNE, HENRY GUSTAVE -	14,066	17th April 1852	Fire-arms, and methods of discharging the same; projectiles.
DAM, FREDERICK - - -	14,272	23d Aug. 1852	Preventing incrustation in boilers.
DAMPIER, CHRISTOPHER ED-[WARD.	8342	14th Jan. 1840	Weighing-machine.
DAMPIER, CHRISTOPHER ED-[WARD.	8924	15th April 1841	Weighing-machines.
DAMPIER, EDWARD - -	2916	12th March 1806	Machinery for rasping, grating, and reducing into small parts or powder, wood, drugs, and other substances, for the use of dyers.
DANBY, GEORGE - - -	96	4th March 1636	Melting and casting copper into ingots so as to make it tough; drawing the same.
DANCE, CHARLES WEBB, SIR -	5977	5th Aug. 1830	Packing and transporting goods.
DANCE, CHARLES WEBB, SIR -	6262	8th April 1832	Steam-boilers.
DANCE, CHARLES WEBB, SIR -	6465	20th Aug. 1833	Boilers, and other apparatus for locomotive carriages.
DANCHELL, FREDERICK LUD-[WIG HAHN.	6779	28th Feb. 1835	Pianofortes.
DANFORTH, THOMAS - -	1047	19th July 1773	Condensing steam arising in distillation, in the worm tube or steam vessel, by keeping cold water applied constantly or otherwise, around the worm.
DANIEL, JAMES - - -	1871	25th April 1792	Machine for felting and making hats.
DANIEL, ROBERT - - -	1141	16th Dec. 1776	Spring-boots.
DANIEL, WILLIAM - - -	696	23d Jan. 1755	Machine worked by water, wind, or horses, for dressing, winnowing, and cleansing flax.
DANIEL, CLISILD - - -	4987	7th July 1824	Weaving woollen-cloth.
DANIELL, FRANCIS - -	9721	4th May 1843	Obtaining lime from substances not hitherto used for the purpose.
DANIELL, FREDERICK - -	5454	1st Feb. 1827	Manufacture of gas.
DANIELL, JOHN FREDERICK -	4528	15th Jan. 1821	Clarifying and refining sugar.
DANIELL, JOSEPH CLISILD -	3348	19th June 1810	Machines named gigs, and shearing-frames, for dressing cloths.
DANIELL, JOSEPH CLISILD -	4391	17th July 1819	Dressing woollen-cloths; preparing and using wire-cards for the purpose.
DANIELL, JOSEPH CLISILD -	5038	20th Nov. 1824	Dressing woollen-cloth.
DANIELL, JOSEPH CLISILD -	5266	13th Oct. 1825	Machinery for weaving woollen-cloth.
DANIELL, JOSEPH CLISILD -	5504	8th June 1827	Preparing wire-cards; dressing woollen and other cloths.
DANIELL, JOSEPH CLISILD -	5598	2nd Jan. 1828	Dressing cloths; and machinery for the purpose.
DANIELL, JOSEPH CLISLID -	5679	5th Aug. 1828	Manufacturing and preparing woollen-cloth.
DANIELL, JOSEPH CLISLID -	5706	18th Sept. 1828	Machinery for dressing woollen-cloths.
DANIELL, JOSEPH CLISLID -	5795	26th May 1829	Machinery for dressing woollen-cloth.

Name of Patentee.	Progressive. Number.	Date.		Subject-matter of Patent.
DANIELL, JOSEPH CLISILD -	5812	8th July	1829	Machinery for dressing woollen-cloth.
DANIELL, JOSEPH CLISILD -	5897	6th Feb.	1830	Machinery for manufacturing woollen-cloths.
DANIELL, JOSEPH CLISILD .	6685	25th Sept.	1834	Manufacturing or preparing woollen-cloth.
DANIELL, JOSEPH CLISILD -	7385	6th June	1837	Stone-masonry.
DANIELL, JOSEPH CLISILD -	7927	9th Jan.	1839	Weaving woollen-cloths, and cloths made of wool together with other materials.
DANIELL, JOSEPH CLISILD -	8409	3rd March	1840	Preparing weft for use in weaving woollen-cloth, and cloths made of wool and other materials.
DANIELL, JOSEPH CLISILD -	9111	7th Oct.	1841	Manufacture of manure, or a composition to be used on land as a manure.
DANIELL, JOSEPH CLISILD -	9309	31st March	1842	Making and preparing food for cattle.
DANIELL, JOSEPH CLISILD -	10,869	10th Oct.	1845	Dressing and finishing woollen and other cloths.
DANIELL, WILLIAM - -	4667	16th April	1822	Rolling iron into bars used for making tin-plates.
DANIELL, WILLIAM - -	9849	22nd July	1843	Rolling iron into plates or sheets.
DANINOS, ALEXANDER - -	5767	5th Feb.	1829	Manufacture of hats and bonnets, in imitation of Leghorn straw hats and bonnets.
DANRE, GEORGE - - -	5860	2nd Nov.	1829	Self-acting air or gas regulator or stop-cock, for governing the flow of air or gas;—applicable to other purposes.
DARBY, JOHN - - -	4412	23d Nov.	1819	Machine and apparatus for a fire burglary alarum.
DARBY, ROBERT - - -	2394	1st May	1800	Making portable ovens.
DARBY, WILLIAM - - -	380	18th April	1707	Casting iron bellied-pots, and other iron bellied-ware.
DARBY, WILLIAM - - -	1509	10th Nov.	1785	Manufacturing spoons and other articles.
DARKER, WILLIAM HILL, junior	8806	21st Jan.	1841	Looms for weaving.
DARKER, WILLIAM HILL, junior	9065	4th Sept.	1841	Looms for weaving.
DARKER, WILLIAM HILL, senior	8806	21st Jan.	1841	Looms for weaving.
DARKER, WILLIAM HILL, senior	9065	4th Sept.	1841	Looms for weaving.
DARLING. WILLIAM - -	11,738	10th June	1847	Moulding and the manufacture of certain articles of cast-iron.
DARLU, PAUL MARIE - -	12,181	8th June	1848	Obtaining motive-power.
DARNELL, JAMES - - -	10,647	1st May	1845	Machinery for beating and brushing carpets.
DARTHEZ, STANISLAUS - -	7891	1st Dec.	1838	Construction and arrangement of axles, axletrees and naves, of wheels for carriages.
DARTNELL, GEORGE RUSSELL	11,590	24th Feb.	1847	Truss for inguinal hernia.
DASHWOOD, JONATHAN GUY -	8856	22nd Feb.	1841	Pumps.
DASHWOOD, JONATHAN GUY -	9170	9th Dec.	1841	Construction of cocks and taps.
DAUBENY, HENRY CHARLES -	8714	25th Nov.	1840	Making paddle-wheels for vessels propelled in the water by steam or other power;—applicable to propel vessels and mills.
DAVENANT, CHARLES - -	254	13th Aug.	1687	Manufacture of milled lead, for sheathing and preservation of ships or other things.
DAVENPORT, JOHN - - -	2946	4th July	1806	Ornamenting glass, to imitate engraving or etching.
DAVEY, GEORGE - - -	8287	2nd Dec.	1839	Applying water-power.
DAVEY, HENRY - - -	6476	28th Sept.	1833	Machinery for preparing linen and cotton rags and other materials, used in the manufacture of paper.

Name of Patentee.	Progressive Number.	Date.	Subject-matter of Patent.
DAVEY, PETER - -	2403	20th May 1800	Fuel.
DAVEY, PETER - - -	4597	18th Oct. 1821	Preparation of coal for fuel.
DAVEY, SIMON - - -	14,065	15th April 1852	Explosive compounds and fusees; also methods of firing the same.
DAVEY, THOMAS - - -	10,928	6th Nov. 1845	Manufacturing the miner's safety fuse.
DAVEY, WILLIAM - - -	9857	31st July 1843	Covering the ridges and hips of roofs of buildings with slate and other materials.
DAVID, EVAN WILLIAM -	9474	22nd Sept. 1842	Machinery for ploughing, harrowing, and raking land, and cutting food for animals.
DAVID, FRANÇOIS MARIUS -	10,031	30th Jan. 1844	Manufacture of gas.
DAVID, PIERRE ISIDOR - -	12,499	28th Feb. 1849	Bleaching cotton.
DAVID, PIERRE ISIDOR - -	14,356	5th Feb. 1853	Bleaching, and apparatus connected therewith.
DAVIDGE, JOSEPH DANIEL -	9851	24th July 1843	Manufacturing certain materials as substitutes for whalebone; machinery for effecting the same.
DAVIDSON, JOHN - - -	2145	7th Nov. 1796	Machine for doubling, twisting or making, reeling and skeining worsted, thread, silk, cotton, and other similar articles.
DAVIDSON, JOHN - - -	8505	12th May 1840	Preserving salt.
DAVIDSON, JOSEPH CHRISTIAN	13,305	2nd Nov. 1850	Lime and other kilns and furnaces.
DAVIDSON, WILLIAM - -	5396	1st Aug. 1826	Process for bleaching or whitening bees'-wax, myrtle-wax, and animal tallow.
DAVIES, CHARLES FREDERICK	3290	20th Dec. 1809	Raising a nap on woollen stocking-pieces; giving transverse elasticity to cassimere and broad-cloth.
DAVIES, DAVID - - -	11,371	17th Sept. 1846	Steps for carriages and for other purposes.
DAVIES, DAVID - - -	12,127	15th April 1848	Construction of the heads of open or close carriages.
DAVIES, DAVID - - -	13,485	31st Jan. 1851	Construction of wheel-carriages; appendages thereto.
DAVIES, GEORGE - - -	12,347	2nd Dec. 1848	Steam-engines.
DAVIES, GEORGE - - -	12,880	10th Dec. 1849	Engines worked by steam, air, water, and other fluids, and whether locomotive, marine or stationary; boilers;—applicable to blowing air and pumping water.
DAVIES, HENRY - - -	7072	26th April 1836	Machinery for supplying water or other fluids to steam-boilers or evaporating-vessels; obtaining mechanical-power by steam; communicating motion to vessels floating on water.
DAVIES, HENRY - - -	7325	15th March 1837	Machinery for obtaining mechanical-power; machinery for impelling or raising fluids.
DAVIES, HENRY - - -	7688	14th June 1838	Engine for obtaining mechanical-power, also for raising or impelling fluids.
DAVIES, HENRY - - -	9124	21st Oct. 1841	Tools for cutting or shaping metals and other substances.
DAVIES, HENRY - - -	9143	9th Nov. 1841	Machinery for applying power to move bodies on land or water.
DAVIES, HENRY - - -	10,024	25th Jan. 1844	Construction of vessels for conveying goods or passengers on water; arrangement of machinery for communicating motion to such vessels.
DAVIES, HENRY - - -	10,261	15th July 1844	Construction of certain steam-engines; application of steam to such engines.

Name of Patentee.	Progressive Number.	Date.	Subject-matter of Patent.
DAVIES, ISAIAH - - -	10,161	27th April 1844	Steam-engines; partly applicable to impelling carriages.
DAVIES, ISAIAH - - -	12,145	2nd May 1848	Steam-engines and locomotive-carriages; in partly applicable to other motive machinery.
DAVIES, JAMES COLLARD -	8515	23rd May 1840	Clock or time-piece.
DAVIES, JOHN - - -	8655	7th Oct. 1840	Machinery for weaving.
DAVIES, JOHN - - -	10,896	25th Oct. 1845	Dyeing or staining woven or piece-goods or fabrics; machinery for the purpose.
DAVIES, JOHN DOBBS - -	2904	23rd Jan. 1806	Saddle-bar named "motion saddle-bar."
DAVIES, JONAH - - -	12,880	10th Dec. 1849	Engines worked by steam, air, water, and other fluids, and whether locomotive, marine, or stationary; boilers;—applicable to blowing air and pumping water.
DAVIES, JOSEPH - - -	7787	30th Aug. 1838	Composition for protecting wood from flame.
DAVIES, JONAH - - -	12,347	2nd Dec. 1848	Steam-engines.
DAVIES, REES - - -	10,236	24th June 1844	Manufacture of iron.
DAVIES, RICHARD - - -	7433	14th Sept. 1837	Earthenware tile, slab, or plate.
DAVIES, SAMUEL - - -	2160	31st Jan. 1797	Harpsichord, grand piano-forte, and square piano-forte.
DAVIES, THOMAS - - -	877	2nd June 1767	Making velvet-shag and brocaded-silk, on a stocking-frame, and either plain, cut, or figured, and in gold and silver.
DAVIES, THOMAS - - -	1195	24th June 1778	Machine for making network with knotted meshes, in silk, thread, cotton, worsted, or other similar materials.
DAVIES, THOMAS - - -	3501	30th Oct. 1811	Construction of buckles.
DAVIES, WILLIAM - - -	7422	24th Aug. 1837	Construction of boilers for the generation of steam, and for heating water or other fluids.
DAVIS, CHARLES FREDERICK -	3327	6th April 1810	Manufacture of woollen-cloth.
DAVIS, DANIEL - - -	2124	4th July 1796	Apparatus for sweeping chimneys and extinguishing fire therein.
DAVIS, DANIEL PAULIN -	2697	11th April 1803	Cleansing and sweeping chimneys.
DAVIS, GEORGE - - -	2306	11th April 1799	Double-chambered lock with cylinders, to which pins are affixed instead of wards.
DAVIS, ISAAC - - - -	9153	11th Nov. 1841	Manufacture of sealing-wax;—applicable to other purposes.
DAVIS, JAMES - - -	1887	6th June 1792	Pianofortes and harpsichords.
DAVIS, JAMES - - -	8040	23d April 1839	Manufacture of soap.
DAVIS, JAMES - - -	8736	16th Dec. 1840	Applying heat to certain steam-boilers.
DAVIS, JOHN - - - -	1464	28th Jan. 1785	Curing smoky chimneys.
DAVIS, JOHN - - - -	1618	11th Aug. 1787	Hanging coaches, vis-à-vis, and other bodies, so as to cause the same to remain upright when overturned.
DAVIS, JOHN - - - -	2537	3d Sept. 1801	Mill for grinding bark.
DAVIS, JOHN - - - -	5635	29th March 1828	Boiling or evaporating solutions of sugar and other liquids.
DAVIS, JOAN - - - -	5785	28th April 1829	Condenser used in apparatus for boiling sugar in vacuo.
DAVIS, JOHN - - - -	10,700	3rd June 1845	Lamps.
DAVIS, MARCUS - - -	9113	7th Oct. 1841	Ascertaining the distances that vehicles travel.
DAVIS, ROBERT - - -	3414	14th March 1811	Composition to be used in manufacturing umbrella and parasol furniture.
DAVIS, SAMSON - - -	4648	12th Feb. 1822	Lock for guns and other fire-arms.

Name of Patentee.	Progressive Number.	Date.		Subject-matter of Patent.
DAVIS, SAMSON - - -	5055	18th Dec.	1824	Guns and other fire-arms.
DAVIS, SAMSON - - -	6046	6th Dec.	1830	Construction of guns and fire-arms.
DAVIS, THOMAS JOHN - -	8593	8th Aug.	1840	Form and combination of blocks for building or paving, and for other purposes.
DAVIS, WILLIAM - - -	3477	7th Aug.	1811	Machine for chopping meat for sausages, and other like purposes.
DAVIS, WILLIAM - - -	4189	19th Dec.	1817	Wire gig-mills for dressing woollen and other cloths.
DAVIS, WILLIAM - - -	4196	15th Jan.	1818	Machines for shearing woollen and other cloths.
DAVIS, WILLIAM - -	4378	19th June	1819	Application of mechanical powers for laying, smoothing, and polishing the pile or face of cloth, and for cleansing such cloth at the same time.
DAVIS, WILLIAM - - -	4379	19th June	1819	Application of pointed wires, or other suitable pointed substances, for raising the pile or face of woollen and other cloths or fabrics.
DAVIS, WILLIAM - - -	4487	11th July	1820	Machinery for shearing woollen and other cloths.
DAVIS, WILLIAM - - -	4820	24th July	1823	Machinery for shearing and dressing woollen and other cloths.
DAVIS, WILLIAM - - -	5159	7th May	1825	Machinery for reducing wool into slivers or threads having more hair points projecting than is usual with worsted.
DAVIS, WILLIAM - - -	6776	25th Feb.	1835	Machinery for dressing woollen or other cloths.
DAVIS, WILLIAM - - -	8059	7th May	1839	Machinery for dressing and cleansing woollen-cloths.
DAVISON, ROBERT - -	1839	26th Nov.	1791	Engine, in place of a steam-engine, to be worked without fire, wind, or water, and with or without a horse.
DAVISON, ROBERT - -	9924	2nd Nov.	1843	Cleansing, purifying and sweetening casks, vats, and other vessels.
DAVISON, ROBERT - -	10,126	28th March	1844	Drying, seasoning, and hardening wood and other articles;—partly applicable to the desiccation of vegetable substances generally.
DAVISON, ROBERT -	11,947	6th Nov.	1847	Application of heat to the preparation, desiccation, and preservation of bread-stuffs, confectionary, pulse, meats, vegetables, and other edible substances.
DAVY, EDWARD - - -	7540	13th Jan.	1838	Saddles and harness for horses; and seats for carriages.
DAVY, EDWARD - - -	7719	4th July	1838	Apparatus for making telegraphic communications or signals by electric-currents;—partly applicable to obtaining, regulating, or measuring electric-currents for other purposes.
DAVY, GEORGE - - -	784	21st Jan.	1763	Making orchil from rock or stone moss.
DAVY, HENRY - - -	11,851	2nd Sept.	1847	Separating copper and other metals from their ores.
DAWBENEY, CLEMENT -	10	11th Dec.	1618	Engine, worked by water, for cutting iron into small bars or rods for making nails.
DAWES, JOHN BYRON -	9320	15th April	1842	Chemical composition for use in preparation of glass or other media of light.
DAWES, JOHN SAMUEL -	6207	22nd Dec.	1831	Manufacture of iron.
DAWES, JOHN SAMUEL -	6374	29th Jan.	1833	Manufacture of iron.

Name of Patentee.	Progressive Number.	Date.	Subject-matter of Patent.
DAWES, JOHN SAMUEL - -	6948	9th Dec. 1835	Manufacture of iron by the application of certain known materials; preparing such materials; recovering certain products in the manufacture of iron.
DAWES, JOHN THOMAS - -	3980	6th Feb. 1816	Steam-engines;—partly applicable to other purposes.
DAWES, THOMAS - - -	1489	16th July 1785	Sun-shade for the outside of windows.
DAWS, ROBERT - - -	5490	28th April 1827	Chairs.
DAWSON, CHARLES - -	12,307	2nd Nov. 1848	Musical instruments; apparatus to be used in connection with musical instruments.
DAWSON, EMERSON - -	4001	23rd March 1816	Grates and stoves, and apparatus for supplying them with fuel.
DAWSON, JAMES - - -	3821	16th July 1814	Producing or communicating motion in or unto bodies wholly or in part surrounded by water or air, by means of the reaction of apparatus on such water or air, or upon both of them.
DAWSON, JAMES - - -	3996	14th March 1816	Producing or communicating motion in or unto bodies wholly or in part surrounded by water or air, by the motion of suitable apparatus upon the said water or air, or upon both of them.
DAWSON, JOHN SOMERS - -	11,318	30th July 1846	Railway-carriages; machinery for working railways;—partly applicable to other carriages, and to the bearings of other machinery.
DAWSON, ROBERT - - -	3463	3rd July 1811	Applying any moving power to machinery; increasing such power; rendering machinery more susceptible of a multiplicity of power.
DAWSON, THOMAS - - -	2661	25th Nov. 1802	Lamp or lantern.
DAWSON, THOMAS - - -	12,818	18th Oct. 1849	Cutting and shaping garments and other articles of dress for the human body.
DAWSON, THOMAS - - -	13,554	13th March 1851	Constructing umbrellas and parasols.
DAWSON, WILLIAM - -	1820	19th July 1791	Machine for making, twisting, and looping open-work bobbin-lace, also lace and open-work, as mits, gloves, caps, handkerchiefs, aprons, stocking-pieces, or other work that may be manufactured on the said machine.
DAY, BENJAMIN AGER - -	3364	18th July 1810	Construction of toast-stands, hearth-brushes, and toasting-forks, or brush and toasting-fork combined.
DAY, BENJAMIN AGER - -	4132	3rd June 1817	Chimney ornaments, which may be used for fire-screens, flower or sweet jars, time-piece cases, candlesticks, toast-stands, and for other purposes.
DAY, BENJAMIN AGER - -	4973	15th June 1824	Manufacturing knobs for drawers, doors, and locks, also knobs of every description.
DAY, BENJAMIN AGER - -	5691	28th Aug. 1828	Making picture-frames.
DAY, GEORGE THOMAS - -	9002	23rd June 1841	Apparatus for creating draft;—applicable to chimneys and to other purposes.
DAY, FRANCIS - - -	1534	27th Feb. 1786	Lengthening hair for making tails, braids, and curls, to adorn the human head; mounting the same.
DAY, FRANCIS - - -	5802	19th June 1829	Musical instruments.
DAY, JAMES - - - -	3072	9th Sept. 1807	Compounding Dantzic spruce or black beer.
DAY, JOHN - - - -	3010	12th Feb. 1807	Engine for loading and unloading vessels, and raising anchors or other weights.

Name of Patentee.	Progressive Number.	Date.	Subject-matter of Patent.
DAY, JOHN - - - -	3022	20th March 1807	Applying friction-boxes with or without a perpetual screw-spindle and cog-wheel, to extend and facilitate the power of engines, cranes, capstans, machines for raising anchors and other great weights or bodies, and to the steerage-wheels of ships.
DAY, JOHN - - - -	4080	14th Nov. 1816	Construction of pianofortes and other keyed musical instruments.
DAY, JOHN - - - -	4861	13th Nov. 1823	Percussion gun-locks for various sorts of fire-arms.
DAY, JOHN - - - -	5207	8th July 1825	Pusher twist or bobbin-net machine.
DAY, JOHN - - - -	6242	15th March 1832	Manufacture of cocks for stopping and drawing off gas and water, and for other purposes.
DAY, JOHN - - - -	6750	22nd Jan. 1835	Construction of railways.
DAY, JOHN - - - -	6880	14th Aug. 1835	Wheel for carriages.
DAY, JOHN ROCK - -	8775	6th Jan. 1841	Construction of collars for horses and other draught animals.
DAY, JOHN WOODHOUSE -	9821	6th July 1843	Apparatus to facilitate the loading of vessels with coal, culm, or cinders.
DAY, PHILIP - - -	1471	4th April 1785	Travelling-trunk, box, or case, which may be converted into a writing or other table, and a seat with folding feet.
DAY, RICHARD KEMSLEY -	12,727	1st Aug. 1849	Manufacture of emery-paper, emery-cloth, and other scouring fabrics.
DAY, SAMUEL - - -	2700	20th April 1803	Timepiece, or "watchman's noctuary and labourer's regulator."
DAY, WILLIAM - - -	4076	1st Nov. 1816	Trunks, and application of machinery to make them contract or expand at pleasure.
DAY, WILLIAM - - -	5410	31st Aug. 1826	Bedsteads;—applicable to other purposes.
DAY, WILLIAM - - -	6246	22nd Mar. 1832	Construction of printing-presses.
DAY, WILLIAM - - -	7814	20th Sept. 1838	Applying and combining timber, and other materials used in the construction of ships or vessels, masts, yards, beams, piers, bridges, and for other purposes.
DAY, WILLIAM ALLAMUS -	3769	20th Dec. 1813	Extracting the gross or mucilaginous matter from whale-oil, produced from Finks or Greenland blubber when boiled.
DAY, WILLIAM CHAMBERS -	12,478	14th Feb. 1849	Machinery for weighing.
DAYMAN, JOHN - - -	4053	3rd Aug. 1816	Coating iron, steel, and other metals or mixture of metals, with tin, lead, copper, brass, or other metals or mixture of metals.
DAYME, LOUIS HENRY DANIEL	3995	14th March 1816	Machine which acts by expansion or contraction of air heated by fire, for raising water, or giving motion to mills or other machines.
DE ANGELY, PAUL - - [D'Angely, Paul.]	13,097	4th June 1850	Construction of privies and urinals; apparatus and machinery for cleansing privies, cesspools, and other places; deodorizing the matter extracted therefrom, and rendering it available for agricultural purposes.
DE ARCY, JOSEPH - - - [D'Arcy, Joseph.]	5719	29th Nov. 1828	Construction of steam-engines, and apparatus connected therewith.
DE ARTENN, JOSE FRANCISCO [CARLOS. [D'Arten, Jose Francisco Carlos.]	8022	5th April 1839	Machinery for transmitting power.

Name of Patentee.	Progressive Number.	Date.	Subject-matter of Patent.
DE ASDA, AUGUSTE VICTOR [JOSEPH. [D'Asda, Auguste Victor Joseph.]	6591	10th April 1834	Pumps.
DE ASDA, AUGUSTE VICTOR [JOSEPH, Baron. [D'Asda, Augsute Victor Joseph, Baron.]	7989	6th March 1839	Producing or affording light, "solar light."
DE BAADER, JOSEPH	3959	14th Nov. 1815	Constructing railroads, and carriages to be used on them.
DE BARROS, IGNACIO	11,880	30th Sept. 1847	Machinery for making lasts for boots and shoes, butts or stocks for fire-arms, and other irregular forms.
DE BARROS, IGNACIO	12,519	14th March 1849	Machinery for making lasts for boots and shoes, butts or stocks for fire-arms, and other irregular forms.
DE BEAUREGARD, FELIX ALEX-[ANDER TESTUD.	12,209	11th July 1848	Generating steam; obtaining power from steam-engines.
DE BERENGER, CHARLES	2949	24th July 1806	Preparing and manufacturing a certain animal substance as a substitute for horse and other hair, for stuffing cushions, mattrasses, carriages, sofas, and chairs, and for other purposes for which flock, wool, or hair are now used.
DE BERENGER, CHARLES RAN-[DOM.	3507	21st Nov. 1811	Producing oil, soap, barilla, and a black colour or pigment.
DE BERENGER, CHARLES RAN-[DOM. [De Berenger, C. R., Baron.]	4990	27th July 1824	Applying percussion for the purpose of igniting charges in fire-arms generally.
DE BERENGER, CHARLES RAN-[DOM. [De Berenger, C. R., Baron.]	5439	20th Dec. 1826	Powder-flasks, horns, or other utensils for carrying gunpowder, to load therefrom guns, pistols, blunderbusses, and other fire-arms.
DE BERENGER, CHARLES RAN-[DOM.	5905	27th Feb. 1830	Fire-arms and other weapons of defence.
DE BERGUE, CHARLES	6714	15th Nov. 1834	Machinery for spinning or twisting cotton, flax, silk, and other fibrous substances.
DE BERGUE, CHARLES	7048	29th March 1836	Machinery for spinning and doubling yarn or thread manufactured from cotton or other fibrous material.
DE BERGUE, CHARLES	8691	7th Nov. 1840	Machinery for making reeds used in weaving.
DE BERGUE, CHARLES	9052	21st Aug. 1841	Axletrees and axletree-boxes.
DE BERGUE, CHARLES	10,782	24th July 1845	Rollers and other machinery or apparatus employed in flattening, preparing, and polishing wire, for the construction or manufacture of reeds for weaving;—the rollers being applicable to other like purposes.
DE BERGUE, CHARLES	11,184	24th April 1846	Atmospheric-railways.
DE BERGUE, CHARLES	11,649	8th April 1847	Wheeled-carriages.
DE BERGUE, CHARLES	11,815	26th July 1847	Buffing and traction apparatus; springs for railway and other carriages.
DE BERGUE, CHARLES	12,013	5th Jan. 1848	Carriages used on railways.
DE BERGUE, CHARLES	12,286	12th Oct. 1848	Bridges, girders, and beams.
DE BERGUE, CHARLES	12,435	23rd Jan. 1849	Steam-engines; pumps; springs for railway and other purposes.
DE BERGUE, CHARLES	13,043	15th April 1850	Locomotive and other steam-engines; buffers for railway purposes.
DE BERGUE, CHARLES	13,493	7th Feb. 1851	The permanent way of railways, and construction of the same.

Name of Patentee.	Progressive Number.	Date.	Subject-matter of Patent.
DE BEURET, EUGENE - -	7766	10th Aug. 1838	Construction of railroads and tramroads, to facilitate the ascent and descent of hills and inclined planes.
DE BISSY, STEPHEN, Baron -	884	11th Nov. 1767	Oar, for men of war, merchantmen, and other rowing vessels.
DE BLEWSTON, FREDERICK -	198	25th Oct. 1677	Melting down, forging, extracting, and reducing iron, and all metals and minerals, with pit-coal and sea-coal, at less expense, and as effectually as with charcoal.
DE BLIGNY, JOSEPHINE JULIE [BESNIER.	8086	3rd June 1839	Umbrellas and parasols.
DE BODE, HENRY, Baron -	7107	4th June 1836	Capstans.
DE BODE, HENRY, Baron -	7379	23rd May 1837	Apparatus for retarding and stopping chain or other cables or ropes, on board ships or vessels.
DE BODE, HENRY, Baron -	8096	8th June 1839	Rendering magnetic-needles less prejudicially influenced by local attraction;—applicable to other magnetic objects for the same purpose.
DE BOUSSOIS, EDWARD JOSEPH [FRANCOIS DUCLOS.	9154	11th Nov. 1841	Manufacture of copper.
DE BOUSSOIS, EDWARD JOSEPH [FRANCOIS DUCLOS.	9764	10th June 1843	Manufacture of lead, tin, tungsten, copper, and zinc, from ores, slags, and other products; and manufacture of their alloys with other metals.
DE BREZA, EUGENE RICHARD [LADISLAS.	7570	20th Feb. 1838	Chemical compound, to render cloth, wood, paper, and other substances, indestructible by fire, and preserve them from the ravages of insects.
DE BRUGES, PIERRE - -	1104	27th Oct. 1775	Making saltpetre.
DE CALCINA, Comte MELANO -	9097	21st Sept. 1841	Paving or covering roads and other ways or surfaces.
DE CAMBIS, LOUIS JOSEPH [MARIE, Marquis.	5372	23rd May 1826	Rotatory steam-engines; apparatus connected therewith.
DE CANOLLE, JEAN - -	1386	12th Sept. 1783	Factitious coal to supply the use of charcoal.
DE CARDONELS, ADAM - -	249	9th Jan. 1686	Making writing and printing paper, and printing His Majesty's Arms thereon.
DE CAVAILLON, FLORENTIN [JOSEPH.	12,718	1st Aug. 1849	Obtaining carbonated hydrogen-gas; applying the products resulting therefrom to various purposes.
DE CHABANNES, JEAN FRE-[DERIC, Marquis.	3875	16th Jan. 1815	Extracting from fuel a larger quantity of caloric than ordinary, and applying it to warm several rooms by one fire.
DE CHABANNES, JEAN FRE-[DERIC, Marquis.	3963	5th Dec. 1815	Conducting air and regulating the temperature in houses and other buildings; warming and cooling air or liquids;—applicable to various purposes.
DE CHABANNES, JEAN FRE-[DERIC, Marquis.	4191	19th Dec. 1817	Constructing pipes or tubes of tin, copper, sheet-lead, sheet-iron, or other metals or mixture of metals capable of being reduced into sheets.
DE CHABANNES, JEAN FRE-[DERIC, Marquis.	4192	19th Dec. 1817	Warming, cooling, or conducting air in houses and other buildings; warming, cooling, evaporating, condensing, and taking the residuum from liquids;—applicable to other purposes.
DE CHABANNES, JEAN FRE-[DERIC, Marquis.	4582	14th Aug. 1821	Method and apparatus for attracting and catching fish.

Name of Patentee.	Progressive Number.	Date.	Subject-matter of Patent.
DE CHANGY, CHARLES ED-[OUARD FRANCIS CONSTANT [PROSPERE.	12,855	20th Nov. 1849	Preparation and manufacture of flax, hemp, and other like fibrous substances.
DE CHAPEAUROUGE, PHILIP [AUGUSTUS.	6614	24th May 1834	Machine or apparatus for producing motive-power.
DE CHAPEAUROUGE, PHILIP [AUGUSTUS.	6802	31st March 1835	Machine or apparatus for producing motive-power.
DE CHARLIEU, ANDRÉ DROUET [De Charlien, André Dronot.]	8941	27th April 1841	Preparation of matters to be consumed in obtaining light; construction of burners for the same.
DE CHARLIEU, ANDRÉ DROUET	10,115	20th March 1844	Rails for railways; and wheels for locomotive-carriages.
DE CHASTEL, CHARLES, Baron	1363	28th April 1783	Machine for separating gold and silver from earth, scoriæ, and impurities, by trituration, mercury, and amalgama.
DE CHATAUVILLARD, LOUIS [ALFRED.	12,613	15th May 1849	Fire-arms, cartridges, bullets, bayonets, and ordnance.
DE CHEMANT, NICHOLAS DU-[BOIS.	1803	11th May 1791	Composition for making artificial teeth; springs for fastening the same.
DE CHEMANT, NICHOLAS DU-[BOIS.	2167	15th Feb. 1797	Table with a stove placed in the centre thereof.
DE CLARRANT, ANTHONY -	259	19th May 1688	Making three sorts of tar or pitch, one for the preservation of wood from putrefaction and worms; another to resist fire and the heat of the sun; and another for the better preservation of ropes.
DE COLMAR, CHARLES XAVIER [THOMAS.	13,504	10th Feb. 1851	Calculating-machine, "arithmometer."
DE CROUY, HENRY, Count -	7902	12th Dec. 1838	Filtration.
DE CROUY, NICOLAS HENRY [JEAN FRANCOIS, Comte.	9678	25th March 1843	Rotary-pumps and rotary steam-engines.
DE DOUHET, GUILLAUME FER-[DINAND.	13,092	1st June 1850	Disoxygenation of certain bodies, and application, separately or simultaneously, of the products therefrom.
DE DUNON, EMILIAN - -	13,628	10th May 1851	Apparatus for measuring persons, and facilitating the fitting of garments.
DE ERESBY, PETER ROBERT [DRUMMOND, Lord WIL-[LOUGHBY.	8160	20th July 1839	Compressing peat.
DE GLIMES, ANTHONY MO-[VILLON.	10,010	13th Jan. 1844	Apparatus for propelling vessels on water; machinery to effect the purpose by manual labour;—applicable to raising heavy bodies, and to other purposes.
DEGOURNAY, JULES ALPHONSE [SIMON.	8358	22nd Jan. 1840	Manufacture of horse-shoes.
DEGRANDE, JOHN ALEXANDER [ALZEAR.	7903	12th Dec. 1838	Production of motive-power; and machinery for applying the same to useful purposes.
DE GRUCHY, CHARLES - -	249	9th Jan. 1686	Making writing and printing paper, and printing His Majesty's arms thereon.
DE HARCOURT, GEORGE RO-[BERT [D'Harcourt, George Robert.]	7771	15th Aug. 1838	Propelling canal-boats, steamers, and other vessels.
DE HARCOURT, GEORGE RO-[BERT [D'Harcourt, George Robert.]	7772	15th Aug. 1838	Manufacture of paper.
DE HARCOURT, GEORGE RO-[BERT [D'Harcourt, George Robert.]	7991	6th March 1839	Artificial granite, stone, marble, or concrete, in which invention neither asphaltic nor bituminous substances are used.

Name of Patentee.	Progressive Number.	Date.	Subject-matter of Patent.
DE HARCOURT, GEORGE RO-[BERT [*D'Harcourt, George Robert.*]	9884	28th Sept. 1843	Sorting, checking, and delivering letters, newspapers, and other articles.
DE HARCOURT, GEORGE RO-[BERT [*D'Harcourt, George Robert.*]	10,367	29th Oct. 1844	Ascertaining and checking the number of checks or tickets which have been used and marked ;—applicable for railway offices and for other purposes.
DE HEINE, AUGUSTUS FREDE-[RICK.	3297	1st Feb. 1810	Printing and stamping presses.
DE HEINE, AUGUSTUS FREDE-[RICK [*De Heine, Augustus.*]	3310	26th Feb. 1810	Apparatus for preserving animal and vegetable food and other perishable articles from decay.
DE HERRYPON, MARTIAL [AUGUSTIN JOSEPH.	8079	25th May 1839	Machine for washing and bleaching wool, cotton, silk, linen, and other fibrous materials, manufactured or unmanufactured.
DE JOUGH, MAURICE - -	3762	29th Nov. 1813	Preparing madder and madder-roots.
DE JOUGH, MAURICE - -	4914	28th Feb. 1824	Constructing and placing a coke-oven under or near to boilers, so as to make the heat from the coke useful for heating the boilers also, and such heat may be excluded if necessary.
DE JOUGH, MAURICE - - [*De Jongh, Maurice.*]	5140	29th March 1825	Spinning-machines, as "mules," "jennies," "slubbers," and other similar machines.
DE JOUGH, MAURICE - - [*De Jongh, Maurice.*]	5432	18th Dec. 1826	Machinery for preparing rovings, and twisting, spinning, and winding fibrous substances.
DE JOUGH, MAURICE - -	5576	4th Dec. 1827	Machines for spinning, doubling, twisting, roving, or preparing cotton and other fibrous substances.
DE LA CHATRE, RAOUL, AN-[NAND JOSEPH JEAN, Comte.	9331	26th April 1842	Preparing surfaces of fabrics to be used in covering roofs, floors, and other surfaces.
DE LA CHAUMETTE, ISAAC -	434	12th Aug. 1721	Cannon, fusees, and pistols; swords which serve for bayonets; powder-flasks; machine to cure smoky chimneys; snuff-boxes; penknife and pocket-knife; buckles; machine for drawing lotteries; two cases of pistols, of which a carbine may be made; turning-mattrass for armies and hospitals; coaches and chaises; preventing shipwreck; bomb or grenado; breast-plates; candlesticks and rings; pocket-scissors; machine for holding glasses at table; picture serving as a tester to a bed and an ornament to a room; lantern; fusee-lock; firing fusees horizontally; double counters for drawing lotteries.
DE LA COURT, ALEXANDER [ALLARD.	5359	6th May 1826	Instrument applicable to the organ of sight.
DE LA CROUEE, JULES THIE-[BALD.	10,114	19th March 1844	Apparatus for purifying, clarifying, and refining vegetable extracts.
DE LA FONS, JOHN - -	2893	19th Nov. 1805	Marine alarum chronometer, for ascertaining the time of a ship's log line running out, the time of the watches on shipboard, and for other purposes.
DE LA FONS, JOHN PALMER -	5219	16th July 1825	Extracting and fixing teeth.
DE LA FONS, JOHN PALMER -	5388	14th July 1826	Securing or mooring ships and other floating bodies, and apparatus for performing the same.
DE LA FONS, JOHN PALMER -	11,283	6th July 1846	Manufacture of locks and other fastenings.

Name of Patentee.	Progressive Number.	Date.	Subject-matter of Patent.
DE LA GARDE, AUGUSTUS, [Count.	5469	20th Feb. 1827	Making paper from the ligneous parts of certain plants produced in preparing them by the rural mechanical-break.
DE LA GARDE, PHILIP CHIL- [WICK.	5914	27th Feb. 1830	Apparatus for fidding and unfidding masts ; masting and rigging vessels.
DE LA MAYNE, THOMAS -	1475	3rd May 1785	Making buttons of burnt earth or porcelain.
DE LA RUE, THOMAS - -	6231	23rd Feb. 1832	Making and ornamenting playing-cards.
DE LA RUE, THOMAS - -	6663	15th Aug. 1834	Manufacturing or preparing embossed paper-hangings.
DE LA RUE, THOMAS - -	8549	20th June 1840	Printing calicoes and other surfaces.
DE LA RUE, THOMAS - -	12,243	15th Aug. 1848	Producing ornamental surfaces on paper and other substances.
DE LA RUE, WARREN - -	10,436	12th Dec. 1844	Covering the surface of paper and other materials with colour and other substances.
DE LA RUE, WARREN - -	10,565	17th March 1845	Manufacture of envelopes.
DE LA RUE, WARREN - -	12,084	8th March 1848	Machinery used in the manufacture of cardboard and paste-board.
DE LA RUE, WARREN - -	12,904	19th Dec. 1849	Manufacturing envelopes.
DE LAVELEYE, CHARLES -	7551	25th Jan. 1838	Manufacture of bricks.
DE LIGNAC, JULES JEAN BAP- [TISTE MARTIN.	11,892	7th Oct. 1847	Preserving milk.
DE LINIERE, FRANCIS XAVIER [DE ARLES.	755	27th Nov. 1760	Pump.
DE LINIERE, FRANCIS XAVIER [DE ARLES.	756	27th Nov. 1760	Pump.
DE LOLME, JOHN LEWIS -	1718	12th Dec. 1789	Instrument by means of which vessels can be made to sail faster, veered about with more facility, made more manageable, and from which an easier landing can be effected.
DE LOLME, JOHN LEWIS -	1991	24th May 1794	Implements for the safety and conveniency of wheel-carriages, and for lessening friction.
DE L'OSIER, GERMAIN LE [NORMAND.	8063	8th May 1839	Machinery for raising water.
DE LOS VALLES, LOUIS AUGUST [DE ST. SYLVAIN, Baron.	8472	15th April 1840	Cleansing, decorating, purifying, and preserving corn and other grain.
DE MAGALHEANS, JOHN HYA- [CINTH.	825	28th March 1765	Instrument for showing the effect of the weight of the atmosphere, with the variation caused by heat and cold; also the quantity of that variation.
DE MAGES, JOSEPH - -	937	7th Nov. 1769	Making baize for the Spanish and Portuguese trade, to imitate French baize.
DE MAY, JAMES - - -	249	9th Jan. 1686	Making writing and printing paper, and printing His Majesty's Arms thereon.
DE MAYERNE, SIR THEODORE [Knight.	81	25th March 1635	Distilling strong-waters, and making vinegars of cider, perry, and buck or French-wheat.
DE MECHENHEIM, LOUIS NI- [CHOLAS.	9373	31st May 1842	Manufacture of iron.
DE MADEIROS, JOHN CAR- [VALHOE.	7581	28th Feb. 1838	Producing gas for illumination ;—apparatus connected with the consumption thereof.
DE MEURATO, DAVID - -	141	4th Feb. 1663	Making and framing sugar-mills.
DE MOLEYNS, FREDERICK -	9053	21st Aug. 1841	Production or development of electricity ;—application of electricity for obtaining illumination and motion.
DE MONTRAVEL, ANTOINE [MAURICE TARDY.	14,031	24th March 1852	Obtaining motive-power ; — machinery employed therein.

Name of Patentee.	Progressive Number	Date.	Subject-matter of Patent.
DE MORNAY, EDWARD - -	13,702	5th Aug. 1851	Machinery for crushing sugar-canes;—and apparatus for evaporating saccharine fluids.
DE NANTEUIL, PIERRE AN-[TOINE AUGUSTE DE LA BARRE.	13,309	2nd Nov. 1850	Propelling carriages.
DE NORMANDY, ALPHONSE [RENE LE MIRE.	8175	1st Aug. 1839	Manufacture of inks and dyes
DE NORMANDY, ALPHONSE [RENE LE MIRE.	9081	8th Sept. 1841	Manufacture of soap.
DE NORMANDY, ALPHONSE [RENE LE MIRE. [De Normandy, A. le Mire.]	10,423	7th Dec. 1844	Purifying lac, and converting lac into shell-lac.
DE NORMANDY, ALPHONSE [RENE LE MIRE. [De Normandy, A. Le Mire.]	11,591	24th Feb. 1847	Manufacture of zinc.
DE NORMANDY, ALPHONSE [RENE LE MIRE.	13,512	12th Feb. 1851	Manufacture of iron coated with other metal (galvanized-iron).
DE NORMANDY, ALPHONSE [RENE LE MIRE.	13,714	7th Aug. 1851	Obtaining fresh water from salt water; concentrating sulphuric-acid.
DE OLSZOWSKI, ANDREW PRUSS [D'Olszowski, Andrew Pruss.]	8742	16th Dec. 1840	Level for ascertaining the horizon, and the several degrees of inclination.
D'ORVILLE, EDWARD - - [D'Orville, Edward.]	13,413	19th Dec. 1850	Finishing thread or yarn.
DE PHILEPSTHAL, PAUL -	2575	26th Jan. 1802	Optical-apparatus, to represent human figures in a dark space or scene.
DE POGGI, ANTHONY CESARI -	2428	24th July 1800	Constructing and using ordnance, both for sea and land.
DE PONS, HENRY FRANCOIS [MARIE.	13,514	17th Feb. 1851	Constructing roads and ways, and pavements of streets; ballast of railways.
DE RIGEL, ANTONIN PIEUX -	7445	14th Oct. 1837	Steam-engines.
DE ROBIEN, LOUIS JOSEPH [FRANCOIS JULIEN, Count.	2071	22nd Oct. 1795	Economical fire-place.
DE ROCHE, RANDOLPH [ISCHIFFELI.	3263	26th Sept. 1809	Brewing.
DE ROSEN, ADOLPHE EUGENE, [Count.	5398	1st Aug. 1826	Engine for communicating power, to answer the purposes of a steam-engine.
DE SAINTE CHARLES, PHIL-[LIPE POIRIER.	10,746	1st July 1845	Production of type for printing; machinery for the same.
DE SARUL, HENRY - - -	3983	20th Feb. 1816	Cylindrical gold and silver sweep and washing machine.
DE SCHELESTADT, EDWARD [LOOS.	9079	8th Sept. 1841	Machinery and process for tanning skins or hides; preparing and operating upon vegetable and other substances.
DE SERIONNE, LOUIS JEAN [JACQUES, Viscount.	12,963	9th Feb. 1850	Manufacture of buttons.
DE SOLA, ANTONIO - -	13,882	24th Dec. 1851	Treatment of copper-minerals.
DE SORAS, GABRIEL - -	5545	21st Aug. 1827	Sizing, glazing, or beautifying materials used in the manufacture of paper, paste-board, Bristol-boards, and other substances.
DE STRUBING, JAMES ULRIC [VAUCHER, Baron.	12,876	3rd Dec. 1849	Axletree-boxes for carriages; bearings of the axles of railways; making an alloy of metal suitable for such purposes.
DE SUARCE, CHARLES GA-[BRIEL, Baron.	7964	11th Feb. 1839	Obtaining dyes, colours, tannin, and acids, from vegetable substances.
DE SUSSEX, FRANCOIS STANI-[LAS MELDON. [De Sussex, Francois Stanilas.]	10,296	29th Aug. 1844	Recovery of manganese used in making bleaching-powder.

Name of Patentee.	Progressive Number.	Date.	Subject-matter of Patent.
DE SUSSEX, FRANCOIS STANI-[LAS MELDON.	11,263	29th June 1846	Manufacture of soda and potash.
DE SUSSEX, FRANCOIS STANI-[LAS MELDON.	11,585	19th Feb. 1847	Manufacture of chlorine, hydro-chloric acid, and nitric-acid; obtaining products therefrom.
DE SUSSEX, FRANCOIS STANI-[LAS MELDON.	11,635	23rd March 1847	Smelting copper and other ores.
DE TAUSCH, FRANCOIS - -	7176	25th Aug. 1836	Machinery for propelling vessels, raising water, and for various other purposes.
DE THIERRY, CHARLES PHILIP, [Baron.	4396	20th Sept. 1819	Bit for horses; "Humane safety Bit."
DE THIVILLE, JOSEPH GASTON [JOHN BAPTISTE.	2406	26th May 1800	Lamp for lighting chambers, rooms, halls, &c.
DE TROISBRIOUX, ALPHONSE -	9327	21st April 1842	Lithographic and other printing presses.
DE URCLE, FELIX VICTOR [CHARLES LEON LEVACHER. [D'Urcle, Felix Victor Charles Leon Levacher]	13,661	12th June 1851	Increasing the produce of Autumn wheat.
DE VARROC, EUGENE - -	9426	23rd July 1842	Apparatus to be applied to chimneys to prevent their taking fire, and to render the sweeping of chimneys to which such apparatus is applied, unnecessary.
DE VAUX, CHARLES GRANT, [Viscount.	3088	9th Dec. 1807	Machine to show the latitude and longitude at sea, also for weighing objects, measuring space, or a ship's course, or keeping account upon dials and cosmographical columns, shewing also the lee-way of a ship;—partly applicable to other purposes.
DE VILLARS, LOUIS FLORENT [DELANNOY.	683	30th May 1753	Making gun-carriages of cast-iron, to be worked by two men instead of eight as heretofore.
DE WARDIN, WINCESLAS LE [Baron DE TRAUX.	12,945	26th Jan. 1850.	Looms for weaving linen, woollen, and cotton cloths; machines for preparing yarns for such cloths before entering the loom; also machine for finishing linen-cloths.
DE WENDEL, CHARLES ALEXIS	13,478	30th Jan. 1851	Process and instruments used for boring the earth and sinking shafts for mining and other purposes; lining such shafts.
DE WITTE, GERARD JOHN -	12,998	7th March 1850	Machinery, apparatus, metallic and other substances, for the purposes of letter-press and other printing.
DE WYDROFF, Baron VICTOR -	9580	29th Dec. 1842	Construction of railways; wheels to run on railways; apparatus for clearing the rails.
DEACON, BENFORD - -	3664	13th March 1813	Applying air for domestic and manufacturing purposes, and employing therein improved fire-places and bricks.
DEACON, HENRY - - -	10,686	22nd May 1845	Constructing, grinding, and smoothing plate-glass, crown-glass, and sheet-glass.
DEACON, HENRY - - -	11,384	24th Sept. 1846	Construction of flattening kilns.
DEACON, JAMES - - -	5753	14th Jan. 1829	Making from horns and hoofs of animals, handles, knobs, curtain-rings, bell-pulls, escutcheons, and finger-plates.
DEACON, JAMES - - -	8706	19th Nov. 1840	Manufacture of glass-chimneys for lamps.
DEACON, THOMAS - - -	5753	14th Jan. 1829	Making from horns and hoofs of animals, handles, knobs, curtain-rings, bell-pulls, escutcheons, and finger-plates.
DEACON, WILLIAM ARCHER -	4403	1st Nov. 1819	Manufacture of boots, shoes, and clogs, by the application of materials hitherto unused for the purpose.

Name of Patentee.	Progres- sive Number.	Date.	Subject-matter of Patent.
DEAKIN, FRANCIS - - -	3603	23rd Oct 1812	Making cases or sheaths for knives, scissors, &c.
DEAKIN, FRANCIS - - -	4724	9th Nov. 1822	Manufacture of holster-cases, cartouch-boxes, and other cases.
DEAKIN, FRANCIS - - -	4759	18th Feb. 1823	Pianofortes and other stringed instruments.
DEAKIN, FRANCIS - - -	4785	22nd April 1823	Manufacturing furniture for mounting umbrellas and parasols.
DEAKIN, THOMAS - - -	3427	1st April 1811	Kitchen ranges and stoves, and mode of setting the same.
DEAKIN, THOMAS - - -	3890	7th March 1815	Portable kitchen.
DEAKIN, THOMAS - - -	3975	15th Jan. 1816	Stove, grate, or fire-place.
DEAKIN, THOMAS - - -	9417	12th July 1842	Making parts of harness and saddlery-furniture.
DEAKIN, THOMAS - - -	11,540	21st Jan. 1847	Construction and arrangement of machinery for cutting, stamping, and pressing.
DEAKIN, THOMAS - - -	13,130	12th June 1850	Machinery and apparatus to be used in rolling metals, and in the manufacturing of metal tubes.
DEAN, ALEXANDER - -	8647	24th Sept. 1840	Mills for reducing grain and other substances to a pulverized state; apparatus for dressing or bolting pulverized substances.
DEAN, JOHN - - - -	8858	23rd Feb. 1841	Preparing skins and other animal substances for obtaining gelatine, size, and glue; preparing skins for tanning.
DEAN, THOMAS MURGATROYD	11,109	25th Feb. 1846	Machinery or apparatus applicable to the furnaces or fire-places of steam-engine or other boilers.
DEAN, WILLIAM - - -	4089	14th Dec. 1816	Machinery for waxing calico or other fabric previous to glazing.
DEANE, CHARLES ANTHONY -	4869	20th Nov. 1823	Apparatus to be worn by persons entering a room filled with smoke or other vapour, for the purpose of extinguishing fire, or extricating persons or property therein.
DEANE, CHARLES ANTHONY -	10,205	30th May 1844	Constructing, propelling, and steering vessels.
DEANE, WILLIAM - - -	481	10th Dec. 1725	Engine to extinguish fires and raise water.
DEARMAN, RICHARD - -	1129	6th July 1776	Making hoes for the American and West Indian plantations.
DEARMAN, RICHARD - -	1214	22nd March 1779	Making mills for grinding malt, wheat, barley, beans, peas, groats, rice, Indian-corn, coffee, pepper, seeds, drugs and all kinds of spice.
DEBAC, PIERRE BARTHELEMY [GUINIBERT.	6652	26th July 1834	Machine for weighing, with the means of keeping a register of the operations of the instrument.
DEBAC, PIERRE BARTHELEMY [GUINIBERT.	7100	18th May 1836	Railways.
DEBAC, PIERRE BARTHELEMY [GUINIBERT.	7373	13th May 1837	Railroads.
DEBAIN, ALEXANDRE - -	11,359	29th Aug. 1846	Keyed musical instruments.
DEBAUFRE, JACOB - -	371	1st May 1704	Working stones, crystal or glass, and other matters different from metal, for use in clock or watch-work and in other engines.
DEBAUFRE, PETER - -	371	1st May 1704	Working stones, crystal or glass, and other matters different from metal, for use in clock or watch-work and in other engines.
DEBAUFRE, PETER - -	922	21st March 1769	Tools for shaving, cutting, and preparing wood for making Leghorn hats and bonnets.

Name of Patentee.	Progressive Number.	Date.	Subject-matter of Patent.
DEEBLE, EDWARD BARNARD -	5522	12th July 1827	Construction and combination of metallic blocks for forming caissons, jetties, piers, quays, embankments, lighthouses, foundations, walls, or other erections to which such blocks may be applicable.
DEELEY, EDWIN - - -	13,711	6th Aug. 1851	Construction of furnaces for the manufacture of glass.
DEELEY, JOSEPH - - -	12,374	16th Dec. 1848	Ovens and furnaces.
DEELEY, RICHARD MOUNTFORD	13,711	6th Aug. 1851	Construction of furnaces for the manufacture of glass.
DEER, EVAN - - - -	815	22nd Sept. 1764	Using refuse of alum or alum-slam, in place of kelp, for fluxing and making green glass, and soap.
DEFRIES, NATHAN - -	7705	27th June 1838	Gas-meters.
DEFRIES, NATHAN - -	9449	18th Aug. 1842	Meters for gas and other fluids.
DEFRIES, NATHAN - -	11,224	27th May 1846	Gas-meters.
DEFRIES, NATHAN - -	12,504	5th March 1849	Applying gas to heat apparatus containing fluids; heating and ventilating buildings; gas-fittings, and apparatus for controlling the passage of gas.
DEFRIES, NATHAN - -	13,414	19th Dec. 1850	Obtaining light and heat; and apparatus connected therewith.
DEGELDEW, CORNELIUS - -	210	4th May 1680	Instruments for recovering from under water ships' guns, or goods wrecked or sunk.
DELABADID, JAMES - -	237	1st Aug. 1684	Napping cloths, friezes, and other woollen manufactures.
DELAHANTE, ALEXIS - -	3655	3rd March 1813	Making a green colour, and its application to useful purposes.
DELAP, ROBERT - - -	2302	6th April 1799	Economical boilers for sundry purposes.
DELAP, ROBERT - - -	4555	1st May 1821	Producing rotary-motion.
DELARUE, EMILIE ALEXIS [FAUQUET, junior.	7819	27th Sept. 1838	Printing and fixing red and other colours in which red forms a constituent part, upon cotton, silk, woollen, and other fabrics.
DELARUE, EMILIE ALEXIS [FAUQUET, junior. [Delarue, Fauquet, junior.]	7880	22nd Nov. 1838	Printing or otherwise applying and fixing the colouring matter of madder, upon cotton, silk, linen, and other fabrics, without dyeing, and by these means producing permanent colours.
DELAVAL, THOMAS - -	846	22nd April 1766	Flux for making glass; making gunpowder from sulphur-stones or brasses found in coal-mines.
DELAVAL, THOMAS - -	870	13th March 1767	Making kelp by burning seaweed, as cut from the rocks, without further preparation.
DELBRUCK, CHARLES - -	8624	10th Sept. 1840	Apparatus for applying combustible gas to the purposes of heat.
DELCAMBRE, ADRIEN - -	8428	13th March 1840	Mode of setting up printing-types.
DELCROIX, FLORIMOND, junior	9817	6th July 1843	Furnaces for locomotive and other engines; apparatus for regulating the escape of steam and the passage of air, in chimneys of furnaces.
DELEMER, ALEXIS - - -	13,622	6th May 1851	Application of colouring matter to linens, cottons, silks, woollens, and other fabrics, also to wefts; machinery for these purposes.
DELVEAN, JAMES - - -	4672	24th April 1822	Harps.
DELFOSSE, MAXIMILIAN FRAN- [COIS JOSEPH.	11,347	25th Aug. 1846	Preventing and removing incrustation in steam-boilers.
DELL, EDWARD - - -	9047	13th Aug. 1841	Magazines and cases for gunpowder.
DELL, EDWARD - - -	10,974	4th Dec. 1845	Apparatus for heating and warming.

Name of Patentee.	Progressive Number.	Date.	Subject-matter of Patent.
DELL, EDWARD CRUMP - -	11,150	25th March 1846	Apparatus for lighting the magazines and other parts of ships ;—applicable to general purposes of lighting buildings, roads, or ways.
DELL, WILLIAM - -	4491	20th July 1820	Gun-barrels.
DELVALLE, JOSEPH - -	5134	25th March 1825	Looms for making cloths, silks, and different kinds of woven stuffs, of various breadths.
DELVIGNE, HENRI GUSTAVE -	14,066	17th April 1852	Fire-arms ; methods of discharging the same.
DEMEUR, JOHN - - -	6256	13th April 1832	Extracting oil from a foreign vegetable kernel ; its application to making candles, soap, and other articles.
DEMONDION, AUGUSTUS -	6137	13th July 1831	Guns, muskets, and other fire-arms ; cartridges to be used therewith ; method of priming ; also machinery for making such fire-arms, cartridges and priming ;—applicable to other purposes.
DEMPSTER, CATHCART - -	2733	30th Aug. 1803	Making canvas or strong cloth of vegetable materials, for sails, tents, packages, and other purposes.
DEMPSTER, CATHCART - -	5252	15th Sept. 1825	Cordage.
DENCH, EDWARD - - -	12,255	26th Aug. 1848	Roofing conservatories, hothouses, and other like structures.
DENISON, JOSEPH WADE -	12,657	12th June 1849	Engines for raising and forcing liquids.
DENISON, SAMUEL - - -	5064	1st Jan. 1825	Machinery for making wove and laid paper.
DENIZE, JOHN BAPTISTE -	2425	16th July 1800	Cement.
DENIZE, JOHN BAPTISTE -	2827	9th March 1805	Procuring a greater quantity of resinous, bituminous, and oily substances from various articles, than has hitherto been usual.
DENLEY, WILLIAM - -	9882	21st Sept. 1843	Construction of fire-places, flues, and chimneys.
DENNE, THOMAS - - -	11,674	27th April 1847	Manufacture of grease or compositions for atmospheric pipes, and for lubricating the axles and moving parts of machinery.
DENNETT, JOHN - - -	7759	2nd Aug. 1838	War-rockets, and apparatus for applying the power of rockets for obtaining communication with stranded ships ; instrument for pointing mortars for the purpose of throwing shells, or firing shot from the same.
DENNISON, JOHN - - -	13,961	9th Feb. 1852	Lubricating-compound.
DENOON, ALEXANDER - -	10,002	1st Jan. 1844	Making carbonate of soda.
DENOON, ALEXANDER - -	10,003	1st Jan. 1844	Making muriate of ammonia.
DENT, EDWARD JOHN - -	7067	23rd April 1836	Balance-springs of chronometers and other time-keepers ; and their adjustment.
DENT, EDWARD JOHN - -	8625	10th Sept. 1840	Clocks and other time-keepers.
DENT, EDWARD JOHN - -	9302	21st March 1842	Chronometers and other time-keepers.
DENT, EDWARD JOHN - -	10,277	30th July 1844	Ship's compasses.
DENT, EDWARD JOHN - -	13,176	17th July 1850	Compasses for navigation, surveying, and other purposes.
DENT, ISAAC - - - -	654	13th March 1750	Making tarrass used in brick and stone work, for building bridges and wharfs.
DENTON, JAMES - - -	11,458	21st Nov. 1846	Parts of machines used in the preparation for the spinning of cotton-wool and other fibrous substances.
DENTON, JAMES - - -	14,241	29th July 1852	Machinery for preparing cotton and other fibrous materials.
DENTON, JOHN BAILEY -	10,147	18th April 1844	Machinery for moulding or shaping clay and other plastic substances, for draining and other purposes.

Name of Patentee.	Progressive Number.	Date.	Subject-matter of Patent.
DENTON, JOSEPH - - -	13,978	23rd Feb. 1852	Machinery or apparatus for manufacturing looped, terry, or other similar fabrics.
DEPLANGUE, AMAND - -	8380	8th Feb. 1840	Looms for weaving.
DEPLEDGE, JOHN - - -	10,967	20th Nov. 1845	Metallic-broacher.
DERBISHIRE, PHILIP - -	5723	4th Dec. 1828	Medicine or embrocation to prevent or alleviate sea-sickness.
DEREHAM, RICHARD - -	202	18th April 1678	Spinning-engine, for linen or worsted thread.
DERHAM, JAMES - - -	12,116	10th April 1848	Machinery for carding, combing, preparing, and spinning cotton-wool, alpaca, mohair, flax, silk, and other fibrous materials.
DERICKSON, CHRISTIAN - -	66	7th Jan. 1634	Making, setting, and framing spring-doors, for the land side of sluices on sandy rivers; making ten mills for raising water, and for draining fens and marsh grounds.
DERING, GEORGE EDWARD -	13,427	27th Dec. 1850	Means and apparatus for communicating intelligence by electricity.
DERODE, AMIE NICOLAS -	13,716	14th Aug. 1851	Process for uniting cast-iron to cast-iron and other metals, and for uniting other metals together,
DEROSNE, CHARLES - -	5878	14th Dec. 1829	Extracting sugar or syrups from cane-juice and other substances; refining sugar and syrups.
DEROSNE, CHARLES - -	6002	29th Sept. 1830	Extracting sugar or syrups from cane-juice and other substances; refining sugar and syrups.
DEROSNE, CHARLES - -	10,389	9th Nov. 1844	Extracting sugar or syrups from cane-juice and other substances; refining sugar and syrups.
DESAGULIERS JOHN THEO- [PHILUS.	430	25th June 1720	Drying malt, hops, starch, and other humid substances; baking, brewing, distilling, boiling, and making salt, by steam.
DESANGES, FRANCIS (Sir) -	9284	7th March 1842	Apparatus for sweeping chimneys or flues, and extinguishing fires therein. (Ramoneur.)
DESBOISSIERRES, NICOLAS [FRANÇOIS CORBIN.	11,097	17th Feb. 1846	Preparing and burning fuel.
DESFORGES, NICHOLAS - -	4300	31st Oct. 1818	Propelling boats and other vessels.
DESGRANDE, JAMES VINCENT -	6334	14th Nov. 1832	Weaving elastic fabrics.
DESGRANDE, JAMES VINCENT -	7643	15th May 1838	Pulpy material for making paper and pasteboard, prepared from substances not hitherto used for the purpose.
DESGRANGES, HIPPOLYTE [PIERRE FRANÇOIS.	10,888	17th Oct. 1845	Manufacturing corks.
DESMOND, WILLIAM - -	2080	15th Jan. 1796	Tanning hides and skins, and rendering more solid and incorruptible in water, certain vegetable and animal substances, as flax, hemp, cotton, silk, hair, wool, &c., also materials made thereof.
DESORMEAUX, DANIEL - -	2884	22nd Oct. 1805	Making candles of wax, spermaceti, and tallow.
DESORMEAUX, JAMES LEWIS -	1728	23rd Feb. 1790	Preventing wringing and crushing of unwrought silk in the process of dyeing.
DESPREZ, JEAN ANDRIEN -	6453	25th July 1833	Manufacturing sulphate of quinine.
DETMOLD, JULIUS ADOLPH -	9911	18th Oct. 1843	Construction and arrangement of furnaces or fire-places, applicable to various purposes.
DETMOLD, JULIUS ADOLPH -	10,689	24th May 1845	Construction of metallic-boats and other vessels having curved surfaces.
DETMOLD, JULIUS ADOLPH -	10,775	21st July 1845	Applying steam as a motive-power.
DETTMER, WILLIAM - -	5548	30th Aug. 1827	Pianofortes.
DEURBROUCQ, DOMINIQUE [PEERRE.	4588	11th Sept. 1821	Apparatus for condensing alcoholic steam arising from spirituous-liquors during fermentation.

Name of Patentee.	Progressive Number.	Date.	Subject-matter of Patent.
DEURBROUCQ, DOMINIQUE [PEERRE.	5368	23rd May 1826	Apparatus for cooling wort or must previous to fermentation; condensing steam during distillation.
DEUTSCHE, CLAUDE EDWARD	9487	8th Oct. 1842	Combining materials for cementing purposes; forming articles from such compositions.
DEVAUX, CHARLES PIERRE -	6901	8th Oct. 1835	Smelting iron-stone or iron-ore.
DEVAUX, CHARLES PIERRE -	7210	13th Oct. 1836	Apparatus for preventing the explosion of boilers or generators of steam.
DEVAUX, CHARLES PIERRE -	7378	23rd May 1837	Apparatus for preventing the explosion of boilers or generators of steam.
DEVENOGE, HENRY ROBERT [SALMON.	5937	8th May 1830	Machinery for making bricks.
DEVERELL, WILLIAM - -	2227	5th April 1798	Pump, or pump-work.
DEVERELL, WILLIAM - -	2878	2nd Sept. 1805	Steam-engine.
DEVERELL, WILLIAM - -	2939	6th June 1806	Giving motion to hammers, stampers, knives, shears and other things, without wheel, pinion, or rotative motion.
DEVEREUX, FRANCIS - -	4885	8th Jan. 1824	Mill or machine for grinding wheat and other articles. "French Military mill."
DEVERILL, HOOTON - -	6587	31st March 1834	Engraving and etching on cylindrical surfaces, for printing and other purposes.
DEVERILL, HOOTON - -	8955	10th May 1841	Machinery for making and ornamenting bobbin-net lace.
DEVILLE, JAMES - - -	6941	3rd Dec. 1835	Production, maintenance, direction or distribution of light;—partly applicable to other p urposes.
DEVILLE, JEROME - - -	7563	8th Feb. 1838	Railroads; and carriages used thereon.
DEVILLE, JEROME - - -	7852	3rd Nov. 1838	Railroads; and carriages used thereon.
DEWEE, JOHN - - -	311	17th Jan. 1693	Engine, consisting of screw-wheels and long tumblers, for raising or lowering heavy weights; also for weighing ships' guns and anchors, and raising heavy stones to the top of buildings; also for craning goods, boring timber, and pounding and grinding minerals or other hard substances.
DEWEY, JAMES - - -	145	22nd April 1664	Making a valuable metal for divers sorts of vessels, from a certain stone mixed with other ingredients.
DEWHURST, DANIEL - -	6954	16th Dec. 1835	Machinery for preparing flax and hemp; machinery for spinning flax, hemp, cotton, silk, and other fibrous substances, by power.
DEWHURST, THOMAS - -	1131	23rd Aug. 1776	Machinery for preparing and spinning cotton.
DEWRANCE, JOHN - -	10,594	7th April 1845	Steam-boilers; construction, composition, and manufacture of bearings, steps, and other rubbing surfaces of steam-engines and other machinery; lubricating the same.
DEXTER, LAMBERT - -	5509	16th June 1827	Machinery for spinning wool, cotton, and other fibrous substances.
DEXTER, WILLIAM BULL -	11,020	24th Dec. 1845	Manufacture of warp fabrics.
DEYERLEIN, JOHANN GEORGE	3319	22nd March 1810	Machine for making bricks and tiles, also for making by means thereof and of clay, loam, or similar materials, mouldings, beads, tubes, gutters, channels or cylinders; to convey water, smoke, steam, or any fluid or soft substance.
DEYERLEIN, JOHANN GEORGE	5290	10th Nov. 1825	Weighing-machines, "German weighbridges."
DEYKIN, JAMES - - -	5062	23rd Dec. 1824	Manufacture of buttons for military, naval, and other uniforms and liveries.
DEYKIN, WILLIAM HENRY -	5062	23rd Dec. 1824	Manufacture of buttons for military, naval, and other uniforms and liveries.
DEZ MAUREL, FRANÇOIS MARIE [AGATHE.	9087	20th Sept. 1841	Buckle.

Name of Patentee.	Progres-sive Number.	Date.		Subject-matter of Patent.
DIBDIN, CHARLES - - -	3124	9th April	1808	Facilitating the learning of music.
DICAS, JOHN - - - -	1259	27th June	1780	Constructing hydrometers with sliding-rules, to ascertain the strength of spirituous liquors, malt worts and wash for fermentation.
DICK, DAVID - - - -	14,129	22nd May	1852	Manufacture and treatment or finishing of textile fabrics and materials.
DICK, MAXWELL - - -	5790	21st May	1829	Railroad; propelling carriages thereon by machinery.
DICK, WILLIAM - - -	13,230	22nd Aug.	1850	Manufacture of steel and gas.
DICKENS, JOHN - - -	463	26th Feb.	1724	Machine and floats for raising water to supply cities, drain mines, water gardens, turn mills, move ships, and for other purposes.
DICKENSON, LYMINGE - -	101	9th Jan.	1636	Taking off the outside of ormer-shells, and covering cloth, taffety, wood, and other stuffs with the same.
DICKIN, THOMAS - - -	3255	8th Aug.	1809	Preparing hemp, flax, hards, short-tow, clearings, and other inferior parts of hemp and flax, alone or mixed with cotton-wool, for the purpose of spinning; also spinning the same.
DICKINS, THOMAS - - -	12,379	21st Dec.	1848	Machinery for warping and beaming yarns or threads of silk or other fibrous materials.
DICKINSON, GEORGE - -	3839	24th Aug.	1814	Machinery for manufacturing paper; apparatus for separating knots and lumps from paper or paper-stuff.
DICKINSON, GEORGE - -	5617	21st Feb.	1828	Making paper by machinery.
DICKINSON, GEORGE - -	6535	28th Dec.	1833	Making paper.
DICKINSON, GEORGE - -	7782	23rd Aug.	1838	Steam-engines.
DICKINSON, GEORGE WASH-[INGTON.	4074	1st Nov.	1816	Preventing leakage in vessels for holding liquids; preventing admission of moisture into packages.
DICKINSON, JOHN - - -	3056	30th June	1807	Machinery for cutting and placing paper.
DICKINSON, JOHN - - -	3080	12th Nov.	1807	Cannon cartridge-paper.
DICKINSON, JOHN - - -	3191	19th Jan.	1809	Machinery for cutting and placing paper; also machinery for manufacturing paper.
DICKINSON, JOHN - - -	3452	21st May	1811	Machinery for making, cutting, and placing paper.
DICKINSON, JOHN - - -	3839	24th Aug.	1814	Machinery for manufacturing paper; apparatus for separating knots and lumps from paper or paper-stuff.
DICKINSON, JOHN - - -	4152	5th Aug.	1817	Manufacturing by means of machinery, paper for copper-plate printing, also papers for writing, drawing, letter-press printing, and a thicker sort for boards similar to card-boards or paste-boards; machinery for cutting paper.
DICKINSON, JOHN - - -	4959	20th May	1824	Cutting cards by machinery; pasting paper together, by machinery.
DICKINSON, JOHN - - -	5754	14th Jan.	1829	Manufacturing paper by machinery; cutting paper into single sheets by machinery.
DICKINSON, JOHN - - -	6008	6th Oct.	1830	Manufacturing paper by machinery.
DICKINSON, JOHN - - -	6209	10th Jan.	1832	Manufacture of paper.
DICKINSON, JOHN - - -	6866	24th July	1835	Manufacture of paper.
DICKINSON, JOHN - - -	8242	17th Oct.	1839	Manufacture of paper.
DICKINSON, JOHN - - -	8751	23rd Dec.	1840	Manufacture of paper.
DICKINSON, JOHN - - -	11,871	23rd Sept.	1847	Manufacture of paper.
DICKINSON, ROBERT - -	860	13th Sept.	1766	Bedstead for invalids, made in such a way that the person lying thereon can be raised into a sitting posture by turning a winch; may also be used as a settee.

Name of Patentee.	Progressive Number.	Date.	Subject-matter of Patent.
DICKINSON, ROBERT - -	2557	10th Nov. 1801	Construction of saddles, harness, and other gear for horses and other animals.
DICKINSON, ROBERT - -	2578	6th Feb. 1802	Fixing to saddles the straps to which the girths are usually made fast.
DICKINSON, ROBERT - -	2648	27th Sept. 1802	Working and making furniture or accoutrements useful or necessary in the employment of horses.
DICKINSON, ROBERT - -	2868	19th July 1805	Sustaining life and combustion under water, and enabling persons to move about under water.
DICKINSON, ROBERT - -	3067	1st Aug. 1807	Machinery for improving turnpike and other roads.
DICKINSON, ROBERT - -	3148	5th July 1808	Machinery for towing, driving, or forcing, and discharging the cargoes of ships and other vessels.
DICKINSON, ROBERT - -	3172	31st Oct. 1808	Stowing ships' cargoes by means of packages, to lessen the expense of stowage, and keep the goods safe.
DICKINSON, ROBERT - -	3231	29th April 1809	Naval-architecture and navigation;—applicable to other purposes.
DICKINSON, ROBERT - -	3538	8th Feb. 1812	Sweetening water and other liquids;—applicable to other purposes.
DICKINSON, ROBERT - -	3637	15th Jan. 1813	Vessels for containing liquids.
DICKINSON, ROBERT - -	3857	28th Nov. 1814	Saddlery.
DICKINSON, ROBERT - -	3858	10th Dec. 1814	Manufacture of barrels and other packages made of iron and other metals.
DICKINSON, ROBERT - -	3866	20th Dec. 1814	Implements for navigation, as a sounder, nun-buoy, and beacon-buoy.
DICKINSON, ROBERT - -	3895	14th March 1815	Making implements for use in various arts of life.
DICKINSON, ROBERT - -	3932	22nd June 1815	Facilitating the propulsion of boats or other vessels through the water; safety of the same.
DICKINSON, ROBERT - -	3970	19th Dec. 1815	Hoops or hooping of barrels.
DICKINSON, ROBERT - -	4094	23rd Jan. 1817	Preparing and paving streets and roads for horses and carriages.
DICKINSON, ROBERT - -	4170	1st Nov. 1817	Sea-beacons and their moorings.
DICKINSON, ROBERT - -	4568	14th July 1821	Constructing vessels or craft.
DICKINSON, ROBERT - -	4827	5th Aug. 1823	Shoeing, stopping, and treatment of, horses' feet.
DICKINSON, ROBERT - -	5008	7th Oct. 1824	Manufacture and construction of metal casks or barrels, for conveyance of goods by sea or otherwise.
DICKINSON, ROBERT - -	5050	7th Dec. 1824	Air-chamber.
DICKINSON, ROBERT - -	5420	8th Dec. 1826	Formation, coating and covering of vessels or packages for containing, preserving, conveying and transporting liquids or solids.
DICKINSON, THOMAS - -	1720	15th Jan. 1790	Engine worked by steam, air, water, or any other elastic or gravitating fluid, for the purpose of moving mills, pumps, and engines of every sort, also for raising or pumping water.
DICKINSON, THOMAS FRIEND -	11,494	15th Dec. 1846	Gas-meters.
DICKINSON, WILLIAM - -	5337	13th Aug. 1827	Buoyant bed or mattrass.
DICKINSON, WILLIAM - -	12,267	11th Sept. 1848	Looms for weaving.
DICKINSON, WILLIAM - -	13,693	17th July 1851	Machinery for manufacturing textile fabrics.

Name of Patentee.	Progressive Number.	Date.	Subject-matter of Patent.
DICKINSON, WILLIAM - -	13,809	13th Nov. 1851	Manufacture of chenille, and other piled fabrics.
DICKSEE, JOHN ROBERT -	10,130	30th March 1844	Manufacture of mosaics.
DICKSON, ISAAC - - -	5726	8th Dec. 1828	Projectile.
DICKSON, JAMES - - -	4415	4th Dec. 1819	Communicating power to machinery, by water, spirits of wine, quicksilver, oil, or fluids.
DICKSON, JAMES HENRY -	11,305	23rd July 1846	Saddles.
DICKSON, JOHN - - -	16	5th July 1620	Backscreen for the ease of invalids troubled with heat in their backs occasioned by continual lying on the same.
DICKSON, JOHN - - -	2249	14th July 1798	Constructing steam-engines, pumps, and other hydraulic machines.
DICKSON, JOHN - - -	3123	29th March 1808	Construction of stop-cocks.
DICKSON, JOHN - - -	7988	6th March 1839	Rotatory steam-engines.
DICKSON, JOHN - - -	9398	21st June 1842	Rotatory engines and boilers; stopping railway-carriages; machinery for propelling vessels;—partly applicable to propelling air and gases.
DICKSON, JONATHAN - -	3181	15th Nov. 1808	Construction of tuns, coolers, vats and backs, used by brewers, distillers, and others.
DICKSON, JONATHAN - -	4541	5th March 1821	Transmitting heat and cold from one body to another, whether solid or fluid.
DICKSON, JONATHAN - -	6381	6th Feb. 1833	Making gas from coal or other substances.
DICKSON, JONATHAN - -	7439	30th Sept. 1837	Steam-engines; generating steam.
DIDOT, AMBROISE FIRMAN -	3845	3rd Oct. 1814	Types for printing.
DIDOT, LEGER - - -	3209	1st March 1809	Construction of umbrellas and parasols.
DIDOT, LEGER - - -	3568	26th May 1812	Machines for making wove and laid paper.
DIDOT, LEGER - - -	3572	2nd June 1812	Candlesticks, snuffers, and candles.
DIDOT, LEGER - - -	3598	25th Sept. 1812	Moulds for making paper.
DIDOT, LEGER - - -	3852	10th Nov. 1814	Illuminating apartments or places by the combination of tallow or other inflammable materials.
DIDOT, LEGER - - -	4126	22nd May 1817	Machines for making wove and laid paper, in continued lengths or separate sheets.
DIGGLE, JAMES - - -	7027	8th March 1836	Steam-engines.
DIGGLE, ROBERT - - -	13,903	20th Jan. 1852	Bleaching and dyeing, also washing, scouring, and other processes connected therewith.
DIGGLE, SQUIRE - - -	10,462	11th Jan. 1845	Looms for weaving.
DIGGLES, GEORGE - - -	4835	19th Aug. 1823	Bit for riding-horses, and for horses in single and double harness.
DIGHT, WILLIAM - - -	1751	11th May 1790	Laying oil-colours in thin layers on canvas, wood, iron, stone, or any similar substance, to imitate marble, for chimney-pieces, pillars, or floorcloths, and for other purposes.
DIGHTON, EDWARD - -	685	22nd Aug. 1753	Manufacturing paper for hanging and ornamenting rooms, and for other purposes.
DIHL, CHRISTOPH - - -	3872	6th Jan. 1815	Making a mastic cement or composition; (" Dihl's Mastic.")
DIHL, CHRISTOPH - - -	3965	5th Dec. 1815	Apparatus for distillation.
DIHL, CHRISTOPH - - -	4033	25th May 1816	Making mastic cement or composition; working and applying the same to use. (" Dihl's Mastic.")

Name of Patentee.	Progressive Number.	Date.	Subject-matter of Patent.
DIMES, WILLIAM - - -	10,988	10th Dec. 1845	Making and fixing window-glass.
DIMMACK, JEREMIAH - -	3569	26th May 1812	Iron in all its stages.
DINSDALE, CUTHBERT - -	13,040	15th April 1850	Making artificial palates and gums; mode of setting or fixing natural or artificial teeth.
DIRCKS, HENRY - - -	8504	12th May 1840	Construction of locomotive steam-engines; wheel for railways and other ways.
DIRCKS, HENRY - - -	10,952	18th Nov. 1845	Obtaining and preparing extracts from certain vegetable matters; apparatus connected therewith; — applicable to other similar purposes.
DIRCKS, HENRY - - -	13,530	24th Feb. 1851	Manufacture of gas-burners; apparatus for heating by gas.
DISCROIZILLES, PAUL - -	5856	7th Oct. 1829	Apparatus for singeing cotton and other fabrics.
DISCROIZILLES, PAUL - - [Descroizilles, Paul.]	5931	24th April 1830	Apparatus for economizing fuel in heating water and air; — applicable to various purposes.
DISMORE, GEORGE - - -	13,802	4th Nov. 1851	Locks.
DITCHBURN, THOMAS JOSEPH	8871	8th March 1841	Ship-building, applicable to steam-boats and boats and vessels of all descriptions.
DIX, ALEXANDER MILLS -	13,929	27th Jan. 1852	Ventilating apartments or buildings; apparatus connected therewith.
DIX, ALEXANDER MILLS -	14,254	7th Aug. 1852	Artificial illumination and apparatus connected therewith; — applicable to heating and other similar purposes.
DIXON, ABRAHAM - - -	5369	23rd May 1826	Combining and displaying the colours of thread with two or more colours, in piece-goods.
DIXON, ALEXANDER - -	7356	29th April 1837	Dyeing by the use of materials not hitherto so employed.
DIXON, ALEXANDER - -	13,295	24th Oct. 1850	Moulding iron and other metals.
DIXON, EDWYN JOHN JEFFERY	13,087	30th May 1850	Manufacture of sinks and other articles of slate or stone.
DIXON, EDWYN JOHN JEFFERY	14,165	12th June 1852	Machinery for quarrying slate and stone; cutting, dressing, planing, framing and otherwise treating slate and stone; apparatus for moving and conveying slate and stone; joining, framing, and connecting the same.
DIXON, HUGH - - -	1515	14th Dec. 1785	Construction of telescopes, microscopes, spectacles, and other optical instruments.
DIXON, JAMES - - -	7356	29th April 1837	Dyeing by the use of materials not hitherto so employed.
DIXON, JOHN - - -	4729	28th Nov. 1822	Cocks for drawing off liquids.
DIXON, JOHN - - -	6047	13th Dec. 1830	Cocks for drawing off liquids.
DIXON, JOHN - - -	10,158	27th April 1844	Heating air for blast-furnaces, and other uses.
DIXON, PHILIP - - -	1987	8th May 1794	Colouring starch for making hair-powder.
DIXON, RICHARD - - -	3950	11th Aug. 1815	Construction of trunks and portmanteaus; application of materials not hitherto used in the construction thereof.
DIXON, THOMAS - - -	11,838	19th Aug. 1847	Steam-engines.
DIXON, WILLIAM - - -	3455	11th June 1811	Machinery for finishing piece-goods, or other flexible articles or materials of the like description, by glazing, burnishing, graining, or making impressions on the surface thereof.

Name of Patentee.	Progressive Number.	Date.	Subject-matter of Patent.
DIXON, WILLIAM - - -	6109	21st April 1831	Tap for fluids, liquids, and gases.
DIZI, FREDERICK - - -	3642	22nd Jan. 1813	Harps.
DIZI, FREDERICK - - - [Dizi, Frederick John.]	4171	1st Nov. 1817	Harps.
DIZI, FREDERICK - - -	4293	31st Aug. 1818	Musical wind-instruments.
DOBBS, EDGAR - - -	3367	2nd Aug. 1810	Compositions for making waterproof cement, mortar, and stucco;—applicable as a colouring wash.
DOBBS, JAMES - - -	3844	23rd Sept. 1814	Manufacture of machines for cutting and gathering-in grain and produce of the earth.
DOBBS, THOMAS - - -	2761	14th May 1804	"Albion metal" for cisterns, coverings or gutters for buildings, boilers, and vats, worms for distillers, and other articles requiring to be made of a flexible or a cheap metallic substance.
DOBBS, THOMAS - - -	4515	9th Dec. 1820	Uniting or plating tin upon lead.
DOBBS, WILLIAM - - -	7716	30th June 1838	Racks and pullies for window-blinds and other like purposes.
DOBINSON, THOMAS STORER -	6292	3rd Aug. 1832	Windlasses. ("Tysack, Dobinson, and Co.'s compound lever windlass.")
DOBITO, MARK - - -	3242	8th June 1809	Plough for under-draining land.
DOBREE, CARTERET PRIAULX -	9761	10th June 1843	Manufacture of fuel.
DOBREE, SAMUEL - - -	10,055	17th Feb. 1844	Manufacture of fuel.
DOBREE, WILLIAM - -	5968	5th Aug. 1830	Safety-boat.
DOBSON, BENJAMIN - -	6552	6th Feb. 1834	Machinery for roving and spinning cotton and other fibrous materials.
DOBSON, JOHN - - -	3442	1st May 1811	Manufacture of rudder-bands and bolts for shipping.
DOBSON, WILLIAM - - -	2662	25th Nov. 1802	Machinery for chasing away flies and venomous insects.
DOCKER, WILLIAM - -	2253	3rd Aug. 1798	Making pipes or tubes of solid blocks of stone.
DOCKREE, JOHN - - -	8877	15th March 1841	Gas-burners.
DOCKSEY, WILLIAM - -	3341	22nd May 1810	Manufacturing ivory-black; pulverizing potters' clays and flints; colouring and glazing materials in kilns, ovens, or furnaces.
DOD, CHARLES - - -	8702	12th Nov. 1840	Process for manufacturing plate-glass; also substances in imitation of marbles, stones, agates, and other minerals, applicable for use or ornament.
DODD, EDWARD - - -	4671	24th April 1822	Pedal-harps.
DODD, EDWARD - - -	5528	25th July 1827	Pianofortes.
DODD, EDWARD - - -	8692	7th Nov. 1840	Pianofortes.
DODD, GEORGE - - -	2825	28th Feb. 1805	Royal York gun-lock, other gun-locks, and locks of all sorts of fire-arms.
DODD, GEORGE - - -	3522	23rd Jan. 1812	Machinery, also the application of steam, to communicate heat and motion to wines, porter, and other liquids and fluids, in cellars and stores.
DODD, GEORGE - - -	3668	16th March 1813	Umbrellas.
DODD, GEORGE - - -	5023	21st Oct. 1824	Fire-extinguishing machinery.

Name of Patentee.	Progressive Number.	Date.		Subject-matter of Patent.
DODD, RALPH　-　-　-	2937	6th June	1806	Applying steam for forcing and raising water and heavy bodies, and for working machinery.
DODD, RALPH　-　-　-	3071	8th Sept.	1807	Still or alembic, with a refrigeratory worm or condenser, and a piston and rod, for distillers, brewers, and others using like machinery.
DODD, RALPH　-　-　-	3141	3rd June	1808	Bridge-floorings or platforms, and fireproof floorings and roofings, for houses, warehouses, and mills.
DODD, RALPH　-　-　- [Dodds, Ralph.]	3887	28th Feb.	1815	Construction of locomotive-engines.
DODD, BARRODALL ROBERT　-	2839	18th April	1805	Construction of fire-places; adapting stoves and grates thereto.
DODD, THOMAS　-　-　-	6337	24th Nov.	1832	Machinery for raising water and other liquids.
DODDS, ISAAC　-　-　-	6470	14th Sept.	1833	Manufacturing valves for steam-engines or steam-apparatus, or for any fluid or gas, and in any situation where valves or sluices may be used; combination of materials for manufacturing such valves.
DODDS, ISAAC　-　-　- [Dodd, Isaac.]	6755	29th Jan.	1835	Machinery for cutting and shaping wood and other materials.
DODDS, ISAAC　-　-　-	6826	30th April	1835	Construction of fire-arms;—partly applicable to the making and using common or other ordnance.
DODDS, ISAAC　-　-　-	8219	16th Sept.	1839	Railways; construction and manufacture of wheels, engines, and machinery to be used thereon.
DODDS, ISAAC　-　-　-	9157	13th Nov.	1841	Supplying gas for lighting towns and other places.
DODGE, GEORGE HENRY　-	11,888	7th Oct.	1847	Machinery for spinning and winding yarn.
DODGE, GEORGE HENRY　-	12,606	10th May	1849	Machinery for spinning and doubling cotton yarns and other fibrous materials; machinery for winding, reeling, balling, and spooling the same.
DODGEON, JOHN　-　-　-	12,036	22nd Jan.	1848	Looms for weaving.
DODGSON, GEORGE　-　-	2260	23rd Aug.	1798	Making pumps and engines for raising and evacuating water or other fluids, and for producing power, particularly adapted for ships and vessels.
DODGSON, GEORGE　-　-	4034	27th May	1816	Simplifying the construction of extinguishing-engines and forcing-pumps.
DODGSON, JOHN WILLIAM　-	5872	17th Nov.	1829	Ships' scuppers;—applicable to other purposes.
DODSON, ARTHUR JOHN　-	14,165	12th June	1852	Machinery for quarrying slate and stone; cutting, dressing, planing, framing, and otherwise treating slate and stone; apparatus for moving and conveying slate and stone; joining, framing, and connecting the same.
DODSON, GEORGE　-　-　-	2337	8th Aug.	1799	Making and casting naves or stocks for wheels, with cast-iron, brass, or mixed metal.
DODSWORTH, CHRISTOPHER　-	268	12th June	1691	Making metals to give window-glass more lustre; making red crystal glass; casting glass.

Name of Patentee.	Progres-sive Number.	Date.	Subject-matter of Patent.
DODSWORTH, ROBERT - -	325	19th Sept. 1693	Manufacturing and ordering roots and barks with other ingredients, for dyeing silks, wrought and unwrought, and woollen and linen cloth, in many colours, in grain and otherwise, with or without fire; also useful for limners and painters, for perforating glass, and for other purposes.
DOE, JOSEPH BOLTON - -	7687	14th June 1838	Apparatus used in the manufacture of soap.
DOLAN, DENIS - - -	10,489	21st Jan. 1845	Manufacture of plastic materials, applicable to decorative purposes, and as a fireproof cement.
DOLBY, CHARLES - -	635	8th Aug. 1748	Dyeing green and blue Saxon colours.
DOLIER, WILLIAM - - -	6182	14th Oct. 1831	Copybook or writing-tablet, and delible ink.
DOLIER, WILLIAM - - -	7786	30th Aug. 1838	Tablet for receiving writings, drawings, or impressions of engravings;—applicable to roads or pavements, and for strengthening and beautifying glass.
DOLIGNON, STEPHEN - -	1175	31st Dec. 1777	Weaving and cutting the brocade floating-silk on the face of velvet-shag, satin-cord, tabby-chain, lustring or mixtures, plain flowered or spotted with plush-tissue, with gold and silver and with silk mixed to form designs; staining and printing the surface of plain and other plush.
DOLIGNON, STEPHEN - -	1809	28th May 1791	Machine for weaving.
DOLLAND, GEORGE - -	3540	19th Feb. 1812	Lighting the binnacle-compass, for steering ships at sea; also ship's binnacles.
DOLLAND, JOHN - - -	721	19th April 1758	Making object-glasses of refracting-telescopes, by compounding mediums of different refractive qualities.
DOLLAND, JOHN - - -	752	2nd Oct. 1760	Quadrant for taking observations at sea.
DOLLAND, PETER - - -	1017	22nd May 1772	Adjusting and improving the glasses of Hadley's quadrant or sextant, placing darkening glasses before or behind the horizon-glasses, in order that images seen by direct vision may occasionally be darkened.
DOLLMAN, THOMAS FRANCIS -	3561	5th May 1812	Elastic round hat, made of beaver, silk, or other materials.
DOMINICETTI, BARTHOLOMEW	882	11th Sept. 1767	Making arbitrarily heated and medicated salubrious baths, pumps, and stoves, both moist and dry.
DOMINICETTI, BARTHOLOMEW	972	6th Dec. 1770	Machine for dressing from one to twenty dishes at once with one fire; also for purifying foul and maggoty water. "The Economist."
DON, JAMES - - - -	6388	21st Feb. 1833	Machinery used in building steam-vessels and steam-carriages;—applicable to other purposes.
DON, THOMAS - - -	5507	15th June 1827	Making shutters and blinds of iron, steel, or other metal, or composition thereof; constructing and fixing the same; uniting in shutters the double properties of shutters and blinds.
DON, THOMAS - - -	6396	8th March 1833	Machinery for preparing farinaceous substances, and making bread.

Name of Patentee.	Progressive Number.	Date.	Subject-matter of Patent.
DON, THOMAS - - -	7245	3rd Dec. 1836	Preparing and drying grain, seeds, or berries; manufacturing them into their several products;—applicable to other purposes.
DONALD, JAMES Mᶜ - -	1699	29th Aug. 1789	Making all kinds of breeches.
DONALD, JAMES Mᶜ - -	12,925	11th Jan. 1850	Applying oil or grease to wheels and axles, and to machinery; connecting the springs of wheel-carriages with the axles or axle-boxes.
DONALDSON, JAMES - -	10,965	20th Nov. 1845	Scouring, bleaching, and washing wool, cotton, silk, and other fibrous substances raw or manufactured.
DONALDSON, JOHN - -	671	25th June 1752	Engine for raising water, draining lands, and for other purposes.
DONALDSON, JOHN - -	1587	1st Feb. 1787	Luminators, candle-moulds, sockets, stands, and other apparatus for making and using luminators.
DONALDSON, JOHN - -	1933	19th Feb. 1793	Preserving animal and vegetable substances.
DONALDSON, JOHN - -	2589	5th March 1802	Making all kinds of glass.
DONCASTER, WILLIAM - -	3827	26th July 1814	Construction, uses, and mode of navigating ships or vessels for marine and inland navigation; abstracting for separate use such powers and machinery as form an hydrostator or mill; easing the draught of carriages; dining table.
DONISTHORPE, GEORGE ED-[MUND.	6806	3rd April 1835	Combing wool and other fibrous substances.
DONISTHORPE, GEORGE ED-[MUND.	8693	7th Nov. 1840	Machinery for combing and preparing wool and other textile substances.
DONISTHORPE, GEORGE ED-[MUND.	9404	6th July 1842	Combing and drawing wool, and certain descriptions of hair.
DONISTHORPE, GEORGE ED-[MUND.	9780	15th June 1843	Combing wool and other fibrous substances.
DONISTHORPE, GEORGE ED-[MUND.	9966	25th Nov. 1843	Combing wool and other fibrous substances.
DONISTHORPE, GEORGE ED-[MUND.	11,743	12th June 1847	Roving and spinning wool and flax; treating wool previous to spinning; heckling flax.
DONISTHORPE, GEORGE ED-[MUND.	12,468	12th Feb. 1849	Apparatus for stopping steam-engines and other first movers.
DONISTHORPE, GEORGE ED-[MUND.	12,603	8th May 1849	Preparing, combing, and heckling fibrous matters.
DONISTHORPE, GEORGE ED-[MUND.	12,712	18th July 1849	Preparing, combing, and spinning wool.
DONISTHORPE, GEORGE ED-[MUND. [Donisthorpe, George Edmond.]	12,849	17th Nov. 1849	Apparatus for stopping steam-engines and other first movers.
DONISTHORPE, GEORGE ED-[MUND. [Donisthorpe, George Edmond,]	12,877	3rd Dec. 1849	Wheels of locomotive-carriages.
DONISTHORPE, GEORGE ED-[MUND. [Donisthorpe, George Edmond.]	13,009	20th March 1850	Preparing and combing wool and other fibrous materials.
DONKIN, BRYAN - - -	2730	3rd Aug. 1803	Producing rotary motion, applicable to useful purposes.
DONKIN, BRYAN - - -	2948	24th July 1806	Combining wheel-work, to produce any velocity between the weight and the first mover.

Name of Patentee.	Progressive Number.	Date.	Subject-matter of Patent.
DONKIN, BRYAN - - -	3118	14th March 1808	Pens.
DONKIN, BRYAN - - -	3455	11th June 1811	Machinery for finishing piece-goods or other flexible articles or materials of the like description, by glazing, burnishing, graining, or making impressions on the surface thereof.
DONKIN, BRYAN - - -	3757	23rd Nov. 1813	Apparatus employed in printing from types, blocks or plates.
DONKIN, BRYAN - - -	3988	2nd March 1816	Effecting certain purposes or processes requiring a higher temperature than that of boiling water.
DONKIN, BRYAN - - - [Donkin, Boyan.]	[4202	17th Jan. 1818	Printing-press, for printing from types, plates, or blocks.
DONKIN, BRYAN - - -	4842	11th Sept. 1823	Removing fibres from thread of flax, cotton, silk, or other fibrous substance composing lace, net, or other similar fabric.
DONKIN, BRYAN - - -	8212	5th Sept. 1839	Making paper by hand or by machinery.
DONKIN, BRYAN - - -	10,932	11th Nov. 1845	Wheels for railway-carriages; mechanical contrivances by which railway-carriages are made to cross from one line of rails to another, and to sidings.
DONKIN, BRYAN - - -	12,964	9th Feb. 1850	Steam-engines; fluid-meter.
DONKIN, JOHN - - -	6725	25th Nov. 1834	Machinery for making paper.
DONKIN, JOHN - - -	11,417	15th Oct. 1846	Manufacture of paper, or machinery employed therein; bleaching paper, linen, and other manufactures in which chloride of lime is employed.
DONLAN, MICHAEL JOSEPH [JOHN.	12,109	4th April 1848	Compounds or mixtures to be used for lubricating machinery.
DONLAN, MICHAEL JOSEPH [JOHN.	14,164	10th June 1852	Treating the seeds of flax and hemp; treatment and preparation of flax and hemp for dressing.
DONNITHORNE, NICHOLAS -	1256	12th June 1780	White composition or marine-metal for sheathing ships and for other purposes, having the quality of not corroding or becoming foul.
DONOVAN, JEREMIAH - -	3756	23rd Nov. 1813	Saponaceous compounds for deterging in sea-water, hard water, and soft water.
DONOVAN, MICHAEL - -	6003	6th Oct. 1830	Lighting places with gas.
DOORNIK, WILLIAM EVERHARD [BARON VAN.	2798	19th Dec. 1804	Compositions, formed by uniting an absorbent or detergent earth with other ingredients, for washing, scouring, and for other purposes.
DOORNIK, WILLIAM EVERHARD [BARON VAN. [Doornik, William Everhard Baron Von.]	3203	7th Feb. 1809	Manufacture of soap, to wash with sea-water, hard water, and soft water.
DOORNIK, WILLIAM EVERHARD [BARON VAN.	3438	27th April 1811	Manufacture of soap, to wash with sea-water, hard water, and soft water.
DOORNIK, WILLIAM EVERHARD [BARON VAN. [Doornik, William Everhard Baron Von.]	3864	20th Dec. 1814	Manufacture of soap.
DORDOY, STEPHEN GEORGE -	8249	31st Oct. 1839	Manufacture of gelatine, size, and glue.
DOREY, JULES FRANÇOIS -	13,798	4th Nov. 1851	Illuminating the dials of clocks and other instruments in which dials are employed.

Name of Patentee.	Progres-sive Number.	Date.	Subject-matter of Patent.
DORILA, ANDREW - - -	877	2nd June 1767	Making velvet-shag, and brocaded silk, plain, cut, figured, and in gold and silver, on a stocking-frame.
DORNEY, THOMAS - - -	72	17th July 1634	Engine for ploughing land without horses or oxen, by the labour of two men to force it, and one to guide the same.
DORNING, HENRY - - -	1º,914	3rd Jan. 1850	Machinery for manufacturing bricks, tiles, and other similar articles, from clay or other plastic materials.
DORR, EBENEZER - - -	10,403	25th Nov. 1844	Manufacture of horse-shoe nails.
DORR, JAMES AUGUSTUS -	10,737	25th June 1845	Machinery for knitting.
DORR, SAMUEL GRISSOULD -	1945	9th April 1793	Machine for shearing cloth and other articles.
DORR, SAMUEL GRISSOULD -	1985	7th May 1794	Grate, range, or stove, with apparatus to be applied thereto to prevent chimneys smoking, and to facilitate the processes of cooking without using charcoal, also adapted to the operations of the washhouse and laundry.
DOTCHIN, SAMUEL - -	9488	13th Oct. 1482	Paving or covering and constructing roads, ways, and other surfaces.
DOUCHE, FELIX - - -	12,062	10th Feb. 1848	Processes and apparatus for preventing the escape of heat through boilers; apparatus for saving and applying the lost heat, and in some cases directing the same.
DOUDNEY, EDWARD PHILLIPS	9634	17th Feb. 1843	Manufacture of dip and mould candles.
DOUDNEY, GEORGE EBENEZER	9634	17th Feb. 1843	Manufacture of dip and mould candles.
DOUGAL, ALEXANDER Mᶜ -	12,333	21st Nov. 1848	Manufacture of sulphuric-acid, nitric-acid, oxalic-acid, chlorine, and sulphur.
DOUGAL, ALEXANDER Mᶜ -	12,529	20th March 1849	Recovering products from water used in washing and treating wool, woollen and cotton fabrics and other substances.
DOUGALL, ALEXANDER Mᶜ -	11,528	14th Jan. 1847	Manufacture of glue; treating products obtained in the manufacture of the same.
DOUGHTY, ROBERT - -	3C9	— 1692	Tanning skins and making imitation Russian leather.
DOUGHTY, WILLIAM - -	3302	12th Feb. 1810	Combination of wheels for gaining mechanical-power.
DOUGLAS, JOHN COOPER -	6508	19th Nov. 1833	Construction of furnaces for generating heat; construction of apparatus for applying heat to various purposes.
DOUGLAS, JOHN COOPER -	6509	19th Nov. 1833	Prevention of the explosion or collapse of steam and other boilers from an excess of internal or external pressure.
DOUGLAS, JOHN COOPER -	6514	21st Nov. 1833	Depriving vegetable juices, also fermented and distilled liquids, of acidity, colouring-matter, and essential-oils.
DOUGLAS, JOHN COOPER -	6585	29th March 1834	Constructing apparatus from which a motive principle of power is obtained; increasing such motive principle, applicable to locomotion, also to stationary machinery, to raising solid or fluid bodies, and to other purposes; constructing apparatus and vehicles to be propelled or worked by such power.

Name of Patentee.	Progressive Number.	Date.	Subject-matter of Patent.
DOUGLAS, JOHN COOPER -	6875	10th Aug. 1835	Ventilating subterraneous and other places; constructing an apparatus in which combustion is carried on; also applying certain fluids to various purposes, and constructing an apparatus or vessel for the appropriation of such fluids.
DOUGLAS, JOSEPH - - - [*Douglass, Joseph.*]	7167	11th Aug 1836	Manufacture of oakum.
DOUGLAS, JOSEPH - - -	11,030	9th Jan. 1846	Patterns used in casting; also casting metals.
DOUGLAS, Sir HOWARD -	3461	2nd July 1811	Reflecting circle or semicircle.
DOUGLASS, ARCHIBALD - -	6414	30th April 1833	Power-looms, and the shuttles used therein.
DOUGLASS, JAMES - - -	2216	20th Feb. 1798	Machine for making or moulding bricks.
DOUGLASS, JAMES - - -	2225	30th March 1798	Machinery for shearing woollen-cloth with shears, knives, and cutters,. put in operation by various powers.
DOUGLASS, JAMES - -	2359	28th Nov. 1799	Apparatus composed of chains, wheels, rollers, and conductors, for lessening friction in raising, lowering, driving, and conducting heavy bodies;—applicable to other purposes.
DOUGLASS, JOSEPH - -	11,186	30th April 1846	Manufacture of yarn, twine, and cordage.
DOUHET, GUILLAUME FER- [DINAND DE.	13,092	1st June 1850	Disoxygenation of certain bodies, and application, separately or simultaneously, of the products therefrom.
DOULL, ALEXANDER - -	11,569	8th Feb. 1847	Railway, steam-boat, and other signals.
DOULL, ALEXANDER - -	13,804	6th Nov. 1851	Railway construction.
DOVER, JOHN - - -	7492	28th Nov. 1837	Filtering fluids.
DOVER, RICHARD - - -	13,775	16th Oct. 1851	Treating sewage, and obtaining products therefrom; combining such products and other matter.
DOVEY, RICHARD - - -	1055	15th Nov. 1773	Making a metal of the colour and in all respects resembling gold.
DOWALL, CHARLES Mᶜ -	13,587	10th April 1851	Construction of time-keepers.
DOWALL, JOHN Mᶜ - -	6606	12th May 1834	Metallic-pistons, pump-buckets, and boilers of steam-engines.
DOWALL, JOHN Mᶜ - -	7133	24th June 1 836	Machinery for sawing timber; applying power to the same.
DOWALL, JOHN Mᶜ - -	14,026	20th March 1852	Cutting wood and other substances; machinery or apparatus employed therein; application of power to the same;—partly applicable to the transmission of power generally.
DOWDING WILLIAM JOHN -	5566	22nd Nov. 1827	Machinery for rolling or rollering wool from the carding-engine.
DOWIE, JAMES - - -	7493	2nd Dec. 1837	Construction of boots and shoes, or other coverings for the human feet.
DOWLING, THOMAS - -	7704	26th June 1838	Preparing metals for the prevention of oxydation.
DOWLING, THOMAS - -	7949	24th Jan. 1839	Preparing metals for the prevention of oxydation.
DOWN, JAMES- - - -	5966	5th Aug. 1830	Making gas for illumination; apparatus for the purpose.
DOWNE, WILLIAM - - -	5408	25th Aug. 1826	Waterclosets.
DOWNER, HENRY - - -	1742	13th April 1790	Spring for shutting doors.
DOWNES, JOHN - - -	872	13th March 1767	Deepening-tool, for deepening clock and watch wheels.

Name of Patentee.	Progressive Number.	Date.	Subject-matter of Patent.
DOWNING, CHARLES - -	5242	15th Aug. 1825	Fowling-pieces and other fire-arms.
DOWNING, GEORGE - -	11,281	6th July 1846	Manufacture of penholders.
DOWNING, HENRY - - -	7237	29th Nov. 1836	Manufacturing rivets, screw-blanks, and other articles.
DOWNTON, JONATHAN - -	5187	18th June 1825	Waterclosets.
DOWNTON, JONATHAN - -	5221	19th July 1825	Pumps.
DOWSE, CHARLES - - -	10,996	10th Dec. 1845	Paper or material.
DOWSE, CHARLES - - -	11,329	11th Aug. 1846	Manufacturing and finishing fabrics, as substitutes for paper.
DOWSE, CHARLES - - -	11,513	31st Dec. 1846	Applying springs to braces, portfolios, hats, and caps, also to memorandum and other books.
DOWSON, EMERSON - -	4001	23rd March 1816	Grates and stoves; apparatus for supplying grates and stoves with fuel.
DOXAT, ALPHONSO - - -	4532	27th Jan. 1821	Combination of mechanical powers, whereby the weight and muscular force of men may be employed to actuate machinery for raising water, and for other purposes.
DOYL, JOHN - - - -	5401	4th Aug. 1826	Apparatus and process for separating salt from sea-water, and thereby rendering it fresh and fit for use.
DOYNE, WILLIAM THOMAS -	13,801	4th Nov. 1851	The permanent way of railways.
DRAKE, FRANCIS HORATIO [NELSON.	5746	18th Dec. 1828	Process for the invention of a particular till.
DRAKE, FRANCIS HORATIO [NELSON.	5820	25th July 1829	Tiles for covering houses and other buildings.
DRAKE, JAMES LAURENCE -	3552	8th April 1812	Preparing isinglass from river and marine fish.
DRAKE, JOHN COLARD - -	8852	18th Feb. 1841	Scales used in drawing and laying down plans.
DRAKE, JOHN COLARD - -	9871	22nd Aug. 1843	Lining walls of houses.
DRAKE, JOHN LOAD - -	7406	19th July 1837	Building ships, steam-vessels and boats, also canal and river barges and lighters.
DRAKE, JOHN LOAD - -	13,736	4th Sept. 1851	Constructing and propelling ships and other vessels.
DRAKE, WILLIAM - - -	6178	7th Oct. 1831	Tanning hides and skins.
DRAKEFORD. EDWARD - -	4993	29th July 1824	Making swifts and apparatus thereto belonging, for the purpose of winding silk and other fibrous materials.
DRAPER, CRESHOLD - -	223	21st Nov. 1682	Making wet docks and harbours to hold ships forty feet above high water; engines to transfer ships from the river Thames or from stocks, into the said harbours, and vice versâ.
DRAPER, SAMUEL - - -	6683	25th Sept. 1834	Manufacture of ornamented bobbin-net lace.
DRAPER, SAMUEL - - -	6907	15th Oct. 1835	Producing plain or ornamental weavings.
DRAPER, SAMUEL - - -	7491	27th Nov. 1837	Producing ornamental lace or weavings.
DRAPER, SAMUEL - - -	8635	21st Sept. 1840	Manufacture of ornamented twist lace and looped fabrics.
DRAY, WILLIAM - - -	13,924	27th Jan. 1852	Reaping-machines.
DRAYTON, THOMAS - - -	9968	25th Nov. 1843	Coating glass with silver, for looking-glasses and other uses.
DRAYTON, THOMAS - - -	12,358	4th Dec. 1848	Silvering glass and other surfaces.

Name of Patentee.	Progressive Number.	Date.	Subject-matter of Patent.
DREDGE, JAMES - - -	7120	17th June 1836	Construction of suspension-chains for bridges, viaducts, aqueducts, and other purposes ; construction of such bridges, viaducts, and aqueducts.
DRESCHKE, THEOPHILE AU- [GUSTE.	11,320	31st July 1846	Keys of pianofortes and other keyed musical instruments.
DREW, JAMES - - - -	7867	8th Nov. 1838	Consuming smoke and economizing fuel in steam-engine or other furnaces or fire places.
DREW, JOSEPH, junior - -	9069	8th Sept. 1841	Machine for rolling and cutting lozenges, also for cutting gun-wads, wafers, and other similar substances.
DREW, THOMAS - - -	10,569	18th March 1845	Production and manufacture of naphtha, pyroligneous acid, or other inflammable matter.
DREWE, JOHN - - -	37	20th Jan. 1627	Engines for conveying water to dry grounds, and for drawing water from mines of tin, lead, copper, and coals, or from other places.
DRIEU, JEROME ANDRÉ - -	12,719	1st Aug. 1849	Manufacture of wearing-apparel ; machinery connected therewith.
DRIGTON, JOHN - - -	208	24th May 1679	Pipes, engines, and vessels (by way of hydragogy), for raising water out of ships and mines, for draining land, and for supplying, even in the drought of summer, all sorts of mills, whether undershot or overshot ; also for raising the Thames water in larger quantity than is now raised by the water-mill houses, without the great charge and labour of men and horses.
DRING, JOHN - - - -	906	25th Nov. 1768	Making ink into a cake or solid body, which is not liable to decay or to lose its quality.
DRING, JOHN - - - -	984	6th Mar. 1771	Compounding roasted coffee, and making the same into a cake, to dissolve in and mix with water without grinding or scraping.
DRING, JOHN - - - -	1725	20th Jan. 1790	Ball-cocks.
DRIVER, JEREMIAH - -	13,957	9th Feb. 1852	Screws.
DRIVER, WILLIAM - - -	1366	3rd May 1783	Engine and wheel-carriage, with suitable machinery and apparatus to break up, raise, load, carry, shoot, and otherwise work, mould, gravel, stones, chalk, and other materials and substances, without manual labour.
DRUKE, JOHN GEORGE - -	3978	3rd Feb. 1816	Expelling the molasses of syrup out of refined sugars.
DRUMMOND, ANTHONY - -	904	28th Oct. 1768	Machine for polishing or planing marble, flagstones, paving and other stones.
DRUMMOND, PETER ROBERT -	13,701	29th July 1851	Churns.
DRURY, DRU - - - -	970	16th Nov. 1770	Making silver and other metallic hafts for knives, forks, and similar articles, by means of two steel or metallic dies.
DRY, JOHN - - - -	9434	2nd Aug. 1842	Thrashing-machines.
DU BOCHET, HENRY - -	9631	11th Feb. 1843	Making pianofortes.
DU BOIS, PHILIP HENRY -	11,448	12th Nov. 1846	Producing ornamental metal surfaces.
DU BOULAY, JOHN - - -	11,565	8th Feb. 1847	Fitting-up granaries and warehouses ; getting into condition and preserving therein grain, pulse, seed, malt, and other perishable articles.
DU BOULAY, THOMAS - -	7420	24th Aug. 1837	Drying and screening malt.

Name of Patentee.	Progressive Number.	Date.	Subject-matter of Patent.
Du Boulay, Thomas - -	11,565	8th Feb. 1847	Fitting-up granaries and warehouses; getting into condition and preserving therein grain, pulse, seed, malt, and other perishable articles.
Du Buisson, Joseph Marie Ursule la Rigandelle.	5902	12th Feb. 1830	Extracting colour from dyewoods and other substances used by dyers.
Du Buisson, Michel Antoine [Bertin Burin.	10,726	23rd June 1845	Distillation of bituminous shistus and other bituminous substances; purification, rectification, and preparation of the productions obtained by such distillation, for various purposes.
Du Columbier, René Joseph, [le Comte.	10,414	22nd Dec. 1844	Machinery for splitting and cutting skins and hides.
Du Crouy, Nicholas Henri [Jean Francois, Comte.	9678	25th March 1843	Rotary-pumps and steam-engines.
Du Fresue, Francis Fandell	211	9th June 1681	Making bay-salt.
Du Manoir, Richard Law- [rence.	366	12th Sept. 1700	Engines, kilns, and other instruments for the making of looking-glass, plate-glass panels, and chimney-pieces for rooms.
Du Maurier, Louis Mathurin [Busson.	7924	3rd Jan. 1839	Construction of springs for carriages.
Du Motay, Cyprien Marie [Jessie.	11,943	4th Nov. 1847	Inlaying and coating metals with various substances.
Duberguet, Francois Justin	12,857	22nd Nov. 1849	Hydro-pneumatic engines.
Dubern, Henry Adolphe -	10,471	16th Jan. 1845	Atmospheric-railways.
Dubison, Peter - - -	400	19th Nov. 1715	Printing, dyeing, or staining calicoes in grain.
Dubochet, Vincent - -	13,057	23rd April 1850	Production of coke and of gas for illumination; regulating the circulation of such gas.
Dubs, Henry - - -	9699	19th April 1843	Boilers.
Duce, Joseph, junior - -	9364	24th May 1842	Lock and key, and slide-bolt for the said lock;—applicable to other purposes.
Ducie, Henry George Fran- [cis, Earl of.	8660	15th Oct. 1840	Machinery for cutting vegetable and other substances.
Duckworth, William - -	13,346	14th Nov. 1850	Manufacture of chicory; machinery or apparatus for the manufacture thereof.
Duclen, Peter - - -	261	4th Nov. 1688	Making, dressing, and instrating black plain silks, as alamodes, ranforsees, and lustrings.
Duclos, Edouard Francois [Joseph.	7448	20th Oct. 1837	Manufacturing iron.
Duclos, Edouard Francois [Joseph.	7662	31st May 1838	Manufacture of zinc, copper, tin, and antimony.
Duclos, Edouard Francois [Joseph.	8149	11th July 1839	Manufacture of sulphur, sulphuric-acid, and sulphate of soda.
Ducoté, Pierré Auguste -	8133	26th June 1839	Printing on paper, calicoes, silks, and other fabrics.
Ducoté, Pierré Auguste -	8278	21st No. 1839	Printing china, porcelain, earthenware, and other similar wares; and printing on paper, calicoes, silks, woollen, oilcloths, leather, and other fabrics; also material to be used in printing.
Ducrest, Charles Lewis -	1662	12th Aug. 1788	Making paper for building houses, bridges, ships, boats, wheel-carriages, sedan-chairs, chairs, tables, and book-cases, either of paper, or of wood and iron covered with paper.

Name of Patentee.	Progressive Number.	Date.		Subject-matter of Patent.
DUDLEY, DUDD - - -	117	2nd May	1638	Making cast-iron and bar-iron, with sea-coal or pit-coal, peat, or turf; refining metals; also mining and working ores of gold, silver, copper, or lead mixed with silver or quicksilver; draining mines and erecting houses, mills, and works for the said purposes.
DUDLEY, EDWARD, Lord - -	18	22nd Feb.	1621	Smelting iron-ore and making cast-iron or bar-iron with sea-coal or pit-coal, in furnaces with bellows.
DUDLEY, THOMAS BARNARD [WILLIAMSON.	4735	16th Dec.	1822	Making malleable cast-metal shoes for draught and riding horses and other animals.
DUDLEY, WILLIAM - - -	1555	5th Aug.	1786	Buckle-chape or fastening for shoes, with a spring-jointed plate, on which may be affixed any rim, ornament, or device.
DUESBURY, WILLIAM - -	5258	29th Sept.	1825	Preparing or manufacturing a white sulphate from impure native sulphate of barytes.
DUESBURY, WILLIAM - -	5797	1st Aug.	1826	Tanning.
DUFF, JOHN - - - -	3288	14th Dec.	1809	Snuffers.
DUFFY, JOHN, junior - -	3776	8th Feb.	1814	Producing patterns on calico or linen cloths, by defending from injury the mordants or colours previously applied to them, when such mordants or colours are passed through solutions of acids, acid-salts, metallic-salts, or combinations of oxymuriatic-acid.
DUFOUR, WILLIAM - -	1652	10th June	1788	Fire-escape.
DUFOUR, WILLIAM - -	1790	24th Jan.	1791	Sliding balcony or fire-escape.
DUGDALE, JOHN - - -	12,625	31st May	1849	Constructing and propelling ships or other vessels.
DUGDALE, RICHARD - -	7944	19th Jan.	1839	Increasing the security, tenacity, and strength of beams, axles, rods, and other articles made of iron and steel.
DUGDALE, RICHARD -	12,418	13th Jan.	1849	Hardening articles composed of iron.
DUJARDIN, PIERRE ANTOINE [JOSEPH.	11,894	7th Oct.	1847	Electro-magnetic telegraphic apparatus.
DUKE, ELIZABETH - -	2603	2nd April	1802	Waterproofing woollen, cotton, and linen cloths, canvas, silk, hats, paper, and other manufactures.
DULEY, JOHN - - -	12,357	2nd Dec.	1848	Construction and arrangement of stoves for cooking, and other purposes.
DUMBELL, JOHN - - -	3106	4th Feb.	1808	Obtaining, producing, using, and cultivating a moving power; communicating motion to engines, pumps, machinery and to mechanical operations in general; forming and using a circular or a to and fro motion, working and applying the same to mills, machinery, ploughs, tools, and carriages. Structure and guidance of carriages, and rendering them less liable to overturn. (George's Wain.")
DUMBELL, JOHN - - -	3166	25th Aug.	1808	Flax-spinning, and making a thread, furniture, frills, or attire called telary-teguments, from silk, wool, cotton, flax, hemp, or tow, or from other articles combined or uncombined; also refabricating or renovating the same; and producing or reproducing a new body from tatters in general.

Name of Patentee.	Progres-sive Number.	Date.	Subject-matter of Patent.
DUMBELL, JOHN - - -	4737	16th Dec. 1822	Organization of vehicles or carriages; also drawing, actuating, accelerating, or moving the same.
DUMENY, CHARLES - -	4929	22nd March 1824	Apparatus containing within itself the means of producing gas from oil and other oleaginous substances; burning such gas for the purpose of affording light, and replacing the gas consumed.
DUMERY, CONSTANT JOUFFROY	8315	16th Dec. 1839	Rotatory-engines to be actuated by steam or water.
DUMESTE, JULIEN FREDERIC [MAILLARD.	6342	7th Dec. 1832	Machine to reduce caoutchouc or india-rubber into elastic thread of different sizes.
DUMESTE, JULIEN FREDERIC [MAILLARD. [Dumeste, Jules Frederick [Maillard.	13,079	22nd May 1850	Reflectors for luminaries.
DUMMLER, ALBERT - -	12,957	31st Jan. 1850	Obtaining fibres from textile plants.
DUMONT, CHRISTOPHER -	8966	22nd May 1841	Manufacture of metallic letters, figures, and other devices.
DUMONT, FRANÇOIS MARCELIN [ARISTIDE.	13,497	7th Feb. 1851	Means and electric-apparatus for transmitting intelligence.
DUMONTIER, CHARLES HECTOR [FRANÇOIS.	10,129	28th March 1844	Construction of lithographic and autographic presses.
DUMOULIN, ALEXIS - -	6838	19th May 1835	Gas-apparatus.
DUNBAR, GEORGE - - -	13,191	23rd July 1850	Suspending carriages.
DUNCAN, CHARLES STEWART -	11,606	3rd March 1847	Public vehicles.
DUNCAN, GEORGE - - -	3662	13th March 1813	Rope-making, and machinery adapted to the purpose.
DUNCAN, GEORGE - - -	11,211	19th May 1846	Making comfits, confectionary, lozenges, and other pan-goods; machinery and apparatus for the manufacture of the same, or other article to which the said machinery may be made applicable.
DUNCAN, GEORGE - - -	12,779	20th Sept. 1849	Railway-breaks.
DUNCAN, GEORGE - - -	13,925	27th Jan. 1852	Manufacture of casks.
DUNCAN, JOHN - - -	2769	30th May 1804	Tambouring or raising flowers, figures, or other ornaments, on muslins, lawns, silks, woollens, or mixed cloths.
DUNCAN, JOHN - - -	8668	2nd Nov. 1840	Machinery for cutting or reaping grass, grain, corn, or other plants or herbs.
DUNCAN, JOHN - - -	9096	21st Sept. 1841	Machinery for driving piles.
DUNCAN, JOHN - - -	9281	7th March 1842	Machinery for excavating soil.
DUNCAN, JOHN - - -	9802	26th June 1843	Casting and constructing type for printing.
DUNCAN, JOHN - - -	12,035	20th Jan. 1848	Tanning hides and skins.
DUNCAN, JOHN WALLACE -	11,271	29th June 1846	Machinery to be used in preparing and spinning cotton and other fibrous substances.
DUNCAN, JOHN WALLACE -	13,738	4th Sept. 1851	Engines for applying the power of steam or other fluids for impelling purposes; manufacture of appliances for transmitting motion.
DUNCOMBE, JOHN - - -	875	18th May 1767	Instrument for measuring standing timber.

Name of Patentee.	Progressive Number.	Date.	Subject-matter of Patent.
DUNCOMBE, JOHN - - -	876	18th May 1767	Machine for turning spits for roasting meat, and to be used instead of a jack, also, if enlarged, will serve for raising water out of mines.
DUNCOMBE, JOHN - - -	3760	25th Nov. 1813	Mathematical and astronomical instruments in their application to surveying and measurement of angles and distances, by an index which ascertains with precision the measurement of any angle, a parallel movement for obtaining the sine and cosine of such angles, and a detached similar movement for measuring the distance of an inaccessible object, at one station and without trigonometrical calculation; also a compass, capable of adjustment to the variation of the magnetic-needle.
DUNCOMBE, Sir SAUNDERS, [Knight.	76	18th Dec. 1634	Engines for raising water out of mines and other places.
DUNDAS, GEORGE - - -	764	3rd Aug. 1761	Machine for platting or weaving whips.
DUNDAS, GEORGE - - -	1288	28th March 1781	Machine for spinning jersey.
DUNDONALD, ARCHIBALD Earl [of.	1291	30th April 1781	Extracting tar, pitch, essential-oils, volatile-alkali, mineral-acids, salts, and cinders, from pit-coal.
DUNDONALD, ARCHIBALD Earl [of.	2015	4th Oct. 1794	Preparing and obtaining alum, or sulphate or vitriol of argil; and other salts, saline matters or substances at the same time.
DUNDONALD, ARCHIBALD Earl [of.	2039	23th Feb. 1795	Preparing and applying certain saline bodies and other substances, as manures or stimulants to the ground, and also destructive of insects.
DUNDONALD, ARCHIBALD Earl │of.	2043	11th March 1795	Disengaging and obtaining mineral or fossil alkali or soda, and a vegetable alkali or potash, from neutral salts or solutions of the same; applying the products to various purposes.
DUNDONALD, ARCHIBALD Earl [of.	2189	16th Aug. 1797	Making or preparing ceruse or white-lead.
DUNDONALD, ARCHIBALD Earl [of.	2211	25th Jan. 1798	Procuring certain neutral salts, substances, and things, and applying those and other neutral salts to valuable purposes.
DUNDONALD, ARCHIBALD Earl [of.	2529	31st July 1801	Preparing a substitute for gum-senegal and other gums extensively employed in certain branches of manufacture.
DUNDONALD, ARCHIBALD Earl [of.	2719	28th June 1803	Treating or preparing hemp and flax so as to aid the heckles in the division of the fibre, and in other operations.
DUNDONALD, ARCHIBALD Earl [of.	2896	19th Nov. 1805	Machinery for spinning cotton-wool, silk, hemp, and flax, and substitutes for hemp and flax.
DUNDONALD, ARCHIBALD Earl [of.	3547	14th March 1812	Preparing and manufacturing alkaline-salts, from vegetables the growth of Great Britain and Ireland.
DUNDONALD, THOMAS Earl of	6530	20th Dec. 1833	Construction and operation of rotary-engines; and apparatus connected therewith.
DUNDONALD, THOMAS Earl of	6923	5th Nov. 1835	Machinery and apparatus applicable to purposes of locomotion.
DUNDONALD, THOMAS Earl of	9593	19th Jan. 1843	Rotatory-engines; apparatus connected with steam-engines; propelling vessels.
DUNDONALD, THOMAS Earl of	10,497	28th Jan. 1845	Rotatory-engine to be impelled by steam;—applicable to other purposes.

Name of Patentee.	Progressive Number.	Date.	Subject-matter of Patent.
DUNDONALD, THOMAS Earl of -	12,064	11th Feb. 1848	Marine steam-boilers; and apparatus connected therewith.
DUNDONALD, THOMAS Earl of -	13,698	22nd July 1851	Construction and manufacture of sewers, drains, water-ways, pipes, reservoirs, and receptacles for liquids or solids; also making columns, pillars, capitals, pedestals, vases and other articles, from a substance never before employed for such purposes.
DUNIN, EMILIAN DE - -	13,628	10th May 1851	Apparatus for measuring persons, and facilitating the fitting of garments.
DUNINGTON, HENRY - -	6833	13th May 1835	Making or manufacturing lace.
DUNINGTON, HENRY - -	7132	22nd June 1836	Making or manufacturing lace.
DUNINGTON, HENRY - -	7801	10th Sept. 1838	Machinery employed in making frame-work knitting, or stocking fabrics.
DUNINGTON, HENRY - -	7826	8th Oct. 1838	Warp-machinery, and fabrics produced by warp-machinery.
DUNINGTON, HENRY - -	8035	16th April 1839	Machinery employed in making frame-work knitting, or stocking fabrics.
DUNINGTON, HENRY - -	8292	2nd Dec. 1839	Machinery for making frame-work knit, or stocking fabrics.
DUNINGTON, HENRY - -	10,088	4th March 1844	Manufacture of fabrics produced in warp and lace machinery.
DUNINGTON, HENRY - -	12,561	3rd April 1849	Manufacture of looped fabrics; making gloves and hatbands.
DUNKIN, ROBERT - - -	2581	19th Feb. 1802	Sailing and navigating certain ships and vessels.
DUNKIN, ROBERT - - -	3645	30th Jan. 1813	Lessening the consumption of steam and fuel in working fire-engines; instruments used for mining, and other purposes.
DUNKIN, THOMAS - - -	6831	13th May 1835	Obtaining or producing duplicate copies of manuscript writings and drawings; and machinery for the purpose.
DUNLOP, ARCHIBALD, junior -	10,641	29th April 1845	Manufacture of ale, porter, and other fermented liquors.
DUNLOP, ARCHIBALD, junior -	10,973	27th Nov. 1845	Manufacture of ale, porter, and other fermented liquors.
DUNLOP, ARCHIBALD, junior -	10,980	4th Dec. 1845	Manufacture of aërated waters.
DUNLOP, CHARLES TENNANT -	11,624	16th March 1847	Manufacture of alkali and chlorine; application of the products resulting therefrom.
DUNN, ARTHUR - - -	7283	17th Jan. 1837	Dissolving silicious matter and compounds of silica; manufacturing soap.
DUNN, ARTHUR - - -	7783	24th Aug. 1838	Manufacture of soap.
DUNN, ARTHUR - - -	9682	28th March 1843	Treating, purifying, and bleaching oils and fatty matters,
DUNN, ARTHUR - - -	9931	9th Nov. 1843	Manufacture of soap.
DUNN, ARTHUR - - -	12,287	12th Oct. 1848	Ascertaining and indicating the temperature and pressure of fluids.
DUNN, ARTHUR - - -	12,740	16th Aug. 1849	Marking soap.
DUNN, DANIEL - - -	5158	30th April 1825	Apparatus for separating infusion of tea or coffee from its grounds or dregs.
DUNN, DANIEL - - -	5363	23rd May 1826	Screw-press, for pressing paper, books, tobacco, or bale-goods, and expressing oil, extracts, and tinctures, and for other purposes.
DUNN, EDWARD - - -	1821	19th July 1791	Construction of saddles, and stirrup-irons.

Name of Patentee.	Progres-sive Number.	Date.	Subject-matter of Patent.
DUNN, EDWARD　-　-　-	13,425	26th Dec.　1850	Engine for producing motive-power by expansion of fluids or gases, caused by the application of caloric.
DUNN, EDWARD　-　-　-	13,571	24th March 1851	Reciprocating and rotary fluid-meters.
DUNN, SAMUEL　-　-　-	6081	21st Feb.　1831	Generating steam.
DUNN, SAMUEL　-　-　-	12,632	5th June　1849	Constructing tunnels; apparatus to be used for such or similar purposes.
DUNN, THOMAS　-　-　-	10,556	13th March 1845	Turn-tables to be used on railways.
DUNN, THOMAS　-　-　-	11,934	2nd Nov.　1847	Manufacturing railway wheels and axles; machinery and apparatus for placing carriages on to a line of rails, for removing them from one line to another, and for turning them.
DUNN, THOMAS　-　-　-	13,355	19th Nov.　1850	Machinery and apparatus for moving engines and carriages from one line of rails to another, and for turning them; for compressing certain substances, and for raising and lowering heavy bodies.
DUNN, WILLIAM BRUCE -　-	1997	28th June 1794	Constructing and working mills.
DUNNAGE, GEORGE　-　-	2022	11th Nov.　1794	Manufacturing waterproof hats, in imitation of beaver-hats.
DUNNAGE, GEORGE　-　-	2273	27th Nov.　1798	Ventilating the crowns of hats.
DUNNAGE, GEORGE　-　-	3823	26th July　1814	Rowing or propelling boats or other vessels.
DUNNICLIFF, JOHN DEARMAN	10,390	13th Nov.　1844	Manufacture of lace and other weavings.
DUNNICLIFF, JOHN DEARMAN	11,020	24th Dec.　1845	Manufacture of warp-fabrics.
DUNNICLIFF, JOHN DEARMAN	12,426	18th Jan.　1849	Dressing or getting-up fabrics of cotton or silk, and cotton and silk combined.
DUNNICLIFF, JOHN DEARMAN	13,122	11th June 1850	Lace and other weaving.
DUNNING, RICHARD　-　-	451	23rd Sept. 1722	Machine, called a poiser, to be fixed to any coach, chariot, or chaise, to prevent the same overturning.
DUNNING, RICHARD　-　-	468	20th May 1724	Floating water-engine to raise or force water; rowing-engine to force ships against wind and tide.
DUPE, WILLIAM　-　-　-	2252	23rd July 1798	Manufacturing bars of a mixture of iron and steel, for double-barrel gun-barrels.
DUPERREY, LOUIS ADOLPHE -	12,845	17th Nov.　1849	Machinery for producing figures in relievo.
DUPIN, NICHOLAS -　-　-	248	9th Jan.　1686	Making writing and printing paper, and printing His Majesty's arms thereon.
DUPRÉ, JAMES FREDERICK　-	9699	19th April 1843	Boilers.
DUPRÉ, WILLIAM HENRY　-	14,071	17th April 1852	Apparatus for preventing smoky chimneys;—applicable to other purposes of ventilation.
DURAFOUR, JEAN MARIE　-	11,941	4th Nov.　1847	Fastening or system of lacing without eyelet-holes.
DURAND, FRANÇOIS　-　-	11,413	15th Oct.　1846	Forming leather into tubes, cylinders, switches, cases, sheaths, hats, and other articles.
DURAND, JOHN NICHOLAS　-	1632	5th Dec.　1787	Prover for spirituous-liquors; tables and calculations thereto belonging.
DURAND, PETER　-　-　-	3372	25th Aug.　1810	Preserving animal and vegetable food and other articles from decay.
DURAND, PETER　-　-　-	3471	3rd Aug.　1811	Lamps, or addition to lamps, for rendering the illumination more soft and agreeable to the eye.
DURAND, PROSPER -　-　-	13,666	17th June 1851	Communicating intelligence.

Name of Patentee.	Progressive Number.	Date.	Subject-matter of Patent.
DURANT, ANGUISH HONOUR [AUGUSTUS.	9284	7th March 1842	Apparatus for sweeping chimneys or flues, and extinguishing fires therein. (Ramoneur.)
DUREUILLE, JEAN BAPTISTE -	13,382	4th Dec. 1850	Manufacture or production of boots and shoes; and materials and machinery to be employed therein.
DURNERIN, JEAN MARIE -	11,036	13th Jan. 1846	Treating fatty matters..
DURRANT, JAMES WILLIAM -	6321	12th Oct. 1832	Securing, combining, and preserving papers, prints, drawings, music, or other similar matters, so as to be easily referred to, or taken asunder and replaced.
DUTHAIS, DANIEL - - -	221	29th July 1682	Waped milled-stockings.
DUTHOIT, ALCIDE MARCELLIN	13,894	12th Jan. 1852	Chemical combination of certain agents for obtaining a new plastic product.
DUTTON, GEORGE HILL - -	10.936	11th Nov. 1845	Conveying intelligence from one part of a railway-train to another.
DUTTON, JAMES - - -	3960	23rd Nov. 1815	Fulling woollen-cloth; fulling-mills for the purpose.
DUTTON, JAMES - - -	5789	19th May 1829	Propelling ships, boats, and other vessels or floating bodies, by steam or other power.
DUTTON, JAMES - - -	6607	13th May 1834	Dressing or finishing woollen-cloths, and apparatus for effecting the same.
DUTTON, JAMES - - -	7565	8th Feb. 1838	Manufacture of woollen-cloth, applying both to weaving and dressing woollen-cloth.
DUVIVION, ANTHONY - -	290	28th Feb. 1692	Machine for making a ship sail against wind and tide.
DUXBURY, HENRY - - -	5716	9th Oct. 1828	Machine for splitting hides and skins.
DUXBURY, JAMES - - -	2459	17th Dec. 1800	Machine to print distinct sprigs or spots on calico, cotton-stuffs, linen, silk, satin, cloth, woollen, baize, or leather. "Double copper cylinder and copper-plate."
DUYCK, JACQUE EDOUARD -	8866	8th March 1841	Manufacture of vinegar; apparatus employed therein.
DWIGHT, JOHN - - -	164	23rd April 1672	Manufacture of transparent earthenware, as porcelain, china, and Persian-ware; also Cologne-ware.
DWIGHT, JOHN - -	234	12th June 1684	Manufacturing earthenwares, as white gorges, marbled porcelain-vessels, statues and figures, and fine stone gorges and vessels; also transparent porcelain, and opaque-red dark coloured porcelain or china and Persian wares, and Cologne or stone-wares.
DWYER, THOMAS - - -	5265	13th Oct. 1825	Manufacturing buttons.
DYAR, HARRISON GREY - - [Dyar, Harrison Gray.]	6157	5th Sept. 1831	Tunnelling.
DYAR, HARRISON GREY - -	7521	23rd Dec. 1837	Manufacture of white-lead.
DYAR, HARRISON GREY - -	7713	30th June 1838	Manufacturing carbonate of soda.
DYAR, HARRISON GREY - -	7878	20th Nov. 1838	Manufacturing zinc.
DYAR, HARRISON GREY - -	8094	6th June 1839	Obtaining sulphur from pyrites or certain native sulphurets.
DYCK, MATHEWE VAN - -	84	14th July 1635	Engines, instruments, and works, for raising ships, vessels or other carriages or things of weight, from out of the sea or any river or deep water; also for draining mines, and raising water to any height.

Name of Patentee.	Progressive Number.	Date.	Subject-matter of Patent.
DYER, CHARLES BUNT	8884	16th March 1841	Obtaining paints or pigments by the combination of mineral solutions with other substances.
DYER, JOHN	6460	13th Aug. 1833	Machine for fulling, thickening, felting, and cleansing woollen-cloth or other fabric.
DYER, JOHN	6912	22nd Oct. 1835	Materials used for fining or clarifying liquids.
DYER, JONAH	3885	21st Feb. 1815	Frame-machine for shearing woollen-cloth.
DYER, JOSEPH	3365	26th July 1810	Machinery for cutting and heading nails and brads made from strips or plates of iron, copper, or other metal capable of being rolled into plates.
DYER, JOSEPH CHESSEBOROUGH	3375	7th Sept. 1810	Machine for cutting furs from the skins or pelts, and cutting the pelts into strips or small pieces.
DYER, JOSEPH CHESSEBOROUGH	3385	1st Oct. 1810	Construction and use of plates and presses, and combining various species of work in the same plate for copper-plate printing, designed to detect counterfeits, for multiplying impressions, and saving labour.
DYER, JOSEPH CHESSEBOROUGH	3420	26th March 1811	Splitting hides, shaving or splitting leather.
DYER, JOSEPH CHESSEBOROUGH	3498	30th Oct. 1811	Machinery to be used and applied in manufacturing cards for carding wool, cotton, silk, flax, tow, and other similar fibrous materials.
DYER, JOSEPH CHESSEBOROUGH	3543	4th March 1812	Machinery for cutting and heading nails from strips or plates of iron, copper, or other metal capable of being rolled into plates.
DYER, JOSEPH CHESSEBOROUGH	3743	1st Nov. 1813	Spinning hemp, flax, grasses, or any substances having length of fibre.
DYER, JOSEPH CHESSEBOROUGH	3798	1st April 1814	Machinery for manufacturing nails.
DYER, JOSEPH CHESSEBOROUGH	3862	15th Dec. 1814	Machinery for manufacturing cards for carding wool, cotton, silk, tow, and other fibrous materials.
DYER, JOSEPH CHESSEBOROUGH	5217	16th July 1825	Conducting to, and winding upon bobbins, rovings of cotton, flax, wool, or other fibrous substances.
DYER, JOSEPH CHESSEBOROUGH	5309	9th Dec. 1825	Machinery for making wire-cards; machine for shaving and preparing leather for the purpose.
DYER, JOSEPH CHESSEBOROUGH	5909	27th Feb. 1830	Machinery for conducting to, and winding upon bobbins or barrels, rovings of cotton, flax, wool, or other fibrous substances.
DYER, JOSEPH CHESSEBOROUGH	6863	17th July 1835	Machinery for winding upon spools, bobbins or barrels, slivers or rovings of cotton-wool, and other fibrous substances.
DYER, REUBEN	11,951	9th Nov. 1847	Two and four wheel carriages.
DYNE, WILLIAM	11,709	22nd May 1847	Apparatus for protecting life and property in cases of shipwreck.
DYSON, JOHN	4266	26th May 1818	Apparatus for the culture and tillage of land.
DYSON, THOMAS	4512	11th Nov. 1820	Plane-irons and turning-chisels.

Name of Patentee.	Progressive Number.	Date.	Subject-matter of Patent.

E.

Name of Patentee.	Progressive Number.	Date.	Subject-matter of Patent.
EAGLES, SAMUEL SALISBURY -	8530	2nd June 1840	Obtaining motive-power.
EARLE, WILLIS - - -	2836	26th March 1805	Constructing and working steam-engines.
EARLE, WILLIS - - -	3095	13th Jan. 1808	Tilling and dressing land; cultivation of plants.
EARNSHAW, RUBEN - -	6821	25th April 1835	Preparing and working wool for making various fabrics.
EAST, FREDERICK WILLIAM -	13,589	15th April 1851	Dressing, embossing and ornamenting leather.
EAST, PETER - - - -	337	20th Oct. 1694	Instrument to be applied to organs, clocks, harpsichords, virginals or similar instruments, to cause the same to chime or play tunes, which may be altered without changing the instrument.
EASTER, JOHN - - -	6651	26th July 1834	Machinery for propelling vessels in water.
EASTON, JOSIAH - - -	5267	13th Oct. 1825	Locomotive or steam carriages; constructing the roads or ways for the same to travel over.
EASTWOOD, JOHN - - -	14,292	16th Sept. 1852	Machinery for combing, drawing, or preparing wool, cotton, silk, hair, and other fibrous materials.
EASUM, ROBERT HAYES -	13,684	3rd July 1851	Manufacture of rope.
EATON, EDWARD WILLIAM -	11,836	19th Aug. 1847	Machinery for preventing accidents on railways.
EATON, JOHN - - - -	2325	4th July 1799	Machinery to be added and affixed to stocking-frames for making elastic cross-stitch platted hose-pieces, gloves, mits, and other articles, with silk or silk platted upon cotton, worsted, or thread, or cotton platted upon worsted, cotton, or thread.
EATON, ROBERT - - -	442	18th April 1722	Chemical preparation and styptic medicine, for stopping external and internal bleedings, and for healing all flesh wounds.
EATON, SAMUEL - - -	1231	28th July 1779	Machine for knitting without jacks or sinkers.
EATON, WILLIAM - - -	4272	18th June 1818	Parts of machinery for roving and spinning cotton and wool.
EATON, WILLIAM - - -	11,452	17th Nov. 1846	Obtaining motive-power.
EATON, WILLIAM - - -	11,574	9th Feb. 1847	Machinery for twisting cotton and other fibrous substances.
EATON, WILLIAM - - -	11,839	19th Aug. 1847	Raising water and other liquids from one level to another.
EATON, WILLIAM - - -	11,984	1st Dec. 1847	Machinery for twisting cotton or other fibrous substances.
ECARNOT, JEAN BAPTISTE -	12,881	10th Dec. 1849	Manufacture of sulphuric, sulphurous, acetic, and oxalic acids and nitrates.
ECCLES, HENRY - -	12,873	3rd Dec. 1849	Machinery for preparing, spinning, and weaving cotton and other fibrous substances.
ECCLES, JOHN - - -	12,117	10th April 1848	Valves or plugs for the passage of water.
ECCLES, JOSEPH - - -	12,368	15th Dec. 1848	Looms for weaving various descriptions of plain and ornamental textile fabrics.
ECCLES, ROBERT - -	4260	9th May 1818	Masts, sails, and rigging of ships or sailing vessels.

Name of Patentee.	Progressive Number.	Date.		Subject-matter of Patent.
ECCLES, SAMUEL - - -	7532	5th Jan.	1838	Power-looms and hand-looms for weaving plain and figured fabrics.
ECCLES, SAMUEL - - -	9798	22nd June	1843	Looms for weaving.
ECCLES, WILLIAM - - -	10,802	5th Aug.	1845	Machinery used in spinning.
ECCLES, WILLIAM - - -	10,832	18th Sept.	1845	Looms for weaving.
ECCLES, WILLIAM - - -	11,602	2nd March	1847	Machinery to be used in spinning.
ECCLES, WILLIAM - - -	12,873	3rd Dec.	1849	Machinery for preparing, spinning, and weaving cotton and other fibrous substances.
ECCLES, WILLIAM - - -	13,259	19th Sept.	1850	Looms for weaving.
ECCLES, WILLIAM, junior -	12,873	3rd Dec.	1849	Machinery for preparing, spinning, and weaving cotton and other fibrous substances.
ECKHARDT, ANTHONY GEORGE	985	23rd March	1771	Rolling parallel ruler, with or without scales; sliding pen and pencil for drawing and dividing lines, circles, and angles, which may be measured, divided, and determined at first sight, also for drawing problems and plans in perspective.
ECKHARDT, ANTHONY GEORGE	995	29th July	1771	Portable table, with double or single folding flaps and feet, also a portable chair, answering all the purposes of tables and chairs, and yet occupying only the compass of a small box.
ECKHARDT, ANTHONY GEORGE	1023	27th Aug.	1772	Water-wheel for draining fens and low lands; water-engine for raising water.
ECKHARDT, ANTHONY GEORGE	1066	28th Feb.	1774	Printing in designs, silks, cottons, muslins, calicoes, and papers.
ECKHARDT, ANTHONY GEORGE	1845	16th Jan.	1792	Laying on or imprinting grounds or coats of composition or paint, upon satin, silk, cotton, linen, velvet, leather, or any kind of cloth, stuff, or paper, for copper-plate printing.
ECKHARDT, ANTHONY GEORGE	2037	31st Jan.	1795	Applying the use of animals to machinery.
ECKHARDT, ANTHONY GEORGE	2156	23rd Jan.	1797	Making candlesticks, lamps, and girandoles, by the use of sliding pillars, comprising the advantage of an extinguisher.
ECKHARDT, ANTHONY GEORGE	2184	4th July	1797	Making draw or bench looms, for the manufacturing of carpets, borders, and other things.
ECKHARDT, ANTHONY GEORGE	2190	17th Aug.	1797	Constructing pumps and engines for evacuating water or other fluids, extinguishing fires, and producing power.
ECKHARDT, ANTHONY GEORGE	2208	16th Jan.	1798	Making chairs, sofas, stools, benches, &c. adapted for rooms or carriages, with backs, seats, and cushions, fixed in such a manner as instantly to change and show two surfaces in one seat; also preserving covers, whereby different surfaces may be introduced in one seat, and so that when one surface is in use the others may be preserved.
ECKHARDT, ANTHONY GEORGE	2267	13th Nov.	1798	Instrument to serve as a standard for regulating the time in musical performances.
ECKHARDT, ANTHONY GEORGE	2344	3rd Oct.	1799	Constructing and moving the back and bottom of fire-grates, combined with cheeks on a new construction, and particularly adapted for kitchen-ranges, effecting a great saving of coals.

Name of Patentee.	Progressive Number.	Date.	Subject-matter of Patent.
ECKHARDT, ANTHONY GEORGE	2998	22nd Dec. 1806	Covering and enclosing books.
ECKHARDT, ANTHONY GEORGE	2999	22nd Dec. 1806	Manufacturing pipes for conveyance of water under ground.
ECKHARDT, ANTHONY GEORGE	3197	28th Jan. 1809	Casting metallic and other bodies together or separately, in moulds, in a fluid state.
ECKHARDT, FRANCIS FRE-[DERICK.	1953	30th April 1793	Preparing, printing, and silvering paper, to resemble damask lace, and various silk stuffs, for hangings and other furniture for rooms.
ECKHARDT, FRANCIS FRE-[DERICK.	1954	30th April 1793	Preparing linen and cotton cloth with a paste to give it a smooth surface and pliable quality, for receiving a coat of water-size colours, and afterwards printing ornaments on the same in silver and gold, or colours, in patterns to resemble damask lace, and other silk stuffs, for hangings and other furniture for rooms.
ECKSTEIN, GEORGE FREDERICK	4561	9th May 1821	Cooking-apparatus.
ECKSTEIN, GEORGE FREDERICK	6108	14th April 1831	Fire-grate.
ECKSTEIN, GEORGE FREDERICK	6485	12th Oct. 1833	Instrument for pointing pencils, and for certain other purposes.
ECROYD, JOHN - - -	5286	8th Nov. 1825	Engine for cutting nails, sprigs, and sparables.
ECROYD, JOHN - - -	12,117	10th April 1848	Valves or plugs for the passage of water.
EDDY, GEORGE W. - - -	11,433	3rd Nov. 1846	Manufacture of cast metal wheels for railway and various other carriages.
EDGE, ERNEST - - -	10,966	20th Nov. 1845	Wheels and axles of engines, tenders, carriages, and waggons, to be used on railways.
EDGE, THOMAS - - -	7215	28th Oct. 1836	Lighting by gas, oil, or spirit lights or lamps.
EDGE, THOMAS - - -	9344	9th May 1842	Apparatus for measuring gas, water, and other fluids.
EDGE, THOMAS - - -	11,516	31st Dec. 1846	Manufacture of gas-meters.
EDGELL, JAMES - - -	776	8th June 1762	Shooting-belt.
EDGELL, JAMES - - -	986	22nd April 1771	Water-engine for extinguishing fires.
EDGELL, JAMES - - -	1079	10th Sept. 1774	Balance-engine for weighing waggons and other carriages, heavy goods, wares, and merchandise.
EDGELL, JAMES - - -	1459	12th Jan. 1785	Axle or centre-pin for wheels of coaches, chaises, waggons, carts, and all other wheel-carriages.
EDGELL, JAMES - - -	2057	20th July 1795	Axles for wheel-carriages.
EDGELL, JAMES - - -	2287	16th Jan. 1799	Metal in lieu of iron.
EDGEWORTH, RICHARD LOVELL	953	5th Feb. 1770	Portable railway or artificial road to move along with any carriage to which it is applied.
EDISBURY, KENRICK - -	193	12th Jan. 1677	Plaster called "Glassis," for paving floors; water-mills for corn.
EDISBURY, KENDRICK - -	277	1st Oct. 1691	Rollers instead of wheels for the bodies of carriages and carts.
EDMESTON, THOMAS - -	13,248	5th Sept. 1850	Machinery or apparatus for scouring, finishing, and stretching woollen, cotton, and other woven fabrics.
EDMONDS, EZEKIEL - -	5303	3rd Dec. 1825	Machines for scribbling and carding sheep's wool, cotton, or any other fibrous articles.
EDMONDS, EZEKIEL - -	13,182	17th July 1850	Manufacture of certain descriptions of woollen fabrics.

Name of Patentee.	Progressive Number.	Date.	Subject-matter of Patent.
EDMONDS, GEORGE - -	6259	13th April 1832	Philosophic alphabet, or arrangement of letters, forms, or figures, by which the articulate sounds of languages may be scientifically denoted.
EDMONDS, THOMAS - -	6609	22nd May 1834	Process and treatment for the preparation of leather, to render it less pervious to water, and better to preserve its pliability.
EDMONDSON, JAMES - -	8048	23rd April 1839	Machinery for the manufacture of wood-screws and screw-bolts.
EDMONDSON, THOMAS -	8266	9th Nov. 1839	Printing-presses.
EDMONDSON, THOMAS -	8538	9th June 1840	Printing-presses.
EDMONDSON, THOMAS -	12,137	27th April 1848	Marking and numbering railway and other tickets or surfaces; arranging and distributing tickets.
EDMONDSON, THOMAS -	13,007	19th March 1850	Manufacture of railway and other tickets; machinery for marking railway and other tickets.
EDMONDSON, WILLIAM -	8048	23rd April 1839	Machinery for the manufacture of wood-screws and screw-bolts.
EDMUNDS, RICHARD - -	8665	22nd Oct. 1840	Machines for preparing and drilling land, and depositing seeds or manure therein.
EDRIDGE, WILLIAM - -	3948	4th Aug. 1815	Engine, pump, or fire-engine.
EDSOR, JAMES - -	13,575	24th March 1851	Safety-hinge and apparatus for the detection of burglars and prevention of burglaries.
EDWARDS, DAVID - -	5105	26th Feb. 1825	Inkstand.
EDWARDS, DAVID OWEN -	12,773	20th Sept. 1849	Application of gas for producing and radiating heat.
EDWARDS, DOWNES - -	8597	8th Aug. 1840	Preserving potatoes and other vegetable substances.
EDWARDS, HENRY HINA -	8679	5th Nov. 1840	Evaporation.
EDWARDS, JAMES - -	1462	28th Jan. 1785	Embellishing books bound in vellum, by making drawings on the vellum.
EDWARDS, JOHN - -	2230	18th April 1798	Instruments for ascertaining the geographical position of vessels at sea.
EDWARDS, JOHN - -	2496	2nd May 1801	Horse-collars.
EDWARDS, JOHN - -	2731	3rd Aug. 1803	Distilling, rectifying, and dyeing.
EDWARDS, JOHN - -	2795	4th Dec. 1804	Fire-places.
EDWARDS, JOHN - -	2845	7th May 1805	Bridles.
EDWARDS, JOHN - -	2847	14th May 1805	Machine for the prevention of drowning. "Life buoy."
EDWARDS, JOHN - -	3952	15th Aug. 1815	Preventing leakage in ships, boats and other vessels.
EDWARDS, JOHN - -	7535	11th Jan. 1838	Instruments used in writing.
EDWARDS, JOHN - -	9149	9th Nov. 1841	Strap or band for driving machinery, and for other purposes.
EDWARDS, JOHN - -	9175	11th Dec. 1841	Giving signals on railways.
EDWARDS, JOSEPH - -	9504	2nd Nov. 1842	Razor-strap and material for covering the same; which material is also applicable to other purposes.
EDWARDS, RICHARD - -	3667	15th March 1813	Extracting arsenic from the ores or other substances in which it is contained, in a purer state than it is at present procured.
EDWARDS, RICHARD - -	6044	6th Dec. 1830	Substitute for glass, sand, emery, and other scouring paper or substances.
EDWARDS, RICHARD - -	8405	29th Feb. 1840	Preparing and combining materials used in lighting or kindling fires.
EDWARDS, SAMUEL - -	13,319	7th Nov. 1850	Obtaining and applying motive-power; pumps.

Name of Patentee.	Progressive Number.	Date.	Subject-matter of Patent.
EDWARDS, TALBOT - - -	405	29th June 1716	Making pitch, tar, and oil from roach or roof stone by fluxing with fire only.
EDWARDS, THOMAS - -	8019	3rd April 1839	Manufacture of hinges.
EDWARDS, THOMAS - -	10,913	3rd Nov. 1845	Steam-engines.
EDWARDS, WILLIAM - -	480	28th June 1725	Making pipes of clay or earth for conveying water under ground from place to place.
EELE, MARTIN - - -	330	29th Jan. 1694	Extracting pitch, tar, and oil out of a certain sort of stone found in England and Wales.
EGAN, JOHN FRANCIS - -	14,233	20th July 1852	Manufacture of sugar.
EGELLS, FRANZ ANTON - -	4608	9th Nov. 1821	Steam-engines.
EGG, DURS - - - -	2692	23rd March 1803	Firearms.
EGG, DURS - - - -	3599	25th Sept. 1812	Construction of firearms and their locks; also apparatus for trying and loading them.
EGG, DURS - - - -	3909	25th April 1815	Aërial conveyances and vessels to be steered by philosophical, chemical, or mechanical means, which means are also applicable to the propelling of vessels through water, and carriages or other conveyances by land.
EGG, JOSEPH - - - -	2440	21st Aug. 1800	Bending steel without heat, applicable to the manufacture of surgical instruments, and to other purposes.
EGG, JOSEPH - - - -	3676	30th March 1813	Applying and improving locks.
EGG, JOSEPH - - - -	4727	26th Nov. 1822	Construction of guns and firearms, on the self priming and detonating principle.
EGG, JOSEPH - - - -	6829	9th May 1835	Firearms.
EGGLESTON, FREDERICK WILLIAM.	9774	15th June 1843	Combustion of fuel and consumption of smoke.
EGINTON, JOHN - - -	1521	— Jan. 1786	Making buttons and button-moulds of wood.
EIFFE. JAMES SWEETMAN -	11,987	8th Dec. 1847	Manufacture of astronomical and other clocks, chronometers, and watches.
ELAM, ALFRED - - -	9093	20th Sept. 1841	Instruments for the relief and cure of procedencia and prolapsus uteri.
ELCE, JOHN - - - -	11,683	4th May 1847	Machinery for preparing and spinning cotton-wool and other fibrous substances.
ELCE, JOHN - - - -	13,990	26th Feb. 1852	Machinery for preparing cotton and other fibrous substances; machinery applicable to looms for weaving; and the tools employed therein.
ELEY, WILLIAM - - -	1427	17th April 1784	Buckles with new joint and spring chape fastenings.
ELIN, JOHN - - - -	1682	28th May 1789	Machinery for cleaning the inside of chimneys.
ELIN, JOHN - - - -	1700	29th Aug. 1789	Shoebuckles.
ELKINGTON, GEORGE RICHARDS	6692	10th Oct. 1834	Making spectacles.
ELKINGTON, GEORGE RICHARDS	7134	24th June 1836	Gilding copper, brass, and other metals or alloy of metals.
ELKINGTON, GEORGE RICHARDS	7742	24th July 1838	Coating and colouring certain metals (covering?).
ELKINGTON, GEORGE RICHARDS	8447	25th March 1840	Coating, covering, or plating certain metals.
ELKINGTON, HENRY - -	7101	23rd May 1836	Rotary steam-engine.
ELKINGTON, HENRY - -	7304	17th Feb. 1837	Coating certain metals with platina; gilding certain metals ⹁ apparatus used in such processes.

Name of Patentee.	Progres- sive Number.	Date.		Subject-matter of Patent.
ELKINGTON, HENRY	7305	17th Feb.	1837	Steam-engines; boilers, and furnaces used therein, and for other purposes.
ELKINGTON, HENRY	7496	4th Dec.	1837	Gilding and silvering metals; vessels or ap- paratus used in such processes, and for other purposes.
ELKINGTON, HENRY	7721	6th July	1838	Engines, to be worked by steam, air, or other fluids.
ELKINGTON, HENRY	8447	25th March	1840	Coating, covering, or plating certain metals.
ELLAND, CHRISTOPHER	22	5th Oct.	1622	Making white and red lead for painters.
ELLEN, SAMUEL	11,735	8th June	1847	Manufacture of losh hide-leather, and other oiled leathers.
ELLERMAN, CHARLES FREDE- [RICK.	11,898	7th Oct.	1847	Disinfecting and rendering inodorous, fecu- lent, excremental, and other matters; re- tarding the putrefaction of animal and vegetable substances; chemical re-agents employed in such processes.
ELLINS, GEORGE	10,542	3rd March	1845	Manufacturing salt; apparatus for the pur- pose.
ELLINS, GEORGE	11,467	1st Dec.	1846	Apparatus for manufacturing salt.
ELLINS, GEORGE	12,099	22nd March	1848	Manufacturing salt; apparatus for the pur- pose.
ELLIS, JOSEPH	3115	7th March	1808	Machines for finishing, glazing, and glossing leather.
ELLIS, RICHARD	1209	30th Jan.	1779	Plating steel or iron with gold or silver.
ELLIS, ROBERT	8935	24th April	1841	Manufacture of iron.
ELLIS, SAMUEL	9797	22nd June	1843	Weighing-machines and turn-tables, to be used on or in connection with railways; weighing-machines to be used in other situations.
ELLIS, SAMUEL	13,123	11th June	1850	Machinery or apparatus applicable to all kinds of carriages used on railways.
ELLIS, THOMAS	7234	24th Nov.	1836	Manufacture of sheets, pipes or tubes and other articles, of lead and other metal.
ELLIS, THOMAS, senior	13,535,	27th Feb.	1851	Machinery to be employed in the manufac- ture of blooms or piles, for railway and other bars or plates of iron.
ELLISON, THOMAS	14,019	8th March	1852	Manufacture of imitation marbles, granites, and all sorts of stones.
ELLISS, EDWARD	5161	14th May	1825	Brick, or substitute for brick, manufactured from a material not hitherto used for or in the making of bricks.
ELLISTON, MATTHEW	325	19th Sept.	1693	Manufacturing and ordering roots and barks with other ingredients, for dyeing silks, wrought and unwrought, and woollen and linen cloth in many colours, in grain and otherwise, with or without fire; also useful for limners and painters, for perforating glass, and for other purposes.
ELLISTON, MATTHEW	326	9th Oct.	1693	Mills moved with jackwork and wheels, to grind corn and move saws by manual labour, without the help of wind or water.
ELLIOT, ARTHUR	13,091	1st June	1850	Machinery for manufacturing woven fabrics.
ELLIOT, EDWARD	9949	18th Nov.	1843	Means of adding power to the steam-engine and other machinery.
ELLIOT, GEORGE	13,465	21st Jan.	1851	Manufacture of alkali.
ELLIOTT, GEORGE	2638	2nd Aug.	1802	Machine for raising water and other fluids.

Name of Patentee.	Progressive Number.	Date.	Subject-matter of Patent.
ELLIOTT, JOHN	659	22nd Jan. 1751	Printing, painting, staining, and colouring flannels and other woollens.
ELLIOTT, JOSEPH MOSELEY	1959	27th June 1793	Machine for working and binding wire, and making moulds used by paper manufacturers; working and binding wire for making sieves, screens, meat-safes, &c.
ELLIOTT, JOSEPH MOSELEY	2759	14th May 1804	Making repeaters, or repeating watches and chronometers.
ELLIOTT, JOSEPH MOSELEY	2983	30th Oct. 1806	Making and constructing repeaters, or repeating watches and timepieces.
ELLIOTT, OBADIAH	2590	9th March 1802	Eccentrical anti-labourist spring curricle-bar for one or more horses.
ELLIOTT, OBADIAH	2846	11th May 1805	Construction of coaches, chariots, barouches, landaus, and other four-wheel carriages.
ELLIOTT, RICHARD	1285	9th March 1781	Covering houses and other buildings with slate.
ELLIOTT, THOMAS	11,605	3rd March 1847	Locomotive and other boilers.
ELLIOTT, WILLIAM	7508	14th Dec. 1837	Manufacture of covered buttons.
ELLIOTT, WILLIAM	9686	4th April 1843	Manufacture of covered buttons.
ELLIOTT, WILLIAM	10,217	4th June 1844	Manufacture of covered buttons.
ELLIOTT, WILLIAM	10,883	16th Oct. 1845	Manufacture of buttons.
ELLIOTT, WILLIAM	13,871	19th Dec. 1851	Manufacture of covered buttons.
ELLIOTT, WILLIAM GILBERT	13,064	27th April 1850	Manufacture of bricks, tiles, and pipes and other articles, from plastic materials.
ELLWOOD, HENRY	13,833	27th Nov. 1851	Manufacture of hats.
ELMS, JAMES	12,542	28th March 1849	Machinery for cutting and tying up firewood.
ELMSLEY, SAMUEL	788	1st April 1763	Preparation for waterproofing woollen-cloths and hats.
ELMSLIE, JAMES AUGUSTUS	13,377	30th Nov. 1850	Sheathing ships; protecting and confining gunpowder and compounds thereof; materials used for such purposes.
ELSDEN, ROBERT	786	9th March 1763	Weaving and quilting in the loom, cloth of linen, woollen, silk, worsted, cotton, and mohair, separately, or mixed or joined together.
ELSE, ARTHUR	1235	29th Oct. 1779	Manufacture of French or wire ground lace.
ELSE, RICHARD	6468	7th Sept. 1833	Drying malt.
ELSE, RICHARD	9071	8th Sept. 1841	Machinery for forcing and raising water and other fluids.
ELSE, RICHARD	9452	18th Aug. 1842	Machinery for forcing and raising water and other fluids.
ELTON, JOHN	501	27th July 1728	Instrument for taking the sun's altitude at sea and on land.
ELVEN, ROBERT NOYES	9997	28th Dec. 1843	Manufacture of boots, shoes, goloshes, and clogs;—applicable to the manufacture of leather-hose and buckets.
ELVEY, JOHN	3512	16th Dec. 1811	Winnowing-machine.
ELVEY, JOHN	7084	7th May 1836	Steam-engines.
ELVEY, JOHN	7524	23rd Dec. 1837	Paddle-wheels.
ELWELL, EDWARD	4836	20th Aug. 1823	Manufacture of spades and shovels.
ELWELL, JOHN	1251	7th April 1780	Making utensils and articles of grain-tin, alone or united with another metal, for the purposes of cooking or confectionery.

Name of Patentee.	Progressive Number.	Date.		Subject-matter of Patent.
ELWICK, JOHN - - -	2420	1st July	1800	Framing together chairs and sofas.
EMANUEL, HENRY - - -	10,809	7th Aug.	1845	Atmospheric railways.
EMBREY, GODWIN - - -	6817	14th April	1835	Ornamenting china, glass, and earthenware.
EMERSON, EDWARD PATRICK -	10,863	9th Oct.	1845	Manufacture of paints, pigments, cements, and other plastic compositions; machinery used in the process;—partly applicable to the manufacture of artificial stone and marble.
EMERSON, JAMES - - -	1297	13th July	1781	Making brass with copper and spelter.
EMERTON, ALEXANDER - -	557	13th June	1737	Covering and painting timbers, planks, and boards of ships, yachts, barges, lighters, boats, or vessels; and timbers, planks, boards, and plastering in buildings, or other things suited to this method.
EMMERSON, BENJAMIN - -	12,650	7th June	1849	Power-looms.
EMMERSON, RICHARD FARGER	8677	3rd Nov.	1840	Applying a coating to the surfaces of iron-pipes and tubes.
EMMOTT, GEORGE - - -	12,190	16th June	1848	Manufacture of fuel; construction and arrangement of furnaces, flues, boilers, ovens, and retorts.
EMPSON, JOHN FIELDING -	10,019	16th Jan.	1844	Construction and manufacture of buttons and other fastenings for dress.
EMPSON, JOHN FIELDING -	13,640	27th May	1851	Manufacture of buttons.
EMSLIE, JAMES ANTHONY -	8386	9th June	1848	Pumps.
ENGLAND, GEORGE - - -	8058	7th May	1839	Screw-jack for raising or moving heavy bodies, vertically and laterally.
ENGLAND, GEORGE - - -	8860	2nd March	1841	Machinery for weaving woollen and other fabrics; twisting, spooling, and warping woollens; manufacture of doeskins.
ENGLISH, WILLIAM CORNE-[LIUS.	3280	28th Nov.	1809	Rendering heated water, steam and air more serviceable for various purposes, especially for working the steam-engine, warming and heating buildings and stoves, as well as vessels and coppers for all purposes.
ENGLISH, WILLIAM OXLEY -	9541	8th Dec.	1842	Purifying spirits of turpentine, spirits of tar, and naphtha.
ENGLISH, WILLIAM OXLEY -	10,406	25th Nov.	1844	Distilling turpentine and tar; rectifying volatile spirits and oils.
ENSOR, THOMAS - - -	9630	11th Feb.	1843	Manufacture of leather gloves.
ERARD, PIERRE - - -	4631	22nd Dec.	1821	Pianofortes and other keyed instruments.
ERARD, PIERRE - - -	4670	24th April	1822	Harps.
ERARD, PIERRE - - -	5065	5th Jan.	1825	Pianofortes.
ERARD, PIERRE - - -	5468	20th Feb.	1827	Construction of pianofortes.
ERARD, PIERRE - - -	6962	18th Dec.	1835	Harps.
ERARD, PIERRE - - -	6971	31st Dec.	1835	Pianofortes and other keyed instruments.
ERARD, PIERRE - - -	8643	24th Sept.	1840	Pianofortes.
ERARD, PIERRE - - -	13,252	12th Sept.	1850	Construction of pianofortes.
ERARD, PIERRE - - -	13,816	15th Nov.	1851	Pianofortes.
ERARD, SEBASTIAN - -	2016	17th Oct.	1794	Construction of harps and pianofortes, applicable to all kinds of instruments where keys are used.
ERARD, SEBASTIAN - -	2502	16th May	1801	Construction of harps and pianofortes.
ERARD, SEBASTIAN - -	2595	24th March	1802	Construction of the harp.
ERARD, SEBASTIAN - -	3170	24th Sept.	1808	Pianofortes and harps.
ERARD, SEBASTIAN - -	3332	2nd May	1810	Pianofortes and harps.

Name of Patentee.	Progres-sive Number.	Date.		Subject-matter of Patent.
ERARD, SEBASTIAN - -	3835	4th Aug.	1814	Musical instruments.
ERAT, JACOB - - -	3693	8th May	1813	Construction of pedal-harps.
ERESBY, PETER ROBERT DRUM-[MOND, Lord WILLOUGHBY [DE.	8160	20th July	1839	Compressing peat.
ERICSSON, JOHN - - -	5763	31st Jan.	1829	Method of converting liquids into vapour or steam.
ERICSSON, JOHN - - -	5903	27th Feb.	1830	Manufacturing salt.
ERICSSON, JOHN - - -	5981	24th July	1830	Engine for communicating power for mechanical purposes.
ERICSSON, JOHN - - -	5995	7th Sept.	1830	Locomotive-engines.
ERICSSON, JOHN - - -	6221	9th Feb.	1832	Engine for communicating power for mechanical purposes.
ERICSSON, JOHN - - -	6409	4th April	1833	Engine for producing motive-power (obtaining an increase of power with a given quantity of fuel).
ERICSSON, JOHN - - -	6691	10th Oct.	1834	Machinery for propelling vessels.
ERICSSON, JOHN - - -	6928	14th Nov.	1835	Instrument for ascertaining the depth of water in seas and rivers.
ERICSSON, JOHN - - -	7149	13th July	1836	Propeller, applicable to steam-navigation.
ERICSSON, JOHN - - -	7153	20th July	1836	Machinery for manufacturing files.
ERICSSON, JOHN - - -	7568	16th Feb.	1838	Steam-engine.
ERICSSON, JOHN - - -	8146	6th July	1839	Steam-engine, applicable to locomotive purposes and steam navigation.
ERMEN, GODFREY - -	13,670	17th June	1851	Method or apparatus for finishing yarns or threads.
ERMEN, GODFREY ANTHONY -	8290	2nd Dec.	1839	Machinery for spinning, doubling or twisting cotton, flax, wool, silk, or other fibrous materials;—partly applicable to machinery in general.
ERMEN, GODFREY ANTHONY -	12,052	8th Feb.	1848	Machinery for twisting cotton or other fibrous substances.
ERNEST, HENRY - - -	8511	13th May	1840	Manufacture of beer-engines.
ERSKINE, THOMAS - - -	797	27th Sept.	1763	Engine for raising water.
ERWOOD, JOHN - - -	12,481	15th Feb.	1849	Manufacture of paper-hangings.
ESCHAUZIER, JACOB SAMUEL -	3629	19th Dec.	1812	Manufacturing, using and applying certain articles by which mariners and other persons may be saved from drowning.
ESDAILE, EDWARD - - -	9929	9th Nov.	1843	Machine for cutting leaves of wood called scaleboard.
ESSEX, JAMES - - -	3008	5th Feb.	1807	Making dyed, botted, or felted wool into mats, rugs, carpets, &c., of various colours, figures, patterns, and sizes for carriages, halls, parlours hearths, and other purposes.
ESSEX, ROBERT - - -	7564	8th Feb.	1838	Construction of paddle-wheels; paddle-boxes of steam vessels.
ESSEX, WILLIAM - - -	7150	13th July	1836	Machinery for producing rotary motion.
ESTIENNE, LEWIS JAMES [ARMAND.	2570	9th Jan.	1802	Reducing human excrement into a powder divested of nauseous smell, for the purpose of fertilising land.
ESTRANGE, FRANCIS L' - -	9992	21st Dec.	1843	Hernial trusses, to prevent the descent of hernia through the internal as well as external ring.
ETCHELLS, MATTHEW - -	1949	18th April 1793		Constructing and combining machinery for twisting and winding upon bobbins, cotton and sheep's wool, while being drawn.

Name of Patentee.	Progressive Number.	Date.		Subject-matter of Patent.
ETHERIDGE, FREDERICK WIL-[LIAM.	9538	3rd Dec.	1842	Manufacture of bricks, tiles, and other similar plastic substances.
ETHERINGTON, JOHN - -	11	12th Jan.	1619	Making an engine for the purpose of making and casting of clay, earthenware-pipes for conveyance of water, monions and transomes for windows, crests for houses, also tiles and paving stones.
ETIENNE, ANDRE - - -	11,068	31st Jan.	1846	Construction of railways; railway-carriages; and means of preventing accidents on railways.
ETIEVANT, STEPHANI - -	11,098	17th Feb.	1846	Stoves.
ETON, EDWARD WILLIAM -	11,836	19th Aug.	1847	Machinery for preventing accidents on railways.
EUGENE, JOHN - - -	573	13th Nov.	1740	Engine for raising water.
EVA, RICHARD - - -	2087	9th Feb.	1796	Instruments for taking observations and altitudes by sea and on land, without dependence on the visible or sensible horizon.
EVANCE, Sir STEPHEN - -	279	— Oct.	1691	Engine for conveying air into a diving-vessel, to enable several persons at the same time to work under water for many hours.
EVANS, ARTHUR - - -	362	10th April	1699	Drawing low wines and spirits from turnips, carrots, and parsnips.
EVANS, DAVID - - -	9921	2nd Nov.	1843	Sweeping and cleansing chimneys and flues; increasing the draft therein; preventing the same from smoking.
EVANS, EDWARD - - -	6638	4th July	1834	Construction and adaptation of metallic packings for the pistons of steam and other engines, also for pumps, and other purposes.
EVANS, EDWARD - - -	11,927	28th Oct.	1847	Wheels for railway and other carriages.
EVANS, EDWARD - - -	12,776	20th Sept.	1849	Steam-engines; pumps.
EVANS, EVAN - - -	8347	24th Sept.	1840	Mills for pulverizing grain and other substances; apparatus for dressing or bolting pulverized substances.
EVANS, FREDERICK JOHN -	13,059	23rd April	1850	Manufacture of gas for illumination and other purposes; preparing materials to be employed in such manufacture; apparatus for manufacturing and using gas; treating certain products resulting from the distillation of coal.
EVANS, FREDERICK JOHN -	13,904	20th Jan.	1852	Manufacture of gas for illumination; purification of gas; treating products arising from the manufacture of gas.
EVANS, GEORGE - - -	8904	29th March	1841	Trusses for the relief of hernia.
EVANS, HUGH - - -	5329	7th Feb.	1826	Rendering ships and other vessels, whether sailing or propelled by steam, safer from leakage, bilging, or letting in water.
EVANS, HUGH - - -	5506	12th June	1827	Table-apparatus for use at sea or in nautical excursions.
EVANS, JOHN - - - -	110	6th Nov.	1637	Engine for drawing and raising water from overflowed grounds, mines, and coal-pits; refining minerals and metals; making and burning bricks, tiles, limestone, chalk, and other materials.
EVANS, JOHN - - - -	5603	15th Jan.	1828	Steam-engines.
EVANS, JOHN - - - -	7961	4th Feb.	1839	Manufacture of paper.
EVANS, JOHN - - - -	8291	2nd Dec.	1839	Chemically preparing and cleansing felts used by paper manufacturers.

Name of Patentee.	Progressive Number.	Date.	Subject-matter of Patent.
Evans, John - - - -	10,806	7th Aug. 1845	Per-azotic product, and its application to the arts.
Evans, Richard - - -	4907	28th Feb. 1824	Roasting coffee and other vegetable substances; machinery employed therein, applicable to the drying, distillation, and decomposition of other mineral, vegetable, and animal substances; examining and regulating the process whilst substances are exposed to the said operations.
Evans, Richard - - -	5315	7th Jan. 1826	Apparatus for, and process of, distillation.
Evans, Robert - - -	407	31st July 1716	Two circular movements performed by endless chains, useful in jackwork, clockwork, and waterworks.
Evans, Samuel - - -	3688	1st May 1813	Working or giving motion to millwork and machinery;—applicable to raising water from mines, and for other purposes.
Evans, Thomas - - -	7590	10th March 1838	Rail for railway purposes; manufacturing and fastening down the same.
Evans, Thomas - - -	8518	28th May 1840	Manufacture of iron and other metals.
Evans, Thomas Moore -	6361	10th Jan. 1833	Machinery for preparing and dressing flax, hemp, and other fibrous materials.
Eve, Adam - - - -	5254	15th Sept. 1825	Manufacturing carpets. "Prince's patent union carpet."
Eve, Joseph - - - -	5297	24th Nov. 1825	Steam-engines.
Everard, Amye - - -	104	19th April 1637	Making tincture of saffron and essence of roses, gilliflowers and the like.
Everest, John - - -	13,395	7th Dec. 1850	Commodes; fixed and portable watercloset.
Everett, George Allen -	13,133	12th June 1850	Manufacture of metal tubes for locomotive, marine, and other boilers.
Everett, Joseph - - -	2717	28th June 1803	Manufacturing an article having the appearance of velvet; "Salisbury Angola Moleskin."
Evers, Samuel - - -	7271	11th Jan. 1837	Manufacture of bars or nuts for screws.
Evers, William - - -	1292	9th May 1781	Warming-pan, of copper and iron and other metals, japanned or otherwise.
Evoy, Henry Mc - - -	8918	5th April 1841	Fastenings for bands, straps, and parts of wearing-apparel.
Evoy, Henry Mc. - - -	11,720	27th May 1847	Manufacture of, and packing hooks and eyes.
Ewart, George - - -	10,915	3rd Nov. 1845	Manufacture of chimney-pots.
Ewart, Peter - - -	3648	20th Feb. 1813	Working weaving-looms by machinery.
Ewart, Peter - - -	4643	29th Jan. 1822	Making coffer-dams.
Ewart, Peter - - -	6505	9th Nov. 1833	Spinning-machine or mule.
Ewbank, Henry - - -	4340	9th Feb. 1819	Machinery for cleaning or dressing paddy or rough rice.
Ewbank, Henry - - -	5472	10th March 1827	Process to be used in the dressing of paddy or rough rice.
Ewbanke, Collowell Henry	197	29th March 1676	Making fire-hearths for ships, of iron, copper, or other metals.
Ewing, Alexander - -	10,292	15th Aug. 1844	Manufacture of crown glass.
Ewing, Charles - -	13,814	15th Nov. 1851	Method of construction applicable to architectural and horticultural purposes.
Ewington, Henry - -	3566	14th May 1812	"Navigator's sector," to find the difference of latitude, departure from the meridian, and distance sailed, with the course; also to solve any problem geometrically, that may be required to show the angles, hypothenuse, perpendicular and base.

Name of Patentee.	Progressive Number.	Date.	Subject-matter of Patent.
EXALL, WILLIAM - - -	11,435	3rd Nov. 1846	Construction of wheels; tools employed therein, and in forming and manufacturing the tires of wheels;—applicable to making metallic rings, bands, hoops, cylinders, and other like articles.
EXALL, WILLIAM - - -	12,080	8th March 1848	Thrashing-machines; steam boilers, engines, and apparatus for driving the same;—applicable also to driving other machinery.
EXALL, WILLIAM - - -	13,836	1st Dec. 1851	Agricultural-implements; steam-engines and boilers for driving the same.
EXALL, WILLIAM - - -	14,090	27th April 1852	Process, composition or combination of materials, also machinery and apparatus for making bread and biscuits, part of which machinery is applicable to mixing and kneading.
EYRE, EDWARD - - -	4791	15th May 1823	Manufacture of fenders of brass, iron, or steel.
EYRE, EDWARD - - -	9855	26th July 1843	Railways; machinery employed thereon.
EYRE, JOSEPH - - -	2456	13th Dec. 1800	Impressing japan on ornamented handles or scales of knives, forks, razors, and other cutlery-ware made of wood, paper, &c., in order to make the same an imitation of tip or horn.
EYRE, KINGSMILL - - -	553	20th March 1736	Making raw-iron, or iron-metal from iron-stone or ore, in air furnaces, with pit-coal.
EYRES, JOHN - - -	77	19th Dec. 1634	Making woollen-cloth waterproof.
EYTON, GEORGE - - -	4133	10th June 1817	Kiln for drying malt, wheat, oats, barley and beans, by means of steam assisted by air.

F.

Name of Patentee.	Progressive Number.	Date.	Subject-matter of Patent.
FABENE, WILLIAM - - -	509	8th May 1729	Remedy for smoky chimneys, by fixing on the top a "mantle-chimney" without doors, made of brick, lime, or other building material.
FABIEN, JOHN FRANCOIS VICTOR.	8335	7th Jan. 1840	Pumps.
FABIEN, JEAN FRANCOIS VICTOR.	8431	16th March 1840	Rotary-engines, worked by steam or other fluids.
FACIO, NICHOLAS - - -	371	1st May 1704	Working stones, crystal, or glass and other matters different from metal, for use in clock or watch work, and in other engines.
FAIRBAIRN, PETER - - -	6741	23rd Dec. 1834	Preparing, slivering, or roving hemp, flax, and other fibrous substances for spinning.
FAIRBAIRN, PETER - - -	7699	22nd June 1838	Looms for weaving ribbons, tapes, and other fabrics.
FAIRBAIRN, PETER - - -	7700	22nd June 1838	Machinery for roving, spinning, doubling and twisting cotton, flax, wool, silk, and other fibrous substances.
FAIRBAIRN, PETER - - -	8568	13th July 1840	Machinery for hecking, combing, preparing, or dressing hemp, flax, and such like textile or fibrous materials.

Name of Patentee.	Progressive Number.	Date.	Subject-matter of Patent.
FAIRBAIRN, PETER - - -	8810	26th Jan. 1841	Drawing flax, hemp, wool, silk, and other fibrous substances.
FAIRBAIRN, PETER - - -	10,518	10th Feb. 1845	Machinery for drawing, roving, and spinning hemp, flax, tow, silk, wool, and other fibrous substances.
FAIRBAIRN, PETER - - -	11,393	2nd Oct. 1846	Machinery for drawing, roving, and spinning flax, hemp, silk, and other fibrous substances.
FAIRBAIRN, PETER - - -	12,299	26th Oct. 1848	Machinery for heckling, carding, drawing, roving, and spinning flax, hemp, tow, silk, and other fibrous substances.
FAIRBAIRN, PETER - -	12,870	3rd Dec. 1849	Machinery for preparing and spinning cotton, flax, and other fibrous substances.
FAIRBAIRN, PETER - -	13,208	31st July 1850	Machinery for preparing, spinning, and weaving cotton, flax, and other fibrous substances; also constructing and applying patterns for moulding, preparatory to casting parts of such machinery; also tools used in making such machinery.
FAIRBAIRN, PETER - -	13,499	10th Feb. 1851	Moulding for the purpose of casting, pipes, railings, gates, agricultural-implements, and other metallic articles; also preparing patterns or models for the same.
FAIRBAIRN, PETER - -	14,124	8th May 1852	Preparing flax and hemp for heckling; machinery for heckling flax, hemp, china-grass, and other vegetable fibrous substances.
FAIRBAIRN, WILLIAM - -	9072	8th Sept. 1841	Construction and arrangement of steam-engines.
FAIRBAIRN, WILLIAM - -	9409	7th July 1842	Construction of metal ships, boats, and other vessels; preparation of metal plates for the purpose.
FAIRBAIRN, WILLIAM - -	10,095	7th March 1844	Propelling vessels by steam-power, and machinery for the purpose.
FAIRBAIRN, WILLIAM - -	10,166	30th April 1844	Stationary steam-boilers; furnaces and flues connected therewith.
FAIRBAIRN, WILLIAM - -	11,401	8th Oct. 1846	Construction of iron beams for the erection of bridges and other structures.
FAIRBAIRN, WILLIAM - -	13,317	7th Nov. 1850	Crane, and other lifting and hoisting machines.
FAIRBANKS, STEPHEN - -	4812	10th July 1823	Construction of locks and other fastenings.
FAIRLES, EDWARD - - -	614	17th Sept. 1745	Furnaces and boilers for making salt from sea-water.
FAIRLESS, NICHOLAS - -	3180	15th Nov. 1808	Windlass; windlass-bits; metallic hawse-hole chamber, for heaving to, and getting on board, ships' anchors.
FAIRMAN, HERMAN WILLIAM	4796	31st May 1823	Rendering leather, linen, flax, sailcloth, and other like articles, waterproof.
FAIRRIE, JOHN - - -	8147	6th July 1839	Making and refining sugar.
FALCONER, WILLIAM - -	9319	13th April 1842	Apparatus for attaching buttons and fasteners to gloves, and parts of garments.
FALKOUS, JOHN - - -	11,494	15th Dec. 1846	Gas-meters.
FALL, ROBERT - - -	844	25th March 1766	Mechanical contrivance for heating fluids.
FALLOWFIELD, WILLIAM -	490	9th Feb. 1727	Smelting or melting down iron ore, and refining and drawing out the same into bar-iron, by means of fuel different from any that has before been used for such purpose.
FANSHAW, JOHN AMERICUS -	9189	16th Dec. 1841	Manufacture of waterproof fabric, applicable for covering and packing bodies, buildings, and goods exposed to water and damp.

Name of Patentee.	Progressive Number.	Date.	Subject-matter of Patent.
FANSHAW, WILLIAM - -	182	30th July 1675	Working and weaving point laces, after the manner of Point de Buise and Point d'Espagne.
FANSHAWE, HENRY RICHARD-[SON.	5238	12th Aug. 1825	Apparatus for spinning, doubling, and twisting or throwing silk.
FANSHAWE, HENRY RICHARD-[SON.	5376	13th June 1826	Winding-machine.
FANSHAWE, HENRY RICHARD-[SON.	8980	10th June 1841	Curing hides and skins; tanning, washing, and cleaning hides, skins, and other matters.
FARADAY, ROBERT - - -	9679	25th March 1843	Ventilating gas-burners, and burners for consuming oil, tallow, and other matters.
FARAM, JOHN - - -	8276	21st Nov. 1839	Constructing, using, and applying railway-switches, for connecting different lines of railways or two distinct railways, and for passing steam and other engines, carriages, and waggons, from one railway to the other; apparatus connected therewith.
FAREY, BARNARD WILLIAM -	12,964	9th Feb. 1850	Steam-engines; fluid meter.
FAREY, JOSEPH - - -	5214	16th July 1825	Lamps.
FARINA, CHARLES - - -	7181	15th Sept. 1836	Mashing-apparatus.
FARINA, CHARLES - - -	7347	18th April 1837	Obtaining fermentable matter from grain; manufacturing the same for various purposes.
FARINA, CHARLES - - -	9324	15th April 1842	Manufacturing soap, candles, and sealing-wax.
FARINA, JEAN ANTOINE -	13,896	13th Jan. 1852	Manufacturing paper.
FARISH, WILLIAM - - -	5698	4th Sept. 1828	Clearing out watercourses.
FARLAND, WILLIAM Mc - -	3189	29th Dec. 1808	Construction of umbrellas and parasols.
FARMER, RICHARD - - -	9758	6th June 1843	Fixed and portable watercloseIS; beds or bedsteads;—partly applicable to raising water.
FARMER, THOMAS - - -	8398	25th Feb. 1840	Obtaining sulphur, sulphurous acids, and other products, from pyrites.
FARMER, THOMAS - - -	10,224	12th June 1844	Ornamenting papier-maché; manufacturing and ornamenting japanned goods generally.
FARMERY, WILLIAM - -	3179	8th Nov. 1808	Machine for preparing, roving, slubbing, spinning, twisting and doubling cotton, flax, hemp, tow, wool, silk, or any other substance, into threads.
FARNSWORTH, JAMES - -	11,408	8th Oct. 1846	Machinery for the manufacture of bricks and tiles.
FARQUHAR, WILLIAM - -	7566	13th Feb. 1838	Generating steam for steam-engines.
FARQUHARSON, FRANCIS -	2215	20th Feb. 1798	Making bricks and tiles; machinery for the purpose.
FARRAND, ROGER - -	1633	5th Dec. 1787	Gilding and ornamenting various goods of British manufacture, in gold and silver leaf, also with yellow and white metal leaf.
FARRAR, RICHARD - -	76	18th Dec. 1634	Engines for raising water out of mines and other places.
FARRE, NICHOLAS LEE - -	2455	12th Dec. 1800	Naval-architecture.
FARRELL, ISAAC - - -	10,394	14th Nov. 1844	Machinery for impelling carriages on railways and tramways, by means of stationary engines or other power; also apparatus connected with the carriages to run on the same.
FARRIES, ARCHIBALD - -	11,841	19th Aug. 1847	Propelling carriages on common roads.

Name of Patentee.	Progressive Number.	Date.		Subject-matter of Patent.
FARROW, BENJAMIN	5097	19th Feb.	1825	Rendering buildings less liable to injury from fire.
FARROW, JACOB	12,622	29th May	1849	Machinery for preparing wool for spinning; machinery for spinning wool and other fibrous substances.
FARTHING, WILLIAM	11,397	8th Oct.	1846	Manufacture of glass.
FARWIG, CARL LUDEWIG	9701	19th April	1843	Gas-meters.
FATTON, FREDERICK LOUIS	4707	27th Sept.	1822	Watches or chronometers.
FAUCETT, BENJAMIN	12,894	15th Dec.	1849	Pigments and paints, and vehicles for painting.
FAUCON, JOSEPH SERAPHIN	11,272	29th June	1846	Combining materials to be employed in fulling cloth.
FAUCON, JOSEPH SERAPHIN [Fancon Joseph Seraphin.]	11,529	14th Jan.	1847	Manufacture of soap.
FAULCONBRIDGE, WILLIAM	12,588	26th April	1849	Manufacture of hose-pipes, driving-bands, and valves for atmospheric railways.
FAULKNER, LOT	8030	11th April	1839	Working pumps or valves;—applicable to fire-engines, and other similar apparatus.
FAULKNER, LOT	13,722	21st Aug.	1851	Method of obtaining and applying motive-power.
FAULKNER, SAMUEL	6874	6th Aug.	1835	Construction of a machine for carding cotton and other fibrous substances.
FAULKNER, SAMUEL	9854	25th July	1843	Machinery for carding cotton and other fibrous substances.
FAVERYEAR, HENRY	4324	24th Dec.	1818	Machine for cutting veneers in wood and other substances.
FAWCETT, WILLIAM	5572	4th Dec.	1827	Apparatus for manufacturing sugar from the canes.
FAWCETT, WILLIAM	6012	20th Oct.	1830	Introducing air into fluids, for the purpose of evaporation.
FAWCETT, WILLIAM	13,952	2nd Feb.	1852	Manufacture of carpets.
FAXON, SAMUEL WALTON	8314	16th Dec.	1839	Apparatus applied to the chimneys of gas or other burners or lamps, to improve combustion.
FAY, ANTHONY	1763	17th July	1790	Tanning leather; construction of tan-yards for the purpose.
FAYNARD, JAMES	1050	3rd Aug.	1773	Powder for stopping violent internal and external bleeding.
FAYRER, ROBERT JOHN	12,923	11th Jan.	1850	Steering-apparatus.
FEARN, AARON	7292	28th Jan.	1837	Dyeing and scouring piece-goods and other fabrics; machinery for the purpose.
FEARNE, CHARLES	951	25th Jan.	1770	Dyeing paper, card-paper, and white leather on the grain side, in various colours.
FEATHER, JOHN	13,957	9th Feb.	1852	Screws.
FEBRUE, PETER LE	62	12th April	1833	Making water-mills on standing waters, lakes and ditches.
FEETHAM, WILLIAM	4680	13th June	1822	Shower-baths.
FELL, JAMES	11,897	7th Oct.	1847	Obtaining and applying motive-power.
FELL, JONATHAN	8186	5th Aug.	1839	Building ships and other vessels.
FELL, RICHARD	6119	24th May	1831	Machinery for raising water; and its application to other purposes.
FELL, RICHARD	10,688	24th May	1845	Generation and application of steam; obtaining and applying motive-power.
FELL, RICHARD	11,897	7th Oct.	1847	Obtaining and applying motive-power.

Name of Patentee.	Progressive Number.	Date.	Subject-matter of Patent.
FELL, RICHARD - - -	13,507	11th Feb. 1851	Obtaining fresh and pure water from salt, sea, and other waters.
FELL, RICHARD - - -	13,714	7th Aug. 1851	Obtaining fresh-water from salt-water; concentrating sulphuric acid.
FELLOWS, THOMAS - - -	6062	18th Jan. 1831	Skates.
FELTON, EDMUND - - -	37	20th Jan. 1627	Engines for conveying water to dry and barren grounds, and for draining mines of tin, lead, copper, or coals.
FELTON, JOHN - - -	5512	28th June 1827	Machine for giving a fine edge to knives, razors, scissors, and other cutlery.
FELTON, JOHN - - -	10,615	15th April 1845	Wafers; and securing letters and notes from being surreptitiously opened.
FELTON, SAMUEL - - -	3284	9th Dec. 1809	Medicinal preparation, as a remedy for gravel and stony concretions, "Mucilage of Marsh Mallows."
FENILLADE, CHARLES WILLIAM	4418	4th Dec. 1819	Instrument for the prevention and remedy of deformity in the human trunk.
FENN, ISAAC - - - -	833	15th July 1765	Portable perambulator or measuring-wheel for surveying.
FENNER, WILLIAM - - -	5358	6th May 1826	Machinery for curing smoky chimneys, also for cleaning foul chimneys.
FENTON, JAMES - - -	10,208	30th May 1844	Combinations or alloys of metal, applicable for various purposes in which brass and copper are usually employed in constructing machinery.
FENTON, JOHN - - -	6803	3rd April 1835	Composition, as a substitute for soap.
FENTON, SAMUEL - - -	7000	10th Feb. 1836	Construction of locks and latches for doors, gates, and other like purposes.
FERANT, MICHEL LOUIS -	11,409	8th Oct. 1846	Treating oils.
FERGUSON, CHARLES AUGUSTUS	5593	22nd Dec. 1827	Construction of made-masts.
FERGUSON, GEORGE - -	3415	14th March 1811	Lamp, with its appendages.
FERGUSON, GEORGE - -	3721	14th July 1813	Beaver-hats.
FERGUSON, JAMES - - -	4594	18th Oct. 1821	Substitutes for certain materials used in printing from stereotype-plates.
FERGUSON, JOSEPH -	6734	23rd Dec. 1834	Combination of processes for dressing or finishing certain goods.
FERGUSON, ROBERT -	10,318	14th Sept. 1844	Printing and calendering.
FERIER, PIERRE JACQUES -	8179	1st Aug. 1839	Construction of vapour and hot air baths.
FERNANDEZ, JAMES BARLOW -	5374	26th May 1826	Construction of blinds or shades for windows, and for other purposes.
FERNIHOUGH, WILLIAM FRAN- [CIS.	13,281	10th Oct. 1850	Locomotive and other steam-engines; obtaining motive-power.
FERRABEE, JOHN - -	6058	23rd Dec. 1830	Machinery for preparing the pile or face of woollen or other cloths.
FERRABEE, JOHN - -	6986	21st Jan. 1836	Power-looms.
FERRABEE, JOHN - -	7584	5th March 1838	Machinery for dressing woollen and other cloths.
FERRERS, THOMAS - -	346	14th Dec. 1695	Damasking and fixing colours in leather, stuffs, cloths, velvets, and hair, on both sides; also making tapestry with grogram yarn.
FERRIS, MATTHEW - -	5311	14th Dec. 1825	Processes or machinery for printing cotton or other fabrics.
FERRYMAN, JOHN BARKE [GUSTAVUS.	11,855	6th Sept. 1847	Handles to be applied to articles containing liquids or other matters liable to be spilt.

Name of Patentee.	Progres-sive Number.	Date.	Subject-matter of Patent.
FERRYMAN, ROBERT [*Ferryman, Reverend Robert.*]	1819	19th July 1791	Locks acting by lever, toothed-wheel and drop, chiefly without springs, simple in principle, and not liable to be injured by accident or friction ; applicable to prisons and other places where strong fastenings are requisite.
FERRYMAN, ROBERT	1957	15th June 1793	Valve-cock.
FERRYMAN, ROBERT	1989	13th May 1794	Bathing-machine, either fixed or moveable, which may be used as a hot or cold bath in salt or fresh water, fitted with a tap to the boiler, a stop to the door, and a scraper.
FERRYMAN, ROBERT	2158	24th Jan. 1797	Machine for blanching, grinding, and dressing corn.
FESEMNEYER, JOHN PHILLIP	3243	15th June 1809	Construction and working of steam and atmospheric engines.
FEUILLADE, LEWIS	1862	29th March 1792	Constructing a machine for removing rocks, raising sunken vessels, cutting canals, also roads or ways through hills, for cleansing and deepening harbours and ports, and for other purposes.
FEUILLET, LOUIS FRANCOIS	8172	1st Aug. 1839	Casting type for printing.
FEVRE, GABRIEL DIDIER	13,525	24th Feb. 1851	Apparatus for manufacturing and containing soda-water and other gaseous liquids ; preserving other substances from evaporation.
FFERGUSON, PATRICK (Captain)	1139	2nd Dec. 1776	Fire-arms, whereby they may be loaded with more expedition, ease, and safety, and fired with greater certainty, possessing also other advantages.
FIELD, ARTHUR	13,696	22nd July 1851	Manufacture of candles, night-lights, and mortars.
FIELD, JOHN	10,729	23rd June 1845	Apparatus for ascertaining the alcoholic strength of liquids.
FIELD, JOHN	14,324	14th Oct. 1852	Transferring and printing.
FIELD, JOSHUA	5021	14th Oct. 1824	Method and apparatus for continually changing the water used in boilers for generating steam, particularly applicable to the boilers of steam-vessels by preventing the deposition of substances contained in the water.
FIELD, JOSHUA	6465	20th Aug. 1833	Boiler and other apparatus for locomotive carriages.
FIELD, JOSHUA	8060	7th May 1839	Construction of marine steam-engines.
FIELD, JOSHUA	8388	22nd March 1841	Connecting and disconnecting from steam-engines the paddle-wheels used for steam navigation.
FIELD, JOSHUA	10,637	24th April 1845	Propelling, and propelling-machinery.
FIELD, OSGOOD	12,640	5th June 1849	Anchors.
FIELDEN, JOSHUA	11,697	8th May 1847	Laying and pressing cotton, silk, wool, flax, and other fibrous matters into cans, baskets, boxes, or other depositories.
FIELDER, FRANK	10,300	29th Aug. 1844	Wirework for the manufacture of paper, and the application thereof to such purposes.
FIELDER, HENRY	11,950	9th Nov. 1847	Construction of iron beams or girders.
FIGGINS, THOMAS	3539	19th Feb. 1812	" Palanquin couch."
FILLIS, WILLIAM	12,110	5th April 1848	Generating, indicating, and applying heat.
FINCH, EDWARD	8901	25th Mar. 1841	Propelling vessels.

Name of Patentee.	Progres- sive Number.	Date.		Subject-matter of Patent.
FINCH, GEORGE - - -	3198	4th Feb.	1809	Manufacturing metal laces to imitate gold and silver laces; manufacturing gold and silver open laces.
FINCH, JOHN - - -	250	25th June	1686	Woven wire-engine for bolting, dressing, sifting, and chaffing meal, and for cleansing dust or dross from metals.
FINCH, JOHN - - -	12,866	28th Nov.	1849	Manufacture of baths and washtubs or wash vessels.
FINCH, WILLIAM - - -	1768	28th July	1790	Machinery put in motion by the force of animals, water, wind, or steam, for making nails and spikes of iron, copper, and other metals.
FINCH, WILLIAM - - -	3433	11th April	1811	Making nails of wrought iron.
FINCH, WILLIAM - - -	4297	12th Oct.	1818	Bridles for horses.
FINCHETT, ARNOLD - -	916	10th Feb.	1769	Purifying oils and scenting them with aro- matic smells.
FINDLAY, JOSEPH - - -	13,030	5th April	1850	Machinery or apparatus for turning, cutting, shaping, or reducing wood or other substances.
FINDLER, THOMAS - - -	11,005	15th Dec.	1845	Construction and operation of parts of flint grinding-mills, and other grinding- mills.
FINDON, JAMES - - -	7068	23rd April	1836	Apparatus for supplying water to water- closets.
FINLAY, JOHN - - -	10,956	18th Nov.	1845	Raising and lowering gas and other lamps, lustres, and chandeliers.
FINLAYSON, CHARLES - -	14,030	22nd Mar.	1852	Flues, heating air, evaporating certain fluids by heated air.
FINLAYSON, JOHN - - -	4852	9th Oct.	1823	Ploughs and harrows.
FINLAYSON, JOHN - - -	4888	15th Jan.	1824	Ploughs and harrows.
FINLAYSON, ROBERT - -	7622	21st April	1838	Harrows.
FINNEMORE, JOSEPH - -	10,005	4th Jan.	1844	Metallic pens; machines for manufacturing metallic pens.
FINZEL, CONRAD WILLIAM -	12,808	12th Oct.	1849	Processes and machinery employed in and applicable to the manufacture of sugar.
FIRCHILD, CHARLES WILLIAM	9294	14th Mar.	1842	Propelling-apparatus for marine and other purposes.
FIRCHILD, CHARLES WILLIAM	10,691	29th May	1845	Machine for cutting, slicing, grinding, and rasping.
FIRCHILD, CHARLES WILLIAM	11,302	23rd July	1846	Engine for obtaining rotary-motion.
FIRMIN, GEORGE JORDAN -	13,676	24th June	1851	Manufacture of oxalate of potash.
FIRMSTONE, THOMAS - -	8328	24th Dec.	1839	Manufacture of salt.
FIRTH, JOSEPH - - -	12,164	26th May	1848	Machinery for twisting and doubling cotton yarns and other fibrous materials.
FISCHER, JOHN - - -	1377	17th June	1783	Geometrical and pedometrical watch.
FISCHER, PIERRE FREDERIC -	6304	8th Sept.	1832	Pianofortes.
FISCHER, PIERRE FREDERICK	6835	13th May	1835	Pianofortes.
FISH, JOHN - - - -	14,279	26th Aug.	1852	Looms for weaving.
FISHER, CHARLES - - -	14,094	29th April	1852	Transferring ornamental designs on to woven or textile fabrics; and apparatus connected therewith.
FISHER, DAVID - - -	7096	17th May	1836	Steam-engines.
FISHER, DAVID - - -	11,909	14th Oct.	1847	Manufacture of boots and shoes.
FISHER, GEORGE - - -	13,045	18th April	1850	Construction and means of applying carriage and certain other springs.

Name of Patentee.	Progressive Number.	Date.		Subject-matter of Patent.
FISHER, HENRY - - -	12,456	8th Feb.	1849	Coke-ovens; machinery and apparatus for working the same or connected therewith; applying parts of coke, or the residual products of coke, to heating and lighting.
FISHER, JACOB JEDDER - -	5145	2nd April	1825	Application of railways, and the machinery to be employed thereon.
FISHER, JOHN - - -	3626	19th Dec.	1812	"Smoke Conductor" of iron, copper, brass, tin or other metallic substance, for preventing chimneys smoking.
FISHER, JOHN - - -	3694	11th May	1813	Gaiters, and mode of fastening the same.
FISHER, JOHN - - -	4811	8th July	1823	Construction of boilers for steam-engines, and for other purposes where steam is required.
FISHER, JOHN - - -	10,424	7th Dec.	1844	Manufacture of figured or ornamented lace or net, and other fabrics.
FISHER, JOHN - - -	10,716	10th June	1845	Manufacture of lace or net, and other fabrics; machinery for figuring or ornamenting lace or net, and other fabrics.
FISHER, JOHN - - -	11,644	29th March	1847	Manufacture of lace or weavings.
FISHER, JOHN - - -	11,663	20th April	1847	Folding certain narrow fabrics.
FISHER, JOSEPH - - -	1156	9th June	1777	Machine for writing or drawing by lines.
FISHER, SAMUEL - - -	12,878	5th Dec.	1849	Railway-carriages, wheels, axles, buffer and draw-springs, and hinges for railway-carriage and other doors.
FISHER, TIMOTHY - - -	10,251	10th July	1844	Locomotive-engines.
FISHWICK, RICHARD - -	1581	15th Jan.	1787	Making white-lead.
FISKE, THOMAS HAMMOND -	7672	5th June	1838	Apparatus for measuring and indicating the depth of water in a ship's hold.
FITCH, MICHAEL - - -	10,322	19th Sept.	1844	Substance for preventing decomposition in provisions; manufacturing the same; condensing and applying a certain gas or fume to certain perishable articles.
FITCH, MICHAEL - - -	12,806	12th Oct.	1849	Baking bread, biscuits, and other matters;—applicable to drying goods.
FITKIN, JOHN - -	3997	14th March	1816	Trusses.
FITKIN, WILLIAM - -	3997	14th March	1816	Trusses.
FITT, JAMES, senior - -	8654	7th Oct.	1840	Construction of machinery for communicating mechanical power.
FITTON, CHARLES - -	7533	11th Jan.	1838	Power-looms.
FITZGERALD, ROBERT - -	226	9th June	1683	Engines for purifying salt and brackish water, making it sweet and fit for drinking and purposes of cooking.
FITZGERALD, WILLIAM - -	1994	2nd June	1794	Apparatus by which ships and vessels may be discharged of water by means of their own motion;—applicable to purposes in pneumatics, hydrostatics and hydraulics.
FITZGERALD, WILLIAM - -	2001	16th July	1794	Apparatus, to be worked by a steam-engine or other first-moving power, for moving barges and other vessels along navigable canals and other waters used for navigation.
FITZGERALD, WILLIAM - -	2288	23rd Jan.	1799	Signal-trumpet.
FITZGERALD, WILLIAM - -	2532	11th Aug.	1801	Mathematical instrument, or "Marine Level" for showing a ship's deviation from the horizontal plane;—applicable in surveying, levelling, and ascertaining vertical and perpendicular situations.

Name of Patentee.	Progressive Number.	Date.	Subject-matter of Patent.
FITZGERALD, WILSON - -	2330	16th July 1799	Producing tallow or fat.
FITZMAURICE, LEWIS ROPER -	5682	11th Aug. 1828	Ship and other pumps;—applicable by certain alterations to turning lathes, and to other purposes.
FITZPATRICK, JOHN - -	8190	10th Aug. 1839	Making thread and linen from a material not hitherto used for that purpose.
FLEET, THOMAS - - -	2014	1st Oct. 1794	Medicine to prevent the rot in sheep, and to check its progress in those already affected.
FLEETWOOD, CHARLES BAGE-[NALL.	4915	28th Feb. 1824	Liquid and composition for waterproofing leather and other articles.
FLEETWOOD, THOMAS - -	359	1st Dec. 1698	Engine with ladles turning circularly on their axes, for draining water.
FLEMING, JOHN - - -	1057	18th Dec. 1773	Machine, actuated by wheels, for pressing sugar-canes, and squeezing the juice therefrom.
FLETCHER, CHARLES - -	7583	5th March 1838	Construction of looms for weaving.
FLETCHER, HENRY - -	11,619	10th March 1847	Apparatus for ascertaining the distance which locomotive engines and carriages have travelled on railways.
FLETCHER, HOWARD - -	4894	19th Jan. 1824	Tanning hides and other skins.
FLETCHER, JAMES - - -	9883	30th March 1843	Machinery for spinning cotton and other fibrous substances.
FLETCHER, JAMES - -	10,674	22nd May 1845	Machinery for preparing, roving, and slubbing cotton and other fibrous substances.
FLETCHER, JAMES - -	12,551	28th March 1849	Machinery, tools or apparatus for turning, boring, planing, and cutting metals and other materials.
FLETCHER, JAMES - -	14,097	29th April 1852	Machinery or apparatus for stretching and drying woven fabrics.
FLETCHER, JOHN - - -	2978	21st Oct. 1806	Composition or " prepared gypsum," to be used as a manure, and for destroying the fly in turnips, also snails, ants, and other insects detrimental to vegetables.
FLETCHER, JOSEPH - -	2902	23rd Jan. 1806	Machine for raising water.
FLETCHER, LAWRENCE WOOD	8327	23d Dec. 1839	Manufacture of woollen and other cloths or fabrics, and their application to useful purposes.
FLETCHER, RICHARD - -	13,671	21st June 1851	Obtaining motive-power.
FLETCHER, SAMUEL - -	4486	11th July 1820	Saddles, saddle-girths, saddle-straps, and saddle-cloths, by the application of materials not hitherto used for the purpose.
FLETCHER, SAMUEL - -	10,160	27th April 1844	Wheels to be used in slubbing or bobbin frames, and in roving or jack frames, and for other purposes ; engine by which such wheels are or may be cut.
FLETCHER, THEODORE - -	11,828	3rd Aug. 1847	Manufacture of specula for various purposes.
FLETCHER, WILLIAM - -	9875	24th Aug. 1843	Securing corks or substitutes for corks in the mouths of bottles and such like vessels, whether earthenware, stoneware, or of glass.
FLETCHER, WILLIAM - -	10,032	30th Jan. 1844	Construction of locks and latches applicable for doors, and for other purposes.
FLIGHT, BENJAMIN - -	3266	26th Sept. 1809	Metal nave, axle and box for wheeled-carriages.
FLIGHT, JOSEPH - - -	1260	27th June 1780	Making a colour for dyers and calico printers.

Name of Patentee.	Progressive Number.	Date.	Subject-matter of Patent.
FLINT, ALFRED - - -	4721	1st Nov. 1822	Machine for scouring, pising, and washing woollen-cloths.
FLINT, ALFRED - - -	5141	29th March 1825	Machinery for raising the wool or pile on woollen or other cloths, by improved application of the teazle or other points;—partly applicable to brushing, smoothing, and dressing such cloths.
FLINT, ANDREW - - -	2892	16th Nov. 1805	Machine which may be used as a steam-engine.
FLOCKTON, WEBSTER - -	6668	23rd Aug. 1834	Manufacturing rosin.
FLOCKTON, WEBSTER - - [Flockton, John Webster.]	7160	3rd Aug. 1836	Preserving timber.
FLOCKTON, WEBSTER - -	10,317	12th Sept. 1844	Machinery for sweeping or cleaning streets, roads, or ways.
FLOWER, VALENTINE - -	469	20th May 1724	Engine and pump with a leverage and a horizontal fly; for raising water without the help of fire.
FLOYD, WILLIAM - - -	2073	3rd Nov. 1795	Bucking-tub or cistern with a furnace affixed to and communicating with the same, for bucking cloth, yarn or other things usually bleached by bucking.
FLUDE, CHARLES - - -	7555	30th Jan. 1838	Applying heat to the manufacture of alkalies and salts, and for smelting and working ores, metals and earths.
FLUDE, CHARLES - - -	7851	3rd Nov. 1838	Applying heat for generating steam, and for general manufacturing and other purposes where heat is required; supplying steam-boilers with hot water.
FLUDE, CHARLES - - -	8166	20th July 1839	White-lead.
FOARD, EDWARD - - -	8794	16th Jan. 1841	Supplying fuel to the fireplaces or grates of steam-engine boilers, brewers' coppers and other furnaces, also to fireplaces for domestic purposes, and generally to the supplying of fuel to fireplaces or furnaces, so as to consume the smoke.
FODEN, THOMAS - - -	2348	4th Nov. 1799	Crystalline size or mixture to be used in sizing and dressing cotton, worsted, and linen yarn.
FODEN, THOMAS - - -	2353	4th Nov. 1799	Loom for warping, dressing, weaving, and piecing silk, cotton, woollen or other yarn.
FOLJAIMBE, JOSEPH - -	518	21st Sept. 1730	Plough.
FÖLSCH, FREDERICK BARTHO-[LOMEW.	3214	4th March 1809	Writing-pen; black writing ink.
FÖLSCH, FREDERICK BARTHO-[LOMEW. [Fölsch, Bartholomew.]	3235	9th May 1809	Writing-pens.
FOLYARTE, RAPHAELL - -	172	25th Nov. 1673	Royal carousal or tournament contrived for amusement, and instruction in horsemanship, as also for running at the ring, throwing the lance, taking up the head and similar exercises, all performed in a straight line.
FONS, JOHN PALMER DE LA -	5219	16th July 1825	Extracting and fixing teeth.
FONS, JOHN PALMER DE LA -	5388	14th July 1826	Securing or mooring ships and other floating bodies; and apparatus for the purpose.
FONS, JOHN PALMER DE LA -	11,283	6th July 1846	Manufacture of locks and other fastenings.
FONTAINEMOREAU, PIERRE [ARMAND Le Comte de.	7635	5th May 1838	Preventing the oxydation of metals.
FONTAINEMOREAU, PIERRE [ARMAND Le Comte de.	7764	6th Aug. 1838	Wool-combing.

Name of Patentee.	Progressive Number.	Date.	Subject-matter of Patent.
FONTAINEMOREAU, PIERRE [ARMAND Le Comte de.	7781	23rd Aug. 1838	Metallic-alloys, as substitutes for zinc, cast iron, copper, and other metals.
FONTAINEMOREAU, PIERRE [ARMAND Le Comte de.	8604	15th Aug. 1840	Covering and coating metals, and alloys of metals.
FONTAINEMOREAU, PIERRE [ARMAND Le Comte de.	8786	14th Jan. 1841	Machinery for carding and spinning wools and hairs. " Filo finisher."
FONTAINEMOREAU, PIERRE [ARMAND Le Comte de.	9587	14th Jan. 1843	Combining clay with other substances, for producing a " ceramic paste" for moulding into various forms ; its application to several purposes.
FONTAINEMOREAU, PIERRE [ARMAND Le Comte de.	9927	4th Nov. 1843	Crane. " Dynamometric crane."
FONTAINEMOREAU, PIERRE [ARMAND Le Comte de.	10,157	27th April 1844	Constructing barometers, and other pneumatic instruments.
FONTAINEMOREAU, PIERRE [ARMAND Le Comte de.	10,187	15th May 1844	Paving and covering roads, and other ways or surfaces.
FONTAINEMOREAU, PIERRE [ARMAND Le Comte de.	10,232	21st June 1844	Locomotion, applicable to railroads and other ways.
FONTAINEMOREAU, PIERRE [ARMAND Le Comte de.	10,282	31st July 1844	Coating or covering metals, and alloys of metals.
FONTAINEMOREAU, PIERRE [ARMAND Le Comte de.	10,559	13th March 1845	Distilling and rectifying ; apparatus for the purpose.
FONTAINEMOREAU, PIERRE [ARMAND Le Comte de.	10,679	22nd May 1845	Dissolving and separating the oxydes from metals and metallic substances.
FONTAINEMOREAU, PIERRE [ARMAND Le Comte de.	10,796	4th Aug. 1845	Medicines or compounds ; application of an instrument to cure certain diseases ; machinery for manufacturing the said instrument
FONTAINEMOREAU, PIERRE [ARMAND Le Comte de.	10,811	9th Aug. 1845	Apparatus for raising and supporting vessels and other floating or sunken bodies, and its application to the preservation of life and property.
FONTAINEMOREAU, PIERRE [ARMANE Le Comte de.	10,931	11th Nov. 1845	Producing artificial fuel.
FONTAINEMOREAU, PIERRE [ARMAND Le Comte de.	11,115	28th Feb. 1846	Manufacturing and glazing cotton-wadding, and its application to the making of mattrasses.
FONTAINEMOREAU, PIERRE [ARMARD Le Comte de.	11,165	15th April 1846	Constructing parts of the harness of horses and other beasts of burden.
FONTAINEMOREAU, PIERRE [ARMAND Le Comte de.	11,365	3rd Sept. 1846	Machines for the manufacture of bricks, and other plastic products.
FONTAINEMOREAU, PIERRE [ARMAND Le Comte de.	11,379	24th Sept. 1846	Manufacturing corks.
FONTAINEMOREAU, PIERRE [ARMAND Le Comte de.	11,550	28th Jan. 1847	Process and apparatus for treating fatty bodies, and the matters producing them ; applicable to the treating of other substances ; process and apparatus for the application of such products.
FONTAINEMOREAU, PIERRE [ARMAND Le Comte de.	11,716	25th May 1847	Machinery for cutting wood ; laying and uniting veneers.
FONTAINEMOREAU, PIERRE [ARMAND Le Comte de.	11,796	17th July 1847	Machinery for preparing cotton and other fibrous substances.
FONTAINEMOREAU, PIERRE [ARMAND Le Comte de.	11,968	18th Nov. 1847	Machinery for making, uniting, and preserving metallic and other tubes or pipes.
FONTAINEMOREAU, PIERRE [ARMAND Le Comte de.	11,969	18th Nov. 1847	Manufacturing braids, plats, fringes, gimps, and other similar articles.
FONTAINEMOREAU, PIERRE	ARMAND Le Comte de.	12,342	25th Nov. 1848	Process of and apparatus for treating fatty bodies ; application of the products to useful purposes.

Name of Patentee.	Progres-sive Number.	Date.	Subject-matter of Patent.
FONTAINEMOREAU, PIERRE [ARMAND Le Comte de.	12,385	21st Dec. 1848	Hygienic apparatus and processes for preventing and curing chronic and other affections, and for preventing or stopping certain epidemic diseases.
FONTAINEMOREAU, PIERRE [ARMAND Le Comte de.	12,523	14th March 1849	Coating or covering metallic and non-metallic bodies.
FONTAINEMOREAU, PIERRE [ARMAND Le Comte de.	12,614	22nd May 1849	Weaving.
FONTAINEMOREAU, PIERRE [ARMAND Le Comte de.	12,801	12th Oct. 1849	Spinning fibrous substances.
FONTAINEMOREAU, PIERRE [ARMAND Le Comte de.	13,060	23rd April 1850	Conducting and consuming smoke ; also disengaging smoke from its deleterious compounds.
FONTAINEMOREAU, PIERRE [ARMAND Le Comte de.	13,061	23rd April 1850	Manufacture of wafers ; machinery or apparatus connected therewith.
FONTAINEMOREAU, PIERRE [ARMAND Le Comte de.	13,111	8th June 1850	Oscillating engines, put in motion by steam and gas, resulting from combustion.
FONTAINEMOREAU, PIERRE [ARMAND Le Comte de.	13,113	11th June 1850	Manufacture of sulphate of soda, muriatic and nitric acids.
FONTAINEMOREAU, PIERRE [ARMAND Le Comte de.	13,543	10th March 1851	Compressing air and gases for obtaining motive-power.
FONTAINEMOREAU, PIERRE [ARMAND Le Comte de.	13,566	24th March 1851	Mills for grinding wheat and other grain.
FONTAINEMOREAU, PIERRE [ARMAND Le Comte de.	13,617	3rd May 1851	Manufacture of fuel.
FONTAINEMOREAU, PIERRE [ARMAND Le Comte de.	13,619	3rd May 1851	Electric-telegraphs.
FONTAINEMOREAU, PIERRE [ARMAND Le Comte de.	13,731	28th Aug. 1851	Apparatus for gas-lighting.
FONTAINEMOREAU, PIERRE [ARMAND Le Comte de.	13,739	4th Sept. 1851	Preserving animal substances from decay by means of a composition, applicable to the cure of certain diseases.
FONTAINEMOREAU, PIERRE [ARMAND Le Comte de.	13,844	8th Dec. 1851	Apparatus for kneading and baking bread, and other articles of food of a similar nature.
FONTAINEMOREAU, PIERRE [ARMAND Le Comte de.	13,900	20th Jan. 1852	Treating fibrous substances.
FONTAINEMOREAU, PIERRE [ARMAND Le Comte de.	13,905	22nd Jan. 1852	Railways, and locomotive-engines;—applicable to every kind of transmission of motion.
FONTAINEMOREAU, PIERRE [ARMAND Le Comte de.	13,916	24th Jan. 1852	Lithographic, typographic, and other printing presses ;—applicable (with modifications) to extracting saccharine, oleaginous, and other matters, and to compressing in general.
FONTAINEMOREAU, PIERRE [ARMAND Le Comte de.	13,984	23rd Feb. 1852	Gas-burners.
FONTAINEMOREAU, PIERRE [ARMAND Le Comte de.	14,245	29th July 1852	Construction of taps and cocks for fluids and liquids.
FONTAINEMOREAU. PIERRE [ARMAND Le Comte de.	14,269	19th Aug. 1852	Cutting shistus for slates.
FONTAINEMOREAU, PIERRE [ARMAND Le Comte de.	14,284	7th Sept. 1852	Producing gas ; and its application to heat and light.
FONTAINEMOREAU, PIERRE [ARMAND Le Comte de.	14,314	7th Oct. 1852	Washing, bleaching, and dyeing flax and hemp ; mixing them with other textile substances.
FONTAINEMOREAU, PIERRE [ARMAND Le Comte de.	14,342	6th Nov. 1852	Manufacture of certain articles of dress.
FONZI, JOSEPH ANGE - -	5841	9th Sept. 1829	Fireplaces.
FOORD, GEORGE - - -	13,751	25th Sept. 1851	Bending and annealing glass.
FOOT, JOSEPH - - -	4886	15th Jan. 1824	Umbrellas.

Name of Patentee.	Progressive Number.	Date.	Subject-matter of Patent.
FOOT, JOSEPH - - -	12,111	5th April 1848	Manufacture of sieves
FOOT, JOSEPH - - -	12,178	8th June 1848	Marking skeins of silk.
FOOT, JOSEPH - - -	13,155	27th June 1850	Bolters.
FOOTE, RICHARD - - -	8508	12th May 1840	Alarums.
FORBES, JOHN - - -	5735	15th Dec. 1828	Burning or consuming smoke.
FORBES, WILLIAM - - -	1381	29th July 1783	Manufacturing bolts and other fastenings for ships.
FORD, CHARLES - - -	11,488	14th Dec. 1846	Manufacture of earthenware; apparatus employed therein;—partly applicable to other purposes.
FORD, EDWARD - - -	126	14th March 1640	Navigating boats, barges, lighters, and other vessels, on rivers or the sea.
FORD, EDWARD - - -	7998	8th March 1839	Manufacture of sulphate of soda and hydrochloric or other acids and alkalies; furnaces and works connected therewith.
FORD, GEORGE HAYWOOD -	13,096	3rd June 1850	Obtaining power.
FORD, JOHN - - -	5654	13th May 1828	Machinery for clearing, opening, scribbling, carding, combing, slubbing, and spinning wool; carding, roving, and spinning cotton, short-stapled flax, hemp, and silk; and for spinning long-stapled flax, hemp, silk, mohair or other fibrous substances, alone or combined.
FORD, RICHARD - - -	935	28th Aug. 1769	Rolling silver, copper, and other metals, of various thicknesses, with the same rollers, and by one operation; drawing wire by means of wheels and a pinion, of various sizes, at one and the same time; and raising by a stamp and press, scale pans, sauce-pans, warming-pans, basins, plate-covers, kettles, ladles, and various other things, out of silver, copper, and other metals.
FORD, RICHARD - - -	2961	30th Aug. 1806	Cordage made by a new process, from old rope or junk, or short ends of new rope, usually converted into oakum, or coarse paper; such process obviating the objections to twice-laid cordage, and producing an article nearly equal to that made from new materials.
FORD, ROBERT - - -	4037	21st Nov. 1816	Medicine for the cure of coughs, colds, asthmas, and consumptions. "Ford's Balsam of Horehound."
FORD, ROBERT - - -	4673	24th April 1822	Chemical liquid or solution of annotto.
FORD, THOMAS - - -	5981	12th Aug. 1830	Medicine for the cure of coughs, colds, asthmas, and consumption. "Ford's Balsam of Horehound."
FORD, WILLIAM - - -	10,276	30th July 1844	Manufacture of tubes for draining land, and for other purposes; drain tiles.
FORD, WILLIAM JOHN -	5549	6th Sept. 1827	Make, use, and application of bridle-bits.
FORDER, AUGUSTUS TURK -	11,062	29th Jan. 1846	Pump or engine for raising and impelling in-elastic fluids, and producing motive power.
FORDER, AUGUSTUS TURK -	14,007	8th March 1852	Fender.
FORDER, WILLIAM - -	2650	2nd Oct. 1802	Diving-machine, to be used in and about the stopping of holes and leaks in ships' bottoms.
FORDYCE, ALEXANDER -	1222	30th April 1779	Making "Glauber salts."
FORDYCE, ALEXANDER -	1303	1st Aug. 1781	Processes by which the alkalies contained in sea-salt, salt-water, rock-salt, salt-springs, and vitriolated tartar are separated from the marine and vitriolic acids.

Name of Patentee.	Progressive Number.	Date.		Subject-matter of Patent.
FORDYCE, GEORGE - - -	1061	27th Jan.	1774	Preparing blood, so as to preserve the qualities useful in sugar making.
FORDYCE, WILLIAM - -	791	29th July	1763	Medicinal composition. " Stomach pill."
FOREMAN, JAMES - - -	10,654	6th May	1845	Construction and manufacture of pipes and tubes, for locomotive purposes, and for the conveyance of water, gas, and other fluids.
FOREMAN, WALTER - -	5004	7th Oct.	1824	Construction of steam-engines.
FORLONG, RICHARD PANNELL	12,459	8th Feb.	1849	Castors for furniture.
FORMAN, WILLIAM MOTTER-[SHAW.	8367	28th Jan.	1840	Stocking-frames; machinery used in framework knitting.
FORREST, THOMAS - - -	1174	16th Dec.	1777	Machine to melt tallow, without any fire touching the same.
FORRESTER, GEORGE - -	6158	5th Sept.	1831	Wheels for carriages and machinery;—applicable to other machinery.
FORRESTER, WILLIAM - -	8424	11th March	1840	Sizing, starching, dressing, and otherwise preparing warps for weaving fabrics; machinery therewith connected.
FORRET, CHARLES HENRY JO-[SEPH.	10,800	4th Aug.	1845	Archimedean screw, called " Davaine's screw."
FORSTER, JAMES - - -	13,154	27th June	1850	Filtering water and other liquids.
FORSTER, JOHN - - -	5234	11th Aug.	1825	Machinery for, and process of, raising the pile on woollen cloths and other fabrics; pressing the same.
FORSTER, JOHN THOMAS -	12,678	27th June	1849	Building ships, boats, and other vessels; manufacture of boxes, packing-cases, roofs, and other things requiring to be made waterproof.
FORSTER, THOMAS - - -	10,092	6th March	1844	Preparing a composition of India-rubber and other matter, for forming articles therefrom, and for coating the surfaces of leather, and woven and other fabrics.
FORSTER, THOMAS - - -	10,407	25th Nov.	1844	Elastic fabrics; making articles from elastic fabrics; weaving fabrics for driving-bands.
FORSTER, THOMAS - - -	11,850	2nd Sept.	1847	Machinery for cutting India-rubber; waterproofing fabrics, and making articles therefrom; dissolving India-rubber and other gums.
FORSTER, THOMAS - - -	11,917	21st Oct.	1847	Combining gutta-percha with certain materials, and applying it to waterproofing fabrics; moulding and finishing the surfaces of various articles made therefrom; also cleansing gutta-percha.
FORSTER, THOMAS - - -	12,136	-27th April	1848	Electric-telegraphs, and apparatus connected therewith.
FORSTER, THOMAS - - -	12,585	26th April	1849	Manufacturing or treating solvents of India-rubber and other gums or substances.
FORSTER, WILLIAM CHARLTON	9089	20th Sept.	1841	Material or compound for preventing damp rising in walls; freeing walls from damp;—applicable to other purposes.
FORSYTH, ALEXANDER JOHN -	3032	11th April	1807	Discharging or giving fire to artillery and other fire-arms; also exploding gunpowder in mines, chambers, cavities, or other places.
FORSYTH, JAMES - - -	14,061	15th April	1852	Machinery for twisting, drawing, doubling and spinning cotton-wool, silk, flax, and other fibrous substances.
FORSYTH, THOMAS - - -	9751	1st June	1843	Machinery for making bricks and tiles.
FORSYTH, THOMAS - - -	10,905	31st Oct.	1845	Giving signals, applicable to the working of railways, and for marine purposes; working railways.

Name of Patentee.	Progressive Number.	Date.	Subject-matter of Patent.
FORSYTH, THOMAS - - -	12,123	15th April 1848	Manufacture of railway-wheels.
FORTUNE, THOMAS - - -	13,187	23rd July 1850	Machinery for manufacturing screws, bolts, rivets, and nails.
FOSSICK, GEORGE - - -	11,605	3rd March 1847	Locomotive and other boilers.
FOSTER, ABRAHAM - - -	845	15th April 1766	Composition for the cure of ague. "Foster's composition."
FOSTER, DAVID GEORGE -	12,236	10th Aug. 1848	Telegraphic communication; apparatus connected therewith;—partly applicable to moving other machinery.
FOSTER, JAMES - - -	4538	20th Feb. 1821	Manufacture of wrought or malleable iron.
FOSTER, JAMES - - -	6300	8th Sept. 1832	Making malleable iron.
FOSTER, JOHN - - -	813	25th May 1764	Inside-seats to coaches, carriages, and chariots, with braces and springs.
FOSTER, JOHN - - -	2361	2nd Dec. 1799	Bracer or sling acting by means of a steel spring, for suspending breeches, pantaloons, or drawers.
FOSTER, WILLIAM AIR - -	11,358	29th Aug. 1846	Making belts for driving machinery, also traces, reins, and other articles of leather, felt, or parchment; machinery for the purpose.
FOTHERGILL, BENJAMIN -	9552	8th Dec. 1842	Mules and other machines for spinning cotton-wool and other fibrous substances.
FOTHERGILL, BENJAMIN -	10,722	17th June 1845	Machinery used in preparing for spinning, and for spinning and doubling cotton-wool and other fibrous substances.
FOTHERGILL, BENJAMIN -	11,243	16th June 1846	Machinery used in the preparation for spinning, and in spinning and doubling cotton-wool and other fibrous substances.
FOTHERGILL, RICHARD -	1946	12th April 1793	Machine for dressing hemp; making and spinning the same into ropes and cordage.
FOTHERGILL, WILLIAM -	3491	23rd Sept. 1811	Making copper-rollers for printing.
FOUCAUD, LEOPOLD - -	6326*	2nd Nov. 1832	Priming percussion locks of guns and pistols. *Note.—*This Patent does not appear in the Record books of the Great Seal Office, hence its omission in the printed Chronological Index just published; it is, however, inserted in the Index purchased from Mr. Woodcroft, and the following is a copy of the title in full :— "An improvement or improvements applicable to the priming of percussion locks of guns and pistols." A communication, 6 months.
FOUGHT, HENRY - - -	888	24th Dec. 1767	Making types for printing musical notes.
FOUILLET, CHARLES MARIE -	11,388	2nd Oct. 1846	Railways.
FOULERTON, JOHN - - -	4040	11th June 1816	Buoys of various kinds, as beacon, can, nun, mooring, and life buoys;—applicable to other purposes.
FOULERTON, ROBERT - -	10,009	13th Jan. 1844	Machinery for moving vessels, and other floating apparatus.
FOULIS, ANDREW - - -	1431	28th April 1784	Printing books by plates, instead of moveable types.
FOULKE, ROGER - - -	117	2nd May 1638	Making cast-iron and bar-iron, with sea-coal or pit-coal, peat or turf; refining metals; also mining and working ores of gold, silver, copper, or lead mixed with silver or quicksilver; draining mines and erecting houses, mills, and works for the said purposes.
FOUQUET, CHARLES LOUIS MA-[THURIN.	10,635	22nd April 1845	Preparation of an artificial vegetable gum, as a substitute for gum-senegal.

Name of Patentee.	Progressive Number.	Date.	Subject-matter of Patent.
FOURDRINIER, EDWARD NEW-[MAN.	6125	20th June 1831	Machine for cutting paper.
FOURDRINIER, EDWARD NEW-[MAN.	8632	17th Sept. 1840	Steam-engines for actuating machinery; apparatus for propelling ships and vessels on water.
FOURDRINIER EDWARD NEW-[MAN.	11,557	1st Feb. 1847	Apparatus used for raising and lowering weights from mines and other places.
FOURDRINIER, GEORGE HENRY	11,313	23rd July 1846	Preparing the materials used in manufacturing earthenware and china; printing the designs for ornamenting the same.
FOURDRINIER, HENRY	2950	24th July 1806	Making a machine for cutting paper.
FOURDRINIER, HENRY	2951	24th July 1806	Making a machine for manufacturing paper of an indefinite length, both laid and wove, with separated moulds.
FOURDRINIER, HENRY	8632	17th Sept. 1840	Steam-engines for actuating machinery; apparatus for propelling ships and vessels on water.
FOURMENT, ADOLPHE	9203	21st Dec. 1841	Castors for cabinet furniture, and for other purposes.
FOURMENTIN, JEAN MARIE	11,710	22nd May 1847	Manufacture of carbonate of lead.
FOURNESS, ROBERT	1640	4th March 1788	Machine for towing ships, sloops, barges, and all other vessels upon the water.
FOURNESS, ROBERT	1674	6th Nov. 1788	Steam or fire engine, with three or more cylinders and appendages.
FOURNESS, WILLIAM	7479	16th Nov. 1837	Ventilating pits, shafts, mines, wells, ships' holds, and all other confined places.
FOUVIELLE, FERDINAND DE	5632	26th March 1828	Filtering-apparatus.
FOWLER JOHN	7831	16th Oct. 1838	Preparing or manufacturing sulphuric-acid.
FOWLER, JOHN, junior	12,989	7th March 1850	Draining land.
FOWLER, JOHN, junior	13,285	17th Oct. 1850	Steam-engines; raising and forcing fluids; irrigating and draining land; machinery for cutting wood for drain-pipes and other uses.
FOWLER, THOMAS	5711	2nd Oct. 1828	Raising and circulating hot water, hot oils, and other hot fluids for domestic and other purposes.
FOWLES, ROBERT	12,050	8th Feb. 1848	Propelling.
FOX, CHARLES	7773	15th Aug. 1838	Arrangement of rails, for causing a train to pass from one line to another.
FOX, CHARLES	11,381	24th Sept. 1846	Machinery for shearing, cutting, and punching metals.
FOX, CHARLES	11,598	24th Feb. 1847	Welding or uniting pieces of metal together; pressing or forming pieces of metal into forms or shapes.
FOX, CHARLES	11,622	15th March 1847	Construction of presses.
FOX, CHARLES	11,631	23rd March 1847	Permanent-way of railways; carriages employed on railways.
FOX, CHARLES	11,694	6th May 1847	Railway chairs and switches; trenails or fastenings; machinery for preparing railway-sleepers.
FOX, FRANCIS	4427	15th Jan. 1820	Discharge of fire-arms and artillery.
FOX, HENRY HAWES	10,047	10th Feb. 1844	Constructing fire-proof floors, ceilings, and roofs.
FOX, JAMES	4339	28th Jan. 1819	Method of diminishing loss in quality and quantity of ardent spirits and other fluids, during the process of distillation and rectification.
FOX, JAMES	5172	14th May 1825	Safe used in the distillation of ardent spirits.

Name of Patentee.	Progressive Number.	Date.	Subject-matter of Patent.
Fox, Robert Were - -	3621	10th Dec. 1812	Steam-engines ; apparatus used with the same.
Fox, Samuel - - - -	14,055	6th April 1852	Umbrellas and parasols.
Foxon, William - - -	1028	5th Dec. 1772	Machine for measuring a ship's way.
Foxwell, Philip - - -	5688	19th Aug. 1828	Machinery for shearing, cropping or cutting, and finishing woollen and other cloths and cassimeres.
Fraissinet ,Frederic Edou- [ard.	7749	26th July 1838	Machinery for propelling vessels by steam.
Frampton, Robert - -	9285	7th March 1842	Construction of hinges.
Franchot, Charles Louis [Felix.	9877	31st Aug. 1843	Connecting and laying pipes or vessels under water to form tunnels for the conveyance of passengers and goods.
Franchot, Charles Louis [Felix.	10,427	12th Dec. 1844	Engine to be worked by air or gases.
Francis, Alfred - - -	9766	10th June 1843	Manufacture of ornamental tiles.
Francis, Charles - - -	3391	8th Oct. 1810	Joining pipes.
Francis, Henry - - -	10,862	9th Oct. 1845	Manufacturing gas.
Francis, Henry - - -	12,403	4th Jan. 1849	Sawing and cutting wood.
Francis, Henry - - -	13,246	5th Sept. 1850	Propelling, steering, and ballasting vessels ; pistons of steam-engines ; fire-bars of furnaces ; sleepers of railways.
Francis, John - - -	1528	31st Jan. 1786	Making buttons of cast-iron ; japanning and painting the same.
Francis, John - - -	4776	12th April 1823	Making a certain article or fabric of silk and worsted.
Francke, Captain Thornesse	48	31st July 1629	Engine for draining mines or low grounds, also for expediting buildings, and for other uses.
Francke, Captain Thornesse	83	25th June 1635	Making furnaces for melting or smelting copper, tin, lead, iron, glass and other minerals ; melting metals for casting ordnance ; kilns for burning bricks, tiles, earthen-pots, and lime.
Franke, Major Thorney -	129	13th July 1660	Hanging and setting brewing-furnaces, and all other boiling furnaces for melting metals and their ores.
Franklin, Francis Mark -	9058	27th Aug. 1841	Manufacturing buttons and fastenings for wearing-apparel.
Franklin, Henry - - -	11,374	17th Sept. 1846	Manufacture of bricks, tiles, and other like articles.
Franklinsky, Joseph Alex- [ander.	13,384	5th Dec. 1850	Public carriages for the conveyance of passengers.
Franks, Robert - - -	4439	18th March 1820	Manufacturing waterproof hats.
Franncke, Sir Leventhprye	84	14th July 1635	Engines, instruments and works for raising ships, vessels, or other carriages or things of weight from out of the sea, or any river or deep water, also for draining mines, and raising water to any height.
Franzoni, Marco Henry -	11,559	1st Feb. 1847	Obtaining and applying motive-power.
Fraser, James - - -	4201	15th Jan. 1818	Cooking-machine, useful for decomposing salt-water, and rendering the same useful to the general purposes of a ship's crew at sea.
Fraser, James - - -	4310	12th Nov. 1818	Junction of tunnels in a steam-boiler, also new flues in such boiler or the furnace connected with its erection, for the purpose of lessening the consumption of fuel, the appearance of smoke, and the trouble of attendance.

Name of Patentee.	Progressive Number.	Date.	Subject-matter of Patent.
FRASER, JAMES - - -	4706	27th Sept. 1822	Ships' cabooses or hearths; and apparatus connected therewith for evaporating and condensing water.
FRASER, JAMES - - -	5338	25th Feb. 1826	Constructing capstans and windlasses.
FRASER, JAMES - - -	5341	4th March 1826	Distilling and rectifying spirits and strong waters.
FRASER, JAMES - - -	5446	11th Jan. 1827	Constructing capstans and windlasses.
FRASER, JAMES - - -	5447	11th Jan. 1827	Constructing boilers for steam-engines.
FRASER, JAMES - - -	5762	27th Jan. 1829	Arrangement of flues to communicate with various parts of culinary apparatus such as steam, soup, and water boilers, ovens, hot plates, hot closets and stewing-stoves, to render them more compact.
FRASER, JAMES - - -	6421	8th May 1833	Steam-boilers and arrangement of the machinery attached thereto as applicable to land carriages.
FRASER, JAMES BRISTOW -	4450	19th April 1820	Hydro-pneumatic apparatus acted upon by a steam-engine, for propelling boats on water, and for other useful purposes.
FRASER, JOHN - - -	3397	15th Oct. 1810	Preparing certain vegetables to be applied in manufacturing hats, bonnets, chair-bottoms, and baskets, and for other purposes.
FRASER, JOHN MATHISON -	13,428	27th Dec. 1850	Manufacture of sugar.
FRASER, JOHN WILLIAM -	6852	22nd June 1835	Apparatus for descending under water.
FRASER, JOHN WILLIAM -	6905	15th Oct. 1835	Raising weights from below water to the surface of the same.
FRASER, JOHN WILLIAM -	6929	14th Nov. 1835	Apparatus for descending under water.
FRASER, JOHN WILLIAM -	7696	22nd June 1838	Raising or floating sunken and stranded vessels and other bodies.
FRASER, JOSEPH - - -	7845	3rd Nov. 1838	Apparatus or machinery to be employed as centreings or supporters in the construction of bridges, arches, tunnels, or in other mining operations.
FRASI, HENRY GEORGE - -	14,091	27th April 1852	Heating and supplying water for baths, and for other uses; construction of water-closets and supplying them with water; cocks for drawing off liquids.
FRAUNCES, JOSEPH - - -	661	27th March 1751	Chemical preparation ("Female strengthening elixir.")
FREARSON, DAVID - - -	1883	21st May 1792	Machinery and operations for saving fuel in the process of evaporating water from solutions of salts, waste leys of soap-makers, and which may also be applicable in other cases where evaporation of water from substances held in solution is required.
FREARSON, HENRY - - -	10,153	23rd April 1844	Manufacture of warp-fabrics.
FREARSON, JOHN - - -	9649	2nd March 1843	Fastenings for wearing-apparel.
FREARSON, JOHN - - -	12,271	21st Sept. 1848	Bending or shaping iron or steel, and other metals.
FREARSON, JOHN - - -	13,853	10th Dec. 1851	Cutting, shaping, and pressing metal and other materials.
FRÉCHE, ARNAUD NICOLAS -	13,220	12th Aug. 1850	Obtaining power.
FREEMAN, CHARLES JOSEPH -	7380	25th May 1837	Rolls for rolling iron or other metals, applicable to rails for roads, and bars of various shapes for other purposes.
FREEMAN, DANIEL - - -	5382	4th July 1826	Measuring for and making collars for horses and other cattle.
FREEMAN, GEORGE - - -	5125	15th March 1825	Machinery for making bobbin net lace.

Name of Patentee.	Progressive Number.	Date.	Subject-matter of Patent.
FREEMAN, GEORGE - • -	6226	22nd Feb. 1832	Machinery for ornamenting and producing devices upon lace net.
FREEMAN, JAMES - • -	946	13th Dec. 1769	Central second stop-watch, vertical or horizontal, without the assistance of a compound motion.
FREEMAN, MARK - • -	3622	10th Sept. 1840	Weighing-machines.
FREEMAN, MARK - • -	9306	21st March 1842	Construction of inkstands.
FREEMAN, MARK - • -	9525	25th Nov. 1842	Candlesticks, apparatus, and instruments employed in the use of candles and rush-lights.
FREEMAN, MARK - • -	9872	22nd Aug. 1843	Card-cases.
FREEMAN, MARK - • -	10,297	29th Aug. 1844	Apparatus called ever-pointed pencils.
FREEMAN, MARK - • -	10,391	14th Nov. 1844	Working or dressing the surface of stone.
FREEMAN, MARK • • -	11,077	11th Feb. 1846	Obtaining and applying motive-power;—partly applicable to regulating and controlling fluids.
FREEMAN, WILLIAM • -	8617	7th Sept. 1840	Paving or covering roads and other ways or surfaces.
FREEMANTLE, WILLIAM • -	1737	24th Mar. 1790	Vertical weight and spring roasting-jack.
FREEMANTLE, WILLIAM -	2741	17th Nov. 1803	Construction of steam-engines.
FREEMONT, SAMUEL LUZ -	12,072	18th Feb. 1848	Manufacture of colours, oils, and varnishes; manufacture of charcoal; treating vegetable substances for, and obtaining extracts therefrom.
FREESE, JAMES - • -	55	8th July 1631	Making engines or water-ploughs for taking up sand, gravel, shelves, and banks, from the river Thames, and other havens, harbours, or rivers; and casting upon land all such sand or gravel; also making wharfs and safe places for the keeping thereof.
FREETH, SAMPSON - • -	903	6th Oct. 1768	Making hand corn-mills for grinding wheat in private families.
FREETH, SAMUEL - • -	903	6th Oct. 1768	Making hand corn-mills for grinding wheat in private families.
FREETH, THOMAS • - •	1690	2nd July 1789	Chape and fastening for buckles.
FRESUE, FRANCIS FANDELL DU	211	9th June 1681	Making salt.
FREUND, CHARLES - • -	5222	26th July 1825	Refining sugar.
FRICKER, THOMAS - • -	2956	1st Aug. 1806	Decorating walls of apartments, in imitation of fine cloth, by means of cementing flock.
FRIEND, RICHARD - • -	3005	29th Jan. 1807	Making and working gun and carronade carriages.
FRITH, JOHN - • -	9961	25th Nov. 1843	Manufacture of cannon.
FRITH, ROBERT - • -	2237	25th May 1798	Dyeing permanent colours on cotton, linen, woollen, and silk, by a chemical method.
FRITH, ROBERT • - -	2786	3rd Oct. 1804	Dyeing cotton-wool twist, weft, and cloth, of a nankeen and a buff colour.
FRITH, ROBERT • - -	4496	9th Oct. 1820	Dyeing and printing fast colours on cottons, linens, silks, mohair, worsted, and woollens, straw, chip, and leghorn.
FROGGART, ROBERT BECK -	13,886	31st Dec. 1851	Preparation of compounds to be used for rendering waterproof and fireproof woven and textile fabrics, paper, leather, wood, or other materials or substances; machinery employed therein.
FROGGOTT, WILLIAM -	14,028	20th Mar. 1852	Process of decorative painting, applicable to rooms, halls, carriages, furniture, and to other purposes.

Name of Patentee.	Progressive Number.	Date.	Subject-matter of Patent.
FROME, FRANCIS - - -	3042	11th May 1807	Portable bootjack, with a guard to prevent accidents to the legs in pulling off boots.
FROMINGS, THOMAS HENRY -	13,777	16th Oct. 1851	Forge-hammers.
FROSCHLE, GEORGE - -	2397	3rd May 1800	Pedal-harp.
FROST, JAMES - - -	1479	9th May 1785	Machine for producing an alternate progressive and retrograde motion, by a continual rotation.
FROST, JAMES - - -	1746	27th April 1790	Constructing, fixing, and arranging window lights and sashes.
FROST, JAMES - - -	3353	22nd June 1810	Lock-cock.
FROST, JAMES - - -	4679	11th June 1822	Cement or artificial stone.
FROST, JAMES - - -	4710	27th Sept. 1822	Casting or constructing foundations, piers, walls, ceilings, arches, columns, pilasters, mouldings, and other enrichments to buildings.
FROST, JAMES - - -	4772	3rd April 1823	Calcining and preparing calcareous and other substances for forming cements.
FROST, JAMES, junior - -	3353	22nd June 1810	Lock-cock.
FROST, ROBERT - - -	1439	28th June 1784	Machine for making figured lace and net work.
FROST, THOMAS - - -	1294	1st June 1781	Machine to be fixed on a stocking frame for making open-work in silk, cotton, thread, worsted, and other materials.
FROST, THOMAS - - -	1439	28th June 1784	Machine for making figured lace and net work.
FROUDE, WILLIAM - -	12,014	5th Jan. 1848	Valves used in closing the tubes of atmospheric railways.
FRY, JOSEPH STOORS - -	2048	7th May 1795	Roasting cocoa-nuts.
FRYE, THOMAS - - -	610	6th Dec. 1744	Manufacturing a material for making a ware to imitate china or porcelain.
FRYE, THOMAS - - -	649	17th Nov. 1749	Making a ware to imitate china or porcelain.
FRYER, JOSEPH - - -	2627	31st May 1802	Machine for cutting, dressing, and finishing woollen cloth.
FRYER, ROBERT - - -	2401	13th May 1800	Mixing seals' wool or down with lambs' wool; preparing it to be carded, roved, and spun into yarn, capable of being woven with silk, linen, woollen, or cotton, into a cloth fit for garments.
FRYER, ROBERT - - -	2417	20th June 1800	Manufacturing, cutting, dressing, dyeing, and finishing cloth.
FRYER, SAMUEL - - -	2401	13th May 1800	Mixing seals' wool or down with lambs' wool; preparing it to be carded, roved, and spun into yarn, capable of being woven with silk, linen, woollen, or cotton, into a cloth fit for garments.
FRYER, THOMAS - - -	810	10th April 1764	Machine for printing, staining, and colouring silks, stuffs, linens, cottons, leather, and paper.
FRYER, THOMAS - - -	2545	30th Oct. 1801	Manufacturing and finishing goods made from cotton, cotton and woollen, cotton and silk, linen and mohair, so as to imitate ermine or fur.
FULCHER, THOMAS - -	2707	28th May 1803	Waterproof composition to imitate Portland stone, for stuccoing and washing new and old stone and brick buildings, and for cementing the joints and tucking.

Name of Patentee.	Progres-sive Number.	Date.	Subject-matter of Patent.
FULLARTON, JAMES - -	2820	9th Feb. 1805	Diving-machine to be used for various purposes.
FULLARTON, WILLIAM - -	1891	19th June 1792	Separating iron from iron-stones and ores; smelting it into pig-iron, and refining it into forged iron.
FULLER, EDWARD IVES - -	12,699	7th July 1849	Metallic springs for carriages.
FULLER, HENRY PETER - -	4357	3rd April 1819	Procuring or preparing sulphate of soda, soda, sub-carbonate of soda, and muriatic acid.
FULLER, JOHN - - -	11,117	5th March 1846	Apparatus for sowing corn or other seed.
FULLER, ROBERT - - -	238	6th Aug. 1684	Making paper and pasteboards in whole sheets without piecing, and for the purpose of hot and cold pressing of cloth.
FULLER, THOMAS - -	4755	18th Feb. 1823	Construction of shafts; attaching them to two-wheeled carriages.
FULLER, THOMAS - -	5513	28th June 1827	Wheeled carriages.
FULLER, THOMAS - -	8836	8th Feb. 1841	Machinery for combing or preparing wool or other fibrous substances.
FULLER, THOMAS - -	9020	7th July 1841	Retarding the progress of carriages under certain circumstances.
FULLER, THOMAS - -	10,369	29th Oct. 1844	Machinery for turning, boring, and cutting metals and other substances.
FULLER, THOMAS - -	12,551	28th	Machinery for turning, boring, planing, and cutting metals and other materials.
FULLER, THOMAS JOHN - -	5859	28th Oct. 1829	Mechanical power applicable to machinery of different descriptions.
FULLER, THOMAS JOHN - -	5943	19th June 1830	Mechanical power applicable to machinery of different descriptions.
FULLER, THOMAS JOHN - -	6190	15th Nov. 1831	Mechanical apparatus for raising water, and for other purposes.
FULLER, THOMAS JOHN - -	6218	31st Jan. 1832	Raising water or other fluids.
FULLER, THOMAS JOHN - -	6568	27th Feb. 1834	Machinery for manufacturing nails.
FULLER, THOMAS JOHN - -	6571	6th March 1834	Shape of nails, spikes, and bolts.
FULLER, THOMAS JOHN - -	7164	9th Aug. 1836	Screen for intercepting the heat arising from boilers and cylinders of steam-engines.
FULLER, WILLIAM COLES -	10,894	23rd Oct. 1845	Construction of carriages for railways.
FULLJAMES, THOMAS - -	13,153	26th June 1850	Machinery or apparatus for raising, lowering, and moving weights or other heavy bodies.
FULLWOOD, MATTHEW - -	5651	6th May 1828	"German cement."
FULTON, ANDREW - - -	14,345	11th Nov. 1852	Hats, and other coverings for the head.
FULTON, JOHN ALEXANDER -	5568	26th Nov. 1827	Preparing or bleaching pepper.
FULTON, JOHN ALEXANDER -	5919	20th March 1830	Preparation of pepper.
FULTON, ROBERT - - -	1988	8th May 1794	Machine or engine for conveying vessels and their cargoes from one level to another on canals, without locks.
FULTON, WILLIAM - - -	1651	23rd May 1788	Using and working pumps on board ship and on land, also rubbing-boards used in bleaching, as well as other similar machines, by means of a cylinder with its appurtenances.
FUNGE, ISAAC - - -	9766	10th June 1843	Manufacture of ornamental tiles.
FURNESS, ROBERT HOPWOOD -	4072	1st Nov. 1816	Obtaining saccharine matter from wheat, rye, oats, barley, bear, or bigg.

Name of Patentee.	Progressive Number.	Date.	Subject-matter of Patent.
FURNESS, WILLIAM - -	12,735	9th Aug. 1849	Machinery for cutting, tenoning, planing, moulding, dovetailing, boring, morticing, tongueing, grooving, and sawing wood; sharpening tools; welding steel to cast iron.
FURNIVAL, JAMES - -	8907	29th March 1841	Unhairing, mastering, and tanning hides and skins with expedition.
FURNIVAL, JOHN BRADFORD -	8087	4th June 1839	Apparatus to prevent persons sinking when in the water.
FURNIVAL, JOHN BRADFORD -	8815	26th Jan. 1841	Evaporating fluids for the manufacture of salt, and for other purposes.
FURNIVAL, JOHN BRADFORD -	9123	20th Oct. 1841	Evaporating fluids for the manufacture of salt, and for other purposes.
FURNIVAL, JOHN EDWARD -	8807	21st Jan. 1841	Construction and application of air-vessels.
FURNIVAL, WILLIAM - -	4879	9th Dec. 1823	Boiler for steam-engines, and for other purposes.
FURNIVAL, WILLIAM - - [*Furneval, William.*]	5046	4th Dec. 1824	Manufacturing salt.
FURNIVAL, WILLIAM - -	5203	8th July 1825	Manufacturing salt.
FURNIVAL, WILLIAM - -	6086	21st Feb. 1831	Evaporating brine.
FUSSELL, JAMES - -	2284	24th Dec. 1798	Balance-engine for raising and lowering boats, barges, or troughs at the locks or falls on inland canals, and for other purposes.
FUSSELL, JAMES - -	2359	28th Nov. 1799	Apparatus of chains, wheels, rollers, and conductors, for lessening friction in raising, lowering, driving, and conducting heavy bodies, and for other purposes.
FUSSELL, JAMES - -	2710	14th June 1803	Working water-wheels, raising water, and in a great measure preventing water-wheels from being flooded, also useful for other purposes.
FUSSELL, JAMES - -	3326	6th April 1810	Making and working forge and other bellows.
FUSSELL, JOHN - -	4999	11th Aug. 1824	Heating woollen-cloth in dressing, to give it a lustre.
FUSSELL, JOHN - -	6968	29th Dec. 1835	Pumps.

G.

◆

Name of Patentee.	Progressive Number.	Date.	Subject-matter of Patent.
GACHET, LOUIS - -	7122	18th June 1836	Machinery for manufacturing velvets and certain other fabrics.
GADD, SAMUEL - -	3145	25th June 1808	Rope-making upon the principle of each strand being composed of two threads twisted together; arrangement of apparatus for carrying the same into effect.
GADESDEN, AUGUSTUS WILLIAM	10,474	16th Jan. 1845	Manufacture of sugar.
GAGE, JEAN PAUL - -	13,484	31st Jan. 1851	Chemical compounds for tissue bandages, wafers, and also for surgical purposes.
GAITTAIT, JOHN - -	1330	19th June 1782	Machine or stink-trap of metal or earthenware to prevent the disagreeable smell from drains.
GALE, JAMES - - -	3160	18th Aug. 1808	Rope-making.
GALE, THOMAS - -	1002	1st Feb. 1772	Bedsteads.

Name of Patentee.	Progressive Number.	Date.		Subject-matter of Patent.
GALE, THOMAS - - -	1334	31st July	1782	Medicine called " Spa elixir."
GALIBERT, ESPRIT - - -	10,602	7th April	1845	Hats.
GALL, JOHN - - -	7282	17th Jan.	1837	Priming fire-arms; applicable to percussion locks.
GALL, WILLIAM - - -	8819	28th Jan.	1841	Construction of locomotive-engines and railway-carriages;—partly applicable to carriages on common roads.
GALL, WILLIAM - - -	8964	22nd May	1841	Construction of inkstands.
GALLAFENT, DANIEL -	3961	25th Nov.	1815	Engine for raising water, and cold and hot liquor of every description.
GALLAFENT, DANIEL, junior -	3961	25th Nov.	1815	Engine for raising water, and cold and hot liquor of every description.
GALLOWAY, ALEXANDER -	3115	7th Mar.	1808	Machines for finishing, glazing, and glossing leather.
GALLOWAY, ALEXANDER -	3143	14th June	1808	Machines for cutting all sorts of fustians, or other goods usually cut, in the manufacture thereof.
GALLOWAY, ALEXANDER -	4253	4th May	1818	Machine for removing the smoke or gases generated in stoves, furnaces, or fire-places; also in certain cases, for directing the heat and applying such smoke or gases to useful purposes.
GALLOWAY, ALEXANDER -	5166	14th May	1825	Machines for forming and moulding bricks, and other bodies made of clay, ⟨r⟩ other plastic substances or materials from which building and other bricks are usually made.
GALLOWAY, ELIJAH - -	5444	29th Dec.	1826	Rotary steam-engines.
GALLOWAY, ELIJAH - -	5805	2nd July	1829	Steam-engines, and machinery for propelling vessels.
GALLOWAY, ELIJAH - -	6212	17th Jan.	1832	Paddle-wheels.
GALLOWAY, ELIJAH - -	6329	7th Nov.	1832	Steam-engines, and apparatus for propelling.
GALLOWAY, ELIJAH - -	6735	23rd Dec.	1834	Steam-engines;—applicable to other purposes.
GALLOWAY, ELIJAH - -	6887	18th Aug.	1835	Paddle-wheels, for propelling vessels.
GALLOWAY, ELIJAH - -	7259	19th Dec.	1836	Cabriolets and omnibuses.
GALLOWAY, ELIJAH - -	8045	23rd April	1839	Steam-engines.
GALLOWAY, ELIJAH - -	8482	23rd April	1840	Steam-engines;—applicable to engines for raising and forcing fluids.
GALLOWAY, ELIJAH - -	8669	2nd Nov.	1840	Propelling railway-carriages.
GALLOWAY, ELIJAH - -	9744	25th May	1843	Machinery for propelling ships and other vessels.
GALLOWAY, ELIJAH - -	10,054	14th Feb.	1844	Combination of materials as a substitute for canvass and other surfaces, as grounds for painting.
GALLOWAY, ELIJAH - -	10,223	12th June	1844	Machinery for connecting axes or shafts, so as to revolve at different velocities.
GALLOWAY, ELIJAH - -	10,606	10th April	1845	Propelling railway-carriages.
GALLOWAY, ELIJAH - -	11,170	18th April	1846	Locomotive-engines.
GALLOWAY, ELIJAH - -	11,485	14th Dec.	1846	Rotary engines; locomotive-carriages; and railways.
GALLOWAY, ELIJAH - -	12,782	20th Sept.	1849	Furnaces.
GALLOWAY, ELIJAH - -	13,545	10th Mar.	1851	Steam-engines.

Name of Patentee.	Progressive Number.	Date.		Subject-matter of Patent.
GALLOWAY, JOHN - - -	9238	27th Jan.	1842	Machinery for cutting, punching, and compressing metals.
GALLOWAY, JOHN - - -	12,244	17th Aug.	1848	Steam-engines.
GALLOWAY, JOHN - - -	13,552	11th Mar.	1851	Steam-engines and boilers.
GALLOWAY, ROBERT - -	14,354	21st Dec.	1852	Manufacturing and refining sugar.
GALLOWAY, WILLIAM - -	9238	27th Jan.	1842	Machinery for cutting, punching, and compressing metals.
GALLOWAY, WILLIAM - -	12,244	17th Aug.	1848	Steam-engines.
GALLOWAY, WILLIAM - -	13,552	11th Mar.	1851	Steam-engines, and boilers.
GALON, THOMAS - - -	5248	27th Aug.	1825	Manufacture of hats.
GALTE, WILLIAM - - -	180	23rd April	1675	Bee-hives, or boxes placed one on another, with holes in the top, and several entrances backwards and forwards, so that the bees can conveniently and constantly pass in and out, the necessity of the bees swarming or being destroyed is thus prevented.
GAMBLE, DOUGLAS PITT -	11,524	11th Jan.	1847	Electric-telegraphs.
GAMBLE, JOHN - - -	2487	20th April	1801	Machine for making paper in single sheets, without seam or joinings, from one to twelve feet wide and upwards, and from one to forty-five feet long.
GAMBLE, JOHN - - -	2708	7th June	1803	Machine for making paper in single sheets, without seam or joinings.
GAMBLE, JOSIAS CHRISTOPHER	5327	7th Feb.	1826	Apparatus for the concentration and crystallization of aluminous and other saline and crystallizable solutions;—partly applicable to evaporation, distillation, and other like purposes.
GAMBLE, JOSIAS CHRISTOPHER	8000	14th Mar.	1839	Apparatus for the manufacture of sulphate of soda, muriatic-acid, chlorine, and chlorides.
GAMBLE, JOSIAS CHRISTOPHER	10,416	4th Dec.	1844	Manufacture of sulphuric-acid.
GAMBLE, SAMUEL - - -	14,292	16th Sept.	1852	Machinery for combing, drawing, or preparing wool, cotton, silk, hair, and other fibrous materials.
GAMMON, WILLIAM - -	6671	1st Sept.	1834	Manufacturing and working plate and other glass.
GANDELL, JOHN HASKINS -	11,138	23rd March	1846	Construction and mode of opening and closing moveable bridges or arches, for carrying railways, tramways, or other ways across canals, docks, or other open cuttings.
GARBUTT, ROBERT - - -	4970	15th June	1824	Apparatus for filing papers and other articles, and protecting them from dust and damage.
GARCKA, GEORGE - - -	1849	4th Feb.	1792	Pianoforte.
GARD, WILLIAM GOSTWYCK -	11,913	21st Oct.	1847	Machinery or implements for boring and sinking.
GARDE, AUGUSTUS Count DE [LA.	5296	24th Nov.	1825	Machinery for breaking or preparing hemp, flax, and other fibrous materials.
GARDE, AUGUSTUS Count DE [LA.	5469	20th Feb.	1827	Making paper from ligneous parts produced from certain textile plants in the process of preparing them, by the rural mechanical break.
GARDE, PHILLIP CHILWELL [DE LA.	5914	27th Feb.	1830	Apparatus for fidding and unfidding masts; masting and rigging vessels.

Name of Patentee.	Progressive Number.	Date.	Subject-matter of Patent.
GARDINER, HENRY - -	2612	15th April 1802	Preventing damage by heat, to corn, seeds, and all other merchandize, in ships or warehouses; improving corn damaged by heat or otherwise.
GARDINER, PERRY G. - -	13,848	8th Dec. 1851	Manufacture of malleable metals into pipes, hollow-shafts, railway-wheels, and other like forms capable of being dressed, turned down, or polished in a lathe.
GARDNER, DENNY - - -	4681	13th June 1822	Stay, for supporting the body under spinal weakness, and correcting deformity of shape.
GARDNER, GEORGE GORHAM -	6074	11th Feb. 1831	Roving-machine.
GARDNER, JAMES - - -	3926	14th June 1815	Machine for cutting hay and straw.
GARDNER, JAMES - - -	4609	9th Nov. 1821	Machine to cut fat and other articles of a like nature, preparatory to melting for making tallow, soap, and candles;—applicable to other similar purposes.
GARDNER, JAMES - - -	6684	25th Sept. 1834	Machines for cutting turnips, mangel-wurzel, and other roots used as food for sheep, cattle, and other animals.
GARDNER, JAMES - - -	7273	11th Jan. 1837	Machinery for cutting turnips, mangel-wurzel, and other roots used as food for sheep, cattle, and other animals.
GARDNER, JAMES - - -	7904	12th Dec. 1838	Machinery for cutting turnips, mangel-wurzel, and other roots used as food for sheep, cattle, and other animals.
GARDNER, JAMES - - -	9500	27th Oct. 1842	Cutting hay, straw, and other vegetable matters for the food of animals.
GARDNER, JAMES - - -	9791	17th June 1843	Cutting hay, straw, and other vegetable matters for the food of animals.
GARDNER, JOHN - - -	12,360	9th Dec. 1848	Girders for bridges and other structures.
GARDNER, JOSEPH - - -	5059	18th Dec. 1824	Machines for shearing or cropping woollen cloths.
GARDNER, JOSEPH - - -	5997	7th Sept. 1830	Fid.
GARDNER, RICHARD - -	5997	7th Sept. 1830	Fid.
GARDNER, ROBERT - - -	1642	4th March 1788	Manufacturing iron, copper, and other metals by a progressively multiplying air-furnace.
GARFORTH, JAMES - - -	10,993	10th Dec. 1845	Machinery for connecting metallic-plates for the construction of boilers, and for other purposes.
GARFORTH, JAMES - - -	13,756	25th Sept. 1851	Locomotive steam-engines.
GARLICK, AARON - - -	2166	7th Feb. 1797	Machine for spinning and roving cotton.
GARNER, SAMUEL - - -	6715	15th Nov. 1834	Multiplying certain drawings, and engravings or impressions.
GARNETT, ABRAHAM - -	5962	24th July 1830	Manufacturing sugar.
GARNETT, JOHN - - -	1580	6th Jan. 1787	Method of reducing the friction of an axis or fulcrum, useful for axles, wheels, beams, levers, pendulums, blocks, pullies, and other instruments that have a partial, total, or repeated revolution or oscillation.
GARNETT, JOHN - - -	9147	9th Nov. 1841	Manufacturing salt from brine.
GARNETT, JOSEPH - - -	7943	19th Jan. 1839	Machinery for carding cotton, flax, wool, or any other fibrous substance.
GARNETT, JOSEPH - - -	9078	8th Sept. 1841	Improvements applicable to yarns and cloth; machinery or apparatus employed in the manufacture of yarns and cloth.

Name of Patentee.	Progressive Number.	Date.	Subject-matter of Patent.
GARNETT, WILLIAM - -	7694	19th June 1838	Machinery for spinning and doubling wool, flax, cotton, silk, and other fibrous materials.
GARNIER, ALPHONSE - -	12,593	28th April 1849	Extracting and preparing colouring matter from orchil.
GARRARD, WILLIAM - -	1286	21st March 1781	Antimeter, or reflecting-sector with its appendages, for measuring angles by land or sea.
GARRATT, FRANCIS - -	2012	29th Sept. 1794	Preparing cocoa-nuts with other ingredients, for making the same into cocoa.
GARRETT, GEORGE - -	611	15th Dec. 1744	Mixing a certain material with silk, for making lutherines. rufferines, prince's stuffs, or prunellas.
GARRETT, RICHARD - -	9389	13th June 1842	Construction of horse-hoes, scarifiers, dragrakes, and drills, for cultivating land.
GARRETT, RICHARD - -	9960	25th Nov. 1843	Machinery for drilling, thrashing, and cutting agricultural produce.
GARRETT, RICHARD - -	12,698	7th July 1849	Horse-hoes, pug-mills, drilling and thrashing machinery; steam-engines and boilers for agricultural purposes.
GARRETT, SPENCER THOMAS -	11,249	22nd June 1846	Cements, bricks, tiles, quarries, slabs, and artificial stones.
GARROD, WILLIAM -	6548	25th Jan. 1834	Manufacture of salt.
GARSED, EDWARD - - -	5168	14th May 1825	Machinery for heckling, combing, or dressing flax, hemp, and other fibrous materials.
GARSED, EDWARD - - -	6278	22nd June 1832	Apparatus for heating, warming, and ventilating drying-houses, rooms, buildings, ships, and mines.
GARTHWAITE, JOHN - -	10,082	27th Feb. 1844	Wire-cards for carding cotton-wool, silk, flax, and other fibrous substances, and producing tow and yarns from hard waste.
GARTON, ROBERT - - -	7550	25th Jan. 1838	Presses.
GARY, WILLIAM MC. - -	11,284	6th July 1846	Lamps, lamp-glasses, candles, and shades.
GASKELL, HOLBROOK - -	12,074	23rd Feb. 1848	Machinery for forging, stamping, and cutting iron, and other substances.
GASKELL, PETER - - -	14,186	24th June 1852	Manufacture of candles.
GASKIN, JOHN SHEAFE -	13,199	31st July 1850	Manufacture of rum.
GASKINS, JOSHUA - - -	241	2nd Oct. 1684	Beautifying cloth, serges, stuffs, and other manufactures, by impressing indented lines resembling the wale of Tabby, and thereby watering, damasking, and flowering the same.
GASTINEAU, JOHN - -	520	9th Oct. 1730	Manufacturing silk mourning-crapes, named Valle Cypres, or Bologna crapes.
GATHERCOLE, JAMES - -	13,917	24th Jan. 1852	Manufacturing and ornamenting envelopes, partly applicable to other stationery; machinery, apparatus, or means to be used therein.
GATLEY, JOSEPH - - -	6752	27th Jan. 1835	Machine for cutting wood and other materials.
GATLING, RICHARD JORDAN -	14,115	4th May 1852	Machinery for seeding grain.
GATTY, FREDERICK ALBERT -	13,124	11th June 1850	Process for obtaining carbonate of soda, and carbonate of potash.
GATWARD, JOSEPH - - -	1570	9th Nov. 1786	Drawing tube spring lock pillar, for umbrellas.

Name of Patentee.	Progressive Number.	Date.	Subject-matter of Patent.
GAUBERT, ETIENNE ROBERT -	8427	13th March 1840	Machinery for distributing types into receptacles, and placing them in order for setting up, after use in printing
GAUCI, PAUL JOSEPH - -	6512	19th Nov. 1833	Pens and pen-holders.
GAUCI, PAUL JOSEPH - -	6678	20th Sept. 1834	Pens and pen-holders.
GAUCI, PAUL JOSEPH - - [Gauci, Joseph.]	8996	21st June 1841	Ink-stands and inkholders.
GAULEY, JAMES WILLIAM MC.	11,162	7th April 1846	Steam-engines.
GAULLIE, ALFRED HENRY -	14,207	6th July 1852	Plastic composition applicable to manufacturing purposes.
GAUNT, THOMAS - - -	6108	14th April 1831	Firegrate.
GAUNT, THOMAS - - -	6251	27th March 1832	Gaiters, or spatterdashes.
GAUNT, THOMAS - - -	6656	12th Aug. 1834	Earthenware pans or basins of waterclosets, and certain other earthenware vessels, to which the same may be applied.
GAUNT, THOMAS - - -	9400	21st June 1842	Applying such power as is or may be used for propelling vessels or carriages, to produce locomotion thereof.
GAUNTLETT, HENRY JOHN -	14,222	15th July 1852	Organs, seraphines, and other similar wind instruments; piano-fortes.
GAUNTLETT, THOMAS - -	4684	26th June 1822	Vapour-baths.
GAUNTLEY, THOMAS - -	7172	15th Aug. 1836	Machinery for making lace and other fabrics. "Warp machinery."
GAURAN, THOMAS MC. - -	8209	26th Aug. 1839	Manufacture of paper from a material not hitherto so employed.
GAURY, JOSEPH - - -	8911	31st March 1841	Parachute to prevent the fall or injury of carriages on the breaking of their axletrees.
GAVIN, ROBERT MC - -	14,335	23rd Oct. 1852	Manufacture of iron for ship-building.
GAYLEARD, JAMES - - -	2678	1st Feb. 1803	Long stays, short stays, and corsets.
GEACH, CHARLES - - -	12,555	2nd April 1849	Manufacturing axletrees for carriages, and other cylindrical and conical shafts (Hardy's Extension).
GEARY, STEPHEN - - -	7654	28th May 1838	Preparation of fuel.
GEARY, STEPHEN - - -	8085	1st June 1839	Paving or covering streets, roads, and other ways.
GEARY, STEPHEN - - -	9836	13th July 1843	Machinery for clearing, cleaning, and watering, and for wholly or partly covering with sand or other materials, roads, streets, or ways;—applicable to other like purposes.
GEARY, STEPHEN - - -	9907	13th Oct. 1843	Construction of panelling and framing for building purposes, cabinet work, and other similar uses.
GEARY, STEPHEN - - -	10,356	17th Oct. 1844	Construction and arrangement of machinery for cleansing, watering, breaking up and raking streets, roads, and other ways.
GEARY, STEPHEN - - -	10,383	7th Nov. 1844	Machinery and arrangements for supply and distribution of water for public and private use, particularly in case of fires.
GEARY, STEPHEN - - -	11,570	8th Feb. 1847	Obtaining and applying motive-power.
GEDDE, JOHN - - -	180	23rd April 1675	Bee-hives or boxes placed one on another with holes in the top, and several entrances backwards and forwards, so that the bees can conveniently and constantly pass in and out, the necessity of the bees swarming or being destroyed is thus prevented.

Name of Patentee.	Progres-sive Number.	Date.	Subject-matter of Patent.
GEDDES, ALEXANDER - -	1046	8th July 1773	Fire-balcony, for rescuing persons from houses when on fire.
GEDGE, JOHN - - - -	11,571	8th Feb. 1847	Machinery used for watering grain.
GEDGE, JOHN - - - -	13,018	23rd March 1850	Lamps and candlesticks.
GEDGE, JOHN - - - -	13,860	17th Dec. 1851	Treatment of certain substances for the production of manures.
GEE, EDWARD - - - -	14,110	1st May 1852	Apparatus for roasting coffee and cocoa.
GEEVES, WILLIAM - - -	7295	2nd Feb. 1837	Steam-engines.
GEEVES, WILLIAM - - -	9361	24th May 1842	Machinery for cutting cork.
GEEVES, WILLIAM - - -	10,048	12th Feb. 1844	Preparing wood for lighting or kindling fires.
GEEVES, WILLIAM - - -	12,721	1st Aug. 1849	Manufacture of boxes for matches, and for other purposes.
GEIB, JOHN - - - -	1571	9th Nov. 1786	Piano-forte and harpsichord.
GEIB, JOHN - - - -	1866	18th April 1792	Musical instrument to be played upon with the fingers, like a piano-forte.
GEITHNER, FREDERICK BEN-[JAMIN.	5584	13th Dec. 1827	Castors for furniture and for other purposes.
GEITHNER, FREDERICK BEN-[JAMIN.	7206	13th Oct. 1836	Drawing or winding-up window and other roller-blinds or maps; — applicable to other purposes.
GEITHNER, FREDERICK BEN-[JAMIN.	13,828	22nd Nov. 1851	Manufacture of castors and legs of furniture.
GELDART, WILLIAM - -	4161	12th Aug. 1817	Mangles.
GELDART, WILLIAM - -	4377	1st June 1819	Heating Dryhouses, Maltkilns, and other buildings requiring heat.
GEMMELL, JOHN - - -	7297	6th Feb. 1837	Steamboats, ships, and other vessels;— partly applicable to other purposes.
GENT, CHARLES - - -	3900	21st Mar. 1815	Swift and apparatus thereto belonging, for winding silk.
GEORGE, JOHN - - -	5590	18th Dec. 1827	Preserving decked ships or vessels from dry rot, and preserving goods on board from damage by heat.
GEORGE, JOSEPH - - -	11,257	22nd June 1846	Construction of houses, buildings, and other erections.
GEORGE, OLIVER ST. - -	6171	28th Sept. 1831	Machinery for acquiring power in tides and currents.
GEORGE, WATKIN - - -	1602	12th May 1787	Destroying friction in wheel-carriages, capstans, and windlasses, also in horizontal, perpendicular, or oblique axes of water-mills and windmills.
GERARD, GUSTAVE EUGENE [MICHEL	13,069	7th May 1850	Dissolving caoutchouc and gutta-percha.
GERARD, JACQUES FRANÇOIS [VICTOR.	6489	19th Oct. 1833	Jacquard looms for weaving figured fabrics.
GERARD, JACQUES FRANÇOIS [VICTOR.	6553	8th Feb. 1834	Finishing silks, woollen-cloths, stuffs, and other substances requiring heat and pressure.
GERARD, JAMES - - -	1369	7th May 1783	Obtaining the mineral and vegetable alkalies contained in rock-salt, brine-salt, salt refined from rock-salt, salt made from sea-water, glauber-salts, and vitriolated-tartar, by separating them from the marine and vitriolic acids.
GERENTE, ALIAS DE CLARRANT [ANTHONY	259	19th May 1688	Making tar or pitch for the preservation of wood from putrefaction and worms, also to resist fire and the heat of the sun, and for the better preservation of ropes.

Name of Patentee.	Progressive Number.	Date.		Subject-matter of Patent.
GERISH, FRANCIS WILLIAM -	7383	30th May	1837	Apparatus for closing doors, gates, and shutters.
GERISH, FRANCIS WILLIAM -	8440	20th Mar.	1840	Locks, keys, and other fastenings for doors, drawers, and other such purposes.
GERISH, FRANCIS WILLIAM -	8599	8th Aug.	1840	Apparatus to be used as a fire-escape;—applicable to other purposes where ladders are used.
GERMAN, THOMAS - - -	2032	12th Jan.	1795	Machine for curing smoky chimneys.
GERMAN, THOMAS - - -	2538	12th Sept.	1801	Easing the labour, and lessening the number of horses in the draft of coaches, carts, waggons, drays, and all land carriages whatsoever.
GEROTHWOHL, JOSEPH MEUCKE	7103	28th May	1836	Filtration.
GERVOY, ANNET - - -	13,970	13th Feb.	1852	Means to prolong the durability of the rails on railways.
GESSWEIN FREDERICK - -	14,212	6th July	1852	Preparing for baking and burning masses of clay; baking and burning the same as thoroughly as a common brick is burned.
GETHEN, THOMAS - - -	4942	15th April	1824	Machinery and process for making metallic rollers, pipes, cylinders, and other articles.
GETHEN, THOMAS - - -	5873	21st Nov.	1829	Dressing woollen-cloths.
GETRICK, FRANCIS MC - -	9604	26th Jan.	1843	Apparatus for preventing engines and carriages from going off the rails on railways, and for removing obstructions thereon.
GETTEN, JOSEPH - - -	8566	11th July	1840	Preparing and purifying whale-oil.
GHIGO, CARLO - - -	5487	24th April	1827	Weaving-machinery.
GIBBINS, JAMES - - -	10,370	31st Oct.	1844	Manufacture of figured or ornamented lace or net of various textures.
GIBBINS, JAMES - - -	10,424	7th Dec.	1844	Manufacture of figured and ornamented lace or net or other fabrics.
GIBBINS, WILLIAM - -	6117	24th May	1831	Converting salt or other water into pure or fresh water.
GIBBON, MARTHA - - -	2457	17th Dec.	1800	Stays for women and others.
GIBBONS, BEVINGTON - -	4587	8th Sept.	1821	Retort for making coal-gas and other gas, and for distillation, evaporation, and concentration of acids, and other substances.
GIBBONS, JAMES - -	6621	5th June	1834	Texture of bobbin-net or twist-net; also machinery to produce lace-net with the said improved texture.
GIBBONS, JAMES - -	9914	21st Oct.	1843	Machinery for reading patterns and stamping them in jacquard cards.
GIBBONS, JAMES - - -	10,370	31st Oct.	1844	Manufacture of figured or ornamented lace or net of various textures.
GIBBONS, JAMES - - -	10,424	7th Dec.	1844	Manufacture of figured or ornamented lace or net and other fabrics.
GIBBONS, JAMES - - -	10,716	10th June	1845	Manufacture of lace or net and other fabrics; machinery for ornamenting lace or net and other fabrics.
GIBBONS, WILLIAM - -	11,860	9th Sept.	1847	Trussing beams and girders.
GIBBS, HENRY - - -	7798	6th Sept.	1838	Perforated button.
GIBBS, JOSEPH - - -	5871	12th Nov.	1829	Machinery for cutting marble, wood, and other substances.
GIBBS, JOSEPH - - -	6032	6th Nov.	1830	Evaporating fluids;—applicable to various purposes.

Name of Patentee.	Progressive Number.	Date.	Subject-matter of Patent.
GIBBS, JOSEPH - - -	6241	8th Mar. 1832	Wheeled-carriages, and constructing the same.
GIBBS, JOSEPH - - -	6310	22nd Sept. 1832	Machinery for cutting-out wood for carriage-wheels, and for cutting and shaping the wheels.
GIBBS, JOSEPH - - -	6318	29th Sept. 1832	Steam-carriages.
GIBBS, JOSEPH - - -	6360	9th Jan. 1833	Dressing or preparing hemp, flax, New-Zealand flax and other like substances, for spinning, paper-making, and other purposes.
GIBBS, JOSEPH - - -	6408	4th April 1833	Apparatus and machinery for exhibiting scenery paintings, or other descriptions of pictures.
GIBBS, JOSEPH - - -	6438	20th June 1833	Construction of railroads, bridges. piers, jetties, and aqueducts ;—partly applicable to other purposes.
GIBBS, JOSEPH - - -	6707	4th Nov. 1834	Carriages, and wheels for carriages.
GIBBS, JOSEPH - - -	6752	27th Jan. 1835	Machinery for cutting wood and other materials.
GIBBS, JOSEPH - - -	8323	21st Dec. 1839	Machinery for preparing fibrous substances for spinning, and mode of spinning the same.
GIBBS, JOSEPH - - -	8945	29th April 1841	Combination of materials for making bricks, tiles, pottery and other such articles ; machinery for and process of burning the same ;—applicable to the burning of other descriptions of bricks, tiles, and pottery.
GIBBS, JOSEPH - - -	8977	5th June 1841	Roads and railways ; propelling carriages thereon.
GIBBS, JOSEPH - - -	13,071	7th May 1850	Artificial stone, mortar, and cements ; modes of manufacturing the same.
GIBBS, JOSEPH - - -	14,358	21st March 1853	Treatment of metals and metalliferous ores.
GIBBS, WILLIAM HENRY -	5369	23rd May 1826	Piece-goods, formed by the combination of threads of two or more colours, the manner of combining and displaying such colours constituting the novelty thereof.
GIBLETT, JOHN - - -	12,467	10th Feb. 1849	Manufacture of woollen-cloth.
GIBSON, JAMES GREEN - -	12,445	27th Jan. 1849	Machines for preparing to be spun, and spinning cotton and other fibrous substances, and for preparing to be woven, and weaving the same when spun.
GIBSON, JOHN - - -	4976	15th June 1824	Manufacture of elastic fabric from whalebone, and from whalebone, hemp and other materials combined, for making elastic bodies for hats, caps, bonnets, and other like articles ; also manufacturing such elastic bodies from the same materials by platting.
GIBSON, JOHN - - -	7228	19th Nov. 1836	Manufacture of silk, and silk in combination with certain other fibrous substances.
GIBSON, JOHN - - -	8641	24th Sept. 1840	Cleaning silk and other fibrous substances.
GIBSON, JOHN BUSHBY - -	9743	25th May 1843	Manufacture of salt.
GIBSON, JOSEPH - - -	9352	23rd May 1842	Axletrees ; axletree-boxes.
GIBSON, JOSEPH, junior - -	10,046	10th Feb. 1844	Ornamenting glass.
GIBSON, MATTHEW - -	11,346	22nd Aug. 1846	Machine for reaping and cutting grass, and for other similar purposes.
GIBSON, MATTHEW - -	13,776	16th Oct. 1851	Machinery for pulverising and preparing land.

213

Name of Patentee.	Progressive Number.	Date.	Subject-matter of Patent.
GIBSON, MATTHEW - -	14,219	15th July 1852	Reaping-machines.
GIBSON, ROBERT - - -	2484	26th Feb. 1801	Windlass for ships, and for other purposes.
GIBSON, ROBERT - - -	5353	27th April 1826	Machinery for making bricks.
GIDDY, OSMAN - -	11,667	20th April 1847	Apparatus for sweeping or cleansing chimneys and flues.
GIEB, JOHN - - -	1571	9th Nov. 1786	Pianofortes and harpsichords.
GIFFIN, THOMAS - -	1067	11th April 1774	Machine for making tin-foil.
GIFFORD, JOHN WALTER DE [LONGUEVILLE.	14,058	6th April 1852	Fire-arms and projectiles.
GIFFORD, NATHANIEL -	284	Nov. 1691	Instruments for making blue, purple, and other coloured paper.
GIFFORD, NATHANIEL -	305	18th Oct. 1692	Beautifying, figuring, imprinting, and embellishing blue and other coloured paper.
GIFFORD, WILLIAM JAMES -	7429	7th Sept. 1837	Paddle-wheels.
GILBEE, WILLIAM ARMAND - [Gilbee William Armand Moreau.]	13,830	22nd Nov. 1851	Process and apparatus for treating fatty or oleaginous matters; manufacture of candles, and other such articles therefrom.
GILBEE, WILLIAM ARMAND -	14,149	1st June 1852	Machinery for cutting corks.
GILBERT, GEORGE, ALEXANDER	8628	10th Sept. 1840	Machinery for obtaining and applying motive-power.
GILBERT, HENRY - - -	11,719	27th May 1847	Apparatus for holding sacks, to facilitate the filling them with corn or other materials.
GILBERT, HENRY - - -	12,133	20th April 1848	Operating in dental surgery; apparatus or instruments to be used therein.
GILBERT, JOHN - - -	9	16th July 1618	Water-plough for taking up sands or banks from the river Thames; engine for raising water.
GILBERT, JOHN - - -	55	8th July 1631	Engines or water-ploughs for taking sand, gravel, shells, and banks out of rivers, harbours, and other places.
GILBERT, THOMAS - - -	3473	7th Aug. 1811	Machinery for the delivery of bricks, tiles, ornaments and other articles made in moulds, after the moulds are filled.
GILBERT, THOMAS WILLIAM -	10,777	21st July 1845	Construction of sails for ships and other vessels.
GILBERTSON, JAMES - -	5601	15th Jan. 1828	Construction of furnaces, so that they may consume their own smoke.
GILCHRIST, ANTHONY -	4060	15th Aug. 1816	Machine for making nails and screws, and for working all metallic substances.
GILCHRIST, WILLIAM - -	1059	14th Jan. 1774	Mill for grinding sugar-canes.
GILCHRIST, WILLIAM -	1128	14th June 1776	Mill for grinding sugar-canes.
GILES, EDWARD GALLEY -	6716	15th Nov. 1834	Apparatus for engraving on copper and other substances.
GILES, ROBERT GOSWELL -	3535	6th Feb. 1812	Cap or cowl to be placed on the tops of chimneys to prevent the smoke being driven down by the wind.
GILL, BENNINGTON - -	4814	15th July 1823	Construction of saws, cleavers, straw-knives or other implements, requiring a metallic back.
GILL, JOHN EDGCUMBE - -	12,113	8th April 1848	Manufacture of manures.
GILL, RICHARD - - -	4818	24th July 1823	Preparing, dressing, and dyeing sheep-skins and lamb-skins with the wool on, for carriages, rooms, and for other purposes.
GILL, THOMAS - - -	2436	2nd Aug. 1800	Rifling the bores or calibres of cannon, and of musket, carbine, gun, and pistol barrels.

Name of Patentee.	Progres-sive Number.	Date.	Subject-matter of Patent.
GILL, THOMAS - - -	4238	14th March 1818	Instruments and apparatus for ascertaining the strength of spirituous liquors and the specific gravity of fluids.
GILL, THOMAS - - -	12,113	8th April 1848	Manufacture of manures.
GILLANDERS, FRANCIS - -	1199	22nd Oct. 1778	Covering artificial teeth, also decayed natural teeth and gums, with a composition that will not corrode, stain, or lose its colour.
GILLARD, JOSEPH PIERRE -	11,080	11th Feb. 1846	Production of heat in general.
GILLARD, JOSEPH PIERRE -	12,858	22nd Nov. 1849	Production of heat and light in general.
GILLESPIE, JOHN PETTY -	5349	25th April 1826	Spring, or combination of springs for forming an elastic resisting medium.
GILLESPIE, ROBERT - -	6805	3rd April 1835	Trusses for the cure of hernia or rupture.
GILLESPIE, WILLIAM - -	14,122	8th May 1852	Instrument or means of ascertaining or setting-off the slope or level of drains, banks, inclines, or works of every description on land or water.
GILLESPY, SAMUEL - -	1092	28th Dec. 1774	Construction of harpsichords, being a mode of putting-on the quills to strike the strings, with a pedal and swell which raises the top, brings on the tone, and swells a new celestial stop.
GILLET, AUGUSTUS WHITING -	6030	4th Nov. 1830	Construction and application of wheels to carriages, or to machines for moving heavy bodies.
GILLET, AUGUSTUS WHITING -	6153	13th Aug. 1831	Instrument to measure, beat, and give the accents in all the modes of time, and in any velocity;—applicable to the teaching of music.
GILLET, HARRIET GRANT -	6279	28th June 1832	Instrument to measure, beat, and give the accents in all the modes of time, and in any velocity;—applicable to the teaching of music.
GILLETT, JOHN - - -	9742	25th May 1843	Machine for cutting or boring ricks.
GILLETT, JOHN - - -	11,172	18th April 1846	Machines for cutting, slicing, and otherwise dividing hay, straw, turnips, and other vegetable substances.
GILLETT, JOHN - - -	11,256	22nd June 1846	Apparatus for protecting property by sounding alarums or giving signals.
GILLETT, JOHN - - -	14,069	17th April 1852	Ploughs.
GILLETT, WILLIAM STEDMAN	6554	8th Feb. 1834	Guns and other small arms.
GILLETT, WILLIAM STEDMAN [Gillett, Stedman.]	7266	21st Dec. 1836	Cabs.
GIBLETT, WILLIAM STEDMAN	7288	19th Jan. 1837,	Trimming and facilitating the progress of vessels in water.
GILLETT, WILLIAM STEDMAN	7300	16th Feb. 1837	Harness for draft and saddle horses.
GILLETT, WILLIAM STEDMAN	12,802	12th Oct. 1849	Packing pistons, stuffing-boxes, slides, and other parts of machinery; forming bearings; making cylinders and other forms of metal.
GILLIES, ALEXANDER - -	1469	22nd March 1785	Clogs.
GILLISPIE, WILLIAM - -	2311	30th April 1799	Printing, colouring, or staining linens, calicoes, or other cloths.
GILLMAN, JOSEPH - - -	4866	18th Nov. 1823	Manufacture of hats and bonnets.
GILLMAN, WILLIAM - -	5427	13th Dec. 1826	Applying heat to certain useful purposes.
GILLOT, BENJAMIN - -	9270	26th Feb. 1842	Heating and ventilating.
GILLOTT, JOSEPH - - -	6169	27th Sept. 1831	Making metallic-pens.
GILLOTT, JOSEPH - -	7321	13th March 1837	Giving elasticity, freedom of action, and durability to pens; also obtaining a flow of ink therefrom.

Name of Patentee.	Progressive Number.	Date.	Subject-matter of Patent.
GILLOTT, JOSEPH - - -	8031	13th April 1839	Engines and carriages to be worked by steam, or other motive-power.
GILLOTT, JOSEPH - - -	12,278	28th Sept. 1848	Ornamenting cylindrical and other surfaces of wood and other materials.
GILLOW, RICHARD - - -	2396	1st May 1800	Constructing dining and other tables.
GILLYON, THOMAS AUGUSTUS [GREGORY.	6491	19th Oct. 1833	Ordnance, and the carriages and projectiles to be used therewith.
GILMAN, WILLIAM - -	5150	13th April 1825	Generating steam; engines worked by steam, or other elastic fluids.
GILMAN, WILLIAM - -	7417	17th Aug. 1837	Steam-boilers, and engines actuated by steam or other power.
GILMORE, JOHN - - -	12,027	17th Jan. 1848	Ventilating ships and other vessels.
GILMOUR, JAMES RICHARD -	4500	20th Oct. 1820	Printing-presses.
GILPIN, GEORGE - - -	3454	11th June 1811	Machine or instrument for combing wool, dressing flax, and preparing them for spinning; construction of a breaking frame for drawing and cleaning wool from the combs; stove heated by fire or steam for heating the said combs.
GILPIN, WILLIAM - - -	3448	16th May 1811	Manufacturing augers.
GILROY, CLINTON GRAY -	7012	25th Feb. 1836	Machinery for weaving plain and figured fabrics.
GIMSON, THOMAS FOSTER -	4859	6th Nov. 1823	Machinery for doubling and twisting cotton, silk, and other fibrous substances.
GIRARD, LOUIS DOMINIQUE -	11,807	20th July 1847	Hydraulic-apparatus;—in part applicable to air-apparatus.
GIROUD, CHARLES LOUIS -	5285	8th Nov. 1825	Chemical substitute for gall-nuts.
GITTINS, WILLIAM - -	6602	6th May 1834	Applying the water used for the purpose of condensation in marine and other steam engines, to the condenser.
GLADSTONE, JAMES - -	4592	20th Sept. 1821	Increasing the strength of timber.
GLADSTONE, JAMES - -	4658	12th March 1822	Chain.
GLADSTONE, JOHN - -	4629	20th Dec. 1821	Construction of steam-vessels; propelling such vessels by steam or other power.
GLADSTONE, THOMAS MURRAY	7616	21st April 1838	Ships' windlasses;—applicable to other purposes.
GLADSTONE, THOMAS MURRAY	9995	28th Dec. 1843	Machines for cutting or shearing iron or other metals; — applicable to other like purposes.
GLADWIN, THOMAS - -	287	2nd Jan. 1692	Engine to clear water out of ships, to quench fires, and to drain mines.
GLASCOTT, GEORGE MINSHAW	4877	9th Dec. 1823	Form of nails used for securing copper and other sheathing on ships, and for other purposes.
GLASGOW, GEORGE - -	772	21st May 1762	Weaving cloth in imitation of women's stitched stays, of linen, thread, silk, or worsted.
GLASGOW, GEORGE - -	786	9th March 1763	Weaving and quilting in the loom, cloth of linen, woollen, silk, worsted, cotton, and mohair, separately or mixed.
GLASGOW, JOHN - - -	12,926	12th Jan. 1850	Machinery for shearing, shaping, punching, and compressing metals.
GALSHAN, ALEXANDER M^c -	12,779	20th Sept. 1849	Construction of railway-breaks.
GLASHEN, STEWART M^c -	14,100	29th April 1852	Application of certain mechanical powers to lifting, removing, and preserving trees, houses, and other bodies.
GLAZEBROOK, JAMES - -	2164	7th Feb. 1797	Working and giving power to machinery by means of air.

Name of Patentee.	Progressive Number.	Date.	Subject-matter of Patent.
GLAZEBROOK, JAMES - -	2504	21st May 1801	Working and giving powers to machinery by means of the properties of airs.
GLENNY, GEORGE - - -	1813	2nd July 1791	Obtaining from wood-ashes a greatly superior quantity of potashes and pearl-ashes than hitherto.
GLENNY, JOSEPH - - -	4412	23rd Nov. 1819	Machine and apparatus to answer the purpose of a fire burglary alarm.
GLENTON, MATTHEW - -	1042	23rd April 1773	Iron-oven, with a grate and regulator, to place behind a common range fire, for culinary purposes.
GLIMES, ANTHONY MOVILLON [De.	10,010	13th Jan. 1844	Apparatus for propelling vessels on water; machinery capable of communicating manual power to work the same;—applicable also for raising heavy bodies and exerting power for other purposes.
GLOVER, EDWARD - - -	3860	10th Dec. 1814	Apparatus for drawing or extracting bolts, nails, &c., and for various other purposes.
GLOVER, FREDERICK AUGUSTUS	8256	2nd Nov. 1839	Instrument for the measurement of angles.
GLOVER, JAMES - - -	13,561	20th March 1851	Rolling and laminating of metals; manufacture of metallic cases and coverings.
GLOVER, JOHN - - -	2384	24th March 1800	Bleaching linen-cloth and other cloths.
GLOVER, WILLIAM HEYWOOD	12,055	8th Feb. 1848	Manufacture of oil from blubber.
GLYDON, GEORGE - - -	13,133	12th June 1850	Manufacture of metal tubes for locomotive, marine, and other boilers.
GLYNN, HENRY - - -	13,717	14th Aug. 1851	Manufacture or treatment of paper or fabrics, to prevent copies or impressions being taken of any writing or printing thereon.
GODARD, JOHN THOMAS [LAURENTE LAMY.	8263	7th Nov. 1839	Looms for weaving, to be worked by steam or other power.
GODBOLD, FRANCIS - -	2729	3rd Aug. 1803	Dice.
GODBOLD, NATHANIEL - -	1476	3rd May 1785	Medicine for the cure of consumption and disease of the lungs. "Godbold's Vegetable Balsam."
GODBOLD, NATHANIEL - -	2275	27th Nov. 1798	Vegetable pill, balsam, and ointment, as remedies for the cure of consumption, scrofula, and gout.
GODDARD, JAMES - - -	3192	23rd Jan. 1809	Machinery for the manufacture of wooden pill-boxes.
GODDARD, LEMUEL - -	10,754	3rd July 1845	Manufacture of candles; preventing them from guttering whilst burning.
GODDARD, ROBERT HENDRICK	6567	27th Feb. 1834	Construction of weighing-machines for ascertaining, registering, and indicating the work done by weighing, measuring, or numbering apparatus.
GODDARD, SAMUEL ASPINWALL [Goddard, Samuel Aspinall.]	7191	22nd Sept. 1836	Locomotive steam-engines and carriages, partly applicable to ordinary steam-engines and to other purposes.
GODDARD, SAMUEL ASPINWALL	7730	11th July 1838	Machinery applicable to locomotion on rail-roads, and to steam-navigation; partly applicable to land or stationary engines.
GODDARD, SAMUEL ASPINWALL	14,087	24th April 1852	Firearms, ordnance, and projectiles to be used with such or the like weapons; machinery or apparatus for the manufacture of parts of such firearms, ordnance, and projectiles.
GODEFROY, PAUL - - -	10,472	16th Jan. 1845	Printing calico and other fabrics.
GODEFROY, PETER AUGUSTIN	12,422	16th Jan. 1849	Dressing and finishing woven fabrics.

Name of Patentee.	Progressive Number.	Date.	Subject-matter of Patent.
GODFREY, AMBROSE - -	458	12th Nov. 1723	Extinguishing fires in houses and ships, by means of casks and other vessels and materials.
GODFREY, SAMUEL - -	2103	6th April 1796	Machine to reduce the labour of animals, when employed in operations of draft or burden.
GODFRY, GEORGE - - -	1712	8th Dec. 1789	Making and annexing the tambourine, tabor, or drum and pipe, to barrel-organs and musical instruments; constructing such barrel-organs and musical instruments, so as to beat and play the said tambourine, tabor or drum and pipe therewith at pleasure.
GODSAL, PHILIP - - -	1353	22nd Jan. 1783	Steps for coaches, chariots, phaetons, and other carriages which let down and take up by the opening and shutting of the door.
GODWIN, JOHN - - -	7021	8th March 1836	Construction of pianofortes.
GODWIN, JOHN - - -	8999	23rd June 1841	Construction of pianofortes.
GODWIN, SAMUEL - - -	2766	30th May 1804	Machines for carding, scribbling, dressing, and brushing wool, and woollen-cloths.
GOLBY, JOHN - - -	1195	24th June 1778	Machine for making network with knotted meshes in silk, thread, cotton, worsted, or any other materials.
GOLD, JOHN - - -	6640	7th July 1834	Cutting, grinding, smoothing, polishing, or otherwise preparing glass-decanters and certain other articles.
GOLD, JOHN - - - -	7177	1st Sept. 1836	Machinery for grinding, smoothing, and polishing plate-glass, marble, slate, and stone, also glass-vessels, spangles, and drops.
GOLD, JOHN - - - -	8470	15th April 1840	Manufacture of decanters and other articles of glass.
GOLDEN, WILLIAM - -	9129	2nd Nov. 1841	Firearms; bullets and other projectiles to be used therewith.
GOLDFINCH, HENRY - -	4548	5th April 1821	Formation of horse-shoes.
GOLDFINCH, WILLIAM - -	2110	24th May 1796	Truss for the cure and prevention of rupture.
GOLDING, ROBERT - - -	1312	1st Jan. 1782	Dyeing, staining, and colouring beaver and stuff hats, green or any other colour, underneath or on one side only.
GOLDNER, STEPHEN - -	8873	8th March 1841	Preserving animal and vegetable substances and fluids.
GOLDSMID, LIONEL CAMPBELL	11,530	14th Jan. 1847	Applying rudders to ships and other vessels.
GOLDSWORTH, JOHN - -	1491	23rd July 1785	Guitars.
GOLIGHTLY, CHARLES - -	8771	4th Jan. 1841	Apparatus for obtaining motive-power.
GOLLOP, JOHN - - -	10,456	11th Jan, 1845	Spring-hinges and spring roller-blinds; applying springs to easy chairs and carriages.
GOMPERTZ, LEWIS - - -	3804	27th April 1814	Carriages, and substitutes for wheels for carriages and other machines.
GONIN, LOUIS SYLVAIN - -	11,502	21st Dec. 1846	Printing stuffs, paper, and other matters.
GOOCH, DANIEL - - -	8520	28th May 1840	Wheels and locomotive-engines to be used on railways.
GOOCH, WILLIAM - - -	5868	6th Nov. 1829	Baths;—the improvements being applicable to other purposes.
GOOD, WILLIAM - - -	3479	9th Sept. 1811	Valves for various purposes.

Name of Patentee.	Progressive Number.	Date.	Subject-matter of Patent.
GOOD, WILLIAM - - -	4390	10th July 1819	Tanning hides and skins; barking or colouring nets, sails, and other articles by the application of certain materials hitherto unused for that purpose.
GOODACRE, ROBERT - -	8629	10th Sept. 1840	Apparatus for raising heavy loads in carts or other receptacles, when it is required that the unloading should take place at any considerable elevation above the ground.
GOODACRE, ROBERT - -	8892	22nd March 1841	Weighing bodies raised by cranes or other elevating machines.
GOODACRE, ROBERT - -	9605	26th Jan. 1843	Weighing-apparatus, applicable to cranes or other elevating machines, whereby the weight of goods may be ascertained while in a state of suspension.
GOODALL, DANIEL - - -	3785	12th March 1814	Manufacturing English crapes from silk, dyed and coloured, either in a raw state or after being thrown or spun; introducing weaving or working into the warp and weft of such crapes, black, white, coloured, and fancy silk, cotton, and worsted, also gold and silver, or other plain or fancy materials.
GOODALL, JONATHAN CHARLES	13,032	5th April 1850	Machinery for cutting paper.
GOODE, BENJAMIN WILLIAM -	13,609	29th April 1851	Chains, chain-pins, swivels, brooches, and other fastenings for wearing-apparel.
GOODE, JOHN - - - -	4838	20th Aug. 1823	Machinery for boring the earth for the purpose of obtaining and raising water.
GOODFELLOW, BENJAMIN -	7912	18th Dec. 1838	Metallic-pistons.
GOODFELLOW, BENJAMIN -	12,762	13th Sept. 1849	Steam-engines.
GOODFELLOW, BENJAMIN -	14,023	11th March 1852	Boilers for generating steam.
GOODFELLOW, GEORGE - -	12,619	24th May 1849	Preparing plastic materials for manufacturing purposes.
GOODFELLOW, THOMAS - -	12,619	24th May 1849	Preparing plastic materials for manufacturing purposes.
GOODIER, JOHN - - -	12,702	9th July 1849	Mills for grinding wheat and other grain.
GOODLET, GEORGE - - -	6266	3rd May 1832	Preparing rough meal from ground wheat or other grain before dressing also rough meal from ground barley, malt, or other grain previous to their being put into the mash-tun for brewing or distilling.
GOODLET, GEORGE - - -	7276	11th Jan. 1837	Distilling spirits from wash and other articles;—also applicable to purposes of rectifying, boiling, and evaporating.
GOODMAN, GEORGE - -	8640	24th Sept. 1840	Manufacture of mourning and other dress pins.
GOODMAN, GEORGE, junior -	14,099	29th April 1852	Ornamenting japanned metal and papier-machè wares.
GOODMAN, JAMES - - -	3595	12th Aug. 1812	Saddles.
GOODMAN, JAMES - - -	4547	5th April 1821	Stirrup-irons.
GOODMAN, WILLIAM - -	4703	27th Sept. 1822	Looms.
GOODRIDGE, RICHARD - -	7691	14th June 1838	Apparatus for lifting and raising fluids on water or on land, and for marine propelling purposes without steam.
GOODSELL, NAMEN - - -	4930	25th March 1824	Machinery for breaking, scutching, and preparing flax and hemp, and for thrashing out the seed thereof;—applicable to thrashing other grain, also for shelling clover and other seeds.

Name of Patentee.	Progressive Number.	Date.	Subject-matter of Patent.
GOODWIN, CHARLES　-　-	3709	26th June 1813	Socket for a candlestick, with springs to hold the candle; also a self-acting extinguisher to be fixed to the candlestick.
GOODWIN, CHARLES　-　-	10,745	30th June 1845	Masts and spars.
GOODWIN, RICHARD　-　-	7627	26th April 1838	Prepared fuel.
GOODWYN, HENRY, junior　-	2171	9th March 1797	Machine and mash-tun for mixing and mashing malt and grain or corn, for brewing or distilling.
GOODYER, JAMES -　-　-	1000	20th Dec. 1771	Making steel directly from pig-iron or cast-iron.
GOOLDING, HENRY -　-　-	2220	10th Mar. 1798	Machine for raising, removing, and carrying earth, stones, rubbish, or any thing of the like nature.
GOOS, FREDERICK　-　-	9359	23rd May 1842	Jacquard-machine to be employed in looms for weaving.
GOOSE, WILLIAM　-　-	12,629	5th June 1849	Machinery for making nails.
GORDELIER, NICHOLAS　-	1524	28th Jan. 1786	Machine for throwing and winding silk and spinning cotton-wool, hemp, and flax.
GORDON, ALEXANDER　-　-	4638	14th Jan. 1822	Construction of lamps; compositions and materials to be burned in the said lamps and which may also be burned in other lamps.
GORDON, ALEXANDER　-　-	6390	21st Feb. 1833	Boilers or generators of steam or vapour; condensing such steam or vapour; also engines worked by steam or vapour for propelling machinery on land and water.
GORDON, ALEXANDER　-　-	6941	3rd Dec. 1835	Production, maintenance, direction, or distribution of light;—partly applicable to other purposes.
GORDON, ALEXANDER　-　-	8082	30th May 1839	Machine for employing steam or other elastic fluid as a motive-power.
GORDON, ALEXANDER　-　-	10,544	3rd Mar. 1845	Producing motive-power by the action or agency of heat; application of that power to purposes of locomotion or navigation.
GORDON, CUTHBERT　-　-	727	12th Aug. 1758	Dye called cudbear.
GORDON, DAVID　-　-　-	4381	19th June 1819	Portable gas-lamp.
GORDON, DAVID　-　-　-	4581	14th Aug. 1821	Construction of wheeled-carriages.
GORDON, DAVID　-　-　-	4586	8th Sept. 1821	Construction of harness for animals of draft and burden.
GORDON, DAVID　-　-　-	4638	14th Jan. 1822	Construction of lamps; compositions, and materials to be burned in the said lamps, and which may be also burned in other lamps.
GORDON, DAVID　-　-　-	4639	14th Jan. 1822	Steam-packets and other vessels;—partly applicable to other naval and marine purposes.
GORDON, DAVID　-　-　-	4940	14th April 1824	Construction of portable gas-lamps.
GORDON, DAVID　-　-　-	5056	18th Dec. 1824	Construction of carriages or other machines to be moved or propelled by mechanical means.
GORDON, DAVID　-　-　-	5111	26th Feb. 1825	Uniting and plating or casting iron with copper, or with any other composition whereof copper is the principal ingredient.
GORDON, GEORGE　-　-	727	12th Aug. 1758	Dye called cudbear.

Name of Patentee.	Progressive Number.	Date.		Subject-matter of Patent.
GORDON, LEWIS DUNBAR [BRODIE.	12,149	9th May	1848	Railways.
GORDON, ROBERT - - -	10,165	30th April	1844	Grinding wheat and other grain; dressing flour or meal;—applicable to grinding cements and other substances.
GORDON, ROBERT - - -	12,580	19th April	1849	Ventilation of mines.
GORDON, Sir ROBERT, Knt. -	252	19th Jan.	1687	Engine for drawing up water, both at the thrusting down and pulling up of the same rod or pump-staff, with valves opening from both sides and fast in the middle.
GORDON, WALTER - - -	1520	23rd Jan.	1786	Purified soap.
GORE, HENRY - - - -	6201	22nd Dec.	1831	Throstle-frames and spinning-frames that operate by spindles, flyers, and bobbins, for spinning yarn or threads.
GORE, SAMUEL - • -	13,593	15th April	1851	Treatment of substances used in the production of gas for giving light and heat; treating some of the products of the said substances; apparatus employed in the manufacture of such gas; discharging and giving motion to gas.
GORE, THOMAS - - -	8908	30th Mar.	1841	Machinery for roving, spinning, and doubling cotton, silk, wool, and other fibrous materials.
GORMAN, WILLIAM - -	14,351	8th Dec.	1852	Obtaining motive-power;—applicable or partly so to measuring and transmitting aëriform bodies and fluids.
GORTON, RICHARD - - -	1804	11th May	1791	Loom or machine to weave woollen, linen, worsted, cotton, and silk goods, and which will work one or more pieces at the same time by hand, steam-engine, or water-machinery.
GOSCHEN, HENRY - - -	7408	19th July	1837	Preparing flax and hemp for spinning.
GOSSAGE, WILLIAM - -	4753	11th Feb.	1823	Portable alarum to be attached to and detached from clocks and watches.
GOSSAGE, WILLIAM - -	5595	2nd Jan.	1828	Construction of cocks for the passage of fluids.
GOSSAGE, WILLIAM - -	7046	29th March	1836	Making ceruse or white-lead.
GOSSAGE, WILLIAM - -	7105	2nd June	1836	Apparatus for evaporating water from saline solutions; construction of stoves for drying salts.
GOSSAGE, WILLIAM - -	7267	24th Dec.	1836	Apparatus for decomposing common salt, and for condensing and using the gaseous product of such decomposition; conducting the process.
GOSSAGE, WILLIAM - -	7284	19th Jan.	1837	Manufacturing oxyde of lead, for making paints, and for other purposes; process of bleaching and purifying oils for mixing paints, also for mixing with other oils and fatty matters.
GOSSAGE, WILLIAM - -	7416	17th Aug.	1837	Processes for the manufacture of alkali from common salt; use of the products obtained therefrom.
GOSSAGE, WILLIAM - -	7636	8th May	1838	Manufacture of sulphuric-acid.
GOSSAGE, WILLIAM - -	7693	18th June	1838	Manufacturing iron.
GOSSAGE, WILLIAM - -	9591	14th Jan.	1843	Treating or reducing ores of zinc; furnaces for the purpose;—in part applicable to other furnaces.
GOSSAGE, WILLIAM - -	10,976	4th Dec.	1845	Obtaining products from certain ores and other compounds of certain metals.

Name of Patentee.	Progressive Number.	Date.	Subject-matter of Patent.
GOSSAGE, WILLIAM HERBERT	13,177	17th July 1850	Obtaining certain metals from some compounds containing such metals; obtaining other products by the use of certain compounds containing metals.
GOSSAGE, WILLIAM HERBERT	13,424	20th Dec. 1850	Concentration of sulphuric-acid and certain other fluids; use of products obtained in manufacturing sulphuric-acid and sulphates.
GOSSET, PIERRE JEAN - -	4882	18th Dec. 1823	Combination of machinery for producing various shapes, patterns, and sizes, from metals and other materials capable of receiving an oval, round, or other form.
GOSSET, PIERRE JEAN BAP- [TISTE VICTOR.	5058	18th Dec. 1824	Construction of looms or machinery for weaving various sorts of cloths or fabrics.
GOTTLIEB, ANDREW - -	5798	1st June 1829	Locks and keys.
GOTTLIEB, VALLENTINE -	1577	19th Dec. 1786	Crane.
GOTTLIEB, VALLENTINE -	1592	1st March 1787	Construction of wheels and axletrees for carriages;—applicable to other machinery.
GOUCHER, JOHN - - -	12,343	25th Nov. 1848	Machine for thrashing corn and other grain.
GOUGH, NATHAN - - -	5628	20th March 1828	Propelling carriages or vessels by steam or other power.
GOUGY, PIERRE FREDERIC -	8308	11th Dec. 1839	Clocks, watches, and other timekeepers.
GOUGY, PIERRE FREDERIC -	11,509	23rd Dec. 1846	Machinery for raising, lifting, and otherwise moving heavy bodies.
GOUGY, PIERRE FREDERIC -	12,443	27th Jan. 1849	Apparatus and machinery for lifting and moving heavy bodies, and for raising and displacing fluids.
GOULD, CHESTER - - -	2405	26th May 1800	Instrument or log for ascertaining a ship's distance at sea.
GOULD, CHESTER - - -	2458	17th Dec. 1800	Instrument or log for ascertaining a ship's distance at sea.
GOULD, CHESTER - - -	2559	17th Nov. 1801	Artificial horizon, to be attached to and used with the quadrant or sextant, for taking altitudes on land or water.
GOULD, CHESTER - - -	2706	28th May 1803	Glass for the use of mariners at sea when heaving the log, in lieu of the common sandglass, and for other uses.
GOULD, CHESTER - - -	2734	3rd Sept. 1803	Hydrometer for ascertaining the strength of spirits, and determining the specific-gravity of fluids.
GOULD, CHESTER - - -	2945	24th June 1806	Machine for roasting meat by the power of steam.
GOULD, CHESTER - - -	3002	24th Jan. 1807	Machine for weighing to the amount of ten tons and upwards, in place of the common steelyard, or beams and weight.
GOULD, CHESTER - - -	3045	26th May 1807	Machine for mangling linen and other articles.
GOULD, CHESTER - - -	3133	17th May 1808	Construction of a machine for washing or cleansing linen and other articles.
GOULDER, STEPHEN - -	803	15th Dec. 1763	Composition for use in making or manufacturing canvas for sailcloth, to prevent the same from mildewing.
GOULDING, JOHN - - -	5355	2nd May 1826	Machines for carding, slubbing, slivering, roving, or spinning wool, cotton, waste-silk, short-staple hemp and flax, or any other substances.
GOULSON, BENJAMIN - -	5877	14th Dec. 1829	Manufacture of farina and sugar from vegetable productions.

Name of Patentee.	Progressive Number.	Date.		Subject-matter of Patent.
GOURNAY, JULES ALPHONSE [SIMON DE.	8358	22nd Jan.	1840	Manufacture of horse-shoes.
GOUT, RALPH - - - -	1710	7th Nov.	1789	Machinery attached to a carriage to measure the distance travelled over, also to afford security.
GOUT, RALPH - - - -	2351	4th Nov.	1799	Pedometers and pedrometrical watches, by the use of which the number of steps the wearer takes when walking may be ascertained, or if affixed to a saddle will indicate the number of paces the horse makes, and when affixed to a curricle or other carriage will also indicate the number of the revolutions of the wheel.
GOVER, JOHN - - - -	2151	8th Dec.	1796	Carriage for cannon.
GOVER, JOHN - - - -	2803	19th Dec.	1804	Construction of a carriage for all sorts of cannon.
GOVER, WILLIAM CLEGG -	2976	15th Oct.	1806	Wheel or purchase for steering ships.
GOVER, WILLIAM CLEGG -	10,085	1st March	1844	Casting-off the sash-lines and weights from window-sashes; taking out window-sashes from their frames without removing the beads.
GOWAN, THOMAS - - -	4860	11th Nov.	1823	Trusses.
GOWER, CHARLES - - -	1864	5th April	1792	Depurating and improving animal oil.
GOWER, RICHARD HALL -	1895	5th July	1792	Perpetual log, or instrument for measuring a ship's way through the water, and for ascertaining the rate of sailing at any time.
GOWER, RICHARD HALL -	2350	4th Nov.	1799	Rigging vessels.
GOWLAND, JAMES - - -	7456	2nd Nov.	1837	Mechanism of timekeepers.
GOYVARTS, MELCHIOR - -	62	12th April	1633	Making water-mills on standing waters, lakes, and ditches.
GRACE, THOMAS - - -	2461	30th Dec.	1800	Making an acid for corroding lead, and for other purposes; preparing and making white lead.
GRAEFER, JOHN - - -	1275	30th Dec.	1780	Drying and preparing green and brown borecole, Scotch or other kale, so that it will retain for a year or a longer period its natural flavour as an excellent food, or its virtue as a preventative of scorbutic disorders.
GRAFTON, CHARLES - -	4601	24th Oct.	1821	Making spirit-black; apparatus for producing the same.
GRAFTON, HENRY - - -	9240	27th Jan.	1842	Preserving animal and vegetable matters.
GRAFTON, HENRY - - -	11,533	16th Jan.	1847	Railway-wheels, and apparatus connected with railway-carriages.
GRAFTON, JOHN - - -	4306	10th Nov.	1818	Making carburetted hydrogen-gas for the purpose of illumination.
GRAFTON, JOHN - - -	4409	18th Nov.	1819	Apparatus for purifying gas used for illumination.
GRAFTON, JOHN - - -	4483	11th July	1820	Distilling-off the products of coal; carbonizing coal in making gas for illumination.
GRAFTON, JOHN - - -	7788	30th Aug.	1838	Construction of retorts and other machinery for making gas from coals and other substances.
GRAFTON, JOHN - - -	9062	4th Sept.	1841	Manufacturing gas.
GRAHAM, AUGUSTUS - -	6054	17th Dec.	1830	Application of spring-carriages.

Name of Patentee.	Progressive Number.	Date.	Subject-matter of Patent.
GRAHAM, CHARLES WILLIAM	10,229	18th June 1844	Manufacturing pathological, anatomical, zoological, geological, botanical, and mineralogical representations in relief, and arranging them for use.
GRAHAM, HUGH - - -	8740	16th Dec. 1840	Preparing designs, and dyeing materials for weaving Kidderminster carpets; producing patterns therein.
GRAHAM, HUGH - - -	8950	6th May 1841	Manufacture of Kidderminster carpeting.
GRAHAM, JAMES - - -	9912	18th Oct. 1843	Construction of pots or vessels and furnaces used in the manufacture of zinc and in other manufactures; treatment of the ores of zinc in the process of manufacturing zinc.
GRAHAM, JAMES - - -	10,524	17th Feb. 1845	Manufacture of zinc, antimony, and brass; casting brass; apparatus for making pots used in such processes.
GRAHAM, JAMES - - -	13,999	8th March 1852	Treating ores containing zinc, and the products obtained therefrom.
GRAHAM, JAMES REGINALD [TORIN.	13,108	7th June 1850	Machinery or apparatus for cleaning, purifying, and drying wheat or other grain or seeds. (Miles Berry's extension.)
GRAHAM, WILLIAM, junior -	6424	22nd May 1833	"Self-acting temple," for use in weaving by power or hand loom.
GRAHAME, THOMAS - -	7092	13th May 1836	Passing boats and other bodies from one level to another.
GRAND, JAMES LE - - -	446	31st May 1722	Preventing the smoking of chimneys and all inconveniences that happen thereto, either from wind, sun, or rain, by causing an attraction of smoke by a method not hitherto practised.
GRAND, JEAN LE - - -	4889	15th Jan. 1824	Fermented liquors, and the various products to be obtained therefrom.
GRANDISON, Viscount GEORGE [Lord.	206	12th Nov. 1678	Melting metallic-ores with sea-coal, turf, peat, or other mixed fuel instead of wood.
GRANHOLM, LEWIS - -	4070	25th Oct. 1816	Rendering articles manufactured of hemp or flax, or hemp and flax mixed, more durable than they now are.
GRANHOLM, LUDWIG - -	4109	11th March 1817	Pressing vegetable and animal products.
GRANHOLM, LUDWIG - -	4150	5th Aug. 1817	Preserving such animal and vegetable substances, separately or mixed, as are fit for the food of man, and for such a time as to render them fit for ship and garrison stores.
GRANNSELL, WILLIAM - -	8102	12th June 1839	Apparatus for drilling corn, grain, pulse, and manure.
GRANT, CHARLES WILLIAM -	7606	26th March 1838	Exhibiting signals for communicating intelligence at sea or on shore.
GRANT, DAVID - - -	3805	27th April 1814	Pump or apparatus for drawing off soda-water and other liquids impregnated with air.
GRANT, DONALD - - -	10,146	18th April 1844	Ventilation of apartments in which gas and other combustible matters are consumed by ignition.
GRANT, HENRY - - -	2598	24th March 1802	Machine for purifying and clarifying water.
GRANT, JAMES - - -	10,174	7th May 1844	Ventilating buildings and other places where a change of air is required.
GRANT, JOHN - - - -	13,298	24th Oct. 1850	Heating and regulating temperature.
GRANT, JOSEPH COOKE - -	9073	8th Sept. 1841	Horse-rakes and hoes.
GRANT, JOSEPH COOKE - -	9820	6th July 1843	Construction of harrows.
GRANT, THOMAS - - -	3317	22nd March 1810	Making paint or varnish from a fossil, for use in painting ships, and in various manufactures.

Name of Patentee.	Progres-sive Number.	Date.	Subject-matter of Patent.
GRANT, THOMAS - - -	3704	31st May 1813	Ingredients for mixing with oil, in preparing and making paint.
GRANT, THOMAS TASSELL -	8569	13th July 1840	Manufacture of fuel.
GRANTHAM, JOHN - - -	7805	13th Sept. 1838	Furnaces for steam-boilers.
GRANTHAM, JOHN - - -	9550	8th Dec. 1842	Construction and arrangement of engines and their appendages for propelling vessels on water.
GRANTHAM, JOHN - - -	12,684	4th July 1849	Sheathing ships and vessels.
GRAS, LOUIS NAPOLEON LE -	12,869	30th Nov. 1849	Separation and disinfection of fecal matters in the manufacture of manure; apparatus employed therein.
GRATRIX, SAMUEL - - -	2331	17th July 1799	Dyeing and staining colours on cotton-cloth, linen-cloth, and cloth of cotton and linen mixed.
GRATRIX, WILLIAM - -	6356	5th Jan. 1833	Imparting to woven-fabrics, or to the yarns or threads of which the same are intended to be composed, the colour necessary to form the required pattern thereon.
GRATRIX, WILLIAM - -	7349	22nd April 1837	Bleaching or cleansing linens, cotton and other fibrous substances; also discharging colours from the same in the raw or manufactured state.
GRATRIX, WILLIAM - -	12,518	14th March 1849	Drying and finishing woven and other fabrics; machinery for the purpose;—partly applicable to stretching woven-fabrics.
GRATRIX, WILLIAM - -	14,159	8th June 1852	Production of designs upon cotton and other fabrics.
GRATRIX, WILLIAM HODGSON	10,878	10th Oct. 1845	Looms for weaving ribbons and other fabrics.
GRATRIX, WILLIAM HODGSON	12,483	28th Feb. 1849	Steam-engines, more particularly marine engines; machinery for propelling vessels.
GRATRIX, WILLIAM HODGSON	13,426	26th Dec. 1850	Manufacturing velvets or other piled fabrics.
GRAULHIE, GERARD - -	4777	16th April 1823	Apparatus capable of being inclined in different degrees, adapted to the conveyance of persons and goods across rivers or ravines, for military and other objects;—applicable to purposes of recreation and exercise.
GRAVES, Captain BENJAMIN -	298	31st May 1692	Engine or diving-habit, by means of which a man may be let down under water, secure from its pressure and with his arms and legs at liberty; also, by the aid of another engine for pumping air, the said person may work under water with freedom and clearness of sight, for an hour at the least.
GRAVES, PIERREPONT - -	6202	22nd Dec. 1831	Making ornamental cotton yarns and threads;—applicable to the making, sewing, or embroidering of cotton and other fabrics.
GRAVIER, JEAN FRANCOIS -	5164	14th May 1825	Regulating the flow of gas from portable reservoirs; increasing the safety of the said reservoirs.
GRAY, JAMES - - - -	951	25th Jan. 1770	Dyeing paper, card-paper, and white leather on the grain side, of various colours.
GRAY, JOHN - - - -	5895	4th Feb. 1830	Preparing and putting on copper-sheathing for vessels.

Name of Patentee.	Progressive Number.	Date.	Subject-matter of Patent.
GRAY, JOHN - - - -	6920	2nd Nov. 1835	Combination of parts forming a furnace for consuming smoke, and economizing fuel;—applicable to steamboats, and to other purposes.
GRAY, JOHN - - - -	7308	17th Feb. 1837	Furnaces for locomotive-engines, and for other purposes.
GRAY, JOHN - - - -	7512	19th Dec. 1837	Steam-engines, and apparatus connected therewith; particularly applicable to marine engines; also to locomotive and stationary steam-engines.
GRAY, JOHN - - - -	7745	26th July 1838	Steam-engines, and apparatus connected therewith; particularly applicable to marine engines; also to locomotive and stationary steam-engines.
GRAY, JOHN THOMAS - -	11,702	14th May 1847	Boot and shoe.
GRAY, JOSEPH - - -	11,339	17th Aug. 1846	Gas-meters.
GRAY, MATTHEW - - -	13,209	31st July 1850	Supplying steam-boilers with water.
GRAY, RICHARD - - -	9006	26th June 1841	Machinery for making lace and other fabrics, traversed, looped, or woven.
GRAY, THOMAS WOOD - -	10,861	9th Oct. 1845	Ports, and apparatus for opening and closing ports of ships or other vessels;—applicable in opening and closing windows, and other instruments having the like movement.
GRAY, THOMAS WOOD - -	12,673	26th June 1849	Waterclosets, pump-cocks, lubricators, and deck-lights.
GRAY, WILLIAM - - -	1401	17th Nov. 1783	Chape for buckles.
GRAYDON, GEORGE - -	4996	5th Aug. 1824	Compass for navigation and other purposes.
GRAYDON, GEORGE - -	8248	24th Oct. 1839	Compass for navigation and other purposes;—partly applicable for measuring angles, and partly to magnetic-compasses for ascertaining true bearings from celestial observations, and for determining the variation of the magnetic-needle, by comparing such bearings with that of the said needle.
GRAYSON, WILLIAM - -	13,838	1st Dec. 1851	Road-measurer (odometer), to be attached to carriages, for showing the distances over which the wheels pass.
GREAVES, EDMUND - -	1241	17th Dec. 1779	Candlestick with a screw-nosle, to raise or lower the candle at pleasure.
GREAVES, EDWARD - -	2780	4th Aug. 1804	Razors.
GREAVES, FRANCIS - -	8540	11th June 1840	Manufacture of knives and forks.
GREAVES, HUGH - - -	11,216	22nd May 1846	Construction of railways; carriages to be used thereon.
GREAVES, WILLIAM - -	4912	28th Feb. 1824	Harness, chiefly applicable to carriages drawn by one horse.
GREAVES, WILLIAM - -	6240	4th Sept. 1832	Construction of fire-engines.
GREEN, ALFRED - - -	9296	15th Mar. 1842	Trusses or surgical bandages.
GREEN, CHARLES - - -	7707	27th June 1838	Manufacture of brass and copper tubing.
GREEN, CHARLES - - -	8838	8th Feb. 1841	Manufacture of brass and copper tubes.
GREEN, CHARLES - - -	12,124	15th April 1848	Manufacture of parts of railway-wheels.
GREEN, CHARLES - - -	12,539	28th Mar. 1849	Manufacture of railway-wheels.
GREEN, CHARLES - - -	13,752	25th Sept. 1851	Manufacture of brass tubes.
GREEN, DARIUS ISAAC - -	10,512	8th Feb. 1845	Raising and moving heavy bodies;—partly applicable amongst other uses, to mines, vessels, and public works.

Name of Patentee.	Progres- sive Number.	Date.		Subject-matter of Patent.
GREEN, EDWARD - - -	10,986	10th Dec.	1845	Economizing fuel, retaining and applying heat for generating steam and heating water.
GREEN, GEORGE JOSEPH -	6671	1st Sept.	1834	Manufacture and working of plate and other glass.
GREEN, GEORGE JOSEPH -ꜟ	10,492	23rd Jan.	1845	Harness or harness-furniture.
GREEN, JOHN - - -	269	12th June	1691	Carriages drawn or driven by man or beast, and on one or more wheels.
GREEN, JOHN - - -	314	31st Jan.	1693	Converting stone and chalk into lime, so that by the heat thereof, water and other liquids may be heated or boiled.
GREEN, JOHN - - -	796	29th July	1763	Fire-alarm.
GREEN, JOHN - - -	1095	8th April	1775	Fire-lock constructed for portability and safety, with the lock so constructed as not to obstruct the sight, having the prime secured against the effects of rain, and so contrived that the barrel can be taken from the lock for the purpose of cleaning the same ; is also provided with a lever that sets the lock in motion, but being removed disengages the action of the gun ; the said fire-lock may be used either to a gun, pistol, cannon, or other fire-arm, with one, two, three, or more barrels.
GREEN, JOHN - - -	4807	26th June	1823	Machines for roving, spinning, and twisting cotton, flax, silk, wool, or other fibrous substances.
GREEN, JOHN - - -	7154	27th July	1836	Forming musical-instruments in which continuous sounds are produced from strings, wires, or springs.
GREEN, JOHN, jun. - - -	9278	7th March	1842	Machinery for cutting turnips, mangel-wurzel, carrots and other roots, for food for horned cattle, horses, and other animals.
GREEN, JOSEPH - - -	1968	9th Dec.	1793	Warming rooms and buildings with hot air of purer quality than hitherto used.
GREEN, JOSEPH - - -	7667	2nd June	1838	Ovens.
GREEN, JOSHUA - - -	1390	2nd Oct.	1783	Machinery for drying and tentering cloths, crapes, cottons, velvets, silk-stuffs, and other woven goods.
GREEN, JOSHUA - - -	1958	18th June	1793	Constructing navigable canals without the use or necessity of locks.
GREEN, JOSHUA - - -	2704	17th May	1803	Manufacturing corded and ribbed shags or plushes composed of different materials.
GREEN, NICHOLAS WHITAKER	12,263	4th Sept.	1848	Manufacture of artificial fuel in blocks or lumps.
GREEN, RADCLIFFE - -	679	30th Mar.	1753	Dyeing and staining leather.
GREEN, RICHARD - - -	3656	3rd Mar.	1813	Stirrup with a spring in the eye and a spring-bottom, for the safety of persons riding on horseback, and to prevent their being dragged in the stirrup.
GREEN, RICHARD - - -	4291	31st Aug.	1818	Spring-billet for harness ; and its application to bridles, heads and reins, bits, sword-belts, gun-springs, and to other purposes.
GREEN, RICHARD - - -	4864	13th Nov.	1823	Constructing gambadoes or mud-boots, and attaching spurs thereto.
GREEN, RICHARD - - -	5769	5th Feb.	1829	Construction of made-masts.
GREEN, THOMAS - - -	13,791	29th Oct.	1851	Moulding, casting, ornamenting, and finishing articles and surfaces.
GREEN, WILLIAM - - -	8959	14th May	1841	Manufacture of iron and steel.

Name of Patentee.	Progressive Number.	Date.	Subject-matter of Patent.
GREEN, WILLIAM - - -	11,121	11th March 1846	Apparatus for facilitating the putting on of boots to the feet.
GREEN, WILLIAM HENRY -	12,507	5th March 1849	Preparation of fuel.
GREEN, WILLIAM HENRY -	13,420	19th Dec. 1850	Preparation of peat and other ligneous and carbonaceous substances; conversion of some of the products derived thereby; mode of their application to the preservation of substances liable to decomposition and destructive agencies;—applicable to other products of a similar nature.
GREEN, WILLIAM PRINGLE -	7193	28th Sept. 1836	Capstans, applicable to ships and to other purposes; method of reducing manual labour in working capstans used at mines.
GREEN, WILLIAM PRINGLE -	7400	10th July 1837	Capstans; and machinery for raising, lowering, and moving ponderous bodies and matters.
GREENALL, JONATHAN - -	760	6th Feb. 1761	Manufacturing salt.
GREENALL, JONATHAN - -	761	6th Feb. 1761	Fire-engine for draining mines, coal-pits, and lands.
GREENBURY, EDWARD - -	99	— 1636	Painting with oil-colours upon woollen-cloth, kerseys, and stuffs for hangings; also on silk for windows.
GREENBURY, RICHARD - -	99	— 1636	Painting with oil-colours upon woollen-cloth, kerseys, and stuffs for hangings; also on silk for windows.
GREENE, JOHN - - -	267	13th April 1691	Carriage, and way of hanging coaches and chariots.
GREENER, WILLIAM - -	11,076	7th Feb. 1846	Ignition and illumination.
GREENFIELD, DANIEL - -	9263	21st Feb. 1842	Making hollow metal-knobs, for the handles of door and other locks.
GREENHOW, CONRAD HAVER-[KAM.	11,026	6th Jan. 1846	Construction of railways and railway-carriages.
GREENHOW, CONRAD HAVER-[KAM.	11,684	4th May 1847	Construction of ships or vessels; propelling ships and vessels.
GREENHOW, CONRAD HAVER-[KAM.	12,417	13th Jan. 1849	Atmospheric-railways.
GREENING, THOMAS - -	464	16th March 1724	Grafting or budding the English elm upon the stock of the Dutch elm.
GREENING, THOMAS NICHOLAS	12,574	17th April 1849	Knives and forks.
GREENOUGH, JAMES - -	6996	5th Feb. 1836	Machinery used in preparing and spinning cotton, silk, wool, and other fibrous material.
GREENOUGH, JOHN JAMES -	13,207	31st July 1850	Obtaining and applying motive-power.
GREENOUGH, JOHN JAMES -	13,361	21st Nov. 1850	Construction of chairs, couches, and seats;— in part applicable where springs for resisting sudden and continuous pressure, and for supporting heavy bodies, are required.
GREENOUGH, JOHN JAMES -	13,613	3rd May 1851	Obtaining and applying motive-power.
GREENOUGH, THOMAS - -	599	9th Feb. 1744	Tincture for cleansing and preserving the teeth, and curing the tooth-ache.
GREENOUGH, THOMAS - -	716	31st Oct. 1757	Remedy for pains and disorders in the stomach, bowels, and other membranous parts of the body.
GREENOUGH, THOMAS - -	810	10th April 1764	Machine for printing, staining, and colouring silks, stuffs, linens, cottons, leather, and paper.
GREENOUGH, THOMAS - -	1206	8th Jan. 1779	Samaritan-water, a remedy for strains, bruises, wounds, and many complaints.

Name of Patentee.	Progressive Number.	Date.		Subject-matter of Patent.
GREENSHILDS, THOMAS - -	10,288	6th Aug.	1844	Manufacturing salt.
GREENSTREET, FRANCIS HAST-[INGS.	12,349	2nd Dec.	1848	Hydraulic-engines.
GREENSTREET, FRANCIS HAST-[INGS.	13,889	31st Dec.	1851	Coating and ornamenting zinc.
GREENSTREET, WILLIAM JAMES	9609	26th Jan.	1843	Machinery for producing or obtaining mo-tive-power.
GREENWAY, CHARLES - -	4265	26th May	1818	Opening raw cotton or cotton-wool, previous to carding and spinning the same.
GREENWAY, CHARLES - -	8211	5th Sept.	1839	Snuffers.
GREENWAY, CHARLES - -	8333	3rd Jan.	1840	Reducing friction in wheels of carriages ;— applicable to bearings and journals of machinery.
GREENWAY, CHARLES - -	13,136	19th June	1850	Ships' and other pumps ; anchors ; propelling vessels.
GREENWOOD, DAVID - -	8250	2nd Nov.	1839	Engines for obtaining power.
GREENWOOD, JOHN - -	5074	11th Jan.	1825	Sawing and cutting timber by machinery.
GREENWOOD, JOHN - -	10757	8th July	1845	Manufacturing certain chemical agents used in dyeing and printing cottons, woollens, and other fabrics.
GREENWOOD, JOHN - -	11,064	29th Jan.	1846	Dyeing turkey-red and other colours.
GREENWOOD, JOHN - -	11,252	22nd June	1846	Dyeing and printing turkey-red and other colours.
GREENWOOD, JOHN - -	11,742	12th June	1847	Certain substances applicable to the manu-facture, scouring, and washing of wool, woollen-fabrics, and other substances.
GREENWOOD, JOHN - -	14,024	15th March	1852	Preparing cotton and other fabrics for dye-ing and printing.
GREENWOOD, JOHN DANFORTH	7580	27th Feb.	1838	Manufacture of cement ; application of ce-ment and other earthy substances for pro-ducing ornamental surfaces.
GREENWOOD, JOHN DANFORTH	8090	4th June	1839	Producing plain and ornamental articles and surfaces from cements or earths, separately or combined with other materials.
GREENWOOD, JOSEPH - -	1333	30th July	1782	Composition made in balls for cleaning leather-breeches, gloves, and other accou-trements.
GREENWOOD, THOMAS - -	4883	27th Dec.	1823	Pattens and clogs, or substitutes for them.
GREENWOOD, THOMAS - -	12,682	4th July	1849	Filtering syrups and other liquors.
GREENWOOD, THOMAS - -	13,794	3rd Nov.	1851	Machinery for drawing and combing wool, silk, flax, hemp, and tow.
GREER, JAMES JOHN - -	9811	1st July	1843	Apparatus for securing or fixing standing-rigging, chains, and other tackle.
GREG, ROBERT HYDE - -	13,712	7th Aug.	1851	Machinery or apparatus for manufacturing weavers' healds or harness.
GREGOR, MALCOLM Mᵒ - -	3189	29th Dec.	1808	Construction of umbrellas and parasols.
GREGOR, MALCOLM Mᶜ - -	3349	19th June	1810	Musical instrument or flute with improved keys ;—applicable to other wind instru-ments.
GREGOR, MALCOLM Mᶜ - -	6698	20th Oct.	1834	Machinery for slubbing, roving, spinning, twisting, and doubling cotton and other fibrous substances.
GREGORY, EDMOND - -	101	9th Jan.	1636	Taking off the outside of ormer-shells, and covering cloth, taffety, wood, and other stuffs with the same.
GREGORY, GEORGE - -	1960	16th Aug.	1793	Heating by steam and in vats, the water and stuffs for paper-making.

Name of Patentee.	Progressive Number.	Date.		Subject-matter of Patent.
GREGORY, HENRY -	752	2nd Oct.	1760	Quadrant for taking observations at sea.
GREGORY, JAMES -	8959	14th May	1841	Manufacture of iron and steel.
GREGORY, JOHN -	595	5th Jan.	1744	Engine for draining fens, and cleansing rivers and wharfs choked with sand or gravel.
GREGORY, JOHN -	3320	22nd March	1810	Tunning ales and beers into casks; cleansing ales and beers.
GREGORY, JOHN -	4332	15th Jan.	1819	Combination of machinery, consisting of a fire-escape, ladder, and apparatus, for the safety of persons and property in case of fire;—applicable to other purposes.
GREGSON, JOHN BRUMWELL -	8748	23rd Dec.	1840	Pigments, and preparation of the sulphates of iron and magnesia.
GREGSON, JOHN BRUMWELL -	10,520	10th Feb.	1845	Manufacture of Epsom-salts and carbonate of lime, called precipitated chalk;—in part applicable to other purposes.
GREGSON, JOSEPH -	4073	1st Nov.	1816	Constructing chimneys, and supplying fires with fuel.
GREGSON, MATTHEW -	2796	4th Dec.	1804	Cleansing feathers for beds, also hair, wool, down, and other the natural covering of birds and animals, from their animal oil.
GREGSON, MATTHEW -	9503	2nd Nov.	1842	Sawing and cutting veneers.
GREIG, THOMAS -	6927	10th Nov.	1835	Embossing and printing at one time, by means of a cylinder, on fabrics of cotton, silk, flax, hemp, and wool, or on paper.
GRELLETT, CHARLES -	8717	25th Nov,	1840	Treating potatoes in order to their being converted into various articles of food; apparatus for drying, applicable to that and to other purposes.
GRELLIER, JAMES -	3205	13th Feb.	1809	Kiln for burning coke and lime, "The Union and Perpetual Kiln."
GRENFELL, GEORGE SAINT [LEGER.	6622	5th June	1834	Construction of saddles.
GRENFELL. JOHN -	2262	10th Oct.	1798	Manufacturing copper and tin-plate vessels.
GRENT, THOMAS -	47	22nd June	1629	Baths termed "circular baths;" engines and instruments necessary for making the same.
GRENT, THOMAS -	59	20th July	1632	Instrument or the "Winds' Majesty" for the more speedy passage of ships or other vessels becalmed upon the sea or rivers; fish-call, or a looking-glass to lure fishes to nets, spears, or hoops; a water-bow or instrument for the preservation of houses or ships from sudden fire; a building mould or stone-press, useful in the building of churches and great houses, for the formation of stone-windows, door-cases, chimney-pieces, &c. without hewing, cutting, sawing, or engraving, and for the formation of bricks, and tiles, smooth on one side, and worked as if carved; a chamber weather-call to be placed in a room or by a bed-side, to cause sleep to fevered invalids; waterwork instrument or a corrected crane for passing wine, oil, or other liquor from one vessel to another without any sucking or forcing by the mouth.
GREW, NEHEMIAH -	354	15th July	1698	Making the salt of purging-waters perfectly fine, in large quantities and cheap, for use as a medicine.

Name of Patentee.	Progressive Number.	Date.	Subject-matter of Patent.
GREY, JOHN - - - -	392	27th June 1712	Engine for weighing and raising weights; engine for raising water to extinguish fires.
GRIERSON, CHARLES - -	2566	19th Dec. 1801	Breech and lock for single and double barrel guns, pistols, and other fire-arms.
GRIESBACH, JOHN HENRY -	11,642	29th Mar. 1847	Construction of railways; engines and carriages to run thereon.
GRIEVE, JOHN - - -	10,357	17th Oct. 1844	Production and use of steam, applicable to steam-engines.
GRIFFIN, CHARLES JAMES [COVERLEY.	12,666	20th June 1849	Military accoutrements.
GRIFFIN, JAMES - - -	5642	26th April 1828	Manufacturing scythe backs, chaff-knife backs, and hay-knife backs.
GRIFFIN, JAMES - - -	9895	5th Oct. 1843	Manufacture of spades, shovels, and such like tools.
GRIFFITH, EDMUND - -	3393	8th Oct. 1810	Manufacture of soap for washing with sea-water, hard-water, and soft-water.
GRIFFITH, EDWARD - -	3274	9th Nov. 1809	Air-tight agitable lamp.
GRIFFITH, JULIUS - - -	4630	20th Dec. 1821	Steam-carriages capable of conveying goods and passengers on common roads, without horses.
GRIFFITH, OWEN - - -	4600	18th Oct. 1821	Making trusses for the cure of ruptures or hernia.
GRIFFITH, WILLIAM - -	3882	7th Feb. 1815	Toast-stand.
GRIFFITHS, HENRY - -	8078	25th May 1839	Producing prints and impressions from steel, copper, and other plates.
GRIFFITHS, PAUL - - -	10,218	4th June 1844	Washing the products evolved from furnaces.
GRIFFITHS, ROBERT - -	6956	16th Dec. 1835	Machinery for making rivet screw-blanks and bolts.
GRIFFITHS, ROBERT - -	7177	1st Sept. 1836	Machinery for grinding, smoothing, and polishing plate-glass, marble, slate, and stone, also glass-vessels, spangles, and drops.
GRIFFITHS, ROBERT - -	7271	11th Jan. 1837	Manufacture of bars or nuts for screws.
GRIFFITHS, ROBERT - -	10,457	11th Jan. 1845	Manufacture of bolts, railway-pins, spikes, and rivets.
GRIFFITHS, ROBERT - -	10,734	23rd June 1845	Construction of parts of apparatus used in propelling carriages and vessels by the atmosphere; propelling carriages and vessels by atmospheric pressure.
GRIFFITHS, ROBERT - -	11,129	11th Mar. 1846	Apparatus applicable to the working of atmospheric and other railways, canals, and mines; transmitting gas for lighting railways and other places.
GRIFFITHS, ROBERT - -	12,769	13th Sept. 1849	Steam-engines; propelling vessels.
GRIFFITHS, ROBERT - -	14,077	20th April 1852	Apparatus for improving and restoring human hair.
GRIFFITHS, THOMAS - -	6557	15th Feb. 1834	Manufacture of tea-kettles and other articles usually made of copper, copper tinned or plated, iron tinned, or any other metal or metals.
GRIFFITHS, THOMAS - -	8833	8th Feb. 1841	Dish-covers made of iron covered with tin.
GRIFFITHS, THOMAS - -	12,778	20th Sept. 1849	Manufacture of teapots and other vessels, and other articles made of stamped metal.
GRIFFITHS, THOMAS FOXALL -	11,073	3rd Feb. 1846	Stamping and shaping sheet-metal.

Name of Patentee.	Progressive Number.	Date.		Subject-matter of Patent.
GRIMBLE, WILLIAM	5167	14th May	1825	Construction of apparatus for distilling spirituous liquors.
GRIME, JEREMIAH	6079	21st Feb.	1831	Dissolving snow and ice on tramways or railways, to facilitate the passage of engines and carriages thereon.
GRIME, JEREMIAH	7317	7th March	1837	Block-printing.
GRIME, JEREMIAH	7571	21st Feb.	1838	Manufacturing wheels, applicable to locomotive-engines, tenders, and carriages, and to running-wheels for other purposes; apparatus for constructing the same.
GRIMMAN, WILLIAM	8473	15th April	1840	Wood-paving.
GRIMSHAW, JOHN	2089	17th Feb.	1796	Vegetable substances to bleach, or assist in bleaching, printed, painted, stained, or dyed cloths, or other materials.
GRIMSHAW, JOHN	2335	2nd Aug.	1799	Manufacture of ropes and cordage.
GRIMSHAW, JOHN	2651	5th Oct.	1802	Machinery for laying ropes.
GRIMSHAW, JOHN	4669	16th April	1822	Stitching, lacing, or manufacturing flat ropes, by means of rotative machines, worked by steam-engines or other rotative power.
GRIMSLEY, THOMAS	10,179	14th May	1844	Constructing a self-supporting fireproof roof and other parts of buildings, with bricks and tiles formed from an improved machine.
GRIMSLEY, THOMAS	12,884	10th Dec.	1849	Manufacture of bricks and tiles.
GRIMWADE, THOMAS SHIPP	11,703	14th May	1847	Treating milk for purposes of nutriment.
GRINDROD, JONATHAN	13,715	14th Aug.	1851	Machinery for communicating motion from steam-engines - or other motive-power; construction of rudders for vessels.
GRIPENBERG, ODERT	11,291	14th July	1846	Machinery for sowing grain and other seeds.
GRISENTHWAITE, WILLIAM	5128	15th March	1825	Air-engines.
GRISENTHWAITE, WILLIAM	5683	11th Aug.	1828	Making sulphate of magnesia, or Epsom-salts.
GRISENTHWAITE, WILLIAM	5906	27th Feb.	1830	Facilitating the draft or propulsion, or both, of wheeled carriages.
GRISENTHWAITE, WILLIAM	5910	27th Feb.	1830	Steam-engines.
GRISSELL, HENRY	10,560	17th March	1845	Weighing-machines; steel-yards.
GRISSELL, HENRY	13,442	11th Jan.	1851	Coating metals with other metals.
GRIST, JOHN	12,224	29th July	1848	Furnaces and fireplaces.
GRITTON, SEPTIMUS	5752	7th Jan.	1829	Constructing paddles to facilitate their motion through water.
GROCOCK, DAVID WINFIELD	10,216	4th June	1844	Machinery for manufacturing framework knitted or netted work.
GRÖLL, CHARLES	3059	13th July	1807	Harps.
GRÖLL, CHARLES	3531	28th Jan.	1812	Constructing musical-instruments, which afford their tones by friction;—applicable to metallic substances.
GRÖLL, CHARLES	3642	22nd Jan.	1813	Harps.
GROOM, JOHN	10,382	7th Nov.	1844	Machinery for preparing, slubbing, and roving cotton-wool, and other fibrous substances.
GROSE, SAMUEL	14,225	15th July	1852	Machinery for reducing and pulverizing ores, minerals, stones, and other substances.
GROSJEAN, JOHN FREDERICK	7450	20th Oct.	1837	Harps;—applicable to other stringed musical instruments.
GROSSE, TOBIAS LE	309		1692	Tanning skins, and making imitation Russia-leather.

Name of Patentee.	Progressive Number.	Date.	Subject-matter of Patent.
GROUT, JOSEPH - - -	4614	13th Nov. 1821	Manufacture of crape.
GROUT, PARFAIT - - -	11,125	11th March 1846	Manufacture of plaster of Paris, lamp-black, and coke.
GROVE, JONATHAN - -	2072	22nd Oct. 1795	Lock for guns or fire-arms.
GROVER, HENRY MONTAGUE -	8013	26th March 1839	Brewing by use of a material not hitherto so used.
GROVER, HENRY MONTAGU -	8499	7th May 1840	Retarding and stopping railway-trains.
GROVER, JOHN - - -	2162	7th Feb. 1797	Constructing and fixing coppers, boilers, and furnaces.
GROVES, JOHN - - -	358	28th Nov. 1698	Drying malt upon iron, or iron tinned.
GROVES, JOHN THOMAS -	3224	3rd April 1809	Constructing buildings to save expense, labour, and time, and to secure the buildings from dry rot.
GROVES, PETER - - -	5383	4th July 1826	Making white-lead.
GROVES, PETER - - -	5385	10th July 1826	Making paint or pigment, by preparing and combining a substance with oil or turpentine and other ingredients.
GRUBB, ROBERT - - -	1158	13th June 1777	Medicine, called "Friar's Drops," for the cure of the venereal disease, scurvy, rheumatism, strangury, and gleets.
GRUBB, ROBERT - - -	1930	15th Jan. 1793	Human restorative or nervous corroborant drops, for invigorating and repairing the tone of the animal fluids and solids, correcting natural irregularities, debilities, or weaknesses, eradicating hypochondriacism and impediments of the animal functions, thus restoring and preserving health and vigour of body, and serenity of mind.
GRUBB, THOMAS - - -	10,549	11th March 1845	Bank-notes; machinery connected therewith;—in part applicable to cheques, bills, and other documents.
GRUBBE, JAMES ANDREW HUNT	5600	9th Jan. 1828	Transmitting-heat wall for the ripening of fruit.
GRUCHY, CHARLES DE - -	249	9th Jan. 1686	Making writing and printing paper, and printing His Majesty's arms thereon.
GRUNDY, EDMUND - - -	12,622	29th May 1849	Machinery for preparing wool for spinning; machinery for spinning wool and other fibrous substances.
GRUNDY, GEORGE - - -	11,562	8th Feb. 1847	Furnaces; flues and tiles used in the construction thereof.
GRYLLS, JOHN - - -	8767	31st Dec. 1840	Machinery used, for raising and lowering weights.
GRYLLS, JOHN ISAIAH -	11,234	2nd June 1846	Locomotive and other engines and carriages.
GRYLLS, THOMAS - - -	2451	15th Nov. 1800	Stop-cock for barrels and other vessels.
GUALTERAI, ANTHONY - -	308	6th Sept. 1744	Producing sweet, fine, and wholesome oil from a vegetable, and which will be especially useful in the manufacturing of wool.
GUBBINS, Major-General JOSEPH	5984	18th Aug. 1830	Propelling and giving motion to machinery.
GUBIN, NICHOLAS - - -	209	6th Dec. 1679	Making Normandy window-glass.
GUERIMAND, JAMES - -	1133	9th Sept. 1776	Machine for measuring a ship's way with more accuracy than the log-line. "Marine Perambulator."
GUERIN, PIERRE RENE -	12,538	28th March 1849	Steering ships and other vessels.
GUEST, BARNETT - - -	1914	30th Oct. 1792	Manufacturing shoes and boots with soles of prepared leather, and fastening them with spring-fastenings.

Name of Patentee.	Progressive Number.	Date.		Subject-matter of Patent.
GUEST, JAMES, jun. - -	8293	2nd Dec.	1839	Locks and other fastenings.
GUEST, JOSEPH MASON - -	3156	30th July	1808	Mill for twisting thread for various purposes.
GUEST, JOSIAH JOHN - -	6379	31st Jan.	1833	Reducing iron-ore and other materials containing iron, to "Finers."
GUEST, Sir JOSIAH JOHN -	8518	28th May	1840	Manufacture of iron and other metals.
GUEST, THOMAS ROBERT -	2510	2nd June	1801	Boxes to contain articles for drawing and painting; arranging colours in the said boxes.
GUESTIER, JAMES - - -	5293	17th Nov.	1825	Making paper from certain substances.
GUICHARD, EDOUARD AUGUSTE [DESIRE.	11,095	17th Feb.	1846	Printing calico and other fabrics.
GUIGUES, EDOUARD - -	10,353	17th Oct.	1844	Printing on leather and skins.
GUILLIOTTE, CLAUDE - -	6073	11th Feb.	1831	Rack applicable to the battens of looms or machinery for weaving plain or figured ribbons.
GUILLOUET, VICTOR HYA- [CINTHE.	13,544	10th March	1851	Processes for increasing, on manufactured fabrics, the several shades of indigo.
GUITARD, CHARLES FREDERICK	9455	31st Aug.	1842	Construction of railways.
GULLETT, CHRISTOPHER -	1044	17th June	1773	Hydraulic-engine, worked by water, for drawing up ores and other weights from mines and other deep places, in lieu of whims and cranes.
GULLETT, CHRISTOPHER - [Gullet, Christopher.]	1460	15th Jan.	1785	"Eölian-Engines" for working pumps, mills, gins, whims, cranes, and other machines, by the power of wind and condensed air, for the purposes of draining and working mines, quarries, and other works, and for raising or forcing water to any height; also for working corn-mills, saw-mills, and other mills, and for other purposes.
GULLETT, CHRISTOPHER -	1944	1st April	1793	Remedy for expelling the gout from the head, stomach, or any vital part, assuaging the paroxysms, and curing the disease, without medicine, plaster, or other application, internally or externally.
GUNBY, DAY - - - -	2248	6th July	1798	Weights, bolts, and springs for desks, tables, chairs, stools, tambour-frames, bedsteads, and various other articles.
GUNBY, JOHN - - -	4908	28th Feb.	1824	Process of preparing a certain material as a substitute for leather.
GUNBY, JOHN - - -	4939	14th April	1824	Manufacturing cases for knives, scissors, and other articles.
GUNBY, JOHN - - -	6072	11th Feb.	1831	Combining glass with metals or other substances, applicable to various useful and ornamental purposes.
GUNDRY, ISRAEL - - -	4405	1st Nov.	1819	Application of certain gases or vapours to certain useful purposes.
GUNN, JAMES - - -	5017	14th Oct.	1824	Wheeled-carriages.
GUNTER, HENRY - - -	8776	6th Jan.	1841	Preserving animal and vegetable substances.
GUNTHER, JOHN HENRY AN- [THONY.	5673	10th July	1828	Piano-fortes.
GUPPY, SAMUEL - - -	2133	19th Aug.	1796	Cutting and heading nails by two several engines.
GUPPY, SAMUEL - - -	2800	19th Dec.	1804	Machines for cutting, heading, and finishing nails; mode of working the same.
GUPPY, SAMUEL - - -	8180	1st Aug.	1839	Process and apparatus used in the manufacture of soap.

Name of Patentee.	Progressive Number.	Date.	Subject-matter of Patent.
GUPPY, SARAH - - -	3405	4th March 1811	Erecting and constructing bridges and railroads without arches or sterlings, whereby the danger of being washed away by floods is avoided.
GUPPY, SARAH - - -	3549	14th March 1812	Tea and coffee urns.
GUPPY. SARAH - - -	6186	27th Oct. 1831	Applying and arranging certain articles, parts or pieces of cabinet work, upholstery, and other articles commonly applied to bedsteads and hangings, also others not hitherto so applied.
GUPPY, THOMAS RICHARD -	5028	4th Nov. 1824	Masting vessels.
GUPPY, THOMAS RICHARD -	5916	6th March 1830	Apparatus for granulating sugar.
GUPPY, THOMAS RICHARD -	9779	15th June 1843	Building metal-ships and other vessels.
GURLT, ADOLF FREDERICK -	13,283	10th Oct. 1850	Extracting silver from argentiferous minerals.
GURNEY, GOLDSWORTHY -	5068	11th Jan. 1825	Finger keyed musical-instrument in the use of which a performer can hold or prolong the notes and increase or modify the tone at pleasure.
GURNEY, GOLDSWORTHY -	5170	14th May 1825	Apparatus for propelling carriages on common roads or on railways.
GURNEY, GOLDSWORTHY -	5270	21st Oct. 1825	Apparatus for raising and generating steam.
GURNEY, GOLDSWORTHY -	5554	11th Oct. 1827	Locomotive-engines and the apparatus connected therewith.
GURNEY, GOLDSWORTHY -	6483	7th Oct. 1833	Musical-instruments.
GURNEY, GOLDSWORTHY -	8098	8th June 1839	Apparatus for producing and distributing light.
GURNEY, GOLDSWORTHY -	8902	25th March 1841	Production and diffusion of light.
GURNEY, GOLDSWORTHY -	9451	18th Aug. 1842	Apparatus for producing, regulating, and dispersing light and heat.
GURNEY, RICHARD - - -	9163	25th Nov. 1841	Cutting wood and incrustating the same so as to present a sure footing for horses, also for other purposes.
GUSTAFSSON, GUSTAF VICTOR	11,294	14th July 1846	Steam-engines.
GUTHARD, DANIEL - -	221	29th July 1682	Manufacture of draped milled-stockings.
GUTHRIE, GEORGE - - -	13,564	24th March 1851	Machinery for digging, tilling, or working land.
GUTTERIDGE, WILLIAM - -	4890	19th Jan. 1824	Clarionet.
GUTTERIDGE, WILLIAM - -	6112	18th May 1834	Apparatus for distilling, and for other purposes.
GUTTERIDGE, WILLIAM - -	6353	21st Dec. 1832	Apparatus for manufacturing and refining sugar and other extracts;—applicable to other purposes.
GUY, JOHN - - - -	5387	14th July 1826	Preparing straw and grass to be used in the manufacture of hats and bonnets.
GUY, WILLIAM AUGUSTUS -	10,203	25th May 1844	Ventilation.
GUYNEMER, CHARLES - -	7025	8th March 1836	Piano-fortes.
GWYNNE, GEORGE - - -	7231	22nd Nov. 1836	Manufacture of sugar.
GWYNNE, GEORGE - - -	8423	10th March 1840	Manufacture of candles; operating upon oils and fats.
GWYNNE, GEORGE - - -	8681	5th Nov. 1840	Manufacture of candles; operating upon oils and fats.
GWYNNE, GEORGE - - -	9944	16th Nov. 1843	Manufacture of candles; apparatus for and processes of treating fatty and other substances for making candles and for other uses.

Name of Patentee.	Progressive Number.	Date.	Subject-matter of Patent.
GWYNNE, GEORGE - - -	10,000	28th Dec. 1843	Manufacture of candles; treating fatty and oily matters to obtain products for the manufacture of candles and for other uses.
GWYNNE, GEORGE - - -	10,191	20th May 1844	Treating certain fatty or oily matters; manufacture of candles and soap.
GWYNNE, GEORGE - - -	10,365	29th Oct. 1844	Manufacture of night-lights.
GWYNNE, GEORGE - - -	10,371	31st Oct. 1844	Treating fatty and oily matters; and making candles.
GWYNNE, GEORGE - - -	10,435	12th Dec. 1844	Treating fatty and oily matters; manufacture of candles.
GWYNNE, GEORGE - - -	10,551	13th March 1845	Manufacture of candles when palm-oil is used.
GWYNNE, GEORGE - - -	10,664	10th May 1845	Treating certain inflammable matters; manufacture of candles and soap.
GWYNNE, GEORGE - - -	10,870	10th Oct. 1845	Manufacture of soap.
GWYNNE, GEORGE - - -	11,008	20th Dec. 1845	Treating inflammable matters; manufacture of candles.
GWYNNE, GEORGE - - -	11,146	25th March 1846	Producing light; materials and apparatus applicable thereto; treating fatty and oily matters.
GWYNNE, GEORGE - - -	12,981	27th Feb. 1850	Manufacture of sugar.
GWYNNE, GEORGE - - -	13,887	31st Dec. 1851	Treating fatty and oily matters; manufacture of lamps, candles, night-lights, and soap.
GWYNNE, JOHN - - -	13,212	5th Aug. 1850	Obtaining motive-power; applying the same to giving motion to machinery.
GWYNNE, JOHN - - -	13,577	31st March 1851	Machinery for pumping, forcing, and exhausting steam, fluids, and gases; adaptation of the same for producing motion, and to the saturation, separation, and decomposition of substances.
GWYNNE, LAWRENCE - -	2940	6th June 1806	Chain and common pumps, whereby the latter will act as a fire-engine for sea and land purposes.
GYE, FREDERICK - - -	10,960	20th Nov. 1845	Moulding sugar.
GYE, FREDERICK, jun. - -	9399	21st June 1842	Binding pamphlets, papers, and other documents.
GYE, FREDERICK, jun. - -	10,999	10th Dec. 1845	Preparing aërated water; vessels to contain aërated and mineral water.

H.

HAACKE, CHRISTIAN WILHEM [BARON VAN.	1015	30th April 1772	Extracting and making (from a certain mineral) tar and oil, intended and used for the bottoms and other parts of ships and navigable vessels; also extracting vitriol, saltpetre, lampblack, and caput-mortuum from the said mineral.
HAACKE, CHRISTIAN WILHEM [BARON VAN.	1049	30th July 1773	Composition for manuring and improving arable land, meadow and pasture ground, ("Baron Van Haake's Composition.")
HAAS, JACOB BERNARD	1385	22nd Aug. 1783	Air-pump.

Name of Patentee.	Progressive Number.	Date.	Subject-matter of Patent.
HACKETT, JOHN - - -	11,989	8th Dec.　1847	Manufacturing pill-boxes.
HACKING, JOSEPH - - -	13,012	23rd March 1850	Steam-engines and apparatus connected therewith.
HACKING, RICHARD - -	8426	13th March 1840	Machinery for drawing, slubbing, roving, and spinning cotton-wool, flax, silk, and other fibrous substances.
HACKING, RICHARD - -	8433	16th March 1840	Machinery for spinning cotton and other fibrous substances.
HACKWOOD, WILLIAM - -	2818	5th Feb.　1805	Making windows and lights.
HACKWORTH, JOHN WESLEY -	12,892	15th Dec.　1849	Locomotive and other engines.
HACKWORTH, THOMAS - -	11,605	3rd March 1847	Locomotive and other boilers.
HACKWORTH, TIMOTHY - -	7233	22nd Nov.　1836	Steam-engines.
HACKWORTH, TIMOTHY - -	12,892	15th Dec.　1849	Locomotive and other engines.
HADDAN, JOHN COOPE - -	7675	7th June　1838	Warming, lighting, and ventilating.
HADDAN, JOHN COOPE - -	7784	25th Aug.　1838	Construction of carriages to be used on railways; method of forming the same into trains.
HADDAN, JOHN COOPE - -	7946	22nd Jan.　1839	Machinery for propelling vessels and boats by steam or other power.
HADDAN, JOHN COOPE - -	8243	17th Oct.　1839	Construction of wheels for carriages to be used on railways.
HADDAN, JOHN COOPE - -	9261	15th Feb.　1842	Steam-engines and railway-carriages.
HADDAN, JOHN COOPE - -	9953	21st Nov.　1843	Manufacturing papier-maché and other articles made of vegetable pulp.
HADDAN, JOHN COOPE - -	10,609	14th April 1845	Preparing sleepers, chairs, and spikes, and constructing wheels for railways.
HADDAN, JOHN COOPE - -	11,649	8th April　1847	Wheeled-carriages; panels and springs for carriages and for other purposes.
HADDAN, JOHN COOPE - -	11,694	6th May　1847	Railway chairs and switches; trenails or fastenings; machinery for preparing railway-sleepers.
HADDAN, JOHN COOPE - -	12,125	15th April 1848	Manufacturing wheels for railways.
HADDAN, JOHN COOPE - -	12,404	5th Jan.　1849	Railway-wheels.
HADDAN, JOHN COOPE - -	13,162	3rd July　1850	Construction of carriages and wheels; brickwork.
HADDAN, JOHN COOPE - -	13,603	26th April 1851	Permanent way of railways; railway and other carriages; manufacture of papier-maché for making carriages and other articles.
HADDEN, ALEXANDER - -	4384	22nd June 1819	Manufacture for carpeting.
HADDEN, JAMES, junior - -	4307	12th Nov.　1818	Preparing, roving, and spinning wool.
HADDOCK, URIAH - - -	4263	19th May　1818	Manufacture of sulphuric-acid.
HADDOCK, URIAH - -	4365	4th May　1819	Producing inflammable gas from pit-coal.
HADDOCK, WILLIAM - -	4012	23rd March 1816	Paint, colour, and cement for painting, colouring, and preserving houses, ships, and other things.
HADEN, BENJAMIN - -	2686	28th Feb.　1803	Manufacturing bagging for packing nails, and for other purposes.
HADEN, GEORGE - - -	5773	2nd March 1829	Machinery for dressing cloths.
HADEN, GEORGE - - -	6561	24th Feb.　1834	Machinery applicable to the manufacturing of woollen-cloth.
HADEN, GEORGE - - -	7827	8th Oct.　1838	Manufacturing soap or composition for the felting and other processes employed in the manufacture of woollen-cloth, and for other purposes.

Name of Patentee.	Progressive Number.	Date.	Subject-matter of Patent.
HADEN, GEORGE - - -	9259	15th Feb. 1842	Apparatus for warming and ventilating buildings.
HADLEY, GILBERT - • -	577	4th June 1741	Piece of ordnance or cannon, to be charged and discharged eight times in a minute.
HADLEY, JOHN - • -	315	3rd March 1693	Obtaining a motive-power from the ebbing and flowing of the water operating on a vessel floating thereon, which by its rising or falling gives motion to mills, engines, &c.; horizontal-wheels, to be moved by water or by wind; raising and letting down vertical-wheels, so as to render them useful at all heights of the water; engines for drawing several machines and carriages, and to be moved by wind instead of horses; measuring time by means of one wheel, and with more accuracy than with a multiplicity of wheels.
HADLEY, JOHN - • -	550	22nd Nov. 1734	Quadrant for taking at sea the altitude of the sun, moon, or stars, and also any other angles; level to be fixed to a quadrant, for taking meridional altitudes at sea.
HADLEY, MOSES - • -	634	12th July 1748	Double concave-boiler, with a flange, for raising steam by fire, to work atmospheric-engines used for raising water, and for other purposes.
HAGEN, THOMAS - • -	9016	7th July 1841	Bagatelle-board.
HAGGAR, MORYS - • -	11,709	22nd May 1847	Apparatus for protecting life and property in cases of shipwreck.
HAGNER, GEORGE FREDERICK	4211	27th Jan. 1818	Manufacturing the pigments called white-lead and verdigris.
HAGUE, CHARLES - • -	10,725	19th June 1845	Machines for slubbing, roving, or preparing to be spun, cotton and other fibrous substances; apparatus for lubricating shafts and bearings in such machines, for the purpose of reducing friction;—applicable to other shafting and machinery.
HAGUE, JOHN - • -	4048	27th July 1816	Expelling molasses or syrup from sugars.
HAGUE, JOHN - • -	4181	28th Nov. 1817	Expelling molasses and syrup from sugars; refining sugars.
HAGUE, JOHN - • -	4453	9th May 1820	Heating hothouses and other buildings; boiling liquids.
HAGUE, JOHN - • -	4466	2nd June 1820	Preparing materials for making pottery-ware, tiles, and bricks.
HAGUE, JOHN - • -	4471	3rd June 1820	Making and constructing steam-engines.
HAGUE, JOHN - • -	4641	29th Jan. 1822	Making metallic pipes, tubes, or cylinders, by the application and arrangement of apparatus of certain machinery and mechanical powers.
HAGUE, JOHN - • -	5546	30th Aug. 1827	Working cranes or tilt-hammers.
HAGUE, JOHN - • -	5725	6th Dec. 1828	Expelling molasses or syrup from sugar.
HAGUE, JOHN - • -	7088	9th May 1836	Raising water from mines, excavations, holds of ships or vessels and from other places, by the application and arrangement of a well-known power; applying such power to certain machinery, for giving motion to the same.
HAGUE, JOHN - • -	7369	10th May 1837	Wheels for carriages.

Name of Patentee.	Progressive Number.	Date.	Subject-matter of Patent.
HAGUE, MATTHEW - - -	12,164	26th May 1848	Machinery for twisting and doubling cotton-yarns and other fibrous materials.
HAGUE, SAMUEL - - -	1777	29th Oct. 1790	Machinery to be added and affixed to a stocking-frame, for making elastic double knit framework pieces, for hose or stockings, waistcoats, breeches, gloves, purses, and various sorts of work, either with silk, cotton, cotton and silk, worsted, worsted and silk, thread, and yarn.
HAHNEMAN, MARIE MELANIE [D'HERVILLY.	11,671	27th April 1847	Instruments for writing.
HAIG, ALEXANDER - - -	10,827	4th Sept. 1845	Machinery for ventilation, and other similar purposes.
HAIG, ALEXANDER - - -	12,760	6th Sept. 1849	Apparatus for exhausting and driving atmospheric-air and other gases, and giving motion to other machinery.
HAIGH, EDWARD - - -	12,152	9th May 1848	Measuring water or other fluid.
HAINES, THOMAS - - -	13,629	10th May 1851	Manufacture of knit and looped fabrics, and raising the pile thereon.
HAINES, JOB - - - -	10,050	13th Feb. 1844	Making or manufacturing links for the construction of flat chains, used for mining and other purposes.
HAINES, MICHAEL JOHN -	12,660	14th June 1849	Manufacturing packing for steam-engines, cylinders, and other purposes ;—partly applicable to manufacturing waterproof fabrics.
HAINES, MICHAEL JOHN -	12,828	2nd Nov. 1849	Manufacturing bands for driving machinery ; hose or pipes and buffers for railway purposes.
HAINES, RICHARD - - -	202	18th April 1678	Spinning-engine for spinning linen and worsted thread.
HAINES, RICHARD - - -	231	6th Feb. 1684	Preparing, improving, and meliorating cyder, perry, and the juice of wildings, crabs, cherries, gooseberries, currants and mulberries, by adding to them spirits of such juices, or other spirits, either with or without sweets or sugars.
HAINES, RICHARD - - -	10,050	13th Feb. 1844	Making or manufacturing links for the construction of flat chains used for mining and other purposes.
HAINSSELIN, PIERRE NICHOLAS	6290	26th July 1832	Machine or motive-power for giving motion to machinery ("Hainsselin's motive-power").
HAKEWILL, JAMES - -	3217	20th March 1809	Construction of tables, chairs, and stools for domestic, military, and naval service ; packing the same.
HALAHAN, THOMAS - -	5379	22nd June 1826	Machinery for working ordnance.
HALE, ELISHA - - -	8016	27th March 1839	Umbrellas and parasols.
HALE, JAMES LYSANDER -	11,426	22nd Oct. 1846	Sewerage and drainage ; apparatus connected therewith ;—in part applicable to steam-engines.
HALE, JAMES WEBSTER - -	10,887	16th Oct. 1845	Machinery for cleaning or freeing wool and other fibrous materials from burs and other extraneous substances.
HALE, JOHN - - -	10,849	2nd Oct. 1845	Guns.
HALE, MICHAEL - - -	254	13th Aug. 1687	Manufacture of milled lead for sheathing and preservation of ships and other articles.
HALE, THOMAS - - -	145	22nd April 1664	Making a valuable metal, as sweet, clean, and wholesome as silver, by mixing a certain stone with chargeable ingredients ; to be used for making various vessels.

Name of Patentee.	Progressive Number.	Date.	Subject-matter of Patent.
HALE, THOMAS - - -	254	13th Aug. 1687	Manufacture of milled lead for sheathing and preservation of ships and other articles.
HALE, WARREN STORMES -	14,215	8th July 1852	Manufacture of night-lights or mortars.
HALE, WILLIAM - - -	5594	22nd Dec. 1827	Machinery for propelling vessels.
HALE, WILLIAM - - -	5879	12th Jan. 1830	Machine for raising and forcing water for propelling vessels.
HALE, WILLIAM - - -	6180	13th Oct. 1831	Machinery for propelling vessels;—applicable for raising or forcing fluids.
HALE, WILLIAM - - -	6649	26th July 1834	Windmills;—applicable to other purposes.
HALE, WILLIAM - - -	6786	11th March 1835	Boilers or apparatus for producing motive-power.
HALE, WILLIAM - - -	7040	22nd March 1836	Machinery applicable to vessels propelled by steam or other power;—partly applicable to other purposes.
HALE, WILLIAM - - -	7586	8th March 1838	Steam-engines and apparatus connected therewith; machinery for propelling vessels.
HALE, WILLIAM - - -	9047	13th Aug. 1841	Cases and magazines for gunpowder.
HALE, WILLIAM - - -	9545	8th Dec. 1842	Producing aërated-liquors.
HALE, WILLIAM - - -	10,008	11th Jan. 1844	Rockets.
HALEY, ABRAHAM - - -	13,349	14th Nov. 1850	Looms for weaving.
HALEY, CHARLES - - -	2132	17th Aug. 1796	Marine time-keeper for ascertaining the longitude at sea.
HALEY, JOSEPH - - -	7331	28th March 1837	Machinery for cutting, planing, and turning metals and other substances.
HALEY, JOSEPH - - -	8768	31st Dec. 1840	Lifting-jack for raising heavy bodies;—applicable to packing or compressing goods or other substances.
HALEY, JOSEPH - - -	9238	27th Jan. 1842	Machinery for cutting, punching, and compressing metals.
HALIBURTON, ALEXANDER -	4231	27th Feb. 1818	Steam-engines and boilers.
HALL, ALFRED - - -	10,845	2nd Oct. 1845	Machinery for making, moulding, or manufacturing bricks, tiles, and other articles from earthy or plastic materials.
HALL, ANDREW - - -	6657	12th Aug. 1834	Construction of looms for weaving by hand or power.
HALL, EDWARD - - -	9212	11th Jan. 1842	Steam-boiler.
HALL, EDWARD - - -	10,943	15th Nov. 1845	Double cylinder condensing-engine.
HALL, GEORGE - - -	1457	29th Nov. 1784	Construction of chapes for shoe and other buckles.
HALL, GEORGE - - -	2561	28th Nov. 1801	Making elastic fastenings for the shoes, &c.
HALL, GEORGE - - -	3361	18th July 1810	Working and making spoons, forks and such other articles of silver, gold, or other metals, as are usually stamped by dies of any description; instruments for the purpose.
HALL, GEORGE FREDERICK -	11,060	29th Jan. 1846	Machinery for writing and booking, numbering, cutting, checking, and expediting the delivery and receipt of pawnbrokers' duplicates, pass-tickets, and other like documents.
HALL, HORACE - - -	3855	17th Nov. 1814	Preparing and spinning hemp, flax, and other substances containing fibre.
HALL, JAMES - - - -	2701	27th April 1803	Looms.
HALL, JAMES - - - -	2728	3rd Aug. 1803	Loom, with a method of perpetually taking away the articles woven therein as they are woven.

Name of Patentee.	Progressive Number.	Date.	Subject-matter of Patent.
HALL, JAMES - - - -	3275	14th Nov. 1809	Making and manufacturing shives or shivers, pulley-wheels, and various other articles, from compositions of earths and minerals, which render them more durable than wood.
HALL, JAMES - - - -	3356	3rd July 1810	Making a material from the twigs or branches of broom, mallows, rushes, and other shrubs of the like species, to be used for the purposes and as a substitute for flax or hemp.
HALL, JAMES - - - -	8349	21st Jan. 1840	Beds, mattrasses, and apparatus applicable to bedsteads, couches, and chairs.
HALL, JAMES - - - -	12,979	25th Feb. 1850	Looms for weaving.
HALL, JAMES, jun. - -	5597	2nd Jan. 1828	Dyeing piece-goods by machinery.
HALL, JOHN - - - -	3146	28th June 1808	Manufacturing ropes and other cordage; coiling lines in whale-boats.
HALL, JOHN - - - -	4787	22nd April 1823	Machinery for expressing oil from linseed, rapeseed, or other oleaginous seeds or substances, by pressure.
HALL, JOHN - - - -	6033	9th Nov. 1830	Machine for manufacturing paper.
HALL, JOHN - - - -	6148	4th Aug. 1831	Machinery used in the manufacture of paper.
HALL, JOHN - - - -	6517	6th Dec. 1833	Filters for sugar and other liquids.
HALL, JOHN - - - -	7155	27th July 1836	Machinery for dressing, getting-up, or finishing large pieces of lace-nets, called bobbin-net, or twist-net, warp-net, and fattings.
HALL, JOHN - - - -	7500	5th Dec. 1837	Machinery whereby cloth or woven fabrics may be stretched and dried in an extended state.
HALL, JOHN - - - -	9168	9th Dec. 1841	Construction of boilers for generating steam; application of steam to mechanical power.
HALL, JOHN HEATON - -	8301	5th Dec. 1839	Preserving and rendering woollen and other fabrics and leather waterproof.
HALL, JOSEPH - - -	2573	16th Jan. 1802	Hammer for guns, pistols, and other fire-arms, which contains the prime and preserves the same from damp.
HALL, JOSEPH - - -	5551	11th Oct. 1827	Manufacturing metallic-cocks for drawing off liquids.
HALL, JOSEPH - - -	7110	7th June 1836	Pumps.
HALL, JOSEPH - - -	7175	17th Aug. 1836	Manufacturing salt.
HALL, JOSEPH - - -	7778	21st Aug. 1838	Making iron.
HALL, JOSEPH - - -	7804	13th Sept. 1838	Manufacture of salt.
HALL, JOSEPH - - -	8784	14th Jan. 1841	Seed and dust disperser;—applicable to the freeing of corn and other plants from insects.
HALL, JOSEPH - - -	9402	6th July 1842	Machinery for tilling land.
HALL, JOSEPH - - -	10,271	24th July 1844	Manufacture of horse-shoe nails.
HALL, RICHARD - - -	5775	10th March 1829	Composition, applicable to certain fabrics or substances from which may be manufactured boots, shoes, and other articles.
HALL, ROBERT - - -	3675	30th March 1813	Machine for dressing, getting-up, or finishing frame-work knitted goods, manufactured on the stocking-frame.
HALL, SAMUEL - - -	3675	30th March 1813	Machine for dressing, getting-up, or finishing frame-work knitted goods, manufactured on the stocking-frame.
HALL, SAMUEL - - -	4177	3rd Nov. 1817	Method of improving thread or yarn of every description, whether vegetable, animal, or other substance.

Name of Patentee.	Progressive Number.	Date.	Subject-matter of Patent.
HALL, SAMUEL - - -	4178	3rd Nov. 1817	Method of improving lace or net, or other fabrics with holes and interstices, made from thread or yarn, whether fabricated from vegetable, animal, or other substances.
HALL, SAMUEL - - -	4559	9th May 1821	Manufacturing starch.
HALL, SAMUEL - - -	4779	18th April 1823	Method of improving lace, net, muslin, calico, and other manufactured goods, whose fabric is composed of holes or interstices; also thread or yarn, whether fabricated from flax, cotton, silk, worsted, or other substance or mixture of substances.
HALL, SAMUEL - - -	4935	8th April 1824	Steam-engine.
HALL, SAMUEL - - -	5207	8th July 1825	Pusher twist or bobbin-net machine.
HALL, SAMUEL - • -	5659	31st May 1828	Generating steam and various gases, to produce motive-power; apparatus for the same and other purposes.
HALL, SAMUEL • - -	6204	22nd Dec. 1831	Piston and valve for steam, gas, and other engines; lubricating the pistons, piston-rods, and valves or cocks of such engines; condensing the steam, and supplying water to the boilers of such engines.
HALL, SAMUEL - - -	6359	9th Jan. 1833	Lubricating the pistons, piston-rods, and valves of steam-engines; condensing the steam of such engines as are worked by a vacuum produced by condensation; a method of condensation applicable to other purposes.
HALL, SAMUEL - - -	6556	13th Feb. 1834	Steam-engines.
HALL, SAMUEL - - -	7135	24th June 1836	Propelling vessels; steam-engines; working parts of the same;—partly applicable to other purposes.
HALL, SAMUEL - - -	7754	30th July 1838	Steam-engines; heating or evaporating fluids or gases; generating steam.
HALL, SAMUEL - - -	8233	7th Oct. 1839	Machinery for propelling.
HALL, SAMUEL - - -	8792	14th Jan. 1841	Combustion of fuel and smoke.
HALL, SAMUEL - - -	9345	9th May 1842	Combustion of fuel and smoke.
HALL, SAMUEL - - -	10,531	20th Feb. 1845	Steam-engines, boilers, furnaces and flues; consuming fuel and preventing smoke; propelling vessels.
HALL, SAMUEL - - -	12,527	19th March 1849	Apparatus for effecting the combustion of fuel, also for consuming smoke, and preventing explosions of steam-boilers.
HALL, SAMUEL - - -	13,444	11th Jan. 1851	Manufacture of starch and gums.
HALL, SAMUEL - - -	14,125	17th May 1852	Construction of cocks, taps, or valves.
HALL, SAMUEL SANDERSON -	7760	3rd Aug. 1838	Preserving certain vegetable substances from decay.
HALL, THOMAS - - -	5551	11th Oct. 1827	Manufacturing metallic-cocks for drawing off liquids.
HALL, THOMAS - - -	7974	21st Feb. 1839	Combination of parts forming a furnace, for consuming smoke and economizing fuel;—applicable to steam-engine boilers and other furnaces.
HALL, THOMAS DEHANY -	4425	18th Dec. 1819	Dyeing cloths and other substances; preparing dyes for that purpose.
HALL, THOMAS YOUNG - -	13,980	23rd Feb. 1852	Screens for screening coal or other substances.

Name of Patentee.	Progressive Number.	Date.	Subject-matter of Patent.
HALL, WALTER　-　-　-	4085	21st Nov. 1816	Making soft lead out of hard lead or slag lead.
HALL, WILLIAM　-　-　-	4444	11th April 1820	Manufacturing hafts, handles, or hilts for knives, forks, swords, or other instruments.
HALL, WILLIAM MATHERS　-	11,253	22nd June 1846	Sliding gas-pendants, lamps, lustres, and chandeliers.
HALL, WILLIAM SANDFORD　-	7519	19th Dec. 1837	Paddle-wheels.
HALL, WILLIAM WILMOT　-	5448	15th Jan. 1827	Engine for moving and propelling ships, boats, carriages, mills, and machinery.
HALLADAY, STEPHEN　-　-	2254	3rd Aug. 1798	Draught or moving of carriages.
HALLAM, EDWARD　-　-	1151	10th April 1777	Engine for spinning, drawing, and twisting cotton-wool, and the wool of sheep, also silk and flax.
HALLEN, HARDING　-　-	13,626	10th May 1851	Gas-burners.
HALLETT, JOHN HOTHERSALL	6771	25th Feb. 1835	Construction of cocks or taps for drawing off fluids.
HALLEWELL, BENJAMIN　-	13,735	4th Sept. 1851	Drying malt.
HALLEY, EDMUND -　-　-	279	7th Oct. 1691	Engine for conveying air into a diving-vessel, to enable several persons at the same time to live and work safely under water for many hours, for the purpose of finding gold, silver, bullion, money, and goods, lost at sea.
HALLEY, WILLIAM　-　-	5115	5th March 1825	Construction of forges; bellows or apparatus to be used therewith or separately.
HALLIDAY, ANDREW PATON -	12,275	28th Sept. 1848	Manufacture of pyroligneous-acid.
HALLIDAY, FRANCIS　-　-	5308	9th Dec. 1825	Machinery to be operated upon by steam.
HALLIDAY, FRANCIS　-　-	5351	25th April 1826	"Wind-guard," or machine for preventing the inconvenience arising from smoke in chimneys.
HALLIDAY, FRANCIS　-　-	5407	25th Aug. 1826	Raising or forcing water.
HALLIDAY, FRANCIS　-　-	5414	4th Oct. 1826	Apparatus used in drawing boots on and off.
HALLIDAY, JOSEPH　-　-	3334	5th May 1810	Bugle-horn.
HALLILEY, EDWARD　-　-	8355	21st Jan. 1840	Machinery for raising pile on woollen and other fabrics.
HALLIWELL, ROBERT　-　-	12,232	8th Aug. 1848	Machinery for preparing and spinning cotton and other fibrous substances.
HALLUM, EPHRAIM　-　-	13,780	22nd Oct. 1851	Machinery for preparing and spinning cotton and other fibrous substances.
HALPIN, GEORGE, junior　-	8689	7th Nov. 1840	Applying air to lamps.
HALSE, NICHOLAS　-　-	85	23rd July 1635	Making kilns for drying malt and hops, with seacoal, turf, or other fuel, without touching smoke, capable also of being used for cooking, drying, and starching at one time with one fire, and thereby lessening the consumption of wood and straw.
HALSTEAD, JAMES -　-　-	6761	9th Feb. 1835	Paddle-wheels for steam-vessels;—applicable to mill-machinery moved by water.
HAM, JOHN　-　-　-　-	5012	7th Oct. 1824	Manufacturing vinegar.
HAM, JOHN　-　-　-　-	5377	13th June 1826	Process for promoting the action of acetic acid on metallic bodies.
HAM, JOHN　-　-　-　-	8144	6th July 1839	Manufacturing cider and perry.
HAMBLIN, Captain ROBERT　-	517	14th July 1730	Distinguishing lights, for the convenience of sailors, to enable them to ascertain their position by night and day.

Name of Patentee.	Progres-sive Number.	Date.		Subject-matter of Patent.
HAMEL, SEPTIMUS -	9543	8th Dec.	1842	Making reels for reeling cotton and linen thread.
HAMELIN, PETER -	4144	19th July	1817	Making a cement or composition for orna-ments and statues, for making and ce-menting artificial bricks, tiles, and stones, and for erecting, covering, and decorating buildings; mixing, working and mould-ing the cement upon any sort of ma-terials, or working and moulding entire substances therewith.
HAMER, JAMES -	9592	19th Jan.	1850	Propelling vessels.
HAMER, JAMES -	10,588	7th April	1845	Enema syringes; stomach and other pumps.
HAMER, WILLIAM -	13,685	3rd July	1851	Looms for weaving.
HAMER, WILLIAM -	13,818	15th Nov.	1851	Weaving textile fabrics.
HAMILTON, ALEXANDER -	27	25th Nov.	1623	Ploughing, harrowing, sowing, seeding, and setting corn and grain.
HAMILTON, JAMES -	593	14th Sept.	1743	Engine for taking fish.
HAMILTON, JAMES -	6531	23rd Dec.	1833	Machinery for sawing, boring, and manu-facturing wood; — applicable to various purposes.
HAMILTON, JAMES -	12,425	18th Jan.	1849	Cutting wood.
HAMILTON, JAMES -	13,264	28th Sept.	1850	Machinery for sawing, boring, and shaping wood.
HAMILTON, JOHN -	13,365	25th Nov.	1850	Warming and ventilating buildings and structures.
HAMILTON, JOSEPH -	3623	16th Dec.	1812	Applying well known principles in the construction and formation of earthen-wares.
HAMILTON, JOSEPH -	3649	20th Feb.	1813	Constructing and connecting earthen build-ing-materials.
HAMILTON, JOSEPH -	3685	28th April	1813	Machine for making bricks, tiles, and earthenwares.
HAMILTON, JOSEPH -	3727	31st July	1813	Application of earths and other materials to useful purposes.
HAMILTON, SAMUEL HAVEN -	11,343	19th Aug.	1846	Machinery for dredging and excavating.
HAMILTON, WILLIAM FRANCIS	3232	4th May	1809	Preparing soda and other mineral-water, spirituous, acetous, saccharine, and aro-matic liquors.
HAMILTON, WILLIAM FRANCIS	3781	12th Feb.	1814	Optical instruments and apparatus.
HAMILTON, WILLIAM FRANCIS	3819	28th June	1814	Making, also preparation of, soda-water and other liquids impregnated with carbonic-acid gas.
HAMILTON, WILLIAM FRANCIS	5291	12th Nov.	1825	Alloys of metals.
HAMME, JOHN ARIENS VAN -	191	27th Oct.	1676	Making tiles, porcelain, and other earthen-ware, in the way practised in Holland.
HAMMICK, THOMAS -	6094	21st March	1831	Rudders for ships; rudder-hangings.
HAMMOND, WILLIAM FREDE-[RICK.	11,764	22nd June	1847	Steam-engine; machinery for propelling.
HAMOND, CHARLES -	3459	27th June	1811	Machine for sawing, cutting, and planing wood.
HAMOND, Sir GRAHAM EDEN, [Bart.	10,349	14th Oct.	1844	Fastening on and reefing paddle-wheel float-boards, or paddles.
HAMPSON, ROBERT -	8534	9th June	1840	Block-printing on woven fabrics of cotton, linen, silk, or woollen, or any two or more of them intermixed; machinery, appa-ratus, and implements for that purpose.
HANBURY, JOHN -	3624	19th Dec.	1812	Weaving Scotch or Kidderminster carpets.

Name of Patentee.	Progressive Number.	Date.	Subject-matter of Patent.
HANCE, WILLIAM - - -	3003	29th Jan. 1807	Waterproofing beaver and other hats.
HANCHETT, JOHN MARTIN -	4775	12th April 1823	Propelling boats and vessels.
HANCHETT, JOHN MARTIN -	5134	25th March 1825	Looms for making cloths, silks, and different kinds of woven stuffs of various breadths.
HANCOCK, CHARLES - -	7552	25th Jan. 1838	Producing figured surfaces, sunk and in relief; printing therefrom; moulding, stamping, and embossing.
HANCOCK, CHARLES - -	9248	8th Feb. 1842	Printing cotton, silk, woollen, and other stuffs.
HANCOCK, CHARLES - -	9622	31st Jan. 1843	Dyeing and staining cotton, woollen, silk, and other fabrics; and rendering them repellent of water and moisture.
HANCOCK, CHARLES - -	10,185	15th May 1844	Cork and other stoppers; composition which may be used in preference to and as a substitute for cork; manufacturing the same into bungs, stoppers, and other articles.
HANCOCK, CHARLES - -	11,032	12th Jan. 1846	Manufacture of gutta-percha; and its applications alone and in combination with other substances.
HANCOCK, CHARLES - -	11,208	15th May 1846	Gutta-percha and its application, alone and in combination with other substances.
HANCOCK, CHARLES - -	11,575	10th Feb. 1847	Preparation of gutta-percha; its application to manufacturing purposes, alone and in combination with other materials;—applicable to other substances.
HANCOCK, CHARLES - -	11,874	24th Sept. 1847	Preparation of gutta-percha; its application to manufacturing purposes, alone and in combination with other materials.
HANCOCK, CHARLES - -	12,153	11th May 1848	Preparations and compounds of gutta-percha; manufacture of articles and fabrics composed of gutta-percha, alone and in combination with other materials.
HANCOCK, CHARLES - -	12,223	29th July 1848	Apparatus and machinery for giving shape and configuration to plastic substances.
HANCOCK, DANIEL - -	389	13th Nov. 1711	Making iron-boxes for the wheels of carriages. "Open Boxes."
HANCOCK, FREDERICK AUGUS-[TUS LAMB.	10,599	7th April 1845	Rotary steam-engine.
HANCOCK, JAMES - - -	8382	8th Feb. 1840	Forming a fabric, applicable to various uses, by combining caoutchouc or certain compounds thereof, with wood, whalebone, or other fibrous materials manufactured for that purpose, or with metallic substances, manufactured or prepared.
HANCOCK, JAMES - - -	8662	15th Oct. 1840	Raising water and other fluids.
HANCOCK, JAMES - - -	8953	6th May 1841	Manufacturing locks, keys, latches, and other fastenings;—in part applicable to taps for drawing off fluids.
HANCOCK, JAMES LAMB -	10,599	7th April 1845	Rotary steam-engine.
HANCOCK, JOHN - - -	3733	25th Aug. 1813	Construction of carriages; application of a material hitherto unused in the construction thereof.
HANCOCK, JOHN CRANG -	1703	9th Sept. 1789	Machine for cleaning, sifting, and dividing wheat, barley, oats, beans, rye, and all other grain and seeds.
HANCOCK, JOHN CRANG -	1743	13th April 1790	Grand pianoforte, with a spring key touch, German-flute, and harp.

Name of Patentee.	Progres-sive Number.	Date.	Subject-matter of Patent.
HANCOCK, JOHN GREGORY -	2069	15th Oct. 1795	Making and constructing the uprights and crossbars for shop and sash windows, panels, frames, and other such uses.
HANCOCK, JOHN GREGORY -	2102	6th April 1796	Ornamenting paper by embossing or enchasing.
HANCOCK, JOHN GREGORY -	2783	14th Sept. 1804	Forcing or working the bolts of presses or engines used for cutting, pressing, and squeezing metals, horn, tortoiseshell, leather, paper, and other substances.
HANCOCK, JOHN GREGORY [GEORGE.	5440	21st Dec. 1826	Elastic rod for umbrellas and other like purposes.
HANCOCK, JOHN WEBSTER -	12,854	17th Nov. 1849	Manufacture of hosiery goods, or articles composed of knitted fabrics.
HANCOCK, JOHN WEBSTER -	13,629	10th May 1851	Manufacture of knit and looped fabrics, and raising pile thereon.
HANCOCK, JOSEPH - -	1772	18th Aug. 1790	Machine for washing, cleansing, and scouring linen, wool, cotton, silk, or any other commodity.
HANCOCK, THOMAS - -	330	29th Jan. 1694	Extracting and making pitch, tar, and oil, out of a certain stone found in England and Wales.
HANCOCK, THOMAS - -	4451	29th April 1820	Application of a certain material to render various parts of dress and other articles more elastic.
HANCOCK, THOMAS - -	4768	22nd March 1823	Preparation of pitch or tar, separately or in union, by an admixture of other ingredients with either or both of them.
HANCOCK, THOMAS - -	5045	29th Nov. 1824	Making an article as a substitute for leather;—applicable to various other purposes.
HANCOCK, THOMAS - -	5120	15th March 1825	Manufacture to be used as a substitute for leather, and otherwise.
HANCOCK, THOMAS - -	5121	15th March 1825	Rendering ships' bottoms, vessels and other utensils of various manufactures, also porous or fibrous substances, impervious to air and water; coating surfaces of metallic and other bodies.
HANCOCK, THOMAS - -	5122	15th March 1815	Preparation or process of making ropes, cordage, and other articles from hemp, flax, and other fibrous substances.
HANCOCK, THOMAS - -	5970	5th Aug. 1830	Manufacture of certain articles of wearing-apparel, fancy ornaments and figures; rendering certain substances impervious to air and water; protecting the same from being injured by air, water, or moisture.
HANCOCK, THOMAS - -	6849	4th June 1835	Air bed-cushions, and other articles made from caoutchouc, or of cloth or other substance coated or lined with caoutchouc.
HANCOCK, THOMAS - -	7344	18th April 1837	Rendering cloth and other fabrics, partially or entirely, impervious to air and water, by means of caoutchouc.
HANCOCK, THOMAS - -	7549	23rd Jan. 1838	Manufacturing or preparing caoutchouc, alone or in combination with other substances.
HANCOCK, THOMAS - -	9952	21st Nov. 1843	Preparation or manufacture of caoutchouc in combination with other substances, suitable for making leather, cloth, and other fabrics water-proof, and for various other purposes for which caoutchouc is employed.

Name of Patentee.	Progressive Number.	Date.	Subject-matter of Patent.
HANCOCK, THOMAS - -	11,135	18th March 1846	Manufacturing and treating articles of caoutchouc, either alone or in combination with other substances ; means employed in their manufacture.
HANCOCK, THOMAS - -	11,455	19th Nov. 1846	Manufacture of articles where India-rubber or gutta-percha is used.
HANCOCK, THOMAS - -	11,938	2nd Nov. 1847	Fabrics elasticated by gutta-percha, or any of the varieties of caoutchouc.
HANCOCK, THOMAS - -	12,007	30th Dec. 1847	Treating or manufacturing gutta-percha, or any of the varieties of caoutchouc.
HANCOCK, THOMAS GREGORY	7732	12th July 1838	Condensing steam in steam-engines, and supplying their boilers with water thereby formed.
HANCOCK, THOMAS GREGORY	8395	22nd Feb. 1840	Cutting corks, and constructing the necks of bottles.
HANCOCK, WALTER - -	5208	16th July 1825	Making pipes or tubes for the passage or conveyance of fluids.
HANCOCK, WALTER - -	5514	4th July 1827	Steam-engines.
HANCOCK, WALTER - -	6364	15th Jan. 1833	Steam-boilers.
HANCOCK, WALTER - -	7037	21st March 1836	Arrangement and combination of certain mechanical means of propelling vessels through water.
HANCOCK, WALTER - -	7990	6th March 1839	Steam boilers and condensers.
HANCOCK, WALTER - -	8785	14th Jan. 1841	Means of preventing accidents on railways.
HANCOCK, WALTER - -	9935	9th Nov. 1843	Manufacture of caoutchouc, and caoutchouc in combination with other substances ; machinery for preparing caoutchouc and other materials.
HANCOCK, WILLIAM - -	7247	7th Dec. 1836	Bookbinding,
HANCOCK, WILLIAM - -	9301	21st March 1842	Combs and brushes.
HANCOCK, WILLIAM - -	11,869	16th Sept. 1847	Bolts, locks, and other fastenings.
HANCOCK, WILLIAM, junior -	8830	3rd Feb. 1841	Fabric, suitable for making friction-gloves, horse-brushes, and other articles requiring a rough surface.
HANCOCK, WILLIAM, junior -	9537	3rd Dec. 1842	Bands, straps, and cords, for driving machinery, and for other mechanical purposes.
HANCOCK, WILLIAM LAMB -	10,599	7th April 1845	Rotary steam-engine.
HANCORNE, EDWARD - -	5717	16th Oct. 1828	Making nails.
HAND, JOHN - - - -	2002	22nd July 1794	Plating and covering with silver, steel-cutlery in general.
HANDCOCK, ELIAS ROBISON -	7835	17th Oct. 1838	Castors for furniture and for other purposes.
HANDCOCK, ELIAS ROBISON -	8745	18th Dec. 1840	Mechanism applicable to turn-tables for changing the position of carriages on railroads ; also applicable to castors for furniture and other purposes.
HANDCOCK, ELIAS ROBISON -	10,316	12th Sept. 1844	Mechanism applicable to a method of propelling vessels on the water.
HANDCOCK, ELIAS ROBISON -	12,282	12th Oct. 1848	Mechanism applicable to impelling and facilitating the propulsion of vessels in the water ;—also applicable to locomotive engines for railways and for other purposes.
HANDFORD, CHARLES - -	8637	21st Sept. 1840	Edible vegetable preparation called Eupooi ; and mode of manufacturing the same.
HANDFORD, THOMAS - -	3600	25th Sept. 1812	Travelling-trunk.
HANDLEY, WILLIAM - -	12,779	20th Sept. 1849	Railway-breaks.

Name of Patentee.	Progres-sive Number.	Date.	Subject-matter of Patent.
HANDS, SAMUEL - - -	1494	4th Aug. 1785	Making hats and caps of copper, tin, and other metals japanned.
HANDS, SAMUEL - - -	1679	2nd May 1789	Making spring shoe-buckles.
HANDS, SAMUEL - - -	1727	23rd Feb. 1790	Ornamenting buckles, straps, coaches, chaises, phaetons, also harness and accoutrements made of leather or paper.
HANKINSON, CHARLES - -	3521	20th Jan. 1812	Tanning leather by the use of pyroligneous or wood-acid.
HANKSBEE, FRANCIS - -	495	3rd Feb. 1728	Manufacturing copper ores, extracting silver from them, and making brass, to be cast into plates, ingots, rods, kettles, and other utensils, in metal moulds, by a new way of mixing the copper with calamy and charcoal, and making brass thereof, without pots.
HANKSBEE, FRANCIS - -	497	9th May 1728	Preserving plank and sheathing of ships, to prevent worms and shell-insects from eating and fouling their bottoms; also enabling ships so sheathed to outsail other ships of the same burden and form.
HANKSBEE, FRANCIS - -	511	16th May 1729	Applying the centrifugal force of a body moving in a curve line, to the moving of all kinds of mechanical and hydraulical engines now in use, or that may be hereafter invented.
HANNAH, JAMES LEE - -	6627	16th June 1834	Surgical-instruments for reducing the stone in the bladder, and enabling the patient to pass it off through the urethra.
HANNAH, JAMES LEE - -	8722	25th Nov. 1840	Fire-escapes.
HANNAY, SAMUEL - - -	1078	1st Sept. 1774	Medicine or liquid for preventing venereal contagion, by outward application.
HANNINGTON, CHARLES MEP-[HAM	6065	22nd Jan. 1831	Apparatus for impressing, stamping, or printing for certain purposes.
HANNUIC, PAUL - - -	8623	10th Sept. 1840	Construction of governors or regulators applicable to steam-engines, and other engines used for obtaining motive-power.
HANSARD, THOMAS CARSON -	4176	1st Nov. 1817	Printing-presses; processes of printing.
HANSCOMB, WILLIAM - -	1666	15th Aug. 1788	Machine for roasting many joints of meat, turkeys, geese, fowls, ducks, &c. both horizontally and vertically, at the same time or separately, and to the weight of one hundred pounds or more, in such manner that several joints may be ready at one time, or progressively one after another, as wanted.
HANSOM, JOSEPH - - -	6733	23rd Dec. 1834	Vehicle for conveying loads on common and other roads.
HANSON, CHARLES - -	7427	31st Aug. 1837	Machinery for making pipes, tubes, and various other articles, from metallic and other substances.
HANSON, CHARLES - -	10,876	10th Oct. 1845	Clocks, watches, or timekeepers.
HANSON, CHARLES - -	13,138	19th June 1850	Steam-engines, steam-boilers, and safety-valves; apparatus and machinery for propelling vessels.
HANSON, EDWARD - - -	10,177	7th May 1844	Consuming tallow and other fatty matters in lamps.
HANSON, GEORGE - - -	8261	7th Nov. 1839	Construction of cocks or taps for drawing off liquids.
HANSON, JOHN - - -	5991	31st Aug. 1830	Locomotive-carriages.

Name of Patentee.	Progressive Number.	Date.	Subject-matter of Patent.
HANSON, JOHN - - -	7427	31st Aug. 1837	Machinery for making pipes, tubes, and various other articles, from metallic and other substances.
HANSON, JOHN - - -	8167	24th July 1839	Apparatus for measuring and registering the quantity of gas, water, and other fluid passed through such apparatus.
HANSON, JOHN - - -	8393	22nd Feb. 1840	Meters for measuring volumes of gas, water, and other fluids when passed through them; construction of valves applicable to such purposes.
HANSON, JOHN - - -	9129	2nd Nov. 1841	Fire-arms, bullets, or other projectiles to be used therewith.
HANWORTH, XR'OFER - -	60	3rd Dec. 1632	Making salt.
HAPPEY, ALEXANDRE - -	7626	25th April 1838	Composition for paving roads, streets, terraces and other places, applicable also for building purposes; apparatus for making the same.
HAPPEY, ALEXANDRE - -	7641	14th May 1838	Extracting tar and bitumen from all matters which contain those substances or either of them.
HARBOTTLE, THOMAS - -	10,084	27th Feb. 1844	Machine for manufacturing boot sole-taps, and also for riveting leather hose-traces, and for other purposes.
HARBY, WILLIAM - - -	1198	13th July 1778	Cemented hair-shag.
HARCOURT, DAVID - -	8240	10th Oct. 1839	Castors for furniture and for other purposes.
HARCOURT, DAVID - -	12,725	1st Aug. 1849	Vices; manufacturing hinges; apparatus for dressing and finishing articles made of metal.
HARCOURT, GEORGE ROBERT D'	7771	15th Aug. 1838	Propelling canal-boats, steamers, and other vessels.
HARCOURT, GEORGE ROBERT D'	7772	15th Aug. 1838	Manufacture of paper.
HARCOURT, GEORGE ROBERT D'	7991	6th March 1839	Artificial granite, stone, marble, or concrete, without asphaltic or bituminous substances.
HARCOURT, GEORGE ROBERT D'	9884	28th Sept. 1843	Sorting, checking, and delivering letters, newspapers, and other articles.
HARCOURT, GEORGE ROBERT D'	10,367	29th Oct. 1844	Ascertaining and checking the number of checks or tickets which have been used and marked, applicable for railway offices.
HARCOURT, JAMES - - -	4481	21st June 1820	Castors applicable to tables and other articles.
HARCOURT, ROBERT - -	12,898	15th Dec. 1849	Knobs, handles, and fastenings for doors and drawers; fastenings to be used for window-sashes, curtain and other rods, and for other purposes.
HARDACRE, HENRY THOMAS -	3573	6th June 1812	Composition to prevent to a great degree, the effects of friction.
HARDACRE, SAMUEL - -	11,645	29th March 1847	Machinery for opening and carding cotton and other fibrous substances, and for grinding the cards of carding-engines.
HARDCASTLE, JAMES - -	10,875	10th Oct. 1845	Method of conveying water.
HARDCASTLE, JAMES - -	10,904	31st Oct. 1845	Scouring, bleaching, preparing, dyeing, and finishing piece-goods, or woven fabrics.
HARDCASTLE, WILLIAM -	3570	26th May 1812	Cranes to prevent accidents arising in the raising or lowering of heavy bodies.
HARDIE, DANIEL - - -	2300	8th March 1799	Cranes for raising and lowering goods into and out of warehouses.

Name of Patentee.	Progres-sive Number.	Date.	Subject-matter of Patent.
HARDIE, DAVID - - -	2383	19th March 1800	Apparatus for weighing.
HARDIE, FEROUSON - -	1827	12th Sept. 1791	Construction of mangles.
HARDING, GUSTAVUS PALMER	13,129	12th June 1850	Manufacture of buttons and other fasten-ings.
HARDING, JAMES DUFFIELD -	6565	27th Feb. 1834	Pencil, pen, and chalk cases or holders.
HARDING, THOMAS RICHARDS	13,289	17th Oct. 1850	Machinery for heckling and carding flax; machinery for combing and drawing wool and other fibrous materials; machinery for making parts of such machines; new arrangement of the steam-engine for driving flax and woollen mills;—also applicable to other purposes.
HARDING, WILLIAM - -	433	17th July 1721	Making sugar-mills, engines, and worms, for making sugar and rum.
HARDMAN, JOHN - - -	7089	10th May 1836	Making and constructing wheels for rail-way-carriages.
HARDMAN, JOHN - - -	7308	21st Feb. 1837	Steam-engines.
HARDMAN, LAURENCE - -	9898	5th Oct. 1843	Machinery to be employed in the manu-facture of sugar.
HARDMAN, ROBERT - -	14,155	5th June 1852	Looms for weaving.
HARDMAN, SAMUEL - -	9057	27th Aug. 1841	Machinery for roving and slubbing cotton and other fibrous substances.
HARDWICK, JOSEPH - -	6346	17th Dec. 1832	Paddle-wheels.
HARDWICK, JOSEPH - -	13,041	15th April 1850	Construction and setting of steam-boilers.
HARDY, CHARLES - - -	13,594	15th April 1851	Manufacture of scythes.
HARDY, HENRY - - -	877	2nd June 1767	Making, upon a stocking-frame, velvet-shag, and brocaded silk, plain, cut, figured, and in gold and silver.
HARDY, JAMES - - -	6637	3rd July 1834	Making axletrees for carriages.
HARDY, JAMES - - -	6807	4th April 1835	Making or manufacturing axletrees for car-riages; also other cylindrical or conical shafts.
HARDY, JAMES - - -	7666	2nd June 1838	Rolling and making shafts, rails, tyre-iron, and various other heavy articles; machinery used in the same.
HARDY, JAMES - - -	10,122	28th March 1844	Welding tubes or hollow rods of malleable iron, by machinery.
HARDY, JAMES - - -	10,710	5th June 1845	Manufacture of metallic tubes or pipes by machinery.
HARDY, JAMES - - -	12,555	2nd April 1849	Manufacturing axletrees for carriages; also other cylindrical and conical shafts, (ex-tension to Geach and Walker for four years from the 4th day of April 1849).
HARDY, ROBERT - - -	4102	20th Feb. 1817	Manufacturing cast-iron bushes or pipe-boxes for chaise, coach, waggon, and all sorts of carriage-wheels.
HARE, RICHARD - - -	1826	12th Sept. 1791	Apparatus for preserving and applying to use the essential oil of hops, and for heating water for brewing, without the application of fire.
HAREWELL, Sir EDMOND -	20	10th May 1622	Making soap, soap-ashes, pot-ashes, and salts for soap.
HARFORD, RICHARD SUMMERS	4634	9th Jan. 1822	Puddling iron.
HARFORD, RICHARD SUMMERS	4663	21st March 1822	Heating-processes in the manufacture of bar, rod, sheet, or other malleable iron.
HARGRAVES, JAMES - -	962	12th June 1770	Making an engine for spinning, drawing, and twisting cotton.

Name of Patentee.	Progressive Number.	Date.	Subject-matter of Patent.
HARGREAVE, JAMES - -	5224	26th July 1825	Machinery used in scribbling and carding wool or other fibrous substances.
HARGREAVES, WILLIAM, junior	13,049	18th April 1850	Means of consuming smoke ;—partly applicable to the generating of steam.
HARLAND, ROBERT - -	12,670	25th June 1849	Construction of railway-carriages.
HARLAND, WILLIAM - -	5592	21st Dec. 1827	Machinery for propelling locomotive carriages ;—applicable to other purposes.
HARLOW, FREDERICK - -	9250	9th Feb. 1842	Paving or covering roads and other surfaces ; machinery for cutting the materials used for the purpose.
HARLOW, FREDERICK - -	10,873	10th Oct. 1845	Atmospheric railways.
HARLOW, JONATHAN - -	9187	16th Dec. 1841	Manufacturing metallic tubes ; joining them or other tubes or pieces for various purposes.
HARLOW, JONATHAN - -	11,705	18th May 1847	Manufacturing bedsteads.
HARLOW, JONATHAN - -	12,838	10th Nov. 1849	Bedsteads.
HARLOW, JONATHAN - -	13,086	30th May 1850	Manufacture of bedsteads and other articles for sitting or reclining on.
HARLOW, SAMUEL BOLTON -	1708	6th Nov. 1789	Making watch-keys, with a spring to preserve the watch from injury when the key is turned the wrong way.
HARMAR, JOHN - - -	1595	20th March 1787	Machine for dressing woollen-cloths, and shearing fustians.
HARMAR, JOHN - - -	1982	29th March 1794	Machine for dressing woollen-cloths, and shearing fustians.
HARPER, THOMAS - - -	4909	28th Feb. 1824	Combining and applying certain kinds of fuel.
HARPER, THOMAS - - -	8073	22nd May 1839	Railways or tramroads.
HARPER, WILLIAM - -	8065	10th May 1839	Stoves and grates.
HARPUR, THOMAS - - -	1343	16th Nov. 1782	Machine for watering yarn or cloth, or whitstering-grounds, crofts, or calico-printing grounds.
HARPER, GEORGE EMANUEL -	4761	18th March 1823	Impelling machinery.
HARPUR, THOMAS - - -	4848	9th Oct. 1823	Combining and using fuel in stoves, furnaces, boilers, and steam-engines.
HARRADINE, JOHN THANG -	11,911	14th Oct. 1847	Instrument for preparing lands in various ways for agricultural purposes.
HARRADINE, JOHN THANG -	12,132	20th April 1848	Mode of fitting certain girths and straps.
HARRATT, CHARLES - -	13,265	28th Sept. 1850	Rolling iron.
HARRIES, JOSEPH - - -	3871	4th Jan. 1815	Necessaries or clothing for the military in general.
HARRINGTON, GEORGE FELLOWS	12,717	1st Aug. 1849	Making artificial teeth, also beds and palates for teeth.
HARRINGTON, JOHN - -	568	8th June 1739	Planting and manufacturing jalap or machoacan ; also the prickly pear or cochineal plant.
HARRINGTON, JOSIAH - -	12,543	28th March 1849	Priming fire-arms ; apparatus for discharging fire-arms.
HARRINGTON, SARAH - -	1100	24th June 1775	Taking and reducing shadows, with appendages and apparatus for taking likenesses, furniture, and decorations, in minature.
HARRINGTON, WILLIAM - -	210	4th March 1680	Tools, engines, or instruments to be used without diving, for weighing or recovering from under water, ships' guns, and goods sunk at sea.

Name of Patentee.	Progressive Number.	Date.	Subject-matter of Patent.
HARRINGTON, WILLIAM - -	4971	15th June 1824	Raft for transporting timber.
HARRIOTT, JOHN - - -	2197	31st Oct. 1797	Cog-wheel, crab, or capstan, with gear to work ships' pumps, engines, and hydraulic machines, and, while working the pumps, engines, or machines, to give a ship way through the water in calms or light winds.
HARRIOTT, JOHN - - -	2610	13th April 1802	Engine for raising and lowering weights, and for working mills.
HARRIOTT, JOHN - - -	2713	14th June 1803	Making and working windlasses.
HARRIOTT, JOHN - - -	3130	10th May 1808	Fire-escapes.
HARRIS, ADOLPHUS OLIVER -	13,422	19th Dec. 1850	Barometers.
HARRIS, GEORGE - - -	2419	1st July 1800	Boxes for snuffs, essences, &c.
HARRIS, GEORGE - - -	5846	15th Sept. 1829	Manufacture of ropes and cordage, canvas and other fabrics, from substances hitherto unused for the purpose.
HARRIS, GEORGE - - -	6429	1st June 1833	Reducing and preparing various vegetable substances, and manufacturing them into articles usually made of hemp and flax.
HARRIS, GEORGE DANIEL -	5606	15th Jan. 1828	Dressing and preparing woollen-yarns; cleansing, dressing, and finishing woollen-cloths; apparatus for the purpose.
HARRIS, GEORGE SAMUEL -	5024	21st Oct. 1824	Machine for giving publicity by day and by night to proclamations, notices, advertisements, and other things to which the same is applicable.
HARRIS, JAMES - - -	4635	9th Jan. 1822	Manufacture of shoes for horses and other cattle.
HARRIS, JOHN - - -	432	7th July 1721	Making and printing globular charts or sea-charts, for use in navigation.
HARRIS, JOHN - - -	521	22nd Oct. 1730	Harpsichord.
HARRIS, JOHN - - -	5064	1st Jan. 1825	Machinery for making wove and laid paper.
HARRIS, JOHN - - -	12,306	2nd Nov. 1848	Founding type, and casting in metal, plaster, and certain other materials.
HARRIS, JOHN DOVE - -	13,044	18th April 1850	Manufacture of looped fabrics.
HARRIS, JOHN RAWLINSON -	4574	26th July 1821	Clearing furs and wools used in the manufacture of hats, from kemps and hairs.
HARRIS, MICHAEL - - -	3265	26th Sept. 1809	Ships' binnacles and compasses; mode of lighting the same.
HARRIS, RICE - - -	8502	12th May 1840	Cylinders, plates, and blocks, used in printing and embossing.
HARRIS, RICHARD - - -	10,133	30th March 1844	Manufacture of looped, woven, and elastic fabrics.
HARRIS, RICHARD - - -	10,388	9th Nov. 1844	Machinery employed in the manufacture of looped fabrics.
HARRIS, THOMAS - - -	580	19th Nov. 1741	Making saltpetre or nitre.
HARRIS, THOMAS - - -	624	3rd Nov. 1747	Machine for raising water.
HARRIS, THOMAS - - -	965	21st July 1770	Watches.
HARRIS, THOMAS - - -	1769	28th July 1790	Apparatus for use in breweries, distilleries, &c. for the purpose of cooling worts of all kinds.
HARRIS, THOMAS - - -	8782	11th Jan. 1841	Horse-shoe.
HARRIS, THOMAS - - -	8931	22nd April 1841	Manufacture of horn-buttons; dies to be used for the purpose.
HARRIS, TIMOTHY - - -	2182	4th July 1797	Manufacturing pins with iron and other metals; making the same white.

Name of Patentee.	Progres-sive Number.	Date.		Subject-matter of Patent.
HARRIS, TIMOTHY - - -	3777	8th Feb.	1814	Machines for ploughing, laying on colours, printing, flocking, and pressing, to produce an even smooth face on paper, silk, linen, woollen, leather, cotton, and various articles.
HARRIS, WILLIAM - - -	218	12th May	1682	Engine for drawing water out of mines.
HARRIS, WILLIAM - - -	3453	21st May	1811	Telescopes and other optical instruments for measuring angles.
HARRIS, WILLIAM - - -	12,470	12th Feb.	1849	Preparing leather.
HARRIS, WILLIAM SMITH -	9543	8th Dec.	1842	Manufacture of reels, for reeling cotton and linen thread.
HARRISON, CHARLES - -	10,098	14th March	1844	Manufacture of cast-iron pipes, and other iron castings.
HARRISON, GEORGE - -	5086	1st Feb.	1825	Making bricks, tiles, and other articles, manufactured with brick-earth.
HARRISON, GEORGE - -	7834	17th Oct.	1831	Supplying air for promoting and supporting the combustion of fire in close stoves and furnaces, and economizing fuel therein.
HARRISON, HENRY - - -	9030	8th Sept.	1841	Means of raising water and other liquids.
HARRISON, JACOB - - -	5387	14th July	1826	Preparing straw and grass to be used in the manufacture of hats and bonnets.
HARRISON, JAMES - - -	10,260	15th July	1844	Machinery for spinning cotton and other fibrous substances.
HARRISON, JOHN - - -	1882	21st May	1792	Washing-engine.
HARRISON, JOHN - - -	13,643	27th May	1851	Manufacture of textile-fabrics; preparation of yarns or threads for weaving.
HARRISON, JOSEPH - -	6007	6th Oct.	1830	Glazing horticultural and other buildings; sash-bars, and rafters.
HARRISON, JOSEPH - -	12,455	6th Feb.	1849	Improvements in and applicable to looms for weaving.
HARRISON, JOSEPH - -	13,843	8th Dec.	1851	Steam-engines and boilers.
HARRISON, SAMUEL - -	7862	8th Nov.	1838	Manufacture of wood-screws.
HARRISON, THOMAS - -	12,553	28th March	1849	Construction of baking-ovens; machinery for working or using the same.
HARRISON, THOMAS ELLIOTT -	7260	21st Dec.	1836	Locomotive-engines.
HARRISON, WILLIAM - -	717	11th Nov.	1757	Coach-springs.
HARRISON, WILLIAM - -	1179	5th Feb.	1778	Making screws, and machines for dividing instruments from the said screws.
HARRISON, WILLIAM - -	12,455	6th Feb.	1849	Improvements in and applicable to looms for weaving.
HARRISON, WILLIAM CURRIE -	8818	28th Jan.	1841	Turning-table for railway purposes.
HARROLD, WILLIAM - -	6363	11th Jan.	1833	Machinery for making paper.
HARRY, WILLIAM - - -	4168	3rd Oct.	1817	Building, constructing, or erecting the roofs or upper parts of furnaces used for the smelting of copper and other ores, or any of their metals, and for other purposes requiring strong fires.
HARSLEBEN, CHARLES - -	5428	13th Dec.	1826	Machinery for facilitating the working of mines, and for facilitating the extraction of diamonds and other precious stones, also gold, silver, and other metals from the ore, the earth, or the sand;— applicable to other purposes.
HARSLEBEN, CHARLES - -	5433	20th Dec.	1826	Constructing or building ships and other vessels, applicable to various purposes; machinery for propelling the same.

Name of Patentee.	Progres-sive Number.	Date.	Subject-matter of Patent.
HARSLEBEN, CHARLES - -	5637	3rd April 1828	Machinery to be used in navigation, chiefly applicable to propelling ships and other floating bodies, also to other purposes.
HARSLEBEN, CHARLES - -	6984	19th Jan. 1836	Machinery and arrangements for propelling vessels and other floating bodies, also carriages on railways as well as on common roads;—partly applicable to other purposes.
HART, JAMES - - - -	12,311	2nd Nov. 1848	Machinery for manufacturing bricks and tiles;—in part applicable to moulding other substances.
HART, JAMES - - - -	13,559	17th March 1851	Manufacture of bricks, tiles, and other articles made from plastic materials; making parts of the machinery used therein.
HART, MOSES - - - -	1709	6th Nov. 1789	Extracting, hardening, purifying, and whitening the bottoms, foots, or flush of whale-oil, or the sediments of seal-oil, or any other fish-oil, chiefly for making candles.
HART, NAPHTALI - - -	2563	3rd Dec. 1801	Instrument or goniometer to measure angles, "Hartesian Goniometer."
HART, SAMUEL - - -	4562	17th May 1821	Springs applicable to various descriptions of carriages.
HART, SIR HENRY - - -	12,187	13th June 1848	Apparatus for preventing what are called smoky chimneys.
HART, WILLIAM - - -	2281	17th Dec. 1798	Apparatus for raising beer, ale, spirituous liquors, &c. from the cellar to the bar or other part of the house, for the use of publicans, brewers, distillers, and others.
HART, WILLIAM HENRY -	3550	24th March 1812	Machine for cutting, cropping, or shearing woollen and other cloths, and the fur from peltry.
HARTAS, ISAAC - - -	13,139	19th June 1850	Machinery for obtaining motive-power.
HARTER, WILLIAM - - -	6976	8th Jan. 1836	Machinery for winding, cleaning, drawing, and doubling hard and soft silk.
HARTES, ISAAC - - -	10,858	9th Oct. 1845	Machinery for rowing, sowing, and manuring land.
HARTES, ISAAC - - -	12,144	2nd May 1848	Machinery for rowing, sowing, and manuring land.
HARTLEY, DAVID - - -	1037	1st April 1773	Securing buildings and ships against accidents from fire.
HARTLEY, DAVID - - -	1687	9th June 1789	Tempering instruments and manufactures of steel.
HARTLEY, EDMUND - -	12,367	11th Dec. 1848	Machinery to be employed in the preparation and spinning of cotton and other fibrous substances.
HARTLEY, JAMES - - -	6702	22nd Oct. 1834	Manufacture of glass.
HARTLEY, JAMES - - -	7886	1st Dec. 1838	Manufacture of glass.
HARTLEY, JAMES - - -	9815	6th July 1843	Manufacture of glass.
HARTLEY, JAMES - - -	11,891	7th Oct. 1847	Manufacture of glass.
HARTLEY, JOHN - - -	3179	8th Nov. 1808	Machine for preparing, roving, slubbing, spinning, twisting, and doubling cotton, flax, hemp, tow, silk, wool, worsted, or any other substances.
HARTLEY, JOHN - - -	6702	22nd Oct. 1834	Manufacture of glass.
HARTLEY, JOHN GALLEY -	7020	8th March 1836	Preparing caoutchouc for various useful purposes.

Name of Patentee.	Progressive Number.	Date.	Subject-matter of Patent.
HARTLEY, JOHN GALLEY -	9773	13th June 1843	Paving and covering streets, roads, or other ways.
HARTLEY, JOHN GEORGE -	7419	22nd Aug. 1837	Application of levers for the purpose of multiplying power.
HARTLEY, WILLIAM - -	12,547	28th March 1849	Steam-engines.
HARTOP, JOHN - - -	2888	7th Nov. 1805	Preparing malleable iron for making bars, sheets, and slit-rods, and manufacturing the same into hoop-iron; preparing all other malleable metals.
HARTREE, WILLIAM - -	11,017	23rd Dec. 1845	Steam-engines; machinery for propelling vessels;—applicable to other purposes.
HARVEY, EDMUND - - -	1638	19th Jan. 1788	Bed-ticking, made of materials never before used for that purpose.
HARVEY, FREDERICK EDWARD	6995	3rd Feb. 1836	Process and machinery for manufacturing metallic-tubes; also machinery for forging or rolling metal for other purposes.
HARVEY, JAMES - - -	8529	2nd June 1840	Paving streets, roads, and ways with blocks of wood; machinery for cutting such blocks.
HARVEY, JAMES - - -	8562	8th July 1840	Extracting sulphur from pyrites and other substances.
HARVEY, JAMES - - -	9583	11th Jan. 1843	Steam-engines.
HARVEY, JAMES - - -	9588	14th Jan. 1843	Paving streets, roads, and other places.
HARVEY, JOSEPH - -	1238	24th Nov. 1799	Piece of machinery to be added to a stocking-frame, for making lace, " Brussels or double ground lace," for shades, aprons, handkerchiefs, caps, mits, gloves, purses, waistcoats, shawls, and other sorts of open work.
HARVEY, JOSEPH - - -	3947	4th Aug. 1815	Machine for striking and finishing leather.
HARVEY, JOSEPH - - -	9848	20th July 1843	Construction of two-wheeled carriages.
HARVEY, NICHOLAS - -	8103	12th June 1839	Valve for machines for raising water and other liquids.
HARVEY, NICHOLAS - -	11,366	3rd Sept. 1846	Filtering water for steam-engines and boilers.
HARVEY, ROBERT - - -	4183	5th Dec. 1817	Making pipes and tubes of porcelain, clay, or other ductile substances.
HARVEY, SAMUEL - - -	10,712	7th June 1845	Sawing-machinery.
HARVEY, WILLIAM - - -	4497	12th Oct. 1820	Manufacture of ropes and bolts by machinery; improvements in the said machinery.
HARVIE, ARTHUR - - -	9512	8th Nov. 1842	Process of vinous fermentation.
HARVIE, JAMES - - -	4494	16th Aug. 1820	Construction of ginning-machines employed in separating cotton-wool from the seeds.
HARVIG, JOHN - - -	9048	21st Aug. 1841	Mode of cutting or working cork for various purposes.
HARVIG, JOHN - - -	9049	21st Aug. 1841	Sculpturing, moulding, engraving, and polishing stone, metals, and other substances.
HARVEY, THOMAS - - -	207	24th Feb. 1679	Engine for drawing Spanish and Swedish iron into rounds, for bolts suitable for shipping and other uses.
HARWOOD, JOHN - - -	9117	7th Oct. 1841	Means of giving expansion to the chest.
HASE, WILLIAM - - -	2501	14th May 1801	Steam-engines.
HASE, WILLIAM - - -	4847	11th Sept. 1823	Constructing mills or machines chiefly applicable to prison discipline.
HASELER, GEORGE CARTER -	9273	3rd March 1842	Tops of scent-bottles.

Name of Patentee.	Progressive Number.	Date.	Subject-matter of Patent.
HASKEW, EDWARD - -	2115	31st May 1796	Machinery for raising and removing earth, sand, gravel or any other things, from the bottom of canals.
HASKINS, HENRY - - -	619	7th Aug. 1746	Extracting a spirit or oil from tar, also producing the finest pitch.
HASLEWOOD, ROGER - -	3787	12th March 1814	Folding-screens to impede the passage of air, smoke, fire, and light;—applicable to fire-places.
HASLUCK, DANIEL SYDNEY -	11,334	13th Aug. 1846	Manufacture of harness for beasts of burden.
HASTIE, ARCHIBALD - -	8550	24th June 1840	Generating and condensing steam; heating, cooling, and evaporating fluids.
HASTIE, JOHN - - -	11,822	29th July 1847	Application of steam-power to turn certain mills or machines with continuous rotatory motion.
HASTINGS, JAMES - -	11,276	30th June 1846	Machine for making bricks and tiles, quarries and cornice-ornaments.
HATCHER, WILLIAM HENRY -	11,634	23rd March 1847	Electric-telegraphs; apparatus connected therewith; electric-clocks and time-keepers.
HATCHETT, JOHN - -	863	21st Nov. 1766	Spring for hanging coaches and other carriages.
HATCHETT, JOHN - -	1085	10th Nov. 1774	Making ornaments, such as arms, supporters, borders, cyphers, and flowers, for coaches and carriages, to be pierced on copper or other metallic or composition plates, and afterwards painted, gilt, glazed, bronzed, inlaid, or coloured, and contrived so as to be put on or taken off as occasion may require.
HATCHETT, JOHN - -	1393	25th Oct. 1783	Coaches and carriages, also coach and carriage bodies.
HATCHETT, JOHN - -	1643	21st March 1788	Carriage for coaches, chariots, vis-a-vis, phaetons, curricles, one horse chaises, &c. drawn on wheels; also sledges without wheels.
HATELEY, JOSEPH - -	895	8th March 1768	Fire-engine with boiler.
HATELEY, JOSEPH - -	1493	3rd Aug. 1785	Rotatory reciprocal fire-engines, for raising or forcing water, drawing coal, iron, and stone, or for other business where mechanic powers are necessary.
HATELEY, JOSEPH - -	1775	16th Oct. 1790	Pneumatic fire-engines, for working mills, rolling metals, raising coals, minerals, and other bodies.
HATELY, JOSEPH - -	2090	19th Feb. 1796	Extracting and making (from vegetable bodies) an astringent acid liquor; applicable to improvements in divers arts and manufactures.
HATELY, JOSEPH - -	2645	31st Aug. 1802	Purifying metals.
HATTERSLEY, WILLIAM - -	10,592	7th April 1845	Construction of pianofortes.
HATTON, LEONARD - -	1125	21st May 1776	Engine for planing boards and fluting wood for columns.
HAUCK, FREDERICK - -	3658	3rd March 1813	Musical-instruments.
HAUGHTON, JOHN - -	8713	24th Nov. 1840	Preventing railway-accidents resulting from one train overtaking another.
HAUGHTON, JOHN - -	8992	19th June 1841	Affixing labels.
HAUGHTON, JOHN - -	9304	21st March 1842	Affixing labels.
HAUGHTON, WILLIAM -	14,154	5th June 1852	Machinery for spinning cotton and other fibrous substances.

Name of Patentee.	Progressive Number.	Date.	Subject-matter of Patent.
HAWE, GEORGE - - -	9343	9th May 1842	Machinery for sweeping and cleaning chimneys and flues.
HAWES, WILLIAM - - -	8101	12th June 1839	Manufacture of soap;—partly applicable to preparing tallow for the manufacture of candles.
HAWKER, PETER - - -	4508	1st Nov. 1820	Instrument to assist in the attainment of proper performance on the pianoforte or other keyed instrument.
HAWKES, GEORGE - - -	2054	2nd June 1795	Manufacture for tanning.
HAWKES, GEORGE - - -	3079	6th Nov. 1807	Making and keeping in repair cast iron wheels for coal-waggons and other carriages.
HAWKES, GEORGE - - -	4856	1st Nov. 1823	Construction of ships' anchors.
HAWKES, GEORGE - - -	4857	1st Nov. 1823	Capstans.
HAWKES, THOMAS - - -	618	26th July 1746	Rendering safe and easy the riding in a chaise, chair or such like vehicle.
HAWKES, WILLIAM - -	3154	25th July 1808	Musical keyed instruments of twelve fixed tones.
HAWKESLEY, JOHN - -	1958	8th June 1793	Machinery for combing and preparing wool, cotton, silk, flax, hemp, and mohair, for spinning.
HAWKESLEY, JOHN - - [Hawksley, John.]	2185	4th July 1797	Combing wool, cotton, silk, flax, hemp, and mohair, or a circular revolving comb-pot to heat the combs used in the combing of wool; also a lasher or layer-on of wool or other materials on combing machines, and a socket or holster in which to place the combs used for drawing off the wool and other materials from such machines.
HAWKINS, BENJAMIN - -	2533	20th Aug. 1801	Floating mill or engine for grinding grain, and to be worked by tides or currents of water.
HAWKINS, CHARLES - -	1098	10th June 1775	Mail pillion.
HAWKINS, EDWARD - -	1189	30th March 1778	Making shaven or bright latten.
HAWKINS, GRIFFIN - -	3447	9th May 1811	Apparatus for the defence of ships against boarding.
HAWKINS, HENRY - - -	1137	19th Nov. 1776	Working an aquarello ground, to be used on copper-plates engraved for printing linen, cottons, muslins, and calicoes, to produce various tints.
HAWKINS, ISAAC - - -	2446	13th Nov. 1800	Invention applicable to musical instruments;—the principles applicable to other machinery.
HAWKINS, ISAAC - - -	2735	24th Sept. 1803	Machinery and methods for writing, painting, drawing, ruling lines, and other things;—the machinery being applicable in part to other purposes.
HAWKINS, JOHN ISAAC - -	3271	2nd Nov. 1809	Instrument or machine applicable in machines as a balance or equipoise.
HAWKINS, JOHN ISAAC - -	4001	23rd March 1816	Grates and stoves; apparatus for supplying grates and stoves with fuel.
HAWKINS, JOHN ISAAC - -	4742	20th Dec. 1822	Pencil-holders or port-crayons; pens for facilitating writing and drawing.
HAWKINS, JOHN ISAAC - -	5277	1st Nov. 1825	Apparatus used in manufacturing and preserving books, whether bound or unbound.
HAWKINS, JOHN ISAAC - -	6574	13th March 1834	Instruments to facilitate the cure of disease, by administering galvanic influence into the human body.

Name of Patentee.	Progressive Number.	Date.	Subject-matter of Patent.
HAWKINS, JOHN ISAAC - -	7142	4th July 1836	Manufacturing iron and steel.
HAWKINS, JOHN ISAAC - -	7194	28th Sept. 1836	Blowing-pipe of blast furnaces and forges.
HAWKINS, JOHN ISAAC - -	7303	16th Feb. 1837	Application of the products of combustion in generating steam and aiding steam for giving motion to steam-engines.
HAWKINS, JOHN ISAAC - -	8598	8th Aug. 1840	Buttons, and mode of affixing them to clothes.
HAWKINS, JOHN ISAAC - -	11,613	10th March 1847	Holding together or filing, letters, music-sheets, newspapers, and other documents.
HAWKINS, RICHARD FRANCIS	2695	5th April 1803	Applying a certain power to work ship and other windlasses, winches, and cranes, also to other purposes.
HAWKINS, RICHARD FRANCIS	3028	8th April 1807	Guns and carronade carriages.
HAWKINS, RICHARD FRANCIS	4028	14th May 1816	Principle for the construction of tunnels or archways under rivers, for the passage of carriages, cattle, and foot passengers; and for other purposes.
HAWKINS, RICHARD FRANCIS	4589	11th Sept. 1821	Construction of anchors.
HAWKINS, STEPHEN - -	4595	18th Oct. 1821	Traps for privies, waterclosets, close-stools, or chamber conveniences to which the same may be applicable.
HAWKINS, STEPHEN - -	6615	24th May 1834	Warming-pans.
HAWKINS, THOMAS - -	13,574	24th March 1851	Brushes.
HAWKS, GEORGE - - -	8243	17th Oct. 1839	Construction of wheels for carriages to be used on railways.
HAWKS, JOHN - - -	4149	5th Aug. 1817	Making iron rails for railways.
HAWKS, JOHN - - -	5672	10th July 1828	Construction of ships' cable and hawser chains.
HAWKS, WILLIAM - -	2776	2nd July 1804	Constructing and making chains for the use of mines, and for other purposes.
HAWKSHAW, JOHN - -	7911	17th Dec. 1838	Mechanism applicable to railways; also to carriages to be used thereon.
HAWLEY, JOHN - - -	8526	1st June 1840	Pianos and harps.
HAWORTH, EDMUND - -	7346	18th April 1837	Machinery or apparatus adapted to facilitate the operation of drying calicoes, muslins, linens, or other similar fabrics. Extension of W. Southworth's patent for five years from 19th of April 1837.
HAWORTH, RICHARD -	10,516	10th Feb. 1845	Steam-engines.
HAWTHORN, ROBERT -	8277	21st Nov. 1839	Boilers for locomotive and other steam-engines, and conveying steam therefrom to the cylinders.
HAWTHORN, ROBERT - [Hawthorne, Robert.]	9691	7th April 1843	Locomotive-engines; partly applicable to other steam-engines.
HAWTHORN, ROBERT -	13,533	24th Feb. 1851	Locomotive-engines; partly applicable to other steam-engines.
HAWTHORN, WILLIAM -	8277	21st Nov. 1839	Boilers for locomotive and other steam-engines; and conveying steam therefrom to the cylinders.
HAWTHORN, WILLIAM - [Hawthorne, William.]	9691	7th April 1843	Locomotive-engines;—partly applicable to other steam-engines.
HAWTHORN, WILLIAM -	13,533	24th Feb. 1851	Locomotive-engines;—partly applicable to other steam-engines.
HAWTHORNTHWAITE, MAT-[THEW	7085	7th May 1836	Producing certain patterns in certain woven goods.
HAXBY, THOMAS - - -	977	28th Dec. 1770	Single harpsichord, answering all the purposes of a double one.

Name of Patentee.	Progressive Number.	Date.	Subject-matter of Patent.
HAXBY, JOSEPH BARBER -	12,070	16th Feb. 1848	Making communications between railway servants, also between passengers and such servants.
HAY, JAMES - - -	8450	25th March 1840	Ploughs, "Belton plough."
HAY, THOMAS - -	6594	17th April 1834	Preparing certain metals applicable to the sheathing the bottoms of ships, and for other purposes.
HAY, WILLIAM JOHN -	9967	25th Nov. 1843	Producing light by percussion, for signals and other purposes.
HAYCRAFT, JOSEPH - -	2224	23rd March 1798	Gun-carriage.
HAYCRAFT, SAMUEL - -	4347	4th March 1819	Manufacturing spoons, forks, and other articles, of silver, iron, or other metal, by the application of certain machinery hitherto unused for the purpose; improvements in such machinery.
HAYCRAFT, WILLIAM TUTIN -	5942	11th June 1830	Steam-engines.
HAYCRAFT, WILLIAM TUTIN -	11,167	15th April 1846	Steam-engines.
HAYDEN, WHITING - -	13,282	10th Oct. 1850	Apparatus for regulating the draught of the sliver, on the machine termed a drawing frame.
HAYES, JAMES - - -	132	16th May 1661	Forcing water by means of bellows not worked by wind, and drawing it up with leather bags linked in the manner of buckets where the bellows cannot be placed together; supplying ships with water, by forcing the same through the bottom or side below the surface of the water; useful also for draining mines, supplying houses, emptying rivers or ponds, and draining and watering grounds.
HAYES, JAMES - - -	139	Aug. 1662	Making ships sail without aid of wind or tide; instrument for taking a ship's course; raising water with springs, for draining mines.
HAYES, JOHN - - - -	2320	18th June 1799	Machines for the cultivation or tillage of land.
HAYES, CLAUDE - -	221	29th July 1682	Manufacture of draped milled stockings.
HAYES, THOMAS - -	1881	19th May 1792	Construction of mangles.
HAYMAN, JAMES - -	10,169	30th April 1844	Construction and arrangement of certain parts of omnibuses and other vehicles.
HAYMAN, GEORGE - -	7364	6th May 1837	Two-wheel carriages.
HAYNE, JOHN - - -	1348	19th Dec. 1782	Laying threads to make several breadths of work in one stocking-frame at the same time; engine for the purpose.
HAYNE, JOHN - - -	1397	14th Nov. 1783	Machine to be fixed to a stocking-frame for making patterns or figures in framework.
HAYNE, JONATHAN - -	6425	25th May 1833	Making metal spoons and other articles.
HAYNE, RICHARD - -	889	24th Dec. 1767	Mill for grinding corn, wheat, and other grain; preparing utensils and materials used in manufactories, and set up and worked in any small room.
HAYNES, JOHN RICHARD -	3975	15th Jan. 1816	Stove, grate, or fireplace.
HAYNES, RICHARD - -	166	3rd Feb. 1672	Cleaning hop-clover from its husk, and from coarse grass or wad.
HAYNES, RICHARD - - - [Haines, Richard.]	231	6th Feb. 1684	Preparing, improving, and meliorating cyder, perry, and the juice or liquors of wildings, crabs, cherries, mulberries, and several other fruits, to strengthen and render them more wholesome.

Name of Patentee.	Progres-sive Number.	Date.	Subject-matter of Patent.
HAYS, CHRISTOPHER DUNKIN	10,244	3rd July 1844	Propelling vessels.
HAYS, CHRISTOPHER DUNKIN	10,995	10th Dec. 1845	Construction and adaptation of apparatus for propelling and steering vessels on water.
HAYTER, WILLIAM - -	758	5th Feb. 1761	Composition for and method of staining leather.
HAYTON, RICHARD - -	5231	8th Aug. 1825	Precipitating copper from cupreous waters flowing from mines or from artificial waters, and reducing some ores to their metallic state.
HAYWARD, FRANCIS - -	1038	1st April 1773	Stuff or cloth made from hemp, linen, or cotton yarn of different colours, and variously figured and striped (" Rensetty "), to be used for clothing, and also for furniture.
HAYWARD, ROBERT - -	584	13th May 1742	Specific powder for the cure of rheumatism, and the relief of gout.
HAYWARD, ROBERT - -	1375	2nd June 1783	Stirrup for saddles, to prevent accidents arising from entangling the foot therein.
HAYWOOD, JOHN - - -	836	7th Jan. 1766	Ring, called a " Lunar or Calendar Ring."
HAYWOOD, JOHN - - -	1107	17th Nov. 1775	Making artificial globes or spheres without being covered with printing or drawing, on paper, parchment, or such like material, to improve astronomy, geography, and navigation.
HAYWOOD, JOHN - - -	1750	8th May 1790	Machine for working mills and engines without the aid of fire, water, or wind, or in aid of all or any of those powers.
HAYWOOD, JOSEPH - -	8832	4th Feb. 1841	Machinery, called stocking-frames.
HAZARD, ERSKINE - - -	5402	12th Aug. 1826	Preparing explosive mixtures, and employing them as a moving power for machinery.
HAZARD, ROBERT - - -	9307	21st March 1842	Apparatus for heating public and private buildings.
HAZARD, ROBERT - - -	9457	3rd Sept. 1842	Ventilating carriages, and cabins of steamboats.
HAZARD, ROBERT - - -	10,206	30th May 1844	Baths.
HAZELDINE, GEORGE - -	9499	27th Oct. 1842	Omnibuses.
HAZELDINE, GEORGE - -	13,189	23rd July 1850	Construction of waggons, carts, and vans.
HAZELDINE, THOMAS - -	11,704	18th May 1847	Construction of furnaces.
HAZEN, CHARLES DRURY -	9930	9th Nov. 1843	Machinery for knitting stockings and other articles.
HAZLEDINE, ANN - - -	3422	26th March 1811	Plough for cultivation of land.
HAZLEDINE, JOHN - -	2244	14th June 1798	Reducing and forming pigs and pieces of iron, copper, brass, and other metals, into bars, plates, and hoops.
HAZLEDINE, JOHN - - [Hazeldine John.]	3389	8th Oct. 1810	Construction of ploughs for the cultivation of land.
HAZLEDINE, WILLIAM - -	4333	15th Jan. 1819	Casting certain kinds of cast-iron vessels.
HAZLEHURST, ISAAC - -	13,655	3rd June 1851	Manufacturing iron.
HEAD, JAMES - - -	4392	27th July 1819	Machine to ascertain the difference of ships' draught of water forward and aft, at sea or in harbour.
HEAD, JOHN - - - -	5029	4th Nov. 1824	Machinery for making cord or platt for boot and stay laces, and other purposes.
HEALE, EDGAR - - -	10,145	18th April 1844	Construction of carriages for conveyance of passengers on roads and railways.

Name of Patentee.	Progres-sive Number.	Date.	Subject-matter of Patent.
HEALEY, JOHN - - -	11,454	17th Nov. [1846	Woven fabric; machinery for producing the same.
HEAME, BENJAMIN - -	1588	1st Feb. 1787	Machine to be worked by the wind, for drawing water, coals, tin, lead, copper, and other materials from mines, also for stamping ores, and for the use of grist or other mills, with sails constructed so as to contract or expand in proportion to the force of wind required, by means of weights, springs, ropes, pulleys, balances, balance-wheels, and other contrivances.
HEAPS, RICHARD - - -	3249	26th July 1809	Forming pipes and other articles in lead, pewter, tin, or metals of that nature.
HEARD, EDWARD - - -	2941	12th June 1806	Obtaining inflammable gas from pit-coals, to burn without producing offensive smell.
HEARD, EDWARD - - -	3731	9th Aug. 1813	Processes for manufacturing glass.
HEARD, EDWARD - - -	4342	9th Feb. 1819	Hardening and improving tallow and other animal fats and oils for making candles.
HEARD, EDWARD - - -	4381	19th June 1819	Portable gas-lamp.
HEARD, EDWARD - - -	5361	8th May 1826	Compositions to be used for washing in sea or other water.
HEARD, EDWARD - - -	5771	12th Feb. 1829	Illumination, or producing artificial light.
HEARD, EDWARD - - -	7756	1st Aug. 1838	Oxydizing lead; converting the same into pigments of white and red lead, and manu-facturing parts of the products into soda.
HEARD, JOHN - - -	4408	4th Nov. 1819	Cookin-gapparatus.
HEARLE, JOHN - - -	6706	3rd Nov. 1834	Engine pumps;—applicable to ships and to other purposes.
HEARN, WILLIAM - - -	7422	24th Aug. 1837	Construction of boilers for the generation of steam, and for heating water or other fluids.
HEATH, JOSIAH MARSHALL -	8021	5th April 1839	Manufacture of iron and steel.
HEATH, JOSIAH MARSHALL -	10,798	4th Aug. 1845	Manufacture of cast-steel.
HEATH, JOSIAH MARSHALL -	12,757	6th Sept. 1849	Manufacture of steel.
HEATH, MATTHEW - -	7144	11th July 1836	Mechanical combinations for obtaining power and velocity;—applicable to propelling vessels, and raising water, also to machinery of various descriptions.
HEATH, MATTHEW - -	7554	27th Jan. 1838	Engines to be worked by steam or other fluids.
HEATH, MATTHEW - -	7767	10th Aug. 1838	Preparing tobacco, and making snuff.
HEATH, MATTHEW - -	7829	11th Oct. 1838	Clarifying and filtering water, beer, wine, and other liquids.
HEATH, ROBERT - - -	10,431	12th Dec. 1844	Heating ovens and kilns used in the manu-facture of china, bricks, tiles, and other articles of earthenware.
HEATH, ROBERT - - -	11,314	27th July 1846	Wheels to be used upon rail and other roads; —applicable to mill-gearing and other purposes.
HEATH, ROBERT - - -	12,025	13th Jan. 1848	Applying and working friction-breaks to engines and carriages to be used on rail-ways.
HEATH, ROBERT - - -	13,140	19th June 1850	Manufacture of iron.
HEATHCOAT, GEORGE -	6267	15th May 1832	Draining and cultivating land; machinery and apparatus applicable thereto.
HEATHCOAT, JOHN - -	3151	14th July 1808	Machine for making bobbin-lace.
HEATHCOAT, JOHN - -	3216	20th March 1809	Machine for making bobbin-lace.

Name of Patentee.	Progres-sive Number.	Date.	Subject-matter of Patent.
HEATHCOAT, JOHN - -	3673	29th March 1813	Machine for making bobbin-lace.
HEATHCOAT, JOHN - - [Heathcoate, John.]	4037	30th May 1816	Stocking-frames.
HEATHCOAT, JOHN - -	4078	1st Nov. 1816	Machinery for making bobbin-net.
HEATHCOAT, JOHN - -	4867	20th Nov. 1823	Machine for the manufacture of a platted substance, composed either of silk, cotton, or other yarn.
HEATHCOAT, JOHN - -	4896	24th Jan. 1824	Figuring or ornamenting various descriptions of goods made of silk, cotton or flax.
HEATHCOAT, JOHN - -	4917	9th March 1824	Manufacturing certain parts of machines used in the manufacture of bobbin-net.
HEATHCOAT, JOHN - -	4918	9th March 1824	Machines for making bobbin-net.; manufacturing certain parts of such machines.
HEATHCOAT, JOHN - -	4919	9th March 1824	Combining machinery used in the manufacture of lace, in weaving and in spinning, worked by power.
HEATHCOAT, JOHN - -	4926	20th March 1824	Machinery used in spinning cotton-wool or silk.
HEATHCOAT, JOHN - -	4966	15th June 1824	Preparing and manufacturing silk for weaving and other purposes.
HEATHCOAT, JOHN - -	5080	12th Jan. 1825	Machinery for making bobbin-net.
HEATHCOAT, JOHN - -	5093	12th Feb. 1825	Manufacturing silk.
HEATHCOAT, JOHN - -	5103	22th Feb. 1825	Producing figures or ornaments on goods manufactured from silk, cotton, flax, thread, or yarn.
HEATHCOAT, JOHN - -	5144	31st March 1825	Figuring or ornamenting various goods manufactured from silk, cotton, flax, or other thread or yarn.
HEATHCOAT, JOHN - -	5200	6th July 1825	Manufacturing thrown silk.
HEATHCOAT, JOHN - -	6173	3rd Oct. 1831	Machinery used in making bobbin or twist lace-net.
HEATHCOAT, JOHN - -	6222	16th Feb. 1832	Ornamenting, embroidering, or working devices upon lace-net and other fabrics.
HEATHCOAT, JOHN - -	6471	14th Sept. 1833	Machinery used in the manufacture of bobbin-net.
HEATHCOAT, JOHN - -	6967	23rd Dec. 1835	Weaving divers goods and wares; machinery applicable thereto.
HEATHCOAT, JOHN - -	7359	4th May 1837	Producing or forming ornaments or ornamented work or figures on gauze, muslin, net, or woven textures; machinery, tools, implements, or apparatus to be used for producing and applying the same.
HEATHCOAT, JOHN - -	9646	28th Feb. 1843	Manufacture of ornamented net or lace.
HEATHCOTE, JOHN - -	2788	17th Oct. 1804	Machinery and apparatus annexed to warp-frames for making thread-lace.
HEATHCOTE, Sir HENRY -	4880	13th Dec. 1823	Stay-sails of ships, and square-rigged vessels.
HEATHORN, CHARLES - -	5034	11th Nov. 1824	Constructing and erecting furnaces or kilns for making lime and coke, by the same heat, in one building.
HEATHORN, JOSEPH LIDWELL	6332	13th Nov. 1832	Rigging for ships and other vessels.
HEATON, EMANUEL - -	3794	23rd March 1814	Locks and breeches of fire-arms, by rendering the pans of locks and communication between the priming and loading of fire-arms waterproof.

Name of Patentee.	Progressive Number.	Date.	Subject-matter of Patent.
HEATON, GEORGE - - -	6006	6th Oct. 1830	Machinery, and the application thereof to steam-engines, for the purpose of propelling and drawing carriages on rail and other roads.
HEATON, GEORGE - - -	11,953	9th Nov. 1847	Locomotive-engines.
HEATON, JOHN - - -	6006	6th Oct. 1830	Machinery and the application thereof to steam-engines for the purpose of propelling and drawing carriages on rail and other roads.
HEATON, JOHN - - -	8700	12th Nov. 1840	Dressing yarns of linen or cotton or both, to be woven into various sorts of cloth.
HEATON, RALPH - - -	2010	5th Sept. 1794	Machine for making metal-shanks for buttons.
HEATON, REUBEN - - -	6006	6th Oct. 1830	Machinery and the application thereof to steam-engines for the purpose of propelling and drawing carriages on rail and other roads.
HEATON, RICHARD - -	1593	10th March 1787	Drill-harrow for sowing and harrowing grain, turnip-seed, rape-seed, or any other seed with regularity, and with the rows from six to thirty-six inches apart.
HEATON, ROWLAND HALL -	8069	20th May 1839	Connecting straps or bands for driving machinery, &c.; apparatus for effecting the same.
HEATON, THOMAS - - -	10,291	15th Aug. 1844	Hydraulic-machinery applicable to raising other liquids.
HEATON, WILLIAM - -	6006	6th Oct. 1830	Machinery and the application thereof to steam-engines for the purpose of propelling and drawing carriages on rail and other roads.
HEBERT, JOHN - - -	7842	3rd Nov. 1838	Apparatus and processes for storing, cleansing, and preserving grain.
HEBERT, LUKE - - -	3158	30th July 1808	Machine for polishing, embossing, and graining leather, and extending and flattening the same.
HEBERT, LUKE - - -	6370	24th Jan. 1833	Apparatus for and process of making bread from grain, and the application of other products for another product thereof, to certain purposes.
HEBERT, LUKE - - -	6388	21st Feb. 1833	Engines and other machinery employed in the construction of steam-vessels and steam-carriages.
HEBERT, LUKE - - -	6878	10th Aug. 1835	Flour-mills.
HEBERT, LUKE - - -	7087	9th May 1836	Horse-collars.
HEBERT, LUKE - - -	7106	2nd June 1836	Machinery and processes for purifying and economizing the manufacture of bread; partly applicable to other purposes.
HEBERT, LUKE - - -	7659	31st May 1838	Soldering metallic substances.
HEBERT, LUKE - - -	7842	3rd Nov. 1838	Apparatus and processes for storing, cleansing, and preserving grain.
HEBERT, LUKE - - -	7856	6th Nov. 1838	Processes for embalming the dead, and for preserving corpses for anatomical purposes.
HEBERT, LUKE - - -	7893	1st Dec. 1838	Fastening trousers and other parts of dress or apparel.
HEBERT, LUKE - - -	8125	22nd June 1839	Apparatus for producing and communicating artificial light.
HEBERT, LUKE - - -	8288	2nd Dec. 1839	Mechanism for and process of packing and pressing various articles of commerce.

Name of Patentee.	Progressive Number.	Date.	Subject-matter of Patent.
HEBERT, LUKE - - -	8420	7th March 1840	Manufacture of coffered spades and shovels, soughing and grafting tools, and other like implements.
HEBERT, LUKE - - -	8606	17th Aug. 1840	Manufacture of needles.
HEBERT, LUKE - - -	9070	8th Sept. 1841	Apparatus and materials used in the manufacture of gas for illumination; apparatus for burning the same.
HEBERT, LUKE - - -	9088	20th Sept. 1841	Machinery for fulling woollen-cloth.
HEBERT, LUKE - - -	9596	19th Jan. 1843	Machines for grinding and for dressing or sifting grain and other substances.
HEBERT, LUKE - - -	12,058	8th Feb. 1848	Mechanism for reducing, grinding, and sifting bark, sugar, coffee, seeds, and other substances.
HEBSON, DOUGLAS - - -	12,652	7th June 1849	Steam-engines.
HECKFORD, NATHAN - -	243	12th Nov. 1684	Making sails to go the horizontal way, for mills, for engines used in draining pits, and for other uses.
HECKFORD, NATHANIEL -	2060	24th Aug. 1795	Machinery for raising and removing earth, sand, gravel, clay, stone, or other things, from the bottom of canals or other places to the surface, or higher if required.
HEDGE, EGBERT - - -	11,577	12th Feb. 1847	Rails for railways; and manner of securing them.
HÉDIARD, ALEXANDER - -	12,973	21st Feb. 1850	Propelling.
HÉDIARD, ALEXANDER - -	13,944	31st Jan. 1852	Propelling and navigating ships, boats, and vessels by steam and other motive-power.
HÉDIARD, ALEXANDER - -	14,017	8th March 1852	Rotary steam-engines.
HEDLEY, THOMAS - - -	9289	8th March 1842	Apparatus for purifying the smoke, gases, and other noxious vapours arising from certain fires, stoves, and furnaces.
HEDLEY, WILLIAM - -	3666	13th March 1813	Mechanical means of conveying carriages laden with coals, minerals, and other things.
HEELEY, CLEMENT - -	7802	10th Sept. 1838	Straps for wearing-apparel.
HEELEY, CLEMENT - -	8938	27th April 1841	Patten and clog ties, and other articles or fastenings of dress.
HEFFER, GEORGE - - -	3627	19th Dec. 1812	Construction of four-wheel carriages.
HEGINBOTHAM, WILLIAM [HOLME.	7560	31st Jan. 1838	Construction of gas-retorts.
HEGINBOTHAM, WILLIAM [HOLME.	7940	17th Jan. 1839	Machinery for propelling boats or other vessels for marine or inland navigation, and worked by steam or other power.
HEGINBOTHAM, JAMES - -	13,381	2nd Dec. 1850	Manufacture of textile fabrics.
HEGNER, JEAN RUDOFF - -	1854	27th Feb. 1792	Pipe made of flaxen-yarn without seam, for conveying water from engines, and for other purposes.
HEILMANN, JOSUÉ - - -	11,103	25th Feb. 1846	Machines used for preparing to be spun cotton-wool, and other fibrous materials.
HEIMANN, JOHN BAPTIST [FRIED WILHELM.	8876	8th March 1841	Manufacture of ropes and cables.
HEINDRYCKX, FLORIDE - -	8934	24th April 1841	Construction and arrangement of fire-places and furnaces, applicable to various purposes.
HEINDRYCKX, FLORIDE - -	13,039	15th April 1850	Propelling.
HEINE, AUGUSTUS FREDERICK [DE.	3297	1st Feb. 1810	Printing and stamping presses.

Name of Patentee.	Progressive Number.	Date.	Subject-matter of Patent.
HEINE, AUGUSTUS FREDERICK [DE. [*Heine, Augustus De.*]	3310	26th Feb. 1810	Apparatus for preserving animal, vegetable, and other perishable food from decay.
HEISCH, PHILIP JACOB - -	5464	20th Feb. 1827	Machinery for spinning cotton.
HELBRONNER, RODOLPHE -	13,196	31st July 1850	Preventing the external air, dust and noise, from entering apartments.
HELBRONNER, RODOLPHE -	13,872	19th Dec. 1851	Apparatus used when obtaining instantaneous light.
HELE, WILLIAM - - -	1672	29th Oct. 1788	Drill-machine for sowing grain or any kind of seeds.
HELLEWELL, JAMES - -	6934	28th Nov. 1835	Process to render the texture of cotton and certain other fabrics impervious to water.
HELLEWELL, JAMES - -	7292	28th Jan. 1837	Dyeing and scouring piece-goods and other fabrics; machinery for the purpose.
HELY, ALFRED AUGUSTUS DE [REGINALD.	12,019	11th Jan. 1848	Bottles or vessels for containing liquids; mode of and machinery for filling and stopping the same.
HEMET, JACOB - - -	1031	22nd Jan. 1773	Essence of pearl and pearl-dentifrice, for preserving the teeth and gums, and remedying the disorders to which they are subject.
HEMING, EDMUND - - -	364	21st June 1699	Sweeping streets, greens and walks; loading the dirt, dust, or soil, also casks of all sorts; artillery carriages, waggons and carts; repairing the highways so as to throw ridges into the ruts.
HEMINGS, EDMUND - -	282	17th Oct. 1691	Tinning iron-plates to equal those made in and brought from Germany.
HEMINGWAY, ROBERT - -	7374	22nd May 1837	Machinery for carding and piecing wool in the process of manufacture in woollen-mills.
HEMMING, JOHN - - -	7207	13th Oct. 1836	Manufacture of white-lead.
HEMMING, JOHN - - -	7713	30th June 1838	Manufacture of carbonate of soda.
HEMMING, JOHN - - -	8154	16th July 1839	Gas-meters.
HEMMONS, JOHN - - -	12,339	23rd Nov. 1848	Manufacture of cocks or valves for drawing off liquids.
HEMPEL, CHARLES FREDERICK	1530	7th Feb. 1786	Proof earthen-cases with heaters of the same composition, for the purpose of warming beds, dishes, plates, &c.; also useful for persons in carriages or churches, enabling them to keep their feet warm.
HEMPEL, FREDERICK - -	6953	15th Dec. 1835	Oxydizing certain animal or vegetable substances; separating their several parts to render them (by means of divers operations, and either separately or in combination with other materials) capable of producing useful articles.
HEMPEL, JOHN FREDERICK [WILLIAM.	7184	15th Sept. 1836	Operating upon certain vegetable and animal substances in the process of manufacturing candles therefrom.
HEMPEL, JOHANNA - -	1776	16th Oct. 1790	Composition made of earth and other materials, and means of manufacturing the same into basins and other vessels; which basins so manufactured have the power of filtering water and other liquids.
HEMSLEY, WILLIAM - -	13,635	15th May 1851	Manufacture of looped fabrics.
HENCKELL, JAMES - - -	2989	20th Nov. 1806	Machine for dressing coffee or barley and other corn, grain, pulse, fruit, seed, and berries.

Name of Patentee.	Progres-sive Number.	Date.	Subject-matter of Patent.
HENDERSON, CHRISTOPHER　-	868	10th Feb.　1767	Medicine named " Beame de Vie;" manufacturing the same from valuable drugs.
HENDERSON, DAVID　-　-	10,713	10th June 1845	Cranes.
HENDERSON, DAVID　-　-	12,537	26th March 1849	Manufacture of metal-castings.
HENDERSON, DONALD　-　-	13,785	23rd Oct.　1851	Apparatus for generating gas, which may be also used for heating and other purposes; apparatus for heating and ventilating.
HENDERSON, JAMES　-　-	12,239	14th Aug.　1848	Machinery for cleansing and polishing rice, pearl-barley, and other grain and seed.
HENDERSON, JOSEPH　-　-	12,568	16th April 1849	Looms for weaving.
HENDERSON, ROBERT　-　-	9173	9th Dec.　1841	Apparatus for heating and lighting apartments, and for other like purposes.
HENDERSON, THOMAS　-　-	1578	19th Dec.　1786	Drawing and taking any visible object to any size, on true mathematical principles.
HENDERSON, WILLIAM -　-	12,102	22nd March 1848	Treating lead and other ores.
HENDLEY, ROBERT　-　-	7753	30th July 1838	Metallic-concrete, capable by means of fire of being cast into various forms, for a variety of purposes for which iron, lead, zinc, copper, and other substances, have heretofore been used.
HENDREY, JAMES -　-　-	6765	16th Feb.　1835	Laying floors in buildings, or a new combination in the construction of such floors.
HENDRIE, ROBERT JAMES, [junior	6265	3rd May　1832	Mode of improving dyed silk.
HENDRIE, ROBERT JAMES	10,938	11th Nov.　1845	Preparation of silk.
HENDRIKS, HERMAN　-　- [Hendricks, Herman.]	6247	22nd March 1832	Manufacturing the prussiates of potash, soda, and iron, construction of apparatus for the purpose; employing prussiate of iron as a substitute for indigo, in dyeing wools, whether in the fleece, skin, spun or woven, also in dyeing silks, cottons, linens, and other substances; arrangement of utensils and machinery to be used in such process.
HENDRIKS, HERMAN　-　-	6492	19th Oct.　1833	Manufacturing prussiate of potash, and prussiate of soda; dyeing blue colours without indigo.
HENDRIKS, HERMAN　-　-	6589	8th April　1834	Dyeing wool and woollen fabrics yellow.
HENDRIKS, HERMAN　-　-	6784	11th March 1835	Dyeing.
HENDRY, THOMAS -　-　-	9453	25th Aug.　1842	Machinery for preparing and combing wool and other fibrous materials.
HENFREY, JOHN　-　-　-	4850	9th Oct.　1823	Machinery for casting types.
HENFREY, JOHN　-　-　-	7840	25th Oct.　1838	Manufacture of hinges or joints; machinery employed therein.
HENLEY, WILLIAM THOMAS -	12,236	10th Aug.　1848	Telegraphic communication; apparatus connected therewith;—in part applicable to the moving of other machines or machinery.
HENNETT, GEORGE　-　-	10,734	23rd June 1845	Construction of parts of apparatus for propelling carriages and vessels by the atmosphere; propelling carriages and vessels by atmospheric pressure.
HENRY, GEORGE PALMER　-	9198	21st Dec.　1841	Apparatus to be applied to the glass-chimneys of gas-burners.
HENRY, JAMES Mᶜ -　-　-	14,234	20th July 1852	Machinery for manufacturing bricks and tiles.

Name of Patentee.	Progressive Number.	Date.	Subject-matter of Patent.
HENRY, MAYER - - -	9859	3rd Aug. 1843	Steam-engines, boilers, and propelling-machinery.
HENRY, MEYER - - -	11,758	19th June 1847	Treating, manuring, or preparing corn, seeds, plants, and trees; fertilizing land.
HENRY, PETER - - -	601	17th Feb. 1744	Chemical preparation for the cure of nervous complaints. "Nervous medicine."
HENRY, SOLOMON - - -	1004	6th Feb. 1772	Machine for giving alarm in houses, in case of fire or burglary.
HENRY, SOLOMON - - -	1080	12th Sept. 1774	Machine for weighing coin, and ascertaining counterfeit coin.
HENRY, SOLOMON - - -	1146	20th Feb. 1777	Machine for watering roads, gardens, and lands.
HENRY, SOLOMON - - -	1226	28th May 1779	Apparatus to act as a universal lock or bolt.
HENRY, SOLOMON - - -	1575	9th Dec. 1786	Instrument to stamp or mark with, which may be composed of various colours, so as not to be counterfeited or forged.
HENRY, WILLIAM - - -	4049	3rd Aug. 1816	Manufacture of sulphate of magnesia, or Epsom salts.
HENSHALL, EDWARD - -	8811	26th Jan. 1841	Manufacturing carpets and hearth-rugs.
HENSHALL, SAMUEL - -	2061	24th Aug. 1795	Constructing and improving corkscrews.
HENSHAW, THOMAS - -	145	22nd April 1664	Making a valuable metal, as sweet, clean, and wholesome as silver, by mixing a certain stone with chargeable ingredients, to be used for making various vessels.
HENSMAN, WILLIAM - -	8760	31st Dec. 1840	Ploughs.
HENSMAN, WILLIAM - -	11,795	17th July 1847	Thrashing-machines.
HENSON, HENRY - -	11,361	31st Aug. 1846	Railways and railway-carriages.
HENSON, HENRY - -	11,438	5th Nov. 1846	Fabric suitable for goods-wrappers, waggon-covers, and other purposes; processes in the manufacture of the same.
HENSON, HENRY HENSON -	12,122	15th April 1848	Railway carriages and waggons; vessels employed for the storing and conveyance of explosive substances.
HENSON, HENRY HENSON -	12,661	14th June 1849	Railways and railway-carriages.
HENSON, SAMUEL - - -	9478	29th Sept. 1842	Apparatus and machinery for conveying letters, goods, and passengers, from place to place through the air.
HENSON, WILLIAM - -	5067	11th Jan. 1825	Machinery for making bobbin-net lace.
HENSON, WILLIAM - -	6354	26th Dec. 1832	Machinery for producing lace in various breadths, with edges or quilling.
HENSON, WILLIAM - -	6355	26th Dec. 1832	Machinery for manufacturing bobbin-net laces.
HENSON, WILLIAM - -	6397	14th March 1833	Machinery for manufacturing bobbin-net lace.
HENSON, WILLIAM - -	8708	19th Nov. 1840	Machinery for making certain fabrics with thread or yarns;—applicable to various useful purposes.
HENSON, WILLIAM - -	10,933	11th Nov. 1845	Machinery for weaving.
HENSON, WILLIAM SAMUEL -	6898	1st Oct. 1835	Machinery used for making bobbin-net lace.
HENSON, WILLIAM SAMUEL -	8849	16th Feb. 1841	Steam-engines.
HENSON, WILLIAM SAMUEL -	11,797	17th July 1847	Construction of razors for shaving.
HENWOOD, WILLIAM - -	11,685	4th May 1847	Propelling vessels, and steering vessels.
HEPBURN, FRANCIS JOHN [SWAINE.	13,669	17th June 1851	Manufacture of carriages and other vehicles.

Name of Patentee.	Progressive Number.	Date.	Subject-matter of Patent.
HEPPENSTALL, JOHN - -	2770	2nd June 1804	Machinery or mill-spinning for spinning cotton-wool, silk, hemp, flax, and substitutes for hemp and flax, and for laying cords, line, twine, and thread.
HEPPENSTALL, JOHN - -	2817	5th Feb. 1805	Slivering and preparing hemp, flax, and substitutes for hemp and flax, previous to spinning.
HEPPENSTALL, THOMAS -	4234	7th March 1818	Machine for cutting or reducing various articles into chaff, as dry fodder for horses and cattle.
HERAPATH, WILLIAM - -	7478	16th Nov. 1837	Tanning.
HERBERT, JOHN - -	5059	18th Dec. 1824	Machines for shearing or cropping woollen-cloths.
HERBERT, THOMAS -	3281	28th Nov. 1809	Rotative pump, or engine for raising and forcing air, water, and other fluids.
HERBERT, WILLIAM -	6399	21st March 1833	Warp-machinery, employed for the manufacture of lace and other substances.
HERIOT, JAMES - -	993	2nd July 1771	Supplying branches, sconces, and lamps, with oil.
HERIOT, JAMES - -	1322	20th March 1782	Mariner's compass, with compass-boxes, pendent or standing, and ventilator to contain either lamp or candle.
HERRADINE, JOHN THANG -	12,132	20th April 1848	Fitting certain girths and straps.
HERRING, MATTHEW -	13,562	24th March 1851	Manufacture of sugar and rum;—partly applicable to evaporation generally.
HERTZ, BRAM - -	12,681	30th June 1849	Fountain-pens.
HERVEY, ROBERT - - -	8309	13th Dec. 1839	Preparing and purifying alum, alumina, aluminous mordants, and other aluminous combinations and solutions, and the application thereof to purposes of manufacture.
HERZ, ADOLPHUS CHARLES [VON.	14,143	29th May 1852	Treating, preparing, and preserving roots and plants; extracting saccharine and other juices from roots and plants; treatment of such juices; processes, machinery, and apparatus employed therein.
HESELTINE, SAMUEL - -	9937	9th Nov. 1843	Engines worked by air or other gases.
HESELTINE, SAMUEL - -	11,014	22nd Dec. 1845	Machinery for dressing stones used in grinding corn, grain, and other substances.
HESELTINE, SAMUEL, junior -	11,398	8th Oct. 1846	Construction of lamps to burn oil.
HESELTINE, SAMUEL, junior -	14,086	24th April 1852	Engines to be worked by air or gases.
HESFORD, JAMES - - -	9718	2nd May 1843	Manufacture of certain bowls or rolls.
HESLOP, ADAM - - -	1760	17th July 1790	Engine for lessening the consumption of steam and fuel in fire-engines or steam-engines.
HESKETH, ROBERT - -	13,955	3rd Feb. 1852	Apparatus for reflecting light into rooms, and other parts of buildings and places.
HESSE, EMANUEL - - -	2426	24th July 1800	Stirrups.
HESTER, JAMES TORRY - -	7258	15th Dec. 1836	Manufacture of chairs.
HETHERINGTON, JOHN - -	10,166	30th April 1844	Stationary steam-boilers; furnaces and flues connected therewith.
HETHERINGTON, JOHN - -	12,870	3rd Dec. 1849	Machinery for preparing and spinning cotton, flax, and other fibrous substances.

Name of Patentee.	Progressive Number.	Date.		Subject-matter of Patent.
HETHERINGTON, JOHN - -	13,208	31st July	1850	Machinery for preparing, spinning, and weaving cotton, flax, and other fibrous substances; constructing, and applying models for moulding, preparatory to casting, parts of such machinery; tools to be used in making such machinery.
HETHERINGTON, JOHN - -	13,499	10th Feb.	1851	Moulding, preparatory to casting pipes, railings, gates, agricultural-implements, and other metallic articles; preparing patterns or models for the same.
HETHERINGTON, WILLIAM -	14,251	3rd Aug.	1852	Machinery for stamping or shaping metals.
HETT, ALEXANDER - -	8360	23rd Jan.	1840	Arrangement and construction of fire-grates or fire-places;—applicable to various purposes.
HEURTELOUP, CHARLES LOUIS [STANISLAS Baron.	6611	22nd May	1834	Fire-arms.
HEURTELOUP, CHARLES LOUIS [STANISLAS Baron.	7980	23rd Feb.	1839	Fire-arms, and balls to be used therewith.
HEURTELOUP, CHARLES LOUIS [STANISLAS Baron.	9084	9th Sept.	1841	Manufacture of continuous priming for certain descriptions of fire-arms; mechanism for applying the same.
HERRYPON, MARSHALL AU-[GUSTIN JOSEPH DE.	8079	25th May	1839	Machine for washing and bleaching wool, cotton, silk, linen, and other fibrous materials, manufactured or unmanufactured.
HEUZE, EDMOND - - -	7820	27th Sept.	1838	Manufacture of dextrine.
HEWES, THOMAS CHUCK -	5756	14th Jan.	1829	Form and construction of windmills, and their sails.
HEWITT, HENRY - - -	7543	18th Jan.	1838	Pills for the cure and amelioration of sciatica, rheumatism, and gout, lumbago, ague, and similar diseases.
HEWITT, DANIEL CHANDLER -	7894	6th Dec.	1838	Musical-instruments.
HEWITT, DANIEL CHANDLER -	10,385	9th Nov.	1844	Stringed and wind musical-instruments.
HEWITT, JOHN - - -	6595	19th April	1834	Combination of materials, forming a substance or compound, to be used with or as a substitute for soap.
HEWITT, JOHN - - -	14,046	27th March	1852	Machinery for spinning, doubling, and twisting, cotton and other fibrous substances.
HEWITT, SAMUEL GEORGE -	12,237	11th Aug.	1848	Construction of certain parts of railways.
HEWLINGS, EDWARD - -	2077	9th Dec.	1795	Machinery for measuring distances, taking altitudes and descents, dimensions of lands, buildings, and other bodies or articles, at one view;—applicable to other purposes.
HEYCOCK, EDWIN - - -	12,943	26th Jan.	1850	Finishing and dressing woollen-cloths.
HEYCOCK, HENRY - - -	11,639	23rd March	1847	Rotary engines, to be worked by steam or other power, applicable to raising or forcing fluids.
HEYCOCK, WILLIAM - -	5201	8th July	1825	Machinery for dressing and finishing cloth.
HEYCOCK, WILLIAM - -	5203	8th July	1825	Machinery for dressing and finishing cloth.
HEYCOCK, WILLIAM - -	5235	11th Aug.	1825	Apparatus to prevent the overturning of coaches, carriages, mails, and other vehicles.
HEYLYN, EDWARD - - -	610	6th Dec.	1744	Manufacturing a certain material for making ware, to equal china or porcelain.
HEYNS, PATRICK - - -	13,319	7th Nov.	1850	Obtaining and applying motive-power; pumps.
HEYS, HENRY - - -	13,091	1st June	1850	Machinery for manufacturing woven fabrics.

Name of Patentee.	Progressive Number.	Date.	Subject-matter of Patent.
HEYS, JOHN - - - -	1036	19th March 1773	Making lees and ashes from marl and other materials, for bleaching cloth and yarn and for the use of soapers, dyers, and others.
HEYS, JOHN - - - -	1371	7th May 1783	Making ashes and lees from straw, turf, lime, dung, dirt of the street, and other waste.
HEYS, THOMAS - - -	1151	10th April 1777	Engine for spinning, drawing, and twisting cotton-wool, the wool of sheep, also silk, and flax.
HEYS, THOMAS - - -	6305	8th Sept. 1832	" Throstles" or machinery for spinning cotton, silk, flax, and other fibrous substances.
HEYTHUYSEN, FREDERIC MIG-[HELLS VAN.	4440	18th March 1820	Making portable machines or instruments of wood, brass, or other metal, which are to be placed on a desk or table, and contrived so as to fold into a small compass if required, the said machines to be used for supporting a silk-shade for the purpose of protecting the eyes from a strong light, added to which is a green, blue, or other coloured glass-reflector, which being placed opposite a window, lamp, or candle will take off the glare from white paper and render print more legible because less dazzling.
HEYTHUYSEN, FREDERIC MIG-[HELLS VAN.	4572	23rd July 1821	Propelling small vessels or boats through water and light carriages over land.
HEYWOOD, BENJAMIN - -	13,506	11th Feb. 1851	Railway and other carriages.
HEYWOOD, EDWIN - - -	12,768	13th Sept. 1849	Plain and ornamental weaving.
HEYWOOD, GEORGE - -	3813	7th June 1814	Turning rolls, or rolling gun and pistol barrels, previous to welding.
HEYWOOD, HENRY - - -	12,037	22nd Jan. 1848	Looms for weaving,
HEYWOOD, JOHN SHARP CRO-[MARTIE.	12,611	15th May 1849	Expressing and treating oils; manufacture of varnishes, pigments, and paints.
HEYWORTH, LAWRENCE - -	7790	30th Aug. 1838	Applying steam-power to the periphery of the movement wheel for locomotion, both on land and water, and for propelling machinery.
HICK, BENJAMIN - - -	6550	25th Jan. 1834	Locomotive steam-carriages;—partly applicable to ordinary carriages and steam-engines for other uses.
HICK, BENJAMIN - - -	6638	4th July 1834	Construction and adaptation of metallic packings for the pistons of steam and other engines, pumps, and for other purposes to which the same may be applied.
HICK, BENJAMIN - - -	6689	8th Oct. 1834	Locomotive steam-carriages;—partly applicable to ordinary carriages, and steam-engines for other uses.
HICK, BENJAMIN - - -	8081	25th May 1839	Machinery for drying cotton, woollen, and other fabrics, also other fibrous substances.
HICK, BENJAMIN, iunior -	8613	27th Aug. 1840	Regulators or governors, for adjusting the speed or rotary motion of steam-engines, water-wheels, also other machinery.
HICK, JOHN - - - -	9971	5th Dec. 1843	Steam-engines; apparatus to be connected therewith for driving machinery;—partly applicable to forcing, lifting, and measuring water.

Name of Patentee.	Progressive Number.	Date.	Subject-matter of Patent.
HICK, JOHN - - - -	10597	7th April 1845	Machinery for cleaning wheat and other grain or seeds from smut and other injurious matters.
HICK, JOHN - - - -	12488	28th Feb. 1849	Steam-engines, more particularly applicable to marine-engines; machinery for propelling vessels.
HICK, JOHN - - - -	13,691	17th July 1851	Steam-boilers or generators.
HICKES, GEORGE - - -	9051	21st Aug. 1841	Machine for cleaning and freeing wool and other fibrous materials, of burs and other extraneous substances.
HICKFORD, GEORGE - -	3343	8th June 1810	Plough for draining land; machines for drawing the same through the ground.
HICKINBOTHAM, DAVID -	9026	13th July 1841	Construction of chimneys, flues, and air-tubes, with the stoves and other apparatus connected therewith, for preventing the escape of smoke into apartments, and for warming and ventilating buildings.
HICKLING, SAMUEL SANDY -	2296	28th Feb. 1799	Beatifying vessels used for chemical, culinary, and other purposes.
HICKMAN, JOHN - - -	12,031	18th Jan. 1848	Constructing and connecting parts of bedsteads, couches, and other articles of furniture; attaching knobs to drawers, doors, and other articles of furniture.
HICKMAN, JOHN - - -	12,821	2nd Nov. 1849	Manufacturing bedsteads, chairs, tables, couches, and tubular or hollow articles.
HICKMAN, JOHN - - -	13,083	25th May 1850	Manufacturing cylindrical or other tubes.
HICKMAN, ROBERT - -	1586	1st Feb. 1787	Manufacturing gilt and plated coat and waistcoat buttons, by uniting (by means of tin or tin and lead mixed) the gilt and plated shells with bottoms of copper, brass, iron, or mixed and compound metals.
HICKS, ROBERT - - -	5131	22nd March 1825	Bath.
HICKS, ROBERT - - -	5944	29th June 1830	Machine to be applied in the process of baking, for the purpose of saving materials.
HICKS, ROBERT - - -	6130	6th July 1831	Culinary-apparatus.
HICKS, ROBERT - - -	6285	19th July 1832	Method of and apparatus for baking bread.
HICKS, ROBERT - - -	6391	21st Feb. 1833	Apparatus for baking bread.
HICKS, ROBERT - - -	9626	11th Feb. 1843	Apparatus for impregnating liquids with gases.
HIGGIN, JAMES - - -	13,662	12th June 1851	Treating and preparing certain colouring matters to be used in dyeing and printing.
HIGGIN, JAMES - - -	14,179	24th June 1852	Bleaching and scouring woven and textile fabrics, and yarns.
HIGGIN, ROBERT - - -	4834	18th Aug. 1823	Consuming smoke.
HIGGINS, BRYAN - - -	874	29th April 1767	Instrument which being made to represent a candle and candlestick, keeps the surface of a column of oil contained therein at nearly an equal distance from the blaze, and renders the light given by oil steady and is also as portable, cleanly, and convenient as candles of tallow or wax.
HIGGINS, BRYAN - - -	1207	18th Jan. 1779	Water cement or stucco, for building, repairing, or plastering walls, and for other purposes.
HIGGINS, BRYAN - - -	1302	31st July 1781	Extracting or producing mineral-alkali, and fixed vegetable-alkali.

Name of Patentee.	Progressive Number.	Date.	Subject-matter of Patent.
HIGGINS, BRYAN - - -	2583	19th Feb. 1802	Apparatus for heating air equally; applying the air so heated with great advantage and economy of fuel, to purposes where stoves and kilns have heretofore been employed.
HIGGINS, JAMES - - -	10,584	2nd April 1845	Machinery for preparing, spinning, and doubling cotton-wool, flax, silk, and similar fibrous materials.
HIGGINS, JAMES - - -	12,785	24th Sept. 1849	Machinery for preparing, spinning, and doubling cotton-wool, flax, silk, and other fibrous materials.
HIGGINS, JAMES - - -	14,203	6th July 1852	Machinery for spinning and doubling cotton and other fibrous substances.
HIGGINS, JOHN - - -	4653	2nd March 1822	Construction of carriages.
HIGGINS, JOHN - - -	6638	4th July 1834	Construction and adaptation of metallic packings for the pistons of steam and other engines, also for pumps and for other purposes.
HIGGINS, JOHN LANE - -	4985	7th July 1824	Construction of the masts, yards, sails, and rigging of ships and smaller vessels; tackle used for working or navigating the same.
HIGGINS, JOHN LANE - -	5333	11th Feb. 1826	Construction of the masts, yards, sails, and rigging of ships and smaller vessels; tackle used for working or navigating the same.
HIGGINS, JOHN LANE - -	5390	14th July 1826	Construction of cat-blocks, and fish-hooks; application thereof.
HIGGINS, JOHN LANE - -	5680	11th Aug. 1828	Wheel carriages.
HIGGINS, JOHN LANE - -	6892	26th Aug. 1835	Construction of vessels for navigation; working the same.
HIGGINS, JOHN LANE - -	11,750	15th June 1847	Construction of winches and windlasses.
HIGGINS, WILLIAM - -	6639	7th July 1834	Machinery used for making twisted rovings and yarn of cotton, flax, silk, wool, and other fibrous substances.
HIGGINSON, FRANCIS - -	9958	21st Nov. 1843	Fastenings for parts of ships and other vessels;—applicable to other building purposes.
HIGGINSON, FRANCIS - -	10 397	21st Nov. 1844	Construction of buildings generally.
HIGGINSON, GEORGE MONTA-[GUE.	4096	1st Feb. 1817	Locks.
HIGGINSON, HENRY - -	3564	9th May 1812	Propelling boats or vessels with the aid of steam or any other power.
HIGGON, JOHN PENTON - -	4980	22nd June 1824	Carving-knives and other edged tools.
HIGGS, JOSEPH - - -	1850	11th Feb. 1792	Bedsteads.
HIGGS, JOSEPH - - -	2007	13th Aug. 1794	Construction of tables, sashes, and shutters; sliding-hinges, applicable to the same and other purposes.
HIGGS, WILLIAM - - -	11,181	28th April 1846	Collecting sewage of cities; treating the same chemically; applying it to agricultural and other purposes.
HIGHAM, JOHN WARD - -	6979	11th Jan. 1836	Tablet for sharpening razors, pen-knives, surgical instruments, chisels, plane-irons, and other instruments, by hones, Turkey-stones, or Welch-stones.
HIGHAM, WILLIAM - -	10,221	6th June 1844	Constructions of boilers for evaporating saline and other solutions, for crystallization.
HIGHTON, EDWARD - -	12,039	25th Jan. 1848	Electric-telegraphs.

Name of Patentee.	Progressive Number.	Date.		Subject-matter of Patent.
HIGHTON, EDWARD - - -	12,959	7th Feb.	1850	Electric-telegraphs, and making telegraphic communications.
HIGHTON, EDWARD - - -	13,938	29th Jan.	1852	Electric-telegraphs.
HIGHTON, HENRY - - -	10,257	10th July	1844	Electrict-elegraphs.
HIGHTON, HENRY - - -	11,070	3rd Feb.	1846	Electric-telegraphs.
HIGHTON, HENRY - - -	12,039	25th Jan.	1848	Electric-telegraphs.
HIGMAN, WILLIAM HENRY -	4580	14th Aug.	1821	Construction of harness.
HIGSON, PETER - - -	10,814	9th Aug.	1845	Machinery for connecting and disconnecting the steam-engine or other motive-power with or from the load or matter to be driven or moved.
HIGTON, PAUL - - -	1429	21st April	1784	Refining, clarifying, or separating oil, gall, dirt and other matters, from lees of pot-ash, pearlash, barilla-ash, or any other fossil, vegetable, or caustic alkali, after being used in bleaching.
HIGTON, PAUL - - -	1532	21st Feb.	1786	Machine for spinning and roving sheep's and lambs' wool for making cloth, or for other purposes where woollen yarn is used.
HILDEYERDE, CHARLES -	147	16th Feb.	1665	Making blue paper used by sugar-bakers and others.
HILAH, SELAH - - -	12,126	15th April	1848	Manufacturing stair-rods.
HILL, AARON - - -	393	23rd Oct.	1713	Expressing oil from the fruit or triangular seed of the beech tree.
HILL, ABRAHAM - - -	143	3rd March	1664	Carriages and coaches with rollers, cranes, and springs; guns and pistols; powder horn; instrument for breaking and dressing hemp and flax; pendulum for measuring time and finding out the longitude at sea.
HILL, ABRAHAM - - -	1843	17th Dec.	1791	Making scythes, with steel-blades and iron or steel backs, fixed on with screws or pins.
HILL, ABRAHAM - - -	1972	18th Dec.	1793	Making steel-knives, with iron-backs, for cutting hay and straw.
HILL, ANTHONY - - -	3825	26th July	1814	Smelting and working iron.
HILL, ANTHONY - - -	4151	5th Aug.	1817	Working iron.
HILL, ARTHUR - - -	9747	27th May	1843	Shower-baths.
HILL, EDWARD - - -	10,181	14th May	1844	Manufacture of railway and other axles, shafts, and bars.
HILL, EDWIN - - -	10,565	17th March	1845	Manufacture of envelopes.
HILL, JAMES - - -	7598	19th March	1838	Apparatus, applicable to machinery used in preparing cotton and other fibrous material for spinning.
HILL, JAMES - - -	11,755	19th June	1847	Machines for preparing, spinning, and doubling cotton-wool and other fibrous substances.
HILL, JAMES - - -	13,173	15th July	1850	Machines for preparing cotton-wool, and other fibrous substances, for spinning and doubling.
HILL, JOHN - - -	363	11th May	1699	Smelting ores in the Hungarian manner, with or without bellows.
HILL, JOHN - - -	5090	3rd Feb.	1825	Locomotive or steam carriage, for conveyance of mails, passengers, and goods.
HILL, JOHN - - -	5405	22nd Aug.	1826	Machinery for propelling locomotive-carriages.

Name of Patentee.	Progressive Number.	Date.		Subject-matter of Patent.
HILL, JOHN - - - -	9625	11th Feb.	1843	Looms for weaving carpets and other fabrics in which raised loops or pile constitute the figure of the fabric.
HILL, JOHN - - - -	11,730	3rd June	1847	Looms for weaving certain kinds of cloth.
HILL, JOHN REED - - -	9976	8th Dec.	1843	Presses for letter-press printing.
HILL, JOHN REED - - -	10,284	2nd Aug.	1844	Presses for letter-press printing.
HILL, JOHN REED - - -	10,841	2nd Oct.	1845	Atmospheric propulsion, applicable to water as well as land carriage.
HILL, JOSEPH - - -	4337	23rd Jan.	1819	Machine or top for the cure of smoky chimneys.
HILL, JOSEPH - - -	10,656	6th May	1845	Manufacturing wire-fabrics for blinds, and other uses.
HILL, LAURENCE - - -	10,007	11th Jan.	1844	Machinery for manufacturing shoes for horses and other animals.
HILL, LAURENCE - - -	11,288	14th July	1846	Manufacture of iron for building ships and other vessels; instruments and machinery to be used in constructing the same.
HILL, LAURENCE - - -	11,920	21st Oct.	1847	Manufacture of sugar.
HILL, LAURENCE - - -	12,457	8th Feb.	1849	Manufacture of iron; machinery for producing the same.
HILL, OLIVER - - -	363	11th May	1699	Smelting ores in the Hungarian manner, with or without bellows.
HILL, RICHARD - - -	6792	18th March	1835	Locks, and staples used therewith.
HILL, ROWLAND - - -	6762	12th Feb.	1835	Letter-press printing, by machinery.
HILL, SAMUEL - - -	3070	26th Aug.	1807	Making iron and steel backs, for fixing upon and using with the blades of scythes and straw and hay knives.
HILL, SAMUEL - - -	3355	3rd July	1810	Joining stone-pipes.
HILL, SAMUEL - - -	8443	25th March	1840	Making bread and biscuit.
HILL, SYMON - - - -	64	30th May	1633	Removing bars or beds of sand and gravel from rivers; obtaining firm foundations under water; draining flat and level grounds, by sluices, channels, or otherwise.
HILL, THOMAS - - -	5160	10th May	1825	Construction of railways and tramroads; carriages to be used thereon and on other roads.
HILL, THOMAS - - -	13,565	24th March	1851	Wrought iron or malleable iron; railway-chairs.
HILL, THOMAS IRVING - -	13,001	9th March	1850	Treatment of copper and other ores, obtaining products therefrom.
HILL, URILE CORELLI - -	11,768	28th June	1847	Method of producing musical sounds.
HILL, WILLIAM HOPKINS -	5104	26th Feb.	1825	Machinery for propelling vessels.
HILLARD, JOHN - - -	7953	29th Jan.	1839	Machinery for making screws.
HILLARY, AUGUSTUS WILLIAM	11,308	23rd July	1846	Manufacture of gas.
HILLCOAT, THOMAS - -	838	28th Jan.	1766	Machine for disengaging horses from coaches, carriages, and other conveyances, on an emergency.
HILLES, MALCOLM WILLIAM -	10,949	18th Nov.	1845	Construction of railways; machinery and apparatus for working carriages thereon.
HILLMAN, THOMAS - -	5645	1st May	1828	Construction and fastening of made-masts.
HILLS, FRANK - - -	7958	29th Jan.	1839	Construction of steam-boilers, and locomotive-engines.
HILLS, FRANK - - -	8495	5th May	1840	Construction of steam-boilers and engines, and locomotive-carriages.

Name of Patentee.	Progressive Number.	Date.	Subject-matter of Patent.
HILLS, FRANK - - -	8925	15th April 1841	Manufacturing sulphuric-acid and carbonate of soda.
HILLS, FRANK - - -	9684	30th March 1843	Steam-boilers; locomotive-carriages.
HILLS, FRANK - - -	10,812	9th Aug. 1845	Purifying gas for illuminating; obtaining a valuable product in the process.
HILLS, FRANK - - -	11,326	11th Aug. 1846	Treating certain gases; manufacturing sulphuric, muriatic, and acetic acids, and salts of potash, soda, and ammonia.
HILLS, FRANK CLARKE -	12,290	19th Oct. 1848	Treating certain salts and gases or vapours.
HILLS, FRANK CLARKE -	12,867	28th Nov. 1849	Compressing peat for making fuel or gas; manufacturing gas; obtaining substances for purifying the same.
HILLS, FRANK CLARKE -	13,093	1st June 1850	Manufacturing and refining sugar.
HILLS, FRANK CLARKE -	13,912	24th Jan. 1852	Manufacturing and purifying certain gases, preparing certain substances for purifying the same.
HILLS, GEORGE - - -	8925	15th April 1841	Manufacturing sulphuric-acid and carbonate of soda.
HILLS, GEORGE - - -	13,093	1st June 1850	Manufacturing and refining sugar.
HILLS, THOMAS - - -	4263	19th May 1818	Manufacture of sulphuric-acid.
HILLS, THOMAS - - -	6389	21st Feb. 1833	Furnaces for steam-boilers, and for other purposes.
HILTON, CHRISTOPHER - -	4401	18th Oct. 1819	Process for improving and finishing manufactured piece-goods.
HILTON, ROBERT - - -	1484	11th June 1785	Furling and unfurling the cloth upon the sails of windmills; raising and lowering the mill-stones in the mill, so as to cause them to grind with greater advantage than heretofore; regulating-nut or wheel for turning the stones.
HILLYARD, NICHOLAS - -	2	1st May 1617	Drawing, engraving, and printing pictures and representations of His Majesty, on paper, parchment, and other suitable materials.
HINCHSLIFFE, JOSEPH - -	2922	26th March 1806	Manufacturing elastic spring trusses for ruptures or rupture bandages.
HIND, ROGER - - -	14,253	7th Aug. 1852	Construction of machinery, applicable to weighing-machines, weigh-bridges, railway-turntables, cranes, and other similar apparatus.
HINDLEY, ALBERT DANIEL -	10,337	3rd Oct. 1844	Manufacture of carpets and other piled fabrics.
HINDLEY, ALBERT DANIEL -	10,658	6th May 1845	Manufacture of carpets and other piled fabrics.
HINDMAN, WILLIAM - -	14,081	22nd April 1852	Generating or producing steam; machinery or apparatus connected therewith.
HINDMARSH, RALPH - -	5459	3rd Feb. 1827	Construction of capstans or windlasses.
HINDMARSH, ROBERT - -	2272	27th Nov. 1798	Applying an elementary or physical power to blast furnaces and other works where power is required.
HINES, HENRY - - -	462	20th Feb. 1724	Raising copper-battery in common battery-mills, cold and without cramping or nailing, for brewing-furnaces, kettles, pots, and such like articles.
HINKS, JAMES - - -	13,665	14th June 1851	Construction of reels of metal, for winding cotton, silk, and other threads; machinery for making the same.

Name of Patentee.	Progressive Number.	Date.		Subject-matter of Patent.
HINKS, JOHN - - -	10,005	4th Jan.	1843	Manufacturing metallic pens; machines for the purpose.
HINKS, JOHN - - -	13,524	24th Feb.	1851	Manufacture of hats, caps, bonnets, and other coverings for the head.
HINKS, JOHN - - -	13,915	24th Jan.	1852	Machinery to be used in the manufacture of nails, rivets, bolts, or pins, and screw blanks.
HINKS, JOHN - - -	14,098	29th April	1852	Compositions; machinery for pressing or moulding the same, applicable to moulding or pressing other substances.
HINLEY, BENJAMIN - -	13,383	5th Dec.	1850	Manufacture of castors.
HINTON, WILLIAM - -	484	21st July	1726	Extracting and calcining the lixiviate salt of ashes of wood and other vegetables.
HIORT, JOHN WILLIAM -	5284	8th Nov.	1825	Chimney or flue for domestic and other purposes.
HIRST, HENRY - - -	5209	16th July	1825	Scribbling and carding sheeps' wool.
HIRST, HENRY - - -	5210	16th July	1825	Construction of looms for weaving woollen-cloths.
HIRST, HENRY - - -	5235	11th Aug.	1825	Apparatus to prevent coaches, carriages, mails, and other vehicles overturning.
HIRST, HENRY - - -	5907	27th Feb.	1830	Manufacturing woollen-cloth.
HIRST, SAMUEL - - -	5774	10th March	1829	Combination of materials for scouring, milling or fulling, cleansing and washing, cloths and other fabrics.
HIRST, WILLIAM - - -	4986	7th July	1824	Machinery for the raising or dressing of cloth.
HIRST, WILLIAM - - -	5070	11th Jan.	1825	Spinning and slubbing machines.
HIRST, WILLIAM - - -	5118	5th March	1825	Cleaning, milling, or fulling cloth.
HIRST, WILLIAM - - -	5209	16th July	1825	Scribbling and carding sheeps' wool.
HIRST, WILLIAM - - -	5218	16th July	1825	Apparatus for giving a new motion to mules and billies.
HIRST, WILLIAM - - -	5225	26th July	1825	Printing or dyeing woollen and other fabrics.
HIRST, WILLIAM - - -	5235	11th Aug.	1825	Apparatus to prevent coaches, carriages, mails, and other vehicles overturning.
HIRST, WILLIAM - - -	5268	21st Oct.	1825	Machinery for the raising and dressing of cloth.
HIRST, WILLIAM - - -	6586	31st March	1834	Machinery for dressing and finishing woollen and other fabrics.
HIRST, WILLIAM - - -	8642	24th Sept.	1840	Manufacture of woollen-cloth and cloth made from wool and other materials.
HIRST, WILLIAM - - -	9109	7th Oct.	1841	Machinery for manufacturing woollen-cloth, and cloth made from wool and other materials.
HIRST, WILLIAM - - -	13,862	19th Dec.	1851	Machinery or apparatus for manufacturing woollen-cloth, and cloth made from wool and other materials.
HITCH, CALEB - - -	5616	21st Feb.	1828	Wall for building purposes.
HITCHCOCK, JAMES - -	1934	27th Feb.	1793	Apparatus, by means of which several prints or drawings may be contained and exhibited in the same frame, and changed or varied at pleasure, and whereby each print will produce the same effect as if contained in a separate frame.
HITCHCOCK, JAMES - -	2442	15th Sept.	1800	Converting skins of parchment and vellum into leather; making such leather waterproof.

Name of Patentee.	Progressive Number.	Date.	Subject-matter of Patent.
HITCHIN, JOHN HARTLEY -	7405	19th July 1837	Construction and arrangement of cranes for lifting and removing goods.
HIVES, JOHN - - - -	3257	12th Aug. 1809	Machine for heckling or dressing hemp, flax, and other materials.
HJORTH, SOREN - - -	12,295	26th Oct. 1848	Use of electro-magnetism; its application as a motive-power;—also applicable to ships, engines, and railways.
HOAKESLY, ROBERT - -	2129	20th July 1796	Making British potash.
HOARD, FRANCIS - - -	7438	30th Sept. 1837	Making sugar.
HOARD, WILLIAM - - -	2528	20th July 1801	Portable machine for manufacturing ropes and cordage of any length in a short space of ground;—particularly adapted to shipping.
HOARE, EDWIN - - -	6899	1st Oct. 1835	Preventing the colour of woollen-cloths becoming darker near the list than in the middle, in the process of heating on rollers, in water or by steam.
HOBART, ANTHONY - -	52	— Sept. 1630	Making white and bay salt with sea-water and brine, without pots, furnaces, or other means as now in use.
HOBART, JOHN - - -	93	13th May 1636	Preventing smoke in brewhouses, dyehouses, and other like places; also preserving caldrons, coppers, boilers, furnaces and other like articles, at half the usual charge.
HOBART, JOHN - - -	94	23rd June 1636	Making and erecting ovens for saving of wood.
HOBBINS, JOHN - - -	4978	22nd June 1824	Gas-apparatus.
HOBBS, ALFRED CHARLES -	13,985	23rd Feb. 1852	Construction of locks and other fastenings.
HOBDAY, SAMUEL - - -	3382	26th Sept. 1810	Lever for making snuffers act without springs.
HOBDAY, SAMUEL - - -	4295	1st Oct. 1818	Principle for making snuffers without spring or lever.
HOBDAY, SAMUEL - - -	4604	1st Nov. 1821	Manufacturing the furniture of umbrellas and parasols; uniting the same together.
HOBDAY, SAMUEL - - -	6120	24th May 1831	Machine, worked by steam;—applicable for the moving of ships, boats, and barges on water, and carriages on the road or on tramways, and, when fixed, is also applicable to all purposes for which steam-engines are now used.
HOBDELL, HENRY BASHARD -	12,092	9th March 1848	Studs and buttons.
HOBLER, FRANCIS - - -	12,408	11th Jan. 1849	Construction of the cylinders or barrels of capstans and windlasses.
HOBLYN, EDWARD ROBERT -	13,412	16th Dec. 1850	Apparatus for condensing and purifying smoke, gases, and other noxious vapours arising from fire-places, furnaces, or chemical works; rendering the products resulting therefrom available for manufacturing colours.
HOBLYN, THOMAS - - -	14,191	28th June 1852	Art of navigation.
HOBSON, CHARLES - -	2842	29th April 1805	Manufacturing zinc into wire, and into vessels and utensils for culinary and other purposes.
HOBSON, CHARLES - -	2849	18th May 1805	Sheathing ships, roofing houses, and lining waterspouts, with a certain material not hitherto used for the purpose.

Name of Patentee.	Progressive Number.	Date.		Subject-matter of Patent.
HOBSON, JOHN - - -	4691	27th July	1822	Series of machinery for shearing, cutting, and finishing woollen-cloths, kersey-meres, and all other descriptions of cloths and piece-goods requiring the shears.
HOBSON, JONATHAN CRIPPS -	5748	23rd Dec.	1828	Table-forks.
HOBSON, JONAS - - -	4691	27th July	1822	Series of machinery for shearing, cutting, and finishing woollen-cloths, kersey-meres, and all other description of cloths and piece-goods requiring the shears.
HOBSON, RICHARD - -	12,900	15th Dec.	1849	Manufacture of horse-shoes; apparatus for taking the measurement of horses' shoes or hoofs.
HOBSON, WILLIAM - - -	5449	15th Jan.	1827	Paving streets, lanes, roads, and carriage-ways.
HOBY, JAMES WARD - -	13,158	3rd July	1850	Construction of parts of the permanent way of railways; shaping iron.
HOBY, JAMES WARD - -	13,394	7th Dec.	1850	Construction of the permanent way of railways.
HODGE, PAUL RAPSEY - -	13,159	3rd July	1850	Certain descriptions of steam-engines; apparatus and management for cultivating and manuring the soil; treating the produce thereof.
HODGE, PAUL RAPSEY - -	14,018	8th Mar.	1852	Construction of railways and railway-carriages;—in part applicable to carriages on common roads.
HODGE, WILLIAM - - -	6286	19th July	1832	Apparatus for dyeing hats.
HODGE, WILLIAM - - -	13,763	2nd Oct.	1851	Manufacture of glass, china, porcelain, earthenware, and artificial stone.
HODGES, JAMES - - -	936	28th Oct.	1769	Making wove-wood hats.
HODGES, JOHN - - -	264	26th June	1690	Melting and refining lead ore in close or reverberatory furnaces, with pit-coal and sea-coal, turf, peat, or other mixed fuel, instead of wood.
HODGES, RICHARD EDWARD -	12,623	29th May	1849	Mechanical purchases;—applicable to projectiles.
HODGES, RICHARD EDWARD -	13,674	24th June	1851	Surgical instruments.
HODGESON, MARMADUKE -	312	31st Jan.	1693	Engine for raising and discharging water, from any depth to any height.
HODGETTS, BOOTH - -	2739	8th Nov.	1803	Machine for rolling iron for shanks, and forming the same into shanks for nails.
HODGHON, READ - - -	499	7th June	1728	Making corf bows of iron, instead of wood as heretofore made, with springs and screws, for drawing up coals from the pit.
HODGKINSON, MATTHEW -	13,303	2nd Nov.	1850	Furnaces or apparatus for smelting ores and minerals; making pig-iron.
HODGSON, JAMES - - -	8586	3rd Aug.	1840	Combining and applying machinery for cutting and planing wood, to produce plain or moulded surfaces.
HODGSON, JOHN THOMAS -	5014	7th Oct.	1824	Construction and manufacture of shoes, or substitutes for shoes, for horses and other cattle; applying the same to the feet.
HODGSON, RICHARD - -	8135	27th June	1839	Forms of materials and substances used for building and paving; their combination for such purposes.
HODGSON, RICHARD - -	9331	26th April	1842	Preparing surfaces of fabrics to be used in covering roofs, floors, and other surfaces.

Name of Patentee.	Progressive Number.	Date.	Subject-matter of Patent.
HODGSON, RICHARD - -	9406	7th July 1842	Obtaining images on metallic and other surfaces.
HODGSON, ROBERT - -	10,034	2nd Feb. 1844	Propelling vessels; machinery for working the same.
HODGSON, WILLIAM - -	1011	3rd April 1772	Composition applicable to the purposes of carving, casting and modelling. "Artificial wood."
HODGSON, WILLIAM - -	14,313	30th Sept. 1852	Manufacture of woven, textile and looped fabrics; machinery employed therein.
HODGSON, GEORGE - - -	1906	30th Aug. 1792	Separating mineral alkali from muriatic-acid as it exists in common salt, also from common salt as it exists in kelp.
HODGSON, GEORGE - - -	2168	23rd Feb. 1797	Separating mineral alkali from muriatic-acid as it exists in common salt, salt-rock brine, sea-water, the neutral salt of natron, soza sal enixon, caput-mortuum, spirits of salts, kelp, and salts obtained from soapers' lees; also separating mineral alkali from common salt as it exists in kelp.
HODSON, GEORGE - - -	2586	27th Feb. 1802	Preparing and making fossil or mineral alkali from various substances.
HODSON, GEORGE - - -	3390	8th Oct. 1810	Separating alkaline salt from the acid as it exists in kelp, black-ashes, soapers' salts, spent lees, and other like articles.
HODSON, WILLIAM - -	10,152	18th April 1844	Machine for making and compressing bricks, tiles, square pavers, and ornamental bricks.
HOE, RICHARD MARCH - -	7683	12th June 1838	Machinery for grinding and polishing metal surfaces.
HOE, RICHARD MARCH - -	7684	12th June 1838	Tools and apparatus for chipping, levelling, smoothing and polishing the surfaces of stone, slate, and other materials.
HOE, RICHARD MARCH - -	7737	18th July 1838	Instrument to determine the latitude and longitude of any place, or the situation of ships at sea, and the dip and variation of the magnetic-needle. "Sherwood's magnetic geometer."
HOFFSTAEDT, AUGUSTUS JOHN	13,558	17th March 1851	Manufacture of dials for clocks, watches, barometers, gas-meters, mariners' compasses, and other articles requiring the same.
HOFLAND, THOMAS - -	2067	28th Sept. 1795	Double beating and graduating loom, for weaving.
HOGAN, THOMAS COCKERELL -	7050	29th March 1836	Hats, caps, and bonnets.
HOHMANN, JOHN GEORGE -	1635	15th Jan. 1788	Machine for making marbles for children.
HOLBECK, LOUIS - - -	8769	31st Dec. 1840	Obtaining oil.
HOLCOMBE, CHARLES THOMAS	8949	6th May 1841	Lubricating-matters, for wheels and axles; applicable also to the bearings or other parts of machinery.
HOLCOMBE, CHARLES THOMAS	9256	15th Feb. 1842	Manufacture of fuel; obtaining products in such manufacture.
HOLCOMBE, CHARLES THOMAS	9489	13th Oct. 1842	Using certain materials as fuel; apparatus for collecting the smoke or soot; application of the products as manure, and for other purposes.
HOLCROFT, GEORGE - -	12,300	26th Oct. 1848	Steam-engines; machinery belonging thereto; construction of boilers, furnaces and flues connected therewith;—applicable to other similar purposes.

Name of Patentee.	Progressive Number.	Date.	Subject-matter of Patent.
HOLCROFT, THOMAS - -	9128	28th Oct. 1841	Portable safety boat or pontoon.
HOLDEN, HENRY - - -	8922	5th April 1841	Trouser-straps.
HOLDEN, ISAAC - - -	11,896	7th Oct. 1847	Carding, preparing, combing and spinning wool and other fibrous substances; making heald and genappe yarns.
HOLDEN, RICHARD - -	4273	18th June 1818	Machinery to communicate power and motion to other machinery requiring reciprocating or alternating motion.
HOLDEN, RICHARD - -	4104	20th Feb. 1817	Machines for producing rotatory and pendulous motion.
HOLDSWORTH, ARTHUR HOWE [Holdworth, Arthur Howe.]	4188	19th Dec. 1817	Gasometers.
HOLDSWORTH, ARTHUR HOWE	6191	19th Nov. 1831	Construction of rudders; application of the same to certain descriptions of ships or vessels.
HOLDSWORTH, ARTHUR HOWE	8350	21st Jan. 1840	Preserving wood from decay.
HOLDSWORTH, ARTHUR HOWE	9388	11th June 1842	Constructing certain parts of ships and vessels; arresting the progress of fire; regulating temperature.
HOLDSWORTH, ARTHUR HOWE	11,356	29th Aug. 1846	Buoys; and giving buoyancy to boats.
HOLDSWORTH, ARTHUR HOWE	12,737	9th Aug. 1849	Construction of marine-boilers, and funnels of steam-boats and vessels.
HOLDSWORTH, RICHARD -	13,002	11th March 1850	Apparatus and machinery for warping worsted, cotton, and other fibrous materials.
HOLDSWORTH, SAMUEL - -	11,396	6th Oct. 1846	Apparatus to be applied to railway-carriages to prevent accidents thereon.
HOLEBROOK, JOSIAH PEARCE -	7579	27th Feb. 1838	Propelling vessels.
HOLEMBERG, SAMUEL -	2521	24th June 1801	Locks and fastenings for general uses.
HOLGATE, GEORGE - -	11,980	25th Nov. 1847	Power-looms.
HOLGATE, WILLIAM - -	13,002	11th March 1850	Apparatus and machinery for warping worsted, cotton, and other fibrous materials.
HOLL, ALFRED - - -	13,219	12th Aug. 1850	Steam-engines.
HOLLAND, GEORGE - -	1670	22nd Sept. 1788	Making stockings, gloves, mits, socks, caps, coats, waistcoats, breeches, cloaks, and other clothing, for persons afflicted with the gout, rheumatism, or other complaints requiring warmth; also making false or downy calves in stockings.
HOLLAND, GEORGE - -	1736	20th March 1790	Manufacture of stockings, gloves, mits, socks, caps, coats, breeches, and other clothing where warmth is required; also of blankets, carpets, and tapestry, in imitation and to answer the purposes of furs and skins of various kinds.
HOLLAND, GEORGE - -	1901	24th July 1792	Manufacturing hosiery and other articles for clothing and coverings.
HOLLAND, GEORGE - -	2422	2nd July 1800	Woollen-yarn, worsted, silk, and other kinds of spun materials, for the purpose of manufacture.
HOLLAND, GEORGE - -	2584	23rd Feb. 1802	Machine, to be added to a stocking-frame, for expediting the manufacturing of fleecy-hosiery and other kinds of hosiery.
HOLLAND, HENRY - - -	8498	7th May 1840	Manufacture of umbrellas and parasols.
HOLLAND, HENRY - - -	13,227	22nd Aug. 1850	Manufacture of umbrellas and parasols.
HOLLAND, JAMES - - -	4965	31st May 1824	Manufacture of boots and shoes.

Name of Patentee.	Progressive Number.	Date.		Subject-matter of Patent.
HOLLAND, JOHN - - -	279	7th Oct.	1691	Engine for conveying air into a diving-vessel, to enable several persons at the same time to work under water for many hours, for the purpose of finding gold, silver, bullion, money, and goods lost at sea.
HOLLAND, JOHN - - -	12,705	18th July	1849	Making steel.
HOLLAND, PHILLIP HENRY -	11,581	16th Feb.	1847	Applying manure to land.
HOLLAND, THOMAS - -	281	17th Oct.	1691	Machine for raising, forcing, and discharging water in great quantities in a short time out of drowned mines, pits, coal-delphs and groves, with their sinks and shafts; also for drains, and supplying pipes with water for cities and towns; submerging dry lands.
HOLLAND, THOMAS - -	410	8th Nov.	1716	Engine for raising a continual flow of water by means of locks and chain-works, with two barrels only; to supply cities, towns, and other places with water at a cheap rate; also to drain lands, mines, &c. and to water barren grounds.
HOLLAND, THOMAS STANHOPE	5591	19th Dec.	1827	Combinations of machinery for generating and communicating power and motion for propelling.
HOLLANDS, WILLIAM EDWARD	12,263	4th Sept.	1848	Manufacture of artificial fuel in blocks or lumps.
HOLLICK, FRANCIS - - -	2229	18th April	1798	Affixing an iron or other comb to the edge or outside of a currycomb, for combing the manes and tails of horses, and for combing dirt from horses and other cattle.
HOLLIDAY, READ - - -	12,015	5th Jan.	1848	Lamps.
HOLLIDAY, READ - - -	12,965	11th Feb.	1850	Lamps.
HOLLINGRAKE, GEORGE - -	4287	7th Aug.	1818	Manufacturing copper or other metal rollers for calico-printing.
HOLLINGRAKE, JAMES - -	4371	15th May	1819	Making and working a manufacture for applying a method of casting metallic substances into various forms with improved closeness and soundness in texture.
HOLLINGS, WILLIAM - -	956	27th April	1770	Dyeing wrought and unwrought woollens, linens, silk, and cotton various colours, by means of a liquor extracted from a red wood growing in the West Indies.
HOLLINGSWORTH, THOMAS -	10,865	9th Oct.	1845	Construction of cases for holding cigars.
HOLLISTER, LAWRENCE - -	2616	5th May	1802	Machinery for improving roads.
HOLLOWAY, HENRY - -	741	14th July	1759	Raising water.
HOLLOWAY, NELSON JOHN -	8192	13th Aug.	1839	Head for carriages.
HOLM, CARL AUGUSTUS -	7918	20th Dec.	1838	Printing.
HOLM, CHARLES AUGUSTUS -	12,382	21st Dec.	1848	Printing.
HOLMAN, CHARLES - -	258	7th Feb.	1688	Powder for making black writing-ink, by mixing with water, beer, ale, or wine.
HOLMAN, JOHN - - -	1132	23rd Aug.	1776	Raising metals and other heavy bodies from mines, by balancing the rope in the shaft; weighing anchors by preventing the cable from surging or sudden running out.
HOLME, PETER - - -	831	18th June	1765	Making alum from liquor produced from copperas materials and uncalcined ore.
HOLME, RICHARD - - -	6503	5th Nov.	1833	Apparatus for and means of generating steam; parts of steam-engines; means of producing heat.

Name of Patentee.	Progressive Number.	Date.	Subject-matter of Patent.
HOLMES, GEORGE - - -	9936	9th Nov. 1843	Furnaces or fire-places.
HOLMES, HENRY - - -	10,188	15th May 1844	Manufacture of bricks, tiles, and other plastic substances.
HOLMES, JOHN - - -	6417	4th May 1833	Metallic shanks for buttons.
HOLMES, JOHN - - -	7055	7th April 1836	Construction of boilers for steam-engines.
HOLMES, JOHN - - -	7869	13th Nov. 1838	Forming moulds for casting in metal, studs, buttons, nails, tacks, and other articles.
HOLMES, JOHN - - -	13,672	24th June 1851	Machinery for cutting and stamping metals.
HOLMES, WILLIAM - - -	516	9th May 1730	Pole-mast vessel, for the more easy catching, preserving, and stowing fish.
HOLMES, WILLIAM DAUBNEY	6283	19th July 1832	Heating houses and other buildings; applying heat to various purposes.
HOLMES, WILLIAM DAUBNEY	8279	23rd Nov. 1839	Construction of iron ships, boats, and other vessels; means for preventing the same from foundering.
HOLMES, WILLIAM DAUBNEY	8583	1st Aug. 1840	Steam-engines; generating and applying steam as a motive-power.
HOLMES, WILLIAM DAUBNEY	8614	3rd Sept. 1840	Naval-architecture; apparatus connected therewith, affording security from shipwreck.
HOLT, ALFRED - - -	14,042	24th March 1852	Preventing and removing the deposit of sand, mud, or silt, in tidal rivers, harbours, docks, basins, or other channels communicating with the sea;—applicable to other rivers or moving waters.
HOLT, JAMES - - -	7421	24th Aug. 1837	Waterclosets.
HOLT, JOHN, junior - -	6263	28th April 1832	Application of a mode of preparing and manufacturing certain fibrous substances.
HOLT, JOHN - - -	12,714	24th July 1849	Machinery for preparing cotton and other fibrous substances; applicable to machinery for weighing.
HOLT, RICHARD - - -	447	31st May 1722	Compound liquid metal, by which artificial stone and marble is made, by casting the same into moulds of any form, as statues and capitals; also for house-work, garden-ornaments, and other sculpture-work.
HOLT, RICHARD - - -	448	13th June 1722	Composition (without clay) for making white-ware, formed and moulded in a new method.
HOLT, RICHARD - - -	6644	12th July 1834	Construction of power-looms for weaving cotton and other fibrous materials into cloth or other fabrics.
HOLT, ROBERT - - -	9132	2nd Nov. 1841	Machinery for the production of rotary motion for obtaining mechanical power;—applicable to raising fluids.
HOLT, SAMUEL - - -	13,572	24th March 1851	Manufacture of textile-fabrics.
HOLT, WILLIAM - - -	12,886	10th Dec. 1849	Construction of the pallets or valves of organ sound-boards or wind-chests;—applicable to various other musical instruments.
HOLTHAM, THOMAS - -	507	10th March 1729	Engine or machine for raising water by alternate expulsion, rarefaction, or exhaustion of air, and pressure of the atmosphere (without the help of fire), for supplying towns and gardens, and emptying or draining mines, pits, docks, and fens.
HOME, JAMES - - -	9861	8th Aug. 1843	Manufacture of horse-shoes.

Name of Patentee.	Progressive Number.	Date.	Subject-matter of Patent.
HOMER, MARK - - -	1010	3rd April 1772	Grate or stove, with its appurtenances, made of metal plated with silver, with or without ornaments of enamel or lapis lazuli.
HOMERSHAM, SAMUEL COLLET	12,341	23rd Nov. 1848	Feeding furnaces with fuel.
HOMFRAY, THOMAS - -	4269	28th May 1818	Bobbin used in spinning and other manufactures.
HOMPESCH, THEOPHILE ANTON WILLHELME, Count of	9080	4th Sept. 1841	Obtaining oils and other products from bituminous matters; rectifying the oils so obtained.
HONIBALL, MARY - - -	14,357	9th Feb. 1853	Anchors (being extension for six years of W. H. Porter's patent, 15th August 1838.)
HOOD, CHARLES - - -	6240	8th March 1832	Machinery for manufacturing stockings, stocking-net, or frame-work knitting, warp-web, warp-net and point-net.
HOOD, CHARLES - - -	8824	1st Feb. 1841	Giving signals.
HOOD, JOHN LIONEL - -	7044	26th March 1836	Manufacturing belts, bands, and straps, to be employed in the place of ropes or chains, and for other purposes.
HOOD, JOHN LIONEL - -	10,056	17th Feb. 1844	Mixture of metals applicable for the manufacture of sheathing for ships and other vessels, also bolts, nails, or other fastenings.
HOOD, JOHN LIONEL - -	10,702	3rd June 1845	Application of motive-power for locomotive and other purposes.
HOOD, WILLIAM JOHN HOBSON	5499	26th May 1827	Pumps or machinery for raising or forcing water, chiefly applicable to ships.
HOOKE, JOHN - - -	283	19th Oct. 1691	Engine made of timber, with glass windows, door, air-pipes, leather sleeves and iron braces affixed, to enable a man to work under water for many hours.
HOOKES, ROBERT - - -	268	12th June 1691	Making metals for the manufacture of glass for windows, also red crystal-glass; casting glass, particularly looking-glass plates.
HOOPER, CHARLES - -	5602	15th Jan. 1828	Machine for shearing and cropping woollen and other cloths.
HOOPER, JOHN - - -	592	21st July 1743	Medicine called " Female Pills."
HOOPER, JOHN - - -	672	1st July 1752	" Child-bed Cordial Powder," also " Strengthening Balsam and Powder," for rickety and weak children.
HOOPER, SAMUEL - - -	1622	17th Sept. 1787	Manufacturing printing paper, particularly for copper-plate printing.
HOOPER, SAMUEL - - -	1723	20th Jan. 1790	Manufacturing from leather, leather-cuttings, shavings or parings, and whit-leather, a leather for covering coaches, chariots, post-chaises, sedan-chairs and trunks, and for making band, hat, and other boxes, waiters, and teatrays, inkstands, inkpots, snuff and tobacco-boxes, mouldings, cornices, ceiling and other ornaments for rooms, also for binding books, and, with some variation in the process, for making paper for copper-plate printing, brown and white-brown paper, and paper for drawing.
HOOPER, STEPHEN - -	1149	14th March 1777	Engine or machine for raising water.

Name of Patentee.	Progres-sive Number.	Date.	Subject-matter of Patent.
HOOPER, STEPHEN - -	1706	29th Oct. 1789	Machinery for regulating the power and motion of wind and other mills, as also the process of grinding and dressing therein, and for regulating all other machinery, where the first motion is un-equal; applicable to other purposes.
HOOPER, STEPHEN - -	2323	26th June 1799	Machine for cleansing rivers, creeks, har-bours, or bars of harbours, also sand-banks or shoals at sea, by the power of the tide or current.
HOOPER, STEPHEN - -	2453	4th Dec. 1800	Method by means of machinery, of cleansing and deepening dry harbours, rivers, creeks, &c.;—partly applicable to other purposes.
HOOPER, STEPHEN - -	2554	10th Nov. 1801	Machinery for cleansing harbours, rivers, &c.
HOOPER, STEPHEN - -	2679	5th Feb. 1803	Machinery for cleansing creeks, bars of harbours, and preventing the formation of bars; method of using the same.
HOOPER, STEPHEN - -	2933	3rd May 1806	Aqueduct, tunnel, or machine, for cleansing docks and other basins of penned water; machinery for cleansing dry and other harbours, rivers, creeks, bars of harbours, and for other purposes.
HOOPER, STEPHEN - -	3206	13th Feb. 1809	Thermometer or machine for ascertaining the heat of bakers' ovens, and for other purposes.
HOOTON, RICHARD - -	4968	15th June 1824	Manufacturing wrought-iron.
HOPE, ISAAC - - - -	6954	16th Dec. 1835	Machinery for preparing flax and hemp; machinery for spinning flax, hemp, cotton, silk and other fibrous substances, by power.
HOPE, JOSEPH - - -	6954	16th Dec. 1835	Machinery for preparing flax and hemp; machinery for spinning flax, hemp, cotton, silk and other fibrous substances, by power.
HOPE, THOMAS - - -	6954	16th Dec. 1835	Machinery for preparing flax and hemp; machinery for spinning flax, hemp, cotton and other fibrous substances, by power.
HOPE, WILLIAM - - -	4767	18th March 1823	Construction of printing-presses.
HOPKINS, JOHN - - -	868	10th Feb. 1767	Medicine named " Beaume de Vie," manu-facturing the same from several valuable drugs.
HOPKINS, JOHN - - -	7121	18th June 1836	Furnaces for steam-engine boilers and other purposes.
HOPKINS, JOHN - - -	19,749	3rd July 1845	Rails and trams for railroads and tramways.
HOPKINS, WILLIAM - -	1122	25th March 1776	Preserving ornaments of stoves or grates from being discoloured or damaged by fire.
HOPKINSON, JOHN - - -	13,652	3rd June 1851	Pianofortes.
HOPKINSON, JOSEPH - -	10,500	28th Jan. 1845	Machinery for raising the nap or pile on woollen, cotton, or other cloths; brushing and cleansing the same.
HOPKINSON, LUKE - -	3329	2nd May 1810	Bridle-bits.
HOPKINSON, WILLIAM - -	4242	8th April 1818	Machine or apparatus for preventing the wheels of waggons, carts, coaches, and other carriages, from coming off by acci-dent. " Wheel Detainer."
HOPPER, THOMAS - - -	4868	20th Nov. 1823	Manufacturing silk-hats.

Name of Patentee.	Progressive Number.	Date.	Subject-matter of Patent.
HORABIN, HENRY - - -	12,946	26th Jan. 1850	Machinery for cutting fustians and certain other fabrics to produce a piled surface.
HORLIAC, LOUIS MATTHIAS -	7147	13th July 1836	Carriages and harness.
HORN, ARCHIBALD - -	9865	15th Aug. 1843	Construction of shutters for windows, and other purposes.
HORN, JOHN - - - -	1424	13th March 1784	Machine for sowing the seed of every species of vegetable with expedition and regularity, and requiring a less quantity of seed to produce a larger crop than by the common mode.
HORN, JOHN - - - -	1498	20th Oct. 1785	Machine, which may be used separately or as an appendage to a plough, for sowing the seed of every species of vegetable with expedition and regularity, and requiring a less quantity of seed to produce a larger crop than by the common mode.
HORN, THOMAS - -	13,549	10th March 1851	Machinery for cleansing carpets, matting, and similar fabrics.
HORNBLOWER, HENRY -	11,770	28th June 1847	Obtaining motive-power.
HORNBLOWER, HENRY -	12,042	25th Jan. 1848	Machinery for exerting motive-power, and for raising and forcing fluids.
HORNBLOWER, JABEZ CARTER	2376	4th Feb. 1800	Glazing calicoes, cottons, muslins, linens, &c.
HORNBLOWER, JETHRO - -	2268	15th Nov. 1798	Making pattens.
HORNBLOWER, JONATHAN -	1298	13th July 1781	Machine or engine for raising water and other liquids by means of fire and steam, and for other purposes.
HORNBLOWER, JONATHAN -	2243	8th June 1798	Machine or engine for raising water by steam and otherwise, also for other purposes.
HORNBLOWER, JONATHAN -	2832	26th March 1805	Steam-wheel or engine for raising water by means of steam, and for various other purposes.
HORNBUCKLE, RICHARD -	944	9th Dec. 1769	Moveable iron-oven, which may be set in any room without danger of fire; also a moveable stove, useful for heating or airing rooms and other places.
HORNBY, WILLIAM HENRY -	6619	27th May 1834	Power-looms to be used in the weaving of cotton, silk, linen, woollen, and other cloths.
HORNBY, WILLIAM HENRY -	8226	26th Sept. 1839	Machinery for sizing and otherwise preparing cotton wool, flax, and other warps for weaving.
HORNE, JAMES - - -	8408	3rd March 1840	Stuffing-boxes of lift-pumps.
HORNE, JAMES - - -	10,452	2nd Jan. 1845	Injecting-instruments;—applicable also to various pneumatic purposes.
HORNE, JOHN - - -	54	24th Jan. 1631	Making sieves of kersey and twill; also beads of bone and wood, also permission to erect houses, engines, or instruments for the making of the same.
HORNE, THOMAS - - -	4765	18th March 1823	Making metallic window-frames and other metallic mouldings for ornamenting furniture.
HORNE, THOMAS - - -	4878	9th Dec. 1823	Manufacture of rack-pullies in brass or other metals.
HORNE, THOMAS - - -	6867	24th July 1835	Manufacturing hinges.
HORNE, THOMAS - - -	8615	3rd Sept. 1840	Manufacturing hinges.
HORNE, THOMAS - - -	11,705	18th May 1847	Manufacturing bedsteads.
HORNE, THOMAS - - -	11,903	14th Oct. 1847	Carriage-windows.

Name of Patentee.	Progressive Number.	Date.	Subject-matter of Patent.
HORNE, WILLIAM - - -	11,727	3rd June 1847	Wheel-carriages.
HORNER, WILLIAM - -	4213	27th Jan. 1818	Machine for acquiring a very high mechanical power in a small compass, with little friction, and without the possibility of running amain when employed in raising or lowering weights.
HORNSBY, RICHARD - -	8281	25th Nov. 1839	Machine for drilling land and sowing grain and seeds, with or without bone or other manure.
HORNSBY, RICHARD - -	13,165	3rd July 1850	Machinery for sowing corn and seeds, and for depositing manure; thrashing-machines; machines for dressing or winnowing corn; steam-engines and boilers for agricultural purposes.
HORNSBY, RICHARD - -	14,196	3rd July 1852	Machinery for thrashing, shaking, riddling, and dressing corn.
HORROCKS, WILLIAM - -	2699	20th April 1803	Looms for weaving cotton and other goods, by steam or water.
HORROCKS, WILLIAM - -	2848	14th May 1805	Machines for weaving cotton and other goods, by hand, steam, water, or other power.
HORROCKS, WILLIAM - -	3728	31st July 1813	Machine for weaving cotton and other goods, by hand, steam, water, or other power.
HORROCKS, WILLIAM - -	4626	14th Dec. 1821	Construction of power-looms for weaving cotton or linen cloth.
HORROCKS, WILLIAM HAR-[WOOD.	4817	24th July 1823	Preparing, cleaning, dressing, and beaming silk-warps;—applicable to beaming other warps.
HORROCKS, WILLIAM HAR-[WOOD.	4966	15th June 1824	Apparatus for giving tension to the warp in looms.
HORSEFIELD, WILLIAM - -	7594	19th March 1838	Construction of mills for grinding corn.
HORSEY, Sir GEORGE, Knight -	117	2nd May 1638	Making cast-iron and bar-iron, with sea-coals, pit-coals, peat, or turf; refining metals; also digging, searching, and working mines of gold, silver, copper, or lead mixed with silver or quicksilver; draining and conveying water to the said mines and pits; erecting houses, mills, and works for the carrying on of the above processes.
HORSFALL, CHARLES HODGSON	10,831	18th Sept. 1845	Manufacture of iron.
HORSFALL, JEREMIAH - -	6949	9th Dec. 1835	Engines used for carding cotton-wool and other fibrous substances.
HORSFALL, WILLIAM - -	8039	20th April 1839	Cards for carding various fibrous substances; part of the improvements may be used as a substitute for leather.
HORSFALL, WILLIAM - -	8651	1st Oct. 1840	Cards for carding cotton-wool, silk, flax, and other fibrous substances.
HORSFALL, WILLIAM JOSEPH	13,008	19th March 1850	Rolling iron and other metals.
HORSLEY, JOHN - - -	1400	15th Nov. 1783	Making plated furniture for fire-stoves and grates, with or without glass ornaments.
HORSLEY, JOHN - - -	11,691	6th May 1847	Preserving animal and vegetable substances.
HORSLEY, JOHN - - -	12,592	26th April 1849	Preventing incrustation in steam and other boilers; purifying, filtering, and rendering water fit for drinking purposes.
HORSMAN, PETER SWIRES -	14,124	8th May 1852	Preparing flax and hemp for heckling; machinery for heckling flax, hemp, china-grass, and other vegetable fibrous substances.

Name of Patentee.	Progressive Number.	Date.	Subject-matter of Patent.
HORTON, DANIEL - - -	6299	7th Sept. 1832	Puddling-furnace, for the better production of manufactured iron in the process of obtaining it from the pig-iron.
HORTON, GEORGE - - -	6299	7th Sept. 1832	Puddling-furnace, for the better production of manufactured iron in the process of obtaining it from the pig-iron.
HORTON, JOHN - - -	4811	8th July 1823	Construction of boilers for steam-engines and for other purposes.
HORTON, JOSHUA - - -	5553	11th Oct. 1827	Making hollow cylinders, guns, ordnance, retorts, and various other articles, of wrought-iron, of steel, or composed of both those metals.
HORTON, JOSHUA - - -	6400	23rd March 1833	Manufacture of wrought-iron chains, applicable to various purposes.
HORTON, JOSHUA - - -	12,974	21st Feb. 1850	Arrangement and construction of gas-holders.
HORTON, JOSHUA - - -	13,436	2nd Jan. 1851	Construction of gas-holders.
HORTON, THOMAS - - -	7997	6th March 1839	Constructing chains for pits, shafts, mines, or other purposes.
HORTON, THOMAS ELLWOOD -	14,064	15th April 1852	Apparatus for heating and evaporating.
HORTON, WILLIAM - -	991	25th June 1771	Machine for making knitted, knotted, or double-looped work, for stocking and breeches pieces, and gloves, of silk, thread, cotton, and worsted, either together or separate.
HORTON, WILLIAM - -	1120	16th March 1776	Machine to be fixed to a stocking-frame, for making knotted and double-looped work.
HORTON, WILLIAM - -	1195	24th June 1778	Machine for making network with knotted meshes, in silk, thread, cotton, worsted, or any other materials of the like nature.
HOSKYNS, CHANDOS - -	10,912	3rd Nov. 1845	Trusses.
HOSKING, JOHN - - -	12,761	6th Sept. 1849	Pavement.
HOSKING, JOHN - - -	13,354	19th Nov. 1850	Valves applicable to pumps; apparatus to regulate the pressure and flow of water or air in and through pipes.
HOSKING, SIMON - - -	4075	1st Nov. 1816	Steam-engine, for drawing water from mines, for working different kinds of machinery, and for other purposes.
HOSMER, JOHN - - -	12,098	16th March 1848	Apparatus for supplying water, and for cleansing drains and sewers.
HOTCHKIS, JOHN - - -	2346	3rd Oct. 1799	Mechanical power for lifting weights, moving ships, weighing anchors, &c.
HOUGHAM, SOLOMON - -	2801	19th Dec. 1804	Spring-clasps for buckles, lockets, and other ornaments of dress.
HOUGHTON, GEORGE - -	7265	21st Dec. 1836	Construction of lamps.
HOUGHTON, JAMES - -	11,753	15th June 1847	Machinery to be used in the preparation and spinning of cotton-wool and other fibrous substances.
HOUGHTON, WILLIAM - -	344	23rd Sept. 1695	Watch or clock, with the balance-wheel flat or hollow to work within and cross the centre of the verge, with teeth like tenter-hooks to move the balance or pendulum, the pallets of the verge to be circular, concave and convex.
HOULDITCH, JOHN - - -	3020	7th March 1807	Construction of four-wheeled carriages.
HOULDSWORTH, HENRY - -	3899	18th March 1815	Discharging the air and condensed steam from pipes for conveying steam for heating buildings.

Name of Patentee.	Progressive Number.	Date.	Subject-matter of Patent.
HOULDSWORTH, HENRY	5316	16th Jan. 1826	Machinery for giving the taking-up or winding-on motion to spools or bobbins or other instruments on which the thread is wound in roving, spinning, and twisting machines.
HOULDSWORTH, HENRY	8626	10th Sept. 1840	Carriages used for conveyance of passengers on railways; seat for such carriages, applicable to other purposes.
HOULDSWORTH, HENRY	13,262	26th Sept. 1850	Manufacture of iron and other metals.
HOULDSWORTH, HENRY	14,161	10th June 1852	Embroidering-machines, and apparatus used in connection therewith.
HOULDSWORTH, HENRY	14,240	27th July 1852	Fixing, extending, and holding cloth to receive embroidery; apparatus applicable thereto.
HOULDSWORTH, JAMES	14,240	27th July 1852	Fixing, extending, and holding cloth to receive embroidery; apparatus applicable thereto.
HOULDSWORTH, JOHN	6951	9th Dec. 1835	Drawing and slubbing frames used in the manufacture of cotton and other fibrous substances.
HOULSTON, JOHN	7575	24th Feb. 1838	Apparatus for stopping or retarding carriages.
HOUSEMAN, HENRY	770	10th March 1762	Gilding, colouring, and marbling paper.
HOUSTON, JOHN	12,085	8th March 1848	Obtaining motive-power by aid of atmospheric air; obtaining combustion.
HOUSTON, JOHN	12,649	7th June 1849	Obtaining motive-power when steam and air are used.
HOUSTOUN, WILLIAM	6747	17th Jan. 1835	Type-founding.
HOUSTOUN, WILLIAM	6800	25th March 1835	Tools, implements or apparatus used in or subservient to letter-press printing.
HOW, ANDREW PEDDIE	12,707	18th July 1849	Instrument for ascertaining the saltness of water in boilers.
HOW, JAMES	2655	30th Oct. 1802	Plough.
HOWARD, ADAM	8974	5th June 1841	Cylindrical printing-machinery, for printing calicoes and other fabrics; apparatus connected therewith;—applicable to other purposes.
HOWARD, APPELLES	6902	8th Oct. 1835	Looms for weaving by hand or other power.
HOWARD, CHARLES	130	27th Oct. 1660	Tanning, tawing, dressing, and preparing raw hides and skins, and making the same into leather.
HOWARD, CHARLES	201	26th March 1678	Preparing and whitening hemp and flax, by the help of liquors and engines, so that they may be made into lighter and stronger cordage, may be spun finer, and woven into cloth without boiling or the use of stiffening.
HOWARD, EDWARD CHARLES	3607	31st Oct. 1812	Preparing and refining sugars.
HOWARD, EDWARD CHARLES	3754	20th Nov. 1813	Preparing and refining sugars.
HOWARD, EDWARD CHARLES	3831	4th Aug. 1814	Separating insoluble substances from fluids in which the same are suspended.
HOWARD, HENRY	239	28th Aug. 1864	Melting or smelting copper-ore, and tin-ore, with sea-coal or pit-coal.
HOWARD, HENRY	12,554	28th March 1849	Glass-making; construction of furnaces for melting and fining the same.
HOWARD, JAMES	13,678	3rd July 1851	Ploughs and other implements or machines used in the cultivation of the soil.

Name of Patentee.	Progres-sive Number.	Date.	Subject-matter of Patent.
HOWARD, JAMES - - -	14,082	22nd April 1852	Chilling cast-iron.
HOWARD, JOHN SCOTT - -	6472	21st Sept. 1833	Roving-frames for roving cotton and other fibrous substances.
HOWARD, JOSEPH - - -	10,534	24th Feb. 1845	Manufacture of silk-plushes, silk-velvets, worsted and other plushes.
HOWARD, SAMUEL - - -	8600	8th Aug. 1840	Boilers and furnaces.
HOWARD, Sir PHILLIP, Knight	154	8th Oct. 1667	Graving, garnishing, and colouring ships and other vessels.
HOWARD, Sir PHILLIP, Knight	158	2nd March 1668	Graving, garnishing, and colouring ships and other vessels, also garnishing, colouring, and varnishing wood, iron, stone, plaster and other things, by a liquor from certain grain growing in England, and mixed with some other ingredients.
HOWARD, STANLEY - -	1927	21st Dec. 1792	Pneumatic kitchen for cooking victuals by steam, being a method of supplying the boiler with water to replace the quantity expended by evaporation, which method may also be applied to a pump.
HOWARD, THOMAS - - -	1202	24th Nov. 1778	Warming-pan of steel or iron.
HOWARD, THOMAS - - -	2508	2nd June 1801	Making British barilla and potash, and obtaining alkali.
HOWARD, THOMAS - - -	5262	13th Oct. 1825	Vapour-engine.
HOWARD, THOMAS - - -	6339	29th Nov. 1832	"Vapour-engine," and its application to steam-engines.
HOWARD, THOMAS - - -	9533	3rd Dec. 1842	Machinery for preparing and spinning cotton-wool, flax, silk, and similar fibrous materials.
HOWARD, THOMAS - - -	10,855	6th Oct. 1845	Rolling iron bars for suspension-bridges, and other purposes.
HOWARD, THOMAS - - -	11,141	25th March 1846	Steam-engine condensers.
HOWARD, WILLIAM - -	3214	4th March 1809	Pen, to promote facility in writing; black writing-ink, the durability of which will not be affected by time or change of climate.
HOWARD, WILLIAM - -	3851	10th Nov. 1814	Apparatus .or gear for working pumps on board ship;—applicable for churning, and other useful purposes on shore.
HOWARD, WILLIAM - -	5913	27th Feb. 1830	Construction of wheels for carriages.
HOWARTH, JOHN - - -	7929	11th Jan. 1839	Machinery for spinning, roving, doubling, and twisting cotton and other fibrous materials.
HOWARTH, ROBERT - -	13,343	14th Nov. 1850	Machinery for raising a nap on cotton, woollen, silk, and other fabrics.
HOWDEN, GORDON - - -	3062	20th July 1807	Girth-pannel, to prevent the saddle from getting forward, upon horses.
HOWDEN, ROBERT - - -	2214	10th Feb. 1798	Portable and moving furnace for heating ovens.
HOWDEN, ROBERT - - -	3358	3rd July 1810	Extracting foul air out of ships, also out of mines and pits, and regulating the degree of heat in ships, mines, and pits; giving heat and a constant succession of fresh air to houses, warehouses, churches, theatres, hothouses, hospitals, workhouses, and other buildings, also to manufactories.
HOWE, JAMES K. - - -	12,139	27th April 1848	Building ships and other vessels.
HOWE, THOMAS - - -	1671	6th Oct. 1788	"Howe's Pectoral Lozenges" of horehound, for the cure of consumptions, asthmas, coughs, and other disorders.

Name of Patentee.	Progressive Number.	Date.	Subject-matter of Patent.
HOWE, WILLIAM - - -	11,086	11th Feb. 1846	Locomotive steam-engines.
HOWELL, GEORGE - - -	11,065	29th Jan. 1846	Coating with a metal the surface of articles of copper, or copper-alloys, or iron, wrought or cast.
HOWELL, JOHN - - -	2113	31st May 1796	Machine for boring wooden water-pipes.
HOWELL, THOMAS - - -	6964	21st Dec. 1835	Musical-instruments.
HOWELL, WILLIAM - -	4236	14th March 1818	Working and getting the main or thick mine of coals.
HOWELL, WILLIAM AUGUSTUS	7080	3rd May 1836	Construction of springs for doors.
HOWELLS, HENRY CHARLES -	10,066	21st Feb. 1844	Fastenings of parts of bedsteads and other frames.
HOWELLS, THOMAS HOSKINS -	13,403	12th Dec. 1850	Gun-carriages.
HOWGATE, JONATHAN - -	4377	1st June 1819	Heating drying-houses, malt-kilns, and other buildings requiring heat.
HOWLAND, CHARLES - -	13,508	11th Feb. 1851	Bell-telegraphs.
HOWLAND, CHARLES - -	13,870	19th Dec. 1851	Apparatus for ascertaining and indicating the supply of water in steam-boilers.
HOWSON, MARY - - -	1685	9th June 1789	Stills and boilers; universal and perpetual principles of saving fuel in heating, boiling, or evaporating fluids.
HOYLE, JOHN - - -	1816	7th July 1791	Communicating heat to hothouses, greenhouses, churches, dwelling-houses, and other buildings.
HUBBALL, THOMAS - -	3593	6th Aug. 1812	Ornamenting japanned, painted, or sized articles of paper, wood, or of any metallic substance; also leather, oil-cloths, and wainscot or plaster walls, or partitions.
HUBBUCK, GEORGE PARKER -	10,558	13th March 1845	Steam-engines, steam-boilers, and machinery for propelling vessels.
HUBIE, WILLIAM -	6271	2nd June 1832	Mangle.
HUCKVALE, THOMAS - -	8397	25th Feb. 1840	Ploughs.
HUCKVALE, THOMAS - -	9092	20th Sept. 1841	Horse-hoes, and apparatus for treating and dressing turnips, to preserve them from insects.
HUCKVALE, THOMAS - -	13,582	2nd April 1851	Treating mangel-wurzel, and making drinks and other preparations therefrom.
HUDDART, GEORGE AUGUSTUS	11,779	3rd July 1847	Apparatus for the cultivation of land.
HUDDART, GEORGE AUGUSTUS	13,240	29th Aug. 1850	Manufacture of cigars; apparatus for smoking cigars.
HUDDART, GEORGE AUGUSTUS	14,236	20th July 1852	Manufacture of cigars.
HUDDART, JOSEPH - -	1952	25th April 1793	Making cables and other cordage.
HUDDART, JOSEPH - -	2339	20th Aug. 1799	Registering or forming the strands in the machinery for manufacturing cordage.
HUDDART, JOSEPH - -	2421	1st July 1800	Tarring and manufacturing cordage.
HUDDART, JOSEPH - -	2784	21st Sept. 1804	Manufacturing and spinning yarn.
HUDDART, JOSEPH - -	2886	30th Oct. 1805	Manufacture of large cables, and cordage in general.
HUDLESTON, LAWSON - -	2462	30th Dec. 1800	Conveying boats or barges from a higher to a lower level, and vice versâ, on canals, &c.
HUDSON, JAMES - - -	6728	4th Dec. 1834	Machinery and apparatus applicable in block-printing on silk, woollen, cotton, and other fabrics, and on paper.
HUDSON, JAMES - - -	13,267	28th Sept. 1850	Printing yarns for, and weaving, carpets and other fabrics.

Name of Patentee.	Progressive Number.	Date.	Subject-matter of Patent.
HUDSON, JOHN - - -	3511	9th Dec. 1811	Composition for printing or painting on paper, linen, stuccoed walls, and boarding, for ornamenting the walls and ceilings of rooms.
HUDSON, WILLIAM - -	4406	1st Nov. 1819	Manufacture of boots and shoes.
HUDSON, WILLIAM - -	12,036	22nd Jan. 1848	Looms for weaving.
HUDSWELL, JOHN - - -	4493	20th July 1820	Manufacture of wafers.
HUGGETT, JAMES - - -	4437	10th Feb. 1820	Machine to be attached to carriages as a substitute for a drag, to regulate the speed, and prevent accidents in going down hill.
HUGHES, EDWARD JOSEPH -	14,256	10th Aug. 1852	Machinery for spinning and weaving cotton-wool and other fibrous substances; machinery for stitching, either plain or ornamentally.
HUGHES, HENRY - - -	100	4th Jan. 1637	Making barilla.
HUGHES, HESKETH - -	10,186	15th May 1844	Machine for crimping, fluting, and quilling muslin and other fabrics.
HUGHES, JOHN - - -	3672	27th March 1813	Apparatus for raising gravel or earth from the bottom of rivers and pits; screening and delivering the same into barges or other receptacles.
HUGHES, JOHN - - -	4843	11th Sept. 1823	Securing the bodies of the dead in coffins.
HUGHES, JOHN GEORGE -	9385	9th June 1842	Application of telegraphic-signals, and mode of applying the same.
HUGHES, JOSEPH - -	9242	29th Jan. 1842	Manufacturing paper.
HUGHES, THOMAS - -	5364	23rd May 1826	Method of restoring foul or smutty wheat, and rendering the same fit for use.
HUGHES, THOMAS - -	7464	7th Nov. 1837	Stocks, cravats, or stiffeners.
HUGUENIN, SIMON - -	2659	13th Nov. 1802	Universal lever, or machine for accelerating motion with little friction.
HULETT, DAVID - - -	12,814	18th Oct. 1849	Gas-meters; gas-regulators.
HULL, ALONZO GRANDISON -	9572	28th Dec. 1842	Electrical apparatus for medical purposes; application thereof to the same purposes.
HULL, ALONZO GRANDISON -	9917	27th Oct. 1843	Manufacturing fermented and distilled liquors.
HULL, AMOS GERALD - -	7112	9th June 1836	Instruments for supporting the prolapsed uterus.
HULMANDEL, CHARLES JOSEPH	6496	28th Oct. 1833	Block-printing, as applied to calico and some other fabrics.
HULLMANDEL, CHARLES JO- [SEPH. [Hallmandel Charles.]	7605	26th March 1838	Preparing surfaces for being corroded with acids, to produce patterns and designs for certain kinds of printing and transparencies.
HULLMANDEL, CHARLES JO- [SEPH.	8683	5th Nov. 1840	New effect of light and shadow, imitating a brush or stump drawing, or both combined, being an impression on paper from a prepared plate or stone; preparing the said plate or stone.
HULLMANDEL, CHARLES JO- [SEPH.	10,675	22nd May 1845	Producing patterns upon earthenware and porcelain.
HULLS, JONATHAN - -	556	21st Dec. 1736	Machine for taking ships and vessels out of and into any harbour or river against wind or tide, or in a calm.
HULLS, JONATHAN - -	686	12th Dec. 1753	Machine for weighing gold coin, rings, &c.; also a sliding-rule, for taking the contents of solids and superficials.

Name of Patentee.	Progressive Number.	Date.	Subject-matter of Patent.
HULME, GEORGE - - -	8971	27th May 1841	Waterclosets.
HULME, JOSEPH - - -	9091	20th Sept. 1841	Machinery for grinding or setting the teeth of cards, or other apparatus employed for carding cotton-wool or other fibrous substances.
HULOT, JACQUES - - -	12,637	5th June 1849	Manufacturing fronts of shirts.
HULSEBERG, WILLIAM HENRY	14,035	24th March 1852	Treatment of wool, hair, feathers, fur, and other fibrous substances; machinery or apparatus for the purpose.
HULTON, JOHN SMITH - -	13,964	12th Feb. 1852	Apparatus used in the bleaching of yarns and goods.
HUME, JAMES - - -	3399	28th Feb. 1811	Sweeping-machines or brushes.
HUMFREY, CHARLES - -	10,268	24th July 1824	Manufacturing candles.
HUMFREY, CHARLES - -	12,390	28th Dec. 1848	Production of light by burning oleic-acid in lamps; construction of lamps, and preparation or manufacture of oleic-acid for that purpose.
HUMFREY, CHARLES - -	13,058	23rd April 1850	Manufacture of candles and oils; treating fatty and oily matters; application of the products of fatty and oily matters.
HUMMEL, JOHN - - -	1167	15th Aug. 1777	Working and knitting framework, milled and napped in imitation of ratteen, and consisting of English or Spanish wool or both mixed, in any colour or pattern.
HUMPHREYS, FRANCIS - -	6801	28th March 1835	Marine steam-engines; applicable to steam-engines for other purposes.
HUMPHREYS, JOHN BARNETT -	7557	30th Jan. 1838	Marine and other steam-engines.
HUMPHREYS, JOHN BARNETT -	8236	10th Oct. 1839	Shipping generally; steam-vessels in particular.
HUMPHRIES, JOHN - - -	8182	1st Aug. 1839	Manufacture of carpets and rugs.
HUMPHRYS, EDWARD - -	12,010	4th Jan. 1848	Steam-engines; engines for raising, exhausting, and forcing fluids.
HUNCLASS, SAMUEL YOUNG -	1721	15th Jan. 1790	Making and rendering elastic and waterproof all sorts of painted, printed, varnished, or japanned linen, cotton, and woollen cloths, stuff, or silk, or any material interwoven therewith.
HUNCLASS, SAMUEL YOUNG -	1919	28th Nov. 1792	Construction of canopy, ceiling, wind-up or draw-up bedsteads, with or without bedding or furniture, for obtaining room.
HUNNYBUN, THOMAS - -	10,959	20th Nov. 1845	Omnibuses.
HUNOUT, AUGUSTIN LOUIS -	5155	23rd April 1825	Artillery, musketry, and other fire-arms.
HUNT, CHRISTOPHER - -	118	17th July 1638	Embroidering or huffling gilded leather on several grounds, for hangings or furniture for houses.
HUNT, HARRIOT BRIDGET -	1280	26th Feb. 1781	Making hats, cloaks, waistcoats, and other things, ornamented with feathers and other materials.
HUNT, JAMES - - -	9243	31st Jan. 1842	Manufacture of bricks.
HUNT, JOHN - - -	8280	23rd Nov. 1839	Propelling and steering vessels.
HUNT, JOHN - - -	11,780	3rd July 1847	Effecting the combustion of gas, oil, camphine, and other substances burned for the production of light.
HUNT, JOHN - - -	13,146	20th June 1850	Forming and moulding plastic substances; machinery and apparatus employed therein.
HUNT, JOHN - - -	14,226	16th July 1852	Machinery for washing and separating ores.

Name of Patentee.	Progressive Number.	Date.	Subject-matter of Patent.
HUNT, JOSEPH - - -	8056	7th May 1839	Manufacture of soda and other valuable products, from common salt.
HUNT, JOSEPH - - -	11,163	9th April 1846	Manufacturing soda.
HUNT, SETH - - - -	4128	22nd May 1817	Escapement for clocks, watches, and chronometers.
HUNT, SETH - - - -	4129	23rd May 1817	Machinery for making pins.
HUNT, THOMAS - - -	14,265	19th Aug. 1852	Fire-arms.
HUNT, THOMAS YATE - -	3735	25th Aug. 1813	Back for scythes, reaping-hooks, straw-knives, and hay-knives.
HUNT, WILLIAM - - -	2336	2nd Aug. 1799	Grinding corn, malt, and other grain, with steel or iron-hardened plates.
HUNT, WILLIAM - - -	3131	10th May 1808	Rolling moulds or plates for trowels, of a square or oblong form, from blister, sheer, or cast steel.
HUNT, WILLIAM - - -	8356	21st Jan. 1840	Manufacture of potash and soda, and their carbonates.
HUNT, WILLIAM - - -	10 469	16th Jan. 1845	Apparatus for burning coal; apparatus for applying heat to effect the evaporation of certain solutions.
HUNT, WILLIAM - - -	12,186	13th June 1848	Apparatus to be used in processes connected with the manufacture of certain metals and salts.
HUNT, WILLIAM - - -	12,193	24th June 1848	Obtaining certain metals from their compounds; obtaining other products by the use of compounds containing metals.
HUNT, WILLIAM - - -	14,312	30th Sept. 1852	Producing or obtaining ammoniacal salts.
HUNTER, EBENEZER - -	6527	20th Dec. 1833	Locks used for fastening and security.
HUNTER, EBENEZER - -	11,523	11th Jan. 1847	Latches, latch-locks, and other locks for fastening.
HUNTER, GEORGE - - -	5280	7th Nov. 1825	Construction, use, and application of wheels.
HUNTER, JAMES - - -	6794	18th March 1835	Facing and dressing certain kinds of stone.
HUNTER, THOMAS - - -	7507	13th Dec. 1837	Machine for boring or perforating stones.
HUNTLEY, HENRY VERE -	7430	7th Sept. 1837	Apparatus for securing ships' masts.
HURD, EDWARD - - -	293	24th March 1692	Lacquering on iron and all other metals, useful for armour, guns, and several other things.
HURLISTON, PETER - -	1052	5th Aug. 1773	Elastic periwig.
HURLOCK, ROBERT ALLEN -	7170	11th Aug. 1836	Axletrees.
HURRY, EDMUND COBB -	2713	14th June 1803	Making and working windlasses.
HURRY, HENRY COLUMBUS -	13,077	22nd May 1850	Lubricating machinery.
HURST, RICHARD - -	12,997	7th March 1850	Looms for weaving; machinery for preparing, balling, and winding warps and yarns.
HURWOOD, GEORGE - -	10,946	14th Oct. 1844	Apparatus for moving and fastening windows.
HURWOOD, GEORGE - -	13,070	7th May 1850	Grinding corn and other substances.
HUTCHISON, GEORGE - -	14,297	18th Sept. 1852	Preparing oils for lubricating and burning.
HUTCHISON, STEPHEN - -	6486	12th Oct. 1833	Machinery for manufacturing gas for illumination; supplying gas to the consumer; construction of gas-burners;—partly applicable to other purposes.
HUTCHISON, STEPHEN - -	9904	12th Oct. 1843	Gas-meters.
HUTCHISON, STEPHEN - -	10,747	2nd July 1845	Gas-meters.
HUTCHISON, WILLIAM - -	9839	13th July 1843	Machinery for cutting marble and other stones.

Name of Patentee.	Progressive Number.	Date.	Subject-matter of Patent.
HUTCHISON, WILLIAM	11,979	25th Nov. 1847	Treating pasteboard and other substances, rendering them compact and impervious to wet, frost, vermin, and other destructive agents.
HUTCHINGS, SAMUEL	2884	22nd Oct. 1805	Making and manufacturing wax, spermaceti, and tallow, candles.
HUTCHINGS, SAMUEL	523	2nd Nov. 1730	Extracting and preserving sulphur contained in mundic.
HUTCHINS, WILLIAM HENRY	8711	21st Nov. 1840	Preventing ships and other vessels from foundering; raising vessels when sunk.
HUTCHINSON, JOHN	5822	30th July 1829	Machinery for spinning cotton, silk, linen, woollen, and other fibrous substances.
HUTCHINSON, SAMUEL	146	20th July 1664	Making and framing boiling vessels for salt-works, and other uses; pots for melting glass-metal and other metals; making pot-ashes with tobacco-stalks, broom-stalks and other vegetables; and joining and mixing the volatile spirits with the fixed spirits in the same; mixing the materials for the purpose of making the salts used for melting down glass-metals firm and lasting.
HUTCHINSON, SAMUEL	192	8th Dec. 1676	Melting lead ore and other metals and minerals with sea-coal and pit-coal.
HUTCHINSON, SAMUEL	1317	18th Jan. 1782	Solid warded lock and key to be applied to locks, to prevent them being picked.
HUTCHINSON, THOMAS	9721	4th May 1843	Obtaining or manufacturing lime from a substance or substances not hitherto used for the purpose.
HUTCHINSON, WILLIAM	8920	5th April 1841	Manufacture of oil-cake or seed-cake.
HUTTON, ARTHUR	13,925	27th Jan. 1852	Manufacture of casks.
HUTTON, JOHN	11,427	22nd Oct. 1846	Chronometers and other time-keepers.
HUTTON, THOMAS	307	— 1692	Mill driven by wind, sails, or water-wheels, for making paper, and with another engine attached, for raising water.
HUTTON, WILLIAM	3252	31st July 1809	Making sickles and reaping-hooks with iron in steel backs fixed upon the blades thereof.
HUXHAM, WILLIAM	4676	4th June 1822	Construction of roofs.
HUXLEY, JOHN EARLE	7791	31st Aug. 1838	Stoves.
HUXLEY, JOHN EARLE, junior	7791	31st Aug. 1838	Stoves.
HYAM, BENJAMIN	13,605	26th April 1851	Fastening down trousers or other articles of wearing-apparel.
HYATT, WILLIAM	7952	29th Jan. 1839	Steam-engines.
HYATT, WILLIAM	14,074	17th April 1852	Obtaining and applying motive power.
HYDE, JAMES	9481	29th Sept. 1842	Machinery used for preparing cotton-wool, silk, flax, and similar fibrous substances for spinning.
HYDE, JOHN	6970	31st Dec. 1835	Machinery for carding cotton and other fibrous substances.
HYDE, JOHN	9481	29th Sept. 1842	Machinery used for preparing cotton-wool, silk, flax, and similar fibrous substances for spinning.
HYDE, JOHN	11,225	28th May 1846	Looms and apparatus connected with looms for weaving.
HYDE, LAURENCE	141	4th Feb. 1663	Making sugar-mills.
HYDE, SIMEON	11,166	15th April 1846	Refrigerators.

Name of Patentee.	Progressive Number.	Date.		Subject-matter of Patent.
HYMANS, MARCUS - - -	2751	7th Feb.	1804	Composition for shaving without the use of razor, soap, or water.
HYNAM, JOHN - - -	13,206	31st July	1850	Machinery for placing splints of wood, also wax, and composition tapers, in frames for dipping.
HYNES, PATRICK SEYTON -	6773	25th Feb.	1835	Wheels, axletrees, and boxes; apparatus for locking carriage-wheels.

I.

IBBETSON, JOHN HOLT - -	4954	15th May	1824	Production of gas.
IBBOTSON, HENRY - -	4728	28th Nov.	1822	Fenders capable of being extended or contracted in length, so as to fit fire-places of different dimensions.
IBOTSON, RICHARD -	5964	29th July	1830	Apparatus for separating the knots from paper-stuff, or pulp used in the manufacture of paper.
IKIN, JAMES - - - -	4210	27th Jan.	1818	Constructing fire or furnace bars or gratings.
ILES, CHARLES - - -	11,140	25th March	1846	Carding dress-fastenings and other articles; fabrics employed for the purpose.
ILES, CHARLES - - -	11,332	11th Aug.	1846	Machinery and apparatus for making dress-fastenings;—partly applicable to other useful purposes.
ILES, CHARLES - - -	12,319	4th Nov.	1848	Manufacture of certain descriptions of dress-fastenings; making up dress-fastenings and other articles for sale.
ILES, CHARLES - - -	12,587	26th April	1849	Manufacture of picture-frames, inkstands, and other articles in dies or moulds; producing ornamental surfaces.
ILETT, JOSEPH - - -	3208	21st Feb.	1809	Producing fast greens on cottons and various other articles.
ILLINGWORTH, DANIEL -	13,236	22nd Aug.	1850	Machinery for preparing wool and hair for the carding, combing, and other manufacturing processes.
IMRAY, WILLIAM - -	13,737	4th Sept.	1851	Manufacture of bricks.
INGLEDEW, JAMES - -	4304	10th Nov.	1818	Effecting a saving of fuel by the application of certain articles hitherto unused for that purpose.
INGLEDEW, JOHN - -	6812	14th April	1835	Metallic safety-wheel and revolving axle.
INGLIS, HUGH - -	10,112	19th March	1844	Locomotive steam-engines effecting a saving of fuel;—applicable to steam-vessels and other purposes; and to increasing the adhesion of wheels of railway engines, carriages, and tenders, upon the lines of rail when the same are in a moist state.
INGLIS, WALTER - - -	2503	21st May	1801	Making saddles.
INGOLD, PIERRE FREDERICK -	9511	8th Nov.	1842	Machinery for making parts of watches and other timekeepers.
INGOLD, PIERRE FREDERICK -	9752	1st June	1843	Machinery for making parts of watches and other timekeepers.

Name of Patentee.	Progressive Number.	Date.	Subject-matter of Patent.
INGOLD, PIERRE FREDERICK -	9993	21st Dec. 1843	Machinery for making parts of watches and other timekeepers, as well as parts of mathematical, optical, astronomical, nautical and musical instruments.
INGRAM, JAMES - - -	2899	26th Nov. 1805	Manufacturing powder sugar from raw sugar alone, or syrup of sugar alone, or both mixed.
INGRAM, THOMAS WELLS -	6296	15th Aug. 1832	Manufacture of certain description of buttons; application of machinery for the purpose.
INGRAM, THOMAS WELLS -	7360	4th May 1837	Manufacture of certain description of buttons; tools used in the manufacture thereof.
INGRAM, THOMAS WELLS -	9110	7th Oct. 1841	Shears and other apparatus for cutting, cropping, and shearing certain substances.
INGRAM, THOMAS WELLS -	9768	10th June 1843	Pressing and embossing wood and other materials, in order to apply the same to useful purposes.
INKSON, JOHN - - -	8487	30th April 1840	Apparatus for consuming gas for the purpose of light.
INNES, JAMES, junior - -	185	12th Nov. 1675	Buoying and raising up ships' ordnance, also treasures and other matters, from the bottom of the sea, by the help of air conveyed under water; new way of diving and living several hours under the water, by curing the air conveyed down for sustenance so as to make it fit for respiring whilst beneath the water; engines and instruments for landing and shipping goods and merchandise.
INSOLE, JAMES - - -	9461	8th Sept. 1842	Manufacture of brushes.
IONS, JAMES - - - -	9218	13th Jan. 1842	Smelting copper-ores.
IRELAND, THOMAS - - -	1136	31st Oct. 1776	Chemical preparation of iron equal in hardness to the best blister-steel, retaining at the same time the toughness and properties of iron.
IREMONGER, RICHARD JOSHUA	7457	4th Nov. 1837	Spring or arrangement of springs for wheel-carriages.
IRVIN, PETER HUNTER -	8989	17th June 1841	Producing light; manufacturing apparatus for the diffusion of light.
IRVIN, THOMAS EUGENE -	8989	17th June 1841	Producing light; manufacturing apparatus for the diffusion of light.
IRVINE, THOMAS JOHNSON -	9777	15th June 1841	Packing-cases, boxes, trunks, portmanteaus, and other articles for containing goods.
IRVING, JOHN ROBERT - -	2826	9th March 1805	Apparatus to determine the specific-gravity of fluid bodies, and the relation that their weight bears to a given measure.
IRVING, WILLIAM - - -	9165	7th Dec. 1841	Manufacture of bricks and tiles.
IRVING, WILLIAM - - -	9380	7th June 1842	Corn-drill or machine for sowing seed or grain.
IRVING, WILLIAM - - -	9962	25th Nov. 1843	Machinery and apparatus for cutting and carving substances to be applied for inlaying and other purposes.
IRVING, WILLIAM - - -	10,517	10th Feb. 1845	Construction of apparatus for cutting ornamental forms, beads, recesses, and mouldings, in wood, stone, and other materials.

Name of Patentee.	Progres-sive Number.	Date.	Subject-matter of Patent.
IRVING, WILLIAM - - -	12,073	23rd Feb. 1848	Apparatus for cutting or carving ornamental forms in wood, stone, and other materials.
IRWIN, CHRISTOPHER - -	731	2nd Sept. 1758	Marine observatory and telescope, and almanack for ascertaining longitude at sea.
IRWIN, JAMES - - -	1035	5th March 1773	Making black-currant drops and lozenges of fruits, for the cure of sore throats, coughs, and hoarseness.
ISAAC, FREDERICK WILLIAM -	6280	28th June 1832	Ornamenting the finger-keys and other parts of pianofortes, organs, and other musical instruments.
ISAAC, JOHN JOHNSTON - -	5670	5th July 1828	Propelling vessels, boats, and other floating bodies.
ISAACS, MOSES - - -	4904	19th Feb. 1824	Construction of machinery, which, when kept in motion by any suitable power or weight, is applicable to obviate concussion by means of preventing counteraction, and by which the friction is converted into a power for propelling carriages on land, vessels on water, and for giving motion to other machinery.
ISBISTER, CALEB - - -	2399	8th May 1800	Manufacture of straw-plait made of split straw, presenting only the outside surface to the eye, and also other plait of split straw laid upon silk, paper, or wood.
ISOARD, MATHIEU FRANCOIS -	10,822	28th Aug. 1845	Obtaining motive-power.
ISHERWOOD, JOHN - -	1669	12th Sept. 1788	Locking the wheels of carts and carriages, particularly those with two wheels,
IVERS, JAMES - - -	10,627	22nd April 1845	Machinery for preparing, roving, and slubbing cotton-wool and other fibrous substances.
IVISON, MICHAEL, WHEEL-[WRIGHT.	7578	24th Feb. 1838	Consuming smoke in furnaces and other places for the purpose of economising fuel; applying air, heated or cold, to blasting or smelting furnaces.
IVISON, MICHAEL WHEEL-[WRIGHT.	7600	26th March 1838	Preparing and spinning silk-waste, wool, flax, and other fibrous substances; discharging gum from silks, raw and manufactured.
IZON, JOHN - - - -	1102	3rd Oct. 1775	Casting hinges ready jointed, or with false knuckles or joints and pins, in cast-iron.
IZON, WILLIAM RETLAND -	7526	4th Jan. 1838	Steam-engines.

J.

Name of Patentee.	Progres-sive Number.	Date.	Subject-matter of Patent.
JACK, CHARLES - - -	14,049	29th March 1852	Machinery for grinding pigments, colours, and other matters.
JACK, RICHARD - - -	656	25th May 1750	Quadrant for taking the altitude of the sun or moon by refraction; also a refracting telescope, with four lenses.
JACKE, JOHN - - - -	21	8th Aug. 1622	Engine for raising water for draining land and mines; engine for turning brooches.

Name of Patentee.	Progressive Number.	Date.	Subject-matter of Patent.
JACKS, JAMES - - -	2603	2nd April 1802	Waterproofing woollen, cotton, and linen-cloths, canvas, silk-hats, paper, and other manufactures.
JACKS, JAMES - - -	3150	11th July 1808	Chemical preparation for preserving woollen and vegetable substances from mildew, rot, or fermentation, and rendering cloths and other fabrics impervious to rain.
JACKS, JAMES - - -	4456	11th May 1820	Preventing mildew in sail-cloth and other canvas, and in other manufactures of vegetable fibre.
JACKSON, BENJAMIN - -	370	8th April 1704	Causing the bodies of coaches, calashes, chaises, waggons and other carriages, to remain erect, even though the wheels or carriages may be overset.
JACKSON, BENJAMIN HABAKUK	399	5th May 1715	Causing the bodies of coaches, calashes, chaises, waggons and other carriages, to remain erect, even though the wheels or carriages may be overset.
JACKSON, BENJAMIN HABAKUK	441	11th April 1722	Machine for swimming, to preserve lives in case of shipwreck or the overturning of boats, and in case of the cramp and other accidents in swimming for pleasure.
JACKSON, CHRISTOPHER -	242	11th Oct. 1684	Making writing and printing-paper.
JACKSON, EDWARD - -	2916	12th March 1806	Machinery for rasping, grating, or reducing into powder, such woods, drugs and other substances, for the use of dyers and others, as cannot easily be pulverized by mere concussion.
JACKSON, EDWARD HENRY -	14,330	21st Oct. 1852	Producing artificial light; and also producing motive-power.
JACKSON, GEORGE - - -	5611	19th Jan. 1828	Machinery for propelling boats and other vessels ;—applicable to water-wheels and other purposes.
JACKSON, GEORGE - - -	13,104	6th June 1850	Heckling-machinery.
JACKSON, HUMPHREY - -	680	5th April 1753	Medicine, called Cordial Bitter Tincture, for the stomach.
JACKSON, HUMPHREY - -	749	26th March 1760	Making isinglass from British materials with which finings are made.
JACKSON, HUMPHREY - -	910	9th Dec. 1768	Hardening wood, and rendering it flexible and tough, also preserving wood from decay, particularly oak and elm planks.
JACKSON, HUMPHREY - -	1188	30th March 1778	Stain, varnish and powder, for beautifying and preserving the colour of wood, particularly mahogany or furniture; likewise useful in polishing and sharpening all fine steel edged instruments.
JACKSON, JAMES - - -	673	3rd July 1752	Medicine, called Oleum Anedinum, or British Balsam of Health.
JACKSON, JOHN - - -	4823	29th July 1823	Construction of locks used for the discharge of guns and other fire-arms, on the detonating principle.
JACKSON, JOHN - - -	7569	16th Feb. 1838	Sawing, planing, tongueing, grooving, and preparing or constructing window-sashes, door and other frames, and ornamental work; machinery and tools to be used in the same.
JACKSON, JOHN - - -	8438	19th March 1840	Manufacture of nails, nuts, bolts, and rivets.
JACKSON, JOHN - - -	11,146	25th March 1846	Producing light; materials and apparatus applicable thereto; treating fatty and oily matters.

Name of Patentee.	Progressive Number.	Date.		Subject-matter of Patent.
JACKSON, JOHN - - -	11,470	1st Dec.	1846	Process of and apparatus for treating fatty and oily matters, and manufacturing candles and night-lights.
JACKSON, JOHN - - -	13,795	3rd Nov.	1851	Presses and matting; process and apparatus for treating fatty and oily matters; manufacture of candles and night-lights.
JACKSON, JOSEPH - - -	112	7th Dec.	1637	Making, casting, and gilding leaden-seals.
JACKSON, JOSEPH - - -	1070	19th May	1774	Working water-mills, or conveying water to the wheels of such mills, and thereby occasioning constant motion in the same, whether at high or low water.
JACKSON, PETER ROTHWELL -	6709	6th Nov.	1834	Hydraulic-presses and pumps.
JACKSON, PETER ROTHWELL -	8148	8th July	1839	Mangling, calendering, glazing, and finishing cotton, linen, woollen, and other goods; machinery for the purpose.
JACKSON, PETER ROTHWELL -	10,073	24th Feb.	1844	Construction and manufacture of wheels, cylinders, hoops, and rollers; machinery connected therewith; steam-valves.
JACKSON, RICHARD - -	3409	7th March	1811	Making the shanks of anchors and other bodies of like form, of wrought-iron, by using one solid core of iron for the centre, with bars of feather-edged iron, so constructed as to save a considerable quantity of iron, coals, and labour, in manufacturing the same.
JACKSON, ROBERT RAYNSFORD	9926	4th Nov.	1843	Machinery for preparing cotton and other fibrous substances for spinning.
JACKSON, ROBINSON - -	9132	2nd Nov.	1841	Machinery for the production of rotary-motion for obtaining mechanical power;—also applicable for raising and impelling fluids.
JACKSON, THOMAS - - -	627	9th Dec.	1747	Tincture for curing burns, scalds, green wounds, old bruises, strains, sprains, rheumatic and other maladies.
JACKSON, THOMAS - - -	766	1st Sept.	1761	Specific, called Imperial Lotion.
JACKSON, THOMAS - - -	5653	13th May	1828	Metal-stud, to be applied to boots, shoes, and other like articles.
JACKSON, WILLIAM - -	1449	20th Aug.	1784	Musical instrument, or British lyre.
JACKSON, WILLIAM - -	1821	19th July	1791	Construction of saddles and stirrup-irons, by which saddles are made to fit either horse, mule, or poney, without injury to the backs of the same.
JACKSON, WILLIAM - -	2149	5th Dec.	1796	Doors, made to shut by themselves without noise, and to exclude wind from the room.
JACKSON, WILLIAM - -	2548	3rd Nov.	1801	Drill, to be fixed to a plough-beam, for drilling or sowing turnips.
JACKSON, WILLIAM - -	5067	11th Jan.	1825	Machinery for making bobbin-net lace.
JACKSON, WILLIAM - -	13,115	11th June	1850	Manufacture of soap, and preparation of materials to be used for this purpose.
JACOB, CHARLES - - -	41	22nd Dec.	1627	Engine for turning mills for grinding corn or grain, tools, metals, bark, and other things.
JACOB, CHARLES - - -	12,495	28th Feb.	1849	Manufacture of earthenware tubes or pipes.
JACOB, GEORGE WILLIAM -	11,446	12th Nov.	1846	Manufacture of printed, patterned, ornamented, coloured, embossed, and moulded surfaces.

Name of Patentee.	Progressive Number.	Date.	Subject-matter of Patent.
JACOB, GEORGE WILLIAM -	11,981	30th Nov. 1847	Manufacture of capsules; application of designs to certain descriptions of surfaces.
JACOB, JOSEPH - - -	932	13th July 1769	Construction of wheel-carriages, by application of united spiral springs, hoop-wheels, and leather boxes.
JACOB, JOSEPH - - -	1355	1st Feb. 1783	Constructing carriage-wheels and wheel-carriages.
JACOB, JOSEPH - - -	2675	20th Jan. 1803	Metal-box for the axletrees of wheel-carriages, mills, engines, and other machines.
JACOB, JOSEPH, junior - -	997	17th Sept. 1771	Construction of wheel-carriages.
JACOB, JOSEPH, junior - -	1065	14th Feb. 1774	Ornamenting carriages, sedan-chairs, buildings, furniture, musical-instruments, books, and toys.
JACOB, WILLIAM COMBAULD -	12,664	20th June 1849	Manufacture of parasols and umbrellas.
JACOBS, MEYER - - -	12,301	2nd Nov. 1848	Manufacture and treatment generally of woven fabrics of all kinds, also stamping the same.
JACOBS, SAMUEL - - -	13,300	24th Oct. 1850	Printing on woollen, cotton, paper, and other substances;—partly applicable to colouring, shading, tinting, or varnishing the same.
JACOMB, CHARLES - - -	5257	15th Sept. 1825	Construction of furnaces, stoves, grates, or fire-places.
JACQUEMART, FRANCOIS CONSTANT.	6011	20th Oct. 1830	Tanning skins.
JACQUESON, ADOLPHE - -	6131	6th July 1831	Machinery applicable to lithographic and other printing.
JAMES, EDWARD - - -	7246	3rd Dec. 1836	Manufacture of liquid and paste blacking, by the introduction of India-rubber, oil, and other articles and things.
JAMES, HENRY - - -	3426	26th March 1811	Navigating, forcing, towing, and hauling boats, barges, and other vessels, on canals, rivers, and other navigable waters, by machinery worked by steam or other power.
JAMES, HENRY - - -	3469	26th July 1811	Manufacture of barrels of fire-arms and artillery.
JAMES, HERBERT GEORGE -	7548	23rd Jan. 1838	Making bread.
JAMES, HERBERT GEORGE -	9464	8th Sept. 1842	Apparatus for weighing.
JAMES, JOHN - - -	4284	24th July 1818	Amorphous metal-plates; also crystallizing or rendering crystallizable the surface of tin-plates, or iron or copper plates tinned ("morphous metal-plates.")
JAMES, JOHN - - -	14,285	9th Sept. 1852	Weighing machines, and weighing cranes.
JAMES, NATHANIEL - -	1454	15th Nov. 1784	Spring trusses for ruptures, both single, double, navel, side, and inguinal.
JAMES, ROBERT - - -	626	13th Nov. 1747	Powder and pill for the cure of fevers and other distempers.
JAMES, ROBERT - - -	1089	25th Nov. 1774	Analeptic pills for the cure of rheumatism, loss of appetite, also for the cure of costiveness, giddiness, flatulency, and all disorders occasioned by a sedentary life.
JAMES, SAMUEL - - -	3744	1st Nov. 1813	Sofa or machine for the ease of invalids and others.
JAMES, THOMAS - - -	13,008	19th March 1850	Rolling iron and other metals.

Name of Patentee.	Progressive Number.	Date.		Subject-matter of Patent.
JAMES, WILLIAM - - -	914	19th Jan.	1769	Crane nook with an iron bar fixed horizontally against the end of the perch in wheel-carriages.
JAMES, WILLIAM - - -	4913	28th Feb.	1824	Construction of railroads and tramroads or ways;—applicable to other useful purposes.
JAMES, WILLIAM HENRY -	4957	15th May	1824	Construction of steam-carriages for the conveyance of persons and goods on highways and turnpike roads.
JAMES, WILLIAM HENRY -	5117	5th March	1825	Railways, and construction of carriages to be employed thereon.
JAMES, WILLIAM HENRY -	5176	31st May	1825	Apparatus for diving under water;—applicable to other purposes.
JAMES, WILLIAM HENRY -	5196	14th June	1825	Boilers for steam-engines.
JAMES, WILLIAM HENRY -	6297	15th Aug.	1832	Construction of steam-carriages, and machinery for propelling the same;—partly applicable to other purposes.
JAMES, WILLIAM HENRY -	7520	22nd Dec.	1837	Telegraphic apparatus, and means of communicating intelligence by signals.
JAMES, WILLIAM HENRY -	7637	8th May	1838	Machines for weighing substances or fluids, and certain additions to such machines;—applicable to other purposes.
JAMES, WILLIAM HENRY -	7854	6th Nov.	1838	Apparatus for heating, generating, and cooling fluids; engines to be actuated by such fluids;—partly applicable to the raising and forcing of fluids.
JAMES, WILLIAM HENRY -	9473	16th Sept.	1842	Railways and carriageways; railway and other carriages; propelling the said carriages;—partly applicable to the reduction of friction in other machines.
JAMES, WILLIAM HENRY -	10,411	2nd Dec.	1844	Carriages for the conveyance of passengers and goods; means of working the same.
JAMES, WILLIAM HENRY -	10,784	25th July	1845	Manufacture of plates and vessels of metal and other substances suitable for heating purposes; means of heating the same.
JAMES, WILLIAM HENRY -	14,283	3rd Sept.	1852	Heating and refrigerating; apparatus connected therewith.
JAMIESON, ALEXANDER - -	10,871	10th Oct.	1845	Dressing ores requiring washing.
JAMIESON, WILLIAM -	12,792	4th Oct.	1849	Looms for weaving.
JAPY, MONNIN - - -	8315	16th Jan.	1839	Rotatory-engines, to be actuated by steam or water.
JAQUIER, JEAN JAQUES -	6156	31st Aug.	1831	Machinery for making paper, "Xeranothlipte."
JAQUIN, CORNELIUS ALFRED -	7722	7th July	1838	Manufacture of buttons.
JAQUIN, CORNELIUS ALFRED -	8314	26th Jan.	1841	Manufacture of covered buttons; preparing metal surfaces for such manufacture, and for other purposes.
JAQUIN, CORNELIUS ALFRED -	13,654	3rd June	1851	Manufacture of nails, pins, tacks, screws, and other similar articles.
JARMIN, GEORGE - -	9254	14th Feb.	1842	Machinery for spinning flax, hemp, and tow.
JARRETT, RICHARD - -	49	21st Jan.	1630	Barrel-engine, for raising water out of mines, graffs, coalpits, or any other place.
JARRIN, WILLIAM ALEXIS -	5539	13th Aug.	1827	Apparatus for cooling liquids.
JARVIE, JAMES - - -	9044	11th Aug.	1841	Machinery for preparing and spinning hemp, flax, wool, and other fibrous materials.
JARVIE, ROBERT - - -	9044	11th Aug.	1841	Machinery for preparing and spinning hemp, flax, wool, and other fibrous materials.

Name of Patentee.	Progressive Number.	Date.	Subject-matter of Patent.
JARVIS, THOMAS - - -	10,593	7th April 1845	Preparing extracts from certain vegetable substances ; apparatus connected therewith ;—applicable to other similar purposes.
JAY, CHARLES - - -	11,881	30th Sept. 1847	Apparatus for evaporating and concentrating saccharine and saline solutions ;—also applicable to the evaporation and concentration of vegetable and other extracts.
JAYET, JEAN - - - -	11,928	28th Oct. 1847	Calculating-machines.
JAYNE, WILLIAM - - -	1791	8th Feb. 1791	Composition for keeping and preserving, for the space of at least two years, the eggs of hens, turkeys, geese, and ducks.
JEAKES, WILLIAM - - -	4687	26th June 1822	Cooking-apparatus.
JEAKES, WILLIAM - - -	4819	24th July 1823	Apparatus for regulating the supply of water in steam-boilers and other vessels.
JEAKES, WILLIAM - - -	7838	22nd Oct. 1838	Applying ventilating-apparatus to stoves conducted on Dr. Arnott's principle.
JEANS, JAMES - - -	2921	21st March 1806	Chain-pumps ; mode of working the same ; wells for receiving such pumps.
JEARRARD, CHARLES - -	5114	5th Mar. 1825	Filtering-apparatus.
JEARRARD, ROBERT WILLIAM	8187	6th Aug. 1839	Retarding wheeled-carriages.
JECKS, ISAAC - - - -	6630	17th June 1834	Apparatus for drawing on boots, and putting them off.
JEFFERIES, HUMPHREY - -	6935	28th Nov. 1835	Buttons.
JEFFERIES, HUMPHREY - -	8932	22nd April 1841	Manufacture of buttons.
JEFFERIES, WILLIAM - -	5250	15th Sept. 1825	Machine for impelling-power without the aid of fire, water, or air.
JEFFERIES, WILLIAM - -	5467	20th Feb. 1827	Calcining and smelting metals and semi-metals, from ores and other matters containing them.
JEFFERIES, WILLIAM - -	8072	22nd May 1839	Smelting and extracting metals from copper and other ores.
JEFFERIES, WILLIAM - -	8557	1st July 1840	Obtaining copper, spelter, and other metals from ores.
JEFFERIS, CHARLES - -	4993	29th July 1824	Making swifts and other apparatus thereto belonging, for winding silk and other fibrous materials.
JEFFERSON, THOMAS - -	3115	7th March 1808	Machines for finishing, glazing, and glossing leather.
JEFFERY, ALFRED - - -	8943	29th April 1841	Defending the sheathing of ships, and protecting their sides and bottoms.
JEFFERY, ALFRED - - -	9323	15th April 1842	Preparing masts, spars, and other wood, for shipbuilding and other purposes.
JEFFERY, ALFRED - - -	10,062	19th Feb. 1844	Treating wood and other substances requiring to be exposed to water.
JEFFERYS, THOMAS - -	1107	17th Nov. 1775	Making artificial globes or spheres without being covered with printing and drawing, on paper, parchment, or any such like material.
JEFFRAY, JAMES - - -	4345	4th Mar. 1819	Machinery for propelling boats, ships, or other floating vessels, by wind, steam, animal strength, of water or other power ;—applicable to other purposes.
JEFFREE, JOHN TRESAHAR -	9216	11th Jan. 1842	Lifting and forcing water and other fluids ;—partly applicable to steam-engines.

Name of Patentee.	Progressive Number.	Date.	Subject-matter of Patent.
JEFFREE, JOHN TRESAHAR -	13,725	21st Aug. 1851	Apparatus for facilitating the combustion of fuel, thereby dispensing with funnels, chimneys, or shafts.
JEFFREYS, GEORGE - -	1797	18th March 1791	Dyeing woollen-cloths, stuffs, and other materials, in various colours, and of any figure, pattern, or design.
JEFFREYS, HUMPHREY - -	2294	12th Feb. 1799	Machinery for raising and conveying coals, ores, or other minerals from mines.
JEFFREYS, HUMPHREY - -	5007	7th Oct. 1824	Flue or chimney for furnaces and other purposes.
JEFFREYS, JULIUS - - -	6988	23rd Jan. 1836	Curing or relieving disorders of the lungs.
JEFFREYS, JULIUS - - -	7603	26th March 1838	Stoves, grates, and furnaces.
JEFFREYS, JULIUS - - -	10,287	6th Aug. 1844	Respirators.
JEEFREYS, JULIUS - - -	11,207	13th May 1846	Steam-engine boilers and furnaces; propelling vessels.
JEFFREYS, JULIUS - - -	12,984	28th Feb. 1850	Preventing or removing affections of the chest.
JEFFRIES, WILLIAM - -	10,164	30th April 1844	Sweeping chimneys; apparatus to prevent chimneys from smoking.
JEKYLL, JOHN - - -	4725	9th Nov. 1822	Steam or vapour-bath.
JELF, Sir JAMES - - -	4741	20th Dec. 1822	Combination of machinery for working marble and other stone, for jambs, mantels, chimney-pieces, and other purposes.
JELLICORSE, JOHN - - -	6216	28th Jan. 1832	Spinning-machinery.
JELOWICKE, EDWARD - -	7031	14th March 1836	Steam-engines.
JENAR, RENÉ FLORENTIN -	5516	4th July 1827	Lamps.
JENAR, RENÉ FLORENTIN -	5519	4th July 1827	Filling with metal or other suitable material the interstices in wire-gauze or other similar substances. "Metallic linen."
JENKINS, GEORGE - - -	13,006	18th March 1850	Producing motive-power.
JENKINS, HENRY - - -	745	31st Jan. 1760	Machine or regulator for discovery of the longitude at sea.
JENKINS, JOHN BORLASE -	11,868	9th Sept. 1847	Manufacture of copper and other metallic cylinders or rollers, for printing silks and other fabrics, and for other purposes; casting metallic cylinders, tubes or rollers, hollow and free from air-bubbles.
JENKINS, MARY - - -	12,009	31st Dec. 1847	Manufacture of pins, hooks, eyes, and other fastenings.
JENKINS. WILLIAM - -	3450	21st May 1811	Manufacturing flat-backed handles and rings, used with or affixed to cabinet and other furniture and things.
JENKINS, WILLIAM - -	3698	22nd May 1813	Manufacturing socket-castors used with or affixed to cabinet and other furniture and things.
JENKINS, WILLIAM WALKER -	3483	9th Sept. 1811	Manufacturing drawer and other knobs used with or affixed to cabinet and other furniture and things.
JENKINS, WILLIAM WALKER -	9054	27th Aug. 1841	Machines for making pins, and sticking them into paper.
JENKINSON, JOHN HENRY -	12,887	12th Dec. 1849	Machinery to be used for preparing, spinning, and doubling cotton-wool, flax, silk, and similar fibrous materials.
JENKINSON, WILLIAM - -	943	6th Dec. 1769	Machine for drawing, raising, or forcing up water from mines, coal-pits, and other places of great depth.

Name of Patentee.	Progressive Number.	Date.	Subject-matter of Patent.
JENKINSON, WILLIAM - -	8910	31st March 1843	Machinery for preparing and spinning flax, silk, and other fibrous substances.
JENKYN, RICHARD - -	8816	26th Jan. 1841	Valves for hydraulic-machines.
JENNENS, AARON - - -	5137	29th March 1825	Preparing and working pearl-shell into various forms, for applying it to ornamental uses in the manufacture of japan-ware and other wares and articles.
JENNENS, THEODORE HILAH -	11,670	24th April 1847	Manufacturing papier-maché articles; ornamenting the same;—applicable for ornamental purposes generally.
JENNENS, WILLIAM (Sir) -	200	25th March 1678	Erecting certain baths to sweat, wash, and bathe in, for preservation of health.
JENNER, STEPHEN - - -	1868	18th April 1792	Escape for horses, to enable them to disengage themselves from their halters when entangled therein.
JENNINGS, HENRY CONSTAN-[TINE.	3629	19th Dec. 1812	Manufacturing, using, and applying certain articles, by means of which, mariners and other persons may be saved from drowning.
JENNINGS, HENRY CONSTAN-[TINE.	4259	7th May 1818	Mariner's compass.
JENNINGS, HENRY CONSTAN-[TINE.	4417	4th Dec. 1819	Substitute for pitch.
JENNINGS, HENRY CONSTAN-[TINE.	4443	11th April 1820	Lock or fastening for general use.
JENNINGS, HENRY CONSTAN-[TINE.	4830	14th Aug. 1823	Machine for preventing the improper escape of gas.
JENNINGS, HENRY CONSTAN-[TINE.	4844	11th Sept. 1823	Instrument to be affixed to a saddle-tree, by the application of which distress to the horse may be avoided.
JENNINGS, HENRY CONSTAN-[TINE.	5272	22nd Oct. 1825	Refining sugar.
JENNINGS, HENRY CONSTAN-[TINE.	11,331	11th Aug. 1846	Machine for evaporating fluids or liquids containing matters to be crystallized or concentrated.
JENNINGS, HENRY CONSTAN-[TINE.	12,503	5th March 1849	Manufacture of vehicles for mixing pigments; manufacture of white-lead.
JENNINGS, HENRY CONSTAN-[TINE.	13,190	23rd July 1850	Rendering canvas and other fabrics and leather waterproof.
JENNINGS, JOHN - - -	11,500	21st Dec. 1846	Machinery for thrashing.
JENNINGS, JOSEPH - - -	8128	22nd June 1839	Obtaining metal from pyrites or mundic.
JENNINGS, JOSIAH GEORGE -	11,728	3rd June 1847	Water-closets; making joints and connections of pipes.
JENNINGS, JOSIAH GEORGE -	12,012	5th Jan. 1848	Cocks or taps for drawing off liquids and gases.
JENNINGS, JOSIAH GEORGE -	14,273	23rd Aug. 1852	Water-closets; traps and valves; pumps.
JENOUR, JOSHUA - - -	5570	28th Nov. 1827	Cartridge or case, and method of enclosing therein shot or other missiles, for loading fire-arms and guns.
JEPSON, JOHN - - -	2283	24th Dec. 1798	Manufacturing hats.
JEROM, SARA - - -	87	31st Oct. 1635	Engine for cutting timber into thin pieces or scales, for making bandboxes, scabbards for swords, and the like.
JEROM, SARA - - - [Jerome, Sara.]	120	20th Oct. 1638	Engine for cutting timber into thin pieces or scales, for making bandboxes, scabbards for swords, and the like.

Name of Patentee.	Progressive Number.	Date.	Subject-matter of Patent.
JESSON, RICHARD - - -	1054	30th Oct. 1773	Making malleable-iron from cast-iron, by the use of coals or coke, without charcoal, mixture of granulations, fluxes, or other infusions.
JESSON, RICHARD - - -	1396	14th Nov. 1783	Making bar-iron from cast-iron, by the use of coals or coke, without charcoal.
JESSOP, SYDNEY - - -	9293	21st March 1842	Preparing wrought-iron intended for wheel-tyre, rails, and certain other articles.
JESSOP, WILLIAM - - -	4770	27th March 1823	Elastic metallic-piston, or packing of pistons, applied to cylinders, externally or internally.
JESSOP, WILLIAM - - -	6433	1st June 1833	Constructing railways.
JEVONS, THOMAS - - -	6903	8th Oct. 1835	Machinery for making bar-iron into shoes for horses, also into shapes for various purposes.
JEWELL, JOSEPH - - -	3081	17th Nov. 1807	Reducing calomel to an impalpable powder, for medicinal use.
JEWERS, DANIEL - - -	647	1st July 1749	Making pearl-ashes.
JEWSBURY, THOMAS - -	2463	16th Jan. 1801	Making paste used in weaving and sizing calico, and for pasting paper, &c.
JOAD, JOHN - - -	1337	19th Sept. 1782	Machine for grinding and polishing glass, and at the same time sifting and serving the sand used for that purpose.
JOBBINS, DANIEL - - -	5361	3rd June 1823	Milling and scouring woollen-cloths and other fabrics, by machinery;—applicable to stocks or fulling-machines.
JOBSON, ROBERT - - -	12,393	28th Dec. 1848	Manufacture of stoves.
JOCELYN, NATHANIEL - -	5825	3rd Aug. 1829	Making blank forms for Bankers' cheques, bills of exchange, promissory notes, and other instruments or securities, to prevent forgeries or alterations.
JOELL, JAMES - - -	298	31st May 1692	Diving-habit, for enabling a man to work one hour under water, by means of an air-pump.
JOEST, WILLIAM - - -	8970	26th May 1841	Propelling vessels.
JOHANNOT, JOSIAS - -	625	3rd Nov. 1747	Making cartridge-paper from the mill, so as not to hold any fire.
JOHANSEN, ANDREW - -	3098	23rd Jan. 1808	Artificial whetstone, or tablet for sharpening all sorts of cutlery. "Cotific Tablet."
JOHN, GEORGE - - -	703	25th Aug. 1755	Raising water by fire.
JOHNES, ROGER - - -	23	23rd Feb. 1623	Making hard and soft soap; burning straw of beans and peas, also kelp, fern, and other vegetables, into ordinary ashes or into potashes for the purpose; use of the assay-glass for trying the lee; saving fuel in the process of boiling the same.
JOHNS, AMBROSE BOWDEN -	2996	22nd Dec. 1806	Compositions; mode of making the same, for covering and facing houses and for other purposes.
JOHNS, AMBROSE BOWDEN -	7885	1st Dec. 1838	Colouring or painting walls and other surfaces.
JOHNS, AMBROSE BOWDEN -	8115	19th Jan. 1839	Colouring walls and other surfaces; preparing materials used for that purpose.
JOHNSON, ALFRED RICHARD -	10,123	28th March 1844	Hats.
JOHNSON, ALFRED RICHARD -	11,246	18th June 1846	Hats, caps, and bonnets.
JOHNSON, ARTHUR HARRY -	11,872	23rd Sept. 1847	Refining silver-lead.

Name of Patentee.	Progressive Number.	Date.	Subject-matter of Patent.
JOHNSON, AUGUSTUS WILLIAM	7714	30th June 1838	Preventing the incrustation of steam-boilers or generators, or evaporating-vessels.
JOHNSON, DENIS - - -	4321	22nd Dec. 1818	Machine for diminishing the labour of walking, and enabling persons to use greater speed.
JOHNSON, EDWARD - -	9806	27th June 1843	Apparatus for bathing.
JOHNSON, GEORGE - -	9738	25th May 1843	Making candles.
JOHNSON, GEORGE FREDERICK	5887	26th Jan. 1830	Machine, or substitute for the drags of carriage-wheels, and for other purposes.
JOHNSON, HENRY - - -	1201	9th Nov. 1778	Printing with types of figures connected so as to prevent the possibility of error.
JOHNSON, HENRY - - -	1266	16th Oct. 1780	Casting and moulding types, for composing and printing with words, sentences, and syllables, instead of single letters.
JOHNSON, HENRY - -- -	2188	26th July 1797	Waterproof compound, and a vegetable liquid, for bleaching and cleansing woollens, linens, cottons, and other articles; also preparing stuffs or cloths made of woollen, linen, cotton, and silk, by the application of the aforesaid composition, to render them impenetrable to wet, as well as elastic and durable.
JOHNSON, JAMES - - -	294	24th March 1692	Invention, whereby one or more men may continue and work under water for a quarter of an hour with freedom and clearness of sight, and with the assistance of others that can swim, may recover and take up any bullion, plate, &c. without diving.
JOHNSON, JAMES - - -	8864	8th March 1841	Machinery for making hosiery.
JOHNSON, JAMES - - -	11,741	12th June 1847	Machinery for the manufacture of rivets, railway or other pins, bolts, nuts, and spikes.
JOHNSON, JAMES - - -	14,106	1st May 1852	Manufacture of hats.
JOHNSON, JOHN - - -	174	27th Feb. 1674	Windmill for raising water to great heights, and draining mines, and grounds, and for other purposes.
JOHNSON, JOHN - - -	958	23rd May 1770	Tanning leather.
JOHNSON, JOHN - - -	1150	29th March 1777	Composition for covering the fronts and tops of houses and buildings, and for ornamenting the same, also for other purposes.
JOHNSON, JOHN - - -	1234	15th Oct. 1779	Securing buildings from fire.
JOHNSON, JOHN - - -	2107	3rd May 1796	Preventing and curing smoky chimneys.
JOHNSON, JOHN - - -	9672	18th March 1843	Photography, and its application to the arts.
JOHNSON, JOHN HENRY -	14,011	8th March 1852	Weaving carpets and other fabrics; machinery or apparatus employed therein.
JOHNSON, JOHN HENRY -	14,206	6th July 1852	Steam-engines.
JOHNSON, JOHN ROBERT -	10,982	6th Dec. 1845	Materials employed in constructing and working atmospheric-railways.
JOHNSON, JOHN ROBERT -	11,006	20th Dec. 1845	Purifying gas; treatment of products of gas-works.
JOHNSON, JOHN ROBERT -	13,287	17th Oct. 1850	Fixing colours in fabrics made of cotton or other fibre.

Name of Patentee.	Progres-sive Number.	Date.	Subject-matter of Patent.
JOHNSON, JOSEPH - - -	3104	28th Jan. 1808	Warming-pans for airing beds, rooms, and carriages, and for other things requiring duration of heat.
JOHNSON, JOSEPH - - -	3377	17th Sept. 1810	" Domestic Telegraph," or machinery for communicating intelligence from one room of a house to another.
JOHNSON, JOSEPH - - -	4778	16th April 1823	Drags for carriages.
JOHNSON, JOSEPH - - -	12,797	12th Oct. 1849	Furnaces, or the means of consuming smoke.
JOHNSON, MATTHEW WARTON	7775	15th Aug. 1838	Construction of coffins.
JOHNSON, RICHARD - -	11,243	16th June 1846	Parts of machinery used in the preparation for spinning, and in spinning and doubling cotton-wool and other fibrous substances.
JOHNSON, RICHARD - -	11,877	30th Sept. 1847	Manufacture of wire-cloth.
JOHNSON, RICHARD - -	12,439	23rd Jan. 1849	Manufacture of malted grain; vinous fermentation; brewing; machinery connected with the above, or similar processes.
JOHNSON, RICHARD - -	13,480	31st Jan. 1851	Annealing articles of iron and other materials.
JOHNSON, THOMAS - -	1060	18th Jan. 1774	Preparation for staining horses and other animals so as to make them match in colour, also for preserving cattle from flies and other insects, and for making such marks on animals as cannot be effaced without injury to the said animals.
JOHNSON, THOMAS - -	2684	28th Feb. 1803	Preparing and dressing cotton-warp.
JOHNSON, THOMAS - -	2771	2nd June 1804	Dressing cotton-warp, also linen, silk, and woollen-warps.
JOHNSON. THOMAS - -	2876	9th Aug. 1805	Loom for weaving cotton and other goods, by power.
JOHNSON, THOMAS - -	3023	23rd March 1807	Machine for weaving yarn.
JOHNSON, THOMAS - -	6579	20th March 1834	Looms for weaving different sorts of cloth.
JOHNSON, THOMAS - -	7628	28th April 1838	Preparing yarn or thread by machinery suitably for warps, in preparation for weaving in looms.
JOHNSON, THOMAS - -	8162	20th July 1839	Machinery for manufacturing shoe-heels and toe-tips.
JOHNSON, THOMAS - -	11,424	22nd Oct. 1846	Machinery for weaving and producing patterns in weaving; machinery for finishing certain woven fabrics.
JOHNSON, WILLIAM - -	688	31st Jan. 1754	Double and single kettles, furnaces, and boilers, made of wrought-iron plate, instead of copper, for the navy.
JOHNSON, WILLIAM - -	1646	15th April 1788	Overcoming resistance in mechanical operations by man or beast.
JOHNSON, WILLIAM - -	2382	19th March 1800	Machine for obtaining a self-moving power, or perpetual motion.
JOHNSON, WILLIAM - -	2411	10th June 1800	Machine for obtaining a self-moving power, or perpetual motion.
JOHNSON, WILLIAM - -	2476	10th Feb. 1801	Machine with a perpetual motion, or mechanical self-moving power.
JOHNSON, WILLIAM - -	3236	15th May 1809	Process for heating fluids, for the purposes of art and manufacture.
JOHNSON, WILLIAM - -	3826	26th July 1814	Making salt.

Name of Patentee.	Progressive Number.	Date.	Subject-matter of Patent.
JOHNSON, WILLIAM - -	4325	24th Dec. 1818	Construction of furnaces or fire-places for heating, boiling, or evaporating water and other liquids ;—applicable to steam-engines, and to other purposes.
JOHNSON, WILLIAM - -	4747	8th Jan. 1823	Saving fuel in obtaining the power of steam for the use of steam-engines.
JOHNSON, WILLIAM - -	4997	5th Aug. 1824	Evaporating fluids for heating horticultural and other buildings ; also heating liquors in distilling, brewing, dyeing, and in making sugar and salt, with reduced expenditure of fuel.
JOHNSON, WILLIAM - -	5431	18th Dec. 1826	Process and apparatus for making salt.
JOHNSON, WILLIAM - -	6888	22nd Aug. 1835	Construction of boots and shoes.
JOHNSON, WILLIAM - -	9781	15th June 1843	Paving or covering roads, streets, and other ways or surfaces.
JOHNSON, WILLIAM - -	10,198	23rd May 1844	Machinery for preparing cotton-wool, flax, and other fibrous substances.
JOHNSON, WILLIAM - -	10,933	20th Nov. 1845	Machinery for preparing cotton and other fibrous substances, for spinning.
JOHNSON, WILLIAM - -	11,465	1st Dec. 1846	Machinery for raising or lifting and lowering weights or ponderous bodies.
JOHNSON, WILLIAM - -	11,472	2nd Dec. 1846	Propelling carriages on railways.
JOHNSON, WILLIAM - -	13,730	28th Aug. 1851	Ascertaining the weight of goods.
JOHNSON, WILLIAM BECKETT	11,740	12th June 1847	Construction of locomotive-engines to be used on rail or other ways ; applicable to carriages used on railways.
JOHNSON, WILLIAM BECKETT	12,083	8th March 1848	Locomotive, stationary, and marine steam-engines.
JOHNSON, WILLIAM BECKETT	13,410	12th Dec. 1850	Steam-engines ; apparatus for generating steam ; applicable to engines where other vapours or gases are used as the motive-power.
JOHNSON, WILLIAM BECKETT	13,959	9th Feb. 1852	Railways ; apparatus for generating steam.
JOHNSTON, ALEXANDER - -	9427	23rd July 1842	Carriages ; applicable to ships and boats, and to other purposes where locomotion is required.
JOHNSTON, DAVID - - -	8161	20th July 1839	Manufacture of hinges.
JOHNSTON, JAMES - - -	8841	8th Feb. 1841	Obtaining motive-power.
JOHNSTON, JAMES - - -	9706	20th April 1843	Construction of steam-boilers, and machinery for propelling vessels.
JOHNSTON, JAMES - - -	10,037	8th Feb. 1844	Steam-boilers.
JOHNSTON, JAMES - - -	10,505	31st Jan. 1845	Processes and machinery for making and refining sugar.
JOHNSTON, JOHN - - -	7675	7th June 1838	Warming, lighting, and ventilating.
JOHNSTON, JOHN - - -	8645	24th Sept. 1840	Machinery for ascertaining the velocity of ships, vessels, carriages and other means of locomotion, or the space passed through by the same ;—partly applicable to the measurement of time.
JOHNSTON, JOHN - - -	10,120	25th March 1844	Manufacture of lamps, and shades for lamps and other lights.
JOHNSTON, ROBERT - -	2226	30th March 1798	Medicine for the cure of rheumatism, palsy, and other complaints. " Whitehead's Improved Essence of Mustard."
JOHNSTON, WILLIAM - -	5392	24th July 1826	Ink-holders.
JOHNSTON, WILLIAM - -	11,490	14th Dec. 1846	Arranging the rails on certain parts of railways.

Name of Patentee.	Progressive Number.	Date.	Subject-matter of Patent.
JOHNSTONE, ANDREW - -	1974	8th Jan. 1794	Making " Jessamine Soap."
JOHNSTONE, CHARLES - -	10,446	21st Dec. 1844	Arrangements for raising ships' anchors, and for other purposes.
JOHNSTONE, JAMES - -	11,722	27th May 1847	Manufacture of sugar.
JOHNSTONE, ROBERT - -	10,025	27th Jan. 1844	Construction of lamps for combustion of naphtha, turpentine, and other resinous oils.
JOLLY, THOMAS WILLIAM -	1220	22nd April 1779	Machine for steering ships by an horizontal wheel, quadrants, pinions, and spindles.
JOLLY, WILLIAM GAIRDNER -	10,299	29th Aug. 1844	Form of tiles for draining; implements for manufacturing the same; mode of manufacture.
JONAS, JONAS - - -	1409	17th Dec. 1783	Sliding lead-pencils.
JONES, ALEXANDER - -	8793	14th Jan. 1841	Manufacture of copper tubes and vessels.
JONES, ARCHIBALD - -	2975	7th Oct. 1806	Discharging colours from shawls and other dyed silks, and silk and worsted of every description, or parts thereof as may be required.
JONES, CHARLES - -	6394	7th March 1833	Percussion-locks applicable to fire-arms.
JONES, CHARLES - -	6436	12th June 1833	Gun and pistol locks.
JONES, EDEN THOMAS - -	10,972	27th Nov. 1845	Apparatus used in the concentration of sulphuric-acid.
JONES, EDMUND JOHN - -	8.44	6th July 1839	Manufacturing cyder and perry.
JONES, EDWARD - - -	1992	27th May 1794	Saddle-tree for the use of ladies, with a steel spring head to fall down, and thereby prevent danger in case of the horse tripping, falling, or running away, contrived so that the rider can disengage herself from the saddle, and prevent her clothes from being entangled in the horn or head of the saddle.
JONES, EDWARD THOMAS -	2083	26th Jan. 1796	Plan for detecting errors in accounts.
JONES, EDWARD - - -	6876	10th Aug. 1835	Machinery for moulding bricks, tiles, and other articles made of brick-earth.
JONES, EVAN - - - -	348	24th Jan. 1696	Engine for raising water out of mines and coalpits; blowing the bellows, and working the hammers in melting and forging iron, copper, and other metals;—applicable to the working of mills, and to other uses.
JONES, EZEKIEL - - -	8988	12th June 1841	Machinery for preparing, slubbing, roving, spinning, and doubling cotton, silk, wool, worsted, flax, and other fibrous substances.
JONES, FRANCIS - - -	830	15th June 1765	Knitting-machine, for making and knitting stockings, stocking-pieces, and other goods usually made on stocking-frames.
JONES, FRANCIS - - -	1096	22nd April 1775	Manufacturing double coarse frame-work stockings, mits, gloves, caps, and pieces for coats, upon a stocking-frame, in gold, silver, silk, and mohair; carding and dressing such goods.
JONES, GEORGE - - -	6300	8th Sept. 1832	Process for making malleable-iron.
JONES, HENRY - - -	6418	4th May 1833	Stretching cloth and keeping it even during the process of weaving, and preserving the selvages.
JONES, HENRY - - -	10,555	13th March 1845	Preparation of flour for certain purposes.

Name of Patentee.	Progressive Number.	Date.	Subject-matter of Patent.
JONES, JAMES - - -	2975	7th Oct. 1806	Discharging colours from shawls and other dyed silks, and silk and worsted of every description, or parts thereof as may be required.
JONES, JAMES - - -	6427	25th May 1833	Making rovings, spinning and doubling cotton, silk, flax, and other fibrous substances.
JONES, JAMES - - -	6699	20th Oct. 1834	Making rovings, spinning and doubling cotton, silk, flax, and other fibrous substances.
JONES, JOHN (Reverend) -	842	25th March 1766	British herb-tobacco.
JONES, JOHN - - - -	1143	4th Jan. 1777	Machine for raising water or other liquid, by rarefied air or steam.
JONES, JOHN - - - -	2813	23rd Jan. 1806	Liquor for printing and dyeing cotton, linen, or woollen.
JONES, JOHN - - - -	3267	28th Sept. 1809	Manufacturing skelps for fire-arms.
JONES, JOHN - - - -	3285	9th Dec. 1809	Machine for preparing and cutting cotton and linen candlewicks.
JONES, JOHN - - - -	3469	26th July 1811	Manufacturing barrels for fire-arms and artillery.
JONES, JOHN - - - -	3484	9th Sept. 1811	Applying the expansive force of air or steam upon a wheel, so as to be the first mover of machinery.
JONES, JOHN - - - -	4229	19th Feb. 1818	Machinery used for dressing woollen and other cloths.
JONES, JOHN - - - -	4897	27th Jan. 1824	Machinery and instruments for dressing and cleansing woollen, cotton, linen, silk, and other cloths or fabrics.
JONES, JOHN - - - -	5709	25th Sept. 1828	Machinery for pressing and finishing woollen-cloths.
JONES, JOHN - - - -	5835	21st Aug. 1829	Machinery for dressing and finishing woollen-cloths.
JONES, JOHN - - - -	6300	8th Sept. 1832	Process for making malleable-iron.
JONES, JOHN - - - -	8051	25th April 1839	Frying and grilling pan, for cooking steaks, chops, and other meats.
JONES, JOHN - - - -	8264	7th Nov. 1839	Table-knife.
JONES, JOHN - - - -	8753	23rd Dec. 1840	Carding-engines for carding wool or other fibrous substances.
JONES, JOHN - - - -	9116	7th Oct. 1841	Steam-engines; obtaining power from the use of steam.
JONES, JOHN - - - -	10,142	10th April 1844	Manufacture of sheaves and shells for blocks, and bolt-rings or washers, for the use of shipwrights and engineers.
JONES, JOHN, junior - -	2911	20th Feb. 1806	Manufacturing barrels for fire-arms.
JONES, JOSEPH - - -	5676	17th July 1828	Smelting copper-ore.
JONES, JOSEPH - - -	6628	16th June 1834	Construction of power-looms; manufacture of certain kinds of corded fustians to be woven in diagonal cords, from cotton-wool and other fibrous materials.
JONES, JOSEPH - - -	13,913	24th Jan. 1852	Furnaces used in the manufacture of iron.
JONES, ORLANDO - - -	7995	6th March 1839	Manufacture of starch; converting the refuse to various purposes.
JONES, ORLANDO - - -	8488	30th April 1840	Treating farinaceous matters to obtain starch and other products; manufacturing starch.
JONES, ROBERT - - -	11,610	10th March 1847	Dressing or finishing goods or fabrics.

Name of Patentee.	Progressive Number.	Date.	Subject-matter of Patent.
JONES, ROBERT GRIFFITH -	5626	13th March 1828	Ornamenting china and other compositions. "Lithophanic translucid or opaque China."
JONES, ROBERT LEWIS - -	11,119	5th March 1846	Reducing charcoal and other similar matters to powder; treating such powder to make it of use in lieu of vegetable-black, lamp-black, and other matters.
JONES, ROWLAND - - -	1941	25th March 1793	Machines for stamping and striping woollen cloths, kerseymeres, silk-velvets, cotton-velvets, velveteens, and thicksets.
JONES, SAMUEL - - -	5732	10th Dec. 1828	Producing instantaneous light.
JONES, SAMUEL - - -	6335	20th Nov. 1832	Apparatus, or parts of apparatus, for producing instantaneous light.
JONES, SAMUEL TONKIN -	7202	6th Oct. 1836	Tanning hides and skins.
JONES, STOPFORD THOMAS -	9043	4th Aug. 1841	Machinery for propelling vessels by steam or other power.
JONES, STOPFORD THOMAS -	11,820	29th July 1847	Steam-engines, machinery for propelling vessels.
JONES, THEODORE - - -	5415	11th Oct. 1826	Wheels for carriages.
JONES, THOMAS - - -	461	28th Jan. 1724	Staining, veining, spotting, clouding, and damasking on wood, stone, and earthenware; also upon linen, silk, canvas, paper, and leather, to imitate marble, porphyry, and other stones and tortoise-shell.
JONES, THOMAS - - -	2830	23rd March 1805	Compositions for making trays, waiters, and various other articles; manufacturing the same by presses or stamps.
JONES, THOMAS - - -	3416	14th March 1811	Machine for cutting corks and bungs.
JONES, THOMAS - - -	3446	9th May 1811	Instrument for dividing lines and distances.
JONES, THOMAS - - -	4256	7th May 1818	Blast-engines and steam-engines.
JONES, THOMAS - - -	6418	4th May 1833	Stretching cloth, and keeping it even during the process of weaving, and preserving the selvages.
JONES, THOMAS - - -	9125	21st Oct. 1841	Construction and arrangement of certain parts of marine and stationary steam-engines.
JONES, THOMAS - - -	11,258	22nd June 1846	Machinery for preparing, slubbing, and roving cotton-wool and other fibrous material.
JONES, THOMAS MORTON -	9913	18th Oct. 1843	Heating liquids and aëriform bodies.
JONES, WILLIAM - - -	2236	8th May 1798	Machine for mixing meal or other substances, with fluids, in order to extract more easily the spirit or essence of the malt, or other substance to be acted upon.
JONES, WILLIAM - - -	4713	18th Oct. 1822	Manufacturing iron.
JONES, WILLIAM - - -	5578	4th Dec. 1827	Machinery for cutting sprigs, brads, and nails.
JONES, WILLIAM - - -	6200	22nd Dec. 1831	Machinery for making pins, rivets, wood-screws, and nails.
JONES, WILLIAM - - -	6513	21st Nov. 1833	Machinery to be used in the manufacture of pins and needles.
JONES, WILLIAM - - -	7492	28th Nov. 1837	Filtering fluids.
JONES, WILLIAM COLEY -	9510	8th Nov. 1842	Treating an unctuous substance to obtain products therefrom for manufacturing candles, and for other purposes.

Name of Patentee.	Progressive Number.	Date.		Subject-matter of Patent.
Jones, William Coley -	9542	8th Dec	1842	Operating on certain organic bodies to obtain products therefrom for manufacturing candles, and for other purposes.
Jones, William Henry -	13,433	28th Dec.	1850	Apparatus to be used when burning candles.
Jones, William Lutwyche -	14,032	24th March	1852	Stoves and other apparatus for heating.
Jonquet, Denis - - -	10,900	31st Oct.	1845	Machinery for preparing skins for tanning and dressing.
Jordan, Edward - - -	4385	22nd June	1819	Water-wheel for draining marsh lands.
Jordan, Edward - - -	4931	27th March	1824	Construction of water-closets; apparatus connected therewith.
Jordan, Edward - - -	5191	18th June	1825	Obtaining power applicable to machinery.
Jordan, James - - -	2109	24th May	1796	Building and constructing bridges, aqueducts, and buildings;—applicable to other purposes.
Jordan, John - - -	12,824	2nd Nov.	1849	Construction of ships and other vessels navigated on water.
Jordan, Thomas - - -	14,217	12th July	1852	Disinfecting essential oils; treating fatty matters obtained from shale, shistus, or other bituminous substances; retorts for distilling such minerals.
Jordan, Thomas Brown -	10,377	2nd Nov.	1844	Manufacture of blocks or surfaces for surface-printing, stamping, embossing, and moulding.
Jordan, Thomas Brown -	10,523	17th Feb.	1845	Machinery and apparatus for cutting, carving, and engraving.
Jordan, Thomas Brown -	11,564	8th Feb.	1847	Machinery for working mouldings.
Jordan, Thomas Brown -	13,728	28th Aug.	1851	Apparatus for cutting, planing, and otherwise working slate, and also for framing and setting the same.
Jordan, William - -	1338	2nd Oct	1782	Constructing wheels of carts, waggons, coaches, and chaises.
Jorden, Edward - - -	61	7th Dec.	1632	Melting tin, lead, iron, and copper ore, with pit-coal, peat, and turf.
Jorden, Edward - - -	3869	24th Dec.	1814	Apparatus for the detection of depredators; "Thieves' alarum."
Jorden, John Stubbs - -	3478	20th Aug.	1811	Glazing hothouses, greenhouses, and all horticultural buildings.
Jorden, John Stubbs - -	3814	7th June	1814	Construction of horticultural buildings; making the lights for the same.
Joret, Julien - - -	3923	8th June	1815	Extracting gold and silver from the cinders of gold-refines and other substances, by machinery.
Josephs, Edward - - -	5745	18th Dec.	1828	Wheels, axletrees, and other parts of carts, waggons, and other conveyances.
Jotham, Thomas - - -	2539	15th Sept.	1801	Machine for raising the pile on woollen, cotton, or other piece-goods preparatory to shearing; dressing or dubbing cloths, either wet or dry, otherwise than by yerencards or pickards.
Jouannin, Jean Baptiste [Francois.	9415	9th July	1842	Apparatus for regulating the speed of steam, air, or water engines.
Jough, Maurice De - -	3762	29th Nov.	1813	Preparing madder and madder-roots.
Jough, Maurice De - -	4914	28th Feb.	1824	Constructing and placing a coke oven under or near to boilers, to make the heat from the coke useful for heating the boilers also, and to exclude such heat if necessary.

Name of Patentee.	Progressive Number.	Date.	Subject-matter of Patent.
JOUGH, MAURICE DE - -	5140	29th March 1825	Spinning-machines, as mules, jennies, slubbers, or other similar machines.
JOUGH, MAURICE DE - -	5432	18th Dec. 1826	Machinery for preparing rovings, and twisting, spinning, and winding fibrous substances.
JOUGH, MALRICE DE - -	5576	4th Dec. 1827	Machines for spinning, doubling, twisting, roving, or preparing cotton and other fibrous substances.
JOURNET, PIERRE - -	8960	19th May 1841	Fire-escapes;—applicable to other useful purposes.
JOURNET, PIERRE - -	9239	27th Jan. 1842	Steam-engines.
JOVER, WILLIAM - -	1095	8th April 1775	Fire-lock constructed for portability and safety, with the lock so concealed as not to obstruct the sight, having the prime secured against the effects of rain, and so contrived that the barrels can be taken from the lock for the purpose of cleaning the same, is also provided with a lever that sets the lock in motion, but, being removed, disengages the action of the gun, the said fire-lock may be used either to a gun, pistol, cannon, or other fire-arm, with one, two, three, or more barrels.
JOWETT, FREDERICK WILLIAM	11,543	23rd Jan. 1847	Telegraphic communication.
JOWETT, HENRY ALFRED -	13,546	10th March 1851	Railway breaks and carriages.
JOWETT, HENRY ALFRED -	13,740	4th Sept. 1851	Hydraulic-telegraphs; making signals.
JOWETT, JOSHUA - -	2762	18th May 1804	Fire-guard stove.
JOWETT, THOMAS - -	12,635	5th June 1849	Stopping power-looms; preventing injury to the cloth or fabric in the course of weaving.
JOYCE, GEORGE - -	337	20th Oct. 1694	Instrument, which being applied to clocks, organs, harpsichords, or any other keyed instrument, will cause the same to chime or play tunes.
JOYCE, JOHN - - -	6234	1st March 1832	Machinery for making nails of iron, copper, and other metals.
JOYCE, JOHN - - -	6315	29th Sept. 1832	Machinery for making nails.
JOYCE, JOHN - - -	6401	28th March 1833	Machinery for making nails.
JOYCE, JOHN - - -	6493	19th Oct. 1833	Machinery for making nails.
JOYCE, STEPHEN - -	8202	21st Aug. 1839	Stoves for warming the air in buildings;—applicable to cooking, or for communicating heat for other useful purposes.
JOYCE, THOMAS - -	7509	16th Dec. 1837	Apparatus for heating churches, warehouses, carriages, and other places requiring artificial heat; fuel to be used therewith.
JOYCE, THOMAS - -	7593	15th March 1838	Apparatus for applying prepared fuel to culinary and domestic purposes.
JOYCE, THOMAS - -	7634	5th May 1838	Applying prepared fuel to the purpose of generating steam and evaporating fluids.
JOYCE, THOMAS - -	7698	22nd June 1838	Erecting, heating, and ventilating buildings.
JOYCE, THOMAS - -	9649	1st Oct. 1840	Article used as a knob for parlour and other doors, bell-pulls, and curtain-pins, and capable of being used for a variety of useful and ornamental purposes.
JOYCE, WILLIAM - -	6298	22nd Aug. 1832	Constructing collars for horses and other animals.
JOYNES, CLEMENT - -	413	17th May 1717	Making starch from potatoes.

Name of Patentee.	Progressive Number.	Date.	Subject-matter of Patent.
JOYNSON, WILLIAM - -	7977	21st Feb. 1839	Manufacture of paper.
JUBB, JOHN - - - -	2038	19th Feb. 1795	Machine for thrashing and winnowing corn and grain.
JUBB, RICHARD - - -	2838	5th April 1805	Making and tuning pedal-harps; tuning violins, and other stringed instruments.
JUBBER, HENRY - - -	9377	2nd June 1842	Kitchen-ranges, and apparatus for cooking.
JUCKES, JOHN - - -	7858	8th Nov. 1838	Steam-engine boilers; apparatus for feeding furnaces and fire-places; combustion of smoke, and gases arising therefrom.
JUCKES, JOHN - - -	8307	9th Dec. 1839	Furnaces or fire-places for the better consuming of fuel.
JUCKES, JOHN - - -	9067	4th Sept. 1841	Furnaces or fire-places.
JUCKES, JOHN - - -	9476	22nd Sept. 1842	Furnaces.
JUCKES, JOHN - - -	12,332	18th Nov. 1848	Furnaces and fire-places.
JUDE, HENRY GARDNER GUION	14,309	30th Sept. 1852	Manufacture of type.
JUDSON, JOSEPH EDWARD -	10,866	9th Oct. 1845	Covering rollers used in spinning cotton and other threads; covering mill-straps.
JUKES, EDWARD - - -	3615	7th Nov. 1812	Shears for pruning trees, gathering fruits, and cutting off injured limbs of trees. "Averruncator."
JUKES, JOSEPH - - -	1665	15th Aug. 1788	Fastenings for shoes, boots, knee-bands, and other purposes, to be used instead of buckles.
JULIAN, DOMINIQUE - -	13,733	4th Sept. 1851	Extracting the colouring properties of madder; rendering useful the water employed in such processes.
JULLION, JAMES THOMAS -	11,425	22nd Oct. 1846	Making certain acids; decomposing certain acids; applying the products resulting therefrom to the production of certain chemical compounds.
JULLION, JAMES THOMAS -	12,028	18th Jan. 1848	Making certain acids and salts; apparatus applicable for the purpose.
JUMP, WILLIAM AINSWORTH -	4967	15th June 1824	Manufacturing salt.
JUMP, WILLIAM AINSWORTH -	6181	14th Oct. 1831	Drawing or extracting salt from salt-pans.
JUNIPER, JOHN - - -	781	11th Nov. 1762	Medicine called Essence of Peppermint.
JUNIPER, WILLIAM -	3092	19th Dec. 1807	Rolls for punching tire and drawing hoops, for stocks of wheels; segment for sweeping and setting the same.
JUNOT, CLAUDE JOSEPH EDMEE [CHAUDRON.	8457	30th March 1840	Purifying and solidifying tallow, grease, oils, and oleaginous substances.
JUPE, ROBERT - - -	6788	11th March 1835	Expanding-table.
JUPE, ROBERT - - -	6904	9th Oct. 1835	Ornamental dessert, flower, and other stands.
JUPE, ROBERT - - -	7189	22nd Sept. 1836	Apparatus applicable to book and other shelves.
JUSTICE, JOHN - - -	3313	6th March 1810	Construction of stove-grates calculated to prevent or cure smoky chimneys.

K.

Name of Patentee.	Progressive Number.	Date.	Subject-matter of Patent.
KAEMMERER, ERNST - -	13,758	25th Sept. 1851	Sowing, depositing, or distributing seeds over land.
KAGENBUSCH, PETER - -	9367	26th May 1842	Dyeing wool, woollen-cloths, cotton-cloths, silks, and other fabrics and materials.
KAGENBUSCH, PETER - -	9492	13th Oct. 1842	Treatment of alum rock or shist; manufacture and application of the products derived therefrom.
KANE, FRANCIS - - -	9283	7th March 1842	Construction of fastenings for parts of bedsteads and other frames.
KANE, FRANCIS - - -	13,213	5th Aug. 1850	Reclining chairs; castors for chairs and other furniture; presses.
KASELOWSKY, FERDINAND -	13,310	2nd Nov. 1850	Machinery for washing, steaming, drying, and finishing cotton, linen, and woollen fabrics.
KAUFFMAN, HENRY - -	3013	20th Feb. 1807	Construction of the flageolet or English flute.
KAY, JAMES - - -	2876	9th Aug. 1805	Loom for weaving cotton and other goods, by power.
KAY, JAMES - - -	2929	17th April 1806	Machine for dressing cotton, silk, and other goods, by power.
KAY, JAMES - - -	5226	26th July 1825	Machinery for preparing and spinning flax, hemp, and other fibrous substances, by power.
KAY, JAMES - - -	6769	24th Feb. 1835	Heckling-machine.
KAY, JAMES - - -	8168	24th July 1839	Machinery for preparing and spinning flax, hemp, and other fibrous substances, by power.
KAY, JOHN - - - -	515	8th May 1730	Engine for making, twisting, and cording mohair and worsted, also twining and dressing thread for tailors and others.
KAY, JOHN - - - -	542	26th May 1733	Machine for opening and dressing wool; shuttle for weaving broad-cloths, broad-baize, sail-cloths, or any other cloths, woollen or linen.
KAY, JOHN - - - -	561	24th June 1738	Machine or upright windmill moved chiefly by the wind, for raising water, applicable to other purposes where force is required; remedying the inconvenience of raising water from a mine or deep pit by buckets.
KAY, JOHN - - - -	612	18th April 1745	Weaving tapes and other narrow goods; kiln for drying malt; saving fuel in the making of salt.
KAYSER, PHILIP JACOB - -	9369	31st May 1842	Construction of lamps.
KAYSER, WILLIAM - -	11,327	11th Aug. 1846	Manufacture of looking-glass.
KEAN, JAMES - - - -	6856	3rd July 1835	Throstle-flyer used in spinning cotton, flax, hemp, wool, silk, and other fibrous substances.
KEARESBY, JOHN (Sir) - -	148	20th Nov. 1665	Making steel.
KEASLEY, THOMAS - -	10,466	11th Jan. 1845	Manufacture of leather; partly applicable to other purposes.

Name of Patentee.	Progressive Number.	Date.	Subject-matter of Patent.
KEATES, WILLIAM - -	13,225	16th Aug. 1850	Machinery for manufacturing rollers and cylinders used for calico printing and other purposes.
KEATING, JOHN - - -	11,079	11th Feb. 1846	Manufacturing cement.
KEDDIE, THOMAS HAMILTON -	2810	19th Jan. 1805	Cartouch-box.
KEEFFE, OWEN O' - - -	801	2nd Dec. 1763	Axletree and box for the same, for coaches and other carriages, so contrived as to supply itself with oil without taking off the wheels.
KEEFFE, OWEN O' - -	811	16th April 1764	Carriage upon which to hang the bodies of coaches and other carriages.
KEEFFE, OWEN O' - -	1101	1st Aug. 1775	Carriage for coaches, chariots, chaises, waggons, and all manner of vehicles, to be used with three or four wheels.
KEELE, EDWARD - -	6623	7th June 1834	Valve and apparatus for close fermenting and cleansing porter, beer, ale, wine, spirits, cyder, and all other saccharine and fermentable fluids.
KEELING, JAMES - -	2117	20th June 1796	A preparation or substitute for white-lead, red-lead, calcined lead, or other similar preparation of lead, for glazing and enamelling earthenwares, porcelain, and chinawares, also useful in the making of glass and enamel.
KEELING, JAMES - -	2127	5th July 1796	Constructing, erecting, and making ovens, kilns, and fire-places, used in baking and hardening porcelain, china, and earthenware.
KEELING, SAMUEL - -	11,756	19th June 1847	Making candlesticks.
KEELY, JOHN, junior - -	9652	2nd March 1843	Machinery for drying or freeing from liquid or moisture, woollen, cotton, silk, and different fibrous materials and other substances, and stretching certain fibrous materials.
KEELY, JOHN, junior - -	11,483	14th Dec. 1846	Dressing or finishing lace and other fabrics.
KEELY, THOMAS - -	12,840	10th Nov. 1849	Looped or elastic fabrics, and articles made therefrom; machinery for producing the improvements; partly applicable to looped fabrics generally.
KEELY, THOMAS - -	13,596	17th April 1851	Machinery for manufacturing textile and woven fabrics and other articles of fibrous materials; improvements in such fabrics and articles.
KEEN, BENJAMIN - -	790	16th June 1763	Composition and varnish for staining, printing, and laying gold, silver, or metal, on woollens, and goods mixed with wool, for wearing-apparel or furniture.
KEEN, WILLIAM - -	589	10th March 1743	Machine for printing or painting landscapes, fruits, and flowers, on silks, cottons, linens, stuffs, woollen-cloths, and other manufactures.
KEENE, CHARLES - -	8441	23rd March 1840	Producing surfaces on leather and fabrics.
KEENE, CHARLES - -	9554	15th Dec. 1842	Manufacture of hose, socks, drawers, gloves, mits, caps, comforters, and cuffs.
KEENE, CHARLES - -	10,692	29th May 1845	Boots, shoes, gaiters, overalls, and other like articles of apparel.
KEENE, RICHARD WYNNE -	7580	27th Feb. 1838	Manufacturing cement; application of cements and other earthy substances, for producing ornamental surfaces.

Name of Patentee.	Progressive Number.	Date.	Subject-matter of Patent.
KEENE, WILLIAM - - -	6919	2nd Nov. 1835	Machinery for sowing corn, grain, and other seed, and manuring land.
KEHLHOFF, FRIEDERIECK -	819	29th Nov. 1764	Making watches.
KEIR, JAMES - - -	1240	10th Dec. 1779	Compound metal, capable of being forged hot or cold, for making bolts, nails, sheathing for ships, and for other purposes.
KEIR, JAMES - - -	2926	3rd April 1806	Manufacturing white-lead.
KEIR, PETER - - -	1585	29th Jan. 1787	Raising the supply of oil in lamps.
KELLOGG, ISAAC - -	3258	21st Aug. 1809	Machine for shearing woollen and other cloths.
KELLY, JASPER AUGUSTUS -	1810	23th May 1791	Saddle-tree and saddle.
KELLY, JASPER AUGUSTUS -	2082	19th Jan. 1796	Construction of harness.
KELLY, JASPER AUGUSTUS -	3516	15th Jan. 1812	Construction of arches, and other erections and buildings. " Moor's Modern Architecture."
KELLY, WILLIAM - -	1879	15th May 1792	Machinery to be applied to spinning-machines.
KEMP, ABRAHAM - -	323	21st July 1693	Making orchil and litmus.
KEMP, GEORGE - -	13,681	3rd July 1851	Obtaining motive-power by means of electro-magnetism.
KEMP, MATTHEW - -	2009	29th Aug. 1794	Machine for grinding and polishing glass, and washing or separating emery, white-lead, colours, and ores.
KEMP, ROBERT - -	9640	21st Feb. 1843	Wood-paving.
KEMP, ROBERT, junior -	4036	27th May 1816	Manufacturing locks and keys.
KEMP, WILLIAM - -	6820	23rd April 1835	Machine for raising sunken vessels.
KEMPELEN, WOLFGANG DE -	1426	10th April 1784	Reaction-machine, set in motion by fire, air, water, or any fluid;—applicable to other machines requiring a moving power.
KEMPEN, PETER VAN -	14,015	8th March 1852	Refrigerator, to be used in brewing, distilling, and other similar purposes.
KEMPSON, WILLIAM -	9544	8th Dec. 1842	Manufacture of muffs, cuffs, ruffs, tippets, mantillas, pellerines, dressing-gowns, boots, shoes, and other articles of wearing-apparel.
KEMPTON, WILLIAM HENRY -	8758	30th Dec. 1840	Cylinders to be used for printing calicoes and other fabrics.
KEMPTON, WILLIAM HENRY -	8766	31st Dec. 1840	Lamps.
KEMPTON, WILLIAM HENRY -	9375	1st June 1842	Manufacture of candles.
KEMPTON, WILLIAM HENRY -	11,636	23rd March 1847	Copying-presses.
KEMPTON, WILLIAM HENRY -	12,320	7th Nov. 1848	Reflectors and apparatus for artificial light.
KENDALL, JOSEPH - -	3712	29th June 1813	Plan for making pill and other small boxes.
KENDALL, JOSEPH - -	3840	8th Sept. 1814	Plan for making pill and other small boxes.
KENDALL, PETER - -	8927	17th April 1841	Connecting and disconnecting locomotive-engines and railway-carriages.
KENDALL, WILLIAM -	1786	8th Dec. 1790	Machine for washing, cleansing, and scouring linen, cotton, or woollen apparel, and household furniture.
KENDREW, JOHN - -	1613	19th June 1787	Machine for spinning yarn from hemp, tow, flax, or wool.
KENDRICK, MATTHEW SAMUEL	8486	28th April 1840	Improvements in lighting, and in lamps.
KENDRICK, WILLIAM - -	4473	6th June 1820	Manufacturing a liquid from materials now considered useless for that purpose; application of the same liquid to tanning hides and other articles.

Name of Patentee.	Progressive Number.	Date.		Subject-matter of Patent.
KENDRICK, WILLIAM - -	4514	5th Dec.	1820	Apparatus for extracting a tanning matter from bark and other substances containing such tanning matter.
KENNEDY, CHARLES - -	5354	29th April	1826	Apparatus used for cupping.
KENNEDY, JAMES - - -	10,143	15th April	1844	Construction of iron and other vessels for navigation on water.
KENNEDY, MATTHEW - -	12,600	3rd May	1849	Packing "cops" of cotton and other fibrous materials; apparatus connected therewith.
KENNEDY, ROBERT ALEXANDER	9726	15th May	1843	Machinery for grinding and sharpening cards used in carding cotton or other fibrous material.
KENNEDY, ROBERT ALEXANDER	13,657	10th June	1851	Machinery applicable to engines for carding cotton and other fibrous substances.
KENNEDY, THOMAS - -	13,899	20th Jan.	1852	Measuring the flow of water and other fluids.
KENNEDY, WILLIAM SADLER -	11,566	8th Feb.	1847	Attaching plain or ornamental surfaces of earthenware, china or glass, to articles made of metal, wood, or other materials.
KENRICK, ARCHIBALD - -	3916	23rd May	1815	Mills for grinding coffee, malt and other articles.
KENRICK, SAMUEL - -	4459	13th May	1820	Tinning cast-iron vessels of capacity.
KENRICK, SAMUEL - -	11,664	20th April	1847	Forming moulds for casting metal.
KENRICK, TIMOTHY -	11,220	26th May	1846	Glazing and enamelling the surfaces of cast-iron.
KENRICK, TIMOTHY -	13,734	4th Sept.	1851	Manufacture of wrought-iron tubes.
KENT, GEORGE - - -	10,225	12th June	1844	Machinery for cleaning, polishing, and sharpening knives, forks, and other articles.
KENT, GEORGE - - -	13,920	24th Jan.	1852	Apparatus for sifting cinders; apparatus for cleaning knives.
KENT, JOHN - - - -	2286	5th Jan.	1799	Applying power to the working of mills and other machinery where power is required.
KENT, JOHN - - - -	3316	12th Mar.	1810	Moving goods or materials to high buildings, or from deep places.
KENT, JOHN - - - -	3357	3rd July	1810	Making artificial stone for various purposes.
KENT, RICHARD - - -	254	13th Aug.	1687	Manufacture of milled lead, for sheathing and preservation of ships or any other thing.
KENT, WILLIAM - - -	2862	2nd July	1805	Candlestick.
KENTISH, RICHARD - -	2885	30th Oct.	1805	Armour-waistcoat as a defence against the bayonet, sword, pike, or any pointed instrument, and in many instances may prevent the infliction of a wound from a musket ball.
KENTISH, THOMAS - -	2725	29th July	1803	Derrick for loading and unloading ships and vessels, and for removing heavy bodies;— applicable to other useful purposes.
KENTISH, THOMAS - -	2910	20th Feb.	1806	Construction of machines for moving, raising or lowering heavy bodies, and weights of all kinds.
KENWORTHY, WILLIAM -	6619	27th May	1834	Power-looms for weaving cotton, linen, silk, woollen and other cloths.
KENWORTHY, WILLIAM -	8226	26th Sept.	1839	Machinery for sizing and otherwise preparing cotton-wool, flax and other warps, for weaving.
KENWORTHY, WILLIAM -	8790	14th Jan.	1841	Machinery for weaving.
KENWORTHY, WILLIAM -	9660	11th March	1843	Beaming or warping-machines.

Name of Patentee.	Progressive Number.	Date.		Subject-matter of Patent.
KENWORTHY, WILLIAM - -	10,428	12th Dec.	1844	Looms for weaving.
KENWORTHY, WILLIAM - -	12,449	31st Jan.	1849	Power-looms for weaving.
KENYON, JAMES - - -	6949	9th Dec.	1835	Engines used for carding cotton-wool and other fibrous substances.
KER, WILLIAM - - -	1136	31st Oct.	1776	Chemical preparation of iron, equal in hardness to the best blister-steel, retaining at the same time the toughness and properties of iron.
KER, WILLIAM - - -	1641	4th March	1788	Brewing ale, beer, porter and other malt-liquors.
KERR, ROBERT - - -	10,681	22nd May	1845	Hand-loom weaving, and improvements for producing double fabric of raised figure-work, by one process of weaving.
KERR, THOMAS - - -	8391	22nd Feb.	1840	Mortar or cement for building, also for mouldings, castings, statuary, tiles, pottery, and for other useful purposes.
KERR, WILLIAM - - -	1551	3rd Aug.	1786	Infusing certain metallic-substances into the body and pores of iron, steel, and other metals, which will effectually secure them from rust or corrosion.
KERROD, SAMUEL - - -	3424	26th March	1811	Cement and size for plastering and stuccoing walls, setting and whitening ceilings, running and whitening cornices and colours to be laid on the stucco in oils and distemper, the whole for finishing the interior of houses.
KERSHAW, JOHN - - -	3779	10th Feb.	1814	Preparing flax for being spun on the like machinery as cotton.
KERSHAW, JOHN - - -	10,843	2nd Oct.	1845	Machinery used in preparing cotton or other fibrous substances for spinning.
KESSELMEYER, CHARLES WILLIAM.	12,309	2nd Nov.	1848	Manufacture of velvets, velveteens and other similar fabrics.
KESSELS, HERMAN - -	7676	7th June	1838	Apparatus for saving lives and property from fire. " The Salvator."
KETTLE, GEORGE - - -	522	22nd Oct.	1730	Making or dyeing men's or women's black hats with ruffs of any colour.
KETTLE, JOHN LUCENA ROSS	9727	16th May	1843	Construction of roads, and carriages to run thereon.
KETTLE, WILLIAM ROBINSON	9210	24th Dec.	1841	Bolts for building and other purposes.
KEUX, JOHN HENRY LE -	9003	23rd June	1841	Line-engraving, and producing impressions therefrom.
KEWLEY, JAMES - - -	4086	21st Nov.	1816	Thermometers.
KEY, JAMES - - - -	2025	25th Nov.	1794	Making ladies' elastic habits and gentlemen's coats, without seams.
KEYLOCK, JOHN - - -	2008	16th Aug.	1794	Fire-extinguisher and fire-guard.
KEYS, JOHN - - - -	7793	31st Aug.	1838	Manufacture of sulphuric-acid from copper-ore, copper-regulus, and sulphuret of zinc.
KIBBLE, JOHN - - -	9918	2nd Nov.	1843	Apparatus for propelling vessels.
KIBBLE, JOHN - - -	10,057	17th Feb.	1844	Transmitting power in working machinery where endless-belts, chains, or straps are or may be used.
KILBY, JOHN - - - -	3920	1st June	1815	Brewing malt-liquors.
KILBY, THOMAS - - -	5807	2nd July	1829	Gas-lamp or burner.
KILNER, WILLIAM - - -	12,583	24th April	1849	Manufacturing railway and other axles and wheels; machinery to be employed in such manufacture.
KIMBALL, NATHANIEL - -	5263	13th Oct.	1825	Converting iron into steel.

Name of Patentee.	Progres-sive Number.	Date.	Subject-matter of Patent.
KIND, CHARLES GOTTHELF -	13,478	30th Jan. 1851	Boring the earth and sinking shafts for mining and other purposes; instruments used; lining such shafts.
KINDER, GEORGE - - -	8059	7th May 1839	Machinery for dressing and cleansing woollen-cloths.
KINDER, ROBERT - - -	3069	19th Dec. 1815	Propelling ships, boats, and other vessels.
KING, EDWARD AUGUSTIN -	10,919	4th Nov. 1845	Obtaining light by electricity.
KING, EDWARD AUGUSTIN -	11,188	30th April 1846	Production of magnetic-electricity.
KING, HENRY - - -	5298	26th Nov. 1825	Fids for top-masts, gallant-masts, bow-sprits, and all other masts to which fids are applied.
KING, HENRY - - -	9138	4th Nov. 1841	Steam-engines and boilers.
KING, JAMES - - - -	1246	4th March 1780	British barilla for manufacturing glass and glass-bottles, also for manufacturing soap and alum.
KING, JOHN - - - -	9005	25th June 1841	Candlesticks and other candle-holders.
KING, JOHN - - - -	9061	4th Sept. 1841	Machinery for making figured fabrics in warp and bobbin-net lace machines.
KING, JOHN - - - -	12,222	26th July 1843	Gas-meters.
KING, ROBERT - - -	543	1st Oct. 1734	Machine for scouring the inside of cast-iron boxes for all manner of carriages.
KING, WILLIAM - - -	2318	17th June 1799	Joints; and applying the same to tea-pots, coffee-pots, coffee-biggins, tea-urns, and other articles.
KING, WILLIAM ROBERT WALE	2934	8th May 1806	Manufacturing tin-plates or iron-plates covered with tin, into covers for dishes and plates.
KING, WILLIAM ROBERT WALE	3593	6th Aug. 1812	Ornamenting japanned, painted, or sized articles of paper, wood, or metallic sub-stance; also leather, oil-cloths, and wain-scot or plaster-walls or partitions.
KING, WILLIAM ROBERT WALE	3669	22nd March 1813	Application of heat to the boiling of water and other fluids; apparatus for the pur-pose.
KING, WILLIAM ROBERT WALE	5506	12th June 1827	Table-apparatus for the use of persons at sea.
KINGDON, KENT - - -	9325	21st April 1842	Impressing and embossing patterns on silk, cotton, and other woven or felted fabrics.
KINGDON, RICHARD - -	8400	25th Feb. 1840	Apparatus for the support of the human body, and correction of curvature of the spine.
KINGSFORD, JAMES - -	13,167	3rd July 1850	Refrigerating and freezing.
KINGSTON, JOHN FILMORE -	6239	8th March 1832	Machinery and apparatus for separating copper, lead, and other ores from earthy and other substances.
KINGSTON, JOHN FILMORE -	6991	28th Jan. 1836	Rotary-engine.
KINGSTON, WILLIAM -	5298	26th Nov. 1825	Fid for top-masts, gallant-masts, bow-sprits, and all other masts to which fids are applied.
KINGSTON, WILLIAM -	5435	20th Dec. 1826	Apparatus for ascertaining the trim and stability of ships or other vessels.
KINLEY, WILLIAM Mᶜ -	8697	10th Nov. 1840	Machinery for measuring, folding, plaiting, or lapping goods or fabrics.
KINSMAN, ISRAEL - - -	11,956	11th Nov. 1847	Construction of rotary-engines to be worked by steam, air, or other elastic fluid.
KINSMAN, ISRAEL - - -	12,394	28th Dec. 1848	Construction of rotary-engines to be worked by steam, air, or other elastic fluid.

Name of Patentee.	Progressive Number.	Date.	Subject-matter of Patent.
KIRBY, JOSEPH - - -	9310	26th Jan. 1843	Apparatus for manufacturing bricks, tiles, and other articles, from clay and earthy materials.
KIRBY, ROBERT - - -	9988	13th Dec. 1843	Materials for and mode of applying coverings to coffins for the dead.
KIRK, HENRY - - -	8455	28th March 1840	Composition, as a substitute for ice, for skating and sliding purposes;—partly applicable to ornamental slabs and mouldings.
KIRK, HENRY - - -	8384	5th Nov. 1840	Application of a composition as a substitute for ice, for skating and sliding purposes.
KIRK, HENRY - - -	9134	2nd Nov. 1841	Substitute for ice for skating and sliding purposes.
KIRK, RUPERT - - -	4674	9th May 1822	Crystallization and evaporation of fluids, by a peculiar application of air, mechanically.
KIRK, RUPERT - - -	4922	20th March 1824	Preparing safflower (carthamas) to preserve its colouring principle from decay or deterioration.
KIRK, SAMUEL - - -	9621	31st Jan. 1843	Machinery for preparing cotton and other fibrous substances for spinning.
KIRK, WHEATLEY - - -	7094	14th May 1836	Pianofortes.
KIRKHAM, JOHN - - -	7387	8th June 1837	Removing the carbonaceous incrustation from retorts used in distilling coal for generating gas.
KIRKHAM, JOHN - - -	8298	4th Dec. 1839	Manufacture of gas for illumination.
KIRKHAM, JOHN - - -	13,740	4th Sept. 1851	Hydraulic-telegraphs; making signals.
KIRKHAM, JOHN - - -	14,238	22nd July 1852	Manufacture of gas for lighting and heating.
KIRKHAM, THOMAS NESHAM -	14,238	22nd July 1852	Manufacture of gas for lighting and heating.
KIRKMAN, CHARLES FELTON -	12,816	18th Oct. 1849	Machinery for twisting cotton-wool or other fibrous substances.
KIRKMAN, CHARLES FELTON -	13,537	28th Feb. 1851	Machinery for spinning or twisting cotton-wool or other fibrous substances.
KIRKMAN, JOSEPH - - -	4038	14th Oct. 1816	Applying an octave stop to pianofortes.
KIRKMAN, JOSEPH - - -	9594	19th Jan. 1843	Action of Pianofortes.
KIRKWOOD, ROBERT - -	2683	28th Feb. 1803	Copper-plate printing-press.
KIRRAGE, WILLIAM - -	9345	25th Feb. 1843	Coffins.
KIRRAGE, WILLIAM - -	11,922	22nd Oct. 1847	Combination of materials for building purposes; application of certain materials for building purposes.
KIRTLEY, MATHEW - -	12,210	11th July 1848	Railway-wheels.
KITCHEN, GEORGE - - -	3489	14th Sept. 1811	Making portable sconces or branches.
KITCHEN, JOHN - - -	6454	25th July 1833	Printing presses.
KITCHEN, WILLIAM HENRY -	5770	7th Feb. 1829	Construction of window-frames, sashes, or casements, shutters, and doors.
KITE, JAMES - - -	10,273	26th July 1844	Constructing chimneys; means used for sweeping the same;—applicable to other like purposes.
KITE, JAMES - - -	11,415	15th Oct. 1846	Steam-engine chimneys; furnaces and flues; vent and exhaust-pipes; machinery connected therewith.
KITSON, RICHARD - -	10,082	27th Feb. 1844	Wire-cards for carding cotton-wool, silk, flax, and other fibrous substances; producing tow and yarns from hard waste.
KITTOE, ROBINSON - - -	3665	13th March 1813	Double coned revolving axle for carriages.

Name of Patentee.	Progressive Number.	Date.	Subject-matter of Patent.
KLEFT, HENRY WILLIAM VAN-[DER.	3824	26th July 1814	Sweetening, purifying, and refining Greenland whale and seal oil.
KLEFT, HENRY WILLIAM VAN-[DER.	3837	17th Aug. 1814	Constructing a walking-staff to contain a pistol, powder, ball, and screw telescope, pen, ink, paper, pencil, knife, and drawing-utensils.
KLŒT, JACQUE - - -	11,093	17th Feb. 1846	Combination of materials as a substitute for leather or for waterproof cloth, and other useful purposes.
KNAB, DAVID CLOVIS - -	12,733	1st Aug. 1849	Apparatus for distilling fatty and oily matters.
KNAPP, WILLIAM HYDE -	12,573	17th April 1849	Preparing wood for matches and fire-wood.
KNAPPE, EDWARD - - -	31	7th Jan. 1625	Axletrees of metal, for coaches, carts, waggons, or other carriages; making the wheels approach to and recede from each other; stopping the hinder wheels from turning; hanging the bodies of carriages by springs of steel; horse-collars and harness.
KNAPTON, WILLIAM - -	12,398	3rd Jan. 1849	Manufacturing gasometers or gas-holders.
KNELLER, WILLIAM GODFREY	3720	14th July 1813	Manufacturing verdigris.
KNELLER, WILLIAM GODFREY	5718	27th Nov. 1828	Evaporating sugar.
KNELLER, WILLIAM GODFREY	6127	29th June 1831	Stills or apparatus for distilling.
KNELLER, WILLIAM GODFREY	6467	24th Aug. 1833	Evaporation.
KNELLER, WILLIAM GODFREY	9569	22nd Dec. 1842	Manufacture of soda; evaporation of brine; concentration and manufacture of sulphuric-acid.
KNELLER, WILLIAM GODFREY	10,100	14th March 1844	Preparation of zinc; combinations of zinc with other metallic bodies.
KNIGHT, CHARLES - - -	7673	7th June 1838	Process and apparatus used in producing coloured impressions on paper, vellum, parchment, and pasteboard, by surface printing.
KNIGHT, GEORGE - - -	11,292	14th July 1846	Excavating and dredging; formation of permanent and temporary harbours, canals, bridges, docks, and similar works; apparatus employed therein.
KNIGHT, GOWIN - - -	750	14th May 1760	Machine window-blind.
KNIGHT, GOWIN - - -	850	10th June 1766	Constructing compasses in general.
KNIGHT, HENRY - - -	5494	28th April 1827	Apparatus for ascertaining the attendance to duty of any watchman or other person;—applicable to other purposes.
KNIGHT, HENRY - - -	12,653	7th June 1849	Apparatus for printing, embossing, pressing, and perforating.
KNIGHT, JAMES - - -	783	13th Dec. 1762	Making and drawing iron and other metals by wood bellows.
KNIGHT, PAUL SLADE - -	4355	3rd April 1819	Fire-engines, pumps, or other engines, in which are used pistons working in barrels or cylinders.
KNIGHT, RICHARD - -	4674	9th May 1822	Process for the more rapid crystallization and evaporation of fluids, at comparative low temperature, by a peculiar mechanical application of air.
KNIGHT, SAMUEL - - -	8449	25th March 1840	Machinery for boiling, bucking, or scouring, for preparing and assisting the process of bleaching and dyeing cotton, linen, and other fabrics and fibrous substances.

Name of Patentee.	Progressive Number.	Date.	Subject-matter of Patent.
KNIGHT, SAMUEL - - -	10,541	3rd March 1845	Machinery for scouring, washing, cleansing, and other similar purposes.
KNIGHT, SAMUEL JOHN -	9767	10th June 1843	Kilns for drying hops, malt, and other substances.
KNIGHT, WILLIAM - -	7723	7th July 1838	Machinery for raising and forcing water and other fluids.
KNIGHT, WILLIAM - -	9011	28th June 1841	Indicator for registering the number of passengers using an omnibus or other passenger vehicle.
KNILL, HENRY - - -	7789	30th Aug. 1838	Cleansing the bottoms of docks, rivers, and other waters.
KNIPE, FRANCIS NOBLE -	1817	7th July 1791	Machine for raising or dispersing water, condensing air, or for other purposes.
KNIPE, FRANCIS NOBLE -	1818	7th July 1791	Application of certain mechanical powers for working rotatory and some other motions.
KNOWELDEN, WILLIAM - -	11,510	31st Dec. 1846	Steam-engines.
KNOWLES, Sir FRANCIS CHARLES	12,687	4th July 1849	Production and manufacture of iron and steel.
KNOWLES, Sir FRANCIS CHARLES	13,331	9th Nov. 1850	Manufacture of charcoal.
KNOWLES, JAMES - - -	2310	27th April 1799	Dressing or preparing skins for the purpose of converting them into leather.
KNOWLES, JAMES - - -	8422	10th March 1840	Arrangement of apparatus for regulating the supply of water to steam-boilers.
KNOWLES, JAMES - - -	10,877	10th Oct. 1845	Machinery for raising coal or other matters from mines;—applicable to other similar purposes.
KNOWLES, JOHN - - -	5982	13th Aug. 1830	Machine for drawing hop-poles out of the ground, previous to picking the hops. "Hop-pole drawer by lever and fulcrum."
KNOWLES, JOHN - - -	14,075	17th April 1852	Machinery for preparing cotton and other fibrous substances, for reversing the direction of motion in, and for regulating the speed of machines.
KNOWLES, MARGARET - -	5809	4th July 1829	Axletrees for, and mode of applying the same to carriages.
KNOWLES, THOMAS - -	6115	23rd May 1831	Machinery by aid of which mules may be worked by power. "Self-acting Mules."
KNOWLES, THOMAS - -	8177	1st Aug. 1839	Machinery used in the preparation of cotton and other fibrous substances.
KNOWLES, WILLIAM - -	1132	23rd Aug. 1776	Raising tin, copper, and other heavy bodies from mines, by balancing the rope in the shaft; also weighing anchors, by preventing the cables from suddenly running out.
KNOWLYS, THOMAS JOHN -	5378	13th June 1826	Manufacture of ornamented metals.
KNOWLYS, THOMAS JOHN -	5397	1st Aug. 1826	Tanning.
KNOWLYS, THOMAS JOHN -	12,110	5th April 1848	Generating, indicating and applying heat.
KNOWLYS, THOMAS JOHN -	12,313	2nd Nov. 1848	Application, removal, and compression, of atmospheric air.
KNOWLYS, THOMAS JOHN -	12,738	9th Aug. 1849	Application and combination of mineral and vegetable products; obtaining products from mineral and vegetable substances; generation and application of heat.
KNOX, GEORGE - - -	12,528	19th Mar. 1849	Railway-carriages.

Name of Patentee.	Progressive Number.	Date.	Subject-matter of Patent.
KNOX, JOHN - - - -	1197	21st July 1778	Plan for assurances on lives of persons from 10 to 80 years of age.
KOBER, CHARLES - - -	8415	7th March 1840	Fixing colour in cloth.
KOENIG, FREDERICK - - [Koeing, Frederick.]	3321	29th March 1810	Printing by machinery.
KOENIG, FREDERICK - -	3496	30th Oct. 1811	Printing by machinery.
KOENIG, FREDERICK - -	3725	23rd July 1813	Printing by machinery.
KOENIG, FREDERICK - -	3868	24th Dec. 1814	Printing by machinery.
KOLLMAN, GEORGE AUGUSTUS	5107	26th Feb. 1825	Mechanism and general construction of pianofortes.
KOLLMAN, GEORGE AUGUSTUS	7069	23rd April 1836	Railway and other locomotive-carriages.
KOLLMAN, GEORGE AUGUSTUS	7979	23rd Feb. 1839	Mechanism and general construction of pianofortes.
KOLLMAN, GEORGE AUGUSTUS	8200	17th Aug. 1839	Railways; locomotive and other carriages.
KOOPS, MATTHIAS - - -	2392	28th April 1800	Extracting inks from printed and written paper, and converting the paper into pulp.
KOOPS, MATTHIAS - - -	2433	2nd Aug. 1800	Manufacturing paper fit for printing and other purposes, from straw, hay, thistles, waste and refuse of hemp and flax, and different kinds of wood and bark.
KOOPS, MATTHIAS - - -	2481	17th Feb. 1801	Manufacturing paper from straw, hay, thistles, waste and refuse of hemp and flax, and different kinds of wood and bark.
KORTRIGHT, LAURENCE -	8885	17th March 1841	Treating and preparing whalebone, and the fins and similar parts of whales, rendering them fit for commercial and other uses.
KOSMAN, THEODORE -	13,799	4th Nov. 1851	Brooches and other dress-fastenings.
KOSSOVITCH, GAETAN -	13,614	3rd May 1851	Rotary steam-engine.
KOSTER, JOHN THEODORE -	2536	31st Aug. 1801	Building carriages.
KOSTER, JOHN THEODORE -	4200	15th Jan. 1818	Constructing wheel-carriages; also making wheels for carriages.
KOYMANS, HENRY ANTHONY -	5319	16th Jan. 1826	Construction and use of apparatus and works for inland navigation.
KREEFT, JOHN CHRISTOPHER [TOBIAS.	6203	22nd Dec. 1831	Apparatus for shaping plates of metal, and for manufacturing various articles therefrom.
KRONHEIM, JOSEPH MARTIN -	10,275	29th July 1844	Stereotyping.
KRUPP, ALFRED - - -	11,353	26th Aug. 1846	Manufacture of spoons, forks and other similar wares; machinery employed therein.
KUFAHL, GEORGE LEOPOLD [LUDWIG.	13,994	3rd March 1852	Fire-arms.
KUPPLER, CONRAD GEORGE -	6861	11th July 1835	Construction of weighing-machines, and other machines used in ascertaining weights.
KURTZ, ANDREW - - -	8688	5th Nov. 1840	Construction of furnaces.
KURTZ, ANDREW - - -	9234	27th Jan. 1842	Manufacture of artificial fuel.
KURTZ, ANDREW - - -	10,053	14th Feb. 1844	Apparatus for drying, evaporating, distilling, torrefying, and calcining.
KURTZ, ANDREW - - -	11,052	20th Jan. 1846	Construction of furnaces and apparatus connected therewith, for evaporating or concentrating sulphuric-acid.
KURTZ, CHARLES - - -	9808	30th June 1843	Lamp for combustion of naphtha, turpentine, and other resinous oils.

Name of Patentee,	Progressive Number.	Date.	Subject-matter of Patent.
KURTZ, CLEMENCE AUGUSTUS	11,514	31st Dec. 1846	Preparing and using indigo in the dyeing and printing of woollen, cotton and other fabrics.
KURTZ, CLEMENCE AUGUSTUS	11,544	26th Jan. 1847	Manufacture of a certain colouring matter to be used in dyeing or printing woollen, cotton, silk and other fabrics.
KURTZ, CLEMENCE AUGUSTUS	11,866	9th Sept. 1847	Preparing and using indigo in the dyeing and printing of woollen, cotton, and other fabrics.
KURTZ, CLEMENCE AUGUSTUS	12,485	28th Feb. 1849	Looms for weaving.
KURTZ, CLEMENCE AUGUSTUS	13,357	19th Nov. 1850	Dyeing.
KURTZ, CLEMENCE AUGUSTUS	14,072	17th April 1852	Preparations of madder-roots and ground madder, also of munjeet in the root and stem.
KYAN, JOHN HOWARD - -	6253	31st March 1832	Preserving certain vegetable substances from decay.
KYAN, JOHN HOWARD - -	6309	22nd Sept. 1832	Preserving paper, canvas, cloth, and cordage used for ships and other purposes, also the raw materials, as hemp, flax or cotton, of which the same may be made.
KYAN, JOHN HOWARD - -	6534	21st Dec. 1833	Combination of machinery for steam-navigation.
KYAN, JOHN HOWARD - -	7001	11th Feb. 1836	Preserving certain vegetable substances from decay.
KYAN, JOHN HOWARD - -	7460	4th Nov. 1837	Extracting ammoniacal salts from liquor produced in the manufacture of coal-gas.
KYAN, JOHN HOWARD - -	7952	29th Jan. 1839	Steam-engines.
KYAN, WILLIAM EDWARD -	11,817	28th July 1847	Consuming the smoke and economizing the fuel of steam-engines, breweries, and manufactories.
KYMER, JOHN - - -	9638	21st Feb. 1843	Burning anthracite or stone-coal and other fuel, for obtaining heat.

L.

LA BLACHE, LOUIS GOY - -	719	12th Nov. 1757	Royal military drops.
LA CHATRE, RAOUL ARMAND [JOSEPH JEAN, Comte DE.	9331	26th April 1842	Preparing surfaces of fabrics for covering roofs, floors, and other surfaces.
LA CHAUMETTE, ISAAC DE -	434	12th Aug. 1721	Cannon, fusees, and pistols; swords which serve for bayonets; powder-flasks; machine to cure smoky chimneys; snuff-boxes; penknife and pocket-knife; buckles; machine for drawing lotteries; two cases of pistols, of which a carbine may be made; turning-mattrass for armies and hospitals; coaches and chaises; preventing shipwreck; bomb or grenade; breastplates; candlesticks and rings; pocket-scissors; machine for holding glasses at table; picture, serving as a tester to a bed, and an ornament to a room; lantern; fusee-lock; firing fusees horizontally; double counters for drawing lotteries.

Name of Patentee.	Progressive Number.	Date.	Subject-matter of Patent.
La Court, Alexander Allard De.	5359	6th May 1826	Instrument for the organ of sight.
La Crouée, Jules Thiebauld De.	10,114	19th March 1844	Apparatus for purifying, clarifying, and refining vegetable extracts.
La Fons, John Palmer De - [Lafons, John De.]	2893	19th Nov. 1805	Marine-alarum; chronometer for ascertaining the time of a ship's log running up, the time of the watches on shipboard, and other purposes.
La Fons, John Palmer De -	5219	16th July 1825	Extracting and method of fixing teeth.
La Fons, John Palmer De -	5388	14th July 1826	Securing or mooring ships and other floating bodies; apparatus for the same.
La Fons, John Palmer De -	11,283	6th July 1846	Manufacture of locks and other fastenings.
La Fount, Moses - - -	2153	23rd Dec. 1796	Plate and hoop or band, to be used in the mounting of glass chandeliers, girandoles, or other lustres.
La Garde, Augustus Count De	5469	20th Feb. 1827	Making paper from ligneous parts produced from certain textile plants in the process of preparing them by the "rural mechanical break," and which substances may be used alone or mixed with other materials.
La Garde, Philip Chilwell De.	5914	27th Feb. 1830	Apparatus for fidding and unfidding masts, and for masting and rigging vessels.
La Lantais, Edouard Loysell De.	10,476	16th Jan. 1845	Making infusions of tea, coffee, and other materials.
La Mayne, Thomas De -	1475	3rd May 1785	Making buttons of burnt earth or porcelain.
La Riviere, Marc - -	5241	15th Aug. 1825	Machine for perforating metal-plates of gold, silver, tin, platina, brass, or copper, and applicable as sieves.
La Riviere, Marc - -	5300	28th Nov. 1825	Machinery to be applied to stamps, fly-presses or other presses, for perforating metal-plates;—applicable to other purposes.
La Riviere, Marc - -	9271	1st March 1842	Machinery for figure-weaving in silk and other fabrics.
La Rue, Thomas De - -	6231	23rd Feb. 1823	Manufacturing and ornamenting playing-cards.
La Rue, Thomas De - -	6663	15th Aug. 1834	Manufacturing or preparing embossed paper-hangings.
La Rue, Thomas De - -	8549	20th June 1840	Printing calicoes and other surfaces.
La Rue, Thomas De - -	12,243	15th Aug. 1848	Producing ornamental surfaces to paper and other substances.
La Rue, Warren De - -	10,436	12th Dec. 1844	Covering the surfaces of paper and other materials with colour, and other substances.
La Rue, Warren De - -	10,565	17th March 1845	Manufacture of envelopes.
La Rue, Warren De - -	12,084	8th March 1848	Manufacture of card-board and pasteboard.
La Rue, Warren De - -	12,904	19th Dec. 1849	Manufacture of envelopes.
Lacey, William - - -	8779	11th Jan. 1841	Combinations of vitrified and metallic substances, applicable to the manufacture of ornaments, and the decoration of domestic articles; also applicable to church-windows and ship lights.
Lachenal, Louis - - -	9066	4th Sept. 1841	Machinery for cutting cork.
Lackerstein, James Frederick.	13,764	9th Oct. 1851	Obtaining motive-power.

Name of Patentee.	Progressive Number.	Date.	Subject-matter of Patent.
LACKERSTEIN, JAMES FREDE-[RICK.	13,868	19th Dec. 1851	Machinery for cutting wood and other substances; manufacture of boxes.
LACON, WILLIAM STIRLING -	13,975	25th Feb. 1852	Suspending ships' boats, and lowering the same into the water.
LACY, CHARLES - - -	4063	30th Sept. 1816	Machinery to be used with machines for making bobbin-lace net.
LACY, HENRY CHARLES - -	5423	18th Nov. 1826	Apparatus on which to suspend carriage-bodies.
LACY, HENRY CHARLES - -	10,467	14th Jan. 1845	Manufacture for and method of sustaining the rails of railways.
LACY, JOHN GEORGE - -	6046	6th Dec. 1830	Construction of guns and fire-arms.
LADD, JOHN - - -	714	9th April 1757	Making waggons and other wheel-carriages.
LADORE, PETER - - -	123	3rd April 1639	Glossing plain and figured satins.
LAINER, JEROME - - -	70	21st May 1634	Affixing wool, silk, and other materials upon linen-cloth, silk, cotton, leather and other substances, with oil, size, and other cements for hangings. "Londrindiana."
LAINTAIS, EDOUARD LOYSEL [DE LA.	10,476	16th Jan. 1845	Making infusions of tea, coffee, and other materials.
LAIRD, JOHN - - -	9830	10th July 1843	Construction of steam and other vessels.
LAIRD, MACGREGOR - -	12,934	19th Jan. 1850	Construction of metallic ships or vessels; materials for coating the bottoms of iron-ships; steering ships.
LAIRD, WILLIAM - - -	13,149	24th June 1850	Life-boats; apparatus for filtering and purifying water.
LAIRD, WILLIAM - - -	13,353	19th Nov. 1850	Machinery for loading and discharging certain descriptions of cargo in ships and other vessels; construction of such vessels.
LAKE, JOHN - - -	10,857	9th Oct. 1845	Propelling.
LAKE, JOHN - - -	13,851	8th Dec. 1851	Propelling on canals or rivers.
LAKIN, ROBERT - - -	11,902	14th Oct. 1847	Machines used for preparing to be spun and spinning cotton and other fibrous substances; preparing to be woven and weaving the same when spun.
LAKIN, ROBERT - - -	12,805	12th Oct. 1849	Machinery used for preparing, spinning, doubling, and weaving cotton and other fibrous substances.
LAMAILLE, PIERRE JULES -	14,350	1st Dec. 1852	Preservation of japanned leather.
LAMB, ALEXANDER - -	5294	17th Nov. 1825	Machinery for preparing, drawing, roving, and spinning flax, hemp, and waste-silk.
LAMB, ANDREW - - -	12,362	9th Dec. 1848	Steam-engines and steam-boilers; apparatus connected therewith.
LAMB, GEORGE AUGUSTUS -	5091	10th Feb. 1825	Composition of malt and hops.
LAMB, JAMES - - -	11,383	24th Sept. 1846	Manufacture of clogs.
LAMB, JAMES - - -	14,337	23rd Oct. 1852	Construction of kilns for burning or calcining cement, chalk, limestone, and other substances; application of the heat therefrom to the generation of steam.
LAMB, JOHN - - -	2952	25th July 1806	Machinery for extracting fresh-water from the salt-water of the ocean, and for other purposes.
LAMB, JOHN - - -	9321	15th April 1842	Engines to be worked by steam, air, gas, or vapours;—applicable to pumps for raising water, air, or other fluids.

Name of Patentee.	Progres-sive Number.	Date.	Subject-matter of Patent.
LAMB, JOSEPH - - -	9978	8th Dec. 1843	Machinery used in preparing and spinning cotton-wool, flax, silk, and other materials.
LAMB, RICHARD - - -	8003	15th March 1839	Apparatus for supplying atmospheric air in the production of light and heat.
LAMBE, THOMAS - - -	2050	12th May 1795	Trusses for persons afflicted with bubonocele and other ruptures.
LAMBERT, CHARLES - -	12,011	5th Jan. 1848	Machinery for making nails.
LAMBERT, FRANCIS - -	4442	11th April 1820	Mounting and producing, also removing, preserving and replacing the figure, in weaving all kinds of lace.
LAMBERT, JOHN - - -	8571	15th July 1840	Manufacture of soap.
LAMBERT, JOSIAS - - -	5779	30th March 1829	Making iron; applicable at the smelting and at subsequent stages, up to the completion of the bars; improving the quality of inferior iron.
LAMBERT, JOSIAS - - -	5893	4th Feb. 1830	Making iron; applicable at the smelting and at subsequent stages, up to the completion of the bars; improving the quality of inferior iron.
LAMBERT, LOUIS - - -	5041	23rd Nov. 1824	Material and manufacture of paper.
LAMBERT, SAMUEL - -	4416	4th Dec. 1819	Mills and navigable bodies; water-wheel;—applicable to mills and navigable rivers.
LAMBERT, SAMUEL - -	6122	2nd June 1831	Throstle-spindles, for spinning and twisting silk, cotton-wool, flax, and other fibrous substances.
LAMBERT, THOMAS - -	9226	15th Jan. 1842	Action of cabinet pianofortes.
LAMBERT, THOMAS - -	9716	29th April 1843	Action of pianofortes.
LAMBERT, THOMAS - -	11,189	30th April 1846	Cocks for drawing off liquids and gases.
LAMBERT, THOMAS - -	13,930	27th Jan. 1852	Pianofortes.
LAMBIE, JAMES - - -	2334	23rd July 1799	Applying additional power to machinery.
LAMENANDE, JEAN LOUIS -	12,214	18th July 1848	Fixing letters of metal on glass, marble, wood, and other substances.
LAMING, JAMES - - -	10,955	18th Nov. 1845	Making the cyanides and ferro-cyanides of potassium and sodium.
LAMING, RICHARD - -	8878	15th March 1841	Production of carbonate of ammonia.
LAMING, RICHARD - -	9832	13th July 1843	Purification and application of ammonia to obtain certain chemical products.
LAMING, RICHARD - -	11,944	4th Nov. 1847	Manufacturing and purifying coal-gas; treating a residual product of such manufacture; preparing materials for purifying gas.
LAMING, RICHARD - -	12,151	9th May 1848	Manufacture of oxalic-acid.
LAMING, RICHARD - -	12,264	4th Sept. 1848	Obtaining sulphur and sulphuric-acid.
LAMING, RICHARD - -	13,059	23rd April 1850	Manufacture of gas for illumination and other purposes; preparing materials for the purpose; apparatus for manufacturing and using gas; treating products of coal distillation;—partly applicable to other purposes.
LAMING, RICHARD - -	14,260	12th Aug. 1852	Manufacture of and burning gas; treatment of the residual products of such manufacture; distillation of coal or other similar substances; cokeing of gas.
LAMPITT, CHARLES - -	10,826	4th Sept. 1845	Dibbling-machines.
LAMPLOUGH, HENRY - -	12,864	24th Nov. 1849	Supplying pure water to cities and towns.

Name of Patentee.	Progressive Number.	Date.	Subject-matter of Patent.
LAMPORT, CHARLES - -	13,125	19th June 1850	Machinery for lifting and moving weights, working chains, and pumping, especially adapted for ships' use.
LAMPORT, CHARLES - -	13,875	19th Dec. 1851	Reefing sails.
LANCASTER, CHARLES WILLIAM.	13,161	3rd July 1850	Manufacture of fire-arms and cannon, and percussion-tubes.
LANCASTER, CHARLES WILLIAM.	13,454	16th Jan. 1851	Manufacture of fire-arms, cannons, and projectiles.
LANCASTER, WILLIAM - -	10,832	18th Sept. 1845	Looms for weaving.
LANCE, WILLIAM - - -	8541	11th June 1840	Apparatus to be used in whale-fishery;—partly applicable, on an increased scale, to motive-power for driving machinery.
LANDELS, JAMES - - -	2647	20th Sept. 1802	Working pumps by machinery.
LANDER, CHARLES - -	1339	25th Oct. 1782	Universal wheel or engine for working machinery requiring power and velocity.
LANDER, WILLIAM - -	2357	9th Nov. 1799	Apparatus for moving the piston-rod of pumps or other engines for raising water.
LANDRETH, JOHN - - -	1596	31st March 1787	Pianoforte, harpsichord, organ, guitar, and other musical instruments.
LANE, EDWARD - - -	3256	9th Aug. 1809	Rotative-engine, worked by steam, for raising water, grinding corn, and for other useful purposes.
LANE, JAMES LEWIS - -	10,560	17th March 1845	Weighing-machines and steel-yards.
LANE, JOHN - - - -	11,748	15th June 1847	Railway carriages and engines.
LANE, JOHN - - - -	12,344	29th Nov. 1848	Engines, boilers, and pumps; railway-carriages; propelling vessels; construction of boats; extinguishing fire; brewing.
LANE, RALPH - - -	343	2nd Aug. 1695	Producing colours in cloths of woollen or silk, simple or compound, in figures, flowers, and other designs.
LANE, TIMOTHY - - -	2511	5th June 1801	Measuring-glasses for compounding medicines.
LANE, URIAH - - -	4719	28th Oct. 1822	Platting straw, for the manufacture of bonnets and other articles therefrom.
LANE, WILLIAM - - -	4585	23rd Aug. 1821	Horizontal roasting-jacks;—applicable to other purposes.
LANE, WILLIAM - - -	5969	5th Aug. 1830	Roving-frames.
LANE, WILLIAM - - -	10,412	2nd Dec. 1844	Scaffolding; applicable also as a fire-escape.
LANG, GILBERT - - -	4246	11th April 1818	Producing the Swiss deep and pale reds by topical mordants and a pale blue discharge on the said reds.
LANG, JAMES - - - -	6168	24th Sept. 1831	Machinery for spreading, drawing, roving, or spinning flax, hemp, and other fibrous substances dressed or undressed.
LANGHAM, JOHN - - -	6348	17th Dec. 1832	Machinery for manufacturing bobbin-net lace.
LANGLEY, JAMES - - -	666	31st Dec. 1751	Oil for giving ease in fits of the gravel and stone, and for other purposes.
LANGMEAD, JOSEPH - -	1361	25th March 1783	Making fire-grates.
LANGMEAD, JOSEPH - -	1419	9th Feb. 1784	Making chimney fronts with grates, for warming rooms.
LANGTON, DANIEL - -	2203	18th Nov. 1797	Lock, springs, and machinery for security to doors and for preventing wet passing under them, also, when applied to the doors of rooms covered with carpets, floor-cloths, or matting, will prevent the cold air from passing under such doors.

Name of Patentee.	Progressive Number.	Date.		Subject-matter of Patent.
LANGTON, JOHN STEPHEN -	5236	11th Aug.	1825	Seasoning timber and other wood.
LANGTON, THOMAS - -	11,930	2nd Nov.	1847	Manufacturing knitted fabrics.
LANGWORTHY, RICHARD -	643	9th May	1749	Machine turned by wind, for raising water, metal ore, or other weight from quarries, pits, or other great depths.
LANOA FRANCOIS MARIE	13,796	3rd Nov.	1851	Apparatus for holding and drawing off aërated-liquors; and machinery for filling vessels with aërated-liquors.
LARBALESTIER, ISABELLA -	10,081	26th Feb.	1844	Making certain skins resemble sable-fur.
LARDY, WILLIAM MAC - -	11,012	22nd Dec.	1845	Machinery applicable to the preparation and spinning of cotton-wool, silk, flax, and other fibrous substances.
LARDY, WILLIAM MAC - -	12,150	9th May	1848	Machinery applicable to the preparation and spinning of cotton-wool, silk, flax, and other fibrous substances.
LARDY, WILLIAM MAC - -	13,127	12th June	1850	Machinery for preparing, spinning, and doubling cotton and other fibrous materials.
LARKIN, MICHAEL - - -	3836	16th Aug.	1814	Windlasses for ships and other vessels.
LARKIN, NATHANIEL JOHN -	7702	23rd June	1838	Machinery for cutting corks and bungs.
LARPENT, Sir GEORGE GERARD [DE HOCHPIED, Bart.	9874	24th Aug.	1843	Preparation of a material from a vegetable substance, and its application for affording light, and for other uses.
LARRAD, CHARLES - -	11,736	8th June	1847	Machinery for cutting wood for the manufacture of bobbins and other articles.
LASSALLE, WILLIAM HENRY -	2928	5th April	1806	Soap.
LASSALLE, WILLIAM HENRY -	4018	23rd April	1816	Construction of gigs and cards used in woollen and other manufactures.
LATHAM, WILLIAM - -	7653	26th May	1838	Machinery for stretching, drying, and finishing woven fabrics.
LATHROP, BENJAMIN - -	12,177	6th June	1848	Wheel for railway purposes.
LAUBEREAU, JOSEPH FRANCOIS	10,830	18th Sept.	1845	Obtaining power.
LAUDET, JEAN BAPTISTE [GEORGES.	14,176	24th June	1852	Locomotive-engines;—partly applicable to other engines.
LAUGHTON, LAURA - -	10,927	6th Nov.	1845	Manufacture of soap.
LAURAGNUIS, Count DE -	849	10th June	1766	Making porcelain-ware.
LAURAS, MICHAEL BERAND -	7334	4th April	1837	Steam-navigation.
LAURENCE, JOHN - - -	2618	10th May	1802	Tanning.
LAURENT, VICTOR HIPPOLYTE	12,639	5th June	1849	Looms for weaving.
LAURIE, ROBERT WILLIAM -	12,701	9th July	1849	Apparatus to be employed for the preservation of life and property;—wholly or partly applicable to articles of furniture, dress, and travelling-apparatus.
LAVELEYE, CHARLES DE -	7551	25th Jan.	1838	Manufacture of bricks.
LAW, ALEXANDER - - -	4554	1st May	1821	Formation of bolts and nails for ship and other fastenings.
LAW, ALEXANDER - - -	4571	17th July	1821	Form of bolts and nails for ship and other fastenings.
LAW, EDWARD - - -	8007	20th March	1839	Evaporating sea-water and other fluids; manufacture of salt.
LAW, JOHN - - - -	11,547	28th Jan.	1847	Yarns, and machinery for manufacturing the same.
LAW, RICHARD - - -	1726	23rd Jan.	1790	Making chapes and shoe-buckles.
LAW, WILLIAM - - -	2111	31st May	1796	Water-closets.
LAWES, JOHN BENNET - -	9353	23rd May	1842	Manures.

Name of Patentee.	Progres-sive Number.	Date.	Subject-matter of Patent.
LAWES, THOMAS - - -	5633	29th March 1828	Thread to be used in the manufacture of bobbin-net lace.
LAWES, THOMAS - - -	5729	10th Dec. 1828	Manufacture of bobbin-net lace.
LAWES, THOMAS - - -	8696	10th Nov. 1840	Process and apparatus for cleansing and dressing feathers.
LAWES, THOMAS - - -	10,706	3rd June 1845	Propelling carriages on rail and other roads, and boats or vessels on canals or rivers.
LAWES, THOMAS - - -	12,633	5th June 1849	Generating steam; obtaining and applying motive-power.
LAWES, THOMAS - - -	13,440	4th Jan. 1851	Generating and applying steam.
LAWRANCE, JOHN - - -	5980	10th Aug. 1830	Apparatus to be affixed to saddles and girths.
LAWRENCE, DAVID - -	5845	15th Sept. 1829	Apparatus to be applied to fowling-pieces and other fire-arms, in place of locks.
LAWRENCE, GEORGE - -	7026	8th March 1836	Screws used for fastening the mouths of mounted inkstands, perfume and other bottles; also fastening the mouths of jars and tumblers.
LAWRENCE, HENRY - -	10,991	10th Dec. 1845	Buckles suitable for harness, and for other purposes.
LAWRENCE, JAMES - -	12,549	28th March 1849	Brewing worts for ale, porter, and other liquors; storing ale, porter, and other liquors.
LAWRENCE, JAMES - -	14,282	26th Aug. 1852	Brewing-apparatus.
LAWRENCE, MORTON WILLIAM	5488	28th April 1827	Refining sugar.
LAWRENCE, MORTON WILLIAM	7587	8th March 1838	Concentrating certain vegetable juices and saccharine solutions.
LAWRENCE, THOMAS - -	832	28th June 1765	Fabric made of silk and worsted, for lining gentlemen's clothes, and for other uses. " Soyelainet."
LAWSON, EDWARD - - -	10,833	18th Sept. 1845	Machinery for preparing and spinning flax and other fibrous substances.
LAWSON, EDWARD - - -	14,301	23rd Sept. 1852	Machinery for scutching and cleaning flax-straw.
LAWSON, JOHN - - -	8332	2nd Jan. 1840	Machinery for spinning, doubling, and twisting flax, wool, silk, cotton, and other fibrous substances.
LAWSON, JOHN - - -	10,144	16th April 1844	Machinery for heckling, dressing, combing, and cleaning flax, wool, silk, and other fibrous substances.
LAWSON, JOHN - - -	11,942	4th Nov. 1847	Machinery for separating burs, seeds, and other foreign matters from wool, cotton, and other fibrous substances.
LAWSON, JOHN - - -	14,301	23rd Sept. 1852	Machinery for scutching and cleaning flax-straw.
LAWSON, SAMUEL - - -	3715	9th Oct. 1828	Machinery for preparing and dressing hemp, flax, silk, and other fibrous substances.
LAWSON, SAMUEL - - -	6464	20th Aug. 1833	Machinery for preparing, drawing, or roving hemp, flax, wool, and other fibrous substances.
LAWSON, SAMUEL - - -	8332	2nd Jan. 1840	Machinery for spinning, doubling and twisting flax, wool, silk, cotton and other fibrous substances.
LAWSON, THOMAS - - -	14,237	21st July 1852	Adaptation and application of a new manufactured material, to certain articles of dress.
LAWTON, JOHN - - -	3891	7th March 1815	Lock and key;—applicable to other purposes.

Name of Patentee.	Progressive Number.	Date.		Subject-matter of Patent.
LAYBOURN, MARK - - -	3087	9th Dec.	1807	Roving-machine for preparing flax, tow, and wool, for spinning.
LAYCOCK, GEORGE - - -	13,837	1st Dec.	1851	Unhairing and tanning skins.
LAYCOCK, THOMAS - - -	891	2nd Jan.	1768	Window-blinds for coaches and other carriages.
LAYCOCK, WILLIAM - -	9699	16th Mar.	1843	Constructing houses and such like buildings.
LE BLON, JAMES CHRISTOPHER	423	5th Feb.	1719	Multiplying pictures and draughts by natural colours, with impression.
LE BLON, JAMES CHRISTOPHER	492	1st May	1727	Weaving tapestry in the loom.
LE BASTIER, JULES - -	12,800	12th Oct.	1849	Machinery for printing.
LE BROCQ, PHILIP - -	1513	5th Dec.	1785	Rearing, cultivating, training, and bringing to perfection all kinds of fruit-trees and plants; protecting their leaves, blossoms, flowers and fruit.
LE BROCQ, PHILIP - - -	1894	5th July	1792	Portable mangles.
LE CAAN, CHARLES - -	3311	26th Feb.	1810	Apparatus to be added to the axletrees and wheels or naves of wheels of carriages, to check their motion.
LE CAPELAIN, PHILIP - -	9030	15th July	1841	Meters for gas and other aëriform fluids.
L'ESTRANGE, FRANCIS - -	9992	21st Dec.	1843	Hernial trusses to prevent the descent of hernia through the internal as well as the external ring.
LE FARRE, NICHOLAS - -	2455	12th Dec.	1800	Naval-architecture.
LE FEBRUE, PETER - -	62	12th April	1633	Erecting water-mills on standing waters, lakes and ditches.
LE GRAND, JAMES - - -	446	31st May	1722	Preventing the smoking of chimneys.
LE GRAND, JEAN - - -	4889	15th Jan.	1824	Fermented liquors, and the various products to be obtained therefrom.
LEACH, EDMUND - - -	8519	28th May	1840	Machinery for carding, doubling and preparing wool, cotton, silk, flax, and other fibrous substances.
LE GRAS, LOUIS NAPOLEON -	12,869	30th Nov.	1849	Separation and disinfection of fecal matters in the manufacture of manure; apparatus employed therein.
LE GROSSE, TOBIAS - -	309	—	1692	Tanning skins for leather, and making imitation Russian leather.
LE KEUX, JOHN HENRY - -	9003	23rd June	1841	Line-engraving and producing impressions therefrom.
LE LIEVRE, HENRY - -	11,714	24th May	1847	Dyeing and stretching silk, and finishing plush.
LE MESURIER, FREDERICK -	7812	13th Sept.	1838	Construction of pumps for raising water or other fluids.
LE MESURIER, HENRY - -	8112	17th June	1839	Pumps.
LE MALT, Chevalier ALEXANDER EDOUARD.	12,219	20th July	1848	Apparatus for lighting by electricity; partly applicable to other uses in electricity.
LE PAIGE, LOUIS - - -	9795	22nd June	1843	Preventing accidents on railways.
LE PETIT, SAMUEL HEARNE -	9213	11th Jan.	1842	Manufacture and supply of gas.
LE SUEUR, CLEMENT - -	14,071	17th April	1852	Apparatus for preventing smoky chimneys;— applicable to other purposes of ventilation.
LEA, ABNER COWELL - -	2569	2nd Jan.	1802	Manufacturing the furniture for umbrellas and parasols.
LEA, THOMAS - - - -	3613	31st Oct.	1812	Making carpets.
LEACH, EDMUND - - -	8198	17th Aug.	1839	Looms for weaving various kinds of cloth.

Name of Patentee.	Progressive Number.	Date.	Subject-matter of Patent.
LEACH, JAMES - - -	13,539	3rd March 1851	Machinery for carding, spinning, doubling, and twisting cotton and other fibrous substances.
LEACH, JOHN - - -	2605	6th April 1802	Applying madder in the dyeing of calicoes, linens, and stuffs.
LEACH, JOHN - - -	2696	7th April 1803	Steam-engine boilers.
LEACH, MATTHEW - -	9919	2nd Nov. 1843	Rotary steam-engines;—applicable to pumps for lifting and forcing water.
LEACH, THOMAS - - -	4718	25th Oct. 1822	Steam-engines, in the application of steam immediately to a wheel instead of the usual process.
LEACH, THOMAS - - -	4833	18th Aug. 1823	Machinery for roving, spinning, and doubling wool, cotton, silk, flax, and other fibrous substances.
LEADBETTER, JAMES - -	11,856	6th Sept. 1847	Machinery for raising water and other fluids.
LEADBETTER, JAMES - -	12,674	26th June 1849	Raising water and other fluids;— applicable to propelling machinery, pumping mines, and for other purposes.
LEAHY, EDMUND - - -	11,040	15th Jan. 1846	Locomotive-carriages, intended to be employed on ordinary roads.
LEAHY, MATTHEW - -	11,439	5th Nov. 1846	Steam-engines.
LEAK, ELIJAH - - -	7376	22nd May 1837	Construction of shutters and sashes for windows of buildings, also applicable to hothouses and other purposes; mode of fitting the same.
LEAKE, JOHN SIMPSON - -	13,749	18th Sept. 1851	Machinery or apparatus employed in the manufacture of salt.
LEAKE, WALTER - - -	677	6th March 1753	Pill. "Health restoring Pill."
LEAN, JOEL - - - -	3621	10th Dec. 1812	Steam-engines, and apparatus to be used with the same.
LEAN, JOEL - - - -	5228	30th July 1825	Machine for effecting an alternating motion between bodies revolving about a common axis; also additional machinery for applying the same to mechanical purposes.
LEAR, PETER - - - -	10,154	23rd April 1844	Machinery for propelling vessels through the water.
LEARY, CONNOR WILLIAM O' -	11,864	9th Sept. 1847	Producing power for the discharge of weapons and missiles, and for other purposes.
LEATHAM, SOLOMON - -	11,579	15th Feb. 1847	Roving and spinning flax and other fibres.
LEATHES, JOHN HAGGERSTON	9845	25th Feb. 1843	Coffins.
LEATHY, WILLIAM - -	5036	11th Nov. 1824	Apparatus used in making bricks; drying bricks by flues and steam.
LECONTE, LOUIS - - -	8563	9th July 1840	Constructing fire-proof buildings.
LECOUR, LOUIS JOSEPH - -	10,473	16th Jan. 1845	Apparatus for moving the warps in looms.
LEDGINGHAM, ROBERT - -	205	4th Oct. 1678	Engines for discharging water out of mines and ships, wetting sails, and quenching fires, and for other purposes.
LEDGINGHAM, ROBERT - -	340	12th July 1695	Making chain-pumps and hand-pumps for ships of war and merchant ships.
LEDRU, HECTOR - - -	13,528	24th March 1851	Heating.
LEDSAM, DANIEL - - -	5578	4th Dec. 1827	Machinery for cutting sprigs, brads, and nails.
LEDSAM, DANIEL - - -	6200	22nd Dec. 1831	Machinery for making pins, rivets, wood-screws, and nails.
LEDSAM, DANIEL - - -	6513	21st Nov. 1833	Machinery to be used in the manufacture of pins and needles.

Name of Patentee.	Progressive Number.	Date.		Subject-matter of Patent.
LEDSAM, JOSEPH FREDERICK -	5178	31st May	1825	Production and purification of coal-gas.
LEDSAM, JOSEPH FREDERICK -	5471	2nd March	1827	Purifying coal-gas.
LEE, EDMUND - - -	615	9th Dec.	1745	Self-regulating wind machine.
LEE, EDWARD - - -	168	26th Feb.	1672	Engines for cutting new rivers; also for deepening, clearing, and removing sand, gravel, and earth in rivers, to make them navigable.
LEE, GEORGE LAWRENCE -	12,366	11th Dec.	1848	Producing ornamental designs.
LEE, GEORGE WILLIAM - -	5787	2nd May	1829	Machinery for spinning cotton and other fibrous substances.
LEE, JAMES - - -	3096	13th Jan.	1808	Preparing certain kinds of hemp.
LEE, JAMES - - -	3574	9th June	1812	Preparing hemp and flax for various uses, by which also other vegetable substances may be made applicable to many purposes for which hemp and flax are now used.
LEE, JAMES - - -	3964	5th Dec.	1815	Preparing hemp and flax for various uses, by which also other vegetable substances may be made applicable to many purposes for which hemp and flax are now used.
LEE, JAMES - - -	4422	13th Dec.	1819	Machinery and process for breaking, cleaning, and preparing flax and hemp for use; also applicable to other vegetable fibrous substances.
LEE, JOHN - - -	2154	23rd Jan.	1797	Mixture of chalk, whiting or lime, with clay, loam, or earth, for making and colouring bricks.
LEE, JOHN - - -	9041	4th Aug.	1841	Manufacture of chlorine.
LEE, JOHN - - -	9432	3rd Aug.	1842	Wheels and axletrees to be used on railways; machinery to prevent carriages running off railways.
LEE, JOHN - - -	10,207	30th May	1844	Obtaining products from sulphurets and other compounds containing sulphur.
LEE, RICHARD EGAN - -	12,703	10th July	1849	Manufacture of bread; machinery and apparatus used therein; also regulating ovens and furnaces;—applicable to other purposes.
LEECH, GEORGE - - -	7173	15th Aug.	1836	Connecting window-sashes and shutters with the lines by which they are hung.
LEEDHAM, WILLIAM - -	1840	26th Nov.	1791	Preventing the splinter-bar of wheel-carriages from being out of order.
LEEMING, JAMES - - -	6760	9th Feb.	1835	Construction of water-wheels and paddle-wheels.
LEES, EDWARD - - -	5086	1st Feb.	1825	Making bricks, tiles, and other articles manufactured with brick-earth.
LEES, EDWARD - - -	5094	19th Feb.	1825	Waterworks, and mode of conveying water for the purpose of flooding and draining lands;—applicable to other purposes.
LEES, JAMES - - - -	7910	17th Dec.	1838	Machinery for spinning, twisting, and doubling cotton, silk, wool, hemp, flax, and other fibrous materials.
LEES, JOSEPH - - -	14,145	29th May	1852	System of preparing, cutting, and engraving rollers used for printing woven and other fabrics.
LEES, SAMUEL - - -	12,234	8th Aug.	1848	Manufacture of malleable iron.
LEES, THOMAS - - -	4596	18th Oct.	1821	Construction of snuffers.

Name of Patentee.	Progressive Number.	Date.	Subject-matter of Patent.
LEESE, JOSEPH, junior - -	8014	26th March 1839	Printing calicoes, muslins, and other woven fabrics ; processes connected therewith.
LEESE, JOSEPH, junior - -	8554	24th June 1840	Printing calicoes and other surfaces.
LEESE, JOSEPH, junior - -	14,145	29th May 1852	Preparing, cutting, and engraving rollers to be used for printing woven and other fabrics ; machinery for printing and washing such fabrics.
LEESON, HENRY BEAUMONT -	9374	1st June 1842	Depositing and manufacturing metals and metallic articles by electro-galvanic agency ; apparatus connected therewith.
LEESON, WILLIAM - - -	5814	8th July 1829	Harness and saddlery ; partly applicable to other purposes.
LEFORT, LOUIS PAUL - -	6423	17th May 1833	Machinery for making bobbin-net lace.
LEGGETT, HENRY HARDING- [HAM.	6515	23rd Nov. 1833	Printing in colours.
LEGGETT, ROBERT - - -	13,065	30th April 1850	Machinery for thrashing and grinding corn, cutting straw and other similar substances ; applying steam-power to such machinery ; machines for depositing seed.
LEGER, MAURICE ST. - -	4262	19th May 1818	Making lime.
LEGUIN, ESTIENNE - -	1753	1st June 1790	Instruments for calculating longitude.
LEIFCHIELD, JOHN - -	10,759	8th July 1845	Manufacture of blue as a substitute for stone-blue.
LEIGH, EVAN - - -	12,708	18th July 1849	Steam-engines, communicating steam or other power for driving machinery.
LEIGH, EVAN - - -	13,027	26th March 1850	Machinery or apparatus for preparing and spinning cotton and other fibrous substances.
LEIGH, JOHN - - -	7.35	28th Feb. 1839	Obtaining white-lead.
LEIGHTON, Sir ELLIS - -	153	3rd July 1667	Engine to be attached to coaches, chariots, waggons, and such like conveyances, to facilitate their motion.
LEIGHTON, THOMAS HODGSON	7061	12th April 1836	Converting sulphate of soda into sub-carbonate of soda, or mineral alkali.
LEIGHTON, THOMAS HODGSON	9639	21st Feb. 1843	Burning anthracite or stone-coal and other fuel, for the purpose of obtaining heat.
LEJEUNE, JULES - - -	9139	4th Nov. 1841	Condensing and collecting the sulphurous and metallic vapours evolved in the treatment of ores by heat.
LEJEUNE, JULES - - -	9430	29th July 1842	Accelerating combustion ;—applicable in place of blowing-machines.
LELLAN, ARCHIBALD M' -	7811	13th Sept. 1838	Springs and braces of wheeled-carriages ; mode of hanging such carriages.
LELLAN, JAMES M' -	8821	30th Jan. 1841	Combination of materials for umbrella and parasol cloth.
LEMAITRE, LOUIS - - -	12,745	16th Aug. 1849	Manufacture of ferrules, for fixing the tubes of locomotive and other boilers.
LEMAN, JAMES - - -	6847	4th June 1835	Making, mixing, compounding, improving, or altering soap.
LEMAN, JAMES - - -	7060	12th April 1836	Manufacture of soap.
LEMOIGN, VICTOR - -	13,704	31st July 1851	Rotary and other engines.
LEMOINE, JULES - - -	14,205	6th July 1852	Composition applicable as varnish for water-proofing fabrics, also to the manufacture of transparent fabrics, to the fixing of colours, and to other purposes.
LENA, INNOCENZO DELLA -	2432	2nd Aug. 1800	Medicine called phlogistical and fixed earth of Mars, for the cure of various diseases.

Name of Patentee.	Progressive Number.	Date.	Subject-matter of Patent.
LENOX, GEORGE WILLIAM -	10,142	10th April 1844	Manufacture of sheaves and shells for blocks, and of bolt-rings or washers, for shipwrights and engineers.
LENOX, GEORGE WILLIAM -	12,985	28th Feb. 1850	Working windlass and other barrels.
LENTZ, ERNST - - -	9765	10th June 1843	Machinery for raising and forcing water and other fluids, and which, when worked by steam or water, may be employed for driving machinery.
LENZ, GOTTLOB FREDERIC -	2486	27th March 1801	Constructing tan-pits for tanning hides and skins, and for striking hides by machinery.
LENZ, GOTTLOB FREDERIC -	2516	18th June 1801	Constructing tan-pits for tanning hides and skins, and for striking hides by machinery.
LEOD, JOHN Mc - - -	5829	12th Aug. 1829	Preparing certain substances so as to produce a substitute for barilla.
LEONARD, ROBERT - -	8491	5th May 1840	Machinery for sawing, rasping, or dividing dye-woods or tanners' bark.
LERAT, CHARLES - - -	948	23rd Dec. 1769	Powders to purify the human blood, and cure rheumatism and several other disorders, "Poudre unique."
LERMITTE, THOMAS - -	3150	11th July 1808	Chemical preparation for preserving woollen and vegetable substances from mildew, rot, or fermentation; also for rendering woollen, cotton, and linen cloths, canvas, silk, leather, hats, and paper, impervious to rain.
LEROW, JOHN ALEXANDER -	13,321	7th Nov. 1850	Sewing-machines.
LEROY, EDOUARD GABRIEL -	13,210	31st July 1850	Locomotive-engines; and means and apparatus employed for generating and condensing the steam to be used therein.
LEROY, NARCISSE - - -	10,408	28th Nov. 1844	Covering the tops of bottles, jars, and other vessels.
LESLIE, JOHN - - -	8303	9th Dec. 1839	Measuring the human figure.
LESLIE, JOHN - - -	10,501	28th Jan. 1845	Stoves, and apparatus used in consuming fuel, and in ventilating.
LESLIE, JOHN - - -	10,977	4th Dec. 1845	Combustion of gas.
LESLIE, JOHN - - -	11,630	22nd March 1847	Combustion of gas for the purposes of light.
LESLIE, ROBERT - - -	1970	13th Dec. 1793	Clocks, watches, and other timekeepers used at sea or on land.
LESNARD, FREDERICK - -	10,642	29th April 1845	Generating steam and evaporating liquids.
LESNARD, FREDERICK - -	11,532	16th Jan. 1847	Obtaining motive-power.
LESTER, SARAH - - -	14,307	30th Sept. 1852	Treating the seeds of flax and hemp; also treating flax and hemp for dressing.
LESTER, WILLIAM - - -	2223	10th March 1798	Harrows.
LESTER, WILLIAM - - -	2375	4th Feb. 1800	Machine for cutting hay and straw into chaff for the use of cattle.
LESTER, WILLIAM - - -	2480	17th Feb. 1801	Machine for cutting hay and straw into chaff.
LESTER, WILLIAM - - -	2629	19th June 1802	Machine for separating corn and seeds from the straw;—partly applicable to other purposes.
LESTER, WILLIAM - - -	2808	16th Jan. 1805	Machine for separating corn, seed, and pulse from the straw and chaff.
LESTER, WILLIAM - - -	2943	19th June 1806	Rotary-motion, or engine to communicate power to machines.

Name of Patentee.	Progres-sive Number.	Date.		Subject-matter of Patent.
LESTER, WILLIAM - - -	3082	21st Nov.	1807	Machine for separating corn, seeds, and pulse from the straw and chaff.
LESTER, WILLIAM - - -	3841	17th Sept.	1814	Machine for separating corn or seeds from the straw and chaff.
LESTER, WILLIAM - - -	4270	2nd June	1818	Increasing and projecting light produced by lamps or by other means.
LETSOME, THOMAS - -	33	8th April	1626	Making steel; apparatus for the purpose.
LEVERS, JOHN - - -	5622	3rd March	1828	Machinery for the manufacture of bobbin-net lace.
LEVERS, JOHN - - -	5741	18th Dec.	1828	Machinery for making bobbin-net lace.
LEVERS, JOHN - - -	5940	8th June	1830	Machinery for making bobbin-net lace.
LEVERS, JOHN - - -	6778	27th Feb.	1835	Machinery for making bobbin-net lace.
LEVY, ISAAC - - -	866	17th Dec.	1766	Floating machine for conveying timber and other materials from one part of the world to another, without shipping.
LEVY, JACOB - - -	1262	5th July	1780	Making (from wheat) semolina from which vermicelli and maccaroni are manufactured.
LEWELL, JOHN - - -	2671	21st Dec.	1802	Register-stoves.
LEWIS, GEORGE - -	11,161	7th April	1846	Construction of shutters and blinds for windows and doors; construction of doors.
LEWIS, ISRAEL - - -	1142	24th Dec.	1776	Making window-curtains with springs.
LEWIS, ISRAEL - - -	1162	14th July	1777	Making festoon window-curtains with springs.
LEWIS, JAMES HEATH - -	10,677	22nd May	1845	Printing.
LEWIS, JAMES HENRY - -	4426	20th Dec.	1819	Pens. "Caligraphic Fountain Pens."
LEWIS, JOHN - - -	690	21st May	1754	Pine varnish for paying ships' sides and masts, and for preventing the decay of timber buildings.
LEWIS, JOHN - - -	2588	27th Feb.	1802	Preventing accidents liable to occur in carriages drawn by horses.
LEWIS, JOHN - - -	3605	31st Oct.	1812	Horse-shoes; shoeing horses.
LEWIS, JOHN - - -	3630	19th Dec.	1812	Smelting copper ore.
LEWIS, JOHN - - -	3723	23rd July	1813	Smelting copper ore.
LEWIS, JOHN - - -	3945	27th July	1815	Shearing-machines.
LEWIS, JOHN - - -	4189	19th Dec.	1817	Wire gig-mills, for dressing woollen and other cloths.
LEWIS, JOHN - - -	4196	15th Jan.	1818	Shearing-machines, for shearing woollen and other cloths.
LEWIS, JOHN - - -	4378	19th June	1819	Application of mechanical powers for laying, smoothing, and polishing the face of woollen or other cloth or fabric, also cleansing such cloth or fabric at the same time.
LEWIS, JOHN - - -	4379	19th June	1819	Application of pointed wires or other pointed substances of a suitable nature, for raising the pile or face of woollen or other cloths or fabrics.
LEWIS JOSEPH - - -	2572	16th Jan.	1802	Dyeing, or a new method of cooling the cloth and other piece-goods, and of applying the fire for heating the boiler or other vessels;—applicable to the heating of other boilers or vessels.
LEWIS, JOSEPH - - -	12,150	9th May	1848	Machinery applicable to the preparation and spinning of cotton-wool, silk, flax, and other fibrous substances.

Name of Patentee.	Progressive Number.	Date.	Subject-matter of Patent.
LEWIS, ROBERT - - -	3679	13th April 1813	Making brass chimney-pieces or chimney-piece frames, plain or ornamental.
LEWIS, THOMAS - - -	1490	16th July 1785	Truss for the cure of ruptures.
LEWIS, THOMAS - - -	12,298	26th Oct. 1848	Machinery to be used in making playing-cards and other cards; also other articles made wholly or in part of paper or paste-board;—partly applicable to other machinery where pressure is required.
LEWIS, WILLIAM - - -	3939	15th July 1815	Erecting racks for racking woollen-cloth and other articles.
LEWIS, WILLIAM - - -	4013	5th April 1816	Machinery for fulling woollen and other cloths.
LEWIS, WILLIAM - - -	4189	19th Dec. 1817	Wire gig-mills for dressing woollen and other cloths.
LEWIS, WILLIAM - - -	4196	15th Jan. 1818	Shearing-machines, for shearing woollen and other cloths.
LEWIS, WILLIAM - - -	4378	19th June 1819	Application of mechanical powers for laying, smoothing, and polishing the face of woollen or other cloth or fabric, also cleansing such cloth or fabric at the same time.
LEWIS, WILLIAM - - -	4379	19th June 1819	Application of pointed wires or other pointed substances of a suitable nature for raising the pile or face of woollen and other cloths or fabrics.
LEWIS, WILLIAM - - -	7148	13th July 1836	Machinery applicable to the dressing of woollen and other cloths.
LEWIS, WILLIAM - - -	7584	5th March 1838	Machinery for dressing woollen and other cloths or fabrics.
LEWTHWAITE, JOHN - -	9260	15th Feb. 1842	Steam-engines and boilers.
LEWTHWAITE, JOHN - -	11,812	23rd July 1847	Numbering-machines.
LEWTY, JAMES WINDEYER -	6478	5th Oct. 1833	Castors.
LARDET, JOHN - - -	1040	3rd April 1773	Cement for building purposes; grease for frictions, for preserving steel and iron, and for other uses.
LIDBETTER, THOMAS - -	10,586	2nd April 1845	Manufacture of salt.
LIDDELL, CHARLES - -	14,343	11th Nov. 1852	Electric-telegraphs.
LIDDELL, JOHN - - -	359	1st Dec. 1698	Engine for draining water, which, with ladles or forcers turning circularly, drives the water to the desired place or height.
LIDDELL, RICHARD - -	682	12th April 1753	Machines or vessels for removing earth, ballast, sand, rubbish, or any other matter.
LIDDELL, RICHARD - -	884	25th Nov. 1766	Discharging coals, culm, corn, merchandize, and other things, out of ships, boats, lighters, or other craft; also measuring or weighing the same.
LIDDELL, THOMAS - - -	10,067	21st Feb. 1844	Apparatus for preventing explosion in steam-boilers.
LIDEL, JOSEPH - - -	7006	17th Feb. 1836	Pianofortes.
LIDELL, THOMAS - - -	111	26th Nov. 1637	Mill for grinding corn.
LIEBHABER, JOSEPH CONRAD [MARIE BARON DE.	10,579	27th March 1845	Blasting rocks and other mineral substances for mining and other purposes; apparatus to be used in such works.
LIEBHABER, JOSEPH CONRAD [MARIE BARON DE. [Liebhaber, Joseph Conrad, Baron de.]	13,344	14th Nov. 1850	Blasting rocks, working marble and stone, and preparing products therefrom.
LIENDU, JOHN, junior - -	13,462	18th Jan. 1851	Purifying or filtering oils and other liquids.

Name of Patentee.	Progressive Number.	Date.	Subject-matter of Patent.
LIGHT, EDWARD - - -	4041	18th June 1816	Harp-lute, or "British Lute Harp."
LIGHT, EDWARD - - -	7168	11th Aug. 1836	Propelling vessels and other floating bodies.
LIGHT, EDWARD - - -	11,802	19th July 1847	Apparatus for supporting persons, boats, and other bodies when in the water.
LIGHTFOOT, JOHN EMANUEL -	13,662	12th June 1851	Treating and preparing certain colouring matters to be used in dyeing and printing.
LIGHTFOOT, THOMAS - -	12,799	12th Oct. 1849	Printing cotton-fabrics.
LIGHTFOOT, THOMAS - -	12,916	3rd Jan. 1850	Printing and dyeing fabrics of cotton and other fibrous materials.
LIGHTFOOT, THOMAS - -	13,778	16th Oct. 1851	Machinery applicable to the manufacture of paper.
LIGHTOLER, TIMOTHY - -	670	9th April 1752	Machine for cutting files.
LIGHTOLLER, RICHARD ASHTON	12,601	3rd May 1849	Machinery for manufacturing bricks and tiles from clay or other plastic materials.
LIGNAC, JULES JEAN BAPTISTE [MARTIN DE.	11,892	7th Oct. 1847	Preserving milk.
LIHON, JOHN - - • -	5781	14th April 1829	Constructing ships' pintals for hanging the rudder.
LIHON, JOHN - - • -	6210	10th Jan. 1832	Constructing capstans.
LEJEUNE, JULES - - •	9139	4th Nov. 1841	Condensing and collecting sulphurous and metallic vapours evolved in treating all kinds of ores by heat.
LILLEY, GEORGE - - -	4413	23rd Nov. 1819	Construction of an engine, wrought by steam or other elastic fluid, for driving mills, and for other purposes.
LILLEY, GEORGE - - -	4450	19th April 1820	Hydro-pneumatic apparatus, acted upon by a steam-engine or other power, for propelling boats or other vessels upon water.
LILLIE, Sir GEORGE SCOTT -	7043	23rd March 1836	Acquiring power for the purpose of propelling carriages, barges, and other contrivances for conveying goods and passengers.
LILLIE, Sir JOHN SCOTT -	8184	1st Aug. 1839	Application of elastic fluids to the working of machinery.
LILLIE, Sir JOHN SCOTT -	9505	2nd Nov. 1842	Roads.
LILLIE, Sir JOHN SCOTT -	11,907	14th Oct. 1847	Machinery;—applicable to tillage, and for other agricultural purposes.
LILLIE, Sir JOHN SCOTT -	13,241	5th Sept. 1850	Application of motive-power.
LILLIE, Sir JOHN SCOTT -	13,765	9th Oct. 1851	Forming or cover'ng roads, floors, doors, and other surfaces.
LILLIE, JOSEPH - - -	12,270	21st Sept. 1848	Machinery, applicable for purifying and cooling liquids, and for purifying, condensing, and cooling gases.
LIN, FRANCIS - - - -	109	6th Sept. 1637	Drawing and working barges and other vessels on rivers, without the use of horses.
LINIKAR, JAMES - - -	3152	14th July 1808	Towing, driving, or forcing ships and other vessels.
LINDEN, DEDERICK WESSEL -	616	1st April 1746	Making saltpetre.
LINDLEY, JAMES - - -	10,012	16th Jan. 1844	Coffins.
LINDLEY, JOHN - • -	4063	30th Sept. 1816	Machinery to be used with machines for making bobbin-lace net.

Name of Patentee.	Progressive Number.	Date.	Subject-matter of Patent.
LINDO, ABRAHAM ALEXANDER	8744	18th Dec. 1840	Means to be applied to railways and carriages thereon, for preventing accidents, and to lessen the injurious effects of accidents, to passengers, goods, and railway-trains.
LINDOPP, THOMAS - - -	1254	4th May 1780	Scoop-saddle, with a cavity for containing apparel under lock and key.
LINDSAY, GEORGE - - -	588	17th Feb. 1743	Portable microscope.
LINDSAY, JOHN - - -	3238	30th May 1809	Telegraph, or apparatus for conveying intelligence by night or by day.
LINDSAY, JOHN - - -	3351	19th June 1810	Boat and apparatus, whereby heavy burdens can be conveyed on shallow water, and on rivers wherein shoals and other difficulties impede navigation;—applicable to other purposes.
LINDSAY, JOHN - - -	5185	14th June 1825	Construction of horse and carriageways of streets, turnpike and other roads; wheels to be used thereon.
LINDSAY, JOHN - - -	8906	29th March 1841	Covers for water-closets, night-stools, and bed-pans.
LINDSEY, ROBERT - - -	93	13th May 1636	Avoiding the annoyance of smoke in brew-houses, dye-houses, and similar places, preserving caldrons, coppers, and the like.
LINDSEY, ROBERT - - -	94	23rd June 1636	Erecting ovens.
LINDSLEE, THOMAS - -	843	25th March 1766	Composition for making fictile-pipes for conducting water and other fictile-wares; making and burning the same.
LINES, EDWARD DUNCOMBE -	12,072	18th Feb. 1848	Manufacture of colours, oils, and varnishes; also charcoal; treating and obtaining extracts from vegetable substances.
LINGFORD, JOHN - - -	3919	1st June 1815	Anatomical self-regulating truss.
LINGFORD, JOHN - - -	4925	20th March 1824	Machinery for making bobbin-net lace.
LINGFORD, JOHN - - -	5025	1st Nov. 1824	Machinery for making bobbin-net lace.
LINGHAM, GEORGE - -	1556	21st Aug. 1786	Manufacturing gloves without side seams; also improvements in sewing or setting on the tops, and in other particulars.
LINGHAM, THOMAS - -	1358	27th Feb. 1783	Cutting and making breeches of leather, velvet, silk, worsted, and other materials.
LINGS, JOHN - - - -	10,781	21st July 1845	Apparatus for the preservation of provisions.
LINIERE, FRANCIS XAVIER DE [ARLES DE.	755	27th Nov. 1760	Pumps.
LINIERE FRANCIS XAVIER DE [ARDES DE.	756	27th Nov. 1760	Pumps.
LINLEY, THOMAS - - -	4740	20th Dec. 1822	Increasing the force or power of bellows.
LINNING, MICHAEL - -	7296	6th Feb. 1837	Operating to convert peat-moss and peat-turf or bog into fuel, and to obtain from it tar, gas, and other substances.
LINTON, GEORGE - - -	4632	22nd Dec. 1821	Propelling machinery without the aid of steam, water, wind, air, or fire.
LINTON, JOHN - - -	6378	29th Jan. 1833	Construction of steam-boilers.
LIPSCOMBE FREDERICK - -	9869	17th Aug. 1843	Railway-carriages; hydrostatic engines;—partly applicable to other engines, and for other purposes.

Name of Patentee.	Progressive Number.	Date.	Subject-matter of Patent.
LISTER, GEORGE - - -	9788	15th June 1843	Covering the cylinders of carding and scribbling engines with wire-cards; condensing the rovings from such engines; also apparatus for grinding or sharpening the points of such cards, which may be also employed for grinding other articles.
LISTER, SAMUEL CUNCLIFFE -	10,102	14th March 1844	Machinery for applying fringes to shawls and other articles.
LISTER, SAMUEL CUNCLIFFE -	10,336	27th Sept, 1844	Preparing and combing wool.
LISTER, SAMUEL CUNCLIFFE -	11,004	12th Dec. 1845	Carding, combing, and spinning wool.
LISTER, SAMUEL CONCLIFFE -	11,469	1st Dec. 1846	Combing wool.
LISTER, SAMUEL CUNCLIFFE -	11,896	7th Oct. 1847	Carding, preparing, combing, and spinning wool and other fibrous substances; making heald and genappe yarns.
LISTER, SAMUEL CUNCLIFFE -	12,029	18th Jan. 1848	Stopping railway and other carriages.
LISTER, SAMUEL CUNCLIFFE -	12,289	19th Oct. 1848	Preparing, heckling, and combing wool and other fibrous substances.
LISTER, SAMUEL CUNCLIFFE -	12,712	18th July 1849	Preparing, combing, and spinning wool.
LISTER, SAMUEL CUNCLIFFE -	13,009	20th March 1850	Preparing and combing wool and other fibrous materials.
LISTER, SAMUEL CUNCLIFFE -	13,532	24th Feb. 1851	Preparing and combing wool and other fibrous materials.
LISTER, SAMUEL CUNCLIFFE -	13,950	2nd Feb. 1852	Preparing and combing wool and other fibrous materials.
LISTER, SAMUEL CUNCLIFFE -	14,135	22nd May 1852	Treating and preparing before being spun, wool, cotton, and other fibrous materials.
LISTER, WILLIAM - - -	4748	16th Jan. 1823	Machinery for, and method of preparing and spinning wool, silk, mohair, or other animal fibre.
LISTON, HENRY - - -	3354	3rd July 1810	Construction of organs.
LISTON, HENRY - - -	3739	23rd Sept. 1813	Ploughs.
LITHERLAND, PETER - -	1830	14th Oct. 1791	Escapement to be applied to watches, clocks, or dials, for use at sea or on land.
LITHERLAND, PETER - -	1889	12th June 1792	Watches, particularly escapements to be applied to them.
LITHERLAND, PETER - -	2430	31st July 1800	Apparatus for keeping musical instruments in tune.
LITHERLAND, PETER - -	2594	24th March 1802	Keeping musical instruments in tune, and preserving the strings from breaking.
LITHERLAND, RICHARD -	4103	20th Feb. 1817	Escapement of watches.
LITTLE, GEORGE - - -	11,576	11th Feb. 1847	Electric-telegraphs; arrangements and apparatus to be used therein and therewith; —partly applicable to time-keepers, and to other purposes.
LITTLE, GEORGE - - -	13,555	14th March 1851	Electric-telegraphs; apparatus to be used in connection therewith;—partly applicable to other purposes.
LITTLE, THOMAS - - -	10,572	20th March 1845	Manufacture of ladies' bonnets or hats.
LITTLE, WILLIAM - - -	11,203	12th May 1846	Machinery for printing.
LITTLE, WILLIAM - - -	12,571	16th April 1849	Manufacture of materials for lubricating machinery.
LITTLEWORT, GEORGE - -	6697	17th Oct. 1834	Watches and clocks.
LITTLEWORT, WILLIAM - -	5388	14th July 1826	Mooring ships and other floating bodies; apparatus for the purpose.

Name of Patentee.	Progres- sive Number.	Date.	Subject-matter of Patent.
LIVESEY, JOHN - - -	6451	18th July 1833	Preparation of hemp, flax, and other fibrous materials, for the manufacture of glazing, friction and mangle bowls, paper-makers' felts, and for other purposes.
LIVESEY, JOHN - - -	13,750	18th Sept. 1851	Manufacture of textile-fabrics; machinery for producing the same.
LIVESEY, JOHN - - -	14,270	19th Aug. 1852	Manufacture of textile-fabrics; machinery for producing such fabrics.
LIVEINGS, THOMAS - -	506	19th Feb. 1729	Making a compound manure for enriching and mending all sorts of land.
LIVINGSTONE, ALEXANDER [SPEED.	11,845	23rd Aug. 1847	Construction of locomotive-engines to be used on railways.
LIVINGSTONE, ALEXANDER [SPEED.	13,450	11th Jan. 1851	Manufacture of fuel.
LIVSEY, JOEL - - - -	7220	10th Nov. 1836	Machinery for spinning, preparing, and doubling cotton and other fibrous substances.
LIZARS, CHARLES - - -	12,890	15th Dec. 1849	Gas-meters.
LLANOS, VALENTINE - -	5734	15th Dec. 1828	Bits.
LLEWELLIN, PETER -	12,339	23rd Nov. 1848	Making cocks or valves for drawing off liquids.
LLOYD, EDMUND - - -	2143	31st Oct. 1796	Tea-kettle or tea-boiler.
LLOYD, EDMUND - - -	5096	19th Feb. 1825	Apparatus from which to feed fires with coals and other fuel.
LLOYD, EDWARD - - -	13,522	24th Feb. 1851	Steam-engines;—applicable wholly or in part to other motive-engines.
LLOYD, FRANCIS - -	2152	13th Dec. 1796	Furnace or fire-place.
LLOYD, FRANCIS -	11,904	14th Oct. 1847	Preparation and manufacture of tobacco.
LLOYD, GEORGE -	12,087	8th March 1848	Furnaces and blowing-machines; engines and machinery for driving the same;—applicable to other purposes where motive power is required.
LLOYD, JOHN WILLIAM -	2988	20th Nov. 1806	Anti-friction rollers or wheels, to assist carriage-wheels.
LLOYD, NATHANIEL - -	8812	26th Jan. 1841	Thickening and preparing colours for printing calicoes and other substances.
LLOYD, OLIVER - - -	114	14th Dec. 1637	Making an engine for working all kinds of mills; also for carriages and wheel-works turned by wind, water, man or beast.
LLOYD, RICHARD - -	13,700	28th July 1851	Steam-engines; heating steam.
LLOYD, ROBERT - - -	4900	19th Feb. 1824	Hat.
LLOYD, ROBERT - - -	5347	18th April 1826	Preparing, combining, and putting together, certain materials for making hats, caps, bonnets, cloaks, coats, and other articles of apparel, and for other purposes.
LLOYD, SAMPSON - - -	11,621	15th March 1847	Making tires or hoops for wheels and other articles made of iron or steel.
LOACH, JOHN - - -	3548	14th March 1812	Manufacturing claw, socket, and other kinds of castors; also knobs and furniture for locks.
LOACH, JOHN - - -	5370	23rd May 1826	Self-acting sash-fastener;—applicable to other purposes.
LOACH, JOHN - - -	7443	5th Oct. 1837	Roller-blind furniture; manufacturing the same.
LOACH, JOHN - - -	8788	14th Jan. 1841	Castors applicable to cabinet furniture and other purposes.

Name of Patentee.	Progressive Number.	Date.		Subject-matter of Patent.
LOACH, JOHN - - - -	10,176	7th May	1844	Corkscrews;—applicable to cocks or taps and valves.
LOACH, JOHN - - - -	11,568	8th Feb.	1847	Fastenings for window-shutters, doors, and tables;—applicable as fastenings generally.
LOAM, MICHAEL - - -	12,406	11th Jan.	1849	Manufacture of fusees.
LOAT, WILLIAM JOHN - -	9585	12th Jan.	1843	Constructing floors and roofs.
LOBB, JOSEPH - - -	4553	1st May	1821	Machine for cutting and preparing ley-ground for tillage, and for renewing grass and other lands without destroying or tearing up the whole of the surface.
LOBB, THEOPHILUS - -	773	21st May	1762	Tincture to preserve the blood from siziness; and a saline scorbutic acrimony.
LOBECK, HENRY LEWIS - -	4506	1st Nov.	1820	Making yeast.
LOCKE, EDWARD - - -	8572	18th July	1840	Rotary-engine.
LOCKETT, JOHN - - -	2423	8th July	1800	Box and axletree for carriages, lathes, and grindstones.
LOCKETT, JOSEPH - - -	5082	14th Jan.	1825	Producing or manufacturing a neb or slot in the roller, shell, or cylinder made of copper or other metal, and used in the printing of calicoes, muslin, cotton, or linen cloth.
LOCKETT, JOSEPH - - -	7455	2nd Oct.	1837	Printing calicoes and other fabrics of cotton, silk, wool, paper, or linen, separately or intermixed.
LOCKETT, JOSEPH - - -	8610	27th Aug.	1840	Manufacturing, preparing, and engraving, cylinders, rollers, or other surfaces, for printing or embossing calicoes or other fabrics.
LOCKETT, JOSEPH - - -	10,432	12th Dec.	1844	Apparatus for preparing metal cylinders to be engraved or turned, for use in printing calicoes or other fabrics.
LOCKHEAD, JAMES - -	12,081	8th March	1848	Ventilation.
LOCKYER, WILLIAM - -	5493	28th April	1827	Manufacture of brushes; also the manufacture of a material, and its application to manufacturing brushes, and for other purposes.
LO DACRE, RICHARD - -	33	8th April	1626	Making steel; apparatus for the purpose.
LODGE, GEORGE - - -	10,309	12th Sept.	1844	Furnaces, fire-bars, hot-air generators, and flues.
LODGE, GEORGE - - -	11,324	10th Aug.	1846	Heating water, generating steam, and saving fuel.
LODGE, JAMES - - -	1230	12th July	1779	Drying, tentering, and setting woollen-goods, after being dyed or whitened by the heat of fires.
LODGE, JOHN BUTLER - -	4478	20th June	1820	Construction and application of spring-trusses or bandages for the relief or cure of hernia.
LODGE, WILLIAM - - -	647	1st July	1749	Making pearl-ashes.
LOESCHMAN, DAVID - -	3250	26th July	1809	Musical scale of keyed-instruments with fixed tones, such as pianos, organs, &c.
LOESCHMAN, DAVID - -	4637	14th Jan.	1822	Keyed musical instrument.
LOFTING, Mr. - - -	319	4th April	1693	Instrument for making thimbles for men, women, and children.
LOFTINGH, JOHN - - -	263	25th Feb.	1690	Engine for quenching and extinguishing fires, unexpectedly arising in dwelling houses, or elsewhere.

Name of Patentee.	Progres-sive Number.	Date.	Subject-matter of Patent.
LOGAN, MICHAEL - - -	2301	8th March 1799	Centrifugal barrel-engine of central force, for raising water and heavy weights from great depths; applicable to all manufactories where power is required.
LOGAN, MICHAEL - - -	2732	5th Aug. 1803	Conservative lock, for use of inland and canal navigation.
LOGAN, MICHAEL - - -	2917	13th March 1806	System of marine, fort, and field artillery.
LOGAN, MICHAEL - - -	3196	26th Jan. 1809	Transcendant ordnance or cannon, for marine, fort, or field service.
LOGAN, MICHAEL - - -	3485	9th Sept. 1811	Instrument for the generation of fire, and for various purposes in chemical and experimental operations.
LOGAN, ROBERT - - -	7934	11th Jan. 1839	Cloth made from cocoa-nut fibre; preparing such fibrous material for the same.
LOGAN, ROBERT - - -	9131	2nd Nov. 1841	Obtaining and preparing the fibres and other products of the cocoa-nut and its husk.
LOGIER, JOHN BERNARD -	3806	28th April 1814	Apparatus to facilitate the acquirement of proper execution on the pianoforte.
LOGOINS, WILLIAM - -	229	15th Nov. 1683	Making several things of iron by mill-work only instead of by hand and hammer, as sheaths and tire for wheels, plates for fenders, half pounds of iron for kettles, and other things in constant use.
LOLME, JOHN LEWIS DE -	1718	12th Dec. 1789	Instrument or method of making a vessel sail faster and keep a truer course, without upsetting, and capable of being veered about from opposite tacks with more speed and in a less space, having the upper parts of the vessel made and the sail hung, so as also to assist in fast sailing, the rudder likewise being sunk deep in the water thereby increases the manageableness of the vessel, which, having the part of its body which is under the water diminished, also affords an easier landing than can be effected with boats in common use on the sea-coast.
LOLME, JOHN LEWIS DE -	1991	24th May 1794	Instruments for the safety and convenience of wheel-carriages, and for lessening friction.
LOMAS, WILIAM - - -	9549	8th Dec. 1842	Manufacture of fringes, cords, and other similar small-wares; machinery for producing the same.
LOMAX, PETER - - -	8116	19th June 1839	Looms for weaving.
LOMAX, WILLIAM ROTHWELL	12,346	29th Nov. 1848	Machine for cutting hay and straw into chaff, and for cutting other vegetable substances.
LOMBE, THOMAS - - -	422	9th Sept. 1718	Three engines, one to wind the finest raw silk, another to spin, and another to twist the finest Italian raw silk into organzine.
LONDON, PHILLIPS - -	3227	19th April 1809	Manufacturing, refining, and purifying muriate of soda or common salt.
LONDON, PHILLIPS - - *[London, Phillips, junior.]*	3227	19th April 1809	Manufacturing, refining, and purifying muriate of soda or common salt.
LONDON, PHILLIPS - -	4432	25th Jan. 1820	Destroying the offensive vapour arising from animal or vegetable matter when heated.

Name of Patentee.	Progres-sive Number.	Date.	Subject-matter of Patent.
LONDON, PHILLIPS - -	4533	3rd Feb. 1821	Application of heat to coppers and other utensils.
LONDON, SAMUEL - - -	448	13th June 1722	Composition or mixture for making white ware, without any sort of clay.
LONG, DANIEL RUTTER -	6711	13th Nov. 1834	Applying certain anti-putrescent and flavouring substances to meat.
LONG, JAMES - - -	12,941	24th Jan. 1850	Instruments and machinery for steering ships;—applicable to vices and other instruments.
LONG, JOHN - - - -	1754	4th June 1790	Utensils or methods to be employed in the essential parts of brewing good malt-liquor stronger and better flavoured, with only the usual quantity of malt and hops; such as extracting the finer parts of the malt and hops, keeping the mash-tun at a proper heat for obtaining the full extract of the malt and the hops, also conveying the worts from the mash-tun to the copper, and a means of cooling the tun if required.
LONG, JOHN - - - -	1769	28th July 1790	Utensil or apparatus to be used in breweries, distilleries, &c., for the purpose of cooling worts of all kinds.
LONG, JOSEPH - - -	12,941	24th Jan. 1850	Instruments and machinery for steering ships;—applicable to vices and other instruments.
LONG, SAMUEL - - -	3259	4th Sept. 1809	Horizontal windmills.
LONG, THOMAS - - -	869	25th Feb. 1767	Machine for blotching, printing, intermixing, and variegating, by means of copper-plates, different colours on calicoes, cottons, lawns, and all other whitstered linens, for furniture, garments, and handkerchiefs.
LONGBOTHAM, JOHN - -	1905	28th July 1792	Supplying water to canals or other cuts, ponds, or sluices.
LONGBOTTOM, JOHN - -	6257	13th April 1832	Machinery and process used in the manufacture of bricks, tiles, bread, biscuits, and other articles made of plastic materials;—partly applicable to other purposes.
LONGBOTTOM, JOHN - -	11,136	18th March 1846	Manufacture of oil-cake; machinery and processes for pressing and moulding the same;—applicable to the manufacture of other articles from plastic materials.
LONGDON, ROBERT, the younger	13,253	12th Sept. 1850	Manufacture of looped fabrics.
LONGFIELD, WILLIAM - -	6674	6th Sept. 1834	Lock or fastening for doors and for other situations where security is required.
LONGHURST, JAMES - -	3849	1st Nov. 1814	Æolian-organ or barrel-organ, with a self-acting swell.
LONGMAID, WILLIAM - -	9496	20th Oct. 1842	Treating ores and other minerals, and obtaining various products therefrom;—partly applicable to the manufacture of alkali.
LONGMAID, WILLIAM - -	10,004	1st Jan. 1844	Manufacture of copper, tin, zinc, and peroxide of iron.
LONGMAID, WILLIAM - -	10,797	4th Aug. 1845	Manufacture of chlorine; treating sulphurous ores and other minerals; obtaining various products therefrom.
LONGMAID, WILLIAM - -	11,484	14th Dec. 1846	Manufacture of alkali and chlorine.
LONGMAID, WILLIAM - -	11,931	2nd Nov. 1847	Manufacture of alkali and chlorine.

Name of Patentee.	Progres-sive Number.	Date.		Subject-matter of Patent.
LONGMAID, WILLIAM - -	12,297	26th Oct.	1848	Treating the oxydes of iron, and obtaining products therefrom.
LONGMAID, WILLIAM - -	12,685	4th July	1849	Manufacture of soap.
LONGMAID, WILLIAM - -	13,630	10th May	1851	Treating ores and minerals, and obtaining products therefrom;—applicable to the manufacture of alkali.
LONGMAID, WILLIAM - -	13,940	30th Jan.	1852	Obtaining gold.
LONGMAN, JOHN - - -	2468	27th Jan.	1801	Construction of barrel-organs.
LONGMORE, JOSIAH - -	2509	2nd June	1801	Patten or clog.
LONGMORE, JOSIAH - -	9719	4th May	1843	Pens, penholders, and pencil-cases;—partly applicable to other purposes.
LONGRIDGE, ROBERT BEWICK	10,513	10th Feb.	1845	Locomotive-engines.
LONGRIDGE, ROBERT BEWICK	11,038	13th Jan.	1846	Locomotive-engines.
LONGSHAW, WILLIAM - -	11,192	5th May	1846	Machinery for spinning and doubling cotton and other fibrous substances.
LONGWORTH, JOHN - -	12,119	10th April	1848	Pickers for power-looms.
LONSDALE, WILLIAM - -	2349	4th Nov.	1799	Weighing anchors; steering ships; weighing and raising heavy burdens on board ships.
LOOS, EDWARD - - -	8107	17th June	1839	Extracting saccharine matters from sugar-canes and other substances of the like nature;—applicable in extracting colouring matter from wood and other substances used in dyeing.
LOOSEMORE, WILLIAM - -	2366	20th Dec.	1799	Manufacturing certain cloth for general uses.
LOOSEY, CHARLES - - -	9191	16th Dec.	1841	Steam-engines;—applicable for raising or forcing water, and propelling vessels.
LO PRESTI, Baron LOUIS -	12,885	10th Dce.	1849	Hydraulic-presses;—applicable wholly or in part to pumps and similar machines.
LORADOUX, AUGUSTE -	13,471	23rd Jan.	1851	Machinery for raising water or other fluids.
LORD, AMBROSE - -	11,260	24th June	1846	Furnaces, and the flues of steam-boilers, for the purpose of consuming the smoke and saving fuel.
LORD, EDWARD - - -	12,476	13th Feb.	1849	Machinery, applicable to the preparation of cotton and other fibrous substances.
LORD, JOHN - - -	10,613	15th April	1845	Supplying steam-boilers with water.
LORD, ROBERT - - -	789	11th April	1763	Machines for forming and repairing roads. " Tectonodes."
LORD, SAMUEL - - -	5234	11th Aug.	1825	Machinery for and process of raising the pile on woollen-cloths and other fabrics; pressing the same.
LORD, THOMAS WILKS -	13,690	17th July	1851	A machine to open and clean tow, waste from flax, and other fibrous substances; piecing straps and belts for driving machinery; machine for effecting the same.
LORD, THOMAS WILKS - [Lord, Thomas Wilkes.]	14,162	10th June	1852	Machinery for spinning, preparing, and heckling flax, tow, hemp, cotton, and other fibrous substances; lubricating such machinery, also other machinery.
LORENT, ABRAHAM ROBERT -	5323	19th Jan.	1826	Applying steam, without pressure, to pans, boilers, coppers, and machinery, to regulate heat in boiling, distilling, evaporating, and warming, also to produce power.
LORENTZ, RICHARD - -	3007	5th Feb.	1807	Instruments to produce instantaneous light, and instantaneous fire.

Name of Patentee.	Progressive Number.	Date.		Subject-matter of Patent.
LORIMIER, ANTHONY - -	10,240	3rd July	1844	Apparatus and means of facilitating drawing from nature or from models.
LORIMIER, ANTHONY - -	12,206	10th July	1848	Combining gutta-percha and caoutchouc with other materials.
LORKIN, JOSIAH - - -	12,775	20th Sept.	1849	Apparatus for beating or triturating viscous or gelatinous substances.
LOSH, JOHN - - - -	6842	30th May	1835	Surface or pattern-roll of surface printing machines; working the said rolls.
LOSH, WILLIAM - - -	3905	8th April	1815	Fire-places or furnaces for heating ovens and boilers, and the water or other liquids in the same, and for converting such liquids into steam for the purpose of working engines, and for other uses.
LOSH, WILLIAM - - -	4067	30th Sept.	1816	Construction of machines, carriages, carriage-wheels, railways and frameways, for facilitating the conveyance of carriages, goods, and materials along the said ways.
LOSH, WILLIAM - - -	4591	14th Sept.	1821	Construction of iron-rails for railways.
LOSH, WILLIAM - - -	5704	18th Sept.	1828	Formation of iron-rails for railroads, and chairs or pedestals upon which the rails may be placed.
LOSH, WILLIAM - - -	5989	31st Aug.	1830	Construction of wheels for carriages to be used on railways.
LOSH, WILLIAM - - -	7523	23rd Dec.	1837	Decomposing muriate of soda or common salt;—partly applicable to the condensing of vapours in other processes.
LOSH, WILLIAM - - -	9009	26th June	1841	Manufacture of railway-wheels.
LOSH, WILLIAM - - -	9335	28th April	1842	Construction of wheels for carriages and locomotive-engines, intended to be employed on railways.
LOSH, WILLIAM - - -	10,058	17th Feb.	1844	Manufacture of metal-chains, for mining and other purposes.
LOSH, WILLIAM - - -	12,265	4th Sept.	1848	Steam-engines.
LOSH, WILLIAM SEPTIMUS -	6646	17th July	1834	Bleaching certain animal fats, and certain animal, vegetable, and fish oils.
LOSH, WILLIAM SEPTIMUS -	8020	3rd April	1839	Reducing metallic-ores.
LOSH, WILLIAM SEPTIMUS -	14,147	29th May	1852	Purification of coal-gas.
LOSH, WILLIAM SEPTIMUS -	14,208	6th July	1852	Obtaining salts of soda.
L'OSIER, GERMAIN LE NORMAND DÉ.	8063	8th May	1839	Machinery for raising water.
LOSVELT, CORNELIUS - -	324	19th Sept.	1693	Engine for raising water, and craning and lifting goods and other things of weight, by an artificial flux and reflux of water.
LOTHIAN, JOHN - - -	8235	10th Oct.	1839	Apparatus for measuring or ascertaining weights, strains, or pressure.
LOTHMAN, CHARLES RUNHOLD	11,521	7th Jan.	1847	Manufacture of white-lead.
LOTT, JAMES - - -	13,813	15th Nov.	1851	Harness and fastenings.
LOUD, THOMAS - - -	2591	9th March	1802	Action and construction of upright pianofortes.
LOUGHTON, JOHN - - -	10,586	2nd April	1845	Manufacture of salt.
LOUIS, ABRAHAM - - -	5731	10th Dec.	1828	Mechanical volti-subito, to assist musical performers in turning over quickly the leaves of music-books.
LOUIS, FELIX HYACINTHE FOLLIET.	12,166	26th May	1848	Preserving certain animal products.

Name of Patentee.	Progressive Number.	Date.		Subject-matter of Patent.
Love, Richard - - -	11,466	1st Dec.	1846	Paving streets, roads, yards, and other surfaces over which carriages and beasts of burden have to pass.
Lovelace, William - -	1001	31st Jan.	1772	Making gut-strings for violins and other musical instruments. "Roman strings."
Lovell, Edward - - -	533	11th Oct.	1731	Styptic for the cure of the bloody flux, diarrhœa, vomiting, and all external and internal bleeding.
Lovi, Isabell - - -	2826	9th March	1805	Apparatus for determining the specific gravity of fluid bodies.
Low, Charles - - -	10,204	25th May	1844	Manufacturing iron and steel.
Low, Charles - - -	11,939	4th Nov.	1847	Manufacture of zinc, copper, tin, and other metals.
Low, Charles - - -	12,389	28th Dec.	1848	Smelting copper-ore.
Low, David - - -	8336	7th Jan.	1840	Machinery for crushing, preparing, and combing flax, hemp, phormium-tenax, and other fibrous substances.
Low, George - - -	13,904	20th Jan.	1852	Manufacture of gas for the purpose of illumination; purification of gas; treating the products arising from the manufacture of gas.
Low, John - - - -	11,594	24th Feb.	1847	Carriages to be used upon railways and other roads.
Lowcock, Henry - - -	9998	28th Dec.	1843	Ploughs.
Lowder, John - - -	4369	11th May	1819	Machines for the preparation of hemp or flax and other fibrous vegetable substances.
Lowe, Benjamin - - -	5386	14th July	1826	Dressing-pins.
Lowe, George - - -	3144	23rd June	1808	Manufacture of a fabric composed of flax and cotton.
Lowe, George - - -	6179	12th Oct.	1831	Manufacture of gas for illumination.
Lowe, George - - -	6276	9th June	1832	Increasing the illuminating power of coal-gas; converting the refuse arising in the manufacture of the same into an article of commerce not before used; also conducting the process of condensation in the manufacture of gas.
Lowe, George - - -	8298	4th Dec.	1839	Manufacture of gas for purposes of illumination.
Lowe, George - - -	8883	16th March	1841	Supplying gas; improving its purity and illuminating power.
Lowe, George - - -	11,238	4th June	1846	Increasing the illuminating power of coal-gas; converting the refuse arising in the manufacture of the same, into an article of commerce not before used; also conducting the process of condensation in the manufacture of gas.
Lowe, George - - -	11,405	8th Oct.	1846	Manufacture of gas; burning gas; manufacture of fuel.
Lowe, James - - - -	7599	24th March	1838	Propelling vessels.
Lowe, James - - -	14,263	19th Aug.	1852	Propelling vessels.
Lowe, Joseph - - -	12,798	12th Oct.	1849	Grates or grids applicable to sewers, drains, and other similar purposes.
Lowndes, Francis - -	2135	9th Sept.	1796	Machine for exercising the joints and muscles of the human body.
Lowndes, John - - -	3504	30th Oct.	1811	Heating baths.
Lowrey, Jane Bentley -	5630	25th March	1828	Manufacture of hats and bonnets.

Name of Patentee.	Progressive Number.	Date.	Subject-matter of Patent.
LOWTHER, WILLIAM - -	700	4th June 1755	Anti-epileptic powders for the cure of apoplexy, epilepsy, convulsions, and several other distempers.
LOWTHER, WILLIAM - -	718	12th Nov. 1757	Medicine which being made into powders, is a cure for nervous and paralytic disorders, and chemically made into drops is an immediate cure for nervous and other pains and weaknesses.
LUCAS, EDWARD - - -	1915	30th Oct. 1792	Fusing ores, metals, and calces of metals.
LUCAS, EDWARD - - -	6384	11th Feb. 1833	Self-acting force and lift-pump.
LUCAS, EDWIN - - -	10,468	16th Jan. 1845	Manufacture of chains.
LUCAS, JOHN ROBERT - -	2812	23rd Jan. 1805	Making, spreading, and flatting German sheet-glass, plate-glass, or other spread glass requiring a polished surface.
LUCAS, JONATHAN - - -	5472	10th March 1827	Process used in the dressing of paddy or rough rice,
LUCAS, JOSEPH - - -	1519	21st Dec. 1785	Convex mirror, lantern, or lamp, for lighting carriages and houses, and for other purposes.
LUCAS, JOSEPH - - -	1963	12th Oct. 1793	Lamps of glass and tin or other metal, also lanterns, burners, and frames with lens glasses.
LUCAS, ROBERT - - -	13,326	7th Nov. 1850	Telegraphic and printing apparatus.
LUCAS, SAMUEL - - -	623	27th July 1747	Erecting salt-pans for the boiling of salt.
LUCAS, SAMUEL - - -	1869	18th April 1792	Bringing iron-ore and calx of iron into a metallic state, without first rendering the same fluid.
LUCAS, SAMUEL - - -	2767	30th May 1804	Separating impurities from cast-iron without fusing the iron; rendering the same malleable.
LUCAS, THOMAS - - -	11,316	29th July 1846	Manufacture of lozenges or sweetmeats.
LUCCOCK, JOHN - - -	2297	28th Feb. 1799	Machine upon hydrostatic principles, for producing mechanical power, applicable to all the purposes of a steam-engine, but without the use of fire, steam, or water-wheel.
LUCENA, JAMES LANCASTER -	9810	1st July 1843	Steam-engines and machinery for propelling vessels;—applicable to other purposes.
LUCKCOCK, JOSEPH - -	4956	15th May 1824	Manufacturing iron.
LUCKCOCK, JOSEPH - -	5153	20th April 1825	Machinery for propelling vessels; applicable to other purposes.
LUCY, WILLIAM - - -	6889	24th Aug. 1835	Steam-engines.
LUCY, WILLIAM - - -	10,697	3rd June 1845	Preparing dough.
LUDLOW, EDWARD - -	2365	20th Dec. 1799	Playing-cards.
LUGG, THOMAS - - -	540	11th May 1733	Preventing the inconveniences arising from the running away of horses with coaches, chariots, chaises, and other four-wheeled carriages.
LUKE, JOHN - - - -	2126	4th July 1796	Machinery for the purpose of lifting, drawing, and conveying loaded and light vessels from one canal or branch of canal to another, on a slope or plain surface, in lieu of stone or other locks.
LUKENS, ISAIAH - - -	5255	15th Sept. 1825	Surgical-instrument for destroying the stone in the bladder without cutting. "Lithontriptor."
LUKIN, LIONEL - - -	1502	2nd Nov. 1785	Construction of boats and small vessels for sailing or rowing, and which will neither overset nor sink.

Name of Patentee.	Progressive Number.	Date.	Subject-matter of Patent.
LUKIN, LIONEL - - -	2534	20th Aug. 1801	Giving power to machinery by the application of air and water.
LUKIN, LIONEL - - -	5532	1st Aug. 1827	Manufacture of collars for draught and carriage horses; and saddles for draught, carriage, and saddle horses.
LUKYN, WILLIAM - - -	7954	29th Jan. 1839	Applying and attaching artificial and natural teeth.
LUMBERT, RICHARD - -	2373	4th Feb. 1800	Plough or machine for draining land.
LUMBERT, RICHARD - -	2897	23rd Nov. 1805	Thrashing-machine; portable windlass for drawing or hauling.
LUMSDEN, ROGER - - -	8523	30th May 1840	Manufacture of iron-knees for ships and vessels.
LUND, BENJAMIN - - -	495	3rd Feb. 1728	Manufacture of copper-ores, extracting silver therefrom, and making brass by mixing the copper with calamy and charcoal, also casting the same into plates, ingots, rods, kettles, and other utensils, by means of metal moulds instead of pots.
LUND, HENRY - - -	10,455	11th Jan. 1845	Manufacture of umbrellas and parasols.
LUND, HENRY - - -	13,610	30th April 1851	Propelling.
LUND, JOHN RICHARD - -	9969	25th Nov. 1843	Construction of compensation balances of chronometers.
LUND, THOMAS - - -	7761	3rd Aug. 1838	Extracting corks from wine and other bottles, with steadiness, facility, and safety.
LUNDHOLM, JOHN FREDERICK	10,871	10th Oct. 1845	Dressing ores requiring washing.
LUSCOMB, EDMUND - -	5306	6th Dec. 1825	Preparing oils extracted from certain vegetable substances; application thereof to gas-light and other purposes.
LUSCOMBE, MATTHEW -	1779	29th Oct. 1790	Composition or " naval black varnish" for paying yards, masts, blocks, and anchors of ships, also ships' bottoms, and for laying on copper for sheathing ships.
LUSHER, DENNIS - - -	11,442	5th Nov. 1846	Machinery for obtaining, applying, accelerating, and retarding motive-power; also for giving notice of alarm in cases of danger.
LUSTY, SAMUEL - - -	14,184	24th June 1852	Manufacturing wire into woven-fabrics and pins.
LUTEL, ELIZABETH OUDINOT	11,549	28th Jan. 1847	Producing a certain texture, elastic in some parts.
LUTTON, JAMES - - -	6380	31st Jan. 1833	Easy chairs.
LUTTON, JAMES - - -	6721	25th Nov. 1834	Castors for furniture.
LUTWYCHE, CHARLES THOMAS	11,215	22nd May 1846	Manufacture of porcelain-buttons.
LUTWYCHE, THOMAS - -	7208	13th Oct. 1836	Construction of apparatus used in the decomposition of common salt; method of using the same.
LYALL, JAMES BAGSTER -	13,604	26th April 1851	Construction of public carriages.
LYDALL, ROBERT - - -	351	4th Sept. 1697	Separating silver from lead, in a close furnace and with sea-coals, also making litharge and red-lead from the lead when so separated.
LYDALL, ROBERT - - -	368	13th June 1702	Smelting and melting black tin, and making the same into merchantable white tin.
LYDALL, ROBERT - - -	374	23rd July 1705	Separating gold and silver from tin, and refining the same; melting and smelting black tin ore, and making the same into white tin.

Name of Patentee.	Progressive Number.	Date.	Subject-matter of Patent.
LYDE, GEORGE - - -	1711	10th Nov. 1789	Coach-trumpet.
LYDE, GEORGE - - -	1841	28th Nov. 1791	Hats. " India summer hats."
LYDFORD, ROBERT - - -	1434	19th May 1784	Box for wheel-carriages, to be placed in the centre of the wheel, and work on the axle-tree.
LYMAN, JOHN CHESTER -	6632	24th June 1831	Hulling and cleansing rice and coffee; bearding and peeling barley.
LYNDSEY, ROBERT - - -	94	23rd June 1636	Making and erecting ovens, so as to economize the consumption of wood.
LYNE, GEORGE HENRY -	5246	23rd Aug. 1825	Machinery for making bricks.
LYON, DAVID - - -	9180	16th Dec. 1841	Cutting, dressing, preparing, and polishing stones, marble, and other substances; forming mouldings and other figures thereon.
LYON, JOSEPH - - -	2999	22nd Dec. 1806	Manufacture of pipes for the conveyance of water under ground.
LYONS, MORRIS - - -	11,632	23rd March 1847	Alloys of metals; deposition of metals.
LYTTLETON, WILLIAM - -	2000	15th July 1794	Machine for giving way to ships and other vessels, during calms and light winds. " Aquatic propeller."

M.

Name of Patentee.	Progressive Number.	Date.	Subject-matter of Patent.
MAAS, JOHANNES AMBROSIUS	3492	23rd Sept. 1811	Making vinegar.
MABERLY, FREDERICK HER-[BERT.	6862	13th July 1835	Propelling vessels.
MABERLY, FREDERICK HER-[BERT.	6999	10th Feb. 1836	Machinery for raking, scraping, and sweeping roads or streets.
MABERLY, FREDERICK HER-[BERT.	10,356	17th Oct. 1844	Construction and arrangement of machinery for clearing, cleansing, watering, breaking up and raking, streets, roads, lands, and other ways.
MABERLY, FREDERICK HER-[BERT.	10,514	10th Feb. 1845	Machinery for stopping or retarding railway or other carriages;—applicable also to engines or wheels.
MABERLY, FREDERICK HER-[BERT.	11,442	5th Nov. 1846	Machinery for obtaining, applying, accelerating, and retarding motive-power, also for giving notice of alarm in cases of danger.
MABERLY, JOHN - - -	3018	7th March 1807	Making and constructing tents, poles and other machinery, so as to expel and carry off noxious and contaminated air by a more effectual ventilation than by the tents in common use.
MABERLY, JOHN - - -	3818	25th June 1814	Securing carriage-glasses.
MABLEY, WILLIAM TUDOR -	8743	17th Dec. 1840	Producing surfaces to be used for printing, embossing, or impressing.
MABLEY, WILLIAM TUDOR -	9357	23rd May 1842	Machinery for making nails.
MABLEY, WILLIAM TUDOR -	10,461	11th Jan. 1845	Manufacture of buttons from horn or hoof; manufacture of articles in dies, from horn or hoof and other matters requiring similar pressure.

Name of Patentee.	Progressive Number.	Date.	Subject-matter of Patent.
MABLEY, WILLIAM TUDOR	13,270	3rd Oct. 1850	Manufacture of soap.
MACADAM, QUINTON	2924	26th March 1806	Dressing yarns for weaving by means of a machine.
MACALPIN, THOMAS [M'Alpin, Thomas.]	13,055	23rd April 1850	Machinery for washing cotton, linen, and other fabrics.
MACALPINE, WILLIAM	13,055	23rd April 1850	Machinery for washing cotton, linen, and other fabrics.
MACANASPIE, PATRICK [M'Anaspie, Patrick.]	14,339	2nd Nov. 1852	Manufacture of Portland-stone, cement and other compositions, for general building purposes and hydraulic-works.
MACBRIDE, JOHN [M'Bride, John.]	9032	21st July 1841	Machinery and apparatus for dressing and weaving cotton, silk, flax, wool, and other fibrous substances.
MACBRIDE, JOHN [M'Bride, John.]	10,259	15th July 1844	Machinery and apparatus for weaving by hand, steam, or other power.
MACBRIDE, JOHN [M'Bride, John.]	11,444	12th Nov. 1846	Weaving.
MACBRIDE, WILLIAM, junior [M'Bride, William, junior.]	12,566	2nd April 1849	Apparatus and process for converting salt-water into fresh water, and in oxygenating water.
MACBRIDE, WILLIAM CARDWELL. [M'Bride, William Cardwell.]	14,172	18th June 1852	Machinery for scutching or otherwise preparing flax and other like fibrous substances.
MACCARTHY, DENIS [M'Carthy, Denis.]	1573	11th Nov. 1786	Compound for covering houses, and for other purposes.
MACCARTHY, DENNIS [M'Carthy, Dennis.]	841	6th March 1766	Composition or cement called Pietra Cotta.
MACCARTHY, DENNIS	4153	5th Aug. 1817	Ploughs.
MACCARTHY, JOHN JAMES [ALEXANDER.	3915	11th May 1815	Pavement or coving, or a method of paving, pitching, or covering streets, roads, and ways.
MACCARTHY, JOHN JAMES [ALEXANDER.	4163	26th Aug. 1817	Road or way for passing across rivers, creeks, and waters, without stopping the navigation thereof, and likewise across ravines, fissures, cliffs, and chasms; constructing arches or apertures for the flowing of water through the same.
MACCARTHY, JOHN JAMES [ALEXANDER. [M'Carthy John James Alexander.]	4239	8th April 1818	Applying granite or other materials in forming pavement, pitching, and covering, for streets, roads, ways, and places.
MACCARTHY, JOHN JAMES [ALEXANDER.	5287	10th Nov. 1825	Pavement, pitching, or covering for streets, roads, ways, and places.
MACCARTHY, JOHN JAMES [ALEXANDER.	11,422	22nd Oct. 1846	Anchors; and fids for masts of vessels.
MACCLELLAN, CAREY [M'Clellan, Carey.]	12,424	16th Jan. 1849	Corn-mill.
MACCONNELL, JAMES EDWARD [M'Connell, James Edward.]	12,231	7th Aug. 1841	Steam-engines; retarding engines and carriages on railways; connecting railway-carriages or waggons together; effecting a communication with different parts of a railway-train by signals or otherwise.
MACCONNELL, JAMES EDWARD [M'Connell, James Edward.]	13,729	28th Aug. 1851	Locomotive steam-engines; and railway axles;—parts of which are applicable to stationary and marine steam-engines.
MACCONNELL, JAMES EDWARD [M'Connell, James Edward.]	14,182	24th June 1852	Steam-engines; boilers and other vessels for containing fluids; railways; materials and apparatus employed therein or connected therewith.

Name of Patentee.	Progressive Number.	Date.	Subject-matter of Patent.
MacConochie, John - - [M'Conochie, John.]	12,089	8th March 1848	Locomotive-engines.
MacConochie, John - - [M'Conochie, John.]	14,189	24th June 1852	Locomotive and other steam-engines and boilers; railways; railway-carriages and appurtenances; machinery for producing parts of the same.
MacCulloch, John - - [M'Culloch, John.]	11,862	9th Sept. 1847	Apparatus for distilling and rectifying.
MacCulloch, Kenneth - [M'Culloch, Kenneth.]	1663	12th Aug. 1788	Mariner's compass.
MacCurdy, John - - [M'Curdy, John.]	4974	15th June 1824	Generating steam.
MacCurdy, John - - [M'Curdy, John.]	5313	27th Dec. 1825	Generating steam.
MacCurdy, John - - [M'Curdy, John.]	5356	6th May 1826	Steam-engines.
MacCurdy, John - - [M'Curdy, John.]	5495	28th April 1827	Rectifying spirits.
MacCurdy, John - - [M'Curdy, John.]	5861	2nd Nov. 1829	Constructing mills and millstones for grinding.
MacCurdy, John - - [M'Curdy, John.]	6368	22nd Jan. 1833	Machinery for acquiring power in rivers and currents.
MacCurdy, John - - [M'Curdy, John.]	6819	23rd April 1835	Generating steam.
MacCurdy, John - - [M'Curdy, John.]	7890	1st Dec. 1838	Generating steam; applying the same to the evaporating and boiling of fluids;—applicable to steam-engines and to other purposes.
MacDonald, James - - [M'Donald, James.]	1699	29th Aug. 1789	Making breeches.
MacDonald, James - - [Macdonald, James.]	6187	31st Oct. 1831	Construction of bridges of iron or other materials;—applicable to piers, railroads, roofs, and other useful purposes.
MacDonald, James - - [Macdonald, James.]	6281	29th June 1832	Construction of railways.
MacDonald, James - - [Macdonald, James.]	6369	24th Jan. 1833	Construction of bridges made of iron or other materials;—applicable to other purposes.
MacDonald, James - - [M'Donald, James.]	12,925	11th Jan. 1850	Applying oil or grease to wheels, axles, and machiney; connecting springs of wheel-carriages with the axle or axle-boxes.
MacDonogh, Montagu - [Macdonogh, Montagu.]	9211	6th Jan. 1842	Spindles, flyers, and bobbins for spinning, twisting, and reeling fibrous or textile substances;—application or adaptation of any or all of them to machinery for the same purposes.
MacDougall, Alexander - [M'Dougall, Alexander.]	10,671	17th May 1845	Working atmospheric-railways.
MacDougall, Alexander - [M'Dougall, Alexander.]	11,523	14th Jan. 1847	Manufacture of glue; treating products obtained in the manufacture of glue.
MacDougall, Alexander - [M'Dougal, Alexander.]	12,333	21st Nov. 1848	Manufacture of sulphuric, nitric, and oxalic acid, chlorine, and sulphur.
MacDougall, Alexander - [M'Dougall, Alexander.]	12,529	20th March 1849	Recovering products from water used for washing and treating wool, woollen, and cotton fabrics, and other substances.
MacDougall, Daniel - [Macdougall, Daniel.]	5869	10th Nov. 1829	Syringes applicable to garden and other purposes.

Name of Patentee.	Progressive Number.	Date.	Subject-matter of Patent.
MacDowal, Charles - - [McDowal, Charles.]	13,587	10th April 1851	Construction of timekeepers.
MacDowall, John - - [McDowall, John.]	6606	12th May 1834	Metallic pistons; pump-buckets; and boilers of steam-engines.
MacDowall, John - - [McDowall, John.]	7133	24th June 1836	Machinery for sawing timber; mode of applying power to the same.
MacDowall, Joseph Eden -	7874	15th Nov. 1838	Manufacture of escapements for chronometers, clocks, and watches.
MacDowall, John - -	14,026	20th March 1852	Cutting wood and other substances; machinery employed therein; application of power to the same;—partly applicable for the transmission of power generally.
MacEvoy, Henry - - [McEvoy, Henry.]	8918	5th April 1841	Fastenings for bands, straps, and parts of wearing apparel.
MacEvoy, Henry - - [McEvoy, Henry.]	11,720	27th May 1847	Manufacture of hooks and eyes, also packing the same.
MacEwan, Alexander [Macewan, Alexander.]	7414	5th Aug. 1837	Process for improving teas as ordinarily imported.
MacFarlane, Malcolm [Macfarlane, Malcolm.]	12,756	30th Aug. 1849	Machinery for drying and finishing woven fabrics.
MacFarlane, William [McFarlane, William.]	3189	29th Dec. 1808	Construction of umbrellas and parasols.
MacFie, Robert Andrew [Macfie, Robert Andrew.]	13,147	24th June 1850	Manufacturing, refining, and preparing sugar; manufacturing and treating animal charcoal.
MacGary, William - - [McGary, William.]	11,284	6th July 1846	Lamps; lamp-glasses; candles and shades.
MacGauley, James William [McGauley, James William.]	11,162	7th April 1846	Steam-engines.
MacGauran, Thomas - [McGauran, Thomas.]	8209	26th Aug. 1839	Manufacture of paper from a material not hitherto so employed.
MacGavin, Robert - [McGavin, Robert.]	14,335	23rd Oct. 1852	Manufacture of iron for ship-building.
MacGetrick, Francis - [McGetrick, Francis.]	9604	26th Jan. 1843	Apparatus for preventing engines and carriages from going off railways, and for removing obstructions on railways.
MacGlashan, Alexander - [McGlashan, Alexander.]	12,779	20th Sept. 1849	Railway-breaks.
MacGlashen, Stewart - [McGlashen, Stewart.]	14,100	29th April 1852	Application of certain mechanical powers to lifting, removing, and preserving trees, houses, and other bodies.
MacGregor, Malcolm - [McGregor, Malcolm.]	3189	29th Dec. 1808	Construction of umbrellas and parasols.
MacGregor, Malcolm -	3349	19th June 1810	Flutes with improved keys; which keys are applicable to various other wind-instruments.
MacGregor, Malcolm - [McGregor, Malcolm.]	6698	20th Oct. 1834	Machines for slubbing, roving, spinning, twisting, and doubling cotton and other fibrous substances.
MacHenry, James -	14,234	20th July 1852	Machinery for manufacturing bricks and tiles.
MacInnes, John - - [McInnes, John.]	5928	24th April 1830	Preparation of certain substances; " British Tapioca," and the cakes and flour to be made from the same.
MacInnes, John - -	8461	31st March 1840	Renovating animal charcoal, after having been used in certain processes or manufactures, so as to render it fit for use a second time.

Name of Patentee.	Progressive Number.	Date.	Subject-matter of Patent.
MacINNES, JOHN [M‘Innes, John.]	9708	20th April 1843	Funnels for conducting liquids into vessels.
MacINNES, JOHN [M‘Innes, John.]	12,831	21st Dec. 1848	Packing lard.
MacINTOSH, CHARLES	4804	17th June 1823	Process and manufacture for rendering the texture of hemp, flax, wool, cotton, silk, and also leather, paper, and other substances, impervious to water and air.
MacINTOSH, CHARLES [M‘Intosh, Charles.]	5173	14th May 1825	Making steel.
MacINTOSH, JOHN [M‘Intosh, John.]	10,189	17th May 1844	Revolving-engines; producing motive-power; propelling vessels.
MacINTOSH, JOHN [M‘Intosh, John.]	10,661	8th May 1845	Preparing materials for colouring and printing calicoes and other fabrics; printing and ornamenting fabrics.
MacINTOSH, JOHN [M‘Intosh, John.]	11,537	19th Jan. 1847	Rotatory engines; moving carriages up inclines; propelling vessels.
MacINTOSH, JOHN	11,763	22nd June 1847	Engines to be worked by steam; propelling carriages and vessels.
MacINTOSH, JOHN	12,533	24th March 1849	Furnaces and machinery for obtaining power; regulating, measuring, and registering the flow of fluids.
MacINTOSH, JOHN [M‘Intosh, John.]	12,196	28th June 1848	Obtaining motive-power.
MacINTOSH, JOHN [Macintosh, John.]	12,968	12th Feb. 1850	Obtaining power in the floating of bodies and in conveying fluids.
MacINTOSH, JOHN [Macintosh, John.]	13,840	4th Dec. 1851	Steam-engines; rigging and propelling vessels, and facilitating their progress through water.
MacINTOSH, JOHN [Macintosh, John.]	14,041	24th March 1852	Ordnance and fire-arms, balls and shells.
MacINTOSH, JOHN [Macintosh, John.]	14,131	22nd May 1852	Manufacture of paper and articles of paper.
MacINTOSH, JOHN [Macintosh, John.]	14,293	18th Sept. 1852	Manufacturing and refining sugar.
MacINTOSH, PETER	1124	1st April 1776	Horizontal windmill with a multiplying power, which mill may be likewise worked by cattle, and the wind power applied to a water-mill.
MacINTOSH, THOMAS SIMMONS. [Mackintosh, Thomas Simmons.]	7437	28th Sept. 1837	Steam-engines.
MacKENZIE, COLIN [Mackenzie, Colin.]	1144	9th Jan. 1777	Axis or spindle to be fixed in cranks and pullies used in bell-hanging and other mechanical operations.
MacKENZIE, COLIN [Mackenzie, Colin.]	1497	19th Oct. 1785	Alarm-clatterer to prevent housebreaking; mode of fixing the same.
MacKENZIE, COLIN [Mackenzie, Colin.]	1823	13th Aug. 1791	Link for chains; making a mooring-chain, ship-cable chain, watch-chain, or any other chain by uniting such links together, and which can be lengthened or shortened by adding or taking away such links without cutting or breaking them.
MacKENZIE, DUNCAN [Mackenzie, Duncan.]	12,229	5th Aug. 1848	Jacquard-machinery for figuring fabrics and tissues; apparatus for transferring designs to the same;—partly applicable to playing musical instruments, composing printing types and other like purposes.

Name of Patentee.	Progressive Number.	Date.	Subject-matter of Patent.
MacKenzie, Duncan - - [Mackenzie, Duncan.]	14,194	29th June 1852	Machinery for reading in and transferring designs, and for cutting, punching, numbering or otherwise preparing, perforated cards, papers, or other materials, for the manufacture of figured textile fabrics by Jacquard or other looms or frames.
MacKenzie, Sir George [Steuart. [Mackenzie, Sir George Stewart.]	10,329	26th Sept. 1844	Manufacture of paper for writing and copying writings; machinery for the purpose; manufacture of a fluid to be used with the improved paper in the manner of ink.
MacKinley, William - - [McKinley, William.]	8697	10th Nov. 1840	Machinery for measuring, folding, plaiting or lapping goods or fabrics.
MacLardy, William - - [McLardy, William.	11,012	22nd Dec. 1845	Machinery applicable to the preparation and spinning of cotton-wool, silk, flax, and other fibrous substances.
MacLardy, William - - [McLardy, William.]	12,150	9th May 1848	Machinery applicable to the preparation and spinning of cotton-wool, silk, flax, and other fibrous substances.
MacLardy, William - - [McLardy, William.]	13,127	12th June 1850	Machinery or apparatus for preparing, spinning, and doubling cotton and other fibrous materials.
MacLellan, Archibald - [McLellan, Archibald.]	7811	13th Sept. 1838	Springs and braces of wheel-carriages; mode of hanging such carriages.
MacLellan, James - -	8821	30th Jan. 1841	Combination of materials for umbrella and parasol cloth.
MacLeod, John - - -	5829	11th Aug. 1829	Preparing certain substances so as to produce barilla, or a substitute for barilla.
MacMahon, William - - [McMahon, William.]	2546	30th Oct. 1801	Machine for gaining speed and power in all mechanical operations by land and water.
MacMillan, Charles - -	5830	11th Aug. 1829	Constructing, forming, or making streets, ways, carriage-roads, and highways in general.
MacMurray, William - [McMurray, William.]	8558	1st July 1840	Manufacture of paper.
MacNab, Andrew - - [McNab, Andrew.]	8956	11th May 1841	Manufacture of bricks.
MacNab, Andrew - - [McNab, Andrew.]	9021	7th July 1841	Construction of meters, or apparatus for measuring water or other fluids.
MacNab, John - - - [McNab, John.]	13,694	17th July 1851	Stretching and drying textile fabrics or materials; machinery employed therein.
MacNair, Archibald - - [McNair, Archibald.]	10,799	4th Aug. 1845	Construction and means of manufacturing apparatus for conducting electricity.
MacNamar, William - - [Macnamar, William.]	4011	23rd March 1816	Manufacturing glass.
MacNamara, Richard - [Macnamara, Richard.]	4616	20th Nov. 1821	Paving, pitching, and covering streets, roads, and other places.
MacNamara, Richard - [Macnamara, Richard.]	7324	15th March 1837	Paving, pitching, or covering streets and other ways;—applicable to other purposes.
MacNaught, William - [McNaught, William.]	11,001	10th Dec. 1845	Steam-engine.
MacNaught, William - [McNaught, William.]	12,988	7th March 1850	Steam-engines, and apparatus for ascertaining and registering the power of the same.
MacNaughtan, James - [Macnaughtan, James.]	2882	27th Sept. 1805	Stove or grate and range, by which rooms will be more effectually warmed, and chimneys prevented from smoking.

Name of Patentee.	Progres-sive Number.	Date.	Subject-matter of Patent.
MacNEE, JAMES - - - [*Macnee, James.*]	**7619**	21st April 1838	Carriages.
MacNEE, JAMES - - - [*Macnee, James.*]	**13,898**	20th Jan. 1852	Manufacture or production of ornamental fabrics.
MacNEIL, JOHN BENJAMIN - [*Macneil, John Benjamin.*]	**5652**	6th May 1828	Preparing and applying materials for making or rendering more durable, roads and other ways;—which materials so prepared are applicable to other purposes.
MacNEILL, JOHN - - - [*Macneill, John.*]	**7077**	3rd May 1836	Making or mending turnpike or common roads.
MacNEILL, JOHN - - - [*Macneill, John.*]	**7278**	11th Jan. 1837	Making or mending turnpike and other roads.
MacNEILL, Sir JOHN - [*Macneill, Sir John.*]	**12,758**	6th Sept. 1849	Locomotive-engines, and construction of railways.
MacNICOLL, JOHN - - [*Macnicoll, John.*]	**13,105**	6th June 1850	Machinery for raising and conveying weights.
MacONIE, PETER - - - [*McOnie, Peter.*]	**9180**	16th Dec. 1841	Cutting, dressing, preparing, and polishing stones, marble, and other substances; forming mouldings and other figures thereon.
MacRAE, ALEXANDER - -	**8329**	24th Dec. 1839	Machinery to be worked by steam or other power for ploughing, harrowing, and other agricultural purposes.
MacRAE, COLIN - - -	**8591**	5th Aug. 1840	Rotary-engines worked by steam, gases, smoke, or heated air; applying the same to useful purposes.
MacSWENY, THOMAS JOHN - [*McSweny, Thomas John.*]	**11,143**	25th March 1846	Steering ships and other vessels.
MACARTAN, FELIX - - -	**7864**	8th Nov. 1838	Treating the waste matters resulting from the washing of wool and woollen fabrics.
MACAULEY, THOMAS - -	**9130**	2nd Nov. 1841	Bed-steps convertible into other useful forms or articles of furniture.
MACCAUD, ETIENNE ABRAM -	**11,421**	22nd Oct. 1846	Lamp and gas burners.
MACERONI, FRANCIS - [*Macerone, Francis.*]	**6449**	18th July 1833	Boilers for generating steam.
MACERONI, FRANCIS - -	**8229**	27th Sept. 1839	Steam-boilers or generators.
MACHABEE, LAURENT - -	**14,156**	8th June 1852	Composition applicable to the coating of wood, metals, and other substances to be preserved from decay.
MACHELL, THOMAS - -	**4288**	24th Aug. 1818	Applying the agency of atmospheric air and liquid or gaseous substances to the human body, externally and internally, for medicinal purposes; employing oil and spirits on similar principles in lamps and other luminous apparatus.
MACHELL, THOMAS - -	**5425**	8th Dec. 1826	Apparatus for the burning of oil and other inflammable substances.
MACHELL, THOMAS - -	**9014**	28th June 1841	Raising and conveying water and other fluids.
MACHINE, JOHN - - -	**13,668**	17th June 1851	Boots and shoes.
MACHINE, WILLIAM - -	**7139**	2nd July 1836	Producing and transferring patterns in one or more colours or metallic preparations, to surfaces of metal, wood, cloth, paper or other suitable substances.
MACINDOE, GEORGE PARK -	**12,822**	2nd Nov. 1849	Machinery applicable to preparing, spinning, and doubling or twisting cotton-wool, silk, flax, and other fibrous substances.
MACKAY, GEORGE - - -	**8493**	5th May 1840	Rotatory-engines.

Name of Patentee.	Progressive Number.	Date.		Subject-matter of Patent.
MACKAY, JOHN - - -	760	6th Feb.	1761	Manufacturing salt.
MACKAY, JOHN - - -	1006	4th March	1772	Making salt from sea-water or brine, by steam.
MACKAY, PETER - - -	5430	13th Dec.	1826	Rendering the names of streets and other inscriptions, more durable and conspicuous.
MACKELCAN, FREDERICK PAYNE	8648	1st Oct.	1840	Thrashing-machinery;—a portion of which may be used as a means of transmitting power to other machinery.
MACKELCAN, FREDERICK PAYNE	8749	23rd Dec.	1840	Tables;—applicable to other articles of furniture.
MACKELL, ROBERT - - -	896	14th March	1768	Machine for dressing wheat, malt and other grain, before they are ground, and cleansing them from sand, dust and smut.
MACKIE, WILLIAM - - -	10,629	22nd April	1845	Window-sashes, and fastenings for window-sashes and shutters.
MADDICK, WILLIAM - -	14,079	20th April	1852	Production of a liquid extract from madder and its preparations, suitable for the purpose of dyeing or printing; treatment of spent madder, garancine or garancaux, or other preparations of madder, to render them again available for the like purposes.
MADDOCK, JOHN - - -	11,107	25th Feb.	1846	Building and constructing kilns or ovens used by potters and manufacturers of china and earthenware.
MADELEY, CHARLES - -	6434	6th June	1833	"Scarifier" or harrow.
MADELEY, WILLIAM - -	3943	27th July	1815	Drilling-machine, for drilling beans, turnips, peas, pulse, corn, and seeds of every description.
MADELEY, WILLIAM - -	5778	28th March	1829	Machine for catching and detaining depredators and trespassers.
MADELEY, WILLIAM - -	7746	26th July	1838	Machinery used for spinning cotton and other fibrous materials of a like nature, and for forming the same into cops upon spindles.
MADIGAN, RICHARD - -	11,852	2nd Sept.	1847	Railway turn-tables.
MADIGAN, RICHARD - -	12,125	15th April	1848	Manufacture of wheels for railways.
MAGALHEANS JOHN HYACINTH [DE.	825	28th March	1765	Instrument for showing the effect of the weight of the atmosphere with the variation caused by heat and cold, also the quantity of that variation.
MAGES, JOSEPH DE - -	937	7th Nov.	1769	Making baize for the Spanish and Portuguese trades to imitate French baize.
MAGNIN, JEAN MARIE - -	12,060	9th Feb.	1848	Machinery for sewing, embroidering, and for making cords or plats.
MAGNUS, GEORGE EUGENE -	8383	8th Feb.	1840	Manufacturing, polishing, and finishing slate; application of the same to domestic and other purposes.
MAGRATH, THOMAS - -	5076	11th Jan.	1825	Composition to preserve animal and vegetable substances.
MAGRATH, THOMAS - -	5077	11th Jan.	1825	Apparatus for conducting and containing water and other fluids, and preserving the same from frost.
MAHON, WILLIAM MC. - -	2546	30th Oct.	1801	Machine for gaining speed and power in all mechanical operations by land and water.

Name of Patentee.	Progres-sive Number.	Date.	Subject-matter of Patent.
MAIBEN, JOHN - - -	3333	2nd May 1810	Apparatus for making carbonated hydrogen-gas from pit-coal, and using the same for lighting mills, factories, houses, shops, lamps, &c., the lights being regulated by siphons.
MAILLARD, NICHOLAS DORAN	12,788	27th Sept. 1849	Obtaining motive-power for giving motion to machinery; propelling vessels.
MAIN DAVID - - - -	13,744	11th Sept. 1851	Steam-engines and furnaces.
MAIN, JOSEPH - - -	4430	15th Jan. 1820	Preparing and spinning wool, cotton, silk, flax, fur, and all other fibrous substances.
MAIN, JOSEPH - - -	4502	20th Oct. 1820	Wheeled-carriages.
MAIN, THOMAS - - -	13,327	8th Nov. 1850	Printing-machinery.
MAIRE, PETER FRANCIS - -	10,803	5th Aug. 1845	Combining iron and other materials for constructing bridges, roofs, arches, floors, and other similar structures.
MAJOR, WILLIAM - - -	12,376	16th Dec. 1848	Looms for weaving certain descriptions of cloth.
MALAM, JAMES - - -	9668	16th Mar. 1843	Manufacture of gas-retorts; and modes of setting the same.
MALAM, JAMES - - -	10,326	26th Sept. 1844	Purifying coal-gas; increasing its illuminating power; preventing its circulation being impeded by frost.
MALAM, JOHN - - -	4286	5th Aug. 1818	Steam-engines.
MALAM, JOHN - - -	4458	11th May 1820	Gas-meters.
MALAM, JOHN - - -	4832	18th Aug. 1823	Applying certain materials for constructing retorts; gas-apparatus.
MALAM, JOHN - - -	6844	2nd June 1835	Gas-meters; apparatus for generating gas for illumination.
MALAM, JOHN - - -	10,844	2nd Oct. 1845	Apparatus for watering, manuring, and drying trees, plants, seeds, and roots, and accelerating and improving their growth.
MALCOMSON, JOSEPH - -	10,770	12th July 1845	Apparatus used for propelling carriages on roads, and vessels on inland waters, by employing atmospheric pressure.
MALINS, WILLIAM - -	10,429	12th Dec. 1844	Constructing roofs and other parts of buildings, of iron or other metals; preparation of materials for constructing the same.
MALINS, WILLIAM - -	10,953	18th Nov. 1845	Constructing roofs and other parts of buildings, of iron or other metal; preparation of materials for constructing the same.
MALINS, WILLIAM - -	11,049	20th Jan. 1846	Construction of buildings.
MALLET, ROBERT - - -	9018	7th July 1841	Protecting cast and wrought iron and steel or other metals from corrosion and oxydation; preventing the "fouling" of iron ships, or other ships, or iron buoys.
MALLET, ROBERT - -	11,318	30th July 1846	Railway-carriages; machinery for working railways;—partly applicable to other carriages, and bearings of other machinery.
MALLET, WILLIAM - -	4519	14th Dec. 1820	Locks applicable to doors, and to other purposes.
MALLET, WILLIAM - -	5971	5th Aug. 1830	Constructing certain descriptions of wheel-barrows.
MALLORY, JAMES - - -	3412	12th March 1811	Making machines for cutting the fur from all peltries, and for shearing cloth.

Name of Patentee.	Progres- sive Number.	Date.	Subject-matter of Patent.
MALLORY, JAMES - - -	3476	7th Aug. 1811	Making a machine for cutting or shearing the nap or wool from broad and narrow cloths.
MALO, CHARLES ADRIEN -	5202	8th July 1825	Composition of wood and other substances.
MALO, GASPARD - - -	13,144	20th June 1850	Propelling vessels.
MALONE, THOMAS AUGUSTINE	12,906	19th Dec. 1849	Photography.
MALTBY, THOMAS - - -	2628	14th June 1802	Stirrup.
MALTBY, WILLIAM - -	8419	7th March 1840	Extracting and concentrating the colour, tannin, and other matter contained in vegetable and animal substances.
MALTBY, WILLIAM - -	11,998	15th Dec. 1847	Manufacture of spirits from grain or other saccharine matters ; apparatus to be used therein.
MALZEL, JOHN - - -	3966	5th Dec. 1815	Musical timekeeper, or " Metronome."
MAN, ROBERT - - -	325	19th Sept. 1693	Manufacturing and ordering roots and barks with other ingredients for dyeing silks, wrought and unwrought, and woollen and linen cloth in many colours, in grain and otherwise, with or without fire ; also useful for limners and painters, for perforating glass, and for other purposes.
MANIOR, LAWRENCE DU -	366	12th Sept. 1700	Engines, kilns, and instruments for the making of large rough looking-glass, plate-glass panels, and chimney pieces for rooms.
MANBY, ARON - - -	3705	31st May 1813	Making the refuse produced in the smelting of iron, into forms which may be used for bricks, quarries, tiles, slates, or stone.
MANBY, AARON - - -	4558	9th May 1821	Manufacturing steam-engines.
MANBY, EDWARD OLIVER -	8062	8th May 1839	Manufacturing gas for the general purposes of illumination.
MANBY, EDWARD OLIVER -	8820	30th Jan. 1841	Construction of puddling, balling, and other reverberatory furnaces, to fit them for burning anthracite, stone-coal, or culm.
MANBY, GEORGE - - -	111	26th Nov. 1637	Making mills for grinding corn, &c.
MANBY, JOHN - - -	8820	30th Jan. 1841	Construction of puddling, balling, and other reverberatory furnaces, to fit them for burning anthracite, stone-coal, or culm.
MANCEAUX, FRANCOIS JULES -	13,934	29th Jan. 1852	Fire-arms, and instruments and apparatus used in connection therewith.
MANDELL, NICHOLAS LEWIS -	392	27th June 1712	Making engines for weighing and raising up weights, also for raising water.
MANDER, JOHN - - -	3705	31st May 1813	Making the refuse produced in the smelting of iron, into forms which may be used for bricks, quarries, tiles, slates, or stone.
MANICLER, NICHOLAS HEGE-[SIPPI.	5345	20th March 1826	Preparation of fatty substances ; and application thereof for giving light.
MANICLER, NICHOLAS HEGE-[SIPPI.	6121	2nd June 1831	Manufacture of useful products from a certain oleaginous substance.
MANIQUET, JEAN BAPTISTE -	10,375	2nd Nov. 1844	Doubling, twisting, and reeling silk, cotton, and other substances.
MANLOVE, THOMAS - -	802	7th Dec. 1763	Making tarrass.
MANLEY, EDWARD - -	3237	30th May 1809	Plough.
MANLEY, EDWARD - -	3595	8th Oct. 1810	Apparatus for writing.
MANLEY, JAMES - - -	2524	1st July 1801	Manufacturing salt.
MANLY, JOHN, junior - -	13,134	12th June 1850	Manufacture of nails.

Name of Patentee.	Progres-sive Number.	Date.	Subject-matter of Patent.
MANN, THOMAS - -	1724	20th Jan. 1790	Instrument to supply the place of an amputated leg, constructed so as to perform the functions of the natural limb in all its joints.
MANN, THOMAS - - -	3398	31st Oct. 1810	Construction of artificial legs.
MANN, WILLIAM - - -	5797	1st June 1829	Communicating power and motion to machinery, carriages, and other locomotive engines, and to ships, vessels, and other floating bodies, by the application of compressed air.
MANNALL, JOHN - - -	1684	9th June 1789	Windlass-wheel to be affixed to a crane, for lifting weights.
MANNERING, GEORGE - -	9080	8th Sept. 1841	Raising water and other liquids.
MANNOURY, PIERRE MATTHEW	8680	5th Nov. 1840	Wind and stringed musical-instruments.
MANSELL, JOSEPH - - -	13,707	31st July 1851	Ornamenting paper and other fabrics.
MANSELL, RICHARD CHRISTO-[PHER.	12,170	1st June 1848	Construction of vehicles used on railways or on common roads.
MANSELL, RICHARD CHRISTO-[PHER.	14,089	24th April 1852	Construction of railways; railway rolling-stock; and machinery for manufacturing the same.
MANSELL, THOMAS - -	9529	3rd Dec. 1842	Machinery for cutting or shaping leather, paper, linen, lastings, silk, and other fabrics.
MANSFIELD, CHARLES BLACH-[FORD.	11,960	11th Nov. 1847	Manufacture and purification of spirituous substances and oils;—applicable to artificial light and various useful arts; application thereof to such purposes; construction of lamps and burners applicable to the combustion of such substances.
MANTELL, JOHN - - -	1155	13th May 1777	Making and refining common and sea-salt for curing fish and flesh and for other purposes; preparing a manure from the offals, and the salt so purified, and which by its attractive quality will impregnate the soil with saltpetre, and so establish perpetual saltpetre mines throughout the kingdom.
MANTON, GEORGE HENRY -	5838	2nd Sept. 1829	Locks on fowling-pieces or fire-arms.
MANTON, GEORGE HENRY -	7965	11th Feb. 1839	Fowling-pieces and other fire-arms.
MANTON, GEORGE HENRY -	12,543	28th March 1849	Priming fire-arms; apparatus for discharging fire-arms.
MANTON, JOHN - - -	2178	12th April 1797	Construction of guns and pistols.
MANTON, JOHN - - -	3286	11th Dec. 1809	Lock for guns and pistols.
MANTON, JOHN - - -	3942	21st July 1815	Construction of hammers and pans for the locks of fowling-pieces and fire-arms.
MANTON, JOHN - - -	4577	30th July 1821	Construction of locks of fowling-pieces and fire-arms.
MANTON, JOHN AUGUSTUS -	6572	13th March 1834	Fire-arms.
MANTON, JOSEPH - - -	1865	18th April 1792	Hammer for the locks of fire-arms; breech for double and single-barrelled guns and pistols.
MANTON, JOSEPH - - -	1893	5th July 1792	Triggers for double and single-barrelled guns and pistols; wadding for the same.
MANTON, JOSEPH - - -	2722	6th July 1803	Hammer for the locks of fowling-pieces and small-arms.
MANTON, JOSEPH - - -	2966	15th Sept. 1806	Double-barrelled guns.
MANTON, JOSEPH - - -	3085	5th Dec. 1807	Timekeepers.

Name of Patentee.	Progressive Number.	Date.	Subject-matter of Patent.
MANTON, JOSEPH - - -	3295	23rd Jan. 1810	Telescopes.
MANTON, JOSEPH - - -	3558	30th April 1812	Guns and pistols.
MANTON, JOSEPH - - -	3985	22th Feb. 1816	Construction and use of certain of the parts of fire-arms; shoeing horses.
MANTON, JOSEPH - - -	4166	26th Sept. 1817	Locks for fire-arms.
MANTON, JOSEPH - - -	4285	3rd Aug. 1818	Primers of fire-arms; construction of certain of the parts of fire-arms.
MANTON, JOSEPH - -	5106	26th Feb. 1825	Fire-arms.
MANTON, JOSEPH -	5135	25th March 1825	Shot.
MANTON, WILLIAM - -	4092	20th Jan. 1817	Application of springs to wheel-carriages.
MANWARING, GEORGE - -	4127	22nd May 1817	Steam-engines.
MANWARING, ISAAC - -	1792	10th Feb. 1791	Pendulum steam-engine with two or more cylinders, to work upon a wheel without a crank, long beam, or lever, and applicable to raising water, working mills, increasing the power of cranes, raising anchors, and assisting the navigation of vessels.
MANWARING, WILLIAM - -	9162	23rd Nov. 1841	Manufacture of sugar.
MAPPLE, HENRY - - -	11,428	27th Oct. 1846	Apparatus for transmitting electricity between distant places; electric-telegraphs.
MAPPLE, HENRY - - -	11,765	23rd June 1847	Communicating intelligence by electricity; apparatus relating thereto.
MAPPLE, HENRY - - -	12,711	18th July 1849	Communicating intelligence by means of electricity; electric-clocks.
MAPPLE, HENRY - - -	13,336	12th Nov. 1850	Electric-telegraphs; apparatus connected therewith.
MAPPLE, JAMES LODGE - -	11,765	23rd June 1847	Communicating intelligence by electricity; apparatus relating thereto.
MARBE, ABRAHAM MOSES -	13,048	18th April 1850	Manufacture of a vegetable fluid to be used in the production of artificial light; lamps or burners for consuming the same; which fluid is also applicable to the manufacture of lacker or varnish.
MARBOT, ANTOINE ADOLPHE [MARCELLIN.	5460	3rd Feb. 1827	Machinery for cutting wood into mouldings, rebates, cornices, or any fluted work.
MARBURY, WILLIAM - -	222	31st July 1682	Making salt; and draining brine-pits.
MARCESCHEAU, ARMAND JEAN [BAPTISTE LOUIS.	14,088	24th April 1852	Conveying letters, letter-bags, and other light parcels and articles.
MARCH, JAMES COLLEY - -	8979	8th June 1841	Producing heat from the combustion of certain kinds of fuel.
MARCH, JOHN - - -	1885	25th May 1792	Coaches, landaus, chariots, berlins, phaetons, post-chaises, and caravans, the bodies of which cannot overturn, and are more safe and convenient than ordinary carriages.
MARCH, RICHARD - - -	991	25th June 1771	Machine for making knitted-work for stockings, breeches-pieces and gloves, of silk, thread, cotton, and worsted.
MARCH, RICHARD - - -	1186	16th March 1778	Machine to be fixed to a stocking-frame for making single and double-cross looped and inlaid work.
MARCH, RICHARD - - -	1236	15th Nov. 1779	Machine for regulating and spinning wool, silk, cotton, flax, hemp, &c.
MARCH, RICHARD - - -	1445	28th July 1784	Machine for maufacturing platted work, plain and figured lace, lines, ropes, and cables, nets, and net-work.
MARCH, RICHARD - - -	1904	28th July 1792	Butter-churn.

Name of Patentee.	Progressive Number.	Date.		Subject-matter of Patent.
MARCH, RICHARD - - -	1911	18th Oct.	1792	Butter-churn.
MARCH, RICHARD - - -	2755	1st May	1804	Double seaming and uniting the insides of stocking-net work together, so as to make the same one compact and elastic body, for cutting into any shape, and converting into articles of hosiery or wearing-apparel.
MARCHANT, WILLOUGHBY -	662	4th April	1751	Making Castile soap.
MARCNARD, DANIEL AUGUSTINE	856	13th Aug.	1766	Machine for making women's mits and gloves.
MARE, CHARLES JOHN - -	13,992	27th Feb.	1852	Constructing iron ships or vessels, and steam-boilers
MARGARY, JOSHUA JOHN LLOYD	7511	19th Dec.	1837	Preserving animal or vegetable substances from decay.
MARGARET, THOMAS - -	2802	19th Dec.	1804	Mills and machinery for throwing, spinning, doubling and twisting thread of silk, cotton, flax, hemp, and other similar articles.
MARIE, DAVID - - -	771	20th April	1762	Constructing and making watches.
MARIE, DAVID - - -	840	6th Feb.	1766	Fire-machine (fire-escape).
MARIE, LEWIS ANNE ST. -	366	12th Sept.	1700	Engines, kilns, and instruments for the making of large rough looking-glass, plate-glass panels, and chimney-pieces for rooms.
MARINO, JOHN ALEXANDER [PHILIP DE VAL.	8126	22nd June	1839	Manufacture of gas; apparatus employed for consuming gas for the purpose of producing light.
MARKLAND, RICHARD - -	12,978	21st Feb.	1850	Method of and machinery for preparing warps for weaving.
MARKS, JOHN - - -	2278	8th Dec.	1798	Making breeches.
MARKWICK, ALFRED - -	11,213	20th May	1846	Manufacture of epithems used for medical and surgical purposes.
MARLOW, RICHARD - -	2251	14th July	1798	Hanging window-sashes and shutters, so as to conceal the appearance of the lines and pullies.
MARNAS, JEAN AIME - -	13,404	12th Dec.	1850	Manufacture of indigo.
MARR, WILLIAM - - -	6555	13th Feb.	1834	Manufacturing copper, iron, tin, and other metal safes, boxes, and repositories, so as to secure against fire the property contained therein.
MARRECO, ANTONIO JOAQUIM [FRIERE.	4114	29th April	1817	Manufacturing an instrument for calculating and ascertaining longitude at sea.
MARRIOTT, HENRY - -	5014	14th Oct.	1824	Water-closets.
MARRIOTT, HENRY - -	5190	18th June	1825	Stoves or grates.
MARRIOTT, HENRY - -	5636	29th March	1828	Hydraulic-machines.
MARSDEN, CHARLES - -	12,784	20th Sept.	1849	Traps to be applied to closets, drains, sewers, and cesspools.
MARSDEN, CHARLES - -	13,341	12th Nov.	1850	Scissors and thimbles.
MARSDEN, CHARLES - -	13,482	31st Jan.	1851	Boots and shoes.
MARSDEN, THOMAS - -	9468	8th Sept.	1842	Machinery for dressing or heckling flax and hemp.
MARSDEN, THOMAS - -	10,001	28th Dec.	1843	Drawing and spinning cotton and other fibrous substances.
MARSDEN, THOMAS - -	11,957	6th Sept.	1847	Machinery for dressing or combing flax, wool, or other fibrous substances.
MARSDEN, THOMAS - -	12,770	13th Sept.	1849	Machinery for heckling, combing, or dressing flax, wool, and other fibrous substances.

Name of Patentee.	Progressive Number.	Date.	Subject-matter of Patent.
MARSDEN, THOMAS - -	13,825	22d Nov. 1851	Machinery for heckling and combing flax and other fibrous materials.
MARSH, JAMES HENRY - -	4551	17th April 1821	Wheeled-carriages.
MARSH, JOHN - - -	12,736	9th Aug. 1849	Manufacture of looped fabrics, stays, and other parts of dress; apparatus for measuring.
MARSH, THOMAS - - -	3488	9th Sept. 1811	Construction of watches.
MARSH, THOMAS - - -	4961	20th May 1824	Making saddles.
MARSHALL, HEZEKIAH - -	8343	14th Jan. 1840	Window-sashes and frames, and fastening for window-sashes.
MARSHALL, JAMES - -	5511	26th June 1827	Mounting cannons or guns for sea or other service.
MARSHALL, JOHN - - -	2393	29th April 1800	Dining and other tables.
MARSHALL, JOHN - - -	2909	14th Feb. 1806	Manufacturing salt.
MARSHALL, JOHN - - -	5876	10th Dec. 1829	Preparing an extract from cocoa. "Marshall's extract of Cocoa."
MARSHALL, JOHN - - -	10,885	16th Oct. 1845	Preparing cocoa and chocolate.
MARSHALL, MARGARET HENRI- [ETTA.	9900	5th Oct. 1843	Plastic composition applicable to the fine arts, and to useful and ornamental purposes.
MARSHALL, MARY - -	235	3rd July 1684	Making, staining, and colouring stuff, so as to resemble tapestry hangings.
MARSHALL, RALPH - -	286	2nd Jan. 1692	Making spinnall yarn.
MARSHALL, RALPH - -	289	22nd Feb. 1692	Making spinnall yarn.
MARSHALL, WILLIAM - -	5640	26th April 1828	Machinery for cutting or shearing and finishing cloth, and other articles manufactured from wool or other raw materials.
MARSLAND, HENRY - -	1126	6th June 1776	Machine for doubling, throwing, and winding yarns of cotton-wool, silk, flax, hemp, or mohair, or of any other materials.
MARSLAND, PETER - -	2869	19th July 1805	Sizing cotton yarn.
MARSLAND, PETER - -	2870	19th July 1805	Dyeing silk, woollen, worsted, mohair, fur, hair, cotton, and linen, in a manufactured or raw state.
MARSLAND, PETER - -	2955	1st Aug. 1806	Weaving cotton, linen, silk, woollen, worsted, and mohair, by machinery.
MARSTON, ISAAC - - -	12,866	28th Nov. 1849	Manufacture of baths and wash-tubs or wash-vessels.
MARSTON, FRANCIS - -	9235	27th Jan. 1842	Apparatus for making calculations.
MARSTON, JOHN - - -	1165	1st Aug. 1777	Stamping upon plated metal, gilt and other metals, also hat and cloak pins, various decorations or devices, for furniture and lock-furniture.
MARTEN, EDWIN - - -	7936	12th Jan. 1839	Laying covering, composed of lead or other metal, on the roof of houses or other buildings with drains, whereby the water is carried off, and rolls and seams rendered unnecessary.
MARTEN, JOHN - - -	428	7th May 1720	Meliorating oils.
MARTIN, BENJAMIN - -	852	5th July 1766	Hydraulic-engine in the nature of a pump for raising water.

Name of Patentee.	Progressive Number.	Date.	Subject-matter of Patent.
MARTIN, BENJAMIN - -	1423	12th March 1784	Medicine for the cure of the hooping-cough and disorders of the stomach and lungs, and which is also an anti-scorbutic. "Anti-pertussis."
MARTIN, EDWARD - - -	2775	23rd June 1804	Making pig-iron and cast-iron from iron-stone, iron-mine, and iron-ore; remelting, preparing, and refining iron by blast, and making the same into bars, by using raw stone coal, and culm.
MARTIN, HENRY - - -	8458	30th March 1840	Preparing surfaces of paper.
MARTIN, JAMES - - -	7016	27th Feb. 1836	Dissolving and preparing caoutchouc or India-rubber, to render it applicable to various purposes.
MARTIN, JOHN - - -	1465	18th Feb. 1785	Roasting-jack, with pullies and other appurtenances. "Tourne-broche."
MARTIN, JOHN - - -	11,700	10th May 1847	Apparatus and means used for draining cities, towns, and other inhabited places, also land.
MARTIN, JOHN - - -	12,201	6th July 1848	Preparing and dressing flax, tow, and other fibrous substances; doubling, drawing, and twisting the same; machinery to be used for such purposes.
MARTIN, JOHN - - -	14,243	29th July 1852	Implements for hoeing.
MARTIN, JOSEPH - - -	13,351	16th Nov. 1850	Machinery and apparatus for cleansing and otherwise treating rice and certain other grains, seeds, and farinaceous substances.
MARTIN, JOSHUA LOVER -	1075	19th July 1774	Spring screw-fastenings for sashes.
MARTIN, JOSHUA LOVER -	1088	25th Nov. 1774	Hadley's quadrant, or sea octant and sextant.
MARTIN, JOSHUA LOVER -	1193	29th May 1778	Chain-belt for securing trunks to carriages, and which is fastened with a lock that cannot be picked.
MARTIN, JOSHUA LOVER -	1316	14th Jan. 1782	Drawing tubes plated with silver or gold on copper or other metal, for the construction of telescopes, perspectives, opera-glasses, and other instruments.
MARTIN, RICHARD FREEN -	6688	8th Oct. 1834	Combining various materials to form stucco, plasters, or cements, and for manufacture of artificial stone, marble, and other like substances used in buildings.
MARTIN, RICHARD FREEN -	8528	2nd June 1840	Manufacture of cement.
MARTIN, THOMAS - - -	2613	19th April 1802	Tanning and dressing hides and skins.
MARTIN, THOMAS - - -	2660	20th Nov. 1802	Applying fire by machinery for heating liquors; applying such heated liquors to use.
MARTIN, THOMAS - - -	4601	24th Oct. 1821	Making fine light black called spirit-black; apparatus for producing the same.
MARTIN, THOMAS - - -	6636	3rd July 1834	Machinery for cutting or preparing slates and similar substances, for various purposes.
MARTIN, THOMAS - - -	10,192	22nd May 1844	Construction of slated roofs, flats, floors, tanks, cisterns, or reservoirs for water; and improvements in pipes, tubes, or channels of the same materials, for conveying water.
MARTIN, THOMAS, junior -	11,972	18th Nov. 1847	Manufacture of drain-tiles and tubes and other articles, from plastic materials.
MARTIN, WILLIAM - -	839	6th Feb. 1766	Making silk-mits and silk-gloves.

Name of Patentee.	Progressive Number.	Date.	Subject-matter of Patent.
MARTIN, WILLIAM - -	2824	19th Feb. 1805	Fastening shoes to the feet of women and children.
MARTIN, WILLIAM - -	12,421	16th Jan. 1849	Machinery for figuring textile fabrics;—partly applicable to playing certain musical instruments, printing, and other like purposes.
MARTINEAU, JOHN - -	4870	20th Nov. 1823	Construction of the furnace of steam-boilers and other vessels, by which fuel is economised and smoke consumed.
MARTINEAU, JOHN - -	5259	6th Oct. 1825	Manufacture of steel.
MARTINEAU, JOHN, junior	3912	8th May 1815	Refining and clarifying certain vegetable substances.
MARTINEAU, PETER, junior -	3912	8th May 1815	Refining and clarifying certain vegetable substances.
MARTINEAU, ROBERT - -	5904	27th Feb. 1830	Cocks for drawing off liquids.
MARTINEAU, ROBERT - -	7650	24th May 1838	Cocks for drawing off liquids.
MARTYN, RICHARD LOMAX -	3499	30th Oct. 1811	"Agricultural Hoe" for hoeing turnips, and for other farming purposes.
MARVIN, RICHARD - -	11,230	28th May 1846	Gratings of metal or wood, for the fronts of houses and general purposes for the admission of light, and for ventilation.
MARWOOD, HUMPHREY - -	295	22nd April 1692	Taking fish by means of a light burning some fathoms under water and another burning above the water, by means of which the fish, within the compass of a league, can be drawn to one place, and thereby more easily taken.
MARYON, ROBERT JAMES -	13,770	10th Oct. 1851	Obtaining and applying motive-power; signalising.
MARX, FRANCIS - - -	9179	16th Dec. 1841	Construction of ships or other vessels; propelling the same.
MASERES, JOHN - - -	1383	9th Aug. 1783	Apparatus whereby persons may escape from houses or buildings, in case of accidents by fire.
MASNATA, DAVID FERDINAND	13,516	18th Feb. 1851	Mechanical system adapted to obtain a new moving power by means of compressed air.
MASON, CHARLES JAMES -	3724	23rd July 1813	Manufacture of English porcelain.
MASON, GEORGE, junior -	10,585	2nd April 1845	Collecting and raising stone or substances from below water.
MASON, ISAAC - - -	3800	7th April 1814	Making stamped fronts for stoves, fenders, tea-trays, mouldings, and other articles, in brass and other metals.
MASON, JAMES - - -	4368	8th May 1819	Working the oar or paddles of boats, barges, ships, and other kind of navigating-vessels.
MASON, JOHN - - -	8196	15th Aug. 1839	Machinery for boring and turning metals and other substances.
MASON, JOHN - - -	9078	8th Sept. 1841	Machinery employed in the manufacture of yarns and cloth; improvements applicable to the same.
MASON, JOHN - - -	12,535	26th March 1849	Machinery for preparing and spinning cotton and other fibrous materials; preparation of yarn; machinery for weaving the same.

Name of Patentee.	Progres- sive Number.	Date.	Subject-matter of Patent.
MASON, JOHN - - -	12,952	29th Jan. 1850	Machinery for preparing, spinning, and weaving cotton and other textile materials; preparing yarns or threads; machinery for the purpose.
MASON, JOHN - - -	13,408	12th Dec. 1850	Preparing cotton and other textile materials for spinning; apparatus for making cards and other parts of preparing-machinery; engines for giving motion to the same;—which engines are applicable in other cases where motive power is required.
MASON, JOHN - - -	14,140	22nd May 1852	Preparing, spinning, twisting, doubling, and weaving cotton-wool and other fibrous materials; apparatus for constructing parts of machines used in such manufactures.
MASON, JOSEPH - - -	257	3rd Oct. 1687	Engine for weaving without the aid of a draw-boy.
MASON, NATHANIEL - -	914	19th Jan. 1769	Crane-nook with an iron bar fixed horizontally against the end of the perch, for coaches, chariots, landaus, and chaises.
MASON, ROBERT - - -	1878	15th May 1792	Medicine for the extirpation of worms and their cause, from the human body; also for the relief and cure of other complaints.
MASON, ROBERT - - -	2685	28th Feb. 1803	Common waggon, which may be separated and used as two carts. "Patent Hampshire waggon."
MASON, SAMUEL - - -	106	18th May 1637	Making and dyeing buckrams and tilletts in whole pieces.
MASON, SAMUEL - - -	9236	27th Jan. 1842	Clogs;—applicable in part to shoes and boots.
MASON, SAMUEL - - -	9782	15th June 1843	Manufacture of boots, shoes, slippers, overalls, and clogs; machinery used in such manufacture; preparation of materials.
MASON, TIMOTHY - - -	6019	20th Oct. 1830	Manufacture of painting-brushes and other brushes;—applicable to various purposes.
MASON, WILLIAM - - -	466	15th April 1724	Machine called a siphon, or an attracting engine that acts without friction or solids, partly by friction and partly by force, of great use for preserving ships of war in engagements, and merchant-ships in diversity of distress at sea; also for draining mines, moors, and marshes, and raising water to extinguish fires.
MASON, WILLIAM - - -	5188	18th June 1825	Axletrees.
MASON, WILLIAM - - -	5451	15th Jan. 1827	Construction of axletrees and boxes for carriages or mail-coaches.
MASON, WILLIAM - - -	5986	24th Aug. 1830	Axletrees, and the boxes applicable thereto.
MASON, WILLIAM - - -	6151	10th Aug. 1831	Construction of wheeled-carriages.
MASON, WILLIAM - - -	6872	7th Aug. 1835	Making fire-arms and artillery.
MASON, WILLIAM - - -	6873	7th Aug. 1835	Manufacture of steam-engines, cylinders, pistons, bearings, pumps, and cocks.
MASON, WILLIAM - - -	6895	24th Sept. 1835	Wheels, boxes, and axletrees of carriages, for carrying persons and goods on common roads, and on railways.
MASSEY, EDWARD - -	2601	24th March 1802	Instrument for taking soundings at sea.
MASSEY, EDWARD - -	2938	6th June 1806	Instrument for taking soundings at sea.
MASSEY, EDWARD - -	3168	24th Sept. 1808	Cock for drawing off liquors.
MASSEY, EDWARD - -	3559	30th April 1812	Construction of chronometers.
MASSEY, EDWARD - -	3854	17th Nov. 1814	Chronometers and pocket-watches.

Name of Patentee.	Progressive Number.	Date	Subject-matter of Patent.
MASSEY, EDWARD - -	4465	19th May 1820	Construction of chronometers and pocket-watches.
MASSEY, EDWARD - -	6512	19th Nov. 1833	Pens and penholders.
MASSEY, EDWARD - -	6678	20th Sept. 1834	Pens and penholders.
MASSEY, EDWARD - -	6731	9th Dec. 1834	Apparatus used for measuring the progress of vessels through the water, and for taking soundings.
MASSEY, EDWARD - -	7113	13th June 1836	Apparatus used for measuring the progress of vessels through the water, and for taking soundings.
MASSEY, EDWARD - -	7807	13th Sept. 1838	Watches, and machines for keeping time.
MASSEY, EDWARD - -	9120	14th Oct. 1841	Watches.
MASSEY, EDWARD - -	10,210	1st June 1844	Apparatus for ascertaining the rate at which vessels are passing through the water; also applicable for ascertaining the rate at which streams are running.
MASSEY, EDWARD - -	12,071	18th Feb. 1848	Logs, and sounding-apparatus.
MASSEY, EDWARD JOHN -	7070	23rd April 1836	Railway and other locomotive carriages.
MASSEY, EDWARD JOHN -	7678	9th June 1838	Chronometers and other time-keepers.
MASSEY, EDWARD JOHN -	12,280	5th Oct. 1848	Apparatus for measuring the speed of vessels and streams, and the depths of water.
MASSEY, FRANCIS JOSEPH -	8947	4th May 1841	Winding-up watches and other time-keepers.
MASSIAH, SELIM RICHARD [ST. CLAIR.	13,218	10th Aug. 1850	Manufacture of artificial marble and stone; treating marble and stone.
MASSIE, ALEXANDER - -	6998	9th Feb. 1836	Construction of paddles or paddle-wheels for propelling vessels;—applicable to the construction of water-wheels for mills.
MASSON, ETIENNE - -	13,338	12th Nov. 1850	Preparation of certain vegetable alimentary substances for provisioning ships and armies, and for other purposes where the said substances are required to be preserved.
MASTERMAN, JOHN - -	5113	5th March 1825	Corking bottles.
MASTERMAN, THOMAS - -	4536	10th Feb. 1821	Machinery for imparting motion, and to be worked by steam and water, without cylinder or piston, also with less loss of power than occurs in working steam-engines now in use.
MASTERMAN, THOMAS - -	5095	19th Feb. 1825	Apparatus for bottling wine, beer, and other liquids, with increased economy and despatch.
MASTERMAN, THOMAS - -	10,071	24th Feb. 1844	" Refrigerator " for the speedy cooling of liquids within certain degrees of temperature.
MASTERS, JOHN - - -	7029	14th March 1836	Essence of anchovies.
MASTERS, JOHN - - -	10,694	31st May 1845	Trouser-fastenings; attaching the same; application of an elastic material to trousers and other articles of dress.
MASTERS, JOHN - - -	12,120	12th April 1848	Dress-fastenings; attaching the same; articles made wholly or in part of certain flexible materials or fabrics.
MASTERS, THOMAS - -	401	25th Nov. 1715	Cleaning and curing Indian-corn.
MASTERS, THOMAS - -	403	18th Feb. 1716	Working and staining in straw and chip, and the plat and leaf of the Palmeta tree; covering and adorning hats and bonnets.
MASTERS, THOMAS - -	9825	6th July 1843	Freezing, cooling, churning, and ice-preserving apparatus, the parts of which may be used either separately or in combination.

Name of Patentee.	Progressive Number.	Date.	Subject-matter of Patent.
MASTERS, THOMAS - -	11,453	17th Nov. 1846	Apparatus and means for cooling liquids and matters; filtering liquids, and preventing them from freezing.
MASTERS, THOMAS - -	12,330	18th Nov. 1848	Apparatus for making aërated waters; apparatus for charging bottles and other vessels with gaseous fluid; bottles or other vessels; apparatus for drawing off liquids; securing corks or stoppers in bottles or other vessels; taps and vent-pegs.
MASTERS, THOMAS - -	12,642	7th June 1849	Construction and arrangement of apparatus for cooking, also for heating, and evaporating fluids; obtaining decoctions and infusions from certain vegetable and animal matters;—applicable to certain chemical processes.
MASTERS, THOMAS - -	13,857	11th Dec. 1851	Retaining and drawing off aërated and other liquids; charging vessels with gaseous fluids;—applicable to vessels for holding solid matters, also as a fastening for utensils and apparatus; holders for cigars.
MATCHAM, GEORGE - -	2676	29th Jan. 1803	Mechanical power for raising great weights, preventing ships from sinking, raising ships when sunk, rendering ships capable of entering rivers, passing bars or shoals, or otherwise moving in shallow water, and for other purposes.
MATCHETT, FREDERICK COOK	9666	16th March 1843	Manufacture of hinges.
MATHER, COLIN - - -	10,752	3rd July 1845	Boring earth, stone, and subterraneous matter; machinery, tools, or apparatus applicable to the same.
MATHER, COLIN - - -	11,183	28th April 1846	Metallic pistons.
MATHER, COLIN - - -	13,310	2nd Nov. 1850	Machinery for washing, steaming, drying, and finishing cotton, linen, and woollen fabrics.
MATHER, COLIN - - -	14,022	11th March 1852	Printing, damping, stiffening, opening, and spreading woven fabrics.
MATHER, HENRY - - -	1633	5th Dec. 1787	Gilding and ornamenting goods of British manufacture, made of cotton, or linen and cotton, also goods made of wool, cotton and wool, or linen and wool, with gold and silver leaf, and with yellow or white Dutch-metal leaf.
MATHER, JAMES, junior - -	13,248	5th Sept. 1850	Machinery or apparatus for scouring, finishing, and stretching woollen, cotton, and other woven fabrics.
MATHER, JOSEPH BIRCH -	7476	14th Nov. 1837	Machinery employed in manufacturing hosiery-goods, or frame-work knitting.
MATHER, WILLIAM - -	10,752	3rd July 1845	Boring earth, stone, and subterraneous matter; machinery, tools, or apparatus applicable to the same.
MATHER, WILLIAM - -	11,183	28th April 1846	Metallic pistons.
MATHER, WILLIAM - -	13,310	2nd Nov. 1850	Machinery for washing, steaming, drying, and finishing cotton, linen, and woollen fabrics.
MATTHEW DANIEL DERING -	3125	27th April 1808	Construction of watches and chronometers.
MATHEW, FELTON - - -	2091	22nd Feb. 1796	Separating beer from the yeast; preserving yeast in any climate.
MATHEW, FELTON - - -	3546	5th March 1812	Manufacturing yeast.

Name of Patentee.	Progres- sive Number.	Date.	Subject-matter of Patent.
MATHEW, NATHANIEL - -	13,019	23rd March 1850	Apparatus for cutting or dressing slates into various shapes and sizes.
MATHEWS, DAVID - - -	3376	7th Sept. 1810	Constructing and building locks with a groin or gothic conic-arch; form of the gates; opening and shutting the same.
MATHEWS, THOMAS - -	346	14th Dec. 1695	Damasking, striking, and fixing colours on both sides, on leather, stuffs, cloths, velvets, and hair; making tapestry with gro-gram yarn.
MATHIEU, FRANCOIS - -	14,300	23rd Sept. 1852	Apparatus for containing, aërating, refrigerating, filtering and drawing off liquids; ornamenting such apparatus.
MATLEY, JAMES - - -	7412	2nd Aug. 1837	"Tiering-machine" to be used by block-printers for supplying colours in the printing of cotton, linen, and woollen-cloths, silks, paper, and other substances, and articles to which block-printing is applied and without manual aid.
MATLEY, JAMES - - -	7485	23rd Nov. 1837	Machinery for the operation of tiering used in printing cotton, linen, woollen, silks, papers, and other articles and substances to which block-printing can be applied.
MATLEY, JAMES - - -	8285	25th Nov. 1839	Instruments for the cutting of cotton or the wicks of lamps.
MATTERFACE, ABRAHAM -	3036	21st April 1807	Construction of a machine for mashing and mixing malt.
MATTHEW JOHN - - -	11,017	23rd Dec. 1845	Steam-engines; machinery for propelling vessels;—applicable to other purposes.
MATTHEWS, GEORGE - -	1276	9th Jan. 1781	Engine to work by the power of fire and steam; and to be used in iron and copper manufactories.
MATTHEWS, GEORGE - -	1360	22nd March 1783	Making cast-iron malleable and suitable for making cannon, wheel-tires, arms to axletrees, anchors, chains, iron mill-work, forge-hammers, bar and chain shot, and iron-rollers.
MATTHEWS, HENRY - -	4312	19th Nov. 1818	Wheeled-carriages.
MATTHEWS, JOHN - - -	12,159	22nd May 1848	Treating malt-liquors and other liquids or fluids; machinery for the purpose.
MATTHEWS, JOHN - - -	13,306	2nd Nov. 1850	Sizing paper.
MATTHEWS, THOMAS GADD -	8491	5th May 1840	Machinery for sawing, rasping, or dividing dye-woods or tanners' bark.
MATTHEY, JAMES FREDERICK	2991	4th Dec. 1806	Fire-arms and guns.
MAUDSLAY, HENRY - -	2872	29th July 1805	Press for printing calicoes and other articles.
MAUDSLAY, HENRY - -	2948	24th July 1806	Combining wheelwork so as to produce any velocity between the weight and first-mover.
MAUDSLAY, HENRY - -	3050	13th June 1807	Construction of steam-engines.
MAUDSLAY, HENRY - -	3117	14th March 1808	Machines for printing calicoes and other articles.
MAUDSLAY, HENRY - -	3538	8th Feb. 1812	Sweetening water and other liquids;—applicable to other purposes.
MAUDSLAY, HENRY - -	5021	14th Oct. 1824	Method and apparatus for continually changing the water in boilers for generating steam; particularly applicable to the boilers of steam-vessels, as it prevents depositions from the water, retains the heat, saves fuel, and renders the boilers more lasting.

Name of Patentee.	Progressive Number.	Date.		Subject-matter of Patent.
MAUDSLAY, JOSEPH - -	5531	1st Aug.	1827	Steam-engines.
MAUDSLAY, JOSEPH - -	6482	7th Oct.	1833	Structure of certain boilers for producing steam for the working of steam-engines.
MAUDSLAY, JOSEPH - -	8060	7th May	1839	Construction of marine steam-engines.
MAUDSLAY, JOSEPH - -	.8881	16th March	1841	Arrangement and combination of certain parts of steam-engines to be used for steam-navigation.
MAUDSLAY, JOSEPH - -	9833	13th July	1843	Machinery used for propelling vessels by steam power.
MAUDSLAY, JOSEPH - -	10,124	28th March	1844	Steam-engines.
MAUDSLAY, JOSEPH - -	10,396	16th Nov.	1844	Steam-engines.
MAUDSLAY, JOSEPH - -	10,637	24th April	1845	Propelling; propelling-machinery.
MAUDSLAY, JOSEPH - -	11,039	13th Jan.	1846	Propelling; propelling-machinery.
MAUDSLAY, JOSEPH - -	11,908	14th Oct.	1847	Manufacture of candles;—partly applicable to other substances capable of being moulded.
MAUDSLAY, JOSEPH - -	12,088	8th March	1848	Obtaining and applying motive-power; machinery and engines employed therein.
MAUDSLAY, JOSEPH - -	13,921	26th Jan.	1852	Steam-engines;—applicable wholly or in part to pumps and other motive machines.
MAUGHAN, JOHN - - -	8639	24th Sept.	1840	Construction of wheeled-carriages.
MAUGHAM, WILLIAM - -	7039	22nd March	1836	Production of chloride of lime and certain other chemical substances.
MAUGHAM, WILLIAM - -	7277	11th Jan.	1837	Manufacture of carbonate of soda.
MAUGHAM, WILLIAM - -	7326	15th March	1837	Manufacture of white-lead.
MAUGHAM, WILLIAM - -	9618	31st Jan.	1843	Preparing aërated water.
MAUGHAM, WILLIAM - -	10,641	29th April	1845	Manufacture of ale, porter, and other fermented liquors.
MAUGHAM, WILLIAM - -	10,973	27th Nov.	1845	Manufacture of ale, porter, and other fermented liquors.
MAULE, JOHN - - -	2186	4th July	1797	Machine for clearing grain from the straw.
MAULE, THOMAS - - -	226	9th June	1683	Engine for rendering salt and brackish water sweet, and fit for drinking, cooking, washing, and other uses.
MAULLIN, RICHARD - -	2379	28th Feb.	1800	Machine to mould patterns for casting wood, bed and other screws of cast iron, brass, or other metallic compositions.
MAUNDRELL, RICHARD - -	225	25th April	1683	Casting and making hollow pewter or block-tin buttons.
MAUNSELL, DANIEL - -	2076	8th Dec.	1795	Horizontal windmill for grinding corn and for other purposes.
MAUNSELL, Sir ROBERT, Knight	24	22nd May	1623	Making glass with sea-coal, pit-coal, or any other fuel, not being timber or wood.
MAUREL, FRANCOIS MARIE [AGATHE DEZ.	9087	20th Sept.	1841	Buckles.
MAUREL, FRANCOIS MARIE [AGATHE DEZ.	10,748	3rd July	1845	Manufacture of soap.
MAURIER, LOUIS MATHURIN [BUSSONDU.	7924	3rd Jan.	1839	Construction of springs for carriages.
MAURRAS, ANDRÉ EUSTACHE [GRATIEN AUGUSTE.	9520	15th Nov.	1842	Process and apparatus for filtering water and other liquids.
MAW, HENRY LISTER - -	6141	20th July	1831	Method of using fuel so as to burn smoke.
MAW, JOHN HORNBY - -	6345	17th Dec.	1832	Form and arrangement of parts of an apparatus for injecting enemata.

Name of Patentee.	Progres-sive Number.	Date.	Subject-matter of Patent.
MAW, JOHN HORNBY - -	11,412	15th Oct. 1846	Manufacture of pens.
MAW, ROBERT - - -	694	26th Nov. 1754	Liquid blue for linens, cottons, &c.
MAXFIELD, THOMAS - -	1436	4th June 1784	Gut strainings for making elastic saddles which will give ease in riding to both rider and horse.
MAXWELL, HENRY - -	5684	13th Aug. 1828	Spring spur-sockets.
MAXWELL, JOHN - - -	1715	8th Dec. 1789	Spring fastening for shoe-buckles.
MAXWELL, STEPHEN - -	1617	1st Aug. 1787	Worm for distillation, with a reservoir at the top for receiving the steam raised from the still.
MAY, CHARLES - - -	8560	6th July 1840	Machinery for cutting and preparing straw, hay, and other vegetable matters.
MAY, CHARLES - - -	8847	15th Feb. 1841	Manufacture of railway-chairs, railway and other pins or bolts, wood fastenings and trenails.
MAY, CHARLES - - -	9842	15th July 1843	Machinery for ploughing and scarifying land and for raking, also machinery used in thrashing, cutting, and grinding for agricultural purposes; construction of whippletrees.
MAY, CHARLES - - -	10,358	22nd Oct. 1844	Working atmospheric-railways; machinery for constructing the apparatus employed therein.
MAY, CHARLES - - -	11,168	15th April 1846	Machinery for punching, rivetting, and shearing metal plates.
MAY, CHARLES - - -	11,641	27th March 1847	Railway-chairs; fastenings used therewith; trenails.
MAY, CHARLES - - -	13,065	30th April 1850	Machinery for thrashing and grinding corn, cutting straw and similar substances; applying steam power to give motion to such machinery; machines for depositing seed.
MAY, CHARLES - - -	13,801	4th Nov. 1851	Permanent-way of railways.
MAY, JAMES DE - - -	249	9th Jan. 1686	Making writing and printing paper; imprinting the royal arms thereon; mills and engines for the purpose.
MAY, STRIBBLEHILL NORWOOD	14,229	20th July 1852	Manufacture of thread, yarn and various textile fabrics, from certain fibrous matters.
MAYBURY, JOHN - - -	6214	24th Jan. 1832	Manufacturing and polishing tinned and iron ladles, spoons, and other articles, for culinary, domestic, and other purposes.
MAYBURY, JOSEPH - -	6214	24th Jan. 1832	Manufacturing and polishing tinned and iron ladles, spoons, and other articles, for culinary, domestic, and other purposes.
MAYBURY, JOSEPH, junior -	6214	24th Jan. 1832	Manufacturing and polishing tinned and iron ladles, spoons, and other articles, for culinary, domestic, and other purposes.
MAYER, ANTONIO JAMES -	11,104	25th Feb. 1846	Wood cutting machines.
MAYER, JAMES - - -	8297	4th Dec. 1839	Machine for cutting splints for matches.
MAYER JOSEPH WICKHAM -	2799	19th Dec. 1804	Bridle-bits.
MAYER, MATTHEW JAMES -	3470	31st July 1811	Construction of the instantaneous light machine.
MAYERNE, Sir THEODORE, [Knight.	81	25th March 1635	Distilling strong waters, and making vinegars of cyder, perry, and buck or French wheat.
MAYHEW, WILLIAM - -	5328	7th Feb. 1826	Manufacture of hats.

Name of Patentee.	Progressive Number.	Date.	Subject-matter of Patent.
MAYNE, THOMAS DE LA	1475	3rd May 1785	Making buttons of burnt earth or porcelain.
MAYO, EDWARD	211	9th June 1681	Making bay salt (licence under Du Fresue's patent).
MAYO, WILLIAM	9713	25th April 1843	Manufacture of aërated liquors; vessels used for containing aërated liquors.
MAYO, WILLIAM	11,223	26th May 1846	Manufacture of aërated liquids; bottling aërated and other liquids.
MAYO, WILLIAM	11,471	1st Dec. 1846	Manufacture of aërated liquids; apparatus used for such manufacture, and in pumping liquids; bottling fluids.
MAYO, WILLIAM	12,976	21st Feb. 1850	Connecting tubes, pipes, and other surfaces of glass and earthenware; connecting other matters with glass and earthenware.
MAYOR, JOHN	4560	9th May 1821	Machinery for raising water. "Hydragogue."
MAZELINE, JEAN BAPTISTE [FRANCOIS.	12,420	16th Jan. 1849	Steam-engines; and machinery for propelling vessels.
MAZZINI, JOSEPH	9731	16th May 1843	Typographical printing, combining the advantage of moveable types with the stereotype process, or substituting for distribution a special font for each new work, by means of a pneumatic-machine for casting, and a uniplane machine for composing.
MEACOCK, JAMES	10,979	4th Dec. 1845	Pulping, dressing, and sorting coffee.
MEACOCK, JAMES	12,121	12th April 1848	Preventing and extinguishing fires in vessels, warehouses, and other buildings.
MEAD, CHARLES ROPER	13,468	21st Jan. 1851	Apparatus for measuring gas, water, and other fluids.
MEAD, THOMAS	1543	20th April 1786	Automaton, or machine on a self-moving principle, which will acquire any degree of velocity desired, and also give motion to any machinery to which it can be applied.
MEAD, THOMAS	1628	15th Nov. 1787	Regulator for furling and unfurling the sails of windmills when at work, for grinding corn and dressing flour and meal.
MEAD, THOMAS	1822	12th Aug. 1791	Reciprocating fire or steam-engine for use in pumps, mills, cranes, carriages, and other purposes where the force of fire or steam is required.
MEAD, THOMAS	1979	6th March 1794	Exerting and putting in motion apparatus, whether pneumatic, chemical, or pneumato-chemical; also continuing the same in motion by the decomposition, recomposition, expansion, and condensation of permanently elastic fluids, and thus producing power sufficient to move machinery, and continue the same in motion.
MEAD, THOMAS	3163	24th Aug. 1808	Making and constructing circular or rotative steam-engines.
MEAD, THOMAS	3686	28th April 1813	Endless chain, with appendages.
MEADE, HENRY MANDEVILLE	10,829	18th Sept. 1845	Distilling from Indian-corn and other grain.
MEADE, HENRY MANDEVILLE	11,007	20th Dec. 1845	Manufacture of bread.
MEADE, HENRY MANDEVIELE	11,169	15th April 1846	Preparing food for animals when Indian-corn is used.
MEADE, JOSEPH FULTON	10,765	12th July 1845	Steam-engines and boilers.

Name of Patentee.	Progressive Number.	Date.	Subject-matter of Patent.
MEADON, JOHN - - -	5574	4th Dec. 1827	Wheels for carriages.
MEADOWS, JOHN - - -	12,791	27th Sept. 1849	Veneering.
MEAKIN, THOMAS - - -	7676	20th Nov. 1838	Looms for weaving; also a new description of fabric to be produced or woven therein.
MEARES, ROBERT - - -	1561	10th Oct. 1786	Swivel and socket for the perches of four-wheeled carriages.
MEARES, ROBERT - - -	2404	20th May 1800	Machine for cutting standing corn, grass, and the like.
MECHI, JOHN JOSEPH - -	8509	12th May 1840	Lighting buildings.
MECHI, JOHN JOSEPH - -	8695	10th Nov. 1840	Apparatus to be applied to lamps, to carry off heat and the products of combustion.
MECKENHEIM, LOUIS NICOLAS [DE.	9373	31st May 1842	Manufacture of iron.
MECKENHEIM, LOUIS NICOLAS [DE.	11,620	10th March 1847	Machines used in the manufacture of nails, screw-blanks, rivets, bolts, and pins.
MEDEIROS, JOHN CARVALHO [DE.	7581	28th Feb. 1838	Producing gas for illumination; apparatus connected with the consumption thereof.
MEDHURST, GEORGE - -	2299	28th Feb. 1799	Condensing wind-engine.
MEDHURST, GEORGE - -	2431	2nd Aug. 1800	Driving carriages without the use of horses.
MEDHURST, GEORGE - -	2467	27th Jan. 1801	Compound crank, for changing a circular motion into a rectilinear motion, and vice versâ;—applicable to various mechanical purposes.
MEDHURST, GEORGE - -	2525	10th July 1801	Machines for washing and wringing linen, woollen, wool, cotton, silk, velvet, or any other commodity.
MEDHURST, GEORGE - -	4164	26th Aug. 1817	Arrangement of implements to form certain apparatus, called "Hydraulic Balance";—applicable to mechanical and hydraulic purposes.
MEDHURST, HENRY - -	12,222	26th July 1848	Gas-meters.
MEDHURST, HENRY - -	13,337	12th Nov. 1850	Gas-meters.
MEDHURST, HENRY - -	14,304	27th Sept. 1852	Water-meters; regulating and ascertaining the supply of water and liquids.
MEE, JOHN - - - -	8975	5th June 1841	Manufacture of looped fabrics.
MEËUS, JOSEPH - - -	10,196	22nd May 1844	Weaving; weaving-machines.
MEGE, JOSEPH - - -	9333	26th April 1842	Making trousers.
MEGGITT, SAMUEL - - -	7140	2nd July 1836	Anchors, and apparatus for fishing the same;—applicable to anchors in common use.
MEIKELAM, ROBERT - -	5375	6th June 1826	Engines moved by the pressure, elasticity, or expansion of steam, gas, or air.
MEIKLE, ANDREW - - -	896	14th March 1768	Machine for dressing wheat, malt, and other grain, and cleansing them from sand, dust, and smut.
MEIKLE, ANDREW - - -	1645	9th April 1788	Machine, which may be worked by cattle, wind, water, or other power, for the purpose of separating corn from the straw.
MEIN, ALEXANDER - -	13,391	7th Dec. 1850	Treating the fleeces of sheep when on the animals.
MEINIG, CHARLES LUDOVIC [AUGUSTUS.	12,847	17th Nov. 1849	Applying galvanism and magnetism to curative and sanatory purposes.
MEINZIES, MICHAEL - -	544	15th Feb. 1734	Thrashing grain with a row of flails fixed in an axis turned backwards and forwards, which thus thrashes the grain on both sides.

Name of Patentee.	Progressive Number.	Date.		Subject-matter of Patent.
MEINZIES, MICHAEL - -	653	9th Feb.	1750	Machine for carrying coals from the coal walls to the bottom of the shaft, and from the mouth of the shaft to the heaps, and for other purposes.
MEINZIES, MICHAEL - -	762	20th May	1761	Working mines of coals and metals.
MELL, JAMES - - -	309		1692	Tanning skins for leather, and making imitation Russian leather.
MELLIER, MARY AMIDÉE [CHARLES.	13,979	23rd Feb.	1852	Manufacture of paper.
MELLING, JOHN - - -	7254	15th Dec.	1836	Locomotive steam-engines to be used on railways or other roads;—partly applicable to stationary engines and machinery in general.
MELLING, JOHN - - -	7410	26th July	1837	Locomotive steam-engines to be used on railways;—partly applicable to stationary steam-engines and machinery in general.
MELLING, THOMAS -	11,199	7th May	1846	Steam-engines, marine, stationary, and locomotive; machinery connected therewith;—partly applicable to regulating the flow of fluids generally.
MELLISH, SAMUEL - -	2672	21st Dec.	1802	"Tatham's clumps" for the purpose of constructing water-pipes, sewers, tunnels, wells, conduits, reservoirs, or other circular walls, shelves, or buildings.
MELLISH, THOMAS ROBERT -	13,229	22nd Aug.	1850	Cutting, staining, silvering, and fixing articles of glass.
MELLISH, THOMAS ROBERT -	13,624	7th May	1851	Instruments and apparatus for the admission of light and air into carriages and buildings; also for the exclusion of light and air from the same; manufacture of reflectors;—partly applicable to the decoration of furniture.
MELLODEW, THOMAS - -	6628	16th June	1834	Construction of power-looms; manufacture of corded fustian or fabric to be woven in diagonal cords, from cotton-wool and other fibrous materials.
MELLODEW, THOMAS - -	7642	15th May	1838	Looms for weaving.
MELLODEW, THOMAS - -	12,309	2nd Nov.	1848	Manufacture of velvets, velveteens, and other similar fabrics.
MELLOR, SAMUEL ANDREW -	5743	18th Dec.	1828	Gig-mills for raising and finishing woollen cloths and other fabrics.
MELVILL, JOHN - - -	1051	5th Aug.	1773	Machine or stove-engine for boiling sugar, soap, or other articles which require to be boiled in large vessels, and for distilling liquors.
MELVILLE, ALEXANDER -	13,215	6th Aug.	1850	Muskets, cannon, and other fire-arms; explosive compositions and instruments.
MELVILLE, FRANCIS - -	5085	18th Jan.	1825	Securing square-pianofortes from injuries arising from the tension of the strings.
MELVILLE, JAMES - -	14,047	29th March	1852	Weaving and printing shawls and other fabrics.
MELVILLE, JOHN - - -	5707	18th Sept.	1828	Propelling vessels.
MELVILLE, JOHN - - -	7562	8th Feb.	1838	Generation of steam; application of steam or other power to navigation.
MELVILLE, JOHN - - -	8805	21st Jan.	1841	Propelling vessels.
MELVILLE, JOHN - - -	9348	11th May	1842	Propelling vessels.
MELVILLE, JOHN - - -	10,168	30th April	1844	Construction of railroads, and mode of working the same.

Name of Patentee.	Progressive Number.	Date.	Subject-matter of Patent.
MELVILLE, JOHN - - -	10,485	21st Jan. 1845	Propelling vessels.
MELVILLE, JOHN - - -	13,179	17th July 1850	Construction of railways, locomotive-engines, and carriages,
MELVILLE, WILLIAM - -	13,445	11th Jan. 1851	Manufacturing and printing carpets and other fabrics.
MENCKE, WILLIAM - -	5681	11th Aug. 1828	Preparing materials, and for manufacturing bricks.
MENDAY, JOSEPH - - -	14,337	23rd Oct. 1852	Construction of kilns for burning or calcining cement, chalk, limestone, and other substances ; application of the heat therefrom to the generation of steam.
MENISH, WILLIAM - - -	1898	5th July 1792	Manufacturing sal-ammoniac, and glauber and other salts.
MENOTTI, CELESTE - -	13,431	27th Dec. 1850	Chemical compositions for rendering cotton, linen, woollen, silk, and other fabrics impervious to water, and for fixing colours in dyeing.
MERCER, JOHN - - -	8183	1st Aug. 1839	Processes to be used in the printing, dyeing, or colouring of cotton, woollen, silk, and other cloths and yarns.
MERCER, JOHN - - -	9517	10th Nov. 1842	Manufacture of articles used in printing and dyeing cotton, silk, woollen, and other fabrics.
MERCER, JOHN - - -	10,757	8th July 1845	Manufacture of certain chemical agents used in dyeing and printing cottons, woollens, and other fabrics.
MERCER, JOHN - - -	11,190	2nd May 1846	Scouring and clearing wool and woollen fabrics, also bleaching and clearing silk, cotton, linen, and other fabrics.
MERCER, JOHN - - -	11,252	22nd June 1846	Dyeing and printing Turkey-red and other colours.
MERCER, JOHN - -	11,742	12th June 1847	Certain substances applicable to the manufacture, scouring, and washing of wool, woollen-fabrics, and other substances.
MERCER, JOHN - -	12,807	12th Oct. 1849	Certain materials used in the processes of dyeing and printing.
MERCER, JOHN - -	13,296	24th Oct. 1850	Preparation of cotton and other fabrics and fibrous materials.
MERCER, JOHN - -	14,024	15th March 1852	Preparing cotton and other fabrics for dyeing and printing.
MERCHANT, ALEXANDER -	138	2nd May 1662	Curing smoky chimneys by altering the course of the smoke towards the top, or by inserting tunnels with checks.
MERCHANT, GEORGE - -	893	29th Feb. 1768	Milling raw hides and skins so as to be equally good for leather as if tanned.
MERCHANT, THOMAS - -	12,670	25th June 1849	Construction of railway-carriages.
MERCIE, CHARLES - - -	2580	6th Feb. 1802	Air-slides, to be fixed to windows, doors, and partitions, to prevent the ingress of air.
MERCIER, SEBASTIAN - -	10,430	12th Dec. 1844	Pianofortes.
MERCY, CHARLES - - -	5249	8th Sept. 1825	Propelling vessels.
MERLIN, JOSEPH - - -	1032	29th Jan. 1773	Spring-jack, having a reflector to increase the heat, and thereby save fuel.
MERLIN, JOSEPH - - -	1081	12th Sept. 1774	Compound harpsichords, with a set of hammers similar to those in a pianoforte, in addition to quills ; adding such hammers to common harpsichords.
MERRICKS, THOMAS - -	1824	16th Aug. 1791	Construction of ploughs.

Name of Patentee.	Progressive Number.	Date.	Subject-matter of Patent.
MERRIMAN, NATHANIEL	2756	8th May 1804	Stove, grate, or range; applicable to those used in churches, chapels, houses, buildings, and rooms.
MERRY, ANTHONY THEOPHILUS	7018	8th March 1836	Application of certain plated white metal to certain manufactures to which it has not hitherto been applied.
MERRY, ANTHONY THEOPHILUS	8890	22nd March 1841	Process for obtaining zinc and lead from their respective ores, and for calcination of other metallic bodies.
MERRY, THOMAS - - -	1380	26th July 1783	Engine to cut, split, and divide asunder the flesh side from the grain side of hides, skins, and leather.
MERRYWEATHER, JOHN - -	4006	23rd March 1316	Propelling boats and vessels.
MERSEY, SAMUEL - - -	4156	7th Aug. 1817	Weaving livery-lace and coach-lace.
MERTENS, ANTOINE - -	9186	16th Dec. 1841	Manufacture of plaited fabrics.
MERTENS, ANTOINE - -	9231	22nd Jan. 1842	Covering surfaces with wood.
MERTIAN, BAZIL LOUIS - -	3820	12th July 1814	Extracting jelly or gelatinous matter from substances capable of affording the same, for use in the arts, or for domestic or other purposes.
MERTIN, JAMES - - -	76	18th Dec. 1634	Making and using engines for raising water out of mines and other places.
MESUIL, EUGENE DU - -	5533	1st Aug. 1827	Stringed musical-instruments.
MESURIER, FREDERICK LE -	7812	13th Sept. 1838	Construction of pumps for raising water or other fluids.
MESSURIER, HENRY LE - -	8112	17th June 1839	Pumps.
METCALF, DAVID - -	10,398	21st Nov. 1844	Manufacturing or preparing a vegetable preparation, applicable to dyeing blue and other colours.
METCALF, JACOB - -	4065	30th Sept. 1816	Tapered hair or head-brush.
METCALFE, JOHN - -	12,232	8th Aug. 1848	Machinery for preparing and spinning cotton and other fibrous substances.
METCALFE, THOMAS -	10,422	7th Dec. 1844	Manufacture of brooms, brushes, or other similar articles.
METCALFE, THOMAS -	10,595	7th April 1845	Propelling carriages;—applicable to driving certain machinery.
METCALFE, THOMAS -	12,279	5th Oct. 1848	Construction of chairs, sofas, and other articles of furniture for sitting upon.
METHLEY, THOMAS CHARLES	9007	26th June 1841	Machinery for raising, lowering, and moving bodies or weights.
METHLEY, WILLOUGHBY -	9007	26th June 1841	Machinery for raising, lowering, and moving bodies or weights.
METTEMBERG, CHEVALIER JO- [SEPH DE.	5112	26th Feb. 1825	Vegetable, mercurial, spirituous preparation; "Quintessence antipsorique, or Mettemberg's Water;" employing the same by cutaneous absorption as a specific and medical cosmetic.
MEURATO, DAVID DE - -	141	4th Feb. 1663	Making and framing sugar-mills.
MEYER, FREDERICK - -	13,081	25th May 1850	Treating fatty, oleaginous, resinous, bituminous, and cerous bodies; manufacture and application of such bodies, their compounds and subsidiary products, with the apparatus to be employed therein; also their application to new and other purposes.

Name of Patentee.	Progressive Number.	Date.	Subject-matter of Patent.
MEYER, HENRY - - -	7833	17th Oct. 1838	Manufacture of lamps.
MEYER, HENRY - - -	13,217	10th Aug. 1850	Power-looms for weaving.
MEYER, MEYER - - -	11,929	2nd Nov. 1847	Manufacture of umbrellas and parasols.
MEYER, PHILIP JAMES - -	2596	24th March 1802	Machines to prevent danger to persons driving in curricles, chaises, or other carriages, in consequence of horses taking fright while harnessed thereto.
MICHAEL, GEORGE - -	4267	26th May 1818	Opening and shutting windows or sashes; application of machinery for opening window-shutters.
MICHAUT, GEORGE AMBROISE	11,997	15th Dec. 1847	Production and application of heat; and manufacture of coke.
MICHELL, JAMES - - -	6853	22nd June 1835	Smelting argentiferous ores.
MICHELL, JOHN - - -	9692	11th April 1843	Extracting copper, iron, lead, bismuth, and other metals or minerals from tin-ore.
MICHELL, JOHN - - -	14,295	18th Sept. 1852	Purifying tin-ores, and separating ores of tin from other minerals.
MICHELL, THOMAS - -	1620	28th Aug. 1787	Raising water and other fluids for the purpose of driving mills and other machines, and watering lands, also draining land and pumping water from ships, extinguishing fires in houses, and for other purposes.
MICHELL, TOBIAS - -	3832	4th Aug. 1814	Machinery for raising water for impelling machinery, and for other purposes.
MICHELL, TOBIAS - -	4877	9th Dec. 1823	Form of nails for securing copper and other sheathing on ships, and for other purposes.
MICHELL, TOBIAS - -	7463	7th Nov. 1837	Washing or purifying smoke and vapours evolved from furnaces.
MICHIELS, GEORGE - -	13,066	30th April 1850	Treating coal; manufacture of gas; apparatus for burning gas.
MICHIELS, GEORGE - -	13,284	17th Oct. 1850	Treating and preparing potatoes for seed.
MIDDLEMORE, WILLIAM -	11,287	13th July 1846	Saddles.
MIDDLETON, EDWARD -	14,087	24th April 1852	Fire-arms, ordnance, and projectiles used with such weapons; machinery for manufacture of parts of such fire-arms, ordnance, and projectiles.
MIDDLETON, HUGH - -	19	2nd July 1621	Winning and draining grounds overflowed with water.
MIDDLETON, THOMAS -	9356	23rd May 1842	Preparing vegetable gelatine or size for paper; also applying the same in the manufacture of paper.
MIDDLETON, THOMAS - -	10,286	5th Aug. 1844	Machinery for the manufacture of artificial fuel.
MIDDLETON, THOMAS - -	10,506	31st Jan. 1845	Machinery for the manufacture of artificial fuel, bricks, tiles, and other similar articles.
MIDGLEY, GEORGE DEAKIN -	7460	4th Nov. 1837	Obtaining ammoniacal-salts from liquor produced in the manufacture of coal-gas.
MIDGLEY, ROBERT - -	5342	4th March 1826	Apparatus for conveying persons and goods across rivers, valleys, and other places.
MIDWORTH, WILLIAM - -	9837	13th July 1843	Construction of street guard-plates for public water-service; constructing the stop-valves or stop-cocks for the same;—applicable to other purposes where the flow of water or other liquid is required to be regulated.

Name of Patentee.	Progres-sive Number.	Date.		Subject-matter of Patent.
MIERS, JOHN - - - -	3495	30th Oct.	1811	Accelerating the evaporation of liquid or fluid bodies, destroying effluvia from spent soap-lees and other liquid, fluid, or solid substance.
MIKOVINIJ, ANTHONY - -	1145	23rd Jan.	1777	Composition for the manufacturing, improving, dressing, and bleaching of hemp, flax, and other vegetable substances, also cloth of hemp and all other cloth and yarn.
MILBOURN, RICHARD - -	3087	9th Dec.	1807	Roving-machine for preparing flax, tow, and wool, for spinning.
MILES, JOHN - - - -	1591	12th Feb.	1787	Lamps.
MILES, THOMAS - - -	4799	3rd June	1823	Machines for shearing or cropping woollen-cloth.
MILL, HENRY - - -	376	12th April	1706	Mathematical instrument, consisting of several springs, for the ease of persons riding in coaches, chaises, and other conveyances.
MILL, HENRY - - -	395	7th Jan.	1714	Impressing or transcribing letters, singly, or progressively one after another, in writing, so neatly as not to be distinguished from print.
MILL, WILLIAM - - -	8636	21st Sept.	1840	Propellers and steam-engines; method of ascertaining and measuring steam-power;— partly applicable to other purposes.
MILL, WILLIAM - - -	11,266	29th June	1846	Instruments used for writing and marking; construction of inkstands.
MILLAR, JOHN - - -	2624	31st May	1802	Tanning leather.
MILLARD, JOHN - - -	3717	14th July	1813	Manufacturing cotton-wool into cloth suitable for the purpose of regulating perspiration.
MILLBOURN, SAMUEL - -	8310	13th Dec.	1839	Manufacture of paper.
MILLBOURN, SAMUEL - -	11,394	3rd Oct.	1846	Manufacture of paper.
MILLER, CHARLES TAVERNER	5896	4th Feb.	1830	Manufacture of candles.
MILLER, DANIEL - - -	12,638	5th June	1849	Drawing ships out of water up an inclined plane.
MILLER, FREDERICK -	14,144	29th May	1852	Apparatus for hatching eggs.
MILLER, GEORGE - - -	3383	1st Oct.	1810	Making military fifes, of substances never before used for that purpose.
MILLER, GEORGE - - -	4750	16th Jan.	1823	Communicating the spiral motion to shot and shells when fired from plain barrels, and igniting by percussion, shells to which the spiral motion has been communicated.
MILLER, GEORGE ALEXANDER	6551	6th Feb.	1834	Lamps.
MILLER, GEORGE ALEXANDER	11,778	3rd July	1847	Lamps.
MILLER, JAMES - - -	3878	28th Jan.	1815	Construction of stills, furnaces, chimneys, and other apparatus connected with distillation.
MILLER, JAMES CAPPLE -	8195	15th Aug.	1839	Printing calicoes, muslins, and other fabrics.
MILLER, JOHN - - -	4	1st July	1617	Making an oil to be used for preventing the formation of rust and canker on armour and arms.
MILLER, JOHN - - -	8043	23rd April	1839	Drilling-machine.
MILLER, JOHN - - -	12,183	13th June	1848	Accelerating menattrite locomotion, in transport machines acting by wheels, on land or water.
MILLER, JOSEPH - - -	9107	29th Sept.	1841	Arrangement and combination of certain parts of steam-engines used for steam-navigation.

379

Name of Patentee.	Progressive Number.	Date.	Subject-matter of Patent.
MILLER, PATRICK - - -	2106	3rd May 1796	Construction of a vessel which will draw less water than any other of the same dimensions, and which cannot founder at sea; method of putting the same into motion, in calms and light winds.
MILLER, ROBERT - - -	2122	28th June 1796	Looms worked by water, steam, horse, or other power, for weaving linen, cotton, and woollen and other cloths.
MILLER, SAMUEL - - -	1108	22nd Nov. 1775	Machine for pumping water out of ships, and for adding velocity to the same by the use of sculls; loading and unloading goods.
MILLER, SAMUEL - - -	1152	11th April 1777	Machine for sawing wood, stone, and ivory.
MILLER, SAMUEL - - -	1545	13th May 1786	Machine for weighing.
MILLER, SAMUEL - - -	1913	26th Oct. 1792	Machine for raising heavy goods.
MILLER, SAMUEL - - -	2047	14th April 1795	Machine and process for preparing cork for ornament and use.
MILLER, SAMUEL - - -	2372	4th Feb. 1800	Machine and process for dividing hard substances, raising heavy weights, and drawing machinery.
MILLER, SAMUEL - - -	2543	13th Oct. 1801	Machine and process for manufacturing materials for securing walls and roofs of houses from lateral pressure and the inclemency of the weather.
MILLER, SAMUEL - - -	2689	16th March 1803	Applying the repelling force of nature to give impulse to any body in motion.
MILLER, SAMUEL - - -	2854	27th May 1805	Machinery to be attached to coaches and other carriages, for the accommodation of passengers.
MILLER, SAMUEL - - -	2887	30th Oct. 1805	Steam-engines.
MILLER, SAMUEL - - -	2926	1st April 1806	Working coal, tin, lead, and other mines.
MILLER, TAVERNER JOHN -	9565	22nd Dec. 1842	Apparatus for supporting a person in bed or when reclining.
MILLER, THOMAS - - -	440	30th March 1722	Burning bricks, tiles, and lime.
MILLER, WILLIAM - - -	4570	17th July 1821	Printing.
MILLER, WILLIAM - - -	8178	1st Aug. 1839	Grates used in steam-engines or other furnaces or fire-places.
MILLICHAP, GEORGE - -	4495	18th Aug. 1820	Axletree and boxes.
MILLICHAP, GEORGE - -	6588	31st March 1834	Locomotive machines or carriages.
MILLICHAP, GEORGE - -	10,405	25th Nov. 1844	Construction of axletrees.
MILLIGAN, ROBERT - -	13,005	18th March 1850	Mode of treating certain floated warp or weft, or both, for producing ornamental fabrics.
MILLIGAN, ROBERT - -	13,607	26th April 1851	Ornamenting certain cloth-fabrics.
MILLIGAN, WILLIAM - -	11,075	4th Feb. 1846	Power-looms.
MILLIGAN, WILLIAM EMERY -	13,874	19th Dec. 1851	Construction of boilers for generating steam.
MILLINGTON, BRYAN - -	13,301	24th Oct. 1850	Corn-cleaning and flour-dressing machines.
MILLINGTON, JOHN - -	3977	1st Feb. 1816	Machinery moved by wind, steam, manual labour, or any process now employed for moving machinery, for propelling boats, barges, and other floating vessels.
MILLS, GEORGE - - -	10,750	3rd July 1845	Springs and elastic power as applicable to railway-carriages and other vehicles, and to other purposes.
MILLS, GEORGE - - -	13,831	22nd Nov. 1851	Steam-engine boilers, and steam propelling-machinery.

Name of Patentee.	Progressive Number.	Date.	Subject-matter of Patent.
MILLS, ISAAC - - - -	456	27th June 1723	Two instruments of iron, to be used in wool-combing and pressing.
MILLS, JOHN - - - -	3894	14th March 1815	Elastic stays for women and children.
MILLS, JOHN - - - -	4796	31st May 1823	Waterproofing leather, linen, flax, sail-cloth, and certain other articles.
MILLS, SAMUEL - - -	7502	9th Dec. 1837	Machinery for rolling metals.
MILLS, THOMAS - - -	13,185	22nd July 1850	Steam-engines and pumps.
MILLS, WILLIAM - - -	5416	18th Oct. 1826	Fire-arms.
MILLS, WILLIAM - - -	9729	16th May 1843	Fastenings for gloves and other wearing-apparel, and mode of attaching the same.
MILNE, BENJAMIN - - -	3386	1st Oct. 1810	Bell and gun alarm.
MILNE, JAMES - - -	5847	15th Sept. 1829	Machine for dressing stones used in masonry, by means of steam, wind, horse, or water-power.
MILNE, JAMES - - -	7734	13th July 1838	Apparatus employed in transmitting gas for the purpose of affording light and heat.
MILNE, JOHN - - - -	827	10th May 1765	Machine or wire-cylinder for dressing flour from wheat, barley, and other grain.
MILNE, JOHN - - - -	968	13th Oct. 1770	Wire-cylinders worked by gear, and used in wind or water-mills, for dressing wheat, barley, and other grain ; also for dressing flour.
MILNE, JOHN - - - -	6133	13th July 1831	Roving-frames and slubbing-frames, used for preparing cotton-wool for spinning.
MILNER, THOMAS - - -	8401	26th Feb. 1840	Boxes, safes, or other depositories for the protection of papers and other materials from fire.
MILNER, WILLIAM - - -	2402	15th May 1800	Making women's pattens.
MILNER, WILLIAM - - -	13,540	3rd March 1851	Boxes, safes, or other depositories for the protection of papers and other materials from fire.
MILNES, JAMES - - -	12,468	12th Feb. 1849	Apparatus used in stopping steam-engines and other first movers.
MILNES, JAMES - - -	12,849	17th Nov. 1849	Apparatus used for stopping steam-engines and other first movers.
MILNES, THOMAS BROWN -	14,261	19th May 1818	Machinery for finishing cotton, Angola, and lambs'-wool stockings, and other frame-work goods ; applying known power for working the same.
MILNES, THOMAS BROWN [Milnes, James Brown.]	6931	14th Nov. 1835	Machinery for embroidering bobbin-net lace or other fabrics made from silk, cotton-wool, flax, or hemp.
MILNES, THOMAS BROWN -	6937	3rd Dec. 1835	Machinery for manufacturing bobbin-net lace.
MILNS, JOHN CLARKSON -	13,449	11th Jan. 1851	Machinery used in spinning, doubling, and weaving cotton, flax, and other fibrous substances.
MILON, MARCEL JEAN - -	11,403	8th Oct. 1846	Making roads and ways,
MILSON, CHARLES - - - [Edward Nelthorpe's Invention.]	195	14th Feb. 1677	Engine or mill for hulling black pepper or barley.
MILTON, JAMES - - -	4278	11th July 1818	Loom-work, whereby figures or flowers can be produced on any fabric during the process of weaving.
MILTON, WILLIAM - - -	2206	23rd Dec. 1797	Ship-building.
MILTON, WILLIAM - - -	2890	16th Nov. 1805	Stage-coaches and other carriages.

Name of Patentee.	Progressive Number.	Date.	Subject-matter of Patent.
MILTON, WILLIAM - - -	3982	10th Feb. 1816	Wheels and perches of carriages.
MILWAIN, JOHN - - -	12,927	12th Jan. 1850	Closing doors, windows, and shutters.
MILLWARD, ARTHUR - -	11,416	15th Oct. 1846	Producing figured surfaces, either sunk or in relief.
MILLWARD, WILLIAM - -	4343	4th March 1819	Skates, and fixing the same on the feet.
MILLWARD, WILLIAM - -	11,632	23rd March 1847	Alloys of metals; deposition of metals.
MILLWARD, WILLIAM - -	13,536	28th Feb. 1851	Electro-magnetic and magneto-electric apparatus.
MINIKEW, THOMAS - -	5700	11th Sept. 1828	Construction of chairs, lounges, sofas, beds, and other articles of furniture, carriages and other vehicles.
MINTER, GEORGE - - -	6034	9th Nov. 1830	Construction and manufacture of chairs. " Minter's reclining Chairs."
MINTER, GEORGE - - -	6188	9th Nov. 1831	Fastenings for dining-tables and for other purposes.
MINTER, GEORGE - - -	10,918	4th Nov. 1845	Construction of easy-chairs.
MINTER, JOHN - - -	6034	9th Nov. 1830	Manufacture of chairs. " Minter's reclining Chairs."
MINTON, HERBERT - -	8124	22nd June 1839	Porcelain.
MINTON, HERBERT - -	13,558	17th March 1851	Manufacture of dials for clocks, watches, barometers, gas-meters, mariners' compasses, and other articles.
MINTON, HERBERT - -	13,608	26th April 1851	Machinery to be employed in the manufacture of tiles, bricks, and other articles, from disintegrated or pulverized clay.
MIRRLEES, JAMES BUCHANAN	13,689	7th July 1851	Machinery for the manufacture of sugar.
MITCHELL, ALEXANDER -	6443	4th July 1833	Dock to facilitate the repairing, building, or retaining of ships and other floating vessels.
MITCHELL, ALEXANDER -	11,777	4th July 1847	Dock to facilitate the repairing, building, or retaining of ships and other floating vessels;—partly applicable to other purposes.
MITCHELL, BENJAMIN - -	12,023	13th Jan. 1848	Manufacture of manure.
MITCHELL, EDWARD - -	13,151	24th June 1850	Fastenings for articles used for writing, drawing, and for other purposes; articles to be used for writing and drawing.
MITCHELL, JAMES - - -	2333	23rd July 1799	Manufacturing cables, hawsers, or shroud-laid ropes, and other cordage.
MITCHELL, JAMES - - -	2592	9th March 1802	Manufacture of cables and hawsers.
MITCHELL, JAMES, senior -	2592	9th March 1802	Manufacture of cables and hawsers.
MITCHELL, JAMES BARR -	12,038	25th Jan. 1848	Manufacture of soda; treating products obtained in such manufacture.
MITCHELL, JOHN - - -	1250	30th March 1780	Rectifying spent lees from which soap has been made, rendering it again fit for use.
MITCHELL, JOHN - - -	9514	8th Nov. 1842	Manufacture of metallic-pens and pen-holders.
MITCHELL, JOHN - - -	12,393	28th Dec. 1848	Smelting copper
MITCHELL, THOMAS - -	9778	15th June 1843	Machine and apparatus for increasing and fastening the gloss of woollen, worsted, and fancy cloths, by the application of steam alone.
MITCHELL, THOMAS - -	13,085	29th May 1850	Machinery or apparatus for preparing, spinning, and weaving cotton-wool and other fibrous materials.
MITCHELL, WILLIAM - -	3660	3rd March 1813	Manufacture of soap.

Name of Patentee.	Progressive Number.	Date.	Subject-matter of Patent.
MITCHELL, WILLIAM - -	3891	7th March 1815	Lock and key applicable to various purposes.
MITCHELL, WILLIAM - -	4698	24th Aug. 1822	Process for manufacturing gold and silver plate, and other plate formed of ductile metals.
MOAT, CROFTON WILLIAM -	7906	17th Dec. 1838	Applying horse-power to carriages on ordinary roads.
MOAT, CROFTON WILLIAM -	8372	5th Feb. 1840	Applying steam-power to carriages on ordinary roads.
MOAT, WILLIAM CROFTON -	9856	26th July 1843	Obtaining aërial locomotion.
MOAT, WILLIAM CROFTON -	12,399	4th Jan. 1849	Engines to be worked by steam, air, or gas.
MOENCK, GUSTAVUS - -	11,985	1st Dec. 1847	Clocks and timekeepers.
MOFFATT, JAMES - - -	5330	3rd June 1828	Apparatus for stoppering and securing chain-cables, also for weighing anchors attached to cables, with or without a messenger.
MOGGRIDGE, WILLIAM HENRY	11,154	31st March 1846	Plates or pieces for the roof and gums of the mouth, for attaching artificial teeth thereto.
MOHUN, HENRY HUNTLEY -	7201	4th Oct. 1836	Manufacture of fuel.
MOHUN, HENRY HUNTLEY -	7861	8th Nov. 1838	Composition and manufacture of fuel; furnaces for consumption of such and other fuel.
MOINAU, AUGUSTE - -	8501	9th May 1840	Construction of timekeepers.
MOINDRON, PHILIPPE MARIE -	8370	31st Jan. 1840	Construction of furnaces and boilers.
MOLE, KEYSER - - -	681	10th April 1753	Bleaching, whitening, and beautifying Leghorn hats.
MOLESWORTH, JOHN - -	1170	29th Sept. 1777	Securing to the purchasers of shares and chances of state-lottery tickets any prize drawn in their favour.
MOLEYNS, FREDERICK DE	9053	21st Aug. 1841	Production or development of electricity; and application of electricity for obtaining light and motion.
MOLINARD, CLAUDE MARIE [HILAIRE.	6410	9th April 1833	Looms for weaving fabrics.
MOLINARD, CLAUDE MARIE [HILAIRE.	6696	17th Oct. 1834	Looms for weaving fabrics.
MOLINE, JOHN SPARKS - -	3795	28th March 1814	Tanning leather.
MOLINEUX, FRANCIS - -	5265	23rd May 1826	Machinery for spinning and twisting silk and wool, and for roving, spinning, and twisting flax, hemp, cotton, and other fibrous substances.
MOLINEUX, FRANCIS - [Molyneux, Francis.]	6001	21st Sept. 1830	Machinery for spinning and twisting silk and wool; also for roving, spinning, and twisting cotton, flax, hemp, and other fibrous substances.
MOLINEUX, FRANCIS - -	6428	25th May 1833	Machinery for making paper.
MOLINEUX, FRANCIS - -	8481	23rd April 1840	Manufacture of candles; means of consuming tallow and other substances for the purposes of affording light.
MOLINEUX, FRANCIS - -	10,570	18th March 1845	Apparatus for cutting and dividing sugar.
MOLL, FRANTZ - - -	6983	19th Jan. 1836	Preserving certain vegetable substances from decay.
MOLLADAY, JOHN, junior -	13,968	12th Feb. 1852	Machinery or apparatus for manufacturing hats or caps.

Name of Patentee.	Progressive Number.	Date.	Subject-matter of Patent.
MOLLARD, DAVID - -	2018	23rd Oct. 1794	Machine for moving heavy articles by raising or lowering them perpendicularly, or (by the addition of a moveable catch-frame) by removing them in an horizontal, oblique, or curvilinear direction, or on inclined planes, or by changing the direction of the motion of the said articles, the weight of the rope or chain, whether long or short, acting equally upon the power working the machine, the same being useful for emptying buckets by the mere motion of the machine, also for loading and unloading ships and land-carriages, raising water, draining and working mines, and cleansing rivers and other places,
MOLLE, FRANÇOIS MARCELLIN	4172	1st Nov. 1817	Propelling boats and other vessels.
MOLLERAT, JEAN BAPTISTE -	6680	25th Sept. 1834	Manufacture of gas for illumination.
MOLLERAT, JEAN BAPTISTE -	7358	2nd May 1837	Manufacture of gas for illumination.
MOLLERSTON, CHARLES [FREDERICK.	2814	23rd Jan. 1805	Chemical composition; applying the same in the preparation of hides, skins, and leather, silks, taffetas, and linen, also to articles made of skins and leather, thereby colouring and giving a gloss to the same, rendering them waterproof and impenetrable to hot or corroding liquors, at the same time preserving them from decay, and keeping them soft and pliable.
MOLLET, JOHN - - -	11,657	15th April 1847	Fire-arms and cartridges.
MOLLETT, ROBERT - -	10,127	28th March 1844	Separating the fatty and oily portions of animal and vegetable substances from the membranous portions of the same.
MOLT, ALEXANDER EDOUARD [LE (Chevalier).	12,219	20th July 1848	Apparatus for lighting by electricity;—partly applicable to other purposes in electricity.
MOLYNEUX, JAMES - -	8738	16th Dec. 1840	Dressing flax and tow.
MOLYNEUX, ROBERT - -	8418	7th March 1840	Chronometers.
MONK, WILLIAM - - -	743	29th Nov. 1759	Axletrees for vehicles.
MONNOYEUR, CLAUDE CELESTIN	3466	22nd July 1811	Process for the purification of ardent spirits.
MONS, WILLIAM - - -	520	9th Oct. 1730	Manufacturing silk mourning-crapes, known as Valle-Cypre or Bologna crapes.
MONTAUBAN, HIPPOLYTE FRAN-[COIS DE BOUFFET.	7581	28th Feb. 1838	Producing gas for illumination; apparatus connected with the consumption thereof.
MONTAUBAN, HIPPOLYTE FRAN-[COIS Marquis de BOUFFET.	7720	4th July 1838	Manufacture of soap.
MONTGOLFIER, PIERRE FRAN-[COIS.	3992	14th March 1816	Machine called " Bellier hydraulique " or hydraulic-ram.
MONTGOLFIER, PIERRE FRAN-[COIS.	3995	14th March 1816	Machine which acts by the expansion or contraction of air heated by fire, applicable to the raising of water or for giving motion to mills or other machines.
MONTGOMERY, CONRAD - -	12,872	3rd Dec. 1849	Brewing, distilling, and rectifying.
MONTGOMERY, CONRAD - -	13,000	7th March 1850	Sawing, cutting, boring, and shaping wood.
MONTGOMERY, JAMES - -	11,221	26th May 1846	Construction of steam-boilers and steam-engines; also steam-vessels and machinery for propelling the same.
MONTGOMERY, JAMES - -	12,018	11th Jan. 1848	Pianofortes and other similar finger-keyed instruments.

Name of Patentee.	Progressive Number.	Date.	Subject-matter of Patent.
MONTGOMERY, ROBERT - -	6261	26th April 1832	Construction of a machine for spinning cotton, silk, flax, and other fibrous substances.
MONTGOMERY, ROBERT - -	8341	11th Jan. 1840	Spinning-machinery, applicable to mules, jennies, slubbers, and other similar mechanism.
MONTMIRAIL, PIERRE DUFAURE [DE.	8527	2nd June 1840	Manufacture of bread.
MONTRAVEL, ANTOINE MAURICE [TARDY DE.	14,031	24th March 1852	Obtaining motive-power; machinery employed therein.
MONZANI, TEBALDO - -	3074	19th Oct. 1807	German-flute.
MONZANI, TEBALDO - -	3586	16th July 1812	Clarionets and German-flutes.
MONZANI, WILLOUGHBY THEO- [BALD.	10,249	3rd July 1844	Construction of boats for the preservation of life and property; apparatus applicable thereto.
MONZANI, WILLOUGHBY THEO- [BALD.	12,242	15th Aug. 1848	Construction of bridges, aqueducts, and roofings.
MOODY, ALEXANDER - -	3719	14th July 1813	Tanning or dressing white, buff, or losh leather.
MOODY, EDMUND - - -	8265	7th Nov. 1839	Machinery for preparing turnips, carrots, parsnips, potatoes, and other bulbous roots, as food for cattle.
MOODY, JOHN - - -	4435	25th Jan. 1820	Inkstand containing carbonaceous and extractive matter in a dry state, from which matter ink may be formed by the addition of water.
MOODY, WILLIAM - - -	578	18th July 1741	Making moccadoes or French carpeting.
MOON, JAMES - - -	9711	25th April 1843	Manufacture of bricks for use in the construction of chimneys and flues.
MOOR, JOHN HENRY - -	10,197	23rd May 1844	Construction of carriages generally.
MOOR, THOMAS - - -	245	13th April 1685	Making alum or alum-glass, for medicinal, chirurgical, metallic, and mineral improvements.
MOORCROFT, WILLIAM - -	2104	16th April 1796	Manufacturing horse-shoes and other articles formed of metals.
MOORCROFT, WILLIAM - -	2398	3rd May 1800	Manufacturing horse-shoes.
MOORE, ALFRED - - -	12.032	18th Jan. 1848	Valves or plugs for the passage of water or other fluids.
MOORE, BRYAN - - -	498	21st May 1728	Engine for boring stone, in either a straight, square, or circular direction or form, for pipes, pumps, and other uses.
MOORE, FRANCIS - - -	921	14th March 1769	Machines made of wood or metal, and worked by fire, water, or air, for the purpose of moving bodies on land or water.
MOORE, FRANCIS - - -	930	19th June 1769	Multiplying levers, to expedite and extend motion and reduce vibration.
MOORE, FRANCIS - - -	933	13th July 1769	Machines made of wood and metal, and moved by power, for the carriage of persons and goods, and for accelerating boats, barges, and other vessels.
MOORE, FRANCIS - - -	961	1st June 1770	Ploughs.
MOORE, FRANCIS - - -	1415	28th Jan. 1784	Four-wheel carriage.
MOORE, FRANCIS - - -	1546	13th June 1786	Coach with two wheels.
MOORE, FRANCIS - - -	1547	13th June 1786	Quadrant or quarter circle and standard, fixed to doors for the purpose of shutting them.

Name of Patentee.	Progressive Number.	Date.	Subject-matter of Patent.
MOORE, GEORGE - - -	443	21st April 1722	Refining copper on the test, by air and blast, with proper furnaces, and with sea coal, whereby the copper is purified and refined at one operation.
MOORE, ISAAC - - -	999	6th Nov. 1771	Casting cases in metal for holding printing-types, for printing on silk, leather, paper, and parchment, together with raised letters for signs and inscriptions; printing-presses.
MOORE, JOHN - - -	3443	1st May 1811	Machine for the manufacture of gold and silver twist, silk, cotton, or thread twisted lace-net similar to lace as made by hand with bobbins on pillows; also making iron, brass, or copper wire-net.
MOORE, JOHN - - -	4516	9th Dec. 1820	Machinery which may be worked by steam, water, or gas, as a moving power.
MOORE, JOHN - - -	5032	6th Nov. 1824	Steam-engines or steam-engine apparatus.
MOORE, JOHN - - -	5853	30th Sept. 1829	Machinery for propelling carriages, ships, vessels or other floating bodies, and for guiding carriages; apparatus for condensing the steam of the engine after it has propelled the steam-engine piston.
MOORE, JOHN - - -	8185	5th Aug. 1839	Steam-engine or steam-engine apparatus.
MOORE, JOHN - - -	14,105	1st May 1852	Nautical instruments applicable for ascertaining and indicating the true spherical course, and the distance between one port and another.
MOORE, MATTHEW - -	646	1st July 1749	Chemical composition of metal, suitable for cannon and other field-arms.
MOORE, ROBERT ROSS ROWEN	12,511	14th March 1849	Manufacture of letters and figures to be applied to shop fronts and other surfaces.
MOORE, THOMAS - - -	7490	27th Nov. 1837	Machinery for frame-work knitting.
MOORE, THOMAS - - -	11,875	30th Sept. 1847	Looms for weaving.
MOORE, THOMAS WILLIAM [CHARMING.	5733	10th Dec. 1828	Combination of machinery for the manufacture of hats or caps.
MOORE, WILLIAM HENRY -	11,230	28th May 1846	Gratings of metal or wood, for the fronts of houses, and for general purposes, for ventilation and the admission of light.
MOORHOUSE, JOHN - - -	2849	18th May 1805	Materials for sheathing ships, roofing houses, and lining water-spouts.
MORDAN, JOHN SAMPSON -	7071	23rd April 1836	Manufacturing triple-pointed pens.
MORAND, SAMUEL - - -	6104	14th April 1831	Stretching-machine.
MORAND, SAMUEL - - -	6593	12th April 1834	Stretching-machine.
MORAND, SAMUEL - - -	8251	2nd Nov. 1839	Machinery for stretching fabrics.
MORAND, SAMUEL - - -	9269	26th Feb. 1842	Machinery for stretching fabrics.
MORAND, SAMUEL - - -	13,475	30th Jan. 1851	Apparatus used when stretching and drying fabrics.
MORDAN, SAMPSON - -	4742	20th Dec. 1822	Pencil-holders or port-crayons; pens for facilitating writing and drawing.
MORDAN, SAMPSON - -	6136	13th July 1831	Writing and drawing-pens and penholders; method of using them.
MORDAN, SAMPSON - -	6163	20th Sept. 1831	Construction of writing-pens and penholders; method of using them.
MORDAUNT, CHARLES LEWIS -	1198	11th Aug. 1778	Preparing cotton, sheep's wool, and flax, for the loom; materials and necessary articles for manufacturing cotton and linen cloth.

Name of Patentee.	Progressive Number.	Date.		Subject-matter of Patent.
MORDAUNT, OCTAVIUS DILL- [INGHAM.	9955	21st Nov.	1843	Apparatus for obtaining the profile of various forms or figures.
MORE, ROBERT - - -	5526	18th July	1827	Preparing and cooling worts or wash from vegetable substances, for the production of spirits.
MORE, ROBERT - - -	5527	18th July	1827	Rendering productive of spirits the refuse arising from distilling.
MOREAU, FELIX - - -	9048	21st Aug.	1841	Cutting cork.
MOREAU, FELIX - - -	9049	21st Aug.	1841	Sculpturing, moulding, engraving, and polishing stone, metals, and other substances.
MOREAU, FELIX - - -	10,479	18th Jan.	1845	Manufacturing corks and similar articles made of cork, wood, or other materials; application of the refuse matters to other purposes.
MOREAU, GABRIEL HIPPOLYTE	9562	21st Dec.	1842	Steam-generators.
MOREAU, GABRIEL HIPPOLYTE	9563	21st Dec.	1842	Propelling vessels.
MOREAU, GABRIEL HIPPOLYTE	10,852	6th Oct.	1845	Steam-carriage.
MORECROFT, WILLIAM - -	1753	8th July	1790	Mechanical crane for lifting and shifting weights.
MORELAND, JOSEPH - -	11,238	29th June	1846	Setting and fixing coppers, stills, and boilers; construction of furnaces.
MOREWOOD, EDMUND - -	9055	27th Aug.	1841	Preserving iron and other metals from oxydation or rust.
MOREWOOD, EDMUND - -	10,222	8th June	1844	Coating iron with other metals.
MOREWOOD, EDMUND - -	10,859	9th Oct.	1845	Manufacture of iron into sheets, plates, and other forms; coating iron; preparing iron for coating, and for other purposes.
MOREWOOD, EDMUND - -	11,390	2nd Oct.	1846	Machinery for separating certain fibrous substances from seed and other extraneous matters.
MOREWOOD, EDMUND - -	11,476	7th Dec.	1846	Manufacturing iron into sheets, plates, and other forms; coating iron; preparing iron for coating and for other purposes.
MOREWOOD, EDMUND - -	13,401	12th Dec.	1850	Coating or covering metals.
MOREWOOD, EDMUND - -	13,971	13th Feb.	1852	Manufacture, shaping, and coating of metals, and in the means of applying heat.
MOREWOOD, EDMUND - -	14,040	24th March	1852	Shaping and coating sheet-metal, and applying the same to building purposes.
MOREWOOD, EDWARD - -	9720	4th May	1843	Coating metals.
MOREY, CHARLES - - -	12,752	30th Aug.	1849	Machinery for sewing, embroidering, and uniting or ornamenting by stitches, various descriptions of textile fabrics.
MOREY, CHARLES - - -	13,627	10th May	1851	Machinery for preparing, dressing, cutting, and shaping stone and other materials for buildings and decorations.
MORFITT, JOHN - - -	5739	15th Dec.	1828	Retorts used by bleachers and makers of oxy-muriate of lime.
MORGAN, DAVID - - -	11,868	9th Sept.	1847	Manufacture of copper and other metallic cylinders for printing silks and other fabrics, and for other similar purposes; casting copper and other metallic cylinders, tubes, and rollers, hollow and free from air-bubbles.
MORGAN, EDMUND - - -	10,863	9th Oct.	1845	Envelope for letters.

Name of Patentee.	Progressive Number.	Date.	Subject-matter of Patent.
MORGAN, JOHN - - -	3628	19th Dec. 1812	Power applicable to propelling vessels and boats of every description, through the water, also to pumping the same.
MORGAN, JOHN - - -	5269	21st Oct. 1825	Consolidated or combined drawing and forcing-pump.
MORGAN, JOHN - - -	11,676	27th April 1847	Machinery for preparing and spinning flax, hemp, and other fibrous substances.
MORGAN, JOSEPH - - -	6610	22nd May 1834	Apparatus used in the manufacture of mould-candles.
MORGAN, JOSEPH - - -	9627	11th Feb. 1843	Manufacture of candles.
MORGAN, JOSEPH - - -	14,186	24th June 1852	Manufacture of candles.
MORGAN, THOMAS - - -	5843	9th Sept. 1829	Preparing iron-plates for tinning.
MORGAN, WILLIAM - -	6075	14th Feb. 1831	Steam-engines.
MORGAN, WILLIAM - -	6544	18th Jan. 1834	Apparatus for heating and ventilating churches, conservatories, houses, and other buildings or places.
MORGAN, WILLIAM -	6573	13th March 1834	Steam-engines.
MORGAN, WILLIAM - -	6753	27th Jan. 1835	Steam-engines.
MORGAN, WILLIAM - -	7848	3rd Nov. 1838	Generation of steam.
MORGAN, WILLIAM - -	9999	28th Dec. 1843	Treating copper-ores;—partly applicable to other ores; construction of furnaces for treating such ores.
MORIDE, EDOUARD - - -	14,311	30th Sept. 1852	Tanning.
MORISON, DAVID - - -	8316	16th Dec. 1839	Printing.
MORISON, JAMES - - -	7019	8th March 1836	Jacquard-machines; ten box lay; reading and stamping-machines used in making shawls and figured work.
MORISON, JAMES - - -	11,821	29th July 1847	Applying power in propelling carriages, and giving motion to machinery.
MORLAND, SIR SAMUEL - -	151	13th Jan. 1667	Making fire-hearths of cast-iron, brass, or copper.
MORLAND, SIR SAMUEL - -	175	14th March 1674	Engines for raising great quantities of water.
MORLEY, HILLDEBRAND -	1315	14th Jan. 1782	Machine for raising and discharging water from holds of ships, mines, and other places, spontaneously, or by the assistance of a small force, and for working mills, or any other purpose requiring like power.
MORLEY, HILLDEBRAND -	1324	15th April 1782	Wheel-engine for giving a constant force and motion to mills, clocks, time-pieces, and other instruments or engines.
MORLEY, HILLDEBRAND -	1325	15th April 1782	Automaton clock or timepiece.
MORLEY, HILLDEBRAND -	1342	5th Nov. 1782	Single and compound timepieces.
MORLEY, PHILEMON AUGUSTINE	8952	6th May 1841	Manufacture of sugar-moulds, dish-covers, and other articles of similar manufacture.
MORLEY, WILLIAM - -	4921	15th March 1824	Machinery for making bobbin-net lace.
MORLEY, WILLIAM - -	5599	9th Jan. 1828	Machinery for making bobbin or twist net lace.
MORNAY, ARISTIDES FRANKLIN	5478	27th March 1827	Preparing for smelting and smelting ores and other substances containing metals.
MORNAY, EDWARD DE -	13,709	5th Aug. 1851	Machinery for crushing sugar-canes; apparatus for evaporating saccharine fluids.
MORRALL, ABEL - - -	7923	3rd Jan. 1839	Making needles; machinery employed therein.

Name of Patentee.	Progressive Number.	Date.	Subject-matter of Patent.
MORRELL, GEORGE FREDERICK	13320	7th Nov. 1850	Obtaining and applying motive-power; pumps.
MORRICE, ROBERT EDMUND -	8241	17th Oct. 1839	Manufacture of boots, shoes, and coverings for the legs.
MORRIS, JAMES - - -	9571	22nd Dec. 1842	Locomotive and other steam-engines.
MORRIS, JOHN - - -	807	28th March 1764	Machine fixed to a stocking-frame to make eyelet-holes in mits, gloves, and other goods usually made on such frames.
MORRIS, JOHN - - -	1282	5th March 1781	Twisting-machine for making Brussels point-lace, and other open-worked lace.
MORRIS, JOHN - - -	1500	28th Oct. 1785	Making window-shutters of wood, iron, tin, and other materials, to slide up and down.
MORRIS, JOHN SHORTER -	3109	4th Feb. 1808	Machine for mangling.
MORRIS, JOHN SHORTER -	3636	15th Jan. 1813	Machine to be used as a crane, or to give a rotary motion to any machine, engine, or mill-work.
MORRIS, ROBERT - -	711	9th Feb. 1757	Fashioning and colouring copper, in imitation of Japan copper.
MORRIS, SAMUEL - - -	14,153	3rd June 1852	Steam-boilers.
MORRIS, STEPHEN - -	7321	13th March 1837	Giving elasticity, freedom of action and durability to certain parts of pens for writing, also obtaining a supply of ink to the same.
MORRIS, THOMAS - - -	807	28th March 1764	Machine fixed to a stocking-frame for making eyelet-holes in mits, gloves, and other goods usually made on such frames.
MORRIS, WILLIAM - - -	10,730	23rd June 1845	Apparatus and machinery for tilling and and draining land.
MORRIS, WILLIAM - -	12,831	2nd Nov. 1849	Preparing clay; manufacture of bricks, tiles, and other articles of clay or brickearth.
MORRISON, JOHN - -	12,278	28th Sept. 1848	Ornamenting cylindrical and other surfaces of wood and other materials.
MORRISON, ÆNEAS - -	3306	22nd Feb. 1810	Machine for conveying persons from the upper part of houses on fire, for lowering goods from warehouses, and for other purposes.
MORRISON, ÆNEAS - -	4350	23rd March 1819	Combination of processes and manufactures for preserving animal and vegetable food.
MORRISON, THOMAS - -	5442	22nd Dec. 1826	Process for rendering boots, shoes, and other articles waterproof.
MORSE, ANNE - - -	1480	13th May 1785	Sandal-clogs.
MORSE, JUSTINIAN - -	527	13th April 1731	Organ with the open diapason in the front, with one or more sets of keys, and the bellows to be worked either with the feet or the hands.
MORSE, SYDNEY EDWARDS -	12,022	13th Jan. 1848	Manufacture of plates or surfaces for printing or embossing.
MORTIMER, HENRY - -	9158	16th Nov. 1841	Covering ways and surfaces; constructing arches.
MORTIMER, JOHN - -	13,392	7th Dec. 1850	Magnetic-needle and mariner's compass.
MORTIMER, JOSEPH HART -	14,183	24th June 1852	Lamps.
MORTON, ALEXANDER - -	11,643	29th March 1847	Printing warps.
MORTON, CHARLES - -	288	22nd Jan. 1692	Engine for beating and pounding or stamping mineral-ores, hemp, and flax; partly applicable to the working of mines and coalpits.

Name of Patentee.	Progres-sive Number.	Date.		Subject-matter of Patent.
MORTON, GEORGE - - -	3958	14th Nov.	1815	Attaching horses to waggons and other four-wheeled carriages.
MORTON, RICHARD - -	2156	23rd Jan.	1797	Making candlesticks, lamps, and girandoles with sliding pillars, and having also an extinguisher.
MORTON, ROBERT - - -	6998	9th Feb.	1836	Construction of paddles or paddle-wheels for propelling vessels;—applicable to the construction of water-wheels for mills.
MORTON, THOMAS - - -	4352	23rd March	1819	Dragging ships out of water on to dry land.
MOSEDALE, WILLIAM - -	5147	2nd April	1825	Collars for draught-horses.
MOSER, ABRAHAM ADOLPH -	6196	15th Dec.	1831	Fire-arms.
MOSLEY, JOHN OSBORNE -	6302	8th Sept.	1832	Making pill and other boxes from pasteboard, paper, or other materials;—applicable to other purposes.
MOSLEY, WILLIAM DARKER -	4920	10th March	1824	Making and working machines used in the manufacture of bobbin-net.
MOSS, ISAAC - - - -	9394	13th June	1842	Manufacture of covered buttons, ornaments, and fastenings for wearing-apparel.
MOSS, THOMAS - - -	10,633	22nd April	1845	Printing and preparing bankers' notes, cheques and other papers, for the prevention of fraud.
MOTAY, CYPRIEN MARIE TESSIE [DU.	9877	31st Aug.	1843	Connecting and laying pipes under water, to form tunnels for the conveyance of passengers and goods.
MOTAY, CYPRIEN MARIE TESSIE [DU.	11,943	4th Nov.	1847	Inlaying and coating metals with various substances.
MOTLEY, THOMAS - - -	3587	22nd July	1812	Manufacture of letters or characters for signs, show-boards, fronts of shops, houses, and other places.
MOTLEY, THOMAS - - -	4264	19th May	1818	Ladders.
MOTLEY, THOMAS - - -	4621	27th Nov.	1821	Construction of candlesticks or lamps; candles to be burnt therein.
MOTLEY, THOMAS - - -	8618	7th Sept.	1840	Apparatus and means of burning concrete fatty matters.
MOTLEY, THOMAS - - -	12,514	14th March	1849	Obtaining and applying motive-power; railroads and other roads; supporting pressure, resisting strain, and protecting against fire.
MOTT, ISAAC HENRY ROBERT	4098	1st Feb.	1817	Producing tones from vibrating substances. "Sostinenti pianoforte."
MOTT, ISAAC HENRY ROBERT	11,180	28th April	1846	Musical instruments.
MOTTE, AUGUSTE - - -	13,581	2nd April	1851	Portmanteaus.
MOUATIS, FRANCIS CLARK -	13,528	24th Feb.	1851	Hydraulic siphon.
MOUATIS, FRANCIS CLARK -	13,885	31st Dec.	1821	Hydraulic siphon.
MOULD, JACOB - - -	5099	19th Feb.	1825	Fire-arms.
MOULDEN, DAVID - - -	12,474	13th Feb.	1849	Machinery for the manufacture of looped fabrics.
MOULT, FRANCIS - - -	406	30th June	1716	Fluxing, separating, and reducing black tin into white tin, by alkaline and saline mixtures.
MOULT, WILLIAM - - -	3810	23rd May	1814	Method of acting upon machinery.
MOULT, WILLIAM - - -	3884	13th Feb.	1815	Evaporation and sublimation.
MOULT, WILLIAM - - -	4057	14th Aug.	1816	Method of acting upon machinery.
MOULT, WILLIAM - - -	4198	15th Jan.	1818	Steam-engines.
MOULT, WILLIAM - - -	5053	9th Dec.	1824	Working water-wheels.

Name of Patentee.	Progressive Number.	Date.	Subject-matter of Patent.
MOULTON, STEPHEN - -	11,567	8th Feb. 1847	Treating caoutchouc with other materials, to produce elastic and impermeable compounds.
MOULTON, STEPHEN - -	11,650	8th April 1847	Construction of bridges.
MOULTON, STEPHEN - -	13,721	14th Aug. 1851	Preparation of gutta-percha and caoutchouc, and the application thereof.
MORVILLON, ANTONIO - -	8046	23rd April 1839	Machinery for propelling ships, boats, and other vessels on water, to supersede paddle-wheels.
MOWATE, CHARLES - -	77	19th Dec. 1634	Making woollen-cloth impenetrable to rain.
MOWATE, JOHN - - -	77	19th Dec. 1634	Making woollen-cloth impenetrable to rain.
MOWBRAY, FREDERICK WIL-[LIAM.	11,982	1st Dec. 1847	Machinery for the manufacture of looped fabrics.
MOWBRAY, FREDERICK WIL-[LIAM.	12,195	27th June 1848	Manufacture of looped fabrics.
MOWBRAY, FREDERICK WIL-[LIAM.	13,563	24th March 1851	Machinery for weaving.
MOWBRAY, GEORGE - -	6392	27th Feb. 1833	Machinery used in the manufacture of bobbin-net lace, for the purpose of producing ornamental lace.
MOWBRAY, GEORGE MORDEY	10,989	10th Dec. 1845	Method of communication between the person in charge of a railway-train, and the controller of its motive-power.
MOWER, SAMUEL - - -	13,918	24th Jan. 1852	Machinery for manufacturing bricks, tiles, or other articles of a similar character.
MOXON, JOHN DOWELL - -	4706	27th Sept. 1822	Ships' hearths; apparatus connected therewith, for evaporating and condensing water.
MOXON, JOHN DOWELL -	4723	9th Nov. 1822	Construction of bridges and works of a similar nature.
MUIR, JOHN - - - -	8210	26th Aug. 1839	Apparatus connected with the discharging-press for conducting, distributing, and applying the discharging and dyeing liquors.
MUIR, MALCOLM - - -	5502	1st June 1827	Machinery for preparing boards for flooring, and other similar purposes.
MUIR, MALCOLM - - -	6199	22nd Dec. 1831	Machinery for preparing boards for flooring, and other purposes.
MUIR, THOMAS - - -	8641	24th Sept. 1840	Cleaning silk and other fibrous substances.
MULBERY, JAMES - - -	12,689	4th July 1849	Slide-valves of steam-engines.
MULLER, JOHN DIETRICK -	1228	16th June 1779	Machine constructed on self-moving principles.
MULLER, WILLIAM - -	3300	12th Feb. 1810	Construction of pumps.
MULLER, WILLIAM - -	5674	10th July 1828	Instrument or apparatus for the purpose of resolving problems in navigation, spherics, and other sciences.
MULLEY, WILLIAM ROBINSON	10,585	2nd April 1845	Collecting and raising stone or other substances from below water.
MULLINER, JOHN - - -	5193	21st June 1825	Loom for weaving tape and other such articles.
MULLINS, JOHN - - -	9501	27th Oct. 1842	Making oxides of metals; separating silver and other metals from their compounds; making salts of lead, and salts of other metals.
MÜNCH, AUGUST - - -	5802	19th June 1829	Musical-instruments.

Name of Patentee.	Progres-sive Number.	Date.	Subject-matter of Patent.
MUNDEE. WILLIAM - -	621	29th April 1747	Cleansing and improving British spirits.
MUNKITTRICK, ALEXANDER -	12,596	1st May 1849	Composition of matter to be used as a substitute for oil in the lubrication of machinery.
MUNN, ROBERT - - -	12,400	4th Jan. 1849	Looms, and apparatus connected with looms, for weaving various textile fabrics.
MUNNS, JOHN - - -	1909	10th Oct. 1792	Carriage-trumpet.
MUNRO, JOHN - - -	4226	12th Feb. 1818	Steam-engines.
MUNTZ, GEORGE FREDERICK - [Muntz, Frederick.	3989	2nd March 1816	Abating smoke, and obtaining a valuable product therefrom.
MUNTZ, GEORGE FREDERICK -	6325	22nd Oct. 1832	Manufacture of metal-plates for sheathing the bottoms of ships, and other such vessels.
MUNTZ, GEORGE FREDERICK -	6347	17th Dec. 1832	Manufacture of bolts and other ships' fastenings.
MUNTZ, GEORGE FREDERICK -	6495	28th Oct. 1833	Manufacture of boilers used for the purpose of generating steam.
MUNTZ, GEORGE FREDERICK -	11,410	15th Oct. 1846	Manufacture of metal-plates for sheathing the bottoms of ships and other vessels.
MUNTZ, GEORGE FREDERICK, [junior.	13,461	18th Jan. 1851	Furnaces for melting metals for the purpose of making brass, yellow metal, and other compound metals.
MUNTZ, GEORGE FREDERICK, [junior.	14,117	8th May 1852	Manufacture of metal-tubes.
MURDOCK, JAMES - - -	8259	7th Nov. 1839	Marine steam-engines.
MURDOCK, JAMES - - -	8749	23rd Dec. 1840	Tables ;—partly applicable to other articles of furniture.
MURDOCK, JAMES - - -	10,137	2nd April 1844	Apparatus and processes for preparing the phormium tenax, or New Zealand flax.
MURDOCK, JAMES - - -	10,148	18th April 1844	Construction of vessels for holding aërated-liquids ; introducing such liquids into the said vessels, and retaining them therein.
MURDOCK, JAMES - - -	10,211	4th June 1844	Manufacture of gas ; apparatus employed therein.
MURDOCK, JAMES - - -	10,532	20th Feb. 1845	Manufacture of gas ; apparatus employed therein.
MURDOCK, JAMES - - -	10,715	10th June 1845	Dyeing.
MURDOCK, JAMES · - -	11,085	11th Feb. 1846	Preparing a certain material for painting.
MURDOCK, JAMES - - -	11,351	25th Aug. 1846	Making a composition or artificial stone applicable to building and other purposes.
MURDOCK, JAMES - - -	11,616	10th March 1847	Preparing and employing certain colours and materials for painting.
MURDOCK, JAMES - - -	11,757	19th June 1847	Manufacturing woven-goods figured on both sides.
MURDOCK, JAMES - - -	11,937	2nd Nov. 1847	Capsules, or small cases for protecting matters enclosed therein from the air ; materials used in the manufacture of the same.
MURDOCK, JAMES - - -	12,730	1st Aug. 1849	Converting sea-water into fresh ; ventilating ships and other vessels ;—also applicable to the evaporation of liquids, and to the concentration and crystallization of syrups and saline solutions.
MURDOCK, JAMES - - -	13,477	30th Jan. 1851	Preserving animal and vegetable substances.
MURDOCK, JAMES - - -	14,209	6th July 1852	Manufacture of certain kinds of woollen fabrics.

Name of Patentee.	Progressive Number.	Date.	Subject-matter of Patent.
MURDOCK, WILLIAM - -	1802	2nd May 1791	Making from the same material, copperas, vitriol, and different sorts of dye-stuffs, paints, and colours; also a composition to preserve ships' bottoms.
MURDOCK, WILLIAM - ·	2340	29th Aug. 1799	Manufacturing and constructing steam-engines.
MURDOCK, WILLIAM - -	3292	15th Jan. 1810	Boring and forming pipes, cylinders, columns, and circular discs, out of solid blocks and slabs of stone.
MURFORD, NICHOLAS - -	60	3rd Dec. 1632	Making salt.
MURLAND, CHARLES - -	10,833	18th Sept. 1845	Machinery for preparing and spinning flax and other fibrous substances.
MURPHY, JAMES - - -	2159	27th Jan. 1797	Tanning hides and skins; construction of tan-pits and utensils appertaining to the same.
MURPHY, JAMES CAVANAH -	3248	26th July 1809	Designing, making, and forming mosaics and ornaments in the Arabian style.
MURPHY, JAMES CAVANAH -	3774	24th Dec. 1813	Arabian method of preserving timber and other substances from corruption or decay.
MURRAY (Sir), JAMES -	9380	23rd May 1842	Combining various materials for the purpose of manure.
MURRAY, JAMES - -	10,139	10th April 1844	Using and applying artificial gas made from coal, oil, or other substances, for lighting and ventilating mines and pits.
MURRAY, JAMES - -	13,548	10th March 1851	Saddlery and harness.
MURRAY, JOHN - -	3287	14th Dec. 1809	Portable stove or furnace made of cast-iron, plate-iron, or other metal.
MURRAY, JOHN - -	7285	19th Jan. 1837	Construction of carriages.
MURRAY, MATTHEW - -	1752	1st June 1790	Machine for spinning yarn from silk, cotton, hemp, tow, flax, and wool.
MURRAY, MATTHEW - -	1971	18th Dec. 1793	Instruments and machines for preparing and spinning flax, hemp, tow, wool, and silk.
MURRAY, MATTHEW - -	2327	16th July 1799	Steam-engines.
MURRAY, MATTHEW - -	2531	11th Aug. 1801	Constructing the air-pump and other parts belonging to steam-engines, so as to increase power and save fuel.
MURRAY, MATTHEW · -	2632	28th June 1802	Combined steam-engines for producing circular powers, and machinery belonging thereto, applicable for drawing coals and other minerals from mines, for spinning cotton, flax, and wool, or for any purpose requiring circular power.
MURRAY, MATTHEW - -	3792	12th March 1814	Construction of hydraulic-presses for pressing cloth and paper, and for other purposes.
MURRAY, ROBERT - - -	1448	20th Aug. 1784	Refining sugar; making sugar from the cane-juice.
MURRAY, THOMAS - -	5	11th Jan. 1618	Making sword-blades, falchions, skeans, and rapier-blades.
MURRAY, WILLIAM - -	2096	8th March 1796	Extracting starch from the horse-chesnut.
MURRAY, WILLIAM Mᶜ - -	8558	1st July 1840	Manufacture of paper.
MUSGRAVE, JOHN - -	3179	8th Nov. 1808	Machine for preparing, roving, slubbing, spinning, twisting, and doubling cotton, flax, hemp, and other substances, preparatory to their being manufactured.
MUSGRAVE, JOSEPH - -	13,864	12th Feb. 1852	Apparatus used in the bleaching of yarns and goods.

Name of Patentee.	Progressive Number.	Date.	Subject-matter of Patent.
MUSHET, DAVID	2447	13th Nov. 1800	Processes applicable to the manufacture of metals from the ore, into bars, ingots, or otherwise, and to the completion of the various articles or utensils usually made of such metals.
MUSHET, DAVID	3944	27th July 1815	Manufacture of iron.
MUSHET, DAVID	4248	18th April 1818	Manufacture of bar or other iron, from refuse, slags, or ashes, produced in smelting copper-ores, and in the manufacture of copper.
MUSHET, DAVID	4697	20th Aug. 1822	Manufacture of iron from certain slags and cinders, produced in the working or making of that metal.
MUSHET, DAVIS	6908	22nd Oct. 1835	Manufacture of bar-iron or malleable iron.
MUSHET, JOHN	5834	20th Aug. 1829	Medicine for gouty affections of the stomach, spasms, cramp, inflammation of the lungs, and other like diseases.
MUSHET, ROBERT	4802	14th June 1823	Process for improving the quality of copper, and of alloyed copper, applicable to the sheathing of ships, and to other purposes.
MUSHET, ROBERT	10,997	10th Dec. 1845	Moulding iron.
MUSHET, WILLIAM	10,997	10th Dec. 1845	Moulding iron.
MUSPRATT, JAMES	10,616	15th April 1845	Manfacture of manure.
MUSSELWHITE, THOMAS	5220	16th July 1825	Construction of collars for horses or other animals.
MUSTON, PAUL ISAAC	6520	11th Dec. 1833	Making white-lead or carbonate of lead.
MYATT, JOHN	6170	27th Sept. 1831	Substitute for pattens or clogs. "Myatt's Health preserver."
MYERS, GEORGE	10,756	8th July 1845	Cutting or carving wood, stone, and other materials.
MYERS, GEORGE DAVIS	11,512	31st Dec. 1846	Making caps, bonnets, book-covers, curtains, and hangings, show-cards, or boards, &c.
MYERS, JOHN FREDERICK	8164	20th July 1839	Construction of certain musical-instruments; partly applicable to pianofortes, seraphines, and certain descriptions of organs.
MYERSCOUGH, THOMAS	8375	5th Feb. 1840	Construction of looms for weaving a new fabric; arrangement of machinery for weaving other woven goods or fabrics.
MYLES, FRANCIS	109	6th Sept. 1637	Drawing and working barges and other vessels, without the use of horses.
MYLNE, GEORGE EDWARD	9915	21st Oct. 1843	Construction of watches.

Name of Patentee	Progressive Number.	Date.		Subject-matter of Patent.

N.

Name of Patentee	Progressive Number.	Date.		Subject-matter of Patent.
NAB, ANDREW Mᶜ - - -	8956	11th May	1841	Manufacture of bricks.
NAB, ANDREW Mᶜ - -	9021	7th July	1841	Construction of meters or apparatus for measuring water or other fluids.
NAB, JOHN Mᶜ - - -	13,694	17th July	1851	Stretching and drying textile fabrics or materials; machinery employed therein.
NAIR, ARCHIBALD Mᶜ - -	10,799	4th Aug.	1845	Construction of and means of manufacturing apparatus for conducting electricity.
NAIRN, WILLIAM - - -	5615	5th Feb.	1828	Propelling vessels through the water by aid of steam or other mechanical force.
NAIRNE, EDWARD - - -	1318	5th Feb.	1782	Electrical-machine, or a method of insulating such machine, and constructing the conductors so that either shocks or sparks may be received from them. "Insulated Medical Electrical-Machine."
NAIRNE, WILLIAM - - -	7366	8th May	1837	Machinery of reels for reeling-yarns.
NAIRNE, WILLIAM - - -	11,124	11th March	1846	Propelling carriages along railways.
NAISH, EDMUND - - -	4221	3rd Feb.	1818	Machinery used for winding cotton.
NAISH, FRANCIS - - -	5867	2nd Nov.	1829	Manufacture or application of silks mixed or combined with other articles.
NAISH, JOHN - - - -	3734	25th Aug.	1813	Making moveable characters for composing names and professions.
NALDER, FRANCIS - - -	11,402	8th Oct.	1846	Manufacture of gloves.
NALDER, JAMES HALL - -	10,742	28th June	1845	Drills for drilling corn, grain, and manure.
NANTEUIL, PIERRE ANTOINE [AUGUSTE DE LA BARRE DE.	13,309	2nd Nov.	1850	Propelling carriages.
NAPIER, DAVID - - -	5713	2nd Oct.	1828	Machinery; applicable to letter-press printing.
NAPIER, DAVID - - -	6010	13th Oct.	1830	Printing and pressing machinery; economising the power applied to the same; also applicable to other purposes.
NAPIER, DAVID - - -	6090	4th March	1831	Machinery for propelling locomotive-carriages.
NAPIER, DAVID - - -	7343	18th April	1837	Letter-press printing.
NAPIER, DAVID - - -	8044	23rd April	1839	Iron steam-boats.
NAPIER, DAVID - - -	8385	12th Feb.	1840	Manufacture of projectiles.
NAPIER, DAVID - - -	8893	22nd March	1841	Propelling vessels.
NAPIER, DAVID - - -	9439	9th Aug.	1842	Steam-engines and steam-boilers.
NAPIER, DAVID - - -	9852	25th July	1843	Boilers or apparatus for generating steam.
NAPIER, DAVID - - -	11,652	8th April	1847	Steam-engines and steam-vessels.
NAPIER, DAVID - - -	12,220	20th July	1848	Mariner's compasses, barometers, and certain other measuring instruments.
NAPIER, DAVID - - -	13,098	4th June	1850	Apparatus for separating fluid from other matters.
NAPIER, DAVID - - -	13,884	31st Dec.	1851	Steam-engines.
NAPIER, JAMES - - -	6090	4th March	1831	Machinery for propelling locomotive-carriages.
NAPIER, JAMES - - -	9693	11th April	1843	Treating fabrics made of fibrous materials, for covering roofs and the bottoms of ships and vessels, and for other uses.

Name of Patentee.	Progressive Number.	Date.	Subject-matter of Patent.
NAPIER, JAMES - - -	10,362	22nd Oct. 1844	Treating mineral-waters to obtain products therefrom ; separating metals from other matters.
NAPIER, JAMES - - -	10,684	22nd May 1845	Treating mineral-waters to obtain products therefrom ; separating metals from other matters.
NAPIER, JAMES - - -	11,301	20th July 1846	Smelting copper-ores.
NAPIER, JAMES - - -	11,600	2nd March 1847	Smelting copper and other ores.
NAPIER, JAMES - - -	12,322	9th Nov. 1848	Manufacture of copper and other metals and alloys of metals.
NAPIER, JAMES MURDOCK -	12,220	20th July 1848	Mariner's compasses, barometers, and certain other measuring instruments.
NAPIER, JAMES MURDOCK -	13,098	4th June 1850	Apparatus for separating fluid from other matters.
NAPIER, WILLIAM - - -	6090	4th March 1831	Machinery for propelling locomotive-carriages.
NARBELL, ISAAC - - -	1225	26th May 1779	Bitumen or fire-mastic for covering or sheathing ships, and preventing the necessity of caulking and careening ; may be also made into cakes to be carried as ballast, and used, when melted, for stopping leaks in the vessel, or for other casualties ; also for lining apparatus for sugar-bakers, brewers, dyers, and tanners, also gutters, troughs, water-pipes, cisterns, baths, bridges, and various parts of buildings, both under and above water ; Egyptian mastic, a cement for building purposes, impervious to water, and a preservative from fire, or, when moulded, may be used as ornaments to buildings ; and, in a dissolved state, will also receive artistic impressions, which become hard in a few hours without the aid of fire, and form a stone equal in appearance to marble.
NASH, EBENEZER - - -	7342	18th April 1837	Manufacturing colouring-matter, and rendering certain colours applicable to dyeing, staining, and writing.
NASH, JOHN - - -	2165	7th Feb. 1797	Constructing bridges of plate-iron, wrought, cast, framed, or put together so as to form hollow bodies, capable of being filled with earth or other materials to make them solid, or, not being filled, to have the semblance of solid bodies.
NASH, JOHN - - -	6257	13th April 1832	Machinery and process used in making tiles, bricks, bread, biscuits and other articles formed of plastic materials.
NASH, MICHAEL - - -	1421	10th March 1784	Making blacking to resist moisture, and preserve leather from the effects of salt-water.
NASH, THEOPHILUS JOHN -	7395	19th June 1837	Manufacturing letters, figures, and other devices having a flat surface, presenting, by the aid of colours, the appearance of projection, and made in metals, wood, or other substances and materials ; also domed letters, figures, and other devices made from the same material, without seam or joint.
NASH, THOMAS - - -	10,023	23rd Jan. 1844	Machinery for the manufacture of paper.
NASH, WILLIAM - - -	7975	21st Feb. 1839	Construction of bridges, viaducts, roofs, and other parts of buildings.

Name of Patentee.	Progressive Number.	Date.	Subject-matter of Patent.
NASH, WILLIAM - - -	7978	23rd Feb. 1839	Machinery for winding, spinning, doubling, and throwing silk and other fibrous materials.
NASMITH, JOHN - - -	387	3rd Oct. 1711	Preparing and fermenting wash from sugar, molasses and grain, for distilling.
NASMYTH, GEORGE - -	12,260	4th Sept. 1848	Construction of fire-proof flooring and roofing;—applicable to the construction of viaducts, &c.
NASMYTH, JAMES - - -	7815	20th Sept. 1838	Machinery for cutting or planing metals and other substances; securing the cottars used in such machinery, and other machinery where keys or cottars are applied.
NASMYTH, JAMES - - -	8023	9th April 1839	Bearings or journals of locomotive and other steam-engines;—applicable to machinery in general.
NASMYTH, JAMES - - -	8299	4th Dec. 1839	Railway-carriages.
NASMYTH, JAMES - - -	9382	9th June 1842	Machinery for forging, stamping, and cutting iron and other substances.
NASMYTH, JAMES - - -	9850	24th July 1843	Machinery for driving piles;—partly applicable to forging or stamping metals and other substances.
NASMYTH, JAMES - - -	10,358	22nd Oct. 1844	Working atmospheric-railways; machinery for constructing the apparatus employed therein.
NASMYTH, JAMES - - -	10,413	2nd Dec. 1844	Machinery for hewing, dressing, splitting, breaking, stamping, crushing, and pressing stone and other materials.
NASMYTH, JAMES - - -	10,643	29th April 1845	Engines for obtaining and applying motive-power.
NASMYTH, JAMES - - -	11,091	16th Feb. 1846	Machines for obtaining and applying motive-power.
NASMYTH, JAMES - - -	12,074	23rd Feb. 1848	Machinery for forging, stamping, and cutting iron and other substances.
NASMYTH, JAMES - - -	12,675	26th June 1849	Communicating and regulating the power for driving machinery employed in manufacturing, dyeing, printing, and finishing textile-fabrics; and apparatus for the purpose.
NASMYTH, JAMES - - -	13,004	12th March 1850	Obtaining and applying heat.
NASMYTH, JAMES - - -	13,261	19th Sept. 1850	Machinery or apparatus for printing calicoes and other surfaces; manufacture of copper and other metallic rollers employed therein; machinery or apparatus connected with such manufacture.
NASMYTH, JAMES - - -	13,608	26th April 1851	Machinery to be employed in the manufacture of tiles, bricks, and other articles, from disintegrated or pulverized clay.
NATION, GEORGE - - -	311	17th Jan. 1693	Engine consisting of screw-wheels and long tumblers for raising or lowering heavy weights, also for weighing ships' guns and anchors, and raising heavy stones to the top of buildings, also for craning goods, boring timber, and pounding and grinding minerals or other hard substances.
NAUGHT, WILLIAM Mᶜ - -	11,001	10th Dec. 1845	Steam-engine.
NAUGHT, WILLIAM Mᶜ - -	12,788	7th March 1850	Steam-engines; and apparatus for ascertaining and registering the power of the same.

Name of Patentee.	Progressive Number.	Date.		Subject-matter of Patent.
NAYLOR, DAVID　-　　-　　-	8057	7th May	1839	Machinery for weaving single, double, or treble cloths, by hand or power.
NAYLOR, DAVID　-　　-　　-	8317	16th Dec.	1839	Machinery for weaving single, double, or treble cloths, by hand or power.
NAYLOR, ISAAC　-　　-　　-	7232	22nd Nov.	1836	Alarm-gun or reporter and detector.
NAYLOR, JOHN　-　　-　　-	1653	30th June	1788	Oven for baking bread and all kinds of victuals.
NAYLOR, JOHN　-　　-　　-	2909	14th Feb.	1806	Manufacturing salt.
NAYLOR, JOHN　-　　-　　-	10,693	31st May	1845	Machinery for crushing, tearing, and pulverizing arable land.
NAYLOR, WILLIAM -　　-　　-	1299	27th July	1781	Tying the spots of silk handkerchiefs, in imitation of India handkerchiefs.
NAYLOR, WILLIAM　　-　　-	2053	2nd June	1795	Cutting straw into chaff; cutting unthrashed grain; cutting wheat, oats, or other grain in the ear, with clover or other grass.
NEADE, WILLIAM -　　-　　-	69	16th May	1634	Making engines for fixing the bow and the pike together; also a quiver for the arrows.
NEADE, WILLIAM junior -　　-	69	16th May	1634	Making engines for fixing the bow and the pike together; also a quiver for the arrows.
NEALE, FRANCIS　-　　-　　-	5751	7th Jan.	1829	Combination of machinery for propelling vessels.
NEALE, JOHN -　　-　　-　　-	605	12th July	1744	Quadrantal planetarian-machine for taking the altitude of the planets or stars.
NEALE, JOHN WILLIAM　　　-	8866	8th March	1841	Manufacture of vinegar; apparatus employed therein.
NEALE, THOMAS　-　　-　　-	186	12th Nov.	1675	Engine or pump for drawing water by the aid of one barrel, for the purpose of draining mines, and for other similar uses.
NEALE, THOMAS　-　　-　　-	270	26th Aug.	1691	Making verdigris, and boiling the same in wooden or other pans; also making such pans or vessels of wood.
NEALE, THOMAS　-　　-　　-	272	15th Sept.	1691	Making steel equivalent to Corinthian steel.
NEALE, THOMAS　-　　-　　-	273	15th Sept.	1691	Making brass, and plates of the same, for kettles and the like, with materials the native growth of this kingdom.
NEALE, THOMAS　-　　-　　-	292	— Feb.	1692	Table for the purpose of playing upon with balls which fit into small hollows; dice cut perfectly square by means of a mould, having spots stained upon them, instead of holes filled with wax.
NEALE, WILLIAM -　　-　　-	4349	13th March	1819	Combination of machinery to increase power, and to be worked by manual labour or other suitable means.
NEAVE, EDWARD　-　　-　　-	4405	1st Nov.	1819	Application of various gases or vapours to certain useful purposes.
NEAVE, JOSIAH　-　　-　　-	4405	1st Nov.	1819	Application of various gases or vapours to certain useful purposes.
NEEDHAM, FRANCIS HENRY [WILLIAM.	5003	7th Oct.	1824	Casting steel.
NEEDHAM, HENRY -　　-　　-	12,432	20th Jan.	1849	Fire-arms.
NEEDHAM, JAMES -　　-　　-	3493	23rd Sept.	1811	Portable apparatus for brewing beer and ale from malt.
NEEDHAM, JAMES -　　-　　-	3575	9th June	1812	Portable apparatus for brewing beer from malt and hops.

Name of Patentee.	Progressive Number.	Date.	Subject-matter of Patent.
NEEDHAM, WILLIAM - -	6049	13th Dec. 1830	Machinery for spinning, doubling, and twisting silk and other fibrous substances.
NEEDHAM, WILLIAM - -	7663	31st May 1838	Machine for spinning, twisting, and doubling silk. "Silk-worm."
NEEDHAM, WILLIAM - -	9801	24th June 1843	Fire-arms.
NEELER, EDMUND - - -	617	3rd April 1746	Medicinal belt.
NEGRETTI, HENRICO ANGELO [LUDOVICO.	14,002	8th March 1852	Thermometers, barometers, gauges, and other instruments for ascertaining and registering the temperature, pressure, density, and specific-gravity of aëriform fluids, and liquid or solid bodies.
NEILSON, JAMES BEAUMONT -	5701	11th Sept. 1823	Application of air to produce heat in fires, forges, or furnaces where bellows and other blowing-apparatus are required.
NEILSON, JAMES BEAUMONT -	8403	29th Feb. 1840	Coating iron to prevent oxydation or corrosion, and for other purposes.
NEILSON, JOHN - - -	4274	22nd June 1818	Tanning and tawing hides and skins; dyeing or colouring leather and other articles.
NEILSON, JOHN - - -	4380	19th June 1819	Tanning and tawing hides and skins; dyeing or colouring leather and other articles.
NEILSON, ROBERT - -	7329	21st March 1837	Machine for preparing and cleaning coffee from the pod or husk, and separating the different qualities, so as to render it better adapted for roasting and for consumption.
NEILSON, WALTER - - -	12,676	26th June 1849	Application of steam for raising, lowering, moving, or transporting heavy bodies.
NEILSON, WILLIAM - -	9180	16th Dec. 1841	Cutting, dressing, preparing, and polishing stone, marble, and other substances; forming mouldings and other figures thereon.
NELME, SAMUEL DOLE - -	10,821	12th Sept. 1774	Alarm, whereby sedan-chairs, coaches, chariots, post-chaises, and other carriages, may be immediately stopped, and their attendants summoned in cases of imminent danger.
NELSON, GEORGE - - -	7375	22nd May 1837	Process for improving the qualities of isinglass.
NELSON, GEORGE - - -	8010	23rd March 1839	Preparing gelatine which has the properties of or resembles glue.
NELSON, JOSEPH - - -	2582	19th Feb. 1802	Manufacturing woollen-cloth.
NELTHORPE, EDWARD - -	195	14th Feb. 1677	Engine or mill for the hulling of black pepper and barley.
NEROT, EDMUND - - -	11,382	24th Sept. 1846	Manufacture of paper.
NESBITT, ALEXANDER - -	4989	27th July 1824	Process by which certain materials may be manufactured into paper or felt, or a substance nearly resembling the same.
NESHAM, WILLIAM TOPLING -	11,259	22nd June 1846	Apparatus and mode of applying power for raising and lowering weights or heavy bodies.
NETTLEFOLD, JOHN SUTTON -	6223	16th Feb. 1832	Table-furniture;—applicable to other purposes.
NEUBERGER, AUGUSTE - -	13,958	9th Feb. 1852	Lamps.
NEUMANN, JOHN PAUL - -	7275	11th Jan. 1837	Manufacture of prussiate of potash and prussiate of soda.

Name of Patentee.	Progressive Number.	Date.	Subject-matter of Patent.
NEVETT, GEORGE - - -	12,908	21st Dec. 1849	Steam-engines ;—applicable to apparatus for regulating, measuring, and registering the flow of liquids and gases.
NEVILL, ALFRED HOOPER -	9677	24th March 1843	Preparing lentils and other matters for food.
NEVILLE, CHARLES - -	604	22nd June 1744	Lime, stucco, plaster, mortar, cement, and manure from cockle, oyster, and other sea shells.
NEVILLE, FREDERICK - -	7898	6th Dec. 1838	Manufacturing coke, whereby the sal-ammoniac, bitumen, gases, and other residual products of coal are separately collected, and the heat employed in the process applied to other purposes.
NEVILLE, JAMES - - -	4058	14th Aug. 1816	Generating power by means of steam or other fluids, elastic or non-elastic, and applying the same for driving machinery;—applicable also to condensing steam and other aqueous-vapours in distillation or evaporation.
NEVILLE, JAMES - - -	4746	8th Jan. 1823	Producing heat, and applying the same to apparatus for roasting, smelting, and melting ores, metals, or other substances ; also to apparatus used in producing steam, distilling, brewing, baking, dyeing, and making sugar and soap, or to other operations where heat is necessary ; constructing and erecting furnaces and reservoirs for the above-named purposes ; also applying heat to furnaces and other apparatus as now erected, so as to save fuel, consume smoke, and to collect and preserve volatile matters contained in ores or other substances.
NEVILLE, JAMES - - -	5002	16th Sept. 1824	Propelling ships, boats, or other vessels.
NEVILLE, JAMES - - -	5344	14th March 1826	Boiler for generating steam with less expenditure of fuel.
NEVILLE, JAMES - - -	5450	15th Jan. 1827	Carriage to be worked or propelled by steam.
NEVILLE, JAMES - - -	5710	25th Sept. 1828	Machine for obtaining mechanical power from falls and running streams of water.
NEVILLE, JAMES - - -	6160	9th Sept. 1831	Apparatus for clarifying water and other fluids.
NEVILLE, JAMES - - -	7428	31st Aug. 1837	Furnace to economize fuel, and consume smoke or gases arising therefrom, applicable for generating steam and heating or evaporating fluids.
NEVILLE, JAMES - - -	9818	6th July 1843	Form and manufacture of horse-shoes.
NEVILLE, JAMES - - -	9840	13th July 1843	Obtaining power by means of gases, applicable to working machinery.
NEVILLE, JAMES - - -	11,918	21st Oct. 1847	Conveying goods and passengers on railroads ;—in part applicable to driving machinery.
NEVILLE, RICHARD JANION -	9909	18th Oct. 1843	Separating certain metals when in certain states of combination with each other.
NEVILLE, WILLIAM - -	3811	26th May 1814	Making hurdles, gates, palisades, verandahs, balustrades, stair-case rails, espalier-frames, and other articles.
NEWALL, ROBERT STIRLING -	8594	7th Aug. 1840	Wire-ropes ; and machinery for making such ropes.

Name of Patentee.	Progressive Number.	Date.	Subject-matter of Patent.
NEWALL, ROBERT STIRLING -	9160	16th Nov. 1841	Manufacture of flat bands.
NEWALL, ROBERT STIRLING -	9656	6th March 1843	Manufacture of wire-ropes; apparatus and arrangements for the manufacture of the same.
NEWALL, ROBERT STIRLING -	11,582	16th Feb. 1847	Locomotive-engines.
NEWALL, ROBERT STIRLING -	11,901	14th Oct. 1847	Machinery for grinding grain, paint, and other substances.
NEWALL, ROBERT STIRLING -	12,274	28th Sept. 1848	Locks, springs, means of fastening and setting up the rigging of ships.
NEWBERRY, JAMES WILMOT -	8294	2nd Dec. 1839	Machinery for dibbling or setting wheat and other grain or seed.
NEWBERRY, WILLIAM -	3105	30th Jan. 1808	Machinery for sawing wood, and splitting or paring skins.
NEWBERY, GEORGE JOHN -	8503	12th May 1840	Rendering silk, cotton, woollen, linen and other fabrics waterproof.
NEWBERY, GEORGE JOHN -	9448	18th Aug. 1842	Producing damask and other surfaces on leather and other fibrous substances and fabrics.
NEWBERY, JOHN - - -	810	10th April 1764	Machine for printing, staining, and colouring silks, stuffs, linens, cottons, leather and paper.
NEWBERY, JOHN - - -	9822	6th July 1843	Manufacture and construction of window blinds, screens, shutters, and other similar articles;—partly applicable to other purposes.
NEWCOMB, JOHN - - -	250	25th June 1686	Woven wire-engine, for bolting, dressing, sifting, and chaffing meal, and cleansing dross from metals.
NEWCOMB, THOMAS - -	12,428	18th Jan. 1849	Furnaces.
NEWCOME, AUGUSTINE - -	1320	9th March 1782	Making wheels for coaches, chaises, and other carriages, the nave and spokes consisting either wholly of iron, or in part of iron, brass, or other metals.
NEWELL, ROBERT - - -	13,595	15th April 1851	Construction of locks.
NEWEY, JAMES GEORGE -	10,247	3rd July 1844	Fastenings for wearing-apparel.
NEWEY, JAMES GEORGE -	12,865	28th Nov. 1849	Manufacture of buttons, studs, and other dress fastenings and ornaments.
NEWINGTON, CHARLES -	10,033	27th Feb. 1844	Apparatus for ascertaining and indicating the time at which a person is present at a particular place.
NEWINGTON, SAMUEL - -	11,986	7th Dec. 1847	Dibbling or sowing seed.
NEWINGTON, SAMUEL - -	12,921	11th Jan. 1850	Sowing, manuring, and cultivating land; implements used therein.
NEWMAN, CHARLES - -	4569	·17th July 1821	Construction of the body and carriage of stage or other coaches.
NEWMAN, HENRY CHARLES [CHRISTIAN.	3021	7th March 1807	Machine applicable to mills in general, but particularly to sugar-mills worked by cattle, videlicet, a ring of wood or iron round the mill, a new construction of the axis in peritrochis and the lever, also a lantern wheel or pinion, the teeth of which turn a cog-wheel on the spindle of the mill, and so constructed as to revolve together, with a rotatory motion round their own axis and a progressive circumvolutionary motion on the ring, and thus constantly act upon and impel the cog-wheel and spindle by their separate and united forces.

Name of Patentee.	Progressive Number.	Date.	Subject-matter of Patent.
NEWMAN, JAMES - - -	10,247	3rd July 1844	Fastenings for wearing-apparel.
NEWMAN, JAMES - - -	12,124	15th April 1848	Manufacture of parts of railway-wheels.
NEWMAN, JAMES - - -	12,539	28th March 1849	Manufacture of railway-wheels.
NEWMAN, JAMES - - -	12,865	28th Nov. 1849	Manufacture of buttons, studs, and other dress fastenings and ornaments.
NEWMAN, JAMES - - -	13,609	29th April 1851	Chains, chain-pins, swivels, brooches and other fastenings for wearing-apparel.
NEWMAN, PAUL - - -	2329	16th July 1799	Figuring or ornamenting cloths or stuffs of woollen, linen, cotton, velvet, silk or satin, or any mixture thereof, by means of pressure, embossment, or otherwise.
NEWMAN, ROBERT - - -	2965	6th Sept. 1806	Construction of ships and other vessels.
NEWMAN, WILLIAM - -	8321	16th Dec. 1839	Mechanism for roller-blinds. "Simcox and Company's patent blind-furniture."
NEWMAN, WILLIAM - -	10,373	2nd Nov. 1844	Window-blinds.
NEWMANN, JOHN PAUL -	6533	21st Dec. 1833	Making leather from hides and skins.
NEWMARCH, BENJAMIN - -	5317	16th Jan. 1826	Exploding fire-arms.
NEWMARCH, BENJAMIN - -	5334	18th Feb. 1826	Suspending and securing windows, gates, doors, shutters, blinds, &c.
NEWMARCH, BENJAMIN - -	5339	25th Feb. 1826	Preserving vessels and other bodies from the effects of external or internal violence on land or water; other improvements connected with the same.
NEWMARCH, BENJAMIN - -	5340	25th Feb. 1826	Preparation for preventing decay in timber or other substances, arising from dry rot or other causes.
NEWMARCH, BENJAMIN - -	5421	7th Nov. 1826	Fire-arms.
NEWSHAM, RICHARD - -	439	26th Dec. 1721	Water-engine for extinguishing fires.
NEWSHAM, RICHARD - -	494	8th June 1727	Stirrup-leathers, stirrups, and housens.
NEWSHAM, RICHARD - -	479	5th June 1725	Engine for extinguishing fires; three inventions for raising water; bush or box for the spindle-neck of a corn-mill to run in.
NEWSON, HENRY - - -	12,336	23rd Nov. 1848	Trusses.
NEWSTEAD, THOMAS - -	2714	18th June 1803	Preparing barilla and kelp, and the neutral salts obtained therefrom.
NEWTON, ALFRED VINCENT -	9985	13th Dec. 1843	Making cyanogen and its compounds, particularly the prussiates of potash and soda.
NEWTON, ALFRED VINCENT -	10,590	7th April 1845	Machinery for forging and stamping metals;—applicable to other purposes.
NEWTON, ALFRED VINCENT -	10,820	28th Aug. 1845	Machinery for manufactuing India-rubber fabrics.
NEWTON, ALFRED VINCENT -	10,839	26th Sept. 1845	Machinery for manufacturing screws.
NEWTON, ALFRED VINCENT -	10,840	26th Sept. 1845	Machinery for manufacturing metal pipes or screws.
NEWTON, ALERED VINCENT -	10,994	10th Dce. 1845	Printing and dyeing various fabrics.
NEWTON, ALFRED VINCENT -	11,013	22nd Dec. 1845	Combing wool.
NEWTON, ALFRED VINCENT -	11,084	11th Feb. 1846	Grinding grain and other substances.
NEWTON, ALFRED VINCENT -	11,196	5th May 1846	Machinery for manufacturing screws.
NEWTON, ALFRED VINCENT -	11,312	23rd July 1846	Manufacture of sugar.
NEWTON, ALFRED VINCENT -	11,380	24th Sept. 1846	Heating, hardening, and tempering various articles made of steel, or steel and iron combined.
NEWTON, ALFRED VINCENT -	11,436	3rd Nov. 1846	Manufacture of driving-bands;—partly applicable to the manufacture of other fabrics.

Name of Patentee.	Progressive Number.	Date.	Subject-matter of Patent.
NEWTON, ALFRED VINCENT -	11,655	15th April 1847	Apparatus to be applied to steam-boilers.
NEWTON, ALFRED VINCENT -	11,675	27th April 1847	Construction of roads or ways; and carriages to be used thereon.
NEWTON, ALFRED VINCENT -	11,793	13th July 1847	Locomotive-engines and carriages employed on railways.
NEWTON, ALFRED VINCENT -	11,824	29th July 1847	Kiln or oven for firing porcelain and other similar ware.
NEWTON, ALFRED VINCENT -	11,893	7th Oct. 1847	Construction of floors and other parts of buildings, also furniture and fittings.
NEWTON, ALFRED VINCENT -	11,906	14th Oct. 1847	Machinery for blooming iron.
NEWTON, ALFRED VINCENT -	12,048	31st Jan. 1848	Machinery for manufacturing shot and other solid balls.
NEWTON, ALFRED VINCENT -	12,254	22nd Aug. 1848	Dressing or cleaning grain, and separating extraneous matters therefrom.
NEWTON, ALFRED VINCENT -	12,310	2nd Nov. 1848	Manufacture of steel.
NEWTON, ALFRED VINCENT -	12,372	16th Dec. 1848	Casting printing-types and other similar raised surfaces; casting quadrats and spaces.
NEWTON, ALFRED VINCENT -	12,524	19th March 1849	Manufacture of piled fabrics.
NEWTON, ALFRED VINCENT -	12,557	2nd April 1849	Separating and assorting solid materials or substances of different specific-gravities.
NEWTON, ALFRED VINCENT -	12,734	9th Aug. 1849	Derricks for raising heavy bodies.
NEWTON, ALFRED VINCENT -	12,749	23rd Aug. 1849	Making and refining sugar.
NEWTON, ALFRED VINCENT -	12,795	5th Oct. 1849	Manufacture of pipes or tubes.
NEWTON, ALFRED VINCENT -	12,846	17th Nov. 1849	Manufacturing leather.
NEWTON, ALFRED VINCENT -	12,971	21st Sept. 1850	Separating and assorting solid materials or substances of different specific-gravities.
NEWTON, ALFRED VINCENT -	13,021	23rd March 1850	Preparation of materials for the production of a composition applicable to the making of buttons, knife and razor handles, and other articles where strength and durability are required.
NEWTON, ALFRED VINCENT -	13,024	26th March 1850	Coupling-joints for pipes.
NEWTON, ALFRED VINCENT -	13,084	28th May 1850	Couplings for carriages, and attachment of wheels to axles.
NEWTON, ALFRED VINCENT -	13,128	12th June 1850	Production of gases, to be used for lighting, heating, and motive-power purposes.
NEWTON, ALFRED VINCENT -	13,170	9th July 1850	Preparation and manufacture of caoutchouc or India-rubber.
NEWTON, ALFRED VINCENT -	13,239	29th Aug. 1850	Cutting types and other irregular figures.
NEWTON, ALFRED VINCENT -	13,263	26th Sept. 1850	Dyeing yarn; and manufacturing certain woven fabrics.
NEWTON, ALFRED VINCENT -	13,358	19th Nov. 1850	Composition applicable to coating of wood, metals, plaster, and other substances which are required to be preserved from decay; may also be used as a pigment or paint.
NEWTON, ALFRED VINCENT -	13,406	12th Dec. 1850	Manufacture of iron-hurdles or fences, or other articles in the construction of which wire-work may be employed.
NEWTON, ALFRED VINCENT -	13,407	12th Dec. 1850	Cutting and dressing stone.
NEWTON, ALFRED VINCENT -	13,430	27th Dec. 1850	Construction of metal-shutters.
NEWTON, ALFRED VINCENT -	13,479	30th Jan. 1851	Manufacturing looped and other woven fabrics.
NEWTON, ALFRED VINCENT -	13,489	3rd Feb. 1851	Communicating intelligence by electricity.

Name of Patentee.	Progres-sive Number.	Date.	Subject-matter of Patent.
NEWTON, ALFRED VINCENT -	13,542	4th March 1851	Preparation of materials for the production of a composition for manufacturing buttons, knife and razor handles, ink-stands, door-knobs, and other articles where hardness, strength, and durability are required.
NEWTON, ALFRED VINCENT -	13,642	27th May 1851	Carbonization of coal; utilization of products disengaged in the operation; improving the quality of the products intended for illuminating purposes; regulating the flow of the same.
NEWTON, ALFRED VINCENT -	13,856	10th Dec. 1851	Dyeing textile fabrics.
NEWTON, ALFRED VINCENT -	13,881	24th Dec. 1851	Separating substances of different specific-gravities.
NEWTON, ALFRED VINCENT -	13,937	29th Jan. 1852	Manufacture of pigments or paints.
NEWTON, ALFRED VINCENT -	13,948	31st Jan. 1852	Machinery for weaving coach-lace, Brussels-tapestry, and velvet, carpeting, and other pile-fabrics.
NEWTON, ALFRED VINCENT -	14,003	8th March 1851	Machinery for combing wool and other fibrous substances.
NEWTON, ALFRED VINCENT -	14,062	15th April 1851	Preventing the incrustation of steam-boilers; —applicable also to the preservation of metals and wood.
NEWTON, ALFRED VINCENT -	14,070	17th April 1852	Manufacture of lenses.
NEWTON, ALFRED VINCENT -	14,084	22nd April 1852	Manufacturing wood-screws; machinery used therein ;—partly applicable to arranging and feeding pins; assorting screws, pins, and other articles of various sizes.
NEWTON, ALFRED VINCENT -	14,085	22nd April 1852	Priming fire-arms.
NEWTON, ALFRED VINCENT -	14,113	1st May 1852	Manufacture of printing-surfaces.
NEWTON, ALFRED VINCENT -	14,137	22nd May 1852	Winnowing-machines.
NEWTON, ALFRED VINCENT -	14,150	1st June 1852	Machinery for propelling vessels; and apparatus to be used in connection therewith.
NEWTON, ALFRED VINCENT -	14,216	10th July 1852	Machinery for cutting soap into slabs, bars, or cakes.
NEWTON, ALFRED VINCENT -	14,252	7th Aug. 1852	Manufacture of metallic-fences;—applicable to the manufacture of verandahs, truss-frames for bridges, and to other analogous manufactures.
NEWTON, ALFRED VINCENT -	14,326	19th Oct. 1852	Manufacturing railway-chairs.
NEWTON, AMBROSE - -	590	4th April 1743	Making alum from the dross or dregs of the liquor from which alum is made.
NEWTON, DAVID - - -	12,230	7th Aug. 1848	Application of glass and glazed surfaces to nautical, architectural, and other similar purposes.
NEWTON, EDWARD - - -	8948	4th May 1841	Producing ornamental or tambour work in the manufacture of gloves.
NEWTON, HENRY - - -	11,873	23rd Sept. 1847	Spinning and doubling cotton and other fibrous substances.
NEWTON, SAMUEL - - -	413	17th May 1717	Making starch from potatoes.
NEWTON, WILLIAM - - -	618	29th July 1749	Machine for drawing coals, stones, water, ore, and other heavy bodies out of pits, mines, and other deep places.
NEWTON, WILLIAM - - -	5605	15th Jan. 1828	Surgical chair-bed, with various appendages.

Name of Patentee.	Progressive Number.	Date.	Subject-matter of Patent.
NEWTON, WILLIAM - -	6295	10th Aug. 1832	Apparatus for producing instantaneous light; means and mechanism used in the manufacture of the same.
NEWTON, WILLIAM - -	6440	20th June 1833	Apparatus for boiling, evaporating, and concentrating syrups for the production of sugar, and also of saline liquors, or for the crystallization of salt;—also applicable to distillation.
NEWTON, WILLIAM - -	6448	11th July 1833	Roving-frames for roving cotton and other fibrous substances.
NEWTON, WILLIAM - -	6774	25th Feb. 1835	Preparing fibrous or textile plants, either indigenous or exotic, to be used in place of flax or hemp.
NEWTON, WILLIAM - -	6787	11th March 1835	Preparing animal milk, and preserving its nutritive properties for any length of time.
NEWTON, WILLIAM - -	7169	11th Aug. 1836	Means of producing instantaneous ignition.
NEWTON, WILLIAM - -	7932	11th Jan. 1839	Machines for drilling land, or sowing grain and seeds.
NEWTON, WILLIAM - -	7941	17th Jan. 1839	Engines to be worked by air or other gases.
NEWTON, WILLIAM - -	8017	27th March 1839	Machinery for cutting and removing earth, applicable to the digging of canals, levelling ground for railroads or ordinary roads, and other similar earth works.
NEWTON, WILLIAM - -	8105	12th June 1839	Medicinal compound or ferruginous preparation. to give tone and vigour to the human system; applicable to weak digestion and diseases called " chlorosis".
NEWTON, WILLIAM - -	8134	27th June 1839	Construction of sun-dials designed to show mean time.
NEWTON, WILLIAM - -	8221	19th Sept. 1839	Machine for weighing.
NEWTON, WILLIAM - -	8246	24th Oct. 1839	Machinery for manufacturing screws.
NEWTON, WILLIAM - -	8442	23rd March 1840	Strengthening and preserving ligneous and textile substances.
NEWTON, WILLIAM - -	8492	5th May 1840	Apparatus and process for producing sculptured forms, figures, or devices, in marble and other hard substances.
NEWTON, WILLIAM - -	8661	15th Oct. 1840	Engines to be worked by air or other gases.
NEWTON, WILLIAM - -	8762	31st Dec. 1840	Rigging of ships and other navigable vessels.
NEWTON, WILLIAM - -	8774	6th Jan. 1841	Looms for weaving.
NEWTON, WILLIAM - -	8781	11th Jan. 1841	Machinery for cleaning wheat and other grain or seeds from smut and other injurious matters.
NEWTON, WILLIAM - -	8854	22nd Feb. 1841	Apparatus for purifying and disinfecting greasy and oily substances, animal and vegetable.
NEWTON, WILLIAM - -	8879	15th March 1841	Machinery for picking and cleaning cotton and wool.
NEWTON, WILLIAM - -	8882	16th March 1841	Spinning and twisting cotton and other materials capable of being spun and twisted.
NEWTON, WILLIAM - -	9036	28th July 1841	Machinery for making pins and pin-nails.
NEWTON, WILLIAM - -	9090	20th Sept. 1841	Machinery for manufacturing felts or felted cloths.
NEWTON, WILLIAM - -	9118	14th Oct. 1841	Engines to be worked by gas, vapour, or steam.
NEWTON, WILLIAM - -	9196	21st Dec. 1841	Cleansing wool; dyeing, washing, and bleaching cotton yarns or fabrics.

Name of Patentee.	Progressive Number.	Date.	Subject-matter of Patent.
NEWTON, WILLIAM - -	9246	8th Feb. 1842	Apparatus to be adapted to lace-making machinery, for producing a novel description of elastic fabric from silk, cotton, woollen, linen, and other fibrous materials.
NEWTON, WILLIAM - -	9265	25th Feb. 1842	Regulating the flow of air and gaseous fluids.
NEWTON, WILLIAM - -	9288	7th March 1842	Machine for weighing.
NEWTON, WILLIAM - -	9638	20th Feb. 1843	Working coal-mines, and quarries of stone, marble, and slate ;—applicable to making tunnels, borings, and to other purposes.
NEWTON, WILLIAM - -	9657	7th March 1843	Machinery for making pins.
NEWTON, WILLIAM - -	9748	30th May 1843	Obtaining copper from copper ores ;—partly applicable to working other metals containing copper ores.
NEWTON, WILLIAM - -	9771	10th June 1843	Preparation of paper designed for bank-notes, government documents, bills, cheques, deeds, and other purposes wherein protection and safety from forgery or counterfeits is required.
NEWTON, WILLIAM - -	9974	5th Dec. 1843	Extracting certain metals from ores and other compounds of the said metals ;—partly applicable to obtaining other products from such compounds.
NEWTON, WILLIAM - -	10,256	10th July 1844	Manufacturing wire from zinc ;—application of the same to various purposes.
NEWTON, WILLIAM - -	10,301	29th Aug. 1844	Apparatus for preventing shocks or accidents on railways.
NEWTON, WILLIAM - -	10,313	12th Sept. 1844	Treating or preparing oil or fatty matter.
NEWTON, WILLIAM - -	10,324	19th Sept. 1844	Machinery to be employed in manufacturing nails, rivets, screws and pins.
NEWTON, WILLIAM - -	10,338	3rd Oct. 1844	Machinery for letter-press printing.
NEWTON, WILLIAM - -	10,703	3rd June 1845	Dyeing yarns and fabrics of cotton, flax and hemp.
NEWTON, WILLIAM - -	10,753	3rd July 1845	Railways ; propelling carriages.
NEWTON, WILLIAM - -	10,815	14th Aug. 1845	Application of machinery and processes for cleaning, softening, dividing, and preparing flax, hemp, and other vegetable fibrous materials.
NEWTON, WILLIAM - -	10,947	17th Nov. 1845	Manufacturing types and other similar raised surfaces for printing.
NEWTON, WILLIAM - -	11,050	20th Jan. 1846	Manufacturing piled fabrics.
NEWTON, WILLIAM - -	11,615	10th March 1847	Engines to be worked by gas, vapour, or steam, either separately or in combination.
NEWTON, WILLIAM - -	11,625	16th March 18	Engines to be worked by gas, vapour, or steam, either separately or in combination.
NEWTON, WILLIAM - -	11,688	4th May 1847	Machinery for letter-press printing.
NEWTON, WILLIAM - -	12,033	18th Jan. 1848	Manufacture of sugar from the cane.
NEWTON, WILLIAM - -	12,134	27th April 1848	Machinery for burring, ginning, and carding wool and cotton or other similar fibrous materials requiring those processes.
NEWTON, WILLIAM - -	12,602	5th May 1849	Jacquard-machine.
NEWTON, WILLIAM - -	13,109	8th June 1850	Manufacture of cords, ropes, bands, strong cloths, quilting, sacks and cushions, and elastic material for stuffing the latter, in which manufacture caoutchouc forms an essential ingredient ;—application of parts of the same to the manufacture of pads, stoppers, tubes, boxes, baskets, coverings, wrappers and other articles of utility.

Name of Patentee.	Progres-sive Number.	Date.	Subject-matter of Patent.
NEWTON, WILLIAM - -	14,092	28th April 1852	Machinery for weaving, colouring and marking fabrics.
NEWTON, WILLIAM EDWARD -	7695	19th June 1838	Diving-apparatus.
NEWTON, WILLIAM EDWARD -	7836	17th Oct. 1838	Construction of bridges, viaducts, piers, roofs, truss-girders and stays.
NEWTON, WILLIAM EDWARD -	7839	22nd Oct. 1838	Preparing substances for the preservation of wood and other material used in constructing houses, ships, and other works.
NEWTON, WILLIAM EDWARD -	8843	15th Feb. 1841	Obtaining a concentrated extract of hops. " Humuline."
NEWTON, WILLIAM EDWARD -	8914	3rd April 1841	Manufacturing lime, cement, artificial stone, and such other compositions, applicable for working under water, and in constructing buildings exposed to damp.
NEWTON, WILLIAM EDWARD -	9019	7th July 1841	Manufacture of fuel.
NEWTON, WILLIAM EDWARD -	9145	9th Nov. 1841	Production of ammonia.
NEWTON, WILLIAM EDWARD -	9178	14th Dec. 1841	Printing or delineating patterns on painted cloths, for floor-cloths, covers, and other uses.
NEWTON, WILLIAM EDWARD -	9195	21st Dec. 1841	Lamps and burners; supplying air and heat thereto for the support of combustion.
NEWTON, WILLIAM EDWARD -	9293	10th March 1842	Boilers, furnaces, and steam-engines.
NEWTON, WILLIAM EDWARD -	9463	8th Sept. 1842	Machinery for making screws, screw-blanks and rivets.
NEWTON, WILLIAM EDWARD -	9490	13th Oct. 1842	Manufacture of artificial fuel.
NEWTON, WILLIAM EDWARD -	9548	8th Dec. 1842	Construction and arrangement of axles and axletrees for carriages, carts, and other vehicles used on rail and other roads.
NEWTON, WILLIAM EDWARD -	9724	15th May 1842	Construction of boxes for the axles or axletrees of locomotive engines and carriages, and for bearings and journals of machinery in general; oiling or lubricating the same.
NEWTON, WILLIAM EDWARD -	9749	30th May 1843	Constructing boats and other vessels.
NEWTON, WILLIAM EDWARD -	9772	10th June 1843	Application of certain volatile liquids for the production of light; lamps and burners for the combustion of the same.
NEWTON, WILLIAM EDWARD -	9783	15th June 1843	Apparatus for propelling vessels.
NEWTON, WILLIAM EDWARD -	9831	13th July 1843	Machine for ploughing, harrowing or tilling land.
NEWTON, WILLIAM EDWARD -	9925	4th Nov. 1843	Furnaces or fire-places.
NEWTON, WILLIAM EDWARD -	9938	16th Nov. 1843	Machinery for preparing and combing wool, hair and other fibrous substances.
NEWTON, WILLIAM EDWARD -	10,016	16th Jan. 1844	Machinery for tracing and copying designs, drawings, and etchings of all kinds, either of the original size, or upon an enlarged or reduced scale.
NEWTON, WILLIAM EDWARD -	10,027	30th Jan. 1844	Preparation of caoutchouc or India-rubber; manufacturing various fabrics of which caoutchouc forms a component part.
NEWTON, WILLIAM EDWARD -	10,C45	8th Feb. 1844	Machinery for obtaining and applying motive-power for propelling and raising heavy bodies.
NEWTON, WILLIAM EDWARD -	10,049	12th Feb. 1844	Furnaces.
NEWTON, WILLIAM EDWARD -	10,821	28th Aug. 1845	Machinery for spinning.
NEWTON, WILLIAM EDWARD -	11,082	11th Feb. 1846	Construction of instruments for ascertaining, registering, and regulating the speed of carriages and machinery.

Name of Patentee.	Progressive Number.	Date.	Subject-matter of Patent.
NEWTON, WILLIAM EDWARD -	11,092	17th Feb. 1846	Manufacture of thread or yarn.
NEWTON, WILLIAM EDWARD -	11,178	28th April 1846	Clocks or timekeepers.
NEWTON, WILLIAM EDWARD -	11,372	17th Sept. 1846	Preserving fruit and vegetables.
NEWTON, WILLIAM EDWARD -	11,578	15th Feb. 1847	Aërial locomotion.
NEWTON, WILLIAM EDWARD -	11,708	22nd May 1847	Apparatus for manufacturing capsules for enclosing medicinal preparations, or other liquid or solid substances.
NEWTON, WILLIAM EDWARD -	11,769	28th June 1847	Manufacturing wheels.
NEWTON, WILLIAM EDWARD -	12,791	12th July 1847	Manufacture of screws.
NEWTON, WILLIAM EDWARD -	11,876	30th Sept. 1847	Machinery for manufacture of nets and netting.
NEWTON, WILLIAM EDWARD -	11,934	16th Nov. 1847	Preparing certain matters to be employed as pigments.
NEWTON, WILLIAM EDWARD -	12,100	22nd March 1848	Coupling-joints for pipes, nozzles, stop-cocks, cylinder-heads, and other apparatus.
NEWTON, WILLIAM EDWARD -	12,204	6th July 1848	Construction of stoves, grates, furnaces, and fire-places.
NEWTON, WILLIAM EDWARD -	12,216	18th July 1848	Machinery for letter-press printing.
NEWTON, WILLIAM EDWARD -	12,395	28th Dec. 1848	Steam-engines.
NEWTON, WILLIAM EDWARD -	12,413	11th Jan. 1849	Construction of wheels.
NEWTON, WILLIAM EDWARD -	12,473	12th Feb. 1849	Engines, principally designed for pumping water.
NEWTON, WILLIAM EDWARD -	12,475	13th Feb. 1849	Machinery for hulling and polishing rice and other grain or seeds.
NEWTON, WILLIAM EDWARD -	12,572	16th April 1849	Machinery for the manufacture of net-lace or other similar fabrics.
NEWTON, WILLIAM EDWARD -	12,577	17th April 1849	Boilers or steam-generators.
NEWTON, WILLIAM EDWARD -	12,634	5th June 1849	Grates, stoves, or fire-places; warming or heating buildings.
NEWTON, WILLIAM EDWARD -	12,748	23rd Aug. 1849	Steam-boilers.
NEWTON, WILLIAM EDWARD -	12,783	20th Sept. 1849	Pumps, and machinery for working the same;—applicable for working other machinery.
NEWTON, WILLIAM EDWARD -	12,786	27th Sept. 1849	Manufacture of knobs for doors, articles of furniture, or other purposes; connecting metallic attachments to articles of glass or other analogous materials.
NEWTON, WILLIAM EDWARD -	12,794	5th Oct. 1849	Machinery for planing, tongueing, and grooving, boards or planks.
NEWTON, WILLIAM EDWARD -	12,834	6th Nov. 1849	Machinery for dressing, shaping, cutting, and drilling or boring rocks or stone;—partly applicable (with certain modifications) to machinery for driving piles.
NEWTON, WILLIAM EDWARD -	12,955	29th Jan. 1850	Machinery for making hat-bodies and other similar articles.
NEWTON, WILLIAM EDWARD -	13,058	23rd April 1850	Casting type.
NEWTON, WILLIAM EDWARD -	13,075	22nd May 1850	Warming and ventilating buildings.
NEWTON, WILLIAM EDWARD -	13,103	6th June 1850	Improvements applicable to boots, shoes, and other coverings for or appliances to the feet.
NEWTON, WILLIAM EDWARD -	13,114	11th June 1850	Machinery for carding-cotton, wool or other fibrous materials; apparatus for preparing or setting the cards of carding-engines.
NEWTON, WILLIAM EDWARD -	13,116	11th June 1850	Rotary-engines.
NEWTON, WILLIAM EDWARD -	13,132	12th June 1850	Construction of railways.

Name of Patentee.	Progressive Number.	Date.	Subject-matter of Patent
NEWTON, WILLIAM EDWARD -	13,192	23rd July 1850	Obtaining, preparing, and applying zinc and other volatile metals and their oxydes, application of zinc or ores containing the same, to the manufacture of certain metals or alloys of metals
NEWTON, WILLIAM EDWARD -	13,193	23rd July 1850	Machinery for cutting files.
NEWTON, WILLIAM EDWARD -	13,232	22nd Aug. 1850	Refining gold.
NEWTON, WILLIAM EDWARD -	13,233	22nd Aug. 1850	Construction of ships' magazines.
NEWTON, WILLIAM EDWARD -	13,234	22nd Aug. 1850	Apparatus for producing ice, and for general refrigerating purposes.
NEWTON, WILLIAM EDWARD -	13,235	22nd Aug. 1850	Construction of ships or vessels; and steam-boilers or generators.
NEWTON, WILLIAM EDWARD -	13,279	10th Oct. 1850	Manufacturing yarns.
NEWTON, WILLIAM EDWARD -	13,397	7th Dec. 1850	Engines to be worked by steam or other power.
NEWTON, WILLIAM EDWARD -	13,498	10th Feb. 1851	Apparatus for milking.
NEWTON, WILLIAM EDWARD -	13,541	4th March 1851	Portable bedsteads and sacking bottoms.
NEWTON, WILLIAM EDWARD -	13,612	3rd May 1851	Manufacture of woven or felted fabrics.
NEWTON, WILLIAM EDWARD -	13,625	8th May 1851	Apparatus for the generation and condensation of steam for various purposes; parts of engines to be worked by steam, air, or gases.
NEWTON, WILLIAM EDWARD -	13,966	12th Feb. 1852	Healds or harness for looms for weaving; machinery for producing the same.
NEWTON, WILLIAM EDWARD -	13,974	23rd Feb. 1851	Manufacture of coke, and application of the gaseous products arising therefrom to useful purposes.
NEWTON, WILLIAM EDWARD -	14,005	8th March 1852	Propelling vessels.
NEWTON, WILLIAM EDWARD -	14,067	17th April 1852	Machinery or apparatus for cutting paper, pasteboard, or other similar substances.
NEWTON, WILLIAM EDWARD -	14,068	17th April 1852	Indicating and regulating the heat, also the height and supply of water in steam-boilers, and apparatus for the purpose;— applicable for heating buildings, furnaces, stoves, fire-places, kilns, and ovens, and for indicating the height and regulating the supply of water in other boilers and vessels.
NEWTON, WILLIAM EDWARD -	14,127	17th May 1852	Construction of docks, basins, railways, and apparatus connected therewith, for raising or removing vessels or ships out of the water, or on to dry land, for the purpose of preserving or repairing the same.
NEWTON, WILLIAM EDWARD -	14,174	19th June 1852	Construction of fences.
NEWTON, WILLIAM EDWARD -	14,249	31st July 1852	Construction of wheels for carriages.
NEWTON, WILLIAM EDWARD -	14,320	11th Oct. 1852	Steam and other gauges.
NEWTON, WILLIAM EDWARD -	14,328	19th Oct. 1852	Machinery or apparatus for sewing.
NEWTON, WILLIAM EDWARD -	14,329	19th Oct. 1852	Apparatus applicable to public carriages, for ascertaining and registering the number of passengers who have travelled therein during a given period, and the distance travelled by each.
NIBLET, DANIEL - - -	430	25th June 1720	Using the steam of boiling liquors for drying malt, hops, starch, and other humid substances, and for baking, brewing, distilling, boiling, and making salt.
NICHOL, JOHN - - -	4584	22nd Aug. 1821	Capstan, windlass, and horses' roller.

Name of Patentee.	Progressive Number.	Date.	Subject-matter of Patent.
NICHOL, WILLIAM - - -	10,018	16th Jan. 1844	Lithographic and other printing-presses.
NICHOLAS, EDWARD - -	4113	19th April 1817	Plough for covering grain with mould, when sown.
NICHOLLS, JOHN - - -	5821	25th July 1829	Lever; application of its power.
NICHOLLS, NICHOLAS - -	283	19th Oct. 1691	Engine, made of timber, with glass windows, door, air-pipes, leather sleeves, and braces affixed, to enable a man to work under water for many hours.
NICHOLLS, ROBERT HAWKINS	11,879	30th Sept. 1847	Machinery for distributing corn and other grain on land; giving motion to agricultural and other machinery.
NICHOLLS, ROBERT HAWKINS	13,600	24th April 1851	Machinery for giving motion to agricultural and other machinery.
NICHOLS, MORGAN - - -	2394	1st May 1800	Making portable ovens.
NICHOLS, SAMUEL - - -	14,270	19th Aug. 1852	Manufacture of textile fabrics; machinery for producing such fabrics.
NICHOLSON, JAMES	831	18th June 1765	Making alum from liquor made from copperas materials and uncalcined ore.
NICHOLSON, JOHN - -	4736	16th Dec. 1822	Apparatus for applying heat to certain instruments of domestic use.
NICHOLSON, ROBERT - -	831	18th June 1765	Making alum from liquor made from copperas materials and uncalcined ore.
NICHOLSON, WILLIAM - -	1159	14th July 1777	Securing the property of persons purchasing shares of State-lottery tickets.
NICHOLSON, WILLIAM - -	1748	29th April 1790	Machine for printing on paper, linen, cotton, woollen, and other articles.
NICHOLSON, WILLIAM - -	2641	14th Aug. 1802	Machinery for manufacturing files.
NICHOLSON, WILLIAM - -	2990	22nd Nov. 1806	Application of steam to useful purposes; apparatus required to effect the same.
NICHOLSON, WILLIAM - -	3514	13th Jan. 1812	Suspending the bodies or principal parts of wheel carriages.
NICHOLSON, WILLIAM - -	5465	20th Feb. 1827	Constructing gasometers.
NICHOLSON, WILLIAM - -	7393	17th June 1837	Construction and arrangement of preparation and spinning-machinery
NICHOLSON, WILLIAM - -	11,118	5th March 1846	Manufacture of glass and other vitreous products.
NICHOLSON, WILLIAM WILKINSON.	12,277	28th Sept. 1848	Machinery for compressing wood and other materials.
NICKELS, BENJAMIN - -	10,061	19th Feb. 1844	Manufacture of elastic fabrics, and rendering them less elastic.
NICKELS, BENJAMIN - -	10,897	27th Oct. 1845	Pianofortes.
NICKELS, CHRISTOPHER -	7213	24th Oct. 1836	Preparing and manufacturing caoutchouc;—applicable to various purposes.
NICKELS, CHRISTOPHER -	7483	21st Nov. 1837	Embossing or impressing the surfaces of leather and other substances;—applicable to various purposes.
NICKELS, CHRISTOPHER -	7515	19th Dec. 1837	Bookbinding;—in part applicable to the cutting of paper for other purposes.
NICKELS, CHRISTOPHER -	7621	21st April 1838	Machinery for covering fibres;—applicable to the manufacture of braid and other fabrics.
NICKELS, CHRISTOPHER -	80,021	15th March 1838	Manufacturing fabrics from linen, woollen, silk, and other fibrous materials.
NICKELS, CHRISTOPHER -	8090	4th June 1839	Producing plain and ornamental articles and surfaces from cements or earths.
NICKELS, CHRISTOPHER -	8171	1st Aug. 1839	Cutting india-rubber.

Name of Patentee.	Progressive Number.	Date.	Subject-matter of Patent.
NICKELS, CHRISTOPHER -	8300	4th Dec. 1839	Propelling carriages.
NICKELS, CHRISTOPHER -	8537	9th June 1840	Manufacture of braids and plaits.
NICKELS, CHRISTOPHER -	8799	19th Jan. 1841	Manufacture of braids and plaits.
NICKELS, CHRISTOPHER -	9012	28th June 1841	Mattrasses, cushions, paddings, or stuffings, and carpet-rugs or other napped fabrics.
NICKELS, CHRISTOPHER -	9252	10th Feb. 1842	Manufacture of plaited fabrics.
NICKELS, CHRISTOPHER	9472	15th Sept. 1842	Fabrics produced by lace-machinery.
NICKELS, CHRISTOPHER	9629	11th Feb. 1843	Manufacture of fabrics made by lace-machinery.
NICKELS, CHRISTOPHER -	9735	22nd May 1843	Manufacture of fabrics made by lace-machinery.
NICKELS, CHRISTOPHER -	9980	8th Dec. 1843	Apparatus for facilitating the cutting or shaping of materials for making gloves and other articles.
NICKELS, CHRISTOPHER -	10,039	8th Feb. 1844	Manufacture of crape, or a substitute for crape.
NICKELS, CHRISTOPHER -	10,061	19th Feb. 1844	Manufacture of elastic fabrics, and rendering them less elastic.
NICKELS, CHRISTOPHER -	10,552	13th March 1845	Manufacture of elastic webs and cords; manufacturing articles from the same.
NICKELS, CHRISTOPHER -	10,673	20th May 1845	Binding and covering books, pamphlets, portfolios, writing-cases, and other articles.
NICKELS, CHRISTOPHER -	11,729	3rd June 1847	Manufacture of woven-fabrics, and giving elasticity to certain articles or fabrics.
NICKELS, CHRISTOPHER -	12,364	9th Dec. 1848	Making gloves and other articles of dress and furniture.
NICKELS, CHRISTOPHER -	12,407	11th Jan. 1849	Preparing and manufacturing india-rubber.
NICKELS, CHRISTOPHER -	12,472	12th Feb. 1849	Manufacture of woollen and other fabrics.
NICKELS, CHRISTOPHER -	12,671	26th June 1849	Manufacture of woollen and other fabrics.
NICKELS, CHRISTOPHER -	12,938	23rd Jan. 1850	Manufacture of woollen and other fabrics.
NICKELS, CHRISTOPHER -	13,384	23rd Nov. 1850	Manufacture of woollen and other fabrics.
NICKELS, CHRISTOPHER -	13,880	24th Dec. 1851	Manufacture of knitted, looped, and other elastic fabrics.
NICKELS, CHRISTOPHER -	14,308	30th Sept. 1852	Weaving.
NICKHOLLS, HENRY - -	2255	3rd Aug. 1798	Machine for lifting, raising, and conveying boats, vessels, or other things from one level to another on canals or rivers, so as to save water and prevent tunnelling.
NICKOLL, SAMUEL WILSON -	6877	10th Aug. 1835	Rendering condensing steam-engines portable, and applicable as a means of general transport on rail and other roads.
NICOL, JOHN M - - -	13,105	6th June 1850	Machinery for raising and conveying water.
NICOLAS, JOHN LEO - -	8331	1st Jan. 1840	Construction and propulsion of carriages on railways or common roads, and through fields for agricultural purposes.
NICOLE, ADOLPHE - - -	10,348	14th Oct. 1844	Chronometers and watches.
NICOLL, HENRY JOHN - -	11,707	22nd May 1847	Garments, pockets, bags, and other receptacles.
NICOLLE, EUGENE - - -	13,915	24th Jan. 1852	Machinery to be used in the manufacture of nails, rivets, bolts, or pins, or screw-blanks.
NICOLLE, EUGENE - - -	14,098	29th April 1852	Compositions; machinery for pressing or moulding the same;—applicable to moulding or pressing other substances.

411

Name of Patentee.	Progressive Number.	Date.	Subject-matter of Patent.
NIELD, JAMES - - -	10,266	24th July 1844	Looms.
NIEPEE, JOSEPH CLAUDE -	4179	25th Nov. 1817	Propelling boats and other vessels ;—applicable to machinery of other descriptions.
NIGHTENGALE, PAUL - -	697	10th Feb. 1755	Making saltpetre from vegetables.
NIGHTINGALE, JAMES - -	12,565	16th April 1849	Machinery for washing and cleansing cotton and other fabrics ; applicable to bleaching, dyeing, printing, and sizing warps and piece-goods.
NIGHTINGALE, THOMAS -	1783	16th Nov. 1790	Machine for calendering, glazing, and dressing muslin, calico, cotton, linen, woollen, silk, paper, gauze, mohair, and other articles.
NIND, PHILIP - - - -	13,416	19th Dec. 1850	Manufacture of sugar; cutting and rasping vegetable substances.
NISBET, ROBERT - - -	11,099	19th Feb. 1846	Locomotive-engines; and railways.
NISBETT, JOHN - - -	9739	25th May 1843	Preparing hides and skins in the manufacture of certain descriptions of leather.
NOAK, JOHN - - -	10,209	1st June 1844	Manufacture of salt; apparatus to be used therein.
NOAK, WALTER - - -	10,209	1st June 1844	Manufacture of salt; apparatus to be used therein.
NOBLE, EDWARD MOORE -	3099	23rd Jan. 1808	Making white-lead.
NOBLE, JAMES - - -	2861	29th June 1805	Discharging wool-combs by separating the tears from the noiles, and drawing what are called slivers from the combs, after or before the combs are worked, or the wool is combed upon the same.
NOBLE, JAMES - - -	6413	25th April 1833	Machine for combing wool and other fibrous materials.
NOBLE, JAMES - - -	6559	20th Feb. 1834	Combing wool.
NOBLE, JAMES - - -	7047	29th March 1836	Combing wool and other fibrous substances.
NOBLE, JAMES - - -	11,508	21st Dec. 1846	Combing wool; preparing wool for combing and carding.
NOBLE, MARK - - -	1416	29th Jan. 1784	Pump for raising water.
NOBLE, MARK - - -	1453	6th Nov. 1784	Machine for raising water.
NOBLE, MARK - - -	1646	15th April 1788	Overcoming resistance in mechanical operations by man or beast.
NOBLE, MARK - - -	2274	27th Nov. 1798	Apparatus for working pumps, engines, or machines in general, whether for sea or land service.
NOBLE, MARK - - -	3037	25th April 1807	Chain-pumps, hand-pumps, and fire-extinguishing engine.
NOBLE, MARK - - -	3289	14th Dec. 1809	Chain and hand-pumps, fire-extinguishing engine, and steam-engine.
NOBLE, PETER - - -	2940	6th June 1806	Chain and common pumps, the latter acting as a fire-engine for sea and land purposes.
NOBLE, WILLIAM ALFRED -	3793	23rd March 1814	Steam and fire engine; connecting steam or water pipes together.
NOBLE, WILLIAM ALFRED -	6603	6th May 1834	Pumps for drawing, raising, forcing, or propelling water and other fluids.
NOBLE, WILLIAM ALFRED -	6727	4th Dec. 1834	Applying the steam to the common and other engines.

Name of Patentee.	Progressive Number.	Date.	Subject-matter of Patent.
NOCK, HENRY - - -	1095	8th April 1775	Firelock constructed for portability and safety with the lock so constructed as not to obstruct the sight, having the prime secured against the effects of rain, and so contrived that the barrel can be taken from the lock for the purpose of cleaning the same, is also provided with a lever that sets the lock in motion, but being removed disengages the action of the gun; the said firelock may be used either to a gun, pistol, cannon, or other fire-arm, with one, two, three, or more barrels.
NOCK, HENRY - - -	1598	25th April 1787	Breeching applicable to guns and other fire-arms.
NOCK, SAMUEL - - -	4054	12th Aug. 1816	Pan of the locks of guns and fire-arms.
NOEL, WILLIAM - - -	9326	21st April 1842	Manufacture of boots and shoes.
NOLAN, FREDERICK -	3183	26th Nov. 1808	Construction of flutes, flageolets, hautboys, and other wind instruments.
NOLTE, VINCENT - -	6563	27th Feb. 1834	Hydraulic power engine.
NOON, THOMAS - - -	2790	30th Oct. 1804	Thrashing-machine with loose beaters.
NOON, THOMAS - - -	3233	4th May 1809	Guns, pistols, and other fire-arms; applicable to cannon and other large guns.
NOONE, GEORGE EDWARD - [Noon, George Edward.]	8588	3rd Aug. 1840	Pumps and engines for drawing beer, cyder, and other fluids.
NOONE, GEORGE EDWARD -	8850	18th Feb. 1841	Dry gas-meters.
NORMAN, GEORGE - - -	13,460	18th Jan. 1851	Cooking and boiling apparatus.
NORMAN, WILLIAM -	11,699	10th May 1847	Construction of expanding or dining tables.
NORMANDY, ALPHONSE RENE [LE MIRE DE.	8175	1st Aug. 1839	Manufacture of inks and dyes.
NORMANDY, ALPHONSE RENE [LE MIRE DE.	9081	8th Sept. 1841	Manufacture of soap.
NORMANDY, ALPHONSE RENE [LE MIRE DE. [Normandy, Alphonse le Mire de.]	10,423	7th Dec. 1844	Purifying lac and converting lac into shellac.
NORMANDY, ALPHONSE RENE [LE MIRE DE. [Normandy, Alphonse le Mire de.]	10,632	22nd April 1845	Dissolving lac and shellac; rendering fabrics waterproof.
NORMANDY, ALPHONSE RENE [LE MIRE DE. [Normandy, Alphonse le Mire de.]	10,743	28th June 1845	Manufacture of thimbles and finger-shields.
NORMANDY, ALPHONSE RENE [LE MIRE DE. [Normandy, Alphonse le Mire de.]	11,591	24th Feb. 1847	Manufacture of zinc.
NORMANDY, ALPHONSE RENE [LE MIRE DE.	13,512	12th Feb. 1851	Manufacture of galvanized iron.
NORMANDY, ALPHONSE RENE [LE MIRE DE.	13,714	7th Aug. 1851	Obtaining fresh-water from salt-water; concentrating sulphuric-acid.
NORMANVILLE, WILLIAM JOHN	12,143	2nd May 1848	Railway or other carriages, being partly new modes of constructing axle-boxes and journals of wheels; lubricating such and other parts of machinery by the introduction of aqueous, alkaline, oleaginous or saponaceous solutions.
NORRIS, EDWIN - - -	6763	12th Feb. 1835	Machine for letter-press printing.
NORRIS, RICHARD STUART -	13,500	10th Feb. 1851	Construction of the permanent-way of railways, also bridges, locks, and other erections wholly or in part constructed of metal; breaks for railway-carriages.

Name of Patentee.	Progressive Number.	Date.	Subject-matter of Patent.
NORRIS, THOMAS - - -	909	7th Dec. 1768	Drops for the cure of fevers and all inflammatory disorders, also beneficial in many chronic disorders.
NORRIS, THOMAS - - -	3381	26th Sept. 1810	Sheathing the bottoms of ships or vessels with certain materials, to serve instead of copper.
NORRIS, WILLIAM - - -	7227	19th Nov. 1836	Manufacture of combs.
NORRIS, WILLIAM - - -	9641	21st Feb. 1843	Coating, with other metals, iron-nails, screws, nuts, bolts, and other articles made of iron.
NORTH, THOMAS - - -	7402	19th July 1837	Manufacture of wire.
NORTH, WILLIAM - - -	5810	4th July 1829	Constructing ceilings and partitions for dwelling-houses, warehouses, workshops, or other buildings.
NORTH, WILLIAM - - -	6373	29th Jan. 1833	Roofing or covering houses or other buildings or places.
NORTH, WILLIAM - - -	9893	5th Oct. 1843	Covering roofs and flats of buildings with slate.
NORTH, WILLIAM - - -	10,393	14th Nov. 1844	Covering roofs and flats with slates.
NORTON, BENJAMIN DAWSON	11,560	1st Feb. 1847	Cranes and other hoisting and lowering machinery.
NORTON, CHARLES - -	3245	20th June 1809	Construction of houses and other buildings, whereby expense will be reduced, and the buildings rendered more secure from fire.
NORTON, EARDLEY - -	987	2nd May 1771	Clock which strikes the hours and parts; also a watch which repeats the hours and parts, and contrived to contain its appendages, as a key, seal, or tricket.
NORTON, FREDERICK WILLIAM	12,545	28th March 1849	Production of figured fabrics.
NORTON, FREDERICK WILLIAM	13,859	16th Dec. 1851	Manufacture or production of plain and figured fabrics.
NORTON, GEORGE JAMES -	10,499	28th Jan. 1845	Cooking-apparatus;—parts of which are applicable to lighting and heating.
NORTON, JAMES - - -	1697	27th Aug. 1789	Box for supplying oil to the wheels of carriages and to other wheels.
NORTON, JAMES - - -	14,171	17th June 1852	Ascertaining and registering the mileage run by vehicles, and the number of persons entering or travelling in vehicles;—applicable to public buildings and other places where tolls are taken.
NORTON, JEHIEL FRANKLING	7525	23rd Dec. 1837	Stoves or furnaces.
NORTON, JEHIEL FORBES -	7825	8th Oct. 1838	Stoves or furnaces : and instruments for making the same.
NORTON, JOHN - - -	820	30th Nov. 1764	Medicine, called "Maredant's Drops."
TON, JOHN - - -	2724	28th July 1803	Construction of a water-mill.
NORTON, JOHN - - -	3060	13th July 1807	Pumps.
NORTON, JOHN - - -	9185	16th Dec. 1841	Sheathing ships and other vessels.
NORTON, JOSEPH - - -	8412	4th March 1840	Looms for weaving figured and twilled fabrics.
NORTON, JOSEPH EMMETT -	12,019	11th Jan. 1848	Bottles or vessels for containing liquids; mode and machinery or apparatus for filling and stopping the same.
NORTON, WILLIAM -	912	21st Dec. 1768	Manufacturing a silk stuff equal to Italian crape and tiffany.
NORVELL, WILLIAM - -	6420	8th May 1833	Machinery for making strands from the yarns and laying ropes by such machinery, at one and the same time.

Name of Patentee.	Progressive Number.	Date.	Subject-matter of Patent.
NORWOOD, RICHARD - -	56	2nd April 1632	Instruments for diving and raising goods out of deep waters.
NOSSITER, CHARLES - -	10,242	3rd July 1844	Tanning hides and skins.
NOSSITER, CHARLES - -	10,874	10th Oct. 1845	Manufacture of leather.
NOTON, THOMAS - -	10,486	21st Jan. 1845	Power-looms for the manufacture of cloth from cotton-wool and other fibrous substances.
NOTT, BENEDICT - -	6205	22nd Dec. 1831	Construction of furnaces for generating heat; apparatus for applying heat to useful purposes.
NOTT, JOEL BENEDICK - -	6026	4th Nov. 1830	Construction of furnaces for generating heat; apparatus for the application of heat to useful purposes.
NOTT, JOHN - - -	11,051	20th Jan. 1846	Communicating intelligence from one place to another.
NOUAILLE, PETER - -	960	25th May 1770	Crossing silk in the throwing, by means of a mechanical and mathematical progressively-moving guider, affixed to the reel upon the silk throwing-mill and which proceeds in a diagonal direction upon the reel, thus making the skein broader, being advantageous not only in dyeing but also in winding and weaving the silk after it has been dyed.
NOUAILLE, PETER - -	1062	27th Jan. 1774	Making silk-strings for stringed musical-instruments.
NOUAILLE, PETER - -	3608	31st Oct. 1812	Saving water in mechanical and hydraulic operations.
NOWELL, CHARLES - -	413	17th May 1717	Making starch from potatoes.
NOWELL, SAMUEL - -	180	23rd April 1675	Beehives or boxes placed one on another, with holes in the top and several entrances backwards and forwards, so that the bees can conveniently and constantly pass in and out, and the necessity of the bees swarming or being destroyed will thus be prevented.
NUGENT, PATRICK ROONEY -	1980	18th March 1794	Instruments whereby the latitude, longitude, and magnetic variation at sea or on shore may be obtained.
NUGENT, PATRICK ROONEY -	2246	27th June 1798	Instruments whereby the latitude and longitude, also the variation and inclination of the needle at sea or on shore, may be obtained.
NUNN, HENRY - -	5125	15th March 1825	Machinery for making bobbin-net lace.
NUNN, HENRY WILLIAM -	6392	27th Feb. 1833	Machinery used in the manufacture of bobbin-net lace for producing ornamented lace.
NUNN, HENRY WILLIAM -	6583	27th March 1834	Manufacturing certain kinds of embroidered lace.
NUNN, HENRY WILLIAM -	6804	3rd April 1835	Manufacturing the ornamented parts of lace; producing ornamented or embroidered lace.
NUNN, HENRY WILLIAM -	7065	21st April 1836	Manufacturing certain kinds of embroidered lace; — partly applicable to other purposes.
NUNN, HENRY WILLIAM -	7527	4th Jan. 1838	Manufacture of certain descriptions of lace and other ornamented fabrics.
NUSSEY, GEORGE - -	7660	31st May 1838	Vegetable preparation, for dyeing blues and other colours.

Name of Patentee.	Progres-sive Number.	Date.		Subject-matter of Patent.
NUTTALL, JOSEPH WILSON -	8922	5th April	1841	Trouser-straps.
NUTTALL, THOMAS - -	476	5th April	1725	Engine for supplying cities, corporations, and towns with water; also for draining tin, lead, and coal mines, lands and marshes; and useful on board ship in case of leakage.
NYE, JOSEPH - - - -	6635	1st July	1834	Construction and application of pumps and machinery for raising fluids, and for other purposes.
NYE, JOSEPH - - -	6843	2nd June	1835	Pumps and instruments for conveying fluids into and withdrawing them from cavities in human and other animal bodies.
NYE, JOSEPH - - -	11,884	7th Oct.	1847	Machinery for driving piles and raising earth and fluids.
NYE, JOSEPH - - -	12,931	17th Jan.	1850	Hydraulic-machinery;—partly applicable to steam-engines and machinery for driving piles.
NYE, JOSEPH - - -	13,333	12th Nov.	1850	Hydraulic-machinery;—partly applicable to steam-engines and machinery for driving piles.
NYE, SAMUEL - - -	6635	1st July	1834	Construction and application of pumps and machinery for raising fluids and for other purposes.
NIREN, JOHN - - -	2880	27th Sept.	1805	Printing fancy patterns on silk and cotton lace-net, to supersede tambouring or working them in colours.
NIREN, JOHN WILLIAM - -	8555	26th June	1840	Manufacture of oxalic-acid.

O.

Name of Patentee.	Progres-sive Number.	Date.		Subject-matter of Patent.
OATES, JOSEPH PIMLOTT -	13,739	9th Oct.	1851	Machinery for the manufacture of bricks, tiles, quarries, and drain-pipes, and such other articles as may be made of clay or other plastic substances.
OATES, JOSEPH PIMLOTT -	14,054	6th April	1852	Machinery for the manufacture of bricks, tiles, quarries, and drain-pipes, and such other articles as may be made of clay or other plastic substances.
OBERLIN, JEAN JACQUES LEO-[POLD.	6545	18th Jan.	1834	Boilers applicable to various purposes.
OCCLESHAW, WILLIAM - -	7494	2nd Dec.	1837	Machinery for manufacturing pipes or tubes and other articles, from lead or other metallic substances.
ODDIE, JOHN - - -	12,455	6th Feb.	1849	Improvements in and applicable to looms for weaving.
ODY, JOHN - - - -	6836	13th May	1835	Construction of waterclosets.
OGDEN, ADAM - - -	10,547	8th March	1845	Machinery for preparing and cleaning wool, cotton, and similar fibrous materials.
OGDEN, ADAM - - -	11,798	17th July	1847	Machinery for cleaning wool, cotton, and similar fibrous substances from burs, motes, and other extraneous matter.
OGDEN, ADAM - - -	13,101	4th June	1850	Machinery for cleaning wool, cotton, and similar fibrous substances from burs, motes, and other extraneous matter.
OGDEN, JAMES - - -	8913	3rd April	1841	Looms for weaving.

Name of Patentee.	Progres-sive Number.	Date.	Subject-matter of Patent.
OGILBY, Colonel BARTHOLO-[MEW.	350	21st April 1697	Engine to prevent the overturning of coaches, carts, or waggons.
OGILVY, CHARLES - - -	5152	20th April 1825	Apparatus for storing gas
OGLE, HENRY MEAD - -	4173	1st Nov. 1817	Tea and coffee pots and biggins.
OGLE, JAMES - - - -	574	24th April 1741	Making salt from sea-water.
OGLE, JAMES - - -	5245	20th Aug. 1825	Fulling-mills, or machinery for fulling and washing woollen-cloths, or other fabrics that require the process of felting or fulling.
OGLE, NATHANIEL - -	5927	14th April 1830	Construction of steam-engine and other boilers or generators; applicable to propelling vessels and locomotive-carriages, and for other purposes.
OGLETHORP, THEOPHILUS -	228	9th June 1683	Engine for rendering salt and brackish water sweet, and fit for drinking, cooking, washing, and other uses.
OGSTON, JAMES - - -	5314	6th Jan. 1826	Construction and manufacture of watches.
O'KEEFFE OWEN - - - [O'Keefe Owen.]	801	2nd Dec. 1763	Axletree and axletree-box for coaches and all other carriages, contrived to supply itself with oil, without taking off the wheels.
O'KEEFFE, OWEN - - -	811	16th April 1764	Carriage upon which to hang the bodies of coaches and other conveyances.
O'KEEFFE, OWEN - - -	1101	1st Aug. 1775	Carriage for coaches, chariots, chaises, waggons, and other vehicles, to be used with three or four wheels.
OKELL, BENJAMIN - -	483	31st March 1726	Drops for rheumatism, stone, gravel, agues, and hysterics. " Dr. Bacon's Pectoral drops."
OLDHAM, ELISHA - - -	8837	8th Feb. 1841	Construction of turn-tables to be used on railways.
OLDHAM, JOHN - - -	4169	10th Oct. 1817	Propelling ships and vessels on seas, rivers, and canals, by the agency of steam.
OLDHAM, JOHN - - -	4429	15th Jan. 1820	Propelling ships and vessels on seas, rivers, and canals, by the agency of steam.
OLDHAM, JOHN - - -	5455	1st Feb. 1827	Construction of wheels designed for driving machinery, to be impelled by water or wind;—applicable to propelling boats and other vessels.
OLDHAM, THOMAS - - -	1368	7th May 1783	Machine for spinning hards or refuse flax, also flax, hemp, or wool.
OLDHAM, THOMAS - - -	9785	15th June 1843	Manufacture of bonnets and hats.
OLDKNOW, JAMES - - -	12,897	15th Dec. 1849	Manufacture of lace and other fabrics.
OLDLAND, GEORGE - -	5960	22nd July 1830	Machinery for shearing and dressing woollen-cloths and other fabrics.
OLDLAND, GEORGE - -	6236	3rd March 1832	Machinery for shearing, dressing, and finishing woollen-cloths and other fabrics.
OLDLAND, GEORGE - -	6327	3rd Nov. 1832	Machinery for preparing, dressing, and finishing woollen-cloth and other fabrics.
OLDMIXON, Lieutenant WILLIAM	8077	22nd May 1839	" Safety decks " for saving human life in cases of disaster at sea.
OLDNER, GEORGE - - -	352	24th Sept. 1697	Preserving ships or vessels for navigation, from foundering at sea or in harbour, by accident or from any other cause.
O'LEARY, CONNOR WILLIAM -	11,834	9th Sept. 1847	Producing power for the discharge of weapons and missiles, and for other purposes.

Name of Patentee.	Progressive Number.	Date.	Subject-matter of Patent.
OLIPHANT, JAMES - -	3703	31st May 1813	Manufacturing military caps.
OLIVER, JOHN - - -	7791	31st Aug. 1838	Stoves.
OLIVER, JULIUS - - -	7289	24th Jan. 1837	Filters employed in sugar refining.
OLIVER, JULIUS - - -	7601	26th March 1838	Filters employed in sugar refining.
OLIVER, LAVER - - -	2727	3rd Aug. 1803	Dining, card, Pembroke and other tables.
OLIVER, PETER - - -	339	6th April 1695	Engine for glazing and smoothing linen-cloth, calico, silks, and stuffs bare of wool, also paper and pasteboard.
OLIVER, RICHARD - - -	6162	17th Sept. 1831	Obtaining impressions from engravings in various colours, and applying the same to earthenware, porcelain, china, glass, and other substances.
OLIVER, ROBERT STEPHEN -	7205	13th Oct. 1836	Manufacture of hats, caps, and bonnets.
OLIVER, SAMUEL BROWN -	12,841	10th Nov. 1849	Dyeing-materials; and dyeing.
OLIVIER, JOSEPH - - -	1253	22nd April 1780	Waterproof hat. " Parapluie."
OLLERENSHAW, EDWARD -	4794	27th May 1823	Dressing or finishing hats, by means of machinery and implements to be used and applied thereto.
OLLIVANT, GEORGE BENT -	8974	5th June 1841	Cylindrical printing-machinery, for printing calicoes and other fabrics; apparatus connected therewith;—also applicable to other purposes.
OMMANEY, HENRY MORTLOCK	13,421	19th Dec. 1850	Manufacture of steel.
ONIE, PETER M^c - - -	9180	16th Dec. 1841	Cutting, dressing, preparing, and polishing stones, marble, and other substances; forming mouldings and other figures thereon.
ONIONS, GEORGE - - -	9017	7th July 1841	Wheels and rails for railway purposes.
ONIONS, JOHN - - -	3340	22nd May 1810	Machine for thrashing corn.
ONIONS, JOHN - - -	9155	11th Nov. 1841	Manufacture of nails, screws, and chains.
ONIONS, JOHN - - -	13,973	14th Feb. 1852	Manufacture of parts of machinery used in paper-making, and certain parts of railways, and railway and other carriages.
ONIONS, PETER - - -	1370	7th May 1783	Working and refining cast or pig iron, and converting the same from a fluid state into wrought-iron.
ONIONS, THOMAS - - -	11,539	21st Jan. 1847	Rotatory steam-engines.
ONIONS, WILLIAM - - -	3524	23rd Jan. 1812	Machine to be wrought by steam or other power.
ONIONS, WILLIAM - - -	13,495	7th Feb. 1851	Manufacture of parts of machinery used in spinning.
ONIONS, WILLIAM - - -	13,496	7th Feb. 1851	Manufacture of steel.
ONIONS, WILLIAM - - -	13,773	16th Oct. 1851	Manufacture of nuts and bolts; of bearings, axles, and bushes; of mills and dies for engravers; of bells, lathe, and other spindles: of weft-forks; of shuttle-tongues and lips for looms; and of agricultural chains, and throstle-bars; by the application of materials not hitherto used for the purpose.
OOST, AUGUSTUS JULIEN VAN	10,853	6th Oct. 1845	Treating seed; preparing materials used for fertilizing land and for aiding vegetation.
OPPENHEIM, MAYER - -	707	28th Nov. 1755	Manufacturing red transparent glass.
OPPENHEIM, MEYER - -	969	20th Oct. 1770	Making opaque or red glass.
ORAM, JOHN - - -	8909	31st March 1841	Machinery for the manufacture of netted fabrics.

Name of Patentee.	Progressive Number.	Date.	Subject-matter of Patent.
ORAM, ROBERT - - -	7405	19th July 1837	Construction and arrangement of cranes for lifting and removing goods.
ORAM, ROBERT - - -	8983	12th June 1841	Hydraulic-presses.
ORAM, THOMAS - - -	7604	26th March 1838	Manufacture of fuel.
ORAM, THOMAS - - -	9705	20th April 1843	Manufacture of fuel; machinery for manufacturing the same.
ORANGE, JOHN EDWARD -	8674	2nd Nov. 1840	Apparatus for serving ropes and cables with yarn.
ORGILL, SIMON - - -	3006	3rd Feb. 1807	Stops for working the bolt-wheels of the machine attached to the warp lace-frame, to give motion to the said machine; and a rotatory spindle, projections, and levers, to be affixed to the frame itself to give motion to the same, for the purpose of manufacturing lace or net-work of various figures and qualities.
ORLEBAR, JOHN - - -	437	26th Sept. 1721	Raising water by the rotation or circular motion of wheels, without lever or crank.
ORME, WILLIAM - - -	8851	18th Feb. 1841	Manufacture of coffered spades and other coffered tools.
ORMEROD, EDWARD - -	12,962	7th Feb. 1850	Apparatus for changing the position of carriages on railways.
ORMEROD, JOHN - -	12,579	19th April 1849	Carding cotton and other fibrous substances.
ORMROD, RICHARD - -	4280	22nd July 1818	Manufacture of copper and other metallic cylinders or rollers, for calico-printing.
ORMROD, RICHARD - -	4633	7th Jan. 1822	Heating liquids in boilers, and thereby increasing the production of steam.
ORR, MATTHEW - - -	5918	20th March 1830	Manufacture of canvass and sail-cloth for making sails.
ORSI, JOSEPH - - -	10,890	23rd Oct. 1845	Sleepers or blocks for supporting railways.
ORSI, JOSEPH - - -	12,103	22nd March 1848	Manufacture of artificial stone, cement, ornamental tiles, bricks, and quarries.
ORSON, EDWARD FORBES -	5708	18th Sept. 1828	Cartridge for sporting purposes.
ORTMAN, ERNEST ADOLPHUS -	7459	4th Nov. 1837	Extracting certain foreign matters from wooden or other porous vessels; turning such matters to useful account, when so extracted.
ORTON, REGINALD - - -	10,898	27th Oct. 1845	Life-boats, life-buoys, and apparatus for conveying persons ashore from wrecked vessels.
ORVILLE, EDWARD D' - -	13,413	19th Dec. 1850	Finishing thread or yarn.
OSBALDESTON, JOHN - -	6958	16th Dec. 1835	Making metal healds for weaving silk, woollen, worsted, cotton, or any other fibrous substance.
OSBALDESTON, JOHN - -	5044	29th Nov. 1824	Making healds to be used in the weaving of cotton, silk, woollen, and other cloths.
OSBALDESTON, JOHN -	9257	15th Feb. 1842	Looms for weaving.
OSBALDESTONE, THOMAS -	89	18th March 1836	Extracting tallow or other liquid substance from bones.
OSBORN, HENRY - - -	3590	5th Aug. 1812	Machine for turning and levelling articles made of iron, preparatory to welding and grinding.
OSBORN, HENRY - - -	3617	28th Nov. 1812	Welding and making cylinders of iron and steel.

Name of Patentee.	Progres-sive Number.	Date.	Subject-matter of Patent.
OSBORN, HENRY - - -	3740	15th Oct. 1813	Making tools for tapering cylinders of iron, steel, or other metal or mixture of metals; also for tapering bars of the same materials.
OSBORN, HENRY - - -	4005	23rd March 1816	Producing cylinders.
OSBORN, JOHN TULLOH - -	11,304	23rd July 1846	Power-machines for tilling, draining, and otherwise cultivating land; mode of working the same.
OSBORN, WILLIAM HENRY -	4105	1st March 1817	Producing cylinders.
OSBORNE, CHARLES - -	8139	2nd July 1839	Construction of cork-screws.
OSBORNE, GEORGE - - -	13,395	7th Dec. 1850	Commodes, and fixed and portable water-closets.
OSBORNE, JOHN JAMES - -	10,470	16th Jan. 1845	Manufacture of iron and steel; furnaces to be employed for such or similar manufacture.
OSBORNE, RICHARD BOYSE -	11,501	21st Dec. 1846	Bridges, roofing, and flooring.
OSIER, GERMAIN LE NORMAND [DE L'.	8063	8th May 1839	Machinery for raising water.
OSLER, THOMAS - - -	3359	5th July 1810	Manufacturing glass or paste drops for chandeliers, lamps, and lustres.
OSLER, THOMAS - - -	5870	10th Nov. 1829	Construction of glass and metal chandeliers, and other articles for ornamental lighting.
OSMOND, GEORGE - - -	10,361	22nd Oct. 1844	Fastenings for doors, drawers, window-sashes, and dining-tables; apparatus for suspending looking-glasses, and other articles.
OTTLEY, RICHARD - - -	2921	21st March 1806	Chain-pumps; mode of working the same; wells for receiving such pumps.
OTWAY, THOMAS - - -	5619	21st Feb. 1828	Stopping horses when running away with riders or carriages.
OULD, HENRY - - - -	1842	17th Dec. 1791	Apparatus to be affixed to Hadley's quadrant, to obtain an artificial horizon.
OUTHETT, JOHN - - -	4351	23rd March 1819	Construction, arrangement, and combination of apparatus used for the production of gas from pit-coal and other substances;—purifying, storing, and delivering the same for illumination; partly applicable to other purposes.
OVEREND, HENRY - - -	2201	9th Nov. 1797	Manufacture of a machine, which may be used as a waggon, cart, or dray, in a more perfect and expeditious manner, and with fewer horses than usual.
OVEREND, JAMES - - -	9843	15th July 1843	Printing fabrics with metallic matters, and finishing silks and other fabrics.
OVEREND, JAMES - - -	10,052	13th Feb. 1844	Printing fabrics with metallic matters, and finishing silks and other fabrics.
OVERING, JOHN - - -	302	20th Sept. 1692	Engine to convey air into pipes by means of bellows, and having plates covered with leather, for securing the head and retaining air about the upper part of the body, for the purpose of enabling a man to see, walk, and work a considerable time under water.
OVERTON, THOMAS - - -	769	10th Feb. 1762	Spring for hanging coaches and other carriages.
OVERTON, WILLIAM - -	8018	3rd April 1839	Machinery for making ships' bread or biscuits.
OVEY, THOMAS - - -	2283	24th Dec. 1798	Manufacturing hats.

Name of Patentee.	Progressive Number.	Date.	Subject-matter of Patent.
OWEN, GEORGE - - -	10,265	20th July 1844	Confining corks in bottles and other vessels of glass, earthenware or stone-ware, containing liquids.
OWEN, WILLIAM - - -	4124	17th May 1817	Portable table or box mangle, for getting up and smoothing linen, cotton, and other articles.
OWEN, WILLIAM - - -	8219	16th Sept. 1839	Railways; construction and manufacture of wheels, engines, and machinery to be used thereon;—partly applicable to other engines; and which wheels, without a flange, may be used on turnpike roads.
OXENHAM, HUGH - - -	1064	10th Feb. 1774	Mangle.
OXENHAM, THOMAS - -	2169	28th Feb. 1797	Portable lever mangle for calendering linen, and cotton, silk, stuffs, and for other purposes where mangles are used.
OXFORD, JOHN - - -	4722	1st Nov. 1822	Preventing premature decay in timber, metallic substances, and canvas.
OXLAND, JOHN - - -	12,590	26th April 1849	Manufacture of sugar.
OXLAND, JOHN - - -	13,634	15th May 1851	Manufacture and refining of sugar.
OXLAND, ROBERT -	10,528	20th Feb. 1845	Manufacture of chlorine.
OXLAND, ROBERT -	11,848	2nd Sept. 1847	Dyeing;—partly applicable to the manufacture of metallic alloys.
OXLAND, ROBERT -	12,590	26th April 1849	Manufacture of sugar.
OXLAND, ROBERT -	13,634	15th May 1851	Manufacture and refining of sugar.
OXLEY, JOSEPH - - -	795	29th July 1763	Machine for drawing coals out of coal-pits, by the help of a fire-engine, also for other purposes.
OXLEY, JOSEPH - - -	871	13th March 1767	Machine or water-wheel for drawing coals by the agency of water, or for other purposes, which machine also counterbalances ropes made use of for such purposes.
OXLEY, THOMAS - - -	10,819	22nd Aug. 1845	Constructing and propelling vessels; machinery connected therewith.

P.

PACE, EDMUND - - -	10,274	26th July 1844	Machinery for figure weaving in silk and other fabrics.
PACE, EDMUND - - -	13,464	21st Jan. 1851	Bedsteads, couches, chairs, and other like articles of furniture.
PACE, JOHN - - -	6506	14th Nov. 1833	Horological machines.
PADDON, JOHN BIRCH -	12,814	18th Oct. 1849	Gas-meters, and gas-regulators.
PAGE, HENRY - - -	9762	10th June 1843	Painting, graining, or decorating, with oil and other colours.
PAGE, HENRY - - -	10,504	30th Jan. 1845	Painting or decorating with oil and other colours.
PAGE, JOHN - - -	1548	22nd June 1786	Machine for extricating persons from buildings on fire, also for extinguishing fires, facilitating repairs, and for other purposes.
PAGE, NICHOLAS - - -	33	8th April 1626	Making steel.

Name of Patentee.	Progressive Number.	Date.	Subject-matter of Patent.
PAGE, THOMAS - - -	13,088	1st June 1850	Construction and means of cleansing sewers.
PAIGE, LOUIS LE - - -	9795	22nd June 1843	Preventing accidents on railways.
PAINE, THOMAS, jun. - .	8638	22nd Sept. 1840	Propelling carriages by atmospheric pressure only, without aid of other power.
PAINE, THOMAS - - -	1667	26th Aug. 1788	Constructing arches, vaulted roofs, and ceilings, either in iron or wood.
PAJON, DANIEL - - -	478	3rd June 1725	Preparation applied to the bottoms of ships to preserve the same from decay, also from worms and other things detrimental to shipping.
PALEY, JOHN, jun. - - -	8954	10th May 1841	Looms for weaving.
PALIN, JOSEPH - - -	14,327	19th Oct. 1852	Brewing; also production of extracts or infusions for other purposes.
PALIN, WILLIAM - - -	229	15th Nov. 1683	Millwork for making iron sheets and tire for wheels, plates for fenders, and half-pounds of iron for kettles, and for other things.
PALLISER, GEORGE - -	11,191	5th May 1846	Outside-seats of carriages.
PALM, JOSEPH BARON - -	14,218	13th July 1852	Baking bricks, tiles, and other kinds of pottery or earthenware.
PALMAERT, JEAN ALBERT -	10,303	29th Aug. 1844	Economizing and applying heat obtained from known processes.
PALMER, ANDREW - - -	23	23rd Feb. 1623	Making hard and soft soap; burning straw of beans and peas, kelp, fern, and other vegetables into ordinary ashes or into potashes, and with the said materials, also of all other vegetables, to make the said soap; using the assay glass to try the lees.
PALMER, CHARLES FIELDING -	12,141	27th April 1848	Chalybeate water.
PALMER, EBENEZER - -	2412	13th June 1800	Metallic hinge or chain for use in the art of binding books.
PALMER, EDWARD - - -	8987	12th June 1841	Producing printing-surfaces, and printing china, pottery-ware, music, maps, and portraits.
PALMER, EDWARD - - -	9227	15th Jan. 1842	Producing printing and embossing surfaces.
PALMER, FREDERICK OCTAVIUS	12,825	2nd Nov. 1849	Manufacture of candles; machinery for manufacturing the same.
PALMER, GEORGE HOLWORTHY	4199	15th Jan. 1818	Purifying certain descriptions of gases.
PALMER, GEORGE HOLWORTHY	4646	12th Feb. 1822	Production of heat by the application of known principles; construction of furnaces of steam-engines and of air-furnaces in general, for the saving of fuel and consumption of smoke.
PALMER, GEORGE HOLWORTHY	5253	15th Sept. 1825	Arrangement of machinery for propelling vessels through the water by steam or any other power
PALMER, GEORGE HOLWORTHY	6161	16th Sept. 1831	Steam-engine and boiler, and machinery connected therewith, applicable to propelling vessels and carriages, and for other purposes.
PALMER, GEORGE HOLWORTHY	7024	8th March 1836	Purification of inflammable gases; apparatus for effecting the same;—applicable to other purposes.
PALMER, GEORGE HOLWORTHY	7703	25th June 1838	Steam-generators, and engines applicable to locomotive and stationary uses; carriages to be used therewith, and otherwise.

Name of Patentee.	Progressive Number.	Date.	Subject-matter of Patent.
PALMER, GEORGE HOLWORTHY	7751	28th July 1838	Preparing, constructing, and adapting certain parts of gas-meters.
PALMER, GEORGE HOLWORTHY	7996	6th March 1839	Gas-meters.
PALMER, GEORGE HOLWORTHY	8047	23rd April 1839	Paddle-wheels for propelling ships, boats, and other vessels navigated by steam or other motive-power.
PALMER, GEORGE HOLWORTHY	8728	28th Nov. 1840	Construction of pistons and valves for retaining and discharging liquids, gases, and steam.
PALMER, GEORGE HOLWORTHY	11,661	17th April 1847	Producing inflammable gases; also arrangement of apparatus employed for the purpose, which apparatus may be applied to other similar purposes.
PALMER, GEORGE HOLWORTHY	12,974	21st Feb. 1850	Arrangement and construction of gas-holders.
PALMER, GEORGE HOLWORTHY	13783	22nd Oct. 1851	Obtaining heat and light.
PALMER, GEORGE VAUGHAN -	5941	8th June 1830	Machine to cut and excavate earth.
PALMER, GEORGE VAUGHAN -	6213	24th Jan. 1832	Machinery for excavating. "Excavating and self-loading cart."
PALMER, HENRY ROBINSON -	4618	22nd Nov. 1821	Construction of railways or tram-roads; and carriages to be used thereon.
PALMER, HENRY ROBINSON -	5786	28th April 1829	Construction of warehouses, sheds, and other buildings intended for the protection of property.
PALMER, HENRY ROBINSON -	6504	7th Nov. 1833	Construction of arches, roofs, and other parts of buildings;—applicable to other purposes.
PALMER, HENRY ROBINSON -	7449	20th Oct. 1837	Giving motion to barges and other vessels on canals.
PALMER, HENRY ROBINSON -	9332	26th April 1842	Construction of roofs and other parts of buildings; application of corrugated plates of metal to certain purposes for which they have not heretofore been used.
PALMER, JAMES - - -	5647	6th May 1828	Moulds or apparatus for making paper.
PALMER, JAMES - - -	13,726	23rd Aug. 1851	Delineating objects; apparatus and materials for the purpose.
PALMER, JARVIS - - -	12,469	12th Feb. 1849	Matches or similar articles for igniting combustible bodies; manufacturing the same, and machinery for the purpose; match and other boxes, and machinery for manufacturing such boxes.
PALMER, JOHN - - -	2241	5th June 1798	Construction of apparatus used for clearing grain from the straw, and pulverizing the same.
PALMER, JOHN - - -	2362	6th Dec. 1799	Machinery for clearing grain from the ear or stalk, and for cutting the straw into provender for cattle, and for other purposes.
PALMER, JOHN - - -	3055	26th June 1807	Constructing and erecting bridges.
PALMER, JOHN CLEAVELAND -	10,564	17th March 1845	Machinery to be used in manufacturing tools for boring wood and various other substances.
PALMER, LANCELOT - -	1544	3rd May 1786	Tea and coffee urn.
PALMER, MATTHEW - -	457	22nd Sept. 1723	Machine to raise water any height out of mines, rivers, pits, pools or concavities.
PALMER, SAMUEL - - -	645	29th June 1749	Horse-bits.
PALMER, THOMAS - - -	10,941	15th Nov. 1845	Mine lifting-machinery;—applicable to other purposes.

Name of Patentee.	Progres-sive Number.	Date.	Subject-matter of Patent.
PALMER, THOMAS.	11,814	24th July 1847	Machinery for making cards; machinery for preparing and spinning cotton and other fibrous materials; also for preparing and dressing yarn, and weaving the same.
PALMER, WALTER OBELL -	12,205	10th July 1848	Machinery for thrashing and dressing corn.
PALMER, WILLIAM - - -	3536	6th Feb. 1812	Machinery or "revolving rollers and revolving roller-wheels," to be applied to wheel-carriages in conjunction with part or instead of any of the present wheels and axle-trees, to facilitate the draught of the same.
PALMER, WILLIAM - - -	4783	22nd April 1823	Machinery for printing or staining paper for paper-hangings.
PALMER, WILLIAM - - -	4816	15th July 1823	Machinery for printing on calico or other woven-fabrics wholly or in part of cotton-wool, linen, or silk.
PALMER, WILLIAM - - -	5979	10th Aug. 1830	Making candles.
PALMER, WILLIAM - - -	6314	29th Sept. 1832	Making candles and candle-sticks.
PALMER, WILLIAM - - -	7411	29th July 1837	Printing pager-hangings.
PALMER, WILLIAM - - -	7726	10th July 1838	Lamps.
PALMER, WILLIAM - - -	8084	1st June 1839	Lamps; and manufacture of candles.
PALMER, WILLIAM - - -	8445	25th March 1840	Manufacture of candles; apparatus for applying light.
PALMER, WILLIAM - - -	8567	11th July 1840	Ploughs.
PALMER, WILLIAM - - -	9146	9th Nov. 1841	Manufacture of candles.
PALMER, WILLIAM - - -	9276	4th March 1842	Construction of candle-lamps.
PALMER, WILLIAM - - -	9277	4th March 1842	Vessels for making infusions or decoctions for culinary purposes; apparatus for measuring or supplying from vessels.
PALMER, WILLIAM - - -	9305	21st March 1842	Manufacture and preparation of pills and some other articles of a medicinal or remedial nature.
PALMER, WILLIAM - - -	9555	15th Dec. 1842	Manufacture of candles.
PALMER, WILLIAM - - -	9602	26th Jan. 1843	Manufacture of candles.
PALMER, WILLIAM - - -	9954	21st Nov. 1843	Manufacture of pills.
PALMER, WILLIAM - - -	10,184	15th May 1844	Manufacture of wicks for candles and lamps; manufacture of candles.
PALMER, WILLIAM - - -	10,540	3rd March 1845	Pressing tallow and other matters and substances and fabrics.
PALMER, WILLIAM - - -	10,695	3rd June 1845	Manufacture of candles and lamps, and shades or chimneys.
PALMER, WILLIAM - - -	10,707	5th June 1845	Working atmospheric-railways; lubricating railway and other machinery.
PALMER, WILLIAM- - -	11,377	17th Sept. 1846	Manufacture of lamps and candlesticks, also gas and other pillars and pipes.
PALMER, WILLIAM - - -	11,414	15th Oct. 1846	Obtaining products from fat or fatty matters; manufacture and packing of the same.
PALMER, WILLIAM - - -	12,077	28th Feb. 1848	Melting fats and manufacturing candles.
PALMER, WILLIAM - - -	12,365	9th Dec. 1848	Manufacture of candles.
PALMER, WILLIAM - - -	12,910	29th Dec. 1849	Manufacture of candles, lamps, and wicks.
PALMER, WILLIAM - - -	13,078	22nd May 1850	Manufacture of candles and candle-wicks; machinery applicable to such matters.
PALMER, WILLIAM - - -	13,329	9th Nov. 1850	Manufacture of candles and night-lights.

Name of Patentee.	Progressive Number.	Date.	Subject-matter of Patent.
PALMER, WILLIAM - - -	14,264	19th Aug. 1852	Manufacture of candles and candle-lamps; packing candles and night-lights.
PALMER, WILLIAM VAUGHAN -	3903	4th April 1815	Twisting and laying hemp, flax, ropes, twine, line, thread, mohair, wool, cotton, silk, and metals, by machinery.
PALTRINERI, JOHN - - -	10,793	30th July 1845	Obtaining and applying motive-power.
PANTER, WILLIAM - - -	1094	31st Jan. 1775	Mill for husking coffee.
PANTER, WILLIAM - - -	4110	11th March 1817	Rotary motion; removing friction in wheel-carriages and machinery of different descriptions.
PANTIN, LEWIS - - -	598	21st Jan. 1744	Engine for raising ballast from the bottom of rivers, and for other purposes.
PAPE, HENRY - - -	8137	2nd July 1839	Stringed musical instruments.
PAPE, HENRY - - -	8823	1st Feb. 1841	Castors.
PAPE, JOHN HENRY - -	9334	28th April 1842	Carriages; and construction of wheels.
PAPE, JOHN HENRY - -	10,668	17th May 1845	Musical instruments.
PAPE, JOHN HENRY - -	13,423	20th Dec. 1850	Musical instruments.
PAPE, JOHN HENRY - -	13,786	23rd Oct. 1851	Ploughs.
PAPPS, DANIEL - -	6055	23rd Dec. 1830	Machinery for dressing or roughing woollen-cloth.
PAPPS, FRANCIS - - -	13,390	7th Dec. 1850	Metallic and other bedsteads, mattrasses, and curtain-rods; coating or covering bedsteads and other articles wholly or partly composed of metal.
PAPPS, THOMAS - - -	4190	19th Dec. 1817	Account-books.
PARADIS, JOSEPH - - -	12,874	3rd Dec. 1849	Manufacture of elastic mattrasses, cushions, and paddings;—partly applicable to other purposes.
PARDOE, THOMAS - - -	3604	23rd Oct. 1812	Making carpeting in pieces of different widths, by which a pattern, figure or flower, is made to extend the whole width of the piece.
PARET, NOEL ETIENNE AIMÉ -	11,431	2nd Nov. 1846	Finishing silk, cotton, and other fabrics; heating apartments.
PARHAM, WILLIAM - -	39	6th Aug. 1627	Engine for earing, ploughing, and tilling land, without the help of oxen or horses.
PARHAM, WILLIAM - -	41	22nd Dec. 1627	Engine for driving mills for grinding corn or grain, tools, metals, bark, and other things.
PARHAM, WILLIAM - -	72	17th July 1634	Engine for ploughing land, without oxen or horses.
PARIS, CHARLES HENRY -	12,437	23rd Jan. 1849	Preventing the oxydation of iron.
PARISH, HENRY HEADLEY -	11,432	3rd Nov. 1846	Supplying and purifying water.
PARISH, HENRY HEADLEY -	12,458	8th Feb. 1849	Safety and other lamps, and gas-burners.
PARKER, ABRAHAM - -	7591	10th March 1838	Instrument for gauging malt, and the fluid or solid contents of casks and other vessels.
PARKER, CHARLES - -	8664	22nd Oct. 1840	Looms for weaving linen and other fabrics, to be worked by hand, steam, water, or other power.
PARKER, EBENEZER - -	3387	8th Oct. 1810	Adjusting-bedstead.
PARKER, FREDERICK - -	8123	22nd June 1839	Revivifying or reburning animal charcoal.
PARKER, FREDERICK - -	12,682	4th July 1849	Filtering syrups and other liquors.

Name of Patentee.	Progressive Number.	Date.	Subject-matter of Patent.
PARKER, JAMES - - -	1806	17th May 1791	Burning bricks and tiles, and calcining chalk, earth-stone, or lime-stone, with a certain material not before used for the purpose.
PARKER, JAMES - - -	2120	28th June 1796	Cement or tarrass to be used in aquatic and other buildings, and stucco-work.
PARKER, JOHN - - -	5367	23rd May 1826	Park or other gates.
PARKER, ROBERT - - -	538	18th Jan. 1733	Machine for showing the increase or decrease of liquor of any sort contained in casks, and for other purposes.
PARKER, ROBERT - - -	5764	31st Jan. 1829	Drag for stage-coaches and other wheel-carriages.
PARKER, ROBERT - - -	6027	4th Nov. 1830	Locomotive and other carriages applicable to rail and other roads ;—also partly applicable for moving bodies on water, and working other machinery.
PARKER, SAMUEL - - -	4475	15th June 1820	Lamp.
PARKER, SAMUEL - - -	4733	10th Dec. 1822	Construction of lamps.
PARKER, SAMUEL - - -	5291	12th Nov. 1825	Certain alloys of metals.
PARKER, SAMUEL - - -	5458	1st Feb. 1827	Construction of lamps.
PARKER, SAMUEL - - -	5947	29th June 1830	Producing mechanical power from chemical agents.
PARKER, SAMUEL - - -	5948	29th June 1830	Lamp.
PARKER, SAMUEL - - -	6362	11th Jan. 1833	Apparatus for making extracts from coffee and other substances.
PARKER, SAMUEL - - -	6811	14th April 1835	Metallic air and water stop and stopper.
PARKER, SAMUEL - - -	7682	12th June 1838	Lamps, and apparatus connected therewith.
PARKER, SAMUEL - - -	7917	20th Dec. 1838	Stoves.
PARKER, SAMUEL - - -	8621	10th Sept. 1840	Apparatus for preserving and purifying oils; apparatus for burning oils, tallow, and gas.
PARKER, THOMAS - - -	49	21st Jan. 1630	Barrel-engine for raising water out of mines, graffs, coal-pits, or any other place.
PARKER, THOMAS - - -	1929	22nd Dec. 1792	Machine to be worked by means of air and water, or by air, fire, and water, to perform work usually done by mills and engines, or by other mechanical powers.
PARKER, THOMAS - - -	2469	3rd Feb. 1801	Preparing and manufacturing flax, hemp, silk, and other materials.
PARKER, THOMAS - - -	2607	8th April 1802	Preparing and manufacturing flax, hemp, silk, and other materials.
PARKER, THOMAS - - -	4296	5th Oct. 1818	Regulating and improving the draught of chimneys.
PARKER, THOMAS - - -	13,651	3rd June 1851	Machinery for opening, cleaning, and preparing fibrous substances, and for manufacturing felted fabrics.
PARKER, THOMAS KNOTT -	14,138	22nd May 1852	Window-sashes.
PARKER, WILLIAM - -	1287	28th March 1781	Making pedestals or supports for candlesticks, lamps, girandoles, chandeliers, epergnes, watches, vases, or urns, of various materials, and variously ornamented.
PARKER, WILLIAM - -	3594	10th Aug. 1812	Manufacture of green paint.
PARKER, WILLIAM - -	6061	15th Jan. 1831	Preparing animal charcoal.

Name of Patentee.	Progressive Number.	Date.	Subject-matter of Patent.
PARKER, WILLIAM - -	6441	26th June 1833	Refining and purifying oils.
PARKER, WILLIAM - -	6442	26th June 1833	Making and refining sugar.
PARKER, WILLIAM PHILLIPS -	11,551	28th Jan. 1847	Bell machinery.
PARKER, WILLIAM PHILLIPS -	11,647	1st April 1847	Manufacture of cigars.
PARKER, WILLIAM PHILLIPS -	11,826	19th July 1847	Manufacture of cigars.
PARKER, WILLIAM PHILLIPS -	12,609	15th May 1849	Construction of pianofortes.
PARKES, ALEXANDER - -	8905	29th March 1841	Production of works of art in metals, by electric deposition.
PARKES, ALEXANDER - -	9807	17th June 1843	Preparing solutions of certain vegetable and animal matters, applicable to preserving wood and other substances.
PARKES, ALEXANDER - -	10,063	21st Feb. 1844	Manufacture of certain alloys or combinations of metals; depositing certain metals.
PARKES, ALEXANDER - -	10,366	29th Oct. 1844	Manufacture of certain alloys or combinations of metals; depositing certain metals.
PARKES, ALEXANDER -	10,860	9th Oct. 1845	Coating or covering certain metals with other metals and alloys; ornamenting the surfaces of metallic articles.
PARKES, ALEXANDER - -	11,147	25th March 1846	Preparation of certain vegetable and animal substances; combinations of the same substances.
PARKES, ALEXANDER - -	11,350	25th Aug. 1846	Manufacture of candles; preparing and combining certain animal, vegetable, and mineral substances applicable to the purpose, and for other uses.
PARKES, ALEXANDER - -	11,971	18th Nov. 1847	Manufacture of metals; coating iron and steel.
PARKES, ALEXANDER - -	12,142	27th April 1848	Manufacture of metals; coating metals.
PARKES, ALEXANDER - -	12,325	11th Nov. 1848	Manufacture of metals, and alloys of metals; treatment of metallic matters with various substances.
PARKES, ALEXANDER - -	12,534	26th March 1849	Deposition and manufacture of certain metals and alloys; treating and working the same;—also applicable to various other purposes.
PARKES, ALEXANDER - -	13,118	11th June 1850	Smelting and treating certain metals; construction and manufacture of furnaces, and the materials to be used for the same, such furnaces and materials being applicable to the treatment of metals and metallic compounds, and to other purposes of a like nature.
PARKES, ALEXANDER - -	13,675	24th June 1851	Separating silver from other metals.
PARKES, ALEXANDER - -	13,746	11th Sept. 1851	Manufacture of copper, and the separation of some other metals therefrom; production of alloys of certain metals.
PARKES, ALEXANDER - -	13,997	8th March 1852	Separating silver from other metals.
PARKES, ALEXANDER - -	14,103	1st May 1852	Obtaining and separating certain metals.
PARKES, HENRY - -	12,325	11th Nov. 1848	Manufacture of metals and alloys of metals; treatment of metallic matters with various substances.
PARKES, HENRY PERSHOUSE -	7166	11th Aug. 1836	Flat pit-chains.
PARKES, HENRY PERSHOUSE -	10,101	14th March 1844	Manufacture of flat pit-chains.
PARKES, JOSEPH - • -	8761	31st Dec. 1840	Manufacture of covered buttons.

Name of Patentee.	Progressive Number.	Date.	Subject-matter of Patent.
PARKES, JOSIAH - - -	4455	9th May 1820	Saving fuel in steam-engines and furnaces; consuming smoke.
PARKES, JOSIAH - - -	4876	4th Dec. 1823	Manufacture of salt.
PARKES, WILLIAM - - -	2535	20th Aug. 1801	Perpetual power, to give motion to machinery.
PARKES, ZACHARIAH - -	9299	21st March 1842	Apparatus for grinding and dressing wheat and other grain.
PARKES, ZACHARIAH Major -	11,214	22nd May 1846	Manufacture of coffins.
PARKHURST, STEPHEN R. -	10,944	17th Nov. 1845	Propelling vessels.
PARKHURST, STEPHEN R. -	11,511	31st Dec. 1846	Carding wool, cotton, and other fibrous substances.
PARKHURST, STEPHEN R. -	11,527	14th Jan. 1847	Rotary-engines
PARKIN, THOMAS - - -	4619	24th Nov. 1821	Printing.
PARKIN, THOMAS - - -	4958	15th May 1824	Machinery applicable to or employed in printing.
PARKIN, THOMAS - - -	5142	30th March 1825	Paving parts of public roads, whereby the draft of waggons, carts, and other carriages, is facilitated.
PARKIN, THOMAS - - -	6940	3rd Dec. 1855	Sleepers or bearers applicable to railroads.
PARKIN, THOMAS - - -	8026	9th April 1839	Railroad and other carriages; wheels for such carriages; roads on which they are to travel.
PARKIN, THOMAS - - -	11,274	29th June 1846	Giving motion to locomotive-carriages; construction of ways, passages, and roads on which they are to travel.
PARKIN, THOMAS WILLIAM -	8694	12th Nov. 1840	Making and working locomotive and other steam-engines.
PARKINSON, ANDREW - -	7051	29th March 1836	Stretcher to be used with hand or power looms.
PARKINSON, FRANK - -	3737	4th Sept. 1813	Still and boiler, to prevent accidents by fire, and to preserve spirits and other articles from waste, in distilling and boiling.
PARKINSON, JOHN - - -	7063	19th April 1836	Block-printing.
PARKINSON, JOHN - - -	12,731	1st Aug. 1849	Machinery for measuring and registering the flow of liquids.
PARKINSON, THOMAS - -	2369	1st Feb. 1800	Hydrostatic-engine for drawing beer or any other liquid out of a cellar or vault, or raising water out of mines, ships, or wells, or for any other purpose.
PARKINSON, THOMAS - -	2568	2nd Jan. 1802	Apparatus to be applied to engines, for conveying fluids therefrom.
PARKINSON, WILLIAM - -	5530	1st Aug. 1827	Constructing and working an engine for producing power and motion.
PARKINSON, WILLIAM - -	12,532	20th March 1849	Gas-meters and water-meters; and instruments for regulating the flow of fluids.
PARLBY, SAMUEL - - -	9990	18th Dec. 1843	Construction of wheels for carriages.
PARLOUR, SAMUEL - - -	6050	13th Dec. 1830	Lamps; "Parlour's improved table-lamp."
PARLOUR, SAMUEL - - -	7052	31st March 1836	Sketching, drawing, or delineating.
PARLOUR, SAMUEL - - -	7671	5th June 1838	Paddle-wheels; communicating rotary motion from steam or other power where change of speed and power are required.

Name of Patentee.	Progressive Number.	Date.	Subject-matter of Patent.
PARLOUR, SAMUEL - - -	10,961	20th Nov. 1845	Propelling vessels.
PARNALL, JOHN - - -	4134	10th June 1817	Tinning sheets or plates of copper, brass, or zinc.
PARNALL, ROBERT - - -	12,842	13th Nov. 1849	Instrument to facilitate the stitching or sewing of woven fabrics.
PARNELL, EDWARD ANDREW -	12,505	5th March 1849	Manufacture of glass; preparation of certain materials to be used therein; — partly applicable to the manufacture of alkalies.
PARNELL, MICHAEL LEOPOLD	13,806	6th Nov. 1851	Locks.
PARR, WILLIAM - - -	2925	26th March 1806	Machine for splitting hides, skins, pelts, or leather.
PARR, WILLIAM - - -	3328	11th April 1810	Gunpowder.
PARR, WILLIAM - - -	5247	27th Aug. 1825	Propelling vessels.
PARR, WILLIAM - - -	5747	22nd Dec. 1828	Producing a reciprocating action by rotatory motion, to be applied to the working of pumps and machinery.
PARR, WILLIAM - - -	5881	18th Jan. 1830	Producing a reciprocating action by rotatory motion, to be applied to the working of pumps, mangles, and all other machinery.
PARRATT, GEORGE FREDERICK	14,126	17th May 1852	Life-rafts.
PARREY, WILLIAM - - -	4557	5th May 1821	Propelling vessels.
PARRIS, RICHARD - - -	14,038	24th March 1852	Machinery or apparatus for cutting and shaping cork.
PARRISH, JOHN - - -	2199	31st Oct. 1797	Rendering woollen-cloths waterproof.
PARRY, FRANCIS CHARLES -	7551	25th Jan. 1838	Manufacture of bricks.
PARRY, HENRY - - -	11,345	20th Aug. 1846	Manufacture of hats.
PARRY, WILLIAM - - -	12,560	3rd April 1849	Shoeing horses; horse-shoes.
PARSEY, ARTHUR - - -	8093	6th June 1839	Obtaining motive-power.
PARSEY, ARTHUR - - -	10,352	17th Oct. 1844	Obtaining motive-power.
PARSONS, ANTHONY - -	547	12th Sept. 1734	Engine for supplying towns, seats, houses, and gardens with water; also for raising water, and ore, coal and other minerals out of mines or pits.
PARSONS, BENJAMIN - -	9929	9th Nov. 1843	Machine for cutting leaves of wood, such as scale-board.
PARSONS, GEORGE - - -	9827	7th July 1843	Portable roof for agricultural and other purposes.
PARSONS, GEORGE - - -	9828	10th July 1843	Machinery for beating, cleansing, and crushing animal and vegetable materials and substances.
PARSONS, JAMES - - -	3451	21st May 1811	Hinges and pullies for doors and windows.
PARSONS, JOHN - - -	8275	21st Nov. 1839	Preventing and curing smoky chimneys.
PARSONS, JOHN - - -	10,136	2nd April 1844	Machinery for cleansing and sweeping chimneys and flues.
PARSONS, JOHN - - -	10,666	10th May 1845	Manufacture of fuel; and apparatus for the use of the same.
PARSONS, PERCIVAL MOSES -	9553	9th Dec. 1842	Steam-engines and boilers, and motive machinery connected therewith.
PARSONS, PERCEVAL MOSES -	12,492	28th Feb. 1849	Railways; railway-engines and carriages, and certain of their appurtenances.
PARSONS, PERCEVAL MOSES -	13,637	19th May 1851	Cranes capable of being used on railways; parts of railways.
PARSONS, THOMAS - - -	6350	20th Dec. 1832	Locks for doors, and for other purposes.

Name of Patentee.	Progressive Number.	Date.	Subject-matter of Patent.
PARSONS, THOMAS - - -	6516	3rd Dec. 1833	Locks for fastenings.
PARSONS, WILLIAM - -	5395	24th July 1826	Ship-building.
PARTINGTON, JOHN - -	13,413	19th Dec. 1850	Finishing thread or yarn.
PARTRIDGE, BENJAMIN - -	1391	3rd Oct. 1783	Spinning and carding short-tow or hards, by means of a spinning and carding engine.
PARTRIDGE, JOHN - - -	1319	4th March 1782	Furnace for smelting and refining tin from the ore.
PARTRIDGE, JOHN - -	3114	3rd March 1808	Register and other stoves.
PARTRIDGE, JOSEPH - -	9425	23rd July 1842	Cleansing wool.
PARTRIDGE, NATHANIEL -	4754	14th Feb. 1823	Setting or fixing steam-boilers or other coppers.
PARTRIDGE, NATHANIEL -	6945	7th Dec. 1835	Application of a composition paste as an anti-attrition for the bearings of wheels and machinery.
PARTRIDGE, NATHANIEL -	6947	8th Dec. 1835	Mixing and preparing oil-paints.
PARTRIDGE, REUBEN - -	9295	14th March 1842	Machinery for splitting and shaping wood into splints for manufacturing matches, also into other similar forms.
PASCAL JEAN LOUIS - -	13,293	24th Oct. 1850	Apparatus for the cure or prevention of smoky chimneys, also for the ventilation of ships, rooms, and buildings.
PASQUIER, STEPHEN - -	2797	19th Dec. 1804	System of writing, printing, engraving, drawing, painting, and stamping certain characters and figures; also using such characters and figures, as well as instruments and machines for facilitating correspondence and other literary operations.
PASS, WILLIAM - - -	4743	20th Dec. 1822	Calcining and smelting various descriptions of ores.
PASSMAN, JOHN - - -	2044	21st March 1795	Machine for combing and heckling or preparing for combing and heckling wool, hemp, flax, silk, hair, or cotton; also machinery for spinning the same or any other material, and which machinery is also adapted for clearing or preparing wool, hemp, flax, silk, hair, or cotton for combing or heckling before spinning.
PASSMAN, JOHN - - -	2177	25th March 1797	Machinery for drawing, roving, and spinning wool, hemp, flax, silk, mohair, or other materials.
PASSMORE, THOMAS - -	2753	9th Feb. 1804	Machine for chopping straw, splitting beans, crushing oats, and grinding malt and barley.
PATERSON, BERTIE - -	7221	12th Nov. 1836	Construction of meters for measuring gas or liquids.
PATERSON, GEORGE BERTIE -	7751	28th July 1838	Preparing, constructing, and adapting certain parts of gas-meters.
PATERSON, GEORGE BERTIE -	7996	6th March 1839	Gas-meters.
PATERSON, GEORGE DACRES -	8682	5th Nov. 1840	Rest for cutting out wooden bowls, and a self-acting rest for other curvilinear turning.
PATERSON, JAMES - - -	12,159	22nd May 1848	Treating malt-liquors and other liquids or fluids; machinery for effecting such treatment.
PATERSON, JOHN - - -	6963	21st Dec. 1835	Propelling vessels and other floating bodies by means of steam or other power.

Name of Patentee.	Progressive Number.	Date.		Subject-matter of Patent.
PATERSON, THOMAS LUCAS -	13,255	12th Sept.	1850	Preparation or manufacture of textile materials, and the finishing of woven fabrics; machinery or apparatus used therein.
PATON, THOMAS - - -	2198	31st Oct.	1797	Press.
PATON, THOMAS - - -	2418	24th June	1800	Construction of mills for grinding sugarcanes.
PATON, THOMAS - - -	3169	24th Sept.	1808	Wheel for various purposes.
PATTEN, ANDREW - - -	3521	20th Jan.	1812	Tanning leather by the use of pyroligneous or wood acid.
PATTENDEN, RICHARD - -	12,941	24th Jan.	1850	Instruments and machinery for steering ships;—applicable to vices and other instruments for obtainig power.
PATTERSON, WILLIAM - -	6839	20th May	1835	Materials for tanning hides and skins, also applicable to other purposes.
PATTERSON, WILLIAM - -	6913	22nd Oct.	1835	Converting skins and hides into leather by the application of matter from a material not hitherto used for the purpose.
PATTINSON, HUGH LEE - -	6497	28th Oct.	1833	Separating silver from lead.
PATTINSON, HUGH LEE - -	8020	3rd April	1839	Reducing metallic-ores.
PATTINSON, HUGH LE - -	8627	10th Sept.	1840	Manufacture of white-lead.
PATTINSON, HUGH LE - -	9102	24th Sept.	1841	Manufacture of white-lead;—partly applicable to the manufacture of magnesia and its salts.
PATTINSON, HUGH LE - -	12,252	22nd Aug.	1848	Manufacture of a certain compound of lead; applying the same and other compounds of lead to various purposes.
PATTINSON, HUGH LE - -	12,479	14th Feb.	1849	Manufacture of a certain compound of lead; applying the same and other compounds of lead to various purposes.
PATTINSON, HUGH LE - -	13,519	18th Feb.	1851	Manufacture of "Pattinson's Oxy-chloride of Lead."
PATTINSON, HUGH LEE - -	14,104	1st May	1852	Smelting certain substances containing lead.
PATTINSON, WATSON - -	11,290	14th July	1846	Manufacture of chlorine.
PATTINSON, WILLIAM WATSON	12,045	27th Jan.	1848	Manufacture of soda.
PATTINSON, WILLIAM WATSON	14,056	6th April	1852	Manufacture of chlorine.
PATTISON, GRANVILLE SHARP	5692	4th Sept.	1828	Applying iron in the sheathing of ships and other vessels, and applying iron bolts, spikes, nails, pintals, braces, and other things used in the construction of the same.
PATTISON, ROBERT THOMSON	12,316	2nd Nov.	1848	Preparation for fixing paint or pigment colours on cotton, linen, woollen, silk, and other woven fabrics.
PATY, THOMAS - - -	3031	11th April	1807	Dyeing, spinning, weaving, and manufacturing East-India sun-hemp into carpets and carpet rug mats.
PAUL, ANDREW - - -	7752	30th July	1838	Hydraulic pump douche, or jet d'eau, for medical lavement.
PAUL, JOHN THEODORE - -	4950	13th May	1824	Generating steam and applying it to useful purposes.
PAUL, JOSEPH - - -	11,818	29th July	1847	Cutting drains in land; raising sub-soils to the surface of land.
PAUL, LEWIS - - - -	562	24th June	1738	Machine for spinning wool and cotton.
PAUL, LEWIS - - - -	636	30th Aug.	1748	Machine for carding wool, cotton, and raw silk.
PAUL, LEWIS - - - -	724	29th June	1758	Machine for spinning wool, cotton, and raw silk.
PAUL, NICHOLAS - - -	2654	30th Oct.	1802	Lamps and reflectors.

Name of Patentee.	Progressive Number.	Date.	Subject-matter of Patent.
PAUL, ONESIPHORUS - -	630	19th March 1748	Preparing cloths intended to be dyed scarlet, to more effectually ground the colours and preserve their beauty, and for other purposes.
PAUL, ROBERT - - -	4562	17th May 1821	Springs applicable to various descriptions of carriages.
PAUL, WILLIAM - - -	2084	4th Feb. 1796	Machine for printing and staining calicoes and other goods.
PAULDEN, THOMAS - -	134	10th Nov. 1661	Making crystal glass.
PAULY, JEAN SAMUEL - -	3833	4th Aug. 1814	Construction and use of fire-arms.
PAULY, JEAN SAMUEL - - [Pauly, Samuel John.]	3909	25th April 1815	Aërial conveyances and vessels, to be steered by chemical or mechanical means.
PAULY, JEAN SAMUEL - - [Pauly, Samuel Jean.]	4000	23rd March 1816	Substance for making coats or other clothing without seams; also covers for umbrellas and hats, likewise mattrasses, seats and cushions filled with atmospheric air.
PAULY, JEAN SAMUEL - -	4026	14th May 1816	Construction and use of fire-arms.
PAULY, JEAN SAMUEL - -	4059	15th Aug. 1816	Machinery for weighing.
PAUWELS, ANTOINE - -	13,057	23rd April 1850	Production of coke and gas for illumination; also regulating the circulation of such gas.
PAWLEY, WILLIAM - -	212	25th June 1681	Draining mines.
PAXON, GEORGE - - -	3597	28th Aug. 1812	Manufacture of bedsteads or bed-frames to relieve the bed-ridden, the ruptured, and sufferers with broken limbs, gout, or any other affliction.
PAXTON, JOSEPH - - -	13,186	22nd July 1850	Roofs.
PAYERNE, PROSPER ANTOINE	9776	15th June 1843	Keeping the air in mines and other confined places in a pure and respirable state.
PAYNE, BENJAMIN MATTHEW	5686	18th Aug. 1828	Weighing-machines.
PAYNE, CHARLES - - -	8658	13th Oct. 1840	Salting animal matters.
PAYNE, CHARLES - - -	9025	9th July 1841	Preserving vegetable matters where metallic and earthy solutions are employed.
PAYNE, CHARLES - - -	11,265	29th June 1846	Preserving vegetable matters.
PAYNE, CHARLES - - -	13,680	3rd July 1851	Drying animal and vegetable substances; also heating and cooling liquids.
PAYNE, CORNELIUS MARCH -	6194	3rd Dec. 1831	Printing silk, cotton, and other goods or fabrics.
PAYNE, DANIEL BEAUMONT -	3330	2nd May 1810	Ascertaining the numbers, dates, and sums in bank bills, notes, and other securities for money; preventing forgeries.
PAYNE, EDWARD JOHN - -	12,643	7th June 1849	Marine-vessels; apparatus for preservation of life; moulding, joining, and finishing hollow and solid figures, made wholly or in part of gums or combinations of gums; dissolving the aforesaid gums; and apparatus or machinery for the purposes.
PAYNE. JOHN - - -	505	21st Nov. 1728	Engine to be moved by the pressure of air into any building where the air is so rarified that the said pressure from without is sufficient to turn wheels for grinding corn, raising water, and performing other operations; applying the heat of fire made of pit-coal or turf to heating at the same time three or more furnaces, coppers, or other vessels for melting metals or metallic ores, drying malt, and for other purposes; also making iron malleable, and drawing the same into bars, by the use of the forge-hammer.

Name of Patentee.	Progressive Number.	Date.	Subject-matter of Patent.
PAYNE, JOHN - - -	555	15th Nov. 1736	Expanding fluids, and rarifying them into an elastic impelling force, sufficient for the turning of engines for raising water, and for other uses; also brewing and distilling by a new form of boiler, still, evaporating vessel, and other necessary things.
PAYNE, JOHN EDWARD HAW-[KINS.	12,646	7th June 1849	Manufacture of coach-lace and other simila looped or cut pile fabrics.
PAYNE, THOMAS - - -	11,322	4th Aug. 1846	Manufacture of rolls for rolling iron and other metals.
PAYNE, WILLIAM - - -	6078	15th Feb. 1831	Pedometer for the waistcoat pocket.
PAYNE, WILLIAM - - -	12,516	14th March 1849	Clocks and watches.
PAYTON, JAMES - - -	1471	30th April 1785	Construction of gloves.
PEACE, HENRY GEORGE - -	5997	7th Sept. 1830	Fids.
PEACE, WILLIAM - - -	12,776	20th Sept. 1849	Steam-engines and pumps.
PEACHE, JAMES - - -	3025	8th April 1807	Floating hollow buoys for supporting mooring chains, cables, ropes, &c.
PEACOCK, JAMES - - -	1844	23rd Dec. 1791	Filtration of water and other fluids.
PEAKE, THOMAS - - -	13,809	13th Nov. 1851	Manufacture of chenille and other piled fabrics.
PEAL, SAMUEL - - -	1801	2nd May 1791	Rendering waterproof all kinds of leather, cotton, linen, and woollen-cloths, silks, stuffs, paper, wood, and other substances.
PEARCE, CHARLES THOMAS -	12,482	16th Feb. 1849	Apparatus for obtaining light by electric agency.
PEARCE, JOHN - - -	2247	30th June 1798	Making and using combs and machines for combing wool.
PEARSALL, THOMAS - -	3503	30th Oct. 1811	Constructing iron-work for certain parts of buildings.
PEARSE, HENRY - - -	10,818	21st Aug. 1845	Manufacture of sugar.
PEARSE, JOHN - - -	4693	27th July 1822	Construction and manufacture of spring-jacks, and their connection with roasting-apparatus.
PEARSE, JOHN - - -	5972	5th Aug. 1830	Making and constructing wheels; application thereof to carriages.
PEARSE, JOHN - - -	6124	7th June 1831	Wheeled carriages; apparatus to be used therewith.
PEARSE, JOHN - - -	7404	19th July 1837	Construction of wheels.
PEARSON, CHARLES - -	5427	13th Dec. 1826	Applying heat to certain purposes.
PEARSON, JAMES - - -	2611	15th April 1802	Machine for beating and dressing cotton-wool or flax.
PEARSON, JAMES - - -	11,885	7th Oct. 1847	Locomotive engines and carriages.
PEARSON, RICHARD - -	7197	28th Sept. 1836	Drags for retarding carriages.
PEARSON, THOMAS - -	2932	30th Aug. 1806	Machinery for cleansing, seasoning, and dressing feathers and other articles.
PEARSON, THOMPSON - -	4505	1st Nov. 1820	Rudders.
PEASE, ROBERT - - -	383	— 1708	Making green oil for use in the woollen manufacture, and for making soft soap, the same oil is also edible.
PEASE, THOMAS - - -	743	29th Nov. 1759	Axletrees.
PEASE, THOMAS - - -	855	5th Aug. 1766	Machine and spring for the purpose of causing coaches, chaises, chariots, or any other vehicle, to hang more steadily.
PECK, DANIEL - - -	375	15th March 1706	Making and refining white salt from sea-water, brine-springs, and rock-salt.

Name of Patentee.	Progres-sive Number.	Date.	Subject-matter of Patent.
PECK, ELISHA - - -	4650	22nd Feb. 1822	Machinery worked by water, for moving mills and other machinery, and for forcing or pumping water.
PECK, WILLIAM BISHOP -	8846	15th Feb. 1841	Four-wheeled carriages.
PECKHAM, JOHN RANDELL -	2709	10th June 1803	Lock for muskets, fusees, carbines, fowling-pieces or pistols.
PECKHAM, RANDALL - -	2280	17th Dec. 1798	Constructing a watch so as to unite it with a mariner's compass. "A polar watch."
PECKITT, WILLIAM - -	1268	22nd Nov. 1780	Composing stained glass with unstained glass, and making the same into sheets, tables, vessels, and ornaments.
PECKSTON, THOMAS - -	9030	15th July 1841	Meters for measuring gas and other aëri-form fluids.
PECQUEUR, ONESIPHORE -	11,413	15th Oct. 1846	Forming leather into tubes, cylinders, switches, cases, sheaths, hats, and other articles.
PECQUEUR, ONESIPHORE -	12,755	30th Aug. 1849	Manufacture of fishing and other nets.
PEDDER, JAMES - - -	6660	13th Aug. 1834	Machinery for making ornamental bobbin-net lace.
PEDDER, JAMES - - -	6778	27th Feb. 1835	Machinery for making bobbin-net lace.
PEDDER, JAMES - - -	7064	21st April 1836	Machinery for making figured or ornamented bobbin-net lace.
PEDDER, JAMES - - -	11,946	6th Nov. 1847	Steam-engines; and propelling.
PEDDER, WILLIAM - -	3073	19th Oct. 1807	Additions to cattle-mills and water-mills for grinding sugar-canes, also to any other machine requiring additional power.
PEEK, JOHN - - - -	3194	23rd Jan. 1809	Machine for casting printing-types.
PEEK, THOMAS - - -	5529	1st Aug. 1827	Construction of a revolving steam-engine.
PEEKE, WILLIAM - - -	6094	21st March 1831	Rudder-hangings, and rudders for ships.
PEEL, DAVID - - - -	13,961	9th Feb. 1852	Lubricating compound.
PEEL, THOMAS - - -	4793	27th May 1823	Rotary-engine.
PEELE, JOHN - - - -	847	10th June 1766	Printing images, songs, maps, landscapes, and sea-pieces, by copper-plates, on linen for handkerchiefs.
PEELE, ROBERT - - -	1212	18th Feb. 1779	Machine for dressing, carding, slubbing, roving, and spinning cotton, silk, worsted, and woollens.
PEET, THOMAS - - -	8425	11th March 1840	Steam-engines.
PEGG, JOHN - - - -	13,646	29th May 1851	Producing corrugated surfaces on leather.
PEGNAULT, MARTIN - -	249	9th Jan. 1686	Making writing and printing paper; im-printing His Majesty's arms thereon; mills and engines for the purposes.
PEIRCE, WILLIAM - - -	8733	9th Dec. 1840	Preparation of wool, both in the raw and manufactured state.
PELLAFINET, ILARIO - -	4545	27th March 1821	Machinery for and method of breaking, bleaching, manufacturing and spinning into thread or yarn, flax, hemp, and other substances.
PELLATT, APSLEY - - -	3058	7th July 1807	Admitting light into the internal parts of ships, vessels, buildings, and other places.
PELLATT, APSLEY - - -	6091	9th March 1831	Forming glass-vessels and utensils with ornamental figured patterns impressed thereon.
PELLATT, APSLEY - - -	10,669	17th May 1845	Manufacture of glass, and casting, rolling, moulding, blowing, and drawing the same.

Name of Patentee.	Progressive Number.	Date.		Subject-matter of Patent.
PELLATT, APSLEY, junior -	4424	18th Dec.	1819	Encrusting into glass-vessels and utensils, figures, arms, crests, or any other ornaments made of composition, metal, or other suitable material.
PELLATT, FREDERICK - -	10,669	17th May	1845	Manufacture of glass, and casting, rolling, moulding, blowing, and drawing the same.
PELLERIN, CHARLES ALEXANDER.	8414	4th March	1840	Wind and stringed musical instruments.
PELLETAN, PIERRE [Pelletan, Pierrie.]	3946	3rd Aug.	1815	Making sulphuric-acid.
PELLETAN, PIERRE [Pelleton, Pierre.]	3998	18th March	1816	Making sulphuric-acid.
PELLETAN, PIERRE - -	9068	6th Sept.	1841	Propelling fluids and vessels.
PELLETAN, PIERRE - -	9506	2nd Nov.	1842	Production of light.
PELLETAN, PIERRE - -	9881	6th Sept.	1843	Production of light.
PELLETIER, JOSEPH - -	6453	25th July	1833	Making sulphate of quinine.
PELTRAU, JOHN - - -	1299	27th July	1781	Tying the spots of silk handkerchiefs, to make them more uniform, like India handkerchiefs.
PEMBERTON, RALPH STEPHEN	5269	21st Oct.	1825	Combined drawing and forcing pump.
PEMBERTON, THOMAS - -	11,108	25th Feb.	1846	Ornamenting window-furniture, and articles of upholstery in general.
PENN, JOHN - - - -	11,017	23rd Dec.	1845	Steam-engines, and machinery for propelling vessels;—applicable to other purposes.
PENN, JOHN - - -	12,386	21st Dec.	1848	Marine steam-engines.
PENN, RICHARD - - -	4237	14th March	1818	Manufacture of ornamented wooden furniture, by the application of machinery.
PENN, THOMAS - - -	2427	24th July	1800	Sinking, locking-up the jacks, pressing, drawing back the needle-bar, and keeping up the jacks, in frames for frame-work knitting of silk, thread, cotton, and worsted.
PENNECK, HENRY - - -	2581	19th Feb.	1802	Sailing and navigating certain ships and vessels.
PENNECK, HENRY - - -	4539	27th Feb.	1821	Machinery for lessening the consumption of fuel in working steam-engines.
PENNINGTON, JOHN - -	1518	19th Dec.	1785	Machine whereby any given number of pumps, sledge-hammers, and other subjects requiring the like powers may be worked with facility.
PENNINGTON, WILLIAM -	657	13th Oct.	1750	Machine for pricking the leathers of wool, silk, cotton, or other cards.
PENNY, JAMES - - -	3712	29th June	1813	Making pill and other small boxes.
PENNY, JAMES - - -	3840	8th Sept.	1814	Making pill and other small boxes.
PENNY, JAMES PARKER -	12,162	26th May	1848	Obtaining copper from copper ores.
PENROSE, WILLIAM - -	4612	10th Nov.	1821	Machinery for propelling vessels; vessels so propelled.
PENTON, GEORGE - - -	2743	19th Nov.	1803	Argand-lamps.
PENWARNE, JOHN - - -	3262	26th Sept.	1809	Giving to statues and other ornamental works in plaster of Paris, an appearance of statuary marble.
PENWARNE, JOHN - - -	4215	31st Jan.	1818	Instrument in lieu of cocks for drawing beer, cyder, and other liquors from casks, and other vessels.
PEOVER, JOSEPH - - -	1314	9th Jan.	1782	Making saddles.
PEPPE, GEORGE TOSCO -	12,983	28th Feb.	1850	Timekeepers.

Name of Patentee.	Progressive Number.	Date.	Subject-matter of Patent.
PEPPER, JOHN - - -	2116	9th June 1796	Kiln for drying malt or any other grain.
PEPPER, JOHN - - -	2140	3rd Oct. 1796	Building ovens and kilns for firing and burning china, earthenware, bricks, tiles, and other earths and compositions.
PEPPERCORNE, GEORGE RYDER	7559	31st Jan. 1838	Machinery to be employed for locomotion on railroads and other roads ;— applicable to other engines for exerting power.
PERCEVAL, ARTHUR PHILIP -	11,175	23rd April 1846	Communicating between places separated by water.
PERCIVALL, WILLIAM - -	5610	19th Jan. 1828	Construction and application of shoes, without nails, to the feet of horses and other animals.
PERCY, JOHN - - -	13,152	24th June 1850	Metallic alloys.
PERCY, JOHN - - -	13,439	2nd Jan. 1851	Metallic alloys.
PERCY, WILLIAM CARTER [STAFFORD.	11,236	2nd June 1846	Manufacture of bricks, tiles, chimney-tops, and other similar articles.
PERCY, WILLIAM CARTER [STAFFORD.	11,682	29th April 1847	Machinery for making and dressing bricks and tiles; sheds and kilns in which bricks and tiles are dried and burnt.
PERING, RICHARD - - -	3726	23rd July 1813	Anchors.
PERING, RICHARD - - -	6004	6th Oct. 1830	Anchors.
PERKINS, ANGIER MARCH -	6146	30th July 1831	Apparatus for heating air in buildings, heating and evaporating fluids, and heating metals.
PERKINS, ANGIER MARCH -	8311	16th Dec. 1839	Apparatus for transmitting heat by circulating water.
PERKINS, ANGIER MARCH -	8804	21st Jan. 1841	Apparatus for heating by the circulation of hot water; construction of pipes for such and other purposes.
PERKINS, ANGIER MARCH -	9664	16th March 1843	Manufacture and melting of iron ;—applicable for evaporating fluids and disinfecting oils.
PERKINS, ANGIER MARCH -	10,778	21st July 1845	Apparatus for heating air in buildings, heating and evaporating fluids, and heating metals.
PERKINS, ANGIER MARCH -	13,492	5th Feb. 1851	Railway axles and boxes.
PERKINS, ANGIER MARCH -	13,509	11th Feb. 1851	Constructing and heating ovens.
PERKINS, BENJAMIN DOUGLAS	2221	10th March 1798	Curing diseases in the human body by drawing pointed metals over the parts affected.
PERKINS, CHARLES - -	8728	28th Nov. 1840	Construction of pistons and valves for retaining and discharging liquids, gases, and steam.
PERKINS, CHRISTOPHER -	1773	19th Aug. 1790	Drill for sowing corn, pulse, and seeds.
PERKINS, CHRISTOPHER -	2821	9th Feb. 1805	Machine for thrashing corn and pulse.
PERKINS, EDWARD EMANUEL	9095	21st Sept. 1841	Manufacture of soap.
PERKINS, EDWARD MOSELEY	13,998	8th March 1852	Manufacture of cast-metal pipes, retorts, or other hollow-castings.
PERKINS, JACOB - - -	4400	11th Oct. 1819	Machinery and implements applicable to ornamental turning and engraving, transferring engraved or other work from the surface of one to another piece of metal, and forming metallic dies and matrices; construction of plates and presses for printing bank-notes and other papers; making dies and presses for coining money, stamping medals, and for other purposes.

Name of Patentee.	Progressive Number.	Date.	Subject-matter of Patent.
PERKINS, JACOB - - -	4470	3rd June 1820	Construction of fixed and portable pumps.
PERKINS, JACOB - - -	4732	10th Dec. 1822	Steam-engines.
PERKINS, JACOB - - -	4792	17th May 1823	Heating, boiling, or evaporating by the steam of fluids, in pans, boilers, or other vessels.
PERKINS, JACOB - - -	4800	5th June 1823	Steam-engines.
PERKINS, JACOB - - -	4870	20th Nov. 1823	Construction of the furnace of steam-boilers and other vessels.
PERKINS, JACOB - - -	4952	15th May 1824	Throwing shells and other projectiles.
PERKINS, JACOB - - -	4998	9th Aug. 1824	Propelling vessels.
PERKINS, JACOB - - -	5237	11th Aug. 1825	Construction of bedsteads, sofas, and other similar articles.
PERKINS, JACOB - - -	5477	22nd March 1827	Construction of steam-engines.
PERKINS, JACOB - - -	5806	2nd July 1829	Machinery for propelling steam-vessels.
PERKINS, JACOB - - -	6128	2nd July 1831	Generating steam.
PERKINS, JACOB - - -	6154	27th Aug. 1831	Generating steam;—applicable to evaporating and boiling fluids for certain purposes.
PERKINS, JACOB - - -	6275	9th June 1832	Blowing and exhausting air;—applicable to various purposes,
PERKINS, JACOB - - -	6326	20th Nov. 1832	Preserving copper in certain cases from the oxydation caused by heat.
PERKINS, JACOB - - -	6662	14th Aug. 1834	Apparatus and means for producing ice; cooling fluids.
PERKINS, JACOB - - -	7059	12th April 1836	Steam-engines; generating steam; evaporating and boiling fluids for certain purposes.
PERKINS, JACOB - - -	7114	13th June 1836	Apparatus for cooking.
PERKINS, JACOB - - -	7242	3rd Dec. 1836	Steam-engines, furnaces, and boilers;—partly applicable to other purposes.
PERKINS, JOHN THOMAS -	10,628	22nd April 1845	Machinery for cutting paper and other fabrics.
PERKINS, STEPHEN HIGGINSON	10,836	18th Sept. 1845	Steam-engine, and its application to steam-navigation.
PERKINS, THOMAS - - -	747	4th March 1760	Geometrical scale-beam engine.
PERKINS, WILLIAM - -	185	12th Nov. 1675	Buoying and raising up ships' ordnance, also treasures and other matters from the bottom of the sea, by the help of air conveyed under water; new way of diving and living several hours under the water, by curing the air conveyed down for sustenance, so as to make it fit for respiring whilst beneath the water; engines and instruments for landing and shipping goods and merchandize.
PERKINS, WILLIAM - -	609	6th Sept. 1744	Machine for grinding corn, drawing coals and great weights out of pits and mines, and draining fenny lands.
PERKINS, WILLIAM - -	658	24th Nov. 1750	Machine for grinding corn, raising water, draining fens, pits, and mines, and for other purposes.
PERKS, JOHN - - - -	4154	5th Aug. 1817	Apparatus for manufacturing, purifying, and storing gas.
PERLBACH, HARRY JOSEPH -	11,811	23rd July 1847	Uniting certain metals and alloys of metals.
PERLEY, CHARLES - - -	13,708	31st July 1851	Construction of capstans for nautical and general purposes.

Name of Patentee.	Progressive Number.	Date.	Subject-matter of Patent.
PERPIGNA, ANTOINE - -	11,270	29th June 1846	Regulators for qualifying the actions of mechanical powers.
PERPIGNA, ANTOINE - -	11,507	21st Dec. 1846	Machinery for platting and braiding.
PERRIER, MICHEL - - -	10,780	20th July 1845	Spinning and twisting cotton, flax, silk, and other fibrous materials.
PERRIER, Sir ANTHONY - -	4604	27th July 1822	Apparatus for distilling, boiling, and concentrating by evaporation, liquids and fluids.
PERRIN, CHARLES HENRI -	9438	8th Aug. 1842	Construction of certain parts of the mechanism used in watches and chronometers; —applicable to some kind of clocks.
PERRIN, JOHN - - -	3096	13th Jan. 1808	Preparing certain kinds of hemp.
PERRING, JOHN - - -	9410	7th July 1842	Wood-paving.
PERROTT, BENJAMIN - -	426	26th March 1720	Furnace for making, melting, and preparing the metal for making glass-wares.
PERROTT, HUMPHREY - -	545	15th Feb. 1734	Furnaces for melting and preparing glass; preserving window-glass when annealing in the kiln.
PERRY, JAMES - - -	5933	24th April 1830	Pens.
PERRY, JAMES - - -	6215	28th Jan. 1832	Pens.
PERRY, JOHN - - - -	7706	27th June 1838	Combs for combing wool.
PERRY, JOHN - - - -	10,433	12th Dec. 1844	Combing wool.
PERRY, JOHN - - - -	11,508	21st Dec. 1846	Combing wool, and preparing wool for combing and carding.
PERRY, STEPHEN - - -	6512	19th Nov. 1833	Pens and penholders.
PERRY, STEPHEN - - -	6678	20th Sept. 1834	Pens and penholders.
PERRY, STEPHEN - - -	10,460	11th Jan. 1845	Application of springs to locks and other fastenings, to paper-holders, candle-lamps, blinds, window-sashes, and doors, and to seats and elastic surfaces for sitting or reclining upon.
PERRY, STEPHEN - - -	10,568	17th March 1845	Springs to be applied to girths, belts, and bandages; manufacture of elastic bands.
PERRY, STEPHEN - - -	11,212	19th May 1846	Manufacture of rings, straps, bands, and bandages, cords and string; and their application to clock-work, locks, and other fastenings, presses for books, paper-holders, candle-lamps, window-sashes, doors, window-blinds, also to seats and surfaces for lying and reclining upon.
PERRY, THOMAS - - -	13,774	16th Oct. 1851	Manufacture of looped fabrics.
PERRYMAN, ELIZABETH - -	3221	29th March 1809	Street and hall lamp; apparatus for trimming, lighting, and cleansing the same.
PERSHOUSE, HENRY - -	4319	10th Dec. 1818	Stamping pans for scales.
PERSHOUSE, HENRY - -	11,016	23rd Dec. 1845	Apparatus used in connection with writing, and in attaching postage-stamps and labels.
PERTINS, MARIE ELIZABETH [ANTOINETTE.	6057	23rd Dec. 1830	Preparation of a coal fitted for refining and purifying sugar and other matters, and restoring the coal after being used.
PETER, JOHN - - - "	10,454	6th Jan. 1845	Flax-spinning and flax-spinning machinery, also applicable to the manufacture of other fibrous substances.
PETHER, HENRY - - -	8042	23rd April 1839	Preparation and combination of earthenware or porcelain for mosaic or tessellated work.
PETHER, WILLIAM - -	2778	4th Aug. 1804	Preventing or curing smoky chimneys.

Name of Patentee.	Progressive Number.	Date.	Subject-matter of Patent.
PETHERICK, THOMAS - -	5935	28th April 1830	Machinery for separating copper, lead and other ores, from earthy and other substances with which they are mixed.
PETHERICK, THOMAS - -	6239	8th March 1832	Machinery and apparatus for separating copper, lead and other ores, from earthy and other substances with which they are mixed.
PETIGARS, JEAN LOUIS AL-[PHONSE.	9101	24th Sept. 1841	Construction of presses.
PETIT, SAMUEL HEARNE LE -	9213	11th Jan. 1842	Manufacture and supply of gas.
PETIT, CLAUDE FRANCOIS JULES	10,021	23rd Jan. 1844	Fastenings for gloves.
PETIT, JEAN JOSEPH HAZARD	11,623	16th March 1847	Manufacture of oils; apparatus for disinfecting and purifying oils and other inflammable or spirituous matters; lamps and gas-burners.
PETITPIERRE, JEAN HENRY -	4923	20th March 1824	Machine for making from one piece of leather without seam or sewing, shoes and slippers, gloves, caps, and hats, cartouche-boxes, sheaths for swords, bayonets, and knives.
PETITPIERRE, HENRY - -	11,671	27th April 1847	Instruments for writing.
PETO, HENRY - - -	5585	13th Dec. 1827	Apparatus for generating power.
PETRIE, GEORGE - - -	11,926	26th Oct. 1847	Electric telegraphic-apparatus.
PETRIE, JAMES - - -	10,193	22nd May 1844	Steam-engines.
PETRIE, JAMES - - -	12,118	10th April 1848	Steam-engines.
PETRIE, JOHN - - -	6452	25th July 1833	Steam-engines.
PETRIE, WILLIAM - -	8937	27th April 1841	Obtaining a moving power by voltaic electricity, applicable to engines and other cases where power is applied.
PETRIE, WILLIAM - -	8991	19th June 1841	Obtaining mechanical power, also applicable for obtaining rapid motion.
PETRIE, WILLIAM - -	12,772	20th Sept. 1849	Electric and galvanic instruments and apparatus, and their application to lighting and motive purposes.
PETRIE, WILLIAM - - -	14,346	13th Nov. 1852	Obtaining and applying electric currents; apparatus employed therein;—partly applicable to refining metals, and production of metallic solutions of certain acids.
PETTIT, GEORGE BROOKS -	12,504	5th March 1849	Applying gas to heat apparatus containing fluids; heating and ventilating buildings; gas fittings, and apparatus for controlling the passage of gas.
PETTIT, GEORGE BROOKS -	14,333	21st Oct. 1852	Obtaining and applying heat and light.
PETTIT, ROBERT - -	8659	15th Oct. 1840	Railroads; carriages and wheels employed thereon.
PETTITT, EDWIN - -	14,061	15th April 1853	Machinery for twisting, drawing, doubling, and spinning cotton-wool, silk, flax, and other fibrous substances.
PETTITT, EDWIN - -	13,082	25th May 1850	Manufacture of glass; forming and ornamenting vessels and articles of glass; construction of furnaces and annealing-kilns.
PETTITT, EDWIN WATKINS [WILLIAM WYNN.	11,297	15th July 1846	Machinery for tilling land.
PETTITT, WILLIAM - -	8525	30th May 1840	Communicating-apparatus, to be applied to railroad-carriages.
PEW, RICHARD - -	4803	17th June 1823	Composition for covering houses and other buildings.

Name of Patentee.	Progres-sive Number.	Date.		Subject-matter of Patent.
PEYN, JAMES - - - -	559	13th Oct.	1737	Worm-pitch, for preserving the timbers and closing the seams of ships and vessels.
PEYRE, FRANCOIS, junior -	7011	23rd Feb.	1836	Economizing fuel in ships' hearths or cooking-apparatus; obtaining distilled water from sea-water;—applicable to generating steam.
PEYTON, RICHARD - - -	11,705	18th May	1847	Manufacture of bedsteads.
PEYTON, THOMAS - - -	98	26th July	1636	Charking sea-coals.
PHELPS, SAMUEL - - -	2942	17th June	1806	Making kelp, barilla or other vegetable or mineral alkali, by fermentation and other means in addition to combustion.
PHELPS, SAMUEL - - -	3100	23rd Jan.	1808	Manufacturing soap.
PHILCOX, GEORGE - - -	8145	6th July	1839	Chronometers, watches, and other time-keepers.
PHILCOX, GEORGE - - -	11,177	25th April	1846	Construction of chronometers and other time-keepers.
PHILEPSTHAL, PAUL DE - -	2575	26th Jan.	1802	Optical apparatus to represent human figures in a dark space or scene.
PHILIPPE, JEAN - - -	1444	20th July	1784	Springs made of tempered steel, either flat or square, for garters, bracelets, boots, &c.
PHILIPPI, FREDERICK THEO-[DORE.	8721	25th Nov.	1840	Printing cotton, silk, and other woven fabrics.
PHILIPPI, FREDERICK THEO-DORE.	9034	21st July	1841	Production of sal-ammoniac; purification of gas for illumination.
PHILIPPI, FREDERICK THEO-[DORE.	11,752	15th June	1847	Machinery for stretching, drying, and finishing woven-fabrics.
PHILIPS, THOMAS (Captain) -	274	15th Sept.	1691	Making moulds for ordnance.
PHILLIPS, CHARLES - -	4394	20th Sept.	1819	Capstans.
PHILLIPS, CHARLES - -	4529	19th Jan.	1821	Apparatus for propelling vessels; construction of vessels so propelled.
PHILLIPS, CHARLES - -	4938	13th July	1824	Tillers and steering-wheels of vessels of various denominations.
PHILLIPS, CHARLES - -	5189	18th June	1825	Construction of a ship's compass.
PHILLIPS, CHARLES - -	5505	8th June	1827	Capstans.
PHILLIPS, CHARLES - -	7152	14th July	1836	Drawing-off beer and other liquors from casks or vessels.
PHILLIPS, CHARLES - -	7556	30th Jan.	1838	Machinery for punching, bending, cutting, and joining metal, and for holding or securing metal to be so operated on;—parts of which machinery are adapted to perform some of these operations on other materials.
PHILLIPS, CHARLES - -	8962	20th May	1841	Reaping and cutting vegetable substances as food for cattle.
PHILLIPS, CHARLES - -	9812	3rd July	1843	Machinery for cutting corn, grass, and other standing or growing crops; machinery for cutting vegetable substances as food for cattle.
PHILLIPS, CHARLES - -	13,164	3rd July	1850	Apparatus for cutting turnips and other similar substances as food for cattle.
PHILLIPS, GEORGE - - -	1487	16th July	1785	Making coats and riding-habits without seams in the back or sides.
PHILLIPS, GEORGE - - -	11,337	17th Aug.	1846	Construction and arrangement of apparatus for supporting garden-pots, and improving the growth of plants.
PHILLIPS, GEORGE - - -	11,965	16th Nov.	1847	Purification of certain oils and spirits.

Name of Patentee.	Progressive Number.	Date.	Subject-matter of Patent.
PHILLIPS, GEORGE - - -	13,747	18th Sept. 1851	Preventing the injurious effects arising from smoking tobacco.
PHILLIPS, HENRY - - -	6884	17th Aug. 1835	Purifying gas for the purpose of illumination.
PHILLIPS, HENRY - - -	9370	31st May 1842	Purifying gas for purposes of light.
PHILLIPS, HENRY - - -	9612	26th Jan. 1843	Removing impurities from coal-gas for the purposes of light.
PHILLIPS, HENRY - - -	10,618	15th April 1845	Purifying gas.
PHILLIPS, JAMES - - -	1481	20th May 1785	Cocks and valves.
PHILLIPS, JOHN - - -	2907	12th Feb. 1806	Construction of tinder-boxes.
PHILLIPS, JOHN - - -	2908	12th Feb. 1806	Chain and apparatus, for straight, square, and parallel stone and marble sawing;—applicable to other purposes.
PHILLIPS, JOHN - - -	3064	28th July 1807	Method of constructing and removing offices, counting-houses and other rooms, with desks, drawing-boards, and other conveniences;—applicable to constructing and removing bridges, cottages, sentry-boxes, and other erections of a large or small extent.
PHILLIPS, JOHN - - -	6087	21st Feb. 1831	Bridles.
PHILLIPS, JOHN LEDYARD -	7198	4th Oct. 1836	Manufacture of woollen-cloths.
PHILLIPS, PEREGRINE - -	6096	21st March 1831	Manufacturing sulphuric-acid, commonly called oil of vitriol.
PHILLIPS, PHILIP WILLIAM -	8846	15th Feb. 1841	Four-wheeled carriages.
PHILLIPS, REUBEN - - -	4142	19th July 1817	Purifying gas for the purpose of illumination.
PHILLIPS, REUBEN - - -	12,007	30th Dec. 1847	Treating or manufacture of gutta-percha or any of the varieties of caoutchouc.
PHILLIPS, RICHARD - -	3848	5th Oct. 1814	Plough.
PHILLIPS, RICHARD - -	6846	4th June 1835	Manufacturing sulphate of soda.
PHILLIPS, ROBERT - -	512	11th July 1729	Curing smoky chimneys; and warming rooms.
PHILLIPS, THOMAS - -	13,599	24th April 1851	Apparatus for heating, ventilating, and cooking by gas.
PHILLIPS, WILLIAM HENRY -	9023	13th July 1841	Construction of chimneys, flues, and air-tubes, with the stoves and apparatus connected therewith, for preventing the escape of smoke into apartments; and for warming and ventilating buildings.
PHILLIPS, WILLIAM HENRY -	10,212	4th June 1844	Apparatus and means for extinguishing fire and saving life and property; obtaining and applying motive-power; propelling.
PHILLIPS, WILLIAM HENRY -	12,570	16th April 1849	Extinguishing fire; preparation of materials for the purpose; saving life and property.
PHILLIPS, WILLIAM HENRY -	14,152	1st June 1852	Decorative illumination; applying light for other purposes.
PHILP, EDWARD DAKIN -	5720	29th Nov. 1828	Apparatus for distilling and rectifying.
PHIPPS, ALFRED JOHN -	9432	1st Aug. 1842	Paving streets, roads, and ways.
PHIPPS, CHRISTOPHER -	5075	11th Jan. 1825	Machinery for making paper.
PHIPPS, CHRISTOPHER -	10,234	21st June 1844	Manufacturing paper; machinery employed therein.
PHIPPS, GEORGE HENRY -	9015	2nd July 1841	Construction of wheels for railway and other carriages.
PHIPPS, GEORGE HENRY -	13,031	5th April 1850	Propelling vessels.

Name of Patentee.	Progressive Number.	Date.	Subject-matter of Patent.
PHIPPS, JOHN - - -	1774	21st Aug. 1790	Preparing paper with lines made and copies set for writing, also outlines for drawing, by means of the watermark.
PHIPPS, JOHN - - -	5075	11th Jan. 1825	Machinery for making paper.
PHIPPS, ROBERT - - -	1569	7th Nov. 1786	Manufacturing silk and mohair, separately or in combination with other materials.
PHIPSON, JOSEPH WEATHERBY	4361	24th April 1819	Making pipes, tubes, or conductors, for gas and other purposes.
PHYSICK, HY. VERNAN - -	10,026	30th Jan. 1844	Machinery for driving piles.
PIAGET, LOUIS HYPOLITE -	11,448	12th Nov. 1846	Producing ornamental metal surfaces.
PICAULT, GUSTAVE FRANCOIS	12,651	7th June 1849	Apparatus for opening oysters.
PICCIOTTO, MOSES HAYM -	12,245	17th Aug. 1848	Purifying and decolourizing certain gums.
PICKARD, JAMES - - -	1263	23rd Aug. 1780	Machine for boring, turning, rolling, grinding corn, and all other sorts of grinding; forging, flatting, and slitting of iron, and other work that a mill is capable of performing by a rotative motion.
PICKEN, GEORGE BUCKNALL -	10,307	12th Sept. 1844	Umbrellas and parasols.
PICKERING, CHARLES WILLIAM [HARRISON.	12,530	20th March 1849	Evaporating brine and certain other fluids.
PICKERING, EXUPERIUS - -	1981	18th March 1794	Machinery for forming and constructing navigable canals;—applicable to other purposes.
PICKERING, GEORGE - -	829	12th June 1765	Making iron-screws for raising and lifting up timber, and for other purposes.
PICKERING, JOHN - - -	920	7th March 1769	Chasing coffin-furniture, ornaments for coaches, chariots, sedans, and other carriages, cabinet-work, and domestic furniture, in gold, silver, brass, tin, and other metals.
PICKERING, JOHN - - -	1058	20th Dec. 1773	Making ornaments with paper to resemble wood-carving, for the inside and outside of buildings and ships, and for furniture.
PICKERING, JOHN - - -	1630	22nd Nov. 1787	Detector or pocket-spring, for preventing the pocket being picked.
PICKERING, PETER - -	5784	28th April 1829	Engine or machinery to be worked by means of fluids, gases, or air, on shore or at sea. "Pickering's Engine."
PICKERING, ROGER - -	629	16th March 1748	Producing a spirit from British materials, to equal French brandy.
PICKERING, THOMAS ABREE -	3809	21st May 1814	Preventing loss of remittances or parcels sent by coach.
PICKERING, WILLIAM - , -	5784	28th April 1829	Engine or machinery to be worked by means of fluids, gases, or air, on shore or at sea. "Pickering's Engine."
PICKERING, WILLIAM - -	8250	2nd Nov. 1839	Engines for obtaining power.
PICKERSGILL, JOHN - -	7178	1st Sept. 1836	Preparing and applying India-rubber to fabrics.
PICKETT, WILLIAM VOSE -	10,175	7th May 1844	Preparing, in metals or other substances, the parts and features of architectural construction and decoration; applying the same in the construction of houses and other buildings.
PICKFORD, MATTHEW - -	4709	29th Sept. 1822	Construction of wheels of carriages, and all other vertical wheels of a certain size.

Name of Patentee.	Progressive Number.	Date.	Subject-matter of Patent.
PICKFORD, SAMUEL - -	11,179	28th April 1846	Apparatus applicable to casks or vessels for preserving ale and other fermented liquors, also for raising or forcing the same for draught.
PICKSTONE, SAMUEL - -	13,449	11th Jan. 1851	Machinery used in spinning, doubling, and weaving cotton, flax, and other fibrous substances.
PICKWORTH, HENRY - -	6990	26th Jan. 1836	Machinery for propelling vessels and other floating bodies moved by steam or other power.
PIDDING, HENRY JAMES -	8228	27th Sept. 1839	Collars for horses and other animals.
PIDDING, WILLIAM - -	11,198	5th May 1846	Process for preserving the flavour of coffee and cocoa, or any preparations thereof, from the effects of the atmosphere.
PIDDING, WILLIAM - -	11,460	21st Nov. 1846	Carriages.
PIDDING, WILLIAM - -	11,561	2nd Feb. 1847	Mode of exhibiting and protecting certain coloured fabrics, ornamental inscriptions, and other designs.
PIDDING, WILLIAM - -	11,588	24th Feb. 1847	Processes for preparing certain vegetable extracts, also preserving the aroma of certain vegetable substances from the atmosphere.
PIDDING, WILLIAM - -	12,562	3rd April 1849	Obtaining perfect combustion; apparatus relating thereto, applicable to furnaces and fire-places of every description.
PIDDING, WILLIAM - -	13,850	8th Dec. 1851	Treatment, manufacture, and application of materials or substances for building purposes.
PIDDING, WILLIAM - -	13,911	24th Jan. 1852	Manufacture, preparation, and combination of materials or substances for production of fuel, and for other purposes to which natural coal can be applied.
PIDDING, WILLIAM - -	14,014	8th March 1852	Mining operations; and machinery or apparatus connected therewith.
PIDDING, WILLIAM - -	14,036	24th March 1852	Construction of vehicles used on railways or on ordinary roads.
PIDGEON, THOMAS - -	2850	18th May 1805	Saddle.
PIERCE, WILLIAM - -	8489	2nd May 1840	Construction of locks and keys.
PIERCE, WILLIAM - -	11,856	6th Sept. 1847	Machinery for raising water and other fluids.
PIERCY, JOHN - -	4077	1st Nov. 1816	Making thimbles.
PIERPOINT, MATTHEW -	11,895	7th Oct. 1847	Distribution of artificial light.
PIERPONT, HEZEKIAH BEERS	2292	5th Feb. 1799	Oil, extracted from certain vegetable substances.
PIERRET, JOSEPH BERROIT -	11,522	11th Jan. 1847	Steam-engines.
PIERSON, JOSIAH GILBERT -	6532	20th Dec. 1833	Construction of bolts and latches to be attached to doors, and other situations requiring a strong fastening.
PIGOT, Sir HUGH - -	7813	13th Sept. 1838	Engines, useful as steam-engines, pumps, or propellers of vessels or machinery.
PIGOTT, RICHARD GREVILLE -	9710	25th April 1843	Apparatus for supporting the human body when immersed in water, to prevent drowning.
PIGGOTT, WILLIAM PETER - [Piggott, Peter.]	10,625	17th April 1845	Mathematical, nautical, optical, and astronomical instruments; manufacturing dials and graduated plates.

Name of Patentee.	Progressive Number.	Date.	Subject-matter of Patent.
PIGGOTT, WILLIAM PETER -	12,059	8th Feb. 1848	Nautical instruments; manufacturing cases for containing instruments, goods, or merchandize.
PIGGOTT, WILLIAM PETER -	12,697	4th July 1849	Electric-batteries; production of light; transmitting intelligence;—partly applicable to other purposes.
PIKE, ANN - - - -	748	26th March 1760	Ointment, as an antidote for the itch and all scorbutic humours.
PILBROW, JAMES - - -	8630	10th Sept. 1840	Steam-engines.
PILBROW, JAMES - - -	9354	23rd May 1842	Steam-engines.
PILBROW, JAMES - - -	9658	7th March 1843	Application of steam, air, and other vaporous and gaseous agents, for the production of motive-power; machinery for the purpose.
PILBROW, JAMES - - -	10,190	17th May 1844	Machinery for propelling carriages on railways and common roads, and vessels on rivers and canals.
PILBROW, JAMES - - -	11,069	31st Jan. 1846	Propelling on land and water.
PILBROW, JAMES - - -	12,108	4th April 1848	Propelling upon railways and canals; machinery for accomplishing the same.
PILBROW, JAMES - - -	13,993	3rd March 1852	Apparatus for supplying the inhabitants of towns and other places with water.
PILCHER, WILLIAM HENRY -	7517	19th Dec. 1837	Construction of docks, and apparatus for repairing ships and vessels.
PILLING, JAMES - - -	13,983	23rd Feb. 1852	Looms for weaving.
PIM, JAMES - - - -	7352	25th April 1837	Propulsion on railways.
PIM, WAKEFIELD - - -	9670	18th March 1843	Construction of buoys or other water-marks.
PIM, WAKEFIELD - - -	12,440	25th Jan. 1849	Propelling ships or vessels.
PIM, WAKEFIELD - - -	13,160	3rd July 1850	Construction of boilers and funnels of steam-engines.
PINCHBACK, JOHN - - -	4363	1st May 1819	Making machines for catching flies and wasps.
PINCHBECK, CHRISTOPHER -	892	29th Feb. 1768	Nozzles and candlesticks.
PINCHBECK, CHRISTOPHER -	899	17th March 1768	Tablets by which persons may secure their thoughts in the dark. "Nocturnal Remembrancer."
PINCHBECK, CHRISTOPHER -	1119	14th March 1776	Addition to snuffers.
PINCHBECK, EDMUND GEORGE	12,453	6th Feb. 1849	Certain parts of steam-engines.
PINCOFFS, SIMON - - -	13,080	23rd May 1850	Ageing process in calico-printing and dyeing;—also applicable to other processes in calico-printing and dyeing.
PINDIN, PHILIP - - -	4359	20th April 1819	Single and double trusses.
PINE, WILLIAM - - -	999	6th Nov. 1771	Casting cases in metal for holding printing-types, for printing on silk, leather, paper, and parchment, together with raised letters for signs; printing-presses.
PINEL, JAMES FRANCIS - -	10,321	19th Sept. 1844	Treating farinaceous substances.
PINEL, JAMES FRANCIS - -	10,648	1st May 1845	Treating farinaceous substances.
PINEL, JAMES FRANCIS - - [Pinel, Jacques Francois.]	11,468	1st Dec. 1846	Grinding wheat and other grain.
PINKUS, HENRY - - - [Pinkins, Henry.]	5541	15th Aug. 1827	Apparatus for generating gas to be applied to lights and other purposes.
PINKUS, HENRY - - -	5563	17th Nov. 1827	Purifying carburetted hydrogen-gas for the purpose of illumination.
PINKUS, HENRY - - -	5926	5th April 1830	Generating gas for illumination; apparatus for the purpose.

Name of Patentee.	Progres-sive Number.	Date.	Subject-matter of Patent.
PINKUS, HENRY - - -	6570	1st March 1834	Apparatus for communicating and transmitting or extending motive-power, for propelling carriages on railways or common roads.
PINKUS, HENRY - - -	6885	17th Aug. 1835	Inland transit applicable to apparatus for communicating and transmitting or extending motive-power, for propelling carriages on railways or roads, and vessels on canals.
PINKUS, HENRY - - -	8207	26th Aug. 1839	Applying motive-power to the impelling of machinery; — also applicable to several other useful purposes.
PINKUS, HENRY - - -	8644	24th Sept. 1840	Applying motive-power to the impelling of machinery, carriages on railways, on common roads or ways and through fields, and vessels afloat; constructing roads or ways on which carriages may be impelled or propelled.
PINKUS, HRNRY - - -	8363	15th Oct. 1840	Combining and applying materials applicable to the formation or construction of roads or ways.
PINKUS, HENRY - - -	8958	14th May 1841	Applying electrical-currents or electricity, either frictional, atmospheric, voltaic, or electro-magnetic.
PINKUS, HENRY - - -	9835	13th July 1843	Applying motive-power in combination with apparatus and machinery, to certain purposes in propelling and applicable to railways, or to ships or other vessels afloat.
PINKUS, HENRY - - -	10,447	27th Dec. 1844	Obtaining and applying motive-power to impelling machinery.
PINTO, FRANCIS - - -	1087	17th Nov. 1774	Pump to be worked by fire; for raising water, draining mines, pits, or marshes, watering meadows, and filling canals; applicable as a ship's pump.
PINTO, FRANCIS - - -	1227	7th June 1779	Preventing and curing smoky chimneys.
PIPER, JOHN - - - -	438	8th Nov. 1721	Compound of prepared chalk and sea-water, as manure for grain, pulse, and grass.
PIPER, THOMAS - - -	8637	22nd Oct. 1840	Wheels for carriages.
PIPER, WILLIAM - - -	3456	11th June 1811	Manufacturing gun-skelps.
PIPER, WILLIAM - - -	4720	1st Nov. 1822	Anchors.
PIPER, WILLIAM - - -	4774	12th April 1823	Preparation of iron for manufacturing chains and chain cables.
PIRNIE, ALEXANDER - -	10,847	2nd Oct. 1845	Steering vessels.
PIRON, LOUIS PROSPER NICO-[LAS DUVAL.	12,566	16th April 1849	Tubes, pipes, flags, and curbs, for pavements and tram roads.
PIRSSON, JOSEPH POOLE -	13,205	31st July 1850	Steam-machinery and apparatus connected therewith.
PITCHER, WILLIAM HENRY -	7517	19th Dec. 1837	Construction of docks; apparatus for repairing ships and vessels.
PITCHER, LEMAN BAKER -	13,759	2nd Oct. 1851	Apparatus for regulating motive-power engines.
PITT, BENJAMIN - - -	10,182	14th May 1844	Construction of locks and latches, spindles and knobs; applicable to doors and other similar purposes.

Name of Patentee.	Progres-sive Number.	Date.	Subject-matter of Patent.
PITT, CHARLES - - -	3913	11th May 1815	Security and safe conveyance of small parcels and remittances of property of every description ; also security in the formation or appendage of shoes.
PITT, GEORGE - - -	223	21st Nov. 1682	Making wet harbours and docks to hold ships from ten to forty feet above high water mark ; also engines and means for raising ships from the river Thames or from stocks, into the said harbours and vice versâ.
PITT, JAMES - - - -	11,867	9th Sept. 1847	Apparatus for holding down trousers.
PITT, JOSEPH - - -	9758	6th June 1843	Improvements applicable to fixed and portable waterclosets, and beds or bedsteads ; —partly applicable to raising and forcing water.
PITTAR, SAMUEL JOHN - -	13,223	13th Aug. 1850	Umbrellas and parasols.
PITTS, MATTHEW - - -	1867	18th April 1792	Steam-engines.
PITTS, MATTHEW - - -	1943	25th March 1793	Steam-engines; method of generating steam; its application to steam-engines or any other purpose where steam is used.
PITTS, NICHOLAS - - -	144	17th April 1664	Making salt by preparing brine of sea water, by means of an artificial furnace.
PLACE, FRANCIS - - -	2920	21st March 1806	Locks for muskets, pistols, fowling-pieces, carriage-guns, and every species of fire-arms.
PLACE, JOHN - - - -	10,527	20th Feb. 1845	Looms for weaving.
PLANT, FREDERICK - -	6538	13th Jan. 1834	Fur-cutting machine.
PLANT, JOHN - -	13,719	14th Aug. 1851	Manufacture of textile fabrics.
PLANT, REUBEN - - -	12,705	18th July 1849	Making bar or wrought iron.
PLASKETT, JOHN - - -	3408	6th March 1811	Manufacturing casks and other vessels, by machinery.
PLATOW, MORITZ - - -	7987	6th March 1839	Pumps for raising or forcing liquids.
PLATOW, MONTZ - - -	8201	17th Aug. 1839	Making decoctions of coffee and other matters.
PLATT, JOHN - - - -	5560	10th Nov. 1827	Machinery for combing wool and other fibrous substances.
PLATT, JOHN - - - -	11,110	25th Feb. 1846	Machinery to be employed in the preparaand spinning of cotton and other fibrous substances.
PLATT, JOHN - - - -	11,525	11th Jan. 1847	Consuming smoke and economizing fuel.
PLATT, JOHN - - - -	11,814	24th July 1847	Machine for making cards, and for preparing and spinning cotton and other fibrous materials, also for preparing and dressing yarn, and weaving the same.
PLATT, JOHN - - - -	13,034	11th April 1850	Machinery for spinning, doubling, and weaving cotton, flax, and other fibrous substances.
PLATT, JOHN - - - -	13,379	2nd Dec. 1850	Machinery for spinning, doubling, and weaving cotton, flax, and other fibrous substances.
PLATT, JOHN - - - -	13,677	3rd July 1851	Looms for weaving.
PLATT, JOHN - - - -	13,784	22nd Oct. 1851	Machinery for the preparation and manufacture of fibrous materials ;—also applicable or partly so for the transmission of fluids and aëriform bodies.

Name of Patentee.	Progressive Number.	Date.		Subject-matter of Patent.
PLATT, MOSES - - -	589	10th March	1743	Machine for printing ornamental designs on silks, cottons, linens, stuffs, woollen-cloths, and other manufactures, for apparel, furniture, or otherwise.
PLAYER, JOHN - - -	7888	1st Dec.	1838	Furnaces and fire-places for consuming anthracite and other fuel, for generating steam, &c.
PLAYFAIR, JAMES - - -	1345	28th Nov.	1782	Shaving-box.
PLAYFAIR, JAMES - - -	1814	2nd July	1791	Constructing locks for navigable canals.
PLAIRFAIR, PATRICK - -	11,920	21st Oct.	1847	Manufacture of sugar.
PLAYFAIR, WILLIAM - -	1309	29tn Dec.	1781	Making tongs, spoons, knives, forks, and medals, out of solid silver or other metals.
PLAYFAIR, WILLIAM - -	1373	24th May	1783	Making bars for sash-windows, of copper, iron, or any mixed metal containing copper, also metallic ornaments and mouldings for grates and fenders, and borders for tea-waiters, trays, and bottle-stands, likewise horse-shoes and curtain-rods of iron.
PLAYFAIR, WILLIAM - -	1408	17th Dec.	1783	Cutting or dividing pieces of metal, and giving them a cylindrical or other uniform shape through their whole length, or making them taper regularly, for the formation of bars, bolts, rods, wire, spade and shovel bits; ornamenting the surfaces of metal for making ornaments for the exterior and interior decoration of houses and furniture, also for coaches, and for other purposes where brass-nails, carved-work, and stucco-work have been commonly used; joining and connecting metal-beads, husks, leaves, or other ornaments consisting of single detached pieces.
PLAYFAIR, WILLIAM - -	1466	26th Feb.	1785	Making buckles of silver or other metal; and plating the surface of copper or other metals with gold or silver.
PLAYFAIR, WILLIAM - -	2455	12th Dec.	1800	Naval-architecture.
PLEASANTS, WILLIAM - -	3226	19th April	1809	Self-mover, or machine which can keep itself in motion.
PLEES, WILLIAM - - -	2649	27th Sept.	1802	Manufacturing paper for various purposes.
PLENEY, JEAN BAPTISTE -	6701	22nd Oct.	1834	Machinery for making articles out of brick and other the like earth.
PLENTY, WILLIAM - - -	2443	18th Oct.	1800	Pump; plough.
PLENTY, WILLIAM - - -	3971	22nd Dec.	1815	Plough or agricultural-implement, answering a two-fold purpose; so that land or ground may be thereby both pared and ploughed.
PLETT, SILVESTER - - -	208	23rd May	1679	Pipes, engines, and vessels (by way of hydragogy) for raising water out of ships and mines, for draining land, and for supplying, even in the drought of summer all sorts of mills, whether undershot or overshot; also for raising the Thames water in larger quantities than is now raised by the water-mill houses, without the great charge and labour of men and horses.
PLEUNIUS, ROGER - - -	581	30th Dec.	1741	Meliorating harpsichords, lyrichords, and spinnets.
PLEUNIUS, ROGER - - - [Plenius, Roger.]	613	10th July	1745	Harpsichords and spinnets.

Name of Patentee.	Progressive Number.	Date.	Subject-matter of Patent.
PLIMLEY, CHARLES - -	3650	20th Feb. 1813	Working steel or iron, or steel joined with iron, into taper forms for the purpose of making files, and for various other purposes.
PLIMLEY, CHARLES - -	4256	7th May 1818	Blast-engines and steam-engines.
PLINTH, CHARLES - - -	3680	13th April 1813	Construction of a vessel, machine, or fountain, used in the manufacture of water impregnated with fixed air, and of artificial mineral and soda waters ; delivery of the same therefrom, also in the delivery of cyder, perry, and other liquids. " Regency Portable Fountain."
PLOWDON, FRANCIS - -	3051	13th June 1807	Preserving meat and other comestible substances, without acid salt, or drying.
PLUCKNETT, THOMAS JAMES -	2483	26th Feb. 1801	Capstans and windlasses for ships and other purposes.
PLUCKNETT, THOMAS JAMES -	2859	15th June 1805	Mowing corn, grass, and other things, by means of a machine moving on wheels, and worked by men or horses.
PLUCKNETT, THOMAS JAMES -	2877	23rd Aug. 1805	Mowing corn, grass, and other things, by means of a machine moving on wheels, and worked by men or horses.
PLUCKNETT, THOMAS JAMES -	2930	17th April 1806	Machine for drilling and dibbling grain and pulse.
PLUMMER, ROBERT - -	12,515	14th March 1849	Machinery, instruments, and processes employed in the preparation and manufacture of flax, and other fibrous materials.
POCOCK, GEORGE - - -	3147	28th June 1808	Geographical slates for the construction of maps.
POCOCK, GEORGE - - -	5420	18th Oct. 1826	Construction of cars and other carriages ; application of a power hitherto unused for that purpose to draw the same ; also applicable to drawing ships and other vessels, for raising weights, and for other purposes.
POCOCK, GEORGE - - -	5894	4th Feb. 1830	Making globes, for astronomical, geographical, and other purposes.
POCOCK, LEWIS - -	14,349	27th Nov. 1852	Rendering sea and other water pure.
POCOCK, WILLIAM - -	2389	23rd April 1800	Machine for raising, lowering, and moving heavy bodies.
POCOCK, WILLIAM - -	2895	19th Nov. 1805	Tables for dining and other uses.
POGGI, ANTHONY CESARI DE -	2428	24th July 1800	Constructing and using ordnance, both for sea and land.
POGGIOLI, PAUL JOSEPH -	14,276	26th Aug. 1852	Medical compound.
POHLE, JOSEPH - - -	875	18th May 1767	Instrument for measuring standing timber.
POHLE, JOSEPH - - -	876	18th May 1767	Machine, instead of a jack, for turning spits used in the roasting of meat ; and, upon an enlarged plan, may be used for drawing water out of mines, and thereby economise the expenses of fuel.
POITTEVIN, JOSEPH HENRY [JEROME.	6865	17th July 1835	Powder to disinfect night-soil and certain other matters, and to facilitate the production of manure.
POLE, WILLIAM - - -	13,119	11th June 1850	Steam-engines.
POLKINGHORNE, JAMES -	10,834	18th Sept. 1845	Treating ores, and separating from them the metals which they contain.

Name of Patentee.	Progressive Number.	Date.	Subject-matter of Patent.
POLLARD, GEORGE - -	4891	19th Jan. 1824	Machinery for levigating or grinding colours used in painting, and which machinery may be worked by any suitable power;—applicable to other purposes.
POLLARD, GEORGE NATHANIEL	3119	14th March 1808	Machinery for grinding, smoothing, and polishing plate and other glass, for looking-glasses, mirrors, and various other articles.
POLLARD, ROBERT - -	12,490	28th Feb. 1849	Machinery for rope-making.
POLLARD, THOMAS HENRY -	6184	19th Oct. 1831	Application of a mechanical apparatus as a smoke conductor in chimneys.
POLLARD, WILLIAM - -	10,121	28th March 1844	Manufacture of ammonia and its compounds.
POLLARD, WILLIAM - -	10,733	23rd June 1845	Production of combustible gases; application of the same as fuel.
POLLOCK, ALLAN - - -	3049	11th June 1807	Stove of a new construction; various improvements applicable to stoves, grates, and fire-places.
POMROY, EBENEZER G -	12,993	7th March 1850	Process of coating iron and other metals with copper and other metallic substances.
POMERY, GEORGE - -	2240	5th June 1798	Apparatus and machinery for the manufacture of tobacco and snuff, and for other purposes.
PONCY, JOHN PETER ISAIE -	8602	13th Aug. 1840	Clocks and chronometers.
PONS, HENRY - - -	13,514	17th Feb. 1851	Constructing roads and ways; pavements of streets; ballast of railways.
PONS, JOSEPH - - -	8120	22nd June 1839	Hardening wood and iron, and rendering wood repulsive of vermin, and proof against dry rot.
PONSFORD, WILLIAM - -	7935	12th Jan. 1839	Manufacture of hats; felt, suitable for hats and other purposes; preparing the materials used in the manufacture of such felt.
PONTIFEX, EDMUND - -	7082	5th May 1836	Making and refining sugar.
PONTIFEX, JOHN - - -	4328	7th Jan. 1819	Raising water for giving motion to machinery, and for other purposes.
PONTIFEX, WILLIAM - -	2269	17th Nov. 1798	Still-head for use in the distilling of all sorts of liquors.
PONTIFEX, WILLIAM - -	4982	1st July 1824	Adjusting or equalising the pressure of fluids or liquids in pipes or tubes; measuring the said fluids or liquids.
PONTIFEX, WILLIAM - -	7889	1st Dec. 1838	Apparatus and materials employed in filtering and clarifying water and other liquids.
PONTIFEX, WILLIAM - -	7964	11th Feb. 1839	Obtaining dyes, colours, tannin, and acids, from vegetable substances.
PONTIFEX, WILLIAM - -	8364	28th Jan. 1840	Treating fluids containing colouring matter, to obtain the colouring matter therefrom.
POOLE, ALFRED - - -	9736	25th May 1843	Drying malt and grain.
POOLE, JAMES - - -	732	21st Dec. 1758	Making coaches, chariots, post-chaises, sedan-chairs and other carriages, and covering them with copper, iron, or brass, instead of leather.
POOLE, JOHN - - -	4050	3rd Aug. 1816	Brass and copper plating, or plating iron or steel with copper or brass, both plain and ornamental; working the same into plates, bars, or other articles.

Name of Patentee.	Progressive Number.	Date.	Subject-matter of Patent.
POOLE, JOHN - - -	4598	18th Oct. 1821	Brass and copper plating, or plating iron or steel with brass or copper, or copper alloyed with other metal or metals, both plain and ornamental, for the purpose of rolling and working into plates, sheets, or bars, and such goods or wares to which the same may be found applicable.
POOLE, JOHN - - -	5381	4th July 1826	Steam-engine boilers or steam-generators; applicable also to the evaporation of other fluids.
POOLE, JOHN DAVID - -	8559	2nd July 1840	Evaporating and distilling water and other fluids.
POOLE, JOHN FRAY - -	11,531	14th Jan. 1847	Machinery for spinning cotton and other fibrous substances.
POOLE, MOSES - - -	4187	15th Dec. 1817	Steam-engines.
POOLE, MOSES - - -	4305	10th Nov. 1818	Application of known materials or cements to the modelling of statues, making slabs, raising or impressing figures, also to covering houses, and in any other manner in which mastic or cement may be applied.
POOLE, MOSES - - -	5183	9th June 1825	Preparation of certain substances for making candles, including a wick peculiarly constructed for the purpose.
POOLE, MOSES - - -	5804	19th June 1829	Machinery for kneading dough.
POOLE, MOSES - - -	5815	8th July 1829	Apparatus for raising or generating steam and currents of air; application thereof to locomotive-engines, and to other purposes.
POOLE, MOSES - - -	5908	27th Feb. 1830	Springs applicable to carriages, and to other purposes.
POOLE, MOSES - - -	5946	29th June 1830	Apparatus used in extracting molasses or syrup from sugar.
POOLE, MOSES - - -	6134	13th July 1831	Steam-engines, and propelling boats and other floating bodies;—applicable to other purposes.
POOLE, MOSES - - -	6981	19th Jan. 1836	Jacquard-looms.
POOLE, MOSES - - -	7182	15th Sept. 1836	Anchors; friction rollers, to facilitate the lowering and raising such and other anchors;—applicable to other purposes.
POOLE, MOSES - - -	7188	21st Sept. 1836	Cabs.
POOLE, MOSES - - -	7240	3rd Dec. 1836	Machinery for generating power applicable to various purposes.
POOLE, MOSES - - -	7286	19th Jan. 1837	Ordnance and other fire-arms.
POOLE, MOSES - - -	7328	21st March 1837	Making fermented liquors.
POOLE, MOSES - - -	7498	5th Dec. 1837	Looms for weaving figured and ornamental fabrics.
POOLE, MOSES - - -	7499	5th Dec. 1837	Printing.
POOLE, MOSES - - -	7574	24th Feb. 1838	Preserving wine and other fermented liquids in bottles.
POOLE, MOSES - - -	7620	21st April 1838	Manufacturing carpets, rugs, and other napped fabrics.
POOLE, MOSES - - -	7857	8th Nov. 1838	Machinery for obtaining rotary-motion.
POOLE, MOSES - - -	7928	11th Jan. 1839	Clogs.
POOLE, MOSES - - -	7960	4th Feb. 1839	Means of conveying and transporting persons and goods from one place to another.

Name of Patentee.	Progressive Number.	Date.		Subject-matter of Patent.
POOLE, MOSES - - -	7970	21st Feb.	1839	Epaulets and ornamental metallic wire-fringes, and other ornamental articles or fabrics of wire.
POOLE, MOSES - - -	7983	28th Feb.	1839	Constructing and applying boxes to wheels.
POOLE, MOSES - - -	7984	28th Feb.	1839	Tanning.
POOLE, MOSES - - -	8067	13th May	1839	Reducing the friction of axletrees, axletree-boxes, and other such moving parts of machinery.
POOLE, MOSES - - -	8088	4th June	1839	Manufacture of soap by the application of materials not hitherto used for that purpose.
POOLE, MOSES - - -	8099	11th June	1839	Printing calicoes and other fabrics.
POOLE, MOSES - - -	8136	29th June	1839	Wheel-carriages; springs.
POOLE, MOSES - - -	8159	20th July	1839	Casting for printing purposes.
POOLE, MOSES - - -	8203	23rd Aug.	1839	Introducing elastic materials into fabrics, to render them elastic or partly elastic.
POOLE, MOSES - - -	8217	11th Sept.	1839	Apparatus applicable to steam-boilers to render them more safe.
POOLE, MOSES - - -	8269	12th Nov.	1839	Making nails, bolts, and spikes.
POOLE, MOSES - - -	8270	12th Nov.	1839	Looms for weaving.
POOLE, MOSES - - -	8304	9th Dec.	1839	Manufacture of caustic soda and carbonate of soda.
POOLE, MOSES - - -	8337	7th Jan.	1840	Obtaining power.
POOLE, MOSES - - -	8368	30th Jan.	1840	Pumps for raising and forcing water and other fluids.
POOLE, MOSES - - -	8435	17th March	1840	Producing and preparing lees for soap-making; manufacture of soap.
POOLE, MOSES - - -	8573	18th July	1840	Fire-arms and apparatus to be used therewith.
POOLE, MOSES - - -	8633	17th Sept.	1840	Preparing materials to facilitate the teaching of writing.
POOLE, MOSES - - -	8857	22nd Feb.	1841	Tanning and dressing or currying skins.
POOLE, MOSES - - -	8898	22nd Mar.	1841	Stretching cloths.
POOLE, MOSES - - -	8951	6th May	1841	Manufacture of fabrics by felting.
POOLE, MOSES - - -	9008	26th June	1841	Producing and applying heat.
POOLE, MOSES - - -	9028	13th July	1841	Steam-baths and other baths.
POOLE, MOSES - - -	9119	14th Oct.	1841	Fire-arms.
POOLE, MOSES - - -	9133	2nd Nov.	1841	Machinery used in the manufacture of bobbin-net or twist-lace.
POOLE, MOSES - - -	9171	9th Dec.	1841	Construction of masts for ships and vessels; applying the shrouds.
POOLE, MOSES - - -	9224	15th Jan.	1842	Construction of locks.
POOLE, MOSES - - -	9264	21st Feb.	1842	Treating, refining, and purifying oils and other similar substances.
POOLE, MOSES - - -	9391	13th June	1842	Obtaining the colouring matter from wool and woollens dyed with indigo.
POOLE, MOSES - - -	9443	11th Aug.	1842	Paving or covering roads and other ways.
POOLE, MOSES - - -	9557	15th Dec.	1842	Dressing mill-stones.
POOLE, MOSES - - -	9694	11th April	1843	Manufacture of ornamented lace or net.
POOLE, MOSES - - -	9717	29th April	1843	Making decoctions of coffee and other matters.
POOLE, MOSES - - -	9741	25th May	1843	Deposition of certain metals; apparatus connected therewith.
POOLE, MOSES - - -	9799	23rd June	1843	Collars for horses and other animals.

Name of Patentee.	Progressive Number.	Date.	Subject-matter of Patent.
POOLE, MOSES - - -	9906	12th Oct. 1843	Enveloping medicine.
POOLE, MOSES - - -	9950	18th Nov. 1843	Manufacture of parts of knives and other cutting instruments.
POOLE, MOSES - - -	9956	21st Nov. 1843	Machine for towing or propelling vessels, and which can also be used as a boat.
POOLE, MOSES - - -	10,107	14th March 1844	Steam-engines, steam-boilers, and furnaces or fire-places.
POOLE, MOSES - - -	10,118	21st March 1844	Dyeing.
POOLE, MOSES - - -	10,226	12th June 1844	Wheels and axles.
POOLE, MOSES - - -	10,252	10th July 1844	Manufacture of paper.
POOLE, MOSES - - -	10,253	10th July 1844	Manufacture of oils by using a material not heretofore employed; obtaining stearine therefrom applicable in the making of candles; manufacture of manure from the residuum of such oils, along with other matters.
POOLE, MOSES - - -	10,298	29th Aug. 1844	Pumps.
POOLE, MOSES - - -	10,363	22nd Oct. 1844	Machinery for emptying privies and cess-pools.
POOLE, MOSES - - -	10,434	12th Dec. 1844	Construction of fids for ships' masts; means for setting up ships' rigging.
POOLE, MOSES - - -	10,451	31st Dec. 1844	Preparing or treating hemp, flax, and other textile plants.
POOLE, MOSES - - -	10,554	13th March 1845	Lithographic-presses.
POOLE, MOSES - - -	10,617	15th April 1845	Construction of taps or cocks.
POOLE, MOSES - - -	10,698	3rd June 1845	Construction of vessels to contain liquids and substances; impregnating liquids with gases; drawing off such liquids, and enclosing such vessels.
POOLE, MOSES - - -	10,727	23rd June 1845	Apparatus for withdrawing air, gases, and other vapours.
POOLE, MOSES - - -	10,851	6th Oct. 1845	Rails for railways.
POOLE, MOSES - - -	10,948	18th Nov. 1845	Raising and transporting earth and other heavy bodies.
POOLE, MOSES - - -	10,971	27th Nov. 1845	Preventing the oxydation of iron in all its stages; also rendering malleable-iron harder and more durable.
POOLE, MOSES - - -	10,978	4th Dec. 1845	Locks.
POOLE, MOSES - - -	11,000	10th Dec. 1845	Apparatus to be used for drawing and marking.
POOLE, MOSES - - -	11,003	12th Dec. 1845	Filling bottles and other vessels; covering, stopping, or securing liquids and other matters in bottles and other vessels.
POOLE, MOSES - - -	11,106	25th Feb. 1846	Cleaning and separating grain and other seeds.
POOLE, MOSES - - -	11,233	2nd June 1846	Making fabrics from fibrous materials.
POOLE, MOSES - - -	11,267	29th June 1846	Regulating the velocity of steam-engines.
POOLE, MOSES - - -	11,338	17th Aug. 1846	Manufacturing terry and cut piled fabrics.
POOLE, MOSES - - -	11,369	10th Sept. 1846	Treating vegetable fibres to render them applicable for the manufacture of paper.
POOLE, MOSES - - -	11,481	14th Dec. 1846	Construction and working of electric-telegraphs; apparatus connected therewith; —partly applicable to other purposes.
POOLE, MOSES - - -	11,503	21st Dec. 1846	Means and apparatus for administering certain matters to the lungs, for medical or surgical purposes.

Name of Patentee.	Progres-sive Number.	Date.		Subject-matter of Patent.
POOLE, MOSES - - -	11,506	21st Dec.	1846	Steam-engines, and machinery for propelling machinery and fluids.
POOLE, MOSES - - -	11,520	7th Jan.	1847	Fish-hooks.
POOLE, MOSES - - -	11,693	6th May	1847	Apparatus for connecting and disconnecting railway-carriages.
POOLE, MOSES - - -	11,712	22nd May	1847	Construction of pneumatic springs and presses.
POOLE, MOSES - - -	11,810	20th July	1847	Manufacture of cast metal, iron, and steel.
POOLE, MOSES - - -	12,161	26th May	1848	Propelling vessels.
POOLE, MOSES - - -	12,233	8th Aug.	1848	Manufacture of casks and other similar vessels, of wood.
POOLE, MOSES - - -	12,321	7th Nov.	1848	Machinery for making nails.
POOLE, MOSES - - -	12,392	28th Dec.	1848	Manufacture of heels for boots and shoes, of swivels, of bag-fastenings, of revolving furniture, and of the connections of pipes for gases and other fluids.
POOLE, MOSES - - -	12,612	15th May	1849	Apparatus for drawing fluids from the human or animal body.
POOLE, MOSES - - -	12,626	2nd June	1849	Brazing, pressing, separating, cleaning, bleaching, and cooling or heating matters; pistons, valves, taps, and spring apparatus.
POOLE, MOSES - - -	13,090	1st June	1850	Machinery for punching metals, construction of springs for carriages, and for other uses.
POOLE, MOSES - - -	13,789	23rd Oct.	1851	Axle-boxes for railway-carriages.
POOLE, MOSES - - -	13,863	19th Dec.	1851	Apparatus for excluding dust and other matters from railway-carriages, and for ventilating such carriages.
POOLE, MOSES - - -	14,052	31st March	1852	Fire-arms.
POOLE, MOSES - - -	14,057	6th April	1852	Covering wires for telegraphic purposes.
POOLE, MOSES - - -	14,201	6th July	1852	Reaping and mowing machines; and pulverizing land.
POOLE, MOSES - - -	14,221	15th July	1852	Boots, shoes, clogs, and similar articles.
POOLE, MOSES - - -	14,299	18th Sept.	1852	Combining caoutchouc with other matters.
POOLE, MOSES - - -	14,306	30th Sept.	1852	Manufacture of combs.
POOLE, MOSES - - -	14,348	27th Nov.	1852	Elastic ribs, sticks, strips and fillets, used in the manufacture of umbrellas, parasols and various other articles, in substitution of whalebone and steel.
POOLE, WILLIAM - - -	5793	26th May	1829	Machinery for propelling vessels, and giving motion to mills and other machinery.
POOLEY, CHARLES - - -	10,575	27th March	1845	Machines used in preparing to be spun, and in spinning cotton-wool and other fibrous substances.
POOLEY, HENRY - - -	11,754	16th June	1847	Weighing-machine.
POPE, CHRISTOPHER - -	4773	8th April	1823	Composition of certain metals for sheathing the bottoms of ships and vessels, roofing houses, or any other purpose for which the same is applicable.
POPE, FRANCIS - - -	7623	24th April	1838	Machinery for manufacturing pins, bolts, nails, and rivets;—applicable to various purposes.
POPE, FRANCIS - - -	8712	24th Nov.	1840	Detaching locomotive and other carriages.
POPE, SAMUEL - - -	530	20th May	1731	Marbling paper by taking off the colours from a body of water prepared after a particular manner.

Name of Patentee.	Progressive Number.	Date.	Subject-matter of Patent.
POPE, THOMAS - - -	11,144	25th March 1846	Apparatus for moving railway-carriages on to railways; machinery for lifting and moving heavy bodies.
POPE, WILLIAM - - -	3751	16th Nov. 1813	Instruments for ascertaining a ship's way at sea, and determining the longitude.
POPE, WILLIAM - - -	3927	14th June 1815	Wheeled-carriages; method of making such carriages move with or without the help of animals;—which methods may be applied to other purposes.
POPE, WILLIAM - - -	5301	3rd Dec. 1825	Wheeled-carriages.
POPE, WILLIAM - - -	5302	3rd Dec. 1825	Making, mixing, compounding, improving or altering the article of soap.
POPE, WILLIAM - - -	9540	6th Dec. 1842	Stoves.
PORRITT, JAMES - - -	12,096	14th March 1848	Carding-engines, for carding wool and other fibrous substances.
PORRITT, SAMUEL - -	10,465	11th Jan. 1845	Machinery for preparing and carding wool.
PORTER, GEORGE RICHARDSON	5609	19th Jan. 1828	Communicating heat for various purposes.
PORTER, JOHN - - -	940	16th Nov. 1769	Machine, on which is fixed a set of sliders, to be attached to a stocking-frame for shading and brocading, working, and making flowers in gold, silver, silk, worsted, cotton, and thread, on silk, thread, cotton, and worsted-pieces, for waistcoats, breeches, stockings, gloves, mits, and all goods made on stocking-frames
PORTER, JOHN - - -	2768	30th May 1804	Lamp upon a new construction.
PORTER, JOHN HENDERSON -	12,091	8th March 1848	Iron girders, beams, trusses, and supports, rendering the floors of buildings fireproof by the use of iron.
PORTER, JOHN HENDERSON -	12,356	2nd Dec. 1848	Applying corrugated iron in the formation of fireproof floors, roofs, and other like structures.
PORTER, ROBERT - - -	5801	13th June 1829	Manufacture of iron heels and tips for boots and shoes.
PORTER, SINCKLER - - -	940	16th Nov. 1769	Machine, on which is fixed a set of sliders to be attached to a stocking-frame, for shading and brocading, working, and making flowers in gold, silver, silk, worsted, cotton, and thread, on silk, thread, cotton, and worsted-pieces, for waistcoats, breeches, stockings, gloves, mits, and all goods made on stocking-frames.
PORTER, THOMAS - - -	278	7th Oct. 1691	Preserving flesh, fowl, fish, and many other things, by liquors or otherwise.
PORTER, WILLIAM HENRY -	7774	15th Aug. 1838	Anchors.
PORTHOUSE, THOMAS - -	1613	19th June 1787	Machine for spinning yarn from hemp, tow, flax, or wool.
PORTHOUSE, THOMAS - -	2787	6th Oct. 1804	Machine for heckling flax and hemp, and at the same time carding the tow.
PORTLOCK, WILLIAM - -	330	29th Jan. 1694	Extracting pitch, tar, and oil, out of a certain kind of stone.
POSTANS, THOMAS - - -	4687	26th June 1822	Cooking-apparatus.
POSTEL, JOHN - - -	3923	8th June 1815	Extracting gold and silver from the cinders of gold-refines and other substances, by machinery.
POSTLETHWAYT, MALACHI -	637	24th Sept. 1748	Casting iron from the iron-stone or ore, and approaching nearer to the toughness and malleability of forged-iron.

Name of Patentee.	Progressive Number.	Date.	Subject-matter of Patent.
POTTER, AMEY - - -	204	4th Oct. 1678	Making Flanders dolberline and all other laces of woollen, to be used for dresses at the burial of the dead.
POTTER, HAROLD - - -	8302	9th Dec. 1839	Printing calicoes, muslins, and other fabrics.
POTTER, HAROLD - - -	11,157	1st April 1846	Printing or staining paper.
POTTER, HAROLD - - -	14,204	6th July 1852	Looms for weaving; manufacture of terry fabrics.
POTTER, JAMES - - -	6098	21st March 1831	Machinery applicable to the spinning or twisting of cotton, flax, silk, wool, and other fibrous materials.
POTTER, JAMES - - -	7263	21st Dec. 1836	Spinning-machinery.
POTTER, JAMES - - -	9366	25th May 1842	Machinery for spinning cotton, flax, and other fibrous substances.
POTTER, JAMES - - -	12,771	13th Sept. 1849	Machinery for spinning and doubling.
POTTER, JAMES - - -	13,644	27th May 1851	Spinning-machines.
POTTER, JOHN - - -	4951	13th May 1824	Looms to be impelled by mechanical power, for weaving figured fabrics of silk, cotton, flax, wool or other materials, or mixtures of the same;—partly applicable to hand-looms.
POTTER, JOHN - - -	6098	21st March 1831	Machinery applicable to the spinning or twisting of cotton, flax, silk, wool, and other fibrous materials.
POTTER, JOHN - - -	7466	9th Nov. 1837	Preparing certain descriptions of warps for the loom.
POTTER, JOHN - - -	8039	20th April 1839	Cards for carding various fibrous substances;—parts of the improvements may be used as a substitute for leather.
POTTER, JOHN GERALD -	14,248	31st July 1852	Manufacture of carpets, rugs, and other similar fabrics.
POTTER, RICHARD - -	1499	28th Oct. 1785	German flute; part of the improvements applicable to other musical wind instruments that are played upon with keys.
POTTER, WILLIAM HENRY -	3136	28th May 1808	German flutes and other wind musical instruments.
POTTER, WILLIAM SIMPSON -	6824	28th April 1835	Rendering fabrics waterproof.
POTTINGER, RICHARD - -	2587	27th Feb. 1802	Apparatus for disengaging horses from carriages in cases of danger.
POTTS, JAMES - - -	2448	15th Nov. 1800	Artificial leg and arm.
POTTS, JOHN - - -	6162	17th Sept. 1831	Obtaining impressions from engravings, in various colours, and applying the same to earthenware, porcelain, china, glass, and other substances.
POTTS, LAURENCE HOLKER -	9642	21st Feb. 1843	Conveying goods, passengers, or intelligence.
POTTS, LAURENCE HOLKER -	9975	5th Dec. 1843	Construction of piers, embankments, breakwaters, and other similar structures.
POTTS, THOMAS - - -	2131	20th July 1796	Machine attached to the stern of any vessel, boat, or barge, for the purpose of moving the same on canals and still waters.
POTTS, THOMAS - - -	3199	4th Feb. 1809	Process of freeing tarred ropes from the tar, and rendering it fit for the use of the manufacturer.
POTTS, THOMAS - - -	3898	14th March 1815	Combining and applying known principles for producing pure and fresh warm air.
POTTS, THOMAS - - -	12,114	10th April 1848	Manufacture of tubular flues of locomotive and other steam-boilers.

Name of Patentee.	Progressive Number.	Date.		Subject-matter of Patent.
POTTS, THOMAS - - -	12,723	1st Aug.	1849	Apparatus used with curtains, blinds, maps, and plans.
POTTS, WILLIAM - - -	8471	15th April	1840	Apparatus for suspending pictures and curtains.
POTTS, WILLIAM WAINWRIGHT	6162	17th Sept.	1831	Obtaining impressions from engravings, in various colours, and applying the same to earthenware, porcelain, china, glass, and other substances.
POTTS, WILLIAM WAINWRIGHT	6938	3rd Dec.	1835	Producing patterns in one or more colours, to be transferred to earthenware, porcelain, china, glass, and other similar substances.
POTTS, WILLIAM WAINWRIGHT	7139	2nd July	1836	Producing and transferring patterns in one or more colours or metallic preparations, to surfaces of metal, wood, cloth, paper, or other suitable substance.
POTTS, WILLIAM WAINWRIGHT	7776	21st Aug.	1838	Machines for printing patterns in one or more colours or metallic preparations, to be transferred to earthenware, porcelain, china, glass, metal, wood, cloth, paper, papier-machè, bone, slate, marble, and other suitable substances.
POUCHANT, DON PEDRO - -	9533	3rd Dec.	1842	Construction of machinery for manufacturing sugar.
POUCHÉE, LOUIS JOHN - -	4826	5th Aug.	1823	Machinery for casting metal types.
POULAIN, JOHN - - -	1496	30th Sept.	1785	Tinning or lining vessels of copper, brass, iron or other metal, especially those for culinary purposes.
POULTON, GEORGE - - -	5517	4th July	1827	Apparatus for writing. "Self-supplying pen."
POUSSETT, FRANCIS - -	332	10th April	1694	Preparing crapes, and other woollen stuffs and silks, before they are dyed, in such manner that any flowers or other figures thus prepared on them will appear in different colours on the same piece, after they have been dyed.
POUSSETT, FRANCIS - -	357	2nd Sept.	1698	Making black silk-crape and white silk-crape.
POWELL, ARTHUR - - -	10,278	30th July	1844	Manufacture of quarries and other panes of glass, for windows.
POWELL, CHARLES - - -	5182	7th June	1825	Blowing-machine.
POWELL, CHARLES - - -	10,605	9th April	1845	Construction of horse-shoes.
POWELL, HENRY BUCKWORTH	10,957	18th Nov.	1845	Carriages to be used on rail and other roads.
POWELL, JOHN - - -	5657	17th May	1828	Apparatus for making moulds or vessels for refining sugar; application of materials hitherto unused for making the said moulds.
POWELL, LANCELOT - -	8935	24th April	1841	Manufacture of iron.
POWELL, NATHANIEL - -	10,278	30th July	1844	Manufacture of quarries and other panes of glass, for windows.
POWELL, SAMUEL - - -	12,550	28th March	1849	Making certain articles of wearing-apparel.
POWELL, THOMAS - - -	5657	17th May	1828	Apparatus for making moulds or vessels for refining sugar; application of materials hitherto unused for making the said moulds.
POWELL, WILLIAM - - -	5657	17th May	1828	Apparatus for making moulds or vessels for refining sugar; application of materials hitherto unused for making the said moulds.

Name of Patentee.	Progressive Number.	Date.		Subject-matter of Patent.
POWER, JAMES - - -	2473	5th Feb.	1801	Portable oven.
POWER, JAMES - - -	2606	7th April	1802	Machine for raising weights, and for other purposes.
POWER, JAMES - - -	10,312	12th Sept.	1844	Manufacture of candles and soap; treating a certain vegetable matter for such manufactures, and for other uses.
POWERS, WILLIAM - - -	900	16th April	1768	Splitting and dividing sheep's pelts and other skins, and rendering the grain and upper part more useful for binding books and for other purposes of trade, while the under part may be wrought into leather.
POWNALL, CHARLES JAMES -	12,848	17th Nov.	1849	Registering the number of passengers entering in or upon conveyances and passage-ways; apparatus for effecting the same.
POWNALL, CHARLES JAMES -	14,224	15th July	1852	Treatment and preparation of flax and other fibrous vegetable substances.
POWNALL, WILLIAM - -	5623	6th March	1828	Making healds for weaving purposes.
POWNALL, ISRAEL - -	391	3rd April	1712	Machine for taking up ballast, sullage, sand, &c.; useful in cleansing rivers, harbours, &c.
POYNTZ, Captain JOHN - -	297	23rd May	1692	Taking up ships, goods, or bullion, that have been sunk at sea or elsewhere.
POYNTZ, Captain JOHN - -	320	17th April	1693	Inventions under water for scouring rivers, harbours, channels, creeks, roads, rivulets, milldams, &c., which are dammed, choked, and almost filled up with sand, mud, gravel, &c.
POYNTZ, Captain JOHN - -	327	24th Oct.	1693	Instruments of wood, iron, steel, and other materials, for raising water for the purpose of performing mill-work, and other work.
PRATT, DANIEL RICE - -	12,138	27th April	1848	Machinery for connecting railway carriages.
PRATT, FELIX EDWARD - -	12,008	31st Dec.	1847	Manufacturing articles composed of earthenware and china.
PRATT, GEORGE WALTER -	12,226	29th July	1848	Manufacture of printing ink.
PRATT, HENRY - - -	2969	2nd Oct.	1806	Toast-stand.
PRATT, HENRY - - -	6035	11th Nov.	1830	Manufacturing quarries applicable to kilns for drying wheat, malt, and other grain, and for various other purposes.
PRATT, HENRY - - -	13,169	9th July	1850	Construction of portmanteaus and travelling-trunks.
PRATT, MAJOR - - -	2098	11th March	1796	Manufacturing a certain composition stone equally applicable in grinding corn and other articles as the millstones now generally used.
PRATT, MAJOR - - -	3309	26th Feb.	1810	Manufacturing machines for performing agricultural operations by mechanical powers.
PRATT, SAMUEL - - -	3914	11th May	1815	Wardrobe-trunk for travellers.
PRATT, SAMUEL - - -	4711	27th Sept.	1822	Straps or bands for securing luggage on coaches, or for securing property generally when placed in exposed situations.
PRATT, SAMUEL - - -	5162	14th May	1825	Combining wood and metal to form rails or rods adapted to the manufacture of bedsteads, cornices, and other works. "Union or compound rods."
PRATT, SAMUEL - - -	5418	18th Oct.	1826	Beds, bedsteads, couches, seats, and other articles of furniture.
PRATT, SAMUEL - - -	5668	25th June	1828	Elastic beds, cushions, seats, pads, and other articles of that kind.

Name of Patentee.	Progressive Number.	Date.		Subject-matter of Patent.
PRATT, SAMUEL - - -	7250	9th Dec.	1836	Construction of knapsacks, portmanteaus, bags, boxes, or cases, for travellers.
PRATT, THOMAS - - -	7981	23rd Feb.	1839	Capstan and winch for purchasing or raising ships' anchors, for drawing coals and other articles out of coal and other mines, and also for drawing and working on railroads, by drawing pullies with flat and round ropes.
PRÉDAVAL, BARTHELEMY [RICHARD COMTE DE	6510	19th Nov.	1833	Engine for producing motive-power.
PREDDY, WILLIAM - - -	12,656	12th June	1849	Watch-keys and other instruments for winding up watches and other time-keepers.
PREECE, JAMES - - -	13,025	26th March	1850	Mills and machinery applicable to the thrashing and grinding of corn, the manufacture of cyder, and other similar purposes.
PRELIER, PAUL GILBERT -	11,773	29th June	1847	Manufacture of dry sulphuric-acid, and smoking or Nordhausen sulphuric-acid.
PRELLER, CHARLES AUGUSTUS	9408	7th July	1842	Machinery for preparing, combing, and drawing wool and goats' hair.
PRELLER, CHARLES AUGUSTUS	14,009	8th March	1852	Preparation and preservation of skins, and animal and vegetable substances.
PRELLER, CHARLES AUGUSTUS	14,292	16th Sept.	1852	Machinery for combing, drawing, or preparing wool, cotton, silk, hair, and other fibrous materials.
PREST, THOMAS - - -	4501	20th Oct.	1820	Movement applied to watches to enable them to be wound up by the pendant knob, without any detached key or winder.
PRESTI, LOUIS BARON LO -	12,885	10th Dec.	1849	Hydraulic-presses ; — applicable to pumps and other like machines.
PRESTON, FRANCIS - - -	11,542	23rd Jan.	1847	Machinery to be used in preparing cotton and other fibrous substances for spinning.
PRESTON, GRANT - - -	3815	7th June	1814	Concavious cabin-stoves.
PRESTON, GRANT - - -	4222	3rd Feb.	1818	Deck glass rim, and safety gate.
PRESTON, GRANT - - -	6269	30th May	1832	Ships' compasses.
PRESTON, THOMAS - -	1045	24th June	1773	Printing colours complete and fixed in the first impression, on silks, satins, woollens, linens, cottons, velvets, and mixed goods, without the process of boiling and bleaching.
PRESTON, THOMAS - -	3101	26th Jan.	1808	Setting boilers for steam-engines, and pans for melting lead, tin, pewter, and other metals of easy fusion ; discharging the same when full ; setting coppers and boilers of every description.
PRESTON, WILLIAM - -	7074	28th April	1836	Printing calicoes and other fabrics.
PRESTWIDGE, GEORGE - -	1368	7th May	1783	Machine for spinning hards or refuse flax ; also for spinning flax, hemp, and wool.
PRETERRE, APOLEON PIERRE -	12.766	13th Sept.	1849	Coffee-pots and tea-pots ; apparatus for cooking ; apparatus for roasting and grinding coffee.
PRETYMAN, ROBERT - -	3722	19th July	1813	Pan touch-hole and pan cover of a gun-lock.
PREWETT, AMBROSE - -	41	22nd Dec.	1627	Engine for driving mills for grinding corn or grain, tools, metal, bark, and other things.
PREWETT, AMBROSE - -	72	17th July	1634	Engine for ploughing land without oxen or horses.

Name of Patentee.	Progres-sive Number.	Date.	Subject-matter of Patent.
PREWETT, JOHN - - -	72	17th July 1634	Engine for ploughing land without oxen or horses.
PRICE, ARTHUR WELLINGTON	11,043	17th Jan. 1846	Construction of anchors.
PRICE, ASTLEY PASTON - -	12,617	24th May 1849	Manufacturing and refining sugar or sac-charine matters.
PRICE, ASTLEY PASTON -	13,254	12th Sept. 1850	Filters.
PRICE, BENJAMIN - - -	754	27th Nov. 1760	Making salt from salt water, salt spring, and rock-salt.
PRICE, CHARLES - - -	3619	4th Dec. 1812	Umbrellas and parasols.
PRICE, CHARLES FOX - -	5833	20th Aug. 1829	Apparatus for communicating heat by means of the circulation of fluids.
PRICE, GEORGE - - -	7690	14th June 1838	Clarifying water and other liquids.
PRICE, HENRY ABBERLEY -	4763	18th March 1823	Apparatus for giving increased effect to paddles used in steam-vessels.
PRICE, HENRY CRUGER -	5833	20th Aug. 1829	Apparatus for communicating heat by means of the circulation of fluids.
PRICE, JOHN - - - -	2021	11th Nov. 1794	Saving water at the locks of navigable canals.
PRICE, JOHN - - - -	4995	5th Aug. 1824	Construction of spinning-machines.
PRICE, JOSEPH - - -	3807	5th May 1814	Methods of making glass.
PRICE, JOSEPH - - -	6766	16th Feb. 1835	Railways, and means of transporting car-riages from one level to another.
PRICE, JOSEPH - - -	7743	26th July 1838	Constructing and adapting boilers for ma-rine, stationary, and locomotive engines; adapting and applying boilers to steam-vessels.
PRICE, RICHARD - - -	3782	12th Feb. 1814	Cooking-apparatus.
PRICE, ROBERT - - -	266	7th Feb. 1691	Making saltpetre.
PRICE, STEPHEN - - -	2981	30th Oct. 1806	Raising a nap or pile on woollen, cotton, and other cloths, by means of a substitute for teasels and cards.
PRICE, STEPHEN - - -	3015	20th Feb. 1807	Raising a nap or pile on woollen, cotton, and other cloths, by means of a substitute for teasels and cards.
PRICE, STEPHEN - - -	3951	12th Aug. 1815	Machine for shearing or cropping woollen or other cloths.
PRICE, STEPHEN - - -	4186	5th Dec. 1817	Substitute for teasels to be used in dressing woollen or other cloth or fabric.
PRICE, THOMAS - - -	3162	24th Aug. 1808	Application of steam for useful purposes; apparatus to effect the same.
PRICE, VINCENT - - -	12,155	11th May 1848	Mechanical arrangement for obtaining and applying motive-power.
PRICHARD, WILLIAM - -	5211	16th July 1825	Looms, and implements connected there-with.
PRICHARD, WILLIAM - -	9412	7th July 1842	Consuming and preventing smoke and economizing fuel, in steam-engines and other furnaces.
PRIDE, WILLIAM - - -	4666	16th April 1822	Self-regulating apparatus for spooling and warping woollen or other warps or chains.
PRIDEAUX, THOMAS SYMES -	11,298	15th July 1846	Machinery for excavating.
PRIDEAUX, THOMAS SYMES -	12,750	30th Aug. 1849	Puddling and other furnaces; steam-boilers.
PRIDEAUX, THOMAS SYMES -	13,432	28th Dec. 1850	Generating and condensing steam; fire-places and furnaces.
PRIESTLY, THOMAS - -	12,887	12th Dec. 1849	Machinery to be used for preparing, spin-ning, and doubling cotton, woollen, flax, silk, and similar fibrous materials.

Name of Patentee.	Progres-sive Number.	Date.	Subject-matter of Patent.
PRIME, ANDREW - - -	352	24th Sept. 1697	Preserving ships or vessels for navigation from foundering at sea or in harbour, by accident or from any other cause.
PRIMEROSE, ANDREW - -	1874	3rd May 1792	Machine for manufacturing feathers into hats, head-dresses, muffs, tippets, and shoes.
PRINCE, JOHN - - -	6782	4th March 1835	Mould and apparatus to be used in making paper.
PRINCE, JOHN DYNELEY -	8183	1st Aug. 1839	Printing, dyeing, and colouring cotton, woollen, silk, or other cloths and yarns.
PRINCE, WILLIAM - - -	890	2nd Jan. 1768	Making starch, with the use of machines, from other ingredients than wheat-flour, pollard, bran, or potatoes.
PRIOR, EDMUND - - -	2354	4th Nov. 1799	Painting and colouring all kinds of leather.
PRIOR, GEORGE - - -	4214	29th Jan. 1818	Detaching the escape-wheel of chronometers from the influence of the friction and in-accuracies of the mainspring, pivots, and teeth of all the other wheels in the machine, during the time of its giving impulses to the balance, whereby its vibra-tions will be more accurately and uniformly supported.
PRIOR, WILLIAM - - -	5780	11th April 1829	Construction and combination of machinery for securing, supporting and striking, top-masts and top-gallant masts of ships and other vessels.
PRIOR, WILLIAM - - -	8092	6th June 1839	Carriages, and axletrees of wheel-carriages.
PRITCHARD, WILLIAM - -	2497	2nd May 1801	Article for hats, soldiers' caps, helmets, &c.
PRITCHARD, WILLIAM - -	4439	18th March 1820	Manufacturing waterproof hats of silk, wool, beaver or other fur, the brims of which are perfectly waterproof and will pre-serve their shape, being stiffened without glue or any material which would prevent the effect of waterproof mixture.
PRITCHARD, WILLIAM - -	4523	22nd Dec. 1820	Apparatus calculated to save fuel, and for the more economical consumption of smoke, in the shutting of fire-doors and air-flues in steam-engine boilers, drying-pans and brewing-pans, and other fire-doors and air-flues.
PRITCHARD, WILLIAM - -	10,308	12th Sept. 1844	Power-looms.
PRITCHET, SAMUEL - -	10,340	3rd Oct. 1844	Cutting and making-up gloves.
PRITTY, THOMAS - - -	2622	20th May 1802	Affixing and hanging certain spring-joints and other apparatus, to doors.
PROCTOR, WILLIAM - -	3149	6th July 1808	Melting and using malleable wrought-iron or steel.
PROCTOR, WILLIAM - -	3215	9th March 1809	Supplying tubes or lamps with oil so as to remove the shade of the vessel containing the oil. " Proctor's spiral argand and candle-lamp."
PROSSER, JOHN - - -	2064	8th Sept. 1795	Smoke-jacks.
PROSSER, JOHN - - -	2454	9th Dec. 1800	Waterproof pan and hammer for gun and pistol-locks; also a breech for gun and pistol barrels.
PROSSER, JOHN - - -	2982	30th Oct. 1806	Smoke or air jacks, applicable to those now in use.
PROSSER, LEMUEL - - -	1160	14th July 1777	Water-closets.
PROSSER, RICHARD - • -	6132	13th July 1831	Manufacturing nails or tacks for ornament-ing boxes and articles of furniture.

Name of Patentee.	Progressive Number.	Date.	Subject-matter of Patent.
PROSSER, RICHARD - -	6775	25th Feb. 1835	Making nails.
PROSSER, RICHARD - -	7969	19th Feb. 1839	Apparatus for generating steam, consuming smoke, and heating apartments.
PROSSER, RICHARD - -	8064	8th May 1839	Machinery for making nails and screws.
PROSSER, RICHARD - -	8454	27th March 1840	Machinery or apparatus for manufacturing pipes.
PROSSER, RICHARD - -	8547	17th June 1840	Apparatus for heating apartments; apparatus for cooking.
PROSSER, RICHARD - -	8548	17th June 1840	Manufacturing buttons from certain materials;—which improvements in manufacturing are applicable, in whole or in part, to the production of knobs, rings, and other articles from the same materials.
PROSSER, RICHARD - -	9707	20th April 1843	Machinery to be used in manufacturing pipes and bars; application of such pipes or bars to various purposes.
PROSSER, RICHARD -	10,649	1st May 1845	Manufacture of metal tubes; machinery and apparatus for producing the same.
PROSSER, RICHARD -	13,035	11th April 1850	Machinery and apparatus for manufacturing metal tubes;—partly applicable for other purposes where pressure is required; also mode of applying metal tubes in steam-boilers or other vessels requiring metal tubes to be applied within them.
PROSSER, RICHARD -	13,238	22nd Aug. 1850	Supplying steam-boilers with water, and clearing out the tubes of steam-boilers.
PROSSER, THOMAS - -	2027	9th Dec. 1794	Machine for letter-press printing.
PROSSER, THOMAS - -	5915	6th March 1830	Construction of window-sashes; hanging the same.
PROSSER, WILLIAM -	9727	16th May 1843	Construction of roads; carriages to run thereon.
PROSSER, WILLIAM, junior -	10,387	9th Nov. 1844	Construction of roads; carriages to run thereon.
PROSSER, WILLIAM -	10,443	18th Dec. 1844	Working atmospheric-railways.
PROSSER, WILLIAM -	10,662	10th May 1845	Railways; propelling railway-carriages.
PROTHEROE, EVAN -	13,067	30th April 1850	Manufacture of oxyde of zinc; making paints from oxyde of zinc.
PROUD, THOMAS - -	1305	22nd Aug. 1781	Drill to be fixed to the side of a common plough-beam, to sow corn and all kinds of seeds.
PROUDFOOT, FRANCIS -	1346	2nd Dec. 1782	Buckles.
PROWETT, WILLIAM -	9183	16th Dec. 1841	Giving signals on railways.
PRUDAY, THOMAS DANSOM -	11,846	26th Aug. 1847	Apparatus for reducing vegetable and other substances to small particles.
PRUNE, ANDREW - -	352	24th Sept. 1697	Preserving ships or vessels for navigation from foundering at sea or in harbour, by accident or from any other cause.
PRUSEN, HILDEBRAND - -	75	19th Nov. 1634	Making or erecting stoves of iron, brick-work and earth, for heating water or other liquor, and for making salt, also for heating hothouses and rooms in dwelling-houses, as well as for drying all sorts of grain and various other articles, with sea-coal, charcoal, peat, turf, or other fuel.
PRYOR, JOSEPH - - -	8817	28th Jan. 1841	Thrashing-machine.
PUCKLE, JAMES - - -	418	15th May 1718	Portable gun, or machine called a defence.

Name of Patentee.	Progres-sive Number.	Date.	Subject-matter of Patent.
PUCKLE, THOMAS - - -	311	17th Jan. 1693	Engine consisting of screw-wheels and long tumblers, for raising or lowering heavy weights; also for weighing ships' guns and anchors, and raising heavy stones to the top of buildings; and for craning goods, bearing timber, and pounding and grinding minerals or other hard substances.
PUCKLE, THOMAS - - -	317	7th March 1693	Making a composition with wood and capable of being run into moulds, in a liquid state, for beautifying rooms, embellishing cabinets, &c.
PUCKRIDGE, FREDERICK -	13,597	17th April 1851	Preparation or manufacture of materials or fabrics, suitable for ornamenting furniture and other articles.
PUGH, JOHN - - - -	3918	26th May 1815	Making salt-pans, thereby saving fuel and labour.
PUGH, SAMUEL - - -	1781	6th Nov. 1790	Preparing oils for manufacturing hard soap with or without tallow or other grease or resin; which preparation may be adapted to several other purposes.
PUIS, PIERRE AUGUSTIN -	12,002	22nd Dec. 1847	Apparatus for raising and lowering heavy bodies in mines.
PULVERMACHER, ISAAC LEWIS	12,899	15th Dec. 1849	Galvanic-batteries; electric-telegraphs; electro-magnetic and magneto-electric machines.
PULVERMACHER, ISAAC LEWIS [*Pulvermacher, Isac Lewis.*]	13,933	29th Jan. 1852	Galvano-electric, magneto-electric, and electro-magnetic apparatus; application thereof to lighting, telegraphic, and motive purposes.
PUMPHREY, JOSIAH - -	8670	2nd Nov. 1840	Machinery to be employed in the manufacture of wire hooks and eyes.
PUMPHREY, JULIUS - -	5765	3rd Feb. 1829	Steam-engines; machinery connected therewith to propel steam-boats and vessels;— partly applicable to other purposes.
PUNSHON, MATTHEW - -	8121	22nd June 1839	Steam-engines; certain parts of which are applicable to steam-engines of ordinary construction.
PURBRICK, ROBERT BAN -	10,557	13th March 1845	Apparatus used in the manufacture of sugar. " Sugar pans or coppers."
PURDEN, FRANCIS - - -	3542	27th Feb. 1812	Horse-boots, for the preservation of sound hoofs, and the restoration of contracted hoofs.
PURKIS, ROBERT ALLÉE -	12,860	24th Nov. 1849	Propelling ships and other vessels; apparatus for ploughing land.
PURNELL, CHARLES - -	12,215	18th July 1848	Apparatus to be applied to vessels loaded with timber and materials having a specific-gravity lighter than water, thereby to rid them of the superincumbent water, enabling them to carry sail, and preventing the necessity of abandonment at sea.
PURNELL, JOHN - - -	854	31st July 1766	Machine for making ships' bolts, round rods of iron and steel, and wires of various sizes.
PURNELL, WILLIAM - -	1608	5th June 1787	Preparing, shingling, and welding iron with pit-coal, from the ore, also cast iron, by the application of a machine constructed to render it of superior quality and in greater quantities, also with a saving of fuel and less waste of metal.
PURT, GEORGE - - -	9545	8th Dec. 1842	Producing aërated liquors.

Name of Patentee.	Progressive Number.	Date.	Subject-matter of Patent.
PUTLAND, HENRY - - -	9314	6th April 1842	Construction and make of driving-reins, harness, bridles, and reins, also bridles and reins for riding.
PYCROFT, JAMES - - -	6135	13th July 1831	Grates and other fire-places.
PYEFINCH, HENRY - -	825	28th March 1765	Instrument for showing the effect of the weight of the atmosphere, with the variation caused by heat and cold, also the quantity of that variation.
PYEFINCH, HENRY - -	976	28th Dec. 1770	Constructing and making refracting-telescopes with object glasses.
PYKE, JAMES - - - -	13,621	3rd May 1851	Manufacture of leather; making boots and shoes.
PYKE, LYON - - - -	2774	20th June 1804	Pencils. "Pyke's patent improved pencils."
PYKE, THOMAS - - -	5165	14th May 1825	Apparatus to prevent the overturning or falling of carriages.

Q.

Name of Patentee.	Progressive Number.	Date.	Subject-matter of Patent.
QUAINTIN, LOUIS - - -	6529	20th Dec. 1833	Construction of carriages.
QUARE, DANIEL - - -	342	2nd Aug. 1695	Making a portable weather-glass or barometer.
QUARRILL, THOMAS - -	5434	20th Dec. 1826	Manufacture of lamps.
QUETIN, LOUIS - - -	5819	25th July 1829	Vehicle, or combination of vehicles, for conveyance of passengers and goods, on a principle of security against overturning or upsetting.
QUICK, JOSEPH - - -	10,521	10th Feb. 1845	Steam-engines.
QUICK, JOSEPH - -	10766	12th July 1845	Combined expansive steam and atmospheric engine.
QUICK, JOSEPH - - -	10,794	31st July 1845	Construction and working of atmospheric-railways.
QUICK, JOSEPH - - -	10,856	9th Oct. 1845	Steam-engines.
QUICK, JOSEPH - - -	11,134	11th March 1846	Construction of railways, and railway carriages and conveyances.
QUIGLAY, WILLIAM - -	8169	25th July 1839	Machinery for manufacturing silk, cotton, woollen, and linen fabrics.
QUINCEY, JOHN HARCOURT -	10,120	25th March 1844	Manufacture of lamps, and shades for lamps and other lights.
QUINCEY, JOHN HARCOURT -	10,335	27th Sept. 1844	Manufacture of blinds and shutters.

Name of Patentee.	Progressive Number.	Date.	Subject-matter of Patent.

R.

Name of Patentee.	Progressive Number.	Date.	Subject-matter of Patent.
RABAUT, LOUIS BERNARD -	4688	26th June 1822	Apparatus for the preparation of coffee or tea.
RABONE, JOSEPH - - -	1582	15th Jan. 1787	Manufacturing coat and waistcoat buttons, plain and figured, from bone and ivory.
RABY, GEORGE - - -	1176	7th Jan. 1778	Instrument, or a silver coin-balance, for detecting base half-crowns, shillings, and sixpences.
RADCLIFF, JOHN - - -	7651	24th May 1838	Removing the fly-droppings, waste, and other matters which fall below the cylinders and beaters in the processes of carding, willowing, devilling, batting, blowing, scutching, opening, or mixing of cotton-wool, silk, flax, wool, or any other fibrous material or substance.
RADCLIFFE, JOHN - - -	7914	19th Dec. 1838	Covering for rollers used in preparing, drawing, slubbing, roving, spinning, twisting, and doubling wool, cotton, flax, silk, mohair, or any other fibrous material or substance.
RADDATZ, JOHN CHARLES [CHRISTOPHER.	5163	14th May 1825	Steam-engines.
RADFORD, JOSEPH - - -	11,948	6th Nov. 1847	Envelopes, wrappers, and covers; machinery and apparatus for the manufacture thereof.
RADLEY, JAMES - - -	6943	4th Dec. 1835	Construction of gauges for indicating or measuring the expansive power of steam, or other elastic vapours or gases used expansively as a medium of power.
RADLEY, WILLIAM - - -	607	19th July 1744	Making salt by means of furnaces.
RADLEY, WILLIAM - - -	941	16th Nov. 1769	Purging and diuretic balls for the cure of several diseases incident to horses.
RADLEY, WILLIAM - - -	1121	19th March 1776	Purging carminative-tincture for the colic, gripes, gout, rheumatism, jaundice, and dropsy.
RADLEY, WILLIAM - - -	10,652	3rd May 1845	Production of gases; their application for illumination; apparatus and machinery used in manufacturing, measuring, and distributing the same.
RADLEY, WILLIAM - - -	13,081	25th May 1850	Treating fatty, oleaginous, resinous, bituminous, and cerous bodies; manufacture and application of such bodies, their compounds and subsidiary products, with the apparatus to be employed therein; also their application to new and other purposes.
RAE, ALEXANDER MAC - -	8329	24th Dec. 1839	Machinery for ploughing, harrowing, and for other agricultural purposes, to work by steam or other power.
RAFFIELD, JOHN - - -	3518	20th Jan. 1812	Apparatus to be attached to fire-stoves for rooms, for the purpose of removing cinders and ashes, and preventing dust arising therefrom.
RAFFIELD, JOHN - - -	4091	10th Jan. 1817	Apparatus to be attached to fire-stoves for rooms, for the purpose of removing cinders and ashes, and for the better prevention of dust; to be used jointly or separately.

Name of Patentee.	Progressive Number.	Date.		Subject-matter of Patent.
RAGON, ADOLPHUS HENRI [ERNESTE.	7849	3rd Nov.	1838	Manufacture of glass, and production of other vitrified matters, applicable to architectural purposes.
RAILTON, JOHN - - -	9339	3rd May	1842	Apparatus for weaving.
RAINES, ROBERT - - -	2792	22nd Nov:	1804	Manufacturing hard glue from tail-fins and other parts of whale-fish.
RALEIGH, Sir CAREY, Knight -	20	10th May	1622	Making soap, also soap-ashes, pot-ashes, and salts for soaps.
RALEY, WILLIAM - - -	2146	8th Nov.	1796	Horizontal turning churn, for churning butter.
RALEY, WILLIAM - - -	2276	8th Dec.	1798	Philosophical furnace and boiler, with an actuating wheel, being an appendage thereto, for drawing foul and inflammable air from pits, mines, &c.
RALLI, PANDIA THEODORE -	9523	25th Nov.	1842	Construction of railway and other carriages; apparatus connected therewith.
RALSTON, GERARD - -	8389	22nd Feb.	1840	Rolling puddle-balls or other masses of iron.
RAMAGE, ADAM - - -	8334	3rd Jan.	1840	Machinery used in the manufacture of paper.
RAMEE, DANIEL - - -	8153	15th July	1839	Paving roads and such like ways.
RAMEL, LOUIS JOSEPH AMANT	7595	19th March	1838	Machinery for excavating and embanking earth for the construction of railways and other works.
RAMINGER, HENRY - -	725	29th June	1758	Machine whereby shot used for fowling, and bullets of lead, are made more exactly round and solid than heretofore.
RAMMELL, THOMAS WEBSTER	11,248	22nd June	1846	Mosaic and tessellated work made of wood.
RAMMELL, THOMAS WEBSTER	11,552	28th Jan.	1847	Preparation and application of cork for linings and other useful purposes.
RAMSAY, ANDREW - - -	5918	20th March	1830	Manufacture of canvas and sail-cloth for making sails.
RAMSAY, JAMES - - -	5918	20th March	1830	Manufacture of canvas and sail-cloth for making sails.
RAMSBOTHAM, HENRY ROBERT	11,461	25th Nov.	1846	Combing wool.
RAMSBOTHAM, HENRY ROBERT	13,013	23rd March	1850	Preparing and combing wool.
RAMSBOTHAM, JAMES - -	1245	23rd Feb.	1780	Printing woollen-cloths, woollen-stuffs, and woollen-mixtures, in water-colours.
RAMSBOTTOM, JOHN - -	6644	12th July	1834	Construction of power-looms for weaving cotton and other fibrous materials into cloth or other fabrics.
RAMSBOTTOM, JOHN - -	6975	6th Jan.	1836	Machinery for roving, spinning, and doubling cotton and other fibrous substances.
RAMSBOTTOM, JOHN - -	12,384	21st Dec.	1848	Railway-wheels and turn-tables;—applicable to shafts or axles driven by steam or other power.
RAMSBOTTOM, JOHN - -	13,781	22nd Oct.	1851	Machinery for measuring and registering the flow of fluids;—applicable to registering the speed of and distance run by vessels in motion, also to obtaining motive power, and to other purposes.
RAMSBOTTOM, WILLIAM -	5813	8th July	1829	Power-looms for weaving cloth.
RAMSDEN, JESSE - - -	1112	30th Dec.	1775	Astronomical equatorial-instrument.
RAMSDEN, JOHN - - -	14,213	6th July	1852	Machinery for cutting screws.
RAMSDEN, NATHAN - -	12,956	31st Jan.	1850	Construction of machines for glazing, embossing, and finishing woven-fabrics and paper.

Name of Patentee,	Progressive Number.	Date.	Subject-matter of Patent.
RAMSEY, DAVID - - -	6	17th Jan. 1618	Engines and other inventions, to plough grounds, whether inland or upland, and to fertilize barren peat and sea-sands; also to raise water, and to make boats on the water move in calms as swiftly as full-sailed boats in great winds, and with more security in storms.
RAMSEY, DAVID - - -	21	8th Aug. 1622	Engine for draining land or mines; engine for turning brooches.
RAMSEY, DAVID - - -	49	21st Jan. 1630	Barrel-engine for raising water out of mines, graffs, coal-pits, or any other place.
RAMSEY, DAVID - - -	50	21st Jan. 1630	Methods of multiplying and making saltpetre in a field of four acres sufficient to serve His Majesty's dominions; raising water from low pits by fire, moving mills on standing-water by continual motion and without the aid of wind, weight, or horse; making tapestry without any weaving-loom or way hitherto in use in this kingdom; making boats, ships, and barges move against the wind and tide; making the earth more fertile; raising water; making copper tough and soft; also hard-copper from soft-copper, and making yellow-wax white.
RAMSEY, DAVID - - -	53	11th Nov. 1630	Separating gold and silver from tin, lead, and copper, and for that purpose to set up engines and instruments.
RAMSEY, DAVID - - -	68	29th Jan. 1634	Dyeing colours with materials of native growth, and without the use of cochineal; sowing corn and grain in a much easier way than now usual; carriage of coaches, carts, drays, and other things going upon wheels.
RAMSEY, DAVID - - -	78	17th Feb. 1635	Heating vessels used by brewers, dyers, soapboilers, salt and saltpetre-makers, as well as drying bricks and tiles, with sea-coals; making and drying tiles, stone jugs, bottles, melting-pots for goldsmiths, and other earthen commodities also with sea-coals.
RAMSEY, DAVID - - -	117	2nd May 1638	Making cast-iron, also plate or bar-iron, and refining all sorts of metals, by means of sea-coal, pit-coal, peat, or turf, with privilege to dig, open, search, or work mines of gold, silver, copper, and lead mixed with silver or quicksilver, to wash, roast, stamp, and melt all such metals or ores, and to refine and extract the gold and silver therefrom; also to drain the said mines, and to erect houses, mills, and works for the above purposes.
RAMSEY, JOHN - - -	6562	26th Feb. 1834	Apparatus for turning over the leaves of music and other books.
RAMUZ, ALEXANDER - -	10,332	27th Sept. 1844	Sofas, wardrobes, ottomans, bedsteads, and other apparatus for reclining or sleeping on; construction of dining and billiard-tables.
RAND, CATER - - -	2289	26th Jan. 1799	Military and naval telescope.
RAND, JOHN - - - -	8863	6th March 1841	Preserving paints and other fluids.
RAND, JOHN - - - -	9480	29th Sept. 1842	Making and closing metallic collapsible vessels.

Name of Patentee.	Progressive Number.	Date.	Subject-matter of Patent.
RAND, JOHN - - - -	9703	20th April 1843	Manufacture of tin-tubes and other soft metal tubes.
RAND, JOHN - - - -	10,589	7th April 1845	Certain stringed and wind musical-instruments.
RANDELL, JOHN REED -	14,319	7th Oct. 1852	Cutting and reaping machines.
RANDOLPH, DAVID MEAD -	3207	21st Feb. 1809	Manufacturing boots, shoes, and other articles, by means of a substitute for thread made of hemp, flax, or other yarns.
RANDOLPH, DAVID MEAD -	3273	6th Nov. 1809	Construction of wheeled-carriages.
RANDS, CHRISTOPHER -	13,867	19th Dec. 1851	Grinding wheat and other grain.
RANGELEY, JOHN - - -	3681	13th April 1813	Constructing and working machines for raising weights, turning machinery of all descriptions, and drawing carriages on railways;—applicable to other purposes.
RANGELEY, JOHN - - -	4021	4th May 1816	Constructing and working engines or machines for lifting or raising weights, turning machinery, and drawing carriages on railways;—applicable to all purposes where mechanical power is required. " Hydro-pneumatic engine."
RANGELEY, JOHN - - -	8410	3rd March 1840	Construction of railways; means of applying power to propelling carriages and machinery.
RANGER, WILLIAM - - -	6341	4th Dec. 1832	Cement or composition. " Ranger's Artificial stone."
RANGER, WILLIAM - - -	6729	4th Dec. 1834	Preparing and combining materials whereby the moulding or forming of blocks, casts, walls, or other aggregates in those said materials may be considerably expedited.
RANKIN, BENJAMIN - -	8939	27th April 1841	Form and combination also mode of making blocks for pavement.
RANKING, JOHN - - -	4855	1st Nov. 1823	Securing property in coaches, travelling carriages, waggons, caravans, &c.
RANSOME, FREDERICK -	10,360	22nd Oct. 1844	Manufacture of artificial stone for grinding and for other purposes.
RANSOME, FREDERICK -	10,665	10th May 1845	Combining small coal and other matters; preserving wood.
RANSOME, FREDERICK -	11,282	6th July 1846	Manufacturing bricks, tiles, pipes, and other articles composed of plastic materials; preparation of plastic materials for the purpose.
RANSOME, FREDERICK -	11,596	24th Feb. 1847	Working coke and other kilns or ovens.
RANSOME, JAMES - - -	4038	1st June 1816	Ploughs.
RANSOME, JAMES - - -	4513	28th Nov. 1820	Ploughs.
RANSOME, JAMES - - -	8847	15th Feb. 1841	Manufacture of railway-chairs, railway and other pins or bolts, and wood fastenings and trenails.
RANSOME, ROBERT - -	1392	25th Oct. 1783	Making and casting iron and other metal plates, for covering houses and other buildings, such plates being superior to tiles, slate, or lead.
RANSOME, ROBERT - - -	1468	18th March 1785	Making plough-shares of cast-iron, which are tempered after a peculiar manner so as to stand the strictest proof.
RANSOME, ROBERT - - -	2736	24th Sept. 1803	Making and tempering cast-iron plough-shares, and other articles of cast-iron, for agricultural purposes.

Name of Patentee.	Progres-sive Number.	Date.	Subject-matter of Patent.
RANSOME, ROBERT - - -	3139	30th May 1808	Wheel and swing plough.
RANSOME, ROBERT - - -	4513	28th Nov. 1820	Ploughs.
RANSOME, ROBERT - - -	6918	2nd Nov. 1835	Manufacturing certain parts of ploughs.
RANSOME, ROBERT - - -	9842	15th July 1843	Machinery and apparatus for ploughing and scarifying land, and for raking; also machinery used in thrashing, cutting, and grinding, for agricultural purposes; construction of whippletrees.
RANSON, ROBERT, GILL - -	8310	13th Dec. 1839	Manufacture of paper.
RANWELL, EBENEZER - -	6998	9th Feb. 1836	Construction of paddles or paddle-wheels for propelling vessels;—applicable to the construction of water-wheels for mills.
RANWELL, WILLIAM - -	6998	9th Feb. 1836	Construction of paddles or paddle-wheels for propelling vessels; applicable to the construction of water-wheels for mills.
RANWELL, WILLIAM - -	9697	13th April 1843	Machinery for indicating the number of persons entering any description of carriage, house, room, chamber, or place, and also the number of passengers and carriages that pass along a bridge or way.
RANYARD, WILLIAM - -	5275	1st Nov. 1825	Circumvolution brush and hander.
RAPBURNE, AARON - -	1	2nd March 1617	Making, describing, carving, graving, and printing, maps of London, Westminster, Bristol, Norwich, Canterbury, Bath, Oxford, Cambridge, and Windsor.
RAPER, HENRY - - -	5510	21st June 1827	System of signals for communicating between ships at sea or other objects distant from each other, by means of flags and pendants in which the colours hitherto used may be dispensed with, also for communicating by night between ships at sea, and other objects distant from each other, by means of light.
RAPER, THOMAS, NICHOLAS - [Raper, Nicholas.]	7364	31st May 1838	Rendering fabrics and leather waterproof.
RAPER, THOMAS NICHOLAS -	7922	3rd Jan. 1839	Rendering fabrics and leather waterproof.
RAPER, THOMAS NICHOLAS -	8158	20th July 1839	Rendering fabrics and leather waterproof.
RAPOZO, FRANCISCO - -	2261	27th Aug. 1798	Construction of steam-engines.
RAPSON, JOHN - - -	3591	5th Aug. 1812	Communicating motion from one axle to another placed at any angle, without the aid of universal joints.
RAPSON, JOHN - - -	6665	23rd Aug. 1834	Apparatus for facilitating the steering of vessels of certain descriptions.
RAPSON, JOHN - - -	8214	9th Sept. 1839	Steering ships and vessels.
RAPSON, JOHN - - -	8678	3rd Nov. 1840	Paddle-wheels for propelling vessels by steam or other power.
RASTRICK, JOHN - - -	1166	8th Aug. 1777	Barrel-churn. " Imperial barrel-churn."
RASTRICK, JOHN U. - -	3799	1st April 1814	Steam-engine.
RATCLIFF, EDMUND - -	10,763	12th July 1845	Furniture of door-locks and latches.
RATCLIFF, JOHN - -	7649	22nd May 1838	Lamp.
RATCLIFF, JOSEPH - -	9039	4th Aug. 1841	Construction and manufacture of hinges for hanging and closing doors.
RATHBORNE, JOHN - - -	25	31st July 1623	Making engines for bolting and dressing meal.
RATHEN, ANTHONY BERNHARD [VON.	8853	22nd Feb. 1841	Fire-grates and parts connected therewith, for furnaces used for heating fluids.

Name of Patentee.	Progressive Number.	Date.	Subject-matter of Patent.
RATHEN, ANTHONY BERNHARD [VON.	9037	28th July 1841	High-pressure and other steam-boilers, combined with a new mode of supplying the same with water.
RATHEN, ANTHONY BERNHARD [VON.	9038	28th July 1841	Propelling locomotive-carriages on railroads and common roads, and vessels on rivers and canals, by power obtained by machinery unconnected with the carriages and vessels to be propelled. "The united stationary and locomotive system."
RATHEN, ANTHONY BERNHARD [VON.	11,800	17th July 1847	Universal wheels or direct rotary-engines, to be worked by steam, air, or other elastic power.
RATHEN, ANTHONY BERNHARD [VON.	11,932	2nd Nov. 1847	Obtaining and applying motive-power.
RATTRAY, WILLIAM	7661	31st May 1838	Manufacture of gelatine, size, and glue.
RAVENSCROFT, GEORGE	176	16th May 1674	Manufacture of chrystalline glass resembling rock-crystal.
RAVENSCROFT, HUMPHREY [WILLIAM.	4636	14th Jan. 1822	Forensic wig, the curls whereof are constructed to supersede the necessity of frizzing, curling, or using hard pomatum, and the tails do not require to be tied.
RAWE, JOHN, junior [Raw, John, junior.]	5923	30th March 1830	Steam-boilers; and a mode of quickening the draft for furnaces connected therewith.
RAWE, JOHN, junior	5956	19th July 1830	Steam-carriages; boilers; producing increased draft.
RAWLE, VALENTINE	1472	16th April 1785	Covering the mitres, angles, or joints of plated wares, with stronger plated metals or solid silver.
RAWLE, WILLIAM	1173	28th Nov. 1777	Machine for the carriage of soldiers' cartridges.
RAWLETT, WILLIAM	8543	13th June 1840	Locks, latches, and other fastenings for doors.
RAWLINS, JAMES	4786	22nd April 1823	Bedstead for invalids.
RAWLINSON, CHARLES	1016	22nd May 1772	Covering buildings with slates laid in such a manner and with such materials that little or no repairs will be needed while the timbers remain good; that the same will resist the effects of wind or weather, will save expense, and not exceed half the weight of the usual method; the pitch of the roof not rising more than one quarter the breadth of the building will also reduce the measurement, and consequently the quantity used, by one ninth part.
RAWLINSON, GEORGE	1099	12th June 1775	Mills for cleansing, splitting, grinding, and dressing beans, peas, wheat, and other grain and flour, and to be worked either by men or horses, wind or water.
RAWLINSON, JAMES	2954	1st Aug. 1806	Trusses or bandages for ruptures.
RAWSON, HENRY	6806	3rd April 1835	Combing wool and other fibrous substances.
RAWSON, HENRY	12,333	21st Nov. 1848	Manufacture of sulphuric, nitric, and oxalic acids, chlorine, and sulphur.
RAWSON, HENRY	14,266	19th Aug. 1852	Preparing and straightening wool and other fibrous materials.
RAY, JOHN	11,782	3rd July 1847	Constructing the interior parts of ships or other vessels, warehouses, and other depôts, to facilitate the delivery of the cargoes or contents thereof.

Name of Patentee.	Progressive Number.	Date.		Subject-matter of Patent.
RAYBOULD, WILLIAM - -	2395	1st May	1800	Candlesticks which will receive and hold firmly candles of various sizes.
RAYBOULD, WILLIAM - -	4108	11th March	1817	Fire-stoves, grates, and ranges.
RAYBOULD, WILLIAM - -	9447	18th Aug.	1842	Soldering-iron.
RAYMONDI, JOSEPH VINCENT [MELCHIOR.	13,932	27th Jan.	1852	Statistic and descriptive maps.
RAYNER, HENRY SAMUEL -	7755	31st July	1838	Machinery for roving, spinning, and twisting cotton, flax, silk, wool, and other fibrous materials.
RAYNER, HENRY SAMUEL -	10,571	18th March	1845	Means of preventing accidents to carriages on railways and common roads.
RAYNER, HENRY SAMUEL -	10,824	4th Sept.	1845	Locomotive-engines.
RAYNER, HENRY SAMUEL -	11,813	23rd July	1847	Propelling on land or water.
RAYNER, JOSEPH - - -	5766	5th Feb.	1829	Apparatus and machinery for conducting heat, and applying the same in the operations of washing, scouring, cleansing, fulling, dressing, dyeing, and finishing woollen-cloths, and calendering, straining, glossing, polishing, and finishing silks, cottons, woollens, and other goods.
RAYNER, JOSEPH - - -	7755	31st July	1838	Machinery for roving, spinning, and twisting cotton, flax, silk, wool, and other fibrous materials.
RAYNER, JOSEPH WHITEHEAD	7755	31st July	1838	Machinery for roving, spinning, and twisting cotton, flax, silk, wool, and other fibrous materials.
RAYNER, SAMUEL - - -	13,387	7th Dec.	1850	Paving.
RAYNHAM, WILLIAM - -	3984	20th Feb.	1816	Composition for making leather and other articles waterproof.
RAYNOR, JOSEPH - - -	3633	1st Jan.	1813	Machinery for roving and spinning cotton, silk, flax, and wool.
READ, JOHN - - - -	3803	18th April	1814	Raising and conveying water, steam, gas, or other fluid, by pipes of purified earth.
READ, JOHN - - - -	4236	14th March	1818	Working or getting the main or thick mine of coals.
READ, JOHN - - - -	4484	11th July	1820	Syringes.
READ, JOHN - - - -	6463	19th Aug.	1833	Machinery or apparatus for raising or forcing fluids.
READ, JOHN - - - -	9314	6th April	1842	Construction and make of driving-reins, harness bridles and reins, also bridles and reins for riding.
READ, JOHN - - - -	9794	21st June	1843	Ploughs for draining, subsoiling, and cultivating land.
READ, JOHN - - - -	10,645	29th April	1845	Machinery for raising and forcing fluids.
READ, JOHN - - - -	11,536	19th Jan.	1847	Cultivation of land.
READ, JOHN - - - -	12,909	29th Dec.	1849	Machinery for extracting fluids from animal, vegetable, and mineral substances; compressing the same.
READE, JOSEPH BANCROFT -	11,474	3rd Dec.	1846	Inks, and processes by which the same are manufactured; application of some of these processes to producing certain salts.
READING, JOHN - - -	10,699	3rd June	1845	Fastenings for articles of dress.
READMAN, JAMES - - -	9280	7th March	1842	Barometers.
REARESBY, Sir JOHN, Baronet -	148	20th Nov.	1665	Making steel.

Name of Patentee.	Progres-sive Number.	Date.	Subject-matter of Patent.
REAVES, JAMES - - -	1279	22nd Feb. 1781	Making table-fork blades both scale and round tangs, with two, three or more prongs; also spring-knife scales from cast-iron alone or mixed with steel or other metal, which by a new system of tempering, renders them sufficiently strong and elastic.
RECORDON, LOUIS - - -	1249	18th March 1780	Making watches to keep time and motion without winding up by key or other manual operation.
REDDELL, ISAAC HADLEY -	2434	2nd Aug. 1800	Constructing carriages for the conveyance of merchandize by land or water, and which carriages may be removed either loaded or unloaded from land to water, and vice versâ.
REDDELL, ISAAC HADLEY -	2435	2nd Aug. 1800	Making stirrups.
REDDELL, ISAAC HADLEY -	2439	13th Aug. 1800	Constructing travelling-carriages.
REDDELL, ISAAC HADLEY -	4035	27th May 1816	Lighting the interior of offices, theatres, buildings, houses, or any place where light may be required.
REDFERN, BARTHOLOMEW -	6053	17th Dec. 1830	Lock break-off and trigger, for fowling-pieces, muskets, rifles, pistols, and small fire-arms.
REDMAN, WILLIAM - -	1261	29th June 1780	Salisbury portable kitchen, for cooking provisions in any room or in the open air, without the assistance of a common fire-place.
REDMAN, WILLIAM - -	1765	28th July 1790	Iron backs, adapted to stoves and grates used in fire-places in rooms, which by rarifying the air in the chimney accelerate and impel the ascension of the smoke, cause the fire to burn freely and clearly, and to give greater heat than in stoves or grates without such backs.
REDMUND, DAVID - - -	3967	9th Dec. 1815	Machine for manufacture of corks and bungs.
REDMUND, DAVID - - -	4607	9th Nov. 1821	Construction of hinges for doors.
REDMUND, DAVID - - -	5193	28th June 1825	Building ships, houses, and other buildings.
REDMUND, DAVID - - -	5443	22nd Dec. 1826	Construction and manufacture of hinges.
REDMUND, DAVID - - -	6322	18th Oct. 1832	Steam-engines.
REDMUND, DAVID - - -	6494	28th Oct. 1833	Steam-carriages;—applicable to other purposes.
REDMUND, DAVID - - -	7612	10th April 1838	Construction and apparatus of steam-boats, or vessels used for war or commerce.
REDMUND, DAVID - - -	9454	25th Aug. 1842	Hinges applicable to suspending or closing doors and gates, and to other purposes.
REDRICH, ROBERT - - -	461	28th Jan. 1724	Staining, veining, spotting, clouding, and otherwise imitating, marble, porphyry, and other rich stones and tortoise shell, on wood, stone, and earthenware, and on goods, wares, utensils and things made from the same; also making, marbling, veining, spotting, staining, clouding, and damasking linen, silks, canvas, paper, and leather.
REDWOOD, THEOPHILUS -	13,442	11th Jan. 1851	Coating metals with other metals.
REECE, REES - - - -	12,436	23rd Jan. 1849	Treating peat and obtaining products therefrom.
REECE, REES - - - -	12,617	24th May 1849	Manufacturing and refining sugar or saccharine matters.

Name of Patentee.	Progressive Number.	Date.	Subject-matter of Patent.
REED, JAMES - - - -	7680	12th June 1838	Joining slate, stone, and marble, for cisterns and for other purposes.
REED, JAMES - - - -	9376	2nd June 1842	Tiles and slating; construction of water-tight joints; covering and casing of buildings and other erections.
REED, JAMES - - - -	10,311	12th Sept. 1844	Manufacture of bricks and tiles, for chimneys and flues and for other purposes.
REED, JOSEPH HAYTHORNE -	13,502	10th Feb. 1851	Saddlery and harness.
REED, JOSEPH HAYTHORNE -	13,945	31st Jan. 1852	Propelling vessels.
REED, STEPHEN - - -	6993	1st Feb. 1836	Two hooks and a bow for corves, baskets, buckets, and other vessels used for conveying loads from one level to another, particularly in mines, pits, wells, shafts, quarries, collieries, warehouses, factories, buildings, and dockyards; also in and about ships, boats, and vessels, and the tackling of the same, and in other cases where cranes, common hooks, and bows are now used.
REED, STEPHEN - - -	10,882	16th Oct. 1845	Railway rails and chairs.
REEDER, JOHN - - -	1559	6th Oct. 1786	Apparatus for clarifying cane-liquor, and drawing off the syrup, in making muscovado sugar.
REEDHEAD, JOHN - -	4557	5th May 1821	Propelling vessels.
REEDHEAD, JOHN - -	5223	26th July 1825	Machinery for propelling vessels, both in marine and inland navigation.
REEDHEAD, JOHN - -	6377	29th Jan. 1833	Construction of coaches, waggons, or other carriages for conveying goods and passengers, to be drawn by horses, steam, or other motive-power.
REEPE, JOHN - - -	313	31st Jan. 1693	Machine for making and twisting whips.
REES, DAVID - - -	6456	7th Aug. 1833	Drags or apparatus to be applied to carriages.
REES, JOHN HUGHES - -	7821	27th Sept. 1838	Machinery applicable to the raising of water, for propelling boats, carriages, and other machinery.
REES, RICHARD - - -	3069	25th Aug. 1807	Trusses.
REES, WILLIAM - - -	13,463	18th Jan. 1851	Preparation of fuel.
REEVE, THOMAS - - -	358	28th Nov. 1698	Drying malt on iron or tinned-iron, with half the usual consumption of fuel, and with a saving of time.
REEVES, CHARLES, junior	13,991	27th Feb. 1852	Manufacture of bayonets, swords, and other cutting instruments.
REEVES, CHRISTOPHER - -	927	8th June 1769	Springs for coaches and other four-wheeled carriages; supporting the bodies of such carriages on the said springs.
REEVES, RICHARD - -	187	18th Nov. 1675	Casting and spreading light by a new and unusual figure of foiled glass, polished without grinding, with pipes of glass to hold candles or lamps.
REHÉ, JOHN HENRY -	10,359	22nd Oct. 1844	Manufacture of starch and farinaceous food.
REHÉ, SAMUEL - - -	2304	11th April 1799	Engine for giving motion to water or other fluids, either for conveying such fluids, or for mechanical purposes.
REID, ANDREW - - -	606	13th July 1744	Making bay-salt by the heat of the sun.
REID, JOHN - - - -	14,030	22nd March 1852	Flues; heating air; evaporating certain fluids by heated air.

Name of Patentee.	Progres-sive Number.	Date.	Subject-matter of Patent.
REID, JOHN PATERSON - -	5482	4th April 1827	Power-looms for weaving cloth of various kinds.
REID, JOHN PATERSON - -	6579	20th March 1834	Looms for weaving different sorts of cloth.
REID, JOHN PATERSON - -	7628	28th April 1838	Preparing, by machinery, yarn or thread for warps, in preparation for weaving in looms.
REID, JOHN PATERSON - -	11,424	22nd Oct. 1846	Machinery for weaving and producing patterns in weaving ; machinery for finishing certain woven-fabrics.
REID, ROBERT - - -	13,038	15th April 1850	Weaving.
REID, WILLIAM - - -	3691	5th May 1813	Instrument for calculating, without reference to tables, various problems in navigation, practical mathematics, and trigonometry, also heights and distances, and embracing every science depending on angles.
REID, WILLIAM - - -	11,974	23rd Nov. 1847	Communicating intelligence by electricity ; instruments and apparatus employed therein.
REID, WILLIAM - - -	14,166	12th June 1852	Electric-telegraphs.
REID, WILLIAM - - -	14,332	21st Oct. 1852	Electric-telegraphs.
REIGNOLDS, HENRY - -	54	24th Jan. 1631	Making kersey and twill sieves, and beads of bone and wood.
REINAGLE, RAMSEY RICHARD	7162	6th Aug. 1836	Construction of carriages for the conveyance of persons, goods, or merchandize.
REINAGLE, RAMSEY RICHARD	7771	15th Aug. 1838	Propelling canal boats, steamers, and other vessels.
REINAGLE, RAMSAY RICHARD	9945	16th Nov. 1843	Applying atmospheric air as a motive-power.
REINECKE, JOHN - - -	1590	3rd Feb. 1787	Machine to be used in all household purposes where boiling is required ; applicable also in the operations of boiling, washing, distilling, and evaporating in manufactories, and in mills and works where the power of steam is employed ; also in heating any liquids, sand, or substance ; in all which operations a considerable saving in fuel will be thereby effected. " British Boiler."
REINHARD, AUGUSTE - -	12,940	24th Jan. 1850	Preparing oils for lubricating purposes ; apparatus for filtering oil and other liquids.
REMINGTON, GEORGE - -	3090	16th Dec. 1807	Tables and couches.
REMINGTON, GEORGE - -	11,340	17th Aug. 1846	Locomotive-engines ;—partly applicable to marine and stationary-engines.
REMINGTON, GEORGE - -	12,163	26th May 1848	Locomotive-engines ; marine and stationary-engines.
REMINGTON, GEORGE - -	12,576	17th April 1849	Locomotive, marine, and stationary steam-engines ; hydraulic and pneumatic-engines.
REMNANT, STEPHEN - -	765	5th Aug. 1761	Gun-carriages of cast-iron.
RÉMOND, AMEDÉE FRANCOIS -	11,609	9th March 1847	Steam-engines.
RÉMOND, AMEDÉE FRANCOIS -	12,493	28th Feb. 1849	Machinery for folding envelopes ; manufacture of envelopes.
RÉMOND, AMEDÉE FRANCOIS -	13,036	15th April 1850	Manufacture of envelopes.
RÉMOND, AMEDÉE FRANCOIS -	13,534	26th Feb. 1851	Manufacture of metallic tubes or pipes, and machinery connected therewith.

Name of Patentee.	Progressive Number.	Date.	Subject-matter of Patent.
RENARD, FRANCOIS AUGUSTIN	11,842	19th Aug. 1847	Preserving and colouring wood.
RENNIE, GEORGE - - -	8286	26th Nov. 1839	Propelling vessels.
RENNIE, HUGH FRANCIS -	8052	30th April 1839	Spinning-frame used for spinning flax, hemp, and tow, upon the wet principle.
RENNIE, JAMES - - -	13,251	5th Sept. 1850	Construction of gas-retorts and furnaces; and apparatus or machinery applicable to the same.
RENNOLDSON, GEORGE - -	5724	4th Dec. 1828	Rotatory steam-engines.
RENSHAW, GEORGE PEARSON	14,181	24th June 1852	Cutting and shaping.
RENSHAW, JONAS - - -	3596	14th Aug. 1812	Making spots in lace or net-work.
RENSHAW, JOSEPH - -	11,254	22nd June 1846	Machinery for finishing velvets and other piled goods or fabrics.
RENTON, JOHN - - -	12,763	13th Sept. 1849	Manufacture of starch and other like articles, from farinaceous and leguminous substances.
RENTZSCH, SIGISMUND - -	3663	13th March 1813	Hydrostatic or pneumatic chronometer.
RESTELL, THOMAS - - -	12,154	11th May 1848	Chronometers, clocks, watches, or other timekeepers.
RESTELL, THOMAS - - -	13,824	22nd Nov. 1851	Locks or fastenings.
RESTELL, THOMAS - - -	13,852	8th Dec. 1851	Locks or fastenings.
RESTELL, THOMAS - - -	14,170	17th June 1852	Construction of lamps and burners.
RETTFORD, RICHARD - -	6732	18th Dec. 1834	Machinery for taking a fac-simile of the human countenance, copy of a bust or sculptured figure, or of a living or other subject. " Physiognotype."
RETTIE, ROBERT - - -	10,068	24th Feb. 844	Grid-irons, frying-pans, and other cooking utensils and heating apparatus.
RETTIE, ROBERT - - -	10,975	4th Dec. 1845	Signalizing or telegraphing on sea or land, by burners with coloured glasses and signal-cards; applicable to railways in all the various departments, as well as for preventing accidents when the train is at full speed, also for showing the state of the tide in harbours, and the diurnal for railways, towns, villages, &c.
RETTIE, ROBERT - - -	11,240	12th June 1846	Manufacture of fuel;—partly applicable to purifying, compressing, and extracting vegetable substances and fluids; machinery to be used for the same.
RETTIE, WILLIAM - - -	14,160	8th June 1852	Lamps and burners; apparatus for ventilating apartments; working signal-lamps.
REVERE, JOHN - - -	5892	28th Jan. 1830	Compound metal or alloy applicable to the sheathing of ships and to other purposes.
REVERE, JOHN - - -	6040	27th Nov. 1830	Protecting iron chain-cables, iron boilers, and iron tanks from corrosion produced by the action of water.
REVERE, JOSEPH WARREN -	3347	19th June 1810	Splitting hides and shaving leather.
REVIS, THOMAS - - -	5671	10th July 1828	Lifting weights.
REWCASTLE, RALPH -	5582	13th Dec. 1827	Ballasting ships or vessels.
REYBURN, ROBERT -	11,244	17th June 1846	Making extracts from animal and vegetable substances.
REYBURN, ROBERT -	14,078	20th April 1852	Printing on silk and other fabrics and yarns.
REYNOLDS, ALFRED -	12,097	14th March 1848	Ornamenting china, earthenware, and glass.
REYNOLDS, JOHN - - -	6357	9th Jan. 1833	Engine and apparatus to be worked by steam and other motive-power.

Name of Patentee.	Progressive Number.	Date.	Subject-matter of Patent.
REYNOLDS, JOHN - - -	6827	5th May 1835	Railways.
REYNOLDS, JOHN - - -	8155	16th July 1839	Manufacture of salt.
REYNOLDS, JOHN WILLIAM [BUCKLE.	10,404	25th Nov. 1844	Obtaining motive-power for working loco-motive-carriages and other machinery.
REYNOLDS, JOSEPH - -	3973	9th Jan. 1816	Construction of wheel-carriages, ploughs, and other instruments used in husbandry, to be moved by steam, heated air, or vapours.
REYNOLDS, JOSEPH - -	13,648	29th May 1851	Manufacturing playing-cards.
REYNOLDS, OLIVER LOUIS -	8719	25th Nov. 1840	Machinery for producing stocking fabric, or frame-work knitting.
REYNOLDS, OSBORNE - -	8940	27th April 1841	Paving streets, roads, and ways.
REYNOLDS, OSBORNE - -	9266	25th Feb. 1842	Covering streets, roads and other ways with wood, enabling horses to pass safely over them.
REYNOLDS, OSBORNE - -	11,837	19th Aug. 1847	Making hop-poles, hurdles, fencing-ropes, basket or wicker-work, and other similar articles.
REYNOLDS, OSBORNE - -	12,552	28th March 1849	Railways.
REYNOLDS, WILLIAM - "	2363	6th Dec. 1799	Preparing iron for the conversion thereof into steel.
REYNOLDSON, GEORGE - -	534	18th Oct. 1731	Machine that gives exactly the way a ship makes, and counts her leeway, tells what speed the winds blow, and proves the different force of current in any depth; also a machine that will retard a ship when driving upon a lee shore where there is no anchorage, or on being forced back in her voyage by contrary winds.
RHAM, WILLIAM LEWIS -	8968	25th May 1841	Machinery for preparing land, and sowing or depositing grain, seeds, and manure.
RHODES, JOSEPH - -	5705	18th Sept. 1828	Machinery for spinning and twisting worsted yarn and other fibrous substances.
RHODES, WILLIAM - -	5039	20th Nov. 1824	Construction of clamps for burning rain bricks.
RHODES, WILLIAM - -	6386	14th Feb. 1833	Manufacture of bricks.
RHODES, WILLIAM - -	7374	22nd May 1837	Machinery for carding and piercing wool in process of manufacture in woollen mills.
RHODES, WILLIAM HENRY ·	12,805	12th Oct. 1849	Machinery used for preparing, spinning, doubling and weaving cotton and other fibrous substances.
RIBRIGHT, THOMAS - -	640	7th Feb. 1749	Making small perspective-glasses with mathematical and other instruments and twees in the same case, with and without microscope or magnifying glasses.
RIBRIGHT, THOMAS - -	1731	2nd March 1790	Instrument to serve as an artificial horizon, by means of which the sun's altitude may be taken at sea, with a Hadley's quadrant, and the latitude found when the real horizon is obscured or invisible.
RICARDO, JOHN LEWIS - -	12,262	4th Sept. 1848	Electric-telegraphs, and apparatus connected therewith.
RICARDO, WALTER - -	14,322	14th Oct. 1852	Gas-burners.
RICCARDS, WILLIAM - -	744	17th Jan. 1760	Making pots and building furnaces for making crown-glass and all sorts of green glass.
RICE, THOMAS - · -	3380	26th Sept. 1810	Burner applicable to all kinds of lamps.

Name of Patentee.	Progressive Number.	Date.	Subject-matter of Patent.
RICHARD, HIPOLYTE AUGUSTE	10,304	5th Sept. 1844	Apparatus for heating and lighting.
RICHARD, WILLIAM - -	4810	5th July 1823	Construction of looms for weaving fabrics composed wholly or partly of woollen, worsted, cotton, linen, silk, or other materials ; machinery and implements for and method of working the same.
RICHARDS, GEORGE - -	3155	30th July 1808	Single and double cannon, carronades or ordnance, muskets and all other kinds of fire-arms; charging or loading the same ; fixing bayonets on fire-arms.
RICHARDS, GEORGE - -	4744	26th Dec. 1822	Grates, stoves, furnaces, and other inventions for the consumption of fuel ; and flues connected with them whereby they are rendered more safe, and the smoke prevented from returning into the rooms; apparatus for cleansing the same.
RICHARDS, HENRY - -	1450	11th Sept. 1784	Machine for spinning and reeling wool, hemp, flax, cotton, silk, and mohair.
RICHARDS (Colonel) JACOB -	335	29th Sept. 1694	Several small engines to be used on board frigates or merchant ships to destroy enemies attempting to board the same.
RICHARDS, JAMES - - -	2391	26th April 1800	Machine for setting grain and seeds.
RICHARDS, JAMES - - -	11,745	12th June 1847	Constructing pistons.
RICHARDS, JAMES WRIGHT -	4911	28th Feb. 1824	Metallic frame and lap, applicable to hot-houses, green-houses, horticultural frames and glasses, sky-lights, and other inclined lights and glasses.
RICHARDS, NICHOLAS - -	7514	19th Dec. 1837	Curing or preventing smoky chimneys;—applicable to ventilation.
RICHARDS, THEOPHILUS -	8592	5th Aug. 1840	Cutting or sawing wood.
RICHARDS, THOMAS - -	9322	15th April 1842	Bookbinding; machinery to be employed therein.
RICHARDS, THOMAS - -	12,986	2nd March 1850	Rollers to be used in the manufacture of silk, cotton, woollen, and other fabrics.
RICHARDS, THOMAS - -	14,225	15th July 1852	Machinery for reducing and pulverizing ores, minerals, stones, and other substances.
RICHARDS, WILLIAM - -	9663	16th March 1843	Manufacture of gas for illumination ; apparatus used when transmitting and measuring gas or other fluids.
RICHARDS, WILLIAM - -	10,096	7th March 1844	Manufacture of gas for illumination ; apparatus used when transmitting and measuring gas.
RICHARDS, WILLIAM WESTLEY	4611	10th Nov. 1821	Construction of gun and pistol locks.
RICHARDS, WILLIAM WESTLEY	6071	11th Feb. 1831	Touch-holes and primers suitable to percussion guns, pistols, and all sorts of arms fired on that principle.
RICHARDS, WILLIAM WESTLEY	7041	22nd March 1836	Primers for discharging fire-arms by means of percussion.
RICHARDS, WILLIAM WESTLEY	7582	2nd March 1838	Primer for fire-arms.
RICHARDS, WILLIAM WESTLEY	9177	14th Dec. 1841	Construction of gun and pistol locks and primers for the discharge of fire-arms.
RICHARDS, WILLIAM WESTLEY	14,027	20th March 1852	Fire-arms ; and means used for discharging the same; also projectiles.
RICHARDSON, ARCHIBALD	7679	12th June 1838	Producing pure spirit from malt and all kinds of grain, and from vegetable substances of every description, containing saccharine matter.

Name of Patentee.	Progressive Number.	Date.	Subject-matter of Patent.
RICHARDSON, CHARLES - -	11,370	10th Sept. 1846	Making and refining sugar; machinery and apparatus employed therein..
RICHARDSON, CHARLES WIL-[LIAM ROWLEY.	6823	28th April 1835	Boilers applicable to steam-engines, and to other purposes.
RICHARDSON, DAVID OLIVER -	5225	26th July 1825	Printing or dyeing woollen and other fabrics.
RICHARDSON, FRANCIS - -	4081	25th May 1816	Locks and barrels of fire-arms; bayonets.
RICHARDSON, HENRY - -	13,520	22nd Feb. 1851	Life-boats.
RICHARDSON, HENRY FRANCIS	8325	21st Dec. 1839	Omnibuses.
RICHARDSON, JOHN - -	2187	4th July 1797	Machine to be applied to glasses and pebbles, for the use of sights in general.
RICHARDSON, JOHN - -	7530	4th Jan. 1838	Covering buildings.
RICHARDSON, JOSEPH - -	13,580	31st March 1851	Dyeing and cleansing piece-goods.
RICHARDSON, ROBERT - -	11,715	24th May 1847	Construction of railways, and engines and carriages used thereon; arrangements for the conveyance, management, and preservation of perishable articles.
RICHARDSON, THOMAS - -	2631	26th June 1802	Preparing, colouring, and uniting the skins of sheep and lambs.
RICHARDSON, THOMAS - -	8305	9th Dec. 1839	Preparation of sulphate of lead, applicable to some of the purposes for which carbonate of lead is applied.
RICHARDSON, THOMAS - -	12,160	26th May 1843	Manufacture of manure.
RICHARDSON, THOMAS - -	12,246	21st Aug. 1848	Condensation of metallic fumes; and manufacture of white-lead.
RICHARDSON, THOMAS - -	12,944	26th Jan. 1850	Manufacture of Epsom and other magnesian salts; also alum, and sulphate of ammonia.
RICHARDSON, THOMAS - -	13,909	23rd Jan. 1852	Manufacture of magnesia and some of its salts.
RICHARDSON, THOMAS - -	14,093	28th April 1852	Treating matters containing lead, tin, antimony, zinc, or silver, and obtaining such metals, or products thereof.
RICHARDSON, WALTER - -	8634	17th Sept. 1840	Tinning metals.
RICHARDSON, WILLIAM HADON	12,189	15th June 1848	Manufacture of tubing.
RICHAULT, GUILLAUME SIMON	9559	15th Dec. 1842	Apparatus for exercising the fingers of the human hand to facilitate their use in playing musical instruments.
RICHMAN, FRANCIS - -	5009	7th Oct. 1824	Construction of fire-escapes;—partly applicable to other purposes.
RICHMOND, JOHN - - -	1313	2nd Jan. 1782	Application of a principle in hydraulics to a machine for raising water out of mines, pits, and wells, and for other purposes.
RICHMOND, JOHN - - -	1441	3rd July 1784	Candlestick with a socket or nosle to fit candles without using paper, and which may be applied to candlesticks already made.
RICHOLD, PETER - - -	7613	10th April 1838	Manufacture of certain pigments or paints, or such like substances.
RICHTER, JOHN - - -	978	28th Dec. 1770	Inlaying scagliola or plaster upon marble and metals, to imitate flowers, birds, &c.
RICHTER, JOHN - - -	3924	10th June 1815	Clarifying and purifying certain fluids; facilitating evaporation; rendering the vapour less noxious.
RICHTER, JOHN - - -	4279	14th July 1818	Utensils used for distillation, evaporation, and condensation.

Name of Patentee.	Progressive Number.	Date.	Subject-matter of Patent.
RICKARDS, CHARLES WILLIAM [ROWLEY.	11,189	30th April 1846	Cocks for drawing off liquids and gases.
RICKETTS, HENRY -	4623	5th Dec. 1821	Manufacturing glass bottles for wine, porter, beer, or cyder.
RIDDETT, GEORGE - - -	11,194	5th May 1846	Reading-tables.
RIDDELL, WILLIAM - -	12,383	21st Dec. 1848	Construction of ever-pointed pencils, writing and drawing instruments, and inkstands.
RIDDLE, GABRIEL - - -	8667	22nd Oct. 1840	Wheels for carriages.
RIDER, BENJAMIN - - -	5675	17th July 1828	Manufacture of hats. " Patent Hat Tips."
RIDER, EMERY - - -	14,230	20th July 1852	Manufacture or treatment of India-rubber and gutta-percha; application thereof.
RIDER, JOB - - - -	2835	26th March 1805	Steam-engines.
RIDER, JOB - - - -	4490	20th July 1820	Producing a concentric and revolving excentric motion, applicable to steam-engines, water-pumps, mills, and other machinery.
RIDGE, JOSEPH - - -	2134	25th Aug. 1796	Making and manufacturing of iron and steel or both united, saws, steel-doctors for printers, plates, beads, mouldings, fender-plates, springs, and other articles.
RIDGE, SAMUEL - - -	1688	20th June 1789	Drill and hoe ploughs.
RIDGE, SAMUEL - - -	1807	24th May 1791	Machines for raising or moving fluids and other bodies by the power or force of wind, steam, manual labour, or any other given power; applicable to many useful purposes.
RIDGWAY, JOHN - - -	5278	1st Nov. 1825	Cock, tap, or valve, for drawing off liquors
RIDGWAY, JOHN - - -	8338	11th Jan. 1840	Moulds used in the manufacture of earthenware, porcelain, and other similar substances, whereby they are rendered more durable.
RIDGWAY, JOHN - - -	8339	11th Jan. 1840	Manufacture of china and earthenware; machinery applicable thereto.
RIDGWAY, JOHN - - -	8340	11th Jan. 1840	Preparing bats of earthenware and porcelain clays; forming them into articles; machinery applicable thereto.
RIDGWAY, JOHN - - -	11,912	21st Oct. 1847	Manufacture of paste-boxes and other similar articles, in china, earthenware, or other plastic materials.
RIDGWAY, JOHN - - -	14,080	20th April 1852	Ornamenting or decorating articles of glass, china, earthenware, and other ceramic manufactures.
RIDGWAY, JONATHAN - -	3322	6th April 1810	Preparing rollers and blocks used for calico-printing.
RIDGWAY, JONATHAN - -	3897	14th March 1815	Casting, and fixing at the same time, metallic types on the surfaces of cylinders or rollers, blocks or plates of metal or having metallic surfaces, for the purpose of printing patterns in cloth made of cotton or linen, or both.
RIDGWAY, JONATHAN - -	3902	4th April 1815	Rollers for printing cotton or linen cloth.
RIDGWAY, JONATHAN - -	3917	26th May 1815	Pumping water or other fluids.
RIDGWAY, WILLIAM - -	5278	1st Nov. 1825	Cock, tap, or valve, for drawing off liquors.
RIDGWAY WILLIAM - -	9450	18th Aug. 1842	Conveying and distributing heat in ovens used by manufacturers of china and earthenware, and brick, tile, and quarry makers.

Name of Patentee.	Progressive Number.	Date.	Subject-matter of Patent.
RIDLEY, HENRY STEPHEN -	13,575	24th March 1851	Safety-hinge, and apparatus for the detection of burglars and prevention of burglaries.
RIDLEY, RALPH ERINGTON -	13,962	9th Feb. 1852	Cutting and reaping machines.
RIDSDALE, JOHN - - -	9482	29th Sept. 1842	Preparing fibrous materials for weaving; sizing warps.
RIEPE, EWALD - - -	12,446	30th Jan. 1849	Manufacture of soap.
RIEPE, EWALD - - -	12,950	29th Jan. 1850	Manufacture of steel.
RIEPE, EWALD - - -	13,385	5th Dec. 1850	Refining steel.
RIGBY, CHARLES JOHN - -	9561	21st Dec. 1842	Manufacture of certain articles in which bristles have been or are used.
RIGBY, EDWARD ROBERT -	9561	21st Dec. 1842	Manufacture of certain articles in which bristles have been or are used.
RIGEL, ANTONIN PIEUX DE -	7445	14th Oct. 1837	Steam-engines.
RIGG, ROBERT - - -	5326	4th Feb. 1826	Condensing-apparatus used with or applied to apparatus for making vinegar.
RILEY, EDWARD - - -	5959	19th July 1830	Process and apparatus for fermenting malt and other liquors.
RILEY, ZACHARIAH - -	5727	10th Dec. 1828	Apparatus to be attached to carriages for the purpose of affording safety in travelling.
RIMINGTON, MICHAEL - -	11,066	31st Jan. 1846	Obtaining and applying motive-power.
RINGEISEN, GEORGE ALOIS -	12,811	12th Oct. 1849	Composition or preparation for destroying vermin.
RINGSTEAD, WILLIAM -	732	21st Dec. 1758	Making coaches, chariots, post-chaises, sedan-chairs, and other carriages, and covering them with copper, iron, or brass, instead of leather.
RIPLEY, HENRY WILLIAM -	13,360	19th Nov. 1850	Dressing and finishing piece-goods.
RIPLEY, THOMAS - - -	447	31st May 1722	Compound liquid metal, which by casting and running in moulds, is formed into statues, columns, and capitals; also house and garden ornaments, and other work, to substitute cut or sculptured work.
RIPPON, JOHN JAMES - -	8547	17th June 1840	Apparatus for heating apartments; apparatus for cooking.
RISHTON, HENRY - - -	13,204	31st July 1850	Water-closets and urinals.
RISTE, JOHN - - - -	5413	4th Oct. 1826	Machinery for making bobbin or twist net.
RITCHIE, ALEXANDER -	7116	13th June 1836	Dressing and finishing woollen-cloths and other woven fabrics.
RITCHIE, CHARLES - -	12,078	2nd March 1848	Locomotive and other engines.
RITCHIE, GEORGE - - -	8653	1st Oct. 1840	Manufacture of boas, muffs, cuffs, flounces, and tippets.
RITCHIE, WILLIAM HENRY -	10,334	27th Sept. 1844	Carding-engines.
RITCHIE, WILLIAM HENRY -	10,342	10th Oct. 1844	Obtaining copper from ores.
RITCHIE, WILLIAM HENRY -	12,648	7th June 1849	Fire-arms.
RITCHIE, WILLIAM HENRY -	13,054	23rd April 1850	Manufacture of copper, brass and other tubes and pipes.
RITCHIE, WILLIAM HENRY -	13,278	10th Oct. 1850	Machinery for preparing and carding fibrous substances.
RITCHIE, WILLIAM HENRY -	13,373	30th Nov. 1850	Stoves.
RITCHIE, WILLIAM HENRY -	13,762	2nd Oct. 1851	Ornamenting glass.
RITTER, WILLIAM - - -	9584	11th Jan. 1843	Crystallizing and purifying sugar.
RITTERBANDT, LOUIS ANTOINE	10,409	2nd Dec. 1844	Preventing and removing incrustation in steam-boilers and steam-generators.

Name of Patentee.	Progressive Number.	Date.	Subject-matter of Patent.
RITTERBANDT, LOUIS ANTOINE	10,672	17th May 1845	Application of heat to boilers for generating steam;—which improvements may be applied to other purposes where heat is required.
RIVIERE, ISAAC - - -	5175	20th May 1825	Construction, arrangement, and simplification of the machinery by which guns, pistols, and other fire-arms are discharged.
RIVIERE, MARC LA - -	5241	15th Aug. 1825	Machine for perforating metal plates of gold, silver, tin, platina, brass, or copper, and applicable as sieves.
RIVIERE, MARC LA - -	5300	28th Nov. 1825	Machinery to be applied to stamps, fly-presses, or other presses for perforating metal plates; applicable to other purposes.
RIVIERE, MARC LA - -	9271	1st March 1842	Machinery for figure-weaving in silk and other fabrics.
RIXON, FREDERICK - -	8093	8th June 1839	Apparatus for producing and distributing light.
RIZ, DANIEL - - - -	1372	17th May 1783	Machine applicable to water-closets, night-tables, or chairs.
RIZ, DAVID - - - -	957	28th April 1770	Lixivium or soap which will wash linen, cotton, woollen, or silk, as effectually as common soap with soft water; also stoves either portable or fixed, for warming rooms, churches, &c.
ROBARTS, GEORGE - - -	13,143	19th June 1850	Clogs and pattens.
ROBATHAN, THOMAS - -	1557	25th Aug. 1786	Bridle-bits, snaffles, and bradoons, for horses and other cattle.
ROBBINS, GEORGE - - -	13,073	7th May 1850	Construction of railway-carriages.
ROBBINS, JOSIAS - - -	2958	20th Aug. 1806	Boilers for manufacturing sugar; mode of fixing the same.
ROBER, CHARLES - - -	8245	19th Oct. 1839	Fixing colour in cloth.
ROBERT, SAMUEL - - -	3083	28th Nov. 1807	Toast-tray.
ROBERTON, JAMES - - -	2437	13th Aug. 1800	Applying steam in the working of steam-engines; constructing furnaces for applying fire to steam-engine boilers, and boilers of every description.
ROBERTON, JOHN - - -	2437	13th Aug. 1800	Applying steam in the working of steam-engines; constructing furnaces for applying fire to steam-engine boilers, and boilers of every description.
ROBERTS, ALEXANDER - -	88	1st Dec. 1635	Making white and red lead, with litharge or lead out of which the silver is first extracted.
ROBERTS, CHARLES - -	10,099	14th March 1844	Manufacture of boot and shoe trees, lasts, and stretchers.
ROBERTS, GEORGE - - -	524	7th Dec. 1730	Improving, graduating, and perfecting metals and their ores, by prepared salts, sulphur, and other ingredients.
ROBERTS, GEORGE - - -	9446	15th Aug. 1842	Construction of lamps.
ROBERTS, GEORGE - - -	10,842	2nd Oct. 1845	Construction of lamps for illumination.
ROBERTS, GEORGE - - -	13,551	10th March 1851	Manufacture of certain yarns of linen, wool, silk, cotton, or other fibrous substances.
ROBERTS, GEORGE - - -	14,215	8th July 1852	Manufacture of night-lights or mortars.
ROBERTS, HENRY - - -	12,896	15th Dec. 1849	Manufacture of bricks and tiles.
ROBERTS, JAMES - - -	2664	29th Nov. 1802	Machinery for dragging or locking the wheels of carriages, and for disengaging the horses therefrom.

Name of Patentee.	Progressive Number.	Date.		Subject-matter of Patent.
ROBERTS, JAMES - - -	2721	6th July	1803	Eradicating smut from wheat.
ROBERTS, JAMES - - -	8533	3rd June	1840	Fastening certain kinds of horn and hoof handles to the instruments requiring the same.
ROBERTS, JAMES - - -	8574	18th July	1840	Apparatus to be applied to the windows of houses or other buildings, for preventing accidents when such windows are being cleaned, also for facilitating the escape of persons from houses on fire.
ROBERTS, JOHN - - -	203	5th June	1678	Grinding, polishing, and diamonding glass plates, for looking-glasses, coaches and other uses, by the motion of water and persons from houses on wheels.
ROBERTS, JOHN - - -	3851	20th Feb.	1813	Concentrating or reducing such parts of malt and hops as are requisite in making ale, beer, and porter.
ROBERTS, JOHN, jun. - -	4334	15th Jan.	1819	Apparatus for preventing the overturning of stage-coaches and other wheeled carriages.
ROBERTS, JOHN - - -	5567	24th Nov.	1827	Argand and other lamps.
ROBERTS, JOHN - - -	7137	27th June	1836	Block-printing.
ROBERTS, JOHN - - -	7913	18th Dec.	1838	Machinery for planing or cutting metals.
ROBERTS, JOHN CRAFT - -	12,076	28th Feb.	1848	Mode of communicating intelligence on railways between the guards or passengers and the engine-driver, by means of electricity and magnetism, combined or not with steam; communicating signals by the same agency, describing the cause of alarm; also communicating intelligence between distant places on the line; mode of securing the passage of electricity for the above purposes.
ROBERTS, JOHN HENRY - -	10,788	29 July	1845	Spirit lamps.
ROBERTS, JOSEPH - -	3801	7th April	1814	Apparatus to be used for map-rollers, carriage-blinds, and other similar objects.
ROBERTS, JOSEPH LINCOLN -	7339	11th April 1837		Looms for weaving.
ROBERTS, JULIUS - - -	14,274	23rd Aug.	1852	Mariner's compass.
ROBERTS, MARTYN JOHN -	9127	26th Oct.	1841	Dyeing various matters, whether the raw material of wool, silk, flax, hemp, cotton, or other similar fibrous substances, or the same in any stage of manufacture; preparation of pigments or painters' colours.
ROBERTS, MARTYN JOHN -	9813	26th Jan.	1843	Dyeing wool and woollen fabrics.
ROBERTS, MARTYN JOHN -	9667	16th March 1843		Composition of ink, blacking, and black paint.
ROBERTS, MARTYN JOHN -	9754	1st June	1843	Machinery for preparing, spinning, and winding wool, cotton, flax, silk, or any other fibrous bodies.
ROBERTS, MARTYN JOHN -	10,498	28th Jan.	1845	Machinery for preparing and winding, and spinning and winding, wool, flax, and other fibrous bodies.
ROBERTS, MARTYN JOHN -	13,943	31st Jan.	1852	Agricultural instruments.
ROBERTS, MARTYN JOHN -	13,963	10th Feb.	1852	Galvanic-batteries; obtaining chemical products therefrom.
ROBERTS, MARTYN JOHN -	14,198	6th July	1852	Production of electric-currents; obtaining light, motion, and chemical products, by electricity;—partly applicable to the manufacture of acids, and the reduction of ores.

Name of Patentee.	Progressive Number.	Date.	Subject-matter of Patent.
ROBERTS, RICHARD - -	4726	14 Nov. 1822	Machinery applicable to the process of weaving plain or figured cloths or fabrics, and which may be applied to looms now in common use; construction of looms for such purpose; working looms either by hand, steam, or other power.
ROBERTS, RICHARD - -	5138	29th March 1825	Machinery used in spinning cotton-wool or other fibrous substances.
ROBERTS, RICHARD - -	5949	1st July 1830	Mechanism employed to render self-acting certain machines for roving, slubbing, or spinning cotton or other fibrous substances.
ROBERTS, RICHARD - -	6258	13th April 1832	Steam-engines; mechanism by means of which the elastic force of steam is made to give impulse to locomotive-carriages.
ROBERTS, RICHARD - -	6536	1st Jan. 1834	Machinery for grinding corn and other materials.
ROBERTS, RICHARD - -	6690	8th Oct. 1834	Machinery for spinning and doubling cotton, silk, flax, and other fibrous materials.
ROBERTS, RICHARDS - -	8012	26th March 1839	Machinery used in spinning cotton-wool or other fibrous substances.
ROBERTS, RICHARD -	10,150	18th April 1844	Machinery for the preparation of cotton and wool; also for spinning and doubling cotton, silk, wool, and other fibrous substances.
ROBERTS, RICHARD - -	11,607	5th March 1847	Machinery for punching and perforating metals.
ROBERTS, RICHARD - -	11,608	5th March 1847	Machinery to perform the processes of beetling, mangling, and the like.
ROBERTS, RICHARD - -	11,747	15th June 1847	Machinery for preparing and spinning cotton and other fibrous substances.
ROBERTS, RICHARD - -	12,207	11th July 1848	Clocks and other time-keepers; machinery for winding-up clocks, hoisting weights, and effecting telegraphic communications.
ROBERTS, RICHARD - -	12,948	29th Jan. 1850	Manufacture of certain textile fabrics; machinery for weaving plain, figured, and looped fabrics; and machinery for cutting velvets and other fabrics.
ROBERTS, RICHARD - -	13,779	17th Oct. 1851	Machinery for regulating and measuring the flow of fluids; also for pumping, forcing, agitating and evaporating fluids, and obtaining motive-power from fluids.
ROBERTS, RICHARD - -	14,130	22nd May 1852	Boats, ships, and other vessels.
ROBERTS, ROBERT - -	8723	25th Nov. 1840	Process for case-hardening iron.
ROBERTS, ROBERT - -	13,754	25th Sept. 1851	Quarrying certain substances.
ROBERTS, SAMUEL - -	1722	15th Jan. 1790	Making candlesticks of white metal plated with silver.
ROBERTS, SAMUEL - -	2210	23rd Jan. 1798	Working, adjusting, supporting, and fixing slide table-candlesticks of silver, silver plated, or other metal.
ROBERTS, SAMUEL - -	2263	30th Oct. 1798	Making nosles of candlesticks.
ROBERTS, SAMUEL - -	3083	28th Nov. 1807	Toast-tray.
ROBERTS, SAMUEL - -	3534	4th Feb. 1812	Working lavers or wash-basins of metal.
ROBERTS, SAMUEL - -	5057	18th Dec. 1824	Manufacture of plated goods of various descriptions.

Name of Patentee.	Progressive Number.	Date.	Subject-matter of Patent.
ROBERTS, SAMUEL　-　-	5963	26th July 1830	Plating or coating copper or brass, or mixture of the same with other metals or materials, with two metals or substances upon each other; making articles or utensils from the said metal when so plated, such as have hitherto been made of silver, or of copper, or brass, or of a mixture of copper and brass, plated or coated with silver only.
ROBERTS, THOMAS　-　-	6758	6th Feb. 1835	Joining pieces of timber end to end, applicable for making masts and topmasts of ships; also for making piles and for other purposes.
ROBERTS, THOMAS ALEXANDER	5156	23rd April 1825	Preserving potatoes and certain other vegetables.
ROBERTS, WILLIAM　-　-	1289	20th April 1781	Cutting and preparing prints or moulds of complete objects and designs; applying the same in printing or staining paper, linen, woollen, cotton, or silk.
ROBERTS, WILLIAM　-　-	1751	11th May 1790	Laying oil-colours in thin layers on canvas, wood, iron, stone, or any similar substance, to imitate marble, for chimney-pieces, pillars, or floor-cloths, and for other purposes.
ROBERTS, WILLIAM　-　-	12,985	28th Feb. 1850	Working windlass and other barrels.
ROBERTSON, ALEXANDER　-	13,561	20th March 1851	Rolling and laminating metals; manufacture of metallic cases and coverings.
ROBERTSON, ARCHIBALD　-	5749	7th Jan. 1829	Construction of paddles for propelling ships, boats, or vessels, on water.
ROBERTSON, JAMES　-　-	11,761	19th June 1847	Manufacture of casks and other wooden vessels; machinery for cutting wood for that and other purposes.
ROBERTSON, JAMES　-　-	12,225	29th July 1848	Manufacture of casks and other wooden vessels; machinery for cutting wood for those purposes.
ROBERTSON, JAMES　-　-	12,308	2nd Nov. 1848	Consuming smoke and other gaseous products arising from fuel and other substances.
ROBERTSON, JAMES　-　-	13,723	21st Aug. 1851	Producing printing-dyes and other substances used in printing;—applicable in part or wholly to other like useful purposes.
ROBERTSON, JOHN　-　-	5696	4th Sept. 1828	Manufacture of hempen rope or cordage.
ROBERTSON, JOHN　-　-	6475	21st Sept. 1833	Machines for spinning or roving cotton; machinery for spinning and roving silk, wool, flax, hemp, or other fibrous substances.
ROBERTSON, JOHN　-　-	7739	18th July 1838	Architecture in all its forms and combinations; also the superficial figures, which may be employed; surfaces of buildings.
ROBERTSON, JOHN　-　-	11,949	9th Nov. 1847	Architecture; elementary method of formation employed in the same;—also applicable for harmonizing formation, as of urns, or vases.
ROBERTSON, JOHN, junior　-	7516	19th Dec. 1837	Architecture as regards its construction, or in the description or properties of the forms and combinations, and of the superficial figures which may be employed in the application of these improvements, being also for supplying forms, figures, or patterns in various arts or manufactures; protecting from decay the interior and exterior surfaces of buildings, and giving them a more finished appearance.

Name of Patentee.	Progressive Number.	Date.	Subject-matter of Patent.
ROBERTSON, JOSEPH CLINTON	8227	27th Sept. 1839	Manufacturing artificial marble.
ROBERTSON, JOSEPH CLINTON	11,098	18th Feb. 1846	Nail-making machinery.
ROBERTSON, JOSEPH CLINTON	11,171	18th April 1846	Manufacture of pins.
ROBERTSON, JOSEPH CLINTON	11,237	4th June 1846	Railways and railway-carriages.
ROBERTSON, JOSEPH CLINTON	11,341	17th Aug. 1846	Constructing boats, ships, and vessels, of wood.
ROBERTSON, JOSEPH CLINTON	11,586	20th Feb. 1847	Distilling and brewing;—application of the materials used therein to other manufacturing purposes.
ROBERTSON, JOSEPH CLINTON	11,858	9th Sept. 1847	Manufacture of metals from their ores.
ROBERTSON, JOSEPH CLINTON	11,993	10th Dec. 1847	Preparation and application of colours for printing stuffs composed of silk, or wool, or a mixture of both.
ROBERTSON, JOSEPH CLINTON	12,034	19th Jan. 1848	Manufacture of textile fabrics, stuffs, and tissues, and of new products obtained by the aid of such improvements.
ROBERTSON, JOSEPH CLINTON	12,203	6th July 1848	Manufacture of gas for illumination; manufacture of the residual products into articles of commerce.
ROBERTSON, JOSEPH CLINTON	13,601	24th April 1851	Musical instruments.
ROBERTSON, MATTHEW	2984	30th Oct. 1806	Constructing and uniting cotton-spinning mule-jennies and stretching-frames, so that a greater number of them, containing any number of spindles, can be wrought at the same time by the same power and person.
ROBERTSON, WILLIAM	11,105	25th Feb. 1846	Machinery for spinning and twisting cotton, silk, wool, flax, and other fibrous substances.
ROBERTSON, WILLIAM	13,106	6th June 1850	Machinery used for spinning and doubling cotton and other fibrous substances.
ROBERTSON, WILLIAM ANGUS [Robertson, Angus.]	7363	6th May 1837	Machinery for sculpturing and otherwise figuring and working marble, stone, alabaster, and other substances suitable for sculpture, and for taking copies of the works produced thereby; process for taking casts of the human face, or other forms.
ROBERTSON, WILLIAM ANGUS	7437	28th Sept. 1837	Steam-engines.
ROBERTSON, WILLIAM ANGUS	7608	4th April 1838	Manufacture of hosiery, shawls, carpets, rugs, blankets, and other fabrics.
ROBIEN, LOUIS JOSEPH FRANCOIS JULIEN Count de.]	2071	22nd Oct. 1795	Economical fire-place.
ROBIN, PAUL	8213	9th Sept. 1839	Spinning.
ROBINSON, ALFRED	6278	22nd June 1832	Apparatus for heating, warming, and ventilating drying-houses, rooms, buildings, ships, and mines.
ROBINSON, ANN	839	6th Feb. 1766	Making silk mits, and silk gloves.
ROBINSON, BENJAMIN	497	9th May 1728	Preserving plank and sheathing of ships from the devastations of worms.
ROBINSON, CHARLES	12,021	13th Jan. 1848	Welded iron pipes or tubes, to be used as the flues of steam-boilers.
ROBINSON, CHARLES ROBERT	11,132	11th March 1846	Machinery for washing and cleansing cotton, linen, or woollen fabrics.
ROBINSON, CHARLES ROBERT	11,139	25th March 1846	Machinery for tiering in the printing of calicoes and other fabrics.

Name of Patentee.	Progressive Number.	Date.	Subject-matter of Patent.
ROBINSON, CHRISTOPHER -	6416	22nd May 1833	Machinery for transferring caloric from aëriform or fluid bodies, to other bodies of the like description;—applicable to other purposes.
ROBINSON, FREDERICK R. -	13,494	7th Feb. 1851	Sewing-machine.
ROBINSON, GEORGE AUGUSTUS	12,703	10th July 1849	Manufacture of bread; machinery and apparatus to be used therein; regulation of ovens and furnaces;—partly applicable to other similar purposes.
ROBINSON, HENRY MARTIN-[SON.	7010	18th Feb. 1836	Lamps.
ROBINSON, HENRY OLIVER -	10,345	10th Oct. 1844	Steam-machinery and apparatus for the manufacture and refining of sugar.
ROBINSON, JAMES - -	5234	11th Aug. 1825	Machinery for and process of raising the pile on woollen-cloths and other fabrics; pressing the same.
ROBINSON, JAMES - -	7709	27th June 1838	Producing by dyeing various figures, or objects of various colours, in woollen, worsted, cotton, silk, and other cloths.
ROBINSON, JAMES - -	8731	2nd Dec. 1840	Sugar-cane mills; apparatus for making sugar.
ROBINSON, JAMES - -	12,751	30th Aug. 1849	Manufacturing orchil and cudbear.
ROBINSON, JAMES HERRING -	1863	29th March 1792	Making alum.
ROBINSON, JOHN - - -	6292	3rd Aug. 1832	Windlasses, or machinery for winding up the cable. "Tysack, Dobinson & Co.'s Compound lever Windlass."
ROBINSON, JOHN - -	7312	23th Feb. 1837	Nipping-lever for causing the rotation of wheels, shafts, or cylinders.
ROBINSON, JOHN - -	8322	16th Dec. 1839	Steering-apparatus.
ROBINSON, JOHN - -	9338	3rd May 1842	Windlasses and capstans.
ROBINSON, JOHN - - -	12,683	4th July 1849	Machinery for moving and raising weights.
ROBINSON, JOHN - - -	13,324	7th Nov. 1850	Lifting and moving fluid and other bodies; apparatus for steering ships and other vessels.
ROBINSON, JOHN - -	14,101	29th April 1852	Machinery for shaping wood into mouldings and other forms.
ROBINSON, JOSEPH -	5579	4th Dec. 1827	Manufacturing brushes; manufacture and application of materials to the manufacture of brushes, and to other purposes.
ROBINSON, JOSEPH - -	9972	5th Dec. 1843	Construction and mode of working engines by the agency of air or gases, for obtaining motive-power.
ROBINSON, JOSEPH - -	13,801	4th Nov. 1851	Permanent-way of railways.
ROBINSON, MARMADUKE -	5975	5th Aug. 1830	Making and purifying sugars.
ROBINSON, MARMADUKE -	6144	27th July 1831	Making and purifying sugars.
ROBINSON, MATTHIAS ARCHI-[BALD.	4837	20th Aug. 1823	Preparing pearl barley and groats from the corns of barley and oats, for making a beverage.
ROBINSON, RICHARD - -	425	24th March 1720	Glazing and painting stone so as to endure the fire, for chimney corner-stones, hearths, and other uses.
ROBINSON, SAMUEL - -	4661	21st March 1822	Machine for shearing and cropping woollen-cloth.
ROBINSON, SOLOMON - -	5508	16th June 1827	Machinery for heckling or dressing and clearing hemp, flax, and tow.
ROBINSON, SOLOMON - -	9468	8th Sept. 1842	Machinery for dressing or heckling flax and hemp.

Name of Patentee.	Progressive Number.	Date.	Subject-matter of Patent.
ROBINSON, THOMAS - -	1267	21st Oct. 1780	Kitchen-range with an oven attached.
ROBINSON, THOMAS - -	3315	12th March 1810	Mashing-machine.
ROBINSON, THOMAS - -	7962	7th Feb. 1839	Rectifying or preparing spirituous liquors in the making of brandy.
ROBINSON, THOMAS - -	8797	19th Jan. 1841	Drying woollen and other fabrics.
ROBINSON, THOMAS - -	8936	27th April 1841	Drying wool, cotton, and other fibrous materials in the manufactured and unmanufactured state.
ROBINSON, THOMAS - -	10,144	16th April 1844	Machinery for heckling, dressing, combing, and cleaning flax, wool, silk, and other fibrous substances.
ROBINSON, THOMAS - -	12.044	27th Jan. 1848	Looms for weaving ribbons and other fabrics.
ROBINSON, THOMAS - -	12,434	23rd Jan. 1849	Machinery for breaking, scutching, cutting, heckling, dressing, combing, carding, and spinning flax, wool, hemp, tow, silk, and other fibrous substances.
ROBINSON, WILLIAM - -	2555	10th Nov. 1801	Making perukes and scalps.
ROBINSON, WILLIAM - -	4353	23rd March 1819	Apparatus to be attached to doors, door-jambs, and hanging-stiles, to keep air from rooms, apartments, or other places.
ROBINSON, WILLIAM - -	5393	24th July 1826	Propelling vessels by steam, on navigable rivers and canals, by moveable apparatus attached to the stern of the vessel.
ROBINSON, WILLIAM - -	13,448	11th Jan. 1851	Machinery for separating corn from straw.
ROBSON, CHRISTOPHER - -	11,457	21st Nov. 1846	Machinery for dressing fruit.
ROBSON, JAMES - - -	11,660	15th April 1847	Instrument for expressing oil from vegetable and other substances; making oil-cake.
ROBSON, JOHN WORDSWORTH	8676	2nd Nov. 1840	Waterclosets.
ROBSON, JOHN WORDSWORTH	9460	8th Sept. 1842	Machinery and apparatus for raising, forcing, conveying, and drawing off liquids.
ROBSON, THOMAS - -	7230	22nd Nov. 1836	Firing signal and other lights.
ROBSON, WILLIAM - - -	4731	10th Dec. 1822	Preventing fraudulent practices on bankers' cheques, bills of exchange and other commercial correspondence.
ROCHAZ, CHARLES ANDRE [FELIX.	12,001	22nd Dec. 1847	Treating zinc ores; manufacturing oxide of zinc.
ROCHAZ, CHARLES ANDRE [FELIX.	12,498	28th Feb. 1849	Manufacture of oxide of zinc; making paints and cements when oxyde of zinc is used.
ROCHE, JAMES - - -	2705	23rd May 1803	Medicine for the cure of the hooping-cough.
ROCHE, RANDOLPH ISCHIFFELI [DE.	3263	26th Sept. 1809	Brewing.
ROCHET, LOUIS THEODORE [MAILLARD.	10,573	20th March 1845	Construction of ovens;—applicable for economizing fuel in furnaces generally.
ROCHFORT, WALTER - -	3480	9th Sept. 1811	Preparing coffee.
ROCK, JAMES, junior -	13,328	9th Nov. 1850	Carriages;—applicable to other machines.
ROCK, JOSEPH, junior -	9578	29th Dec. 1842	Construction of locks.
ROCK, JOSEPH, junior -	9965	25th Nov. 1843	Locks and latches.
ROCK, RICHARD - -	665	17th Oct. 1751	Compound medicine or anti-venereal cathartic electuary.
ROCKE, WILLIAM - -	9458	3rd Sept. 1842	Manufacture of mineral colours.
ROCKE, WILLIAM - -	11,970	18th Nov. 1847	Treating and applying wrought-iron.
RODDA, RICHARD - -	7765	7th Aug. 1838	Furnaces, fire-places, and stoves, for the saving of fuel; applying them to the generation of steam, smelting metals, and other works.

Name of Patentee.	Progressive Number.	Date.	Subject-matter of Patent.
RODGER, WILLIAM - -	4420	4th Dec. 1819	Substitutes for anchors. "Block anchor."
RODGER, WILLIAM - -	5625	13th March 1828	Anchors.
RODGER, WILLIAM - -	5836	21st Aug. 1829	Construction of anchors.
RODGER, WILLIAM - -	5854	30th Sept. 1829	Construction of cat-head stoppers.
RODGER, WILLIAM - -	6455	26th July 1833	Anchors.
RODGER, WILLIAM - -	11,210	18th May 1846	Anchors.
RODGERS, GEORGE - -	5748	23rd Dec. 1828	Table-forks.
RODGERS, GEORGE - -	6062	18th Jan. 1831	Skates.
RODGERS, GEORGE - -	6407	4th April 1833	Buttons.
RODGERS, JOHN - -	6062	18th Jan. 1831	Skates.
RODGERS, JOHN HENRY -	8068	13th May 1839	Clasps or fastenings, and connecting-pieces, principally applicable to certain articles of dress.
RODGERS, JULIAN EDWARD [DISBROWE.	9586	12th Jan. 1843	Separation of sulphur from various mineral substances.
RODGERS, JULIAN EDWARD [DESBROWE.	12,724	1st Aug. 1849	Manufacture of white-lead.
RODHAM, CUTHBERT - -	9289	8th March 1842	Apparatus for purifying the smoke, gases, and other vapours arising from fires, stoves, and furnaces.
RODHAM, RICHARD - -	13,412	16th Dec. 1850	Apparatus for condensing and purifying the smoke, gases, and other vapours arising from fire-places, furnaces, or works; rendering the products available for the manufacture of colours.
RODWAY, HENRY BARRON -	9286	7th March 1842	Manufacture of horse-shoes.
ROE, FREEMAN - -	7398	7th July 1837	Water-closets.
ROE, FREEMAN - -	10,634	22nd April 1845	Manufacture of pipes for conveying water and other fluids.
ROE, RICHARD - -	7391	17th June 1837	Machinery for making bricks, tiles, and other articles made from earthy materials.
ROE, THOMAS - - -	9914	21st Oct. 1843	Machinery used for reading patterns, and stamping them in Jacquard-cards.
ROE, THOMAS - - -	10,716	10th June 1845	Manufacture of lace or net and other fabrics; machinery for ornamenting lace or net and other fabrics.
ROE, WILLIAM - -	1216	27th March 1779	Calcining or burning poor copper and lead ores.
ROEBUCK, JOHN - -	780	25th Oct. 1762	Making malleable iron from pig metal or sow metal.
ROEBUCK, JOHN - -	3044	14th May 1807	Machine called the "Caledonian Balance."
ROEDERER, CHARLES ADOLPHE	8025	9th April 1839	Manufacturing or preparing chemical salts called acetates.
ROEHN, AUGUSTUS - -	12,729	1st Aug. 1849	Making roads and ways; covering the floors of court-yards, buildings, and other similar places.
ROGERS, ABRAHAM - -	4007	23rd March 1816	Effecting a saving of fuel by a mode of setting and heating boilers of steam-engines and other bodies; heating stoves, drying-houses, manufactories, and other buildings; and also burning grapes.
ROGERS, GEORGE - -	9720	4th May 1843	Processes for coating metals.
ROGERS, GEORGE - -	10,222	8th June 1844	Coating iron with other metals.

Name of Patentee.	Progressive Number.	Date.	Subject-matter of Patent.
ROGERS, GEORGE - - -	10,859	9th Oct. 1845	Manufacture of iron into sheets, plates, and other forms; coating iron; preparing iron for coating and for other purposes.
ROGERS, GEORGE - - -	11,476	7th Dec. 1846	Manufacture of iron into sheets, plates, and other forms; coating iron; preparing iron for coating and for other purposes.
ROGERS, GEORGE - - -	13,401	12th Dec. 1850	Coating or covering metals.
ROGERS, GEORGE - - -	13,971	13th Feb. 1852	Manufacture, shaping, and coating of metals; and means of applying heat.
ROGERS, GEORGE - - -	14,040	24th March 1852	Shaping, coating, and applying sheet metal to building purposes.
ROGERS, JAMES - - -	4924	20th March 1824	Instruments for ascertaining the cubic contents of standing timber.
ROGERS, JASPER WHEELER -	12,169	1st June 1848	Methods and machinery for the preparation of peat as a fuel, and in combination, as a compost or manure.
ROGERS, JASPER WHEELER -	13,258	19th Sept. 1850	Preparation of peat, and manufacture of the same, into fuel and charcoal.
ROGERS, JOHN - - -	6860	10th July 1835	Paddle-wheels.
ROGERS, JOHN SWARBRECK -	3767	14th Dec. 1813	Spinning or making a species of wool into yarn, either by itself or with any other material.
ROGERS, ROBERT - - -	4831	18th Aug. 1823	Lanyard for the shrouds and other rigging of ships and other vessels; apparatus for setting up the same.
ROGERS, STEPHEN - - -	8218	16th Sept. 1839	Building the walls of houses and other edifices.
ROGERS, THOMAS - - -	470	24th Oct. 1724	Steel-worm or rolling-spring to be used in coaches, chariots, or other carriages.
ROGERS, THOMAS - - -	1568	7th Nov. 1786	Ornamenting chimney-pieces, looking-glasses, picture-frames and other kinds of furniture, with carved and moulded glass in relief, plain or coloured;—applicable to many other purposes.
ROGERS, THOMAS - - -	3618	28th Nov. 1812	Constructing wheels for carriages.
ROGERS, THOMAS - - -	3625	19th Dec. 1812	Applying manual powers to the crane, pile-driver, and other machinery.
ROGERS, THOMAS - - -	3747	1st Nov. 1813	Flour for bread, pastry and other purposes.
ROGERS, THOMAS - - -	4745	26th Dec. 1822	Apparatus for attaching trousers and gaiters to boots and shoes.
ROGERS, THOMAS - - -	4766	18th March 1823	Stays or bodices;—also applicable to boots.
ROGERSON, JOHN - - -	5268	21st Oct. 1825	Machinery for raising and dressing cloth.
ROGERSON, ROGER - - -	1269	5th Dec. 1780	Machine called a laundry, for washing and pressing linen and wearing-apparel.
ROHDE, MAJOR - - -	4447	15th April 1820	Extracting the molasses or syrup from muscovado or other sugar.
ROLFE, THOMAS HALL - -	5831	11th Aug. 1829	Self-acting pianofortes.
ROLFE, WILLIAM - - -	2160	31st Jan. 1797	Harpsichords, grand pianofortes, and square pianofortes.
ROLFFS, ERNEST - - -	14,022	11th March 1852	Printing, damping, stiffening, opening, and spreading woven-fabrics.
ROLINSON, SOLOMON - -	9673	20th March 1843	Manufacture of shot.
ROLLINSON, MARK - - -	11,201	7th May 1846	Steam-engines.

Name of Patentee.	Progressive Number.	Date.	Subject-matter of Patent.
ROLT, JOHN - - - -	9470	15th Sept. 1842	Saddles.
ROMAN, MARCEL - - -	6511	19th Nov. 1833	Apparatus employed in throwing or winding silk or other threads.
ROMBLEY, JOHN - - -	11,404	8th Oct. 1846	Capstans and windlasses.
RONALD, JOHN - - -	10,418	5th Dec. 1844	Apparatus for boiling sugar-cane juice, and other liquids.
RONALDS, FRANCIS -	5132	23rd March 1825	Tracing-apparatus, to facilitate the drawing from nature.
RONALDS, HUGH - -	4205	23rd Jan. 1818	Making leather.
RONDONI, JEAN - -	3876	20th Jan. 1815	Construction of dioptric telescopes.
ROOF, WILLIAM BROWN -	12,273	21st Sept. 1848	Construction of respirators.
ROOKS, RICHARD - -	76	18th Dec. 1634	Making and using engines for raising water out of mines and other places.
ROOSE, JAMES - - -	9723	9th May 1843	Manufacturing welded iron-tubes.
ROOSE, JAMES - - -	9947	18th Nov. 1843	Manufacturing gun-barrels and ordnance.
ROOSE, JAMES - - -	11,360	29th Aug. 1846	Manufacture of welded iron-tubes.
ROOSE, JAMES - - -	12,189	15th June 1848	Manufacture of tubing.
ROOTSEY, SAMUEL - -	11,432	3rd Nov. 1846	Supplying and purifying water.
ROPER, CHARLES ROBERT -	10,630	22nd April 1845	Manufacture of gelatine.
ROSE, AARON - - -	13,299	24th Oct. 1850	Manufacturing twisted gun and pistol barrels.
ROSE, ADOLPHE EUGENE Count [DE.	5398	1st Aug. 1826	Engine for communicating power, to answer the purposes of a steam-engine.
ROSE, ALEXANDER FERRIER -	12,715	24th July 1849	Process of printing; machinery employed therein.
ROSE, EDWIN - - -	10,502	28th Jan. 1845	Manufacture of grain into flour or meal.
ROSE, EDWIN - - -	13,615	3rd May 1851	Boilers for generating steam.
ROSE, JOHN - - - -	1621	17th Sept. 1787	Preparing steel, and ornamenting the same in the several articles of steel buttons, buckles, sword-hilts, toys, and other steel work.
ROSE, JOHN - - - -	3423	26th March 1811	Conveying vessels of any burden through the water, without the help of oars or sails.
ROSE, JOHN MITCHELL - -	6338	27th Nov. 1832	Construction of flutes.
ROSE, JOHN MITCHELL - -	11,853	6th Sept. 1847	Flutes, clarionets, and other similar wind-instruments.
ROSELEUR, ALFRED GUILL-[AUME.	13,020	23rd March 1850	Coating or covering metals with tin.
ROSENBORG, FREDERICK -	7572	22nd Feb. 1838	Machinery for shearing, cropping, dressing, and finishing woollen and other cloths.
ROSENBORG, FREDERICK -	8726	27th Nov. 1840	Arranging and setting up types for printing.
ROSENBORG, FREDERICK -	9300	21st March 1842	Arranging and setting up types for printing.
ROSENBORG, FREDERICK -	10,610	15th April 1845	Machinery for cutting and shaping wood and other materials into various forms; cleaning the surfaces of such forms or figures.
ROSENBORG, FREDERICK -	10,721	12th June 1845	Construction of machinery for propelling vessels; steering vessels.
ROSENBORG, FREDERICK -	10,844	2nd Oct. 1845	Apparatus for watering, manuring, and drying trees, plants, seeds, and roots, and for accelerating their growth.
ROSENBORG, FREDERICK -	13,000	7th March 1850	Sawing, cutting, boring, and shaping wood.
ROSENBORG, FREDERICK -	13,687	5th July 1851	Manufacture of casks, barrels, and other like articles; machinery employed therein.

Name of Patentee.	Progres-sive Number.	Date.	Subject-matter of Patent.
Ross, Alexander - -	2665	29th Nov. 1802	Perukes or wigs.
Ross, Daniel - - -	11,059	27th Jan. 1846	Manufacture of hats.
Ross, Henry - - -	7362	6th May 1837	Combing wool and goat's-hair.
Ross, Henry - - -	7740	18th July 1838	Machinery for combing and drawing wool and certain descriptions of hair.
Ross, Henry - - -	9121	15th Oct. 1841	Combing and drawing wool and certain descriptions of hair.
Ross, Henry - - -	9636	17th Feb. 1843	Combing and drawing wool and other fibrous substances.
Ross, James Moore - -	5760	19th Jan. 1829	Tap or cock for drawing off liquids.
Ross, Jesse - - -	5098	19th Feb. 1825	Apparatus for combing and straightening wool, cotton, and other like fibrous substances.
Ross, Jesse - - -	9142	9th Nov. 1841	Wool-combing apparatus.
Ross, Jesse - - -	12,211	11th July 1848	Apparatus for dibbling and for other agricultural purposes ;—partly applicable to propelling vessels.
Ross, Jesse - - -	13,553	13th March 1851	Machinery and apparatus for combing wool and other fibrous substances; applying or working the same.
Ross, John - - -	7395	19th June 1837	Manufacturing letters, figures, and other devices having a flat surface, presenting, by the aid of colours, the appearance of projection, and made in metals, wood, or other substances and materials; also domed letters, figures, and other devices made from the same materials, without seam or joint.
Ross, John - - -	10,463	11th Jan. 1845	Machinery for platting or braiding straw, grass, and other materials, for making tuscan or leghorn hats and bonnets.
Ross, Thomas - - -	9916	27th Oct. 1843	Machinery for manufacturing elastic braid.
Ross, Thomas - - -	13,047	18th April 1850	Machinery for raising the pile upon woven and felted fabrics.
Ross, William - - -	1195	24th June 1778	Machine for making net-work with knotted meshes, in silk, thread, cotton, worsted, or other similar materials.
Rosse, James - - -	88	1st Dec. 1635	Making white and red lead, with litharge or lead out of which the silver is first extracted.
Rosse, Michael - - -	294	24th March 1692	Invention, whereby one or more men may continue and work under water for a quarter of an hour with freedom and clearness of sight, and, with the assistance of others that can swim, may recover and take up any bullion, plate, &c. without diving.
Rosser, Archibald Richard [Francis.	7413	2nd Aug. 1837	Preparing manure ; cultivation of land.
Rostill, William - -	4444	11th April 1820	Making hafts, handles, or hilts for knives, forks, swords, or any other instruments to which hafts, handles, or hilts are necessary.
Rostron, John - - -	8055	30th April 1839	Construction of looms for weaving.
Rostron, John - - -	8933	22nd April 1841	Looms for weaving.
Rotch, Benjamin - -	4025	11th May 1816	Flexible elastic horse-shoe.
Rotch, Benjamin - -	4839	21st Aug. 1823	Fid for the upper masts of ships and other vessels.

Name of Patentee.	Progressive Number.	Date.	Subject-matter of Patent.
ROTCH, BENJAMIN - -	5474	22nd March 1827	Diagonal prop for transferring perpendicular to lateral pressure.
ROTCH, BENJAMIN - -	5922	20th March 1830	Guards or protections for horses' feet and legs.
ROTCH, BENJAMIN - -	13,231	22nd Aug. 1850	Factitious saltpetre; obtaining the same.
ROTCH, THOMAS DICKASON -	13,023	26th March 1850	Separating matters usually found combined in certain saccharine, saline, and ligneous substances.
ROTCH, THOMAS DICKASON -	13,197	31st July 1850	Manufacture of soap.
ROTCH, THOMAS DICKASON -	13,517	18th Feb. 1851	Centrifugal apparatus for separating fluid from other matters.
ROTHSCHILD, ANTHONY NA- [THAN DE.	11,182	28th April 1846	Heating apartments and buildings.
ROTHWELL, JOHN - - -	1512	19th Nov. 1785	Construction and principle of valve water-cocks.
ROTHWELL, JOHN - - -	5318	16th Jan. 1826	Healds or harness for weaving purposes.
ROTHWELL, JOHN - -	9509	5th Nov. 1842	Composition and preparation to promote the ignition and combustion of fuel in stoves, furnaces, and grates.
ROTISPEN, ARNOLD - - [Rotsipen, Arnold.]	44	13th July 1628	Making gowns.
ROTISPEN, ARNOLD -	71	24th June 1634	Making twenty-one several engines and instruments, for His Majesty's particular service.
ROTTON, OTTO - - -	9328	26th April 1842	Machinery for spinning cotton-wool, silk, and other fibrous substances.
ROUND, GEORGE - - -	7712	30th June 1838	Manufacture of certain parts of gun and pistol locks.
ROUQUETTE, HENRY PHILIP -	8451	25th March 1840	Pigment.
ROUS, THOMAS - - -	35	24th Oct. 1626	Making stone pots, stone jugs, and stone bottles.
ROUSE, WILLIAM - -	10,072	24th Feb. 1844	Carriages and parts of carriages, applicable to various purposes.
ROUSSEAU, ALEXANDER - -	9258	15th Feb. 1842	Fire-arms.
ROUTLEDGE, JOSHUA - -	4232	27th Feb. 1818	Rotative steam-engine.
ROUTLEDGE, THOMAS - -	7259	19th Dec. 1836	Cabriolets and omnibuses
ROUX, ALBERT - - -	4275	30th June 1818	Locks.
ROW, WILLIAM - - -	2250	14th July 1798	Mineral lamp-black.
ROWAN, WILLIAM - - -	9928	7th Nov. 1843	Axles.
ROWBOTHAM, HENRY - -	8812	26th Jan. 1841	Thickening and preparing colours for printing calicoes and other substances.
ROWBOTHAM, JAMES - -	4900	19th Feb. 1824	Hats.
ROWBOTHAM, JAMES - -	5347	18th April 1826	Preparing, combing, or putting together certain materials for making hats, caps, bonnets, cloaks, coats, &c., for wearing-apparel in general, also for other purposes.
ROWE, ISAAC - - - -	537	21st Aug. 1732	Extracting a spirit from blackberries, equal to French brandy.
ROWE, ISAAC - - -	620	21st March 1747	Machine with pumps, without box or sucker, for drawing water from great depths, and for other purposes.
ROWE, JACOB - - - -	431	20th Oct. 1720	Instrument for taking altitudes at sea; machine for diving.

Name of Patentee.	Progres-sive Number.	Date.	Subject-matter of Patent.
ROWE, JACOB - - - -	485	21st July 1726	Pumping water without the least friction, and without the suckers touching the sides of the pump, thus reducing the power now requisite in raising water, all which is effected by means of a power derived from a screw contrived suddenly to fly up and down, whereby several pumps may be worked at the same time; also a method of exhausting air out of vessels, or making a vacuum, and thereby causing a sudden rise of water.
ROWE, JACOB - - - -	486	21st July 1726	Engine for raising water; saving fuel in heating vessels containing water.
ROWE, JACOB - - - -	543	1st Feb. 1734	Cancelling the friction of the wheel, pully, balance, and pendulum, in land carriages drawn on wheels, by which engines will be worked with much less power; additional contrivance, causing the same power to act more swiftly, and to lift greater weight.
ROWE, JOHN - - - -	715	27th May 1757	Mill for grinding mineral ores.
ROWE, JOHN WESTAWAY -	1749	29th April 1790	Engine to be worked by the power of steam.
ROWE, JOSHUA - - -	4252	4th May 1818	Processes applicable to the printing of cotton and other cloths, and to other purposes.
ROWE, LAWRENCE - - -	8033	16th April 1839	Manufacture of sulphate of soda.
ROWE, WILLIAM - - -	12,405	11th Jan. 1849	Uniting pipes, tubes, or channels, formed of glass, earthenware, or other similar materials.
ROWLAND, DAVID - - -	6528	20th Dec. 1833	Manufacture of sextants, quadrants, circles, and other instruments used in taking observations and surveys.
ROWLAND, EDWARD - -	1981	18th March 1794	Machinery for forming and constructing navigable canals.
ROWLAND, JAMES - - -	5830	11th Aug. 1829	Constructing streets, ways, carriage-roads, and highways in general.
ROWLAND, RICHARD - -	3525	23rd Jan. 1812	Ships' steering-wheel, compasses, and binnacles; lighting the same with lamp or candle; preserving the candles in hot climates.
ROWLANDSON, THOMAS - -	12,497	28th Feb. 1849	Treatment of certain mineral waters, to obtain products therefrom; obtaining metals from certain compounds containing those metals; also obtaining other products by the use of certain compounds containing metals.
ROWLEY, CHARLES - -	8354	21st Jan. 1840	Cutting out, stamping, and piercing buttons, shells, and backs for buttons, washers, or other articles, from metal plate; machinery and tools for the purpose.
ROWLEY, CHARLES - -	9058	27th Aug. 1841	Manufacture of buttons and fastenings for wearing-apparel.
ROWLEY, CHARLES - -	9519	15th Nov. 1842	Manufacture of perforated metal buttons.
ROWLEY, CHARLES - -	11,088	11th Feb. 1846	Buttons and other fastenings for wearing-apparel; machinery for the manufacture of parts of the said fastenings.
ROWLEY, CHARLES - -	12,257	28th Aug. 1848	Manufacture of buttons.

Name of Patentee.	Progres-sive Number.	Date.	Subject-matter of Patent.
ROWLEY, CHARLES - -	12,796	12th Oct. 1849	Apparatus for weaving ; articles to be attached to dresses.
ROWLEY, CHARLES - -	13,371	30th Nov. 1850	Manufacture of dress-pins and other dress fastenings and ornaments.
ROWLEY, EDMUND BUTLER -	7513	19th Dec. 1837	Locomotive-engines, tenders, and carriages, to be used on railways ;—applicable to other purposes.
ROWLEY, EDMUND BUTLER -	8015	26th March 1839	Steam-engines applicable to locomotive, marine, and stationary purposes.
ROWLEY, GEORGE WILLIAM -	11,665	20th April 1847	Construction of carriages ; apparatus to be used with omnibuses and other carriages.
ROWLEY, JAMES - - -	1012	7th April 1772	Making playing-cards, printed from engravings on copper, in oil-colours, with a peculiar ink capable of receiving a polish.
ROWNING, JOHN - - -	535	11th Jan. 1732	Clock which with one set of wheels strikes the hours and quarters, or the past hours with each quarter.
ROWNTREE, THOMAS - -	1714	8th Dec. 1789	Construction of waterclosets ;—applicable to other purposes.
ROWNTREE, THOMAS - -	1730	23rd Feb. 1790	Construction of locks and other fastenings.
ROWNTREE, THOMAS - -	2231	1st May 1798	Applying fire for heating boilers and other vessels ;—applicable to other purposes.
ROWNTREE, THOMAS - -	2754	23rd March 1804	Machine for agitating and separating certain mixtures.
ROWNTREE, THOMAS - -	2841	25th April 1805	Axletree and box for carriages.
ROXBY, ROBERT BENTON -	4695	31st July 1822	Quadrants.
ROYAL, GEORGE - - -	6097	21st March 1831	Making iron pipes, tubes, or cylinders.
ROYCE, GEORGE - - -	12,086	8th March 1848	Machinery for depositing, cleansing, and grinding corn and seed.
ROYCE, GEORGE - - -	13,405	12th Dec. 1850	Grinding, dressing, and cleaning corn and seed.
ROYDS, JOHN - - -	1564	18th Oct. 1786	Machines for roving, slubbing, and spinning woollen, worsted, and linen yarn.
ROYLANCE, JOSEPH - -	1438	19th June 1784	Machine for raising ships and other vessels sunk in deep waters.
ROYLE, GEORGE - - -	10,621	17th April 1845	Locomotive, marine, steam, gas, and other tubes.
ROYLE, VERNON - - -	5276	1st Nov. 1825	Machinery for clearing and spinning silk.
ROYSTON, JAMES - - -	2987	6th Nov. 1806	System of card-making for carding wool and tow, by a method of cutting teeth for the purpose.
RUBERY, JOHN JEREMIAH -	7053	7th April 1836	Manufacturing umbrella and parasol stretchers.
RUBERY, JOHN JEREMIAH -	7475	14th Nov. 1837	Manufacture of umbrella furniture.
RUBERY, JOHN JEREMIAH -	9223	13th Jan. 1842	Manufacture of a certain part of umbrella and parasol furniture.
RUBERY, JOHN JEREMIAH -	10,415	2nd Dec. 1844	Manufacture of umbrellas and parasols.
RUDALL, GEORGE - - -	6338	27th Nov. 1832	Construction of flutes.
RUDDER, ENOCH WILLIAM -	5904	27th Feb. 1830	Cocks for drawing off liquids.
RUDDER, WILLIAM - -	2088	16th Feb. 1796	Making cocks for drawing ale and other fluids from barrels and all kinds of vessels, so as to prevent leakage by the application of collars of leather or cork to the plug.

Name of Patentee.	Progressive Number.	Date.	Subject-matter of Patent.
RUDDER, WILLIAM - -	3500	30th Oct 1811	Construction of cocks for drawing off ale, porter, beer, cyder, wine, water and other liquids and fluids.
RUDDER, WILLIAM -	5083	18th Jan. 1825	Cocks for drawing off liquids.
RUDDER, WILLIAM - -	5980	10th Aug. 1830	Apparatus to be affixed to saddles and girths.
RUDGE, EDMUND, junior -	8381	8th Feb. 1840	Obtaining power for locomotive and other purposes; and applying the same.
RUDSON, JOHN - - -	46	13th April 1629	Making white and bay salt of sea-water, sea-sand, and other materials.
RUE, THOMAS DE LA - -	6231	23rd Feb. 1832	Manufacturing and ornamenting playing-cards.
RUE, THOMAS DE LA -	6663	15th Aug. 1834	Manufacturing or preparing embossed paper-hangings.
RUE, THOMAS DE LA -	8549	20th June 1840	Printing calicoes and other surfaces.
RUE, THOMAS DE LA -	12,243	15th Aug. 1848	Producing ornamental surfaces on paper and other substances.
RUE, WARREN DE LA - -	10,436	12th Dec. 1844	Covering the surfaces of paper and other materials with colour and other substances
RUE, WARREN DE LA - -	10,565	17th March 1845	Manufacture of envelopes.
RUE, WARREN DE LA -	12,084	8th March 1848	Machinery used in the manufacture of cardboard and pasteboard.
RUE, WARREN DE LA -	12,904	19th Dec. 1849	Manufacturing envelopes.
RUFFORD, FRANCIS TONGUE -	12,866	28th Nov. 1849	Manufacture of baths and wash-tubs or wash-vessels.
RUMSEY, JAMES - - -	1673	6th Nov. 1788	Constructing boilers for distillation and for other objects, also for steam-engines.
RUMSEY, JAMES - - -	1738	24th March 1790	Applying the power of water, air, and steam, for milling and giving motion to machines, and for advantageous management of shipping and vessels of all kinds used on water.
RUMSEY, JAMES - - -	1825	25th Aug. 1791	Applying the power of steam and of water for milling and giving motion to machines.
RUMSEY, JAMES - - -	1903	24th July 1792	Raising water and other fluids, or applying their force to milling or moving machinery.
RUNSOME, FREDERICK - -	10,665	10th May 1845	Combining small coal and other matters; preserving wood.
RUPERT, His Highness Prince -	161	1st Dec. 1670	Converting into steel, tools, files, and other instruments forged in soft iron, also iron wire; softening cast-iron, and tincturing copper upon iron.
RUPERT, His Highness Prince -	162	8th Jan. 1671	Authority to take security from, and to administer an oath to workmen, not to divulge the preceding patent (see 161).
RUSH, HENRY SAMUEL - -	9579	29th Dec. 1842	Apparatus for containing matches used for obtaining instantaneous light.
RUSHER, PHILIP - - -	2620	20th May 1802	Printing-types.
RUSHTON, THOMAS LEVER -	10,233	21st June 1844	Manufacture of iron.
RUSSEL, JOHN - - -	11,023	30th Dec. 1845	Manufacture of glass-tiles.
RUSSELL, HENRY HEATHCOTE	10,983	6th Dec. 1845	Constructing suspension bridges and viaducts.
RUSSELL, JAMES - -	4892	19th Jan. 1824	Manufacture of tubes for gas, and for other purposes.

Name of Patentee.	Progressive Number.	Date.	Subject-matter of Patent.
RUSSELL, JAMES - - -	7982	26th Feb. 1839	Manufacturing tubes for gas, and for other purposes. (C. Whitehouse's extension for six years from 26th February 1839.)
RUSSELL, JOHN - - -	2144	5th Nov. 1796	Apparatus to exhibit the phenomena of the moon. "Selenographia."
RUSSELL, JOHN JAMES - -	10,272	24th July 1844	Manufacture of welded iron tubes.
RUSSELL, JOHN JAMES - -	12,970	21st Feb. 1850	Obtaining cadmium and other metals and products from ores or matters containing them.
RUSSELL, JOHN JAMES - -	14,133	22nd May 1852	Coating metal-tubes.
RUSSELL, JOHN SCOTT -	6462	14th Aug. 1833	Construction of vessels for sustaining the pressure of fluids; boilers and machinery of steam-engines; application of the same to locomotive purposes.
RUSSELL, JOHN SCOTT -	13,276	10th Oct. 1850	Construction of ships or vessels propelled by paddle-wheels, with a view to better arming the same.
RUSSELL, RICHARD - -	744	17th Jan. 1760	Making pots and building furnaces for the making of crown-glass, plate-glass, and all sorts of green glass.
RUSSELL, RICHARD, senior -	929	9th June 1769	Making furnaces for making glass without the use of pots.
RUSSELL, RICHARD, junior -	929	9th June 1769	Making furnaces for making glass without the use of pots.
RUSSELL, THOMAS - - -	10,454	6th Jan. 1845	Flax-spinning and machinery for the same;— applicable to the manufacture of other fibrous substances.
RUSSELL, THOMAS HENRY -	7081	3rd May 1836	Manufacturing welded iron tubes.
RUSSELL, THOMAS HENRY -	9287	7th March 1842	Manufacture of welded iron-tubing.
RUSSELL, THOMAS HENRY -	10,272	24th July 1844	Manufacture of welded iron tubes.
RUSSELL, THOMAS HENRY -	10,816	14th Aug. 1845	Manufacture of welded iron tubes.
RUSSELL, THOMAS HENRY -	12,526	19th March 1849	Coating iron and certain other metals, and alloys of metals.
RUSSELL, THOMAS HENRY -	12,970	21st Feb. 1850	Obtaining cadmium and other metals and products from ores or matters containing them.
RUSSELL, WILLIAM - -	4083	19th Nov. 1816	Cocks and vents for brewers, distillers, private families, &c.
RUSSELL, WILLIAM - -	12,047	29th Jan. 1848	Preparation of bar-iron used in the manufacture of certain kinds of rod-iron.
RUTHERFORD, WILLIAM -	6105	14th April 1831	Combination of apparatus used or applied to locks and other fastenings.
RUTHVEN, JOHN - - -	3746	1st Nov. 1813	Press for printing from types, blocks, or other surfaces.
RUTHVEN, JOHN - - -	4322	23rd Dec. 1818	Drag for coaches, carriages, or other vehicles.
RUTHVEN, JOHN - - -	4656	2nd March 1822	Procuring a mechanical power.
RUTHVEN, JOHN - - -	5965	5th Aug. 1830	Machinery for navigating vessels, and propelling carriages.
RUTHVEN, JOHN - - -	6822	28th April 1835	Cutting wood by certain improved instruments.
RUTHVEN, JOHN - - -	7209	13th Oct. 1836	Formation of rails or rods for making railways; method of fixing or joining them.
RUTHVEN, JOHN - - -	8006	20th March 1839	Boilers for generating steam, economizing fuel, and propelling vessels by steam; ventilating vessels;—applicable to mines and buildings.

Name of Patentee.	Progressive Number.	Date.	Subject-matter of Patent.
RUTHVEN, JOHN - - -	12,569	16th April 1849	Preserving lives and property from water and fire; producing pressure for various purposes.
RUTHVEN, JOHN - - -	12,739	10th Aug. 1849	Propelling and navigating ships, vessels, or boats, by steam and other powers.
RUTHVEN, MORRIS WEST -	8006	20th March 1839	Boilers for generating steam, economizing fuel, and propelling vessels by steam; ventilating vessels;—applicable to mines and buildings.
RUTHVEN, MORRIS WEST -	8896	22nd March 1841	Increasing the power of certain media when acted upon by rotary fans or similar apparatus.
RUTT, JOHN TOWILL - -	3278	21st Nov. 1809	Construction of machines for making cards for carding wool, cotton, flax, silk, and other substances.
RUTT, JOHN TOWILL - -	3388	8th Oct. 1810	Apparatus to be used with machines for making fillet, sheet, and hard cards, for carding wool, flax, silk, and other substances.
RUTT, WILLIAM - - -	4375	24th May 1819	Printing-machines.
RUTTER, JOHN OBADIAH NEW- [ALL.	6404	30th March 1833	Process for generating heat, applicable to heating of boilers and retorts, and to other purposes.
RUTTER, JOHN OBADIAH NEW- [ALL.	11,762	22nd June 1847	Apparatus for conveying intelligence.
RUXTON, THOMAS - - -	4027	14th May 1816	Lock for fastening doors, gates, drawers, desks, trunks, boxes, portmanteaus, and other things.
RUZÉ, LOUIS VICTOR - -	14,132	22nd May 1852	Manufacture of hat plush, and other similar silk cloths.
RYALLS, THOMAS - - -	4934	8th April 1824	Apparatus for shaving. " Useful and elegant facilitator."
RYAN, JAMES - - - -	2822	12th Feb. 1805	Apparatus for boring the earth for coal or other substances;—applicable to sinking wells, giving vent to water in bogs, draining mines and grounds, ventilating pits, and to other purposes.
RYAN, JOHN - - - -	729	16th Aug. 1758	Safe, expeditious, and effectual cure of the venereal disease.
RYAN, JOHN - - - -	779	20th Aug. 1762	Medicine called " Dr. Ryan's White drops."
RYAN, JOHN - - - -	10,419	7th Dec. 1844	Construction of casks, barrels, or other vessels for containing wine, beer, and fermented or other liquids liable to fermentation or decomposition from exposure to the atmosphere.
RYAN, JOHN - - - -	11,420	17th Oct. 1846	Preservation of organic and other substances.
RYDER, SAMUEL - - -	5157	28th April 1825	Apparatus for affixing the pole to carriages.
RYDER, WILLIAM - - -	8835	8th Feb. 1841	Apparatus for forging, drawing, moulding, or forming spindles, rollers, bolts, and various other like articles, in metal.
RYDER, WILLIAM - - -	11,489	14th Dec. 1846	Apparatus employed in the manufacture of rollers used in machinery for preparing and spinning cotton and other fibrous substances.
RYLAND, THOMAS - - -	3635	15th Jan. 1813	Fender for fire-places.
RYLAND, THOMAS HENRY -	8005	18th March 1839	Manufacture of screws for wood, in iron, brass, copper, or mixed metal. " Wood screws."

Name of Patentee.	Progressive Number.	Date.	Subject-matter of Patent.
RYLES, AARON - - -	9141	9th Nov. 1841	Operating in certain processes for ornamenting glass.
RYLEY, EDWARD - - -	2562	28th Nov. 1801	Moveable keys for pianofortes, organs, and other instruments.
RYLEY, THOMAS - - -	531	1st June 1731	Compounds of sundry wholesome ingredients for feeding swine.
RYMER, JAMES - - -	1900	24th July 1792	Medicine, or cardiac and nervous tincture, for the relief and cure of disorders of the head, stomach, and bowels, the symptoms of the atonic gout, affections of the nervous system, relaxation and debility of the muscular and vascular systems, and the cure and prevention of infection from fevers prevailing in prisons, hospitals, ships, hot and unhealthy climates, and in other places.
RYMER, JAMES MALCOLM -	8485	23rd April 1840	Castors for furniture;—applicable to other purposes.

S.

Name of Patentee.	Progressive Number.	Date.	Subject-matter of Patent.
SABART, ANTHONY - -	52	— Sept. 1630	Making white and bay salt with sea-water and brine, and without pans or furnaces.
SABATIER, WILLIAM - -	2125	4th July 1796	Retaining cotton, tobacco, hemp, flax, hops, hay and other articles in nearly the same compass into which they can be compressed by machinery, without being liable to any material expansion after they are removed from such machinery.
SABBERTON, JAMES -	8452	26th March 1840	Fastening, to attach straps to the bottoms of trousers.
SADLER, JAMES - -	1812	10th June 1791	Engine for lessening the consumption of steam and fuel in steam or fire-engines.
SADLER, JOHN - -	4524	3rd Jan. 1821	Manufacturing white-lead.
SADLER, JOHN HARVEY -	5177	31st May 1825	Power-loom, for weaving silk, cotton, linen, wool, flax, and hemp, and mixtures thereof.
SADLER, JOHN HARVEY -	5581	13th Dec. 1827	Power-looms, for weaving silk, cotton, linen, wool, flax, and hemp, and all mixtures thereof.
SADLER, JOHN HARVEY -	5951	1st July 1830	Looms.
SADLER, JOHN HARVEY -	11,788	7th July 1847	Constructing bridges, aqueducts, and similar structures.
SAGE, SAMUEL - -	622	12th May 1747	Machine for cutting tobacco.
SAGER, WILLIAM - - -	12,269	15th Sept. 1848	Means and apparatus for effecting the conveyance of goods, passengers and correspondence, by land or water, and for other purposes.
SAILLANT, ALEXANDER JULES, [junior.	14,120	8th May 1852	Manufacture of articles of dress.
SAINT, THOMAS - - -	1761	17th July 1790	Composition of the nature of japan or varnish.

Name of Patentee.	Progressive Number.	Date.		Subject-matter of Patent.
SAINT, THOMAS - - -	1764	17th July	1790	Making and completing shoes, boots, spatter-dashes, clogs, and other articles, by means of tools or machines for the purpose.
SAINT, THOMAS - - -	2670	21st Dec.	1802	Increasing the effect of steam-engines, and saving fuel in the working thereof.
ST. CHARLES, PHILLIPPE [POIRIER DE.	10,746	1st July	1845	Production of type for printing, and machinery employed for the same.
ST. CLAIR, BOWER - - -	10,740	26th June	1845	Manufacture of sugar.
ST. GEORGE, OLIVER - -	6171	28th Sept.	1831	Machinery for acquiring power in tides or currents.
ST. JOHN, JOHN RANSOME -	13,429	27th Dec.	1850	Construction of compasses; apparatus for ascertaining and registering the velocity of ships or vessels moving through the water.
ST. JOHN, JOHN RANSOME -	13,469	21st Jan.	1851	Manufacturing soap, and apparatus for the purpose.
ST. LEGER MAURICE - -	4262	19th May	1818	Making lime.
ST. MARIE LEWIS ANNE -	366	12th Sept.	1700	Engines, kilns, and instruments for the making of looking-glass, plate-glass panels, and chimney-pieces for rooms.
SAINTMARC, JEAN JACQUES -	5197	28th June	1825	Process of and apparatus for distilling.
SALEMBIER, HYPOLITE LOUIS [FRANCOIS.	10,817	14th Aug.	1845	Manufacture and refining of sugar.
SALISBURY, WILLIAM - -	4292	31st Aug.	1818	Machine for preparing hemp, flax, and other vegetable fibrous substances.
SALMEN, SAMUEL - - -	11,958	11th Nov.	1847	Rendering certain materials applicable as a substitute for leather, paper, papier-mâché and oil-cloth, in various articles of manufacture.
SALMON, ROBERT - - -	2095	8th March	1796	Construction of certain machines for weighing goods, carriages, waggons, &c.
SALMON, ROBERT - - -	2970	2nd Oct.	1806	Trusses for cure of ruptures.
SALMON, ROBERT - - -	3402	4th March	1811	Instruments for the relief of hernia. "Salmon's new Royal Patent artificial Abdomens."
SALMON, ROBERT - - -	3614	31st Oct.	1812	Guards and shades for windows.
SALMON, ROBERT - - -	3838	23rd Aug.	1814	Construction of machines for making hay.
SALMON, ROBERT - - -	3859	10th Dec.	1814	Movements and combinations of wheels for working cranes, mills, and machinery, portable or fixed.
SALMON, ROBERT - - -	4047	27th July	1816	Construction of machines for making hay. "Salmon's New Patent self-adjusting and manageable Hay Machines."
SALMON, ROBERT - - -	4061	19th Aug.	1816	Instruments for complaints in the urethra and bladder.
SALMON, ROBERT - - -	4121	17th May	1817	Apparatus for the more safe, pleasant, and economical use of candles; also apparatus now in use for part of the same ends.
SALMON, ROBERT - - -	4331	15th Jan.	1819	Apparatus for cooling, condensing, and ventilating worts, liquors, and all other fluids or solid matters.
SALMON, ROBERT - - -	4526	15th Jan.	1821	Construction of instruments for the relief of hernia and prolapsus. "Scientific-principled, variable, secure, light, easy, elegant, cheap, and durable trusses."
SALMON, THOMAS - - -	5816	9th July	1829	Malt-kiln.

Name of Patentee.	Progressive Number.	Date.	Subject-matter of Patent.
SALTER, GEORGE - - -	7724	9th July 1838	Apparatus for weighing.
SALTER, ROGER GEORGE -	12,140	27th April 1848	Carts for the distribution of liquid substances; construction of drains, sewers, and cesspools; cleansing the same.
SALTER, SAMUEL - - -	3093	19th Dec. 1807	Apparatus for drying malt or hops, or any kind of grain.
SALTER, THOMAS FISHER -	8011	23rd March 1839	Machine for winnowing and dressing corn and other grain.
SALZEDE, CHARLES DE LA -	11,878	30th Sept. 1847	Brassing and bronzing the surface of steel, iron, zinc, lead, and tin.
SAMBOURNE, THOMAS - -	300	4th July 1692	Exercise called Fives.
SAMPSON, JOSEPH STACEY -	2108	24th May 1796	Cutting up tallow, fat, spermaceti and wax, for melting; making the same into candles.
SAMPSON, WILLIAM - -	2906	12th Feb. 1806	Application of power employed mechanically, especially as adapted to the use of cranks and fly-wheels, or other contrivances producing similar effects.
SAMPSON, WILLIAM - -	2974	7th Oct. 1806	Method of working mills, pumps and other machinery, by the impulse of wind.
SAMPSON, WILLIAM - -	3847	3rd Oct. 1814	Raising water.
SAMPSON, WILLIAM - -	4235	14th March 1818	Pumps;—applicable to various descriptions of machinery.
SAMUDA, JACOB - - -	9829	10th July 1843	Construction of steam-engines;—applicable to steam-navigation.
SAMUDA, JACOB - - -	10,167	30th April 1844	Manufacture and arrangement of parts and apparatus for the construction and working of atmospheric-railways.
SAMUDA, JOSEPH - - -	12,655	9th June 1849	Obtaining motive-power; machinery employed therein, and which may be used for raising liquids.
SAMUDA, JOSEPH D'AGUILAR -	10,167	30th April 1844	Manufacture and arrangement of parts and apparatus for the construction and working of atmospheric-railways.
SAMUEL, JAMES - - -	13,029	5th April 1850	Construction of railways and steam-engines; machinery for the same.
SAMUEL, MOSES - - -	1376	6th June 1783	Alarum-gun for preventing houses and other places from being broken into.
SAMUEL, SAMUEL - - -	998	2nd Nov. 1771	Dyeing and staining goat-skins, kid, calf-skins, sheep-skins, lamb-skins, and hides, with various colours.
SAMUELL, EDWARD - -	7873	13th Nov. 1838	Manufacture of soda.
SAMUELSON, ALEXANDER -	13,472	23rd Jan. 1851	Apparatus for cutting turnips, carrots, mangel-wurzel, and other vegetables.
SANDEMAN, HECTOR - -	11,827	31st July 1847	Materials and processes employed in dressing, clearing, scouring, and bleaching certain textile fabrics.
SANDEMAN, PATRICK - -	10,772	21st July 1845	Coffins.
SANDERS, BENJAMIN, senior -	3748	4th Nov. 1813	Manufacturing buttons.
SANDERS, JOHN - - -	8587	3rd Aug. 1840	Ploughs.
SANDERS, JOHN - - -	9474	22nd Sept. 1842	Machinery for ploughing, harrowing, and raking land, and cutting food for animals.
SANDERS, JOSEPH - - -	8106	12th June 1839	Lock and key.
SANDERS, JOSEPH - - -	8903	29th March 1841	Locks.
SANDERSON, CHARLES - -	5693	4th Sept. 1828	Making sheer-steel.
SANDERSON, CHARLES - -	7828	11th Oct. 1838	Process of melting iron ores.

Name of Patentee.	Progressive Number.	Date.		Subject-matter of Patent.
SANDERSON, CHARLES - -	10,921	4th Nov.	1845	Combining steel and iron into bars for wheel-tires, and for other purposes.
SANDERSON, GEORGE - -	763	25th June	1761	Tools and engines for preparing, stamping, fixing, turning, cutting, and finishing divers parts of a watch.
SANDERSON, GEORGE - -	777	25th June	1762	Lunar and calendar watch-key.
SANDERSON, MATTHEW - -	1084	27th Oct.	1774	Ingredients, which being mixed with metallic earths or clays and poor flinty sulphurous and stubborn ores of lead and copper and slag, and brought into a state of fusion, occasion the metallic particles thereof to be precipitated, and will smelt and extract double the usual quantity of metal from a like quantity of the same materials, by means of a high-blast furnace, blown with two or three large or hollow iron cylindrical bellows, worked by a water-wheel.
SANDERSON, MATTHEW - -	1203	21st Dec.	1778	Extracting mineral súlphur from pyrites, also from copper and lead ores ; separating its acid, and rendering it useful for medicinal purposes.
SANDERSON, MATTHEW - -	1243	5th Feb.	1780	Extracting alum, sulphur, and white and green vitriols from lead-glitter, blue-stone, and iron-ores, also blue-vitriol from copper-ore ; refining and separating their metallic contents, by a blast-furnace ; rendering their refuse useful in paintings, and in other purposes.
SANDERSON, WILLIAM - -	9347	9th May	1842	Weaving fabrics to be used for covering buttons.
SANDIFORD, ROBERT - -	7701	22nd June	1838	Block-printing, and certain arrangements connected therewith.
SANDILANDS, [The Honourable] [ROBERT.	1657	30th June	1788	Sward-cutter, or machine for bringing old grass-lands into tillage.
SANDS, THOMAS - - -	6039	20th Nov.	1830	Spinning-machines.
SANDYS, THOMAS - - -	1606	19th May	1787	Machine for throwing and organzining silk, and for throwing and twisting mohair, worsted, thread, cotton, hemp, flax, and gold and silver cords.
SANFORD, ISAAC - - -	2368	20th Jan.	1800	Manufacturing bricks, tiles, and pottery-ware in general, and discharging the moulds used therein.
SANFORD, ISAAC - - -	2558	14th Nov.	1801	Machine for cropping or shearing woollen, cotton, linen, silk, and other cloths made with a nap requiring cropping or shearing.
SANFORD, ISAAC - - -	2981	30th Oct.	1806	Raising a nap or pile on woollen, cotton, and other cloths, by means of a substitute for teasels and cards.
SANFORD, ISAAC - - -	3015	20th Feb.	1807	Raising a nap or pile on woollen, cotton, and other cloths, by means of a substitute for teasels and cards.
SANG, FREDERICK - - -	14,211	6th July	1852	Machinery for cutting, sawing, grinding, and polishing.
SANG, FREDERICK - - -	14,291	16th Sept.	1852	Floating and moving vessels, vehicles and other bodies, on and over water.
SANGSTER, WILLIAM - -	10,035	6th Feb.	1844	Umbrellas and parasols.
SANGSTER, WILLIAM - -	12,056	8th Feb.	1848	Umbrellas and parasols.
SANKEY, WILLIAM STEVENS [VILLIERS.	10,529	20th Feb.	1845	Fastening and securing letters, packets, and dispatches.

Name of Patentee.	Progressive Number.	Date.	Subject-matter of Patent.
SANXTER, WILLIAM - -	2238	25th May 1798	Plough for paring land.
SARJANT, WILLIAM LUCAS -	10,030	30th Jan. 1844	Manufacture of barrels for fire-arms.
SARTORIS, URBANUS - -	4107	11th March 1817	Construction and use of fire-arms.
SARTORIS, URBANUS - -	4281	22nd July 1818	Producing ignition in fire-arms by the condensation of atmospheric-air.
SARTORIS, URBANUS - -	4336	23rd Jan. 1819	Construction and use of fire-arms.
SARUL, HENRY DE - -	3983	20th Feb. 1816	Cylindrical gold and silver sweep and washing machine.
SATCHELL, RICHARD - -	12,540	28th March 1849	Machinery for depositing seeds, and hoeing and working land.
SAUL, JOHN - - - -	13,242	5th Sept. 1850	Machinery for spinning and twisting cotton and other fibrous substances.
SAUNDER, GEORGE - -	8294	2nd Dec. 1839	Machinery for dibbling or setting wheat and other grain or seed.
SAUNDERS, BENJAMIN - -	5264	13th Oct. 1825	Constructing or making buttons.
SAUNDERS, EDMUND - -	1329	2nd May 1782	Composition called naval black varnish, for paying yards, top-masts, bowsprits, bends, blocks, anchors, &c. of ships, instead of tar and lamp black.
SAUNDERS, JAMES FERGUSON	6893	1st Sept. 1835	Clarifying raw cane-juice, and other vegetable and saccharine juices; bleaching such raw juices.
SAUNDERS, JAMES FERGUSON	8037	20th April 1839	Manufacture of certain kinds of paper-mill-board, papier-mâché, and other matters produced from paper-pulp.
SAUNDERS, JONATHAN - -	9894	5th Oct. 1843	Manufacture of tires of railway and other wheels; manufacture of railway and other axles.
SAUNDERS, WILLIAM - -	1503	3rd Nov. 1785	Dressing and preparing leather with turned feet, for boots, half-boots, spatterdashes, or gaiters: making such articles without any seam in the instep; preparing leather for shoes, and making shoes without any heel seam, or side seam.
SAUNDERS, WILLIAM - -	8589	3rd Aug. 1840	Paving streets, roads, and ways.
SAUNDERS, WILLIAM - -	9268	25th Feb. 1842	Apparatus employed in roasting and baking animal food.
SAUNDERS, WILLIAM - -	10,111	19th March 1844	Apparatus for modifying temperature in the condensation of vapours, and cooling or heating of liquids and fluids.
SAUNDERS, WILLIAM - -	13,145	20th June 1850	Sawing; and sawing-machinery.
SAUTTER, CHARLES MAURICE [ELIZEE.	9558	15th Dec. 1842	Manufacture of sulphuric-acid.
SAUTTER, CHARLES MAURICE [ELIZEE.	9734	22nd May 1843	Manufacture of borax.
SAUTTER, CHARLES MAURICE [ELIZEE.	10,238	26th June 1844	Pianofortes.
SAUVAGE, JOHN AUGUSTIN [ALEXIS.	11,315	27th July 1846	Condensing the steam of steam-engines; and supplying water to steam-engine boilers.
SAVAGE, EDWARD - - -	3401	4th March 1811	Machine for washing and bleaching linen and other articles, and for cooking by means of steam.
SAVAGE, GEORGE - - -	3102	26th Jan. 1808	Regulating and equalizing the power of the main-spring in watches or other machines for measuring time.

Name of Patentee.	Progressive Number.	Date.	Subject-matter of Patent.
SAVERY, THOMAS - - -	347	10th Jan. 1696	Mill-work to grind and polish looking-glass, and coach-glass plates, and marble stones; also for rowing ships.
SAVERY, THOMAS - - -	356	25th July 1698	Raising water and giving motion to mill-works by the impellent force of fire, useful for draining mines, serving towns with water, and working all kinds of mills in cases where there is neither water nor constant wind.
SAVERY, THOMAS - - -	379	— 1706	Making double-hand bellows for producing a continual blast by the power of springs and screws, sufficient to melt any sort of metal in a common wood or coal fire, and thus preclude the necessity of making assay furnaces.
SAVIGNY, JOHN HORATIO -	1458	4th Dec. 1784	Making skates, and fixing them on.
SAVIGNY, JOHN HORATIO -	1716	8th Dec. 1789	Razor.
SAVIGNY, JOHN HORATIO -	2387	31st March 1800	Surgical instrument called a "Tourniquet."
SAVILE, HENRY - - -	248	30th Nov. 1685	Carts, waggons, and carriages going on two wheels (applying a third wheel, along with other additions).
SAVORY, THOMAS FIELD -	3954	23rd Aug. 1815	Seidlitz Powders.
SAVOYE, CLAUDE MARIE -	6195	15th Dec. 1831	Mills for grinding or reducing grain and other substances.
SAWBRIDGE, WILLIAM - -	4366	6th May 1819	Engine-looms for weaving figured ribbons.
SAWDON, THOMAS - - -	2637	23rd July 1802	Machine for cutting straw as fodder for cattle.
SAWTON, SAMUEL - - -	210	4th March 1680	Instruments to be used without diving, for recovering from under water, ships guns, or goods wrecked or sunk.
SAXELBYE, JOHN SWIFT -	2758	14th May 1804	Making white-lead.
SAXTON, JOSEPH - - -	6351	20th Dec. 1832	Propelling carriages; and propelling vessels for inland navigation.
SAXTON, JOSEPH - - -	6682	25th Sept. 1834	Printing-presses, and presses for certain other purposes.
SAYER, EDWARD - - -	365	18th May 1700	Engines, kilns, and other tools for making looking-glass plates, and plates for panels of rooms, and chimney-pieces.
SAYNER, GEORGE - - -	5074	11th Jan. 1825	Sawing and cutting wood and timber by machinery.
SCAMBLER, JOHN - - -	3571	2nd June 1812	Manufacturing needles.
SCAMP, WILLIAM - - -	8848	16th Feb. 1841	Application of machinery to steam-vessels, for the removal of sand, mud, soil, and other matters from the sea, rivers, docks, harbours, and other bodies of water.
SCANDALARUS, NICHOLAS -	80	10th March 1635	Making salt, with power to erect works for the purpose on waste land near the sea coasts.
SCANTLEBURY, RICHARD -	2101	17th March 1796	Bucket and clack for raising and lifting or drawing water or other liquids.
SCANTLEBURY, RICHARD -	3210	1st March 1809	Machine to counterbalance the weight of water or other fluids to be lifted by any steam or waterengine.
SCARTH, MICHAEL - - -	2785	21st Sept. 1804	Manufacturing sail-cloth.
SCARTH, ROBERT - - -	7013	26th Feb. 1836	Manufacturing or preparing a certain substance from materials not hitherto used for that purpose, for dyeing blue and other colours.

Name of Patentee.	Progressive Number.	Date.		Subject-matter of Patent.
SCARTH, WILLIAM GILYARD -	7013	26th Feb.	1836	Manufacturing or preparing a certain substance from materials not hitherto used for that purpose, applicable for dyeing blue and other colours.
SCATLIFF, DANIEL - - -	752	2nd Oct.	1760	Quadrant for taking observations at sea.
SCATTERGOOD, JOHN - -	6902	8th Oct.	1835	Looms for weaving by hand or other power.
SCHAFHAUTL, CHARLES - -	6837	13th May	1835	Manufacture of malleable iron.
SCHAFHAUTL, CHARLES - -	7003	16th Feb.	1836	Steam generator.
SCHAFHAUTL, CHARLES - -	7022	8th March	1836	Gear for obtaining a continuous rotary action.
SCHAFHAUTL, CHARLES - -	7117	13th June	1836	Apparatus for puddling iron.
SCHAFHAUTL, CHARLES - -	7994	6th March	1839	Smelting copper ore.
SCHAFHAUTL, CHARLES - - [Schafhœutl, Charles.]	8820	30th Jan.	1841	Construction of puddling, balling, and other reverberatory furnaces, for the purpose of enabling anthracite, stone-coal or culm to be used therein as fuel.
SCHALLER, JOSEPH - -	5360	6th May	1826	Construction of clogs, pattens, or substitutes for the same.
SCHEFFER, JOHN - - -	4389	8th July	1819	Instrument for writing. " Pennographic or writing instrument."
SCHELESTADT, EDWARD LOOS [DE	9079	8th Sept.	1841	Machinery for and process of tanning skins or hides, and preparing or operating upon vegetable or other substances.
SCHENCK, ROBERT BRETT -	11,450	17th Nov.	1846	Preparation of hemp and flax.
SCHICK, ANTHONY - -	3577	25th June	1812	Roasting coffee.
SCHIELE, CHRISTIAN - -	11,717	27th May	1847	Machinery for condensing steam ;—applicable to other purposes.
SCHIELE, CHRISTIAN - -	12,338	23rd Nov.	1848	Construction of cocks or valves ;—applicable for reducing the friction of axles, journals, bearings, and other rubbing surfaces in machinery.
SCHIELE, CHRISTIAN - -	13,784	22nd Oct.	1851	Machinery for the preparation and manufacture of fibrous materials ;—partly applicable for the transmission of fluids and aëriform bodies.
SCHIELE, CHRISTIAN - -	13,965	12th Feb.	1852	Obtaining and applying motive-power.
SCHLESINGER, JOSEPH - -	9420	16th July	1842	Inkstands ; instruments for filing or holding papers and other articles.
SCHLESINGER, JOSEPH WILLIAM	14,227	20th July	1852	Fire-arms, cartridges ; and manufacture of powder.
SCHLOSS, HENRY - - -	11,033	12th Jan.	1846	Instruments for producing ignition.
SCHMALCALDER, CHARLES -	3000	22nd Dec.	1806	Delineator, for taking, tracing and cutting out profiles, also copying and tracing reversely, on copper, brass, wood, and other articles, landscapes, prospects, or any object standing perpendicularly, also pictures, drawings, prints, plans, and public characters.
SCHMALCALDER, CHARLES AUGUSTUS [Schmacalder, Charles Augustus.]	3545	5th March	1812	Mathematical instruments.
SCHMETTAN, SAMUEL - -	384	12th July	1709	Making salt.
SCHMIDT, CARL FREDERICK -	790	16th June	1763	Composition and varnish made with oils and other things, for staining, printing, and laying gold, silver, or metal, on woollens, worsteds, and goods mixed with wool, for apparel and furniture.

Name of Patentee.	Progressive Number.	Date.	Subject-matter of Patent.
SCHMIDT, JOHN - - -	3185	20th Dec. 1808	Phantasmagoric chronometer or nocturnal dial, representing or making visible at night on an enlarged scale, the dial of a watch against the wall of the room, the reflection obtained by a light and optical apparatus being sufficient at the same time to give the room a pleasing illumination; the dial may be constructed of any watch or time-piece, but is rendered more simple and useful by the adoption of an instrument or "mysterious circulator," which requires only one hand to show seconds, minutes, and hours, which also may, with little alteration, be made to represent an orrery.
SCHMIDT, JOHN GOTTLIEB [FREDERIC	2868	19th July 1805	Sustaining life and combustion under water, and enabling persons to move about under water.
SCHNEBLY, WILLIAM - -	10,488	21st Jan. 1845	Machinery for letter-press or surface printing.
SCHOFIELD, JONATHAN - -	4933	7th April 1824	Manufacture of a fabric named "British cachemere."
SCHOFIELD, JOSEPH - -	8198	17th Aug. 1839	Looms for weaving various kinds of cloth.
SCHOFIELD, THOMAS - -	12,946	26th Jan. 1850	Machinery for cutting fustians and certain other fabrics, to produce a piled surface.
SCHOLEFIELD, GEORGE - -	5627	13th March 1828	Looms for weaving woollen, linen, cotton, silk, and other cloths.
SCHOLEFIELD, GEORGE - -	6718	20th Nov. 1834	Apparatus for cutting the pile of fustians, and other fabrics manufactured of cotton-wool and other fibrous materials.
SCHOLEFIELD, GEORGE - -	10,924	4th Nov. 1845	Machinery to be employed for lithographic printing.
SCHOMBERG, CHARLES LOUIS-	9100	23rd Sept. 1841	Manufacture of certain glass.
SCHOTTLAENDER, JULIUS -	9982	8th Dec. 1843	Deposition of metals upon various felted and other fabrics.
SCHRODER, HERMAN - -	5000	11th Aug. 1824	Filter.
SCHRODER, HERMAN - -	8675	2nd Nov. 1840	Filters.
SCHRODER, HERMAN - -	13,591	15th April 1851	Manufacturing and refining sugar.
SCHROTH, CLAUDE - -	7589	10th March 1838	Preparing, pressing, and embossing the surface of leather.
SCHROTH, CLAUDE - -	7725	9th July 1838	Manufacturing the tools employed in the process of pressing or embossing the surface of leather or other substances.
SCHROTH, CLAUDE - -	8132	26th June 1839	Embossing on leather or such like materials; means for effecting the same; making tools used therein.
SCHUNK, EDWARD - -	12,345	29th Nov. 1848	Manufacture of malleable iron, and treating other products obtained in the process.
SCHWABE, LOUIS - -	6066	22nd Jan. 1831	Processes and apparatus for preparing, beaming, printing, and weaving, yarns of cotton, silk, woollen and other fibrous substances, so that figures printed on them may be preserved when woven into cloth or other fabric.
SCHWARTZ, HENRY WILLIAM	12,148	4th May 1848	Steam-engines.
SCHWARTZ, THEODORE - -	6890	24th Aug. 1835	Practical application of known principles to produce mechanical power.
SCHWIERS, CONRADUS - -	1745	21st April 1790	Self-moving principle, or perpetual motion.
SCHWIESO, JOHN CHARLES -	5404	22nd Aug. 1826	Certain stringed musical instruments.

Name of Patentee.	Progressive Number.	Date.		Subject-matter of Patent.
SCHWIESO, JOHN CHARLES -	6069	2nd Feb.	1831	Pianofortes and other stringed instruments.
SCHWIESO, JOHN CHARLES -	8163	20th July	1839	Construction of locks.
SCHWIESO, JOHN CHARLES -	8861	2nd March	1841	Constructing elastic seats or surfaces of furniture.
SCOBELL, FRANCIS - -	467	20th May	1724	Engine and slope, or declining-wheel, for raising water, working mills, and other useful purposes.
SCOFFERN, JOHN - - -	11,991	8th Dec.	1847	Manufacture and refining of sugar.
SCOFFERN, JOHN - - -	12,977	21st Feb.	1850	Manufacture and refining of sugar; treatment and use of matters obtained in such manufacture; construction of valves used in such and other manufactures.
SCOTT, ALEXANDER - -	2552	10th Nov.	1801	Making pianofortes.
SCOTT, ANTHONY - - -	5534	4th Aug.	1827	Apparatus for preventing the boilers of steam-engines and other vessels becoming foul, and for cleaning the same.
SCOTT, DANIEL - - -	1006	4th March	1772	Making salt from sea-water or brine, by steam.
SCOTT, GEORGE - - -	917	16th Feb.	1769	Boiler, pot, or utensil of metal, for dressing ships' provisions with sea-water or other water, and purifying the same; also extracting broths or soups.
SCOTT, GEORGE - - -	3730	9th Aug.	1813	Machine for cutting out wearing-apparel and other articles and things.
SCOTT, GEORGE - - -	5920	20th March	1830	Windlasses and relative machinery, applicable to naval purposes.
SCOTT, GEORGE - - -	9098	23rd Sept.	1841	Flour-mills.
SCOTT, GEORGE - - -	9942	16th Nov.	1843	Manufacture, purification, and combustion of gas or gases.
SCOTT, HENRY, junior - -	7205	13th Oct.	1836	Manufacture of hats, caps, or bonnets.
SCOTT, HENRY - - -	8770	31st Dec.	1840	Manufacture of ink or writing-fluids.
SCOTT, JAMES - - -	4448	15th April	1820	Combining, adjusting, and applying certain mechanic powers and modifications thereof, or an " Accelerating lever-motion," applicable to many purposes.
SCOTT, JAMES - - -	4457	11th May	1820	Combining, adjusting, and applying by machinery certain mechanical powers and modifications thereof, in cases where power and velocity are required.
SCOTT, JAMES - - -	13,330	9th Nov.	1850	Docks, slips, and apparatus connected therewith.
SCOTT, JOHN - - -	822	23rd Jan.	1765	Making glass from one single material; making pig-iron from one certain material.
SCOTT, JOHN - - -	2552	10th Nov.	1801	Making pianofortes.
SCOTT, JOHN - - -	2672	21st Dec.	1802	"Tatham's clumps," for constructing water-pipes, sewers, tunnels, wells, conduits, reservoirs, or other circular walls, shells, or buildings.
SCOTT, JOHN - - -	4209	23rd Jan.	1818	Steam-boats, and machinery for propelling the same.
SCOTT, JOHN HARRISON -	9403	6th July	1842	Metal pipes; and the manufacture thereof.
SCOTT, JOSEPH - - -	8840	8th Feb.	1841	Constructing railways; and propelling carriages thereon;—applicable to raising and lowering weights.
SCOTT, LANGSTON - -	13,194	24th July	1850	Preparing certain matters to be used as pigments.

Name of Patentee.	Progressive Number.	Date.	Subject-matter of Patent.
SCOTT, MICHAEL - - -	13,792	30th Oct. 1851	Punching, riveting, bending, and shearing metals; building and constructing ships and vessels.
SCOTT, RICHARD - - -	2477	10th Feb. 1801	Preserving papers and other property from injury by fire.
SCOTT, ROBERT - - -	2552	10th Nov. 1801	Making pianofortes.
SCOTT, THOMAS - - -	2995	13th Dec. 1806	Flageolet, so constructed that two parts of a musical composition may be played thereon at one time.
SCOTT, THOMAS - - -	3314	12th March 1810	German flute, clarionet, and hautboy.
SCOTT, URIAH - - -	14,010	8th March 1852	Wheels and springs, and spring-bearings for carriages.
SCOTT, WILLIAM - -	1960	16th Aug. 1793	Heating the water and stuffs for making paper, in vats, and by steam.
SCOTT, WILLIAM - -	2875	9th Aug. 1805	Manufacture of and working various kinds of glass.
SCOTT, WILLIAM CHARLES -	13,812	15th Nov. 1851	Construction of omnibuses and other public and private carriages.
SCOTTHORN, ROBERT - -	11,627	17th March 1847	Engines for obtaining and applying motive-power.
SCRIVENOR, HARRY - -	6328	6th Nov. 1832	Construction of iron railways.
SCULTHORPE, GEORGE KING -	5811	4th July 1829	Axle-trees; coach and other springs.
SCULTHORPE, GEORGE KING -	9834	13th July 1843	Method of fastening and securing bedsteads.
SEALY, JOHN - - -	9534	3rd Dec. 1842	Tile.
SEARELL, ALLEN - -	13,790	23rd Oct. 1851	Sawing-machinery.
SEARLE, CHARLES - -	7652	24th May 1838	Aërated waters.
SEARLE, CHARLES - -	9383	9th June 1842	Preparation of tea, coffee, cocoa, and milk.
SEARLE, CHARLES - -	10,813	9th Aug. 1845	Stoves.
SEARLE, HENRY - - -	214	29th Aug. 1681	Making pitch and tar out of pit-coals.
SEARLE, HENRY - - -	215	29th Aug. 1681	Engine to raise and throw out water from deep mines.
SEARLE, THOMAS - - -	6693	11th Oct. 1834	Boilers for generating steam.
SEARLES, JAMES STURMAN -	1837	26th Nov. 1791	Gun-triggers.
SEARLES, JAMES STURMAN -	2744	3rd Dec. 1803	Fire-arms, or defensive instruments.
SEARLES, MICHAEL -	1115	30th Jan. 1776	Pinion and rack for pumps, and for water and fire-engines.
SEARS, MATTHEW URLWIN -	12,920	11th Jan. 1850	Construction of guns and cannons; manufacture of cartridges for the loading thereof.
SEATON, RICHARD - -	3380	26th Sept. 1810	Burners for lamps.
SEATON, THOMAS - -	5279	7th Nov. 1825	Wheeled carriages.
SEATON, WILLIAM - -	12,168	30th May 1848	Closing tubes, and preventing and removing incrustation in boilers.
SEAWARD, JOHN - -	4356	3rd April 1819	Producing steam for working steam-engines and other apparatus.
SEAWARD, JOHN - -	5274	1st Nov. 1825	Propelling boats, craft and all other kind of vessels, on canals, rivers, and other shallow waters.
SEAWARD, JOHN - -	5694	4th Sept. 1828	Propelling carriages on land, and ships, boats, and other vessels, on water.
SEAWARD, JOHN - -	7588	10th March 1838	Steam-engines.
SEAWARD, JOHN - -	9046	13th Aug. 1841	Steam-engines.
SEAWARD, JOHN - -	10,511	5th Feb. 1845	Steam propelling-machinery.

Name of Patentee.	Progres-sive Number.	Date.	Subject-matter of Patent.
SEAWARD, JOHN - - -	11,034	12th Jan. 1846	Steam-engines, and machinery for propelling.
SEAWARD, SAMUEL - -	5274	1st Nov. 1825	Propelling boats, craft and all other kind of vessels, on canals, rivers, and other shallow waters.
SEAWARD, SAMUEL - -	5694	4th Sept. 1828	Propelling carriages on land, and ships, boats, and other vessels on water.
SEAWARD, SAMUEL - -	6080	15th Jan. 1831	Apparatus for economizing steam, and for other purposes; application thereof to the boilers of steam-engines used on board packet-boats and other vessels.
SEAWARD, SAMUEL - -	6695	17th Oct. 1834	Construction of steam-engines.
SEAWARD, SAMUEL - -	7646	21st May 1838	Steam-engines.
SEAWARD, SAMUEL - -	8436	17th March 1840	Construction of steam-engines; application of steam-engines to propelling ships and other vessels.
SEAWARD, SAMUEL - -	9046	13th Aug. 1841	Steam-engines.
SEDDON, JOSHUA - -	10,687	24th May 1845	Constructing the flues and interior arrangements of ovens and kilns used in the manufacture of china and earthenware.
SEDGIER, HENRY - - -	860	13th Sept. 1766	Bedstead for invalids, made in such a way that the person lying thereon can be raised into a sitting posture by turning a winch; may also be used as a settee.
SEDGWICK, MARY - - -	4224	10th Feb. 1818	Products from the refuse, slime, or wash of starch.
SEDGWICK. WILLIAM - -	641	23rd Feb. 1749	Making sal-ammoniac.
SEEBOHM, BENJAMIN -	10,417	4th Dec. 1844	Manufacturing certain descriptions of chains.
SEED, WILLIAM - - -	11,293	14th July 1846	Machinery for preparing, slubbing, and roving cotton and other fibrous substances.
SEEGERS, THEODORUS CORNE-[LIUS.	12,082	8th March 1848	Construction of railway-carriages.
SEELY, CHARLES - - -	13,033	5th April 1850	Grinding wheat and other grain.
SEELY, CHARLES - - -	14,063	15th April 1852	Manufacture of flour.
SEGUNDO, JUAN JOSE - -	6597	22nd April 1834	Apparatus applicable to side-saddles, for security of persons riding.
SEIDLER, CHARLES - -	5437	20th Dec. 1826	Drawing water out of mines, wells, pits, and other places.
SELBY, GEORGE - - -	10,546	8th March 1845	Manufacture of pipes or tubes which are formed by welding skelps of wrought-iron.
SELBY, ROBERT - -	6352	20th Dec. 1832	Making bedsteads, sofas, couches, and other articles.
SELDEN, DAVID - - -	6088	26th Feb. 1831	Machinery to give a degree of consistency to rovings of cotton and other fibrous substances, and to wind the same on to bobbins, barrels, or spools.
SELDEN, DAVID - - -	6152	11th Aug. 1831	Metallic mills for grinding coffee, corn, drugs, paints, and various other materials.
SELDEN, DAVID - - -	6192	22nd Nov. 1831	Carding and slubbing engine, for wool and other fibrous substances.
SELLARS, WILLIAM - -	2034	19th Jan. 1795	Preparing and spinning flax, hemp, tow, and other things, by heckles and machines worked by water, steam, horse-mills, or other moving power.

Name of Patentee.	Progressive Number.	Date.	Subject-matter of Patent.
SELLARS, WILLIAM - -	2172	11th March 1797	Making and working machines for drawing out wool or flax combed by hand, into slivers, and which machines may be worked by water, steam, horse-mills, or other moving power.
SELLARS, WILLIAM - -	2228	18th April 1798	Making and working machines for preparing and spinning wool, cotton, flax, hemp and other materials, without drums or belts, and which machines may be worked by water, steam, horse-mills, or other moving power.
SELLARS, WILLIAM - -	3812	7th June 1814	Spinning and laying ropes, twine, line, thread, mohair, wool, cotton, and silk, by machinery.
SELLER, JOHN - - -	10,483	21st Jan. 1845	Machinery to be used for drain-cutting and subsoiling.
SELLER, WILLIAM - - -	2515	18th June 1801	Machinery for diminishing friction and communicating rotátory motion from one wheel to another by cranks, applicable to wind or water drainage mills, for raising water, and for other purposes. "Alternate relieving cranks."
SELLERS, JOHN, junior - -	10,563	17th March 1845	Looms for weaving.
SELLIGUE, FELICITE RAISON -	12,147	4th May 1848	Propelling; machinery employed therein.
SEMEINS, EDWARD - -	417	15th Jan. 1718	Use of certain vegetables of American growth, for making potashes.
SENEFELDER, JOHN ALOYSIUS	2518	20th June 1801	Printing on paper, linen, cotton, woollen, and other articles.
SENEX, JOHN - - -	432	7th July 1721	Making and printing globular charts or sea-charts, for use in navigation.
SENIOR, GEORGE - - -	11,367	3rd Sept. 1846	Washing, cleansing, scouring, and bleaching silk, cotton-wool, and fibrous substances generally; also dyeing, combing, carding, spinning, felting, or otherwise treating or preparing fibrous substances.
SEPPINGS, Sir ROBERT, Knight	5324	19th Jan. 1826	Construction of made masts and made bow-sprits.
SEPPINGS, Sir ROBERT, Knight	5357	6th May 1826	Construction of fids or apparatus for striking top-masts and top-gallant-masts in ships.
SERBAT, LOUIS - - -	11,145	25th March 1846	Constructing roofs of houses, buildings, sheds, and all other erections.
SERIONNE, LOUIS JEAN, [JACQUES, Viscount de.	12,963	9th Feb. 1850	Manufacture of buttons; apparatus and machinery used therein.
SERNY, JOHN BAPTIST - -	3602	25th Sept. 1812	Raising sunken vessels and other matters; machinery used for such purposes.
SERVANT, JOHN - - -	4161	12th Aug. 1817	Mangles.
SERVANT, JOHN - - -	4377	1st June 1819	Heating dry-houses, malt-kilns, and other buildings.
SERVICE, GRACE ELIZABETH -	3930	17th June 1815	Manufacturing straw with gauze net-web and other similar articles, for making hats and bonnets, and other articles.
SERVILL, SAMUEL - - -	4863	13th Nov. 1823	Dressing woollen or other cloths.
SEVERNE, JOSEPH - - -	1516	19th Dec. 1785	Remedy for the ague. "Aromatic ague cake."
SEVILL, SAMUEL - - -	5564	20th Nov. 1827	Raising the pile of woollen and other cloths, and dressing such cloths.
SEVILLE, THOMAS - - -	9494	20th Oct. 1842	Machinery used in the preparing and spinning of cotton, flax, and other fibrous substances.

Name of Patentee.	Progressive Number.	Date.	Subject-matter of Patent.
SEWARD, ABRAHAM - -	3212	1st March 1809	Hook for bearing up the heads of horses in drawing carriages.
SEWARD, CHARLES - -	3184	26th Nov. 1808	Construction of lamps.
SEWARD, CHARLES - -	3251	26th July 1809	Street lamp and burner, and lantern-head for street and other lamps and lanterns.
SEWELL, ROBERT - -	7280	11th Jan. 1837	Manufacture of white-lead.
SEWELL, THOMAS ROBERT -	6936	2nd Dec. 1835	Machinery for making bobbin-net lace.
SEWELL, THOMAS ROBERT -	7736	14th July 1838	Manufacture of white-lead.
SEWELL, THOMAS ROBERT -	8765	31st Dec. 1840	Obtaining carbonic-acid from certain mineral substances.
SEWELL, THOMAS ROBERT -	12,030	18th Jan. 1848	Preparing flour.
SEYBEL, JULIUS - - -	9310	31st March 1842	Manufacture of sulphate of soda and chlorine.
SEYFFERT, FREDERICK WILLIAM	4317	5th Dec. 1818	Watches and clocks.
SEYMOUR, BENJAMIN - -	1442	3rd July 1784	Re-manufacturing cordage ; also making new ropes and twice-laid ropes, by spinning the yarns together without knots, and laying and closing them with more regularity and expedition.
SEYMOUR, BENJAMIN - -	1537	4th March 1786	Machine for manufacturing twine, cable, and other cordage.
SEYMOUR, GEORGE - -	10,484	21st Jan. 1845	Manufacture of covered buttons.
SEYMOUR, JOHN - -	10,109	14th March 1844	Safety-bolt and tumbler for the locks of certain kinds of fire-arms.
SEYMOUR, THOMAS - -	10,109	14th March 1844	Safety-bolt and tumbler, for the locks of certain kinds of fire-arms.
SEYRIG, JOHANN GOTTLOB -	7567	16th Feb. 1838	Extracting liquids or moisture from woollen, cotton, and other stuffs and substances, in the manufactured or unmanufactured state.
SEYRIG, JOHANN GOTTLOB -	10,494	25th Jan. 1845	Machines for scouring, bleaching, and dyeing ; machines used in filtering and drying substances.
SEYRIG, JOHANN GOTTLOB -	11,695	6th May 1847	Propelling on land and on water.
SHACKLETON, THOMAS - -	2916	12th March 1806	Machinery for rasping, grating, and reducing into small parts or powder, wood, drugs, and other substances for the use of dyers.
SHAIRP, ALEXANDER - -	14,316	7th Oct. 1852	Cutting and slicing machine.
SHAKESPEAR, WILLIAM - -	3359	5th July 1810	Manufacturing glass or paste drops for chandeliers, lamps, and lustres.
SHALDERS, WILLIAM - -	5149	12th April 1825	Gravitating expressing fountain, for raising and conveying water, or any other fluid.
SHALES, ROBERT - - -	249	9th Jan. 1686	Making writing and printing paper ; imprinting His Majesty's arms thereon ; mills and engines for the purpose.
SHALLCROSS, JOHN - -	361	10th March 1699	Tiles or bricks for the floors of kilns for drying malt, oats, or other grain.
SHALLCROSS, JOHN - -	367	4th July 1701	Covering for houses, made of clay, and resembling a flat board, about fourteen inches long and twelve inches broad, with a rib on both sides about half an inch in height ; two of these boards being placed together, and the ribs fastened with a small hollow cap, each board folding about two inches over the other, form a close, tight, and safe covering, which will be also much lighter than those now used.

Name of Patentee.	Progres-sive Number.	Date.	Subject-matter of Patent.
SHALLCROSS, WILLIAM THOMAS	6358	9th Jan. 1833	Looms, or machines for weaving cotton, linen, silk, woollen, and other fibrous cloths and substances.
SHAND, WILLIAM - - -	4039	1st June 1816	Construction of artificial legs and feet made of leather and wood, acting by a lever and a spiral spring.
SHAND, WILLIAM - - -	5828	10th Aug. 1829	Distillation.
SHAND, WILLIAM - - -	5837	21st Aug. 1829	Distillation and evaporation.
SHAND, WILLIAM - - -	5945	29th June 1830	Purifying and whitening sugar, or other saccharine matter.
SHANKLAND, ALEXANDER [BEATTIE. [Shankland, Alexandre Beattie.]	6228	23rd Feb. 1632	Cutting, working, and planing wood, minerals, and metals, by means of machinery.
SHANKLAND, ALEXANDER [BEATTIE.	6255	13th April 1832	Spinning flax and hemp by means of machinery.
SHANKLAND, ALEXANDER [BEATTIE.	6282	5th July 1832	Spinning wool.
SHANKLAND, ALEXANDER [BEATTIE.	6604	6th May 1834	Machine for cutting wood into certain defined forms for various purposes.
SHANKS, ALEXANDER, junior -	6745	15th Jan. 1835	Machinery for preparing and dressing hemp and other fibrous substances.
SHANKS, ANDREW - - -	12,509	14th March 1849	Mode of giving form to certain metals when in a fluid or molten state.
SHANKS, JAMES - - -	8973	27th May 1841	Manufacture of carbonate of soda.
SHANKSTER, JOHN - - -	1514	9th Dec. 1785	Making wheeled-carriages for coaches, phaetons, chaises, waggons, drays, field-pieces, and other conveyances, with boxes and axletrees whereby the greater part of the friction attending boxes and axletrees is taken off, thus rendering the carriages lighter and more easy for work and draught, they also do not require grease; applicable for hydraulic, steam, or other engines, mills and machinery where spindles and axletrees are used, and which do not work on centre-points.
SHANKSTER, JOHN - - -	1623	6th Oct. 1787	Hanging coaches, chariots, phaetons, calashes, gigs, chaises, and other carriages, for the security of persons riding therein.
SHANNON, MICHAEL - -	3318	22nd March 1810	Brewing.
SHANNON, RICHARD - -	1223	10th May 1779	Making and preparing potashes and pearl-ashes of materials not before used for the purpose; furnaces for facilitating the process.
SHANNON, RICHARD - -	2212	1st Feb. 1798	Process of brewing, distilling, boiling, and evaporating, and of raising and condensing steam or vapour from aqueous, spirituous, saccharine, and saline fluids, which expedites the process, improves the quality, and saves time and fuel.
SHANNON, RICHARD - -	2245	19th June 1798	Process of fermentation; brewing-utensils and pneumatic-apparatus for the purpose.
SHAPPLE, HENRY - - -	12,711	18th July 1849	Communicating intelligence by means of electricity; electric-clocks.
SHARP, CLEMENT - - -	2322	26th June 1799	Making cards for carding cotton-wool, silk, and other things.
SHARP, DAVID WILKINSON -	7558	30th Jan. 1838	Machinery for warping worsted, linen, cotton, silk, or woollen yarns.

Name of Patentee.	Progres-sive Number.	Date.		Subject-matter of Patent.
SHARP, GEORGE ANTHONY -	5525	18th July	1827	Tableurn.
SHARP, JAMES - - -	1304	21st Aug.	1781	Stove or grate.
SHARP, JOHN - - - -	7204	8th Oct.	1836	Machinery for converting ropes into tow; machinery for preparing hemp or flax for spinning;—partly applicable to the pre-paring of cotton-wool and silk for spin-ning.
SHARP, JOSEPH BUDWORTH -	6012	20th Oct.	1830	Introducing air into fluids for the purpose of evaporation.
SHARP, THOMAS - - -	6536	1st Jan.	1834	Machinery for grinding corn and other materials.
SHARP, THOMAS - - -	6690	8th Oct.	1834	Machinery for spinning and doubling cot-ton, silk, flax, and other fibrous mate-rials.
SHARP, WILLIAM DOUGLAS -	8411	3rd March	1840	Machinery for preparing, spinning, and doubling cotton, flax, wool, and other fibrous substances.
SHARPE, EDMUND - - -	13,102	5th June	1850	Railway-carriages.
SHARPE, HENRY - - -	7078	3rd May	1836	Sawing wood and other materials.
SHARPE, SAMUEL - - -	17	15th July	1620	Making camlets after the Turkish manner.
SHARPE, WILLIAM - - -	5689	19th Aug.	1828	Machinery for spinning or roving cotton, silk, wool, or other fibrous substances.
SHARPE, WILLIAM - - -	7256	15th Dec.	1836	Treatment of cotton-wool, in preparation for manufacturing the same into yarn or thread.
SHARPEY, Sir ROBERT KNIGHT	52	— Sept.	1630	Making white and bay salt with sea-water and brine, without pans or furnaces.
SHARPLES, JAMES - - -	1829	12th Oct.	1791	Appropriating certain mechanical powers to the reduction of friction in shafts, pivots, gudgeons, cranks, rollers, axles, and axle-trees.
SHARPLES JAMES - - -	2576	28th Jan.	1802	Mechanical power applicable to steam-engines;—partly applicable to other pur-poses.
SHARPLES JAMES - - -	2794	24th Nov.	1804	Combinations and arrangements of imple-ments and mechanical powers; also prin-ciples and forms of tables used in survey-ing.
SHAW, ABRAHAM - - -	3846	3rd Oct.	1814	Apparatus for cutting window-glass, also plate and sheet glass.
SHAW, BENJAMIN - - -	11,130	11th March	1846	Preparing for spinning worsted and other yarns.
SHAW, BENJAMIN LEDGER -	7470	14th Nov.	1837	Preparing woollen and other warps.
SHAW, BENJAMIN LEDGER -	7681	12th June	1838	Preparing wool for manufacturing, also manufacture and finishing of, woollen cloths;—partly applicable to the weaving and stretching of other fabrics.
SHAW, BENJAMIN LEDGER -	13,491	5th Feb.	1851	Cleaning and preparing wool and other fibrous or textile materials; manufacture of coloured yarns of wool and other fibres; weaving.
SHAW, DAVID - - -	7470	14th Nov.	1837	Preparing woollen and other warps.
SHAW, EDMUND - - -	7432	14th Sept.	1837	Manufacture of paper by the application of a certain vegetable substance not hitherto used for the purpose.
SHAW, EDMUND - - -	7633	5th May	1838	Manufacture of paper and paper-boards.
SHAW, GEORGE - - -	14,352	17th Dec.	1852	Machinery for making envelopes and bags.

Name of Patentee.	Progressive Number.	Date.	Subject-matter of Patent.
SHAW, JAMES - - -	10,235	24th June 1844	Manufacture of metal dish-covers and metal dishes.
SHAW, JAMES HENRY - -	8993	19th June 1841	Setting wheat and other seeds.
SHAW, JOHN - - - -	4482	21st June 1820	Making bricks by machinery.
SHAW, JOHN - - - -	5013	7th Oct. 1824	Transverse spring-slides for trumpets, trombones, French horns, bugles, and every other musical instrument of the like nature.
SHAW, JOHN - - - -	7318	7th March 1837	Machinery used in preparing wool and the waste of cotton-wool for spinning.
SHAW, JOHN - - - -	7892	1st Dec. 1838	Arrangement and construction of wind musical instruments.
SHAW, JOHN - - - -	10,771	12th July 1845	Hydro-pneumatic engine.
SHAW, JOHN - - • -	11,486	14th Dec. 1846	Machinery for carding, drawing slubbing, and roving cotton-wool and other fibrous substances.
SHAW, JOHN - - - -	12,728	1st Aug. 1849	Air-guns.
SHAW, JOHN - - - -	14,231	20th July 1852	Machinery for carding cotton-wool, flax and other fibrous materials.
SHAW, JOSEPH - - -	13,211	3rd Aug. 1850	Constructing and working certain parts of railways.
SHAW, JOSHUA - - -	3906	15th April 1815	Glaziers' diamond.
SHAW, JOSHUA - - -	8704	17th Nov. 1840	Discharging ordnance, muskets, fowling-pieces, and other fire-arms.
SHAW, RICHARD - - -	11,916	21st Oct. 1847	Manufacture of wrought-iron railway-bars, and railway-chairs.
SHAW, RICHARD - - -	12,249	21st Aug. 1848	Manufacture of iron and tire bars, round-bars, square-bars, and flat-bars, T-iron, angle-iron, and trough-iron.
SHAW, ROBERT - - -	12,441	25th Jan. 1849	Machinery for preparing, spinning, and doubling cotton-wool, flax, silk, and similar fibrous materials.
SHAW, THOMAS SILVER -	10,714	10th June 1845	Construction of roasting-jacks.
SHAW, WILLIAM - - -	10,543	3rd March 1845	Machine for paging books and numbering documents consecutively or otherwise, printing words, dates, marks, numbers, or impressions.
SHAW, WILLIAM ROBINSON -	9620	31st Jan. 1843	Supplying steam-boilers with water.
SHAWE, JOHN - - -	95	5th July 1845	Manuring and improving grounds.
SHAWE, JOHN - - -	251	23rd Nov. 1686	Making, marbling, rounding, and finishing mantel-pieces for chimneys, to imitate marble.
SHAWE, RALPH - - -	541	24th May 1733	Composition of various minerals, earth, clay, and other earthy substances mixed together, for making a ware of a chocolate colour, striped with white outside and inside, resembling brown china-ware, and glazed with salt.
SHEAF, HORATIO SYDNEY -	10,767	12th Feb. 1845	Obtaining and applying motive-power.
SHEARMAN, JOHN HENRY -	10,600	7th April 1845	Separating and extracting grease, oil, and oleaginous matter, from water in which any such matter may be contained, particularly the water used in cleansing wool, spun wool, and woollen-cloth.
SHEARS, DANIEL TOWERS -	4175	1st Nov. 1817	Machine for cooling liquids; applicable to the condensation of vapour, and may be of utility in condensing spirits in the process of distillation, and cooling worts, beer, and other liquids.

Name of Patentee.	Progressive Number.	Date.	Subject-matter of Patent.
SHEARS, DANIEL TOWERS -	5005	7th Oct. 1824	Making spelter or zinc.
SHEARS, DANIEL TOWERS -	5925	31st March 1830	Apparatus used in distilling; also process of distilling and rectifying.
SHEARS, DANIEL TOWERS -	11,022	24th Dec. 1845	Treatment of zinc ores for the purpose of producing zinc ingots;—applicable to the reduction of other ores and metals.
SHEARS, DANIEL TOWERS -	11,534	19th Jan. 1847	Treatment of zinc ores for the purpose of producing zinc ingots; applicable to the reduction of other ores and metals.
SHEARS, DANIEL TOWERS -	13,286	17th Oct. 1850	Manufacture and refining of sugar.
SHEARS, JAMES HENRY -	5005	7th Oct. 1824	Making spelter or zinc.
SHEE, JOSEPH - - -	6598	22nd April 1834	Distillation.
SHEFFIELD, WILLIAM EVETTS	3612	31st Oct. 1812	Apparatus and furnaces for separating metallic and other substances from their ores, or other matters combined or united with them; application of the same.
SHEFFIELD, WILLIAM EVETTS [Sheffield, William Evett.]	3843	23rd Sept. 1814	Making copper and its compounds, and other metallic substances.
SHELDON, RICHARD - -	455	27th May 1723	Machine and engine for preserving, securing, and bagging hops.
SHELDON, WILLIAM - -	10,064	21st Feb. 1844	Manufacture of buttons, japanners' ware, and articles in substitution of papier-mâché.
SHELDRAKE, TIMOTHY - -	2157	24th Jan. 1797	Curing deformities of children and others, arising from distortion in the form or combination of bones in the deformed part.
SHELDRAKE, TIMOTHY - -	3458	15th June 1811	Wheels which when combined will constitute a moving power of great force, and being applied to machinery worked by steam, wind, water, or other power, will greatly increase such power, and may also be used in machinery instead of wheels and pinions as now used, producing less friction and greater velocity, also a saving of time and of the moving power.
SHENCK, ROBERT BRETT -	11,450	17th Nov. 1846	Preparation of hemp and flax.
SHENTON, JOHN SNELSON -	5521	12th July 1827	Mechanism of waterclosets.
SHEPARD, EDWARD - -	11,200	7th May 1846	Gates, doors, shutters, windows, and other articles of the like construction, and fastenings to be attached thereto.
SHEPARD, EDWARD CLARENCE	13,302	24th Oct. 1850	Electro-magnetic apparatus, suitable for the production of motive-power, heat, and light.
SHEPARD, EDWARD CLARENCE	13,727	28th Aug. 1851	Obtaining and applying motive-power.
SHEPARD, EDWARD CLARENCE	14,197	6th July 1852	Electro-magnetic apparatus, suitable for the production of motive-power, heat, and light.
SHEPHERD, CHARLES - -	12,567	16th April 1849	Working clocks and other timekeepers, telegraphs, and machinery, by electricity.
SHEPHERD, GEORGE - -	13,363	23rd Nov. 1850	Means or appliances used in conveying telegraphic intelligence between different places.
SHEPHERD, JOSEPH - -	12,962	7th Feb. 1850	Apparatus for changing the position of carriages on railways.
SHEPHERD, WILLIAM - -	9948	18th Nov. 1843	Four-port slide-valve controller, for reversing steam-engines, and for working steam expansively in the cylinder.

Name of Patentee.	Progressive Number.	Date.	Subject-matter of Patent.
SHEPHERD, WILLIAM - -	10,626	19th April 1845	Printing calicoes and other surfaces.
SHEPLEY, GEORGE - - -	1074	27th June 1774	Mill-stones placed horizontally, and worked with wind or water, for grinding bark for tanning leather, Brazil-wood, logwood, madder, fustic, indigo, saltpetre, and all other woods, drugs, roots, minerals, and colours used in dyeing.
SHEPLEY, JOSEPH - - -	5079	11th Jan. 1825	Construction of a machine for throstle and water spinning of yarn from cotton, flax, silk, wool, or other fibrous materials.
SHEPPARD, EDWARD - -	5141	29th March 1825	Machinery for raising the wool or pile on woollen or other cloths, by means of the teasel or other points.
SHEPPARD, EDWIN - - -	10,044	8th Feb. 1844	Machinery for planing, sawing, and cutting wood and other substances.
SHEPPARD, GEORGE - -	13,810	13th Nov. 1851	Construction of apparatus for grinding grain and other substances.
SHEPPARD, RICHARD - -	6881	17th Aug. 1835	Tiles for covering roofs.
SHERIDAN, CHARLES - -	7274	11th Jan. 1837	Manufacture of soda.
SHERIDAN, JOHN JOSEPH [CHARLES.	6673	6th Sept. 1834	Processes of saccharine, vinous, and acetous fermentation.
SHERIDAN, JOHN JOSEPH [CHARLES.	6783	9th March 1835	Processes of saccharine, vinous, and acetous fermentation.
SHERIDAN, JOHN JOSEPH [CHARLES.	6894	17th Sept. 1835	Manufacture of soap.
SHERIDAN, JOHN JOSEPH [CHARLES.	6932	17th Nov. 1835	Processes of saccharine, vinous, and acetous fermentation.
SHERIDAN, JOHN JOSEPH [CHARLES.	7211	20th Oct. 1836	Processes of saccharine, vinous, and acetous fermentation.
SHERIDAN, JOHN JOSEPH [CHARLES.	7420	24th Aug. 1837	Drying and screening malt.
SHERIDAN, JOHN JOSEPH CHARLES.	7426	31st Aug. 1837	Manufacture of soda.
SHERIDAN, JOHN JOSEPH [CHARLES.	7822	27th Sept. 1838	Manufacture of soap.
SHERRARD, WILLIAM - -	261	4th Nov. 1688	Making, dressing, and instrating black plain silks, as alamodes, ranforsees, and lute-strings.
SHERSON, ROBERT - -	1256	12th June 1780	White composition, " Marine metal," for sheathing ships, and for other valuable purposes.
SHERWIN, WILLIAM - -	190	15th Aug. 1676	Printing broad calico and Scotch-cloth, with a double-necked rolling press.
SHEWARD, WILLIAM - -	1097	10th June 1775	Making needles.
SHEWARD, WILLIAM - -	1683	9th June 1789	Finishing, effecting, and completing the eye of a needle, to prevent it cutting the thread.
SHIELS, CHARLES - -	5973	5th Aug. 1830	Preparing and cleansing rice.
SHIERS, RICHARD - -	13,381	2nd Dec. 1850	Manufacture of textile fabrics.
SHILLIBEER, GEORGE - -	9086	20th Sept. 1841	Construction of hearses, mourning and other carriages.
SHILTON, WILLIAM - -	6405	3rd April 1833	Machine for cutting files and rasps.
SHIMWELL, ISAAC - -	9549	8th Dec. 1842	Manufacture of fringes, cords, and other similar wares; machinery for producing the same.
SHIPLEY, JOHN GEORGE -	9484	6th Oct. 1842	Saddles.

Name of Patentee.	Progressive Number.	Date.	Subject-matter of Patent.
SHIPMAN, WILLIAM - -	28	22nd Jan. 1624	Raising and preparing madder for dyeing.
SHIPTON, JAMES ALFRED -	12,240	14th Aug. 1848	Steam-engines.
SHOOLBRED, ANDREW - -	5243	18th Aug. 1825	Substitute for back stays and braces.
SHOOLBRIDGE, GEORGE - -	4436	5th Feb. 1820	Substitute for flax or hemp; manufacturing the same.
SHOOLBRIDGE, WILLIAM -	4436	5th Feb. 1820	Substitute for flax or hemp; manufacturing the same.
SHORE, JOSEPH - - -	8407	3rd March 1840	Preserving and covering certain metals and alloys of metals.
SHORE, THOMAS - - -	13,348	14th Nov. 1850	Dressing flour.
SHORES, JEFFREY - - -	6022	1st Nov. 1830	Tackle and other hooks. "Self-relieving hooks."
SHORLAND, WILLIAM - -	1693	30th July 1789	Regular rotatory motion, the machinery of which is to be put in operation by a steam-engine, without crank or cog-wheel, and to be fixed upon new invented gudgeons and brasses.
SHORLAND, WILLIAM - -	1794	3rd March 1791	Mill, machine or machinery with double power overshot wheels, and floodgates, calculated to prevent mills and other works driven by water from being flooded or impeded by back water, and is suitable for grinding grain, and powdering or whitening sugar, and may be worked by water, wind, manual labour, steam, or by horses or other cattle.
SHORT, THOMAS - - -	1069	27th April 1774	Making reflecting telescopes with more than two specula, to be used by the same person at the same time, whereby their magnifying power and uses are increased, also two persons are enabled to view the same object at the same time, and with the same telescope.
SHORTER, EDWARD - -	2266	10th Nov. 1798	Facilitating the draught of carriages, fixing carriage bodies, tents and marquees.
SHORTER, EDWARD - -	2371	1st Feb. 1800	Machine for working and causing the progressive motion of ships and vessels, without sails or oars.
SHORTER, EDWARD - -	2690	21st March 1803	Apparatus for working pumps.
SHORTER, EDWARD - -	2807	16th Jan. 1805	Mechanical apparatus for raising ballast;—applicable to other purposes.
SHORTER, EDWARD - -	3075	19th Oct. 1807	Jack for roasting meat.
SHORTER, EDWARD - -	3567	19th May 1812	Construction of tunnels and subterraneous passages.
SHORTER, EDWARD - -	4143	19th July 1817	Construction of wheeled-carriages.
SHORTHOUSE, SAMUEL -	4407	1st Nov. 1819	Machine to cut straw.
SHOTBOLT, JOHN - - -	13	23rd May 1619	Engines for making and repairing highways, roads, mounds, and banks of the sea, great rivers, and other waters; also making, sinking, and repairing ponds, drains, rivers, and watercourses.
SHOTWELL, WILLIAM - -	3035	21st April 1807	Machine for bleaching, washing, and cleansing linen and other articles that can be so operated on by hand.
SHOTWELL, WILLIAM - -	3142	14th June 1808	Manufacture of mustard.
SHOVE, GEORGE - - -	12,817	18th Oct. 1849	Manufacturing ornamented surfaces when glass and other substances are used.

Name of Patentee.	Progressive Number.	Date.	Subject-matter of Patent.
SHOWBRIDGE, JAMES - -	2763	18th May 1804	Shield or protection for the human body against sword, bayonet, or pike, also proof against musket ball.
SHRAPNEL, HENRY - -	6675	6th Sept. 1834	Fire-arms; ammunition for the same.
SHRAPNELL, HENRY NEED- [HAM SCROPE.	7287	19th Jan. 1837	Snuffers.
SHRAPNELL, HENRY NEED- [HAM SCROPE.	8224	26th Sept. 1839	Cork-screws.
SHRAPNEL, HENRY NEEDHAM [SCROPE.	14,271	23rd Aug. 1852	Ordnance and fire-arms, cartridges, and ammunition or projectiles ; mode of making up or preparing the same.
SHRAPNEL, HENRY NEEDHAM [SCROPE.	14,333	23rd Oct. 1852	Extracting gold and other metals from mineral and earthy substances.
SHUDI, BURKAT - - -	947	18th Dec. 1769	Machinery to improve harpsichords.
SHULDHAM, MOLYNEUX -	5205	8th July 1825	Setting, working, reefing, and furling the sails of boats, ships, and other vessels.
SHURMUR, THOMAS - -	1998	15th July 1794	Water-engine for raising water or working mills.
SHUTE, THOMAS ROCK - -	6882	17th Aug. 1835	Spinning and doubling organzine silk.
SHUTE, THOMAS ROCK - -	12,891	15th Dec. 1849	Spinning, doubling, and throwing organzine silk.
SHUTTLEWORTH, EDWARD -	414	12th July 1717	Machine for drawing water out of coal-pits, salt-pits, copper and lead mines.
SHUTTLEWORTH, HENRY -	7418	21st Aug. 1837	Machinery and combinations of machinery for making pins.
SHUTTLEWORTH, JOHN GEORGE	8156	18th July 1839	Obtaining a rotary motion from the rectilinear motion of the piston-rod of a steam or other similar engine.
SHUTTLEWORTH, JOHN GEORGE	8539	9th June 1840	Railway and other propulsion.
SHYRIN, JOSEPH - - -	476	5th April 1725	Engine for supplying cities, corporations, and towns with water, and for draining mines, overflowed lands, and marshes.
SIBLY, EBENEZER - - -	2049	7th May 1795	Re-animating tincture, a medicine of great efficacy in the cure of cutaneous diseases, impurities of the blood, debility, disorders of the stomach and bowels, inflammatory and rheumatic disorders; an efficacious stiptic in cases of violent bleeding, also if outwardly applied will heal wounds, and is a preventive of mortification. " Re-animating solar tincture."
SIBTHORP, HENRY - - -	86	2nd Oct. 1635	Making ovens for the use of bakers, cooks, and others, and in such a manner that they may be heated with sea-coal or other coal.
SICARD, PIERRE AMABLE DE [ST. SIMON.	14,281	26th Aug. 1852	Enabling persons to remain under water, and in noxious vapours.
SICCAMA, ABEL - - -	10,553	13th March 1845	Flutes and other wind instruments.
SIDELEY, JOSHUA, junior -	13,016	23rd March 1850	Ships' fittings.
SIDDON, WILLIAM - - -	2173	14th March 1797	Screwing and fastening hammer-springs and sear-springs to gun-locks and pistol-locks.
SIDEBOTHAM, PETER - -	1523	23rd Jan. 1786	Instrument to give alarm in case of accidental or other fire.
SIDEBOTTOM, JAMES - -	9000	23rd June 1841	Machinery for preparing cotton and other fibrous substances for spinning.
SIDEBOTTOM, JOE - - -	12,915	3rd Jan. 1850	Steam-engines.

Name of Patentee.	Progres-sive Number.	Date.	Subject-matter of Patent.
SIDEBOTTOM, JOHN - -	13,126	11th June 1850	Looms for weaving.
SIDGIER, HENRY - - -	1331	4th July 1782	Machine for washing wearing-apparel, lace, linen, and every other thing which re-requires washing.
SIEBE, AUGUSTUS - - -	4358	5th April 1819	Weighing-machine.
SIEBE, AUGUSTUS - - -	5636	29th March 1828	Hydraulic-machines.
SIEBE, AUGUSTUS - - -	14,112	1st May 1852	Machinery for manufacturing paper.
SIEGNETTE, LOUIS ELIZEE -	7036	21st March 1836	Preserving animal and vegetable substances.
SIEMENS, CHARLES WILLIAM	11,021	24th Dec. 1845	Steam-engines; regulating the power and velocity of machines for communicating power.
SIEMENS, CHARLES WILLIAM	12,006	22nd Dec. 1847	Engines to be worked by steam and other fluids.
SIEMENS, CHARLES WILLIAM	12,531	20th March 1849	Engines to be worked by steam and other fluids; evaporating liquids.
SIEMENS, CHARLES WILLIAM	14,060	15th April 1852	Fluid-meter.
SIEMENS, ERNST WERNER -	13,062	23rd April 1850	Electric-telegraphs.
SIEVIER, ROBERT WILLIAM -	5911	27th Feb. 1830	Construction of rudders for navigating vessels.
SIEVIER, ROBERT WILLIAM -	6193	1st Dec. 1831	Manufacture of cables, ropes, whale-fishing and other lines, lath and rigger-bands, bags, and purses.
SIEVIER, ROBERT WILLIAM -	6366	17th Jan. 1833	Manufacture of elastic goods or fabrics.
SIEVIER, ROBERT WILLIAM -	6946	7th Dec. 1835	Waterproof cloth or fabric, elastic or non-elastic;—applicable to various purposes; also waterproof hats or caps.
SIEVIER, ROBERT WILLIAM -	7015	27th Feb. 1836	Dissolving and preparing caoutchouc or India-rubber for various purposes.
SIEVIER, ROBERT WILLIAM -	7763	6th Aug. 1838	Looms for weaving; method of producing figured goods or fabrics.
SIEVIER, ROBERT WILLIAM -	7816	20th Sept. 1838	Rigger-pully; bands for driving machinery, and ropes and lines for other purposes.
SIEVIER, ROBERT WILLIAM -	9491	13th Oct. 1842	Looms for weaving; mode of producing plain or figured goods or fabrics.
SIEVIER, ROBERT WILLIAM -	10,305	5th Sept. 1844	Looms for weaving; mode of producing plain or figured goods or fabrics.
SIEVIER, ROBERT WILLIAM -	11,202	12th May 1846	Printing.
SIEVIER, ROBERT WILLIAM -	11,790	12th July 1847	Materials for purifying or decolourizing bodies, which materials may also be employed as manure and pigments, and for other purposes.
SIEVIER, ROBERT WILLIAM -	11,799	17th July 1847	Stamping, marking, cutting, embossing, or printing.
SIEVIER, ROBERT WILLIAM -	12,292	19th Oct. 1848	Means of warping and weaving plain and figured fabrics.
SIEVIER, ROBERT WILLIAM -	13,467	21st Jan. 1851	Weaving and printing or staining textile goods or fabrics.
SIEVIER, ROBERT WILLIAM -	13,650	29th May 1851	Weaving and printing textile fabrics.
SIEVIER, ROBERT WILLIAM -	14,327	19th Oct. 1852	Brewing; also production of extracts or in-fusions for other purposes.
SIGMOND, JOSEPH - -	2452	20th Nov. 1800	Lotion and dentifrice for preserving and beautifying the teeth and gums. " British Imperial Lotion and Dentifrice."
SILCOCK, JAMES - - -	10,033	31st Jan. 1844	Planes.
SILVESTER, CHARLES - -	3931	22nd June 1815	Texture of bobbin-lace.

Name of Patentee.	Progres-sive Number.	Date.	Subject-matter of Patent.
SILVESTER, EDWARD - -	3490	14th Sept. 1811	Drag to be applied to the wheels of carriages.
SILVESTER, GEORGE - -	1890	14th June 1792	Construction of windmills and watermills.
SILVESTER, JOHN - - -	2170	9th March 1797	Mashing and mixing malt and grain used for brewing and distilling, by means of machinery.
SILVESTER, JOHN - - -	7976	21st Feb. 1839	Arrangement and construction of apparatus for hanging and closing doors.
SILVESTER, JOHN - - -	13,181	17th July 1850	Straightening, flattening, setting, and shaping hardened steel.
SILVESTRI, GIACOMO - -	10,596	7th April 1845	Preserving animal and vegetable substances from decay.
SIMCOX, GEORGE PRICE -	11,963	16th Nov. 1847	Manufacture of carpets and other similar articles.
SIMISTER, JAMES - - -	5744	18th Dec. 1828	Weaving or preparing a cloth or fabric, and application thereof to making stays and other articles of dress.
SIMISTER, JAMES - - -	11,834	5th Aug. 1847	Manufacture of stays and belts.
SIMISTER, RICHARD - -	6740	23rd Dec. 1834	Pens of steel or other elastic metal.
SIMMONDS, GEORGE - -	2765	19th May 1804	Manufacturing hats, bonnets, and other articles, of paper, and rendering the same waterproof.
SIMMONS, BENJAMIN - -	7023	8th March 1836	Retorts, stills, and other chemical apparatus, and the machinery connected therewith.
SIMMONS, EDWARD ROBERT -	9137	2nd Nov. 1841	Apparatus for preventing splashing in walking.
SIMMONS, JOHN LINTORN [ARABIN.	14,095	29th April 1852	Manufacture of ordnance; construction and manufacture of carriages, and traversing-apparatus for manœuvring the same.
SIMMONS, WILLIAM - -	4030	14th May 1816	Keyed instruments, as organs, pianofortes, harpsichords, or any instrument to which keys can or may be fixed.
SIMMONS, WILLIAM - -	10,751	3rd July 1845	Hats, caps, and bonnets.
SIMONS, EDWARD - - -	13,922	27th Jan. 1852	Lighting.
SIMPKIN, CHARLES - -	1925	19th Dec. 1792	Construction of engines used for extinguishing fires.
SIMPSON, ALEXANDER HO-[RATIO.	8687	5th Nov. 1840	Machine or apparatus to be used as a moveable observatory or telegraph, as a moveable platform for repairing the interior and exterior of buildings, and as a fire-escape.
SIMPSON, ALEXANDER HO-RATIO.]	8732	9th Dec. 1840	Apparatus for working pumps.
SIMPSON, ALEXANDRE HO-[RATIO.	8989	17th June 1841	Producing light; manufacturing apparatus for the diffusion of light.
SIMPSON, ALFRED - - -	10,310	12th Sept. 1844	Manufacture of hats.
SIMPSON, EDWARD - - -	2399	8th May 1800	Manufacture of straw-plat.
SIMPSON, GEORGE - - -	12,585	26th April 1849	Treating solvents of India-rubber and of other gums or substances.
SIMPSON, GEORGE - - -	12,631	5th June 1849	Machinery, apparatus, or means of raising, lowering, supporting, moving, or transporting heavy bodies.
SIMPSON, GEORGE - - -	12,936	19th Jan. 1850	Machinery, apparatus, or means of raising, lowering, supporting, moving, or transporting heavy bodies.

Name of Patentee.	Progressive Number.	Date.	Subject-matter of Patent.
SIMPSON, GEORGE - - -	13,377	30th Nov. 1850	Sheathing ships; protecting and confining gunpowder and compounds thereof; materials used for such purposes.
SIMPSON, JAMES - - -	4341	9th Feb. 1819	Method of conveying gas for illumination, to the burners, and at the same time suspending the burners or lamps, lustres or other frames in which burners are placed.
SIMPSON, JAMES - - -	4566	3rd July 1821	Manufacture of snuffers.
SIMPSON, JAMES - - -	11,594	24th Feb. 1847	Carriages to be used upon railways;—partly applicable to other roads.
SIMPSON, JEREMIAH - -	10,687	24th May 1845	Constructing the flues and interior arrangements of ovens and kilns used in the manufacture of china and earthenware.
SIMPSON, JOHN - - -	3581	16th July 1812	Cleaning, gunning, and scouring whalebone.
SIMPSON, JOHN - - -	3582	16th July 1812	Construction of lamps. "Palmer's Birmingham economic Lamps."
SIMPSON, JOHN - - -	4227	16th Feb. 1818	Constructing and making spring-hooks or woodcock-eyes used for coach-harness; which principle of spring is also applicable to harness buckles, territs, hooks, and harness and spring swivels.
SIMPSON, JOHN - - -	4329	15th Jan. 1819	Constructing and making harness for horses and other animals used for drawing carriages. "Release-harness."
SIMPSON, JOHN - - -	10,848	2nd Oct. 1845	Obtaining and applying motive-power.
SIMPSON, JOSEPH - - -	12,240	14th Aug. 1848	Steam-engines.
SIMPSON, LIGHTLY - - -	6952	10th Dec. 1835	Preparation of certain colours to be used for printing cotton and other fabrics.
SIMPSON, MICHAEL HODGE -	7005	17th Feb. 1836	Machinery for heckling or combing and preparing hemp, flax, tow, and other vegetable fibrous substances, also waste silk.
SIMPSON, RICHARD - -	6620	3rd June 1834	Machinery for roving and slubbing cotton and wool.
SIMPSON, RICHARD - -	10,769	12th July 1845	Bleaching yarns and fabrics.
SIMPSON, ROBERT - - -	2309	23rd April 1799	Instrument to extract teeth in a perpendicular direction.
SIMPSON, SAMUEL - - -	546	15th March 1734	Extracting oil or grease from the flesh of swine, for use in the woollen manufacture.
SIMPSON, THOMAS - - -	1562	10th Oct. 1786	Composition, called "British smalts, or Powder-blue."
SIMPSON, THOMAS - - -	9650	2nd March 1843	Buckles.
SIMPSON, THOMAS BARTLETT	11,386	25th Sept. 1846	Propelling; machinery connected therewith.
SIMPSON, WILLIAM - -	6828	9th May 1835	Safety-drag or lever-slide for carriages.
SIMPSON, WILLIAM HENRY -	4138	10th July 1817	Machinery for spinning wool, cotton, and other fibrous substances.
SIMS, JAMES - - - -	8942	29th April 1841	Steam-engines.
SIMS, JAMES - - - -	11,859	9th Sept. 1847	Steam-engines.
SIMSON, JOHN - - -	11,247	20th June 1846	Machinery for preparing and spinning flax and other fibrous materials.

Name of Patentee.	Progressive Number.	Date.	Subject-matter of Patent.
SINCLAIR, JOHN - - -	4411	18th Nov. 1819	Manufacture of shawls, plaids, and other articles in which coloured threads are wrought into flowers and other fancy figures in weaving, and whether of silk, cotton, worsted, lint, hemp, or other materials or mixtures thereof.
SINCLAIR, JOHN JAMES - -	10,773	21st July 1845	Producing glossy surfaces on paper and similar materials.
SINCLAIR, WILLIAM - -	13,807	13th Nov. 1851	Locks.
SINCLAR, GEORGE - -	444	16th May 1722	Raising and cultivating in the American plantations, the plants which produce balsam of tolu, pero, and capair, dragon's blood, coloquintida, scammony, rhubarb, contraherba, coffee, alkermes, jalap, gutta-gamba, Jesuits' balsam, ipecacuanha, and agarie; breeding and curing cochineal, and cultivating plants upon which such insects feed.
SINGER, ALFRED - - -	8042	23rd April 1839	Preparation and combination of earthenware or porcelain, for mosaic or tessellated work.
SINGLETON, GEORGE - -	1780	6th Nov. 1790	Machine for glazing linens, cottons, calicoes, muslin, stuffs of linen and cotton, buckrams, and other articles of British manufacture, as well as those of India.
SISCO, ANTOINE DOMINIQUE -	13,817	15th Nov. 1851	Manufacture of chains; combining iron with other metal, applicable to such and other manufactures.
SITLINTON, THOMAS - -	5213	16th July 1825	Machinery for shearing or cropping woollen or other cloths.
SIX, ALEXANDRE - - -	13,567	24th March 1851	Bleaching flax and hemp.
SIX, HENRI - - - -	13,567	24th March 1851	Bleaching flax and hemp.
SKAIFE, JOSEPH - - -	14,202	6th July 1852	Mills for grinding.
SKENE, ANDREW MOTZ, (Lieutenant.)	5587	15th Dec. 1827	Propelling vessels through the water: working under-shot water-mills.
SKENE, GEORGE ROBERT -	11,646	31st March 1847	Making and refining infusions and decoctions.
SKERTCHLEY, JOSEPH - -	12,197	30th June 1848	Bricks; manufacture of tobacco-pipes and other like articles.
SKEYS, JOHN - - -	1506	7th Nov. 1785	Pump.
SKIDMORE, JOHN - - -	1552	5th Aug. 1786	Ornamenting stove-grates, fire-irons, chimney pieces and panels, the interior of houses and ships, the outside of coaches and other carriages, cabinets and furniture, japan, china, and earthenware, with foil, stones, paste, glass, and compositions used in the jewellery trade.
SKIDMORE, JOHN - - -	2337	8th Aug. 1799	Making and casting with cast-iron, brass or mixed metal, naves and stocks for carriage-wheels.
SKIN, JAMES - - -	6381	6th Feb. 1833	Making gas from coal or other substances.
SKIN, JOHN - - - -	240	16th Sept. 1684	Casting worms for alembics and stills, and other uses, in tin and copper.
SKINNER, GEORGE - - -	10,968	20th Nov. 1845	Manufacture of earthenware pastes and vitrious bodies; composition and material for the same, with mode of combination; which improvements, compositions, and combinations are also applicable to the manufacture of slabs, tiles, and pavements, and for other purposes.

Name of Patentee.	Progressive Number.	Date.	Subject-matter of Patent.
SKINNER, JOSEPH - - -	6969	29th Dec. 1835	Machinery for cutting wood for veneers and other purposes.
SKINNER, THOMAS - -	13,718	14th Aug. 1851	Producing ornamental surfaces on metal and other materials.
SKRINE, JULIAN - - -	8053	30th April 1839	Manufacture of forks, spoons, coins, and medals.
SLACK, ELIJAH - - -	12,628	2nd June 1849	Preparation of materials to be used in the manufacture of textile fabrics.
SLACK, JOHN - - -	12,972	21st Feb. 1850	Manufacture of textile goods or fabrics; machinery connected therewith.
SLADE, JACOB TILTON -	6724	25th Nov. 1834	Metallic sheathing for the bottoms of ships or vessels.
SLADE, JACOB TILTON -	6978	11th Jan. 1836	Machinery for raising earth, and for other purposes.
SLADE, JACOB TILTON -	7844	3rd Nov. 1838	Pumps for liquids or aëriform fluids.
SLADEN, WILLIAM - -	2004	29th July 1794	Machinery for removing and conveying earth, stones, mud, sand, ballast or any other thing, on level ground, and for emptying, raising, and conveying the same out of canals, rivers, ponds, pits, holes or foundations of houses, also for lowering the same from eminences and heights;—applicable to other purposes.
SLAGG, RICHARD - - -	5371	23rd May 1826	Manufacture of springs, chiefly applicable to carriages.
SLARK, JOHN, junior -	6657	12th Aug. 1834	Construction of looms for weaving by hand or power.
SLATE, ARCHIBALD -	12,918	3rd Jan. 1850	Manufacture of iron pipes or tubes.
SLATE, ARCHIBALD -	13,308	2nd Nov. 1850	Canal navigation.
SLATE, ARCHIBALD -	13,641	27th May 1851	Steam-engines and steam-boilers; passages and valves for the induction, eduction, and working of fluids.
SLATE, JOHN - - -	13,312	2nd Nov. 1850	Stoves and furnaces, chimney-pots and regulators.
SLATER, JAMES - - -	6103	2nd April 1831	Generating steam or vapour applicable as a moving power; machinery employed for the purpose.
SLATER, JAMES - - -	6669	23rd Aug. 1834	Machinery for bleaching linen and cotton goods.
SLATER, JAMES - - -	7467	11th Nov. 1837	Steam-engines; boilers and furnaces used for the generation of steam or for other purposes.
SLATER, JAMES - - -	13,434	28th Dec. 1850	Machinery for stretching and opening textile or woven fabrics.
SLATER, JOHN - - -	1433	29th April 1784	Machine for printing three or more colours on cottons, linens, silks, woollen-cloth, or other manufactured goods.
SLATER, JOHN - - -	2748	19th Jan. 1804	Manufacture of cables, shrouds, stays, and other articles for rigging ships, of materials not before used.
SLATER, JOHN - - -	2843	2nd May 1805	Sawing-mills, or machines for sawing timber.
SLATER, JOHN - - -	3301	12th Feb. 1810	Hanging grindstones, so as to secure them from breaking in the centre.
SLATER. JOHN - - -	3790	12th March 1814	Steam-boiler, and apparatus for washing, steaming, cleansing, and whitening clothes and cloths, and for warming laundries, closets, and other places.

Name of Patentee.	Progressive Number.	Date.	Subject-matter of Patent.
SLATER, JOHN - - -	4579	4th Aug. 1821	Making kitchen-ranges, and apparatus for cooking and other purposes.
SLATER, JOHN - - -	4872	22nd Nov. 1823	Machinery to facilitate the operation of cutting or grinding wool or cotton from the surfaces of cloths, kerseymeres, cotton cloths, or mixtures of the same; also for removing hair or fur from skins.
SLATER, JOHN - - -	5740	15th Dec. 1828	Axletrees and boxes for carriage-wheels.
SLATER, JOHN NUTTALL -	13,434	28th Dec. 1850	Machinery for stretching and opening textile or woven fabrics.
SLATER, JOSEPH - - -	2183	4th July 1797	Machine for finishing bleached, dyed, and printed muslins.
SLAUGHTER, EDWARD -	9274	4th March 1842	Construction of iron-wheels for railway and other carriages.
SLAUGHTER, EDWARD -	11,801	19th July 1847	Locomotive-engines.
SLAUGHTER, EDWARD -	12,433	23rd Jan. 1849	Marine steam-engines.
SLEATH, JOHN - -	1912	18th Oct. 1792	Manufacture of springs for trusses, and the coverings thereof, which method of manufacturing springs is applicable to steel backs, and to other purposes.
SLEDDON, FRANCIS -	7668	2nd June 1838	Machinery for spinning and doubling cotton, silk, flax, wool, and other fibrous substances.
SLEDDON, FRANCIS, junior -	8827	2nd Feb. 1841	Machinery for roving, slubbing, and spinning cotton and other fibrous substances.
SLEIGH, ADDERLEY WILLCOCKS	9247	8th Feb. 1842	Effecting and forming sheltered floating harbours of safety, by the employment of buoyant sea barriers;—applicable for the formation of breakwaters, floating-bridges, and other erections.
SLEIGH, WILLIAM WILLCOCKS	10,425	7th Dec. 1844	Hydro-mechanic apparatus, which, by a combination of hydraulic and mechanical apparatus, will, on known philosophical principles, supersede the use of fire and steam in working and propelling machinery and engines.
SLEIGH, WILLIAM WILLCOCKS	10,711	7th June 1845	Hydro-mechanic apparatus for producing motive-power.
SLEIGH, WILLIAM WILLCOCKS	12,463	8th Feb. 1849	Preventing injuries to persons and property from the sudden stoppage of railroad-carriages.
SLEIGH, WILLIAM WILLCOCKS	14,016	8th March 1852	A counteracting reaction motive-power engine.
SLOCUM, SAMUEL - - -	6577	18th March 1834	Machinery for making nails.
SLOCUM, SAMUEL - - -	6578	18th March 1834	Machinery for making pins.
SLOCUM, SAMUEL - - -	6768	18th Feb. 1835	Machinery for making nails.
SLOCUM, SAMUEL - - -	6911	22nd Oct. 1835	Machinery for making pins.
SLOMAN, CHARLTON HENRY -	11,921	21st Oct. 1847	Apparatus used for ironing.
SMALL, JAMES - - -	1164	1st Aug. 1777	Window-lath for curtains, also for bedsteads.
SMALL, JOHN - - -	7860	8th Nov. 1838	Filtering liquids.
SMALL, JOHN - - -	7883	1st Dec. 1838	Application of certain fibrous materials to the manufacture of thread or yarn and paper.
SMALL, WILLIAM - - -	1048	22nd July 1773	Constructing time-pieces.
SMALLWOOD, EDWARD -	9606	26th Jan. 1843	Covering roads, ways, and other surfaces.
SMART, GEORGE - - -	2415	17th June 1800	Method of combining masts, yards, bowsprits, &c. hollow, so as to give them lightness and strength;—applicable to other purposes.

Name of Patentee.	Progressive Number.	Date.		Subject-matter of Patent.
SMART, GEORGE - - -	3562	5th May	1812	Preparing timber to prevent the same from shrinking.
SMART, GEORGE - - -	3796	1st April	1814	Machinery for grinding corn and various other articles.
SMART, GEORGE - - -	4688	4th July	1822	Manufacture of chains. "Mathematical Chains."
SMART, HENRY - - -	4821	24th July	1823	Construction of pianofortes.
SMART, JAMES - - -	1873	26th April	1792	Making plough-shares and share-beds.
SMART, NEVIL - - -	7434	21st Sept.	1837	Preparing the materials for making bricks ;—applicable to other purposes.
SMART, ROBERT - - -	9759	8th June	1843	Paddle-wheels.
SMART, WALTER, junior - -	11,497	21st Dec.	1846	Lithographic printing-press.
SMARTFOOT, FRANCIS - -	262	8th Nov.	1689	Weighing and taking up ships' guns and goods lost at sea ; engine to enable a man to breathe under water with a pair of lungs fixed to his back as he swims.
SMEATON, JOHN - - -	1597	4th April	1787	Machine to be used in extracting oil from seeds.
SMEDLEY, THOMAS - -	8464	4th April	1840	Manufacture of tubes, pipes, and cylinders.
SMETHURST, JAMES - -	1831	18th Oct.	1791	Making a lamp and burner ; also making, moulding, and forming glass lenses.
SMETHURST, JAMES - -	2450	15th Nov.	1800	Lamp-burner.
SMETHURST, JAMES - -	2654	30th Oct.	1802	Lamps and reflectors.
SMETHURST, JAMES - -	3411	11th March	1811	Lamps.
SMETHURST, JAMES - -	5557	6th Nov.	1827	Lamps.
SMETHWICK, FRANCIS - -	149	14th May	1666	Grinding optical glasses in figures which are not spherical.
SMITH, ADDISON - - -	1359	13th March	1783	Constructing spectacles ; grinding and applying glasses for the purpose.
SMITH, ALEXANDER - -	4879	9th Dec.	1823	Boiler for steam-engines, and for other purposes.
SMITH, ANDREW - - -	5507	15th June	1827	Making shutters and blinds of iron, steel, or any other metal or composition thereof ; constructing and fixing the same ; uniting in shutters the properties of shutters and blinds.
SMITH, ANDREW - - -	5770	7th Feb.	1829	Construction of window-frames, sashes, or casements, shutters and doors, designed for security against burglars, as well as to exclude the weather.
SMITH, ANDREW - - -	6063	22nd Jan.	1831	Machinery for propelling boats and other vessels on water ; constructing boats or vessels for carrying such machinery,
SMITH, ANDREW - - -	6477	5th Oct.	1833	Springs for doors, and for other purposes.
SMITH, ANDREW - - -	6612	24th May	1834	Preparing phormium tenax, hemp, flax, and other fibrous substances, and rendering the same fit for heckling and spinning.
SMITH, ANDREW - - -	6743	12th Jan.	1835	Standing-rigging for ships and vessels ; method of fitting and using the same.
SMITH, ANDREW - - -	6793	18th March	1835	Printing-machines.
SMITH, ANDREW - - -	7002	12th Feb.	1836	Engines for exerting power for driving machinery, and for raising and lowering heavy bodies.
SMITH, ANDREW - - -	7044	26th March	1836	Manufacture of belts, bands, and straps, to be employed in the place of ropes or chains.

Name of Patentee.	Progres-sive Number.	Date.	Subject-matter of Patent.
SMITH, ANDREW - - -	7261	21st Dec. 1836	Construction of standing-rigging and stays for ships and vessels; method of fitting and using the same; construction of chains; machinery for making such rigging and chains.
SMITH, ANDREW - - -	7916	20th Dec. 1838	Apparatus for heating fluids, and generating steam.
SMITH, ANDREW - - -	8009	20th March 1839	Manufacture of ropes for cables, and for other purposes.
SMITH, ANDREW - - -	8595	7th Aug. 1840	Carriage-wheels; rails and chairs for railways.
SMITH, ANDREW - - -	9031	21st July 1841	Arrangement and construction of engines to be worked by steam or other fluids; applicable to the raising of water and other fluids.
SMITH, ANDREW - - -	11,083	11th Feb. 1846	Coating or covering metals to prevent oxydation.
SMITH, ANDREW - - -	11,538	21st Jan. 1847	Warping or hauling vessels.
SMITH, ANDREW - - -	11,727	3rd June 1847	Wheel-carriages.
SMITH, ANDREW - - -	12,620	24th May 1849	Machinery for the manufacture of rope or cordage; modes of fitting and using the same.
SMITH, ANTHONY FORESTER -	310	— — 1692	Boiling and heating water and other liquor; melting and refining sugars and other things usually operated on by means of fire.
SMITH, ARCHIBALD -	14,021	8th March 1852	Electric and electro-magnetic telegraph apparatus; machinery for and method of making and laying down submarine, submerged, and other such lines
SMITH, ARTHUR - - -	10,893	23rd Oct. 1845	Manufacture of soda-ash.
SMITH, BENJAMIN - - -	8868	8th March 1841	Apparatus for making salt from brine.
SMITH, BROOKE - - - [Smith, Brook.]	7650	24th May 1838	Cocks for drawing off liquids.
SMITH, BROOKE - - -	11,919	21st Oct. 1847	Apparatus for filtering.
SMITH, CHARLES - - -	1308	24th Dec. 1781	Machine for dressing or bolting flour and meal.
SMITH, CHARLES - - -	1680	9th May 1789	Machine for making thread used in manufacturing bone-lace, called mechlin long dozen and bell.
SMITH, CHARLES - - -	4330	15th Jan. 1819	Form of making up superfine oil and water colours for drawing and painting, and for other purposes.
SMITH, CHARLES - - -	8607	27th Aug. 1840	Manufacture of lime and cements or compositions.
SMITH, CHARLES - - -	9521	17th Nov. 1842	Manufacture and application of bricks, tiles, and other plastic articles; cements to be used with the same for building and for other purposes.
SMITH, CHARLES - - -	10,374	2nd Nov. 1844	Construction and application of a variety of cooking, culinary, and domestic articles and utensils, some of which are applicable to cleaning and a variety of other purposes.
SMITH, CHARLES - - -	11,149	25th March 1846	Utensils for cooking and for culinary purposes; methods of heating and suspending articles of domestic use.
SMITH, CHARLES JAMES -	10,667	14th May 1845	Artillery, guns, pistols, and other fire-arms; apparatus to be used therewith.

Name of Patentee.	Progres-sive Number.	Date.	Subject-matter of Patent.
SMITH, CHARLOTTE - -	12,607	14th May 1849	Certain articles of wearing-apparel.
SMITH, COLLIN - - -	6219	31st Jan. 1832	Apparatus for regulating the course and action of fluids and liquors ;—applicable to various purposes.
SMITH, DAVID - - -	12,624	29th May 1849	Manufacture of certain articles in lead.
SMITH, EDWARD - -	1256	12th June 1780	White composition, " Marine Metal," for sheathing ships and for other valuable purposes.
SMITH, EDWARD - - -	12,375	16th Dec. 1848	Window-blinds; and springs applicable to window-blinds, doors, and other purposes.
SMITH, EDWARD N. - -	13,175	17th July 1850	Machine to fold paper.
SMITH, EGERTON - - -	2512	5th June 1801	Tuning and keeping in tune musical and stringed instruments in general.
SMITH, EGERTON - - -	3265	26th Sept. 1809	Ships' binnacles and compasses; and mode of lighting the same.
SMITH, ENOS - - - -	956	27th April 1770	Dyeing wrought and unwrought woollens, linens, silks and cottons, with a liquid extracted from a red wood growing in the West Indies.
SMITH, FRANCIS - - -	6412	15th April 1833	Machinery for manufacturing bobbin-net lace.
SMITH, FRANCIS - - -	7219	8th Nov. 1836	Machinery for making bobbin-net or twist lace.
SMITH, FRANCIS - - -	8362	28th Jan. 1840	Machinery for manufacture of figured bobbin-net or lace.
SMITH, FRANCIS PETTIT - -	7104	31st May 1836	Propeller for steam and other vessels.
SMITH, GEORGE - - -	7870	13th Nov. 1838	Vessels to be propelled by steam or other power; construction and arrangement of machinery for propelling.
SMITH, GEORGE - - -	10,928	6th Nov. 1845	Manufacture of the miner's safety-fuze.
SMITH, GEORGE - - -	11,447	12th Nov. 1846	Safety-fuze.
SMITH, GEORGE - - -	13,243	5th Sept. 1850	Steam-engines; supplying boilers of steam-engines ;—partly applicable to other similar purposes.
SMITH, HELSON - - -	13,926	27th Jan. 1852	Construction of violins and other similar stringed musical instruments.
SMITH, HENRY - - -	2658	11th Nov. 1802	Vessel or barrel for the safe carriage and conveyance of gunpowder.
SMITH, HENRY - - -	8446	25th March 1840	Gas-burners and lamps.
SMITH, HENRY - - -	9291	10th March 1842	Construction of wheels and breaks for carriages.
SMITH, HENRY - - -	9838	13th July 1843	Apparatus for fastening doors; also apparatus for giving action to alarums.
SMITH, HRNRY - - -	10,241	3rd July 1844	Construction and arrangement of hand-rakes and horse-rakes; machinery for cutting vegetable substances.
SMITH, HENRY - - -	10,808	7th Aug. 1845	Manufacture of wheels for railways, and springs for railway and other carriages ; axle-guards for railway-carriages.
SMITH, HENRY - - -	11,638	23rd March 1847	Machine for cutting and separating vegetable substances; construction of machines for dibbling and sowing seed, and distributing vegetable substances and manure over land ;—partly applicable to wheeled carriages in general.
SMITH, HENRY - - -	12,266	5th Sept. 1848	Manufacture of railway-wheels.

Name of Patentee.	Progres- sive Number.	Date.		Subject-matter of Patent.
SMITH, HENRY WILLIAM -	5259	6th Oct.	1825	Manufacture of steel.
SMITH, JAMES - - -	160	22nd Sept.	1670	Planting and making madder.
SMITH, JAMES - - -	1908	7th Sept.	1792	Construction of fastenings for shoes and spurs;—applicable to other purposes where buckles are used.
SMITH, JAMES - - -	3865	20th Dec.	1814	Self-acting sash-fastening.
SMITH, JAMES - - -	4552	18th April	1821	Machinery employed for shearing or cropping woollen-cloth.
SMITH, JAMES - - -	4805	19th June	1823	Apparatus for applying steam to the boiling and concentrating of solutions, crystallizing muriate of soda from brines containing that salt, melting and refining tallow and oils, boiling of sugar, distilling, and other similar purposes,
SMITH, JAMES - - -	6560	20th Feb.	1834	Machinery used in preparing and spinning cotton, flax, wool, and other fibrous materials.
SMITH, JAMES - - -	6564	27th Feb.	1834	Machinery for carding cotton, flax, wool, silk, and other fibrous materials.
SMITH, JAMES - - -	6863	17th July	1835	Machinery for winding upon spools, bobbins, or barrels, slivers or rovings of cotton-wool and other fibrous substances.
SMITH, JAMES - - -	8054	30th April	1839	Machinery for spinning and twisting wool and other similar fibrous substances.
SMITH, JAMES - - -	8237	10th Oct.	1839	Self-acting temple applicable to looms for working fabrics, and moved by hand or power.
SMITH, JAMES - - -	8238	10th Oct.	1839	Canal navigation.
SMITH, JAMES - - -	8796	19th Jan.	1841	Preparing, spinning, and weaving cotton, silk, wool, and other fibrous substances; measuring and folding woven fabrics; machines for these purposes.
SMITH, JAMES - - -	9313	6th April	1842	Preparing and spinning cotton-wool, flax, hemp, and other fibrous substances.
SMITH, JAMES - - -	9523	25th Nov.	1842	Weaving ribbons and other ornamental fabrics.
SMITH, JAMES - - -	10,080	24th Feb.	1844	Slubbing, spinning, twisting, and doubling cotton and other fibrous substances.
SMITH, JAMES - - -	10,299	29th Aug.	1844	Form of tiles for draining; implements for manufacturing the same; mode of manufacture.
SMITH, JAMES - - -	10,420	7th Dec.	1844	Printing or ornamenting various fabrics.
SMITH, JAMES - - -	12,902	19th Dec.	1849	Treating the fleeces of sheep when on the animals.
SMITH, JAMES ELNATHAN -	7217	8th Nov.	1836	Railways; and locomotive-carriages to work on such railways.
SMITH, JAMES, junior - -	6412	15th April	1833	Machinery for manufacturing bobbin-net lace.
SMITH, JAMES, junior - -	7219	8th Nov.	1836	Machinery for making bobbin-net or twist lace.
SMITH, JAMES, junior - -	8362	28th Jan.	1840	Machinery for manufacture of figured bobbin-net or lace.
SMITH, JESSE - - -	9144	9th Nov.	1841	Construction of locks and latches applicable for doors and other purposes.
SMITH, JOACHIM - - -	887	18th Dec.	1767	Compound preparation for preserving the bottoms of ships and other vessels from being eaten into by worms and other insects.

Name of Patentee.	Progressive Number.	Date.		Subject-matter of Patent.
SMITH, JOACHIM - - -	915	6th Feb.	1769	Making candlesticks, sconces, and lamps.
SMITH, JOACHIM - - -	1043	15th May	1773	Machine for conveying persons and valuables out of houses when such houses are on fire.
SMITH, JOHN - - -	959	25th May	1770	Manufacturing gold and silver buttons, and studs set with stones, paste, &c. by making the cups out of a solid piece of gold or silver, without soldering, and with a new letter-link to distinguish them from others.
SMITH, JOHN - - -	1356	12th Feb.	1783	Printing by wooden or metal blocks and metal-plates, on linens, cottons, calicoes, stuffs, paper, woollen-cloths, silks, silk and stuff gauzes, muslins, or any other species of goods.
SMITH, JOHN - - -	3652	24th Feb.	1813	Construction and manufacture of iron and other chains.
SMITH, JOHN - - -	4360	20th April	1819	Making arms or axle-trees for coaches, carts, waggons, and other carriages.
SMITH, JOHN - - -	5799	4th June	1829	Machinery for dressing flour.
SMITH, JOHN - - -	6182	14th Oct.	1831	Copy-book or writing-tablet, and delible-ink to be used therewith.
SMITH, JOHN - - -	6613	24th May	1834	Weaving-machinery.
SMITH, JOHN - - -	6737	23rd Dec.	1834	Chisels or instruments for cutting or dressing stone and certain other substances.
SMITH, JOHN - - -	6980	14th Jan.	1836	Tentering, stretching, or keeping out cloth to its width, (made either of cotton, silk, wool, or any other fibrous substances) by machinery.
SMITH, JOHN - - -	7165	10th Aug.	1836	Tentering, stretching, or keeping out cloth to its width, (made either of cotton, silk, wool, or any other fibrous substances) by machinery.
SMITH, JOHN - - -	7192	22nd Sept.	1836	Machinery for dressing worsted and other woven fabrics.
SMITH, JOHN - - -	10,149	18th April	1844	Machinery for tentering and stretching cloths or fabrics.
SMITH, JOHN - - -	10,347	14th Oct.	1844	Manufacture of fabrics suitable for ornament or dress.
SMITH, JOHN - - -	10,490	21st Jan.	1845	Means and apparatus for shaping hats.
SMITH, JOHN - - -	12,471	12th Feb.	1849	Manufacture of paper and cardboard; producing water-marks thereon; apparatus and machinery for such purposes.
SMITH, JOHN - - -	12,510	14th March	1849	Manufacture of flour, applicable to the making of bread, biscuits, and pastry.
SMITH, JOHN - - -	14,044	25th March	1852	Locomotive and other steam-engines.
SMITH, JOHN BURNS - -	6980	14th Jan.	1836	Tentering, stretching, or keeping out cloth to its width (made either of cotton, silk, wool, or any other fibrous substances) by machinery.
SMITH, JOHN BURNS - -	7075	30th April	1836	Machinery for roving, spinning, and twisting cotton and other fibrous substances.
SMITH, JOHN BURNS - -	7165	10th Aug.	1835	Tentering, stretching, or keeping out cloth to its width (made either of cotton, silk, wool, or any other fibrous substances) by machinery.
SMITH, JOHN BURNS - -	8272	16th Nov.	1839	Machinery for preparing, roving, spinning, and twisting, cotton and other fibrous substances.

Name of Patentee.	Progressive Number.	Date.	Subject-matter of Patent.
SMITH, JOHN BURNS - -	9760	8th June 1843	Machinery for preparing, carding, roving, and spinning, cotton and other fibrous substances.
SMITH, JOHN FREDERICK -	4647	12th Feb. 1822	Dressing piece-goods made from silk or worsted, or both.
SMITH, JOHN FREDERICK -	5071	11th Jan. 1825	Preparation or manufacture of slivers or tops from wool, or wool and cotton, or other suitable fibrous materials.
SMITH, JOHN FREDERICK -	5072	11th Jan. 1825	Dressing and finishing woollen-cloths.
SMITH, JOHN FREDERICK -	5196	21st June 1825	Machinery for drawing, roving, spinning, and doubling, cotton-wool and other fibrous substances.
SMITH, JOHN FREDERICK -	5320	19th Jan. 1826	Drawing, roving, spinning, and doubling, wool, cotton, and other fibrous substances.
SMITH, JOHN FREDERICK -	5901	12th Feb. 1830	Preparing or finishing piece-goods made from wool, silk, or other fibrous materials.
SMITH, JOSEPH - - -	2345	3rd Oct. 1799	Internal bracings of pianofortes, to admit the introduction of a drum, tabor, or tambourine, into the internal part of the instrument.
SMITH, JOSEPH - - -	2642	19th Aug. 1802	Fixing and setting an alarum or alarm bell for purposes of alarm, and for awaking families in case of fire.
SMITH, JOSEPH - - -	3652	24th Feb. 1813	Construction and manufacture of iron and other chains.
SMITH, JOSEPH - - -	3822	16th July 1814	Spring-hinge for doors and gates.
SMITH, JOSEPH - - -	4689	4th July 1822	Steam-engine boilers.
SMITH, JOSEPH - - -	5373	23rd May 1826	Stocking-frames; making stockings and other goods usually made on the stocking-frame.
SMITH, JOSEPH DENHAM -	7477	16th Nov. 1837	Manufacture of glass.
SMITH, JUNIUS - - -	4752	20th Jan. 1823	Machine for washing, cleansing, and whitening cotton, linen, silk, and woollen garments or piece-goods.
SMITH, JUNIUS - - -	8716	25th Nov. 1840	Furnaces.
SMITH, JUNIUS - - -	9122	20th Oct. 1841	Machinery for manufacturing cloths of wool and other fibrous substances.
SMITH, JUNIUS - - -	9756	3rd June 1843	Machinery for sawing wood.
SMITH, LEAPRIDGE - -	5983	18th Aug. 1830	Mode of applying size to paper.
SMITH, LUKE - - -	6613	24th May 1834	Weaving-machinery.
SMITH, LUKE - - -	9940	16th Nov. 1843	Looms for weaving various kinds of fabrics.
SMITH, LUKE - - -	13,633	14th May 1851	Fabrics; weaving; machinery and apparatus for winding, weaving, cutting, and printing.
SMITH, MARK - - -	12,156	11th May 1848	Looms for weaving.
SMITH, MARK - - -	12,952	29th Jan. 1850	Machinery for preparing, spinning, and weaving cotton and other textile materials; preparing yarns or threads; machinery employed for those purposes.
SMITH, MARK - - -	13,633	14th May 1851	Fabrics; weaving; machinery and apparatus for winding, weaving, cutting, and printing.
SMITH, MARSHALL - -	317	7th March 1693	Making a composition with wood, and capable of being run into moulds, in a liquid state, for beautifying rooms, embellishing cabinets, &c.

Name of Patentee.	Progres-sive Number.	Date.	Subject-matter of Patent.
SMITH, MARSHALL - - [Smith, Marshal.]	421	23rd May 1718	Machine for grinding colours to be used in painting; also for grinding looking-glass and polishing marble; and for pounding and sifting colours, ores, and all hard substances usually ground with a muller on a flat stone, by a motion imitating that of the hands.
SMITH, MATTHEW - -	13,633	14th May 1851	Fabrics; weaving; machinery and apparatus for winding, weaving, cutting, and printing
SMITH, MATTHEW - -	14,204	6th July 1852	Looms for weaving; manufacture of terry fabrics.
SMITH, MATTHEW - -	14,248	31st July 1852	Manufacture of carpets, rugs, and other similar fabrics.
SMITH, NATHAN - -	787	15th March 1763	Composition to be used as the groundwork in making painted floor-cloths; machine to apply the same.
SMITH, NATHAN - -	2271	20th Nov. 1798	Making a vapour-bath or vessel, of different sizes and shapes, by uniting thereto an air-pump or exhauster, for curing and relieving the gout, and inflammatory disorders incident to the human body.
SMITH, NATHANIEL -	4223	5th Feb. 1818	Winnowing-machines.
SMITH, OCTAVIUS HENRY -	10,245	3rd July 1844	Steam-engines, boilers, and condensers.
SMITH, PHILIP - -	11,015	22nd Dec. 1845	Locks, latches, and other similar fastenings.
SMITH, RICHARD - -	3901	29th March 1815	Smelting iron, lead, and copper ores, and other minerals or metallic substances; refining crude iron, lead, copper, gold, silver, tin, and other metals and metallic bodies; making and manufacturing iron.
SMITH, RICHARD - -	8426	13th March 1840	Machinery for drawing, slubbing, roving, and spinning, cotton-wool, flax, silk, and other fibrous substances.
SMITH, RICHARD - -	8433	16th March 1840	Machinery for spinning cotton and other fibrous substances.
SMITH, RICHARD - -	12,929	17th Jan. 1850	Looms for weaving.
SMITH, ROBERT - -	4246	11th April 1818	Producing the Swiss deep and pale reds by topical mordants, and a pale blue discharge on the said reds.
SMITH, ROBERT - -	6457	10th Aug. 1833	Rail for railways.
SMITH, ROBERT - -	7126	22nd June 1836	Means of connecting metallic plates for the construction of boilers, and for other purposes.
SMITH, ROBERT - -	7302	16th Feb. 1837	Means of connecting metallic plates for the construction of boilers, and for other purposes.
SMITH, ROBERT ANGUS -	12,291	19th Oct. 1848	Application and preparation of coal-tar.
SMITH, ROBERT JOHN -	13,895	13th Jan. 1852	Machinery or apparatus for steering ships and other vessels.
SMITH, SAMUEL - -	3620	9th Dec. 1812	Escapement for watches.
SMITH, SAMUEL -	5978	7th Aug. 1830	Touch-hole applied to fire-arms for firing the same by percussion; cap to contain the priming.
SMITH, SAMUEL -	7377	23rd May 1837	Machinery for combing or clearing sheep's wool and goats' hair.
SMITH, SAMUEL JOHN -	3936	29th June 1815	Staining, printing or dyeing, on silk, woollen, cotton-yarn, or goods manufactured of cotton.

Name of Patentee.	Progressive Number.	Date.	Subject-matter of Patent.
SMITH, SAMUEL SIDNEY -	8173	1st Aug. 1839	Machinery for raising water.
SMITH, SAMUEL WAGSTAFF -	7625	24th April 1838	Regulating the heat of furnaces for smelting iron;—applicable to retorts for generating gas.
SMITH, SAMUEL WAGSTAFF -	8535	9th June 1840	Apparatus for supplying and consuming gas.
SMITH, SETH - - - -	5999	14th Sept. 1830	Chimneys for dwelling-houses and other houses and buildings.
SMITH, STANHOPE BAYNES -	12,654	7th June 1849	Depositing metals; obtaining motive-power; —partly applicable to similar purposes.
SMITH, SYDNEY - - - [Smith, Sidney.]	10,170	30th April 1844	Apparatus for making gas for illumination.
SMITH, SYDNEY - - -	11,711	22nd May 1847	Apparatus for determining the pressure of steam in boilers, and regulating the dampers of a furnace.
SMITH, SYDNEY - - -	13,878	22nd Dec. 1851	Indicating the height of water in steam-boilers.
SMITH, THEOPHILUS - -	8844	15th Feb. 1841	Ploughs.
SMITH, THOMAS - - -	411	16th Feb. 1717	Expressing a sweet oil from four seeds the growth of Great Britain, useful to soap-makers and to the clothing trades.
SMITH, THOMAS - - -	475	11th Feb. 1725	Engine for rowing ships ahead with oars, against wind and tide, or stemming a current, carrying ships of war in or out of harbours or line of battle, useful for fire ships or bomb vessels, for approaching or leaving ships becalmed at sea or having lost their masts, also useful for packets and cruizers, and for suppressing pirates and smugglers.
SMITH, THOMAS - - -	650	6th Dec. 1749	Medicinal snuff, useful in curing hypochondriacism, imposthumations, agues in the head, ejection of polypi, and various other indispositions.
SMITH, THOMAS - - -	1558	29th Sept. 1786	Applying springs to saddles, stirrups, martingale rings, whips, caps, buckles for belts, bridle-bits, territs for harness, squares for stable collar-reins, trusses, or bandages, and milking pails.
SMITH, THOMAS - - -	3140	3rd June 1808	Steam-engines.
SMITH, THOMAS - - -	5728	10th Dec. 1828	Machinery for scraping, sweeping, cleaning, and watering streets, roads, and other ways.
SMITH, THOMAS - - -	5755	14th Jan. 1829	Piece of machinery to combine with parts of the steam-engine, or with pumps, fire-engines, water-wheels, air-pumps, condensers, and blowing-machines.
SMITH, THOMAS - - -	7997	6th March 1839	Making chains for pits, shafts, mines, or for other purposes.
SMITH, THOMAS - - -	9272	1st March 1842	Water-closets.
SMITH, THOMAS - - -	10,717	10th June 1845	Suspending carriages; construction of wheels for carriages.
SMITH, THOMAS MOSDELL -	14,107	1st May 1852	Manufacture of wax candles.
SMITH, WILLIAM - - -	3588	28th July 1812	Gun or pistol lock.
SMITH, WILLIAM - - -	5470	20th Feb. 1827	Manufacturing cutlery and other articles of hardware, by means of rollers.
SMITH, WILLIAM - - -	7377	23rd May 1837	Machinery for combing or clearing sheep's wool and goats' hair.

Name of Patentee.	Progressive Number.	Date.	Subject-matter of Patent.
SMITH, WILLIAM - - -	9479	29th Sept. 1842	Treating certain animal matters to obtain products applicable to the making of candles, and to other purposes.
SMITH, WILLIAM - - -	10,535	3rd March 1845	Gas-meters and gas-meter cases.
SMITH, WILLIAM - - -	11,269	29th June 1846	Gas-meters.
SMITH, WILLIAM - - -	13,271	3rd Oct. 1850	Producing and applying heat; engines to be worked by steam or other elastic fluid, which engines are also applicable as pumps.
SMITH, WILLIAM - - -	13,599	24th April 1851	Apparatus for heating, ventilating, and cooking, by gas.
SMITH, WILLIAM - - -	13,618	3rd May 1851	Locomotive and other engines; carriages used on railways.
SMITH, WILLIAM - - -	13,809	13th Nov. 1851	Manufacture of chenille and other piled fabrics.
SMITH, WILLIAM - - -	13,936	29th Jan. 1852	Apparatus for cutting or breaking lump-sugar and other vegetable substances.
SMITH, WILLIAM - - -	14,021	8th March 1852	Electric and electro-magnetic telegraph apparatus; machinery for and method of making and laying down submarine, submerged, and other such lines.
SMITH, WILLIAM - - -	14,296	18th Sept. 1852	Machinery for reaping.
SMITH, WILLIAM HENRY -	8521	28th May 1840	Mode of resisting shocks to railway carriages and trains; connecting and disconnecting railway-carriages; application of springs to carriages.
SMITH, WILLIAM HENRY -	9202	21st Dec. 1841	Construction and manufacture of connectors or fastenings applicable to garments and to other uses.
SMITH, WILLIAM HENRY -	9674	21st March 1843	Breakwaters, beacons, and sound alarms; landing or transmitting persons and goods over or through strata or obstructions; may be used either separately or in combination.
SMITH, WILLIAM HENRY -	9698	19th April 1843	Construction and manufacture of gloves, mits, and cuffs, and fastenings for the same; applicable to articles of dress generally.
SMITH, WILLIAM HENRY -	10,509	4th Feb. 1845	Construction of boots, shoes, and other coverings for the legs and feet; apparatus for fastening the same.
SMITH, WILLIAM HENRY -	12,630	5th June 1849	Breakwaters, beacons, and moorings;—partly applicable to other purposes.
SMYTH, JAMES - - -	9943	16th Nov. 1843	Construction of drills for sowing grain, seeds, and manure.
SMYTH, THOMAS - - -	2424	16th July 1800	Preparing colours in cakes and powder, from logwood and other vegetable substances, for dyeing and painting.
SMYTHE, BENJAMIN - -	4071	1st Nov. 1816	Apparatus for propelling vessels, boats, barges, and rafts; also mill-wheels, and other revolving power.
SNEATH, CHARLES - - -	8859	23rd Feb. 1841	Machinery for manufacturing stockings, or other kinds of loop-work.
SNEATH, WILLIAM - - -	6084	21st Feb. 1831	Machinery for making, figuring, or ornamenting lace or net, and such other articles to which the said machinery may be applicable.
SNEATH, WILLIAM - - -	6208	31st Dec. 1831	Machinery for manufacture of bobbin-net lace.

Name of Patentee.	Progressive Number.	Date.	Subject-matter of Patent.
SNEATH, WILLIAM - - -	7079	3rd May 1836	Machinery by aid of which thread-work ornaments of certain kinds can be formed in net or lace, by bobbin-net machinery.
SNEATH, WILLIAM - - -	7326	28th Nov. 1836	Producing embroidery or ornaments on muslins, silks, and certain other fabrics.
SNELL, EDMUND - - -	9951	21st Nov. 1843	Manufacture of soap.
SNELL, WILLIAM - - -	9589	14th Jan. 1843	Machinery for the manufacture of farina.
SNELLING, ROBERT - -	260	8th Sept. 1688	Compound metal which can be drawn fine enough to spin and weave into all sorts of stuffs; also fit for several other uses.
SNODGRASS, NEIL - - -	7323	15th March 1837	Steam-engines, and other mechanism of steam-boats.
SNOWDEN, ROBERT - -	11,599	25th Feb. 1847	Treating or dressing coffee, to render it more wholesome for use.
SNOWDEN, WILLIAM - -	4079	1st Nov. 1816	Apparatus to be applied to carriages, to prevent them being overturned.
SNOWDEN, WILLIAM FRANCIS	3108	4th Feb. 1808	Engine for cutting hay and straw into chaff, and for cutting other articles.
SNOWDEN, WILLIAM FRANCIS	3551	28th March 1812	Mangles.
SNOWDEN, WILLIAM FRANCIS	5060	18th Dec. 1824	Wheelway and its carriages, for conveyance of passengers along roads, rail and other ways, either on a level or inclined plane; — applicable to other purposes.
SNOWDON, THOMAS - -	12,454	6th Feb. 1849	Machinery for moulding and pressing artificial fuel and bricks.
SNOXELL, WILLIAM - -	10,508	4th Feb. 1845	Roller-blinds and shutters.
SNYDER, SIMON - - -	10,744	28th June 1845	Tanning hides and skins.
SOAMES, JAMES, jun. - -	5842	9th Sept. 1829	Manufacture of a material produced from a vegetable substance; application thereof for affording light, and for other uses.
SOAMES, JAMES, jun. - -	5863	2nd Nov. 1829	Manufacture of a material produced from a vegetable substance; application thereof for affording light, and for other uses.
SOLA, ANTONIO DE - -	13,882	24th Dec. 1851	Treatment of copper minerals.
SOLDI, JOHN BAPTIST - -	9896	5th Oct. 1843	Apparatus for measuring persons' heads, and for fitting and retaining hats, caps, and bonnets, according to such measure.
SOLOMONS, ABRAHAM - -	11,737	10th June 1847	Manufacture of charcoal and other fuel.
SOLOMONS, ABRAHAM - -	12,165	26th May 1848	Manufacture of gas, tar, charcoal, and certain acids.
SOLOMONS, ELIAS - - -	6224	16th Feb. 1832	Preparing certain transparent substances for spectacles and for other purposes.
SOLOMONS, GEORGE - -	6224	16th Feb. 1832	Preparing certain transparent substances for spectacles and for other purposes.
SOMERS, BENJAMIN - -	5492	28th April 1827	Furnaces for smelting different kinds of metals, ores, and slags.
SOMERS, NATHANIEL - -	233	6th March 1684	Grinding logwood and other wood, for dyeing.
SOMERTON, WILLIAM - -	1258	14th June 1780	Making friction-boxes, collars or rundles, for wheels or axletrees of coaches and other carriages; also for gougings, arbours, spindles, pins, screws, hinges, and other purposes in housework, millwork, shipwork, and in engines, and machines of every kind.
SOMERVILLE, JOHN, Rev. -	5026	4th Nov. 1824	Method of preventing the accidental discharge of fowling-pieces or other firearms.

Name of Patentee.	Progressive Number.	Date.	Subject-matter of Patent.
SOMERVILLE, JOHN, Rev. - [Somerville, John.]	6825	28th April 1835	Construction of guns or muskets, and other such fire-arms.
SOMERVILLE, JOHN SOUTHEY [LORD.	2579	6th Feb. 1802	Double-furrowed plough.
SOMES, SAMUEL FRANCIS -	4715	18th Oct. 1822	Construction of anchors.
SOMMELET, HUBERT - -	13,772	10th Oct. 1851	Manufacture of scissors.
SORAS, GABRIEL DE -	5545	21st Aug. 1827	Sizing, glazing, or beautifying materials used in manufacturing paper, pasteboard, Bristol-board, and other substances.
SORBY, JOHN, jun. - - -	3513	19th Dec. 1811	Making sheep or wool shears, glovers' shears, and horse-shears.
SORBY, JOHN, jun. - - -	4010	23rd March 1816	Making augurs, to be used by shipwrights, millwrights, carpenters, and other artificers.
SOROCOLD, GEORGE - -	369	1st Jan. 1703	Cutting and sawing boards, timber, and stone; also twisting ropes, cords, and cables, by horse or water power.
SOULAS, ACHILLE, ELIE JOSH.	8894	22nd March 1841	Apparatus for regulating the flow of fluids.
SOUTER, JAMES - - -	13,861	17th Dec. 1851	Manufacture of papier-mâché, and articles made therefrom; manufacture of buttons, studs, and other articles where metal and glass are combined.
SOUTHALL, THOMAS - -	10,038	8th Feb. 1844	Manufacture of iron and steel.
SOUTHAM, WILLIAM - -	7537	11th Jan. 1838	Machinery for drying corn and other grain, and seeds.
SOUTHCOMBE, BENJAMIN -	3004	29th Jan. 1807	Making flexible or malleable metallic plates into convex or concave forms, or hollow shapes.
SOUTHGATE, JOHN - - -	594	17th Nov. 1743	Bringing malt liquor to much greater perfection by means of floors of brass, copper, and lead, for curing and preparing malt.
SOUTHWELL, WILLIAM - -	2017	18th Oct. 1794	Construction of pianofortes.
SOUTHWELL, WILLIAM - -	2264	8th Nov. 1798	Action and construction of pianofortes, and other musical instruments.
SOUTHWELL, WILLIAM - -	3029	8th April 1807	Cabinet pianofortes.
SOUTHWELL, WILLIAM - -	3403	4th March 1811	Construction of pianofortes.
SOUTHWELL, WILLIAM - -	4546	5th April 1821	Cabinet pianofortes.
SOUTHWELL, WILLIAM - -	7424	24th Aug. 1837	Pianofortes.
SOUTHWORTH, EBENEZER -	11,418	15th Oct. 1846	Engines to be worked by steam and other power, and applicable to raising or forcing water, the propulsion of vessels, and other similar purposes.
SOUTHWORTH, THOMAS -	2746	31st Dec. 1803	Heating pans, vats, cisterns, and other vessels used for various manufactories, and for working steam-engines.
SOUTHWORTH, WILLIAM -	4780	19th April 1823	Apparatus adapted to facilitate the drying of calicoes, muslins, linens, and other similar fabrics.
SOUTHWORTH, WILLIAM -	7346	18th April 1837	Machinery or apparatus adapted to facilitate the operation of drying calicoes, muslins, linens, or other similar fabrics. (Extension to E. Haworth for 5 years from 18th April 1837.)
SOUTTER, JAMES - - -	11,116	2nd March 1846	Pump applicable to steam-engines and to other purposes.
SOUTTER, JAMES - - -	11,764	22nd June 1847	Steam-engines, and machinery for propelling.

Name of Patentee.	Progressive Number.	Date.	Subject-matter of Patent.
SOWARD, GEORGE JAMES -	11,959	11th Nov. 1847	Suspending window-sashes, shutters, and blinds; construction of frames for the same.
SOWERBY, JAMES WILLIAM -	5150	13th April 1825	Generating steam; engines to be worked by steam, or other elastic fluids.
SOWERBY, THOMAS - -	4699	29th Aug. 1822	Chain suitable for ships' cables, and for other purposes.
SOWERBY, THOMAS - -	5031	6th Nov. 1824	Air-furnace, for melting metallic substances.
SOWERBY, THOMAS - -	5518	4th July 1827	Construction of ships' windlasses.
SOWLER, JOHN - - -	1114	13th Jan. 1776	Making pan-tiles, and plain or flat tiles.
SPACKMAN, JOSEPH - -	821	5th Dec. 1764	Turning ovals in pewter, also in English-china, and all other earthenwares.
SPARKE, JONATHAN - -	8483	23rd April 1840	Processes of smelting lead-ores.
SPARKES, SAMUEL - -	8769	10th June 1843	Machinery for carding wool, cotton, and other fibrous materials.
SPARKHALL, ALEXANDER -	1411	19th Dec. 1783	Machine for safely escaping from houses in case of fire.
SPARKS, JONATHAN - -	13,787	23rd Oct. 1851	Substitutes for laced stockings or bandages for the leg.
SPARRE, JULIUS FREDERICK [PHILIP LUDWIG VON.	14,228	20th July 1852	Separating substances of different specific gravities; machinery and apparatus employed therein.
SPARROW, JOSEPH - -	1964	16th Oct. 1793	Method of raising, removing, and delivering earth or water, by which rivers, canals, or fish-ponds may be made or emptied, also for raising coals, limestone, and other stones, out of any boat, barge, or vessel, in a navigable river or canal, and delivering the same upon the wharf or shore, or into any waggon, cart, or other carriage; engine or machine for these purposes.
SPEAR, JOHN - - -	8705	17th Nov. 1840	Apparatus for cutting and shaping metals and other substances.
SPEAR, JOHN - - -	11,681	29th April 1847	Pianofortes, and the musical scale of notes in use for such instruments; apparatus to facilitate the action of the fingers on the keys of pianofortes.
SPEARS, ALEXANDER - -	9980	6th Sept. 1843	Glass-bottles for wine and other liquids.
SPEARS, JAMES - - -	2062	28th Aug. 1795	Construction of locks.
SPEER, WILLIAM - - -	2640	2nd Aug. 1802	Construction of hydrometers.
SPEER, WILLIAM - - -	2994	13th Dec. 1806	Purifying, refining, &c., fish-oils and other oils; converting and applying to use the unrefined parts thereof.
SPEER, WILLIAM - - -	3325	6th April 1810	Increasing the inflammability and combustibility of oils used for burning, and improving the light obtained therefrom, particularly applicable to oils refined according to the patent process.
SPENCE, GEORGE - - -	635	8th Aug. 1748	Dyeing green and blue Saxon colours.
SPENCE, PETER - - -	7156	27th July 1836	Manufacture of Prussian-blue, prussiate of potash, and plaster of Paris.
SPENCE, PETER - - -	10,970	27th Nov. 1845	Manufacture of copperas and alum.
SPENCE, PETER - - -	13,335	12th Nov. 1850	Manufacture of alum and certain alkaline salts; manufacture of cement;—in part applicable in obtaining volatile liquids.
SPENCELEY, JOHN - - -	11,053	20th Jan. 1846	Construction of ships and other vessels; apparatus to be attached to the same.

Name of Patentee.	Progres-sive Number.	Date.		Subject-matter of Patent.
SPENCER, ARNOLD - - -	36	3rd Jan.	1627	Cutting, contriving, erecting, perfecting, and making locks, sluices, bridges and dams, for making rivers and streams navigable, with power to pass and row upon the same with boats, keels, and other vessels, and to collect tolls from all persons passing down the same.
SPENCER, ARNOLD - - -	122	11th Dec.	1638	Cutting, contriving, framing, erecting, and perfecting locks, sluices, bridges, cuts, and dams, for making rivers and streams navigable, with power to collect tolls from all persons passing down the same.
SPENCER, GEORGE - - -	10,458	11th Jan.	1845	Propelling vessels on inland waters.
SPENCER, GEORGE - - -	13,951	2nd Feb.	1852	Springs of railway carriages, trucks, and waggons.
SPENCER, HENRY - - -	14,267	19th Aug.	1852	Machinery or apparatus for preparing, spinning and weaving, cotton, and other fibrous substances.
SPENCER, HERBERT - -	11,692	6th May	1847	Machinery for planing and sawing wood.
SPENCER, JEREMIAH - -	4316	5th Dec.	1818	Fire-grates by which the combustion of smoke is more easily effected.
SPENCER, JOHN - - -	2517	20th June	1801	Making horse-shoe nails.
SPENCER, JOHN - - -	3622	14th Dec.	1812	Setting up salt-pans.
SPENCER, JOHN - - -	10,399	23rd Nov.	1844	Manufacturing or preparing plates of iron or other metal for roofing, and for other purposes.
SPENCER, JOSEPH - -	4932	7th April	1824	Construction of furnaces or forges for preparing iron or steel, and for manufacturing nails and other articles from the said materials.
SPENCER, THOMAS - -	8326	21st Dec.	1839	Machinery for making wire-cards for carding cotton, silk, wool, and other fibrous substances.
SPENCER, THOMAS - -	8556	26th June	1840	Twisting machinery used for roving, spinning, and doubling cotton-wool, silk, flax, and other fibrous substances.
SPENCER, THOMAS - -	8656	7th Oct.	1840	Process of engraving on metals by means of voltaic electricity.
SPENCER, THOMAS - -	8865	8th March	1841	Manufacture of picture and other frames and cornices;—applicable to other useful and decorative purposes.
SPENCER, THOMAS - -	12,115	10th April	1848	Machinery for the manufacture of pipes or tubes from clay or other plastic materials;—partly applicable to the manufacture of hollow earthenware.
SPERSHOTT, JAMES - -	3009	7th Feb.	1807	Manufacture of earthenware.
SPIBY, WILLIAM - -	11,156	1st April	1846	Construction of furnaces used for heating water and other fluids.
SPICER, CHARLES WILLIAM -	10,128	28th March	1844	Portable life-preserver and swimming-belt. "Nautilus."
SPILLER, JOEL - - -	4916	6th March	1824	Machinery to be employed in the working of pumps.
SPILLER, JOEL - - -	6897	24th Sept.	1835	Boilers for generating steam, or heating water or other fluids.
SPILLER, JOEL - - -	12,951	29th Jan.	1850	Cleaning and grinding wheat.
SPILSBURY, FRANCIS - -	1848	4th Feb.	1792	Medicine for eradicating scorbutic disorders. "Anti-scorbutic Drops."

Name of Patentee.	Progressive Number.	Date.	Subject-matter of Patent.
SPILSBURY, FRANCIS GYBBON [Spilsbury, Francis Gybson.]	4784	22nd April 1823	Tanning.
SPILSBURY, FRANCIS GYBBON	5069	11th Jan. 1825	Weaving.
SPILSBURY, FRANCIS GYBBON	7038	22nd March 1836	Machinery for stamping-up and compressing metals or other substances.
SPILSBURY, FRANCIS GYBBON	7277	11th Jan. 1837	Manufacture of carbonate of soda.
SPILSBURY, FRANCIS GYBBON	8234	7th Oct. 1839	Paints or pigments and vehicles ; modes of applying the same.
SPILSBURY, FRANCIS GYBBON	12,314	2nd Nov. 1848	Paints and pigments.
SPINKS, JOHN, junior	9515	8th Nov. 1842	Apparatus for giving elasticity to certain parts of railway and other carriages.
SPINNEY, THOMAS	6123	4th June 1831	Apparatus for manufacturing gas for illumination.
SPINNEY, THOMAS	6333	13th Nov. 1832	Earthenware retort for generating gas for illumination.
SPINNEY, THOMAS	6422	11th May 1833	Combination of materials for the manufacture of crucibles, melting-pots, and fire-bricks.
SPIRES, NEHEMIAH	1181	17th Feb. 1778	Preparing essences from vegetables.
SPIVEY, CHARLES	671	25th June 1752	Engine for raising water, draining lands, and for other purposes.
SPONG, WILLIAM	5542	15th Aug. 1827	Diminishing friction in wheeled-carriages, water-wheels, and other rotatory parts of machinery.
SPRATLEY, WILLIAM	3770	20th Dec. 1813	Axle-trees of wheels for carriages.
SPRAY, FREDERICK GEORGE	12,908	21st Dec. 1849	Steam-engines, parts of the arrangements of which may be applied to apparatus for regulating, measuring, and registering the flow of liquids.
SPRIGG, JAMES, senior	4845	11th Sept. 1823	Manufacture of grates, fenders, and fire-iron rests.
SPRINGALL, JOHN	6395	7th March 1833	Corn-stack stand.
SPRINGALL, JOHN	6918	2nd Nov. 1835	Manufacturing certain parts of ploughs.
SPRINGALL, JOHN	7293	31st Jan. 1837	Shoes for horses and other animals.
SPROULE, MATTHEW	11,611	10th March 1847	Steam-engines.
SPURGIN, JOHN	7054	7th April 1836	Ladder or machinery applicable to the working of mines, and to other useful purposes.
SPURGIN, JOHN	7368	8th May 1837	Means of propelling vessels through water ;— partly applicable to other useful purposes.
SPURGIN, JOHN	12,106	27th March 1848	Manufacture of metallic pens.
SQUIRE, JOHN	6449	18th July 1833	Boilers for generating steam.
SQUIRE, JOHN	9159	16th Nov. 1841	Construction of steam-boilers or generators.
SQUIRE, JOHN	9564	21st Dec. 1842	Steam-boilers or generators.
SQUIRE, THOMAS	10,368	29th Oct. 1844	Tanning hides and skins.
SQUIRE, WILLIAM	1290	23rd April 1781	Spring-truss for the relief of persons afflicted with ruptures.
SQUIRE, WILLIAM	13,947	31st Jan. 1852	Construction of pianofortes.
SQUIRES, WILLIAM WEST-[BROOKE.	11,999	18th Dec. 1847	Modes of producing a vacuum ; may also be applied to pneumatic, hydraulic, and hydrostatic apparatus, and to machinery for obtaining motive-power.
STABLE, WILLIAM	1451	27th Sept. 1784	Making gloves, fastening them by a new method, and making them fit close to the wrist.

Name of Patentee.	Progressive Number.	Date.	Subject-matter of Patent.
STACE, WILLIAM - - -	10,135	2nd April 1844	Applying power for drawing or working ploughs and other implements and carriages used for agricultural purposes.
STACEY, GEORGE - - -	13,910	24th Jan. 1852	Machinery for reaping, mowing, and delivering dry or green crops.
STACEY, WILLIAM - - -	12,447	30th Jan. 1849	Heating and boiling liquids.
STAFFORD, DANIEL - -	5063	24th Dec. 1824	Carriages.
STAFFORD, DANIEL - -	7919	21st Dec. 1838	Carriages. (*Extension for 7 years from the 24th December* 1838.)
STAFFORD, DANIEL - -	10,250	3rd July 1844	Apparatus for preventing smoky chimneys or flues, and for extinction of fires in chimneys or flues.
STAFFORD, DOMINICK - -	6501	2nd Nov. 1833	Fuel.
STAGG, JOSEPH DICKINSON -	9920	2nd Nov. 1843	Collecting, condensing, and purifying the fumes of lead, copper, and other ores and metals, also the particles of such ores and metals arising from the roasting, smelting, or manufacturing thereof, likewise the noxious smoke, gases, salts and acids soluble and absorbable in water, and generated in treating and working such ores and metals.
STAINFORD, THOMAS - -	5246	23rd Aug. 1825	Machinery for making bricks.
STAINMARC, JEAN JACQUES -	4928	20th March 1824	Process of and apparatus for distiliing.
STAITE, WILLIAM EDWARDS -	10,285	3rd Aug. 1844	Processes and apparatus for preparing extracts and essences of vegetable and animal substances.
STAITE, WILLIAM EDWARDS -	11,076	7th Feb. 1846	Means of ignition and illumination.
STAITE, WILLIAM EDWARDS -	11,449	12th Nov. 1846	Lighting.
STAITE, WILLIAM EDWARDS -	11,783	3rd July 1847	Lighting; and apparatus connected therewith.
STAITE, WILLIAM EDWARDS -	12,212	12th July 1848	Construction of galvanic-batteries; formation of magnets; application of electricity and magnetism for lighting and signalizing; mode of employing galvanic-batteries for obtaining chemical products.
STAITE, WILLIAM EDWARDS -	12,772	20th Sept. 1849	Electric and galvanic instruments and apparatus; and their application to lighting and motive purposes.
STAITE, WILLIAM EDWARDS -	12,987	4th March 1850	Pipes for smoking, and apparatus connected therewith.
STAMMERS, WILLIAM - -	504	4th Nov. 1728	Ingredient to rectify spirits distilled from malt, molasses, and other liquors.
STAMP, ROBERT - - -	5292	17th Nov. 1825	Working, weaving, or preparing, silk and other fibrous materials used in making hats, bonnets, shawls, and other articles.
STAMP, ROBERT - - -	12,005	22nd Dec. 1847	Manufacture of fabrics to be used for covering hats, caps, and bonnets, which fabrics may be used for other articles of wearing-apparel.
STANBRIDGE, JOHN WILLIAM	11,089	11th Feb. 1846	Manufacture of certain descriptions of silks and other fabrics.
STANCLIFFE, JOHN - - -	3323	6th April 1810	Apparatus for the combination and condensation of gases and vapours;—applicable to processes of distillation.
STANDAGE, PETER - - -	2034	19th Jan. 1795	Preparing and spinning flax, hemp, tow, and other things, by heckles and machines worked by water, steam, or horse-mills, and which will be of great utility in manufacturing linen, sail-cloth, cordage, and several other things.

Name of Patentee.	Progressive Number.	Date.	Subject-matter of Patent.
STANHOPE, CHARLES Earl -	1732	13th March 1790	Constructing ships and vessels ; moving and conducting them without help of sails, and against wind, waves, current, or tide.
STANHOPE, CHARLES EARL -	1771	17th Aug. 1790	Moving ships and vessels against wind, waves, current, or tide.
STANHOPE, CHARLES EARL -	2527	20th July 1801	Burning chalk, marble and limestone, into lime.
STANHOPE, CHARLES EARL -	3011	16th Feb. 1807	Form, construction, and manner of building and fitting-out ships and vessels for the purpose of navigation, so as to counteract the danger arising from submarine bombs or explosions.
STANLEY, JOHN - - -	4692	27th July 1822	Machinery for supplying furnaces with fuel, reducing the consumption thereof, and the appearance of smoke, also saving labour.
STANLEY, JOHN - - -	6703	22nd Oct. 1834	Grates or apparatus applicable to steam-engines, or to other purposes ; apparatus for feeding the same with fuel ;—applicable conjointly or separately, to other purposes.
STANLEY, ROBERT JOHN -	3038	28th April 1807	Tanning leather (except backs and bins,) without the use or application of bark or mineral astringent.
STANNING, Sir NICHOLAS, [Knight.	170	30th May 1673	Melting, casting, refining, and forging iron and other metals, with turf and peat charked.
STANSBURY, ABRAHAM OGIER [D'	2851	18th May 1805	Locks and keys.
STANSFELD, HAMER - -	7066	23rd April 1836	Machinery for generating power, applicable to various purposes.
STANSFELD, HAMER - -	7130	22nd June 1836	Machinery for preparing certain threads or yarns, and for weaving certain fabrics.
STANSFELD, HAMER - -	7269	30th Dec. 1836	Application of certain machinery of a tappet and lever action, to produce a vertical or horizontal movement through the medium of ropes or bands working over, under, or round, pullies.
STANSFELD, HAMER - -	7471	14th Nov. 1837	Machinery of a tappet and lever action, to produce a vertical or horizontal movement through the medium of ropes or bands working over, under, or round, pullies.
STANSFELD, THOMAS WOLRICH	4810	5th July 1823	Construction of looms for weaving fabrics composed wholly or partly of woollen, worsted, cotton, linen, silk, or other material ; machinery and implements for and method of working the same.
STANSFELD, THOMAS WOLRICH	4991	27th July 1824	Power-looms ; and the preparation of warps for the same.
STANSFELD, THOMAS WOLRICH	5211	16th July 1825	Looms, and implements connected therewith.
STANSFELD, SAMUEL - -	2192	13th Sept. 1797	Machine for roving and spinning cotton, flax, hemp, worsted yarn, &c., and doubling and twisting silk, cotton, and thread, capable of being applied to other purposes.
STANTON, JACOB - - -	2058	29th July 1795	Machine for the relief of persons with a fractured leg or thigh.

Name of Patentee.	Progressive Number.	Date.	Subject-matter of Patent.
STANYFORTH, DISNEY - -	518	21st Sept. 1730	Ploughs.
STAPLETON, JOHN - - -	285	7th Dec. 1691	Making, by way of translocation, a fine metal both white and yellow, and which is also easily malleable. " Nuremberg metal."
STAPLETON, JOHN - - -	318	17th March 1693	Engine contrived so as to admit of a person enclosed in it walking under water; forcing air into any depth of water to supply the said person, and to cause a lamp to burn while under water; also an engine which will float on the water in the most violent storms, but if inverted and supplied with air, will enable a person enclosed therein to sink to the bottom and ascend again without injury; purifying the air to make the same again serviceable for respiration, so that a man in either of the said engines may remain a long time under water without other air than what the engines contain.
STAPLEY, EDWARD MAITLAND	14,200	6th July 1852	Cutting mouldings, grooves, tongues, and other forms; planing wood.
STARK, CHARLES SIGISMOND -	646	1st July 1749	Chemical composition of metal suitable for cannon and other field-arms.
STARKEY, GEORGE - - -	980	17th Jan. 1771	Preparing glass, stones, shell, coral, horn, and bone, for painting and gilding.
STARKEY, SAMUEL - - -	14,247	31st July 1852	Machinery for washing minerals, and separating them from other substances.
STARKEY, THOMAS - - -	9188	16th Dec. 1841	Percussion-caps for discharging fire-arms.
STARR, CHARLES - - -	13,166	3rd July 1850	Book-binding.
STARR, FRANCIS - - -	11,825	29th July 1847	Jet for delivery of water and other fluids. " Protean Jet."
STARTIN, JAMES - - -	10,623	17th April 1845	Boiling liquors;—applicable to many purposes of domestic use, particularly tea or table urns.
STATHAM, ENOCH - - -	13,826	22nd Nov. 1851	Manufacture of lace and other fabrics.
STATHAM, JAMES - - -	9497	20th Oct. 1842	Construction of locks for Venetian-blinds used in carriages.
STATHAM, THOMAS - - -	13,821	20th Nov. 1851	Piano-fortes.
STATON, THOMAS - - -	2257	7th Aug. 1798	Apparatus for raising beer, ale, wine, spirits, oil, or other liquids, from cellars or other low places to a more elevated situation.
STEAD, DAVID - - -	7645	19th May 1838	Making and paving streets, ways, roads, courts and bridges, with timber or wooden blocks.
STEAD, DAVID - - -	8041	23rd April 1839	Making and paving streets, ways, roads, paths, courts, and bridges, with timber or wooden blocks.
STEAD, JAMES - - -	5742	18th Dec. 1828	Paddle-wheels for propelling steam-packets and other vessels.
STEAD, JOHN - - -	3204	9th Feb. 1809	Manufacturing cards for carding and spinning flax, tow, wool, cotton, and silk, combining the quality of a fine card with the strength of a coarse one.
STEAD, JOHN - - -	3991	14th March 1816	Stage-coaches or other coaches or carriages.
STEAD, PATRICK - - -	9475	22nd Sept. 1842	Manufacture of malt.
STEAD, WILLIAM - - -	5742	18th Dec. 1828	Paddle-wheels for propelling steam-packets and other vessels.
STEBBING, GEORGE - - -	3363	18th July 1810	Action of sea and land compasses.

Name of Patentee.	Progres-sive Number.	Date.	Subject-matter of Patent.
STEBBING, GEORGE - -	5435	20th Dec. 1826	Apparatus for ascertaining the trim and sta-bility of ships or other vessels.
STEDMAN, JOHN - - -	1350	13th Jan. 1783	Shoe and buckle.
STEDMAN, JOHN ` - - -	1410	19th Dec. 1783	Fastenings for shoe-buckles, knee-buckles, stock-buckles, and other kind of buckles.
STEDMAN, JOHN - - -	1510	17th Nov. 1785	Sympathetic hinges and quadrants to be used with folding doors, gates, and shutters; fastenings for the same.
STEDMAN, JOHN - - -	1655	30th June 1788	Buckle-chape or fastening for shoes.
STEDMAN, JOHN - - -	3135	24th May 1808	Pattens and clogs.
STEDMAN, WILLIAM - -	1604	19th May 1787	Philosophical fire-alarms to be applied to houses and other buildings.
STEDMAN, JOHN - - -	2141	25th Oct. 1796	Machine for thrashing corn.
STEEL, ENOCH - - -	12,202	6th July 1848	Manufacture of tobacco-pipes.
STEEL, JAMES - - -	12,650	7th June 1849	Power-looms.
STEEL, JOSEPH - - -	2901	17th Dec. 1805	Species of cloths, fustians, calicoes, cambrics, lawns, striped cottons, and other articles manufactured with cotton-wool and flax mixed and spun together.
STEEL, WILLIAM - - -	3187	29th Dec. 1808	Machine for making white salt.
STEELE, JEREMIAH - -	3537	8th Feb. 1812	Apparatus for distilling and rectifying spirits, also method of working the same.
STEELE, JOSEPH - - -	13,216	9th Aug. 1850	Coating and impregnating metals and me-tallic articles.
STEELE, PATRICK SANDERSON	8373	5th Feb. 1840	Kitchen-ranges; apparatus for raising the temperature of water, for baths and for other uses.
STEELE, Sir RICHARD, Knight -	419	21st May 1718	Vessel for conveying fish, alive and in health.
STEELE, THOMAS - - -	5273	28th Oct. 1825	Construction of diving-bells.
STEELE, WILKINSON - -	8373	5th Feb. 1840	Kitchen-ranges; apparatus for raising the temperature of water, for baths and for other uses.
STEEN, ROBERT - - -	4537	20th Feb. 1821	Steam-engines.
STEENSTRUP, PAUL - -	5580	11th Dec. 1827	Machinery for propelling vessels;—appli-cable to other purposes.
STEERS, EDWARD - - -	2380	19th March 1800	Machine to be applied to boats or vessels for the purpose of moving them along with ease and celerity.
STEERS, EDWARD - - -	2805	19th Dec. 1804	Engine producing a force by the impetus which the parts of a fluid body have to an equal altitude, applicable to the work-ing of all sorts of machinery.
STEERS, EDWARD - - -	3211	1st March 1809	Method, directed by machinery, of using the screw, by which its mechanical power or its motion is increased.
STEERS, EDWARD - - -	3788	12th March 1814	Rendering stoppers of bottles, jars, &c. air-tight.
STEIN, ROBERT - - -	4537	20th Feb. 1821	Steam-engines.
STEIN, ROBERT - - -	4865	13th Nov. 1823	Construction of blast-furnaces and apparatus connected therewith, adapted to save fuel.
STEIN, ROBERT - - -	5583	13th Dec. 1827	Applying heat for distillation.
STEIN, ROBERT - - -	5721	4th Dec. 1828	Distillation.
STEIN, ROBERT - - -	6419	7th May 1833	Steam-engine on the rotary principle.
STEIN, ROBERT - - -	6666	23rd Aug. 1834	Certain engines to be worked by steam.

Name of Patentee.	Progressive Number.	Date.	Subject-matter of Patent.
STEINER, FREDERICK - -	6270	2nd June 1832	Process or processes by which spent madder can be made to yield a great quantity of colouring matter; dyeing with the same, various colours, all descriptions of cotton, linen, wool, silk, or any mixture of them; improving dyeing madders that have not been previously used.
STEINER, FREDERICK - -	8801	19th Jan. 1841	Looms for weaving and cutting asunder double-piled cloths; machine for winding weft to be used thereon.
STEINER, FREDERICK - -	9860	8th Aug. 1843	Manufacture of garancine.
STEINER, FREDERICK - -	10,392	14th Nov. 1844	Colouring-matter to be used in dyeing certain colours on cotton, woollen, silk, and linen fabrics.
STEINER, FREDERICK - -	11,863	9th Sept. 1847	Manufacture of sugar.
STEINER, FREDERICK - -	12,621	24th May 1849	Processes and apparatus to be used in the Turkey-red dye on cotton and its fabrics.
STEINHAUSER, JOHN LE-[BERECHT. [Steinhœuser, John Leberecht.]	3533	4th Feb. 1812	Fire-screens, music-stands, reading-desks, and candelabra.
STEINHAUSER, JOHN LE-[BERECHT.	4008	23rd March 1816	Castors or rollers for tables, sofas, bedsteads, and other articles.
STEINHAUSER, JOHN LE-[BERECHT.	4428	15th Jan. 1820	Portable lanterns or lamps;—applicable to various purposes.
STEINHAUSER, JOHN LE-[BERECHT. [Steinhaueser, John Leberecht.]	8460	31st March 1840	Spinning and doubling wool, cotton, silk, and other fibrous materials.
STEINKAMP, JOHANN ARNOLD	12,218	18th July 1848	Manufacture of sugar from the cane; refining raw sugar.
STEINKELLER, PETER - -	7367	8th May 1837	Plates or tiles of zinc or other proper metal or mixture; applicable to roofs or other parts of buildings.
STELL, ANNE - - - -	926	23rd May 1769	Preventing the dangers arising to equestrians from their hanging by the foot in the stirrup, in case of falling or being thrown from their horses.
STELL, JOSEPH - - -	612	18th April 1745	Weaving tapes and other goods in narrow breadths; kiln for drying malt; saving fuel in making common salt.
STELL, JOSEPH - - -	753	22nd Oct. 1760	Weaving figured and flowered silk-ribbons and other sorts of figured and flowered goods.
STENSON, JOSEPH - - -	12,217	18th July 1848	Steam-engines and boilers;—partly applicable to other motive machinery.
STENSON, JOSEPH - - -	13,883	27th Dec. 1851	Manufacture of iron; steam-apparatus used therein;—partly applicable to evaporative and motive purposes generally.
STENSON, WILLIAM - -	4017	11th April 1816	Engine to be worked by steam or other power.
STEPHENS, EDWARD - -	2677	29th Jan. 1803	Furnace-stove or fire-place, which is conveniently applicable to the burning of limestone, at the same time that it is used for heating corn-kilns, &c.
STEPHENS, HENRY - -	7333	28th March 1837	Ink-stands or ink-holders, and pens for writing.
STEPHENS, HENRY - -	7342	18th April 1837	Manufacturing colouring-matter, and rendering certain colours applicable to dyeing, staining, and writing.

Name of Patentee.	Progressive Number.	Date.		Subject-matter of Patent.
STEPHENS, HENRY - -	13,148	24th June	1850	Ever-pointed pencils, pens, and penholders.
STEPHENS, JOHN - - -	13,501	10th Feb.	1851	Thrashing-machinery.
STEPHENS, JOHN - - -	13,967	12th Feb.	1852	Obtaining and applying motive-power.
STEPHENS, THOMAS - -	634	12th July	1748	Double-concave boiler, with a flange, for raising steam by fire, to work engines for raising water.
STEPHENSON, DAVID -	558	17th June	1737	Method for the improvement of mechanics and hydraulics, by diminishing friction, generating and producing motion and power in solid and fluid bodies, collecting the force of fluids already in a state of motion, and communicating the motion and power thus generated, to all kinds of machines, particularly to those for raising water.
STEPHENSON, FREDERICK -	10,108	14th March	1844	Book-binding and apparatus for cutting books or other folded paper;—in part applicable to pen-holders.
STEPHENSON, GEORGE - -	3887	28th Feb.	1815	Construction of locomotive-engines.
STEPHENSON, GEORGE - -	4067	30th Sept.	1816	Facilitating the conveyance of carriages, goods, and materials, along railways and frameways, by improvements in the construction of the machine, carriages, carriage-wheels, railways, and frameways employed for that purpose.
STEPHENSON, GEORGE - -	4662	21st March	1822	Steam-engines.
STEPHENSON, GEORGE - -	6111	30th April	1831	Constructing wheels for railway-carriages.
STEPHENSON, GEORGE - -	11,086	11th Feb.	1846	Locomotive steam-engines.
STEPHENSON, JOSEPH - -	3312	27th Feb.	1810	Machine for filtering and purifying water.
STEPHENSON, ROBERT - -	5325	23rd Jan.	1826	Axletrees to remedy the extra friction on curves, to waggons, carts, cars, and carriages used on railroads, tramways, and other public roads.
STEPHENSON, ROBERT - -	6092	11th March	1831	Axles and bearings at the centre of wheels for carriages to travel on edge railways.
STEPHENSON, ROBERT - -	6372	26th Jan.	1833	Locomotive steam-engines.
STEPHENSON, ROBERT - -	6484	7th Oct.	1833	Locomotive steam-engines.
STEPHENSON, ROBERT - -	6524	11th Dec.	1833	Mode of supporting the iron-rails for edge-railways.
STEPHENSON, ROBERT - -	8998	23rd June	1841	Arrangement and combination of the parts of locomotive-engines.
STEPHENSON, ROWLAND MAC-[DONALD.	8404	29th Feb.	1840	Method of adjusting, shifting, and working theatrical scenery and apparatus.
STERLINGUE, ETIENNE - -	9079	8th Sept.	1841	Machinery for and process of tanning skins or hides; preparing or operating upon vegetable and other substances.
STEVELLY, JOHN - -	10,087	2nd March	1844	Steam-engines.
STEVENS, ALEXANDER - -	8707	19th Nov.	1840	Machinery to be used as a universal chuck, for turning and boring purposes.
STEVENS, ALFRED - - -	11,725	29th May	1847	Preparation of certain substances for making various glutinous compounds.
STEVENS, BENJAMIN - -	3921	3rd June	1815	Making marine-soap, and domestic hard and soft soap.
STEVENS, FRANCIS BOWES -	11,746	12th June	1847	Applying means and apparatus to ships and vessels to improve their speed.
STEVENS, FRANCIS WORRELL -	8274	19th Nov.	1839	Apparatus for propelling boats and other vessels on water.

Name of Patentee.	Progressive Number.	Date.	Subject-matter of Patent.
STEVENS, GEORGE - - -	6353	21st Dec. 1832	Apparatus for the manufacture and refining of sugar and other extracts;—applicable to other purposes.
STEVENS, GEORGE - - -	7947	22nd Jan. 1839	Stoves.
STEVENS, GEORGE - - -	9574	28th Dec. 1842	Manufacture of sugar and the products of sugar.
STEVENS, JAMES - - -	11,612	10th March 1847	Apparatus for conveying signals or communications between distant places;—partly applicable to lamps and burners.
STEVENS, JAMES - - -	14,083	22nd April 1852	Lamp-glasses.
STEVENS, JOHN - - -	2464	16th Jan. 1801	Making bricks.
STEVENS, JOHN COX - -	2855	31st May 1805	Generating steam.
STEVENS, JOHN LEE - -	5588	18th Dec. 1827	Propelling vessels through the water by aid of steam or other power; its application to other purposes.
STEVENS, JOHN LEE - -	6126	22nd June 1831	Mangles.
STEVENS, JOHN LEE - -	9005	25th June 1841	Candlesticks and other candle-holders.
STEVENS, JOHN LEE - -	13,835	27th Nov. 1851	Propelling vessels on water.
STEVENSON, DAVID - -	7313	2nd March 1837	Preparing writing-paper from which writing-ink cannot be expunged or abstracted without detection.
STEVENSON, JAMES - -	6822	28th April 1835	Cutting wood by certain improved instruments.
STEVENSON, JOHN - -	2556	10th Nov. 1801	Stoving and drying tobacco and the preparation for snuffs.
STEVENSON, JOHN - -	13,010	23rd March 1850	Machinery for spinning flax and other substances.
STEVENSON, RALPH - -	5917	6th March 1830	Machinery for making quarries, bricks, tiles and other articles, from clay or other suitable materials.
STEVENSON, WALTER HART -	2023	15th Nov. 1794	Machines to heckle, dress, and prepare flax and hemp, by water, steam, horse-mills, or any other power, for spinning.
STEVENSON, WILLIAM HENRY	10,889	23rd Oct. 1845	Machinery to be used in dyeing or staining.
STEVENSON, WILLIAM SHARPE	11,651	8th April 1847	Regulating the generation of steam in steam-boilers.
STEWARD, JOHN - - -	8737	16th Dec. 1840	Construction of pianofortes, harpsichords, and other similar stringed musical instruments.
STEWARD, JOHN - - -	9023	7th July 1841	Construction of pianofortes.
STEWART, ALEXANDER - -	14,290	10th Sept. 1852	Manufacture or production of ornamental fabrics.
STEWART, CHARLES - -	3339	22nd May 1810	Construction of dining and other tables.
STEWART, DAVID - - -	2549	3rd Nov. 1801	Ventilating dwelling-houses, theatres, hospitals and other buildings; ventilating, heating, and constructing buildings for preserving trees, plants, shrubs, flowers, fruits, roots, and vegetables, thereby reducing the consumption of fuel, simplifying the mode of management, and rendering the production of fruits and flowers more certain.
STEWART, DAVID - - -	3417	22nd March 1811	Rendering dwelling-houses, theatres, hospitals, prisons, shipping, horticultural, and other buildings, air and water-tight as far as relates to the glazing, by means of a lap made of copper or any other metal, or some metal prepared by machinery for that purpose.

Name of Patentee.	Progressive Number.	Date.	Subject-matter of Patent.
STEWART, DAVID YOOLOW -	11,296	14th July 1846	Moulding iron and brass.
STEWART, DAVID YOOLOW -	12,402	4th Jan. 1849	Manufacture of moulds and cores for casting iron and other substances.
STEWART, JAMES - - -	5475	22nd March 1827	Pianofortes, and mode of stringing the same.
STEWART, JAMES - - -	5865	2nd Nov. 1829	Piano-fortes.
STEWART, JAMES - - -	6744	15th Jan. 1835	Mechanism of horizontal, grand, and square pianofortes.
STEWART, JAMES - - -	9150	11th Nov. 1841	Action of horizontal pianofortes.
STEWART, JAMES - - -	9182	16th Dec. 1841	Construction of castors.
STEWART, JAMES - - -	9362	24th May 1842	Hinges for pianofortes, and for other purposes.
STEWART, JAMES - - -	9716	29th April 1843	Action of pianofortes.
STEWART, JOHN - - -	859	6th Sept. 1766	Machine to be worked by the power of such common fire-engines as are used in raising water out of mines.
STEWART, WILLIAM - -	3103	26th Jan. 1808	Making bricks and tiles.
STIERBA, JOHANN - - -	14,139	22nd May 1852	Furnaces; treating and utilizing certain products of combustion.
STIRLING, JAMES - - -	5456	1st Feb. 1827	Air-engines for the moving of machinery.
STIRLING, JAMES - - -	8652	1st Oct. 1840	Air-engines.
STIRLING, JOHN DAVIE MOR- [RIES.	11,262	29th June 1846	Certain alloys and metallic compounds; method of welding the same and other metals.
STIRLING, JOHN DAVIE MOR- [RIES.	12,288	12th Oct. 1848	Manufacture of iron and metallic compounds.
STIRLING, JOHN DAVIE MOR- [RIES. [Stirling, John Davie Morris.]	13486	31st Jan. 1851	Manufacture of metallic sheets; coating metals; metallic compounds; welding.
STIRLING, JOHN DAVIE MOR- [RIES.	13,877	22nd Dec. 1851	Alloys and combinations of metals.
STIRLING, ROBERT - - -	4081	16th Nov. 1816	Diminishing consumption of fuel; engine capable of being applied to the moving of machinery.
STIRLING, ROBERT - - -	5456	1st Feb. 1827	Air-engines for the moving of machinery.
STIRLING, ROBERT - - -	8652	1st Oct. 1840	Air-engines.
STIRLING, THOMAS - -	5685	16th Aug. 1828	Filtering apparatus or machines.
STIRLING, THOMAS - -	8439	20th March 1840	Manufacture of fuel.
STIRRAT, JAMES - - -	9099	23rd Sept. 1841	Rotary-machines, to be worked by water.
STOCKER, ALEXANDER - -	5885	26th Jan. 1830	Cock for drawing liquor from casks.
STOCKER, ALEXANDER - -	6323	22nd Oct. 1832	Manufacturing iron and other metal tips for the heels and toes of shoes, chain-links, and other articles.
STOCKER, ALEXANDER - -	6816	14th April 1835	Machinery for manufacturing horse-shoes and certain other articles.
STOCKER, ALEXANDER - -	7136	25th June 1836	Machinery for making files.
STOCKER, ALEXANDER - -	7237	29th Nov. 1836	Manufacture of rivets, screw-blanks and other articles.
STOCKER, ALEXANDER SOUTH- [WOOD.	7802	10th Sept. 1838	Straps for wearing-apparel.
STOCKER, ALEXANDER SOUTH- [WOOD.	8162	20th July 1839	Machinery for manufacturing shoe-heels and toe-tips.
STOCKER, ALEXANDER SOUTH- [WOOD.	8453	27th March 1840	Manufacturing tubes applicable to gas, and to other purposes.

Name of Patentee.	Progressive Number.	Date.		Subject-matter of Patent.
STOCKER, ALEXANDER SOUTH-[WOOD.	8536	9th June	1840	Manufacture of tubes for gas and for other purposes.
STOCKER, ALEXANDER SOUTH-[WOOD.	8938	27th April	1841	Patten and clogties, and other articles or fastenings of dress.
STOCKER, ALEXANDER SOUTH-[WOOD.	9933	8th Dec.	1843	Manufacture of glass and other vessels, so that corks for the same are more easily applied; apparatus for extracting such corks when required to be released.
STOCKER, ALEXANDER SOUTH-[WOOD.	10,449	30th Dec.	1844	Bottles, jars, pots, and other similar vessels; manufacturing, stoppering, and covering the same.
STOCKER, ALEXANDER SOUTH-[WOOD.	11,228	28th May	1846	Manufacturing bottles and other similar vessels; stopping or covering the same; application of the whole or part of the articles used.
STOCKER, ALEXANDER SOUTH-[WOOD.	12,146	4th May	1848	Time-teachers and boxes; show-cards, and holders for matches, pens, pins, needles, and other articles; manufacturing the same.
STOCKER, ALEXANDER SOUTH-[WOOD.	13,832	25th Nov.	1851	Stoppering of bottles, jars, pots, or other similar receptacles.
STOCKER, EDWARD - -	10,5E9	18th March	1845	Production and manufacture of naphtha, pyroligneous-acid, or other inflammable matter.
STOCKER, GEORGE - - -	5885	26th Jan.	1830	Cock for drawing liquor from casks.
STOCKER, GEORGE - - -	8024	9th April	1839	Guns, pistols, and other fire-arms.
STOCKER, GEORGE - - -	8063	13th May	1839	Cocks or apparatus for drawing off liquids.
STOCKER, GEORGE - - -	9105	28th Sept.	1841	Machinery and apparatus for raising, forcing, conveying, and drawing off liquids.
STOCKER, SAMUEL - - -	7315	4th March	1837	Pumps.
STOCKER, SAMUEL - - -	7777	21st Aug.	1838	Chimneys for dwelling-houses; apparatus for scraping, sweeping, or cleaning chimneys; manufacture of such apparatus and the materials of which such chimneys are formed.
STOCKER, SAMUEL - - -	8216	11th Sept.	1839	Beer, cyder, and spirit engines.
STOCKER, SAMUEL - - -	9105	28th Sept.	1841	Machinery and apparatus for raising, forcing, conveying and drawing off liquids.
STOCKER, SAMUEL - - -	10,608	10th April	1845	Machinery or apparatus for lifting, forcing, or conveying liquids in vessels for holding liquids; waterclosets.
STOCKER, SAMUEL - - -	12,852	17th Nov.	1849	Beer-engines, beer-measures, and tobacco-boxes.
STOCKER, WILLIAM - -	3701	25th May	1813	Cock, made of metal and wood, for drawing liquor from casks.
STOCKER, WILLIAM - -	3775	10th Jan.	1814	Cock made of metal and wood, for drawing liquor from casks.
STOCKER, WILLIAM SOUTH-[WOOD.	6323	22nd Oct.	1832	Machinery for manufacturing iron and other metal tips for the heels and toes of shoes, also for chain-links, and other articles.
STOCKER, WILLIAM SOUTH-[WOOD.	7143	7th July	1836	Machinery applicable to making nails and to other purposes.
STOCKER, WILLIAM SOUTH-[WOOD.	8531	2nd June	1840	Machinery applicable to making nails, pins, and rivets.
STOCKWELL, JOHN - - -	3435	24th April	1811	Manufacturing shag-tobacco.
STODART, ROBERT - - -	1172	21st Nov.	1777	Grand pianoforte with an octave swell.
STODART, WILLIAM - - -	2028	12th Jan.	1795	Upright grand pianofortes.

Name of Patentee.	Progressive Number.	Date.	Subject-matter of Patent.
STOKES, JAMES - - -	5555	11th Oct. 1827	Making, boiling, burning, clarifying, or preparing raw or muscovado bastard sugar and molasses.
STOKES, SAMUEL - - -	11,789	10th July 1847	Machine for tracing or engraving from solid bodies or subjects in relief.
STOKES, THOMAS HERVEY -	1627	6th Nov. 1787	Raising oil in lamps to supply the wick.
STOKOE, JAMES - - -	10,785	25th July 1845	Purifying the vapours arising from smelting and other furnaces; recovering useful matters therefrom.
STOKOE, THOMAS - - -	648	29th July 1749	Machine for drawing coals, stone, water, ore and other heavy bodies, out of pits, mines, and other places of great depth.
STOKOE, THOMAS - - -	883	2nd Nov. 1767	Machine for drawing coals, stones, earth, rubbish and water, from coal-pits and other pits to the bank, and conveying the same and other heavy burdens to any distance.
STOLLE, EDWARD - - -	7573	24th Feb. 1838	Making sugar from sugar-cane; refining sugar.
STOLLMEYER, CONRAD FREDE-[RICK.	9085	17th Sept. 1841	Obtaining and applying motive-power by means of winds and waves, for propelling vessels on water, and driving machinery.
STONE, AMASA - - -	6704	23rd Oct. 1834	Power and other looms; weaving silk, hempen, cotton, woollen, and other cloth.
STONE, BENJAMIN - - -	97	9th July 1636	Making sword-blades, falchions, skeans, rapier-blades, and blasts serving as rests for muskets, by the help of mills.
STONE, CHARLES WILLIAM -	7200	4th Oct. 1836	Harness for weaving purposes; apparatus for making the same.
STONE, WILLIAM - - -	1832	18th Oct. 1791	Applying heat arising from coke-ovens to the distillation of volatile alkali, evaporation of saline solutions, exsiccation of chrystalline solutions, sublimation of sal-ammoniac, and to other purposes.
STONE, WILLIAM - - -	4122	17th May 1817	Application of apparatus for converting the fuel used for heating retorts of gas-light apparatus, into coke or charcoal.
STONE, WILLIAM - - -	8348	21st Jan. 1840	Manufacture of wine.
STONES, WILLIAM - - -	13,521	24th Feb. 1851	Manufacture of safety-paper for banker's cheques, bills of exchange, and for other like purposes.
STONES, WILLIAM BENSON -	12,990	7th March 1850	Treating peat and other carbonaceous and ligneous matters so as to obtain products therefrom.
STONES, WILLIAM BENSON - [Stones, Benson.]	13,590	15th April 1851	Use and treatment of peat and its products, and other carbonaceous matters; also apparatus applicable to such and other chemical purposes.
STOPFORD, JOSHUA - - -	3659	3rd March 1813	Mangles.
STOPPORTON, JOHN - -	13,131	12th June 1850	Propelling vessels.
STORCK, PETER - - -	2715	21st June 1803	Substitute for brewers' yeast.
STORER, JOSEPH - - -	8164	20th July 1839	Construction of certain musical instruments; partly applicable to pianofortes, seraphines, and certain descriptions of organs.

Name of Patentee.	Progressive Number.	Date.	Subject-matter of Patent.
STORER, JOSEPH - - -	11,261	27th June 1846	Organs, seraphines, and other " free-reed " instruments ;— partly applicable to pianofortes.
STORER, WILLIAM - - -	1068	14th April 1774	Making, chasing or embossing in lead, girondoles, frames for pier-glasses, tablets, friezes and brackets for chimney-pieces and rooms; hardening the same, and rendering them as durable as if made of copper.
STORER, WILLIAM - - -	1183	4th March 1778	Optical instrument or accurate delineator, entirely obviating the defects of the camera-obscura, being used without the assistance of the sun in the day-time, and also by candle-light, for drawing the human face, inside of rooms or buildings, also perspectives, landscapes, foliage and fibres of trees and flowers, exactly representing the true outlines, lights, shades, and colours.
STORER, WILLIAM - - -	1252	10th April 1780	Telescopes, microscopes, spectacles, opera-glasses, and other optical instruments.
STORER, WILLIAM - - -	1407	12th Dec. 1783	Preparing and making optic glasses (" Syllepsis glasses "); application thereof to optical instruments in general.
STOREY, EDWARD - - -	736	3rd Feb. 1759	Medicine or worm-destroying cakes. " Rotulæ Anthelminthicæ."
STOREY, JAMES [Story, James.]	994	18th July 1771	Machine for pumping water out of ships, mines or pits, and which by the force of one pound weight will raise fifty pounds as many feet as the one pound descends; will also enable one man to pump as much water as has been hitherto by thirty, may also be used for supplying towns with water, grinding malt and corn, working forge hammers, and slitting iron.
STOREY, JAMES - - -	1529	4th Feb. 1786	Machine for drawing coals, lead, tin and other materials, out of mines.
STOREY, JAMES - - -	1601	10th May 1787	Machine for drawing and raising water out of mines, and for other purposes.
STOREY, WILLIAM - - -	5774	10th March 1829	Materials in combination, suitable for scouring, milling or fulling, cleansing and washing cloths and other fabrics.
STOTHERT, HENRY - - -	6736	23rd Dec. 1834	Ships' hearths or cabouses.
STOTHERT, HENRY - - -	14,073	17th April 1852	Manufacture of manure.
STOTHERT, HENRY ASPREY -	5481	4th April 1827	Ploughs.
STOUGHTON, RICHARD - -	390	3rd April 1712	Restorative cordial and medicine. " Stomachic Tincture" or " Bitter Drops."
STOVEL, JOSEPH - - -	12,820	18th Oct. 1849	Coats ;—partly applicable to sleeves of other garments.
STOW, GARDNER - - -	11,687	4th May 1847	Construction of steam-vessels, and apparatus for propelling ships and other vessels.
STOW, GARDNER - - -	12,020	11th Jan. 1848	Apparatus for propelling ships and other vessels.
STOWE, HENRY MILLS - -	12.662	20th June 1849	Blocks and sheaves.
STOWELL, ANN MARIA - -	10,572	20th March 1845	Manufacture of ladies bonnets or hats.
STRACEY, EDWARD - - -	3193	23rd Jan. 1809	Hanging the bodies and constructing the perches of four-wheeled carriages; constructing perch-bolts and collar-braces.

Name of Patentee.	Progressive Number.	Date.	Subject-matter of Patent.
STRACH, HOWARD - -	75	19th Nov. 1634	Making or erecting stoves of iron-work, brickwork and earth, for heating water or other liquor, and for making salt, also for heating hothouses and rooms in dwelling-houses, as well as for drying all sorts of grain and various other articles, with sea-coal, charcoal, peat, turf or other fuel.
STRACHAN, WILLIAM - -	3486	9th Sept. 1811	Preparing ore of cobalt for various purposes.
STRACHAN, WILLIAM - -	3494	1st Oct. 1811	Making salt.
STRACHAN, WILLIAM - -	5665	12th June 1828	Manufacturing alum.
STRAKER, GEORGE - - -	5818	25th July 1829	Ships' windlasses.
STRAKER, GEORGE - - -	10,043	8th Feb. 1844	Ships' windlasses.
STRAND, LOUIS FRANCOIS -	11.784	3rd July 1847	Manufacture of various articles from cork.
STRATTON, BENJAMIN TUCKER	10,283	1st Aug. 1844	Welding sheet-iron for ship building and for other uses.
STRATTON, BENJAMIN TUCKER	11,648	6th April 1847	Railways; wheels and other parts of carriages for railways and common roads, partly applicable in the construction of ships and vessels; machinery for manufacturing parts of the same.
STRATTON, GEORGE - -	1985	7th May 1794	Grate, range, or stove, with apparatus to be applied thereto to prevent chimneys smoking, and to facilitate the processes of cooking without using charcoal, also adapted to the operations of the wash-house and laundry.
STRATTON, GEORGE - -	2522	26th June 1801	Machines for cooking; fire-places.
STRATTON, GEORGE - -	4147	5th Aug. 1817	Fire-places; heating and ventilating buildings.
STRATTON, GEORGE - -	4657	2nd March 1822	Consuming smoke.
STRATTON, GEORGE - -	5690	28th Aug. 1828	Warming and ventilating churches, hot-houses and other buildings;—applicable to other purposes.
STRATTON, WILLIAM - -	4184	5th Dec. 1817	Gas-apparatus.
STRATTON, WILLIAM - -	5462	12th Feb. 1827	Apparatus for heating air by means of steam.
STREET, JOHN - - -	3449	21st May 1811	Making and working bellows.
STREET, JOHN - - -	3949	11th Aug. 1815	Making and working bellows.
STREET, JOHN - - -	5967	5th Aug. 1830	Obtaining a rotatory motion by means of water, steam, gas, or other vapour, applicable to giving blast to furnaces and forges, also to other purposes where a constant blast is required.
STREET, ROBERT - - -	1983	7th May 1794	Producing an inflammable vapour force by means of liquid, air, fire and flame, for giving motion to engines, pumps, and machinery.
STREETS, JOHN, junior - -	6748	22nd Jan. 1835	Warp-machinery employed in the manufacture of lace and other fabrics.
STRICKLAND, EDWARD - -	1550	4th July 1786	Machine to prevent fire and house-breaking;—applicable to other purposes.
STRICKLAND, THOMAS, Sir [Knight.	148	20th Nov. 1665	Making steel.

Name of Patentee.	Progressive Number.	Date.	Subject-matter of Patent.
STRINGER, RICHARD - -	1796	18th March 1791	Chemical preparation for curing scurvy on the gums, fastening the teeth, causing the gums (when parted from the teeth) to grow up, and giving them a firmness and beautiful red colour, also for stopping the progress of teeth which are decaying, and preventing their being offensive. " Essence of Myrrh."
STRODE, BERNARD - -	189	21st June 1676	Engines with leather pipes, for raising water for drenching fires, draining mines, and divers other uses.
STRODE, BERNARD - -	260	8th Sept. 1688	Compound metal which can be drawn fine enough to spin and weave into all sorts of stuffs, and fit for several other uses.
STRODE, THOMAS - - -	1867	18th April 1792	Steam-engines.
STRODE, THOMAS - - -	2610	13th April 1802	Engine for raising and lowering weights, working mills, and other similar purposes.
STROMBON, ISAAC - - -	6198	17th Dec. 1831	Medicinal composition or embrocation, for the cure of external and internal complaints.
STRONG, JOHN - - -	2114	31st May 1796	Construction of piston-cylinders, suction chambers and valves.
STRONG, THEODORE FREDE-[RICK.	9104	28th Sept. 1841	Locks and latches.
STRUBING, JAMES ULRIC [VAUCHER, Baron de.	12,876	3rd Dec. 1849	Manufacture of axletree boxes for carriages, and bearings of the axles of railways; making an alloy of metals for the purpose.
STRUTT, ANTHONY RADFORD -	4402	18th Oct. 1819	Construction of locks and latches.
STRUTT, JEDEDIAH - -	722	19th April 1758	Machine furnished with a set of turning-needles, and to be fixed to a stocking-frame for making turned ribbed-stockings, pieces, and other goods usually manufactured upon stocking-frames.
STRUTT, JEDEDIAH - -	734	10th Jan. 1759	Machine furnished with a set of turning-needles, and to be fixed to a stocking-frame for making turned ribbed-stockings, pieces, and other goods usually manufactured upon stocking-frames.
STRUTT, JEDEDIAH - -	964	19th July 1770	Machine for roasting, boiling, and baking, consisting of a portable fire-stove, an air-jack, and a meat-screen, to be used in the field, in ships, and houses, where they may be separately used.
STRUTT, JOSEPH - - -	964	19th July 1770	Machine for roasting, boiling, and baking, consisting of a portable fire-stove, an air-jack, and a meat-screen, to be used in the field, in ships, and houses, where they may be separately used.
STRUVE, WILLIAM PRICE -	11,127	11th March 1846	Ventilating mines.
STRUVE, WILLIAM PRICE - [Struve, Price.]	11,406	8th Oct. 1846	Railway transit; moving or raising weights.
STUARD, JAMES - - -	954	15th March 1770	Windlass to raise heavy weights on board ships and vessels.
STUARD, JAMES - - -	1740	31st March 1790	Reducing friction.
STUARD, JAMES - - -	2086	4th Feb. 1796	Anchors for ships and vessels.
STUARD, JAMES - - -	2723	27th July 1803	Strengthening ships or floating vessels.
STUART, FERDINAND SMYTH -	3254	4th Aug. 1809	Substitute for Peruvian bark.

Name of Patentee.	Progres-sive Number.	Date.	Subject-matter of Patent.
STUART, PETER - - -	3307	26th Feb. 1810	Engraving and printing maps of counties, also charts or designs, music, and mathe-matical diagrams or figures, on wood, metal or other substance, to be thrown off in a common printing-press, either for books, newspapers, or other printed papers.
STUART, ROBERT - - -	2377	19th Feb. 1800	Starching and preparing cotton-yarn in the cop, so that it may be at once warped without any intermediate process, which cotton-yarn so prepared in the cop, is at once fitted for the purpose of weft.
STUBB, JOSEPH - - -	8764	31st Dec. 1840	Construction of screw-wrenchers and span-ners, for screwing and unscrewing nuts and bolts.
STUBBINS, JOHN - - -	9532	3rd Dec. 1842	Combinations of machinery to be employed for manufacturing parts of articles in stocking or lace fabrics.
STUBBS, HENRY - - -	3394	8th Oct. 1810	Grand imperial aulœum, from three to eighteen or twenty feet wide, without seam, and any length, for decorating rooms, as, for drapery curtains and fringes, chairs, sofas, tables, -&c., or finished on one side, for hangings, borders, and other species of decorations.
STUBBS, HENRY - - -	4294	7th Sept. 1818	Moveable heel, for boots, shoes, and for other purposes.
STUBBS, WILLIAM - - -	11,234	2nd June 1846	Locomotive and other engines and car-riages.
STUCKEY, WILLIAM HENRY -	9419	12th July 1842	Pneumatic-engine for producing motive-power.
STUCKEY, WILLIAM HENRY -	9539	3rd Dec. 1842	Filtering water and other fluids.
STUDLEY, FRANCIS - - -	10,069	24th Feb. 1844	Mill for grinding grain with or without sifter or dresser, and for cobbing, bruising, crushing, splitting or dividing, seed, pulse, berries, or other articles.
STUMPFF, JOHANN ANDREAS -	7971	21st Feb. 1839	Grand and other pianofortes.
STURGEON, THOMAS WILLIAM	3406	6th March 1811	Castors.
STURGEON, THOMAS WILLIAM	3428	1st April 1811	Micrometers.
STURGES, RICHARD FORD -	9441	10th Aug. 1842	Manufacture of Britannia metal and plated wares.
STURGES, RICHARD FORD -	11,378	17th Sept. 1846	Filtering-apparatus; apparatus for making tea-pots and other vessels of metal.
STURGES, RICHARD FORD -	11,919	21st Oct. 1847	Apparatus for filtering.
STURGES, RICHARD FORD -	12,480	14th Feb. 1849	Manufacture of candlesticks and lamp pillars.
STURGES, RICHARD FORD -	12,838	10th Nov. 1849	Bedsteads.
STURGES, RICHARD FORD -	13,914	24th Jan. 1852	Ornamenting metallic surfaces.
STURGES, RICHARD FORD -	14,148	29th May 1852	Ornamental fabric.
STURGES, RUSSELL - -	13,989	25th Feb. 1852	Weaving-looms.
STURTEVANT, CHARLES TURNER	5794	26th May 1829	Manufacturing soap.
STURTEVANT, RICHARD LAW-[RENCE	8870	8th March 1841	Manufacture of soap.
STYLES, WILLIAM - - -	4309	12th Nov. 1818	Machinery for sifting cinders, and then dis-charging them into a convenient receptacle; —applicable to other useful purposes.
SUARCE, CHARLES GABRIEL [BARON DE	7964	11th Feb. 1839	Obtaining dyes, colours, tannin and acids, from vegetable substances.

Name of Patentee.	Progres-sive Number.	Date.	Subject-matter of Patent.
SUEUR, CLEMENT LE - -	14,071	17th April 1852	Apparatus for preventing smoky chimneys; —applicable to other purposes of ventilation.
SULCLIFFE, JOHN - - -	6552	6th Feb. 1834	Machinery for roving and spinning cotton and other fibrous materials.
SULLIVAN, GEORGE - -	7243	3rd Dec. 1836	Machinery for measuring fluids.
SUMMERS, JAMES - - -	1828	6th Oct. 1791	Constructing a steam-engine by which may be worked mills for grinding, rolling, cutting, and turning, or any other machine that can be wrought by water, by means of a new figure called the sub-supra.
SUMMERS, THOMAS SEDGWICK	12,700	9th July 1849	Fastenings for the mouths of sacks and bags.
SUMMERS, WILLIAM, jun. -	3742	1st Nov. 1813	Raising hot water from a lower to an upper level, for baths, manufactories, and for other useful purposes.
SUMMERS, WILLIAM ALLTOFT	5927	14th April 1830	Construction of steam-engine and other boilers or generators, applicable to propelling vessels, locomotive-carriages, and to other purposes.
SUMMERS, WILLIAM ALLTOFT	12,362	9th Dec. 1848	Steam-engines and steam-boilers; apparatus connected therewith.
SUMNER, WILLIAM - -	6070	3rd Feb. 1831	Machinery for making bobbin-net.
SUNDERLAND, THOMAS - -	5151	20th April 1825	Combination of fuel.
SUNDERLAND, THOMAS - -	6526	19th Dec. 1833	Propelling vessels.
SUNDERLAND, THOMAS - -	9598	19th Jan. 1843	Moving floating bodies through water and air; accelerating the flow of water, air and other fluids, through shafts, pipes and other channels.
SURMAN, JOHN - - -	5953	6th July 1830	Bits for horses and other animals.
SURREY, JAMES - - -	4840	4th Sept. 1823	Applying heat for producing steam and for other purposes, thereby lessening the expense of fuel.
SURREY, JAMES - - -	7179	1st Sept. 1836	Application of a principle by which mechanical power may be obtained or applied.
SUSSEX, FRANCIS STANILAS [MELDON DE [Sussex, Francois Stanislas de.]	10,296	29th Aug. 1844	Recovery of manganese used in making bleaching-powder.
SUSSEX, FRANCIS STANILAS [MELDON DE	11,263	29th June 1846	Manufacture of soda and potash.
SUSSEX, FRANCIS STANILAS [MELDON DE	11,585	19th Feb. 1847	Manufacture of chlorine, hydro-chloric acid and nitric-acid; obtaining products therefrom.
SUSSEX, FRANCIS STANILAS [MELDON DE	11,635	23rd March 1847	Smelting copper and other ores.
SUTCLIFF, ROBERT - -	1488	16th July 1785	Die for stamping and ornamenting the hafts or handles of knives and forks made of silver, silver-plated, or other metal.
SUTCLIFF, ROBERT - - -	1505	7th Nov. 1785	Die for stamping and ornamenting the hafts or handles of knives and forks made of silver, silver plated, or other metal.
SUTCLIFFE, JAMES - - -	8247	24th Oct. 1839	Machinery for raising and forcing water or other fluids, and increasing the power of water on water-wheels and other machinery.
SUTCLIFFE, ROBERT - -	12,605	8th May 1849	Machinery for spinning cotton, silk, and other fibrous substances.

Name of Patentee.	Progressive Number.	Date.	Subject-matter of Patent.
SUTCLIFFE, WILLIAM - -	10,231	19th June 1844	Preparing, dyeing, sizing or dressing, drying, and winding, yarns and manufactured fabrics of wool, flax, cotton and other fibrous materials.
SUTHERLAND, JOHN - -	3583	16th July 1812	Construction of copper stills and intermediate condensers.
SUTHERLAND, JOHN - -	3771	20th Dec. 1813	Construction of copper and iron sugar-pans, and sugar-boilers; hanging the same; construction of furnaces in which the same ought to be placed.
SUTHERLAND, JOHN - -	4233	7th March 1818	Construction of an apparatus for purifying liquids.
SUTTILL, WILLIAM - -	5294	17th Nov. 1825	Machinery for preparing, drawing, roving, and spinning flax, hemp, and waste silk.
SUTTILL, WILLIAM - -	8810	26th Jan. 1841	Drawing flax, hemp, wool, silk, and other fibrous substances.
SUTTON, DANIEL - - -	857	13th Aug. 1766	Specific medicine to produce a favourable species of the small-pox.
SUTTON, JOHN - - -	8282	25th Nov. 1839	Obtaining power.
SUTTON, RALPH - - -	2973	7th Oct. 1806	Apparatus for cooking by steam or water.
SUTTON, RALPH - - -	3462	2nd July 1811	Self-acting curtain or window-blind rack.
SUTTON, RALPH - - -	3773	24th Dec. 1813	Security to prevent accidental discharges of fowling-pieces, which is unconnected with the lock, and applicable to all kinds of fire-arms.
SUTTON, ROBERT - - -	857	13th Aug. 1766	Specific medicine to produce a favourable species of the small-pox.
SUTTON, ROBERT - - -	2438	13th Aug. 1800	Sails for windmills.
SUTTON, SAMUEL - - -	602	16th March 1744	Extracting foul air out of ships.
SUTTON, WILLIAM - - -	275	— Sept. 1691	Ordering linen and woollen cloths and other manufactures, silks, stuffs, hats, and leather, thereby making them waterproof, and preventing moths and mildew in the same.
SUWERKROP, JOHN HILLARY -	5048	4th Dec. 1824	Portable mineral or river water bath and linen-warmer; apparatus connected therewith, for filtering and heating water.
SUXSPEACH, JOHN - -	676	19th Feb. 1753	Instrument called "The Catholic Organon," or "Universal sliding Foot-rule."
SWAIN, SAMPSON - - -	774	21st May 1762	Machine, furnace, and fire-engine, for smelting and refining metals, and for other purposes.
SWAIN, WILLIAM - - -	12,213	18th July 1848	Kilns for burning bricks, tiles, and other earthen substances.
SWAINE, EDWARD SCHMIDT -	4851	9th Oct. 1823	Producing and preserving artificial mineral waters; machinery to effect the same.
SWAINE, EDWARD SCHMIDT -	7384	6th June 1837	Producing and preserving artificial mineral waters; machinery to effect the same.
SWAN, ALEXANDER -	12,517	14th March 1849	Heating-apparatus; applying hot and warm air to manufacturing and other purposes.
SWAN, JOHN - - - -	6316	29th Sept. 1832	Brewing.
SWAN, JOSEPH - - -	14,180	24th June 1852	Production of figured surfaces; printing; machinery used therein.
SWARBRICK, JOHN - - -	14,136	22nd May 1852	Manufacturing retorts used for gas and for other purposes; apparatus connected therewith.

Name of Patentee.	Progres-sive Number.	Date.		Subject-matter of Patent.
SWEETAPPLE, THOMAS - -	7897	6th Dec.	1838	Machinery for making paper.
SWEETNAM, RICHARD - -	2007	13th Aug.	1794	Construction of tables, sashes, shutters, and sliding hinges applicable to such shutters;—and which improvements may be adapted to other purposes.
SWENY, THOMAS JOHN Mc -	11,143	25th March	1846	Steering ships and other vessels.
SWINBORNE, GEORGE PHIL-[BRICK.	11,975	24th Nov.	1847	Manufacture of gelatinous substances; apparatus to be used therein.
SWINBURNE, ROBERT WALTER	7141	4th July	1836	Manufacture of plate-glass.
SWINBURNE, ROBERT WALTER	7257	15th Dec.	1836	Manufacture of plate-glass.
SWINBURNE, THOMAS - -	7810	13th Sept.	1838	Water-closets and other conveniences of the kind.
SWINBURNE, THOMAS - -	11,024	3rd Jan.	1846	Railways; and means of propelling and carrying thereon.
SWINDELLS, JOHN - - -	7264	21st Dec.	1836	Effecting the decomposition of muriate of soda or common salt.
SWINDELLS, JOHN - - -	8036	16th April	1839	Manufacture of prussiate of potash and prussiate of soda.
SWINDELLS, JOHN - - -	8773	6th Jan.	1841	Manufacture of artificial stone, cement, stucco, and other similar compositions.
SWINDELLS, JOHN - - -	10,227	12th June	1844	Preparation of various substances for dyeing and producing colour; application and use of chemical compounds for the purpose.
SWINDELLS, JOHN - - -	13,342	14th Nov.	1850	Obtaining products from ores and other matters containing metals; preparation and application of such products for bleaching, printing, dyeing, and colour making.
SWINTON, WILLIAM - -	1338	2nd Oct.	1782	Making and constructing wheels of carts, waggons, coaches, and chaises.
SYEDS, JOHN - - - -	1789	21st Jan.	1791	Quadrant for determining altitudes at sea when no horizon can be found, and for more easily ascertaining the longitude.
SYEDS, JOHN - - - -	2883	7th Oct.	1805	Steering amplitude or azimuth compass and scale, for finding and working the course of ships.
SYEDS, JOHN - - - -	3052	16th June	1807	Construction of a machine for making rope or cordage, either shroud or cable laid; manufacturing the same.
SYKES, JOHN - - - -	10,547	8th March	1845	Machinery for preparing and cleaning wool, cotton, and similar fibrous materials.
SYKES, JOHN - - - -	11,798	17th July	1847	Machinery for cleaning wool, cotton, and similar fibrous substances from burs, motes, and other extraneous matter.
SYKES, JOHN - - - -	13,101	4th June	1850	Machinery for cleaning wool, cotton, and similar fibrous substances, from burs, motes, and other extraneous matters.
SYKES THOMAS - - -	1978	4th Feb.	1794	Lock instrument, or machine with one trigger or bolt, whereby both locks affixed to fire-arms with double barrels may be fired without a side motion, or other inconvenience.
SYKES, THOMAS - - -	3828	4th Aug.	1814	Construction of guns, pistols, and other fire-arms, and of implements used for loading them.
SYKES, WILLIAM - - -	8375	5th Feb.	1840	Construction of looms for weaving a new fabric; arrangement of machinery to produce other woven goods or fabrics.

Name of Patentee.	Progressive Number.	Date.	Subject-matter of Patent.
SYKES, WILLIAM	13,011	23rd March 1850	Manufacture of candles and wicks.
SYLVANUS, GEORGE	322	— April 1693	Making a mixture of wax and other ingredients, for beautifying and preserving leather, and being used for coaches, will preserve them much better than anything now used, and will also prevent any wet entering into boots or shoes.
SYLVESTER, CHARLES	2842	29th April 1805	Manufacturing zinc into wire, and into vessels and utensils for culinary and other purposes.
SYLVESTER, CHARLES	2849	18th May 1805	Sheathing ships, roofing houses, and lining water-spouts, with a material not before used.
SYLVESTER, JOHN	6273	5th June 1832	Apparatus for raising the temperature of air, in order to warm and ventilate buildings.
SYLVESTER, JOHN	6789	11th March 1835	Apparatus used in the communication or transmission of heat to aëriform, liquid, and solid bodies.
SYLVESTER, JOHN	8406	3rd March 1840	Construction of doors and frames for closing the openings of fire-places, ash-pits, flues, chimneys, and retorts.
SYLVESTER, JOHN	9681	28th March 1843	Producing ornamental surfaces on or with iron, applicable in the manufacture of stoves and other uses; modifying the transmission of heat.
SYLVESTER, JOHN	9986	13th Dec. 1843	Applying heat to brine or other matters contained in vessels.
SYLVESTER, JOHN	10,639	29th April 1845	Stoves and fire-places.
SYMES, EDWARD BOWLES	4613	10th Nov. 1821	Expanding hydrostatic-piston to resist the pressure of certain fluids, and to slide in an imperfect cylinder.
SYMES, WILLIAM	10,755	3rd July 1845	Apparatus for dividing lump-sugar.
SYMINGTON, ANDREW	6631	23rd June 1834	Paddle-wheel for propulsion of vessels and for other motive purposes.
SYMINGTON, WILLIAM	1610	5th June 1787	Steam-engine.
SYMINGTON, WILLIAM	2544	14th Oct. 1801	Constructing steam-engines; applying their power for producing rotatory and other motions without the interposition of lever or beam.
SYMINGTON, WILLIAM	6631	23rd June 1834	Paddle-wheel for propulsion of vessels and for other motive purposes.
SYMINGTON, WILLIAM	6925	7th Nov. 1835	Machinery for propelling vessels by steam;—partly applicable to motive machinery of other descriptions, whether actuated by steam or other motive power.
SYMINGTON, WILLIAM	9924	2nd Nov. 1843	Cleansing, purifying and sweetening, casks, vats, and other vessels.
SYMINGTON, WILLIAM	10.126	28th March 1844	Drying, seasoning, and hardening wood and other articles;—partly applicable to the desiccation of vegetable substances generally.
SYMINGTON, WILLIAM	11,947	6th Nov. 1847	Application of heat to the preparation, desiccation and preservation, of bread stuffs, confectionery, pulse, meats, vegetables, and other edible substances.
SYMINGTON, WILLIAM	14,030	22nd March 1852	Flues; heating air; evaporating certain fluids by heated air.
SYMONS, ALEXANDER	11,751	15th June 1847	Railway carriages; preventing accidents on railways; ascertaining the speed of carriages.

Name of Patentee.	Progressive Number.	Date.		Subject-matter of Patent.

T.

—◆—

Name of Patentee.	Progressive Number.	Date.		Subject-matter of Patent.
TAAFFE, JAMES - - -	8585	1st Aug.	1840	Roofing and slating houses and other buildings.
TABBERER THOMAS PARKER -	13,253	12th Sept.	1850	Manufacture of looped fabrics.
TABERNACLE, GEORGE - -	12,699	7th July	1849	Metallic springs for carriages.
TABOR, JAMES ASHWELL -	5312	14th Dec.	1825	Indicating the depth of water in ships and vessels.
TACHET, CLAUDE FRANCOIS -	13,815	15th Nov.	1851	Preparing wood to prevent its warping or shrinking.
TAFT, THOMAS - - -	4155	5th Aug.	1817	Bridle and other reins affixed to bits or other things; also bridle-bits and leather sliding loops, to act with reins and bits.
TAFT, WILLIAM - - -	5759	17th Jan.	1829	Harness and saddlery;—partly applicable to other purposes.
TAIT, WILLIAM IRONSIDE -	12,361	9th Dec.	1848	Producing outlines on paper, pasteboard, parchment, papier-mâché, and other like fabrics.
TAITE, JOSEPH - - -	3455	11th June	1811	Machinery for finishing piece-goods, or other flexible articles or materials of the like description, by glazing, burnishing, graining, or making impressions on the surface thereof.
TALBOT, JOHN - - -	1194	3rd June	1778	Machine to be used in the working of steel, iron, brass, and copper, hot or cold.
TALBOT WILLIAM HENRY FOX	8650	1st Oct.	1840	Producing or obtaining motive-power.
TALBOT, WILLIAM HENRY FOX	8842	8th Feb.	1841	Obtaining pictures or representations of objects.
TALBOT, WILLIAM HENRY FOX	9167	9th Dec.	1841	Coating or covering metals with other metals, and colouring metallic surfaces.
TALBOT, WILLIAM HENRY FOX	9528	25th Nov.	1842	Coating or covering metals with other metals.
TALBOT, WILLIAM HENRY FOX	9753	1st June	1843	Photography.
TALBOT, WILLIAM HENRY FOX	10,539	3rd March	1845	Obtaining motive-power; application of motive-power to railways.
TALBOT, WILLIAM HENRY FOX	11,475	7th Dec.	1846	Obtaining and applying motive-power.
TALBOT, WILLIAM HENRY FOX [Talbot, Henry Fox.]	12,906	19th Dec.	1849	Photography.
TALBOT, WILLIAM HENRY FOX	13,664	12th June	1851	Photography.
TALL, JOSEPH - - -	11,804	19th July	1847	Apparatus for setting saws.
TANN, EDWARD - - -	9963	25th Nov.	1843	Locks and latches, iron rooms, doors, safes, chests, and other repositories.
TANN, EDWARD, junior - -	9983	25th Nov.	1843	Locks and latches, iron rooms, doors, safes, chests, and other repositories.
TANN, JOHN - - -	9963	25th Nov.	1843	Locks and latches, iron rooms, doors, safes, chests, and other repositories.
TANNER, FRANCIS - - -	597	19th Jan.	1744	Pills for curing the gout and rheumatism.
TANNER, WILLIAM - -	14,199	6th July	1852	Dressing leather
TAPPAN, JOHN - - -	9725	15th May	1843	Machinery for preparing and spinning hemp and other fibrous materials.

Name of Patentee.	Progressive Number.	Date.	Subject-matter of Patent.
Tappan, John - - -	9750	30th May 1843	Apparatus applicable to flues or chimneys, for increasing the draft and promoting combustion of fuel.
Tappan, John - - -	9770	10th June 1843	Apparatus for grinding and polishing cutlery and other articles.
Tardieu, Jacques Leon -	14,302	23rd Sept. 1852	Colouring of photographical images.
Target, Felix Napoleon -	9522	25th Nov. 1842	Refining or manufacturing sugar.
Tarling, Henry James -	12,992	7th March 1850	Manufacture of fuel and manure, and deodorizing and disinfecting materials.
Tarlton, Gilbert - -	5079	11th Jan. 1825	Construction of a machine for throstle and water spinning of yarn from cotton, flax, silk, wool, or other fibrous substances.
Tarner, Julien Augustus -	7544	18th Jan. 1838	Propelling vessels through water.
Tarrant, John Kent - -	1182	28th Feb. 1778	Painting, spangling, gilding and silvering glass, for ornamenting carriages, sedan-chairs, buildings, furniture, musical instruments, or any other matters.
Tarver, James - - -	10,487	21st Jan. 1845	Machinery for cutting, grinding, and dressing vegetable substances.
Tasker, Jane - - -	386	2nd Aug. 1709	Working and making flask-cases, covering and casing flask-glasses with flags, rushes, and straw.
Tate, George - - -	13,638	22nd May 1851	Construction of dwelling-houses and other buildings, including floating vessels; adaptation and manufacture of materials for such uses.
Tate, James - - -	1467	26th Feb. 1785	Candlesticks, and nosles for sconces, chandeliers, girandoles, and other things used for holding candles.
Tate, James - - -	1501	2nd Nov. 1785	Cocks or valves.
Tate, James - - -	1589	1st Feb. 1787	Fire-grate and utensils for cooking, boiling, and warming all sorts of fluids.
Tate, James - - -	1734	13th March 1790	Machine for raising ballast, discharging cargoes of ships, and for other useful purposes.
Tate, James - - -	1859	2nd March 1792	Machine with utensils for cooking.
Tate, James - - -	1995	17th June 1794	Applying fire to the coppers of brewers and distillers; managing the same.
Tate, James - - -	2150	5th Dec. 1796	Machine for cooking.
Tate, James - - -	2630	26th June 1802	Construction of wheel-carriages.
Tate, Paul - - - -	1938	15th March 1793	Spinning-machine.
Tatham, John - - -	299	28th June 1692	Copper-boiler and wooden-vessel for brewing and distilling liquors and spirits.
Tatham, John - - -	6407	4th April 1833	Buttons.
Tatham, John - - -	10,106	14th March 1844	Machinery to be employed in the preparation and spinning of cotton-wool and other fibrous substances.
Tatham, John - - -	11,271	29th June 1846	Machinery to be used in the preparation and spinning of cotton and other fibrous substances.
Tatham, John - - -	13,072	7th May 1850	Machinery and operations connected with the manufacture of cotton-wool, silk, and other fibrous substances and fabrics; application of certain materials to the manufacture of textile fabrics.
Tatham, John - - -	13,313	2nd Nov. 1850	Manufacture of cotton and other fibrous materials, and fabrics composed of such materials.

Name of Patentee.	Progressive Number.	Date.	Subject-matter of Patent.
TATHAM, JOHN - - -	13,435	2nd Jan. 1851	Steam-engines; apparatus for generating and indicating the pressure of steam, and filtering water for boilers; also improvements applicable to steam-vessels or ships.
TATHAM, WILLIAM - -	2672	21st Dec. 1802	"Tatham's Clumps," for the purpose of constructing water-pipes, sewers, tunnels, wells, conduits, reservoirs, or other circular walls, shelves, or buildings.
TATTERSALL EDMUND - -	11,915	21st Oct. 1847	Making communications from one part of a railway-train to another.
TATTON, FREDERICK LOUIS -	4645	9th Feb. 1822	Astronomical instrument or watch, by which the time of the day, the progress of the celestial bodies, as well as of carriages, horses or other animals, may be correctly ascertained.
TAUNTON, WILLIAM GEORGE [HENRY.	9176	11th Dec. 1841	Machinery for raising weights.
TAUNTON, WILLIAM GEORGE [HENRY. [Taunton, George Henry.]	10,495	25th Jan. 1845	Machinery for revolving windlasses, barrels, spindles, and shafts, and for pumping.
TAUNTON, WILLIAM GEORGE [HENRY.	12,933	17th Jan. 1850	Obtaining and applying motive-power; means to ascertain the strength of chains, and ships' cables.
TAURINES, JEAN MARIÉ -	13,457	16th Jan. 1851	Machinery and apparatus for measuring and regulating the working of engines.
TAUSCH, FRANCOIS DE - -	7176	25th Aug. 1836	Machinery for propelling vessels, raising water, and for various other purposes.
TAYLER, EDMUND - -	8957	11th May 1841	Construction of carriages used on railroads.
TAYLER, JOHN - - -	12,997	7th March 1850	Looms for weaving; and machinery for preparing, balling and winding, warps and yarns.
TAYLER, JOSEPH NEEDHAM -	7718	4th July 1838	Abating or lessening the mischief arising from the force of the waves, and reducing waves to broken water, thereby preventing injury to breakwaters, mole-heads, piers, fortifications, lighthouses, docks, wharfs, landing-places, embankments, bridges; also adding security and defence to harbours and other places exposed to the action of the water.
TAYLER, JOSEPH NEEDHAM -	8377	8th Feb. 1840	Steam-boats and vessels, making the power of the steam-engine applicable to new and useful purposes of navigation.
TAYLER, JOSEPH NEEDHAM -	9674	21st March 1843	Breakwaters, beacons, and sound-alarms; landing or transmitting persons and goods over or through strata or obstructions, all of which improvements may be used either separately or in combination.
TAYLER, JOSEPH NEEDHAM -	11,151	25th March 1846	Propelling vessels; constructing vessels to be used in combination with machinery for removing sand-banks and other obstructions to navigation;—partly applicable to railways, or carriages on common roads.
TAYLEUR, CHARLES - -	9699	19th April 1843	Boilers.
TAYLOR, ALLEN - - -	3532	28th Jan. 1812	Engine for manufacturing grain into flour, meal, &c.
TAYLOR, ALLEN - - -	3961	25th Nov. 1815	Engine for raising water, cold and hot liquor of every description.

Name of Patentee.	Progressive Number.	Date.	Subject-matter of Patent.
TAYLOR, BENJAMIN - -	4216	31st Jan. 1818	Loom, to work by the power from a steam-engine, to weave figures or flowers on twilled or plain cloth, in either silk, cotton, linen, or worsted, or any of them intermixed.
TAYLOR, CHARLES - -	1007	14th March 1772	Machine for stamping and printing paper, silk, woollen, cotton and linen cloths, and other fabrics of silk, wool, cotton, or linen.
TAYLOR, CLEMENT - - -	1872	25th April 1792	Decomposing or removing all colours in linens and cottons, and whitening all other kinds of linens and cottons in different stages of the paper manufacture.
TAYLOR, DAVID - - -	1456	26th Nov. 1784	Buckle-chape or shoe-fastening.
TAYLOR, DANIEL FOOT - -	7418	21st Aug. 1837	Machinery and combination of machinery for making pins.
TAYLOR, ELIZABETH - -	782	6th Dec. 1762	Set of engines, tools, instruments and other apparatus, for making blocks, sheaves, and pins.
TAYLOR, ENOCH - - -	5655	13th May 1828	Paper-making, so far as relates to the cutting.
TAYLOR, FRANCIS - - -	10,804	6th Aug. 1845	Giving alarm in case of fire; and extinguishing fire.
TAYLOR, GEORGE - - -	1872	25th April 1792	Decomposing or removing all colours in linens and cottons, and whitening all other kinds of linens and cottons, in different stages of the paper manufacture.
TAYLOR, GEORGE - - -	11,733	3rd June 1847	Construction of engines and carriages to be used on railways.
TAYLOR, GEORGE - - -	11,961	13th Nov. 1847	Apparatus for sweeping and cleansing chimneys, funnels, flues, drains, and other places.
TAYLOR. HENRY - - -	1022	11th Aug. 1772	Producing an essence or extract from which fine spruce-beer can be made.
TAYLOR, HENRY - - -	4268	26th May 1818	Apparatus for catching and destroying rats and other vermin.
TAYLOR, HENRY AUGUSTUS -	8516	28th May 1840	Manufacture of braids and plats.
TAYLOR, HENRY BORRISKILL -	10,384	7th Nov. 1844	Apparatus for transmitting light from lamp and other burners.
TAYLOR, HERBERT - -	13,556	15th March 1851	Manufacture of carbonates and oxydes of barytes and strontia; also sulphur or sulphuric-acid from sulphates of the same; manufacture of carbonates and oxydes of soda and potassa.
TAYLOR, ISAAC - - -	12,248	21st Aug. 1848	Preparing and engraving surfaces; construction of cylinders adapted for engraving; machinery for printing and ornamenting surfaces.
TAYLOR, ISAAC, junior - -	5040	20th Nov. 1824	Cock or tap for drawing off liquids.
TAYLOR, JAMES - - -	693	3rd July 1754	Engine for spinning cotton-wool into yarn.
TAYLOR, JAMES - - -	934	4th Aug. 1769	Machine for raising weight or water.
TAYLOR, JAMES - - -	4751	16th Jan. 1823	Constructing the bottoms of merchant-ships, and placing the pumps so as to prevent damage to the cargo by the bilge water.
TAYLOR, JAMES - - -	10,879	10th Oct. 1845	Manufacture of carpets, rugs, and piled fabrics.

Name of Patentee.	Progressive Number.	Date.	Subject-matter of Patent.
TAYLOR, JAMES - - -	11,548	28th Jan. 1847	Apparatus for boring into the earth.
TAYLOR, JAMES - - -	12,355	2nd Dec. 1848	Propelling ships and other vessels.
TAYLOR, JANET - - -	6582	27th March 1834	Instruments for measuring angles and distances, applicable to nautical and other purposes.
TAYLOR, JEREMIAH - -	705	20th Oct. 1755	Cordial draught for the cholic and other griping pains.
TAYLOR, JOB - - - -	8220	19th Sept. 1839	Machinery for cutting or forming ornamental mouldings or devices, in wood and other materials.
TAYLOR, JOHN - - -	465	11th April 1724	Engine which works by means of suction; forming pumps by means of a screw or worm, for drawing water from mines or pits to a considerable height.
TAYLOR, JOHN - - -	3432	11th April 1811	Construction of wheels for carriages.
TAYLOR, JOHN - - -	3517	20th Jan. 1812	Machine and rods for cutting, spreading and preparing, wicks for dip-candles.
TAYLOR, JOHN - - -	3929	14th June 1815	Producing gas to be used for the purpose of affording light.
TAYLOR, JOHN - - -	3933	22nd June 1815	Purifying and refining sugar.
TAYLOR, JOHN - - -	10,201	23rd May 1844	Mechanical combinations for economizing power and fuel in the use of steam-engines.
TAYLOR, JOHN - - -	10,614	15th April 1845	Separating metals from each other, and from certain combinations with other substances.
TAYLOR, JOHN - - -	11,239	6th June 1846	Flour-mills; and machinery connected therewith.
TAYLOR, JOHN - - -	11,407	8th Oct. 1846	Manufacture of explosive compounds.
TAYLOR, JOHN - - -	12,344	29th Nov. 1848	Engines, boilers, and pumps; railway-carriages; propelling vessels; construction of boats; extinguishing fire; brewing.
TAYLOR, JOHN - - -	12,464	8th Feb. 1849	Constructing and fencing walls.
TAYLOR, JOHN GEORGE -	13,415	19th Dec. 1850	Manufacture of dress and other pins, also other dress-fastenings and ornaments.
TAYLOR, JONATHAN - -	1232	10th Aug. 1779	Casting oval-bellied cast-iron pots, and pots and saucepans with a bead or rim round the top; annealing, turning, tinning, and finishing the same.
TAYLOR, JOSEPH - - -	576	29th May 1741	Hydraulic mechanism or water-machine, for raising water out of wells, and carrying the same to any height required.
TAYLOR, JOSEPH - - -	3842	23rd Sept. 1814	Loom to be used in weaving cotton, linen, worsted, silk or other cloth, or cloth made of any two or more of the said materials.
TAYLOR, JOSEPH - - -	3880	4th Feb. 1815	Loom to be used in weaving cotton, worsted, silk or other cloth, or cloth made of any two or more of the said materials.
TAYLOR, JOSEPH - - -	4788	29th April 1823	Apparatus to facilitate or improve the spinning, doubling, and throwing of silk, cotton-wool or flax, or mixtures of the same.
TAYLOR, JOSEPH - - -	11,689	4th May 1847	Construction and manufacture of wheels for railway and other carriages.
TAYLOR, JOSEPH ALEXANDER	5240	13th Aug. 1825	Polishing-apparatus for household purposes.
TAYLOR, JOSEPH ALEXANDER	6272	5th June 1832	Whip-stick, or cane to be used when riding.

Name of Patentee.	Progressive Number.	Date.		Subject-matter of Patent.
TAYLOR, JOSEPH JEPSON [ODDY.	7629	1st May	1838	Propelling ships and other vessels in water.
TAYLOR, JOSEPH JEPSON [ODDY.	14,118	8th May	1852	Ships, boats, and vessels, and certain articles of ship's furniture.
TAYLOR, JOSEPH JEPSON ODDY	14,214	6th July	1852	Propelling ships and other vessels on water. (*Extension for four years from 1st May 1852.*)
TAYLOR, JOSIAH - - -	9172	9th Dec.	1841	Construction of lamps.
TAYLOR, NATHANIEL FORTESCUE.	9449	18th Aug.	1842	Meters for gas and other fluids.
TAYLOR, NATHANIEL FORTESCUE.	10,440	18th Dec.	1844	Apparatus for measuring gas.
TAYLOR, NATHANIEL FORTESCUE.	11,883	7th Oct.	1847	Machinery for printing and staining paper and other fabrics.
TAYLOR, PETER - - -	3842	23rd Sept.	1814	Loom to be used in weaving cotton, worsted, silk or other cloth, or cloth made of any two or more of the said materials.
TAYLOR, PETER - - -	3880	4th Feb.	1815	Loom to be used in weaving cotton, worsted, silk or other cloth, or cloth made of any two or more of the said materials.
TAYLOR, PETER - - -	5334	29th March	1828	Machinery for heckling dressing, or combing flax, hemp, tow, and other fibrous materials.
TAYLOR, PETER - - -	7884	1st Dec.	1838	Machinery for propelling vessels, carriages, and machinery;—partly applicable to raising water.
TAYLOR, PETER - - -	11,044	20th Jan.	1846	Machinery for propelling vessels, carriages, and machinery;—partly applicable to drawing and propelling fluids; construction of vessels.
TAYLOR, PHILIP - - -	4032	25th May	1816	Applying heat to liquors used in the processes of brewing, distilling, and sugar-refining.
TAYLOR, PHILIP - - -	4197	15th Jan.	1818	Applying heat in certain processes; refrigerators.
TAYLOR, PHILIP - - -	4975	15th June	1824	Apparatus for producing gas from various substances.
TAYLOR, PHILIP - - -	4983	3rd July	1824	Steam-engines.
TAYLOR, PHILIP - - -	5244	18th Aug.	1825	Making iron.
TAYLOR, SAMUEL - - -	453	6th Feb.	1723	Engine for stamping and dressing thread.
TAYLOR, SAMUEL LAWRENCE -	8587	3rd Aug.	1840	Ploughs.
TAYLOR, SAMUEL LAWRENCE -	9474	22nd Sept.	1842	Machinery for ploughing, harrowing and raking land, and for cutting food for animals.
TAYLOR, STEPHEN - - -	11,994	10th Dec.	1847	Construction of fire-arms, and cartridges for charging the same.
TAYLOR, STEPHEN - - -	14,289	10th Sept.	1852	Construction of fire-arms, and cartridges for charging the same.
TAYLOR, THOMAS - - -	1192	16th May	1778	Making lace and open-work in silk, cotton, thread, and worsted; engine with a set of working-needles affixed; fixing such engine to a stocking-frame for lace and open-work mits, gloves, caps, handkerchiefs, aprons, stocking-pieces and other things worked upon the stocking-frame.
TAYLOR, THOMAS - - -	7086	7th May	1836	Saddles for riding.

Name of Patentee.	Progressive Number.	Date.	Subject-matter of Patent.
TAYLOR, THOMAS - - -	10,891	23rd Oct. 1845	Machinery for sawing timber.
TAYLOR, THOMAS - - -	13,768	9th Oct. 1851	Apparatus for measuring water and other fluids.
TAYLOR, WALTER - - -	1109	28th Nov. 1775	Construction of wheels for carriages, or improvements in the boxes, naves, and spokes, and in securing the rims thereof, thereby occasioning a less amount of friction.
TAYLOR, WALTER - - -	1110	28th Nov. 1775	Bushing cast-iron or metal shivers for ships' blocks and other things.
TAYLOR, WALTER - - -	1295	5th June 1781	Construction of shivers or pullies for ships' blocks.
TAYLOR, WALTER - - -	1567	30th Oct. 1786	Construction of machines for grinding grain, also starch for hair-powder, and all matters where stones are used; likewise for coating or bushing and greasing shivers and pullies of all kinds.
TAYLOR, WALTER - - -	1704	19th Sept. 1789	Construction of pumps, the chambers, pistons and boxes thereunto belonging, so as to prevent their being choked with gravel, sand, and filth.
TAYLOR, WALTER - - -	2217	28th Feb. 1798	Construction of machines for raising water and clearing ships of the same, also for taking off the pressure of the atmosphere from the tops of chimneys to prevent what are commonly called smoky chimneys.
TAYLOR, WILLIAM - - -	830	15th June 1765	Knitting-machine for making and knitting stockings, stocking-pieces, and other goods.
TAYLOR, WILLIAM - - -	1988	6th Nov. 1793	Air-furnace.
TAYLOR, WILLIAM - - -	3475	7th Aug. 1811	Apparatus to be attached to the axletree and nave of wheel-carriages for checking their motion.
TAYLOR, WILLIAM - - -	4504	23rd Oct. 1820	Furnaces for smelting iron and other ores.
TAYLOR, WILLIAM - - -	5958	19th July 1830	Boilers and apparatus connected therewith;—applicable to steam-engines and to other purposes.
TAYLOR, WILLIAM - - -	7072	26th April 1836	Machinery for supplying water or other fluids to steam-boilers or evaporating-vessels; also for obtaining mechanical power by steam; and for communicating motion to vessels floating on water.
TAYLOR, WILLIAM - - -	9659	8th March 1843	Manufacture of bricks and tiles.
TAYLOR, WILLIAM - - -	10,155	24th April 1844	Manufacture of axle-pullies, and pegs or pins for hanging hats or other garments thereon.
TAYLOR, WILLIAM - - -	10,262	15th July 1844	Manufacture of oil from a vegetable not hitherto so used.
TAYLOR, WILLIAM - - -	11,074	3rd Feb. 1846	Consuming smoke and economizing fuel.
TAYLOR, WILLIAM - - -	12,158	18th May 1848	Bending flat plates of malleable metals or mixtures of metals into the form of tubes, by machinery.
TAYLOR, WILLIAM - - -	12,986	2nd March 1850	Rollers to be used in the manufacture of silk, cotton, woollen, and other fabrics.
TAYLOR, WILLIAM GARNETT -	9844	15th July 1843	Machinery for spinning cotton and other fibrous substances; preparing and dressing yarn for weaving.
TAYLOR, WILLIAM GARNETT -	11,074	3rd Feb. 1846	Consuming smoke and economizing fuel.
TAYLOR, WILLIAM GARNETT -	12,859	24th Nov. 1849	Lint and linting-machines.

Name of Patentee.	Progressive Number.	Date.	Subject-matter of Patent.
TAYLOR, WILLIAM HANNIS -	8255	2nd Nov. 1839	Obtaining power by means of electro-magnetism.
TAYLOR, WILLIAM HANNIS -	8512	20th May 1840	Mode of forming or manufacturing staves, shingles, and laths; and machinery used for that purpose.
TAYLOR, WILLIAM HANNIS -	8976	5th June 1841	Propelling-machinery.
TAYLOR, WILLIAM HANNIS -	10,453	2nd Jan. 1845	Propelling.
TAYLOR, WILLIAM HANNIS -	11,009	20th Dec. 1845	Propelling.
TAYLOR, WILLIAM WILKINSON	6330	8th Nov. 1832	Cloth for the sails of ships and other vessels.
TAYLOR, WILLIAM WILKINSON	8825	1st Feb. 1841	Buffing-apparatus for railway purposes.
TEAGLE, ROBERT - - -	11,440	5th Nov. 1846	Chimney-pots and apparatus for cleansing chimneys.
TEAGUE, MOSES - - -	6211	17th Jan. 1832	Making and smelting pig-iron.
TEALDI, PETER ASCANIUS -	7186	15th Sept. 1836	Vegetable acid, which may be employed in various manufactures, and in culinary or other purposes; process of obtaining the same.
TEBAY, JOHN - - - -	12,999	7th March 1850	Meter for registering the flow of water and other fluids.
TEBBUTT, THOMAS RAINFORTH	7531	5th Jan. 1838	Manufacture of oxydes of lead and carbonate of lead.
TEBBUTT, THOMAS RAINFORTH	7538	11th Jan. 1838	Manufacture of hydrate and carbonate of soda, from chloride of sodium; applicable to the making of soap, and glass, and for other useful purposes.
TEE, EDWARD PEARSON - -	7968	11th Feb. 1839	Weaving linen and other fabrics.
TEETON, THOMAS - - -	482	15th Dec. 1725	Machine for throwing and manufacturing fine single and double raw-silk.
TEISSIER, JEAN ANTOINE -	5251	15th Sept. 1825	Steam-engines.
TEISSIER, JOHN BAPTISTE [SIMEON.	10,578	27th March 1845	Propelling vessels, carriages, and agricultural machines.
TEISSIER, SIMEON - - -	4469	3rd June 1820	Propelling vessels.
TELFER, WILLIAM - - -	2469	3rd Feb. 1801	Preparing and manufacturing flax, hemp, silk, and other materials.
TELFER, WILLIAM - - -	2607	8th April 1802	Preparing and manufacturing flax, hemp, silk, and other materials.
TEMPLEMAN, JAMES - -	1707	6th Nov. 1789	Making locks to discharge double-barrel guns and pistols, by means of one trigger, without discharging both barrels at the same instant, which may be discharged either in immediate succession to or at any distant period from each other.
TEMPLETON, ARCHIBALD -	9169	9th Dec. 1841	Method of preparing silk and other fibrous substances for spinning.
TEMPLETON, JAMES - -	8169	25th July 1839	Manufacturing silk, cotton, woollen, and linen fabrics.
TEMPLETON, JAMES - -	12,954	29th Jan. 1850	Manufacturing figured fabrics, principally designed for the production of carpets.
TEMPLETON, JOHN SAMUEL -	10,761	12th July 1845	Propelling carriages on railways.
TEMPLETON, JOHN SAMUEL -	11,114	27th Feb. 1846	Propelling carriages on railways; propelling vessels.
TENCATE, JOHN - - -	1648	5th May 1788	Horse-pump, calculated to raise from ten to one hundred hogsheads per minute, on the principle of a fulcrum balance, worked by a castor-wheel, performing a double attraction in the same revolution.

Name of Patentee.	Progressive Number.	Date.	Subject-matter of Patent.
TENNANT, CHARLES - -	2209	23rd Jan. 1798	Method of using lime, strontites, and barytes, carbonated or calcined, instead of alkaline substances, for neutralizing the oxygenated muriatic-acid used in bleaching; also using the above earths in other parts of the process of bleaching.
TENNANT, CHARLES - -	2312	30th April 1799	Method of preparing the oxygenated calcareous earths, strontites, barytes, and magnesia, in a dry, undissolved, or powdery form; applying such earths either in the above state or dissolved, for the purpose of removing colours from vegetable or animal substances.
TENNANT, GEORGE - -	3143	14th June 1808	Machine for cutting fustian, velvet, velveret, and every species of fustian, velveret, and velveteen, also velvet-plush, and other cloth or goods made of cotton, silk, woollen, or any mixture of the same, usually cut in the manufacture thereof.
TENNANT, JOHN - - -	6488	19th Oct. 1833	Apparatus to produce or evolve chlorine for manufacturing purposes.
TENNANT, MATTHEW BAILEY	9604	26th Jan. 1843	Apparatus for preventing engines and carriages going off railways, and for removing obstructions on railways.
TENNENT, ROBERT BOWMAN -	14,303	24th Sept. 1852	Pulping cherry-coffee; machinery applicable thereto.
TENNESON, HENRY QUENTIN -	7447	19th Oct. 1837	Construction of portable vessels for containing gas; machinery for compressing gas therein; apparatus for regulating the supply of gas, either from a portable vessel, or from a fixed pipe communicating with an ordinary gasometer.
TERRY, ALEXANDER ROBERT -	12,759	6th Sept. 1849	Manufacture or preparation of fire-wood.
TERRY, CHARLES - - -	6403	28th March 1833	Producing leather from hides and skins.
TERRY, CHARLES - - -	6441	26th June 1833	Refining and purifying oils.
TERRY, CHARLES - - -	6442	26th June 1833	Making and refining sugar.
TESCHEMACHER, JOHN ROGER	1808	24th May 1791	Producing steam by means of a machine, to be used in engines instead of the common boiler; also applying the same machine in working engines of every description where steam is used.
TESCHEMACHER, JOHN ROGER	1917	6th Nov. 1792	Machine for spinning and roving wool, silk, cotton, flax, hemp, and other materials.
TESHMAKER, JOHN ENGLEBERT	288	2nd Jan. 1962	Making spinnall yarn.
TETLEY, CHARLES - - -	9809	30th June 1843	Construction of boilers or generators for producing steam.
TETLEY, CHARLES - -	11,081	11th Feb. 1846	Machinery for raising and impelling water and other liquids, thereby to obtain mechanical power.
TETLOW, JAMES - - -	5020	14th Oct. 1824	Power-looms for weaving various articles.
TETLOW, JOHN - - -	963	15th June 1770	Machine for ruling paper for music and other purposes. " Tetlow."
TEYCHENNE, FRANÇOIS - -	11,325	10th Aug. 1846	Treating stone to render it hard and impermeable; colouring the same.
THACHER, THOMAS - -	5993	7th Sept. 1830	Elastic self adapting saddle.
THACKERAY, JOHN - - -	9225	15th Jan. 1842	Process of preparing and gassing thread or yarn.
THACKRAH, JOSEPH - -	4883	27th Dec. 1823	Pattens and clogs.

Name of Patentee.	Progressive Number.	Date.		Subject-matter of Patent.
THACKRAH, JOHN - - -	3699	22nd May	1813	Enclosing a seat in a portable stool-stick.
THATCHER, CHARLES - -	9456	31st Aug.	1842	Drags or breaks, to be applied to the wheels of carriages generally.
THATCHER, THOMAS - -	9456	31st Aug.	1842	Drags or breaks, to be applied to the wheels of carriages generally.
THENNEMAN, SYMON - -	336	17th Oct.	1694	Printing upon oil-cloth and leather, gold and silver flowers and other figures in various colours.
THIERRY, Baron CHARLES [PHILIP DE.	4396	20th Sept.	1819	Bit for coach and bridle uses. "The Humane Safety Bit."
THIERS, PIERRE LOUIS THI- [MOTÉ.	11,518	7th Jan.	1847	Instrument for drawing off milk from the breasts of women, and for raising and protecting the nipple both before and after childbirth.
THIN, JOHN - - - -	5087	1st Feb.	1825	Constructing a roasting-jack.
THIRION, PIERRE - - -	10,704	3rd June	1845	Dressing furs and skins.
THIRLWALL, THOMAS - -	9166	8th Sept.	1842	Lubricating the piston-rods of steam-engines and of other machinery.
THIVILLE, JOSEPH GASTON [JOHN BAPTISTE DE.	2406	26th May	1800	Lamp or light for lighting chambers, rooms, halls, &c.
THIVILLE, JOSEPH GASTON [JOHN BAPTISTE DE.	2472	5th Feb.	1801	Method of giving an independent moving power to machines, by means of hydraulic engines ; constructing and employing several of their parts, such as wheels, pistons, and apparatus for reducing friction.
THOELDEN, AUGUSTUS FREDE- [RICK.	2653	30th Oct.	1802	Mechanical apparatus for supporting the human body.
THOM, JAMES - - -	4431	15th Jan.	1820	Pianofortes.
THOM, JOHN - - - -	12,610	15th May	1849	Cleansing, scouring, or bleaching silk, woollen, cotton and other woven fabrics and yarns ; ageing fabrics and yarns when printed.
THOMAS, ANTHONY - -	3121	26th March	1803	Manufacturing hats, bonnets, and other articles of the like description.
THOMAS, CHARLES - -	14,109	1st May	1852	Manufacture of soap.
THOMAS, DAVID - - -	3138	30th May	1808	Perforated vessel, percolator and frame, for preparing potable coffee.
THOMAS, DAVID - - -	3674	30th March	1813	Burning animal bones to extract the fat or grease ; likewise extracting the spirituous quality therefrom ; reducing the remaining or dry parts for making ivory black.
THOMAS, EDWARD - - -	7014	26th Feb.	1836	Bedsteads, and apparatus to be used with or for bedsteads.
THOMAS, FRANCIS - - -	1157	10th June	1777	Machine for separating metal from slags.
THOMAS, GILBERT, Captain -	181	11th June	1675	Making stone-blue, flat indigo and powder-blue, out of the useless dust or powder of indigo.
THOMAS, JAMES LEONARD [CLEMENT.	7392	17th June	1837	Steam-engines and steam-generators.
THOMAS, JOHN - - -	2614	26th April	1802	Machine for batting and cleaning wool, cotton, and flax, preparatory to carding and spinning.
THOMAS, JOSEPH - - -	10,380	5th Nov.	1844	Tube.
THOMAS, MATTHEW - -	4838	26th Jan.	1819	Ploughs ; and a propelling power applicable to ploughs and other implements and machines.

Name of Patentee.	Progressive Number.	Date.		Subject-matter of Patent.
THOMAS, PHILIP - - -	4090	19th Dec.	1816	Chains manufactured in a particular manner by a new process ; apparatus and improvements in performing and executing the same.
THOMAS, RICHARD HANDLEY	13,140	19th June	1850	Manufacture of iron.
THOMAS, ROBERT - - -	7677	7th June	1838	Apparatus to be attached to carriages for stopping the horses or checking their speed.
THOMAS, WILLIAM - - -	4553	1st May	1821	Machine for cutting and preparing lay-ground for tillage ; and for renewing grass and other lands, without destroying or tearing up the whole of the surface thereof.
THOMAS, WILLIAM -	9379	6th Sept.	1843	Fastening for wearing-apparel, also applicable as a fastening to portmanteaus, bags, boxes, books, and other things.
THOMAS, WILLIAM - -	10,339	3rd Oct.	1844	Looms.
THOMAS, WILLIAM - -	10,895	24th Oct.	1845	Construction of umbrellas and parasols.
THOMAS, WILLIAM - -	10,925	4th Nov.	1845	Apparatus for impregnating liquids with gases.
THOMAS, WILLIAM - -	11,299	15th July	1846	Frames, locks and fastenings, for carpet-bags and purses ;—partly applicable to all other locks.
THOMAS, WILLIAM - -	11,434	1st Dec.	1846	Machinery for sewing or stitching various fabrics.
THOMAS, WILLIAM - -	11,925	26th Oct.	1847	Construction of stays ; and machinery for the manufacture of stays ;—partly applicable to other species of weaving.
THOMAS, WILLIAM - -	12,221	26th July	1848	Manufacture of stays, boots, and shoes ; fastening and connecting fabrics and garments.
THOMAS, WILLIAM - -	12,401	4th Jan.	1849	Manufacture of window-blinds.
THOMAS, WILLIAM - -	12,736	9th Aug.	1849	Manufacture of looped fabrics, stays, and other parts of dress ; — apparatus for measuring.
THOMAS, WILLIAM - -	13,805	6th Nov.	1851	Construction of apparatus and machinery for economizing fuel in the generation of steam ; machinery for propelling on land and water.
THOMASON, EDWARD - -	2142	25th Oct.	1796	Steps for coaches, chariots, gigs, and other carriages.
THOMASON, EDWARD - -	2282	22nd Dec.	1798	Making steps for coaches, chariots, landaus, &c.
THOMASON, EDWARD - -	2360	28th Nov.	1799	Mechanism of the cocks of gun-locks, applicable to all kinds of fire-arms.
THOMASON, EDWARD -	2617	7th May	1802	Corkscrews.
THOMASON, EDWARD - -	2738	31st Oct.	1803	Making hearth-brushes.
THOMASON, EDWARD -	2750	7th Feb.	1804	Making pikes.
THOMASON, EDWARD -	3171	8th Oct.	1808	Construction of umbrellas and parasols.
THOMASON, EDWARD -	3715	3rd July	1813	Construction of whips.
THOMASON, EDWARD - -	5422	9th Nov.	1826	Construction of medals, tokens, and coins.
THOMASON, HENRY BOTFIELD	4492	20th July	1820	Manufacturing table-knives, dessert-knives, fruit-knives, pocket-knives, scissors, razors, and surgical-instruments.
THOMASON, PHILLIS BOWN -	3228	19th April	1809	Making umbrellas and parasols.

Name of Patentee.	Progressive Number.	Date.	Subject-matter of Patent.
THOMPSON, ARCHIBALD - -	2553	10th Nov. 1801	Machinery for spinning rope-yarn or sail-cloth-yarn, and for laying or making ropes and other cordage.
THOMPSON, BENJAMIN - -	4602	24th Oct. 1821	Facilitating the conveyance of carriages along iron and wood railways, tramways, and other roads.
THOMPSON, BENJAMIN - -	12,722	1st Aug. 1849	Manufacture of iron.
THOMPSON, FRANCIS - -	1884	25th May 1792	Steam-engines.
THOMPSON, FREDERICK PHILIP	13,949	2nd Feb. 1852	Filtering and preserving water.
THOMPSON, GEORGE - -	13,222	12th Aug. 1850	Machinery and apparatus for cutting, digging, or turning up earth;—applicable to agricultural purposes.
THOMPSON, GEORGE ALEX-[ANDER.	3244	15th June 1809	Instrument for cutting the wick of a lighted candle and keeping the same in trim and of a proper length.
THOMPSON, GEORGE ALEX-[ANDER.	3440	1st May 1811	Machine for dragging, locking, and scotching the wheels of carriages.
THOMPSON, GEORGE ALEX-[ANDER.	11,101	25th Feb. 1846	Propelling vessels.
THOMPSON, ISAAC - - -	298	31st May 1692	Diving-habit, for enabling a man to work one hour under water, by means of an air-pump.
THOMPSON, JAMES - - -	3830	4th Aug. 1814	Method of assisting to render a ship, vessel, or craft governable in all her movements.
THOMPSON, JAMES - - -	10,444	20th Dec. 1844	Preparation and application of various farinaceous products; machinery used in manufacturing the same.
THOMPSON, JAMES - - -	11,278	6th July 1846	Machinery for obtaining motive-power;—partly applicable for other useful purposes.
THOMPSON, JAMES - - -	13,842	5th Dec. 1851	Means of and apparatus for heating ovens.
THOMPSON, JAMES WILLIAM -	8320	16th Dec. 1839	Construction of bedsteads, partly applicable to the use of invalids.
THOMPSON, JOHN - - -	412	8th March 1717	Floating-engine for grinding corn and bolting the flour by force of water.
THOMPSON, JOHN - - -	655	6th April 1750	Chair or carriage for one person to travel in, furnished with one wheel, and a harness for the horse to draw the same.
THOMPSON, JOHN - - -	1522	23rd Jan. 1786	Medicine or concentrated balsam of arquebusade, an antiseptic chemical preparation, useful in the cure of fractures, dislocations, and wounds, also bilious complaints, the dropsy, gravel and worms. " Baume d'arquebusade concentre."
THOMPSON, JOHN - - -	1566	30th Oct. 1786	Medicine or concentrated balsam of arquebusade, an antiseptic chemical preparation, useful in the cure of fractures, dislocations, and wounds, also bilious complaints, the dropsy, gravel, and worms. " Baume d'arquebusade concentre."
THOMPSON, JOHN - - -	4397	20th Sept. 1819	Method of extracting iron from ore.
THOMPSON, JOHN - - -	4655	2nd March 1822	Forming or preparing steel for the manufacture of coach-springs.
THOMPSON, JOHN - - -	5051	9th Dec. 1824	Making cast-steel.
THOMPSON, JOHN - - -	5192	21st June 1825	Producing steam, applicable to steam-engines or other purposes.
THOMPSON, JOHN - - -	6393	28th Feb. 1833	Steam-engine.

Name of Patentee.	Progressive Number.	Date.	Subject-matter of Patent.
THOMPSON, JOHN - - -	9730	16th May 1843	Bedsteads and couches for invalids.
THOMPSON, JOHN THOMAS -	3560	30th April 1812	Making iron bedsteads and testers.
THOMPSON, JOHN THOMAS -	5403	17th Aug. 1826	Manufacturing metallic-tubes; applying them to the construction of the metallic-tube and other bedsteads.
THOMPSON, ROGER - - -	3592	5th Aug. 1812	Working two or more pumps, for delivering water out of leaky ships, stone-quarries, or mines, with half the usual manual force.
THOMPSON, TULLY - -	7872	13th Nov. 1838	Additions to locks or fastenings for doors of buildings and of cabinets, and for drawers, chests, and other receptacles.
THOMPSON, SIMEON - -	2815	23rd Jan. 1805	Bushels and other measures for measuring coals, grain, seed, and other dry measurable commodities.
THOMPSON, SIMEON - -	3218	20th March 1809	Machinery for raising, lowering, drawing, driving, forcing, impressing or moving bodies, substances, materials, fluids, articles or commodities.
THOMPSON, SIMON - -	5912	27th Feb. 1830	Pianofortes.
THOMPSON, THOMAS - -	9573	28th Dec. 1842	Weaving figured fabrics.
THOMPSON, THOMAS HARCOURT	12,584	26th April 1849	Apparatus for preventing the rise of effluvium from drains, sewers, cesspools and other places; apparatus and machinery for regulating the level of waters in rivers, reservoirs, and canals.
THOMPSON, WARDHAUGH -	1583	15th Jan. 1787	Instrument for tuning harpsichords, pianofortes, spinnets, organs, guitars, and various other musical instruments.
THOMPSON, WILLIAM - -	8878	8th Jan. 1841	Constructing and mounting various kinds of brushes and brooms.
THOMPSON, WILLIAM - -	14,046	27th March 1852	Machinery for spinning, doubling, and twisting cotton and other fibrous substances.
THOMPSON, WILLIAM CORS-[CADEN.	10,964	20th Nov. 1845	Machinery for propelling vessels on water.
THOMSON, ANTONY TODD -	8872	8th March 1841	Manufacturing calomel and corrosive sublimate.
THOMSON, ARCHIBALD - -	3014	20th Feb. 1807	Certain parts of mill-spinning, for spinning wool or cotton.
THOMSON, ARCHIBALD - -	3024	2nd April 1807	Certain parts of mill-spinning, for spinning wool or cotton.
THOMSON, ARCHIBALD - -	3202	7th Feb. 1809	Machines applicable to various kinds of spinning.
THOMSON, ARCHIBALD - -	4120	17th May 1817	Machine for cutting corks.
THOMSON, DAVID - - -	13,119	11th June 1850	Steam-engines.
THOMSON, FRANCIS HAY -	12,521	14th March 1849	Smelting copper or other ores.
THOMSON, FREDERICK HALE -	12,905	19th Dec. 1849	Manufacture of inkstands, mustard-pots, and other vessels of glass.
THOMSON, FREDERICK HALE -	13,229	22nd Aug. 1850	Cutting, staining, silvering, and fixing articles of glass.
THOMSON, FREDERICK HALE -	13,751	25th Sept. 1851	Bending and annealing glass.
THOMSON, GEORGE - -	11,672	27th April 1847	Machinery for sawing wood and other substances.
THOMSON, GEORGE - -	12,542	28th March 1849	Machinery for cutting and tying up firewood.

Name of Patentee.	Progressive Number.	Date.	Subject-matter of Patent.
THOMSON, HENRY - - -	3077	30th Oct. 1807	Impregnating Cheltenham or other natural medicinal waters, denominated " Mineral Waters," with gas or aëriform fluid, and adding other substances to or combining the same with such waters.
THOMSON, JAMES - - -	2712	14th June 1803	Hanging bells, window-curtains, window and other blinds.
THOMSON, JAMES - - -	3654	3rd March 1813	Producing patterns on cloth previously dyed Turkey-red, and made of cotton or linen, or both.
THOMSON, JAMES - - -	3784	9th March 1814	Construction of fire-arms and the locks to fire-arms.
THOMSON, JAMES - - -	3881	4th Feb. 1815	Process of printing cloth made of cotton or linen, or both.
THOMSON, JAMES - - -	6076	14th Feb. 1831	Making or producing printing-types.
THOMSON, JAMES - - -	13,153	3rd July 1850	Hydraulic machinery and steam-engines.
THOMSON, KEITH NORMAN -	6664	23rd Aug. 1834	Machinery for cutting or making corks and bungs.
THOMSON, ROBERT WILLIAM -	10,990	10th Dec. 1845	Carriage-wheels ;—applicable to other rolling bodies.
THOMSON, ROBERT WILLIAM -	12,691	4th July 1849	Writing and drawing instruments.
THOMSON, SAMUEL - -	3111	3rd March 1808	Frame for stretching leather, and cloth of linen, cotton, woollen, or a mixture of either, and whether brown, bleached, printed, stained or dyed, also all descriptions of piece-goods.
THOMSON, SARAH - - -	4370	15th May 1819	Machine for cutting corks.
THOMSON, WILLIAM - -	11,160	7th April 1846	Machinery for operating upon wool and other fibrous materials intended to be wrought into felted fabrics.
THORBURN, JAMES - -	8834	8th Feb. 1841	Machinery for producing knitted fabrics.
THORBURN, JAMES - -	9075	8th Sept. 1841	Machinery for producing knitted fabrics.
THORNEYCROFT, GEORGE BEN-[JAMIN.	9617	31st Jan. 1843	Furnaces used for the manufacture of iron; mode of manufacturing iron.
THORNEYCROFT, GEORGE BEN-[JAMIN.	9998	28th Dec. 1843	Machine for rolling, squeezing, or compressing puddled balls of iron, and for crushing or grinding other substances.
THORNEYCROFT, GEORGE BEN-[JAMIN.	11,721	27th May 1847	Manufacture of rails for railroads.
THORNEYCROFT, GEORGE BEN-[JAMIN.	12,672	26th June 1849	Manufacturing railway tires, axles, and other iron where great strength and durability is required.
THORNEYCROFT, GEORGE BEN-[JAMIN.	13,400	12th Dec. 1850	Manufacture of crank-axles.
THORNHILL, ELIAS - -	529	20th May 1731	Making the rim or edge of coal-waggon wheels, with iron or steel, and with iron-ribs, bolts, rivets, and screws.
THORNHILL, JOHN - -	7534	11th Jan. 1838	Manufacture of lace.
THORNHILL, JOSEPH - -	806	15th March 1764	Horizontal wheel.
THORNOFF, VAN - - -	1461	28th Jan. 1785	Machine for digging up ground.
THORNTON, ALBERT - -	13,629	10th May 1851	Manufacture of knitted and looped fabrics; raising pile thereon.
THORNTON, GEORGE - -	8750	23rd Dec. 1840	Railways, locomotive-engines, and carriages.
THORNTON, JAMES - - -	13,629	10th May 1851	Manufacture of knitted and looped fabrics; raising pile thereon.

Name of Patentee.	Progressive Number.	Date.	Subject-matter of Patent.
THORNTON, JAMES - -	13,873	19th Dec. 1851	Manufacture of meshed and looped fabrics and other weavings; raising pile on looped fabrics and other weavings.
THORNTON, JOHN - - -	13,873	19th Dec. 1851	Manufacture of meshed and looped fabrics and other weavings; raising pile on looped fabrics and other weavings.
THORNTON, ROBERT -	1190	15th April 1778	Reducing malt and hops into a solid essence or extract, for making beer at sea and in distant climates.
THORNTON, SAMUEL - -	12,231	7th Aug. 1848	Steam-engines; retarding engines and carriages on railways; connecting railway-carriages or waggons together; effecting a communication with different parts of a railway, train by signals or otherwise.
THORNTON, WILLIAM CARR -	9207	21st Dec. 1841	Machinery for making cards for carding cotton and other fibrous substances.
THOROLD, WILLIAM - -	12,024	13th Jan. 1848	Turn-tables.
THORP, WILLIAM - - -	7876	20th Nov. 1838	Looms for weaving; also a new description of fabric to be produced or woven therein.
THORPE, FRANCIS - -	7644	15th May 1838	Machinery for heckling, preparing, or dressing hemp, flax, and other similar fibrous materials.
THORPE, PEGRAM - - -	799	3rd Nov. 1763	Machine for making sashes with plate-iron.
THOUVOIS, PETER - -	873	26th March 1767	Machine for working cranes made use of in landing goods and merchandize out of vessels and other craft.
THREADGOLD, WILLIAM -	4023	4th May 1816	Apparatus to prevent obstruction to the passage of smoke in and through chimneys.
THRELFUL, RICHARD - -	6552	6th Feb. 1834	Machinery for roving and spinning cotton and other fibrous materials.
THUNDER, EDWARD - -	1770	10th Aug. 1790	Machine for mangling and washing articles of linen, wool, silk or cotton, that will bear washing;—applicable to other useful purposes.
THUNDER, EDWARD - -	2811	23rd Jan. 1805	Mode of keeping in tune pianofortes, harpsichords, spinnets, and other stringed instruments.
THURGOOD, RICHARD IRELAND	1538	11th March 1786	Construction of spurs.
THURLOW, EDWARD THOMAS, [Lord.	9575	29th Dec. 1842	Bits for horses and other animals.
THURMAN, WILLIAM - -	11,300	18th July 1846	Manufacture of gloves, stockings, and other hosiery-goods.
THURSTON, JOHN - -	10,574	26th March 1845	Parts of billiard-tables.
THWAITES, THOMAS - -	459	5th Dec. 1723	Engines to spin and mix in the first thread, wool, flax, cotton, &c. into a fine thread, by certain multiplying wheels.
TIBBITS, WILLIAM BULLOCK -	11,637	23rd March 1847	Obtaining and applying motive-power.
TIBBITS, WILLIAM BULLOCK -	12,303	2nd Nov. 1848	Obtaining, applying, and controlling motive-power;—partly applicable to the raising and forcing of liquids.
TICKELL, HENRY - -	2413	13th June 1800	Dissolving and extracting the virtues and preserving the essential oil of hops, malt, and other vegetables used in brewing, distilling, &c.

Name of Patentee.	Progressive Number.	Date.	Subject-matter of Patent.
TICKELL, HENRY - - -	2495	2nd May 1801	Apparatus or refrigerator for cooling the worts, or other fermented, fermentable, or other liquors, or dissolved animal or vegetable substances, used in the process of brewing, distilling, vinegar-making, sugar-refining, chemistry, or other manufactures of a similar nature.
TICKELL, JOHN AMBROSE -	3714	1st July 1813	Alarum and machinery for discovering depredators in a house or premises.
TICKELL, JOHN AMBROSE -	4454	9th May 1820	Cement to be used in aquatic and other buildings; stucco-work produced by the use and application of a mineral substance.
TICKELL, WILLIAM - -	1554	5th Aug. 1786	Chemical medicine, Spiritus ethereus anodynus, or " Anodyne ethereal Spirit.
TIDMARSH, JOSEPH - -	2298	28th Feb. 1799	Article for use as a substitute for paint, or to mix with paint.
TIELENS, JOHN ANTHONY -	8985	12th June 1841	Apparatus for knitting.
TIELENS, JOHN ANTHONY -	9317	7th April 1842	Apparatus for knitting.
TIFFEREAU, CYPRIEN THEO-[DORE.	13,268	3rd Oct. 1850	Hydraulic clocks.
TIGAN, PINNOCK - - -	6540	13th Jan. 1834	Construction and arrangement of iron and other metal wheels for carriages.
TIGERE, GABRIEL - - -	4131	3rd June 1817	Manufacturing writing-paper so that writing cannot be extracted or discharged therefrom.
TILDESLEY, JAMES - - -	8903	29th March 1841	Locks.
TILGHMAN, RICHARD ALBERT	11,555	1st Feb. 1847	Manufacture of certain acids, alkalies, and alkaline salts.
TILGHMAN, RICHARD ALBERT	11,556	1st Feb. 1847	Manufacture of certain alkaline salts.
TILLETT, GEORGE - - -	11,035	13th Jan. 1846	Stoves and fire-places.
TILLOCH, ALEXANDER - -	1431	28th April 1784	Printing books by plates instead of moveable types, by which a greater degree of accuracy, correctness and elegance, will be obtained.
TILLOCH, ALEXANDER - -	3161	20th Aug. 1808	Apparatus to be employed as a moving-power to drive machinery and mill-work;—applicable to other useful purposes.
TILLOCH, ALEXANDER - -	5066	11th Jan. 1825	Steam-engine or apparatus connected therewith; — also applicable to other useful purposes.
TILSON, THOMAS - - -	140	19th Oct. 1662	Making crystal-glass and looking-glass plates.
TILSTONE, JOSEPH - - -	1976	16th Jan. 1794	Material article in the making of hats.
TILT, JOSEPH - - - -	5483	4th April 1827	Salt-pans; mode of applying heat to brine.
TIMBRELL, ANDREW - -	4520	22nd Dec. 1820	Rudder and steerage of a ship or vessel.
TIMMINGS, JOHN - - -	832	28th June 1765	Goods composed of a mixture of silk and worsted, for lining clothes and for other uses.
TIMMINS, JAMES - - -	2030	12th Jan. 1795	Manufacturing cocks for drawing off ale, beer, or any other liquid.
TIMMINS, JAMES - - -	3678	7th April 1813	Making and erecting hothouses, horticultural buildings, pine-pits, cucumber-lights, sashes, and church-windows.
TIMMIS, EBENEZER - -	9530	3rd Dec. 1842	Apparatus used for arresting the progress of and for extinguishing fire.
TINDALL, THOMAS - - -	3817	18th June 1814	Steam-engine with appendages thereto; mode of applying the same to driving all kinds of carriages and machinery.

Name of Patentee.	Progressive Number.	Date.	Subject-matter of Patent.
TINDALL, WILLIAM - -	9230	19th Jan. 1842	Manufacturing from a vegetable substance, materials applicable for affording light and for other uses.
TINDALL, WILLIAM - -	9696	11th April 1843	Manufacture of candles.
TIPPETT, THOMAS - - -	5714	9th Oct. 1828	Construction and mode of working engines with steam and air; boiler or generator of steam; application of such engine to propelling vessels and other floating bodies.
TITLEY, CHARLES - - -	9809	30th June 1843	Construction of boilers or generators for producing steam.
TIZARD, WILLIAM LITTELL -	8921	5th April 1841	Apparatus for brewing.
TIZARD, WILLIAM LITTELL -	14,119	8th May 1852	Machinery, apparatus, and processes for the preparation of grain, and for its conversion into liquors, whether malt, saccharine, vinous, alcoholic or acetous.
TOBIAS, MORRIS - - -	3584	16th July 1812	Binnacle time-piece or timekeeper.
TODD, BRERETON - - -	12,982	27th Feb. 1850	Manufacture of arsenic, sulphuric-acid, and oxyde of antimony, from copper and other ores, also the oxyde of zinc.
TODD, FRANCIS - - -	8575	27th July 1840	Obtaining silver from ores and other matters containing it.
TODD, JOHN - - - ..	2698	14th April 1803	Weaving cloths and stuffs of wool, cotton, linen, silk, and worsted; machines used in weaving by means of looms wrought by water, steam-engines, horses or other power.
TODD, JOHN - - - -	11,490	14th Dec. 1846	Arranging the rails on certain parts of railways.
TODD, MELCHER GARNER	8787	14th Jan. 1841	Form of apparatus for the distillation and rectification of spirits.
TODD, THOMAS	1605	19th May 1787	Machine for washing and ironing linen, &c.
TODD, THOMAS	1691	7th July 1789	Machine for making screws and nuts, and boxes for screws.
TODD, THOMAS -	2180	9th May 1797	Hydraulic-pump or machine for raising water by apparatus shown in the drawing.
TODD, THOMAS - - -	2512	5th June 1801	Tuning and keeping in tune, musical and stringed instruments in general.
TODD, THOMAS - - -	3710	29th June 1813	Machine for separating corn, grain and seeds, from the straw.
TODD, THOMAS - - -	4257	7th May 1818	Rolling iron, and making wire nails, brads, and screws.
TODD, THOMAS - - -	4873	22nd Nov. 1823	Producing tone upon musical instruments of various descriptions.
TODD, THOMAS - -	8223	19th Sept. 1839	Propelling vessels.
TODD, WILLIAM - - -	11,595	24th Feb. 1847	Sizing and dressing yarns; machinery for performing the same.
TOGOOD, THOMAS - - - [Toogood, Thomas.]	132	16th May 1661	Forcing water by means of bellows not worked by wind, and drawing it up with leather-bags linked in the manner of buckets where the bellows cannot be placed together; supplying ships with water by forcing the same through the bottom or side below the surface of the water, useful also for draining mines, supplying houses, emptying rivers or ponds, and draining and watering grounds.

Name of Patentee.	Progressive Number.	Date.	Subject-matter of Patent.
TOGOOD, THOMAS [*Toogood, Thomas.*]	139	— Aug. 1662	Making ships sail without aid of wind or tide; instrument for taking a ship's course; raising water with springs which may be of use for draining mines.
TOGOOD, THOMAS	142	2nd Dec. 1663	Engine made of ropes or chains with cross-staves fixed on them, and having certain instruments placed on the staves, which (by means of valves) emit air and yet retain water, applicable to the draining of mines and pits; exhaling or draining away water in pipes without the help of suckers or buckets.
TOGOOD, THOMAS	173	24th Feb. 1674	Cleaning the streets, and carrying away the dirt by a more easy way than formerly known.
TOGOOD, THOMAS	179	20th April 1675	Engine with pipes and bags, for raising water, and in which all friction is removed, applicable for the draining of mines, pumping ships, and watering grounds; tingeing silks, cottons and stuffs, by way of impression and otherwise, in figures and landscapes, for furniture hangings or similar articles.
TOLSTOY, PAUL DE	13,356	19th Nov. 1850	Dredging-machines.
TOMES, JOHN	10,538	3rd March 1845	Making artificial teeth, gums, and palates.
TOMKINSON, RICHARD	2953	1st Aug. 1806	Machine for making white salt; preparing brine for making white salt.
TOMLINSON, RICHARD JONES	3750	13th Nov. 1813	Constructing the coverings of the roofs or of other surfaces of buildings, external or internal.
TOMLINSON, RICHARD JONES	3883	9th Feb. 1815	Method of framing the roofs of buildings, or the parts thereof.
TOMLINSON, RICHARD JONES	4556	3rd May 1821	Rafter for roofs, or beam for other purposes.
TOMLINSON, RICHARD JONES	5299	26th Nov. 1825	Frame-work for bedsteads and for other purposes.
TOMLYN, GEORGE	128	5th Feb. 1660	Way to text and flourish in vellum and parchment, in black and white.
TOMLYN, GEORGE	137	28th March 1662	Printing with a roller, printing-press, and engraven plates, on vellum and parchment, His Majesty's name, and also the name of his consort, the Queen, with the imperial arms and badges of every of them.
TOMPION, THOMAS	344	23rd Sept. 1695	Watch and clock making.
TOMPSON, GEORGE	5199	28th June 1825	Construction of riding-saddles.
TOMPSON, WILLIAM	3188	29th Dec. 1808	Lock, which acts in a perpendicular and then in a horizontal direction, with springs and tumblers, one part being at liberty whilst the other is in motion, the bolts of which lock return into the body thereof when it is unlocked.
TONGE, DANIEL	4943	15th April 1824	Apparatus for reefing sails.
TONGE, ELIZA	11,775	3rd July 1847	Ornamenting glass.
TONGUE, CORNELIUS	6879	25th Sept. 1834	Apparatus for preventing accidents to travelling-carriages of various descriptions.
TONKIN, ENOCH	3999	20th March 1816	Globe reflecting-stove for light and heat.
TOOKE, NICHOLAS	491	14th April 1727	Composition to flux and make glass.
TOOKEY, THOMAS	103	10th Feb. 1637	Making lamps, and mills for making oil to be used in lamps.

Name of Patentee.	Progres-sive Number.	Date.		Subject-matter of Patent.
TOOTH, WILLIAM - - -	12,465	8th Feb.	1849	Water-closets and chimney-pieces; machinery for the preparation of clays and other materials; manufacture of earthenware articles.
TOPHAM, OVID - - -	6959	16th Dec.	1835	Dressing, starching, cleaning and drying, lace or net.
TOPHAM, OVID - - -	7442	5th Oct.	1837	Construction of sluice-cocks for waterworks;— also applicable to steam, gas, and other purposes.
TOPHAM, OVID - - -	9197	21st Dec.	1841	Apparatus or means for extinguishing fire in houses or other buildings.
TOPHAM, THOMAS - - -	12,041	25th Jan.	1848	Manufacture of time-tables.
TOPLIS, WILLIAM - -	1955	8th June	1793	Machinery for combing and preparing wool, cotton, silk, flax, hemp, and mohair, for the purpose of spinning.
TORASSA, JOHN BAPTISTE -	6520	11th Dec.	1833	Making white-lead or carbonate of lead.
TOREY, WILLIAM SWIFT -	4510	1st Nov.	1820	Drills, to be affixed to ploughs.
TORKINGTON, JOHN -	12,809	12th Oct.	1849	Construction of chairs for railways.
TORR, GEORGE - -	13,954	3rd Feb.	1852	Reburning animal charcoal.
TORRENS, ROBERT - -	5844	9th Sept.	1829	Apparatus for communicating power and motion.
TORROP, JAMES SMITH -	11,990	8th Dec.	1847	Machinery for time-signals.
TOTHILL, RICHARD -	11,698	8th May	1847	Preparing, constructing, and draining land; implements to be used therein.
TOTTIE, WILLIAM - -	12,068	14th Feb.	1848	Distilling.
TOUCHE, JOSEPH - -	11,187	30th April	1846	Lamps.
TOUKS, JOHN - - -	3137	28th May	1808	Method and process in the manufacture of nails.
TOUSSAINT, HENRY FRANCOIS	14,286	10th Sept.	1852	Obtaining a product from the wood of the cactus.
TOWERS, JOHN - -	4045	11th July	1816	Tincture for the cure and relief of coughs, asthmas, and diseases of the lungs and chest. "Towers' new London Cough Tincture."
TOWGOOD, MATTHEW - -	5983	18th Aug.	1830	Mode of applying size to paper.
TOWGOOD, MATTHEW - -	6245	15th March	1832	Cutting paper.
TOWNEND, CHARLES - -	10,094	6th March	1844	Process whereby cotton fabrics are made repellant to water and mildew, and any unpleasant smell is prevented in such fabrics.
TOWNEND, ENOCH - -	14,158	8th June	1852	Manufacture of textile fabrics.
TOWNLEY, CHARLES GOSTLING	3159	9th Aug.	1808	Key for regulating the tone of flutes or other musical instrument capable of the improvement, by causing the bore to lengthen or contract at pleasure.
TOWNLEY, CHARLES GOSTLING	3182	26th Nov.	1808	Musical instruments.
TOWNLEY, MARY - - -	3345	8th June	1810	Prevention or cure of smoky chimneys.
TOWNSEND, MATTHEW -	11,899	7th Oct.	1847	Manufacture of looped or knitted fabrics.
TOWNSEND, MATTHEW -	12,474	13th Feb.	1849	Machinery for the manufacture of looped fabrics.
TOWNSHEND, GEORGE -	8944	29th April	1841	Machinery for cutting certain vegetable substances.
TOY, ALFRED - - -	10,177	7th May	1844	Consuming tallow and other fatty matters, in lamps.
TRAIL, ARCHIBALD -	10,079	24th Feb.	1844	Manufacture of sails for ships and other vessels.

Name of Patentee.	Progressive Number.	Date.		Subject-matter of Patent.
TRANT, PATRICK - - -	199	7th Dec.	1677	Making hard-soap, as Venetian, Marseilles, Castille, and other hard-soaps.
TRANT, PATRICK - - -	226	9th June	1683	Engine for rendering salt and brackish water sweet and fit for drinking, cooking, washing, and other uses.
TRATTLES, MATTHEW - -	13,198	31st July	1850	Saw-sets, mallets, and other tools; apparatus and machinery for manufacturing the same.
TRAVIS, EDWIN - - -	8570	15th July	1840	Machinery for preparing cotton and other fibrous materials for spinning.
TRAVIS, EDWIN - - -	11,978	25th Nov.	1847	Looms for weaving.
TRAVIS, JACOB - - -	6499	1st Nov.	1833	Machinery for spinning wool, cotton, hemp, flax, or other fibrous materials.
TRAVIS, JAMES - - -	2003	29th July	1794	Mode of and apparatus for stiffening cotton twist or weft.
TRAVIS, JOHN - - -	6313	29th Sept.	1832	Machinery for roving cotton and other fibrous substances.
TRAVIS, JOHN - - -	12,381	21st Dec.	1848	Packing lard.
TREADWELL, DANIEL -	4433	25th Jan.	1820	Construction of printing-presses.
TREDENHAM, JOHN - -	218	12th May	1682	Engine for drawing water out of mines.
TREDWELL, RICHARD -	738	21st Feb.	1759	Ribbed-spring for hanging coaches and other carriages.
TREDWELL, RICHARD -	768	10th Feb.	1762	Iron machine for moulding and setting all kinds of springs for hanging coaches and other carriages.
TREDWELL, RICHARD -	769	10th Feb.	1762	Spring for hanging coaches and other carriages.
TREDWELL, RICHARD -	792	29th July	1763	Making springs for hanging coaches and other carriages.
TREDWELL, RICHARD -	816	29th Occ.	1764	Springs for saddles, pillions and their stirrups.
TREDWELL, RICHARD -	861	8th Nov.	1766	Making springs for coaches and other carriages, with a worm and pin, and with or without a plate fixed, to answer many useful purposes.
TREEBY, JOHN WRIGHT -	14,288	10th Sept.	1852	Regulating the flow of fluids.
TREFFRY, RICHARD - -	7741	23rd July	1838	Preserving certain animal and vegetable substances from decay; apparatus for and mode of impregnating substances to be preserved.
TREFUSIS, JAMES - -	280	17th Oct.	1691	Engine, consisting of covering-vessels and pipes, to enable men to work under water for several hours without any want of air.
TREMEERE, JAMES - -	2541	5th Oct.	1801	Working barges and other vessels.
TRENGROUSE, JAMES -	415	17th July	1717	Vehicles or wheel-carriages, "double or single runners," which will not overturn even on bad roads; engines to prevent coaches, waggons and other wheeled-carriages, from overturning.
TRENT, EDWIN WARD -	9297	21st March	1842	Preparing oakum and other fibrous substances for calking ships and other vessels.
TRENTAM, THOMAS - -	1096	22nd April	1775	Manufacturing double coarse frame-work stockings, mits, gloves, caps, and pieces for coats, waistcoats and breeches, on a stocking-frame, in gold, silver, silk, mohair, cotton, thread, worsted, or yarn; carding, shearing, trimming, and dressing such double coarse frame-work goods.

Name of Patentee.	Progressive Number.	Date.	Subject-matter of Patent.
TRETHEWEY, SAMUEL - -	10,76e	12th July 1845	Combined expansive steam and atmospheric engine.
TRETTON, JOHN - - -	3278	21st Nov. 1809	Construction of machines for making cards for carding wool, cotton, flax, silk, and all substances capable of being carded.
TRETTON, JOHN - - -	3388	8th Oct. 1810	Apparatus to machines for making fillet, sheet, and hard cards, for carding wool, cotton, flax, silk, and all substances capable of being carded.
TREVITHICK, RICHARD - -	2599	24th March 1802	Construction of steam-engines; application thereof for driving carriages, and for other purposes.
TREVITHICK, RICHARD - -	3148	5th July 1808	Machinery for towing, driving, or forcing, and discharging ships and other vessels of their cargoes.
TREVITHICK, RICHARD - -	3172	31st Oct. 1808	Stowing ships' cargoes by means of packages, to lessen expense of stowage, and keep the goods safe.
TREVITHICK, RICHARD - -	3231	29th April 1809	Naval architecture and navigation ;—applicable to other purposes.
TREVITHICK, RICHARD - -	3922	6th June 1815	High-pressure steam-engine; and application thereof, with or without other machinery, to useful purposes.
TREVITHICK, RICHARD - -	6082	21st Feb. 1831	Steam-engine.
TREVITHICK, RICHARD - -	6083	21st Feb. 1831	Apparatus for heating apartments.
TREVITHICK, RICHARD - -	6308	22nd Sept. 1832	Steam-engine; application of steam-power to navigation and locomotion.
TREWHITT, HENRY - -	8295	4th Dec. 1839	Fabrication of china-earthenware; machinery applicable thereto.
TREWHITT, HENRY - -	8593	7th Aug. 1840	Applying the power of steam-engines to paddle-shafts used in propelling vessels.
TREWHITT, HENRY - -	12,627	2nd June 1849	Locomotive, marine, and stationary engines; connecting-apparatus of marine engines.
TREWREN, JOHN - - -	218	12th May 1682	Engine for drawing water out of mines.
TRIAT, ANTOINE HYPPOLITE -	10,578	27th March 1845	Propelling vessels, carriages, and agricultural machines.
TRIEWALD, MARTIN - -	449	29th June 1722	Machine for drawing water out of mines and collieries, by the power of the atmosphere.
TRIPP, ROBERT - - -	4056	14th Aug. 1816	Hussar-garter, with elastic springs and fastenings; elastic springs for pantaloons and other articles.
TRIPPETT, WILLIAM LIVER-[SIDGE.	9311	31st March 1842	Looms for weaving by hand or by power.
TRITTON, HENRY - - -	4140	15th July 1817	Apparatus for distilling.
TRITTON, HENRY - - -	4393	11th Aug. 1819	Apparatus for filtration.
TRITTON, HENRY - - -	4414	4th Dec. 1819	Method of producing rotatory motion,
TROISBRIOUX, ALPHONSE DE -	9327	21st April 1842	Lithographic and other printing presses.
TROTMAN, SANDERS - -	13,960	9th Feb. 1852	Fountains.
TROTMAN, JOHN - - -	14,076	20th April 1852	Anchors.
TROTTER, JOHN - - -	2889	14th Nov. 1805	Rotatory engine for applying the power of fluids as first movers.
TROTTER, JOHN - - -	3404	4th March 1811	Musical instruments.

Name of Patentee.	Progressive Number.	Date.	Subject-matter of Patent.
TROTTER, JOHN - - -	3465	19th July 1811	Application of steam and other powers to useful purposes, by means of suitable apparatus.
TROUBAT, FELIX - - -	8582	1st Aug. 1840	Manufacture of vinegar.
TROUGHTON, EDWARD - -	1644	1st April 1788	Method of framing (composed of double parallel flat bars connected by cocks or pillars) to be used in the construction of octants, sextants, quadrants, and of all other nautical and astronomical instruments whose limbs are formed of a circle or part of a circle.
TROUGHTON, NICHOLAS -	6203	8th Sept. 1832	Preparing materials for and producing a cement applicable to building and other purposes, " Metallic Cement."
TROUGHTON, NICHOLAS -	6930	14th Nov. 1835	Finishing ornamental walls and other ornamental surfaces.
TROUGHTON, NICHOLAS -	6965	22nd Dec. 1835	Process of obtaining copper from copper ores.
TROUGHTON, NICHOLAS -	7779	21st Aug. 1838	Process of obtaining copper from copper ores.
TROUGHTON, NICHOLAS -	8075	22nd May 1839	Obtaining copper from ores.
TROUGHTON, NICHOLAS -	8073	22nd May 1839	Manufacture of zinc.
TROUGHTON, NICHOLAS -	9800	23rd June 1843	Dressing ores requiring washing.
TRUELOCK, WILLIAM - -	228	1st Nov. 1683	Engine applied to si ps to show the number of leagues sailed.
TRUEMAN, ALFRED -	13,993	4th March 1852	Obtaining copper from ores.
TRUMAN EDWIN THOMAS -	12,241	15th Aug. 1848	Constructing and fixing artificial teeth and gums, and supplying deficiencies of the mouth.
TRUMAN, THOMAS - - -	10,515	10th Feb. 1845	Apparatus for filtering and purifying water.
TRUSLER, JOHN - - -	1169	16th Sept. 1777	Snuffers that will not drop the wick.
TRUSTED, CHARLES - -	2148	24th Nov. 1796	Time-repeater to be applied to watches, for striking the hours and quarters.
TUCK, EDMUND - - -	9379	4th June 1842	Covering or plating with silver, various metals and metallic alloys.
TUCK, JOSEPH HENRY - -	7409	25th July 1837	Machinery for manufacturing candles.
TUCK, JOSEPH HENRY - -	9462	8th Sept. 1842	Machinery for manufacturing candles.
TUCK, JOSEPH HENRY - -	11,626	16th March 1847	Apparatus for ventilating buildings, carriages, chimneys, and other places where a change of air is required.
TUCKER, HIRAM - - -	12,830	2nd Nov. 1849	Manufacture of mantel-pieces.
TUCKER, JAMES - - -	1902	24th July 1792	Register stoves.
TUCKER, JOHN - - -	2051	12th May 1795	Tanning and making leather.
TUCKER, JOHN - - -	5339	9th Sept. 1829	Construction of cannon.
TUCKER, JOHN - - -	5864	2nd Nov. 1829	Exploding shot or projectile.
TUCKER, JOHN - - -	13,095	1st June 1850	Steam-boilers ; gearing, cleansing, and propelling vessels.
TUCKER, JOHN JERVIS -	6749	22nd Jan. 1835	Urns to be used for tea, and coffee, and for other purposes.
TUCKETT, JOHN DEBELL -	12,819	18th Oct. 1849	Method of preparing by the application of artificial agency, a manure called superphosphate of lime, without using any acids in the decomposition of the various substances of which the manures now in use are made.

Name of Patentee.	Progressive Number.	Date.		Subject-matter of Patent.
TUELY, CHARLES - - -	4603	1st Nov.	1821	Improvements applicable to window-sashes either single or double, also to hung, fixed, or sliding sashes and casements, and to window shutters, and window-blinds.
TUFTS, OTIS - - - -	10,587	2nd April	1845	Mode of building hulls and decks of ships, boats, and other vessels, made of iron or other suitable metal.
TUITE, JOHN - - -	549	21st Nov.	1734	Engine for making stone water-pipes.
TUITE, JOHN - - - -	585	30th July	1742	Water-engine for draining lands and mines, supplying towns with water, and saving ships from danger arising from leaks.
TUITE, JOHN - - - -	671	25th June	1752	Engine for raising water, draining land, and for other purposes.
TULK, JOHN AUGUSTUS - -	8206	26th Aug.	1839	Manufacture of iron.
TULL, JOHN - - - -	570	13th May	1740	Sedan-chair fixed upon a wheel-carriage and springs, to be drawn by horses.
TULLOCH, JAMES - - -	4936	12th April	1824	Machinery to be employed for sawing and grooving marble and other stone, or in producing grooves or mouldings thereon.
TUNNICLIFFE, JOHN - -	9161	20th Nov.	1841	Building and constructing ovens used by potters and china manufacturers in the firing of their wares.
TUNSTALL, WILLIAM - -	2356	9th Nov.	1799	Hand-engine or machine for thrashing all kind of grain.
TUPPER, ARTHUR CHILVER -	9662	16th March	1843	Means of applying carpets and other covering to stairs and steps; construction of stairs and steps.
TUPPER, CHARLES WILLIAM -	13,512	12th Feb.	1851	Manufacture of iron coated with other metal. (Galvanized Iron.)
TURCK, HERMANN - - -	13,972	14th Feb.	1852	Manufacture of resin oil.
TURLINGTON, ROBERT - -	598	18th Jan.	1744	Specific balsam, or " Balsam of Life."
TURNBULL, ALEXANDER -	10,331	26th Sept.	1844	Tanning hides and skins; extracting and separating the catechuic acid from the tannic acid in catechu used in tanning.
TURNBULL, JOHN - - -	2449	15th Nov.	1800	Processes and apparatus applicable to the bleaching and purifying, washing and cleansing of cotton, flax, hemp, and wool, and to the purifying goods made of cotton, flax, hemp, silk, and wool.
TURNBULL, JOHN - - -	9722	6th May	1843	Manufacture of horse-shoes.
TURNER, ARCHIBALD - -	8799	19th Jan.	1841	Manufacture of braids and plats.
TURNER, ARCHIBALD - -	9436	3rd Aug.	1842	Manufacture of muffs, tippets, ruffs, mantillas, cloaks, shawls, capes, pellerines, boas, cuffs, slippers, and shoes.
TURNER, ARCHIBALD - -	13,388	7th Dec.	1850	Applying heat for generating steam for motive-power and for other purposes; generating heat; heating and evaporating fluids.
TURNER, CHARLES - - -	4326	4th Jan.	1819	Curing raw hides and skins by the application of materials hitherto unused for the purpose.
TURNER, EDWARD - - -	5945	29th June	1830	Purifying and whitening sugar or other saccharine matter.
TURNER, EDWIN - - -	8561	6th July	1840	Improvements applicable to locomotive and other steam-engines.

Name of Patentee.	Progressive Number.	Date.	Subject-matter of Patent.
TURNER, GEORGE - - -	10,293	22nd Aug. 1844	Directing the passage of and otherwise dealing with the noxious vapours and other matters arising from chemical works.
TURNER, GEORGE WILLIAM -	6095	21st March 1831	Machine for making paper.
TURNER, JAMES - - -	1281	26th Feb. 1781	Producing a yellow colour for painting in oil or water; making white lead; separating mineral-alkali from common salt, all in one single process.
TURNER, JAMES - - -	5119	9th March 1825	Construction of windows, casements, folding sashes and doors, which are hung so as to exclude rain and wind, and to afford ventilation.
TURNER, JAMES - - -	9519	15th Nov. 1842	Manufacture of perforated metal-buttons.
TURNER, JOHN - - -	2367	9th Jan. 1800	Manufacturing porcelain and earthenware.
TURNER, JOHN - - -	4182	5th Dec. 1817	Plating copper or brass or mixture of copper and brass, with gold or alloy; preparation of the same for rolling into sheets.
TURNER, JOHN - - -	4945	27th April 1824	Machine for crimping, plaiting and goffering linen, muslins, frills, and other articles.
TURNER, JOHN - - -	13,041	15th April 1850	Construction and setting of steam-boilers.
TURNER, JOSEPH - - -	4014	8th April 1816	Rotary-engine; and application thereof with or without other machinery, to useful purposes.
TURNER, MILES - - -	4822	24th July 1823	Process to be used in the bleaching of linen or cotton yarn or cloth.
TURNER, RICHARD - - -	11,496	15th Dec. 1846	Construction of roofs of railway-stations, and roofs and floors of other buildings.
TURNER, ROBERT - - -	1147	28th Feb. 1777	Making pan-tiles and plain or flat tiles to equal Dutch grey tiles.
TURNER, THOMAS - - -	2277	8th Dec. 1798	Construction of locks.
TURNER, WILLIAM - - -	2367	9th Jan. 1800	Manufacturing porcelain and earthenware.
TURNER, WILLIAM - - -	2408	30th May 1800	Machine to be applied to and adopted in the construction of wheel-carriages, for increasing the power of the draught.
TURNER, WILLIAM - - -	3400	4th March 1811	Pike or halberd with cuteaus.
TURNER, WILLIAM - - -	5147	2nd April 1825	Collars for draught-horses.
TURNER, WILLIAM ALLEN -	14,000	8th March 1852	Manufacture of flocked fabrics.
TURNER, WILTON GEORGE -	8124	22nd June 1839	Porcelain.
TURNER, WILTON GEORGE -	9486	8th Oct. 1842	Manufacture of alum.
TURNER, WILTON GEORGE -	10,097	11th March 1844	Manufacturing salts of ammonia and compounds of cyanogen, from a substance not hitherto used for such purposes.
TURNER, WILTON GEORGE -	10,580	27th March 1845	Manufacture of caustic alkalies, soda and potash, and their carbonates; manufacture of the ferro-cyanates of potash or soda.
TURNER, WILTON GEORGE -	11,019	24th Dec. 1845	Mode of treating guano for obtaining chemical compounds therefrom.
TURRILL, FRANCIS - - -	3986	2nd March 1816	Wheel-guard.
TURTON, JOHN - - -	979	2nd Jan. 1771	Method of making maneelas with cast-iron.
TURTON, THOMAS BURDETT -	12,173	1st June 1848	Machinery for bending and fitting plates or bars of steel, iron and other materials, for locomotive-engine and carriage springs, and for other purposes.

Name of Patentee.	Progres-sive Number.	Date.	Subject-matter of Patent.
TUTIN, WILLIAM - - -	1019	13th June 1772	Japanning mourning-buckles of a blue cast or colour.
TUTTON, JOHN - - -	12,363	9th Dec. 1848	Construction and arrangement of certain parts of buildings.
TUXFORD, WESTON - -	13,168	4th July 1850	Machinery for crushing land and shaking straw; applying steam-powers to agricultural machinery.
TUXFORD, WILLIAM WEDD -	5954	6th July 1830	Machine for cleansing or purifying wheat, grain, or other substances.
TWEEDDALE, GEORGE, Marquis [of.	7253	9th Dec. 1836	Making tiles for draining; also house-tiles, flat roofing-tiles, and bricks.
TWEEDDALE, GEORGE, Marquis [of.	7757	1st Aug. 1838	Making tiles for draining; also house-tiles, flat roofing-tiles, and bricks.
TWELLS, THOMAS - -	13,858	15th Dec. 1851	Manufacture of looped fabrics.
TWIGG, GEORGE - -	14,277	26th Aug. 1852	Manufacture of buttons and other dress fastenings; machinery and apparatus used therein.
TWISDEN, JOHN - -	6648	24th July 1834	Inland navigation.
TYER, EDWARD - -	13,906	22nd Jan. 1852	Means of communication by electricity; and apparatus connected therewith.
TYER, GEORGE - -	4251	2nd May 1818	Chain-pump.
TYERS, ROBERT JOHN -	4782	22nd April 1823	Apparatus to be attached to boots, shoes, and other covering for the feet, for the purpose of travelling or pleasure.
TYERS, WILLIAM LONG -	6866	24th July 1835	Manufacture of paper.
TYLEE, JAMES - -	1654	30th June 1788	Shoe, slipper, and buckle to be affixed thereto and worn therewith.
TYLEE, JAMES - -	1741	1st April 1790	Fastenings for shoe, knee, boot, and other buckles.
TYLER, JOHN TALBOT -	12,442	25th Jan. 1849	Hats, caps, and hat-cases.
TYLOR, ALFRED - -	14,091	27th April 1852	Heating and supplying water for baths and other uses; construction of water-closets, and supplying them with water; cocks for drawing off liquids.
TYLOR, HAYWARD - - [Tyler, Hayward.]	5852	23rd Sept. 1829	Construction of water-closets.
TYLOR, HAYWARD - - [Tyler, Hayward.]	8421	7th March 1840	Machinery for impregnating liquids with gas; bottles for retaining, keeping, and preserving such liquids; filling and closing such bottles.
TYLOR, HENRY - -	10,583	29th March 1845	Fabrics used for and applicable to certain screens, blinds, and other like purposes.
TYLOR, JOHN - - -	1352	20th Jan. 1783	Tinning or lining tea and coffee urns and other copper vessels.
TYNDALE, MATTHEW, junior -	438	8th Nov. 1721	Compound of prepared chalk and sea-water, to increase the crops of grain, pulse, and grass.
TYNDALL, THOMAS - -	5577	4th Dec. 1827	Making buttons; and machinery for the purpose.
TYNDALL, THOMAS - -	5589	18th Dec. 1827	Machinery for making nails, brads, and screws.
TYPPER, ROBERT - -	34	5th Sept. 1626	Draining marshes, whether fresh or salt.
TYRER, THOMAS - -	1311	1st Jan. 1782	Horizontal escapement for a watch, to act with two wheels.
TYRON, WILLIAM - -	4348	13th March 1819	Construction of pumps, and machinery for working the same.

Name of Patentee.	Progres-sive Number.	Date.	Subject-matter of Patent.
TYRRELL, JOHN - - -	6038	13th Nov. 1830	Method and apparatus for setting sums, for the purpose of teaching some of the rules of arithmetic.
TYRRELL, JOHN - - -	11,890	7th Oct. 1847	Manufacture of elastic fabrics from vulcanized india-rubber, gutta-percha, or certain fibrous materials.
TYRRELL, SAMUEL - - -	3764	4th Dec. 1813	Broad-cast sowing-machine.
TYSACK, BENJAMIN COWLE -	6292	3rd Aug. 1832	Windlasses, or machinery for winding up the cable. "Compound Lever-windlass."
TYSON, JOSEPH WASHINGTON	10,718	10th June 1845	Fire-arms and ordnance.
TYSSEN, FRANCIS - - -	279	— Oct. 1691	Engine for conveying air into a diving-vessel, to enable several persons at the same time to work under water for many hours.
TYZACKE, JOHN - - -	271	22nd Aug. 1691	Engine to be used in oiling and dressing leather and cloth; applicable to raising water, washing clothes, milling sugar-canes, pounding minerals, pounding and bruising all sorts of goods, pounding charcoal to make powder of, and pounding and making rags fit for making paper, and for other similar purposes.
TYZACKE, JOHN - - -	309	18th — 1692	Tanning skins for leather, and making imitation Russian leather.
TYZACKE, JOHN - - -	331	12th Feb. 1694	Night-engine, which being placed in a convenient situation in any house, will give timely notice to the inhabitants in case of an attempt to break in, and thereby prevent robberies and murders.

U.

Name of Patentee.	Progres-sive Number.	Date.	Subject-matter of Patent.
UDNEY, JOHN - - -	5757	14th Jan. 1829	Steam-engine.
ULLMER, EDWIN - - -	13,511	12th Feb. 1851	Printing-presses.
ULRICH, JOHN GOTTLIEB -	5136	26th March 1825	Chronometers.
ULRICH, JOHN GOTTLIEB -	5639	19th April 1828	Chronometers.
ULRICH, JOHN GOTTLIEB -	6064	22nd Jan. 1831	Chronometers.
ULRICH, JOHN GOTTLIEB -	7350	22nd April 1837	Chronometers.
UNDERDOWN, ABRAHAM -	2806	21st Dec. 1804	Method of making flour without grain.
UNDERHAY, FREDERICK GEORGE	10,650	3rd May 1845	Taps and valves.
UNDERHAY, FREDERICK GEORGE	14,001	8th March 1852	Apparatus for regulating the supply of water to water-closets and other vessels; taps or cocks for drawing off liquids.
UNDERHILL, JOHN -	5536	13th Aug. 1827	Machinery for passing boats or other floating bodies from a higher to a lower level, or vice versâ.
UNDERHILL, WALTER -	156	5th Feb. 1668	Method of bringing salmon alive and well-conditioned from Newcastle and other places to London.
UNDERHILL, WALTER, junior -	156	5th Feb. 1668	Method of bringing salmon alive and well-conditioned from Newcastle and other places to London.

Name of Patentee.	Progressive Number.	Date.	Subject-matter of Patent.
UNDERWOOD, FRANCIS - -	1091	14th Dec. 1774	Casting and working into frames a composition instead of wood, iron, brass, and copper, for sash and other frames.
UNDERWOOD, FRANCIS - -	1327	20th April 1782	Making and ornamenting railings, ballustrades and panels, for staircases, altars, or any parts of churches and buildings; also making and ornamenting chimney-pieces.
UNSWORTH, HUGH - -	8612	27th Aug. 1840	Machinery for mangling, drying, damping, and finishing, woven goods or fabrics.
UNSWORTH, THOMAS - -	10,379	2nd Nov. 1844	Manufacture of elastic fabrics.
UNSWORTH, WILLIAM - -	8476	16th April 1840	Tag for laces.
UNSWORTH, WILLIAM - -	11,148	25th March 1846	Looms for weaving.
UNWIN, SAMUEL - - -	1009	23rd March 1772	Machine for winding, doubling, and running silk, thread, cotton, or worsted, also linen, woollen, and other yarns.
UNWIN, SAMUEL - - -	1257	14th June 1780	Process for or mode of rendering soap-suds used in scouring, cleansing, or discharging, again available for the same purposes, and for making soap therefrom.
UPTON, GEORGE - - -	5567	24th Nov. 1827	Argand and other lamps.
UPTON, JOHN - - -	7458	4th Nov. 1837	Generating steam-power, and applying the same to ploughing, harrowing, and other agricultural purposes.
URCLE, FELIX CHARLES VICTOR LEON, or LEVACHER, D.	13,661	12th June 1851	Increasing the produce of autumn wheat.
URE, ANDREW - - -	6014	20th Oct. 1830	Apparatus for regulating temperature in vaporization, distillation, and other processes.
URE, ANDREW - - -	6015	20th Oct. 1830	Cleansing raw or coarse sugar.
URE, ANDREW - - -	6016	20th Oct. 1830	Air-stove apparatus for the exhalation and condensation of vapours.
URE, ANDREW - - -	6101	31st March 1831	Apparatus for distilling.
URE, ANDREW - - -	6165	22nd Sept. 1831	Apparatus for evaporating syrups and saccharine juices.
URE, ANDREW - - -	6439	20th June 1833	Apparatus for evaporating syrups and saccharine juices;—applicable to other purposes.
URWIN, ROBERT - -	8576	29th July 1840	Steam-engines.
URWIN, ROBERT - - -	12,410	11th Jan. 1849	Steam-engines;—applicable to pumps and to other machines not worked by steam-power.
USHER, JAMES - - -	12,710	18th July 1849	Machinery for tilling land.
USTER, HENRY LAWRENCE TOBIAS TSCHUDY VON -	11,232	2nd June 1846	Machinery for measuring and indicating the distance travelled by wheel-carriages.
UZIELLI, MATTHEW - -	5952	6th July 1830	Preparation of certain metallic substances, and application thereof to the sheathing of ships, and for other purposes.
UZIELLI, MATTHEW - -	7715	30th June 1838	Locks or fastenings.
UZIELLI, MATTHEW - -	7972	21st Feb. 1839	Locks or fastenings.
UZIELLI, MATTHEW - -	8199	17th Aug. 1839	Impregnating wood or timber with chemical materials.
UZIELLI, MATTHEW - -	8780	11th Jan. 1841	Impregnating and preserving wood and timber.

Name of Patentee.	Progres-sive Number.	Date.	Subject-matter of Patent.

V.

Name of Patentee.	Progres-sive Number.	Date.	Subject-matter of Patent.
VAILE, HENRY PURSER - -	7487	25th Nov. 1837	Rails for railroads.
VAILE, HENRY PURSER - -	9567	22nd Dec. 1842	Combining mechanical instruments for obtaining power.
VAILE, HENRY PURSER - -	9987	13th Dec. 1843	Manufacturing metal combined with other matters, for the covering of floors and other surfaces.
VALCK, ETIENNE JOSEPH HA- [NON.	12,958	31st Jan. 1850	Grinding.
VALE, THOMAS - - -	7506	13th Dec. 1837	Hinges.
VALENTINE, CHARLES - -	3219	20th March 1809	Mode of ornamenting and painting japanned and varnished wares of metal, wood, paper, or any other composition, and various other articles.
VALLANCE, JOHN - - -	4479	20th June 1820	Method and apparatus for freeing rooms and buildings from excessive heat, and for keeping them constantly cool.
VALLANCE, JOHN - - -	4480	20th June 1820	Method and apparatus for packing and pre-serving hops.
VALLANCE, JOHN - - -	4564	19th June 1821	Method and apparatus for freeing rooms and buildings from excessive heat, and for keeping them constantly cool.
VALLANCE, JOHN - - -	4884	1st Jan. 1824	Freezing water.
VALLANCE, JOHN - - -	4905	19th Feb. 1824	Means of intercourse by which persons may be conveyed, goods transported, or intel-ligence communicated from place to place, with greater expedition than by means of steam-carriages, steam-vessels, or carriages drawn by animals.
VALLANCE, JOHN - - -	5001	28th Aug. 1824	Abstracting or carrying off the caloric of fluidity from congealing water; pro-ducing intense cold; its application to medical, chemical, or mechanical pur-poses.
VALLANCE, JOHN, junior -	3778	8th Feb. 1814	Apparatus for cooling the worts, wash, &c. of brewers, vinegar-makers, and distillers.
VALLANCE, JOHN, junior -	3867	20th Dec. 1814	Apparatus for and method of constructing and securing brewers' vats or store-casks.
VALLANCE, PHILIP - -	10,135	2nd April 1844	Applying power for drawing or working ploughs and other agricultural implements and carriages.
VALLAURI, JOHN BAPTISTE -	10,533	24th Feb. 1845	Lamps and wicks.
VALLES, LOUIS AUGUST DE [ST. SYLVAN BARON DE LOS.	8472	15th April 1840	Cleansing, decorating, purifying, and pre-serving corn and other grain.
VALLET, LOUIS FELIX - -	4146	5th Aug. 1817	Manufacture of an ornamental surface to metals or metallic compositions.
VALLOTTON, PETER - -	971	16th Nov. 1770	Manufacture of stocking or hose gloves, night-caps, waistcoat or breeches pieces, to be wove on a stocking-frame, or knit with needles.
VALOIS, ALPHONSE HUMBERT [JEAN FRANCOIS.	6830	13th May 1835	Producing engravings, etchings, or reliefs on metallic plates; apparatus used in the same.

Name of Patentee.	Progres-sive Number.	Date.	Subject-matter of Patent.
VANBUTCHELL, MARTIN -	1404	1st Dec. 1783	Spring-bands or fastenings for the apparel or furniture of man or beast.
VANCOUVER, JOHN - -	2636	23rd July 1802	Materials capable of being rendered useful as a substitute for soap.
VANCOUVER, JOHN - -	3808	17th May 1814	Method of painting walls of apartments and other surfaces, by the preparation, use and application of certain materials.
VAN, DAALEN JAMES - -	353	25th Feb. 1698	Engine or carriage with four wheels and double-troubles which open in the middle, shoot the load at once, and return into their places again.
VANDEBROOK, JAMES - -	80	10th March 1635	Making salt.
VANDELEUR, HENRY SEYMOUR [MOORE.	8313	16th Dec. 1839	Paving or covering roads and other ways.
VANDENANKER, PETER - -	259	19th May 1688	Making tar or pitch, for the preservation of wood from putrifaction and worms, also to resist fire and the heat of the sun, and for the better preservation of ropes.
VAN, DYCK MATTHEWE -	84	14th July 1635	Engines, instruments, and works, for recovering ships, vessels, and other things of weight out of the sea or from under water, also for draining mines and raising water.
VANEF, JANE - - -	580	15th Dec. 1737	Joint-hoops for convenience of ladies when entering coaches or chairs.
VAN, HAACKE CHRISTIAN [WILHEM BARON.	1015	30th April 1772	Extracting mineral-tar and mineral-oil from a certain mineral, also vitriol, salt-petre, lampblack and caput-mortuum.
VAN, HAACKE CHRISTIAN [WILHEM BARON.	1049	30th July 1773	Composition for manuring and improving arable-land, meadow and pasture ground. "Brown Van Haacke's Composition."
VAN, HAMME JOHN ARIENS -	191	27th Oct. 1676	Making tiles, porcelain, and other earthenware, in the same manner as practised in Holland.
VAN, HEYTHUYSEN FREDERIC [MIGHELLS.	4440	18th March 1820	Making portable machines to be placed on a desk or table, to support a silk shade for protection of the eyes.
VAN, HEYTHUYSEN FREDERIC [MIGHELLS.	4572	23rd July 1821	Propelling small vessels or boats through water, and light carriages over land.
VAN, OOST AUGUSTUS JULIEN	10,853	6th Oct. 1845	Treating seeds and preparing materials used in fertilizing land and for aiding vegetation.
VAN, THORNHOFF - - -	1461	28th Jan. 1785	Machine for digging-up ground.
VAN, WART HENRY - -	3173	31st Oct. 1808	Machine for manufacturing thimbles.
VAN WOLFEN, JOHN CASPER -	65	1st Oct. 1633	Charking coals, and dressing and qualifying them for melting and making iron and other metals.
VARDY, JAMES - - -	8074	22nd May 1839	Rolling iron.
VARDY, JAMES - - -	8201	17th Aug. 1839	Making decoctions of coffee and other matters.
VARDY, THOMAS - - -	6047	13th Dec. 1830	Cocks for drawing off liquids.
VARICAS, ROBERT - - -	8191	10th Aug. 1839	Rendering fabrics and leather waterproof.
VARICAS, ROBERT - - -	8429	16th March 1840	Rendering fabrics and leather waterproof.
VARILLAT, JEAN JULES - -	13,178	17th July 1850	Extraction and preparation of colouring, tanning, and saccharine matters, from vegetable substances; apparatus employed therein.

Name of Patentee.	Progressive Number.	Date.	Subject-matter of Patent.
VARILLAT, JEAN JULES - - [*Varillat, William Jean Jules.*]	13,745	11th Sept. 1851	Extraction and preparation of colouring, tanning, and saccharine matters, from vegetable substances; apparatus to be employed therein.
VARLEY, CORNELIUS - -	3430	5th April 1811	Telescope with a table or stand, for viewing distant objects, and for other purposes.
VARLEY, EDMONDSON - -	9336	28th April 1842	Steam-engines.
VARLEY, JOHN - - -	8867	8th March 1841	Carriages.
VARLEY, JOHN - - -	9336	28th April 1842	Steam-engines.
VARLEY, JOHN - - -	10,731	23rd June 1845	Atmospheric system of propulsion;—applicable to other motive purposes.
VARLEY, JOHN - - -	11,077	11th Feb. 1846	Obtaining and applying motive-power;—partly applicable to regulating and controlling fluids.
VARLEY, JOHN - - -	12,238	14th Aug. 1848	Steam-engines.
VARLEY, JOHN - - -	13,012	23rd March 1850	Steam-engines; apparatus connected therewith.
VARLEY, RICHARD - - -	2100	17th March 1796	Carding, roving and spinning, cotton, silk and wool; making cards and other parts of machinery for those purposes.
VARLEY, RICHARD - - -	2181	29th May 1797	Perpetual moving-power.
VARLEY, RICHARD - - -	3360	7th July 1810	Machinery for roving, spinning, doubling and twisting cotton, silk, flax, wool, mohair, and other materials used in the manufacture of twist and other yarn.
VARLEY, SAMUEL - - -	13,697	22nd July 1851	Retarding and stopping railway-carriages; making communications between guards and engine-drivers on railways.
VARLEY, WILLIAM - - -	4072	1st Nov. 1816	Obtaining saccharine matter from wheat, rye, oats, and barley-bear or bigg.
VARNHARM, ARTHUR - -	10,507	4th Feb. 1845	Manufacture of paper, to prevent fraud. "Safety and protective Paper."
VARNISH, EDWARD - -	12,905	19th Dec. 1849	Manufacture of ink-stands, mustard-pots and other vessels, of glass.
VARROC, EUGENE DE -	9426	23rd July 1842	Apparatus to be applied to chimneys, to prevent them taking fire, and to render sweeping unnecessary.
VARTY, JONATHAN - - -	3378	17th Sept. 1810	Axle-trees of carriages.
VAUCHER, JAMES ULRICH -	7800	8th Sept. 1838	Fire-engines, watering-engines, and other hydraulic machines and apparatus, for raising or propelling water and other fluids;—partly applicable to steam-engines.
VAUDELIN, LAZARE FRANCOIS	14,195	30th June 1852	Obtaining wool, silk, and cotton, from old fabrics, in a condition to be again used.
VAUGHAN, GEORGE - -	3261	23rd Sept. 1809	Process of refining sugars.
VAUGHAN, GEORGE - -	4518	14th Dec. 1820	Blowing-machine, for fusing and heating metals, smelting ores, and supplying blast for other purposes.
VAUGHAN, GEORGE - -	4946	1st May 1824	Steam-engines.
VAUGHAN, GEORGE - -	5883	23rd Jan. 1830	Pump for raising water or other fluids.
VAUGHAN, PHILIP - - -	2008	12th Aug. 1794	Axle-trees, axle-arms, and boxes, for light and heavy wheel-carriages.
VAUX, CHARLES GRANT, Viscount DE.	3088	9th Dec. 1807	Machine to show the latitude and longitude at sea, also for weighing objects, measuring space or a ship's course, or keeping accounts upon dials and cosmographical columns, showing also the leeway of a ship;—partly applicable to other purposes.

Name of Patentee.	Progressive Number.	Date.		Subject-matter of Patent.
Vaux, Christopher - -	10,319	19th Sept.	1844	Apparatus for bathing.
Vaux, Christopher - -	10,934	11th Nov.	1845	Machinery for tilling land.
Vaux, Christopher - -	10,951	18th Nov.	1845	Machinery for preventing accidents to carriages and passengers on railways.
Vaux, Christopher - -	11,206	13th May	1846	Apparatus employed when transmitting and drawing beer and ale.
Vaux, Christopher - -	11,563	8th Feb.	1847	Storing and supplying beer, ale, and porter.
Vaux, John - - -	10,823	4th Sept.	1845	Apparatus for warming boots and shoes.
Vaux, Thomas - -	7118	13th June	1836	Constructing and applying a revolving harrow for agricultural purposes.
Vaux, Thomas - -	7446	14th Oct.	1837	Tilling and fertilizing land.
Vaux, Thomas - -	7624	24th April	1838	Tilling and fertilizing land.
Vaux, Thomas - -	7905	15th Dec.	1838	Tilling and fertilizing land.
Vaux, Thomas - -	8798	19th Jan.	1841	Horse-shoes.
Vaux, Thomas - -	11,131	11th March	1846	Manufacture of horse-shoes and horse-shoe nails.
Vavasor, James - -	424	7th Sept.	1719	Method of ticketing, marking, and staining horses, to prevent their being stolen.
Vavasour, Lady Ann -	9405	7th July	1842	Machinery for tilling land.
Vazie, Robert - -	1384	16th Aug.	1783	Method of using steam in aid of fire, in obtaining salts of all kinds;—may be used in various kinds of chemistry.
Vazie, Robert - -	1931	15th Jan.	1793	Saddle or pad to be fixed on a horse or other animal, by two girths, one on each side of the saddle.
Vazie, Robert - -	2466	23rd Jan.	1801	Constructing, construction and application of a gun, by removing the touch-hole from the side to the centre of the butt-end of the barrel.
Vazie, Robert - -	2986	6th Nov.	1806	Measures and machinery to be used in making bricks and earthenware; also carriages for removing the said articles.
Vazie, Robert - -	3516	15th Jan.	1812	Construction or formation of arches and other erections and buildings. "Moore's Modern Architecture."
Vazie, Robert - -	4700	3rd Sept.	1822	Compounding different species of metals.
Vazie, Robert - -	5523	12th July	1827	Processes, utensils, apparatus, and machinery applicable to the preparing, extracting, and preserving of food, and to other purposes.
Veale, Richard Rowe -	12,789	27th Sept.	1849	Preparing for pulverization, flint-stone, china-stone, ores, minerals, spars, sands, earths, and other substances.
Venables, John - -	9161	20th Nov.	1841	Building and constructing ovens used by potters and china-manufacturers, in the firing of their wares.
Venden, Edward - -	10,959	20th Nov.	1845	Omnibuses.
Ventura, Angela Benedetto	5618	21st Feb.	1828	Harp, lute, and Spanish guitar.
Verdure, Pierre Jean Isidore.	7951	25th Jan.	1839	Manufacture of starch; machinery for preparing for manufacturing starch; employing refuse matters obtained in such manufacture.
Vere, William - - -	4808	30th June	1823	Manufacture of inflammable gas.
Verity, James - - -	9814	3rd July	1843	Heels and soles of boots and shoes.

Name of Patentee.	Progressive Number.	Date.	Subject-matter of Patent.
VERNATT, Sir PHILLIBERT, [Knight.	91	22nd April 1636	Making, melting, smelting, casting, founding, producing, fining, and annealing, beating or working, iron, steel, brass, copper, or other metals, and casting ordnance or other like works, with a fire of sea-coal, pit-coal, or stone-coal, without charking or mixing the same with charcoal, or by use of any other fuel, except wood or fuel made from wood.
VERNATT, Sir PHILLIBERT, [Knight. [Vernatt, Sir Filibert Knight.]	113	12th Dec. 1637	Making good and merchantable tough iron according to the nature of the mine, with sea-coal or peat, and with one-fifth of the expense of charcoal as now used.
VERNATTY, JOHN - - -	. 227	1st Aug. 1683	Lighting streets and passages by lamps and lanterns.
VERNET, LEWIS - - -	12,582	24th April 1849	Preserving certain vegetable and animal substances from destruction by worms, decay, and fire.
VERNON, JOSEPH - - -	3705	31st May 1813	Making the scoria produced in smelting iron, into forms for use in place of brick, quarry, tile, slate, or other stone.
VERNON, THOMAS -	10,143	15th April 1844	Building or construction of iron and other vessels for navigation.
VERNUM, GEORGE -	12,182	10th June 1848	Steam-engine, which may be also worked by air and other fluids.
VERO, JAMES - - -	13,524	24th Feb. 1851	Manufacture of hats, caps, bonnets, and other coverings for the head.
VIBART, JAMES - - -	10,314	12th Sept. 1844	Obtaining and applying power for working or driving thrashing-machines, mills, chaff-cutters, and other machines.
VICKERS, BENJAMIN -	11,492	14th Dec. 1846	Mechanical chirographer, or machine for delineating letters, figures, and other characters.
VICKERS, EDWARD -	11,535	19th Jan. 1847	Machinery for cutting files.
VICKERS, WILLIAM -	1168	1st Sept. 1777	Machine for preparing and spinning flax, hemp, tow, silk, cotton-wool, and sheep's wool.
VICKERS, WILLIAM -	6864	17th July 1835	Machinery for preparing or shaping steel for the manufacture of files and rasps.
VICKERS, WILLIAM -	7992	6th March 1839	Obtaining tractive-power from carriage-wheels.
VICKERS, WILLIAM -	8129	25th June 1839	Manufacture of cast-steel.
VICKERS, WILLIAM -	11,042	17th Jan. 1846	Manufacturing lace and other fabrics by lace-machinery.
VICKERS, WILLIAM -	11,759	19th June 1847	Manufacture of iron.
VICTOR, DUCHEMAN -	7597	19th March 1838	Rotary-engines to be worked by steam or other aëriform fluids.
VIDIE, LUCIEN - -	12,826	2nd Nov. 1849	Conveyances on land and water.
VIDIE, LUCIEN - -	13,332	9th Nov. 1850	Measuring the pressure of air, steam, gas, and liquids.
VIDLER, JOHN - - -	2020	5th Nov. 1794	Bending timber without injury to the grain, for circular work.
VIDOCQ, EUGENE FRANCOIS -	10,958	20th Nov. 1845	Combining materials to be employed in the manufacture of tea-trays, boxes, trunks, tables, and other like articles.
VIEYRES, ANTOINE -	9066	4th Sept. 1841	Machinery for cutting cork.
VIEYRES, ANTOINE -	10,323	19th Sept. 1844	Manufacture of cut nails.
VIGERS, WILLIAM REVELL -	9413	7th July 1842	Keeping the air pure in confined places, and enabling persons to work under water.

Name of Patentee.	Progressive Number.	Date.		Subject-matter of Patent.
VIGNOELS, CHARLES BLACKER	5995	7th Sept.	1830	Locomotive-engines.
VIGNOLES, CHARLES, junior -	11,323	4th Aug.	1846	Employing steam as a motive power.
VIGURS, HENRY - - -	13,797	4th Nov.	1851	Buffers, grease-boxes, axle-boxes, springs, and appendages, to railway-engines and carriages.
VILLERS, LOUIS FLORENT [DELANNOIJ, DE.	683	30th May	1753	Making gun-carriages of cast-iron, to be worked by two men instead of eight as heretofore.
VINCENT, HENRY - - -	215	29th Aug.	1681	Engine to raise and throw out water from deep mines.
VINEY, JAMES - - -	4948	6th May	1824	Water-closets.
VINEY, JAMES - - -	4962	22nd May	1824	Method of supplying water or fluids for domestic or other purposes.
VINEY, JAMES - - -	5420	18th Oct.	1826	Construction of cars or other carriages, and application of a power to draw the same;—applicable to drawing ships and other vessels, raising weights, and to other purposes.
VINEY, JAMES - - -	5862	2nd Nov.	1829	Steam-boilers and carriages, or apparatus connected therewith.
VINGOE, HENRY - - -	9984	8th Dec.	1843	Apparatus for planting or setting, drilling, or dibbling corn, grain, seed, pulse, or manure;—partly applicable to the construction of wheels and carriages.
VINGOE, WILLIAM HENRY -	9984	8th Dec.	1843	Apparatus for planting or setting, drilling, or dibbling corn, grain, seed, pulse, or manure;—partly applicable to the construction of wheels and carriages.
VINT, HENRY - - -	6857	9th July	1835	Paddle-wheels.
VINT, HENRY - - -	11,854	6th Sept.	1847	Propelling ships and other vessels.
VIOLETTE, FRANCOIS CON-[STANT MAGLIORE	9709	22nd April	1843	Warming the interior of railroad and other carriages.
VIVIAN, ALEXANDER - -	9964	25th Nov.	1843	Apparatus for dressing ores.
VIVIAN, ANDREW - - -	2599	24th March	1802	Construction of steam-engines; application thereof for driving carriages, and for other purposes.
VIVIAN, CHARLES - - -	218	12th May	1682	Engine for drawing water out of mines.
VIVIAN, HENRY HUSSEY -	9591	14th Jan.	1843	Treating or reducing ores of zinc; furnaces for reducing ores of zinc;—partly applicable to other furnaces.
VIVIAN, HENRY HUSSEY -	13,800	4th Nov.	1851	Obtaining nickel and cobalt.
VIVYAN, HANNYBALL - -	67	14th Jan.	1634	Engine for drawing and draining water, and raising weights, from tin-mines or other places.
VIZARD, GEORGE - - -	4535	3rd Feb.	1821	Process of dressing and polishing goods of woollen manufacture.
VOGEL, KASIMIR - - -	11,617	10th March	1847	Making weavers' harness; machinery for the production of the same.
VON DOORNIK, WILLIAM EVER-[HARD BARON [Van Doornik, William Everhard Baron.]	2798	19th Dec.	1804	Composition of absorbent or detergent earths with other ingredients, for purposes for which soaps or detergent earths are used.
VON DOORNIK, WILLIAM EVER-[HARD BARON	3203	7th Feb.	1809	Manufacture of soap to wash with sea or other water.

Name of Patentee.	Progressive Number.	Date.	Subject-matter of Patent.
VON DOORNIK, WILLIAM EVERHARD BARON [Van Doornik, William Everhard Baron.]	3438	27th April 1811	Manufacture of soap to wash with sea or other water.
VON DOORNIK, WILLIAM EVERHARD BARON [Von Doornick, William Everhard Baron.]	3864	20th Dec. 1814	Manufacture of soap.
VON HERZ, ADOLPHUS CHARLES	14,143	29th May 1852	Treating, preparing and preserving roots and plants; extracting juices from the same, and treatment of such juices; processes, machinery, and apparatus employed therein.
VON RATHEN, ANTHONY BERNHARD	8853	22nd Feb. 1841	Fire-grates and parts connected therewith, for furnaces for heating fluids.
VON RATHEN, ANTHONY BERNHARD	9037	28th July 1841	High-pressure and other steam-boilers; and mode of supplying them with water.
VON RATHEN, ANTHONY BERNHARD	9038	28th July 1841	Propelling locomotive-carriages on railroads and common roads, and vessels on rivers and canals, by power obtained by machinery unconnected with the carriages and vessels to be propelled. "The United Stationary and Locomotive systems."
VON RATHEN, ANTHONY BERNHARD	11,932	2nd Nov. 1847	Obtaining and applying motive-power.
VON SPARRE, JULIUS FRIEDRICH PHILIPP LUDWIG	14,228	20th July 1852	Separating substances of different specific gravities; machinery and apparatus employed therein.
VON USTER, HENRY LAURENCE TOBIAS TSCHUDY	11,232	2nd June 1846	Machinery for measuring and indicating the distance travelled by wheel-carriages.
VON WINIWARTER JOSEPH MAXIMILIAN RITTER	13,935	29th Jan. 1852	Locks of fire-arms and cannon; gun-matches, or mode of igniting gunpowder in guns; machinery for manufacturing the same.
VOUILLON, FRANCIS [Vouillon Francois.]	8097	8th June 1839	Manufacture of ornamental woven fabrics.
VOUILLON, FRANCIS	12,546	28th March 1849	Making hats, caps, and bonnets.
VOYEZ, GEORGE HENRY	13,893	7th Dec. 1850	Manufacture of paper-hangings.
VREEM, WILLIAM	430	25th June 1720	Making the steam of boiling liquors useful for drying malt, hops, starch, and other humid substances, and for baking, brewing, distilling, boiling, and making salt, and for other purposes.
VRIES, JOHN HENRY	13,120	11th June 1850	Working engines by atmospheric air.
VULDY, JOHN BAPTISTE	12,777	20th Sept. 1849	Giving a gloss to dyed silk in skeins or hanks.
VULLIAMY, BENJAMIN	1886	6th June 1792	Building two-wheel carriages; harness for the horses drawing such carriages.

Name of Patentee.	Progressive Number.	Date.	Subject-matter of Patent.

W.

Name of Patentee.	Progressive Number.	Date.	Subject-matter of Patent.
WADDELL, ROBERT - -	13,117	11th June 1850	Steam-engines.
WADDINGTON, NATHAN -	8813	26th Jan. 1841	Construction of steam-boilers; furnaces for heating the same.
WADDINGTON, RICHARD -	7089	10th May 1836	Making and constructing wheels for railway-carriages.
WADE, THOMAS - - -	3366	26th July 1810	Process of imitating lapis-lazuli, jasper, and various sorts of marble and other stones, for purposes of sculpture, also mosaic work used in the manufacture of chimney-pieces and slabs, and for other purposes where marbles are applied.
WADHAM, JOHN - - -	1076	27th July 1774	Tea-fountain, constructed to answer the purpose of a tea-pot and urn.
WADSWORTH, GEORGE - -	11,118	5th March 1846	Manufacture of glass and other vitreous products.
WAGONER, FREDERICKE -	119	18th July 1638	Smelting lead-ore.
WAGSTAFF, HENRY GRAHAM -	13,901	20th Jan. 1852	Manufacture of candles.
WAHL, THEOBALD - - -	8252	2nd Nov. 1839	Boilers applicable to locomotive and other engines.
WAINE, GABRIEL - - -	301	9th Aug. 1692	Making pitch and tar.
WAKE, JAMES, junior - -	9469	9th Sept. 1842	Propelling vessels.
WAKEFIELD, BENJAMIN -	8354	21st Jan. 1840	Cutting-out, stamping or forming, and piercing buttons, shells, button-backs and other articles from metal plate; machinery and tools for those purposes.
WAKEFIELD, BENJAMIN -	9210	24th Dec. 1841	An improved bolt for building and other purposes.
WAKEFIELD, JOHN - -	4472	6th June 1820	Construction of furnaces for boilers; feeding the same with fuel.
WAKEFIELD, JOHN - -	8710	21st Nov. 1840	Manufacture of hat bodies.
WAKEFIELD, RICHARD - -	989	2nd May 1771	Tuning and keeping in tune harpsichords, spinnets, forte-pianos, &c.
WAKEFIELD, ROBERT - -	1116	22nd Feb. 1776	Medicinal compound powders for the relief of children afflicted with gripes and convulsions.
WAKEFIELD, THOMAS - -	2506	2nd June 1801	Refining sugar.
WALCOTT, WILLIAM - -	184	28th Oct. 1675	Purifying corrupted water, and making sea-water fresh, clear, and wholesome.
WALDRON, THOMAS - -	1483	4th June 1785	Construction of bedsteads by putting them together without screws and nuts.
WALE, JOSEPH - - -	8351	21st Jan. 1840	Machinery for making frame-work knitting or stocking-fabrics.
WALE, JOSEPH - - -	8619	7th Sept. 1840	Machinery employed in frame-work knitting or stocking-fabrics.
WALFORD, THOMAS - -	638	18th Nov. 1748	Engine or machine for platting.
WALFORD, THOMAS - -	1171	8th Oct. 1777	Engine for platting and interweaving laces, curtain and other lines, both round and flat, also various other articles.
WALKER, ADAM - - -	1020	29th July 1772	Method of producing continued tones from the wire-strings of an harpsichord. "Cœlestina."

Name of Patentee.	Progres-sive Number.	Date.	Subject-matter of Patent.
WALKER, ADAM - - -	1533	21st Feb. 1786	Empyreal air-stove for purifying the air of churches, theatres, gaols, sick and other rooms, and enclosed buildings.
WALKER, ARTHUR ELDRED -	8344	18th Jan. 1840	Engraving by machinery.
WALKER, ARTHUR ELDRED -	11,025	6th Jan. 1846	Machinery for sewing.
WALKER, BERNARD PEARD -	10,091	6th March 1844	Machinery for making nails.
WALKER, BERNARD PEARD -	14,298	18th Sept. 1852	Manufacture of screws and screw-keys; construction of bridges;—applicable to floorings, roofings, and paving.
WALKER, DEANE SAMUEL -	12,191	24th June 1848	Manufacture of bands or straps for hats, caps, shoes and stocks.
WALKER, EDWARD - -	2500	12th May 1801	Portable stove or kitchen for dressing and cooking victuals.
WALKER, EDWARD LESLEY -	10,868	10th Oct. 1845	Pianofortes.
WALKER, FRANCIS PRIME, junior	9342	9th May 1842	Manufacture of candles and candlesticks; apparatus connected therewith.
WALKER, HENRY - - -	2130	20th July 1796	Architecture of houses and other buildings.
WALKER, HENRY - - -	12,370	16th Dec. 1848	Processes of manufacturing needles.
WALKER, JAMES - - -	1611	12th June 1787	Working and mashing malt and other articles, in mash-tuns;—the principle of which is applicable to many other purposes.
WALKER, JAMES - - -	3373	7th Sept. 1810	Machine or vessel for the safe conveyance of gunpowder, and for its preservation from injury by damp.
WALKER, JAMES - - -	3585	16th July 1812	Tubular metallic-vessel, and the application thereof to the preservation of fluids and other things.
WALKER, JOHN - - -	1127	7th June 1776	Spring-saddle and stirrups.
WALKER, JOHN - - -	2547	3rd Nov. 1801	Method of making and manufacturing men's hats and caps, rendering them perfectly waterproof, also all kinds of leather, cotton, linen, silk, stuffs, pasteboard and other manufactures and substances, for the purpose of being worked-up into shoes, boots, women's hats and bonnets and other wearing-apparel, and to be used on all occasions where a power of repelling wet or moisture may be required.
WALKER, JOHN - - -	4119	13th May 1817	Separating or extracting molasses or treacle from Muscovado brown or new sugar.
WALKER, JOHN - - -	5562	17th Nov. 1827	Castor for furniture.
WALKER, JOHN - - -	5936	4th May 1830	Cock for fluids.
WALKER, JOHN - - -	7299	16th Feb. 1837	Heating coppers, stills, and boilers.
WALKER, JOHN - - -	8071	22nd May 1839	Coke-ovens.
WALKER, JOHN - - -	8869	8th March 1841	Hydraulic apparatus.
WALKER, JOHN - - -	11,054	20th Jan. 1846	Weaving piled or napped cloths or fabrics; machinery for cutting the pile or nap of the same.
WALKER, JOHN - - -	11,669	22nd April 1847	Certain hydraulic and pneumatic machines; application of steam or other power thereto.
WALKER, JOSEPH - -	14,338	2nd Nov. 1852	Treating cotton-seeds and obtaining products therefrom; processes and machinery employed therein;—partly applicable to distillation.
WALKER, JOSEPH, junior -	14,141	25th May 1852	Vacuum-pans for the evaporation and crystallization of saccharine or other solutions.

Name of Patentee.	Progressive Number.	Date.	Subject-matter of Patent.
WALKER, JOSHUA - - -	1542	11th April 1786	Construction of cocks and valves.
WALKER, Lieut.-Col. LESLIE -	6005	6th Oct. 1830	Apparatus to effect the escape and preservation of persons and property in case of fire, or in other circumstances.
WALKER, MARK - - -	5715	9th Oct. 1828	Machinery for preparing and dressing hemp, flax, silk, and other fibrous substances.
WALKER, MARK - - -	11,121	11th March 1846	Apparatus for facilitating the putting on of boots.
WALKER, PETER - - -	7658	31st May 1838	Apparatus to be used in cleansing beer or other fermented liquors.
WALKER, RALPH - - -	2957	9th Aug. 1806	Making ropes and cordage.
WALKER, RICHARD - -	6633	26th June 1834	Wadding for fire-arms.
WALKER, RICHARD - -	11,545	26th Jan. 1847	Apparatus for the manufacture of gas for illumination;—applicable to the manufacture of other products of distillation.
WALKER, ROBERT - - -	706	29th Oct. 1755	Medicine called " Jesuits' Drops."
WALKER, ROBERT - - -	2657	6th Nov. 1802	Dining-tables.
WALKER, ROBERT - - -	10,437	18th Dec. 1844	Apparatus for riddling coals at collieries.
WALKER, SAMUEL - - -	5772	20th Feb. 1829	Apparatus applicable to machinery for dressing woollen or other cloths. "Operameter."
WALKER, SAMUEL - - -	6233	1st March 1832	Gig-machines for dressing woollen-cloths.
WALKER, SAMUEL - - -	7572	22nd Feb. 1838	Machinery for shearing or cropping and dressing and finishing woollen and other cloths.
WALKER, SAMUEL, junior -	13,573	24th March 1851	Manufacture of metallic tubes.
WALKER, THOMAS, junior -	1007	14th March 1772	Machine for stamping and printing paper, silk, woollen, cotton, and linen cloths, and other fabrics of silk, wool, cotton, or linen.
WALKER, THOMAS - - -	3689	5th May 1813	Construction of a horizontal windmill;—applicable to machinery worked by wind.
WALKER, THOMAS - - -	6855	3rd July 1835	Extinguishers to candles; application of such extinguishers to candles and candlesticks.
WALKER, THOMAS - - -	7665	31st May 1838	Steam-engines.
WALKER, THOMAS - - -	8031	13th April 1839	Engines and carriages to be worked by steam or other motive-power.
WALKER, THOMAS - - -	8065	10th May 1839	Stoves and grates.
WALKER, THOMAS - - -	8497	7th May 1840	Apparatus applicable to feeding-machinery employed in carding, scrubbing, or teazing fibrous materials.
WALKER, THOMAS - - -	8990	18th June 1841	Steam-engines.
WALKER, THOMAS - - -	9440	9th Aug. 1842	Stoves.
WALKER, THOMAS - - -	9493	20th Oct. 1842	Woollen carding-engines.
WALKER, THOMAS - - -	10,750	3rd July 1845	Springs and elastic power as applicable to railway-carriages and other vehicles, and to other articles and purposes.
WALKER, THOMAS - - -	11,251	22nd June 1846	Ships' logs and sounding-machines.
WALKER, THOMAS - - -	11,973	20th Nov. 1847	Decorating articles of earthenware and china.
WALKER, THOMAS - - -	12,555	2nd April 1849	Manufacturing axletrees for carriages and other cylindrical and conical shafts. (J. Hardy's extension for four years from the 4th April 1849.)

Name of Patentee.	Progressive Number.	Date.	Subject-matter of Patent.
WALKER, THOMAS - - -	12,709	18th July 1849	Boots and shoes; manufacture of parts of boots and shoes, clogs, and goloshes.
WALKER, THOMAS - - -	13,028	28th March 1850	Manufacture of sheets or plates of iron for certain purposes.
WALKER, THOMAS - - -	13,983	23rd Feb. 1852	Steam-engines.
WALKER, THOMAS - - -	14,095	29th April 1852	Manufacture of ordnance; construction and manufacture of carriages, and traversing apparatus for manœuvring the same.
WALKER, WILLIAM - -	818	14th Nov. 1764	Marine collar and belt.
WALKER, WILLIAM - -	5233	10th Aug. 1825	Building or constructing ships or other vessels.
WALKER, WILLIAM - -	8997	23rd June 1841	Manufacture of the detached lever watch.
WALKER, WILLIAM - -	9653	2nd March 1843	Manufacture of springs and axles for carriages.
WALKER, WILLIAM - -	12,412	11th Jan. 1849	Machinery or apparatus for cleansing roads or ways;—applicable to other similar purposes.
WALKER, WILLIAM - -	13,932	23rd Feb. 1852	Ascertaining and indicating the deviations or errors of the Mariner's Compass.
WALKER, WILLIAM, junior -	10,183	15th May 1844	Warming and ventilating apartments and buildings.
WALKER, WILLIAM JAMES -	11,933	2nd Nov. 1847	Weaving.
WALKINSHAW, JOHN - -	775	21st May 1762	Engine for working mines and coalpits, for raising water, and for other purposes.
WALKINSHAW, JOHN - -	6457	10th Aug. 1833	Rail for railways.
WALL, ARTHUR - - -	8490	2nd May 1840	Composition for the prevention of corrosion in metals, and for other purposes.
WALL, ARTHUR - - -	9946	18th Nov. 1843	Manufacture of iron.
WALL, ARTHUR - - -	10,159	27th April 1844	Manufacture of steel, copper, and other metals.
WALL, ARTHUR - - -	10,441	18th Dec. 1844	Manufacture of steel, copper, and other metals.
WALL, ARTHUR - - -	11,910	14th Oct. 1847	Apparatus for and methods of separating oxydes from their compounds, and from each other.
WALL, EDWARD - - -	4373	18th May 1819	Stage-coaches and other descriptions of carriages.
WALL, GEORGE, junior - -	8339	11th Jan. 1840	Manufacture of china and earthenware; apparatus or machinery applicable thereto.
WALL, GEORGE, junior - -	8340	11th Jan. 1840	Preparing bats of earthenware and porcelain clays, and forming them into articles of earthenware and porcelain; machinery and apparatus applicable thereto.
WALL, GEORGE, junior - -	9901	5th Oct. 1843	Processes of manufacturing earthenware, china, and other substances; machinery applicable to such manufactures.
WALL, WILLIAM - - -	4097	1st Feb. 1817	Horizontal escapement for watches.
WALLACE, ELIZABETH - -	12,075	28th Feb. 1848	Facing, figuring, designating, decorating, planning, and otherwise fitting-up houses and other buildings;—partly applicable to articles of furniture.
WALLACE, JOHN - - -	6102	31st March 1831	Safety-hearth for the use of vessels.
WALLER, FRANCIS HENRY -	11,583	16th Feb. 1847	Apparatus for making and filtering infusions of coffee and other articles.
WALLER, HENRY - - -	10,907	31st Oct. 1845	Sluice-cocks.

Name of Patentee.	Progressive Number.	Date.	Subject-matter of Patent.
WALLER, RALPH KNOWLES -	10,438	18th Dec. 1844	Manufacture of platted wicks; manufacture of candles.
WALLER, RICHARD　-　-	9804	27th June 1843	Locomotive carriages, steam-boilers and engines.
WALLER, THOMAS -　-　-	5335	18th Feb. 1826	Manufacture of straw-plat for making bonnets, hats, and other articles.
WALLERAND, LOUIS JOSEPH -	10,448	30th Dec. 1844	Dyeing or staining various kinds of fabrics.
WALLIS, CHARLES JAMES　-	14,187	24th June 1852	Machinery for crushing, pulverizing, and grinding stone, quartz, and other substances.
WALLIS, JOHN　-　-　-	77	19th Dec. 1634	Making woollen-cloth impenetrable to rain.
WALLSON, FRANCIS　-　-	158	2nd March 1668	Graving, garnishing, and colouring ships, barges, and other vessels; also garnishing, colouring, and varnishing iron, stone, plaster, and other things, by a liquor drawn from a certain grain and some other ingredients.
WALMSLEY, EDWARD　-　-	12,135	27th April 1848	Apparatus for preventing the explosion of steam-boilers.
WALMSLEY, JOHN -　-　-	6244	15th March 1832	Machine for cutting off the hair or fur from beaver and other skins.
WALMSLEY, JOHN -　-　-	6703	22nd Oct. 1834	Grates or apparatus applicable to steam-engines, or for other purposes; apparatus for feeding the same with fuel;—which said apparatus, jointly or separately, is applicable to other purposes.
WALMSLEY, THOMAS　-　-	6048	13th Dec. 1830	Manufacture of cotton, linen, silk and other fibrous substances, into fabrics applicable to various purposes.
WALMSLEY, WILLIAM　-　-	2633	2nd July 1802	Machine for batting and opening cotton-wool, sheep's-wool, tow, hemp, and flax.
WALTER, JOHN WINTER　-	9732	16th May 1843	Manufacture of gloves.
WALTER, ROBERT, junior　-	9733	18th May 1843	Propelling ships and boats.
WALTERS, GREGORY SEALE -	9676	24th March 1843	Manufacture of chlorine and chlorides; obtaining the oxydes and per-oxydes of manganese in the residuary liquids.
WALTERS, JOHN　-　-　-	3850	7th Nov. 1814	Construction and fastening of frame-timbers or binds of ships or vessels, whether building or under repair.
WALTERS, JOHN　-　-　-	13,724	21st Aug. 1851	Knives and forks.
WALTHER, DAVID -　-　-	8752	23rd Dec. 1840	Purifying vegetable and animal oils, fats, and tallows, to render them suitable for making soap, or for burning in lamps, and for other purposes;—partly applicable to the purifying of the mineral oil or spirit called naphtha.
WALTHER, PHILIP -　-　-	9902	12th Oct. 1843	Construction of steam-engines.
WALTON, FREDERICK　-　-	11,592	24th Feb. 1847	Coating, covering, and ornamenting the surfaces of articles made of wrought-iron or other metal, and which may be used in substitution of japanning, tinning, or other modes now in use.
WALTON, HUMPHREY　-　-	1607	25th May 1787	Pianofortes and other musical instruments.
WALTON, JAMES　-　-　-	6541	14th Jan. 1834	Machinery for facilitating the operations of raising, dressing, and cropping the pile of woollen and other fabrics.
WALTON, JAMES　-　-　-	6584	27th March 1834	Cards for carding wool, cotton, silk, and other fibrous substances, and for raising the pile of woollen and other cloths.

Name of Patentee.	Progressive Number.	Date.	Subject-matter of Patent.
WALTON, JAMES - - -	6710	12th Nov. 1834	Machinery used for raising the pile of woollen and other cloths.
WALTON, JAMES - - -	6915	23rd Oct. 1835	Dressing, finishing, and setting the face on woollen or other cloths.
WALTON, JAMES - - -	7327	21st March 1837	Machinery for manufacturing and finishing woollen and other cloths.
WALTON, JAMES - - -	7818	21st Sept. 1838	Machinery for making wire-cards for carding cotton-wool, silk, tow, and other fibrous substances.
WALTON, JAMES - - -	8507	12th May 1840	Manufacture of beds, mattresses, pillows, cushions, pads, and other articles; materials for packing.
WALTON, SAMUEL - - -	156	5th Feb. 1668	Bringing salmon alive and well conditioned from Newcastle and other places to London.
WANSBROUGH, JAMES - -	11,512	31st Dec. 1846	Manufacture of caps, bonnets, book-covers, curtains and hangings, show-cards, theatrical decorations, labels, and coffins.
WANSBROUGH, JAMES - -	14,000	8th March 1852	Manufacture of flocked fabrics.
WANT, RICHARD - - -	12,182	10th June 1848	Steam-engine, may also be worked by air and other fluids.
WAPSHARE, JAMES - -	7808	13th Sept. 1838	Application of heat for drying wool, woollen-yarn, woollen-cloths, and other articles; also improvements connected with the use of the press in the process of dressing woollen-cloths.
WARBURTON, HENRY - -	4046	27th July 1816	Distilling certain animal, vegetable, and mineral substances; manufacturing the products thereof.
WARBURTON, JAMES - -	13,794	3rd Nov. 1851	Machinery for drawing and combing wool, silk, flax, hemp, and tow.
WARBURTON, JOHN - -	11,400	8th Oct. 1846	Machinery for preparing, slubbing, and roving cotton-wool, and other fibrous materials.
WARBURTON, PETER - -	3304	13th Feb. 1810	Decorating china, porcelain, earthenware, and glass, with gold, silver, platina, or other metals, pure or fluxed with lead or other substance, which method leaves the metals in their metallic state after being burned.
WARBURTON, WILLIAM - -	9459	8th Sept. 1842	Construction of carriages; apparatus for retarding the progress of the same.
WARCUP, WILLIAM - -	4625	10th Dec. 1821	Machine for washing linen, cotton, or woollen cloths, either as piece-goods, or when made into articles for use.
WARCUP, WILLIAM - -	4771	3rd April 1823	Construction of mangles.
WARCUP, WILLIAM - -	11,330	11th Aug. 1846	Manufacture and arrangement of parts of, and apparatus for the construction and working of atmospheric railways.
WARD, CHARLES WILLIAM -	1861	15th March 1792	Method of changing the smoke arising from combustion, into various useful materials.
WARD, CORNELIUS - - -	7505	9th Dec. 1837	Drums.
WARD, CORNELIUS - - -	9229	18th Jan. 1842	Flutes.
WARD, FREDERICK OLDFIELD	7546	20th Jan. 1838	Clothes-brushes and other brushes.
WARD, FREDERICK OLDFIELD	9525	25th Nov. 1842	Candle-sticks, apparatus, and instruments, employed in the use of candles and rush-lights.

Name of Patentee.	Progressive Number.	Date.	Subject-matter of Patent.
WARD, FREDERICE OLDFIELD	10,949	18th Nov. 1845	Construction of railways; machinery and apparatus for working carriages thereon.
WARD, JAMES - - -	188	18th Dec. 1675	Engine for pumping water; waterworks and mills for draining grounds and raising water for the use of cities, towns, or castles.
WARD, JAMES - - -	6658	12th Aug. 1834	Apparatus for ventilating buildings and other places.
WARD, JOHN - - -	1219	10th April 1779	Manufacturing goods of linen, cotton and other commodities, upon a stocking-frame by double cross-stitch or basket-work inlaid with gold and silver, for coats, waistcoats and breeches, and for stockings, gloves, and other apparel.
WARD, JOHN - - -	4862	13th Nov. 1823	Construction of locks and other fastenings.
WARD, JOHN - - -	12,268	14th Sept. 1848	Manufacture of tubes; manufacture of certain articles made in part of tubes.
WARD, JOHN SHARRER - -	2460	30th Dec. 1800	Machine for doubling silk, cotton, flax, hemp, or worsted yarn or other threads.
WARD, JOSHUA - - -	644	23rd June 1749	Making a liquor and spirit of sulphur with brimstone and saltpetre.
WARD, PETER - - -	10,089	4th March 1844	Combining matters for washing and cleansing.
WARD, PETER - - -	11,279	6th July 1846	Manufacture of certain salts of soda and magnesia.
WARD, WILLIAM - - -	409	14th Sept. 1716	Making and setting vessels used in making salt, alum, copperas, and other things where large furnaces are required.
WARD, WILLIAM - - -	10,216	4th June 1844	Machinery for the manufacture of framework, knitted, or netted work.
WARD, WILLIAM SYKES -	10,736	25th June 1845	Exhausting air from tubes or vessels, for the purpose of working atmospheric railways, and for other purposes.
WARD, WILLIAM SYKES -	11,849	2nd Sept. 1847	Communicating motive-power, applicable for working signals and breaks on railways, also communicating intelligence, signals, and motive-power, by the agency of voltaic-electricity.
WARDEN, ALEXANDER JOHN-[STON.	14,178	24th June 1852	Manufacture of certain descriptions of carpets.
WARDEN, WILLIAM - -	1962	2nd Oct. 1793	Extract or preparation of or from bark, for use in tanning and in other processes.
WARDEN, WINCESLAS LE BARON [DE TRAUX DE.	12,945	26th Jan. 1850	Looms for weaving linen, woollen, and cotton cloths; machinery for preparing yarns for such cloths before entering the looms; machine for finishing linen-cloth.
WARDOER, Sir EDWARD, Knight	58	11th June 1632	Making saltpetre.
WARDROPER, WILLIAM - -	9973	5th Dec. 1843	Forms or constructions of hooks and eyes for fastening dresses, and for other uses.
WARE, GEORGE - - -	3283	5th Dec. 1809	Apparatus for the support and exercise of the human frame, and for the prevention of bodily deformity.
WARHURST, JOHN - - -	14,081	22nd April 1852	Generating or producing steam; machinery and apparatus connected therewith.
WARING, GEORGE - - -	2492	28th April 1801	Making soap of a peculiar quality.
WARING, THOMAS - - -	1639	5th Feb. 1788	Manufacture of long-bows; machines for the purpose.
WARINGTON, ROBERT - -	8880	16th March 1841	Operations of tanning.

Name of Patentee.	Progressive Number.	Date.	Subject-matter of Patent.
WARINGTON, ROBERT - -	11,142	25th March 1846	Operation of tanning.
WARK, Rev. DAVID - - -	834	27th July 1765	Composition or stone-paste made with oils and other things, for covering walls, roofs, and domes, and for other purposes.
WARLICH, FERDINAND CHARLES	9705	20th April 1843	Manufacture of fuel; machinery for manufacturing the same.
WARLICH, FERDINAND CHARLES	9892	5th Oct. 1843	Manufacture of fuel.
WARLICH, FERDINAND CHARLES [Warlick, Ferdinand Charles.]	11,159	7th April 1846	Manufacture of fuel.
WARMINGTON, JOHN - -	9713	25th April 1843	Manufacture of aërated liquors; vessels used for containing aërated liquors.
WARMONT, VICTOR EMILE -	13,304	2nd Nov. 1850	Dyeing wool and other fibrous materials and fabrics.
WARNE, JAMES - - -	6647	17th July 1834	Machinery for raising, drawing, or forcing beer, ale, and other liquids or fluids.
WARNE, THOMAS - -	10,279	30th July 1844	Machinery for raising, drawing, or forcing beer, ale, or other liquids or fluids.
WARNER, EDWARD, junior -	2720	29th June 1803	Air-lamp.
WARNER, HENRY - -	6240	8th March 1832	Machinery for manufacturing stockings, stocking-net, knitting-warp, web-warp, net, and point-net.
WARNER, HENRY - - -	8832	4th Feb. 1841	Stocking-frame or frame-work knitting-machinery.
WARNER, JOHN, junior - -	6371	24th Jan. 1833	Processes in giving a metallic coating to various articles of commerce.
WARRELL, WILLIAM - -	4331	15th Jan. 1819	Cooling, condensing, and ventilating worts, liquors, and other fluids or solid matters; apparatus for the purpose.
WARREN, JAMES - -	9042	4th Aug. 1841	Machine for making screws.
WARREN, JAMES - - -	11,363	31st Aug. 1846	Manufacture of cast-screws.
WARREN, JAMES - - -	12,242	15th Aug. 1848	Construction of bridges, aqueducts, and roofings.
WARREN, JAMES - - -	13,760	2nd Oct. 1851	Improvements applicable to railways and railway carriages; paving.
WARREN, JAMES - - -	14,298	18th Sept. 1852	Manufacture of screws and screw-keys; construction of bridges;—applicable to floorings, roofings, and paving.
WARREN, JOHN - - -	3167	15th Sept. 1808	Apparatus to prevent chimneys from smoking, and to extinguish fires in grates or stoves without causing dust or smoke.
WARREN, JOHN CRABB BLAIR	11,282	6th July 1846	Manufacture of bricks, tiles, pipes, and other articles composed of plastic materials; preparation of plastic materials for such purposes.
WARREN, JOSEPH - - -	9341	9th May 1842	Ploughs.
WARREN, RICHARD - -	1029	17th Dec. 1772	Medicinal and chemical mixture or composition from divers salutary ingredients.
WARREN, RICHARD - -	1283	9th March 1781	Method of preparing leather gloves with flowers, fruits, and vegetables, to prevent the hands and arms from chapping.
WARREN, WILLIAM - -	5332	11th Feb. 1826	Process of extracting quinine and cinchonine from Peruvian bark; preparing salts of the same.
WARRICK, JOHN - - -	6960	16th Dec. 1835	Lock and key.
WARRICK, JOHN - - -	9282	7th March 1842	Apparatus to show the presence of bi-carburetted hydrogen gas in mines, wells, houses, buildings, rooms or vaults. " Gasoscope."

Name of Patentee.	Progressive Number.	Date.	Subject-matter of Patent.
WARRINER, THOMAS - - -	12,393	28th Dec. 1848	Smelting copper.
WARRINGTON, ROBERT - -	11,120	5th March 1846	Preserving animal and vegetable substances.
WARRIS, WILLIAM - -	2779	4th Aug. 1804	Mounting opera glasses.
WART, HENRY VAN - -	3173	31st Oct. 1808	Making a machine for manufacturing thimbles for the sails of ships and vessels, and for rigging, also for other purposes.
WART, HENRY VAN - -	7191	22nd Sept. 1836	Locomotive steam engines and carriages;—partly applicable to ordinary steam-engines, and for other purposes.
WART, HENRY VAN - -	7730	11th July 1838	Apparatus applicable to locomotion on rail-roads, and to steam navigation;—partly applicable to land or stationary engines.
WARTER, JOHN - - -	254	13th Aug. 1687	Manufacture of milled lead for sheathing and preservation of ships or any other thing.
WARWICK, CHARLES - -	13,112	8th June 1850	Apparatus for taking up the work of certain descriptions of knitting-machinery.
WASBOROUGH, MATTHEW -	1213	10th March 1779	Machine, which when applied to a steam-engine or any perpendicular motion, either by means of levers or any reciprocal movement, will cause such movement to become circular, without the medium of a water-wheel, for grinding wheat and other grain, and for grinding, rolling, hammering, and other uses in mechanical operations, also for moving, in a direct position, ships or vessels against tide or wind, and where human or animal strength is inadequate.
WASON, PETER RIGBY - -	5702	15th Sept. 1828	Stick sealing-wax.
WASS, JOSEPH - - -	4682	15th June 1822	Preventing the effects on vegetation and animal life caused by fumes arising from smelting lead ore and other minerals.
WASS, JOSEPH - - -	6502	5th Nov. 1833	Certain mechanical powers which may be applied to various purposes.
WASS, ROBERT - - -	3276	21st Nov. 1809	Construction of hafts or handles for razors.
WATERHOUSE, THOMAS -	9363	24th May 1842	Machinery for carding cotton-wool, flax, silk, and similar fibrous materials.
WATERHOUSE, THOMAS -	11,618	10th March 1847	Railway-engines and tenders, and other railway-carriages.
WATERLOW, ALBERT CRACKELL	12,913	3rd Jan. 1850	Means and apparatus for obtaining copies of writings, drawings, and other designs.
WATERS, JOHN - - -	1284	9th March 1781	Pistol with a bayonet.
WATERS, RICHARD - -	3457	14th June 1811	Method of manufacturing pottery-ware.
WATERS, WILLIAM - -	3391	8th Oct. 1810	Joining pipes.
WATERSTONE, JOHN JAMES -	7399	10th July 1837	Intercepting and directing currents and waves of water.
WATERTON, HENRY - -	8608	27th Aug. 1840	Manufacture of sal-ammoniac.
WATERTON, HENRY - -	9222	13th Jan. 1842	Manufacture of salt.
WATKINS, JOHN - - -	334	27th April 1694	Smelting or melting down tin-ore, and making the same into merchantable tin, by the use of pit-coal and sea-coal, without charcoal or wood.
WATKINS, WILLIAM - -	116	6th April 1638	Burning tiles with sea-coals.
WATLINGTON, JOHN - -	436	9th Sept. 1721	Engine for cutting the wool from beaver, coney, and hare skins, for making hats.

Name of Patentee.	Progres-sive Number.	Date.	Subject-matter of Patent.
WATNEY, ALFRED - - -	10,917	3rd Nov. 1845	Manufacture of horse-shoes, and applying shoes to horses and other animals.
WATNEY, DANIEL - - -	12,284	12th Oct. 1848	Machinery for drilling metals and other substances.
WATSON, BARCLAY FAR-[QUHARSON.	7907	17th Dec. 1838	Crushing or preparing New Zealand flax.
WATSON, CAROLINE - -	11,673	27th April 1847	Apparatus for filtering.
WATSON, CHRISTOPHER -	1504	4th Nov. 1785	Floating dock for docking ships, in rivers, harbours, or at sea, and where there is no tide.
WATSON, FRANCIS - -	145	22nd April 1664	Making a valuable metal for divers sorts of vessels, from a certain stone mixed with other ingredients.
WATSON, FRANCIS - -	154	8th Oct. 1667	Graving, garnishing, and colouring ships and other vessels.
WATSON, FREDERICK - -	13,456	16th Jan. 1851	Sails, rigging, and ships' fittings; machinery and apparatus employed therein.
WATSON, HENRY - - -	664	11th Oct. 1751	Machine for cutting or sawing marble and stone, and for facing and polishing the same.
WATSON, HENRY - - -	11,027	6th Jan. 1846	Withdrawing air and vapours from furnaces or other apparatus; condensing and employing such vapours.
WATSON, HENRY - - -	12,804	12th Oct. 1849	Valves and cocks.
WATSON, HENRY HOUGH -	8465	6th April 1840	Manufacture of sulphuric-acid, crystallized soda, and soda-ash; and the recovery of a residium or residua, applicable to various purposes.
WATSON, HENRY HOUGH -	9194	21st Dec. 1841	Dressing, stiffening, and finishing cotton and other fibrous substances, also textile and other fabrics;—applicable to the manufacture of paper, and processes in printing calicoes and other goods.
WATSON, HENRY HOUGH -	9396	21st June 1842	Bleaching, changing the colours, and otherwise preparing, purifying, and refining tallow and other substances, mixtures, compounds and manufactures.
WATSON, JOHN - - -	3132	10th May 1808	Soap-making.
WATSON, JOHN - - -	9208	23rd Dec. 1841	Construction of filters used in the manufacture of sugar.
WATSON, JOHN - - -	11,498	21st Dec. 1846	Weaving by jacquard-looms by power.
WATSON, JOHN - - -	12,066	14th Feb. 1848	Manufacture of gas.
WATSON, JOHN RICHARD -	11,766	24th June 1847	Instrument for registering angles at sea.
WATSON, RALPH - - -	6230	23rd Feb. 1832	Lamp.
WATSON, RICHARD, junior -	9371	31st May 1842	Draining land, embankments, and cuttings of railways, and other engineering works.
WATSON, SAMUEL - - -	1090	26th Nov. 1774	Hand-mill, made of stone or marble, for grinding and preparing wheat, malt, oats, peas, beans and other grain, and for other purposes, and which may be worked by animal and other power.
WATSON, THOMAS - - -	1387	12th Sept. 1783	Purging-paste for horses and dogs.
WATSON, THOMAS - - -	7611	10th April 1838	Stoves.
WATSON, THOMAS - - -	13,380	2nd Dec. 1850	Manufacture of hat-plush; also machinery employed in such manufacture.
WATSON, WILLIAM - -	7102	24th May 1836	Dyeing hats by the application of certain chemical matters never before applied to that purpose.

Name of Patentee.	Progressive Number.	Date.	Subject-matter of Patent.
WATSON, WILLIAM - -	7124	18th June 1836	Manufacture of sugar from beet-root and other substances.
WATSON, WILLIAM - -	8104	12th June 1839	Construction of ships;—applicable to all sea-going vessels; construction of boats and other vessels for use on canals, and for inland navigation.
WATSON, WILLIAM, junior -	7865	8th Nov. 1838	Manufacture of materials used in the dyeing of blue and other colours.
WATSON, WILLIAM, junior -	7877	20th Nov. 1838	Manufacture of liquid ammonia to make it applicable to dyeing, scouring, and other manufacturing purposes.
WATSON, WILLIAM, junior -	9910	18th Oct. 1843	Ventilating houses and other buildings.
WATSON, WILLIAM, junior -	10,017	16th Jan. 1844	Manufacture of sulphate, muriate, and other salts of ammonia.
WATSON, WILLIAM, junior -	13,100	4th June 1850	Preparation and manufacture of various materials to be used in the processes of dyeing, printing, and colouring.
WATT, CHARLES - - -	4299	31st Oct. 1818	Gilding and preparing quills and pens by manual labour and chemical operations.
WATT, CHARLES - - -	6311	27th Sept. 1832	Process of preparing tallow and stuff from fatty materials, and refining the same for the manufacture of candles, and for other purposes.
WATT, CHARLES - - -	7028	8th March 1836	Preparing, purifying, and refining tallow stuff, fatty materials, and animal and vegetable oils, for various purposes.
WATT, CHARLES - - -	7531	5th Jan. 1838	Manufacture of the oxydes of lead, also carbonate of lead.
WATT, CHARLES - - -	7538	11th Jan. 1838	Manufacture of the hydrate and carbonate of soda, from the chloride of sodium;—applicable to the manufacture of soap and glass, and to other purposes.
WATT, CHARLES - - -	13,755	25th Sept. 1851	Decomposing saline and other substances, and separating their component parts or some of them, from each other; forming certain compounds or combinations of substances; also separating metals and freeing them from their impurities.
WATT, JAMES - - -	913	5th Jan. 1769	Method of lessening the consumption of steam and fuel in fire-engines.
WATT, JAMES - - -	1244	14th Feb. 1780	Copying letters and other writings.
WATT, JAMES - - -	1306	25th Oct. 1781	Applying the reciprocating motion of steam-engines to procure a circular motion round an axis, for working mills and other machinery.
WATT, JAMES - - -	1321	12th March 1782	Steam or fire engines for raising water, and for other mechanical purposes; mechanism applicable to the same.
WATT, JAMES - - -	1432	28th April 1784	Fire and steam engines; and machines worked or moved by the same.
WATT, JAMES - - -	1485	14th June 1785	Constructing furnaces or fire-places for heating, boiling, or evaporating water and other liquids;—applicable to steam-engines and to other purposes; and also for heating and smelting metals and their ores.
WATT, JOHN JAMES - -	5643	29th April 1828	Application of a certain chemical agent for destroying animal poison, and for preventing the disease consequent thereon.

Name of Patentee.	Progressive Number.	Date.	Subject-matter of Patent.
WATT, WILLIAM - - -	13,244	5th Sept. 1850	Inland navigation;—applicable generally to raising, lowering, and transmitting heavy bodies.
WATT, WILLIAM - - -	14,128	22nd May 1852	Treatment and preparation of flax or other fibrous substances; application of some of the products to certain purposes.
WATTEEU, FRANCIS - -	10,395	16th Nov. 1844	Preventing incrustation in steam-boilers and steam-generators.
WATTERSON, CHARLES -	10,178	8th May 1844	Manufacture of soap.
WATTS, HARRY - - -	2195	19th Oct. 1797	Implement for draining land.
WATTS, JOHN - - -	554	22nd May 1736	New form wherein to build the body or lower works of a ship or other marine vessel.
WATTS, JOSEPH - - -	2293	5th Feb. 1799	Tawing, dressing, or converting skins into gloves and mittens, without lime and bran.
WATTS, NATHANIEL -	1629	22nd Nov. 1787	Dyeing in boiling liquors, woollen-cloth or articles composed chiefly of woollen, in various devices, representing scrolls, lines, and other forms, which is effected by certain frames and moulds made of hard metals.
WATTS, RICHARD - -	4463	15th May 1820	Inking printing-types, with rollers; placing and conveying paper on types; inking with a cylinder.
WATTS, WILLIAM - -	1347	10th Dec. 1782	Making small shot solid throughout, perfectly globular in form, and without the imperfections usual in shot as hitherto manufactured.
WATTS, WILLIAM - -	3264	26th Sept. 1809	Combining and disposing machinery, and applying the power of wind, water, and cattle thereto, so as to affect improvements on mills.
WAUD, EDWARD - - -	11,952	9th Nov. 1847	Construction of machinery for preparing and spinning alpaca, mohair, wool, flax, and other fibrous materials.
WAYCOTT, PETER - -	6126	22nd June 1831	Mangles.
WAYNE, RALPH - - -	135	19th March 1662	Method to save coals or other fuel, in boiling brine and making it into salt.
WAYT, JOHN - - -	488	16th Jan. 1727	Method to save coals or other fuel, in boiling brine and making it into salt.
WAYTE, JAMES WILLS - [Wayte, James Wells.]	5776	19th March 1829	Printing-machinery.
WAYTE, JAMES WILLS -	8984	12th June 1841	Machinery for letter-press printing.
WAYTE, JAMES WILLS -	11,628	18th March 1847	Self-feeding furnaces adapted for both land and marine purposes.
WEALE, JOHN - - -	215	29th Aug. 1681	Engine to raise and throw out water from deep mines.
WEALE, SAMUEL - -	215	29th Aug. 1681	Engine to raise and throw out water from deep mines.
WEALE, SAMUEL - -	283	19th Oct. 1691	Engine made of timber with glass-windows, a door, air-pipes, leather-sleeves, and braces affixed thereto, to enable a man to work under water for many hours.
WEALE, SAMUEL - -	288	22nd Jan. 1692	Engine for beating and pounding, or stamping, mineral ores, hemp, and flax;—partly applicable to the working of mines and coal-pits.

Name of Patentee.	Progressive Number.	Date.	Subject-matter of Patent.
WEALE, SAMUEL - - -	325	19th Sept. 1693	Manufacturing and ordering roots and barks, with other ingredients, for dyeing silks, wrought and unwrought, and woollen and linen cloth, in many colours in grain and otherwise, with or without fire; also useful for limners and painters, for perforating glass, and for other purposes.
WEARE, ROBERT - - -	11,776	3rd July 1847	Clocks or time-keepers.
WEARE, ROBERT - - -	12,697	4th July 1849	Electric-batteries; and production of light; also mode of transmitting or communicating intelligence;—partly applicable to other purposes.
WEARE, ROBERT - - -	13,142	19th June 1850	Means and apparatus for extinguishing fire; galvanic-batteries.
WEARE, ROBERT - - -	14,257	12th Aug. 1852	Galvanic-batteries.
WEARN, ROGER - - -	1758	8th July 1790	Heating the boilers of steam-engines with a smaller quantity of fuel than now used; also calcining ores by the fires in such boilers.
WEATHERLEY, HENRY OSWALD	5169	14th May 1825	Machinery for splitting, rending asunder, cutting or cleaving wood, and forming and securing the same in bundles.
WEATHERSTONE, JOHN - -	10,525	20th Feb. 1845	Dibbling-machinery for planting seed or grain.
WEAVER, CHARLES - -	3555	15th April 1812	Machine for heading pins.
WEBB, BENEDICT - - -	30	16th Dec. 1624	Making oil of rape-seed and other like seeds sown in England or Wales.
WEBB, JOHN - - - -	805	8th March 1764	Crane for landing and shipping goods and merchandize, and for other purposes.
WEBB, JOHN - - - -	1417	4th Feb. 1784	Method of making a more easy and perfect division in stocking frame-work manufactures.
WEBB, JOHN - - - -	3278	21st Nov. 1809	Constructing machines for making cards for carding wool, cotton, flax, silk, and other substances.
WEBB, JOHN - - - -	3388	8th Oct. 1810	Apparatus to machines for making fillet, sheet, and hard cards, used for carding wool, cotton, flax, silk, and other substances.
WEBB, JOHN - - - -	3576	13th June 1812	Making rugs, carpets, or other articles of furniture or dress, consisting of carded-wool or other substance capable of being carded, and interwoven to form a firm texture, or consisting of worsted or other spun-yarn of any number of colours formed into a figure in imitation of needle-work, on the surface of any piece of goods woven on the common loom, without passing the threads through the reeds, and with or without the aforesaid carded substances.
WEBB, JOSEPH - - -	8174	1st Aug. 1839	Machinery for raising the pile of woollen and other cloths.
WEBB, RICHARD - - -	2042	28th Feb. 1795	Construction of guns and other fire-arms.
WEBB, THOMAS - - -	11,998	15th Dec. 1847	Manufacture of spirits from grain or other saccharine matters; apparatus to be used therein.
WEBB, WILLIAM - - -	87	31st Oct. 1635	Making an engine for cutting timber into thin pieces or scales, for making scabbards for swords and the like.

Name of Patentee.	Progressive Number.	Date.	Subject-matter of Patent.
WEBLEY, PHILIP - - -	13,611	30th April 1851	Manufacture of boots and shoes, rendering the same waterproof; also machinery and materials to be used therein.
WEBSTER, ALPHONSUS WILLIAM.	7033	17th March 1836	Instrument to be applied to the ear to assist in hearing.
WEBSTER, HENRY - - -	14,142	25th May 1852	Regulating the draft in chimneys or flues.
WEBSTER, JAMES - - -	11,843	19th Aug. 1847	Atmospheric-buffer to be applied to carriages and other vehicles travelling on railways.
WEBSTER, JAMES - - -	12,460	8th Feb. 1849	Apparatus for manufacturing gas.
WEBSTER, JAMES - - -	12,967	12th Feb. 1850	Production of gas for the purposes of light.
WEBSTER, JAMES - - -	13,510	11th Feb. 1851	Construction and means of applying carriage and other springs.
WEBSTER, JAMES - - -	13,854	10th Dec. 1851	Drying gloves and other articles of hosiery.
WEBSTER, ROBERT - - -	1021	31st July 1772	Repeating watch.
WEBSTER, ROBERT - - -	1856	2nd March 1792	Mill or machine for washing and cleansing articles hitherto washed by hand.
WEBSTER, ROBERT - - -	3515	13th Jan. 1812	Portable mangle.
WEBSTER, WILLIAM - -	4590	14th Sept. 1821	Mechanism of and appertaining to "Forsyth's Roller Magazine," for the discharge of fire-arms by percussion.
WEBSTER, WILLIAM HENRY [BAILEY.	8478	16th April 1840	Preparing skins and other animal matters for tanning; manufacture of gelatine.
WEBSTER, WILLIAM HENRY [BAILEY.	8718	25th Nov. 1840	Preparing skins and other animal matters for tanning; manufacture of gelatine.
WEDGWOOD, JOSIAH - -	939	16th Nov. 1769	Ornamenting earthen and porcelain ware with an encaustic gold bronze, together with the peculiar encaustic painting in various colours, in imitation of Etruscan and Roman earthenware.
WEDGWOOD, RALPH - -	2137	3rd Oct. 1796	Making earthenware.
WEDGWOOD, RALPH - -	2138	3rd Oct. 1796	Composition for making glass.
WEDGWOOD, RALPH - -	2139	3rd Oct. 1796	Stove.
WEDGWOOD, RALPH - -	2972	7th Oct. 1806	Apparatus for producing duplicates of writings.
WEDGWOOD, RALPH - -	3110	22nd Feb. 1808	Apparatus for producing several original writings or drawings at one and the same time. "Manifold writer."
WEDGWOOD, RALPH - -	3362	18th July 1810	New character for language, numbers, and music; method of applying the same.
WEDLAKE, ROBERT - -	6284	19th July 1832	Ploughs, particularly the shares applicable to the same and to other ploughs.
WEDLAKE, THOMAS - -	4135	5th July 1817	Ploughs.
WEDLAKE, THOMAS - -	6284	19th July 1832	Ploughs, particularly the shares applicable to the same and to other ploughs.
WEDLAKE, THOMAS - -	9813	3rd July 1843	Machinery for making hay;—applicable to other agricultural purposes.
WEEKES, JOSEPH - - -	2409	10th June 1800	Set of machinery for a tannery.
WEEKES, WILLIAM - -	6796	25th March 1835	Machinery for cleansing, plaining, polishing, and dressing woollen and other cloths.
WEEKES, WILLIAM - -	7338	4th April 1837	Dressing or finishing woollen and other cloths or fabrics.
WEEKS, EDWARD - - -	3120	17th March 1808	Forcing-frame, for raising and forcing cucumbers and various fruits and plants requiring artificial heat.

Name of Patentee.	Progressive Number.	Date.	Subject-matter of Patent.
WEEKS, EDWARD - - -	5832	14th Aug. 1829	Raising, lowering, or conveying heated water or other fluids to various distances.
WEEKS, EDWARD - - -	6677	20th Sept. 1834	Kitchen or other grates or ranges. "Weeks' Cooking apparatus."
WEEMS, JOHN - - -	13,365	25th Nov. 1850	Warming and ventilating buildings and structures.
WEEMS, JOHN - - -	14,344	11th Nov. 1822	Manufacture or production of metallic pipes and sheets.
WEGUELIN, JOHN CHRISTOPHER	635	8th Aug. 1748	Dyeing green and blue Saxon colours.
WEIGER, JOSEPH - - -	10,426	12th Dec. 1844	Amalgamation, alloying and soldering of certain metals.
WEIGHT, JOSEPH - - -	9109	7th Oct. 1841	Machinery for manufacturing woollen-cloth, and cloth made from wool and other materials.
WEIGHTMAN, RICHARD - -	2056	1st July 1795	Stove or grate.
WEILD, WILLIAM - - -	9614	28th Jan. 1843	Windows, blinds, and curtains;—partly applicable to doors.
WEILD, WILLIAM - - -	11,389	2nd Oct. 1846	Certain mills for grinding; manufacture of certain parts of mills.
WEILD, WILLIAM - - -	12,315	2nd Nov. 1848	Machinery for spinning cotton and other fibrous substances.
WEILD, WILLIAM - - -	13,505	11th Feb. 1851	Machinery for turning and burnishing.
WEISE, WILLIAM PHILIP -	5018	14th Oct. 1824	Preparing and making waterproof cloth and other materials for the manufacture of hats, bonnets, caps, and wearing-apparel.
WEISEHAMER, JEREMIAH -	385	26th July 1709	Mill or engine for grinding or pressing sugar-canes.
WEISENTHAL, CHARLES FREDE-[RICK.	701	24th June 1755	Working fine thread in needle-work, after the manner of Dresden needle-work.
WEISS, FREDERICK -	13,827	22nd Nov. 1851	Surgical instruments, scissors, and other like cutting instruments.
WEISS, FREDERICK FOVEAUX -	5558	6th Nov. 1827	Construction of spurs.
WEISS, JOHN - - - -	5061	18th Dec. 1824	Exhausting, injecting, or condensing pumps or syringes, and apparatus connected therewith;—applicable to other purposes.
WEISS, JOHN - - - -	5612	26th Jan. 1828	Instruments for bleeding horses and other animals.
WELCH, EDWARD - - -	9108	30th Sept. 1841	Construction of bricks.
WELCH, EDWARD - - -	13,022	23rd March 1850	Fire-places and flues; apparatus connected therewith.
WELCH, FREDERICK ISAAC -	9923	2nd Nov. 1843	Manufacture of leather.
WELCH, JOHN - - -	4052	3rd Aug. 1816	Making rollers used in spinning wool, cotton, silk, flax, tow, or other fibrous substances.
WELCH, JOHN WHITE - -	9033	21st July 1841	Reverberatory furnace to be used in the smelting of copper or other ores.
WELCH, THOMAS - - -	6480	5th Oct. 1833	Method of taking-up for power and hand-looms.
WELCH, THOMAS - - -	8933	22nd April 1841	Looms for weaving.
WELD, JOSEPH - - -	4185	5th Dec. 1817	Machine for separating corn, grain, and seeds from the straw.
WELDON, JAMES - - -	2205	22nd Dec. 1797	Machine or mill for breaking, grinding, and pulverizing patched or chopped bark, for tanning; also breaking, grinding, and pulverizing different kinds of wood and other hard substances.

Name of Patentee.	Progres- sive Number.	Date.	Subject-matter of Patent.
WELDON, JAMES - - -	2475	10th Feb. 1801	Machine or mill for grinding bark and other articles;—applicable to other purposes.
WELDON, JAMES - - -	3374	7th Sept. 1810	Mill or machine for grinding bark and other articles;—applicable to other purposes.
WELDON, PATRICK - -	1033	2nd March 1773	Bleaching and whitening linen and yarn, by a composition.
WELDON, ROBERT - -	1892	19th June 1792	Machine for conveying vessels or other weights from an upper to a lower level and vice versâ, on canals, and for raising or lowering weights in other situations.
WELLER, RICHARD - -	10,577	27th March 1845	Manufacture of drain and other tiles and pipes.
WELLER, WILLIAM - -	2414	17th June 1800	Manufacturing and engraving copper-plates for printing policies.
WELLS, GEORGE - - -	10,005	4th Jan. 1844	Manufacture of metallic pens; machine for making metallic pens.
WELLS, GEORGE - - -	11,945	4th Nov. 1847	Machine for causing a communication between the guards and engine-drivers of railway-carriages, while travelling; also communication between vessels at sea and the shore, and for other purposes. "Atmospheric Signal by land or water."
WELLS, HENRY AUGUSTUS -	7222	15th Nov. 1836	Manufacture of hats.
WELLS, HENRY AUGUSTUS -	7397	30th June 1837	Manufacture of hats.
WELLS, HENRY AUGUSTUS -	8887	17th March 1841	Machinery for driving piles.
WELLS, HENRY AUGUSTUS -	8926	17th April 1841	Manufacture of woollen-cloths.
WELLS, JOHN - - -	167	15th Feb. 1672	Engine for teaching to perform by artificial horses, the usual exercises of a complete horseman, namely, running at the ring, throwing the lance, shooting the pistol, and taking up the head.
WELLS, JOHN - - -	8757	30th Dec. 1840	Manufacture of coke.
WELLS, JOSEPH - - -	4964	25th May 1824	Machine for dressing, stiffening, and drying cotton and other warps at the time the loom is working, with the motion of the loom or other machinery.
WELLS, STEPHEN - -	2604	3rd April 1802	Hinges.
WELLS, THOMAS - - -	3241	8th June 1809	Making and constructing barrel-cocks and water-cocks.
WELLS, THOMAS - - -	10,670	17th May 1845	Construction of timber and other jacks and floor-cramps.
WELLS, WILLIAM - - -	6237	8th March 1832	Making and constructing gig or raising machines, for raising the nap or pile of and for brushing and dressing woollen-cloths.
WELLS, WILLIAM - - -	6718	20th Nov. 1834	Apparatus for cutting the pile of fustians and other fabrics manufactured of cotton-wool and other fibrous materials.
WELLS, WILLIAM - - -	7532	5th Jan. 1838	Power-looms and hand-looms for weaving plain and figured fabrics.
WEMIS, JAMES - - -	136	24th March 1662	Making light ordnance; performing by one or two men the motions caused by the force of water, wind, or horses.
WENDEL, CHARLES ALEXIS, [DE.	13,478	30th Jan. 1851	Process and instruments used for boring the earth and sinking shafts for mining and other purposes; lining such shafts.

Name of Patentee.	Progressive Number.	Date.	Subject-matter of Patent.
WENNINGTON. WILLIAM VIN- [CENT.	11,047	20th Jan. 1846	Cutting plate and sheet iron.
WENTWORTH, JOHN JAMES -	12,284	12th Oct. 1848	Machinery for drilling metals and other substances.
WERNINCK, HENRY HOPE -	6167	24th Sept. 1831	Apparatus for or methods of preserving persons and property, when in danger by shipwreck or otherwise, by speedily converting ordinary boats into life-boats; also other apparatus or means for the same object.
WERTHEIMBER, DAVID ISAAC	9316	28th Jan. 1843	Calculating-machines;—partly applicable to purposes where wheel-work is required.
WERTHEIMER, JOHN - -	8117	20th June 1839	Preserving animal and vegetable substances and liquids.
WERTHEIMER, JOHN - -	8222	19th Sept. 1839	Producing ornamental raised surfaces on paper.
WERTHEIMER, JOHN - -	8378	8th Feb. 1840	Preserving animal and vegetable substances and liquids.
WERTHEIMER, JOHN - -	8874	8th March 1841	Preserving animal and vegetable substances and liquids.
WESSELS, HART - - -	742	23rd July 1759	Medicine called "Tinctura Embryonum."
WEST, BENJAMIN - -	10,881	16th Oct. 1845	Covering or stoppering the tops of bottles, jars, pots, and other similar vessels.
WEST, CHARLES ROBERT -	2918	18th March 1806	Day or night telescopes.
WEST, DANIEL - - -	3994	14th March 1816	Producing power and motion, and applying the same to presses, and other mechanical apparatus.
WEST, GEORGE - - -	667	1st Jan. 1752	Composition "West's Pectoral Elixir."
WEST, HENRY FREDERICK -	11,362	31st Aug. 1846	Securing corks in bottles, jars, and other vessels, to contain liquids and other matters; bottles and other vessels.
WEST, JAMES ATKINSON -	4100	6th Feb. 1817	Lustres, chandeliers, lanterns, and lamps; conveying gas to the same.
WEST, JOHN - - - -	6730	9th Dec. 1834	Forges.
WEST, WILLIAM - - -	3994	14th March 1816	Producing power and motion, and applying the same to presses and other mechanical apparatus.
WEST, WILLIAM - - -	8103	12th June 1839	Valve for machines for raising water and other liquids.
WESTBY, FRANCIS - - -	5649	6th May 1828	Apparatus to be used for whetting or sharpening the edges of the blades of knives and other instruments.
WESTBY, FRANCIS - - -	5875	26th Nov. 1829	Apparatus to be used for whetting or sharpening the edges of the blades of razors, penknives, and other instruments.
WESTBY, WILLIAM - -	92	25th April 1636	Making pan-tiles or Flanders tiles.
WESTENHOLZ, FREDERIC LEWIS	9853	25th July 1843	Double-centred steam-engine.
WESTERN, CHARLES CALLIS [BARON	7847	3rd Nov. 1838	Drills for drilling corn, grain, seeds, pulse, and manure.
WESTFIELD, ROBERT - -	3732	9th Aug. 1813	Horizontal watches.
WESTHEAD, EDWARD - -	12,502	3rd March 1849	Manufacture of waddings.
WESTHEAD, JOSHUA PROCTOR	6114	23rd May 1831	Manufacture of smallwares.
WESTHEAD, JOSHUA PROCTOR	6896	24th Sept. 1835	Manufacture of smallwares; arrangement of machinery for covering or forming a case around wire, cord, gut, thread or other substance, to render the same applicable to various purposes.

Name of Patentee.	Progressive Number.	Date.		Subject-matter of Patent.
WESTHEAD, JOSHUA PROCTOR	7004	16th Feb.	1836	Cutting caoutchouc, india-rubber, leather, hides, and similar substances, to render them applicable to various purposes.
WESTHEAD, JOSHUA PROCTOR	8091	4th June	1839	Construction of stays or corsets.
WESTHEAD, JOSHUA PROCTOR	9922	2nd Nov.	1843	Fabrics; modifications of machinery for making the same;—which said modifications are applicable to woven fabrics.
WESTHEAD, JOSHUA PROCTOR	11,940	4th Nov.	1847	Treating india-rubber.
WESTHEAD, JOSHUA PROCTOR	12,179	8th June	1848	Manufacturing fur into fabrics.
WESTLY, WILLIAM KING	5409	30th Aug.	1826	Machinery for heckling or dressing, breaking, scutching, and cleaning hemp, flax, and other fibrous substances.
WESTLY, WILLIAM KING [Westley, William King.]	6464	20th Aug.	1833	Machinery for preparing, drawing, or roving hemp, flax, wool, and other fibrous substances.
WESTLY, WILLIAM KING	8789	14th Jan.	1841	Carding, combing, straightening, cleaning, and preparing for spinning, hemp, flax, and other fibrous sbstances.
WESTMACOTT, HENRY SEYMOUR	11,231	30th May	1846	Construction of rotatory steam-engines.
WESTON, JASPER	7309	23rd Feb.	1837	Certain wheeled-carriages.
WESTON, JOHN	12,069	16th Feb.	1848	Obtaining and applying motive-power.
WESTON, (Sir) RICHARD KNT.	107	21st July	1637	Making Castille or Venice soap.
WESTRUP, THOMAS	6117	24th May	1831	Converting salt or other water into pure or fresh water.
WESTRUP, WALTER	12,939	24th Jan.	1850	Cleaning and grinding corn or grain, and dressing meal or flour.
WESTWOOD, JOHN	1398	15th Nov.	1783	Hardening and stiffening copper, and reducing the same from large masses to any diameter and of any length and form, by the use of grooved rollers; also hardening and stiffening brass, iron, steel, mixed and compound metals that will bear drawing or beating out by forge or hammer in either a hot, warm, or cold state.
WESTWOOD, JOHN	3738	4th Sept.	1813	Embossing ivory by pressure.
WESTWOOD, OBADIAH	1576	14th Dec.	1786	Making trays, waiters, card-pans, caddies, dressing-boxes, bottle-stands, ink-stands, coat, breast and other buttons, frames for pictures and other things, mouldings, and ornaments for rooms and ceilings and for other purposes.
WESTWOOD, ROBERT	5850	23rd Sept.	1829	Watches and time-keepers.
WETTERSTEDT, BARON CHARLES	5662	4th June	1828	Liquid or composition for waterproofing and strengthening leather.
WETTERSTEDT, BARON CHARLES	6129	6th July	1831	Composition or combination of materials for sheathing, painting, or preserving ships' bottoms, and for other purposes.
WETTERSTEDT, BARON CHARLES	8601	11th Aug.	1840	Preserving vegetable, animal, and other substances from ignition and decay.
WETTERSTEDT, BARON CHARLES	11,434	3rd Nov.	1846	Manufacture of sheet-metal for sheathing, and for other purposes; preventing the corrosion of metal; preserving wood and other materials.
WETTERSTEDT, BARON CHARLES	13,732	4th Sept.	1851	Preserving animal and vegetable substances.
WETZLAR, GODFREY	9340	7th May	1842	Rendering fabrics waterproof.
WHALEY, THOMAS	12,601	3rd May	1849	Machinery for manufacturing bricks and tiles from clay or other plastic materials.

Name of Patentee.	Progressive Number.	Date.	Subject-matter of Patent.
WHALLEY, JOHN - - -	10,968	20th Nov. 1845	Manufacture of earthenware-pastes and vitrous bodies; composition and material for the same, with mode of combination;—which improvements, compositions, and combinations, are also applicable to the manufacture of slabs, tiles, and pavements, and for other purposes.
WHALLEY, PETER - - -	224	23rd March 1683	Pump or engine.
WHARTON, EMANUEL - -	10,108	14th March 1844	Steam-engines;—applicable to other motive-engines, and to machines for raising or impelling fluids.
WHARTON, GOODWIN - -	185	12th Nov. 1675	Buoying and raising up ships' ordnance, also treasures and other matters from the bottom of the sea, by the help of air conveyed under water; new way of diving and living several hours under the water, by curing the air conveyed down for sustenance, so as to make it fit for respiring whilst beneath the water; engines and instruments for landing and shipping goods and merchandise.
WHARTON, GOODWIN - -	189	21st June 1676	Engines with leather-pipes for raising water for drenching fires, draining mines, and divers other uses.
WHARTON, WILLIAM - -	11,087	11th Feb. 1846	Straps and bands.
WHARTON, WILLIAM - -	12,369	16th Dec. 1848	Construction of vehicles used on railways or on other roads and ways.
WHARTON, WILLIAM LLOYD -	6217	30th Jan. 1832	Engines for raising or forcing water by the pressure and condensation of steam.
WHATELEY, GEORGE - -	905	8th Nov. 1768	Plating silver upon metal-wire, and gold upon silver wire, and drawing the same into very fine wire to make thread, lace, fringe, and tinsel.
WHATELEY, GEORGE - -	908	6th Dec. 1768	Plating silver upon metal-wire, and gold upon silver-plated wire, and drawing the same into very fine wire to make thread, lace, fringe, and tinsel.
WHATMORE, EDWARD - -	1364	3rd May 1783	Machine to convey persons and goods from the windows of houses and other buildings when on fire, and to raise firemen and other persons and goods from the ground to the tops of houses and other buildings, also to gather fruit from trees, without help of ladders or scaffolds.
WHEATLEY, FRANCIS - -	14,025	15th March 1852	Safety cab-omnibus.
WHEATLEY, JOHN - -	3396	15th Oct. 1810	Axle-tree for wheels of carriages, wrought or cast iron boxes and cast-iron stocks to receive the spokes.
WHEATSTONE, CHARLES -	5803	19th June 1829	Construction of wind musical-instruments.
WHEATSTONE, CHARLES -	7154	27th July 1836	Method of forming musical-instruments in which continuous sounds are produced from strings, wires, or springs.
WHEATSTONE, CHARLES -	7390	12th June 1837	Giving signals and sounding alarums at distant places, by means of electric-currents transmitted through metallic-circuits.
WHEATSTONE, CHARLES -	8345	21st Jan. 1840	Giving signals and sounding. alarums at distant places, by means of electric-currents transmitted through metallic-circuits.

Name of Patentee.	Progres-sive Number.	Date.	Subject-matter of Patent.
WHEATSTONE, CHARLES　-	9022	7th July　1841	Producing, regulating, and applying electric-currents.
WHEATSTONE, CHARLES　-	10,041	8th Feb.　1844	Concertina and other musical-instruments in which the sounds are produced by the action of wind on vibratory springs.
WHEATSTONE, CHARLES　-	10,655	6th May　1845	Electric-telegraphs and apparatus relating thereto ;—in part applicable to other purposes.
WHEATSTONE, WILLIAM　-	4994	29th July　1824	Augmenting the tones of pianofortes, organs, and euphonons.
WHEELER, CHARLES　-　-	11,056	22nd Jan.　1846	Construction and working of railways.
WHEELER, DANIEL　-　-	4112	28th March 1817	Method of drying and preparing malt.
WHEELER, EDMUND　-　-	11,787	3rd July　1847	Valves for steam and other engines.
WHEELER, JOSHUA　-　-	632	27th June　1748	Preparing woollen-cloth and hats to keep out a day's or a week's rain, without impairing their beauty or strength.
WHEELER, ROBERT　-　-	5565	22nd Nov. 1827	Refrigerators for cooling fluids.
WHEELER, WILLIAM　-　-	127	24th June　1642	Raising water to great heights to bore timber with a wooden auger ; laying piles without driving ; raising weights.
WHEELEY, JOHN -　-　-	10,439	18th Dec.　1844	Manufacture of iron spoons.
WHEILDON, ISAAC -　-　-	2105	26th April 1796	Making and working presses, particularly packing presses and hot presses.
WHELDON, WILLIAM　-　-	12,261	4th Sept.　1848	Pumps or machinery for raising or forcing fluids.
WHELE, EDWIN　-　-　-	7758	2nd Aug.　1838	Manufacture of candles.
WHELE, EDWIN　-　-　-	9689	6th April　1843	Machinery for preparing wicks used in the making of candles.
WHIFFEM, THOMAS　-　-	12,969	21st Feb.　1850	Machinery for registering the delivery of goods.
WHILE, JOHN　-　-　-	9106	29th Sept. 1841	Horse-hoe, for use in agricultural purposes.
WHISHAW, FRANCIS　-　-	12,079	8th March 1848	Manufacture of pipes of earthenware, pottery, and glass ; certain applications and arrangements thereof.
WHITAKER, FRANCIS BURDETT	8763	31st Dec.　1840	Machinery for drawing cotton and other fibrous substances ;—applicable to warping and dressing yarns of the same.
WHITAKER, JAMES -　-　-	5486	24th April 1827	Machinery for piecing cardings from carding-engines, and for drawing, slubbing, and spinning wool and cotton.
WHITAKER, JAMES -　-　-	6625	12th June　1834	Engines used for carding wool.
WHITAKER, RICHARD　-　-	9059	4th Sept.　1841	Cutting the edges of books, and paper for other purposes ; impressing ornaments, letters and figures, on the binding of books and on other surfaces.
WHITBOURN, JAMES　-　-	4709	27th Sept. 1822	Construction of wheels of carriages, and all other vertical wheels of a certain size.
WHITBY, JAMES　-　-　-	2537	3rd Sept.　1801	Mill for grinding bark.
WHITCHER, JOHN -　-　-	4709	27th Sept. 1822	Construction of wheels of carriages, and all other vertical wheels of a certain size.
WHITCHER, JOHN -　-　-	7218	8th Nov.　1836	Drags, or apparatus applicable to carriages.
WHITE, CHARLES -　-　-	8004	18th March 1839	Ploughs.
WHITE, CHARLES -　-　-	8108	17th June　1839	Ploughs, harrows, scarifiers, cultivators, and horse-hoes.

Name of Patentee.	Progres-sive Number.	Date.	Subject-matter of Patent.
WHITE, CHARLES - - -	8517	28th May 1840	Ploughs and certain other agricultural implements.
WHITE, CHARLES - - -	9654	2nd March 1843	Machinery for raising and forcing fluids.
WHITE, DAVID BLAIR - -	12,919	8th Jan. 1850	Ballasting and stowing cargo in ships and other vessels.
WHITE, ELIHU - - -	2979	23rd Oct. 1806	Machine for founding types, letters, spaces and quadrats, used in printing.
WHITE, GEORGE - - -	3520	20th Jan. 1812	Preventing accidents from carriages.
WHITE, HENRY - - -	473	23rd Dec. 1724	Engine for raising and discharging water in and out of ships.
WHITE, JAMES - - -	1650	20th May 1788	Mechanical motion to be applied to clocks and time-pieces, jacks for roasting, and cranes for raising weights, also to other purposes.
WHITE, JAMES - - -	4485	11th July 1820	Machinery for preparing and spinning wool, cotton, and other fibrous substances, and uniting several threads into one; combinations of the same with other machinery.
WHITE, JAMES - - -	5559	8th Nov. 1827	Apparatus for filtering. "Artificial Spring."
WHITE, JAMES - - -	7199	4th Oct. 1836	Railways.
WHITE, JAMES - - -	8267	12th Nov. 1839	Machinery for moulding clay into the form of bricks and tiles, also for mixing and moulding other substances.
WHITE, JAMES - - -	13,201	31st July 1850	Machinery for bruising, crushing, and expressing juice from certain vegetable substances.
WHITE, JOHN - - -	278	7th Oct. 1691	Preserving flesh, fowl, fish and many other things, by liquors or otherwise.
WHITE, JOHN - - -	644	23rd June 1749	Making a liquor and spirit of sulphur with brimstone and saltpetre.
WHITE, JOHN - - -	2450	15th Nov. 1800	Lamp-burner.
WHITE, JOHN - - -	3269	29th Sept. 1809	Substance capable of being converted into statues, artificial-stone, bricks, tiles, and other descriptions of pottery.
WHITE, JOHN - - -	3653	3rd March 1813	Machine for cooking without wood or coal.
WHITE, JOHN - - -	3870	27th Dec. 1814	Making candles.
WHITE, JOHN - - -	4887	15th Jan. 1824	Floating breakwater.
WHITE, JOHN - - - [White, John, junior.]	5031	6th Nov. 1824	Air-furnace, for melting or fusing metallic substances.
WHITE, JOHN - - -	5457	1st Feb. 1827	Construction of pistons or buckets for pumps.
WHITE, JOHN - - -	6319	10th Oct. 1832	Construction of pumps or engines for raising water and other fluids.
WHITE, JOHN - - -	6402	28th March 1833	Machinery to be worked by steam or other power;—applicable to raising water and to other purposes.
WHITE, JOHN - - -	7119	15th June 1836	Rotatory steam-engine;—applicable to other purposes.
WHITE, JOHN - - -	7510	19th Dec. 1837	Apparatus usually employed in lathes for turning metals and other substances.
WHITE, JOHN - - -	7692	18th June 1838	Construction of railroads, bridges, and viaducts.
WHITE, JOHN - - -	7823	27th Sept. 1838	Construction of ovens and heated air-stoves.
WHITE, JOHN - - -	8484	23rd April 1840	Vices.

Name of Patentee.	Progressive Number.	Date.	Subject-matter of Patent.
WHITE, JOHN - - -	10,969	27th Nov. 1845	Apparatus for raising and forcing water.
WHITE, JOHN - - -	14,034	24th March 1852	Ship-building.
WHITE, JOSEPH - - -	3768	14th Dec. 1813	Steam-engines.
WHITE, PHILLIP - - -	74	12th Sept. 1634	Making iron-chains for mooring ships.
WHITE, ROBERT - - -	7473	14th Nov. 1837	Manufacture of ornamental lace.
WHITE, ROBERT - - -	14,034	24th March 1852	Ship-building.
WHITE, SAMUEL WHITE -	8303	9th Dec. 1839	Preventing persons from being drowned.
WHITE, STEPHEN - - -	11,654	15th April 1847	Means of producing gas, both as to apparatus and materials from which the gas is produced.
WHITE, STEPHEN - - -	12,536	26th March 1849	Manufacture of gases; the application thereof for heating and consuming smoke; also furnaces for economizing heat; and apparatus for the consumption of gases.
WHITE, THOMAS ANGEL -	2464	16th Jan. 1801	Making bricks.
WHITE, WILLIAM - - -	767	25th Jan. 1762	White crucibles, for melting metals and salts.
WHITE, WILLIAM - - -	1681	12th May 1789	Machine for expelling foul air from mines, ships, jails, hospitals, chambers, or other close places.
WHITE, WILLIAM - - -	5328	7th Feb. 1826	Manufacture of hats.
WHITECHURCH, JOHN - -	5129	17th March 1825	Hinges for doors, cupboards, and sashes of houses, also for book-cases, and show-cases;—applicable to all purposes where hinges are used.
WHITECHURCH, RICHARD -	5129	17th March 1825	Hinges for doors, cupboards, and sashes of houses, also for book-cases, and show-cases;—applicable to all purposes where hinges are used.
WHITEHEAD, JAMES HEY-[WOOD.	8672	2nd Nov. 1840	Manufacture of woollen-belts, bands, or driving-straps.
WHITEHEAD, JAMES HEY-[WOOD.	13,254	12th Sept. 1850	Filters.
WHITEHEAD, JOHN - -	6922	5th Nov. 1835	Scouring and cleansing.
WHITEHEAD, JOHN - -	10,290	15th Aug. 1844	Process of finishing fustians or beaverteens, satin-tops, or other similar cotton fabrics.
WHITEHEAD, JOHN - -	10,872	10th Oct. 1845	Machinery for combing, heckling, and straightening wool, flax, tow, and other fibrous substances.
WHITEHEAD, JOHN - -	12,603	8th May 1849	Preparing, combing, and heckling fibrous matters.
WHITEHEAD, JOHN - -	13,903	20th Jan. 1852	Bleaching and dyeing, washing, scouring, and other processes connected therewith.
WHITEHEAD, JOHN - -	14,050	29th March 1852	Machinery for preparing, combing, and drawing wool, silk, cotton, and other fibrous substances.
WHITEHEAD, JOHN DICKEN -	5738	15th Dec. 1828	Making cartridges for sporting and for other purposes.
WHITEHOUSE, CORNELIUS -	5109	26th Feb. 1825	Manufacturing tubes for gas and for other purposes.
WHITEHOUSE, CORNELIUS -	7982	26th Feb. 1839	Manufacturing tubes for gas and for other purposes. (*Extension to James Russell for 6 years from the 26th February 1839, and assigned to him.*)
WHITEHOUSE, CORNELIUS -	9287	7th March 1842	Manufacture of welded iron-tubing.

Name of Patentee.	Progressive Number.	Date.	Subject-matter of Patent.
WHITEHOUSE, CORNELIUS -	10,696	3rd June 1845	Machinery for welding and hammering; manufacture of gun-barrels and other tubes.
WHITEHOUSE, ISAAC - -	1077	31st Aug. 1774	Method of making buttons, studs, bracelets, necklaces, lockets, rings, watch-chains, boxes and trinkets.
WHITEHOUSE, ISAAC - -	1584	23rd Jan. 1787	Plates and dishes for table-service; plates and dishes as substitutes for water-plates and dishes; and plates as substitutes for warming-pans or bed-pans.
WHITEHOUSE, JOHN - -	8366	28th Jan. 1840	Preparing and rolling iron and other metals or alloys for the manufacture of certain articles of commerce.
WHITEHOUSE, JOHN - -	8969	25th May 1841	Making boilers to be used in marine steam-engines.
WHITEHOUSE, JOHN, junior -	8620	7th Sept. 1840	Construction of spring-hinges and door-springs.
WHITEHOUSE, THOMAS - -	1102	3rd Oct. 1775	Cast hinges ready jointed, or with false knuckles and pins in cast-iron.
WHITELAW, ALEXANDER -	12,508	7th March 1849	Manufacturing iron.
WHITELAW, GEORGE - -	8845	15th Feb. 1841	Propelling vessels through the water; steam-engine when used in connection therewith;—partly applicable to other purposes.
WHITELAW, JAMES - -	8061	7th May 1839	Rotary machine to be worked by the pressure and reaction of a column of water, and which may be used as a steam-engine; also a water meter and a machine for raising water by its centrifugal force.
WHITELAW, JAMES - -	8845	15th Feb. 1841	Propelling vessels through the water; steam-engine when used in connection therewith;—partly applicable to other purposes.
WHITELAW, JAMES - -	9099	23rd Sept. 1841	Rotary machines to be worked by water.
WHITELAW, JAMES - -	13,706	31st July 1851	Steam-engines.
WHITELEY, JOHN - -	8262	7th Nov. 1839	Warp-machinery.
WHITELEY, NATHAN - -	10,500	28th Jan. 1845	Machinery for raising the nap or pile on woollen, cotton, or other cloths, also for brushing and cleaning the same.
WHITELEY, THOMAS - -	6748	22nd Jan. 1835	Warp-machinery employed in the manufacture of lace and other fabrics.
WHITELEY, THOMAS - -	8262	7th Nov. 1839	Warp-machinery.
WHITESIDE, ROBERT - -	6719	20th Nov. 1834	Wheels of steam-carriages: and machinery for propelling such carriages;—applicable to other purposes.
WHITFIELD, ROBERT - -	7474	14th Nov. 1837	Composition, called " Indelible safety and durable black fluid writing-ink."
WHITFIELD, SAMUEL - -	3195	23rd Jan. 1809	Application of stamps, dies and piercing tools, to the manufacture of ears, handles and bewells for culinary articles of every description, and whether in wood, iron, brass, copper, tin, silver or mixed metals.
WHITFIELD, SAMUEL - -	3687	28th April 1813	Mountings for culinary and other utensils.
WHITFIELD, THOMAS BRAD-[SHAW.	7314	4th March 1837	Producing parallel motion to the piston-rods of pumps for lamps and other purposes;—applicable to machinery in general where parallel motion is required.
WHITFIELD, WILLIAM - -	3553	15th April 1812	One side compound lever steel-yard.
WHITFIELD, WILLIAM - -	3802	9th April 1814	Carriages.

Name of Patentee.	Progressive Number.	Date.	Subject-matter of Patent.
WHITFIELD, WILLIAM - -	5321	19th Jan. 1826	Manufacture of handles for saucepans, kettles and other culinary vessels, also tea-kettle handle straps and other articles.
WHITFORD, SAMUEL - -	7712	30th June 1838	Making certain parts of gun and pistol locks.
WHITHAM, GEORGE - -	4243	8th April 1818	Machinery for grinding, glazing, and dressing small cotton and woollen spindles for use in spinning-machines.
WHITHAM, WILLIAM - -	7938	15th Jan. 1839	Engines to be worked by steam, water, or other fluids.
WHITING, HENRY - - -	10,732	23rd June 1845	Apparatus for shaping the brims of hats.
WHITING, JOHN - - -	4318	5th Dec. 1818	Window-shutter.
WHITING, JOHN - - -	5445	9th Jan. 1827	Window-sashes and frames.
WHITING, JOHN - - -	7076	3rd May 1836	Preparing certain farinaceous food.
WHITLAW, CHARLES - -	5336	18th Feb. 1826	Administering medicines by the agency of steam or vapour.
WHITLEY, JAMES - - -	11,803	19th July 1847	Washing, scouring and drying wool, alpaca, mohair, cotton and other fibrous substances.
WHITLOCK, WILLIAM - -	1011	5th April 1772	Composition or " Artificial wood," applicable for the purposes of carving, casting and modelling.
WHITLOW, CHARLES - -	3925	14th June 1815	Making certain manufactures from certain American plants.
WHITMORE, Captain THOMAS -	108	28th July 1637	Making vitriol out of copper-ore, preparing and drawing water from copper-ore, by which to make copper out of iron, also preparing any manner of ore so as by water to separate the silver therefrom without melting.
WHITMORE, Captain THOMAS -	113	12th Dec. 1637	Making good and merchantable tough iron according to the nature of the mine, with sea-coal or peat, and with one fifth of the expense of charcoal as now used.
WHITMORE, WILLIAM - -	1705	29th Oct. 1789	Pumping ships and vessels under way, by means of wheels and other machinery, without manual labour.
WHITMORE, WILLIAM - -	1782	16th Nov. 1790	Making the shanks or eyes for buttons, by the application of rollers, presses and other implements.
WHITMORE, WILLIAM - -	1877	15th May 1792	Machine for mashing malt and other grain, to be worked by steam, water, wind, horses, or other power.
WHITMORE, WILLIAM - -	2079	4th Jan. 1796	Weighing-machines.
WHITMORE, WILLIAM - -	3371	14th Aug. 1810	Magnetic-toy to facilitate the teaching of children to spell, read and cypher, in any tongue.
WHITTAKER, JOHN WILLIAM-[SON.	8069	20th May 1839	Uniting straps or bands for driving machinery, and for other purposes; apparatus for effecting the same.
WHITTINGTON, WILLIAM -	1986	7th May 1794	Machine for roasting meat or other food.
WHITTINGTON, WILLIAM -	2118	28th June 1796	Portable baking-stove.
WHITTLE, THOMAS - -	4183	10th June 1817	Kiln for drying malt, wheat, oats, barley, and other substances, by means of steam aided by air.
WHITTMORE, AMOS - -	2322	26th June 1799	Making cards for carding cotton-wool, silk, and other things.

Name of Patentee.	Progressive Number.	Date.	Subject-matter of Patent.
WHITTON, JOHN - - -	2400	10th May 1800	Lead-saccharum for the use of calico-printers, and for other useful purposes.
WHITWORTH, CHARLES FRE-[DERICK.	12,483	17th Feb. 1849	Preventing accidents on railways.
WHITWORTH, JAMES - -	9126	21st Oct. 1841	Looms for weaving.
WHITWORTH, JOHN - -	1755	8th July 1790	Plating silver upon pure or block tin, and making therewith silver-plated goods and wares.
WHITWORTH, JOSEPH - -	6566	27th Feb. 1834	Machinery for cutting screws.
WHITWORTH, JOSEPH - -	6813	14th April 1835	Machinery for spinning and doubling cotton, flax, wool, silk, and other fibrous substances.
WHITWORTH, JOSEPH - -	6850	11th June 1835	Tools or apparatus for turning, boring, planing, and cutting metals and other materials.
WHITWORTH, JOSEPH - -	6926	10th Nov. 1835	Machinery for knitting and producing a fabric similar to that of knitted stockings.
WHITWORTH, JOSEPH - -	7095	17th May 1836	Machinery for spinning and doubling cotton-wool and other fibrous substances.
WHITWORTH, JOSEPH - -	7226	19th Nov. 1836	Machinery for spinning and doubling cotton-wool and other fibrous substances.
WHITWORTH, JOSEPH - -	7332	28th March 1837	Tools or apparatus for turning, boring, planing, and cutting metals and other materials.
WHITWORTH, JOSEPH - -	7441	5th Oct. 1837	Tools or apparatus for turning, boring, planing, and cutting metals and other materials.
WHITWORTH, JOSEPH - -	7453	2nd Nov. 1837	Locomotive and other steam-engines.
WHITWORTH, JOSEPH - -	8188	7th Aug. 1839	Tools or apparatus for planing, boring, and cutting metals or other substances.
WHITWORTH, JOSEPH - -	8475	15th April 1840	Apparatus for cleaning and repairing roads or ways; — applicable to other purposes.
WHITWORTH, JOSEPH - -	8705	17th Nov. 1840	Tools or apparatus for cutting and shaping metals and other substances.
WHITWORTH, JOSEPH - -	9433	2nd Aug. 1842	Machinery for cleaning roads;—applicable to other purposes.
WHITWORTH, JOSEPH - -	11,504	21st Dec. 1846	Machinery for knitting.
WHITWORTH, JOSEPH - -	12,907	19th Dec. 1849	Machinery for cutting metals; machinery applicable to agricultural and sanitary purposes.
WHITWORTH, THOMAS SCHO-[FIELD.	10,537	3rd March 1845	Machinery for preparing, spinning and doubling cotton-wool, flax, silk, and other fibrous materials.
WHITWORTH, THOMAS SCHO-[FIELD.	10,584	2nd April 1845	Machinery for preparing, spinning, and doubling cotton-wool, flax, silk, and other fibrous materials.
WHITWORTH, THOMAS SCHO-[FIELD.	12,785	24th Sept. 1849	Machinery for preparing, spinning, and doubling cotton-wool, flax, silk, and other fibrous materials.
WHITWORTH, THOMAS SCHO-[FIELD.	14,203	6th July 1852	Machinery for spinning and doubling cotton and other fibrous substances.
WHYTOCK, PATRICK - -	2913	8th March 1806	Manufacture of piece-goods composed of cotton, flax, hemp, or a mixture of any two of them, so as to resist the rotting action of wet or moisture.

Name of Patentee.	Progres-sive Number.	Date.		Subject-matter of Patent.
WHYTOCK, RICHARD - -	6307	8th Sept.	1832	Manufacture to facilitate the production of regular figures or patterns on different fabrics, particularly velvet, velvet-pile, and Brussels, Wilton, and Turkey carpets.
WHYTOCK, RICHARD - -	7986	1st March	1839	Process and apparatus for the production of regular figures or patterns in carpets and other fabrics.
WHYTOCK, RICHARD - -	11,328	11th Aug.	1846	Manufacture to facilitate the production of regular figures or patterns on different fabrics, particularly velvet, velvet-pile, and Brussels, Wilton, and Turkey carpets.
WHYTOCK, RICHARD - -	13,834	27th Nov.	1851	Applying colours to yarns or threads, and weaving or producing fabrics when coloured or partly coloured yarns or threads are employed.
WICKENS, HENRY - - -	14,246	31st July	1852	Obtaining motive-power.
WICKES, JOHN BAPTIST -	8524	30th May	1840	Machinery employed in frame-work knitting or stocking fabrics.
WICKES, JOHN BAPTIST -	9883	21st Sept.	1843	Machinery employed in the manufacture of frame-work knitted and looped fabrics.
WICKHAM, THOMAS - -	4769	24th March	1823	Compound paste and liquid for improving and colouring lace, net, and other manu-factured articles of flax, cotton-wool, silk, or other animal or vegetable sub-stance, and whether composed of in-terstices, or open or close work, and to be applied in dressing or getting up the same.
WICKHAM, THOMAS - -	4846	11th Sept.	1823	Prepared rice, for use in all cases where starch is applied.
WICKSTEED, THOMAS - -	13,526	24th Feb.	1851	Manufacture of manure; machinery to be used therein.
WIESMANN, WILLIAM - -	8271	16th Nov.	1839	Making alum.
WIGFULL, THOMAS - -	2055	2nd June	1795	Machine for separating grain from the straw and refuse, and which may be worked by hand or cattle, or by the alteration of its outward apparatus may be worked by any power.
WIGGIN, HENRY - - -	13,152	24th June	1850	Metallic alloys.
WIGGIN, HENRY - - -	13,439	2nd Jan.	1851	Metallic alloys.
WIGLEY, THOMAS - - -	6437	20th June	1833	Pulp-strainer, to be used in making paper.
WIGSTON, WILLIAM - -	4829	11th Aug.	1823	Steam-engines.
WIGSTON, WILLIAM - -	6458	12th Aug.	1833	Apparatus for consuming smoke;—appli-cable to the furnaces of steam-boilers, and to furnaces for other purposes.
WIGSTON, WILLIAM - -	8839	8th Feb.	1841	Apparatus for conveying signals or tele-graphic communication.
WILCOCK, JOSEPH - - -	11,744	12th June	1847	Ventilation of mines.
WILCOX, ANN - - -	2365	20th Dec.	1799	Playing-cards. " Brilliant new invented Knight's Cards."
WILD, CHARLES HEARD -	9524	25th Nov.	1842	Constructing floors for fire-proof buildings.
WILD, CHARLES HEARD -	9535	3rd Dec.	1842	Switch for railway purposes.
WILD, CHARLES HEARD -	11,597	24th Feb.	1847	Constructing parts of railways.
WILD, CHARLES HEARD -	13,226	17th Aug.	1850	Structures for retaining water.
WILD, WILLIAM - -	11,391	2nd Oct.	1846	Machinery for manufacturing barrels and other vessels of capacity.

Name of Patentee.	Progressive Number.	Date.	Subject-matter of Patent.
WILD, WILLIAM - - -	12,371	16th Dec. 1848	Rotary steam-engines.
WILDE, ARNOLD - - -	2033	19th Jan. 1795	Making and manufacturing plane-irons, scythes, sickles, hay-knives, and other edge-tools, from a preparation of cast-steel and iron united and incorporated together by fire.
WILDE, ARNOLD - - -	2134	25th Aug. 1796	Making and manufacturing from iron and steel, or both united, saws, steel-doctors for printers, plates, beads, mouldings, fender-plates, springs, and other articles.
WILDE, JOHN - - -	6926	10th Nov. 1835	Machinery for knitting and producing a fabric similar to that of knitted stockings.
WILDE, WILLIAM - - -	2479	17th Feb. 1801	Machinery to be annexed to harrows.
WILDER, RICHARD - -	519	21st Sept. 1730	Inventions in the art of throwing silk, as supplying the place of the hand in winding, and the need of the lead in throwing; two machines for twisting threads three together; another machine with bobbins fitted thereto, to double raw silk on the spindle as the same moves round in throwing; a frame and bobbins, put on the spindle for throwing single and double raw silk; and a foot-wheel for the more even and perfect drawing of single raw silk.
WILDES, GEORGE - - -	8735	16th Dec. 1840	Manufacture of white-lead.
WILDES, GEORGE - - -	9064	4th Sept. 1841	Manufacture of white-lead.
WILDES, GEORGE WASHING- [TON.	6411	15th April 1833	Machinery for cutting marble and other stones, and cutting or forming mouldings in grooves thereon.
WILDEY, HENRY - - -	952	26th Jan. 1770	Axletree with a washer, box, and collars, to be fixed on the arms of the axletree, and, by jack-wheels enclosed in the said box is applicable to common axletrees now in use, but not upon centres.
WILDEY, HENRY - - -	1942	25th March 1793	Wheel-iron for a coach, chariot, chaise, phaeton, or any other four-wheeled carriage, improved by means of a screwed box, nut, or eye, which, passing through the wheel and being screwed on the fore axletree, and also to the inside of the splinter-bar, by aid of a screwed box end, will keep the same in its proper position, and prevent the fore wheels coming off while in action; axletree double box for wheeled-carriages, constructed to contain and supply itself with oil for several months, without having to be taken off for the purpose of being oiled.
WILDEY, HENRY - - -	2307	16th April 1799	Applying springs to the poles or shafts of two-wheeled carriages. "Anti-Mobile."
WILDGOOSE, THOMAS - -	6	17th Jan. 1618	Engines and other inventions to plough grounds, whether inland or upland, and to fertilize barren peats and sea-sands; also to raise water, and to make boats on the water move in calms as swiftly as full-sailed boats in great winds, and with more security in storms.
WILDING, HENRY - - -	12,690	4th July 1849	Engines and machinery for obtaining and applying motive-power.

Name of Patentee.	Progressive Number.	Date.	Subject-matter of Patent.
WILDSMITH, JAMES HENRY [STAPLE.	12,380	21st Dec. 1848	Purification of naphtha, pyroligneous-acid, eupion, and other products of the destructive distillation of wood, peat, and other vegetable matters, and of acetate of lime and shale; purification of coal-tar and mineral naphtha, also spirit, being the products of fermentation.
WILKES, CHARLES - -	3713	29th June 1813	Naves and centres of wheels for carriages; and centres for wheels of machinery for various purposes.
WILKES, JOHN - - -	2526	10th July 1801	Making self-acting cylindrical spring snuffers.
WILKES, JOHN ASTON - -	4066	30th Sept. 1816	Manufacturing glass icicles, spangles, and other ornamental glass, with loops of the same material.
WILKES, JOSEPH - - -	2463	16th Jan. 1801	Making paste to be used in weaving and sizing calico, and for pasting paper, &c.
WILKES, SAMUEL - - -	8352	21st Jan. 1840	Manufacture of hinges.
WILKES, SAMUEL - - -	8477	16th April 1840	Manufacture of vices.
WILKES, SAMUEL - - -	10,638	26th April 1845	Manufacture of hinges.
WILKES, SAMUEL - - -	12,604	8th May 1849	Manufacture of knobs, handles, and spindles for the same, for doors and other purposes; locks.
WILKES, SAMUEL - - -	13,865	19th Dec. 1851	Manufacture of kettles, saucepans, and other cooking-vessels.
WILKEY, JOHN FRY - -	9483	29th Sept. 1842	Carriages.
WILKIE, JOHN - - -	8861	2nd March 1841	Constructing elastic seats or surfaces of furniture.
WILKIE, JOHN - - -	10,199	23rd May 1844	Machinery for working wood into the various forms required for making doors, window-shutters, window-sashes, mouldings, and floorings, and for other purposes.
WILKINS, ALEXANDER - -	12,447	30th Jan. 1849	Heating and boiling liquids.
WILKINS, EDWARD - -	10,678	22nd May 1845	Manufacture of leather.
WILKINS, EDWARD - -	13,631	13th May 1851	Labels or tickets.
WILKINS, JOHN WALKER -	11,218	26th May 1846	Water-closets.
WILKINS, STEPHEN - -	2314	25th May 1799	Composition of a gum to be used in calico printing.
WILKINS, WILLIAM CRANE -	8486	28th April 1840	Lighting and lamps.
WILKINS, WILLIAM CRANE -	11,429	29th Oct. 1846	Lamps and apparatus connected therewith;—partly applicable to the raising of water.
WILKINS, WILLIAM CRANE -	13,003	11th March 1850	Ventilating; heating and lighting; lamps and candlesticks; manufacture of candles; apparatus for such purposes.
WILKINS, WILLIAM CRANE -	13,318	7th Nov. 1850	Lighting; apparatus for lighthouses, signal, floating, and harbour lights.
WILKINS, WILLIAM CRANE -	13,649	29th May 1851	Railway buffers.
WILKINSON, CHARLES HUN- [NINGS.	4587	8th Sept. 1821	Retort or vessel for making coal and other gas, and for distillation, evaporation, and concentration of acids and other substances.
WILKINSON, DAVID - -	10,867	10th Oct. 1845	Obtaining motive-power.
WILKINSON, ENOCH - -	11,573	9th Feb. 1847	Looms for weaving.
WILKINSON, GEORGE - -	13,995	4th March 1852	Ships' pumps, and other pumps.
WILKINSON, HENRY - -	8119	22nd June 1839	Fire-arms.

Name of Patentee.	Progressive Number.	Date.	Subject-matter of Patent.
WILKINSON, HENRY - -	9174	9th Dec. 1841	Machinery to be used in constructing buildings, and in raising and lowering weights and materials.
WILKINSON, HENRY - -	9372	31st May 1842	Unloading shipping, especially "colliers."
WILKINSON, ISAAC - -	565	8th July 1738	Cast metallic boxes, made of iron, bell-metal, brass, or other mixed metal, for smoothing linen; bellows of cast metal for forges, furnaces, or any other works.
WILKINSON, ISAAC - -	675	24th Jan. 1753	Cast metallic rolls for crushing, flattening, bruising or grinding malt, oats, beans, or any kind of grain.
WILKINSON, ISAAC - -	713	12th March 1757	Machine or bellows to be wrought by water or fire engines.
WILKINSON, ISAAC - -	723	21st April 1758	Casting guns or cannon, fire-engines, cylinders, pipes, sugar-rolls, and such like instruments.
WILKINSON, JEPTHA AVERY -	4162	23rd Aug. 1817	Application of machinery for manufacture of weavers' reeds, by water and other power.
WILKINSON, JOHN - - -	824	7th Feb. 1765	Medicated baths constructed on frames for floating on water; floats made of cork, in the form of a seaman's waistcoat, to be used to prevent drowning.
WILKINSON, JOHN - - -	1063	27th Jan. 1774	Casting and boring iron guns or cannon.
WILKINSON, JOHN - - -	1694	30th July 1789	Making cannon or other ordnance with metal, together with its shot, shell, or arrow.
WILKINSON, JOHN - - -	1733	13th March 1790	Apparatus for preserving the lives of mariners and others in cases of shipwreck, and in all situations where people are exposed to the danger of drowning.
WILKINSON, JOHN - - -	1735	13th March 1790	Method of making lead-pipes.
WILKINSON, JOHN - - -	1857	2nd March 1792	Rolling or flatting iron and other metals, by means of steam-engines or any other power.
WILKINSON, JOHN - -	1993	2nd June 1794	Making cast-metal or pig-iron from the ore, for the purpose of making it into bar or malleable iron.
WILKINSON, JOHN - -	2316	28th May 1799	Boilers applicable to salt-pans or any other purpose.
WILKINSON, JOHN - -	2321	18th June 1799	Making ceruse or white-lead.
WILKINSON, JOHN - -	3097	23rd Jan. 1808	Making cast-iron from the ore, which when made into bar-iron equals that from Sweden.
WILKINSON, JOSIAH - -	10,984	8th Dec. 1845	Filtering water and other fluids.
WILKINSON, SAMUEL - -	5211	16th July 1825	Looms and implements connected therewith.
WILKINSON, SAMUEL - -	5235	11th Aug. 1825	Apparatus for preventing coaches, carriages, mails, and other vehicles from overturning.
WILKINSON, SAMUEL - -	5575	4th Dec. 1827	Mangle. "Bullman's patent Cabinet Mangle."
WILKINSON, SAMUEL - -	10,624	17th April 1845	Machine for washing, wringing, and mangling.
WILKINSON, SMITH - -	124	8th Feb. 1640	Making candles, taps, links, and torches, with oil and other things.
WILKINSON, THOMAS - -	7809	13th Sept. 1838	Construction of tramways or railways; and carriages to be used thereon.

Name of Patentee.	Progres-sive Number.	Date.	Subject-matter of Patent.
WILKINSON, WILLIAM - -	2873	9th Aug. 1805	Pantiles for covering houses and other buildings.
WILKINSON, WILLIAM - -	3634	5th Jan. 1813	Making horse-shears, wool-shears, and glovers' shears.
WILKINSON, WILLIAM - -	6845	2nd June 1835	Machinery by which steam-power is applied to give motion to ships or other floating vessels in or through water.
WILKINSON, WILLIAM - -	12,329	16th Nov. 1848	Construction of coke-ovens; machinery to be connected therewith.
WILKINSON, WILLIAM - -	12,387	21st Dec. 1848	Construction and manufacture of vices.
WILKINSON, WILLIAM - -	12,840	10th Nov. 1849	Looped or elastic fabrics and articles made therefrom; machinery for producing the same;—applicable in whole or in part to the manufacture of looped fabrics generally.
WILKINSON, WILLIAM - -	13,596	17th April 1851	Machinery for manufacturing textile and woven fabrics, and other articles of fibrous or filamentous materials; textile and other fabrics.
WILKS, CHARLES - - -	3749	9th Nov. 1813	Constructing four-wheeled carriages; facilitating the turning thereof without having recourse to locks, or without the necessity of making the fore-wheels lower than the hinder, or of raising the bodies of such carriages higher than usual.
WILKS, JAMES - - -	5286	8th Nov. 1825	Engine for cutting nails, sprigs, and sparables.
WILKS, JOHN - - - -	396	2nd April 1714	Engine or mill for grinding wood dry for the purposes of dyeing.
WILKS, JOHN - - - -	5934	28th April 1830	Parts of apparatus for making paper by machinery.
WILKS, JOSEPH BROWNE -	5399	2nd Aug. 1826	Producing steam for steam-engines and for other purposes.
WILKS, JOSEPH BROWNE -	9687	4th April 1843	Treating oils obtained from certain vegetable matters.
WILKS, JOSEPH BROWNE -	11,774	3rd July 1847	Manufacturing oil from certain nuts, and producing a vegetable substance; application thereof for giving light and for other uses.
WILKS, MATTHIAS - - -	3229	20th April 1809	Compound substance or cake for feeding horses and other animals.
WILKS, MATTHIAS - - -	4739	20th Dec. 1822	Refining oil produced from seed.
WILKS, SAMUEL - - -	8225	26th Sept. 1839	Boxes and pins or screws for vices and presses.
WILLAN, ROBERT - - -	13,693	17th July 1851	Machinery or apparatus for manufacturing textile-fabrics.
WILLANS, PETER - - -	5245	20th Aug. 1825	Fulling-mills or machinery for fulling and washing woollen cloths or other fabrics requiring the processes of felting or fulling.
WILLCOX, RICHARD - -	2493	30th April 1801	Fire or steam engine and furnace.
WILLCOX, RICHARD - -	2574	23rd Jan. 1802	Steam-engine furnace, or boiler and air-pump.
WILLCOX, RICHARD - -	2804	19th Dec. 1804	Machinery for cutting, stripping, or plucking furs of beavers and seals, also wool, hair, &c. from skins now cut and stripped by hand; preparing and cleansing such skins.
WILLCOX, RICHARD - -	2915	8th March 1806	Machinery for glazing and graining leather.
WILLCOX, RICHARD - -	2936	21st May 1806	Steam-engines.

Name of Patentee.	Progressive Number.	Date.	Subject-matter of Patent.
WILLCOX, RICHARD　-　-	3112	3rd March 1808	Machinery or apparatus whereby objects in the sea or clear water, can be discerned from the surface; raising, suspending, and towing into harbour ships or vessels that may be sunk at sea; removing sunken rocks or other obstructions in rivers, harbours, and channels.
WILLCOX, RICHARD　-　-	3222	3rd April　1809	Machinery for accelerating the making of felt or stuff hats, and for cutting fur from skins of animals.
WILLCOX, RICHARD　-　-	3223	3rd April　1809	Machinery for facilitating the making of stuff, wool and other hats and bonnets felted.
WILLCOX, THOMAS　-　-	3697	22nd May 1813	Machine for the prevention and cure of smoky chimneys, and which consists of a hollow cap of copper or other metallic substance or of clay, with a funnel to carry off the smoke; this machine when fixed on the top of a chimney with two or more courses of brickwork, will prevent smoke being driven back into the room, by excluding wind from the orifice of the chimney, and promoting draft by means of a continual accumulation of rarefied air in the cavity of the cap.
WILLCOX, THOMAS　-　-	4362	28th April 1819	Pneumatic-stove, for heating atmospheric air, and diffusing the same through houses, hot-houses, green-houses, and other buildings.
WILLDAY, SAMUEL　-　-	918	21st Feb.　1769	Machine for drying malt with coal or other fuel without communicating any unpleasant taste or flavour to the malt.
WILLIAMES, PRYCE BUCKLEY	10,302	29th Aug. 1844	Manufacture of artificial stone.
WILLIAMES, PRYCE BUCKLEY	10,562	17th March 1845	Manufacture of artificial stone.
WILLIAMS, [Sir] ABRAHAM, [Knight.	65	1st Oct.　1633	Charking coals, dressing and qualifying them for smelting and making iron and other metals.
WILLIAMS, CHARLES　-　-	3368	2nd Aug.　1810	Machine for grinding or cutting malt, splitting beans or any other kind of grain, and various other articles.
WILLIAMS, CHARLES JAMES [BLASINS.	7956	29th Jan.　1839	Two-wheeled carriages.
WILLIAMS, CHARLES WYE　-	7468	11th Nov. 1837	Means of preparing peat-moss or bog, to render it applicable for several useful purposes, particularly for fuel.
WILLIAMS, CHARLES WYE　-	7744	26th July 1838	Means of preparing peat-moss or bog, to render it applicable for several useful purposes, particularly for fuel.
WILLIAMS, CHARLES WYE　-	7770	14th Aug.　1838	Mode of purifying and preparing turpentine, resin, pitch, tar, or other bituminous matters, to increase their power of giving out light and heat either when distilled or burnt as fuel.
WILLIAMS, CHARLES WYE　-	8118	22nd June 1839	Boilers and furnaces for economizing fuel and heat.
WILLIAMS, CHARLES WYE　-	8703	17th Nov. 1840	Construction of furnaces and boilers.
WILLIAMS, CHARLES WYE　-	9215	11th Jan.　1842	Construction of furnaces; effecting combustion of the inflammable gases from coal.

Name of Patentee.	Progressive Number.	Date.		Subject-matter of Patent.
WILLIAMS, CHARLES WYE	9244	31st Jan.	1842	Making and moulding bricks, artificial fuel, and other substances.
WILLIAMS, DANIEL	9393	13th June	1842	Covering ridges and hips of the roofs of buildings.
WILLIAMS, DAVID LLOYD	13,396	7th Dec.	1850	Furnaces.
WILLIAMS, EDMUND WILLIAM	4386	26th June	1819	Distilling.
WILLIAMS, FITZWALTER	6474	21st Sept.	1833	Composition or liquid for polishing furniture and other articles. "Williams' French Polish reviver."
WILLIAMS, GEORGE	12,416	13th Jan.	1849	Preparing puddling-furnaces used in the manufacture of iron.
WILLIAMS, HERBERT READ	7973	21st Feb.	1839	Trusses and surgical bandages.
WILLIAMS, JAMES HENRY	13,291	17th Oct.	1850	Manufacture of buttons.
WILLIAMS, JOHN	20	10th May	1622	Making soap, also soap-ashes, pot-ashes, and salts for soaps.
WILLIAMS, JOHN	225	25th April	1683	Casting and making hollow pewter or block-tin buttons.
WILLIAMS, JOHN	295	22nd April	1692	Taking fish by means of a light burning some fathoms under water, and another burning above the water, by means of which the fish within the compass of a league can be drawn to one place, and thereby more easily taken.
WILLIAMS, JOHN	308	— —	1692	Engine for carrying four men fifteen fathoms or more under the surface the sea, whereby they may work twelve hours under water without danger.
WILLIAMS, JOHN	2355	4th Nov.	1799	Binding books.
WILLIAMS, JOHN	2600	24th March	1802	Disengaging horses from carriages.
WILLIAMS, JOHN	3086	9th Dec.	1807	Covering and enclosing carriages.
WILLIAMS, JOHN	3091	19th Dec.	1807	Method of preserving the equilibrium of carriages and vehicles, and preventing them overturning.
WILLIAMS, JOHN	3344	8th June	1810	Apparatus to be applied to and used with wheel-carriages.
WILLIAMS, JOHN	4716	18th Oct.	1822	Method to prevent the frequent removal of the pavement and carriage-paths for laying down and taking up pipes, and for other purposes.
WILLIAMS, JOHN	5352	27th April	1826	Ships'-hearths, and apparatus for cooking by steam.
WILLIAMS, JOHN	5401	4th Aug.	1826	Apparatus and process for separating salt from sea-water, and rendering it fresh and fit for use.
WILLIAMS, JOSEPH	306	2nd Dec.	1692	Engine, consisting of screws, wheels, and wrenches, for drawing and raising great weights; useful in raising minerals, buildings, and merchants' goods, loading and unloading ships, &c.
WILLIAMS, JOSEPH	2355	4th Nov.	1799	Binding books.
WILLIAMS, JOSEPH	9147	9th Nov.	1841	Manufacturing salt from brine.
WILLIAMS, ORLANDO HARRIS	5750	7th Jan.	1829	Paddles and machinery for propelling ships and other vessels on water.
WILLIAMS, OWEN	9040	4th Aug.	1841	Propelling vessels.
WILLIAMS, OWEN	13,941	31st Jan.	1852	Preparing compositions to be used in railway and other structures, in lieu of iron, wood, and stone.

Name of Patentee.	Progres-sive Number.	Date.	Subject-matter of Patent.
WILLIAMS, PETER - - -	5245	20th Aug. 1825	Fulling-mills or machinery for fulling and washing woollen-cloths, or such other fabrics as require the process of felting or fulling.
WILLIAMS, PETER - - -	5994	7th Sept. 1830	Apparatus or contrivance for preventing accidents in carriages, gigs, and other vehicles, by instantly liberating horses or other animals from the same when in danger or otherwise; locking and securing the wheels in like cases.
WILLIAMS, RICHARD - -	823	29th Jan. 1765	Making a fine, thin, and light cloth of silk and wool, with the appearance of super-fine Spanish cloth and superfine Irish ratteen.
WILLIAMS, RICHARD - -	880	14th July 1767	Making fire-stoves and registers.
WILLIAMS, RICHARD - -	1024	15th Oct. 1772	Manufacturing goods with cotton-weft on woollen, linen, or cotton warps, and dres-sing such goods with a long shag on their surface.
WILLIAMS, RICHARD - -	1272	11th Dec. 1780	Mortar or stucco for the use and purposes of building.
WILLIAMS, RICHARD - -	4118	13th May 1817	Manufacturing cards for dressing woollen-cloths.
WILLIAMS, RICHARD - -	5736	15th Dec. 1828	Application of elastic and dense fluids to the propelling of machinery of various descriptions.
WILLIAMS, RICHARD - -	6089	28th Feb. 1831	Steam-engines.
WILLIAMS, ROWLAND - -	9502	27th Oct. 1842	Machinery for raising, shearing, and finish-ing velvets and other piled goods, by power.
WILLIAMS, SAMUEL - -	3027	8th April 1807	Machinery for spinning wool, cotton, hemp, and other filamentous substances.
WILLIAMS, THOMAS - -	835	3rd Dec. 1765	Medicine called essence of flowers of Ben-zoin, or pulmonic drops.
WILLIAMS, THOMAS' - -	1191	7th May 1778	Smelting copper-ore whereby the arsenic is extracted from the metal, and it is brought to fine copper with less trouble and ex-pense than by the common process.
WILLIAMS, THOMAS - -	9350	17th May 1842	Churn.
WILLIAMS, THOMAS - -	10,987	10th Dec. 1845	Wrenches or spanners.
WILLIAMS, THOMAS ROBINSON	5215	16th July 1825	Lancet.
WILLIAMS, THOMAS ROBINSON	5411	19th Sept. 1826	Machine for separating burs or other sub-stances from wool, hair or fur.
WILLIAMS, THOMAS ROBINSON	5412	19th Sept. 1826	Manufacturing hats and caps with the assistance of machinery.
WILLIAMS, THOMAS ROBINSON	5699	11th Sept. 1828	Making hats, caps and bonnets, and cover-ing them with silk and other materials, by aid of machinery.
WILLIAMS, THOMAS ROBINSON	5791	23rd May 1829	Manufacturing felt or a substance in the nature thereof, applicable to covering the bottoms of vessels.
WILLIAMS, THOMAS ROBINSON	5899	6th Feb. 1830	Power-looms applicable to weaving wire and other materials.
WILLIAMS, THOMAS ROBINSON	6387	14th Feb. 1833	Combination of fibrous materials forming, by means of machinery, artificial skins, applicable to the purposes for which skins, leather, vellum and parchment are used.

Name of Patentee.	Progressive Number.	Date.	Subject-matter of Patent.
WILLIAMS, THOMAS ROBINSON	7901	12th Dec. 1838	Machinery for spinning, twisting or curling, and weaving horse-hair and other hairs, as well as various fibrous substances.
WILLIAMS, THOMAS ROBINSON	8230	28th Sept. 1839	Manufacture of flexible fibrous substances or compositions applicable to covering buildings and other useful purposes; machinery used therein.
WILLIAMS, THOMAS ROBINSON	8387	14th Feb. 1840	Manufacture of woollen and other fabrics, or fabrics of which wool or fur form a principal component part; machinery employed for the purpose.
WILLIAMS, THOMAS ROBINSON	8474	15th April 1840	Obtaining power from steam and elastic vapours or fluids; means employed in generating the same; using these improvements in conjunction with distillation or evaporation, and for other useful purposes.
WILLIAMS, THOMAS ROBINSON	8611	27th Aug. 1840	Measuring the velocities with which ships or other vessels or bodies move in fluids; ascertaining the velocities of fluids in motion.
WILLIAMS, THOMAS ROBINSON	8646	24th Sept. 1840	Manufacture of woollen fabrics or fabrics of which wools, furs, or hairs are the principal components; machinery used therein.
WILLIAMS, THOMAS ROBINSON	10,591	7th April 1845	Preparation and manufacture of certain fibrous and other materials, for the production of a fabric to be used in lieu of horse-hair seating and cloth.
WILLIAMS, THOMAS ROBINSON	10,774	21st July 1845	Process and machinery for rendering paper and wrappers waterproof.
WILLIAMS, WALTER	98	26th July 1636	Charking sea-coals.
WILLIAMS, WILLIAM	1148	6th March 1776	Composition of gold, silver and metal, for making coat and waistcoat-buttons.
WILLIAMS, WILLIAM	3667	15th March 1813	Certain process for extracting arsenic from ores or other substances containing it.
WILLIAMS, WILLIAM	6594	17th April 1834	Preparing certain metals applicable to sheathing the bottoms of ships, and to other purposes.
WILLIAMS, WILLIAM	8587	3rd Aug. 1840	Ploughs.
WILLIAMS, WILLIAM	9474	22nd Sept. 1842	Machinery for ploughing, harrowing and raking land, and cutting food for animals.
WILLIAMS, WILLIAM	12,711	18th July 1849	Communicating intelligence by means of electricity; electric-clocks.
WILLIAMS, WILLIAM	12,991	7th March 1850	Electric and magnetic apparatus for indicating and communicating intelligence.
WILLIAMS, WILLIAM MORRETT	8181	1st Aug. 1839	Lock and key.
WILLIAMS, WILLIAM MORRETT	8402	27th Feb. 1840	Lock and key.
WILLIAMS, WILLIAM MORRETT	9395	13th June 1842	Construction of locks and keys.
WILLIAMSON, JAMES	821	5th Dec. 1764	Turning ovals in pewter, English-china and all earthenwares.
WILLIAMSON, SAMUEL	2992	4th Dec. 1806	Weaving cotton, silk, woollen, worsted and mohair, separately or together, by looms.
WILLIAMSON, WILLIAM	1910	18th Oct. 1792	Fire or steam engine for draining and working mines, working mills, turning wheels or raising water.
WILLIS, ABRAHAM	3407	6th March 1811	Method of producing steel toys, as barbers' curling-irons, sugar-nippers, snuffers, and other articles.

Name of Patentee.	Progres-sive Number.	Date.	Subject-matter of Patent.
WILLIS, HENRY - - -	13,538	28th Feb. 1851	Construction of organs.
WILLIS, JOSEPH - - -	1503	3rd Nov. 1785	Dressing and preparing leather with turned feet, for boots, half-boots, spatterdashes or gaiters; making such articles without any seam in the instep; preparing leather for shoes, and making shoes without any heel-seam or side-seam.
WILLIS, RICHARD - - -	29	4th March 1624	Three engines for drawing and draining water out of mines, minerals and coal-pits; and for raising and bringing water into towns, castles, and houses.
WILLIS, ROBERT - - -	4343	13th Feb. 1819	Pedal-harp,
WILLIS, ROBERT - - -	8384	12th Feb. 1840	Apparatus for weighing.
WILLIS, THOMAS - - -	10,720	12th June 1845	Machinery for spinning, doubling, and winding cotton, silk, woollen, and linen yarns.
WILLIS, THOMAS - - -	14,151	1st June 1852	Machinery for winding yarns or threads; looms for weaving.
WILLMORE, JOSEPH - -	3137	28th May 1808	Method and processes in the manufacture of nails.
WILLMORE, THOMAS - -	2497	2nd May 1801	Article for hats, soldiers' caps, helmets, &c.
WILLOUGHBY, FRANCES -	1855	27th Feb. 1792	Machine for thrashing corn.
WILLOUGHBY, Lord FRANCIS	141	4th Feb. 1663	Making and framing sugar-mills.
WILLOUGHBY, MONCREIFFE -	4806	26th June 1823	Construction of vessels.
WILLSON, HUGH BOWLSBY -	13,811	13th Nov. 1851	Construction of rails for railways.
WILLSON, JAMES - - -	1897	5th July 1792	Construction of fire-arms for the better protection of the powder in bad weather.
WILLSON, JAMES - - -	2070	22nd Oct. 1795	Preventing the effects of moisture on the human body, and facilitating relief in inflammatory and spasmodic complaints arising from it and other causes.
WILLSON, ISAAC - - -	3763	29th Nov. 1813	Stove-grates to prevent smoky rooms, and for obtaining increased heat from the same quantity of fuel.
WILMOT, EDWARD COKE -	3068	10th Aug. 1807	Instrument for warming beds;—applicable to various other purposes.
WILMOT, EDWARD COKE -	10,325	26th Sept. 1844	Apparatus for warming beds, persons, carriages, and rooms.
WILMOT, JOHN - - -	3104	28th Jan. 1808	Warming-pans applicable for airing and warming beds, rooms, or carriages, and for other purposes requiring a long and protracted heat.
WILMS, HENRY - - -	4116	8th May 1817	Artificial leg, arm, and hand.
WILSON, ALEXANDER - -	2865	3rd July 1805	Shot-belts, powder-flasks, and fire-arms.
WILSON, ALEXANDER - -	10,787	29th July 1845	Spinning hemp and flax, and other fibrous materials.
WILSON, ALFRED - - -	13,017	23rd March 1850	Ventilator.
WILSON, BENJAMIN - -	4206	23rd Jan. 1818	Machine for breaking, swingling, and preparing flax or hemp.
WILSON, CHARLES - -	6629	17th June 1834	Machinery used in the preparation for spinning of wool and other fibrous substances.
WILSON, CHARLES ROBERT -	2674	20th Jan. 1803	Apparatus for stopping ungovernable horses.
WILSON, CHRISTOPHER -	2068	15th Oct. 1795	Combining timbers applicable to naval architecture, and all large works composed of wood.

Name of Patentee.	Progres-sive Number.	Date.	Subject-matter of Patent.
WILSON, CHRISTOPHER -	2593	9th March 1802	Obtaining a vacuum or vacua for gaining powers applicable to hydraulic, pneumatic, and mechanical machines or engines, or any others where fluids, steam, or vapour may be used or applied.
WILSON, CHRISTOPHER -	2964	30th Aug. 1806	System of naval architecture.
WILSON, DANIEL - - -	4029	14th May 1816	Apparatus to be employed in the distillation of animal, vegetable, and mineral substances, and in various other processes
WILSON, DANIEL - - -	4095	23rd Jan. 1817	Process of boiling and refining sugar.
WILSON, DANIEL - - -	4106	1st March 1817	Gas-light apparatus and processes; philosophical instruments.
WILSON, DANIEL - - -	4220	3rd Feb. 1818	Process of boiling and refining sugar.
WILSON, DAVID - - -	13,795	3rd Nov. 1851	Presses and matting; process of and apparatus for treating fatty and oily matters; manufacture of candles and night-lights.
WILSON, EDWARD BROWN -	10,480	18th Jan. 1845	Machinery for twisting, roving, and spinning cotton, flax, silk, wool, and other fibrous substances.
WILSON, EDWARD BROWN -	10,954	18th Nov. 1845	Apparatus applicable to swivel-bridges and turn-tables.
WILSON, EDWARD GRIBBEN -	12,228	1st Aug. 1848	Construction of tin-drums or rollers used in machinery for drawing, spinning, doubling, twisting, and throwing cotton-wool, silk, flax, and other fibrous substances.
WILSON, ELIEZER CHATER -	7697	22nd June 1838	Evaporation.
WILSON, GEORGE - - -	1852	11th Feb. 1792	Instrument calculated to detect and prevent delay in delivery of letters and parcels; "Post and Commercial time marker."
WILSON, GEORGE - - -	8318	16th Dec. 1839	Steam-whistles, adapted for locomotive-engines and boilers, and for other purposes.
WILSON, GEORGE - - -	8353	21st Jan. 1840	Paper cutting-machine.
WILSON, GEORGE - - -	10,230	19th June 1844	Cutting paper for manufacture of envelopes, and for other purposes.
WILSON, GEORGE - - -	13,690	17th July 1851	Machine to open and clean tow, and tow-waste from flax, hemp, and other similar fibrous substances; improved mode of piecing straps and belts of driving-machinery; machine for effecting the same.
WILSON, GENERAL GEORGE -	10,269	24th July 1844	Construction of chimneys and flues, furnaces, stoves, grates, or fire-places generally.
WILSON, GEORGE FERGUSSON	9542	8th Dec. 1842	Operating on certain organic bodies or substances, to obtain products therefrom for the manufacture of candles, and for other purposes.
WILSON, GEORGE FERGUSSON	9944	16th Nov. 1843	Manufacture of candles; apparatus for and process of treating fatty and other substances for making candles, and for other uses.
WILSON, GEORGE FERGUSSON	10,000	28th Dec. 1843	Manufacture of candles; treating fatty and oily matters to obtain products for the manufacture of candles, and for other uses.
WILSON, GEORGE FERGUSSON	10,191	20th May 1844	Treating certain fatty and oily matters; manufacture of candles and soap.

Name of Patentee.	Progressive Number.	Date.	Subject-matter of Patent.
WILSON, GEORGE FERGUSSON	10,365	29th Oct. 1844	Manufacture of night-lights.
WILSON, GEORGE FERGUSSON	10,371	31st Oct. 1844	Treating fatty and oily matters; and manufacture of candles.
WILSON, GEORGE FERGUSSON	10,435	12th Dec. 1844	Treating fatty and oily matters; and manufacture of candles.
WILSON, GEORGE FERGUSSON	10,551	13th March 1845	Manufacture of candles when palm oil is used.
WILSON, GEORGE FERGUSSON	10,664	10th May 1845	Treating certain inflammable matters; and manufacture of candles and soap.
WILSON, GEORGE FERGUSSON	10,870	10th Oct. 1845	Manufacture of soap.
WILSON, GEORGE FERGUSSON	11,008	20th Dec. 1845	Treating inflammable matters; and manufacture of candles.
WILSON, GEORGE FERGUSSON	11,146	25th March 1846	Producing light; materials and apparatus applicable thereto; treating fatty and oily matters.
WILSON, GEORGE FERGUSSON	11,470	1st Dec. 1846	Process of and apparatus for treating fatty and oily matters; and manufacturing candles and night-lights.
WILSON, GEORGE FERGUSSON	11,633	23rd March 1847	Production of light; manufacture or preparation of materials applicable thereto.
WILSON, GEORGE FERGUSSON	12,040	25th Jan. 1848	Treating and manufacturing certain fatty or oily matters; manufacturing candles and night-lights.
WILSON, GEORGE FERGUSSON	12,390	28th Dec. 1848	Production of light by burning oleic-acid in lamps; construction of lamps; manufacture or preparation of oleic-acid for that purpose.
WILSON, GEORGE FERGUSSON	12,501	28th Feb. 1849	Separating the more liquid from the more solid parts of fatty and oily matters; separating the same from foreign matters.
WILSON, GEORGE FERGUSSON	12,512	14th March 1849	Manufacture of candles and night-lights.
WILSON, GEORGE FERGUSSON	13,795	3rd Nov. 1851	Presses and matting; process of and apparatus for treating fatty and oily matters; manufacture of candles and night-lights.
WILSON, GEORGE FERGUSSON	13,837	31st Dec. 1851	Treating fatty and oily matters; manufacture of lamps, candles, night-lights, and soap.
WILSON, GEORGE FERGUSSON	13,907	22nd Jan. 1852	Preparation of wool for the manufacture of woollen and other fabrics; obtaining materials to be used for the purpose.
WILSON, HENRY - - -	432	7th July 1721	Making and printing globular charts or sea-charts for use in navigation.
WILSON, HENRY - - -	12,272	21st Sept. 1848	Manufacture of chisels and gouges.
WILSON, JACOB - - -	3910	27th April 1815	Bedsteads and bed-furniture.
WILSON, JACOB - - -	4828	11th Aug. 1823	Construction and manufacture of window-blinds.
WILSON, JACOB - - -	9346	9th May 1842	Bedsteads.
WILSON, JAMES - - -	12,594	1st May 1849	Trusses.
WILSON, JAMES BUCK - -	12,835	8th Nov. 1849	Wire-ropes.
WILSON, JAMES GODFREY -	12,562	3rd April 1849	Obtaining perfect combustion, and apparatus relating thereto;—applicable to furnaces and fire-places of every description.
WILSON, JAMES GODFREY -	12,595	1st May 1849	Manufacture of glass; machinery and apparatus connected therewith.
WILSON, JAMES PILLANS -	10,294	29th Aug. 1844	Treating fatty and oily matters; manufacture of candles.

Name of Patentee.	Progressive Number.	Data.	Subject-matter of Patent.
WILSON, JAMES PILLANS -	10,306	9th Sept. 1844	Treating fatty and oily matters; manufacture of candles.
WILSON, JAMES PILLANS -	10,365	29th Oct. 1844	Manufacture of night-lights.
WILSON, JAMES PILLANS -	10,371	31st Oct. 1844	Treating fatty and oily matters; and manufacture of candles.
WILSON, JAMES PILLANS -	10,435	12th Dec. 1844	Treating fatty and oily matters; and manufacture of candles.
WILSON, JAMES PILLANS -	10,551	13th March 1845	Manufacture of candles when palm oil is used.
WILSON, JAMES PILLANS -	10,664	10th May 1845	Treating certain inflammable matters; and manufacture of candles and soap.
WILSON, JAMES PILLANS -	10,870	10th Oct. 1845	Manufacture of soap.
WILSON, JAMES PILLANS -	11,008	20th Dec. 1845	Treating inflammable matters; manufacture of candles.
WILSON, JAMES PILLANS -	11,146	25th March 1846	Producing light; materials and apparatus applicable thereto; treating fatty and oily matters.
WILSON, JAMES PILLANS -	13,907	22nd Jan. 1852	Preparation of wool for the manufacture of woollen and other fabrics; obtaining materials to be used for the purpose.
WILSON, JAMES PILLANS -	14,294	18th Sept. 1852	Manufacture of cloths; preparation of wool for the manufacture of woollen and other fabrics; preparation of materials to be used for these purposes.
WILSON, JAMES THOMSON -	12,541	28th March 1849	Manufacture of sulphuric-acid and alum.
WILSON, JAMES THOMSON -	13,389	7th Dec. 1850	Manufacture of alum; and obtaining ammonia.
WILSON, JOHN - - -	1701	29th Aug. 1789	Platting goods manufactured on the stocking-frame, by a machine to be annexed to the frame for that purpose.
WILSON, JOHN - - -	2626	31st May 1802	Purifying, clarifying, reducing, separating, and decompounding fluids.
WILSON, JOHN - - -	7879	22nd Nov. 1838	Process of manufacturing alkali from common salt.
WILSON, JOHN - - -	8399	25th Feb. 1840	Process of manufacturing carbonate of soda.
WILSON, JOHN - - -	8656	7th Oct. 1840	Process of engraving on metals by means of voltaic electricity.
WILSON, JOHN CHARLES -	14,334	21st Oct. 1852	Machinery and process employed on and for the manufacture of flax and other fibrous vegetable substances.
WILSON, JOHN HEWITSON -	4866	18th Nov. 1823	Manufacture of hats and bonnets.
WILSON, MELVIL - -	5436	20th Dec. 1826	Machinery for cleaning rice.
WILSON, MELVIL - -	5898	6th Feb. 1830	Method of preparing and cleansing paddy or rough rice.
WILSON, RICHARD - -	7091	12th May 1836	Manufacturing fire-places, slabs, columns, monuments, and cornices.
WILSON, RICHARD - -	10,200	23rd May 1844	Manufacture of tiles.
WILSON, ROBERT - - -	9164	2nd Dec. 1841	Manufacture of leather.
WILSON, ROBERT - - -	9570	22nd Dec. 1842	Locomotive and other steam-engines.
WILSON, ROBERT - - -	11,399	8th Oct. 1846	Looms for weaving velvets and other piled goods; machinery for cutting the pile or nap of the same.

Name of Patentee.	Progressive Number.	Date.	Subject-matter of Patent.
WILSON, ROBERT - - -	11,767	26th June 1847	Machinery and the arrangements thereof, for forging, stamping, punching, cutting, and pressing, metals and other substances.
WILSON, ROBERT - - -	12,026	13th Jan. 1848	Certain kinds of rotatory-engines worked by steam or other elastic fluids; — partly applicable to rotatory-engines worked by water or wind; safety valves for steam-boilers.
WILSON, ROBERT - - -	12,644	7th June 1849	Steam-engines and boilers; methods of preventing accidents in working the same.
WILSON, ROBERT CHRISSOP -	7433	14th Sept. 1837	An earthenware tile, slab, or plate.
WILSON, STEPHEN - - -	4543	8th March 1821	Machinery for weaving figured goods.
WILSON, STEPHEN - - -	4714	18th Oct. 1822	Manufacture of worsted.
WILSON, STEPHEN - - -	4795	31st May 1823	Machinery for weaving and winding.
WILSON, STEPHEN - - -	5010	7th Oct. 1824	Machinery for making velvets and other cut works.
WILSON, STEPHEN - - -	5042	25th Nov. 1824	Manufacture of stuffs with transparent and coloured figures. " Diaphane Stuffs."
WILSON, THOMAS - - -	1278	16th Feb. 1781	Medicinal composition, as a remedy for agues and intermittent fevers.
WILSON, THOMAS - - -	2635	23rd July 1802	Uniting, combining, and connecting metallic patent-blocks for the construction of arches.
WILSON, WILLIAM - - -	2494	30th April 1801	Making, adjusting, and stamping scale-weights.
WILSON, WILLIAM - - -	5515	4th July 1827	Means of extracting spirits and other solvents used in dissolving gums and other articles, for stiffening hats, hat-bodies, bonnets, caps, and divers articles of merchandise; converting into use such spirits after rectification.
WILSON, WILLIAM - - -	9874	24th Aug. 1843	Preparation of a material produced from a vegetable substance; and its application for affording light and for other uses.
WILSON, WILLIAM - - -	12,677	27th June 1849	Cutting plastic tubes or tiles.
WILSON, WILLIAM GILMOUR -	10,640	29th April 1845	Construction of wheels for carriages.
WILSON, WILLIAM GILMOUR -	12,397	30th Dec. 1848	Formation of moulds and cores of moulds for casting iron and other substances.
WILTON, RICHARD - - -	17	15th July 1620	Making camlets after the Turkish manner.
WIMSHURST, HENRY - -	8671	2nd Nov. 1840	Steam-vessels; communicating power to propellors of steam-vessels; shipping and unshipping propellers.
WIMSHURST, HENRY - -	13,340	12th Nov. 1850	Steam-engines, propelling; construction of ships and vessels.
WINANS, ROSS - -	5796	30th May 1829	Diminishing friction in wheeled-carriages to be used on rail and other roads;—applicable to other purposes.
WINBALL, SAMUEL - -	333	10th April 1694	Diving-machine, whereby persons may descend twenty fathoms or more in the sea, and remain twenty-four hours.
WINCH, ROBERT - • -	4273	18th June 1818	Machinery to communicate power and motion to other machinery requiring reciprocating or alternating motion.

Name of Patentee.	Progressive Number.	Date.	Subject-matter of Patent.
WINCH, ROBERT - - -	4464	18th May 1820	Machines or presses, chiefly applicable to printing.
WINCH, ROBERT - - -	5116	5th March 1825	Rotatory pumps, for raising and forcing water or other liquids.
WINCH, ROBERT - - -	6067	29th Jan. 1831	Printing-machines.
WINCHESTER, JAMES - -	9530	15th Dec. 1741	Steam-boilers ; and methods of applying steam or other power to locomotive purposes.
WINDLE, HENRY CHRISTOPHER	7321	13th March 1837	Means of giving elasticity, freedom of action, and durability to certain parts of pens or instruments for writing ; also obtaining a supply and flow of ink to the same.
WINDSOR, THOMAS LORD -	223	21st Nov. 1682	Making wet harbours and docks, to hold ships from ten to forty feet above high water mark ; also engines and means for raising ships from the river Thames, or from stocks, into the said harbours, and vice versâ.
WINFIELD, ROBERT WALTER - [Winfield, Robert Water.]	5573	4th Dec. 1827	Tubes or rods, produced by a new method of manufacture; manufacturing the same into part of bedsteads and other articles.
WINFIELD, ROBERT WALTER - [Wingfield Robert Water.]	6206	22nd Dec. 1831	Construction of bedsteads ;—applicable to other articles.
WINFIELD, ROBERT WALTER -	8891	22nd March 1841	Metallic bedsteads ; — applicable to other articles of metallic furniture.
WINFIELD, ROBERT WALTER -	12,268	14th Sept. 1848	Manufacture of tubes ; manufacture of certain articles made in part of tubes.
WINFIELD, ROBERT WALTER -	12,302	2nd Nov. 1848	Construction and manufacture of metallic bedsteads, couches, and sofas.
WINFIELD, ROBERT WALTER -	13,576	25th March 1851	Bedsteads and couches, or articles for sitting, lying, or reclining upon.
WINGFIELD, SAMUEL - -	1389	2nd Oct. 1783	Machine for cooking.
WINIWATER, JOSEPH MAXI- [MILIAN RETTER VON.	13,935	29th Jan. 1852	Locks of fire-arms and cannon ; gun-matches, or mode of igniting gunpowder in guns; machinery for manufacturing the same.
WINKLES, BENJAMIN - -	8542	11th June 1840	Arrangement and construction of paddle-wheels and water-wheels.
WINLAW, WILLIAM - -	1486	21st June 1785	Mill for separating the grain from the ears of corn.
WINN, JOHN - - - -	879	4th July 1767	Machine, in case of a ship being in distress on a lee shore, where a boat cannot live, and for other purposes.
WINROW, JOHN - - -	7866	8th Nov. 1838	Means of and apparatus for destroying weeds and insects in land.
WINSLOW, GEORGE - -	11,419	15th Oct. 1846	Machinery for manufacturing files and rasps.
WINSLOW, GEORGE - -	11,786	3rd July 1847	Machinery for manufacturing files and rasps.
WINSLOW, JOHN FLACK - -	14,051	31st March 1852	Machinery for blooming iron.
WINSOR, FREDERICK ALBERT [Winsor, Frederic Albert.]	2764	18th May 1804	Oven, stove, or apparatus for extracting inflammable air, oil, pitch, tar, and acids from all kinds of fuel, and reducing the same into coke and charcoal.

Name of Patentee.	Progres-sive Number.	Date.	Subject-matter of Patent.
WINSOR, FREDERICK ALBERT - [*Winsor, Frederic Albert.*]	3016	20th Feb. 1807	Oven, stove, furnace, or apparatus for extracting inflammable air and oil from fuel, for acetous and ammoniacal liquors, reducing fuel into coke and charcoal; purifying such air or gas of its odour during a state of combustion.
WINSOR, FREDERICK ALBERT -	3113	3rd March 1808	Oven, stove, or apparatus for carbonizing raw fuel and combustibles, and reducing them into superior fuel of coke and charcoal; extracting during the same process the oil, acids, and gas; and extracting and refining all the inflammable air or gas, so as to deprive it of all disagreeable odour during combustion, and render it fit for human respiration when diluted with atmospheric air.
WINSOR, FREDERICK ALBERT -	3200	7th Feb. 1809	Oven, stove, or apparatus for carbonizing raw fuel and combustibles, and reducing them into superior fuel of coke and charcoal; extracting during the same process the oil, acids, and gas; and extracting and refining all the inflammable air and gas, so as to deprive it of all disagreeable odour during combustion, and render it fit for human respiration when diluted with atmospheric air.
WINSOR, FREDERICK ALBERT -	3253	3rd Aug. 1809	Fixed and moveable telegraphic lighthouse, for signals and intelligence, in rain, storm, and darkness.
WINSOR, FREDERICK ALBERT -	3510	4th Dec. 1811	Employing raw and refined sugars in the composition of sundry articles.
WINSOR, FREDERICK ALBERT -	9600	26th Jan. 1843	Apparatus for the production of light.
WINSOR, WILLIAM - - -	8394	22nd Feb. 1840	Preserving and using colours.
WINSPEAR, JOHN - - -	9715	27th April 1843	Reefing certain sails of ships and other vessels.
WINTER, FREDERICK - -	14,242	29th July 1852	Construction of machinery for supplying rotatory motion to carriages, vessels, and water-mills.
WINTER, GEORGE - - -	1563	18th Oct. 1786	Machine for drilling seeds, being more expeditious and regular, and requiring a less quantity of seed, is also capable of being regulated so as to increase or decrease the quantity of seed sown.
WINTER, HENRY - - -	11,996	15th Dec. 1847	Manufacture of rope, cord, line, and twine.
WINTER, HENRY JULIUS -	3861	12th Dec. 1814	Giving effect to various operating processes.
WINTER, JAMES - - -	3012	20th Feb. 1807	Machine for sewing and pointing leather-gloves.
WINTER, JAMES - - -	4627	19th Dec. 1821	Machine for sewing and pointing leather-gloves.
WINTER, JAMES, junior - -	10,412	2nd Dec. 1844	Scaffolding;—applicable also as a fire-escape for saving life and property.
WINTER, JAMES, senior - -	10,412	2nd Dec. 1844	Scaffolding;—applicable also as a fire-escape for saving life and property.
WINTER, JOHN - - -	4511	7th Nov. 1820	Chimney-caps, and application thereof.
WINTER, JOHN, junior - -	4111	18th March 1817	Joining and combining horn and tortoise-shell by heat and pressure, giving it the appearance of tortoiseshell with the strength and elasticity of horn, for manufacturing hair combs, ornamental and other combs, snuff-boxes, and other small boxes.

Name of Patentee.	Progressive Number.	Date.	Subject-matter of Patent.
WINTER, JOSEPH - - -	7686	14th June 1838	Painting or otherwise ornamenting the surfaces of leather, silk, cotton, or linen; applicable to the manufacture of gloves, stockings, and such like articles.
WINTER, RICHARD - - -	13,157	3rd July 1850	Metallic-vessels for measuring and holding liquids.
WINTER, ROBERT - - -	4781	22nd April 1823	Conducting the process of distillation.
WINTER, THOMAS - - -	326	9th Oct. 1693	Mill moved with jackwork and wheels, to grind corn and move saws by manual labour without the help of wind or water.
WINTER, THOMAS - - -	752	2nd Oct. 1760	Quadrant for taking observations at sea.
WINTER, THOMAS - - -	2507	2nd June 1801	Manufacture for covering the floors of rooms, and for covering and packing goods, useful also for other purposes.
WINTERBORN, JOHN - -	8967	22nd May 1841	Machinery to facilitate the removal of persons and property from premises, in case of fire;—applicable to raising and lowering weights, to assist servants cleaning windows, and as a substitute for scaffolding.
WINTERBOTTOM, ROBERT -	465	11th April 1724	Engine which works by means of suction; forming pumps by means of a screw or worm, for drawing water from mines or pits to a considerable height.
WINWOOD, DANIEL - -	1273	13th Dec. 1780	Manufacturing buckle-chapes.
WINWOOD, DANIEL - -	1293	28th May 1781	Making and fixing together buckle-chapes and tongues.
WIRE, DAVID WILLIAM - -	11,995	15th Dec. 1847	Manufacture of candles and other like articles used for affording light.
WISE, ANN - - - -	9841	13th July 1843	Construction of stays and umbilical belts.
WISE, CHARLES - - -	5545	21st Aug. 1827	Sizing, glazing, or beautifying the materials used in the manufacture of paper, pasteboard, Bristol-board, and other substances.
WISE, JOHN - - - -	571	7th Aug. 1740	Machine for the more extensive application of the fire-engine.
WISE, SAMUEL - - -	897	14th March 1768	Machine or engine for raising water out of mines and wells, and for draining lands.
WISE, SAMUEL - - -	925	11th May 1769	Machine which, when fixed to a stocking-frame, will make any sort of work usually manufactured on such frames.
WISE, STACEY - - -	5545	21st Aug. 1827	Sizing, glazing, or beautifying the materials used in the manufacture of paper, pasteboard, Bristol-board, and other substances.
WISEMAN, BENJAMIN - -	1399	15th Nov. 1783	Sails for windmills, with horizontal levers.
WISKER, JOHN - - -	6523	11th Dec. 1833	Machinery for grinding covers or stoppers for jars, bottles, and other vessels made of china, stone, or other earthenware.
WITHERBY, HENRY EDWARD -	2867	19th July 1805	Apparatus for purifying and improving water and other liquors, by filtration.
WITHERBY, THOMAS - -	2520	23rd June 1801	Pump; and method of working machinery.
WITHERELL, GEORGE -	11,823	29th July 1847	Manufacturing and working iron for various purposes.
WITHERS, JOHN - -	9939	16th Nov. 1843	Manufacture of glass.
WITTE, GERARD JOHN DE -	12,998	7th March 1850	Machinery, apparatus, metallic and other substances, for the purposes of letter-press and other printing.

Name of Patentee.	Progressive Number.	Date.	Subject-matter of Patent.
WITTERSTEDT, Baron CHARLES	8601	11th Aug. 1840	Preserving vegetable, animal and other substances, from ignition and decay.
WITTY, RICHARD - - -	3305	14th Feb. 1810	Making, arranging, and combining certain parts of rotative steam-engines, so as to dispense with the most complex parts of steam-engines as now used;—applicable to giving motion to all sorts of machinery.
WITTY, RICHARD - - -	3497	30th Oct. 1811	Construction of steam-engines.
WITTY, RICHARD - - -	3707	5th June 1813	Steam-engines; and tools useful in making parts of the same.
WITTY, RICHARD - - -	4498	16th Oct. 1820	Pumps for raising and conveying water and other liquids; applying a certain principle to ships' pumps; useful also for other purposes.
WITTY, RICHARD - - -	5133	25th March 1825	Lighting by gas.
WITTY, RICHARD - - -	5227	30th July 1825	Chimney for argand and other burners.
WITTY, RICHARD - - -	5427	13th Dec. 1826	Methods of applying heat to certain useful purposes.
WITTY, RICHARD - - -	5663	10th June 1828	Apparatus for making and supplying coal-gas for useful purposes.
WITTY, RICHARD - - -	6052	13th Dec. 1830	Apparatus for propelling carriages, boats, or vessels, and for other purposes, by the power of steam.
WITTY, RICHARD - - -	6681	25th Sept. 1834	Saving fuel and burning smoke; applicable to furnaces and stoves.
WITTY, RICHARD - - -	6942	3rd Dec. 1835	Method of arranging and combining certain materials used in constructing houses, bridges, and other buildings, whereby superior strength and durability will be obtained.
WITTY, WILLIAM - - -	6653	26th July 1834	Methods of abstracting heat from steam and other vapours and fluids; applicable to stills, breweries, and to other useful purposes.
WOLCOTT, ALEXANDEE SIMON	9672	18th March 1843	Photography, and application of the same to the arts.
WOLCOTT, ALEXANDER SIMON	10,228	18th June 1844	Roving and spinning cotton-wool and other fibrous substances.
WOLF, ROBERT - - -	6780	2nd March 1835	Construction of the sounding body of pianofortes on the principle of acoustics.
WOLFEN, JOHN JASPER -	4	1st July 1617	Making a certain oil to keep armour and arms from rust and canker.
WOLFEN, JOHN JASPER -	40	8th Dec. 1627	Engines, instruments and devices, for making and preparing certain stuffs and skins to hold out wet or rain.
WOLFEN, JOHN JASPER, Van -	65	1st Oct. 1633	Charking coals, dressing and qualifying them for smelting and making iron and other metals.
WOLFERSTAN, THOMAS - -	9632	11th Feb. 1843	Axletrees and axletree boxes.
WOLFF, ERNST - - -	6519	7th Dec. 1833	Mode of supplying stoves with heated air, without bellows or blow-pipe.
WOLFF, ERNST - - -	6546	23rd Jan. 1834	Means of supplying heated air in order to support combustion in enclosed fireplaces.
WOLFF, ERNST - - - [Wolf, Ernst.]	6600	26th April 1834	Steam-engines.

Name of Patentee.	Progressive Number.	Date.	Subject-matter of Patent.
WOLLASTON, AUGUSTIN -	404	25th June 1716	Extracting a sweet oil from an English vegetable, for use in the woollen manufacture, soap-making, leather-trades, &c.
WOLLASTON, CHARLTON JAMES	9858	1st Aug. 1843	Machinery for cutting marble and stone.
WOLLASTON, HENRY SEPTI-[MUS HYDE.	4675	4th June 1822	Bolt or fastening particularly applicable as a night-bolt.
WOLLASTON, WILLIAM HYDE	2752	9th Feb. 1804	Improvement in spectacles, by the application of concavo-convex glasses.
WOLLASTON, WILLIAM HYDE	2993	4th Dec. 1806	Instrument whereby a person may draw in perspective, or copy or reduce, any print or drawing.
WOLLER, SAMSON - - -	12,598	3rd May 1849	Machinery or apparatus for weaving.
WOLVERSON, JOSEPH - -	8543	13th June 1840	Locks, latches, and other fastenings for doors.
WOOD, CHARLES - - -	794	29th July 1763	Making fused or cast also cinder-iron malleable, with raw pit-coal.
WOOD, CHARLES - - -	6093	11th March 1831	Machinery for spinning cotton, silk, flax, wool, and other fibrous substances, and for throwing, doubling, and twisting threads and yarns.
WOOD, CONIAH - - -	1018	22nd May 1772	Machine or engine for spinning wool and Jersey-tow and flax into thread or yarn, and for spinning many threads at one and the same time on a number of spools.
WOOD, ENOCH - - -	3066	30th July 1807	Applying power for raising water from a lower to a higher level.
WOOD, FRANCIS - - -	489	21st Jan. 1727	Separating iron from iron-stone or iron-mine by means of sea or pit coal in an air-furnace, and thereby rendering the same as good as iron made with charcoal, and at the same time effecting a saving in the consumption of wood.
WOOD, GEORGE - - -	15	25th Oct. 1619	Printing on linen-cloth.
WOOD, HENRY - - -	739	25th May 1759	Fire-engine.
WOOD, HENRY - - -	2308	20th April 1799	Machine whereby the possessor thereof is enabled to publish to every one viewing the same, several purposes intended to be performed by him at any future given period of time, or within certain given intervals, with great ease and celerity, and without being subject to error. "Time setter."
WOOD, HENRY WALKER -	6520	11th Dec. 1833	Making white-lead or carbonate of lead.
WOOD, HENRY WALKER -	6795	18th March 1835	Obtaining certain oils.
WOOD, HENRY WALKER -	7097	17th May 1836	Locomotive-apparatus.
WOOD, HENRY WALKER -	8724	25th Nov. 1840	Producing an uneven surface in wood and other substances.
WOOD, HENRY WALKER -	13,386	7th Dec. 1850	Manufacture of fuel.
WOOD, JAMES - - -	1744	21st April 1790	Machines for washing and wringing linen, woollen, wool, cotton, silk, velvet, or any other commodity requiring washing, cleansing, or scouring.
WOOD, JAMES - - -	2381	19th March 1800	Clarionets;—in part applicable to wind-instruments played on with keys.
WOOD, JAMES - - -	3797	1st April 1814	German flute;— applicable also to the clarionet and bassoon.

Name of Patentee.	Progres-sive Number.	Date.	Subject-matter of Patent.
WOOD, JAMES - - -	4423	18th Dec. 1819	Formation and position of the long keys, B *natural* and C *sharp*, used on the clarionet, for the more easily fingering the same.
WOOD, JOHN - - - -	759	5th Feb. 1761	Making malleable iron from pig or sow metal.
WOOD, JOHN - - - -	778	6th July 1762	Warming beds by a warming-pan, without fire.
WOOD, JOHN - - - -	794	29th July 1763	Making fused or cast, also cinder iron malleable, with raw pit-coal.
WOOD JOHN - - - -	2711	14th June 1803	Machines for spinning and reeling cotton.
WOOD, JOHN - - - -	2747	10th Jan. 1804	Machine for spinning cotton, silk, and wool.
WOOD, JOHN - - - -	3779	10th Feb. 1814	Preparing flax for the purpose of being spun on the like machinery as cotton.
WOOD, JOHN - - - -	3879	4th Feb. 1815	Machinery used for preparing and spinning cotton-wool and various other articles.
WOOD, JOHN - - - -	3987	2nd March 1816	Machines applicable to every description of spinning.
WOOD, JOHN - - - -	4986	7th July 1824	Machinery for raising or dressing cloth.
WOOD, JOHN - - - -	5118	5th March 1825	Cleaning, milling, or fulling cloth.
WOOD, JOHN - - - -	5268	21st Oct. 1825	Machinery for raising and dressing cloth.
WOOD, JOHN - - - -	8319	16th Dec. 1839	Process in the application and laying on of the substances used in the printing, colouring, tinting, and ornamenting of china, porcelain, earthen and other similar wares, whereby such wares may be ornamented with various devices, and a variety of colours painted, shaded, mixed, and blended together in the same design and burnt into the substance of the wares; by a single process in the enamelling kiln.
WOOD, JOHN - - - -	8864	14th Aug. 1843	Machinery for lessening a ship's draft of water;—applicable to raising vessels or other heavy bodies, and for securing or supporting the same.
WOOD, JOHN - - - -	11,603	2nd March 1847	Machinery for spinning fibrous substances.
WOOD, MATTHEW - - -	2625	31st May 1802	Preparing a colour from malt, for the purpose of colouring spirits, wines, and other liquors.
WOOD, PETER - - -	13,399	11th Dec. 1850	Figuring and ornamenting woven fabrics; machinery employed therein.
WOOD, PETER - - -	13,523	24th Feb 1851	Printing, staining, figuring, and ornamenting woven and textile fabrics, wood, leather, or any other material; machinery employed therein.
WOOD, RICHARD - - -	6118	24th May 1831	Inking-apparatus to be used with certain descriptions of printing-presses.
WOOD, SUTTON THOMAS -	1447	20th Aug. 1784	Steam-engines; adapting and connecting boilers used in brewing, to any engines worked by steam and air, so as to render the steam produced from the boiling worts and the steam produced in brewing, capable of working those engines known by the name of fire or steam-engines.

Name of Patentee.	Progressive Number.	Date.	Subject-matter of Patent.
WOOD, SUTTON THOMAS -	1455	17th Nov. 1784	Application of steam; method of using the water produced from condensed steam, and applying the water to other purposes than that of working the steam-engine; also heating and applying water for brewing and distilling; constructing and adapting coppers, boilers, tubes, and other hollow bodies for heating water and worts; and rendering the same air-tight.
WOOD, SUTTON THOMAS -	1492	27th July 1785	Distilling, rectifying, refining, and preparing spirits, oils, sugars, salts, and other substances and solutions by steam.
WOOD, SUTTON THOMAS -	1860	15th March 1792	Weaving-engine or machine, rendering the same capable of being worked by or connected with wind, water, steam, fire, or air engines, also to engines worked by horse or any other power; and improvements on the engine or machine where manual labour only is applied.
WOOD, THOMAS - - -	1130	15th July 1776	Machine for carding and roving silk, cotton, and sheep's wool.
WOOD, THOMAS - - -	8657	7th Oct. 1840	Paving streets, roads, bridges, squares, paths, and such like ways.
WOOD, THOMAS - - -	11,348	25th Aug. 1846	Passenger-carriages.
WOOD, WILLIAM - - -	502	18th Sept. 1828	Making raw iron or iron metal, prepared in an air furnace with pit-coal immediately from iron-ore.
WOOD, WILLIAM - - -	3892	9th March 1815	Manufacture of materials, and the application thereof to making ships and vessels water-tight and seaworthy. "Adhesive Felt."
WOOD, WILLIAM - - -	5348	22nd April 1826	Apparatus for destroying fire-damp.
WOOD, WILLIAM - - -	6056	23rd Dec. 1830	Application of a battering-ram to the purpose of working coal in mines.
WOOD, WILLIAM - - -	8553	24th June 1840	Looms for weaving carpets and other fabrics.
WOOD, WILLIAM - - -	8806	21st Jan. 1841	Looms for weaving.
WOOD, WILLIAM - - -	9065	4th Sept. 1841	Looms for weaving.
WOOD, WILLIAM - - -	9329	26th April 1842	Weaving carpeting, and other figured fabrics.
WOOD, WILLIAM - - -	10,421	7th Dec. 1844	Printing, dyeing, staining, or producing marks or patterns in or upon woven, felted, and other fabrics.
WOOD, WILLIAM - - -	12,167	30th May 1848	Weaving carpets; printing carpets and other fabrics.
WOOD, WILLIAM - - -	12,937	23rd Jan. 1850	Manufacture of carpets and other fabrics.
WOOD, WILLIAM - - -	13,277	10th Oct. 1850	Manufacture of carpets and other fabrics.
WOOD, WILLIAM - - -	13,841	4th Dec. 1851	Manufacture and ornamenting of carpets, rugs, and other fabrics.
WOOD, WILLIAM - - -	14,108	1st May 1852	Manufacture of carpets and other fabrics; apparatus connected therewith.
WOOD, WILTON - - -	7750	26th July 1838	Making bands and tackling to be used in driving, turning, or carrying machinery.
WOODBRIDGE, FREDERICK -	13,247	5th Sept. 1850	Machinery for manufacturing rivets, bolts, and screw-blanks.
WOODBRIDGE, THOMAS - -	11,731	3rd June 1847	Steam-engines.
WOODCOCK, ALONZO BUONA-[PARTE.	10,877	10th Oct. 1845	Machinery or apparatus to be employed for raising coal or other matters from mines;—also applicable to raising or lowering men or animals, and to other purposes.

Name of Patentee.	Progressive Number.	Date.	Subject-matter of Patent.
WOODCOCK, ALONZO BUONA-[PARTE.	12,253	22nd Aug. 1848	Steam-engines; apparatus for raising, forcing, and conveying water and other fluids.
WOODCOCK, JOHN - - -	9381	7th June 1842	Construction of steam-engines.
WOODCROFT, BENNET - -	5424	18th Nov. 1826	Wheels and paddles for propelling boats and vessels.
WOODCROFT, BENNET - -	5480	31st March 1827	Processes and apparatus for printing and preparing for manufacture, yarns of linen, cotton, silk, woollen, or any other fibrous material.
WOODCROFT, BENNET - -	6250	22nd March 1832	Construction and adaptation of a revolving spiral paddle for propelling boats and other vessels on water.
WOODCROFT, BENNET - -	6848	4th June 1835	Printing calicoes and other fabrics, whether manufactured of cotton, silk, wool, or linen, or of all or any two or three of those materials.
WOODCROFT, BENNET - -	6939	3rd Dec. 1835	Printing calicoes and other fabrics, whether manufactured of cotton, silk, wool, or linen, or of all or any two or three of those materials.
WOODCROFT, BENNET - -	7138	2nd July 1836	Mode of printing certain colours on calico and other fabrics.
WOODCROFT, BENNET - -	7268	24th Dec. 1836	Mode of printing certain colours on calico and other fabrics.
WOODCROFT, BENNET - -	7529	4th Jan. 1838	Construction of looms for weaving various sorts of cloths, which looms may be set in motion by any adequate power.
WOODCROFT, BENNET - -	10,051	13th Feb. 1844	Propelling vessels.
WOODCROFT, BENNET - -	11,137	21st March 1846	Construction and adaptation of a revolving spiral paddle for propelling boats and other vessels on water. (*Extension for 6 years from the 22nd day of March* 1846.)
WOODCROFT, BENNET - -	11,250	22nd June 1846	Mode of printing certain colours on calico and other fabrics.
WOODCROFT, BENNET - -	13,476	30th Jan. 1851	Machinery for propelling vessels.
WOODCROFT, BENNET - -	14,359	26th July 1853	Construction of looms for weaving various sorts of cloths, which looms may be set in motion by any adequate power. (*Extension for seven years from the 4th day of January* 1852.)
WOODFALL, HENRY - -	11,395	3rd Oct. 1846	Machinery for making paper.
WOODHOUSE, JOHN - -	2912	20th Feb. 1806	Canals.
WOODHOUSE, JOHN - -	3324	6th April 1810	Canals.
WOODHOUSE, JOHN - -	4015	9th April 1816	Forming the ground for roads and pavements; paving and repairing old pavements and roads.
WOODHOUSE, JONATHAN -	2682	28th Feb. 1803	Forming a cast-iron rail or plate, for making railroads for the working and running of waggons and other carriages on public and other roads; fastening such rail or plate on such roads.
WOODHOUSE, ROGER - -	460	27th Jan. 1724	Rendering cast-iron malleable by means of coals without coking.
WOODIN, DENNIS - - -	10,581	27th March 1845	Forms of shoes for horses or other animals, and process of accomplishing the same.
WOODLEY, WILLIAM - -	8150	13th July 1839	Propelling vessels and carriages, and other machinery.
WOODMAN, JAMES - -	5476	22nd March 1827	Shaving-brushes and other brushes;—applicable to other purposes.

Name of Patentee.	Progressive Number.	Date.	Subject-matter of Patent.
WOODMAN, RICHARD - -	3392	8th Oct. 1810	Manufacturing boots, shoes, and other articles.
WOODMAN, WILLIAM - -	4841	11th Sept. 1823	Horse-shoe denominated " Bevilled heeled expanding Shoe."
WOODROFFE, GEORGE - -	477	26th April 1725	Machine or water-engine for clearing and taking out dust and soil from wheat or other grain.
WOODS, CHARLES - - -	9314	6th April 1842	Construction and make of driving-reins, harness bridles and reins, and bridles and reins for riding.
WOODS, EDWARD - - -	2338	13th Aug. 1799	Machinery for slitting, fashioning, pointing, sinking down, bottoming and founding of ivory, bone, horn, tortoise-shell and box combs ; and for cutting fustians.
WOODS, EDWARD - - -	12,679	28th June 1849	Turn-tables.
WOODS, FRANCIS FREDERICK -	13,374	30th Nov. 1850	Paving.
WOODS, GEORGE - - -	2718	28th June 1803	Constructing harps, harpsichords, pianofortes, violins, guitars, and other stringed musical instruments.
WOODS, JAMES - - -	3040	9th May 1807	Machine for churning milk and cream ; may be used as a pump.
WOODS, JOSEPH - - -	8963	22nd May 1841	Locomotive-engines ; machinery for the production of rotatory motion for obtaining mechanical power ;—also applicable for raising or impelling fluids.
WOODS, JOSEPH - - -	10,151	18th April 1844	Regulating the power and velocity of machines for communicating power.
WOODS, JOSEPH - - -	10,219	6th June 1844	Producing designs and copies ; and multiplying impressions either of printed or written surfaces.
WOODS, JOSEPH - - -	11,662	20th April 1847	Springs for supporting heavy bodies, and resisting sudden and continuous pressure.
WOODS, JOSEPH - - -	12,716	24th July 1849	Bleaching certain organic substances ; and manufacture of certain products therefrom.
WOODS, THOMAS - - -	13,576	25th March 1851	Bedsteads and couches, or articles for sitting, lying, and reclining upon.
WOODS, WILLIAM - - -	2099	17th March 1796	Hand-pump for raising water out of ships and other places.
WOODS, WILLIAM - - -	6320	11th Oct. 1832	Construction of metal pens.
WOODWORTH, ARAD - -	13,918	24th Jan. 1852	Machinery for manufacturing bricks, tiles, and other articles of a similar character.
WOODYATT, THOMAS MAYOS -	7862	8th Nov. 1838	Manufacture of wood-screws.
WOOLLAM, JOSEPH GRUNDY -	8913	3rd April 1841	Looms for weaving.
WOOLLAMS, JOSEPH - -	4477	20th June 1820	Teeth or cogs formed on or applied to wheels, pinions and other mechanical agents, for communicating or restraining motion.
WOOLLAMS, JOSEPH - -	4730	5th Dec. 1822	Wheeled-carriages to counteract the falling and facilitate the labour of animals attached to them, also to render persons and property in and near them secure from injury.
WOOLLAMS, JOSEPH - -	7235	24th Nov. 1836	Obtaining power and motion from known sources.
WOOLLAMS, JOSEPH - -	7381	30th May 1837	Obtaining power and motion from known sources.
WOOLLATT, WILLIAM - -	722	19th April 1758	Machine furnished with a set of turning-needles, and to be fixed to a stocking-frame for making turned ribbed-stockings, pieces, and other goods usually manufactured upon stocking-frames.

Name of Patentee.	Progressive Number.	Date.	Subject-matter of Patent.
WOOLLATT, WILLIAM - - [Woollat, William.]	734	10th Jan. 1759	Machine furnished with a set of turning-needles, and to be fixed to a stocking-frame for making turned ribbed-stockings, pieces, and other goods usually manufactured upon stocking-frames.
WOOLLERY, EDWARD - -	1034	2nd March 1773	Mill for grinding sugar-canes.
WOOLLETT, ALFRED - -	12,559	3rd April 1849	Gun-carriages.
WOOLLEY, EDWARD - -	4303	10th Nov. 1818	Machinery to make wood-screw forgings.
WOOLLEY, FLETCHER - -	7223	15th Nov. 1836	Preparation of materials to be used as a substitute for bees-wax;—partly applicable to other purposes.
WOOLLEY, THOMAS - -	11,285	8th July 1846	Pianofortes.
WOOLF, ARTHUR - - -	2726	29th July 1803	Apparatus for converting water or other liquids into vapour or steam, for working steam-engines, and heating water or other liquids.
WOOLF, ARTHUR - - -	2772	7th June 1804	Construction of steam-engines.
WOOLF, ARTHUR - - -	2863	2nd July 1805	Steam-engines.
WOOLF, ARTHUR - - -	3346	9th June 1810	Construction and working of steam-engines.
WOOLRICH, JOHN - - -	7131	22nd June 1836	Producing or making carbonate of barytes.
WOOLRICH, JOHN - - -	7830	11th Oct. 1838	Process of manufacturing white-lead.
WOOLRICH, JOHN STEPHEN -	9431	1st Aug. 1842	Coating with metal the surface of articles formed of metal or metallic alloys.
WOOLRICH, JOHN STEPHEN -	12,526	19th March 1849	Coating iron and certain other metals and alloys of metals.
WOOLRICH, JOHN STEPHEN -	12,970	21st Feb. 1850	Obtaining cadmium and other metals and products, from ores or matters containing them.
WOOLRYCHE, THOMAS BEST -	12,038	25th Jan. 1848	Manufacture of soda; treating products obtained in such manufacture.
WOOLSTENHOLME, JAMES -	1123	25th March 1776	Velveteens.
WOONE, GODFREY - - -	7389	12th June 1837	Forming plates with raised surfaces thereon, for printing impressions on different substances.
WOONE, GODFREY - - -	11,122	11th March 1846	Engraving in relief.
WORBY, WILLIAM - - -	9842	15th July 1843	Machinery and apparatus for ploughing and scarifying land and for raking; machinery and apparatus for thrashing, cutting and grinding for agricultural purposes; construction of whippletrees.
WORBY, WILLIAM - - -	10,237	24th June 1844	Manufacture of bricks, tiles, and other articles from plastic materials.
WORCESTER, EDWARD, Marquis [of.	131	8th Feb. 1661	Making a watch or clock to go for several weeks without spring, chain, or other method of winding-up; making guns or pistols answer fire to the tenth part of a minute, with a flask contrived for the purpose; engine applicable to a coach whereby the horses may be instantaneously disengaged in cases of emergency; invention to make a boat move to any part of the compass, whichever way the stream runs or the wind blows, the motive-power at the same time being obtained from such stream or wind, a steersman being the only requisite, the force of the stream or wind also being made to perform the work of a watermill or windmill while the boat stays to be loaded or unloaded.

Name of Patentee.	Progressive Number.	Date.	Subject-matter of Patent.
WORDSWORTH, JOHN - -	3987	2nd March 1816	Machines applicable to every description of spinning.
WORDSWORTH, JOSHUA - -	6287	26th July 1832	Machinery for preparing, drawing, roving, and spinning flax, hemp, wool, and other fibrous materials.
WORDSWORTH, JOSHUA - -	6518	6th Dec. 1832	Machinery for heckling flax, hemp, and other fibrous substances.
WORDSWORTH, JOSHUA - -	7657	31st May 1838	Machinery for heckling and dressing flax, hemp, and other fibrous materials.
WORDSWORTH, JOSHUA - -	9254	14th Feb. 1842	Machinery for spinning flax, hemp, and tow.
WORKMAN, JAMES - - -	474	10th Feb. 1725	Machine for making chocolate.
WORKMAN, JOHN - - -	13,703	31st July 1851	Manufacture of bricks, tiles, and other articles made of like materials.
WORMALD, JOHN - - -	13,748	18th Sept. 1851	Machinery or apparatus for spinning and doubling cotton-wool, silk, flax, and other fibrous substances.
WORNUM, ROBERT - - -	3419	26th March 1811	Upright pianoforte.
WORNUM, ROBERT - - -	4460	13th April 1820	Pianofortes and certain other stringed instruments.
WORNUM, ROBERT - - -	5384	4th July 1826	Pianofortes.
WORNUM, ROBERT - - -	5678	24th July 1828	Upright pianofortes.
WORNUM, ROBERT - - -	9262	15th Feb. 1842	Action of pianofortes.
WORSDELL, NATHANIEL -	7528	4th Jan. 1838	Apparatus to facilitate the conveyance of mail-bags and other parcels on railways or roads.
WORSDELL, THOMAS - -	10,892	23rd Oct. 1845	Apparatus to be attached to and employed in connection with railway-carriages.
WORSDELL, THOMAS - -	12,853	17th Nov. 1849	Manufacture of envelopes and cases; tools and machinery used therein.
WORSLEY, FREDERICK CAYLEY	7968	14th Feb. 1839	Locomotive engines and carriages.
WORSLEY, OTNELL - -	115	15th Feb. 1637	Setting and planting carrot roots and carrot seeds.
WORTH, JOHN - - -	990	28th May 1771	Cement for paying the sides and bottoms of ships for preserving them from worms, and for preserving buildings, &c. made of wood and exposed to the weather.
WORTH, JOHN SWAIN - -	7931	11th Jan. 1839	Machine for preparing and cleaning wool for manufacturing purposes.
WORTH, JOHN SWAIN - -	8239	10th Oct. 1839	Rotatory-engines, to be worked by steam and other fluids;—applicable for pumping water and other liquids.
WORTH, JOHN SWAIN - -	8578	29th July 1840	Machinery for cutting vegetable substances.
WORTHEIMER, JOHN - -	8874	8th March 1841	Preserving animal and vegetable substances and liquids.
WORTHINGTON, ROGER - -	1245	23rd Feb. 1780	Printing in water-colours, woollen-cloths, stuffs, and mixtures.
WORTHINGTON, THOMAS -	5193	21st June 1825	Loom or machine for weaving or manufacturing tape and other such articles.
WORTON, JAMES - - -	13,861	17th Dec. 1851	Manufacture of papier-mâché and articles made therefrom; manufacture of buttons, studs, and other articles where metal and glass are combined.
WRAGG, JONATHAN - -	13,606	26th April 1851	Railway and other carriages.
WREN, BENJAMIN - - -	12,774	20th Sept. 1849	Cleansing and treating certain descriptions of wheat.

Name of Patentee.	Progressive Number.	Date.	Subject-matter of Patent.
WRIGG, HENRY - - -	11,373	17th Sept. 1846	Means of diminishing draft and friction in carriages and other conveyances.
WRIGGLESWORTH, JAMES -	10,410	2nd Dec. 1844	Steel-pens.
WRIGHT, ALEXANDER - -	10,355	17th Oct. 1844	Apparatus for measuring gas, water, and other fluids; means of manufacturing the same.
WRIGHT, CHARLES - -	11,217	22nd May 1846	Manufacture of boots and shoes.
WRIGHT, GABRIEL - -	1229	25th June 1779	Azimuth and amplitude compass and quadrant, for use in navigation and practical astronomy.
WRIGHT, GABRIEL - -	1815	5th July 1791	Making magnetical-compasses, commonly called azimuth, amplitude, steering, and hanging compasses, for use in navigation, marine-surveying, &c.
WRIGHT, GABRIEL - -	2081	19th Jan. 1796	Azimuth and amplitude compasses, or adding to the same a reflecting quadrant and horizon, to enable a person without assistance, to take the azimuth of celestial objects and their altitudes at the same time, in every latitude or in any altitude of the object; method of stopping the card of the compass, and reading off the degrees and minutes from the vernier with or without the card being stopped; apparatus for mechanically working and solving the problems for finding the magnetic and true azimuths of objects taken by the compass.
WRIGHT, GEORGE (Sir) - -	2837	30th March 1805	Cutting pillars or tubes, either cylindrical or conical, out of solid stone, wood, or other materials.
WRIGHT, GEORGE - - -	14,004	8th March 1852	Stoves, grates, or fire-places.
WRIGHT, HENRY - - -	757	11th Dec. 1760	Medicine, called "Royal Clove drops."
WRIGHT, HENRY - - -	1956	8th June 1793	Machinery for combing and preparing wool, cotton, silk, flax, hemp and mohair, for spinning.
WRIGHT, JAMES - - -	5783	28th April 1829	Condensing the gases produced by the decomposition of muriate of soda and certain other substances;—applicable to other purposes.
WRIGHT, JERVAS - - -	1446	30th July 1784	Machine for sowing wheat, beans, peas, and other grain and seed, which machine may be fixed to a plough or otherwise.
WRIGHT, JOHN - - -	687	22nd Jan. 1754	Coaches and other wheel-carriages.
WRIGHT, JOHN - - -	709	27th May 1756	Raising steam for working fire-engines.
WRIGHT, JOHN - - -	1054	30th Oct. 1773	Making malleable iron from cast-iron or other cast metal, with raw coals or coke, without charcoal, granulations, mixture of fluxes, or other infusions.
WRIGHT, JOHN - - -	1614	3rd July 1787	Drill-plough, for sowing pulse, grain, and seeds.
WRIGHT, JOHN - - -	5556	11th Oct. 1827	Window-sashes.
WRIGHT, JOHN - - -	8114	18th June 1839	Mixing or alloying iron with other metals, applicable to the manufacture of links for chains and rings; machinery for effecting such manufacture.
WRIGHT, JOHN - - -	9819	6th July 1843	Boots and shoes, and other coverings for the feet.
WRIGHT, JOHN - - -	12,285	12th Oct. 1848	Generating steam and evaporating fluids.

Name of Patentee.	Progressive Number.	Date.	Subject-matter of Patent.
WRIGHT, JOSEPH - - -	8899	22nd March 1841	Apparatus used for dragging or skidding wheels of wheeled-carriages.
WRIGHT, JOSEPH - - -	10,173	7th May 1844	Railway and other carriages.
WRIGHT, JOSEPH - - -	11,101	25th Feb. 1846	Propelling vessels.
WRIGHT, LEMUEL WELLMAN - [*Wright, Samuel Wellman.*]	4507	1st Nov. 1820	Combination of machinery for making bricks and tiles.
WRIGHT, LEMUEL WELLMAN - [*Wright, Samuel Willman.*]	4955	15th May 1824	Machinery for making pins, also combinations of such machinery.
WRIGHT, LEMUEL WELLMAN -	5154	20th April 1825	Machinery for washing, cleansing, or bleaching linens, cottons, and other fabrics, goods, or fibrous substances.
WRIGHT, LEMUEL WELLMAN -	5271	21st Oct. 1825	Construction of steam-engines.
WRIGHT, LEMUEL WELLMAN -	5400	2nd Aug. 1826	Construction of trucks or carriages applicable to useful purposes.
WRIGHT, LEMUEL WELLMAN -	5473	17th March 1827	Combination and arrangement of machinery for making metal-screws.
WRIGHT, LEMUEL WELLMAN -	5543	17th Aug. 1827	Construction of cranes.
WRIGHT, LEMUEL WELLMAN -	5544	21st Aug. 1827	Machinery for cutting tobacco.
WRIGHT, LEMUEL WELLMAN -	5638	15th April 1828	Construction of wheel-carriages; machinery for propelling, drawing, or moving wheel-carriages.
WRIGHT, LEMUEL WELLMAN -	5703	18th Sept. 1828	Machinery for making screws.
WRIGHT, LEMUEL WELLMAN -	6525	16th Dec. 1833	Combination and arrangement of machinery, whereby certain known agents may be employed in producing power; and mode for effecting the same, applicable to various useful purposes.
WRIGHT, LEMUEL WELLMAN -	6642	10th July 1834	Machinery for cutting tobacco;—applicable to other useful purposes.
WRIGHT, LEMUEL WELLMAN -	6655	9th Aug. 1834	Machinery for refrigerating fluids.
WRIGHT, LEMUEL WELLMAN -	6713	15th Nov. 1834	Machinery for making paper.
WRIGHT, LEMUEL WELLMAN -	7251	9th Dec. 1836	Machinery for bleaching or cleansing linens, cottons, or other fabrics, goods, or other fibrous substances.
WRIGHT, LEMUEL WELLMAN -	7348	20th April 1837	Machinery for bleaching or cleansing linens, cottons, or other fabrics, goods, or other fibrous substances.
WRIGHT, LEMUEL WELLMAN -	8028	9th April 1839	Machinery for washing, cleansing, or bleaching linens, cottons, and other fabrics, goods, or fibrous substances.
WRIGHT, LEMUEL WELLMAN -	9787	15th June 1843	Machinery for bleaching various fibrous substances; machinery for converting the same into paper.
WRIGHT, LEMUEL WELLMAN -	11,686	4th May 1847	Apparatus for sweeping or cleansing chimneys and flues, and for other similar purposes.
WRIGHT, LEMUEL WELLMAN -	12,448	30th Jan. 1849	Preparing fibrous substances for spinning; machinery and apparatus connected therewith.
WRIGHT, PETER - - -	6645	17th July 1834	Spinning, twisting, and twining cotton, flax, silk, wool, or any other suitable substances.
WRIGHT, PETER - - -	12,259	31st Aug. 1848	Manufacture of vice-boxes; machinery for effecting the same.
WRIGHT, PETER - - -	13,902	20th Jan. 1852	Manufacture of anvils.
WRIGHT, RICHARD - -	4088	10th Dec. 1816	Constructing and propelling ships and other vessels.

Name of Patentee.	Progressive Number.	Date.	Subject-matter of Patent
WRIGHT, RICHARD - -	4311	14th Nov. 1818	Construction of steam-engines; and the subsequent use of steam.
WRIGHT, RICHARD - -	4606	9th Nov. 1821	Process of distillation.
WRIGHT, RICHARD - -	9819	6th July 1843	Boots and shoes, and other similar coverings for the feet.
WRIGHT, RICHARD - -	10,950	18th Nov. 1845	Refining sugar.
WRIGHT, RICHARD - -	11,280	6th July 1846	Refining sugar.
WRIGHT, SAMUEL - - -	5890	26th Jan. 1830	Manufacture of ornamental tiles, bricks, and quarries, for floors, pavements, and for other purposes.
WRIGHT, SAMUEL - • -	10,022	23rd Jan. 1844	Manufacture of ornamental tiles, bricks, and quarries for floor-pavements, and for other purposes.
WRIGHT, STEPHEN - -	699	2nd April 1755	Weighing a ship's anchor at sea; working the pumps of a ship.
WRIGHT, THEODORE LYMAN -	6973	31st Dec. 1835	Apparatus for cleansing, purifying, and preparing feathers and down, for domestic uses; process of effecting the same.
WRIGHT, THOMAS - - -	1003	4th Feb. 1772	Construction of guns and all other fire-arms.
WRIGHT, THOMAS - -	1135	25th Oct. 1776	Mill for squeezing or grinding sugar-canes.
WRIGHT, THOMAS - -	1307	8th Nov. 1781	Making coffins in cast-iron and other metals; and preserving the same.
WRIGHT, THOMAS - -	1354	1st Feb. 1783	Watch or timekeeper.
WRIGHT, THOMAS - -	2489	25th April 1801	Making hand stone cornmills for grinding wheat and other grain into flour.
WRIGHT, THOMAS - -	3766	9th Dec. 1813	Making a composition or mixture for dyeing scarlet and other colours.
WRIGHT, THOMAS - -	8900	22nd March 1841	Certain improvements applicable to railway and other carriages.
WRIGHT, THOMAS - -	9204	21st Dec. 1841	Applying electricity to control railway-engines and carriages; to mark time; to give signals, and print intelligence at distant places.
WRIGHT, THOMAS - -	10,548	10th March 1845	Apparatus for the production and diffusion of light.
WRIGHT, WILLIAM - -	684	1st Aug. 1753	Medicine called " Cordial mixture," for women in labour.
WRIGHT, WILLIAM - -	7127	22nd June 1836	Twisting-machinery used in the preparation for spinning or twisting cotton, flax, silk, wool, hemp, and other fibrous substances.
WRIGHT, WILLIAM - -	10,006	11th Jan. 1844	Rendering leather, skins, or hides, impervious to wet, more flexible, and more durable.
WRIGHT, WILLIAM EVATT -	6293	4th Aug. 1832	Construction of tea and coffee urns and other utensils of that description.
WRIGHT, WILLIAM EVATT -	6751	27th Jan. 1835	Tea and coffee urns and tea-kettles.
WRIGHT, WILLIAM EVATT -	6879	12th Aug. 1835	Box for holding coals.
WRIGHTON, RICHARD - -	12,000	22nd Dec. 1847	Apparatus to be applied to railway carriages and engines.
WRIGLEY, MILES - - -	12,411	11th Jan. 1849	Making yeast or barm.
WRIGLEY, THOMAS - -	9513	8th Nov. 1842	Machinery for manufacturing paper.
WROUGHTON, EDWARD - -	14,270	19th Aug. 1852	Manufacture of textile fabrics; machinery for producing such fabrics.
WROUGHTON, THOMAS - -	11,354	26th Aug. 1846	Apparatus and instruments for ventilation and respiration.

Name of Patentee.	Progressive Number.	Date.	Subject-matter of Patent.
WYATT, CHARLES - - -	1739	31st March 1790	Covering and combining copper or brass sheets or plates with a metallic or semi-metallic substance, to prevent corrosion.
WYATT, CHARLES - - -	1805	11th May 1791	Making pipes and spouts for conveying water and other liquids; making troughs and cistern-heads for receiving or holding water;—applicable to other purposes.
WYATT, CHARLES - - -	2639	2nd Aug. 1802	Apparatus for and mode of distilling and drying coffee and sugar.
WYATT, CHARLES - - -	2745	21st Dec. 1803	Process of purifying ardent spirits.
WYATT, CHARLES - - -	3706	5th June 1813	Casing or facing brick and other buildings with stone.
WYATT, CHARLES - - -	4130	3rd June 1817	Preventing any disadvantageous accumulation of heat in manufacturing and refining sugar.
WYATT, JOB - - - -	751	14th May 1760	Cutting screws of iron, called wood-screws.
WYATT, JOHN - - -	1609	5th June 1787	Powder to be used where the mixture of oil or oily substances with acetous or watery liquors is required.
WYATT, JOHN FRANCIS - -	3863	15th Dec. 1814	Bricks or blocks adapted for the fronts of houses and other buildings, giving them the appearance of stone; brick or block applicable to a new method of blonding brickwork; blocks or slabs for paving floors and facing or lining walls instead of ashler, and which will resemble marble or stone, and may also be applied to steps, stairs, or other parts of buildings.
WYATT, MATTHEW - -	2669	21st Dec. 1802	Fire-grate.
WYATT, MATTHEW COTES -	4218	3rd Feb. 1818	Safeguard to prevent the accidental movement forward of the cock of a gun, pistol, or other fire-arm, towards the hammer.
WYATT, SAMUEL - - -	2410	10th June 1800	Making and constructing bridges, warehouses, and other buildings, without the use of wood.
WYATT, WALTER HENRY -	3001	15th Jan. 1807	Facilitating the chemical action between copper and saline substances, so as to produce improvements in separating gold and silver from copper plated or united with either of those metals; manufacturing sulphate of copper; and making colours for painting.
WYATT, WILLIAM - - -	751	14th May 1760	Cutting screws of iron, called wood-screws.
WYATT, WILLIAM - - -	12,813	18th Oct. 1849	Coating the surfaces of pumps, pipes, cisterns and other articles of iron.
WYCH, THOMAS EYRE - -	14,263	19th Aug. 1852	Propelling vessels.
WYCHERLEY, GEORGE - -	5049	4th Dec. 1824	Making and constructing saddles and side-saddles.
WYDROFF, Baron VICTOR DE -	9580	29th Dec. 1842	Construction of railways, wheels to run on railways, and apparatus for clearing the rails.
WYKE, GEORGE - - -	2894	19th Nov. 1805	Working pumps by machinery.
WYKE, GEORGE - - -	3303	12th Feb. 1810	Construction of wheel-carriages.
WYKE, GEORGE - - -	4143	19th July 1817	Construction of wheeled-carriages.
WYKE, GEORGE - - -	4235	14th March 1818	Pumps;—applicable to machinery of various descriptions.

Name of Patentee.	Progressive Number.	Date.	Subject-matter of Patent.
WYLAM, WILLIAM - - -	9796	22nd June 1843	Manufacture or preparation of fuel.
WYLAM, WILLIAM - - -	10,603	7th April 1845	Artificial fuel; machinery for manufacturing the same.
WYLAM WILLIAM - - -	10,612	15th April 1845	Hydraulic-presses, and machinery connected therewith.
WYLD, OBADIAH - - -	551	17th March 1735	Making or preparing paper, linen, canvas, and such like substances, so as neither to flame nor retain fire, also to resist moisture and damp, thus rendering them suitable for making cartridges, also for hangings for rooms, or for other purposes.
WYLDE, ELISHA - - -	7484	21st Nov. 1837	Locomotive and other engines.
WYLDE, ELISHA - - -	8694	12th Nov. 1840	Making and working locomotive and other steam-engines.
WYLDE, ELISHA - - -	14,064	15th April 1852	Apparatus for heating and evaporating.
WYLDE, JAMES, junior - -	12,986	2nd March 1850	Rollers to be used in the manufacture of silk, cotton, woollen, and other fabrics.
WYLDER, EDWYN - - -	13,148	24th June 1850	Ever-pointed pencils, pens, and pen-holders.
WYNDUS, EDWARD - - -	232	27th Feb. 1684	Increasing light by means of extraordinary glasses and lamps, for the improvement of ships' lanterns, lighthouses, diffusing light in mines, and other uses where light and heat are required.
WYNN, WILLIAM - - -	7336	4th April 1837	Apparatus for diminishing the evaporation of vinous, alcoholic, acetic, and other volatile vapours, and preventing the absorption of noxious effluvia in vinous, spirituous, acetous, and other fluids, such as wines, spirits, malt-liquors, cyder, perry, and vinegar.
WYOTT, HUGH - - -	43	24th May 1628	Means for the safe transport of horses and cattle to and from any of His Majesty's dominions.
WYTHES, GEORGE - - -	12,893	15th Dec. 1849	Apparatus for receiving and retaining the rails of railways.

Y.

Name of Patentee.	Progressive Number.	Date.	Subject-matter of Patent.
YANDALL, JAMES - - -	5406	24th Aug. 1826	Apparatus for cooling and heating fluids.
YARDLEY, CHARLES - -	4654	2nd March 1822	Manufacturing glue from bones, by means of steam.
YARNOLD, JOHN - - -	355	19th July 1698	Draining mines, meres, and marshes; raising water for supplying towns, villages, and houses.
YATES, DAVID - - -	1647	22nd April 1788	Machine for glazing or polishing cottons, linens, and mixtures, or cloth made either of cotton or linen, or of cotton and linen mixed, or of other materials, and of any breadth to two yards wide.
YATES, GEORGE - - -	800	10th Nov. 1763	Machine, which, being placed upon a stove or in a chimney, will prevent such chimney smoking.

Name of Patentee.	Progres-sive Number.	Date.		Subject-matter of Patent.
YATES, JAMES - - -	1658	8th July	1788	Multiplying engravings or chasings on metals;—applicable to ornaments on coaches and coach-harness, and to many other purposes where chasings are required.
YATES, JAMES - - -	8142	3rd July	1839	Framing raised or projecting letters, mouldings, figures, or other ornamental work, for external decoration of buildings and for other purposes.
YATES, JAMES - - -	8152	13th July	1839	Construction of cupel-furnaces for melting metals.
YATES, JAMES - - -	8244	19th Oct.	1839	Construction of furnaces.
YATES, JAMES - - -	11,482	14th Dec.	1846	Construction of blast-furnaces.
YATES, JOHN - - -	5884	26th Jan.	1830	Process for giving a metallic surface to cotton, silk, linen, and other fabrics.
YATES, JOHN - - -	7252	9th Dec.	1836	Tramroads or railways; wheels or other parts of carriages to be worked thereon.
YATES, THOMAS - - -	8260	7th Nov.	1839	Construction of looms for weaving; application of the same to produce certain descriptions of goods or fabrics by steam or other power.
YATES, THOMAS - - -	11,443	12th Nov.	1846	Time-keepers.
YATES, WILLIAM - - -	10,489	21st Jan.	1845	Plastic manufacture or composition, part of which is applicable to decorative and useful purposes, and part as a fire-proof cement or plastic.
YATES, WILLIAM THOMAS -	6547	23rd Jan.	1834	Boilers for steam-engines and other uses.
YELLDALL, ANTHONY - -	2013	30th Sept.	1794	Acromatic belt, which, being applied to the human body, effects the cure of gout, rheumatism, and other diseases.
YERBURY, FRANCIS - -	858	26th Aug.	1766	Making thin superfine cloths.
YETTS, WILLIAM - -	4910	28th Feb.	1824	Apparatus to be applied to a windlass.
YETTS, WILLIAM - - -	7396	19th June	1837	Calking ships and other vessels.
YGLESIAS, JOSEPH RAMON -	10,940	13th Nov.	1845	Application and combination of mechanical arrangements for augmenting the power of first-moving machines or engines.
YLERY, CHARLES - - -	11,368	10th Sept.	1846	Ascertaining and regulating the speed and times of railway-trains.
YONGE, JOHN GREENHILL -	862	21st Nov.	1766	Constructing sugar-mills, by the application of friction-wheels to diminish the resistance arising by friction.
YORK, JOHN OLIVER - -	9200	21st Dec.	1841	Construction of railway axles and wheels.
YORK, JOHN OLIVER - -	9485	8th Oct.	1842	Manufacture of axles for railway-wheels.
YORK, JOHN OLIVER - -	9781	15th June	1843	Paving or covering roads, streets, and other ways or surfaces.
YORK, JOHN OLIVER - -	12,334	21st Nov.	1848	Manufacture of metallic tubes.
YORK, JOHN OLIVER - -	13,297	24th Oct.	1850	Generating steam in locomotive, marine, and other boilers.
YORKE, HENRY - - -	109	6th Sept.	1637	Drawing and working barges and other vessels on rivers, without the use of horses.
YOUIL, JOHN - - -	13,074	8th May	1850	Machinery or apparatus for washing, cleansing, filling and corking bottles and other vessels.
YOULDON, EDMUND - -	6654	5th Aug.	1834	Preventing or curing smoky chimneys.

Name of Patentee.	Progressive Number.	Date.	Subject-matter of Patent.
YOUNG, ANN - - - -	2485	16th March 1801	Apparatus consisting of an oblong box, which, when opened, presents two tables, and having dice-pins, counters, &c. contained within the same, by means of which six different games may be played for the amusement of children, and at the same time as an exercise in the fundamental principles of music, particularly the keys or modulations major and minor, signatures, intervals, and chords and discords with their resolutions, also the rules of thorough bass.
YOUNG, GEORGE - - -	3962	5th Dec. 1815	Making a peculiar species of canvas for military and other purposes.
YOUNG, GEORGE JOHNSON ·	5667	21st June 1828	Machine for giving additional purchase or power in working ships' windlasses and capstans.
YOUNG, GEORGE JOHNSON - [Young, George Johnston.]	9688	5th April 1843	Construction of capstans.
YOUNG, GEORGE LINDSAY -	8324	21st Dec. 1839	Surface for paper, mill-board, or card-board, vellum, and parchment.
YOUNG, HENRY BURGESS -	12,256	28th Aug. 1848	Smelting and refining lead-ores.
YOUNG, JAMES - - -	7231	22nd Nov. 1836	Manufacture of sugars.
YOUNG, JAMES - - -	9156	11th Nov. 1841	Manufacture of ammonia and salts of ammonia; apparatus for combining ammonia, carbonic-acid and other gases, with liquids.
YOUNG, JAMES - - -	12,359	9th Dec. 1848	Preparation of certain materials used in dyeing and printing.
YOUNG, JAMES - - -	12,744	16th Aug. 1849	Treating certain ores and otner matters containing metals; obtaining products therefrom.
YOUNG, JAMES - - -	13,292	17th Oct. 1850	Treating certain bituminous mineral substances; and obtaining products therefrom.
YOUNG, JAMES HADDEN -	8428	13th March 1840	Setting up printing-types.
YOUNG, JOHN - - -	5171	14th May 1825	Construction of locks for doors and for other purposes.
YOUNG, JOHN - - -	5880	18th Jan. 1830	Locks and other securities, applicable to doors and to other purposes.
YOUNG, JOHN - - -	6143	27th July 1831	Locks and latches, with regard to the security of the same, and construction of the exterior and interior parts thereof.
YOUNG, JOHN - - -	6580	20th March 1834	Manufacturing and forming iron for hoops of casks and other purposes.
YOUNG, JOHN - - -	7109	7th June 1836	Manufacturing metallic hinges for doors, and for other purposes.
YOUNG, JOHN - - -	7125	21st June 1836	Manufacturing boxes and pullies for window-sashes and for other purposes.
YOUNG, JOHN - - -	8605	17th Aug. 1840	Manufacture or construction of knobs, handles, frames, tablets, boxes, and other ornamental articles, for decoration of houses and furniture.
YOUNG, PETER - - -	6176	6th Oct. 1831	Manufacturing mangel-wurzel for producing various known articles of commerce.
YOUNG, PETER - - -	6249	22nd March 1832	Manufacturing mangel-wurzel for producing certain known articles of commerce.
YOUNG, ROBERT - - -	2470	3rd Feb. 1801	Fire-stove or grate.

Name of Patentee.	Progres- sive Number.	Date.	Subject-matter of Patent.
YOUNG, THOMAS - - -	8468	13th April 1840	Lamps.
YOUNG, THOMAS - - -	8829	3rd Feb. 1841	Furnaces or fire-places.
YOUNG, THOMAS - - -	9024	9th July 1841	Lamps.
YOUNG, THOMAS - - -	9867	15th Aug. 1843	Obtaining power.
YOUNG, THOMAS - - -	11,772	29th June 1847	Card-cases, and retaining or fastening papers, deeds, and fabrics.
YOUNG, WALTER - - -	14,012	8th March 1852	Steam-engines.
YOUNG, WILLIAM - - -	9368	28th May 1842	Lamps and candlesticks.
YOUNG, WILLIAM - - -	9989	14th Dec. 1843	Manufacture of lamps and gas-burners.
YOUNG, WILLIAM - - -	10,799	4th Aug. 1845	Construction and means of manufacturing apparatus for conducting electricity.
YOUNG, WILLIAM - - -	12,247	21st Aug. 1848	Closing spirit and other cans or vessels.
YOUNG, WILLIAM - - -	12,256	28th Aug. 1848	Smelting and refining lead-ores.
YOUNG, WILLIAM - - -	12,353	2nd Dec. 1848	Machinery for winding, balling, or spooling thread, yarn, or other fibrous materials. .
YOUNG, WILLIAM TANNER -	6481	7th Oct. 1833	Apparatus for equalizing draft, applicable to towing barges and other floating bodies on water, and drawing carriages on land.
YOUNG, WILLIAM WESTON -	5047	4th Dec. 1824	Manufacturing salt;—partly applicable to other useful purposes.
YOUNGER, RICHARD -	2740	12th Nov. 1803	Extracting worts from malt, barley, and other grains and substances.
YOUNIE, JAMES - -	3220	28th March 1809	Machine to be applied to stoves or grates, for preventing accidents by fire, and whereby fires may be put out with safety and facility.
YOUNIE, JAMES - - -	4009	23rd March 1816	Prevention or cure of smoky chimneys.
YULE, ADAM - - - -	12,726	1st Aug. 1849	Preparation of materials for coating ships and other vessels.
YULE, JOHN - - - -	7224	15th Nov. 1836	Rotatory engines.
YULE, JOHN - - - -	11,829	3rd Aug. 1847	Chairs used on railways; and fixing the same.
YULE, WILLIAM TRUEMAN -	10,493	28th Jan. 1845	Preserving animal and vegetable matters.

Z.

Name of Patentee.	Progres- sive Number.	Date.	Subject-matter of Patent.
ZACHARIAH, LEVY - - -	5362	8th May 1826	Combination of materials to be used as fuel.
ZAMBEAU, JOSEPH - -	7915	19th Dec. 1838	Rotatory engines.
ZAMBEAU, JOSEPH - - [Zambdaux, Joseph.]	10,735	25th June 1845	Atmospheric-railways.
ZAMBRA, JOSEPH WARREN -	14,002	8th March 1852	Thermometers, barometers, gauges, and other instruments for ascertaining and register- ing the temperature, pressure, density, and specific-gravity of aëriform, liquid, and solid bodies.
ZANDER, HENRIK - -	8111	17th June 1839	Steam-engines, steam-boilers, and con- densers.

Name of Patentee.	Progressive Number.	Date.		Subject-matter of Patent.
ZANDER, HENRIK - - -	8138	2nd July	1839	Manufacture of paper.
ZANDER, HENRIK - - -	9516	8th Nov.	1842	Steam-engines, boilers, and furnaces; feeding and working the same; machinery for applying steam-power to propelling purposes.
ZEITTER, JACOB FREDERICK -	6498	1st Nov.	1833	Pianofortes and other stringed musical instruments.
ZERMAN, JEAN NAPOLEON -	12,057	8th Feb.	1848	Ships and other vessels.
ZINCKE, FREDERIC BURT -	7249	9th Dec.	1836	Preparing or manufacturing the leaf of a certain plant, so as to produce a fibrous substance not hitherto used in manufactures; application of the same to various purposes.
ZINK, JACOB - - - -	3519	20th Jan.	1812	Manufacturing verdigris. " British Verdigris.
ZOMER, PETER - - -	691	23rd May	1754	Method of making black train-oil and fish-glue.